Iceland,
Greenland
& the Faroe Islands

Deanna Swaney

Iceland, Greenland & the Faroe Islands

3rd edition

Published by
Lonely Planet Publications
Head Office: PO Box 617, Hawthorn, Vic 3122, Australia
Branches: 155 Filbert St, Suite 251, Oakland, CA 94607, USA
              10 Barley Mow Passage, Chiswick, London W4 4PH, UK
              71 bis rue du Cardinal Lemoine, 75005 Paris, France

Printed by
Colorcraft Ltd, Hong Kong
Printed in China

Photographs by
Deanna Swaney
Graeme Cornwallis
Adrian Smith
Front cover: Late sun on Kong Oscars Havn, Tasiilaq, East Greenland (Deanna Swaney)

First Published
February 1991

This Edition
June 1997

National Library of Australia Cataloguing in Publication Data

Swaney, Deanna
Iceland, Greenland & the Faroe Islands

3rd ed.
Includes index
ISBN 0 86442 453 1.

1. Iceland - Guidebooks. 2. Greenland - Guidebooks. 3. Faroe Islands - Guidebooks.
I. Title. (Lonely Planet travel survival kit)

914.91045

text & maps © Lonely Planet 1997
photos © photographers as indicated 1997

Deanna Swaney

An incurable travel addict, Deanna escaped encroaching yuppiedom in the vibrant heart of mid-town Anchorage, Alaska, and made a break for South America to write Lonely Planet's *Bolivia – travel survival kit*. Subsequent wanderings led through an erratic circuit of wildlife encounters and island paradises – Arctic and tropical – and resulted in four more travel survival kits: *Tonga*; *Samoa*; *Zimbabwe, Botswana & Namibia* and the 1st edition of this book.

She has also worked on LP's *Brazil*; *Mauritius, Réunion & Seychelles*; *Madagascar & Comoros*; and *Southern Africa*, and contributed to shoestring guides to Africa, South America and Scandinavia.

Graeme Cornwallis

Graeme updated the Faroe Islands chapters of this book. Born and raised in Edinburgh, he later wandered around Scotland before coming to rest in Glasgow. While studying astronomy at Glasgow University, he developed a passion for peaks – particularly the Scottish Munros – and eventually bagged all 599 summits over 3000 ft in Britain and Ireland at least once. He has travelled extensively in Scandinavia as well as Asia, North America and the Pacific. In winter, he teaches mathematics and physics, and his summers are spent tramping, tripping and battling deluges, blizzards and gale-force winds in various parts of the world.

From the Authors

From Deanna There are lots of people to thank for their generous help and/or company during the update for this edition. For the Iceland portion: Graeme Cornwallis, Scotland, for assistance, company and friendship, even when the climate conspired against us; Irene McLean, Scotland, for help with articles; Jean Keizer & Resi Botteram, Netherlands, for their bright companionship, information on Siglufjörður, Húsavík and Hveragerði, and fond Melbourne reminiscing; Jón Illugason, Reykjahlíð, for arranging super trips through Jökulsárgljúfur and Gjástykki; Ásdis Illugadóttir, in Reykjahlíð,

for good chats and lots of coffee; Pizza 67 in Fellabær, for the best pizza in the North Atlantic; Karen Erlingsdóttir, Egilsstaðir, for good guidance and the loan of her bicycle; Bergsveinn Ólafsson, Stafafell, for his enthusiasm and hospitality; James & Wendy Bohannon of San Jose, California, for a helpful email; Rev Patrick Jörðsvín Buck, Kentucky, USA, for the lowdown on Ásatrú; Hrefna Hilmisdóttir, Heimaey, who provided good new information and helped sort out a mapping mess. Þórhallur Vilhjálmsson provided good fun and lots of insight on the Icelandic interior, particularly Kverkfjöll.

For the Greenland update I must thank: Gunnar Már & Stein Lárusson at Icelandair in Reykjavík, for their kind help in organising the Tasiilaq trip; Yew Lin, Hotel Angmagssalik, for a typically wonderful stay in his fair town; Hans Christian Florian

Sørensen, Tasiilaq (whose son is destined for greatness!); Jacky Simoud, Qassiarssuk, who was a relaxed and friendly face in Narsarsuaq; Maya Borritsø, Copenhagen, who provided some good Greenland background; Søren Thalund, Nuuk, for an early-morning dockside meeting and subsequent info and support; René Nielsen, Nanortalik, for his help, enthusiasm and friendship on various occasions; Preben Ingemann, Sisimiut, for his valuable time at short notice; Robert and Thrine in Ilulissat, Arne Niemann, Uummannaq, and Strange Filskov, Ilulissat, for updated information; Jørgen Lindgreen, Tasiilaq, for update materials and an enlightened attitude toward tourism in the hub of East Greenland; and Wayne Phair, Australia, for help in Tasiilaq.

Norbert Schürer, at Duke University, North Carolina, was a great travelling companion and contributed text on Greenland's economy and politics, several book reviews, the section on Greenlandic literature, and the Pittufik aside in the North-West Greenland chapter. Frank Smits, Eindhoven, Netherlands, provided astute and well-expressed observations for the South Greenland, Disko Bay and North-West Greenland chapters.

I'd also like to thank Ernst Schürer, Pennsylvania, for fine company and superhuman patience and endurance; Fin & Trish Perry, Massachusetts, for happy times in North-West Greenland and an introduction to Rockwell Kent; Ian Wilton, Shaftesbury, for long-suffering assistance; Dr Mark Nuttall at the University of Aberdeen, for all the long and enlightening Greenland conversations.

As always, for their continuing help and support, I send love and thanks to Earl Swaney in Fresno, Robert Strauss in Kyre Park, Jonny Morland of TINSTAR Bug-Free software; and Dave Dault and Keith & Holly Hawkings, back home in Anchorage.

From Graeme Thanks to Annika Joensen, Oda Andreasen, Ingigerñ á Trøñni and the other members of staff at Kunningarstovan (Tórshavn); Harald Petersen (Klaksvík); Irene McLean (Glasgow); Ian Wilton (Dorset); Deanna Swaney (Alaska); and John Gasbarre (Maine). Their help is greatly appreciated.

From the Publisher

This 3rd edition was edited by Paul Harding with help from Craig MacKenzie and Liz Filleul. Jane Fitzpatrick, Chris Wyness, Katie Cody, Lyn McGaurr and Mary Neighbour assisted with the proofing, and Sharon Benson helped with the index. Jacqui Saunders handled the mapping and design, aided by Rachel Black, Louise Klep and Tamsin Wilson. Marcel Gaston chipped in with the climate charts and Lou Callan tidied up the language sections. Cover design was by David Kemp and Michael Signal.

Thanks

Many thanks to the travellers who used the last edition and wrote to us with helpful hints, advice and interesting anecdotes. Your names appear in the back of this book.

Warning & Request

Things change – prices go up, schedules change, good places go bad and bad places go bankrupt – nothing stays the same. So, if you find things better or worse, recently opened or long since closed, please tell us and help make the next edition even more accurate and useful.

We value all of the feedback we receive from travellers. Julie Young coordinates a small team who read and acknowledge every letter, postcard and email, and ensure that every morsel of information finds its way to the appropriate authors, editors and publishers. Everyone who writes to us will find their name in the next edition of the appropriate guide and will also receive a free subscription to our quarterly newsletter, *Planet Talk*. The very best contributions will be rewarded with a free Lonely Planet guide.

Excerpts from your correspondence may appear in updates (which we add to the end pages of reprints); new editions of this guide; in our newsletter, *Planet Talk*; or in the Postcards section of our Web site – so please let us know if you don't want your letter published or your name acknowledged.

Contents

WEST CENTRAL ICELAND 135

SOUTH CENTRAL ICELAND 160

THE WESTFJORDS 201

NORTH CENTRAL ICELAND 221

AKUREYRI 235

NORTH-EAST ICELAND 254

EAST ICELAND 285

Boxed Asides

Map Legend

BOUNDARIES

───────────── International Boundary
───────────── Regional Boundary

ROUTES

──────────── Freeway
──────────── Highway
──────────── Major Road
── ── ── ── Unsealed Road or Track
──────────── City Road
──────────── City Street
┼┼┼┼┼┼┼┼┼┼┼ Railway
─ ─ ─ ─ ─ ─ Underground Railway
──────────── Tram
─ · ─ · ─ · ─ Walking Track
· · · · · · · · · · · Walking Tour
─ ─ ─ ─ ─ ─ Ferry Route
┼┼┼┼┼┼┼┼┼┼┼ Cable Car or Chairlift

AREA FEATURES

Parks
Built-Up Area
Pedestrian Mall
Market
+ + + + + + Cemetery
Reef
Glacier or Ice
Rocks

HYDROGRAPHIC FEATURES

Coastline
River, Creek
Intermittent River or Creek
Rapids, Waterfalls
Lake, Intermittent Lake
Canal
Swamp

SYMBOLS

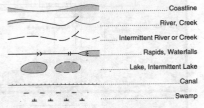

✪ CAPITAL		National Capital
◉ Capital		Regional Capital
◍ CITY		Major City
● City		City
● Town		Town
● Village		Village

▪	▼	Place to Stay, Place to Eat
☕	▯	Cafe, Pub or Bar
✉	☎	Post Office, Telephone
❶	⑤	Tourist Information, Bank
⊙	℗	Transport, Parking
🏛	⌂	Museum, Youth Hostel
⌗	⚊	Caravan Park, Camping Ground
✝	✚	Church, Cathedral
☪	✡	Mosque, Synagogue
⌸	⚏	Buddhist Temple, Hindu Temple
✚	★	Hospital, Police Station

◌	⛽	Embassy, Petrol Station
✈	✛	Airport, Airfield
▭	✿	Swimming Pool, Gardens
❖	🐘	Shopping Centre, Zoo
⚘	⊓	Winery or Vineyard, Picnic Site
←	A25	One Way Street, Route Number
⛪	⚑	Stately Home, Monument
⛨	▣	Castle, Tomb
⌒	⌂	Cave, Hut or Chalet
▲	☀	Mountain or Hill, Lookout
⛨	⤨	Lighthouse, Shipwreck
)(	◎	Pass, Spring
🏊	🏄	Beach, Surf Beach
	∴	Archaeological Site or Ruins
		Ancient or City Wall
		Cliff or Escarpment, Tunnel
		Railway Station

Note: not all symbols displayed above appear in this book

Map Index

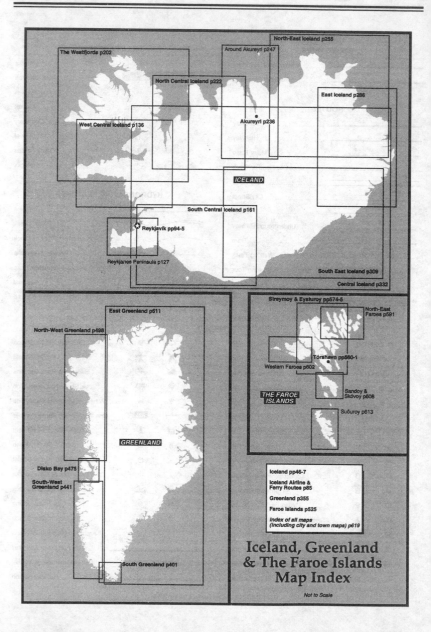

The Westfjords p202

North-East Iceland p255

Around Akureyri p247

North Central Iceland p222

East Iceland p286

West Central Iceland p136

Akureyri p236

ICELAND

South Central Iceland p161

Reykjavík pp94-5

Reykjanes Peninsula p127

South East Iceland p309

Central Iceland p332

East Greenland p511

Streymoy & Eysturoy pp574-5

North-East Faroes p591

North-West Greenland p498

Tórshavn pp560-1

Western Faroes p602

THE FAROE ISLANDS

Sandoy & Skúvoy p608

Suðuroy p613

GREENLAND

Disko Bay p475

South-West Greenland p441

South Greenland p401

Iceland pp46-7

Iceland Airline &
Ferry Routes p85

Greenland p355

Faroe Islands p525

Index of all maps
(including city and town maps) p619

Iceland, Greenland & The Faroe Islands Map Index

Not to Scale

Introduction

As far as travellers are concerned, the North Atlantic countries have historically been places to fly over quickly or to touch down in briefly while flying between North America and Europe. Few who'd spent a two-hour stopover gazing at the barren lava fields around Iceland's Keflavík international airport, or looked down on Greenland's seemingly dimensionless icecap, could ever have imagined visiting those places on purpose.

To some extent this is still true, but it won't be for long. As more and more visitors spend time seeing the wonders of Iceland, Greenland and the Faroe Islands, word will get around and many more visitors will keep arriving.

Culturally, Iceland, Greenland and the Faroes – collectively known as West Norden

– form an arc of stepping stones between Scotland and Canada and provide an intercontinental link as wide as the Atlantic itself. The region is the meeting place of the Inuit peoples who settled from the west, and the Norse who arrived (albeit much later) from the east and actually pressed on as far as eastern North America.

Iceland is, of course, the best known and most visited of the three countries, due to Icelandair's inexpensive flights between New York and Luxembourg. Its wild volcanic landscapes, its mountains, glaciers, hot springs, geysers and waterfalls, combined with its rich history, literature and folklore, will provide endless options for motivated visitors.

Greenland, the world's largest island (that is, if you exclude the island-continent of

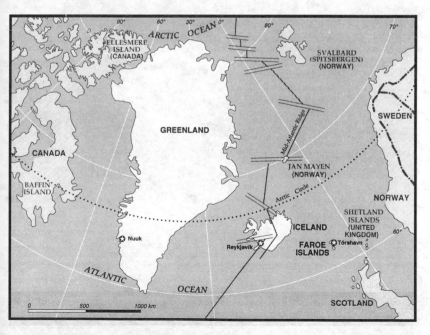

Australia), defies description. It also exemplifies what is perhaps the most successful meeting of European and indigenous cultures in the colonial world. Its friendly people, their resourceful and practical traditions and the haunting beauty of their land will never be forgotten by anyone who experiences them first-hand.

The Faroe Islands, now an independent nation within the Kingdom of Denmark, lie halfway between Iceland and Shetland but remain little known to outsiders. The 18 islands of the Faroes are steep, rocky remnants of an old volcanic plateau rising precipitously out of the often stormy Atlantic. Here the forces of nature, the old Norse tradition and today's technology join to create a part of modern Europe superimposed on a stunning backdrop.

It seems that seasoned travellers often put off visiting the North Atlantic countries until last due to their perceived remoteness and their reputation as money-munchers. The truth is, however, that they're close to both Europe and the USA, lying along the main transatlantic routes. Reykjavík, the closest European city to New York, is closer to London than London is to Athens or Helsinki. As for the expenses, shoestring travellers with time, patience and energy can visit and enjoy themselves. The major attractions of the region – the fresh air, the wilderness, the wildlife and the sense of history – are all free and awaiting discovery.

Facts about the Region

HISTORY
Early Perceptions
Between 330 and 325 BC, the Greek navigator Pytheas embarked on a voyage from Massilia (Marseille), through the Pillars of Heracles, and then northward to investigate trade routes to the amber and tin markets of northern Europe. In the process, he circumnavigated Britain, 'discovered' the Orkneys (and possibly the Shetlands), and visited the west coast of Norway.

In his report on the journey, Pytheas mentioned the island of Ultima Thule, six days' sailing north of Britain, beyond which the sea congealed into a viscous jelly. This was almost certainly a reference to Iceland. Given the description, it seems unlikely he actually visited the island, but it is significant that the Celts or the Norse knew of its existence at such an early date.

Non-Nordic European perceptions of the North Atlantic region both before and after Pytheas' journey, however, were even more shrouded in rumour and myth. The great northern ocean, *oceanus innavigabilis*, or the Hyperborean Sea, was a place of maelstrom where the fierce winds of Boreas howled through the Rhipaean mountains and guarded idyllic lands of plenty like Vinland, the Elysian fields, Avalon, the Hesperides and a host of other enigmatic, but mythical, locales. The borders of paradise were inhabited, they believed, by barbaric dog-headed people (the Cynocephali and the Scythians) who ate raw meat and behaved like bears.

To venture northward, they presumed, would invite all sorts of grisly eventualities. Their fears of the irksome, unknown entities were overcome by economic opportunism when amber and tin deposits beckoned.

The Monks
Some of the myths were dispelled during the 6th century when Ireland was seized by the religious fervour that accompanied its adoption of Roman Christianity; the first Irish monks set sail for fabled lands to the northwest. Some were hermits in search of a solitary environment for religious contemplation. Others undoubtedly observed sea birds flying in from the north-west and concluded that countries awaiting Christian enlightenment lay in that direction.

While some of the Irish zealots were settlers, some were merely voyagers. In the early 6th century the Irish abbot St Brendan embarked on a seven year voyage through the region in a *curraugh*, an open skin-boat. Unfortunately, the account of his journey, *Navigatio Sancti Brendani Abbatis*, wasn't written down until the 9th century and the time lapse surely caused some distortion of fact. Although no conclusive proof of his itinerary has been established, his mentions of 'sheep islands', the 'paradise of birds', 'flaming mountains' and 'crystal columns' have been construed as references to the Faroes, Iceland and the Greenland icebergs. Some traditions state (although they are hardly backed by evidence) that St Brendan and later voyagers pushed on to eastern Canada and even made their way up the St Lawrence River toward the North American heartland.

Others brought back to Ireland tales of the land of Thule where there was no daylight in winter, but on summer nights, according to the clergyman Dicuil in 825, 'whatever task a man wishes to perform, even picking lice from his shirt, he can manage as well as in clear daylight'. This almost certainly describes Iceland and its midnight sun.

To the first monks to settle in the Faroes and Iceland (around the year 700), it would have been apparent that the islands were uninhabited and therefore more suitable as a hermitage than a mission. They built monasteries along the coast, and it's likely that some remained in Iceland and the Faroes and mixed with the Norse people who began arriving in the early 9th century. Nordic accounts, however, state that these *papar* ('fathers') fled during the period of Norse settlement.

The Norse

Although much Faroese and Icelandic national pride is derived from notions that they're 'children of the Vikings', most North Atlantic Norse settlers were ordinary Scandinavian citizens: farmers, herders, merchants and opportunists. The reasons for the westward expansion were undoubtedly complex but Scandinavian politics and tyranny, population growth, shipbuilding prowess, commercial potential and even sheer boredom and wanderlust have been cited as catalysts of the Nordic 'explosion' that nurtured both the Viking rampages and the westward migrations.

Icelandic tradition, however, officially credits the Norse settlement of Iceland and the Faroes to a single mainland phenomenon. From the middle to late 9th century, the tyrannical Harald Haarfager (Harald Fine-hair, or Fairhair), the king of Vestfold district of south-eastern Norway, was taken with expansionist aspirations. In 890, he won a significant naval victory at Hafrsfjord (Stavanger), and the deposed chieftains and landowners chose to flee rather than submit. Many wound up in Iceland and the Faroes,

some via the Orkneys and Shetlands, which in turn also fell to the indefatigable King Harald.

Much of Europe at this time was being subjected to Nordic mischief and entrepreneurial spirit. Storming through the British Isles, sacking, looting, plundering and murdering, the Viking hordes struck terror wherever they went and, by the middle of the 9th century, they controlled most coastal regions of Britain and Ireland. Over the next 200 years they raided their way across the continent as far east as the Volga and south to the Mediterranean and north Africa. They might have continued in both directions had King Harald Hardraada (Harald Hard-Ruler) not fallen to the Saxons in 1066.

Throughout the Viking Age (800-1066), violent Norse advances were marked by an exodus into the North Atlantic, not only of Scandinavians but also of Britons, Westmen (Irish) and Scots who had intermarried with the fleeing victims of Nordic despotism. Slaves and kinsfolk also migrated with these mixed families, introducing a heterogeneous stock into Iceland and the Faroes.

The sagas (fact-based literary accounts of the Settlement and subsequent development of these new lands which will be discussed in the Literature section), written down mostly after the Viking Age had passed, have much to say about events in the colonies. The opening lines of the *Færeyingar Saga* are:

There was a man called Grim Kamban. It was he who first colonised the Faroe Islands in the time of Harald Haarfager. There were many people at that time who fled from the tyranny of the King, of whom some settled down in the Faroes and made their abode there; but others sought out other deserted countries.

Another work, the Icelandic *Landnámabók* or *The Book of Settlement*, explains the renaming of Thule far less romantically:

...at a place called Vatnsfjörður on Barðaströnd... the fjord teemed with fish of all kinds ...The spring was extremely cold. Flóki climbed a high mountain and looked north towards the coast, and saw a fjord full of drift-ice; so they called the country Ice-land and that has been its name ever since.

Norse carving   Inuit figurine

Norse Seafaring

Realising the vast distances covered by the early voyagers through difficult seas, one can only wonder what sort of ships and technology the Norse people used to travel so far abroad through uncharted territory.

Archaeological evidence indicates that Viking longboats, low vessels over 30m long, were used primarily in war and raiding. The majority of the settlers travelled in smaller cargo boats called *knerrir* (singular: *knörr*). These sturdy little craft, scarcely 18m in length with little freeboard, were designed to carry great loads. Journeys in them must have been crowded, uncomfortable and often frightening.

Perhaps the most interesting aspect of these early voyages, however, is the method of navigation employed. The sagas mention a mysterious device known as a *solarsteinn* which allowed navigation even when the sky was overcast or the sun was below the horizon and celestial navigation was impossible.

It is now generally agreed that the 'sunstone' was a crystal of cordierite, which is found in Scandinavia and has natural polarising qualities. When observed from below and rotated, light passing through the crystal is polarised blue when the long axis is pointed toward the source of the sunlight.

This same principle is used today. Jet planes flying over the polar regions, where magnetic compasses are unusable and celestial navigation is difficult, use a sky compass which determines the position of the sun by filtering sunlight through an artificial polarising lens. ■

In the *Íslendingabók*, the *Book of the Icelanders*, the earliest settlement of that island is also recounted:

A Norwegian called Ingólfur is reliably reported to have been the first man to leave Norway for Iceland ... He settled in the south, at Reykjavík.

The Settlement of Greenland by the Norse people is dealt with in two works, the *Saga of Eiríkur Rauðe* or *Erik's Saga* and the *Grænlendinga Saga* or *Tale of the Greenlanders*.

The first European contact with Greenland was probably in the 10th century by Norwegian Gunnbjörn Ulfsson. It was first colonised from the east in 982 by Eiríkur Rauðe, an exile from Iceland and a murderer. After bestowing the island's lovely name, which has come to be regarded as the world's first great real-estate scam, he returned to Iceland and enticed 500 other settlers to bring their expertise and livestock and follow him.

They established two settlements, the Østerbygd or 'eastern settlement' on Eiríks Fjord in south Greenland and the Vesturbygd or 'western settlement' several hundred km north near the present-day Greenlandic capital, Nuuk. The *skrælings* (Eskimos) they encountered appeared to be far less advanced than modern archaeology indicates the Thule people were. Based on this, it can be assumed that southern Greenland at the time was inhabited by survivors from earlier Eskimo cultures, who possibly resettled from Labrador or North Greenland at some time before the arrival of the Thule people.

Forays from these two colonies led to the European 'discovery' of Helluland (the 'land of flat stones', probably Baffin Island), Markland (the 'land of woods', most likely Newfoundland or Labrador) and Vinland (the 'land of wine', probably somewhere between Newfoundland and New Jersey). Eiríkur's son, Leif the Lucky, set foot in the New World as early as the year 999. Europeans had reached the Americas, but permanent settlement was thwarted by the skrælings, who were anything but welcoming. For the continuing story on the Nordic presence, see the individual History sections for each country.

Later European Exploration

Between the 13th and 15th centuries, European knowledge of North Atlantic geography extended as far north as Iceland.

Although Europeans had colonised and occupied Greenland in the late 10th century, the place had been effectively forgotten and, unknown to most people, the Greenland colonies had disappeared. On maps, this island was normally represented as a vast peninsula connected to the Scandinavian mainland.

Although fishing boats from the British Isles were already reaping the harvests of Newfoundland at the time, John Cabot's voyage to that coast in 1497 was considered a mission of discovery. Potential colonies and the possible existence of a North-West Passage to the trading grounds of the East Indies were too much for the Britons to ignore. It didn't take long for much of the rest of Europe – the French, Portuguese, Spanish and Italians – to show interest in becoming the first to make something of it.

The Portuguese, suspecting that Cabot's landfall may have been east of the Pope's line of demarcation (making it Portuguese territory), sent João Fernandes, a *lavrador* or private landholder, to determine its position. In 1500, he happened instead upon southern Greenland, which he modestly named Lavrador, after himself. Later, a confused cartographer evidently shifted the name south-westward to present-day Labrador. For more on later attempts to navigate the presumed North-West Passage, see History in the Facts about Greenland chapter.

GEOGRAPHY

Iceland, Greenland and the Faroe Islands all lie in the North Atlantic Ocean, north-west of Europe and north-east of the North American mainland.

Iceland is just south of the Arctic Circle, roughly three-quarters of the distance from New York to London along the Great Circle Route, while the 18 main islands of the Faroes lie about halfway between Iceland and Scotland. Greenland, the most northerly country in the world, sits midway between Iceland and the Canadian Arctic archipelago.

GEOLOGY

Overall, the character of the North Atlantic landscape is steep and rugged, but its geology displays the most spectacular chronological range on earth. The planet's oldest rocks – up to 3.7 billion years old – are found in the mountains around Nuuk, in south-west Greenland. On the other end of the scale, the Icelandic lava fields continue to grow as numerous volcanoes spew new material fresh from deep within the earth.

In 1620, Sir Francis Bacon glanced at the most recent map of the Atlantic region and noticed that the eastern coast of South America and the western coast of Africa seemed to fit together like bits of a jigsaw puzzle. This curiosity has now been conclusively ascribed to plate tectonics, which describes the lateral motion of continents on 'plates' of the earth's crust.

The theory attributes plate movement to the creation and destruction of crust along plate boundaries. In zones of thin or weak crust, molten rock (magma) from deep within the earth forces its way upward, spreading the surface plates apart. To compensate, deep-sea trenches form on opposite plate boundaries where one plate is forced to slide beneath another and is destroyed by heat. Most of the earth's vulcanism and seismic activity occur, not surprisingly, on or very near these plate boundaries.

Running the length of the Atlantic Ocean from north to south, the 18,000 km Mid-Atlantic Ridge is one such boundary. Activity along it cause the plates containing North America and Eurasia to move apart at a rate of several cm a year.

In hot spots along the ridge, islands occur. The largest and most notable is Iceland, cleanly cut into north-west and south-east halves by the resulting system of fissures and volcanoes. This zone is so active that one-third of all the lava to surface on earth in the last 1000 years is of Icelandic origin. The youngest rocks lie along this rift zone while the east and west coasts are up to 16 million years old.

The Faroe Islands are eroded remains of an old volcanic plateau of the Mid-Atlantic Ridge, subsequently forced away from it as part of the Eurasian plate.

Greenland, on the other hand, consists

Glacier & Ice Glossary

Glaciers and icecaps dominate much of the scene in Iceland and Greenland. The following is a list of terms relating to these icy phenomena:

arête – a sharp ridge between two valley glaciers

bergschrund – the crevasse at the top of a valley glacier separating the moving ice from the parent icefield

bergy bits – icebergs rising less than five metres above the surface of the sea

calving – breaking off of icebergs from tidewater glaciers

cirque – an amphitheatre scoured out by a glacier

crevasse – a fissure in moving ice caused by various strains which may be hidden under snow

dead glacier – a valley glacier that stops short of the sea

erratic – a stone or boulder which clearly was transported from somewhere else, possibly by a glacier

fast ice – solid pack ice

firn limit – the highest level on a glacier to which the snow melts each year. The snow that remains above this limit is called *firn*.

frazil – needle-shaped ice crystals which form a slush in the sea

glacial flour – the fine, talcum-like silt that flows in glacial streams and is deposited in glacial river valleys. It is formed by abrasion of ice on rock.

growler – small iceberg which is difficult to see, floating just on the surface, thereby causing a hazard to boats

hanging valley – a valley formed when a tributary valley glacier flows into a larger valley glacier

horn – the sharp peak that remains after glaciers have scoured all faces of a mountain

hummock – place where ice floes have piled atop one another

icecap or *icefield* – a stable zone of accumulation and compression of snow and ice and a source of valley glaciers. An icecap generally covers a larger area than an icefield. When the entire interior of a landmass is covered by an icecap (as in Greenland or Antarctica), it's known as a *continental glacier*.

ice floe – a flat chunk of floating sea-ice, normally pack ice, but it may also refer to a small iceberg

jökulhlaup – a sudden and often catastrophic release of water from a glacier caused by a broken ice dam or by glacial lifting due to volcanic activity beneath the ice

moraine – deposit of material transported by a glacier. Rock and silt pushed ahead of the glacier is called a *terminal moraine*, that deposited along the sides is a *lateral moraine*, and in the centre of a glacier, it's called a *medial moraine*.

moulin – a pond or a stream inside a glacier, often evidenced by a deep round hole in the ice

névé – hard granular snow on the upper part of a glacier that hasn't yet turned to ice

nilas – thin crust of sea-ice that moves up and down with wave motion but doesn't break

nunatak – a mountain peak that protrudes through a glacier or icecap

pack ice – floating ice formed by frozen seawater, which often creates an impenetrable barrier to navigation

piedmont glacier – a slumped glacier at the foot of a steep slope caused by the confluence of two or more valley glaciers

polynya – area of open water surrounded by pack ice

postholing – what hikers do when crossing fields of melting snow, sinking up to their thighs on every step

roche moutonée – a glacier-scoured boulder, so named because they often look like sheep grazing on the mountainsides

sastrugi – wind-blown furrows in snow

suncup – mushroom-shaped snow formation caused by irregular melting on sunny slopes

tarn – a lake in a cirque

tide crack – a crack separating sea-ice from the shore, caused by rise and fall of the tide

tidewater glacier – a valley glacier that flows into the sea and calves icebergs

valley glacier – a river of ice which flows downward through a valley from an icefield or icecap ■

mostly of rock first deposited as sediment very early in the Earth's history. Subsequent forces of heat, vulcanism, ice, pressure, weathering and plate motion have tortured and drastically altered both the shape and structure of the land. Most of coastal Greenland today is comprised of gneiss and marble (metamorphosed granite and limestone) and several types of true granite. Due to a pronounced lack of topsoil and vegetation, dramatic evidence of crustal folding and fracturing is evident on the surface.

Glaciers & Ice

Much of the North Atlantic landscape has been carved and shaped by rivers of ice flowing down from permanent icecaps. Icecaps are formed as snow piles up over millennia in an area where it's never allowed to melt. It's slowly compressed, from bottom to top, into ice. When the weight of the ice becomes so great that the underlying land cannot support it, the land beneath the centre compresses and the ice around the edges begins to flow downward in glaciers – rivers of ice – which may reach the sea and form icebergs.

Beginning three million years ago, during the Pleistocene epoch, the northern hemisphere experienced a Great Ice Age. On Greenland, it left a vast continental icecap measuring 2500 km from north to south, 1000 km from east to west and up to three km thick. Its great weight has caused the island's surface to sink to over 3000m below sea level; without this burden, the island would resemble an immense bowl. In fact, there's so much water in the Greenland icecap that if it were to melt, sea level would rise by at least six metres.

On the other hand, only parts of Iceland's icecap remain. They weren't formed during the Great Ice Age but in a cool period beginning 2500 years ago, and today cover only about 10% of the country. The largest, Vatnajökull, covers 8000 sq km. The Faroe Islands, which were subject to glaciation in the past, are now ice-free. See also the glossary of terms aside.

CLIMATE

The North Atlantic has the reputation of having an unpleasant climate, which it almost lives up to. While Iceland and the Faroes aren't as cold as their latitudes might suggest and some fine days can be expected at any time of year, the weather could be described as fickle at best.

Due to the Gulf Stream and the prevailing south-westerly winds which carry warm tropical air and moisture northward, the stormiest conditions are found in the Faroe Islands and the southern and western coasts of Iceland. However, Iceland and the Faroes enjoy mild temperatures year round. In January, the daily mean temperature in Reykjavík is 1°C and in July, it's 11°C. At Tórshavn, the average January and July tem-

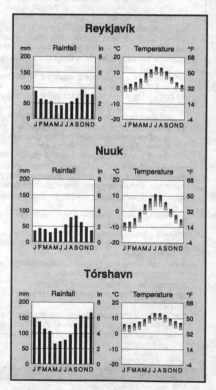

peratures are 3°C and 11°C, respectively. Although Greenland and the Icelandic interior experience more dramatic temperature variations, they enjoy much more stable weather conditions.

In Greenland, which is not affected by the Gulf Stream, summer daytime average temperatures range from -5°C in the north to 20°C in the south. During the winter, temperatures of -50°C and lower are not uncommon, although the far south may only occasionally experience such extreme cold. These periods of high pressure, dominated by the polar continental air mass, bring the calmest and clearest weather in the North Atlantic.

ECOLOGY & ENVIRONMENT

In North Atlantic countries, it's possible to be environmentally conscious without really trying. Iceland, Greenland and the Faroes have small populations, little heavy industry and a lot of wind to blow away anything that might taint the fresh, clean air.

The most populous country, Iceland, has the added advantage of ample natural geothermal and hydroelectric energy, which means that the use of nuclear power or fossil fuels is unnecessary for the generation of heat or electricity.

One of the greatest environmental concerns in Iceland at present is the erosion caused by overgrazing of sheep, which chew vegetation down to the roots and expose the underlying soil to the forces of water and the fierce winds. In parts of the country, particularly around lake Mývatn, the results are most dramatic; the typically high winds create growing patches of scarred silt between platforms and tussocks of grass and tundra. There have been attempts to control the problem by limiting the numbers of sheep allowed on affected land, but it's too soon to know whether they're working.

Due to the low populations, small markets for recycled products and high transport costs, substantial recycling programmes aren't yet viable in the region. However, in Greenland and the Faroes, beer and soft drinks are available almost exclusively in returnable bottles, which are collected and shipped off to Denmark for re-use. In Iceland and the Faroes, rubbish is trucked well out of sight, while in Greenland, what doesn't wind up on the ground or in the wind, the streams or the sea is taken to large dumps and burnt.

For some guidelines visitors can use to help minimise their own environmental impact, see the Minimum Impact Camping section (under Camping) in the Iceland Facts for the Visitor chapter. For details on North Atlantic attitudes toward wildlife and hunting, see the following sections of the book: the Grindadráp aside in Facts About the Faroe Islands chapter; the Whaling Issue aside in the Facts About Iceland chapter; Relation to Nature in the Arts & Culture section of the Facts About Greenland chapter; and Traditional Foods in the Greenland Facts for the Visitor chapter.

ARCTIC PHENOMENA
The Aurora Borealis

There are few sights as mesmerising as an undulating aurora. Although these appear in many forms – pillars, streaks, wisps and haloes of vibrating light – they're most memorable when they appear as pale curtains wafting on a gentle breeze. Most often, the Arctic aurora appears as a faint green or light rose but, in periods of extreme activity, can change to yellow or crimson.

The visible aurora borealis, or northern lights (in the southern hemisphere they're called aurora australis), are caused by streams of charged particles from the sun, the solar winds, flowing past and elongating the earth's magnetic field in the polar regions. Because the field curves downward in a halo surrounding the magnetic poles, the charged particles are drawn earthward. Their interaction with electrons in nitrogen and oxygen atoms in the upper atmosphere (about 160 km above the surface) releases the energy creating the visible aurora. During periods of high activity, a single auroral storm can produce a trillion watts of electricity with a current of one million amps.

The Inuit call the lights *arsarnerit* ('to

play with a ball') as they were thought to be ancestors playing ball with a walrus skull. It was believed that the lights could be attracted by whistling or repelled by barking like a dog! They also attach spiritual significance to the lights, and some believe that they represent the capering of unborn children; some consider them gifts from the dead to light the long polar nights and others believe they're a storehouse of events past and future.

Although science dismisses it as imagination, most people report that the aurora is often accompanied by a crackling or whirring sound. Don't feel unbalanced if you hear it; it may be imaginary – that's the sort of sound you'd *expect* to hear during such a dramatic display – but as an Alaskan, I'll vouch that it's a very convincing illusion.

The best time of year to catch the northern lights in the North Atlantic is from October to March, although you may also see them as early as August in South Greenland. North Greenland is actually too far north to catch the most dramatic activity.

Fata Morgana & Mirages

If the aurora inspires wonder, the Fata Morgana and related phenomena common in the polar regions may inspire a visit to a psychiatrist. The clear and pure Arctic air does not cause distant features to appear out of focus. As a result, depth perception becomes impossible and the world takes on a strangely two-dimensional aspect where distances are indeterminable. An amusing example of distance distortion is described in the enigmatic book *Arctic Dreams*, by Barry Lopez:

A Swedish explorer had all but completed a written description in his notebook of a craggy headland with two unusually symmetrical valley glaciers, the whole of it a part of a large island, when he discovered what he was looking at was a walrus.

Fata Morgana, a special type of mirage, is also common in the vast expanses of sand, ice and tundra found in the Arctic. Early explorers laid down on maps and charts

careful documentation of islands, headlands and mountain ranges that were never seen again.

Fata Morganas are apparently caused by reflections off water, ice and snow, and when combined with temperature inversions, create the illusion of solid, well-defined features where there are none. On clear days along the *sandur* of northern Iceland, you'll often see non-existent archipelagos of craggy islands resting on the horizon. It's difficult indeed to convince yourself, even with an accurate map, that they aren't really there!

Also unsettling are the sightings of ships, large cities and forests where there could clearly be none. Normal visibility at sea is just under 18 km but, in the Arctic, sightings of islands and features hundreds of kilometres distant are frequently reported.

Midnight Sun & Polar Night

Because the earth is tilted on its axis, the polar regions are constantly facing the sun at their respective summer solstices and are tilted away from it in the winter. The Arctic and Antarctic circles, at $66\frac{1}{2}°$ north and south latitude respectively, are the southern and northern limits of constant daylight on the longest day of the year.

In the North Atlantic, the northern three quarters of Greenland and part of the Icelandic island of Grímsey lie north of the Arctic Circle but in regions immediately to the south, including Iceland and the Faroes, the summer sun is never far below the horizon. Between May and early August, no place in the region experiences true darkness. In northern Iceland, for example, the first stars aren't visible until mid-August. Although many visitors initially find it difficult to sleep while the sun is shining brightly outside, most people quickly get used to it, even if that simply means joining the locals in their summer nocturnal hyperactivity.

Conversely, winters here are dark and dreary with only a few hours of twilight to break the long polar night. In northern Greenland, not even a twilight glow can be seen for several weeks in December and most communities make a ritual of formally welcoming the sun the first time it peeks above the southern horizon. In Iceland, the depression which accompanies the long, dark nights is known as *skammdegis-þunglyndi*.

RELIGION

Inuit Religion

The Inuit people may have believed that Europeans were the product of a union between Inuit women and dogs, but that didn't prevent them accepting the outsiders' relatively simplistic religion. South Greenland was converted to Christianity over two centuries ago and most of the rest of Greenland had converted by the early 20th century. However, Greenlanders still adhere to certain aspects of their traditional shamanistic religion, especially in times of hardship.

Even before Christianity arrived, the Inuit believed in the existence of an all-pervading soul or a 'breath', that survived death. The souls of those whose bodies lay on the earth were relegated to the cold and unpleasant sky, while those who were thrown into the sea lived underground in warm, rich hunting grounds. The Middle Eastern notion that hell is a hot place must have inspired both amusement and confusion in Arctic dwellers!

Early Inuit religion was also characterised by belief in familiar spirits who helped or hindered individuals. The Inuit did not fear death but they did fear the *toornot*, the spirits of the dead; the *tupilat*, the hideous creatures that populate nightmares; and the *qivittoq*, the glacier spirits which could take possession of a person who reported seeing one.

Hunters believed that the earth and its creatures should be treated with respect, believing not that a successful hunter had conquered an animal, but that the animal had willingly sacrificed its life. Success in hunting was monitored by a water spirit, an old woman who sat by the shore and would punish blundering humans by combing her hair over the surface of the water, thus preventing seals from surfacing. The services of an *angaqqoq*, or shaman, were required to rectify the problem.

The Inuit also lived in fear of upsetting the *sila*, the delicate natural balance of the universe. For example, to kill an animal that had been inhabited by a *toornoq* (singular of 'toornot') would indicate such a blunder, and only with the death of the hunter could the balance be restored.

Regarding the mourning of the dead, all sorts of taboos had to be followed to the letter, lest the deceased return to administer justice to the guilty party. They also believed justice was inevitable for anyone who had mistreated or dealt badly with that person when he or she was still alive. Those living in fear of the wrath of the dead often became withdrawn, depressed and even suicidal.

Menstruating and pregnant women were also expected to follow a rather oppressive code of behaviour. Women who had miscarried or borne children prematurely were forbidden for a year to mention animals or wear boots while eating. They could not sleep with their husband, nor report the presence of strangers with their voice. All these restrictions were observed in order to appease spirits and thereby preserve balance.

Sickness was often attributed to the presence of *perlussuaq*, an evil spirit which took possession of respiration and upset balance. Medical treatment was fairly simple; the angaqqoq would examine the patient, then determine whether they would live or die. Those who were pronounced doomed simply gave up hope and died. Others followed the angaqqoq's prescriptions, which almost invariably involved eating, sleeping, sexual habits and payment for medical services.

Norse Religion

If you've studied European mythology (or read a few *Hagar the Horrible* comic strips), you'll be familiar with the pantheon of Norse deities. Although there were many gods and godlike beings, the Norse trinity consisted of Þór, to most Icelanders the king of the gods; Óðinn, the god of war and poetry; and Freyr, the god of fertility and sensuous pleasure.

Óðinn was the patron god of the Viking hordes and the *skáld* ('court poet'). He was

Ásatrú – An Ancient Religion Reborn

Ásatrú, which means 'faith in the Æsir', the gods of pre-Christian Scandinavia, has its origins in the ancient religions of most Germanic peoples – Goths, Germans, Dutch, Frisian, Anglo-Saxons, etc – and also appears as far away as India, as described in the *Rig Veda*. The medieval Icelandic text, the *Galdrabók*, reveals that people were calling upon the Æsir long after Christianity was adopted by most Germanic peoples. As late as the 1800s, the Lapps (Saami) people openly worshipped the god Þor, to whom they'd been introduced by their Scandinavian neighbours in the pre-Christian period.

Modern Ásatrú, which is open to anyone, regardless of race, ethnic origin or sexual orientation, was organised in the 1970s, almost simultaneously in Iceland, the USA and the UK.

The main gods and goddesses of Ásatrú, which are all considered friendly, practicable, dependable and approachable, include Þor, the god of thunder and friend of the common folk; Oðinn (or Allfather), the chief god, poet and wandering wizard; Tyr, the god of war and justice; Ingvi Frey, the god of peace, fertility and nature (the British images of the 'Green Man' are likely linked to Freyr); Baldur, the bleeding god; Heimdall, the Watchman of Ásgard; Frigga, wife of Oðinn and mother of all the gods and humanity; Freya, the goddess of fertility, love, magic and war; Idunna, the goddess of renewal; Hela, who rules over the place between death and rebirth or reincarnation; Nerthus, the Mother Earth goddess, who is mentioned in Tacitus' *Germania*. Followers also revere the spirits of nature *(landvættir)* and various guardian spirits, such as the Disir and Alfar (elves).

The two main rituals of Ásatrú are *blót*, or 'sacrifice', and *sumbel*, the 'toast'. While scholars debate whether or not the former is derived from *blóð*, or 'blood', modern Ásatrú followers sacrifice mead (honey-wine), beer or cider. The liquid is consecrated to the god or goddess being honoured, and drinking a portion of it signifies communion with that particular deity. The rest is poured out as a libation. The sumbel, a ritualised toasting to the gods, is made in three rounds. The first goes to the god Oðinn, who won the mead of poetry from the Giant Suttung. It's also wise to pour a few drops for Loki, the trickster, to ward off nasty surprises. The second round is to the ancestors and honourable dead, and the third round is open to whoever one wishes to honour.

Magical work is a part of the spiritual life of many practitioners of Ásatrú. Magic involves working with natural but unseen forces, including those embodied in the runes, the early Germanic alphabet, as well as the *galdra* (spellcraft) and *seiðr* (shamanism). Magic can help foresee the probable course of events, effect healing and assist us in our endeavours, but is no substitute for more down-to-earth methods.

While devoid of rigid dogma, Ásatrú is by no means amoral. It is in fact founded on the Nine Noble Virtues: courage, truth, honour, loyalty, hospitality, industriousness, perseverance, self-discipline and self-reliance. From these, individuals can decide upon the appropriate course of action in any situation and honour themselves, their families, their communities and their gods by striving to do what is right. The gods organised the universe from chaotic material (represented by the body of the dead giant Ymir). The remaining chaos allows for a random factor, which helps the universe to keep evolving. Not even the gods are all-powerful, so perfection is neither required nor respected!

Writings which are held in high esteem include the medieval Icelandic texts, the Elder (Poetic) and Younger (Prose) Eddas, although their myths are not interpreted literally. For a scholarly outline of Ásatrú, see *Myth & Religion of the North* by EOG Turville-Petre; *Teutonic Religion* and *Teutonic Magic*, by Kveldulf Gundarsson (Llewellyn Publications, PO Box 64383-K069, St Paul, MN 55164, USA); or any of the several works on the subject by HR Ellis Davidson. For further information on Ásatrú, check out the Ásatrú newsletter 'The Update', 1200 Madison, Box 657, Denver, CO 80206, USA; call up the Internet website users.aol.com/jordsvin/kindred/kindred.htm; or contact one of the following:

Reverend Patrick Jörðsvín Buck, Assistant goði, Hammerstead Kindred, PO Box 22379, Lexington, KY 40522-2379, USA (email: jordsvin@aol.com)
Jenny Blain, 1075 Wellington St, Halifax, Nova Scotia B3H 3A1, Canada
Yves Kodratoff, Bat A1, Vignes de Bures, F-91940 Les Ulis, France
Heidenische Gemeinschaft, Postfach 442, D-12114 Berlin, Germany
Jón Ingvar Jónsson, Storhólt 33, 105 Reykjavík, Iceland
Ring of Troth, PO Box 415, Flushing, NY 11358, USA

Reverend Patrick Jörðsvín Buck

traditionally depicted as a brooding and intimidating presence, the one who doled out both victory in battle and literary talent.

On the mainland, where Óðinn was the highest-ranking deity, but in Iceland, Greenland and the Faroes – which were less concerned with war and raiding – Þór took precedence. This rowdy and rather slow-minded god of the common people controlled thunder, wind, storm, and natural disaster, and fended off malevolent outsiders. He was depicted as a burly, red-haired, red-bearded dolt (in a film he'd be played by Arnold Schwarzenegger!) who rumbled through the heavens in a goat-drawn chariot.

Freyr and his twin sister Freyja, the children of the sea god Njörður, served as the god and goddess of fertility and sexuality. Freyr was the one who brought springtime with its romantic implications to both the human and animal world and was in charge of the perpetuation of all species.

The Icelandic congregation was formerly led by the late skald, sheep-farmer and *allsherjagoði* (supreme chieftan), Sveinbjörn Beinteinsson, who died in 1995.

Christianity

According to *Færeyingar Saga*, which was written in Iceland in the 13th century, the Faroe Islands officially converted to Christianity around the year 1000 and the first bishopric was set up at Kirkjubøur on the island of Streymoy. Due to the scanty accounts of this period, however, little is known about the conversion or the church administration there.

In Iceland, the sagas provide a great deal of information about the early religious state. Before the official conversion by government decree, there were quite a few Christians living in the country, most of them immigrants from the British Isles and the Orkneys.

The story of Iceland's first Christian mission, which was organised by a farm boy from Stóra-Giljá, is fancifully recounted in the *Tale of Þorvaldur Far-Farer*. Þorvaldur, a sort of Nordic Robin Hood, was a Viking mercenary who donated all his plunder to the poor. He became a Christian in Germany and persuaded Bishop Frederick of Saxony to return with him to Iceland and bring the gospel to the Icelanders.

True to saga form, the Bishop was beset with protests from the incumbent Icelandic deities. Icelanders accused him of homosexuality and forced him to go home. Þorvaldur left Iceland on a pilgrimage to Jerusalem and went from there to Constantinople where he was appointed overlord to the kings of Russia by the Byzantine emperor.

In the late 10th century Denmark peacefully became Christian, but Norway's conversion was quite another story. In 994, during the siege of London, the ruthless Viking prince Olaf Tryggvason, who aspired to the throne of Norway, accepted the new religion. Upon his return home, he usurped power and mercilessly threatened and tortured his subjects into wholesale conversion. He then turned to his next conversion project, Iceland, where several people who resisted were declared criminals and sentenced to execution. However, some Icelandic Christians successfully pleaded for another chance for their pagan countryfolk.

Traditionally, the date of the decree that officially converted Iceland to Christianity has been given as 1000, but research has determined that it probably occurred in 999 and was a political decision. In the Icelandic *Alþing* (parliament) the Christians and pagans had been polarising into two radically opposite factions, threatening to divide the country politically if not geographically. In the session of 999, Þorgeir the Law-speaker appealed for moderation on both sides in the interest of national unity.

In the *Íslendingabók*, the account of the early Icelanders, Ari the Learned (Ari Þorgilsson) writes:

It was...decreed that everyone...should be Christian, and that those who had not yet been baptised should receive baptism.

But the old laws should stand...Also, people could make sacrifices (to the old gods) in private if they wished to, but sacrificing would be subject to a criminal sentence if it were done in public before witnesses...

Greenland's conversion by Danish missionaries happened relatively recently. In 1728, the 'Greenland Apostle' Hans Egede set up a mission and trading station in Godthåb (Nuuk). His mission and that of a rival church, the Moravian Mission, began operating in 1733 and were enormously successful in converting the Greenlanders.

Hans Egede left Greenland in 1736 after his wife, Gertrude Rask, died in an epidemic. His efforts there, however, had toppled the first domino and, 200 years later, all of Greenland was Christianised.

Today, as in mainland Scandinavia, all three North Atlantic countries officially belong to the Protestant Lutheran church.

Regional Facts for the Visitor

PLANNING
What to Bring

The amount of stuff you'll need to carry on a North Atlantic trip will be determined by your budget and your intended activities. Those who want to travel cheaply will unfortunately need to load themselves down with a lot of things that more upmarket travellers won't need to worry about – a good case for bringing a vehicle where applicable. Under ideal circumstances, such things as tents, stoves and cooking implements can be divided among members of a group, but lone travellers may find themselves struggling beneath a good deal of weight.

Some general items which will be required by almost everyone (except those staying in hotels and eating in restaurants) include a synthetic-fibre sleeping bag preferably rated to at least -10°C; a Swiss army-style knife; a towel; a torch (flashlight); a water bottle (at least one litre); lighters or waterproof matches; a couple of thick paperbacks to read during inclement weather (English-language books are very expensive in Iceland and the Faroes and practically unavailable in Greenland); a copy of medical and optical prescriptions; and any film or camera equipment that may be needed.

Clothing Warm clothing will be of utmost importance to everyone. Given the range of weather possibilities (yes, including warm and sunny!), the layering method seems to work best.

The items on the following list should be sufficient to keep you comfortable anywhere in the region between May and September (winter travellers will obviously need to prepare for severe Arctic conditions):

- thermal underwear made of polypropylene or similar material
- several pairs of thick wool and/or polypro socks
- heavy windproof ski gloves
- high-protection sunglasses
- wool hat with ear protection
- a T-shirt or two
- at least one woollen pullover
- hiking shorts (canvas or polyester)
- wool shirt and trousers (jeans are comfortable when dry, but cumbersome and uncomfortable when wet!)
- windproof and waterproof jacket and trousers – Gore Tex may not provide sufficient protection. As disagreeable as it can be, light treated nylon is probably better, although it can trap sweat and cause chills when removed.
- strong hiking shoes with ankle support or (preferably) boots
- swimsuit – Iceland has numerous hot springs and thermally heated swimming pools. Greenland has hot springs as well.

Camping Equipment Apart from the previously mentioned sleeping bag, campers should carry:

- a tent – easily assembled (due to wind), sturdy, waterproofed and preferably free-standing. It's a good idea to get one with some kind of annexe (vestibule) outside for storage of wet clothing, boots and cooking implements.
- a light stove and aluminium fuel bottle – a Peak II, an MSR mountain stove, a Whisperlite or other multi-fuel stove, or an alcohol stove would be preferable to butane stoves which are rather unstable and don't work well in wind. In Greenland, butane cartridges are very hard to come by.
- cooking pots, cups and utensils – a nesting kit is probably the best way to go if you want to keep weight and volume to a minimum.
- waterproof ground cover or space blanket

If you plan on trekking, add the following items:

- gaiters
- compass and magnetic deviation figures – this is vital in the far north since deviation from magnetic north in the region can be as high as 80°
- fishing line, hook and lures (especially for Greenland)
- medical kit (see Health section)
- applicable maps

VISAS & DOCUMENTS
Passport
All overseas visitors – apart from citizens of Scandinavia – must carry a current passport from their country of citizenship, which must be produced when changing currency at banks or hotels. Visa details are provided in the Facts for the Visitor chapters for the individual countries.

Photocopies
When it comes to passports, identification and other valuable documents, it's wise to prepare for the worst. Even if your passport is registered with your embassy, keep separate records of your passport number and issue date, and photocopies of the pages with the passport number, name, photograph, place issued and expiration date. It's also wise to have copies of visas and your birth certificate, if possible.

While you're compiling that information, also photocopy your travellers' cheque receipt slips, health and travel insurance policies and addresses, personal contact addresses, credit card numbers and airline tickets and keep all that material separate from your passport and money.

Travel Insurance
All travellers should consider buying a travel insurance policy, which will provide some sense of security in the case of a medical emergency or the loss or theft of money or belongings. It may seem an expensive luxury, but if you can't afford a travel health insurance policy, you probably can't afford a medical emergency abroad, either. Travel health insurance policies (see under Health in this chapter) can normally be extended to include baggage, flight departure insurance and a range of other options. It's sensible to buy your policy as early as possible. If you wait until the week of departure, you may find, for example, that you're not covered for delays caused by industrial action.

Some policies are very good value, but to find them, you'll have to do a great deal of shopping around. Long-term or frequent travellers can generally find something for under US$200 per year, but these will normally be from a general business insurance company rather than one specialising in travel. Note, however, that such inexpensive policies may exclude travel to the USA (where health care costs are extremely high) and may offer very limited baggage protection. Always read the fine print!

When you do need to make a claim on your travel insurance, you must produce proof of the value of any items lost or stolen (purchase receipts are best). In the case of medical claims, you'll need detailed medical reports and receipts for amounts paid. If you're claiming on a trip cancelled by circumstances beyond your control (illness, airline bankruptcy, industrial action, etc), you must produce all flight tickets purchased, tour agency receipts and itinerary and proof of whatever glitch caused your trip to be cancelled.

If you're taking an organised tour, the company will normally encourage you to purchase their own travel insurance policy, which may or may not be a good deal. Bear in mind that some unscrupulous companies – particularly in Europe – manage to keep their tour prices low and appealing by requiring overpriced travel insurance as part of the package.

Driving Licence
Car hire agencies in Iceland and the Faroes will accept your home driving licence.

MONEY
Costs
Because just about everything must be imported, food, accommodation and transport prices in the North Atlantic are high – only Japan depletes travel budgets faster than Iceland. While expense-account travellers or anyone happy to drop US$500 a day will find joy, those with lesser means who want a stress-free North Atlantic holiday will have to put in some effort.

The lowest average price for a single hotel room in Reykjavík or Tórshavn, for example, is US$90; in Nuuk you'll pay from US$110 to $170, while hotels in smaller

Greenlandic towns average around US$100. A restaurant meal in Iceland, Greenland or the Faroes, typically including some sort of meat or fish dish, a soup or a salad, a spoonful of tinned vegies and a potato or two, will average US$12 to $20. Bus travel in Iceland costs about US$10 per hour; a 15 minute domestic flight in Greenland may cost up to US$200, and fares on certain domestic routes break the US$1000 mark!

In Iceland and the Faroes, if you can forego some comforts and sleep in youth hostels, eat at snack bars and travel on bus passes, you can probably keep expenses down to around US$35 per day. Rock-bottom budget travel in the North Atlantic is only possible with near total exposure to the elements. To get by on less than US$10 to $15 per day, you'll have to camp (at least part of the time away from organised sites), cook your own meals and hitchhike, cycle or walk vast distances. In roadless Greenland, youth hostels and snack-bar meals cost only slightly more than in Iceland, but it's impossible to avoid the high transportation costs short of bringing your own sea kayak or just concentrating on only one area (getting around on foot or on short-haul ferry routes).

Europeans bringing a private vehicle to Iceland or the Faroes, especially a campervan or caravan, can enjoy a bit more comfort and still keep within a reasonable budget. Petrol prices are around US$1.20 per litre, but the sting of fuel costs may be minimised by sharing rides and expenses with other travellers.

In most cases, holders of student cards are entitled to discounts on entrance fees and some transport fares. In Iceland, students and holders of Iceland bus passes receive 10% discount on campground fees, ferries and sometimes even hotel and restaurant charges. These discounts aren't advertised, so it pays to ask in each case.

Tipping
Tipping is not required anywhere in the North Atlantic. Finer restaurants automatically add a service charge to the bill, but those who may feel compelled to tip for particularly good or friendly service will not be refused.

PHOTOGRAPHY & VIDEO
Photographers worldwide sing the praises of the magical Arctic light. The crystalline air combined with the long, red rays cast by a low sun create excellent effects on film. Add spectacular scenery and colourful human aspects and you have a photographer's paradise. There are quite a few tour companies that offer photography tours and instruction, so check with your travel agent or a tourist office if you're interested.

Film and photographic equipment and camera repairs, especially in Iceland, are quite expensive so it would be wise to bring a supply from home (twice as much as you plan to need!) and try to use restraint in the face of celluloid-swallowing scenery.

Film is readily available only during shopping hours in Reykjavík, Akureyri, Tórshavn and several towns in Greenland. In smaller towns and villages supplies and variety of film will be limited. Film processing is available in Iceland and the Faroes but, for Kodachrome and other films requiring specialised processing, wait until you get home.

Due to the clear Arctic light and glare from water, ice and snow, photographers may want to use a UV filter or a skylight filter and a lens shade. In the winter, especially in Greenland, mechanical cameras should be polar oiled so the mechanism doesn't freeze up. In temperatures below about -20°C, electronic cameras may fail altogether.

As usual, subjects for interesting people-pictures are to be found throughout the region and most individuals will enjoy being photographed. As a courtesy, however, it's a good idea to ask before snapping away.

Especially in Greenland, since much of your sightseeing will be done aboard ship and since wildlife normally keeps its distance, it's a good idea to bring a telephoto or zoom lens if you hope for any recognisable shots. Conversely, there will also be plenty of opportunities in all three countries to use a wide-angle 28 mm lens for broad vistas, dramatic skies and urban landscapes.

TIME
The following charts show the time differences (in hours) between the North Atlantic countries and London, New York, Los Angeles and Sydney. The time changes normally take place around the 25th of October and March.

From 25 October to 24 March

	London	NY	LA	Sydney
Greenland	+2	-2	-5	+14
Iceland	0	-5	-8	+11
Faroes	0	-5	-8	+11

From 25 March to 24 October

	London	NY	LA	Sydney
Greenland	+3	-3	-6	+13
Iceland	+1	-4	-7	+10
Faroes	+1	-5	-8	+9

ELECTRICITY
Outlets in the North Atlantic are 220V, 50 cycles AC, so North American appliances will require a transformer. Prongs on foreign equipment may also have to be adapted before they can be used. In the Faroes, most plugs have two round pins and in Iceland, either two round pins or two slanted prongs.

The only exceptions are in Greenland, around the US base at Thule (Pituffik) and the former US base at Kangerlussuaq, where the voltage is 110V.

HEALTH
North Atlantic residents enjoy one of the world's most pollution-free environments and healthiest – although admittedly often unpleasant – climates. Combine these factors with their excellent health-care systems and you come up with an average lifespan in Iceland of 80.3 years for women and 75.7 years for men, the second greatest in the world (the healthy Japanese average 81 years for women and 78 years for men).

Travellers face few health hazards in the North Atlantic, and anyone who does suffer an injury or get sick during their visit should have no problem finding high-quality medical assistance – provided they aren't stuck in the wilderness somewhere.

Travel Health Insurance
Iceland and the Faroe Islands have reciprocal health-care agreements; these also extend to citizens of the UK, Norway, Denmark, Finland and Sweden, entitling them to free health care. Local rates for ambulance services and prescriptions still apply. Citizens of other countries only pay minimal charges for medical services and non-discounted rates on prescriptions.

Greenland extends free health care to everyone, regardless of citizenship, but dental care is not included and prescription medicines may be unavailable in smaller towns and villages.

Even for those who are entitled to free treatment, it's a good idea to take out a travel insurance policy to cover theft, loss and medical problems. There is a wide variety of policies available and your travel agent will make recommendations. The international student travel policies handled by STA Travel or other student travel organisations are usually good value. Some policies offer lower and higher medical expenses options but the higher one is chiefly for countries like the USA with extremely high medical costs.

- Some policies specifically exclude 'dangerous activities' which can include mountain climbing, motorcycling and even trekking. If these activities are on your agenda, you don't want that sort of policy.
- You may prefer a policy which pays doctors or hospitals directly rather than requiring you to pay now and claim later. If you do have to claim later, make sure you keep all documentation. Some policies ask you to call back (reverse charges) to a centre in your home country where an immediate assessment of your problem is made.
- Check if the policy covers ambulances or an emergency flight home. If you have to stretch out, you will need more than one seat and somebody will have to pay for it!

Medical Kit
Especially for those who plan to venture

away from roads and populated areas, it is wise to carry a small, straightforward medical kit. A suggested kit list includes:

- paracetamol (called acetominophen in North America) tablets for pain or fever
- antihistamine (such as Benadryl) – useful as a decongestant for colds, allergies, to ease the itch from insect bites or stings or to help prevent motion sickness
- antibiotics – useful if you are travelling in the wilderness but they must be prescribed and you should carry the prescription with you
- kaolin and pectin preparation and Imodium or Lomotil for bouts of giardia or stomach upset. Imodium and Lomotil should only be used in emergency situations, such as when you are suffering from diarrhoea and must travel for long periods on public transport.
- rehydration mixture – for treatment of severe diarrhoea. This is particularly important if travelling with children.
- antiseptic, mercurochrome and antibiotic powder or similar 'dry' spray – for cuts and grazes
- calamine lotion – to ease irritation from bites and stings
- bandages and Band-aids – for minor injuries
- scissors, tweezers and a thermometer – mercury thermometers are prohibited by airlines
- insect repellent, sun block, chap stick and water purification tablets
- space blanket – to be used for warmth or as an emergency signal

Water Purification

The water from taps in all three countries is safe to drink and, for the most part, surface water is potable except in urban areas. Water from glacial rivers may appear murky but you may drink it, if necessary, in small quantities. The murk is actually fine particles of silt scoured from the rock by the glacier and drinking too much of this has been known to clog up internal plumbing.

Those who are concerned about contamination, however, should purify their drinking water. The simplest way is to thoroughly boil it. Technically this means for 10 minutes although most people can't be bothered to wait that long. Remember that at higher altitudes water boils at lower temperatures so germs are less likely to be killed.

Simple filtering will not remove all organisms so, if you cannot boil water, it may be

treated chemically. Chlorine tablets (Puritabs, Steritabs or other brand names) will kill many but not all organisms. Iodine is very effective in purifying water and is available in tablet form (Potable Aqua) but follow the directions carefully and remember that too much iodine can be harmful.

If you can't find tablets, tincture of iodine (2%) or iodine crystals can be used. Two drops of tincture of iodine per litre of clear water is the recommended dosage. The water should then be left to stand for 30 minutes. Iodine crystals can also be used to purify water but this is a more complicated process as you have to first prepare a saturated iodine solution. Iodine loses its effectiveness if exposed to air or damp, so keep it in a tightly sealed container. Flavoured powder or lemon juice will disguise the taste of treated water and is an especially good idea if you're hiking with children.

Giardia

Although most unpopulated lands in Iceland, the Faroes and far southern Greenland serve as sheep pastures, there seems to be very little giardia; however, while most people have no problems drinking untreated surface water, there is still a possibility of contracting it.

Giardia, sometimes called 'beaver fever', is an intestinal parasite that lives in the faeces of humans and animals and is normally contracted through drinking water. Problems can start several weeks after you have been exposed to the parasite and symptoms may sometimes remit for a few days and then return; this can go on for several weeks or even longer.

The first signs are a swelling of the stomach, pale-coloured faeces, diarrhoea, frequent gas and headache, followed by nausea and depression. Many doctors recommend Flagyl (metronidazole) tablets (250 mg) twice daily for three days – these should be taken only under medical supervision. However, Flagyl can cause side-effects and some doctors prefer to treat giardiasis with two grams of Tinaba or Fasigyn (tinadazole), taken in one fell swoop to knock the bug out hard and fast. If it doesn't work the first time, the treatment can be repeated for up to three days. Broad-spectrum antibiotics are of no use in treating giardia.

Sunburn & Windburn

Sunburn and windburn should be primary concerns for anyone planning to spend time trekking or travelling over snow and ice. The sun will burn you even if you feel cold and the wind will cause dehydration and chafing of skin. Use a good sunblock and a moisture cream on exposed skin, even on cloudy days. A hat provides added protection and zinc oxide or some other barrier cream for your nose and lips is recommended.

Reflection and glare from ice and snow can cause snow blindness, so high-protection sunglasses are essential for any sort of glacier visit or ski trip.

Hypothermia

Perhaps the most dangerous health threat in the Arctic regions is hypothermia. This occurs when the body loses heat faster than it can produce it and the core temperature falls. It is surprisingly easy to progress from very cold to dangerously cold due to a combination of wind, wet clothing, fatigue and hunger, even if the air temperature is above freezing. It is best to dress in layers; silk, wool and polypropylene are all good insulating materials. A hat is important as a lot of heat is lost through the scalp. A strong, waterproof and windproof outer layer is essential since keeping dry is of utmost importance. Carry basic supplies including food containing simple sugars to generate heat quickly and be sure that plenty of fluids are always available.

Symptoms of hypothermia are: exhaustion; numb skin (particularly toes and fingers); shivering; slurred speech; irrational, confused or violent behaviour; lethargy; stumbling; dizzy spells; muscle cramps and violent bursts of energy. Irrationality may include sufferers claiming they are warm and trying to remove clothing.

To treat hypothermia: first get out of the wind and/or rain; if possible, remove wet clothing and replace with dry, warm clothing; drink hot liquids, not alcohol; and eat some high-calorie, easily digestible food. This should be enough for the early stages of hypothermia but, if it has gone further, it may be necessary to place the victim in a warm sleeping bag and get in with them.

Do not rub the patient, or place them near a fire, or remove wet clothing while they're exposed to wind. If possible, place them in a warm (not hot) bath but, if that is not available, remember that the body heat of another person is immediately more important than medical attention, so do not leave the victim alone under any circumstances.

Rabies

Rabies exists in Greenland and is caused by a bite or scratch from an infected animal. Dogs are noted carriers. Any bite, scratch or even lick from a mammal should be cleaned immediately and thoroughly. Scrub with soap in running water, then clean with an alcohol solution. If there is any possibility that the animal is infected, medical help should be sought immediately. Even if the animal is not rabid, all bites should be treated seriously as they can become infected or can result in tetanus. A rabies vaccination is now available.

Bugs

In its sheer density of bugs and pests, the Arctic rivals the Amazon. What the bug season lacks in length, it makes up for in numbers. Especially in Greenland, tundra bogs turn into nurseries for zillions of mosquitoes. If you venture outdoors in less than 20 knots of wind, you may be overwhelmed by the scourge of the Arctic. (In Alaska, caribou have been driven to insanity and death by the whining swarms.)

Don't be caught out without some sort of protection! Long sleeves and trousers are not enough. Mozzies love ears, eyes and noses and, although Iceland's mosquitoes are actually midges and some don't bite, the Greenland variety are perfectly happy to drill anywhere and through anything. A few hardy individuals have even been known to penetrate denim jeans. Some shops and hotels in Greenland sell head-nets but, to protect the rest of your body, the best solution is something containing a good percentage of diethylmetatoluamide (DEET) which is nasty stuff to put on your skin but eminently preferable to battling those swarms of mosquitoes.

Sexually Transmitted Diseases

Nowhere in the North Atlantic is there a negative stigma attached to sexual promiscuity and, in Greenland, the custom of 'wife-swapping' is happily practised. A male Greenlander will in some cases present his wife for a night as a gift to another man and may be rather offended if the intended receiver refuses his hospitality. Those who would accept such offers should be aware, however, that sexually transmitted diseases are rampant in Greenland and precautions should be taken.

Gonorrhoea and syphilis are the most common sexually transmitted diseases and, while abstinence is the only 100% preventative, the use of condoms is also effective. Symptoms can include sores, blisters, or rashes around the genitals and discharges or pain when urinating. These symptoms may be less marked or not observed at all in women. Often the symptoms of syphilis, in particular, will eventually disappear completely but the disease continues and can cause severe problems in later years. Treatment of gonorrhoea and syphilis is with antibiotics.

There are numerous other sexually transmitted diseases, most of which have effective treatments. There is currently no cure for herpes or AIDS. The latter is most often spread by male homosexual intercourse, blood transfusions and injections with shared needles, although heterosexual AIDS is on the increase and everyone is at risk. There is no place in the North Atlantic which yet has a serious AIDS problem (although there have been confirmed cases in all three countries; in late 1992, Iceland alone counted 72 cases) or unsanitary medical equipment, but due precautions are still advised. In Iceland, condoms are called *verja* or *smokkur* and are available from chemists.

Motion Sickness

Since a great deal of North Atlantic travel is by boat or ship and much of the overland travel is on rough, unsurfaced roads, those prone to motion sickness may have problems.

Eating lightly before and during a trip will reduce the chances of motion sickness. If you know you are likely to be affected, try to find a place that minimises disturbance – near the wing on aircraft, close to midships on boats and near the centre on buses. Fresh air almost always helps, but reading or cigarette smoking (or even being around some else's smoke) normally makes matters worse.

Commercial motion-sickness preparations, which can cause drowsiness, have to be taken before the trip – it's too late after you've begun feeling ill. Dramamine tablets should be taken three hours before departure. Ginger is an excellent natural preventative and is available in capsule form.

WOMEN TRAVELLERS

Women travelling alone in Iceland, Greenland and the Faroe Islands will most likely have fewer problems than they would travelling in their home country. Women, accompanied or not, who venture into an Icelandic disco should be prepared to witness and participate in some fairly unrestrained behaviour.

Women hitchhikers, especially those travelling on their own, will not encounter any difficulties if they use common sense and aren't afraid of refusing lifts which may appear suspect. Since alcoholism is a problem in all three countries, you may want to make certain of the driver's sobriety before climbing aboard.

DANGERS & ANNOYANCES

In Iceland, Greenland and the Faroe Islands – where petty larceny merits front-page headlines, police don't carry guns (police aren't even visible most of the time), parents park their children in prams on the street while they shop, and most people are too reserved even to speak to strangers let alone hassle them – there are few dangers and annoyances to contend with. In fact, Iceland actually lets its prisoners go home on public holidays.

Although (or because) it's strictly controlled in Iceland and the Faroes and marginally regulated in Greenland, alcohol is a problem in all three countries. On Friday and Saturday nights (or in Greenland, after work on pay day) you'd be hard-pressed to find someone who isn't affected by it, but alcohol-related violence is almost unheard of. The exceptions seem to be in Nuuk, where social or political dissatisfaction fuelled by alcohol sometimes yields unpleasant results, and in east Greenland around the town of Ittoqqoortoormiit, where serious violence seems to erupt with some frequency. If you sense problems, you'd do well to keep a low profile.

BUSINESS HOURS

Normal weekday shopping hours are from 9 am to 5 or 5.30 pm, although some shops may open at 8 am and close at 4 pm or even remain open later. On Saturday, shops normally open at 9 or 10 am and close at noon or 1 pm. Petrol stations and kiosks, which are similar to US convenience stores or Aussie milk bars, are normally open on weekday evenings until 10 or 11 pm, and also on Saturday afternoon and Sunday. Tourist-oriented souvenir shops generally stay open longer than other shops.

Post office hours vary, but most Icelandic post offices are open from 8.30 am to 4.30 pm on weekdays. Village post offices in the Faroes often close for a one to three-hour lunch break and post offices in Greenland are open very limited hours, especially in smaller towns.

Banks are open from 9 am to 4 pm on weekdays in Iceland and the Faroes and from 10 am to 3 pm in Greenland. Faroese banks stay open until 6 pm on Thursday.

Getting There & Away

AIR

The popularity of the North Atlantic region, especially Iceland, as an adventure-travel destination is mushrooming and the travel industry can scarcely keep up with it. At present there are no earth-shaking bargain fares to or between points in the North Atlantic, and the only way to keep transport costs down is to make plans as far in advance as possible, shop around for cheap fares and buy tickets at least 30 days prior to departure.

It can be difficult to reschedule tickets with Icelandair, Iceland's national carrier, so it's best to buy a ticket only when you're certain you won't need to change it.

Buying Tickets

Your plane ticket will probably be the single most expensive item in your budget. There are lots of airlines and travel agents vying for your business, and it's worth putting aside a few hours to research the market. Start early: the cheapest tickets must be purchased months in advance, and popular flights sell out early. Talk to other travellers and watch newspaper and magazine ads (including the ethnic press of the destination country). Then phone around travel agents. (Airlines can supply routing and timetable information, but unless there's a price war on, they don't offer the cheapest tickets.) Determine the fare, the route, the allowable duration of the journey and any ticket restrictions before deciding which is best.

You may opt to sacrifice the bargains and play it safe with a better-known agent. Firms such as STA, with offices worldwide, Council Travel in the USA or Travel CUTS in Canada offer good fares to most destinations and won't disappear overnight, leaving you clutching a receipt for a nonexistent ticket.

Once you have your ticket, photocopy it or copy down the number, the flight number and other details, and keep the information safe and separate from the ticket. If the ticket is lost or stolen, this will help you get a replacement.

Travellers with Special Needs

If you have any special needs – you've broken a leg, you're vegetarian, travelling in a wheelchair, taking the baby, terrified of flying – let the airline know as soon as possible so they can make appropriate arrangements. Then remind them when reconfirming your booking (at least 72 hours before departure) and again when checking in at the airport. It may also be worth ringing the airlines before making your booking to find out how they can handle your particular needs.

Europe

You'll find the best deals listed in the travel sections of the Saturday and Sunday editions of London newspapers. However, don't take travel agency advertised fares as gospel truth. To comply with advertising laws in the UK, companies must be able to offer *some* tickets at their cheapest quoted price, but they may only have one or two of them per week. If you're not one of the lucky punters, you may be looking at higher fares. Start looking for deals well in advance of your intended departure so you can get a fair idea of what's available.

Discount Travel Agencies Especially in London, a growing slate of travel agencies offer good deals on long-haul travel. Look' for travel agents' ads in the Sunday papers, travel magazines and listings magazines. The following are good places to initiate your price comparisons:

France
Council Travel, Rue St Augustine, 2ème, Paris
  (☎ 01 42 66 20 87)
  22 Rue des Pyramides, 1ère, Paris
  (☎ 01 44 55 55 44)

Ireland
USIT Travel, 19 Aston Quay, Dublin
(☎ 01-679 8833)
UK
Bridge the World, 52 Chalk Farm Rd, Camden Town,
London NW1 8AN (☎ 0171-911 0900;
fax 0171-916 1724)
Quest Worldwide, 29 Castle St, Kingston, Surrey KT1
1ST (☎ 0181-547 3322)
STA Travel, 86 Old Brompton Rd, London SW7
(☎ 0171-937 9962)
117 Euston Rd, London NW1 2SX
(☎ 0171-937 9921 for Europe)
Trailfinders, 42-48 Earls Court Rd, London W8
(☎ 0171-938 3366)
194 Kensington High St, London W8
(☎ 0171-938 3939)
Travel Bug, 125A Gloucester Rd, London SW7 4SF
(☎ 0171-835 2000)
597 Cheetham Hill Rd, Manchester M8 5EJ
(☎ 0161-721 4000)
Travel Mood, 246 Edgware Rd, London W2 1DS
(☎ 0171-258 0280)

Routes & Fares Regular flights take off for
the North Atlantic region from major European cities, but again it pays to book ahead.

Iceland Icelandair flies between Keflavík
(the airport for Reykjavík) and Luxembourg,
Glasgow, London, Paris, Frankfurt, Vienna,
Copenhagen, Gothenburg, Stockholm, Oslo,
Bergen and Vágar (Faroe Islands). It also has
connections to and from other European
cities. In the high season, the Copenhagen
flight operates daily. Twice weekly, it continues to Narsarsuaq, Greenland, and once
weekly, it connects with the Faroe Islands
flight.

Icelandair promotes its European hub,
Luxembourg, with some zeal, and runs buses
between that city and Frankfurt, Karlsruhe,
Stuttgart, Düsseldorf and other cities, as well
as offering discounted rail tickets between
Luxembourg and Amsterdam, Berlin,
London, Paris, Madrid, Rome, Zürich and so
forth.

In summer, the least expensive return
tickets to Keflavík are Apex fares from
Glasgow, which start at US$464. From Lux-
embourg or London, they start at US$584,
must be purchased 30 days in advance and
you're limited to a seven to 30-day stay.

Special discounted tickets issued by an Icelandic agency (such as Samvinn Travel
(☎ 569 1010; fax 552 7796), Austurstræti 12,
101 Reykjavík) start at as little as US$304
return from London, provided you stay more
than three days and less than one month. For
more than one month stay, the return fare
starts at US$381.

Unless you use a travel agent that can
organise special ferry/flight packages (ferry
companies can offer suggestions), you won't
save anything by taking the ferry one-way
and returning on the plane, as the one-way
fare costs more than a return fare (the airline
thus avoids refunding unused portions of
tickets).

An alternative to Icelandair is the charter
company Trans-Avia (☎ 560 9270), Ístravel,
Gnoðarvogur 44, Reykjavík, which charges
as little as US$292 return from Amsterdam.

Greenland International travel to Greenland
is through one of six airports: Narsarsuaq in
South Greenland; Nuuk (the capital) or
Kangerlussuaq (Søndre Strømfjord) in
South-West Greenland; Pituffik (Thule Air
Base) in North-West Greenland; and
Kulusuk in East Greenland. Charter flights
may also use the airports at Nerlerit Inaat
(Constable Pynt) or Mesters Vig in North-
East Greenland.

Note that Narsarsuaq, which sees a good
measure of fog and misty weather, lacks the
most sophisticated radar and planes must
make a visual approach; don't be surprised
if your Narsarsuaq flight is diverted to more
high-tech and climatically stable
Kangerlussuaq. When this happens, airlines
now pay passengers' expenses at Kangerlussuaq.

In the summer, Icelandair flies on Monday
and Thursday between Keflavík and Narsarsuaq; the cheapest excursion fare is
around US$560 return for stays of up to 28
days; for longer stays, the two-hour flight
costs a whopping US$960 return. (Icelandair
justifies this by maintaining that only
expense-account business travellers stay
more than four weeks; they've forgotten
about backpackers and guidebook authors!)

Tickets must be purchased at least 30 days in advance.

In the summer Icelandair offers several weekly excursion flights between Reykjavík and East Greenland for US$418. You can opt for a day tour, which amounts to four hours on Kulusuk Island (including a tour of Kulusuk village, three km from the airport), or continue to Ammassalik by helicopter (Dkr800 return) for two to five days before returning to Iceland.

Icelandair may not carry transit passengers to Kulusuk, so if you're continuing from Kulusuk to West Greenland, you must use Flugfélag Norðurlands, Grønlandsfly (Greenlandair), or the charter airline Íslandsflug, from Reykjavík or Keflavík, via Kulusuk, to Kangerlussuaq or Nuuk. The one-way/return fares between Keflavík and either Nuuk or Kangerlussuaq are Dkr3780/7560. Between Keflavík and Kulusuk costs Dkr2260/4520 one-way/return.

For groups, charter flights to Kulusuk, Nerlerit Inaat and Mesters Vig, among other Greenland destinations, can be arranged with Flugfélag Norðurlands (☎ 461 2100; fax 461 2106), Akureyri or Íslandsflug (☎ 661 6060; fax 662 3537), Reykjavík City Airport, 101 Reykjavík.

From 15 June to 15 August, SAS has three weekly flights between Copenhagen and Kangerlussuaq (Dkr7720 return). Alternatively, you can fly with SAS between Copenhagen and Pituffik every second week for Dkr7720 (note that Thule airbase permits are required and that only 14 'tourist' tickets are available on each flight). Student fares for these flights start at Dkr5790 return.

The Faroes Icelandair flies to the Faroes from Glasgow weekly from May to September, and to Reykjavík two or three times weekly. Another option is fly with Maersk or Atlantic Airways from Copenhagen. Maersk uses Boeing 737s and Atlantic Airways flies British Aerospace high-wing jets. Both airlines have daily flights between Copenhagen and Vágar, except in mid-winter, when the number of flights varies. In the summer, they also fly from Billund airport or Århus (Denmark) once or twice weekly.

The discounted Icelandair Apex fare for Glasgow to Vágar return is UK£198. Copenhagen to Vágar return is Dkr2670 with Maersk and Dkr2550 with Atlantic Airways. For these tickets, you must stay one Saturday night and up to one month in the Faroes, and tickets cannot be changed or refunded. Otherwise, non-discounted return fares are UK£398 with Icelandair, and Dkr4080 with both Maersk and Atlantic Airways. If you're flying from Copenhagen to the Faroes on Friday or Saturday and returning on Sunday or Monday, you can fly for just Dkr2085 return with Maersk and Dkr1995 with Atlantic Airways. Special fares are available for students, pensioners and groups.

North America

In the USA, check for cheap tickets in the Sunday travel sections of major newspapers, such as the *Los Angeles Times*, *San Francisco Examiner* or *Chronicle* on the west coast, and the *New York Times* on the east coast. The student travel agencies – STA or Council Travel – are also worth a try, but you must often produce proof of student status and in some cases, must also be under 26 years of age to qualify for discounted fares.

North America is a newcomer to the bucket-shop traditions of Europe and Asia so ticket availability and the attached restrictions must be weighed against what is offered on the standard Apex or full economy (coach class) tickets.

In Canada, Travel CUTS has offices in all major cities. The *Toronto Globe & Mail* carries travel agents' ads.

Discount Travel Agencies Although North Americans won't get the great deals available in London, some discount agencies keep a lookout for the best airfare bargains. To comply with regulations, these are sometimes associated with travel clubs.

CHA, 3333 River Rd, Vanier, Ottawa, Ontario K1L 8H9

Canadian International Student Services, 80 Richmond St West 1202 Toronto, Ontario M5H 2A4 (☎ 416-364 2738)
Council on International Educational Exchange, 205 East 42nd St, New York, NY 10017
*STA Travel*166 Geary St, Suite 702, San Francisco, CA 94108 (☎ 415-391 8407)
411 Santa Monica Blvd, Santa Monica, CA 90401 (☎ 310-394 5126)
10 Downing St, New York, NY 10017 (☎ 212-627 3111)

Routes & Fares Anything cheaper than standard tourist or economy fares must be purchased at least 14 to 30 days prior to departure. Due to competition between carriers and governmental red tape in determining fare structures, flights originating in the USA are subject to numerous restrictions and regulations. This is especially true of bargain tickets.

Furthermore, departure and return dates must be fixed in advance, and tickets are subject to minimum and maximum stay requirements: usually seven days and six months, respectively. It's often cheaper to purchase a return ticket and trash the return portion than pay the one-way fare. Tickets which allow an open return date within a 12-month period are generally not available in the USA, and you'll pay penalties of up to 50% to change the return booking.

Iceland In high season (24 May to 3 October), Icelandair flies daily between Keflavík and New York JFK and several times weekly between Keflavík and Washington/Baltimore, Orlando, Fort Lauderdale, Boston and Halifax.

Once weekly, their flight between Reykjavík and New York JFK connects with the flight between Keflavík and the Faroe Islands. The fare between New York and Luxembourg is US$388 return with 30-day advance purchase, a minimum stay of 14 days and a maximum of 30 days. Longer stays may dramatically increase the fare. The return fare between New York and Reykjavík is US$580 with the same purchase and stay restrictions as from New York to Luxembourg.

Although the days of the bargain basement Iceland stopover are over for the time being, passengers on Icelandair's trans-Atlantic routes between New York and Copenhagen or Luxembourg may still take a one to three-day Iceland stopover. These include bus transfers between Keflavík and Reykjavík; a two-hour Reykjavík city tour and one to three nights at the Hotel Loftleiðir or Hotel Esja in Reykjavík. Stopovers are free for Saga Class (business class) passengers while economy class passengers pay US$70/120/165 per person (when two people are travelling together) for one/two/three nights. Those travelling alone pay about 50% more.

Greenland The easiest way to Greenland from North America is to fly to Reykjavík or Copenhagen and work out your route from there (see Europe). The alternative is to fly with Air Canada or First Air to Iqaluit, on Canada's Baffin Island, then take First Air's Monday or Thursday (high season) flight to Kangerlussuaq and Nuuk (approximately C$360 one way). For details, contact First Air (☎ 613-521 5435; fax 613-738 0694), 100 Thad Johnson Rd, Gloucester, Ontario K1V 0R1. From within Canada, use the toll-free number ☎ 800-267 1247.

Australasia
From Australia and New Zealand your trip will have to be routed through either the USA or Europe. Currently, there are no Round the World (RTW) tickets that include Iceland, Greenland or the Faroe Islands, so your best option is a RTW ticket that includes New York or London, to which you can add a side trip to Iceland, Greenland or the Faroes. Typical RTW ticket prices range from A$2000 to A$3000.

Discount Travel Agencies In Australia and New Zealand, inexpensive travel is dominated by STA, which has branches in all capital cities and on most university campuses. Here are the addresses of main offices

1A Lee St, Railway Square, Sydney, NSW
(☎ 02-9212 1255)
25 Rundle St, Adelaide, SA (☎ 08-8223 2426)
111-117 Adelaide St, Brisbane, Qld
(☎ 07-9221 3722)
222 Faraday St, Carlton, Victoria, 3053
(☎ 03-934 92411)
53 Market St, Fremantle, WA (☎ 08-9430 5553)
10 High St, Auckland (☎ 9-309 9995)

SEA
Ferry

A pleasant way to travel between Britain, Denmark or Norway and Iceland or the Faroes is by ferry. It takes more time and isn't really economical, but it can be enjoyable and also allows you to bring your own vehicle.

The ferries, run by Smyril Line, operate from late May to early September. The *Norröna* (*Norröna* in Icelandic) sails from Esbjerg, in south-western Denmark, on Saturday at 10 pm and arrives in Tórshavn, Faroe Islands, at 10 am on Monday. There, Iceland-bound passengers must disembark while the ship does a run to Bergen, Norway, to pick up more passengers. It leaves Bergen at 3 pm on Tuesday, arriving in Tórshavn at 11 am on Wednesday. At 3 pm Wednesday, it gathers Iceland-bound passengers and sails overnight to Seyðisfjörður, arriving at 7 am on Thursday. On the return journey, it sails from Seyðisfjörður at 11 am Thursday, arriving in Tórshavn at 6 am on Friday and sailing for Esbjerg at 8.30 am to begin another circuit.

Smyril Line no longer has a bus service from Copenhagen to Esbjerg, but rail services are convenient and pull right into the ferry terminal – so don't get off at the Esbjerg central station!

Iceland-bound passengers coming from Denmark may not remain on board while the ship sails to Norway, which means spending two nights in the Faroe Islands en route. However, if you want more than two days in the Faroes, you'll have to break your journey at Tórshavn and pay for two sectors. The normal deck fare from Esbjerg to Seyðisfjörður (including a couchette) is US$280 one-way. Esbjerg to Tórshavn is

US$221 and from Tórshavn to Seyðisfjörður is US$207, adding up to US$428 for the entire trip. Good discounts are available to student card holders.

To take a vehicle up to five metres long, you'll pay about 75% of the deck-class passenger fare. Motorcycles cost US$116 from Denmark to Iceland and bicycles are US$15. Above deck class are three classes of cabins and a luxury suite. The ship also has a bar, cafeteria, restaurant, disco, casino and duty-free shops.

For information, schedules and fare lists, contact: Smyril Line (☎ 15900; fax 15707), J Broncksgøta 37, Postbox 370, FR-110 Tórshavn, Faroe Islands. In the UK, contact P&O Scottish Ferries (☎ 01224-572615; fax 01224-574411), PO Box 5, Jamieson's Quay, Aberdeen, AB9 8DL, Scotland.

From the UK, you can take Strandfaraskip Landsins' ferry *Smyril*, which sails twice weekly from 14 June to 18 August (once weekly at other times) between Aberdeen (Scotland) and Tórshavn. In summer it leaves Aberdeen on Thursday and Sunday and arrives in Tórshavn on Friday and Monday, respectively. The Monday sailing continues to Klaksvík; then on Tuesday, it sails from Klaksvík to Tórshavn, via Drelnes (Suðuroy). That afternoon, it sails from Tórshavn to Aberdeen, arriving the following day. The Friday sailing from Tórshavn arrives in Aberdeen on Saturday morning.

In the high season, the one-way deck class fare is US$105, with 25% discount for student card holders. For a cabin, you'll pay from US$193 to US$263. Transport of vehicles up to five metres long costs US$105. For information contact: Strandfaraskip Landsins (☎ 14550; fax 18140), Yviri við Strond 6, PO Box 88, FR-110 Tórshavn, Faroe Islands. Their UK agent is P&O Ferries, whose contact details are given earlier in this section.

There are no regular ferries between Greenland and Iceland, the Faroes or mainland Europe. However, the Greenland tourist boat *Disko* makes an annual maintenance run between Greenland and Ålborg, Denmark, and also sails to the Antarctic. It isn't exactly an ocean liner but if you're interested, passage may be booked through KNI Shipping, Grønlandshavnen, Rederiafdelingen, Ålborg, Denmark.

Similarly, the Vestmannaeyjar ferry, *Herjólfur*, sails between Reykjavík and Kristiansund, Norway, for repairs in September and returns in October. Prospective passengers must book well in advance, as the fare is just Ikr8000 each way. For information contact *Herjólfur* (☎ 481 2800; fax 481 2991), Heimaey, Vestmannaeyjar, Iceland.

Cargo Ship

The Icelandic cargo-shipper, Eimskip, accepts passengers on its vessel *Brúarfoss*, which sails every second Thursday from Reykjavík to the Faroe Islands and Hamburg, and returns via Denmark, Sweden, Norway and the Faroes. A double cabin and full board on the four day run from Hamburg to Reykjavík costs Ikr27,400. To transport a car under five metres long costs Ikr22,500. Contact Eimskip (☎ 569 7100; email: mottaka@eimskip.is), Posthússtræti 2, 101 Reykjavík, or their sales agent Úrval-Útsýn Travel (☎ 569 9300; fax 588 0202), Lágmúli 4, 108 Reykjavík.

The Samskip line, which has its UK base in Hull, charges Ikr15,000 for deck class between Reykjavík and Hull, but the facilities are very basic.

Faroe Ship Cargo & Passenger Line operates between Tórshavn, Lysekil and Varberg (Sweden), and Fredericia and Copenhagen (Denmark) weekly year-round. Ships carry a maximum of 12 passengers but places are available only at the captain's discretion and no advance reservations are taken. For information, contact them at Eystara Bryggja (☎ 11225; fax 15707), PO Box 47, FR-100 Tórshavn, Faroe Islands.

Cruise Ship

If you're dreaming of an Arctic cruise, a growing number of ships – many using icebreakers registered in the former Soviet Union – are calling in at Iceland and Greenland. Some of them are trans-Atlantic crossings with stops in these northern countries and others are bona fide Arctic cruises, which may also take in Svalbard, Jan Mayen, or the Russian or Canadian Arctic archipelagoes. Contact the following companies for a list of their sales agents (the company name is followed by the name of the ship):

Princess Cruises, *Royal Princess*, 10100 Santa Monica Blvd, Los Angeles, CA 90067, USA

Cunard Royal Viking, *Vistafjord*, 555 5th Ave, New York, NY 10017, USA

Special Expeditions, *Polaris*, 720 5th Ave, New York, NY 10017, USA

Far East Shipping Co, *Kapitan Khlebnikov*, 15 ulitsa 25 Oktyabrya, Vladivostok 690019, Russia

Murmansk Shipping Co, *Alla Tarasova*, 15 ulitsa Kominterna, Murmansk 183636, Russia

Noble Caledonia, *Alla Tarasova*, 11 Charles St, Mayfair, London W1X 8LE, UK

CTC Cruise Lines, *Azerbaydzhan*, 1 Regnet St, London SW1Y 4NN, UK

Black Sea Shipping Co, *Fyodr Dostoyevsky*, 1 ulitsa Lastochkina, Odessa 270026, Ukraine

Yacht

Anyone considering a North Atlantic cruise in a private yacht will need a copy of *Faroes, Iceland & Greenland Cruising Notes* (Imray, Laurie Norie & Wilson Ltd, St Ives, Cambridgeshire, UK), by RCC Pilotage Foundation and Oz Robinson. It contains invaluable information on ports, soundings and facilities for pilots and sailors. Marine charts for all three countries may be ordered from Iver C Weilbach & Co (☎ & fax 45-33 13 59 27), Toldbodgade 35, PO Box 1560, DK-1253 Copenhagen K, Denmark.

ORGANISED TOURS

There are two types of tour companies: overseas agents who book transportation and hotels, and cobble together itineraries in conjunction with locally-based operators, who actually provide the tours. (Within Iceland, Greenland and the Faroes, there are quite a few of these tour companies, most of which run their trips in small coaches, minibuses or 4WD vehicles.)

If you're going the package route, it always pays to shop around for deals; especially in Europe, it's becoming popular to look for late bookings, which are available at a fraction of the normal price. The best place to begin is the travel sections of weekend newspapers. In some cases, there are special late bookings counters at international airports.

If you prefer not to organise everything beforehand, you can always book your flights and hotels for the first few nights, then join tours locally (local operators are listed under Organised Tours in the Getting Around chapters for each country). Naturally, time flexibility is essential.

It's impossible to include a comprehensive list of North Atlantic operators, but the following companies run a range of tours, from hiking and camping excursions to four-star packages:

Australia

Bentours, 32-34 Bridge St, Sydney 2000, NSW (☎ 02-9241 1353; fax 02-9251 1574) Bentours offers a range of tours covering the highlights of Iceland and Greenland including guided excursions, horse tours and camping and dogsledding tours.

Belgium

Joker Tourism, Avenue Verdilaan 25, 1080 Brussels (☎ 02-426 2303; fax 02-426 0360) This company runs budget adventure camping tours in Iceland; if you want good value and a real hands-on experience, this is the way to go.

Canada

Black Feather-Trailhead, 40 East Wellington St, Toronto, Ontario M5E 1C7 (☎ 416)-862 0881), or 1341 Wellington St, Ottawa, Ontario K1Y 3B8 (☎ 613-722-9717) This experienced outfit is one of the only companies operating kayaking tours in Greenland. It appears to have scaled down operations, but still operates trips in South and South-West Greenland.

Travcoa, 112 St Clair Ave W, Suite 400, Toronto, Ontario M4V 2Y3 (☎ 416-927 9610) Travcoa organises hotel-based tours to Greenland and the Faroe Islands for those who are after some standard of comfort.

Viking Tours, 77 4th Avenue, Box 1080, Gimli, Manitoba R0C 1BQ (☎ 204-42 5114; fax 204-642 8457) This tour operator specialising in Iceland is located in the heart of North America's largest Icelandic community. What better qualifications could they have?

Denmark

Arctic Adventure, 30 Reventlowsgade, DK-1651 Copenhagen V (☎ 33 25 32 21; fax 33 25 63 08) Arctic Adventure offers well organised hotel-based tours around Reykjavík, South Greenland and Disko Bay. They also concoct painless winter (April to May) dogsledding tours in north-west Greenland and Disko Bay.

Greenland Travel (Grønlands Rejsebureau), Gammel Mønt 12, PO Box 130, DK-1004, Copenhagen K (☎ 33 13 10 11; fax 33 13 85 92) This agency, which is affiliated with Greenland Home Rule government, is the only real source of help for independent travellers in Greenland. They arrange hotel-based tours, book ferries and flights, and conduct 'Green Tours': multi-day hiking, dogsledding and mountain-biking tours inherited from the former backpackers' agency, DVL Rejser. The guides, most of whom speak English, German and Danish, are friendly and well-informed volunteers who scout out and organise their own routes and hikes. The result is a slate of refreshingly original options.

France

Grand Nord Grand Large, 15 Rue du Cardinal Lemoine, 75005 Paris (☎ 01 40 46 05 14; fax 01 43 26 73 20) This innovative company operates adventurous sea-kayak tours which will take you to remote and difficult-to-visit places under your own steam.

Germany

Arktis Reisen Schehle, Bahnhofstrasse 12-II, D-87435 Kempten (☎ 0831-521 5964; fax 0831-521 5951) This company's comprehensive list of tours thoroughly covers all areas of Greenland and all styles of travel – especially hiking. They also offer tours to other polar regions, including Canada, Alaska, Svalbard and Antarctica.

Ísland Reisen, Rheinbabenallee 27, D-14199 Berlin (☎ 030-823 1435; fax 030-823 1405) This company specialises in individual itineraries in Iceland, Greenland and the Faroes.

UK

Arctic Experience, 29 Nork Way, Banstead, Surrey SM7 1PB (☎ 01737-218800; fax 01737-362341) This friendly agency is one of the most popular British tour operators to Iceland, Greenland, the Faroes and around Scandinavia. The itineraries concentrate on highlights, but they do offer winter tours and can book Icelandic summer cottages. They've also started up Iceland High Adventures, featuring mountaineering, glacier travel, ice-climbing, and other activity-oriented trips.

Arcturus Expeditions Limited, PO Box 850, Gartocharn, Alexandria, Dunbartonshire G83 8RL (☎ & fax 01389-830204) One of Britain's most inventive operators, Arcturus does hiking and trekking tours to far-flung areas of Greenland, including Qaanaaq and the North-East Greenland National Park, as well as trips to Antarctica, Arctic Siberia, northern Canada, Alaska, Spitsbergen and every other cold and frosty place you could name. This company will take you beyond even the unbeaten track!

DA Study Tours, Williamton House, Low Causeway, Culross KY12 8HL, Fife (☎ 01383-882200; fax 01383-881550) This company specialises in Scandinavia, including Iceland, Greenland and the Faroes. Among the programmes are eight-day tours to Snæfellsnes, Þingvellir and Gullfoss; or to Iceland and Ammassalik, East Greenland, as well as seven-day Faroes tours.

David Oswin Expeditions, Millgarth, Kirklinton, Carlisle CA6 6DW, Cumbria (☎ 01228-75518; fax 01228-75427) With more than 15 years of experience in Iceland and Greenland, David Oswin is now the foremost UK specialist in North Atlantic photographic tours. New programmes include two-week photo tours in Iceland and East Greenland; and winter camping tours in Iceland.

David Sayers Travel, Andrew Brock Travel Ltd, 54 High St East, Uppingham, Rutland LE15 9PZ (☎ 01572-821330; fax 01572-821072) This company specialises in botanical and wildlife tours and runs a pleasantly different Iceland tour, which takes in several lesser-known sites of interest.

Dick Phillips, Whitehall House, Nenthead, Alston, Cumbria CA9 3PS (☎ 01434-381440) Dick Phillips probably knows Iceland better than anyone else in Britain, with decades of experience leading hiking, trekking and skiing trips through the island's remotest areas. The rates are very reasonable but the trips are rigorous and not for anyone who wishes to be pampered.

Discover the World, The Flatt Lodge, Bewcastle, near Carlisle, Cumbria CA6 6PH (☎ 016977-48361; fax 016977-48327) This conservation-minded agency offers weekend whale-watching trips in south-east Iceland. These mini-tours also include a visit to the Vatnajökull icecap.

Goodwood Travel, Flights of Fantasy, Concord House, Stour St, Canterbury, Kent CT1 2NZ (☎ 01227-763336; fax 01227-762417) If you have a spare £2495, this company will take you to Greenland (Kangerlussuaq) on the Concorde for three days of icy adventure in Ilulissat.

High Places, Globe Works, Penistone Road, Sheffield S6 3AE (☎ 0114-275 7500; fax 0114-275 3870; email: highpl@globalnet.co.uk) This company offers all-season trekking, skiing and camping excursions through isolated and little-visited corners of Iceland. Their speciality is winter nordic skiing trips in northern and eastern Iceland.

Mountain & Wildlife Ventures, Compston Rd, Ambleside, Cumbria LA22 9DJ (☎ 015394-33285; fax 015394-34065) Although their emphasis is on mainland Scandinavia, this experienced company operates adventurous trekking and skiing expeditions in the Cape Farewell region of south Greenland, including trips onto the inland ice.

Naturetrek, Chautara, Bighton, near Alresford, Hampshire SO24 9RB (☎ 01962-733051; fax 01962-733368) This wildlife specialist operates original tours to Iceland, and concentrates on birdwatching around Mývatn. It's worth contacting them for their catalogue alone, which is full of lovely wildlife sketches.

Regent Holidays, Regent House, 31A High Street, Shanklin, Isle of Wight PO37 6JW (☎ 01983-864212; fax 01983-864197) Regent Holidays offers comprehensive packages to Iceland, Greenland and the Faroe Islands.

Sovereign Scanscape, Astral Towers, Betts Way, Crawley, West Sussex RH10 2GX (☎ 01293-599922; fax 01293-543414) This company offers a variety of packages including hotel-based tours around Iceland, as well as some which include easy day-walks (ambitiously called 'trekking' in their brochure). They also do extensions to Ammassalik and Disko Bay in Greenland.

Twickers World, 20/22 Church St, Twickenham TW1 3NW (☎ 0181-892 7606; fax 0181-892 8061) This packager cobbles together a range of highlight holidays in Iceland, Greenland and the Faroe Islands.

Wild Oceans, Wildwings, International House, Bank Rd, Bristol BS15 2LX (☎ 0117-984 8040; fax 0117-967 4444) This company, which does whale and dolphin-watching expeditions around the world, runs an Iceland, Greenland and Spitsbergen cruise aboard the *Professor Molchanov*. Prices run from £1115 to £2275.

Worldsaway, 101 Eden Vale Rd, Westbury, Wiltshire BA13 3QX (☎ 01373-858956; fax 01373-858351) This company does moderate hiking and mountain biking tours through the Icelandic highlights, as well as guided trips with easy day-hiking options.

USA

Scantours, 1535 Sixth St, Suite 205, Santa Monica, CA 90401 (☎ 213-451 0911; fax 213-395 2013) Scantours does hotel-based excursions to Iceland and Greenland. As with many operators, they aren't too imaginative, but will show you the sights in a measure of comfort.

Travcoa, S.E. Bristol 2350, Santa Ana Heights, CA 92707 (☎ 714-476 2800; fax 714-476 2538) As with its Canadian branch, the American arm of Travcoa provides short hotel-based highlights tours in Greenland and the Faroes.

HISTORY

Early Settlement

Iceland

Facts about Iceland

Nearly every travel article and TV programme ever written about Iceland has trundled out the overworked description of the country as the 'land of fire and ice', so I'll spare you the cliché. What must be said is that the island with the chilly name – the most isolated nation in the Western world – is rapidly becoming one of Europe's hottest travel destinations and, once you've seen it, you won't wonder why.

Nowhere on earth are the forces of nature more evident than here, where glaciers, hot springs, geysers, active volcanoes, icecaps, tundra, snow-capped peaks, vast lava deserts, waterfalls and active volcanic craters vie for the visitor's attention. On the cliffs that gird much of the coastline are some of the world's most crowded sea-bird colonies, and in the summer, the lakes and marshes teem with nesting waterfowl. Superimposed on this wilderness is a tough and independent society, descendants of the farmers and warriors who fled the tyranny of medieval Scandinavia to settle a new and empty country.

The island also provided a backdrop for the sagas, considered by literature enthusiasts to be the finest of all Western medieval works. Iceland has been inhabited for over 1100 years and the tales of battle, love, revenge and counter-revenge come to life in locales that have changed little since the days of Egill Skallagrímsson and Auður the Deep-Minded.

If it all sounds appealing, there's one catch; Iceland's prices are Europe's highest and if you require hotels, top-class restaurants and hire cars, you'll need an expense account or a very thick wallet indeed. Comfortable middle-range travel in Iceland costs the equivalent of upper range in much of Asia, Australasia and North America; budget travel would be considered middle-range anywhere else; and real shoestring travel requires more effort and greater exposure to the elements than many people are prepared to handle. Still, if you allow lots of time and are equipped for camping, self-catering, and hitching, hiking or biking, you can stay an entire summer in Iceland for little more than you'd spend in such traditional budget destinations as Thailand or Morocco.

HISTORY
Early Settlement
After the Irish monks (see the Facts about the Region chapter), who regarded the island as a sort of hermitage until the early 9th century, Iceland's first permanent settlers came from Norway. The Age of Settlement is traditionally defined as the period between 870 and 930 when political strife on the Scandinavian mainland caused many to flee.

Modern Icelanders maintain that the human history of Iceland was faithfully chronicled from the beginning (modern scholars may disagree). The *Íslendingabók*, which was written by a 12th-century scholar, Ari Þorgilsson (Ari the Learned), about 250 years after the fact, provides a historical nar-

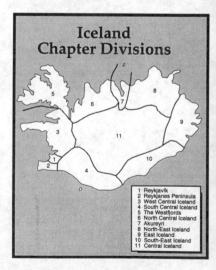

Iceland Chapter Divisions

1 Reykjavík
2 Reykjanes Peninsula
3 West Central Iceland
4 South Central Iceland
5 The Westfjords
6 North Central Iceland
7 Akureyri
8 North-East Iceland
9 East Iceland
10 South-East Iceland
11 Central Iceland

rative. The more detailed *Landnámabók*, a comprehensive account of the Settlement probably compiled from several sources also by Ari the Learned, includes a wealth of information about that era.

It's likely the Norse accidentally discovered Iceland after being blown off course en route to the Faroes. The first arrival, the Swede Naddoddur, landed on the east coast around 850 and named the place Snæland ('snow land') before backtracking to his original destination.

Iceland's second visitor, Garðar Svavarsson, came in search of Naddoddur's reported discovery, Snæland. He circumnavigated it then settled in for the winter at Húsavík on the north coast. When he left in the spring, some of his crew remained, probably invol-

untarily, thereby becoming the island's first residents.

Around 860, the Norwegian Flóki Vilgerðarson uprooted his farm and family and headed for Snæland. He navigated with ravens which, after some trial and error, led him to his destination. This odd practice provided his nickname, Hrafna-Flóki or 'Raven's Flóki'.

Hrafna-Flóki sailed to Vatnsfjörður on the west coast but quickly became disenchanted with the place. Upon seeing icebergs floating in the fjord, he renamed the place Ísland ('ice land'), which he perhaps considered even less flattering than 'Snæland', and returned to Norway. Apparently he reconsidered his position at some point, because he did return to Iceland some years later and settled in the Skagafjörður district on the north coast.

Credit for the first intentional settlement, according to the *Íslendingabók*, goes to a Norwegian called Ingólfur Arnarson, who set up housekeeping in 874 at a place he called Reykjavík ('smoky bay'), after the steam from thermal springs there. Ingólfur was a true Viking who'd had his day in the British Isles; he and his blood-brother Hjörleifur were forced to flee Norway after they encountered some social difficulties there. Hjörleifur settled near the present town of Vík but was murdered by his servants shortly thereafter.

As for Ingólfur, the site of his homestead was determined by the custom of the day, which required well-born intending settlers to toss their high-seat pillars, a symbol of authority and part of a Norse chieftain's pagan paraphernalia, into the sea as they approached land. Tradition and prudence dictated that they build their homes at the place where the gods chose to bring the pillars ashore. At times, settlement necessitated years of searching the coastline for stray pillars.

While Ingólfur Arnarson and his descendants came to control the entire south-western part of Iceland, other settlers were arriving from the mainland. By the time Ingólfur's son Þorsteinn reached adulthood, the island was dotted with farms, and people

Statue of Ingólfur Arnarson

ICELAND

ICELAND

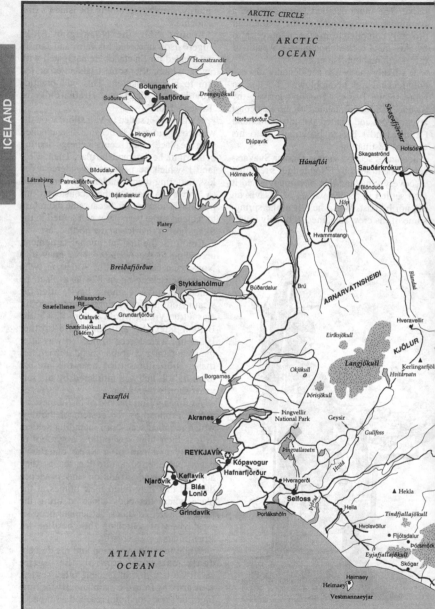

ICELAND

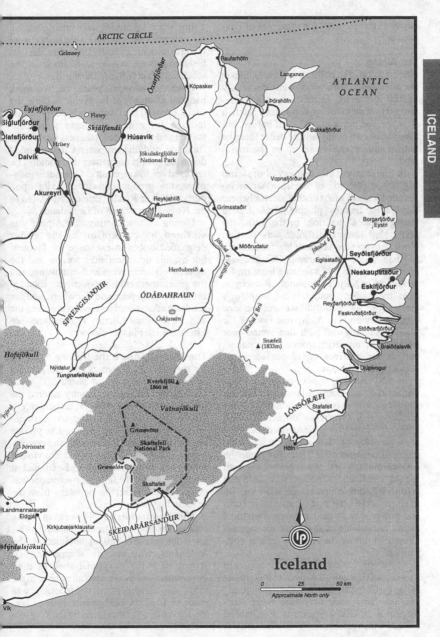

ICELAND

began to feel the need for some sort of government.

The Alþing

After rejecting the political strife at home on the mainland, Icelanders were decidedly against monarchy, so they set up a parliamentary system of government. Such a structure had never proved itself before, but they reasoned it could only be better than the fearful and oppressive set-up on the mainland.

In the early 10th century, Þorsteinn Ingólfsson (the son of Ingólfur Arnarson) founded Iceland's first district assembly near Reykjavík, thereby placing himself in a strong political position. In the 920s, the self-styled lawyer Úlfljótur was sent to Norway to prepare a code of law for Iceland.

At the same time, Grímur Geitskör was commissioned to find a suitable location for an Alþing, or National Assembly. Bláskógar, near the eastern boundary of Ingólfur's estate, with its beautiful lake and wooded plain, seemed ideal. Along one side of the plain was a long cliff with an elevated base (the Mid-Atlantic Rift) from where speakers and representatives could preside over people gathered below.

In 930, Bláskógar was renamed Þingvellir, the 'assembly plains'. Þorsteinn Ingólfsson received the honorary title *allsherjargoði* (supreme chieftain) and Úlfljótur himself was designated the first *lögsögumaður* or 'law-speaker', who was required to memorise and annually recite the entire law of the land. It was him, along with the 48 chieftains or *goðar*, who held the actual legislative power. In addition, 96 advisers served the central assembly. Judicial power was divided between four local courts around the country and the Appeal Court met during the Alþing's annual convention.

At the convention of 999 (some maintain it was 1000) came the decree that made Iceland a Christian nation. Although the conversion came under pressure from Norwegian King Olaf Tryggvason, it provided Iceland with a semblance of national unity at a time when squabbles were arising among the country's leaders, and allegiances were being questioned. Shortly thereafter, the first bishoprics were set up at Skálholt in the south-west and Hólar in the north.

Over the following years, the two-week national assembly at Þingvellir became the social event of the year. Single people came looking for mates, marriages were contracted and solemnised, business deals were finalised and the Appeals Court handed down judgments on matters that couldn't be resolved in lower courts. One such judgment, the pronouncement of exile upon outlaw Eiríkur Rauðe (Eric the Red), led to the Norse colonisation of Greenland.

During its first century, the Alþing was strained by corruption as the goðar demanded bribes in exchange for favours, but by this time, Icelandic society and the agrarian economy were well-established and the government held. Schools were founded at the two bishoprics and elsewhere, and the resulting educational awareness prepared the way for the great Literary Era to come (see Literature later in this chapter).

The Sturlung Age & the Decline

By the early 13th century, the enlightened period of peace that had lasted 200 years came to an end and the country entered the infamous Sturlung Age, a turbulent era graphically recounted in the tragic three-volume *Sturlunga Saga*. Viking-like private armies ravaged the countryside and competition between politicians turned into violent feuds and power struggles. Even had it wanted to do so, the failing government was powerless to protect the populace from the ensuing mayhem.

The opportunistic Norwegian King Hákon Hákonarson regarded the strife as his invitation to take control of the situation. The Icelanders, who saw no alternative, dissolved all but a superficial shell of their government and swore their allegiance to the king. An agreement of confederacy was made in 1262. In 1281, a new code of law, the Jónsbók, was introduced by the king and Iceland was thereby absorbed.

Norway immediately set about appointing Norwegian bishops to Hólar and Skálholt and imposed excessive taxes. Contention flared anew as former chieftains quibbled over high offices, particularly that of *járl* (earl), an honour that fell to the ruthless scoundrel Gissur Þorvaldsson, who in 1241 murdered Snorri Sturluson, Iceland's best known historian and writer. The governorship of Iceland was actually leased for three-year periods to the highest Norwegian bidder and with that office came the power to extract revenue in any efficient manner.

To add insult to injury, in 1300, 1341 and 1389, the volcano Mt Hekla in south Iceland erupted violently, causing death and destruction of property. Recurring epidemics plagued the country throughout the century and the Black Death that struck Norway in 1349 effectively cut off trade and supplies from the mainland.

The Kalmar Union of Norway, Sweden and Denmark at the end of the 14th century brought Iceland, still a province of Norway, under Danish rule. Disputes between church and state resulted in the Reformation of 1550. The Danish government seized church property and imposed Lutheranism. When the stubborn Catholic bishop of Hólar, Jón Arason, resisted and gained a following, he and his two sons were taken to Skálholt and executed.

Toward the end of the 16th century, Iceland was plagued by yet more natural disasters. Four consecutive severe winters led to widespread crop failure and 9000 Icelanders starved to death while thousands more were uprooted from their homes.

In 1602, the Danish king imposed a trade monopoly whereby Swedish and Danish firms were given exclusive trading rights in Iceland for 12-year periods. This resulted in large-scale extortion, importation of spoilt or inferior goods and yet more suffering.

Throughout the 17th and 18th centuries, disaster continued in the form of natural catastrophes and British, Spanish and Arab piracy of Iceland-bound trading ships. Hekla erupted continuously for seven months in 1636 and then again in 1693; Katla erupted violently in 1660 and 1755; and Öræfi, in Vatnajökull, went off in 1727. In 1783, Lakagígar (Laki) erupted continuously for 10 months and devastated much of southeast Iceland, resulting in a poisonous haze that destroyed pastures and crops. Nearly 75% of Iceland's livestock and 20% of the human population died in the resulting famine. The already suffering Icelandic population was then further marginalised by earthquakes and another spell of severe winters.

Independence

Five centuries of oppression under foreign rule had taken its toll on the Icelanders. By the early 1800s, a growing sense of Icelandic nationalism was perceived in Copenhagen, but an ongoing liberalisation process in Europe prevented Denmark from tightening its grip. Jón Sigurðsson, an Icelandic scholar, successfully lobbied for restoration of free trade in 1855. By 1874, Iceland had drafted a constitution and was at last permitted to handle its own domestic matters without interference from the mainland.

The Act of Union, which was signed in 1918, effectively released Iceland from Danish rule, making it an independent state within the Kingdom of Denmark, with Copenhagen retaining responsibility for defence and foreign affairs. The Act of Union was to be valid until 1940 when the Alþing could request a review of Iceland's status.

On 9 April 1940, Denmark was occupied by Germany. Since the Kingdom was in no position to continue overseeing Iceland's defence and foreign affairs, the Alþing took control of its own foreign relations. A year later, on 17 May 1941, the Icelanders requested complete independence. The formal establishment of the Republic of Iceland took place at Þingvellir on 17 June 1944.

Post-Independence

After the occupation of Denmark and Iceland's declaration of sovereignty in 1940, the island's vulnerability became a matter of concern for the Allied powers. They knew Iceland had no military forces whatsoever and was unprepared to defend its strategic position in the case of German aggression. Britain, which would have been most vulnerable to a German-controlled Iceland, sent in forces to occupy the island.

Iceland grudgingly accepted this help but was pleased to find that British construction projects and spending bolstered the economy. When the British troops withdrew in 1941, the government allowed American troops to move in, presumably only for the remainder of the war. They stayed on, however, and in 1946 asked to be allowed 99-year leases on three bases in Iceland. The far-seeing Alþing rejected the request but innocently consented to the US use of Keflavík international airport as a refuelling and staging point for cargo aircraft flying between Europe and North America.

When the North Atlantic Treaty Organisation (NATO) was formed in 1949, Iceland was pressured into becoming a founding member by other Scandinavian states, but only on the condition that under no circumstances would foreign military troops be based there during peacetime.

By 1951, however, the US military had completely taken over Keflavík international airport with no intention of budging. They justified their actions by indicating that Iceland required US protection from the Soviet troops that had invaded North Korea. The Alþing, however, wasn't notified of their intentions until the camel had settled comfortably in the tent, so to speak.

When the Icelanders realised what was happening, they were predictably unhappy but were powerless to evict the Americans, whose numbers and military technology at Keflavík continued to increase over the next four decades. Currently, growing numbers of Icelanders are becoming more adamant in their demands that the 'Yankees go home'.

Since developments in Eastern Europe in the early 1990s could potentially weaken the influence of NATO, they may soon have their way. The selection of Reykjavík for the 1986 summit between Mikhail Gorbachev and Ronald Reagan was enthusiastically accepted by Icelanders as a sign of warmer relations between the superpowers.

Current Trends

Iceland's only international disputes to date have concerned fishing rights. Collectively known as the 'cod wars', they involved British fishing vessels violating Iceland's increasing self-declared territorial waters.

In 1901, Britain and Denmark reduced the extent of the country's offshore fishing rights to less than four miles. In 1952, Iceland increased the limit to four miles offshore but expanded it to 12 miles in 1958, 50 miles in 1972 and finally 200 miles in 1975. The wars were characterised mainly by clashes between Icelandic gunships and British warships and, in 1976, a stop-gap agreement was made with Britain. Since then British fishing boats have respected the 200-mile limit, and no new violence has erupted. There have, however, been clashes between environmental organisations, especially Greenpeace, and the Icelandic whaling industry, which faces increasing world opposition.

Natural disasters, like those of the 16th and 17th centuries, continue to occur in modern Iceland but better communications and a more urban population have reduced their impact considerably. In 1963, the island of Surtsey appeared out of the sea in a submarine eruption just south-west of Vestmannaeyjar. Ten years later, the island of Heimaey, also in Vestmannaeyjar, experienced a terrible eruption that created a new mountain, buried most of the village of 5200 people and threatened to cut off the harbour. In a matter of hours, the island was evacuated and the cleanup began.

Furthermore, Mt Hekla has erupted (with little damage or destruction) as recently as 1991, the Krafla fissure north of Mývatn has experienced a lot of volcanic activity, and in late 1996, Grímsvötn went off and released the largest *jökulhlaup* (flooding caused by volcanic eruption beneath an icecap) of the 20th century (see the South-East Iceland chapter).

As in the rest of Europe, Iceland's current

The Whaling Issue

In 1992, Iceland made its controversial decision to leave the International Whaling Commission (IWC), calling the organisation 'anachronistic and ineffective' and claiming that it had been 'taken over by radical nations' such as Australia and New Zealand which want to permanently halt all whaling for any purpose. Shortly thereafter, it joined Norway, Greenland and the Faroe Islands to form a new organisation, the North Atlantic Marine Mammal Commission (NAMMCO), which extended membership invitations to Canada and Russia and took on Japan as an official observer at meetings.

NAMMCO's self-proclaimed objective is to oversee 'the conservation, rational management and study of marine mammals'. In reality, what that spells is the 'development' of marine mammal 'resources', including seals and both baleen and toothed whales. By withdrawing from the IWC, Iceland has forfeited even its annual 'scientific' quota of 400 whales, which it had used as a pretext for continued commercial whaling and export to the lucrative Japanese market.

NAMMCO has agreed to uphold the United Nations Law of the Sea (UNCLOS) but isn't able to explain how it can uphold the UNCLOS clause that outlines 'the responsibility of the International Whaling Commission for the conservation of whale stocks and the regulation of whaling ...' (To complicate matters further, neither Norway nor Denmark, which represents Greenland and the Faroe Islands in international affairs, has ever ratified UNCLOS!)

Because of the confusion, members cannot agree on whether they have authority to set 'harvest' quotas for specific species. For example, Norway and Iceland have found that numbers of some species, particularly minke and fin whales, have recovered sufficiently that carefully managed 'harvests' would be sustainable. Much of the rest of the world (including the IWC) disagrees and Norway, especially, is under international pressure to re-think its position.

NAMMCO countries are also concerned that competition between marine mammals and commercial vessels may be partially to blame for the present slumps in their fish stocks. (In fact, many individual fishing people blame the current slump in cod stocks not on their own over-exploitation but on Canada's decision to stop taking juvenile seals along the Newfoundland coast! There isn't a marine biologist anywhere who would give the notion a second thought, but you'll hear it repeated again and again across the North Atlantic.) Similarly, Iceland and other North Atlantic countries so fear international human competition in their fisheries that they won't consider membership in the EU.

Whether NAMMCO will ever be recognised as anything more serious than a gang of rebellious nations chafing to resume commercial whaling remains to be seen. Norway's fragile export industry is especially vulnerable to international boycott, so it's unlikely that NAMMCO will make any drastic moves which would polarise the international community against it. ∎

ICELAND

situation is one of economic decline and the country is becoming increasingly indebted while the fishing industry languishes in the slumps. The problem stems primarily from fishing quotas, which in 1992-93 were reduced by 22.5% to allow overfished stocks to regenerate. As a result, in October 1992 unemployment stood at 3% (a previously unheard-of level in Iceland).

Furthermore, the króna was devalued by 6% to relieve pressure caused by turmoil in international currency markets. In January 1993, Iceland approved a European Economic Area agreement between the European Community and the European Free Trade Association (to which it belongs), but only after the agreement conceded to Iceland's demands for restrictions on fishing in its waters. In August 1993, fisheries minister Þorsteinn Pálsson unsuccessfully tried to prevent 20 disgruntled Icelandic trawlers (10% of the fishing fleet) setting off on an expedition to the Barents Sea, which has traditionally been fished by Norway.

GEOGRAPHY

With an area of 103,000 sq km, Iceland is the second largest island in Europe. The southeast coast is 798 km from Scotland, the eastern end is 970 km from Norway and the Westfjords lie 287 km east of Greenland.

The main island, which extends 500 km east to west and 300 km north to south, is roughly duck-shaped, with the head in the Westfjords. Although the northernmost point of the mainland extends to within a few hundred metres of the Arctic Circle, the island of Grímsey off the north coast actually straddles it.

Most of Iceland, a real juvenile among the world's land masses, is characterised by desert plateaus (52%), lava fields (11%), sandur or 'sand deltas' (4%) and glacial icecaps (12%). Over half the country lies above 400m, which is more significant than it sounds given the northerly latitude. The highest point, Hvannadalshnúkur, rises 2119m beneath the glacier Öræfajökull. Only 21% of the land, all near the coast, is considered arable and habitable. The bulk of Iceland's population and agriculture is concentrated in the south-west between Reykjavík and Vík.

GEOLOGY

Volcanic and geothermal features – geysers, thermal springs, fumaroles, lava flows, mudpots, craters, calderas and igneous plugs – figure prominently in the landscape. Currently active volcanoes include Eldfell and Surtsey in Vestmannaeyjar, Hekla in the south-west, Katla beneath the glacier Mýrdalsjökull, Grimsvötn and Öræfi (in Öræfajökull) beneath Vatnajökull and Krafla at lake Mývatn. In addition to the volcanoes themselves, Iceland has around 250 geothermal areas and a total of around 780 individual hot springs with average water temperatures of about 75°C.

Volcano Glossary

aa – sharp, rough and chunky lava from gaseous and explosive magma. (Icelandic: *apalhraun*)

basalt – a rock material that flows smoothly in lava form. Some of the most interesting rock formations in Iceland are columns of basalt cooled into rosette patterns and polygonal shapes

bombs – chunks of volcanic ejecta that cool and solidify in mid-flight

caldera – the often immense depression formed by the collapse of a volcanic cone into its magma chamber

dyke – a vertical intrusion of igneous material up through cracks in horizontal rock layers

fissure – a break or fracture in the earth's crust where vulcanism may occur

graben – a valley formed by spreading and subsidence of surface material

hornitos – small vertical tubes produced in lava by a strong ejection of gases from beneath the surface

laccolith – a mushroom-shaped dome of igneous material that has flowed upward through rock layers and then spread out horizontally, often causing hills to appear on the surface

lava cave or *lava tube* – a tunnel or cavern caused by a lava stream flowing beneath an already solidified surface. (Icelandic: *hellir*)

maar – a lake in a volcanic explosion crater

magma – molten rock before it reaches the surface and becomes lava

obsidian – naturally formed volcanic glass

pahoehoe – ropy, smooth-flowing lava derived from non-gaseous magma. (Icelandic: *helluhraun*)

pillow lava – lava formed in underwater or subglacial eruptions. It is squeezed out like toothpaste in pillow-like bulbs and solidifies immediately.

plug – material that has solidified in volcanic vents and is revealed by erosion

pseudocraters – small craters formed by steam explosions when molten material flows into a body of water

pumice – solidified lava froth. Pumice is so light and porous it will float on water.

rhyolite – light-coloured acid lava solidified into beautifully variegated rock

scoria – porous and glassy black or red volcanic gravel formed in fountain-like eruptions

shield volcano – flattish cones of oozing pahoehoe lava. The name was derived from the classic example, Skjaldbreiður (meaning 'white shield'), near Þingvellir.

sill – a finger or vein of molten material that squeezes between existing rock layers and solidifies

solfatara – a volcanic vent emitting only gases, primarily such acidic gases as sulphur dioxide and hydrochloric acid. Solfataras are often characterised by sulphur-encrusted earth and boiling mud.

table mountain – the result of an eruption inside a glacier which subsequently retreats or melts. Material flows upward and solidifies as in a mould, giving many table mountains their characteristic 'birthday cake' shapes. (Icelandic: *móberg* or *stapi*)

tephra – a collective term for all types of materials ejected from a volcano and transported through the air

CLIMATE

The warm waters of the Gulf Stream and the prevailing south-westerly winds from the tropical Atlantic combine to give the southern and western coasts of Iceland milder winter temperatures than those of New York or Zürich.

The unfortunate side of this incoming warmth is that it combines with relatively

Average Rainfall and Temperature

	Precipitation (mm)			Temperature (°C)		
City	Annual	Jan	July	Annual	Jan	July
Reykjavík	799	68	51	4.3	-0.9	10.6
Stykkishólmur	756	64	50	3.6	-1.8	10.1
Akureyri	470	53	28	3.4	-2.4	10.7
Vík	2300	179	162	5.3	0.9	0.7
Heimaey	1713	145	89	4.8	1.1	9.6

ICELAND

cold polar seas and mountainous coastlines to form condensation and, alas, rain. In January, Reykjavík enjoys an average of only three sunny days. In July, one fine day is the norm. Periods of fierce, wind-driven rain (or wet snow in winter) alternate with partial clearing, drizzle, gales and fog to create a distinctively miserable climate. It's mostly a matter of 'if you don't like the weather now, wait five minutes – it will probably get worse'.

Don't despair, however. As you move north and east in Iceland, the chances of fine weather increase. It's sunniest around Akureyri and Mývatn in the central north and warmest around Egilsstaðir in the east. Neither place, however, seems to be free of the relentless wind that makes even 25°C weather feel uncomfortably chilly.

While they're more prone to clear weather than the coastal areas, the interior deserts experience other problems. Blizzards may occur at any time of year and icy, shrieking winds whip up dust and sand into swirling, gritty and opaque maelstroms. Similar conditions can occur on the sandur of the northern and southern coasts. Especially if you're trapped in a tent or out-of-doors – which is often the case in these remote regions – such times do not pleasant memories make!

The phone number for the weather forecast in English is (☎ 902 0600-44).

FLORA & FAUNA
Flora
One of the first things visitors notice about Iceland is the notable shortage of trees. As they say, if you're lost in an Icelandic forest, just stand up! Nevertheless, in Reykjavík's Háskólabíó cinema is an enormous cross-section of a 1300-year-old California redwood, which was a gift from the US to Iceland on the 1000th anniversary of the Alþing. An accompanying sign asserts that Iceland also had redwood trees at one time.

This may seem remarkable given the country's present tree situation, but even the sagas record that newly-discovered Iceland was 'wooded from the sea to the mountains'. While this may seem to be evidence of deforestation on a vast scale, it's also significant that the Old Norse word við, for 'woods', was the same as the word for 'willow', and it's conceivable that the first settlers actually encountered nothing but ground-hugging dwarf willows, which still grow all over Iceland.

On the other hand, if the island really was wooded, the forests were clearly wiped out by early inhabitants, who would have cut them for fuel and allowed their sheep to nibble down the tender new shoots of young trees. If so, much of the tundra, grassland and desert we see today were created when wind and water erosion stripped away the newly-exposed soil (vulcanism and jökulhlaups also played their part in the devastation). Thanks to massive reafforestation schemes, however, the country now enjoys several recreational forests and stands of scrubby birch.

New lava flows in southern and eastern Iceland are first colonised by mosses while those in the east and at higher elevations are first colonised by lichen. The coastal areas are characterised by low grasses, bogs and marshlands. At higher elevations, the ground is covered with both hard and soft or boggy tundra, the latter occurring in areas of still

ICELAND

water where vegetation grows in odd tussocks.

Some flowering plants, many of them European, have managed to take root in Iceland. The arctic fireweed grows around riverbeds, while in northern Iceland you'll find arctic harebell, upright primrose and mountain heath. The northern green orchid can be found in the grassy lowlands, along with varieties of saxifrage and daisy.

Fauna

The only land mammal indigenous to Iceland is the Arctic fox. Polar bears, which occasionally drift across from Greenland on ice floes, would be indigenous if they weren't considered undesirable immigrants. Bears in Iceland have a very short life expectancy, thanks mainly to armed sheep-farmers. In the summer of 1993 a weary bear whose ice floe had apparently melted from beneath him was strangled and hauled ashore by the crew of a fishing boat while swimming off Ísafjörður. The report in the local paper was met with consternation by the general public both in Iceland and abroad.

Introduced animals include reindeer, mink, field mice and several species of rat. Icelandic seas are rich in marine mammals

The storm petrel is common in Iceland

including the common and grey seals and 17 species of whale.

Birds are the real wealth of Icelandic fauna. Most impressive for their sheer numbers are the sea-bird colonies – gannets, guillemots, razorbills, kittiwakes, fulmars and puffins – that reach saturation point on high coastal cliffs. Less numerous sea birds include wood sandpipers, Arctic terns, skuas, Manx shearwaters, golden plovers, storm petrels and Leach's petrels. In addition, there are many species of ducks, rock ptarmigans, whooping swans, redwings, two species of owl, divers and gyrfalcons. Threatened and endangered species include the white-tailed eagle, water rail, grey phalarope, little auk and Slavonian grebe.

Freshwater fish are limited to eels, salmon, trout and Arctic char. The seas around Iceland, which provide the country with most of its export income, are rich in cod, halibut, shrimp, catfish, lemon sole, herring, lobster, haddock and whiting, to name but a few.

National Parks & Nature Reserves

Icelandic national parks and reserves are administered by the Nature Conservation Council, Náttúruverndarráð (☎ 562 7855; fax 562 7790), Hverfisgata 26, Hlemmur 3, Reykjavík. The office is open weekdays from 9 am to 4 pm.

As yet, there are only three fully fledged national parks – Þingvellir (South Central Iceland), Skaftafell (South-East Iceland) and Jökulsárgljúfur – but there is also a large number of other nature reserves: nature parks, natural monuments, landscape reserves and wildlife reserves, making 59 entities in all.

GOVERNMENT & POLITICS

Since 1944, Iceland has been a democratic republic with a president elected to four-year terms by majority vote. Presidential duties are similar to those of the monarch in a constitutional monarchy. Legislative powers rest with the parliament, or Alþing, today comprised of 63 members elected to four-year terms from eight electoral districts.

Executive functions are performed by the prime minister and a cabinet of ministers who are automatically given a seat in the Alþing. Every citizen over 18 years of age has the right to vote.

Major political parties in Iceland include the conservative Independence Party, or Sjálfstæðisflokkurinn (39.7%), led by Prime Minister David Oddson; the centrist, agrarian Progressive Party, or Framsóknarflokkurinn (23.8%); the Social Democratic Party, or Alþýðuflokkurinn (11.1%); the socialist People's Alliance, or Alþýðubandalag (14.25%); and the Women's Alliance, or Samtök um Kvennalista (4.75%). There is also the Peoples' Movement (6.4%), and the Social Democratic Alliance which held no parliamentary seats after the 1995 election.

Vigdís Finnbogadóttir, the first woman elected to the presidency of a democratic country, held office from 1980 until she stood down in 1996 and Ólafur Ragnar Grímsson was elected. After the 1995 parliamentary election, there was little change in the distribution of support for the four main political parties, and the tradition of coalition government continues.

Local Government
The country is divided into 23 counties or *sýslur*, each with a main town or *kaupstaður*. The sýslur are in turn divided into 200 *hreppur*, or rural districts.

ECONOMY
Iceland's economy is more or less dependent on fish. A nationwide fleet of 900 vessels employs 5% of Iceland's workforce while fish processing occupies another 8%. Of the total annual catch, which averages about 1.6 million tonnes, 97% is for the export market in the form of fresh, frozen or salted fish, fish products, shellfish and tinned seafood. This amounts to over 70% of the total Gross National Product (GNP), representing around US$1000 million and making it the 15th largest fishing industry in the world.

In addition to commercial fishing, aquaculture (particularly of salmon) is becoming increasingly important. Trout farming comes in a distant second.

Export agriculture is limited to animal products, primarily lamb and wool although some cheese is also exported. All agricultural exports combined, however, represent less than 2% of the GNP excluding manufactured woollens.

Other significant industries include geothermal power, aluminium manufacturing, diatomite mining and processing, and manufacturing of equipment for fishing and fish-processing.

Tourism, of course, is an important source of foreign revenue. The number of tourists visiting Iceland each year is increasing and the industry hasn't really been able to keep abreast of it. Although official arrival figures are higher because returning Icelanders and transit passengers are counted, it is estimated that 130,000 foreigners visited Iceland in 1987 and double that in 1989. This trend is continuing through the 1990s.

Historically, inflation has been a problem in Iceland but in recent years it's been kept down to about 16% annually. Unemployment only runs to 3%, however, and there is actually a labour shortage. Many people choose to work two or more jobs in order to maintain a high standard of living and Icelandic children normally start their first job around the age of eight years. During summer school holidays, children are employed in construction, public maintenance and gardening. The government requires half their income to be put away for future educational purposes.

POPULATION & PEOPLE
Because most Icelanders are descended from the early Scandinavian and Celtic settlers, Iceland is the least purely Scandinavian of all the Nordic countries. Immigration is strictly controlled and most foreigners living in the country are either temporary workers or spouses of Icelandic citizens.

Befitting people living on a remote island, Icelanders are generally self-confident, self-reliant and reserved – qualities which gregarious visitors may often find unsettling.

What's in a Name?

Icelanders' names are constructed using the patronymic system. That is, a person receives a Christian name from their parents and their surname is constructed from their father's (or occasionally their mother's) Christian name. Girls add the suffix *dóttir*, meaning 'daughter', to the patronymic and boys add *son*. Therefore, Jón, the son of Einar, would be called Jón Einarsson and his sister, Guðrun, would be called Guðrun Einarsdóttir. This means Icelandic family members will probably only have the same surnames if they're sisters or brothers.

Icelandic telephone directories are alphabetised by Christian name rather than patronymic so the aforementioned Guðrun would be listed before Jón.

Only about 10% of Icelanders actually have family names, most of them dating back to early Settlement times. They are rarely used, however, and the government is trying to do away with them altogether in the hope of homogenising the system. Currently, nobody is permitted to take a new family name nor can they adopt the family name of their spouse.

It is also forbidden to bestow non-Icelandic or foreign-sounding names upon Icelandic children. In fact, even foreign immigrants must take on Icelandic names before citizenship will be granted. The only exception ever made was for conductor Vladimir Ashkenazy (which led a subsequent immigrant to request the new Icelandic name 'Vladimir Ashkenazy'!). ■

However, once you've passed that initial barrier, Icelanders are some of the friendliest folks you'll ever meet – and on Friday and Saturday nights, watch out. You'll be astounded by the transformation that takes place when Icelanders decide to party!

The population, just under 266,000, is increasing by only about 1.5% annually. Around 170,000 people, well over half the total population, live in the Reykjavík metropolitan area which is growing at a rate of about 3% annually, mostly due to continuous migration from the countryside. About 25,000 Icelanders live on farms scattered around the country while the rest live in cities and villages of 200 or more people.

Statistically, everyone is literate and the average life expectancy – 75.7 years for men and 80.3 for women – is the second highest in the world (after Japan). The birth rate is high – 17.2 births per thousand women – and, thanks to a lack of social stigma, over 70% of firstborn children are to unmarried parents.

ARTS
Literature
Although there was no written literature in Iceland prior to the 12th century, the bulk of medieval Icelandic literature consists of either Scandinavian poetry composed before Settlement or works based upon historical events during the first 250 years of Icelandic history.

While traditional Norwegian poetry eventually disappeared in its country of origin, the most popular works were carried to Iceland by early settlers and were preserved and written down during the great Literary Era of the 12th and 13th centuries.

The first literary tradition to emerge from Iceland was poetry. Most of the early themes probably came from mainland Scandinavia even before the settlement of Iceland, but weren't actually written down until the period of literary awareness in the 12th century.

The body of Icelandic poetry was divided into two categories: Eddic poetry, to modern ears actually more like free-metre prose, and Skaldic poetry, written by court poets employing a unique and well-defined syntax and vocabulary.

Eddic Poetry The Eddic poems are subdivided into three classes: the Mythical, the Gnomic and the Heroic. It is assumed that the name of the genre originated with the title of the compilation, known as the *Elder* or *Poetic Edda*. Some scholars believe it was derived from Oddi, the place where Snorri Sturluson was educated. Others more logically see it taken from the word *óðr*, which means simply 'poetry'.

The Eddic poems were composed in free variable metres with a structure very similar to that of early Germanic poetry and were based on Germanic legends and heroic traditions. Mythical poetry was based on the dialogue and antics of the Nordic gods and was probably promoted as an intended affront to growing Christian sentiments in Norway. Gnomic poetry consists of one major work, the *Hávamál*, which both promotes and optimistically extols the virtues of the common life. The Heroic Eddic poems are similar in form, subject matter and even characters to early Germanic works such as the *Nibelungenlied*.

Skaldic Poetry Skaldic poetry was developed and composed by Norwegian court poets, or *skalds*, in veneration of heroic deeds by the Scandinavian kings, but as the genre grew in popularity, other themes were introduced. It probably first appeared in western Norway and has a more intricately defined structure than Eddic poetry.

The most renowned skald was Egill Skallagrímsson, an Icelandic Viking who had run foul of King Harald Haarfager's eldest son, King Eirík Blood-Axe of York. After being captured and sentenced to death at York in 948, Egill managed to compose an ode to the king who had condemned him. The flattered monarch released Egill unharmed and his poem is now known as the *Höfuðlausn*, or 'head ransom'

The Skaldic poems are far more descriptive than the Eddic, which are predominantly dialogue, and concern themselves more with the graphic details of battle, an element lacking even in the Heroic Eddas. They also employ *kennings*, vocabulary and descriptions that fitted the metrical requirements and could add colour and interest to the prose. Blood, for instance, is referred to as 'wound dew'. An arm may have been described as a 'hawk's perch' and eyes as 'jewels of the head'. The battle itself was often referred to as 'the Valkyries' glorious song'.

The Sagas Without doubt, the most popular early works to come out of Iceland were the sagas. Literally translated into Old English, the word *saga* means 'saw', referring to something said (as in 'an old saw'), and is from the same root as 'sage'. Like the Eddas and unlike the Skaldic poems, most of the sagas were written anonymously. *Egils Saga*, however, has been attributed to Snorri Sturluson of Borgarfjörður.

During the Saga Age of the late 12th to late 13th centuries, epic tales of early settlement, romance, dispute and development of Iceland were recorded and sprinkled liberally and artistically with dramatic licence. They provided both entertainment and a sense of cultural heritage for Icelandic commoners. Through the difficult years to come, especially on cold winter nights, Icelanders gathered in farmhouses for *kvöldvaka*, or 'evening vigil', a time of socialising and saga reading. While the men spun horsehair ropes and women spun wool or knitted, a family member would read the sagas and recite *rímur*, which were later reworkings of old material back into verse.

There were several types of sagas written in medieval Europe but Iceland was primarily concerned with 'family sagas', tales of early Icelandic settlers and their struggles, battles, heroics, human relations, religion and occupations. While they are obviously derived from nearly equal parts of fact and fabrication, the historical information and the entertainment they have provided over the ages have set them apart as the most developed form of medieval European literature.

One of the best known, *Egils Saga*, is a biography of the Viking skald, Egill Skallagrímsson. Other favourite works include the saga of Grettir the Strong, *Grettis Saga*, about a superhuman outlaw; *Laxdæla Saga*, the tragic account of a family in northwest Iceland; and *Njáls Saga*, whose relatively endearing characters make it the most popular of all.

The family sagas were originally told in Old Norse, which was the common language of Scandinavia. While Norwegian, Danish and Swedish have developed through the

ICELAND

centuries and felt the influence of other languages, Icelandic has hardly changed since Viking times, and Icelanders of all ages read the sagas in their original form for both historical and entertainment value.

Modern Literature Currently, Iceland publishes the greatest number of books per capita in the world – mostly translated works of foreign authors – in hopes of keeping its language alive. It also has made some significant contributions to modern literature. During the late 1800s, Jón Sveinsson (nicknamed Nonni), a priest from Akureyri, wrote a vast body of juvenile literature in German that was subsequently translated into 40 languages. Just after him, Jóhann Sigurjónsson wrote *Eyvind of the Hills*, the biography of the 18th-century outlaw Fjalla-Eyvindar which was later made into a film. The best known Icelandic writer of the current

century is Nobel Prize winner Halldór Laxness (see boxed aside).

Music

Pop Music Iceland's move into the international pop music scene first came in 1986 when the Sugarcubes arrived on the scene. Anyone who'd visited Iceland in the previous five years wouldn't have been so surprised by their appearance, since from the early '80s there were lots of spiky-topped teenagers with multicoloured hair wandering in the streets of Reykjavík. Many seemed to be members of some garage band or other, and frequently put on fairly wild shows in little halls. All this activity certainly wasn't listed as one of the country's prime tourist attractions. Eventually though, it all came together in the form of the Sugarcubes, who formed their own recording label, Bad Taste. They have now disbanded, but individual

Halldór Laxness

Halldór Laxness was born in Reykjavík in 1902 but, at the age of three, moved with his family to the farm Laxness, from which he took his *nom de plume*.

In 1919, he began the travelling that would shape much of his later life. After wandering and writing around Scandinavia, he went to Germany, converted to Catholicism and joined a monastery in Luxembourg. There he wrote his first novel, *Under the Holy Mountain*, but soon became disillusioned with an ascetic's life. After returning slowly to Iceland for a brief respite, he went to Italy where he wrote of his disaffection with the church and his increasingly leftist leanings in *The Great Weaver from Kashmir*.

When the work reached Iceland it was highly acclaimed but, by this time, Laxness had gone to Canada, where he decided to have a go at the fledgling film industry in Hollywood, USA. There he wrote one of his best-known works, *Salka-Valka*, as a screenplay. It was during this stay in America during the Great Depression of the 1930s that he became a Communist sympathiser. Quickly finding himself facing deportation from the USA, he bought a ticket to Germany.

Laxness became so absorbed with the Communist Party that he attended the 1937 purge trials in Moscow and deliberately misrepresented them in his writings (by his own later admission) lest he in any way defame the system in which he had placed all hope and trust.

Most of Laxness' work during his Communist days reflected everyday life in Iceland, often with thinly disguised autobiographical details. *Independent People* describes the harsh conditions under which the average Icelanders lived, especially the common folk on the farms and in fishing villages. Quite a few Icelanders disputed his observations, but their complaints were often motivated by national pride and their reluctance to publicise Iceland's relative backwardness.

His other major novels based on Icelandic life include *The Fish Can Sing* and *The Atom Station*. The former is an exposé of life on the farm and the latter, written almost prophetically in 1948, is about the American military presence in Iceland, conflicting political ideologies and the threat of nuclear proliferation. In 1955, Laxness won the Nobel Prize for Literature.

By 1962, Laxness had settled back in Reykjavík. Apparently mellowed by his experiences with extremism on both ends of the spectrum, he wrote *A Poet's Time*, which recanted everything he'd ever written praising the Communist Party. ∎

members are pursuing their own careers, most notably lead singer Björk who broke into the international pop charts with her album *Debut* in 1993.

Several other Icelandic 'post punk' pop groups have since been digging in, earning their reputations and rites of passage orchestrating Reykjavík's typically obstreperous Friday nights. Such groups as Reptile, Ham and Bless, all of which appeared on the Sugarcubes' album *World Domination or Death*, have all performed internationally and are now moving in their own directions.

So far, Reptile has been one of the most successful internationally, with its hybrid hard-rock music derived by adding saxophone and violin accompaniment to the standard guitar, bass and drums. Their LP *Fame & Fossils* received favourable reviews.

Before you go to Iceland, Icelandic pop music can be most readily sampled by listening to *World Domination or Death*, or anything by Iceland's most renowned export, Björk, whose lively and wholly original style has gained a worldwide following. Do try to visit a few pubs or catch some garage performances.

Traditional Music As for traditional music, Iceland has hundreds of little ditties which most Icelanders learn before school-age and are still singing with relish in their old age. They're dredged up whenever an occasion brings the generations together – family parties, outings, camping, etc. The two favourites (which you'll hear exhaustively) seem to be *Á Sprengisandur*, a cowboy song about sheep herders and outlaws in the desert interior; and a tear-jerking lullaby based on a legend about the wife of outlaw Fjalla Eyvindar, who threw her starving baby into a waterfall.

Several collections of traditional Icelandic music are available on cassettes or compact discs from Reykjavík music shops and souvenir shops around the country.

LANGUAGE

Icelandic is a Germanic language, one of the family which includes German, Dutch and all the Scandinavian languages except Finnish. Its closest 'living relative', so to speak, is Faroese, which is also derived from Old Norse with few changes.

The country is so protective of its linguistic heritage that it refuses to cannibalise foreign words for new technology, other discoveries, or concepts. There is a central committee in Reykjavík whose responsibility it is to invent new Icelandic words which refer to such things. The Icelandic word for 'computer', for example, is *tölva*, a combination of the words *tala* ('number') and *völva* ('prophet').

Those who speak mainland Scandinavian languages will probably be able to recognise some word similarities and even follow the gist of an Icelandic conversation.

Foreigners who feel uncomfortable dealing in gestures or fractured attempts at local languages have nothing to fear. The second language of most young Icelanders is Danish (and therefore, Swedish and Norwegian, to some degree) followed by English and German. After those, some people go on to learn French, Italian or Spanish. Other Icelanders will normally know enough English and German to do business and exchange pleasantries.

If you'd like to acquire a working vocabulary and learn basic grammatical constructions, one and two-week courses are offered in Reykjavík during the summer months. For more information contact Mímir (☎ 551 0004), Ánanaust 15, Reykjavík, Iceland. Self-taught correspondence courses are available from Bréfaskólinn (☎ 562 9750; fax 562 9752; email brefask@ismennt.is), at Hlemmur 5, 105 Reykjavík. You may also want to check out Lonely Planet's *Scandinavian phrase-book*, which includes a range of useful Icelandic phrases.

Since Icelandic grammar is very complicated, I will spare you (and myself!) a rundown of its finer points. One thing to remember, however, is that proper names are declined as well as common nouns. This can lead to a great deal of confusion, especially when you're trying to read bus timetables and find names of towns spelt several different ways. For example, the sign that welcomes visitors to the town of Höfn in the south-east reads *Velkomin til Hafnar*. Hafnar is the dative of Höfn.

Pronunciation

Emphasis is always placed on the first syllable of a word.

Vowels

a	as in 'f**a**ther'
á	as in 'c**ow**'
e	as in 'g**e**t' (sometimes as in 'f**ea**r')
é	as in 'y**e**t'
i	as in 'l**i**ttle'
í	as in 's**ee**'
o	as in 'c**au**ght'
ó	as in 'st**o**ry'
ö	as in 'f**e**rn', but no 'r' sound
u	as in German 'St**ü**ck', something like a cross between 'w**o**rd' and 'k**oo**k'
ú	as in 'sc**oo**p'
y	as in 'rh**y**thm'
ý	as in 'm**i**rror'
æ	as in 'cr**y**'
au	as in French '**oei**l'. In English, the closest approximation would be as in 'b**oy**'.
ey, ei	as in 'r**ai**n'

Consonants

Consonants are pronounced as in English with the exception of the following:

ð, Ð	as in '**th**e'
þ, Þ	as in 'too**th**'
dj	as in '**j**uice'
f	as in '**f**arm' except before **l** or **n** when it's as p in 'a**p**ple'
hl	as in 'c**l**oud'
hr	as in 'c**r**own'
hv	as in 'wor**k**force'
j	as in '**y**es'
k	if doubled or followed by an **l** or **n**, it is aspirated slightly. There is no equivalent in English. The same for **p** and **t** when followed by **l** or **n**.
ll	as in 'li**ttl**e'
rl	as in 'yo**del**'; the **r** is a quick tap of the tongue on the roof of the mouth
rn	as in 'gar**den**'; again, a quick tap of the tongue on the roof of the mouth
r	as in 'ma**tt**er'
tn, fn	at the end of a word are either silent or almost silent

Basics

Yes.	*Já/Já Já.*
No.	*Nei.*
Hello.	*Góðan dag.*
Good evening.	*Gott kvöld.*
Goodbye.	*Bless.*
Thank you.	*Takk fyrir.*
Cheers!	*Skál!*
What time is it?	*Hvað er klukkan?*
Do you speak English?	*Talarðu ensku?*

Small Talk

How are you?	*Hvernig gengur/ Hvað segirdu gott?*
I'm fine.	*Allt fínt.*
What is your name?	*Hvað heitir þú?*
My name is ...	*Ég heiti ...*
Where are you staying?	*Hvar býrð þú hér?*
I am staying at ...	*Ég bý á ...*
Where are you from?	*Hvaðan ert þú?*
I am from ...	*Ég er frá ...*
I don't understand.	*Ég skil ekki.*
Can I have a room?	*Get ég fengið herbergi?*

Around Town

OPEN	OPIÐ
CLOSED	LOKAÐ
FORBIDDEN	BÖNNUÐ

Where is the ...?	*Hvar er ...?*
toilet	*snyrting*
bus terminal	*umferðarmiðstöð*
train station	*lestarstöð*
ticket office	*miðasala*
airport	*flúgvöllur*
ferry	*ferja*

Is it far from/near here?
Er það langt héðan?
Could you write the address please?
Gætir þú skrifað niður heimilisfangið?
I'd like to change some travellers' cheques.
Ég vil fá þessar ávísanir innleystar.
What is the exchange rate?
Hvad er gengid?
How much is it?
Hvad kostar þetta?
I like this.
Mér líkar þetta.
I would like ...
Gæti ég fengið ...

return ticket	*miða báðar leiðir*
one-way ticket	*miða aðra leiðina*
1st class	*fyrsta farrými*
2nd class	*annað farrými*

Accommodation & Food

Do you have any rooms available?
Eru herbergi laus?
Can I see it?
Má ég sjá herbergið?
Does it include breakfast?
Er morgunmatur innifalinn?

guesthouse	*gistiheimili*
sleeping-bag	*svefnpokapláss*
campground	*tjaldstæði*
youth hostel	*farfuglaheimili*
single room	*einstaklingsherbergi*
double room	*tveggjamannaher*

I am a vegetarian.
Ég er grænmetisæta.
Is service included in the bill?
Er þjónusta innifalin?

beer	*bjór*
biscuit	*smákaka*
bread	*brauð*
butter	*smjór*
cereal	*kornflögur*
chicken	*kjúklingur*
chips/fries	*franskar kartöflur*
coffee	*kaffi*
drinks	*drykkir*
egg	*egg*

fish	*fiskur*
fruit	*ávöxtur*
lamb	*lambakjót*
meat	*kjöt*
meat items	*kjótréttir*
menu	*matsedill*
milk	*mjólk*
onion	*laukur*
potato	*kartafla*
salad	*salat*
sandwich	*samloku*
sausage	*pylsur*
soup	*súpa*
sugar	*sykur*
tea	*te*
water	*vatn*

Geographical Features

Most Icelandic place names are derived from some natural or man-made feature. If you learn the following Icelandic words, you will often be able to tell something about a place merely by glancing at its name. The name of the town *Vík í Mýrdal*, for example, means 'bay of the marshy valley', the iceberg lake *Jökulsárlón* is the 'glacial river lagoon', and the resort town *Laugarvatn* is the 'hot springs lake'.

á	river
ás	small hill or ridge
alda	ridge
bær	farm or village
bjarg	cliff
borg	outcrop
botn	end of a fjord or a valley headwall
brekka	hillside
breið	broad
brú	bridge
bunga	rounded knoll
dalur	valley
djúp	large fjord
drangur	sea stack
dyngja	dome
ey	island
eyri	spit
fell	hill
fjall	mountain

ICELAND

ICELAND

fjlót	large river	*vellir*	plains
fjörður	fjord	*vík*	bay
flói	gulf or bight	*vogur*	cove
foss	waterfall	*völlur*	plain or field
gerði	garden, greenery		
gígur	crater		
gil	ravine or gorge	**Countries**	
grunn	shoal	Australia	*Ástralia*
gjá	fissure	Canada	*Kanada*
hagi	pasture	Denmark	*Danmörk*
háls	saddle or pass	France	*Frakkland*
heiði	heath or moor	Germany	*Þýskaland*
hellir	cave	Italy	*Ítalía*
hlið	slope	New Zealand	*Nýja-Sjáland*
hnúkur	peak	Norway	*Noregur*
höfði	headland	Spain	*Spánn*
höfn	harbour	Sweden	*Svíþjóð*
hólar	small hillocks	UK	*Stóra-Bretland*
hólmur	islet	USA	*Bandaríkin*
holt	rocky hill or outcrop		
hraun	lava field	**Days**	

Days

Although in English, Tuesday, Wednesday, Thursday and Friday are named for the Norse gods Týr, Oðinn, Þór and Freyr, respectively, in Iceland an early Christian bishop, Jón Árason, did away with the traditional names posthaste. Icelandic now uses far more mundane names for their days of the week – 'third day' for Tuesday, 'mid-week' for Wednesday, 'wash day' for Saturday and that sort of thing. Days and months are never capitalised in Icelandic.

hryggur	ridge		
hver	hot spring or fumarole		
jökul	glacier		
jökulsá	glacial river		
klettur	rocks		
kvísl	river		
lækur	stream	Sunday	*sunnudagur*
laug	warm spring	Monday	*mánudagur*
lindir	springs	Tuesday	*þriðjudagur*
lón	lagoon	Wednesday	*miðvikudagur*
mörk	woods	Thursday	*fimmtudagur*
múli	promontory	Friday	*föstudagur*
mýri	marsh	Saturday	*laugardagur*
nes	peninsula		
öræfi	desert or wasteland	today	*í dag*
reykur	steam	tomorrow	*á morgun*
rif	rock reef		
sandur	sandy delta	**Numbers**	
skarð	mountain pass	0	*núll*
skógur	woods	1	*einn*
slétta	flats	2	*tveir*
staður	parish	3	*þrír*
strönd	beach	4	*fjórir*
tangi	slender peninsula, spit		
tindur	summit		
tjörn	pond		
tungur	tongue		
vað	ford		
vatn	lake		

5	*fimm*	22	*tuttugu og tveir*
6	*sex*	30	*þrjátíu*
7	*sjö*	31	*þrjátíu og einn*
8	*átta*	40	*fjörutíu*
9	*níu*	50	*fimmtíu*
10	*tíu*	60	*sextíu*
11	*ellefu*	70	*sjötíu*
12	*tólf*	80	*áttatíu*
13	*þrettán*	90	*níutíu*
14	*fjórtán*	100	*hundrað*
15	*fimmtán*	101	*hundrað og einn*
16	*sextán*	200	*tvö hundrað*
17	*seytján*	300	*þrjú hundrað*
18	*átján*	1000	*þúsund*
19	*nítján*	10,000	*tíu þúsund*
20	*tuttugu*	100,000	*hundrað þúsund*
21	*tuttugu og einn*	1,000,000	*milljón*

ICELAND

Facts for the Visitor

PLANNING

When to Go

Every year around the end of August, someone puts on the brakes and Icelandic tourism grinds slowly to a halt. Hotels close, youth hostels and campgrounds shut down and buses stop running. Many late-summer travellers discover that the most popular attractions are practically inaccessible by 15 September, and by 30 September, it seems the country has gone into hibernation. Although this is likely to change in coming years, it's wise to plan your holiday with this in mind.

'Anti-cyclical' winter visits to Iceland are gaining popularity, especially during the Christmas season when Reykjavík, in partic-ular, puts on its festive best (see boxed aside). Around the coast, the Gulf Stream keeps winter temperatures mostly above freezing, despite the long hours of darkness, and there's lots of snow for nordic and alpine skiing. However, as previously noted, few buses are running and most tourist facilities are closed from September to May, so winter options outside Reykjavík and Akureyri are as yet quite limited.

Maps

Landmælingar Íslands (the Iceland Geodetic Survey), with its monopoly on map produc-tion in Iceland, offers high quality topo-graphic sheets, a small road atlas, and various thematic maps.

Off-Season Iceland

Why, you might ask, would anyone consider visiting Iceland in winter? It's a question the Icelandic tourist industry would probably like you to consider, because they'd seriously love to attract off-season visitors for a glimpse of the real Iceland. After all, winter takes up more than half the year on this northerly island! In fact, several tour companies offer special winter packages (a recommended one is Guðmundur Jónasson Travel).

Of course, there are drawbacks to a winter visit, mainly that many hotels, museums and sites of interest are closed and most bus lines stop running from 15 September to 15 May. Even museums which stay open all year normally close between Christmas and mid-January. The winter dampness may be uncomfortable, but thanks to the Gulf Stream, Iceland isn't as cold as you'd think in winter – in fact, it's warmer than most of Europe or North America – but it is dark. In Reykjavík at Christmas, the sun doesn't rise until noon and slips back below the horizon at around 2 pm.

On the other hand, winter visitors won't face tourist crowds, and can get great off-season hotel deals. What's more, the hot springs and geothermal sites – the Blue Lagoon, for example – are all the more appealing at this time of year. Horse riding trips over bleak snow-covered landscapes can be magical and the skiing is fine and uncrowded. The best resort is Hlíðarfjall near Akureyri, but you'll also find decent conditions at Bláfjöll (near Reykjavík), Siglufjörður, Húsavík, Ísafjörður, Seyðisfjörður and other places.

Iceland's winter highlight, however, is the Christmas and New Year season in Reykjavík, which is celebrated to excess. Be sure to sample the vile *jólaöl* (Christmas beer) and learn the tale of the 12 troublesome Christmas lads (see Grýla under Hveragerði, in the South Central Iceland chapter). From Christmas Eve to the Twelfth Night, enormous bonfires rage around the city and restaurants and clubs put on special feasts and fares. Votive candles are placed everywhere – hotel lobbies, restaurant tables and on gates and window sills. Every town has an enormous Christmas tree decorated with coloured lights, and even the churchyard tombstones are festooned with lights. On New Year's Eve, Reykjavík celebrates beneath a rain of fireworks from 6 pm to 4 am.

And even if you miss the holiday season, you're sure to be treated to the best winter light show of all, the aurora borealis. ∎

DEANNA SWANEY

DEANNA SWANEY

DEANNA SWANEY

DEANNA SWANEY

DEANNA SWANEY

A: Arctic cotton, Nanortalik
B: Harebells, Narsarsuaq
C: Spring flowers, Qassiarsuk

D: Glacier buttercups, Kulusuk Island
E: Autumn leaves, Þórsmörk

DEANNA SWANEY

DEANNA SWANEY

DEANNA SWANEY

Left: Clam boat at Hornvík, Hornstrandir, Westfjords, Iceland
Right: Strokkur geyser, Geysir, South Central Iceland
Bottom: Colourful harbour at Húsavík, North-East Iceland

The best general country map is the *Ferðakort* (touring map), at a scale of 1:500,000. Other useful LÍ maps include the 1:5000 map of Reykjavík, the 1:25,000 map of Skaftafell and Þingvellir, the 1:50,000 map of Hekla, Mývatn, and Vestmannaeyjar, and the 1:100,000 coverage of Hornstrandir and the trek from Landmannalaugar to Þórsmörk and Skógar. There are also three topographic series: 1:25,000, 1:50,000 and 1:100,000, which cover all of Iceland and are useful for hikers.

They also publish touring atlases and special theme maps (population distribution, geology, vegetation, hydrography, etc). Maps are available from their office about one km east of the city centre (take bus No 5). For a catalogue, pricelist and order form, contact Landmælingar Íslands (☎ 533 4000; 533 4011), Laugavegur 178, PO Box 5060, 125 Reykjavík. In the summer, it's open 9 am to 6 pm Monday to Friday. Maps are also sold at Mál og Menning, Laugavegur 18, Reykjavík.

HIGHLIGHTS

Iceland's main draw for visitors is undoubtedly its natural beauty, clean air and wide untrampled spaces, and the following list of popular sites certainly reflects that. After each attraction, the relevant chapter is included in brackets.

1. Mývatn & Krafla (North-East Iceland) – most of Iceland's geological phenomena are represented at Mývatn and the region offers some of the country's best weather. The centrepiece is a lovely blue lake teeming with bird life.
2. Landmannalaugar (Central Iceland) – incredible mountains of variegated rhyolite, lava flows, hot springs, and lots of trekking routes characterise this remote oasis in the interior.
3. Skaftafell (South-East Iceland) – Skaftafell National Park is known for its green moorlands and numerous waterfalls with their backdrop of rugged snow-capped peaks and glaciers.
4. Jökulsárgljúfur National Park & Dettifoss (North-East Iceland) – at Jökulsárgljúfur you'll find Iceland's largest canyon, lush vegetation, bizarre basalt formations, lush springs and fabulous waterfalls; Dettifoss, at the southern end of the park, is Europe's most powerful waterfall.

5. Þórsmörk (South Central Iceland) – this popular valley is characterised by beautiful woodlands, glaciers, braided rivers and rugged peaks studded with hoodoo formations.
6. Vestmannaeyjar (South Central Iceland) – one of the most geologically active areas in the world, these islands well illustrate Iceland's volcanic history. They're also known for their profuse bird life and laid-back atmosphere.
7. Gullfoss & Geysir (South Central Iceland) – these are Iceland's most visited tourist attractions. Gullfoss is a much photographed two-tiered waterfall and Geysir contains the country's best examples of spouting hot springs.
8. Cities & Towns – Akureyri (Akureyri) is Iceland's most livable city with well-kept gardens and a fine summer climate. Other appealing towns include Hafnarfjörður (Reykjavík), Ísafjörður (Westfjords) and – perhaps the nicest of all – Siglufjörður (North Central Iceland).
9. Lónsöræfi (South-East Iceland) – this vast trekking area offers numerous remote routes and spectacular rhyolite scenery.
10. *Runtur* (Reykjavík) – How can you dance until dawn if it never gets dark – or if the sun rises at noon, as it does in December? Icelanders have found a way around the conundrum – on weekends, anyway – and it's non-stop partying! For a unique cultural experience, try a Friday night pub crawl with the beautiful youth through Reykjavík's most 'in' bars and discos.

TOURIST OFFICES
Local Tourist Offices

Icelandic tourist information offices are mostly very helpful and can load you down with more booklets, brochures and maps than anyone would want to cart around. Employees normally speak Scandinavian languages, English and German. There may be someone who speaks French as well, and an Italian or Spanish-speaker.

A valuable free publication is *Around Iceland*, which is published annually. It contains lots of colour photos and information on most communities, services and sites of interest. In the Icelandic version, *A Ferð um Ísland*, the photos are replaced with useful maps.

There are information offices in Reykjavík as well as cities and towns around the country. The main office is the Upplýsingamiðstöð Ferðamála, Iceland

ICELAND

Information Centre (☎ 562 3045; fax 562 4749), Bankastræti 2, 101 Reykjavík. The Ferðamálaraϑ Íslands, or Iceland Tourist Board (☎ 552 7488; fax 562 4749) is at Laekjargata 3, Gimli, 101 Reykjavík.

Information and services are free but a fee may be charged for phone calls made on your behalf, and they charge Ikr400 per tour, hotel or transport booking. National park brochures and commercial maps are sold at bookshop prices.

Campgrounds and youth hostels can also provide tourist information, including budget options.

Scattered around the country, you'll find computerised information terminals, known as *Ask*, which provide information in five languages. However, there are still quite a few bugs and the information on offer is rather sketchy.

Tourist Offices Abroad
For trip planning information, contact one of the following offices:

Denmark
> Vester Farimagsgade 1, DK-1606, Copenhagen V (☎ 33-12 33 88; fax 33-93 86 11)

France
> 9 Boulevard des Capucines, F-75002 Paris (☎ 01 47 42 54 87; fax 01 42 65 17 52)

Germany
> Stadtmitte, Karl-Ulrichstr 11, D-6078 Neu-Isenberg 1 (☎ 6102-254484; fax 6102-254570)
> Rossmarkt 10, D-60313 Frankfurt a/M 1 (☎ 069-299978; fax 069-283872)

Japan
> 6th Floor Harada Building, No 1-1-15, Asakusabashi, Taitoh-Ku, Tokyo 111 (☎ 03-5820 0773; fax 03-5820 0780)

Switzerland
> Siewerdstr 9, 8050 Zürich (☎ 01-312 7373; fax 01-312 7374)

UK
> 172 Tottenham Court Rd, 3rd Floor, London W1P 9LG (☎ 0171-388 4499; fax 0171-387 5711)

USA
> 655 Third Avenue, New York, NY 10017 (☎ 212-949 2333; fax 212-983 5260)
> 610B Fifth Ave, Rockefeller Centre, New York, NY 10020 (☎ 212-967 8888; fax 212-330 1456)

VISAS & DOCUMENTS
Visas
Citizens of Austria, Belgium, France, Germany, Italy, Liechtenstein, Luxembourg, the Netherlands and Switzerland need only a valid identity card to enter Iceland for tourist visits. Norwegians, Swedes, Danes, Faroese and Finns must only carry proof of citizenship when entering Iceland from another Nordic country.

Other Western Europeans and citizens many other countries including Australia, New Zealand, Japan, Canada and the USA, need just a valid passport to enter as tourists. Others need a visa from an Icelandic consulate before arriving.

Tourist visits of up to 90 days during any nine-month period are normally granted if you can show proof of sufficient funds for your visit. Officials are fairly liberal with this requirement – they're used to shoestring travellers – but they may ask to see an onward ticket if they think you may run short of cash. Lengths of stay can be easily extended at police stations.

EMBASSIES
Icelandic Embassies Abroad
Here's a partial list of Icelandic embassies in other countries:

Denmark
> Islands Ambassade, Dantes Plads 3, DK-1556 Copenhagen V (☎ 31-159604; fax 31-930506)

France
> Ambassade d'Islande, 124 Boulevard Haussmann, F-75008 Paris (☎ 01 45 22 81 54; fax 01 42 93 42 95)

Germany
> Isländische Botschaft, Kronprinzenstrasse 6, D-53173 Bonn 2 (☎ 0228-364021; fax 0228-361398)

UK
> Embassy of Iceland, 1 Eaton Terrace, London SW1 8EY (☎ 0171-730 5131; fax 0171-730 1683)

USA
> Embassy of Iceland, 2022 Connecticut Ave NW, Washington, DC 20008 (☎ 202-265 6653; 202-265 6656)
> Consulate of Iceland, 370 Lexington Ave, New York, NY 10017 (☎ 212- 686 4100; fax 212-532 4138)

Foreign Embassies in Iceland

All of the following embassies and consulates are in Reykjavík.

Canada
  Suðurlandsbraut 10 (☎ 568 0820)
Denmark
  Hverfisgata 29 (☎ 562 1230)
France
  Túngata 22 (☎ 551 7621)
Germany
  Túngata 18 (☎ 551 9535)
Irish Republic
  Þverholt 17-21 (☎ 552 6300)
UK
  Laufásvegur 49 (☎ 551 5883)
USA
  Laufásvegur 21 (☎ 552 9100)

CUSTOMS

Visitors may import up to 10 kg of food worth up to Ikr4000 provided it doesn't include eggs, meat or dairy products. This is probably worth taking advantage of if you need freeze-dried stuff for an expedition.

To prevent contamination of Icelandic waters by foreign fish diseases, recreational fishing equipment – lines, rubber boots and waders – requires a certificate from a veterinarian in your home country stating that it has been disinfected for at least 10 minutes by immersion in a 2% formaldehyde solution. Alternatively, officials can disinfect the gear for a fee when you arrive. Riding clothing and equipment are subject to similar regulations.

Travellers over 20 years old can import duty-free one litre of wine (less than 21% alcohol content) plus one of the following: one litre of spirits (less than 50%), six litres of foreign beer or eight litres of Icelandic beer. Those over 16 years old can bring in 200 cigarettes or 250g of tobacco products.

Icelandic customs forbid the import of firearms, narcotics, radios or telephones without special permission from the Customs Department, Ríkistollstjöri (☎ 560 0300), Tryggvagata 19, 15 Reykjavík. In the case of firearms, permission must be granted by the Chief of Police. Plant importers must carry a plant hygiene certificate for each plant from the country of origin, as well as a

permit from the Icelandic Ministry of Agriculture (☎ 560 9750; fax 552 1160), Rauðarárstígur 25, 150 Reykjavík. Animals (including guide dogs) are admitted only with permission from the Chief Veterinarian; contact the Ministry of Agriculture for details.

MONEY

Currency

The Icelandic unit of currency is the *króna* (Ikr) which is equal to 100 *aurar*. Notes come in 500, 1000, 2000 and 5000 krónur denominations. Coins come in one, five, 10, 50 and 100 krónur denominations. You may also occasionally encounter five, 10 and 50 aurar denominations, which are practically worthless. Inflation is currently negligible.

Credit Cards

Icelanders are plastic mad and use cards even for small purchases, so it's no surprise that major credit cards (Visa, MasterCard, Diners Club, American Express, Eurocard, etc) are accepted in most places. Credit card cash advances are available from banks and ATMs (as yet found only in banks). Eurocard (☎ 568 7899, emergency ☎ 568 5542); Visa (☎ 567 1700); American Express (☎ 569 9300, UK emergency ☎ 44-273-551 1111); and Diners Club (☎ 568 6111) all have offices in Reykjavík.

Currency Exchange

Approximate exchange rates are as follows:

Australia	A$1	=	53.24
Canada	C$1	=	51.71
Denmark	Dkr1	=	11.07
France	FF1	=	12.50
Germany	DM1	=	42.20
Japan	¥100	=	56.00
New Zealand	NZ$1	=	47.97
Norway	Nkr1	=	10.76
UK	£1	=	114.17
USA	US$1	=	69.94

Changing Money

Foreign-denomination travellers' cheques, postal cheques and banknotes may be exchanged for Icelandic currency at any bank. Some banks charge a commission of about Ikr150 per transaction, regardless of the amount changed, but Landsbanki Íslands takes no commission on foreign exchange. Cash US$, Danish kroner, Deutschmarks and other major currencies are accepted in many shops catering to tourists. Eurocheques are also accepted but they yield only about 75% of their face value and aren't recommended for travel in Iceland.

After-hours currency exchange is available at Keflavík international airport (open daily 6.30 am to 6.30 pm), and at The Change Group in Reykjavík, with outlets at the main tourist office and the Austurstraeti McDonald's restaurant. Consider however, that the latter charges a punitive commission of 6.75% during banking hours and 8.75% on evenings and weekends. Hotels also exchange foreign currency, but generally offer lower rates than the banks.

Taxes & Refunds

The Icelandic VAT (*söluskattur*) is 24.5% and is included in marked prices. When it was first introduced in 1990, such items as water, electricity, books and newspapers were exempted, but in 1993 the tax was extended to printed matter. On 1 January 1994, 14% VAT was added to accommodation, transport and other tourism-related goods and services.

The 1988 VAT rebate legislation, however, relieves some of the sting, but purchases must be from specially-designated shops and amount to more than Ikr5000 per sales ticket. They must also be exported within 30 days of purchase. Participating shops display a sign saying 'Iceland Tax-Free Shopping' (which is a misnomer, since only 60% to 75% of the tax is refunded).

To collect your refund, fill out a refund voucher at the time of purchase. These must be presented along with all items purchased (except woollens, which may be packed in your luggage) at the Keflavík international airport duty-free shop at your time of departure. The refund is made in US$.

If you're leaving on the Seyðisfjörður ferry, show the items and voucher to the customs official, who will stamp your voucher to verify that it has left the country. You can then apply for your refund (which will be made in US$) through Iceland Tax-Free Shopping, PO Box 1200, 235 Keflavík, Iceland. The claims must be made within three months of your departure.

Business Investments For information on business opportunities or investment in Iceland, contact the Association of Icelandic Importers, Exporters & Wholesale Traders (☎ 588 6666; fax 568 8441), Kringlan 7, 103 Reykjavík; and/or the Trade Council of Iceland (☎ 511 4000; fax 511 4040), 1 Hallveigarstígur, Reykjavík. Call up www.icetrade.is for Internet information.

POST & COMMUNICATIONS

The Icelandic postal system (Póstur og Sími, or 'Post & Telephone') is both reliable and efficient, and rates are comparable to those in other Western European countries. Express Mail Service is available from the post office, but the speediest way to go is DHL Worldwide Express (☎ 568 9822), Skeifun 7, 108 Reykjavík.

Poste restante is available in all cities and villages but the central post office on Pósthússtræti in Reykjavík is best set up to handle it. Tell potential correspondents to capitalise your surname and send mail to Poste Restante, Central Post Office, Reykjavík, Iceland.

Postal Rates

Letters or postcards weighing up to 20g, within Iceland, cost Ikr35. To Europe, airmail letters up to 20g cost Ikr45; for 20 to 50g, they're Ikr85, and up to 100g, Ikr90. To elsewhere, letters and postcards up to 20/50g cost Ikr65/125. Second (B) class mail is slightly cheaper.

Overseas parcels up to two kg can go at letter rates; over that limit, they require more elaborate customs forms.

Telephone

Public telephone offices normally occupy

the same buildings as post offices under the name Póstur og Sími. Iceland also has two types of public pay phones: coin-operated and card-operated. Phone cards cost Ikr500 and are sold at post offices and telephone offices.

Direct dialling is available via satellite for international calls and reverse charge services are available to many countries. The lowest overseas rates apply on weekends and between 11 pm and 8 am on weekdays. For international calling, first dial the international access code (☎ 00 from anywhere except Skaftafell, where it's ☎ 90), then the country code (listed in telephone directories), the area or city code, and the telephone number.

Iceland no longer uses STD (trunk dialling) codes. To phone from outside Iceland, dial only the country code (☎ 354) and the seven-digit phone number.

Special services in Iceland are available on the following numbers: operator assistance (☎ 09); national directory assistance (☎ 03); international directory assistance (☎ 08); international call bookings (☎ 02); and mobile phone access codes (☎ 85) or (☎ 89).

Fax
Public fax services are provided at most telephone offices. The public fax number in Reykjavík is (354) 550 7089 or 550 7589. For receiving faxes, the fee is Ikr160 for the first page and Ikr85 for each subsequent page.

BOOKS
Iceland enjoys 100% literacy and, since most people speak both English and German as well as Icelandic, Icelanders have access to much of the world's literature. Since Iceland publishes more books per capita than any other country and imports many foreign publications, a good variety of books is available and bookshops are very common, particularly in Reykjavík.

Essentially all Icelandic bookshops sell some foreign-language titles, but all books, even paperbacks, are very expensive. There are a couple of second-hand bookshops, however, where you can pick up a cheap paperback for Ikr100 or Ikr200.

You can spend hours perusing the Iceland-related publications alone. In Reykjavík, Mál og Menning publishes and distributes free of charge a complete bibliography of books on Iceland. To order a copy, contact the Mál og Menning (☎ 552 4240; fax 562 3523), 'Books on Iceland', Laugavegur 18, 101 Reykjavík Iceland.

Lonely Planet
If you're doing a grand tour around Scandinavia, look for Lonely Planet's *Scandinavian & Baltic Europe on a Shoestring*.

Other Guides
The excellent *Visitors' Key to Iceland* (Íslenska Bókaútgáfan, 1996), formerly published as the *Iceland Road Guide*, deals mainly with attractions on or near the road system. Once you're used to the format, a wealth of information can be gleaned. It's geared toward car travellers, but bus passengers will also enjoy the titbits about farms and natural features along the way.

History & Society
An exhaustive list of history and society titles is available in Iceland, but those listed here may also be found overseas.

Northern Sphinx – Iceland & the Icelanders from the Settlement to the Present (McGill Queen's University Press, 1977) by Sigurður A Magnússon, may be dated, but it's an easily digestible account of Iceland's people, places, history and issues.

Daughter of Fire – A Portrait of Iceland (Little, Brown, & Co, 1976) by Katherine Scherman, is a creatively written and loosely organised description of Iceland and its history in travelogue format.

Iceland Saga (The Bodley Head, 1987) by Magnús Magnússon, offers an entertaining introduction to Icelandic history and literature, and explains well numerous saga events and settings.

A Xenophobe's Guide to the Icelanders (Ravette Books, 1994) by Richard Sale presents a humorous approach to the quirky side of Icelandic culture.

Travel

The early travelogue, *Letters from High Latitudes* (The Merlin Press London, 1989), by Lord Dufferin, is an account of the voyage of the sailing schooner *Foam* to Iceland, Jan Mayen, and Svalbard in 1856. Written in a state of wide-eyed wonder, it will certainly help renew your enthusiasm on dreary days!

First published in 1937, *Letters from Iceland* by WH Auden & Louis MacNeice, is an irreverent and facetious collection of poems, letters and narrative about a journey by the two poets as young men. It has now become a travellers' classic. An update on this tale is provided in *Moon Country – Further Reports from Iceland* by Simon Armitage and Glyn Maxwell (Faber & Faber, London, 1996). In this unconventional travel book, two modern-day bards follow in the footsteps of Auden and MacNeice, with similarly ludicrous results.

Also entertaining is the well-written and often side-splitting *Last Places – A Journey in the North* (Houghton Mifflin Co, Boston, 1990) by Lawrence Millman. This entertaining and well-written travelogue recounts a hilarious four-month journey from Scotland to Newfoundland via the Faroes, Iceland and Greenland

Literature

The best overall work on Icelandic literature is *The History of Icelandic Literature* (John Hopkins Press, 1957) by Stefán Einarsson.

Many of the Sagas, Iceland's body of medieval literature, are available in translation. Since most are anonymous works, they're normally found in libraries and bookshops under the names of their translators, in most cases Magnús Magnússon, Hermann Pálsson, or both. The more popular available titles include *Hrafnkels Saga, Egils Saga, Laxdæla Saga, Haralds Saga, Grettis Saga, The Vinland Sagas* and *Njáls Saga*.

Iceland's Nobel Prize winning author Halldór Laxness has written a great body of work, much of which has been translated into English and other European languages. His most highly acclaimed novels are *The Atom Station, Salka-Valka, The Fish Can Sing* and

Independent People (see boxed aside in Facts about the Country chapter).

Another solid favourite with Iceland-bound travellers is Jules Verne's *Journey to the Centre of the Earth*. It includes descriptions of Reykjavík and Snæfellsjökull, the icy volcano which served as the gateway to the centre of the earth.

Souvenir Books

Among the best coffee-table books are *Iceland – the Exotic North* by the Swiss photographer Max Schmid, and the fabulous Mál og Menning publication, *Iceland*, a stunning collection of ethereal aerials by Klaus D Franke.

Language

To learn a bit of Icelandic, there's a new self-taught course, complete with cassettes, called *Icelandic for Beginners*. Written by Stanislaw Bartoszek and Anh-Dao Tran (who are probably not Icelandic!), it is available from Reykjavík bookshops or directly from the publisher, Bréfaskólinn (☎ 562 9750; fax 562 9752), Nóatún 17, 105 Reykjavík. The text costs Ikr2300 and the cassettes, Ikr1300.

Less expensive is *Icelandic in Easy Stages* (Bókaútgáfan Mímir, 1975) by Einar Pálsson (1975). It's distributed by the publisher at Sóvallagata 28, 101 Reykjavík.

Also look for Lonely Planet's *Scandinavian Phrasebook*, which includes sections on Icelandic and Faroese, as well as Swedish, Danish, Norwegian and Finnish.

Natural History & Outdoors

A good source for books and field guides on flora, fauna, geology, trekking and travel in Iceland, Greenland and the Faroes is Subbuteo Natural History Books Ltd (☎ 01352-756551; fax 01352-756004; email sales@subbooks.demon.co.uk), Pistyll Farm, Nercwys, near Mold, Flintshire, North Wales CH7 4EW.

Guides to nature and outdoor activities include:

Field Key to Flowering Plants of Iceland (Thule Press, 1979) by Pat Wolseley. This is the best all-round field guide to Icelandic flowers.

Guide to the Geology of Iceland (Örn og Örlygur Press) by Ari Trausti Guðmundsson and Halldór Kjartansson. This is an excellent introduction to the complex geological forces at work in Iceland. It explains in lay terminology the geological history and composition of Iceland's most prominent attractions.

Gönguleiðir á Íslandi (Örn og Örlygur Press) by Einar Guðjohnsen and others. Several books in this series of walking and trekking guides have been translated into English. They're written by knowledgeable Icelandic hiking buffs, and visitors will also find them useful – even those in Icelandic – for the route maps if nothing else.

NEWSPAPERS & MAGAZINES

The only English-language newspaper, *News From Iceland*, is published monthly primarily for second and third generation Icelandic emigrants to Britain, the USA and Canada. The same publisher also produces *Iceland Business*, dealing with economy and commerce, and the glossy quarterly magazine *Iceland Review*, with light articles about the Icelandic people, culture, history and nature. To subscribe to any of these publications, contact Iceland Review/News from Iceland (☎ 567 5700; fax 567 4066), Höfðabakki 9, PO Box 12122, 132 Reykjavík, Iceland. The annual subscription rate for *News from Iceland* is US$28 to Europe and US$35 elsewhere; for *Iceland Review*, it's US$29.50, and for *Iceland Business*, US$29.95, to anywhere in the world.

A variety of German and English language periodicals, including the news magazines *Time*, *Newsweek*, *The Economist* and *Der Spiegel*, is available at Eymundsson and Mál og Menning in Reykjavík and at Bókaverslunin Edda in Akureyri.

RADIO & TV

The catalyst for the development of Icelandic radio and television was American propaganda, broadcast from Keflavík as early as 1961. It bombarded the people with the US military's one-sided view of the world and was so effective at manipulating public opinion that the Icelandic government decided to offer more objective, alternative broadcasting.

Until 1988, Iceland had only one radio station and one TV station, both state-operated, but now there are several competing independent stations. On radio, a variety of formats is broadcast on FM at 93.5 and 99.9 (both state stations), and at 98.9 and 102.2.

Daily at 8.55 am from 1 June to 31 August, the Icelandic National Broadcasting Service broadcasts news in English on channel 1 and at FM 93.5 and FM 92.4 in Reykjavík and FM 91.6 in Akureyri. For a recording of this broadcast, phone (☎ 515 3690). Daily at 7 pm, station FM 90.9 broadcasts news from the BBC. For all-day English language radio programming, including domestic and international news and weather, tune into Keflavík Military Radio at AM 1485.

One TV station operates during afternoon and evening hours, even on Thursdays (until recently, Thursday was TV-free in Iceland). Most programmes deal with Icelandic themes but prime time is dominated by subtitled British, American and Scandinavian programming.

ONLINE SERVICES

On weekdays, you can call up daily news from Iceland on the Iceland Review home page at www.centrum.is/icerev/. The latest news items are available at www.centrum.is/news.

You can access the catalogue of the National Library and Archives, as well as other information, through www.bok.hi.is (email lbs@bok.hi.is).

LAUNDRY

The Icelandic word for self-service laundrette is *þvottahús* but they are thin on the ground and limited to a couple of locations in Reykjavík. The campgrounds in both Reykjavík and Akureyri have machines which can be used by guests, but in July and August you'll wait in long queues to use them. However, all hotels have laundry services and most towns have expensive laundries which will clean your clothes in 24 hours.

HEALTH

Iceland has no private medical services; they are available only from the National Health system. By reciprocal agreement, citizens of Nordic countries and the UK are automatically covered by Icelandic National Health. Other travellers need private or travellers' health insurance coverage. Dental care, however, is handled privately, but charges are lower than in the USA and comparable to those in most European countries. See the Health section in the Regional Facts for the Visitor chapter for more information.

GAY & LESBIAN TRAVELLERS

Iceland has a relatively open gay scene, particularly in Reykjavík, and only in some rural areas will a gay or lesbian couple draw any second glances. Gay travellers may wish to contact the local special interest organisation, Samtökin '78 (☎ 91-28539), Lindargata 49, 101 Reykjavík. It's open on Tuesday from 6 to 8 pm and Thursday from 9 to 11 pm.

DISABLED TRAVELLERS

When it comes to access for disabled travellers, Iceland is more or less on a par with other European countries. Most kerbs have wheelchair ramps, most restaurants have disabled toilets and some hotels have specially accessible rooms. Using public transport, however, will prove more of a challenge, as none of the city or long-distance buses are equipped with lifts and only the ferry Baldur has facilities for wheelchairs.

The best source of information for prospective disabled travellers to Iceland is the Icelandic League of Handicapped Persons (☎ 551 2517), Hátún 10, Reykjavík. They can provide information on tour companies, hotels, guesthouses, restaurants and other businesses which provide services for disabled travellers. Once you're in the country, pick up the brochure 'Hotels & Guesthouses/Wining & Dining', which describes facilities provided by various hotels and restaurants.

For general travel guidelines, disabled travellers in the USA can contact the Society for the Advancement of Travel for the Handicapped (☎ 212-447 7284), 347 Fifth Ave No 610, New York, NY 10016. Mobility International (☎ 541-343 1284) PO Box 10767, Eugene, offers international educational exchanges and can also assist and advise travellers with special needs. In the UK, try RADAR, the Royal Association for Disability & Rehabilitation (☎ 0171-250 3222), 12 City Forum, 250 City Rd, London EC1V 8AF, which produces the book *Holidays & Travel Abroad: A Guide for Disabled People*.

PUBLIC HOLIDAYS & SPECIAL EVENTS

Public holidays in Iceland include:

1 January
New Year's Day
March or April
Maundy Thursday, Good Friday, Easter Sunday, Easter Monday
21 April
First Day of Summer
1 May
Labour Day
12 May
Ascension Day
May
Whitsunday, Whitmonday
17 June
Independence Day
First week in August
Shop & Office Workers' Holiday
24 December (afternoon)
Christmas Eve
25 December
Christmas Day
26 December
Boxing Day
31 December (afternoon)
New Year's Eve

Special Events

Pre-Lenten celebrations include *Bolludagur*, the Monday before Shrove Tuesday, when children receive *bollur* or cream buns by pestering adults with coloured sticks. Shrove Tuesday (Mardi Gras) itself is called *Sprengidagur* (Explosion Day!), but instead of pigging out on junk food, Icelanders serve a traditional meal of salted mutton and pea soup. On *Öskudagur* or Ash Wednesday, children are again given licence to menace adults, collecting money for goodies and tying small sacks of ash on their backs.

Icelanders also celebrate a movable feast called *Þorrablót*, which has origins in old Norse custom (perhaps in anticipation of the feast that warriors expected in Valhalla?). Each community selects a day and organises its individual celebrations, normally sometime in February. Traditional Icelandic delicacies feature prominently.

The largest annual nationwide festival is Independence Day on 17 June, commemorating Iceland's full independence from the Danish crown in 1944. Reykjavík stages the biggest celebration, with parades, street music and dancing, outdoor theatre, colourful costumes and general merriment. Tradition has it that the sun doesn't shine on this day, perhaps a psychological concession to what normally happens anyway. On 1 December, Icelanders also commemorate the day in 1918 when Iceland initially became an independent state within the Kingdom of Denmark.

Sometime during the first week in June is *Sjómannadagurinn*, or Sailors' Day, when sailors all take a holiday and the Seamen's Union sponsors celebrations in every port city. In small coastal towns, this is often the greatest party of the year (surpassing even Independence Day – probably because it comes first!). Competitions include rowing and swimming contests, tugs-of-war, sea rescue etc, and medals are awarded for the past year's rescue operations.

Midsummer is observed on 24 June in Iceland, and although it's lower-key than on the Scandinavian mainland, it's a good excuse for more drunken partying and few miss the opportunity. Tradition has it that the Midsummer Night's dew has magical healing powers and that to roll naked in it will cure 19 different health problems. If you want to try it, however, be warned that there's no darkness on Midsummer Night, so you may be open to public scrutiny. Also around Midsummer, the foundings of the ancient bishoprics of Skálholt and Hólar are commemorated with solemn services in those locations.

Oddly, the first day of summer, or *Sumardagurinn Fyrsti*, is celebrated somewhat prematurely on the third Thursday in April. In Reykjavík, this is marked with a carnival-type bash. The first day of winter, *Fyrsti Vetrardagur*, occurs on the third Saturday of October but it typically inspires little merriment.

A real earth-shaking festival, *Þjóðhátíð Vestmannaeyja*, takes place in early August in Vestmannaeyjar. Islanders light immense bonfires, camp outdoors, dance, sing, eat and hold sports matches to honour the day in 1874 when foul weather prevented them joining the mainland's celebration of Iceland's constitution. A phenomenal amount of alcohol keeps festivities rolling along merrily.

On the same weekend (or in some years on an adjacent weekend), other Icelanders get their turn at bacchanalian revelry with *Verslunarmannahelgi*, when people escape to natural beauty spots and turn them into jungles of cars, tents and caravans. They barbecue enormous quantities of meat, then launch into a repertoire of traditional folk songs and proceed to drink themselves into varying degrees of unconsciousness. Although it can be fun, things easily get out of hand (on one occasion in my experience, people took to overturning their friends' vehicles in the river Krossá at Þórsmörk!), so this may not be an ideal weekend to visit the national parks.

In September, a two-week event is the *réttir*, in which farmers join forces to corral a million sheep, which have spent the summer grazing in the highlands. This event is typically accompanied by much rural camaraderie and festivity.

Every year, Iceland stages several arts and music festivals and sports tournaments, and also hosts an international chess tournament, but dates vary from year to year.

ACTIVITIES
Hiking & Trekking
Most visitors to Iceland know that the best

ICELAND

way to see the country is on foot, whether on an afternoon hike or on a longer wilderness trek. The opportunities are unlimited and although the weather may prove a nuisance at times, it's all part of experiencing Iceland on its own terms.

In the highlands, the best months for walking are July and August, since late or early snow is a real possibility, and in some places, it never melts. Even during the summer, weather conditions can change in minutes. For a list of recommended hiking and trekking equipment, see What to Bring in the Regional Facts for the Visitor chapter.

For walking over lava fields, strong boots are essential; anything less can be torn to shreds on the rough, jagged rock. When walking with children, especially in fissured areas like Mývatn and Þingvellir, beware of even small cracks in the earth which can be hundreds of metres deep.

Apart from nature reserves and privately-owned land, you're free to camp practically anywhere in Iceland. To camp on a private farm, ask the owner's permission before setting up and wherever you camp, take care to keep toilet activities away from streams and surface water, and use biodegradable soaps for washing up. Due to the shortage of natural fuels and environmental impact, campfires are discouraged and in some places prohibited. Hikers should carry a stove and enough fuel for their entire trip.

Iceland's largest outdoor equipment shop is Skátabúðin (☎ 561 2045) at Snorrabraut 60 in Reykjavík. You can hire camping or skiing equipment from the two rental shops beside the BSÍ bus terminal in Reykjavík. You can also visit the factory outlet of Iceland's own outdoor company, 66° N, near the Hlemmur bus terminal in Reykjavík.

Mountaineering

Unfortunately for rock climbers, Iceland's young and crumbly rock formations don't lend themselves well to technical rock climbing, but experienced mountaineers and ice climbers will find lots of scope for adventure. Anywhere on the ice, however, dangerous crevasses may lurk beneath snow

---

Crossing Streams

Trekkers and mountaineers in Iceland and Greenland will invariably face unbridged rivers but in most cases they needn't be put off. The sun and heat of the day melt snow and glacial ice and cause water levels to rise, so the best time to cross is early in the morning, preferably no sooner than 24 hours after a rainstorm.

Remember that constricted rivers passing through narrow passages run deep, so the widest ford is likely to be the shallowest. The swiftest and strongest current is found near the centre of straight stretches and at the outside of bends. Observe the character of the water as it flows and choose a spot with as much slack water as possible.

Never try to cross just above a waterfall and avoid crossing streams in flood – identifiable by dirty, smooth-running water carrying lots of debris and vegetation. A smooth surface suggests that the river is too deep to be crossed on foot. Anything over thigh deep shouldn't be considered crossable without experience and extra equipment.

Before attempting to cross deep or swift-running streams, be sure that you can jettison your pack in midstream if necessary. Put anything that mustn't get wet inside sturdy waterproof bags. Unhitch the waist belt and loosen shoulder straps, remove any bulky clothing that will inhibit swimming, and remove long trousers. Lone hikers should use a hiking staff to probe the river bottom for the best route and to steady themselves in the current.

Never try to cross a stream barefoot. While crossing, face upstream and avoid looking down or you may risk losing your balance. Two hikers can steady each other by resting their arms on each other's shoulders. More than two hikers should cross forming a wedge pointed upstream, with the people behind holding the waist and shoulder of the person at the head of the wedge.

If you do fall while crossing, don't try to stand up. Remove your pack (but don't let go of it), roll over onto your back, and point your feet downstream, then try to work your way to a shallow eddy or to the shore. ■

bridges and even innocent-looking snowfields may overlie rock and ice fissures, so technical expertise and equipment are essential. Crampons, ropes and ice axes are needed for any walk on glacial ice and clothing must be able to withstand extreme conditions, especially on alpine climbs.

Before setting off, check weather conditions and forecasts and leave details of your planned itinerary and estimated time of return with a hut warden or campground attendant. Alternatively, register your trip with the Icelandic touring club, Ferðafélag Íslands (☎ 568 2533; fax 568 2535), Mörkin 6, 108 Reykjavík; or the Icelandic alpine club, Íslenski Alpaklubburinn (☎ 567 2773), PO Box 4186, Reykjavík. Report both your departure and return and, if your plans change, notify them as soon as possible.

For wilderness travel, carry a large-scale map of the applicable area, a compass, a medical kit and a space blanket, in addition to sufficient food and warm clothing. If you're mounting a serious expedition from the UK, contact the Expedition Advisory Centre (☎ 0171-581 2057), Royal Geographical Society, 1 Kensington Gore, London SW7 2AR, for information, advice and planning.

Fishing

Fishing is popular not only with Icelanders but with visitors as well, and everyone seems to be after salmon. However, the glossy brochures omit only one detail about salmon fishing in Iceland: that Icelandic salmon privately caught may well be the most expensive fish on earth. A licence for one day of salmon fishing on some rivers may cost up to – sit down, fish fans! – Ikr150,000. That's per *day* and doesn't include a guide, transportation or equipment hire, just the licence. The least expensive salmon rivers, under some circumstances, cost as little as Ikr20,000 per day but you must book well in advance.

Those whose finances don't run so high, however, can fish for rainbow trout, sea trout and Arctic char on a more reasonably priced voucher system. Some lakes and streams produce more fish and are therefore dearer than others. Most fishing in Iceland is on private farms and fishing time should be booked in advance.

For information, consult the *Veiðiflakkarinn* (Iceland Fishing Guide), which is written in English and Icelandic and is sold for Ikr975 at Icelandic Farm Holidays (☎ 562 3640; fax 562 3644), Hafnarstræti 1, Ingólfstorg, 107 Reykjavík. Another publication, *Veiði Sumar*, is published annually and distributed free of charge. It's mostly in Icelandic, but is still useful for the maps of main fishing regions.

For information on angling and permit details, contact the Angling Club of Reykjavík (☎ 568 6050), Háaleitisbraut 68, 103 Reykjavík or Veiðidivon, Mörkin 6, 108 Reykjavík (☎ 568 7090).

Fishing tackle, outdoor clothing and other equipment are sold at Veiðimadurinn at Hafnarstræti 5 or Veiðihúsið at Nóatún 17, both in Reykjavík. There are special disinfection requirements for fishing equipment brought from overseas; see Customs earlier in this chapter.

Golf

In recent years, golf has become increasingly popular in Iceland and there are now more than 25 courses around the country, five of which are 18-hole. For information, contact the Icelandic Golf Club, Golfsamband Íslands (☎ 568 6686), PO Box 1076, 101 Reykjavík. There are also a number of minigolf courses, charging around Ikr200 per game.

In late June, Akureyri stages the novel Arctic Open, an all-night 'midnight sun' golf tournament attracting amateurs and professionals from around the world. Participation costs US$200 per player with a handicap limit of 28 for men and 36 for women. For entry information, contact the Iceland Tourist Board (☎ 562 3300; fax 562 5895), Skógarhlíð 18, 101 Reykjavík. Other information is available from the Akureyri Golf Club (☎ 96-22974), PO Box 896, 602 Akureyri.

The Icelandic Horse

The Icelandic horse *(Equus scandinavicus)*, which has been prominent in the development of Iceland, is small (about 133 cm high) and weighs between 390 and 400 kg, but it's a sturdy animal perfectly suited to the rough Icelandic terrain.

The first horses were introduced by the early settlers, and since no other horses have been imported recently, the breeding stock remains pure. From the first years of Settlement to the early part of this century, these horses were the primary form of transportation in the country. Horsefights were organised as a source of entertainment and the meat was consumed as a staple and used in pagan rituals. As a result, horsemeat was later banned by the Christian church.

Although the horse's utilitarian value has diminished in recent years, it continues to play a role in the autumn sheep round-up and is still used recreationally. Like some Mongolian breeds, it has five gaits: *fet* (walk), *brokk* (trot), *stökk* (gallop), *skeið* (pace) and the famous *tölt* (running walk), which is so smooth and steady that the rider scarcely notices any motion. ■

Swimming

Thanks to Iceland's abundance of geothermal heat, swimming is a national institution. Nearly every city and village has at least one public swimming pool (*sundlaug* or *sundhöll*) and many cold, rainy and windy afternoons are passed in swirling warm waters with a good book or good company. Most pools also offer saunas and jacuzzis of varying temperatures. A session in the pool and/or jacuzzi costs around Ikr180; showers only are Ikr110. *Sund Sumar*, a complete guide to Iceland's swimming pools, is distributed free at the tourist office in Reykjavík.

Skiing

Skiers will find that Iceland offers several little-known slopes and some pleasant no-frills skiing. In the winter, nordic skiing is possible almost anywhere, and in highland areas it lasts until early July. The main drawback is the limited winter transport.

Reykjavík and Akureyri both have relatively well-organised downhill resorts where you'll spend around Ikr1200 for combination day and evening lift tickets. The slopes at Bláfjöll near Reykjavík are served by regular buses from the BSÍ terminal, but weather conditions vary.

Conditions are more reliable at Hlíðarfjall near Akureyri, with runs of up to 2½ km, and sleeping-bag accommodation is available at the slopes.

There are also more basic resorts at Ísafjörður and Siglufjörður, as well as a small summer ski school at Kerlingarfjöll near Hofsjökull in central Iceland.

River Rafting

Only a handful of commercial operations have discovered Iceland's whitewater potential. Most prominent are the Hvitá (see Geysir in the South Central Iceland chapter) and several rivers in North Central Iceland: the Hjaltadalsá, Blandaá, Jökusá Vestari and Jökulsá Austari (see Sauðárkrókur in the North Central Iceland chapter).

Horse Riding

Riding is an integral part of the traditional Icelandic scene, and the naturally gentle Icelandic horse (see boxed aside) provides excellent riding opportunities, even for visitors with no riding experience. Farmhouse accommodation, tour agencies, and individual farmers hire horses and lead riding expeditions through wild and otherwise inaccessible corners of Iceland. Horse tours normally cost around Ikr9000 per day, including tent or hut accommodation. If you'd prefer just a few hours' riding, the standard price is Ikr1200 per hour. Note that foreign riding clothing or equipment (saddles, bridles, etc) must be disinfected upon entry into the country.

The following list includes some of the

best operators offering short-term horse hire, as well as longer horse-riding tours:

Adventure Tours, Jóhann Pétur, Skeifan 18, 108 Reykjavík (☎ 588 9550; fax 588 9551)

Arinbjörn Jóhannsson, Brekkulækur, Miðfjörður, 531 Hvammstangi (☎ 451 2938; fax 451 2998)

Eld-Hestar, Laugaskarð, Hveragerði (☎ 483 4884)

Engimýri, Þórunn & Harald Jespersen, Öxnadalur, 601 Akureyri (☎ 462 6838; fax 462 6938)

Hestaleiga Brattholt, Biskupstungur, 801 Selfoss (☎ 486 8941)

Hestaleiga Reykjakot, Hveragerði (☎ 483 4462; fax 483 4911; Internet www.smart.is/hr/)

Hestasport, Raftahlíð 20, 550 Sauðárkrókur (☎ 453 5066; fax 453 6004; email hestact@ks.is)

Húsey, Örn Þorleifsson, Hróarstunga, 701 Egilsstaðir (☎ 471 3010; fax 471 3009)

Íshestar, Bæjarhraun 2, 220 Hafnarfjörður (☎ 565 3044; fax 565 2113)

Jöklahestar, Norður-Hvammur, 871 Vík (☎ & fax 487 1267)

Polar Hestar, Stefán Kristjánsson, Grýtubakki II, Grenivík, 601 Akureyri (☎ 463 3179; fax 463 3144)

Safari Hestar, Skútustaðir, Mývatnssveit (☎ 464 4279)

Topp-Hestar, PO Box 98, Furuhlíð1, 550 Sauðárkrókur (☎ 453 5828; fax 453 5858)

WORK

The official policy in Iceland is against employing foreigners, but that doesn't mean that some companies aren't still willing to hire outsiders to do the drudge work. Working in Icelandic canneries and fish-processing plants or on fishing boats used to be popular with Europeans during the summer holidays, but with cod stocks dropping, many fishing boats are lying idle and lots of Icelandic fisherfolk are finding it hard to make a living, so finding lucrative work isn't as casual as it once was.

The highest paying jobs are on fishing boats, but these jobs are hard to get and often go to the boat owners' friends and relatives. Foreigners will probably find themselves slopping fish guts eight hours a day for wages only slightly higher than could be earned at more pleasant jobs at home (and well below what the average Icelander earns). Some hard-to-fill jobs may improve their appeal by including food and/or accommodation.

If you're determined to get into the fishing industry, your best chances are in late winter and early spring. For other types of work, Icelandic embassies abroad keep lists of businesses looking for seasonal employees, and can provide up-to-date information.

Technically, prospective workers need a job-offer before arriving in Iceland. Once you have a job, you may then apply to the Ministry of Social Affairs (☎ 560 9100) for the necessary work permit, but the paperwork must be processed while you're outside Iceland. Alternatively, you can find a job in Iceland, then have the potential employer submit the paperwork while you return home and wait for the results. Employers can sometimes convey a sense of urgency that will help hasten the procedure. Once a work permit is issued, long-term workers must then apply to the Immigration Office (☎ 569 9065) for a residence permit.

ACCOMMODATION
Camping

For strict budgets, camping offers the most effective relief from Iceland's high accommodation prices. A tent also offers flexibility, as it allows you to set up housekeeping anywhere outside populated areas. Although camping is permitted in most rural areas of the sparsely-populated Iceland, permission is necessary to camp on farms or private property.

The need for a stable, seam-sealed, well-constructed and durable tent cannot be stressed enough. Few people can imagine the sort of destruction that can befall tents in the wrath of a North Atlantic storm:

When we arrived at Jökulsárlón, the wind was coming from the west so we put our tent in a sheltered area. During the night, the wind changed direction and began blowing from the north, that is from the icecap towards the sea. It was more than a wind; it was nearly a hurricane. Our tent could hardly stand it and our friend's tent crashed down. We had to resort to the emergency hut one km east of the lake.
Cristina & Luco Rosso, Germany

There are organised campgrounds (*tjaldstæði*) scattered around the country.

ICELAND

Amenities vary – some provide washing machines, cooking facilities, hot showers and common rooms; others have only a cold-water tap and a pit toilet.

Charges per night in organised sites depend on the number of tents and people. In the best-organised sites, you'll pay around Ikr250 per tent or caravan (camper) plus Ikr150 to Ikr250 for each person in the group. In some small Icelandic settlements, local governments maintain basic campsites to promote tourism and charge only nominal fees.

A scarcity of firewood in the essentially treeless North Atlantic means that campers should bring their own stove for cooking. Butane cartridges for Bluet stoves are available in Iceland and the Faroes in shops and petrol stations. Unleaded petrol (blýlaust) is available throughout Iceland. Shellite or white gas is called white spirits or hreinsað bensín and is sold at some Icelandic petrol stations. Super-refined Coleman fuel may be purchased at the outdoor equipment shop Skátabúðin in Reykjavík as well as the Laugardalur campground in Reykjavík. A bright pink fuel called T-Ketene or rauðsprit comes in one-litre bottles and is sold at camping supply shops.

Kerosene (known locally as petroleum, steinólíu or ljósólíu) works in Peak II stoves and MSR mountain stoves (and with some difficulty in Whisperlites) and is available at some petrol stations and ironmongers (hardware stores). Methylated spirits is expensive and sold only at chemists and State Monopoly shops.

The following guidelines are recommended for those camping in the wilderness or other fragile areas of Iceland, Greenland and the Faroes:

- Select a well-drained camp site and, especially if it's raining, use a plastic or other waterproof groundsheet to prevent having to dig trenches.
- Along popular routes, set up camp in established sites.
- Bio-degradable items may be buried but anything with food residue should be carried out – including cigarette butts – lest it be dug up and scattered by animals.

- Use established toilet facilities if they are available. Otherwise, select a site at least 50 metres from water sources and bury wastes in the cat-hole you dig, which should be at least several inches deep. If possible, burn the used toilet paper or bury it well.
- Use only bio-degradable soap products (you'll probably have to carry them from home) and, to avoid thermal pollution, use natural temperature water where possible. When washing up dishes with hot water, either let it cool to outdoor temperature before pouring it out or dump it in a gravelly, non-vegetated place away from natural water sources.
- Wash dishes and brush your teeth well away from watercourses.
- When building a fire, try to select an established site and keep fires as small as possible. Use only driftwood or plant material which is already dead or fallen and, when you're finished, make sure ashes are cool and buried before leaving.'

HI Hostels

Budget travellers will probably be pleased to hear that Iceland has a good network of hostels or farfuglaheimili (literally, this translates as 'little home for migrating birds'), which is administered by the Bandalag Islenskra Farfuglar, or Icelandic Hostelling Association (☎ 553 8110; fax 567 9201), Sundlaugavegur 34, PO Box 1045, 121 Reykjavík.

Nearly all the hostels offer hot water, cooking facilities, luggage storage and opportunities to meet other travellers. With only a couple of notable exceptions (such as Reykjavík), sleeping bags are welcome and guests need not provide or hire sleeping sheets. Some still have curfews, but they seem to have little effect on the noise levels in the light nights of high summer.

If you're planning lots of hostel visits, it's wise to join Hostelling International and take advantage of the lower member rates (Ikr1000 per night). In Iceland, non-members who wish to join may pick up an International Guest Card; after six nights at non-member rates (Ikr1250 per night), you're eligible for the lower member rates.

Guesthouses

Iceland has many types of gistiheimilið (guesthouse). Some are simply private homes which let out rooms to bring in extra cash; others are quite elaborate. Most guesthouses offer single and double rooms with a common bath but some even rent out self-contained flats for up to three or four persons. Some offer hostel-style sleeping-bag accommodation, which is just a soft and dry spot (with facilities close at hand) where you can roll out a sleeping bag. In some cases, a continental breakfast is included in the price.

Given the range of possibilities, it is difficult to generalise about prices. In Icelandic guesthouses, sleeping-bag accommodation averages Ikr1400, double rooms range from Ikr3000 to Ikr6000 and self-contained units normally cost between Ikr5000 and Ikr9000 per night. Rooms are always cheaper if booked in advance through an overseas travel agent. Most Icelandic guesthouses are only open seasonally.

Edda Hotels & Summer Hotels

Edda hotels is a chain of summer hotels operated around Iceland by the Iceland Tourist Bureau. Most of them are school dormitories used as hotels during summer holidays only. All have adjoining restaurants and most have geothermally heated swimming pools. Some offer sleeping-bag accommodation or dormitory facilities in addition to conventional hotel lodging, although many lack private baths.

Single/double rooms in an Edda hotel cost Ikr3150/4150. Sleeping-bag or dormitory accommodation, where available, cost from Ikr750 per person for a mattress on a schoolroom floor to Ikr1500 per person for a dorm room. In addition to the official Edda hotels, several other summer hotels around Iceland also occupy school dormitories.

Marginal savings on bed and breakfast at Edda hotels and some other summer hotels are available by pre-purchasing Open Edda Hotel Vouchers from Ferðaskrifstofa Íslands (☎ 562 3300; fax 562 5895), the Iceland Tourist Board, at Skógarhlíð 18 in Reykjavík. However, the vouchers do not guarantee vacancies.

Farmhouse Accommodation

A growing number of Icelandic farmers are opening their homes to summer visitors who'd like to enjoy a bit of country life. Every farm is named and some of those open to guests date back to Settlement times and are mentioned in the sagas.

Possibilities range from working farms to places which have been specifically converted into tourist accommodation, and standards may be anything from a campsite or sleeping-bag accommodation to made-up rooms with private facilities. Unless you're taking the sleeping bag option, farmhouse accommodation cannot really be considered a budget alternative to other guesthouses, but you'll gain another perspective of Iceland.

Some places offer meal plans and others just have cooking facilities. Many also organise horse rentals or guided horse tours. From September to May, accommodation must be pre-booked. Official prices are:

breakfast – Ikr700
lunch – Ikr950
dinner – Ikr1400
sleeping-bag accommodation (bed) – Ikr1350
cottage (four to six people weekly rate) – Ikr19,000 to Ikr39,000
cottage (four to six people daily rate) – Ikr4400 to Ikr6100
bed linen (daily) – Ikr600
child rate – half price
horse rental (hourly) – Ikr1350

For more information, contact Ferðaþjónusta Bænda (☎ 562 3640; fax 562 3644; email ifh@centrum.is), Icelandic Farm Holidays, Bændahöllin, Ingólfstorg, 107 Reykjavík.

They can also provide information on joining a réttir, or autumn roundup (see Special Events). Alternatively, you may be able to make arrangements directly with individual farmers.

Summer Houses

A national institution with Icelanders is the summer house, and they're found by the hundreds in beauty spots around the country. Particular favourites are the Laugarvatn area in South Central Iceland and Húsafell in Upper Borgarfjörður. During the high season, some of these country cottages are rented to visitors for anywhere from Ikr30,000 to Ikr45,000 per week. Low season rates are about 60% of that. For information and a catalogue of houses, contact Icelandic Summer Houses (☎ 482 1666; fax 482 2807), Suðurgarður Ltd, Austurvegur 22, 800 Selfoss.

Hotels

Every major city and town has at least one upmarket hotel. While most are fairly sterile and characterless, they are comfortable and most have all the amenities including restaurants, pubs, private baths, telephones and television. However, those in need of such creature comforts will pay dearly and the money will go very quickly.

The average price of a double room in Reykjavík, for example, is around Ikr9000 to Ikr10,000 in a mid-range hotel and from Ikr11,000 to Ikr15,000 in a business travellers' hotel. Hotels in smaller towns are normally a bit cheaper but may lack some of the amenities available in the capital.

Mountain Huts

In Iceland you'll find mountain huts (*áfangastaðir á fjöllum*) of varying quality along popular walking tracks and routes around the country. Ferðafélag Íslands (☎ 568 2533; fax 568 2535) – the Icelandic Touring Club – and a couple of smaller local clubs maintain a system of mountain huts (*sæluhús*) in remote areas. Although several, such as those at Landmannalaugar and Þórsmörk, are accessible by 4WD vehicle, most are in wilderness areas and access requires at least a day's walking from roads or populated areas.

Several of the huts offer cooking facilities but accommodation is always dormitory-style and guests must supply their own sleeping bags and food. Huts on the popular Landmannalaugar to Þórsmörk route should be reserved and paid for in advance through the club office in Reykjavík, but it's a good idea to book all huts in advance.

The huts are open to anyone. In the more rudimentary ones, Icelandic Touring Club members pay Ikr550 per night while non-members pay Ikr 750 or Ikr800. In the posher places with running water and cooking facilities, members pay Ikr750 and non-members Ikr1150. If you're planning lots of hut-hopping, club membership may be worthwhile. For information, write to Ferðafélag Íslands, Mörkin 6, Reykjavík, Iceland.

Another Icelandic touring company, Útivist (☎ 561 4330; fax 561 4606), at Hallveigarstígur 1 in Reykjavík operates a hut at Goðaland near Þórsmörk and a posh new mountain hut at Fimmvörðuháls along the route to Skógar.

Other Icelandic hiking clubs which own huts include Jöklarannsóknafélagið (☎ 552 8544) Reykjavík; Austurleið (☎ 813717), Smiðshöfða 14, 112 Reykjavík; and Ferðafélag Akureyrar (☎ 96-22720), Strandgata 3, 600 Akureyri.

Emergency Huts

The Slysavarnafélag Íslands (Lifesaving Association) and the Vegamálaskrifstofan (Icelandic Automobile Association) have set up a series of orange emergency huts in places subject to life-threatening weather conditions, the former on remote coastlines and the latter on high mountain passes. They are stocked with food, fuel and blankets and are open to anyone facing an emergency. Law forbids the use of these huts for any other purpose. Users must sign the hut guestbook and detail which items have been used so they may be replaced for future users.

FOOD

You can minimise the sting of Iceland's food prices by self-catering and eating seafood products. The least expensive prepared foods are available at snack kiosks and petrol stations (as they'd say in the USA, 'Eat Here, Get Gas'). In fact, in many towns and villages, petrol station grills are the only place to buy a meal for yourself, as well as your car. For a hot dog with chips and trimmings, you'll pay around Ikr300; for anything more substantial, plan on Ikr500 to Ikr700.

Some upmarket restaurants offer a *Tilboðsréttir* ('discount menu', or 'tourist menu'), scaled-down meals designed to take some of the sting out of dining at high-priced restaurants. These range from Ikr800 to 1000 for lunch and Ikr1100 to 1700 for dinner. However, less-pretentious places serve better food for similar or lower prices.

Self-Catering

Every town and village has at least one *kaupfélagið*, or cooperative supermarket – your key to inexpensive dining in Iceland. Hagkaup is the largest and most economical chain, with stores in south-western Iceland and Akureyri.

Iceland produces few of its own consumer goods, so groceries must be imported from all over the world. Although prices are roughly twice what you'd pay in North America, Australia or Europe, tinned fish and coffee are cheap!

Icelandic greenhouse produce is very good but imported vegies may be past their peak when they hit the supermarkets. Street stands offer the best value for fresh fruit and vegetables.

Supermarkets are open during normal shopping hours. In the evening, on Saturday afternoon and on Sunday you'll have to resort to smaller and higher priced convenience stores. Petrol stations normally sell basic groceries also.

Dairy Products Many travellers in Iceland find themselves unable to distinguish between the numerous dairy products available. Many come in similar packaging and the Icelandic words printed on them offer few clues as to exactly what is inside. The following list may help:

ab mjólk – acidophilus/bacillus milk
G-mjólk – UHT milk
G-rjómi – UHT cream
ídýfa – sour-cream dip
jógúrt – yoghurt
kotasæla – cottage cheese
lettmjólk – low-fat milk
mysa – whey
nymjólk – whole milk
rjómaskyr – skyr mixed with cream
rjómi – cream
skyr – yoghurt-like concoction made from yeast culture, sometimes mixed with fruit flavours
smjör – butter
smjörliki – margarine
smjörvi – low-fat butter mixed with oil to make it creamy
syrmjólk – thick, smooth sour milk
þykkmjólk – creamy yoghurt
undan renna – skim milk

Fast Food

Apart from the two McDonald's in Reykjavík and a few Kentucky Fried clones, fast food hasn't yet made the big time – but it's coming. The least expensive eateries, invariably associated with petrol stations, serve chips, hot dogs, sandwiches, doughnuts, ice cream and coffee, and there are numerous snack bars and kiosks where you can grab some instant sustenance.

In larger towns and cities, you'll find street kiosks selling the same things as well as pizza, pastries and other pre-packaged pop-it-in-the-microwave items.

Smorgasbord

In Reykjavík and Akureyri, several good-value restaurants offer all the bread, soup and salad you can eat for around Ikr800. One suspects that Iceland caught on to US-style salad bars when greens-starved foreigners resorted to nibbling on the grass. Although Icelanders still aren't big salad fans, these places are growing more popular with young Icelanders and travellers alike.

Cafés & Pubs

Reykjavík and several other towns have small and intimate pub-style cafés where you can drink beer, eat a relatively inexpensive meal, or just sit, talk and drink coffee for hours on end without attracting comment. Some may seem pretentious, but the decor is almost always interesting or unusual and there's often tasteful 60s and 70s music playing in the background. The typically creative menus include some of the best inexpensive meals in Iceland. Expect to pay

ICELAND

around Ikr800 for a light but filling meal with juice or a soft drink.

Restaurants

The word 'restaurant' in Iceland refers almost exclusively to an upmarket eatery. Most towns have at least one restaurant but, in smaller places, it's probably drab and associated with the hotel. Some ethnic restaurants offer inexpensive specials, but generally restaurant meals start at around Ikr1200 and average Ikr1600 to Ikr2200 per person. Order wine and the total spirals even higher, then add the service charge and it's halfway into orbit.

A typical restaurant meal in Iceland consists of some meat dish (beef, lamb, chicken or fish), boiled potatoes bathing in an anonymous sauce, tinned colour-enhanced vegetables (peas and baby carrots feature prominently) and a brothy soup (it's a challenge to distinguish between curry, cream of chicken, or the ubiquitous cream of asparagus). There may also be some sort of green garnish, often cabbage-based.

Lunches, especially in hotel restaurants, may be served cafeteria-style, or they'll feature a 'daily special', with a selection of greens, fruit, breads and pastries on the side.

When it comes to pepping up food, there's little imagination. About the only spices you're likely to encounter are ground paprika (on the chips) and a sprinkle or two of dried parsley. Typically, it doesn't exactly burst with flavour and if you prefer something more exciting, you'll have to resort to self-catering or find an ethnic restaurant that's willing to add extra zing to their normally Iceland-adjusted fare. In Reykjavík, there's an increasing number of such places, including Thai, Italian, Mexican, Japanese, Indian and Chinese.

Traditional Foods

Although many of Iceland's traditional delicacies may remind you of the nightmare feast in *Indiana Jones & the Temple of Doom*, some are better than they sound.

The glaring exception is *hákarl*, putrefied shark meat which has been buried in sand and gravel for three to six months to ensure sufficient decomposition. It can be left anywhere, because even carrion birds won't touch it. Similarly, few foreigners ever come to appreciate its appeal to Icelanders, partially because it reeks like a cross between ammonia (some would say stale piss) and week-old 'road kill'. I once managed to swallow a diminutive chunk and there are no words to describe the taste, so you'll just have to try it for yourself. Suffice it to say that after trying the hákarl, you'll be able to enjoy almost anything, especially the shot of *brennivín* administered as an antidote.

So how about *súrsaðir hrútspungar*, rams' testicles pickled in whey and pressed into a cake? Or *svið*, singed sheep's head (complete with eyes but minus the brain) sawn in two, boiled and eaten either fresh or pickled? According to tourist officials, 'The tongue is excellent and the eye is actually better than it sounds'. When the meat is removed from the bone and pressed into gelatinous loaves and pickled in whey, it's known as *sviðasulta* (head cheese).

But that's not all; you haven't lived until you've tried *slátur* (yes, it means 'slaughter'), a mish-mash of sheep leftovers tied up in a sheep stomach and cooked. One form is known as *blóðmör*, sheep's blood pudding packed in suet and sewn up in the diaphragm or stomach. In another variation, *lifrapylsa*, sheep's liver rather than blood is used.

Moving toward the less bizarre, Icelanders make a staple of *harðfiskur*, haddock which is cleaned and dried in the open air until it has become dehydrated and brittle. It is torn into strips and eaten with butter as a snack. On Christmas Day, they traditionally serve *hangikjöt* or 'hung meat' – which is normally smoked lamb – and *flatkökur*, unleavened bread charred on a grill or griddle without fat. Traditional Christmas Eve fare is *rjúpa*, tough, well-ripened ptarmigan served in milk gravy.

As you'd expect, fish is also prominent in the Icelandic diet. Types which frequently pop up on menus include *bleikja* (char); *steinbítur* (catfish); *ýsa* (haddock); *lúða* (halibut); *sandhverfa* (turbot); *skarkoli* (plaice); *sild* (herring); *skata* (skate); *skötuselur* (monkfish) and of course *þorskur* (cod). During the summer, you can sometimes get *silungur* (trout) and *lax* (salmon). Wild salmon is called *villtur* and farmed salmon is *eldislax*.

Icelanders also eat broiled *lundi*, or puffin, a charmingly awkward little bird which resembles a cross between a penguin and a toucan. The meat looks and tastes a bit like calf's liver. If you haven't any objections to trying them, whale blubber, whale steaks and seal meat are also occasionally available.

The unique Icelandic treat is *skyr*, a delicious concoction made of pasteurised skim milk and a bacteria culture similar to that used to make sourdough. It was originally brought from Scandinavia at the time of Settlement and has become a national institution. Despite its rich and decadent flavour, it's actually low in fat and is often mixed with sugar, fruit flavours and milk to give it a creamy, yoghurt-like texture.

DRINKS
Non-Alcoholic Drinks
Coffee is a national institution in Iceland and coffee imports apparently enjoy a low-tax import status, because half a kg costs only around Ikr125. A cup of coffee costs anywhere from Ikr80 to Ikr150, but you'll normally get at least two refills without extra charge. Anything cheaper than this is probably instant.

The only traditional non-alcoholic drink (although it may be spiked with alcohol) is *jólaöl* or 'Christmas brew', which is fortunately served only around Christmas. British journalist Tony Moore has described the taste as 'de-alcoholised Guinness seasoned with Marmite'. Yuck.

Alcohol
When it comes to alcohol, Iceland is what is popularly referred to as a 'nanny state', in which horrific taxes are levied on alcohol in hopes of discouraging excessive consumption. If you want to see how successful this

policy has been, take a look around Reykjavík on a Friday night.

Heavy alcohol controls date back to the early part of this century, and in 1912, Iceland set the international prohibition bandwagon rolling by outlawing alcohol in any form. In 1933, wine and spirits were legalised but, as a consolation to the temperance crowd, beer with greater than 2.2% alcohol remained illegal. For the next 50 years, beer was either smuggled in or clandestinely brewed at home.

In response, several Reykjavík pubs took to spiking the watery local brew with vodka and began serving it on tap. This stuff flowed freely until September 1985, when a new law banned the mixture. The nation gathered in protest, held mock funerals and sang dirges for the swill that had become a national staple, but the government was not swayed. In a surprise development in 1988, however, a vote was taken to legalise real beer in a year's time. On 1 March 1989, known affectionately as *Bjórdagurinn*, or 'beer day', Icelanders were able to purchase beer with alcohol content greater than 2.2% legally for the first time since 1912.

Today, you must be at least 20 years old to buy beer, wine or spirits, and alcohol is available only from licensed bars, restaurants and *áfengisbúðar*, or State Monopoly shops. These shops open for very limited hours: from 2 to 6 pm Monday to Thursday, 11.30 am to 6 pm on Friday, and not at all on weekends. There are four shops in Reykjavík and others in larger towns around the country. In petrol stations and corner shops, you can readily buy the weak and inexpensive 2.2% swill known as Pilsner (or the rather nauseating Malt Extract), for just Ikr90 to Ikr120 per 350 ml can. However, it packs about as much punch as lemonade and can't be drunk fast enough to have any effect.

Alcohol prices in Iceland are still rather high. In restaurants, a glass of house wine or a shot of spirits costs from Ikr350 to Ikr500. A 350 ml bottle of beer or a 500 ml glass of draught beer falls in the same range, but can go as high as Ikr600 in trendy pubs. The cheapest 350/750 ml bottle of red table wine

ICELAND

starts at around Ikr900/1800. In State Monopoly shops, a 750 ml bottle of a decent Australian or Chilean wine goes for around Ikr900 to Ikr1200.

Iceland may well be the only country which allows travellers to purchase duty-free goods upon arrival. As a gift for Icelandic friends, in most cases nothing will be more appreciated than a bottle of wine or spirits from your duty-free allowance. For more information, see Customs earlier in this chapter.

The traditional Icelandic alcoholic brew is *brennivín* (meaning 'burnt wine'), a sort of schnapps made from potatoes and flavoured with caraway. Its nickname *svarti dauði*, or 'black death', may offer some clues about its character but it's actually quite good. It can also be a blessing since it's normally administered therapeutically to those who manage to choke down a bite of the previously mentioned hákarl.

Note that drink-driving laws are strict and some people may reach the legal limit of 0.05% blood alcohol content after only one drink.

THINGS TO BUY

One souvenir everyone seems to end up with is a warm and woolly Icelandic jumper, known in Icelandic as a *lopapeysa*. It's often said you can identify tourists in the street because few Icelanders actually wear them as everyday attire.

The jumpers come in hundreds of different colours and patterns. The traditional ones are thicker and come in white and blue, violet or earth tones. Not surprisingly, the demand for these is highest and they are therefore more expensive than more delicate pastel fashion sweaters.

Most souvenir woollens shops offer tax-free shopping (see Money earlier in this chapter) and competitive prices. Expect to pay at least Ikr5500 for a traditional patterned sweater of good quality. They also sell a very reasonably priced selection of woollen scarves, socks, hats and gloves. Factory outlets, such as Iceland Wool, at Þinghóltstræti 30 in Reykjavík, and Álafoss, in Mosfellsbær (15 km from Reykjavík), are generally a bit cheaper than in-town tourist shops, such as the Icelandic Handicrafts Centre, Rammagerðin and Álafossbúðin.

The Handknitting Association of Iceland (☎ 552 1890) has a shop at Skólavörðustígur 19 in Reykjavík, which offers very good value on traditional jumpers. Most of their merchandise is handknitted by locals to earn extra money in their spare time and quality is generally very good.

Rock-bottom prices, however, can be found in the street stalls on Austurstræti. Although quality is not consistent, you'll be able to find some garments that are as good as those in the shops for Ikr2900 to Ikr3200. The best indication of high-quality work is the tightness of knit around the underarm, which should not separate when the sleeve is raised.

Iceland's beautiful stamps are a favourite with collectors. For details, contact Postphil (☎ 558 6051), the national philatelic service, at Ármuli 25 in Reykjavík. They also have a desk at the GPO in Reykjavík.

If you prefer something totally unique, check out Iceherbs (☎ 567 4488; fax 587 7409), on Keldnaholt in Reykjavík, which markets a range of health-oriented products derived from Icelandic moss (*Cetraria islandica*), locally known as *fjallagrös*. The range includes skin cream, vitamin supplements (moss is rich in fibre, iron and calcium), throat lozenges, and milled moss (for use in tea or cakes).

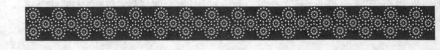

Getting Around

AIR

Iceland's domestic airline, Flugleiðir, has operated jointly with the national flag carrier Icelandair since 1973. In winter, when snow and ice inhibit overland travel, it provides the country's only reliable transport. Flugleiðir has even carried herds of sheep as air freight from remote pastures to winter corrals!

In summer, Flugleiðir has daily flights between Reykjavík and Akureyri, Egilsstaðir, Grímsey, Höfn, Ísafjörður and Vestmannaeyjar. It also flies between Reykjavík and Húsavík, Sauðárkrókur, Patreksfjörður and Þingeyri two to six times a week. Since inclement weather can postpone or cancel flights, flexibility is essential; don't book a flight back from Vestmannaeyjar to Reykjavík the afternoon before you're scheduled to fly to Europe!

Domestic flights may seem expensive, but when you compare them with bus fares and consider the time you're saving, they look much better. The regular airfare between Reykjavík and Akureyri, for example, is less than twice the bus fare and the flight takes just one hour compared with 10 hours.

Non-advertised discounted seats are available on some flights, and a range of air passes are also available. The Holiday Air Rover offers a round routing from Reykjavík to Reykjavík via Akureyri, Egilsstaðir, Höfn and Ísafjörður, but it must be completed within 30 days. Another good deal is the Holiday Unlimited Air Pass, which offers unlimited domestic flights within a 12-day period. However, bookings are available only within 24 hours of departure. There are also the Holiday Flight Pass and Maxi-Flight

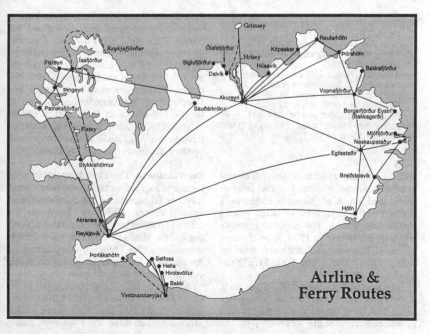

Airline & Ferry Routes

85

Pass, which are valid for two/four domestic flights within 30 days. Note that the last three options must be purchased outside Iceland.

Some gaps in the Flugleiðir timetable are filled by Flugfélag Norðurlands (☎ 461 2100; fax 461 2106), based at Akureyri airport. It connects Akureyri with north-eastern Iceland as well as Ísafjörður and Reykjavík. A third airline, Flugfélag Austurlands (☎ 471 1122), at Egilsstaðir airport, links Egilsstaðir with Reykjavík and several Eastfjords towns.

Air Charters & Air Sightseeing

Íslandsflug operates flightseeing day-tours and 'scheduled' charter flights between Reykjavík, Mývatn, Vestmannaeyjar and other places for reasonable rates. Flugfélag Norðurlands specialises in charter flights to East Greenland, and other charter airlines organise custom tours for groups. The larger operations offer seven, nine and 15-passenger charter flights anywhere in the country:

Flugfélag Norðurlands, Akureyri airport, Akureyri (☎ 461 2100; fax 461 2106)
Flugfélag Vestmannaeyja, Hella (☎ 481 3255)
Íslandsflug, Reykjavík city airport, Reykjavík (☎ 561 6060; fax 562 3537)
Jórvík Aviation, Hangar 31D, Reykjavík airport, PO Box 5308, 125 Reykjavík (☎ & fax 562 5101)
Leiguflug Líó, Reykjavík airport, PO Box 291, 121 Reykjavík (☎ 562 8011; fax 552 8420)
Mýflug Air, Reykjahlíð airport (☎ 454 4107)
Reynisflug, Vík í Mýrdal (☎ 487 1243; fax 487 1303)
Sportflug, Reykjavík (☎ 552 2730)

BUS

Iceland is small and has a well developed public transport system, but the interior routes and much of National Highway 1 (known as the Hringbraut or 'Ring Road') remain unsurfaced. The national highway was only completed in 1974, in celebration of the 1100th year of Settlement, with the bridging of the river Skeiðará near Skaftafell.

Bifreiðastöð Íslands (just BSÍ if you're in a hurry), a consortium of Iceland's long-distance bus lines, covers the country with a comprehensive route network. In the

summer, it allows you to cover from a quarter to one third of the distance around the island in one day, but on minor routes you may wait several days for connections. Although for years it was practically unobtainable, the *Leiðabók* (bus timetable) is now free to everyone.

On 15 September, however, most buses stop running until early June. Interior routes rarely open before July and close again by mid-September, but in high snowfall years, some may not open at all.

Bus Passes

BSÍ offers three bus passes: the Hringmiði ('ring pass'), or Full-Circle Pass; the Tímamiði ('time pass'), better known as Omnibuspass; and the Highland Pass. Bus passes may be booked and paid for outside Iceland at discounted rates; you'll receive a voucher which can be exchanged for a pass either at the ferry terminal in Seyðisfjörður or the BSÍ terminal in Reykjavík.

Full-Circle Pass The Full-Circle Pass is valid in the summer and allows one full circuit of the Ring Road in either direction, stopping as many times as you like. At Ikr12,000, it's only a slight discount on the normal fare, but it entitles you to 10% discount at campgrounds, farmhouses and sleeping-bag accommodation, as well as ferries. For a total of Ikr19,900, it can be extended to include a trip to Ísafjörður and through the Westfjords. It also offers unadvertised discounts on some organised tours.

Omnibuspass The Omnibuspass is good for one to four weeks and allows unrestricted travel on all but interior bus routes and other special routes. However, discounts are offered on some bus tours, pro-rated according to the distance covered on regularly scheduled routes. Omnibuspass is also good for the same ferry and accommodation discounts as the Full-Circle Pass.

A one-week Omnibuspass costs Ikr14,000, two weeks Ikr18,500, three weeks Ikr23,500 and four weeks costs Ikr26,500. The three and four-week passes are good value, but with the one and two-week passes you'd have to do a lot of travelling to get your money's worth.

Highland Pass The Highland Pass costs Ikr18,900 and is actually a book of 15 vouchers for bus trips through the Icelandic Highlands. Each route takes a set number of vouchers. On some routes, if it's used in conjunction with an Omnibuspass (or a Full Circle Pass, if the route replaces a section of the Ring Road), fewer vouchers are required. For example, the Kjölur Route normally requires four vouchers, but with Omnibuspass, it takes just one. The Fjallabak Route normally takes four, but with Omnibuspass, it's only two. The Kverkfjöll trip, on the other hand, requires nine vouchers with or without a bus pass. Unused vouchers may be cashed in at about 90% of their value, so plan your trip carefully.

TAXI
Taxis carrying up to five passengers and an English, German or Scandinavian-speaking driver may be hired for sightseeing at Ikr60 per km or Ikr2300 per hour. They can be arranged through any taxi service.

CAR & MOTORCYCLE
Private Vehicles
It's easy to bring a vehicle – a car, caravan, or motorcycle – on the ferry from Europe. Drivers must carry the vehicle's registration, proof of international insurance valid in Iceland (the 'green card'), and a driving licence from their home country. After the vehicle is inspected, a temporary motor vehicle import permit will be issued. Vehicles can't exceed 2½m in width or 13m in length. Those which carry 15 or more passengers aren't permitted to tow trailers.

Vehicles cannot be sold in Iceland without payment of import duty and you can import no more than 200l of fuel in the tank. Those who are employed in Iceland must pay the duty regardless of the length of stay.

As in Europe and North America, driving is on the right hand side. Seat-belt use in the front and back seats is compulsory and head-lights must be on at all times. Be especially cautious when animals are visible on or beside the road; when animals and cars meet, the driver is liable to claims for compensation by the owner of the animal. When you see the warning sign 'Blindhæð', indicating a blind summit, slow down and keep well to the right. There's often no warning of what lurks over the summit but it could well be a sharp turn that can't be taken at high speed (and some curves are flanked by nasty drop-offs or solid rock walls!).

Most Icelandic roads and highways aren't suitable for high-speed travel so it's better not to be in a hurry. You can get up to about 90 km/h on surfaced roads, but gravel will slow you down considerably. The official speed limit on unpaved roads is 80 km/h (unfortunately, this is universally ignored). Because of excessive dust and flying rocks, some sort of headlight and radiator protection is advisable and all vehicles must be fitted with mudflaps. In urban areas, the speed limit is 50 km/h. Drink-driving laws are strict and the legal limit is 0.05% blood alcohol content.

Rental
Even the Sultan of Brunei would think twice before hiring a car in Iceland. Firstly, the cheapest classes cost around Ikr3500 per day, which may seem tenable until you add in Ikr25 per km, 24.5% VAT, compulsory insurance and some of the world's dearest petrol. The cheapest 4WD costs at least Ikr5000 per day plus all the extras. Some firms offer package deals which include tax and 100 km per day. Generally, the smaller local rental agencies are a bit cheaper than the big international chains.

Currently, the best deal is with the Spanish-Icelandic Hasso-Ísland, which charges Ikr3200 per day, including tax and insurance, plus Ikr700 per day for unlimited km. Also good value is Bónus Car Rental, which charges Ikr3600 per day, including tax and 100 km free.

Note that most agencies require you to be at least 23 years old to hire a car. The following is a list of prominent agencies:

Ág, Tangarhöfði 8-12, 112 Reykjavík (☎ 587 5504; fax 587 5544)

ALP, Hlaðbrekka 2, Kópavogur (☎ 554 3300). There are also offices at the BSÍ terminal in Reykjavik (☎ 551 7570) and Keflavík (☎ 425 0760)

Bílaleiga, Dalshraun 9, 220 Hafnarfjörður (☎ 565 3800; fax 565 3801)

Bónus, Sæviðarsund 84, Reykjavík (☎ & fax 568 8377)

Budget, Ármúli 1, 108 Reykjavík (☎ 588 0880; fax 488 1881)

Corona, Reykjavík (☎ 587 6700)

Geysir, Suðurlandsbraut 16, Reykjavík (☎ 568 8888)

Gullviðis, Glerárgata 36, 600 Akureyri (☎ 462 3400)

Hasso-Ísland, Sigurður S Bjarnarson, Hringbraut 62, Reykjavík (☎ 555 3340; fax 555 3330)

InterRent Europcar, Skeifan 9, Reykjavík (☎ 568 6915; fax 568 8663). There are also offices at Tryggvabraut 14, Akureyri (☎ 461 3000; fax 462 6476); Keflavík airport (☎ 425 0300); Fálkakletti 1, Borgarnes (☎ 437 1618); Olís, Blönduós (☎ 452 4350); Furuhlíð 1, Sauðárkrókur; (☎ 453 5828); Olís, Fellibær, Egilsstaðir (☎ 471 1623); Hólabraut 14, Höfn (☎ 478 1303); Fagraholt 9, Ísafjörður (☎ 456 4072); and Vestmannaeyjar airport (☎ 481 3050)

Icelandair/Hertz, Flugvallavegur, Reykjavík (☎ 505 0600; fax 505 0650). Other offices are in Keflavík (☎ 425 0221); Akureyri (☎ 461 1005); Egilsstaðir (☎ 471 1210); Höfn (☎ 478 1250); and Vestmannaeyjar (☎ 481 3300)

RVS/Avis, Sigtún 5, Reykjavík (☎ 562 4433; fax 562 3590). This agency also has offices at Strandgata 25, Akureyri (☎ 461 2428; fax 462 3899); Langanesvegur 29, Þórshöfn (☎ 468 1175); Olís, Höfn (☎ 478 1260); and Keflavík airport (☎ 562 4423)

SH Car Hire, Nýbýlavegur 32, Kópavogur (☎ 554 5477; fax 554 5519)

SI Car Rental, Stóragerði 25, 108 Reykjavík (☎ 557 4233; fax 588 6550)

Stolpi, Þjóðbraut 1, Akranes (☎ 431 2622)

Driving in the Interior

For independent travel on the F-numbered highways in the Icelandic interior, you need a reliable 4WD vehicle. Also, bear in mind that there are only three petrol stations (Hveravellir, Kerlingarfjöll and Versalir) and no repair services anywhere in the interior. Note that driving off designated F-numbered routes is prohibited.

A suggested spares or repair kit includes extra oil, brake fluid, several jerry cans of petrol, sealing compound for the radiator and petrol tank, a distributor cap, rotor arm, condenser, fuel filter, fan belt, spare tyre, a puncture repair kit, spark plugs, insulated wire, fuses and headlamps. Tool kits should include a tow rope, shovel, crowbar, applicable sockets and wrenches, a jack, torch, batteries, flares, fire extinguisher and emergency rations. And of course, you'll need the expertise to identify all this stuff and fix any mechanical problems!

In the interior, the greatest threats to vehicles are unbridged rivers *(óbrúaðar ár).* Glacial rivers frequently change course and the best ford sites vary. Tyre marks leading into the water don't mean that a river can be crossed. Note that the widest fords can be the shallowest and are more likely to be gravelly and therefore more favourable than sandy fords.

For any ford more than axle-deep, wade into the river (if it's feasible) and check the depth and condition of the riverbed before attempting to drive across. Carry a pole to steady yourself and to test the current and bottom conditions, and always face upstream while wading. If the water is fast or deep, use a flotation device and a lifeline. Before driving into water more than calf-deep, cover the distributor and ignition system with a woollen rag, and switch off the headlights. Don't stop in midstream unless you can't continue and want to reverse out.

Note that heavy rains cause water levels to rise and warmer days bring on heavy glacial melting. In either case, otherwise placid streams may become uncrossable torrents with little warning. If a river is carrying lots of vegetation or you can hear rocks being swept along the riverbed, don't attempt to cross. Wait for the water level to subside.

Another driving hazard is drifting, wind-blown sand. During storms, tracks may disappear into sand drifts and even 4WD vehicles can become bogged. In affected areas, it's best to travel in convoy and carry a good tow rope. You'll also need large-scale maps, a compass, extra rations and a shovel, as well as protection for your eyes and skin from all the grit.

For further information about driving in

the interior, tourist offices distribute several pamphlets: *Some Things You Must Know When Driving in Iceland, Traffic Signs in Iceland, How to Travel in the Interior of Iceland, The Art of Driving on Icelandic Roads, Off-Road Driving in Iceland* and *Fjallvegir/Mountain Roads*. This last one identifies the anticipated summer opening of each interior route.

BICYCLE

Hard-core cyclists will find a challenge in Iceland, and an increasing number of visitors are trying it and having a great time. At its worst, cycling in Iceland is an exercise in masochism; winds blow almost incessantly, many roads are unsurfaced, hills are steep, river crossings can be hazardous, sandstorms are rife, inclement weather is a fact of life and intimidating vehicles howl past in clouds of dust and gravel. In short, if you want to have a pleasant experience, prepare to pack up your bike and travel by bus when the going gets miserable.

The following readers' letters offer some solid advice:

If you don't mind the wind, rain and cold and if you are well trained – and of course if you have the time – discovering Iceland by bicycle is a great experience and we really recommend it! We used our normal 10-speed bicycles (not mountain bikes), which are more or less okay if you don't go into the interior and stay only on numbered routes.

And when you're fed up with cycling, you can easily use the public buses to cover the longest distances and take your bike along. You need to pay an additional ticket for the bike; we paid Ikr400 from Höfn to Mývatn and Ikr700 from Akureyri to Borgarnes. If there is no place for the bike on the bus, BSÍ will send it to you with the next bus.

It's very important to take as many replacement parts and tools with you as possible because (1) there are no bicycle workshops outside Reykjavík (at least we didn't see any) and (2) applying to auto workshops can be very expensive – about Ikr1500 per hour for (in our case unsuccessful) work!

Among the surprises we found in Iceland was the wind; it can be so strong that you can be blown off the road, as I was between Jökulsárlón and Höfn. When planning your tour, you can assume that the winds come mainly from the west. However, locally they also blow down from the mountains to the valleys. This means that along the coast roads, you'll have crosswinds. When the wind comes from the north, this means bad weather in the north (we had snow in Akureyri) and better weather in the south. And vice versa; a south-west wind brings ugly weather in the south and nice days in the north.

Cristina & Luco Rosso, Germany

We are crazy about mountain bikes and northern countries and have crossed Iceland from north to south with our bikes. It was the greatest experience of our lives but also one of the most difficult. Everything remains in our minds – every stone, flower and bird discovered on this beautiful island.

Of course, the weather, the wind and the sand can be horrid, but Iceland is a place for adventurous bikers and a paradise for those who search for challenging conditions and few people on the track. We have travelled from Akureyri to Landmannalaugar, across from Mývatn to Herðubreið, Askja and Nýidalur, crossing the Ódáðahraun and Sprengisandur deserts. Tracks were very difficult with lots of sand, sharp lava and great distances without buildings or people. So it was necessary to be self-sufficient for food, although water was available most of the time from rivers.

To cross rivers with bikes, be very careful. The stream takes the bike with it. It's better with two people so you can pass one bike across. The water is very cold and it's horrid to bike with wet socks and shoes; you're sure to be frozen. We have used plastic sandals to cross rivers. They protect us against stones in the water and are light in the luggage.

Don't carry too many clothes – they're heavy and washing is easy in Iceland. When biking, we wore thermal underwear, polar fleece and waterproof jackets and trousers. The sun may also be very harsh in the desert so have a cap and sun cream for your face and lips. The most important thing, however, is to have waterproof luggage. We used waterproof bags available in sport shops and after biking the whole day in the rain, it's a matter of life or death to sleep in a dry sleeping bag!

Nicole & Jean-Bernard Feller, Switzerland

Transporting Bicycles

Domestic airlines normally accept bicycles as checked luggage and provide bike bags free. You must remove the pedals and front wheel and turn the handlebars sideways.

Bicycles may be carried on long-distance buses if there is space, and some buses even have racks on the front for carrying bicycles. For trips of under 100 km, you'll pay Ikr350; over 100 km, it's Ikr500, even with a bus pass. Space shortages generally only occur in late July and early August, when there are lots of cyclists around.

ICELAND

Bicycle Rental

Bicycle hire is available from tourist offices, hotels, hostels or guesthouses in Mývatn, Reykjavík, Akureyri and a growing number of other places. Standard charges are Ikr1000 to Ikr1500 per day, plus deposit.

BSÍ, the long-distance bus company hires 18-speed mountain bikes, including a pump, water bottle, lock and repair kit, for Ikr1100 per day, Ikr6300 per week and Ikr19,500 for four weeks. Holders of a valid Omnibuspass receive a 50% discount (logical since bike-riding cuts into time spent on buses!) and Full-Circle Pass holders get 20% off. However, rental of BSÍ bikes doesn't guarantee bicycle space on BSÍ buses!

Icelandic Mountain Bike Club

To learn about cycling in Iceland as Icelanders do it, contact the Icelandic mountain bike club, Íslenska Fjallhjólaklúbbsins (☎ & fax 562 0099), PO Box 5193, 125 Reykjavík. Between late May and early September, the club organises cycling trips around the country, and visitors are welcome to join in.

HITCHING

Summer hitching in Iceland is possible but inconsistent and provides scope for meeting some interesting, down-to-earth and normally reserved locals, especially as you move away from Reykjavík.

Although traffic isn't exactly heavy in Iceland, patient hitchers will eventually get a lift. The longest waits may be expected in the Westfjords, Snæfellsnes and the area around Höfn. Generally, the thinner the traffic, the higher your chances of getting a ride if something does come along.

Note that many Icelandic cars are small (although there are some monster American cars out there!) and most drivers are on trips themselves, so avoid hitching in groups of more than two people. Naturally, a lot of visible luggage will put people off stopping for you, but intending hitchers should nevertheless be equipped with the whole gamut of warm, windproof and waterproof clothing. A backpack, a sleeping bag, food and a tent are essential for hitching in remote areas. Mark

Crawford writes: 'A woolly hat and a silly grin are also vital components in a hitcher's repertoire'.

Although Iceland is one of the safest countries in the world, hitching isn't a totally safe way of getting around in any country and just because we explain how hitching works, doesn't mean we recommend it. Women should generally avoid hitching alone and shouldn't be afraid to refuse lifts which may seem suspicious.

BOAT
Ferry

Major Icelandic ferries include the *Akraborg*, which connects Reykjavík and Akranes; the *Herjólfur*, between Þorlákshöfn and Vestmannaeyjar; the *Baldur*, between Stykkishólmur, Flatey, and Brjánslækur; the *Sævar*, between Arskógssand and Hrísey; the *Sæfari*, between Akureyri, Hrísey, Dalvík and Grímsey; the *Anný*, between Neskaupstaður and Mjóifjörður; and the *Fagranes*, between Ísafjörður, Jökulfjörður, Ísafjarðardjúp and Hornstrandir. The first three are car ferries, and the *Fagranes* and *Sæfari* run in the summer only. A small ferry also connects Reykjavík's Sundahöfn harbour with Viðey island.

If you're prone to seasickness, take precautions on the notoriously quease-inspiring Vestmannaeyjar route. In bad weather, the Hornstrandir and Grímsey routes can also be rough.

Ferry schedules are designed to coincide with bus arrival and departure times, and are outlined in the *Leiðabók* bus timetable and the BSÍ tour listing. Holders of bus passes and student cards are eligible for a 10% discount on fares.

LOCAL TRANSPORT
City Buses

Reykjavík has a good system of city buses costing Ikr120 per ride. Other cities and towns with municipal bus services include Kópavogur, Hafnarfjörður, Akureyri and Ísafjörður.

ICELAND

Thumbing through Iceland

Hitchhiking may not be the safest way to travel, but 75-year-old Australian traveller Margaret Penman found it was a great way of getting around Iceland. Here's her story...

Iceland is the most dramatic and beautiful of all the 49 countries I have hitchhiked in. Having an intense interest in Vikings, I read two Icelandic sagas, written almost 1000 years ago, and they and Lonely Planet set the scene.

Practically everyone I met spoke fluent English and the Icelanders are the most friendly people. I had no difficulty hitching along the Ring Road that runs around the island. I went in June and sometimes, especially on the south road, there would be only one or two cars an hour, but I was always picked up.

At 75, I didn't climb the mountains and glaciers, but many kind drivers took me to out-of-the-way places. The three youth hostels I stayed in were great, but usually I was taken to private homes by friendly strangers. I tasted a lot of their food, mostly delicious, but an unforgettable mouthful of rotten shark (eaten raw after having been buried for three months) rather evened the score.

From Reykjavík, I headed out to Snaefellsness along bone-shaking roads with tantalising views of the huge glacier shrouded in mist. I didn't get to the top – I had already fallen head first into the snow from a snowmobile while racing up a mountain! Hitching back was easy; I just went where the cars went and saw many interesting places. I walked around the huge, weird lava rocks, the setting for Jules Verne's *Journey to the Centre of the Earth*, and heard stories of trolls and berserkers.

Having an urge to see and photograph puffins, I went by ferry to Heimaey (Westmen Islands). In my quest, I accidentally left the path and was stuck on a cliff for two and a half hours. I watched my bag of food slide over the steep cliff to the rocks and sea below and waited in the chilly winds until I was rescued. The casual Icelandic comment was that 'many people fall over the cliffs each year'.

The day before I left I had a swim in the mineral waters of the Blue Lagoon. It wasn't blue on the day I went; it was a grey and steamy witches' cauldron, but the water was warm. I hitched there; two lifts and about half a minute between cars, which was lucky because the weather was dreadful, the wind so strong that I had to hold onto a post at the side of the road. I was driven back to Reykjavík by a family who rescued me when I slithered on the stones in the lagoon.

Margaret Penman

ORGANISED TOURS

Some independent travellers may find the idea of joining a group tour rather disagreeable, but in Iceland, many of the best sights are in remote areas not served by public transport. Unless you have a private vehicle or an inclination toward long hikes, hitches or cycles, tours provide the best and easiest way to reach out-of-the-way attractions and beauty spots.

In many cases, the word 'tour' is used rather informally in Iceland, and low profile options are available. These tours, which include those run by BSÍ affiliates, are more like ordinary coach services, except that they stop at points of interest for photos and walks. Only a few of these tours include a guide or meals, and participants may leave and rejoin the tour as many times as they like, as long as pick-up arrangements are made in advance.

Alternatively, lots of local operators run specialist tours involving outdoor pursuits ranging from trekking and cycling to horse-riding, snowmobiling, whitewater rafting and photography packages.

There are also more upmarket guided bus tours which hit the sites of interest. You can keep costs to a minimum by opting for a tour which involves camping or sleeping in huts or hostels, and requires you to participate in camp chores. Alternatively, you can select an all-inclusive deluxe tour which is 1st class in every respect.

The following local operators offer a growing choice of tours. For addresses of agencies and packagers outside Iceland, see Organised Tours in the Getting There & Away chapter:

Austurlands Travel, Stangarhylur 3A, PO Box 9088, 129 Reykjavík (☎ 567 8545; fax 587 0036) Austurlands runs comprehensive hiking, bird-watching, mountain-biking and adventure tours all over Iceland. Guides speak English, German and French.

BSÍ Travel, Umferðarmiðstödin, Vatnsmýrarveg 10, 101 Reykjavík (☎ 552 2300; fax 552 9973). This consortium of bus operators is also a travel agency which organises tours all over the country, many incorporating scheduled bus services. Many tours can be booked on the spot or just a couple of days in advance; the biggest drawback is the minimum participation requirement which means that many scheduled tours never run. Each week there's a Tour of the Week, which is available at a considerable discount.

Erlingsson Naturreisen, Austurstræti 17, PO Box 1325, 101 Reykjavík (☎ 551 9700; fax 551 9703) This friendly German-oriented company specialises in hiking tours through far-flung parts of Iceland. They combine adventure travel on foot with comfortable accommodation.

Icelandic Highland Travel, Lækjargata 3, PO Box 1622, Reykjavík (☎ 552 2225). Strenuous highland expeditions and skiing, geology, mountainbiking and trekking tours.

Fjallaleiðsögumenn, Suðurlandsbraut 30, Reykjavík (☎ 854 2959; fax 551 1392) Better known as 'Iceland Guides', this private guides' association will take you anywhere you might want to go. It's best known for leading Vatnajökull expeditions and climbs of Hvannadalshnúkur, Iceland's highest peak. Individual guides are well versed in Icelandic history and geology and typically speak several foreign languages.

Ferðafélag Íslands, Mörkin 6, 101 Reykjavík (☎ 568 2533; fax 568 2535). The Icelandic Touring Club leads summer trekking trips along the most interesting tracks and routes around the country. Accommodation is normally in mountain huts and tents.

Guðmundur Jónasson Travel, Borgartún 34, 105 Reykjavík (☎ 511 1515; fax 511 1511). This ever-popular company offers bus and camping tours with light hiking. They're an excellent

option for active people who'd rather not make their own arrangements. The 12-day highland walking adventures are especially recommended. They also run winter tours.

Mountaineers, Reykjavík (☎ 488 5550; fax 488 5540) Mountaineers specialises in adventure tours in western Iceland, and also guides hunting tours and believe it or not, scuba diving in the sea or in volcanic lakes and hot springs.

Mountain Taxi Adventure Tours, Kristján Kristjánsson, Lindarbær, Reykholt 320, Borgarfjörður (☎ 436 1117; fax 435 1479) This company runs mountain 4WD tours around upper Borgarfjörður and Arnarvatnsheiði.

Reykjavík Excursions, Bankastræti 2, Reykjavík (☎ 562 4422; fax 562 4450) Reykjavík's most popular day tour agency caters mainly to packaged tourists, but works well for maximising the sites in a minimum of time. Tours are pricey and with all the fleeting stops, you may feel as if you're on an assembly line, but then, you wanted to do it quickly...

Úrval Útsyn, Lágmúli 4, 101 Reykjavík (☎ 569 9300; fax 557 1233) This is the American Express representative in Iceland. It cobbles together Iceland tours, but they're sold mainly through outside travel agencies and not directly. The main office is at Álfabakki 16, outside the Reykjavík city centre.

Útivist, Hallveigarstígur 1, Reykjavík (☎ 561 4330; fax 561 4606) Known in English as the Outdoor Life & Touring Club, this excellent organisation promotes outdoor appreciation in Iceland. Its tours are actually more like friendly trekking trips and cover just about every corner of Iceland.

Vestfjarðarleið, Sætún 4, 105 Reykjavík (☎ 562 9950; fax 562 9912) This friendly company runs recommended day trips to Þórsmörk and offers a taste of the Icelandic countryside on fishing and riding tours at the farm Hjalli, in Kjós, Hvalfjörður.

Reykjavík

Reykjavík, the world's northernmost capital city and home to 170,000 of Iceland's 266,000 people, may be less vibrant than other European capitals, but politically, socially, culturally, economically and psychologically, it dominates the country.

Reykjavík hasn't always been a big smoke. According to one account, as recently as 1806 the city had only 300 inhabitants – 27 of whom were in prison for public inebriation. Only 100 years ago, most of the Icelandic population lived on family farms and the country's shift from predominantly rural to decidedly urban happened very quickly. Even today, many Reykjavík residents are transplanted from somewhere else.

Like many North American and Australian cities, Reykjavík is unconsolidated, reflecting rapid growth and the lack of an overall city plan. Construction is constant, and if urban drift continues and Reykjavík keeps growing at its present pace of 2000 persons annually, it will usurp even more of Iceland's identity in coming years.

Unfortunately for the Reykjavík tourism concerns, most visitors come to Iceland for its glaciers, waterfalls, geysers and mountains. But nearly everyone has to pass through it several times on their Iceland circuit, and awaiting them is the usual gamut of museums, churches and cultural activities befitting a capital city. After weeks of facing the elements in the great outdoors, the idea of cinemas, bookshops, discos and coffee shops, and warm, dry days in museums may appeal even to die-hard nature freaks.

History

Reykjavík was the first place in Iceland to be intentionally settled. The first settler, Ingólfur Arnarson, tossed his high-seat pillars overboard in 874 and built his farm at the place where they washed ashore, between the small lake Tjörn ('the pond') and the sea, where Aðalstræti now intersects with Suðurgata. He called the place Reyk-

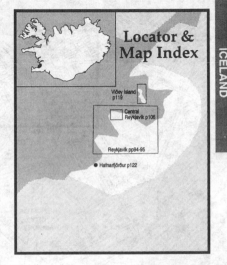

Locator & Map Index

Viðey Island p119

Central Reykjavík p106

Reykjavík pp94-95

● Hafnarfjörður p122

ICELAND

javík, or 'smoky bay', after the steam rising from the earth. Ingólfur claimed the entire south-west corner of the island, then set about planting his hayfields at Austurvöllur, the present town square.

As other settlers arrived, Reykjavík grew and Ingólfur's descendants multiplied. In 1226, an Augustinian monastery was constructed on the offshore island of Viðey and began to accumulate land and power. The manor farm of Bessastaðir, now the official residence of Iceland's head of state, became crown property when Iceland was absorbed by Norway in 1262 and by 1613, when the government took over the Viðey monastery, a small fishing village had already begun to develop.

In the mid-1700s, sheriff and businessman Skúli Magnússon decided to establish local industries in the hope that Iceland could overcome the trade barriers imposed by the Danish Trade Monopoly of 1602. In 1752, he set up weaving, tanning, rope-making and

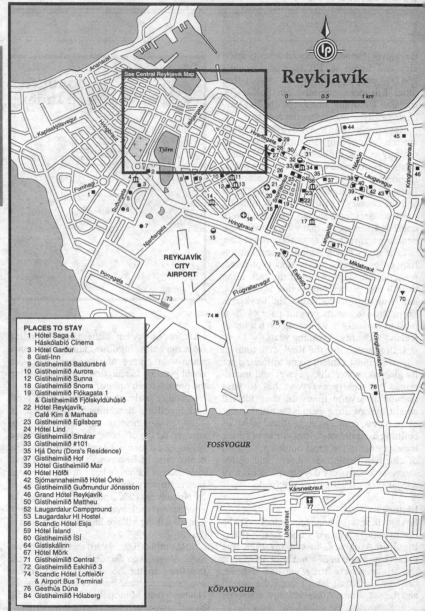

Reykjavík

See Central Reykjavík Map

0   0.5   1 km

REYKJAVÍK
CITY
AIRPORT

FOSSVOGUR

KÓPAVOGUR

Kársnesbraut

PLACES TO STAY
1 Hótel Saga &
   Háskólabíó Cinema
3 Hótel Garður
8 Gisti-Inn
9 Gistiheimilið Baldursbrá
10 Gistiheimilið Aurora
12 Gistiheimilið Sunna
18 Gistiheimilið Snorra
19 Gistiheimilið Flókagata 1
   & Gistiheimilið Fjölskylduhúsið
22 Hótel Reykjavík,
   Café Kim & Marhaba
23 Gistiheimilið Egilsborg
24 Hótel Lind
26 Gistiheimilið Smárar
33 Gistiheimilið #101
35 Hjá Doru (Dora's Residence)
37 Gistiheimilið Hof
39 Hótel Gistiheimilið Mar
40 Hótel Höfði
42 Sjómannaheimilið Hótel Örkin
45 Gistiheimilið Guðmundur Jónasson
46 Grand Hótel Reykjavík
50 Gistiheimilið Mattheu
52 Laugardalur Campground
53 Laugardalur HI Hostel
56 Scandic Hótel Esja
59 Hótel Ísland
60 Gistiheimilið ÍSÍ
64 Gistiskálinn
67 Hótel Mörk
71 Gistiheimilið Central
72 Gistiheimilið Eskihlíð 3
74 Scandic Hótel Loftleiðir
   & Airport Bus Terminal
76 Gesthús Dúna
84 Gistiheimilið Hólaberg

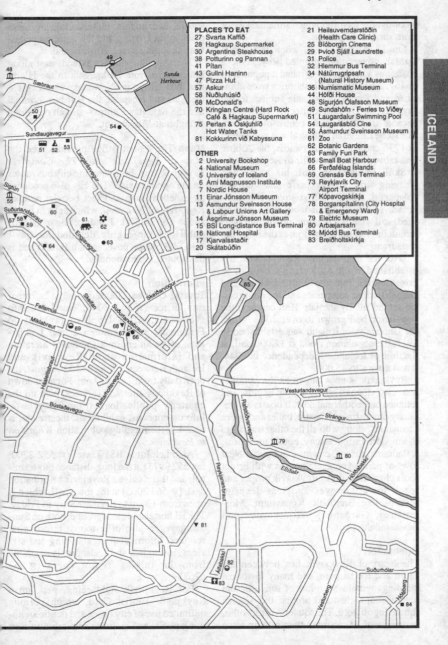

ICELAND

PLACES TO EAT
27 Svarta Kaffið
28 Hagkaup Supermarket
30 Argentina Steakhouse
38 Potturinn og Pannan
41 Pítan
43 Gullni Haninn
47 Pizza Hut
57 Askur
58 Nuðluhúsið
68 McDonald's
70 Kringlan Centre (Hard Rock
   Café & Hagkaup Supermarket)
75 Perlan & Óskjuhlíð
   Hot Water Tanks
81 Kokkurinn við Kabyssuna

OTHER
2 University Bookshop
4 National Museum
5 University of Iceland
6 Árni Magnusson Institute
7 Nordic House
11 Einar Jónsson Museum
13 Ásmundur Sveinsson House
   & Labour Unions Art Gallery
14 Ásgrímur Jónsson Museum
15 BSÍ Long-distance Bus Terminal
16 National Hospital
17 Kjarvalsstaðir
20 Skátabúðin

21 Heilsuverndarstöðin
   (Health Care Clinic)
25 Bíóborgin Cinema
29 Þvíoð Sjálf Laundrette
31 Police
32 Hlemmur Bus Terminal
34 Nátúrrugripsafn
   (Natural History Museum)
36 Numismatic Museum
44 Höfði House
48 Sigurjón Ólafsson Museum
49 Sundahöfn - Ferries to Viðey
51 Laugardalur Swimming Pool
54 Laugarásbíó Cine
55 Ásmundur Sveinsson Museum
61 Zoo
62 Botanic Gardens
63 Family Fun Park
65 Small Boat Harbour
66 Ferðafélag Íslands
69 Grensás Bus Terminal
73 Reykjavík City
   Airport Terminal
77 Kópavogskirkja
78 Borgarspítalinn (City Hospital
   & Emergency Ward)
79 Electric Museum
80 Árbæjarsafn
82 Mjódd Bus Terminal
83 Breiðholtskirkja

wool-dyeing factories which attracted labour from surrounding farms.

On 18 August 1786, when the Royal Danish government granted Reykjavík a charter as a market town, it had a population of 167. After the rural bishoprics were abolished and Iceland was made subject to the Protestant Danish church, Reykjavík became the theological centre of Iceland. The stone Lutheran cathedral was completed in 1796 and, shortly afterwards, the Alþing was moved from Þingvellir to Reykjavík.

Skúli Magnússon built his home and weaving firm in Reykjavík and laid out Aðalstræti, the city's first street. His businesses eventually failed but his weaving shed still stands (it burnt down and was rebuilt in 1764) and now houses the Fógetinn restaurant.

Over the next century, Reykjavík firmly established itself as Iceland's capital. A prison and the Supreme Court were built, and Danish trading companies and the bourgeoisie settled in. By the late 19th century, the population had grown to over 2000. When the University of Iceland was established in 1911, the population stood at 12,000 and, at the time of Icelandic independence in 1944, it had grown to 45,000.

Reykjavík is now known as the 'smokeless city' thanks to its ample winds and reliance on geothermal heat. It boasts a symphony orchestra and theatre, ballet and opera companies, along with all the other trappings of a modern European city: hotels, museums, restaurants, discos, cinemas and pubs. Neat rows of painted concrete houses with bright roofs climb the hills of Reykjavík proper and reach toward greyer and less-descript suburbs like Breiðholt, Kópavogur, Mosfellsbær, Garðabær, Seltjarnarnes and Bessastaðahreppur.

Orientation

The heart of Reykjavík lies between the Tjörn and the harbour, and many historical buildings remain, with lots of souvenir and tourist shops clustered around the sunken square Ingólfstorg. The square Austurvöllur, is more a quiet city park than a main town square, and in fact, more socialising takes place in Lækjartorg and the adjacent pedestrian shopping street, Austurstræti.

The shopping district extends east along Laugavegur from Lækjargata to the Hlemmur bus terminus. Newer developments – the National Hospital, the BSÍ bus terminal and the Kringlan Centre – stretch out along Hringbraut-Miklabraut.

Maps The tourist office provides free the *Map of Reykjavík* and *The Complete Reykjavík Map*, both showing city bus routes on the opposite side. The city also produces an excellent map and fact booklet entitled *Reykjavík og Nágrenni*, which sells in bookshops for Ikr500. Landmælingar Íslands publishes the highly detailed *Reykjavík* 1:15,000, which costs around Ikr600 and is distributed internationally.

Information

Tourist Offices The main tourist information office (☎ 562 3045; email tourinfo @mmedia.is), or Upplýsinga Miðstöð Ferðamála, at Bankastræti 2 near Lækjargata, offers an enormous range of literature and information about Reykjavík and Iceland. Between 1 June and 31 August, it's open daily from 7 am to 7 pm. For a rundown of Reykjavík sites and services, pick up the quarterly publication, *Around Reykjavík*. Info on concerts, exhibitions, theatre etc, is found in the monthly publication *What's on in Reykjavík*.

Also helpful is BSÍ Travel (☎ 552 2300; fax 552 9973) at the long-distance bus terminal, and there's also a Reykjavík information desk (☎ 563 2005) at the town hall, which is open from 10 am to 6 pm Monday to Friday. The HI hostel and campground, both on Sundlaugavegur, also offer tourist information services. Information on shopping and services, in English and Icelandic, is available from the Talking Yellow Pages (☎ 562 6262).

For Reykjavík sightseeing, pick up a Reykjavík Tourist Card, which permits unlimited use of city buses and public swimming pools, and includes admission to four

Top: Krísuvík geothermal area, Reykjanesfólkvangur, Iceland
Middle: Split icebergs approaching the sea
Bottom: Reykjadalur, near Hveragerði, South Central Iceland

DEANNA SWANEY

DEANNA SWANEY

DEANNA SWANEY

Top: Ólafsfjörður, North Central Iceland
Middle: Highlands around Akureyri seen from Mt Sulur
Bottom: Mural on Tryggvagata, Reykjavík

city museums. It costs Ikr600/800/1000 for one/two/three days and is sold at both city tourist offices. A Museum Card, which includes admission to the National Museum, the Nesstofa (Medical Museum) and the Icelandic Maritime Museum (Hafnarfjörður) costs Ikr300 – half the full admission charges.

Money For currency exchange, banks offer the best deals on cash or travellers' cheques. Landsbanki Ísland and Íslandsbanki both offer good rates and neither charges commission (the former provides free coffee while you wait). You can also pick up Danish kroner for travel to Greenland or the Faroes.

In summer, Búnaðarbanki Íslands in the Kringlan Centre is open weekdays from 9.30 am to 6 pm and on Saturday from 10 am to 4 pm. In the evening and on weekends, your best option is to change money at major hotels.

The Change Group, with outlets in the main tourist office and the Austurstræti McDonald's, is a last resort option, as its rates are lower than in banks and out of banking hours it charges a punitive 8.75% commission. During bank hours, it's 6.75%. From May to September, the outlets are open from 8.30 am to 8 pm. ATMs, which are found only at banks, accept MasterCard, Visa and Cirrus.

Post & Communications The main post office, on the corner of Posthússtræti and the Austurstræti pedestrian mall, is open weekdays from 8.30 am to 4.30 pm, and from June to August it's open on Saturday from 10 am to 2 pm. There's also a sub-station in the BSÍ terminal, open from noon to 6 pm on weekdays and 9 am to 1 pm on Saturday. The post office at Kringlan Centre opens weekdays from 8.30 am to 6 pm and Saturday from 10 am to 4 pm. For courier packages, DHL Worldwide Express (☎ 568 9822) is at Skeifan 7, near the Grensás city bus terminus.

The telephone exchange, near Austurvöllur, is open Monday to Friday from 9 am to 6 pm for local or overseas calls, faxes (fax 550 7089 or 550 7579) and telephone cards. Local calls are charged a Ikr35 connection fee. Public phones at the Lækjartorg bus terminal are available from 6 am (7 am on Sunday) to 11 pm.

Travel Agencies BSÍ Travel (☎ 552 2300; fax 552 9973) at the long-distance bus terminal is good for organising excursions from town and for travel within Iceland. In summer, it's open 7.30 am to 7 pm Sunday to Friday and 7.30 am to 2 pm Saturday.

Farmhouse accommodation around the country can be organised by Ferðaþjónusta Bænda (☎ 562 3640; fax 562 3644), Icelandic Farm Holidays, on Ingólfstorg. The American Express representative is Úrval-Útsyn Travel (☎ 569 9300; fax 657 0202; email urval@skima.is) at Lágmúli 4, but it doesn't change travellers' cheques.

Bookshops For a range of topographic maps and foreign-language books and periodicals, your best options are Eymundsson in Austurstræti and Mál og Menning at Laugavegur 18. Both offer a selection of books on Icelandic topics, including souvenir books, sagas and guidebooks in English, German, French, Italian and Icelandic. Mál og Menning distributes the free bibliography *Books on Iceland*.

For classical literature and textbooks, check out the University Bookshop on Hringbraut near Tjarnargata. For used paperbacks at reasonable prices, see the friendly second-hand book dealer at Vesturgata 17.

Libraries The Icelandic National Library (☎ 563 5600), Arngrímsgata 3, near the National Museum, is open from 9 am to 5 pm weekdays and 1 to 5 pm on Saturday. Reykjavík also has a city library, at Þingholtsstræti 29, and a university library on the campus.

Cultural Centres The following cultural centres sponsor socials, show films and have libraries where you can catch up on news from home:

Alliance Française (☎ 552 3870), Vesturgata 2, open 3 to 6 pm weekdays

American Library (☎ 562 1022), Laugavegur 26, open 11.30 am to 5.45 pm weekdays

Goethe Institut (☎ 551 6061), Tryggvagata 26, open 2 to 6 pm from Monday to Thursday

Nordic House, (☎ 551 7030), Sæmundagata and Hringbraut, open 1 to 7 pm Monday to Saturday and 2 to 5 pm on Sunday

Laundry The Þvioð Sjálf Laundrette, at Barónsstígur 3 and Þvottahúsið at Vesturgata 12, are open 8 am to 10 pm Monday to Friday, 8 am to 5 pm on Saturday and 11 am to 3 pm on Sunday. The latter has a pick-up service (☎ 562 7878). The campground in Laugardalur also has self-service washing machines.

Medical Services Medical help is available at the city hospital on weekdays from 8 am to 5 pm (☎ 569 6600). Non-emergency care after hours is available at the clinic, Heilsuverndarstöðin (☎ 552 1230) at Barónsstígur 47. Dispensaries, listed under *apótek* in the yellow pages, have a roster for 24-hour openings. To learn which one currently has the shift, check daily papers or phone (☎ 551 8888).

Emergency All emergency services – police, ambulance and fire brigade – are accessed by dialling ☎ 112. For around-the-clock emergency medical services, go to the emergency ward *(slysadeild)* at the Borgarspítalinn (☎ 569 6600). The Womens' Crisis Centre (☎ 611205) is available 24 hours a day.

Film & Photography For Kodak products, there are several shops on Laugavegur and another in the Kringlan Centre. A 36-exposure roll of Kodachrome 64 is around Ikr1600, including processing. Fuji film is available at Midbæjarmynðir, Lækjargata 2. A 36-exposure roll of Fujichrome 100 costs Ikr900 and Fujichrome Velvia 50 costs Ikr1020.

Left Luggage The left-luggage storage at the BSÍ terminal is open weekdays from 7.30 am to 9.30 pm, on Saturday from 7.30 am to 2.30 pm, and on Sunday, in summer only, from 5 to 7 pm. The youth hostel and campground offer left-luggage service for guests, but the former charges a nominal fee.

Outdoor Equipment Climbing, camping and fishing equipment and repairs are available from Skátabúðin (☎ 561 2045) at Snorrabraut 60. It also sells white gas, butane cartridges and other stove fuels. Iceland's own outdoor equipment company, *66° North*, has a factory outlet near the Hlemmur bus terminal. Immediately north of the main harbour at Eyjaslöð 7 is another outdoor shop, Seglagerðin Áegir (☎ 511 2200).

You can hire tents, sleeping bags, backpacks, stoves, and cooking and ski equipment from Sport-Leigan Rent-a-Tent (☎ 551 9800) and ALP Camping Gear Rental (☎ 551 7570), both beside the BSÍ bus terminal. Sleeping bags and two-person tents average Ikr1300 and Ikr3300 per week, respectively.

Old Town

Old Town includes the area bordered by Tjörn, Lækjargata, the harbour and the suburb of Seltjarnarnes, including the east bank of Tjörn and both sides of Lækjargata.

The Harbour During the 18th century, Hafnarstræti ran alongside the harbour, but as the city grew, land was reclaimed and Tryggvagata and new piers were added. The houses on the south side of Hafnarstræti were used by Danish traders during the Trade Monopoly from 1602 to 1855.

In the area are lots of tourist shops selling woollens, pottery and souvenirs. The Icelandic Handicrafts Centre has carved wooden falcons which commemorate the real ones captured by the Danish king for gifts to friends and nobles. The birds were stored in this building awaiting shipment to the mainland.

Often, restored or replica wooden sailing ships moor in the harbour and add interest and colour to this rustic area.

Dómkirkjan In 1796, after the Danish king Christian VII abolished the Catholic bishoprics at Hólar and Skálholt and replaced them with a Lutheran diocese centred in Reykjavík, he built the Dómkirkjan to serve as the new heart of Christian Iceland. Over the years, this rather ordinary stone structure has undergone several renovations and become a bit drabber, especially after the addition of corrugated iron sides. It's open to visitors from 10 am to 4 pm daily except Wednesday and Saturday. On Wednesday, it's open from 11.30 am to 12.30 pm, with an organ recital at 12.10 pm.

Tjörn The name means simply 'the pond', and it was around this pleasant lake that old Reykjavík grew up. Over 40 species of birds frequent the area, including the original intrepid traveller, the Arctic tern. It's relaxing for reading or feeding the ducks and geese, and the park at the southern end has jogging and bike trails, a fountain and gardens planted with colourful flowers. The octagonal gazebo, Hljómskálinn, was built in 1922 as a rehearsal hall for the Reykjavík Brass Band.

Ráðhús (Town Hall) At the northern end of the Tjörn is Reykjavík's post-modern town hall, which was inaugurated on 14 April, 1992. While it's certainly bold, many people consider it an intrusion in the heart of the historical city. The main hall contains a tourist information desk, a café, an immense raised relief map of Iceland and a gallery of surreal photos depicting some of Iceland's more adverse natural aspects. It's open Monday to Friday from 8.20 am to 10 pm and on weekends from noon to 6 pm.

National Museum The National Museum on Hringbraut is obligatory viewing for anyone interested in Norse culture and Icelandic history. The museum was founded in 1863 and was installed in its present location in 1950. Unfortunately, the bored guards seem to believe that all visitors are possible perpetrators of the next great museum heist.

On the upper floor are religious and folk relics and tools from the period of Settlement. The most renowned is the Valþjófsstaður church door, which was carved around 1200 and depicts a Norse battle scene. In the basement are nautical and agricultural tools and models, including fishing boats and a collection of ingenious farm implements.

It's open daily, except Monday, from 11 am to 4 pm from 15 May to 15 September. The rest of the year, it's open from noon to 4 pm on Tuesday, Thursday and weekends. Admission is Ikr200.

Árni Magnússon Institute Saga enthusiasts shouldn't miss the Árni Magnússon Institute (☎ 525 4010), behind the National Museum. In the late 17th century, Árni Magnússon became secretary of Royal Archives in Copenhagen and in 1701 was appointed Professor of Danish Antiquities. In 1702, when collecting Icelandic vellums was all the rage, the king sent him to Iceland for 10 years to track down, beg and buy every scrap of vellum he could find for the Danish government. His uncanny abilities resulted in a massive collection which he carried back to Denmark and deposited in university storerooms. When the great Copenhagen fire of 20 October 1728 threatened the university, he personally rushed in to save the precious vellums from the flames. Despite his efforts, much of the collection was lost and he died 15 months later, lamenting his failure to preserve all the manuscripts.

On 21 April, 1971, the remaining works, including famous ones like the *Landnámabók*, the *Íslendingabók* and *Njáls Saga*, were graciously returned from Denmark to independent Iceland – a cause for national celebration. Most were placed in the Árni Magnússon Institute which was built specifically to house them. The institute is open from 2 to 4 pm on Tuesday, Thursday and Saturday; admission is Ikr300. You'll also find a small vellum display in the foyer of the National Library.

Kolaportið Flea Market Iceland's largest flea market was once held in the Kolaportið

ICELAND

parking garage beneath the National Bank of Iceland, but it became so popular that a dedicated building was constructed a block away. Between 10 am and 4 pm on Saturday and 11 am and 5 pm on Sunday, anyone can set up a booth and sell just about anything they'd like. It's good for inexpensive clothing and you can also riffle through heaps of second-hand stuff ranging from books and phonograph records to lampshades and ashtrays.

Stjórnarráðið The plain white building across Lækjargata from Lækjartorg contains the offices of the president and prime minister. This is one of Reykjavík's oldest buildings, originally built as a jail in the 1700s. Overlooking it on Arnarhóll, or 'eagle hill', stands a statue of the first settler, Ingólfur Arnarson.

Bernhöftstorfan Bernhöftstorfan, the set of rustic old wooden buildings between Stjórnarráðið and the old Grammar School, have altered little since the mid-1800s. The oldest buildings – the houses at Bankastræti 2 and Amtmannsstígur 1 – date to the late 18th century when Reykjavík first became Iceland's capital. They were renovated between 1979 and 1989 and now hold the tourist office, Reykjavík Excursions, the Lækjarbrekka restaurant and other businesses.

The Alþing The grey basalt building south of Austurvöllur, built in 1881, houses the Alþing, or parliament. It lost legislative powers in 1262 when Iceland joined the Kingdom of Norway (and subsequently Denmark), but the body wasn't actually abolished and was first moved from Þingvellir to Reykjavík in 1798. Its legislative powers were regained in 1845.

The Alþing is now comprised of 63 members from five political parties and serves as the national law-making body. Sessions begin on 1 October each year, when a president is elected to act as chief executive of the Alþing. Meetings, which are open to the public, are held from Monday to Wednesday at 1.30 pm and on Thursday at 10.30 am.

The present building is too small for the growing government and a new building is being planned.

Austurvöllur Reykjavík's old town square (the 'eastern field') is the site of Ingólfur Arnarson's hayfields, and his track down to the harbour followed the same route as present-day Aðalstræti. Today, Austurvöllur is a quiet grassy park surrounded by small restaurants and shops. The statue in the square is of Icelandic nationalist and scholar Jón Sigurðsson who lobbied in Copenhagen in 1855 for the restoration of free trade and first called for Icelandic independence. This was achieved in 1944 on 17 June, which was selected because it was his birthday.

Fógetinn Constructed around 1752, Fógeti ('sheriff') Skúli Magnússon's weaving shed at Aðalstræti 10 is the oldest building in Reykjavík. Skúli's competitive businesses helped break the Danish Trade Monopoly which had caused so much economic strife in Iceland. Although the shed burnt down in 1764, it was immediately rebuilt on the same foundation. It now houses the small and popular restaurant Fógetinn. There's also a statue of Skúli Magnússon on Aðalstræti.

New Reykjavík
Modern Reykjavík has sprawled eastward from Old Town across the low hills and beyond Elliðaár, the salmon stream that brings a touch of the countryside to Iceland's only cloverleaf junction.

Hallgrímskirkja People either love it or hate it, but they certainly can't miss it. Hallgrímskirkja, at the top of Skólavörðustígur, is certainly Reykjavík's most imposing structure and is visible from over 20 km away. First begun in the late 1940s, it was completed in 1974 and it doesn't take an architect to identify its obvious resemblance to a mountain of basaltic lava. The church was named in honour of Reverend Hallgrímur

Pétursson, who was the author of the hymnal *50 Passíusálmar* (50 Passion Hymns).

The stark, light-filled interior merits a look, but most people are interested in the view from the 75m tower, which is reached by lift for Ikr200. In summer, it's open daily from 10 am to 6 pm. On Sunday at 8.30 pm in July and August, organ recitals are held to help pay for the pipe organ inaugurated in December 1992; admission is Ikr500.

The statue of Leifur Eiríksson, by Alexander Stirling Calder, identifies him as the 'Son of Iceland, Discoverer of Vinland'. It was presented to Iceland by the USA in 1930 on the 1000th anniversary of the Alþing.

Ásmundur Sveinsson Museum Born in rural Iceland in 1893, Ásmundur Sveinsson came to Reykjavík to learn woodcarving and wound up in Copenhagen and Paris studying sculpting instead. Most of his themes came from Icelandic sagas and folklore and were interpreted in massive but graceful concrete abstractions.

Most visitors first experience the gallery devoted to his work from bus No 5 between the campground and the city centre and wonder what the hell it is. This igloo-shaped building on Sigtún was designed by the sculptor himself, but one wonders who is responsible for the igloo bus stop shelter in front of it! The exhibit is open daily from 10 am to 4 pm from 1 May to 30 September and other times from 1 to 4 pm. Admission is Ikr200.

Ásmundur Sveinsson House & Labour Unions Art Gallery Not to be confused with his gallery, this house at Freyjugata 41 opposite Hallgrímskirkja is owned by the Association of Icelandic Architects and used for artistic exhibitions. It was designed in 1933 by Ásmundur Sveinsson in collaboration with architect Sigurður Guðmundsson. Although avant-garde in its day, it now seems relatively unobtrusive.

The building now houses the Icelandic Labour Unions Art Gallery (☎ 511 5353). It may not be earthshaking but the visiting exhibitions are normally worthwhile and

there's a range of amateur – and occasionally inspired – artwork. It's open daily from 2 to 7 pm. Admission is free.

National Gallery of Iceland The National Gallery is in the modernistic building – originally built as an ice house – behind Fríkirkjan church near Tjörn. The standing collection is rather sparse – only a few of the 5000 pieces are on display – but visiting exhibitions by Icelandic artists make it worthwhile. It's open daily, except Monday, from noon to 6 pm (but is closed from 16 December to 14 January). Admission is free except for special exhibitions, which cost Ikr300.

Volcano Show If you're headed for Vestmannaeyjar or Mývatn, the Volcano Show on Hellusund will provide a grounding in those places and their geological histories. In addition, it illustrates the volcanic spectre under which Icelanders live.

For over 40 years, Vilhjálmur and Ósvaldur Knudsen have rushed to the scenes of major volcanic eruptions in Iceland and filmed the greatest action, including the award-winning *Birth of an Island* about Surtsey in Vestmannaeyjar.

The 2½-hour shows (in English) begin at 10 am, and 3 and 8 pm daily in the summer. French and German programmes are shown at 12.30 pm and 5.30 pm, respectively. Admission is Ikr850.

Öskjuhlið If you're wondering why your hot showers smell a bit sulphuric, the answer is at Öskjuhlið. This group of tanks, east of the city airport, stores hot water fresh from the centre of the earth. Perched atop the tanks is the swish restaurant *Perlan* (The Pearl), which is now a city landmark. To get there, take bus No 7 from Lækjartorg.

Kjarvalsstaðir Kjarvalsstaðir (☎ 552 6131; email kjarvalsst@centrum.is), in Miklatún Park, is dedicated to the work of Iceland's most popular artist, Jóhannes Kjarval. He was born in 1885, and as a young man went to work on a fishing trawler. Some of his co-workers recognised his artistic talent and organised a lottery to pay for his study abroad. Although he was rejected by the Royal Academy of Arts in London, he absorbed the master works in the British museums and entered the Academy of Fine Arts in Copenhagen.

Kjarval's surrealistic style is Iceland's ethereal landscapes. When observed at close range, it may appear rather haphazard, but from five metres away, the magic appears.

In addition to the Kjarval salon, there's a second hall which is used for visiting exhibitions. Kjarvalsstaðir is open from 10 am to 6 pm daily. Admission costs Ikr300.

Einar Jónsson Museum Near Hallgríms-kirkja on Njarðargata is the cube-shaped

Statue of Jón Sigurðsson

Einar Jónsson Museum, a worthwhile exhibit of work by Iceland's foremost modern sculptor. The building, which was designed by Jónsson himself in 1923 and subsidised by the government, reflects the mysticism that characterises his work. To find inspiration for his fantastic art, which dealt mostly with political and religious themes, he lived in a self-imposed state of seclusion. His only non-mystical work, a statue of Jón Sigurðsson, stands in Austurvöllur square. From 1 June to 15 September, the museum is open daily, except Monday, from 1.30 to 4 pm. Admission is Ikr200.

Nordic House Iceland's Nordic House (☎ 551 7030), south of Tjörn, was designed by architect Alvar Aalto and serves as a Scandinavian cultural centre. It offers travelling exhibitions, concerts, lectures, films based on Nordic themes and a library of Scandinavian literature. The cafeteria is open every day from 9 am to 7 pm (on Sunday from noon to 7 pm) and the exhibition hall from 2 to 7 pm daily when exhibitions are being shown.

Sigurjón Ólafsson Museum Born in 1908, Sigurjón Ólafsson studied in Denmark and became a sensitive, if not prolific, sculptor and portraitist. A standing collection of his work is on display at Laugarnestangi 70 near Héðinsgata, two blocks seaward from Laugardalur and the city campground. From June to August, it's open from Monday to Thursday from 8 to 10 pm and on Saturday and Sunday from 2 to 6 pm. Admission is Ikr200. Concerts catering to a range of musical tastes are held on Tuesday evenings at 8.30 pm.

Natural History Museum The Nátúr-rugripsafn Reykjavíkur, at Hlemmtorg, isn't Iceland's most exciting museum, but it's worth a look if you're keen on Icelandic geology, fauna and flora. It's open on Sunday, Tuesday, Thursday and Saturday from 1.30 to 4 pm. Admission is free.

Numismatic Museum Set up as a joint project by the National Bank of Iceland and the Central Bank of Iceland, the Numismatic Museum at Einholt 4 near Kjarvalsstadíir houses a collection of Icelandic and other notes and coins. It's open from 2 to 4 pm on Sunday and other times by arrangement (☎ 569 9600).

Höfði House The Höfði House, used for official receptions and city social functions, looks across the bay at 914m Mt Esja. It was catapulted to dubious fame as the official meeting place of the superpowers in the non-eventful 1986 Reagan-Gorbachev summit and is now often known as the 'Reagan-Gorbachev House'. The building is also reputedly haunted by ghosts of the Icelandic past, and may provide unique face-to-face encounters with history. If you're curious as to what those Viking high-seat pillars looked like, at least as far as sculptor Sigurjón Ólafsson was concerned, check the sculpture out the front.

Viking Ship On the shore near the bay end of Klapparstígur stands the sculpture *Sun-Craft*, by Jón Gunnar Árnason, which was apparently intended to resemble a Viking ship. It's rather porous, however, and more strongly suggests an immense 10-legged bug that has just crawled out of the sea to greet the city with open mandibles. It certainly merits a photo.

Ásgrímur Jónsson Museum Ásgrímur Jónsson, born in 1876, was the first great Icelandic landscape painter. He was educated in Copenhagen and showed so much promise that the Icelandic parliament voted him a grant to study painting in Italy. There he was attracted to Impressionism, which was reflected in his work ever after. In his will, he bequeathed about half of his art to the Icelandic government, which set up a museum in his former home at Bergstaðastræti 74. From June to August, it's open daily, except Monday, from 1.30 to 4 pm. Admission is free.

Botanic Gardens These small botanic gardens, which contain 65% of all plant species occurring naturally in the country, are good for a pleasant evening stroll, especially from the nearby campground and HI hostel. The relief carving is a portrait of Eiríkur Hjartarson, who owned the area and began planting trees there in 1929. It was purchased by the city in 1955. In summer, a small kiosk serves coffee and waffles for good prices. From 15 April to 30 September, the gardens are open weekdays from 8 am to 10 pm and weekends from 10 am to 10 pm.

Fjölskyldugarðurinn & Húsdýragarðurinn The Icelandic names may sound intimidating, but this family fun park and zoo in Laugardular is quite popular with Icelanders. The zoo, which is mainly for children, houses all sorts of Icelandic farm animals as well as birds, seals and reindeer. The family fun park is designed around Nordic and Viking themes and includes a large sandbox with kid-sized earth-moving equipment, go-cart tracks, a driving course which teaches the fundamentals in mini-cars, a cycling course, mini-golf, a fort, an outlaw hideout and a duck pond with a replica of a Viking longship.

From 1 June to 31 August, the parks are open daily from 10 am to 9 pm. Admission to both parks is Ikr300 for adults.

Árbæjarsafn The 12.5 hectare farm at Árbær was first mentioned in literary sources in the mid-15th century. It was originally purchased by the city in 1906 to secure rights to the Elliðaár river valley and served as an inn until the 1930s and as an open-air museum in 1957. It includes a growing collection of old homes and buildings from around the country which illustrate life in early Iceland.

Besides the farm, there is a variety of exhibits outlining the development of public services, transport systems and emergency services in Reykjavík. The turf church, which dates from 1842, was moved from Skagafjörður in 1960. In front of the farm is the sculpture *Woman Churning Milk* by

ICELAND

Ásmundur Sveinsson. Special events are held throughout the summer.

From 27 May to 1 September it's open daily, except Monday, from 10 am to 6 pm. On Mondays from 21 June, it's also open to passengers on the museum bus. At other times, visits are by arrangement only (☎ 577 1111). Admission is Ikr300; take bus No 10 from Hlemmur or bus No 110 from Lækjartorg (weekdays only).

Elliðaár This is Reykjavík's salmon river – in early August you can watch the leaping salmon making their way upstream to spawn. If it weren't for the noisy cloverleaf junction nearby, it would be easy to forget you're in the city while you sit, relax on the grass and watch the tumbling water. It's about a 45-minute walk from central Reykjavík. You can also take bus No 10 from Hlemmur or bus No 100 from Lækjargata.

Electric Museum This museum, dedicated to the electrification of Reykjavík and the development of hydroelectric power in Iceland, is at the Elliðaár power station on Rafstöðvarvegur, not far from Árbæjarsafn. It's open on Sunday from 2 to 4 pm and other times by prior arrangement (☎ 567 9009), and every day for passengers of the museum bus. Admission is free.

Heiðmörk Heiðmörk ('heath woods') is a 2800 hectare city park spreading out southeast of Elliðavatn lake, immediately east of Reykjavík. It's very popular with city-dwellers who visit on weekends to take advantage of the hiking tracks, picnic sites and ample vegetation.

There's now a car-free hiking and cycling track running from Seltjarnarnes to Heiðmörk, but there's no public transport into the park. The closest access from Reykjavík is from the corner of Suðurlandsvegur and Norðurás, accessible on bus No 16. From there, it's a two km walk to the park entrance. Alternatively, you can reach the western end of the park by taking bus No 142 from Mjódd to Vífilsstaðir in Garðabær. From there, it's just a short walk to Vífilsstaðavatn lake at the

park entrance. See also Organised Tours later in this section.

Sports

You can play squash and racquetball at Veggsport (☎ 551 9011) at Seljavegur 2, open on weekdays from 11.30 am to 1.30 pm and from 4 to 10 pm. Games cost Ikr600 per person including use of the sauna, gym and training room. Bowling is available at Keilusalurinn Öskjuhlíð (☎ 562 1599) beside the Hótel Loftleiðir. It's open daily from noon to 12.30 am.

In August, the city stages a marathon, half-marathon, 10 km run and a 7.5 km fun run along courses through Reykjavík and Seltjarnarnes. The full marathon is open to entrants over 18 years and costs US$25 to enter. Half-marathon runners must be over 16 and pay US$22. The fun run and 10 km run have no age limits and cost US$13 and US$16 respectively. Pre-registration is mandatory and prices include a carbohydrate-loading pasta party the night before. For more information, contact the Iceland Travel Bureau (☎ 562 3300; fax 562 5895), Reykjavík Marathon, Skógarhlíð 18, 101 Reykjavík.

Swimming

Admission to Reykjavík pools is Ikr150 for adults, and most hire towels and swimming costumes. In summer, most pools are open Monday to Friday from 7 am to 10 pm and on weekends from 8 am to 8.30 pm. Intercity and national swimming events take place at the Laugardalur pool (bus No 5 from Lækjartorg or Hlemmur), which also has jacuzzis, a steam bath, solarium, mud baths and a large waterslide.

Other city pools include Vesturbæjar (bus No 4 from Lækjartorg or Hlemmur), on Hofsvallagata; Sundhöll Reykjavíkur (bus No 1 from Lækjartorg by day or bus No 17 on weekends and evenings) on Barónsstigur; Fjölbraut Breiðholt (bus No 112 from Lækjartorg or No 12 from Hlemmur) at Austurberg 5; and Seltjarnarnes (bus No 3 from Lækjartorg) on Suðurströnd. You'll find other pools in Mosfellsbær, Kópavogur, Garðabær and Hafnarfjörður.

Organised Tours

Several companies offer excursions around the city, its hinterlands and further afield. One of the most popular is Reykjavík Excursions (☎ 562 4422; fax 562 4450), at Bankastræti 2, which runs lots of day tours: the Golden Circle (Ikr4600), city tours (Ikr1800), Grindavík and the Blue Lagoon (Ikr3500), Krísuvík (Ikr6000), Kaldidalur (Ikr5400), Þjórsárdalur (Ikr6000), Heiðmörk & Bláfjöll (Ikr2500), and lots of other possibilities.

BSÍ (☎ 552 2300; fax 552 9973), at the long-distance bus terminal, offers a variety of tours during the tourist season, some departing daily. These include the popular Golden Circle Tour (Ikr4500, including hotel pick-up), city tours (Ikr1700), Krísuvík (Ikr3200), Heiðmörk & Bláfjöll (Ikr2400), Lundey Island (Ikr3700), whale-watching tours to Eldey Island (Ikr5200), and many more, which are outlined in the brochure *Iceland Summer*. You can join a tour by turning up at BSÍ at the time of departure, but it's best to book, since tours may be cancelled if there are insufficient bookings. The more popular tours are described under individual destinations.

Blueland Tours (☎ 551 2542) offers daily five-hour hiking and fishing excursions around Heiðmörk for Ikr4900, including refreshments and fishing equipment rental.

In July and August, Iceland Nature Tours (☎ 564 2060), at Dalvegur 22 in Kópavogur, offers four-hour guided hiking tours to Mt Esja for Ikr950. They leave daily from the Reykjavík BSÍ terminal at noon; hotel pick-up is available.

The MS *Andrea* (☎ & fax 555 4630) does four-hour fishing and sightseeing cruises from Ægisgarður wharf, Reykjavíkurhöfn, at 10 am daily in summer. Trips cost Ikr4000 and include use of fishing equipment and a fish grill-up.

For other possibilities, see Organised Tours in the Iceland Getting Around chapter.

Special Events

From early June to early July in even-numbered years, the city holds the Reykjavík International Arts Festival, featuring films, dance, theatre, concerts and art exhibitions from around Iceland, Europe and elsewhere. In relevant years, information is available online at www.saga.is/artfest.

In late September, Reykjavík holds a Jazz Festival, attracting musicians from around the country and abroad.

Places to Stay – bottom end

Thanks to Reykjavík's increasing popularity, budget travellers now have numerous accommodation options, but in July or August, finding a bed at the HI hostel or an inexpensive guesthouse may be difficult. To avoid risking literally being left out in the cold, bring a tent or make advance bookings.

Camping The popular *Laugardalur Campground* in Laugardalur covers an immense bit of real estate, but at the height of summer you'll be lucky to find enough space for a tent. In spite of the crowds, the friendly attendants, Kristian and Árni, maintain a mellow attitude and one can only admire their patience with questions they must hear hundreds of times a day.

The campground is open from 15 May to 15 September (that may be extended to 30 September by the time you read this). Camping costs Ikr250 per person plus Ikr250 per tent; if you show this book at the desk, you'll get a 10% discount. Cooking and laundry facilities and hot showers are available at a nominal extra charge. From 15 June to 31 August, a free shuttle bus runs every morning at 7 am from the campground to the BSÍ terminal and from 15 June to 15 September, a Flybus runs to Keflavík airport (Ikr600) at 4.45 am.

Hostels The friendly *Laugardalur HI Hostel* (☎ 553 8110; fax 588 9201), beside the campground at Sundlaugavegur 34, is a 15-minute bus ride (bus No 5) from Lækjartorg and a Ikr600 taxi ride from the BSÍ terminal.

ICELAND

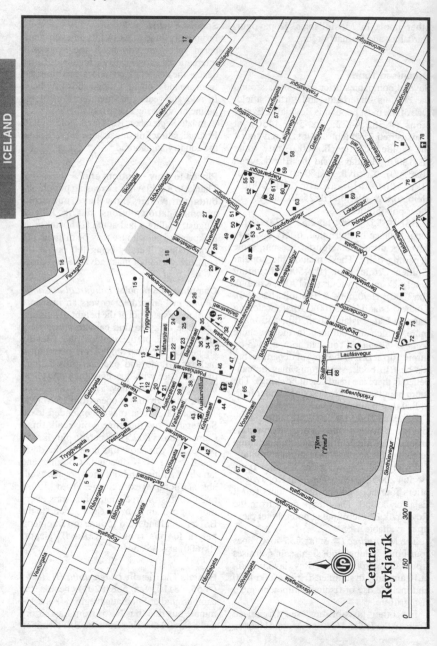

Central
Reykjavík

The hostel is closed from 20 December to 5 January.

In July and August, advance booking is essential, but if you have another option, such as a tent, you can turn up in the evening and hope there has been a cancellation. IYHF members pay Ikr1000 per night and non-members Ikr1250. Breakfast is available for an extra charge.

Thanks to night-time security, the midnight closing no longer precludes romps in Reykjavík's late summer sun or weekend merriment. However, combine the eight-bed dorms with the light nights, the airport bus at 4.45 am and the BSÍ terminal bus at 7 am and you get one of the noisiest hostels you'll ever visit. A pair of earplugs will go a long way.

Sleeping-Bag Accommodation Lots of Reykjavík guesthouses also offer budget sleeping-bag accommodation. See under Places to Stay – middle.

Places to Stay – middle

Guesthouses Most *gistiheimili* (guesthouses) charge Ikr4000 to Ikr7000 for comfortable, but hardly elegant, accommodation. There is now a host of choices, with more springing up every day. Many also serve breakfast, which is either included in the room rate or costs around Ikr500 extra.

PLACES TO STAY

- 4 Gistiheimilið Víkingur
- 6 Hótel City
- 7 Gistiheimilið Ísafold
- 42 Salvation Army Guesthouse
- 46 Hótel Borg
- 63 Hótel Jörd
- 69 Gistiheimilið Svala
- 70 Hótel Óðinsvé
- 74 Hótel Holt
- 76 Gistiheimilið Svanurinn
- 77 Hótel Leifur Eiríksson

PLACES TO EAT

- 1 Amigo's
- 2 Jónatan Livingston Mávur
- 3 Naust
- 11 Pizza 67 & Goethe Institut
- 13 Svarta Pannan
- 14 Hornið & Djúpið
- 19 Ingólfstorg & Hlölla Bátar
- 20 Dubliner
- 21 Subway
- 23 10-11 Supermarket
- 28 Samurai
- 29 Café Sólon Íslandus
- 30 Caruso
- 32 Bernhöftstorfan – Lækjarbrekka, Myllan & Humarhúsið
- 33 Kína Húsið
- 34 Café Ópera, Café Romance, Café Sport, & Tunglið Disco
- 36 McDonald's
- 38 Café Paris
- 40 Kaffi Austurstræti & Bítlaklubbarinn
- 41 Fógetinn
- 47 Skólabrú
- 48 Græni Kosturinn
- 50 Ítalía
- 51 Thailandi & Me Nam Khwai
- 52 Indo-Kina
- 53 Gott í Gogginn
- 54 Asía
- 57 Austur India Fjelagið
- 58 Sjanghæ
- 60 Pasta Basta
- 61 Á Næstu Grösum
- 65 Við Tjörnina
- 75 Eld-Smiðjan Pizzeria

OTHER

- 5 Second-hand Bookshop
- 8 Alliance Française
- 9 Glaumbar
- 10 Gaukur á Stöng
- 12 Ferðaþjónusta Bænda (Farmhouse Accommodation Agency)
- 15 Kólaportið Flea Market
- 16 *Akraborg* Ferry to Akranes
- 17 Viking Ship Sculpture
- 18 Arnarhóll & Ingólfur Arnarson Statue
- 22 Post Office (GPO)
- 24 Lækjartorg Bus Terminal
- 25 Lækjartorg
- 26 Stjórnaráðið (Government House)
- 27 National Theatre
- 31 Tourist Office & Reykjavík Excursions
- 35 Miðbærmyndir Photographic Shop
- 37 Sigfús Eymundsson Bookshop
- 39 State Monopoly Shop
- 43 Telephone Office
- 44 Alþing
- 45 Dómkirkjan
- 49 Icelandair
- 55 Borgarhjól Bicycle Rental
- 56 Bíóbarinn & Café List
- 59 Club 22
- 62 Mál og Menning Bookshop
- 64 Útivist Travel Agency
- 66 Ráðhús (Town Hall)
- 67 Tjarnarbíó (Light Nights)
- 68 National Gallery of Iceland
- 71 USA Embassy
- 72 UK Embassy
- 73 Volcano Show
- 78 Hallgrímskirkja

Some guesthouses offer sleeping-bag accommodation and others have only private rooms. In addition, numerous private homes let out rooms during peak periods.

One of the most popular guesthouses is *Salvation Army Guest House* (☎ 561 3203; fax 561 3315), or Hjálpræðisherinn, at Kirkjustræti 2. Don't be put off by the name – it's not a hostel for down-and-outs. Rather, it offers clean single/double rooms for Ikr2200/3000 without bathroom, and sleeping-bag accommodation for Ikr1100/1300 without/with blankets. For some travellers, the central location makes it preferable to the HI hostel.

Also well-known is *Gistiheimilið Guðmundur Jónasson* (☎ 511 1500; fax 515 1511) at Borgartún 34, between the centre and Laugardalur. It's run mainly for guests of Guðmundur Jónasson tours, but anyone is welcome when there's space available. Rooms are comfortable, but a bit stark. With shower and washbasin, they cost Ikr4230/6000 for singles/doubles. Single/double sleeping-bag accommodation is Ikr2600/3700. All options include breakfast.

A good central place is *Gistiheimilið Svala* (☎ 562 3544; fax 562 3650) at Skólavörðustígur 30, in a quiet, nice-looking old house. For single/double rooms the charge is Ikr4050/6100; sleeping-bag accommodation in the attic costs Ikr1400. Also central is *Gistiheimilið #101* (☎ 562 6101; fax 562 6105), at Laugavegur 101, east of the shopping district, which has single/double rooms without bath for Ikr5800/7800, including breakfast. *Gistiheimilið Eskihlíð 3* (☎ 552 4030; fax 552 8030), at (you guessed it) Eskihlíð 3, is convenient to the BSÍ terminal. Singles/doubles cost Ikr4500/5800.

In the former HI hostel at Laufásvegur 41, the Fischer family has set up the eight-room *Gistiheimilið Baldursbrá* (☎ 552 6646; fax 562 6647). Single/double rooms cost Ikr5200/7150. Sleeping-bag accommodation costs Ikr1625. All rates include breakfast.

Pleasantly located near the Tjörn, *Gisti-Inn* (☎ & fax 561 3005), at Sóleyjargata 11, is a nice residence in a leafy part of town.

Singles/doubles cost Ikr5850/7800 without bath and Ikr10,075 for a double with shower, all including breakfast.

The recommended *Gistiheimilið Aurora* (☎ 552 5515; fax 551 4894), at Freyjugata 24, which is popular with French tour groups, charges Ikr1000 for pleasant sleeping bag accommodation. It's open 15 June to 15 September and French is spoken.

More basic is *Gistiheimilið Central* (☎ 552 2822; fax 562 3535), at Bólstaðarhlíð 8 near Kjarvalsstaðir, which is run by Ms Guðrun Kjartansdóttir. Sleeping-bag accommodation costs Ikr1250 and single/double rooms are a bargain at Ikr2700/3800, with use of kitchen facilities. The quiet and centrally-located *Gistiheimilið Svanurinn* (☎ 552 5318; fax 562 5166), at Lokastígur 24a, near Hallgrímskirkja, charges Ikr3520/4560 for single/double accommodation.

Gistiskálinn (☎ & fax 568 3188), at Ármúli 17a, about midway between Kringlan and Laugardalur, charges Ikr1300 for sleeping-bag accommodation.

The bright and comfy *Gistiheimilið Egilsborg* (☎ 561 2600; fax 561 2636), Þverholt 20, also lies just east of the centre. Phone for pickup at the BSÍ terminal or Hótel Loftleiðir. Single/double rooms without bath cost Ikr4420/6300.

Another nice convenient place is *Gistiheimilið Hof* (☎ 551 6239; fax 561 6239) at Brautarholt 4, just a couple of blocks from the Hlemmur bus terminal. Single/double rooms with breakfast cost Ikr4350/6250 and sleeping-bag accommodation (without breakfast) is Ikr1400.

Guesthouse Smárar (☎ 562 3330; fax 562 3331) at Snorrabraut 52, near the Hlemmur bus terminal, accommodates up to 18 guests. Single/double rooms cost Ikr3800/5500 and sleeping-bag accommodation is Ikr1500, including a buffet breakfast at any time you decide to roll out of bed.

Nearby is *Gistiheimilið Flókagata 1* (☎ 552 1155; fax 568 0236), at Flókagata 1, which costs Ikr3800/5500 for single/double rooms and Ikr1900 for sleeping-bag accommodation. For the same rates, you can also stay a hop down the street at *Gistiheimilið*

Fjölskylduhúsið (☎ 551 9828; fax 551 2448), at Flókagata 5.

In spite of its name, *Hótel Gistiheimilið Mar* (☎ 552 5599; fax 562 5599), at Brautarholt 22, about 10 minutes walk from Hlemmur, is more guesthouse than hotel. Single/double rooms with washbasin and shared facilities cost Ikr4225/6175. Another guesthouse with high aspirations is the even more basic *Hótel Jörd* (☎ 562 1739; fax 562 1735) at Skólavörðustígur 13a, which charges Ikr2860/4355 for single/double rooms and Ikr390 for breakfast.

Gistiheimilið Snorra (☎ 552 0598; fax 551 8945), at Snorrabraut 61, has singles/doubles for Ikr4680/6370 and sleeping-bag accommodation in double rooms for Ikr1500. Kitchen facilities are available. *Gistiheimilið Sunna* (☎ 896 5070; fax 551 6388), half a block from Hallgrímskirkja at Þórsgata 26, charges Ikr3970/5900 for single/double rooms with breakfast. Non-smoking rooms are available.

The new and popular *Gesthús Dúna* (☎ 588 2100; fax 588 2102), at Suðurhlíð 35d, midway between Reykjavík and Kópavogur, has B&B (without bath) for Ikr4500/6500 single/double. Sleeping-bag accommodation costs Ikr1500.

At Mörkin 8 is the budget-friendly *Hótel Mörk Guesthouse* (☎ 568 3600; fax 568 3606), which has double flats for Ikr6500 and sleeping-bag accommodation for Ikr900.

For a quiet retreat far from the crowds, try *Gistiheimilið Hólaberg* (☎ 567 0980; fax 557 3620), a smart suburban home at Hólaberg 80 in Breiðholt. Single/double rooms cost Ikr3770/5500 and sleeping-bag accommodation is Ikr1300. If you're booked in, free pick-up is provided from the BSÍ terminal or Hótel Loftleiðir, and groups can be picked up from Keflavík. Otherwise, take bus No 12 from Hlemmur or No 112 from Lækjartorg.

A novelty option is *Gistiheimilið ÍSÍ* (☎ 581 3377; fax 567 8848) at the Íþróttamiðstöðin Laugardal (Laugardalur Sports Centre). For single/double rooms with private shower they charge Ikr4225/5525, with breakfast. Double self-catering apartments are available at *Hótel Baron* (☎ 562 3204; fax 562 3779), Barónsstígur 2-4, for Ikr6240 to Ikr9425 per night.

Others include *Gistiheimilið Víkingur* (☎ & fax 562 1290) at Ránargata 12, which charges Ikr4875/5460 for single/double rooms, with breakfast; the stately *Gisti heimilið Ísafold* (☎ 561 2294; fax 562 9965), in the heart of old Reykjavík at Bárugata 11, charging Ikr4550/6370 for single/double rooms with breakfast; *Gistiheimilið Mattheu* (☎ 553 3207), Bugðulækur 13; and *Gisti heimilið Sigrún Ólafsdóttir* (☎ 562 2240), at Skeggjagata 1. The last two charge Ikr3575/5000 for singles/doubles with breakfast.

In addition to the guesthouses, a number of private individuals rent rooms to travellers, providing a personable alternative to formal accommodation. Most are open in the summer only. Single/double rates are set at Ikr3575/5000:

Anna Sigurðardóttir, Tryggvagata 14, (☎ 561 4590; fax 562 8409)
Arnar Jónsson, Óðinsgata 9, (☎ & fax 552 2313)
Ingabjörg Sigurbjörnsdóttir, Laugavegur 49, (☎ 551 4170)
Ruth Þorsteinsson, Vesturbrún 16, (☎ 553 8534)
Hjördís Oddgeirsdóttir, Otrateigur 46, (☎ 553 0343)
Hólmfríður Guðmundsdóttir, Skólavörðustígur 16-4h, (☎ 562 5482)
Magdalena Sigurðardóttir, Fjólugata 11, (☎ 562 6201)
Þórunn Ragnarsdóttir, Norðurbrún 30, (☎ 581 2474)
Jóna Guðlaugsdóttir, Safamýri 77, (☎ 553 7654)
Ásgeir Guðlaugsson, Urðarstekkur 5, (☎ 557 4996; fax 567 0036)
Ingibjörg Ingimundardóttir, Samtún 4, (☎ 551 1835)
Steingerður Þorsteinsdóttir, Rauðalækur 14, (☎ 553 5683)
Kristín Tómasdóttir, Melhagi 5, (☎ 551 7869)
Ruth Sigurðardóttir, Kúrland 19, (☎ 553 7005)
Svanfríður Ingvarsdóttir, Urðarstekkur 12, (☎ 557 4095)

Hotels With only a few exceptions, anything called a 'hotel' refers to an upmarket establishment. One budget option is *Hótel City* (☎ 511 1155; fax 552 9040) at Ránargata 4a, which charges Ikr5100 for a small single room with communal bath. Single/double rooms with shower cost Ikr6300/10,000.

ICELAND

However, the restaurant isn't too hot. Cheaper is *Hótel Höfði* (☎ 552 6210; fax 562 3986) at Skipholt 27. Single/double rooms with television start at Ikr3700/4700, with breakfast.

The stark *Hótel Reykjavík* (☎ 562 6250; fax 562 6350), at Rauðarárstígur 37, charges Ikr11,700/16,000 for single/double rooms with shower. A relatively affordable and recommended option is *Hótel Leifur Eiríksson* (☎ 562 0800; fax 562 0804), opposite Hallgrímskirkja at Skólavörðustígur 45. Rates for single/double rooms are Ikr7550/10,200, including breakfast.

At Laugavegur 140 is the simple *Hótel Hjá Doru* (☎ 562 3204; fax 562 3779), also known as *Dorás Residence*. Single/double rooms with showers start at Ikr7540/10,200. In a similar range is *Hótel Óðinsvé* (☎ 552 5640; fax 552 9613), at Þórsgata 1, which costs Ikr8700/10,200 for single/double rooms with shower and washbasin, including breakfast.

Iceland's only seamen's home, *Sjómannaheimilið Hótel Örkin* (☎ 568 0777; fax 568 9747), Brautarholt 29, offers 20 rooms with television and sea views for a relatively good price: Ikr5720/7400 for singles/doubles with breakfast. It's not licensed to sell alcohol.

Reykjavík's summer hotel, *Hótel Garður* (☎ 551 5656; fax 562 4004), is a 44-room residence hall on the university campus. It's open from June to late August and costs Ikr5480/6450 for singles/doubles with shared bath, including breakfast. Sleepingbag accommodation in two-bed rooms is Ikr1950.

Places to Stay – top end

Generally considered Iceland's finest hotel, *Hótel Saga* (☎ 552 9900; fax 562 3980), at Hagatorg 1, offers a grand view and all the trappings of an international-class hotel – a pool, penthouse restaurant, health club, two bars, shops, convention facilities etc. Single/double rooms start at Ikr11,400/14,950 with a shower and Ikr12,090/15,600 with full bath.

Icelandair also runs two hotels. The rather stuffy *Scandic Hótel Esja* (☎ 505 0940; fax 505 0955), at Suðurlandsbraut 2, isn't exactly central but it's comfy and cheaper than the Hótel Saga. The *Hótel Loftleiðir* (☎ 505 0900; fax 505 0905), where delayed flight passengers almost invariably wind up, is also convenient for catching early morning buses to Keflavík airport. It has a swimming pool, massage room, sauna, bank, restaurants, shops and conference facilities. The interesting sculpture out the front is *Through the Sound Barrier*, by Ásmundur Sveinsson. At either hotel, single/double rooms with shower cost Ikr11,000/14.500; with bath, they're Ikr13,200/17,400.

At Rauðarárstígur 18, at the eastern end of the shopping district, is *Hótel Lind* (☎ 562 3350; fax 562 3351). Single/double rooms with shower and breakfast cost Ikr8385/11,440.

The less-than-central *Hótel Ísland* (☎ 568 8999; fax 568 9957), at Ármúli 9, may have international-class amenities, but the rooms look a bit too much like the US$24.95 American chain, *Motel 6*, to justify Ikr11,400/14,950 for a single/double with shower or Ikr12,090/15,600 with bath.

A pleasant and central upmarket choice is *Hótel Holt* (☎ 552 5700; fax 562 3025) at Bergstaðastræti 37. Even if you're not looking for a room, stop by to see the collection of Icelandic artwork decorating the lobby and hallways. Single/double rooms start at Ikr11,865/13,650 with shower.

The *Grand Hótel Reykjavík* (☎ 568 9000; fax 568 0675), at Sigtún 38, formerly the Holiday Inn, is one of Reykjavík's finest luxury hotels, but it's not central. Single/double rooms with full bath cost Ikr11,700/15,925, including breakfast. When space is available, last-minute bookings score substantial discounts.

Right in the centre of things at Pósthússtræti 11 is *Hótel Borg* (☎ 551 1440; fax 551 1420), a pleasant older hotel with single/double rooms for Ikr10,900/13,900 with bath and breakfast. It's now run by the owner of the Hard Rock Café and has recently been remodelled in a retro 1930s decor, to reflect the era in which it was built.

Places to Eat

Self-Catering The least expensive super-market chain is *Hagkaup* with stores in the Kringlan Centre and on Laugavegur, near Snorrabraut. Both have bargain salad bars for Ikr198/299/499 for small/medium/large serves, but they're only open weekdays until 7 pm and weekends until 5 pm. Later at night or on weekends, try the *10-11* supermarket on Austurstræti, which is open from 10 am to 11 pm daily, or the higher-priced convenience stores scattered around residential areas.

A good place for baked goods is the half-price *bakery* on Suðurlandsbraut, which is open daily. The shop *Osta-Búðin*, at Skólavörðustígur 8, sells a variety of domestic and imported cheeses.

For beer, wine and spirits, Reykjavík has six State Monopoly stores. The most accessible are at Austurstræti 10 and in the Kringlan Centre.

Fast Food & Pizza For a quick bite on the run, you can buy chips, hot dogs, pizza, soft drinks and other snacks around Lækjartorg and the Austurstræti mall for around Ikr250 to Ikr300. Moving slightly upscale is *Hlölla Bátar*, in the middle of Ingólfstorg, which is a locally popular place for quick eats. *Gott í Gogginn*, at Laugavegur 2, does a range of quick takeaway snacks, from pasta and baguette sandwiches to nachos, burritos and pizza – a sort of European Union hybrid.

At *Svarta Pannan*, on Tryggvagata, you'll find fried chicken, fish & chips, burgers etc for Ikr400 to Ikr700. For a change from the same old snack foods, try the delicious pitta sandwiches at *Pítan*, Skipholt 50c, which also does burgers, fish & chips, chicken and vegetable kebabs for Ikr400 to Ikr700.

For quick, inexpensive and fabulous Thai takeaway, go to *Thailandi* (☎ 551 7627) (note the Pepsi sign in Thai script). You'll pay Ikr400 to Ikr900 for a range of mild to spicy set dishes; if you like heat, the beef in Panang chilli and coconut creme is tops. Ask for a *stimpilkort* which is good for a free meal after you've eaten there five times. In summer, it's open daily from 10.30 am to 10 pm.

An alternative for quick Thai takeaways – but not as good as Thailandi – is *Nuðluhúsið*, with two locations, one just off Laugavegur and the other on Suðurlandsbraut, within easy walking distance of the campground and HI Hostel. They're open from 11.30 am to 9 pm Monday to Thursday, on Friday and Saturday from 5 to 10 pm, and on Sunday from 5 to 9 pm. Main curry dishes start at under Ikr500.

Eld-Smiðjan (☎ 562 3838), at Bragagata 38a, serves up pizzas baked in a birchwood-fired oven; free deliveries are available until 11.30 pm nightly.

The US chain *Pizza Hut* at the Hótel Esja offers a self-serve salad bar, pizzas, pasta, beer and wine. You'll spend around Ikr1500 for a full meal, with alcohol. It's always overflowing with locals and is convenient to the HI hostel and campground. The branch also offers free delivery for orders over Ikr1000.

Pizza 67, at Tryggvagata 26, is a super hippie-theme pizza-pub, where small pizzas with names like Woodstock, Rolling Stones, Highway 49, Sergeant Pepper's, Flower Power and TNT (all manner of chilli peppers plus tabasco sauce!) cost around Ikr700.

With burgers, it pays to be careful. The best are found in pubs and cafés, while those fried up at food stalls and kiosks may well be small, gristly blends of dubious beef bits and unspecified cereals. If there's comfort in consistent and familiar standards – which are actually higher than most people realise – check out the world's two most expensive *McDonald's*, on Austurstræti and at the corner of Suðurlandsbraut and Skeiðarvogur. A *McGoðborgari* ('Quarter Pounder') with *McFranskar* (fries) and a medium coke will set you back Ikr599.

Also making its Reykjavík debut is the 'submarine' (baguette) sandwich specialist, *Subway*. It serves both hot and cold sandwiches. There are two locations, one on Austurstræti and the other at Suðurlandsbraut 46.

The old *Myllan* bakery, in a historical

building beside the Restaurant Lækjar-brekka (see Fine Dining section), serves up coffee and pastries in the afternoon. A number of small cafeterias, some in museums, offer limited à la carte snacks and rich desserts. More down-to-earth is the *cafeteria* in the BSÍ long-distance bus terminal.

Cafés & Pubs For good food and lively atmosphere, nothing beats Reykjavík's small coffee shops and pub-style cafés. Naturally, most places are busiest on weekends. After 10 pm on Friday or Saturday night, expect queues, and if there's live music, you'll also pay a cover charge of around Ikr1000 per person. Don't bother arriving until 11 pm, when the action starts heating up.

A rightfully popular place is *Gaukur á Stöng* (☎ 551 1556) at Tryggvagata 22. It's said that this is where Iceland's famous vodka-spiked beer originated and it's become almost legendary for its daring. On Friday or Saturday nights things start winding up at about midnight and maintain fever pitch until closing time at 3 am. Even weeknights can get interesting. As a restaurant, it's also recommended for its excellent fresh fish.

For a less rollicking time, try the *Djúpið* at Hafnarstræti 15 in the cellar of the *Hornið* restaurant. It's open only on Friday and Saturday nights and is a good place to chat. Alternatively, you can return to the early days of Hollywood at the *Bíóbarinn* (☎ 551 8222), at Klapparstígur 26.

At the wonderful new *Dubliner* (☎ 511 3233), run by an Irishman who migrated from one Emerald Isle to another, the Guinness, Jameson's, and Irish stew are served up with an authentic measure of blarney. There's also a collection of Irish and Icelandic literature to fill up those rainy afternoons sipping coffee or Guinness.

Café Ópera (☎ 552 9499) at Lækjargata 2 is a good place for nicely priced fish dishes and more expensive steaks, barbecues and other meat standards. There's piano music nightly. Next door there's the more mood-conscious *Café Romance* (☎ 562 4045), which tries very hard to live up to its name

and set the stage for *l'amour*. The live piano music is gentle and an open fire and soft candlelight keep everything nice and cosy. This is more a pub than a café but meals are available. In the same building is *Café Sport*, which naturally features a sports theme.

Reykjavík's *Hard Rock Cafe* (☎ 568 9888), at Kringlan Centre, has the Hard Rock's standard repertoire of earthy slogans and rides its trendy reputation as far as possible. Some people just go to buy the T-shirt, but several affordable dishes are now available: charbroiled salmon for Ikr1190, a chef's salad for Ikr895 and a small order of spare ribs for Ikr1195. Deluxe burgers of various descriptions cost from Ikr690 to Ikr990.

Coffee is an Icelandic staple, particularly in Reykjavík, and you'll find loads of places to linger over a cuppa. If it's windy and pouring rain, you can dream of the Costa del Sol at *Café List* (☎ 562 5059), Klapparstígur 26, with a Spanish-style bar serving tapas, cakes, breads and Mediterranean meals. On weekends, it stays lively until 3 am.

Kaffi Austurstræti at Austurstræti 6 has great value daily specials (normally soup and a main fish course) for Ikr700 to Ikr800. You can also get pasta dishes (Ikr600 to Ikr800) and a superb Peruvian-style ceviche for Ikr570. It's open to 1 am on weekdays and 3 am on weekends. For info on the *Bítal-klubbarinn* downstairs, see Entertainment, later in this chapter.

Highly recommended is the funky *Svarta Kaffið* at Laugavegur 54, which serves up great light meals – salads, sandwiches and homemade soup in bread roll bowls – as well as Iceland's best-value draught beer (Ikr350 for a half litre) from 6 to 9 pm.

At the popular but slightly stuffy *Café Paris*, at Austurstræti 14, you'll get a cafetière for Ikr180 and light continental lunches for Ikr400 to Ikr600.

If you wish to discuss Andy Warhol, Karl Marx or Halldór Laxness over a cappuccino, visit Iceland's only bohemian café, *Café Sólon Íslandus* (☎ 551 2666), at Bankastræti 7. It's a simple and pleasant place to chat, and upstairs there's a gallery of local art and a small concert venue. It's open from 10 am to 1 am weekdays, and until 3 am on weekends.

For more on pubs and music, see under Pubs in the Entertainment section, later in this chapter.

Foreign Cuisine For a city of its size, Reykjavík has a fair number of restaurants serving reasonable ethnic cuisines (see also Fast Food & Pizza earlier in this section). However, thanks to the Icelanders' typically cautious approach to spicy foods, dishes that would otherwise be hot or strongly flavoured dishes are generally toned down.

Ítalía (☎ 562 4630), Laugavegur 11, has pasta dishes for Ikr1000 to Ikr1200 and pizzas for around Ikr1200. In the evening, it lays on an Italian buffet for Ikr1500. Also central is *Caruso* (☎ 552 4555) at the corner of Þinghóltstræti and Laugavegur, which does seafood buffets and Italian cuisine. *Pasta Basta* (☎ 561 3131), at Klapparstígur 38, has a generous buffet lunch, including soup, bread, homemade pasta, vegetables and salads for just Ikr790.

Sjanghæ (☎ 551 6513), at Laugavegur 28, serves Westernised Mandarin Chinese dishes; evening meals cost from Ikr1300 to Ikr1800. It's open every day for lunch and dinner. For Chinese, Thai, Malaysian and Japanese options, there's *Asía* (☎ 562 6210) at Laugavegur 10. Lunch specials cost around Ikr450. The *Indo-Kina*, also on Laugavegur, serves up good value Vietnamese and other South-East Asian specials. With two or more people, hearty combination meals are available for under Ikr1000. A basic Chinese option is *Kína Húsið* (☎ 551 1014) at Lækjargata 8. Great value lunch specials start at under Ikr500.

Reykjavík also has a new Japanese restaurant, *Samurai* (☎ 551 7776), at Ingólfsstræti 1a. The extensive menu includes fish and vegetable tempura starting at Ikr820 and nine-piece sushi specials starting at Ikr1440.

For Asian cuisine that claims to be Korean, there's *Café Kim* (☎ 562 6259), in the Hótel Reykjavík. The food's not bad but it's expensive and not really Korean. Note that evening specials are available only for two or more people dining together. In the same building is the *Marhaba* (☎ 562 6766) Lebanese restaurant, which does renowned Middle Eastern cuisine, complete with a belly dancer.

Iceland's best Thai restaurant, the *Me Nam Khwai* (☎ 551 8111), on Smiðjustígur just off Laugavegur, is affiliated with the equally excellent Thailandi takeaway (see under Fast Food & Pizza earlier in this section). It's open Thursday to Sunday from 6 to 10 pm.

Austur Indía Fjelagið (☎ 552 1630), at Hverfisgata 56, serves up genuine Indian fare prepared by a chef with 20 years experience in Bombay, Delhi, Madras and Bangalore. The menu includes dishes from most regions of India.

For excellent and reasonably genuine Mexican food, *Amigo's* (☎ 511 1333), at Tryggvagata 8, is highly recommended. It's open daily for lunch and dinner until 1 am on weekdays and 3 am on Saturday and Sunday. There's also a bar.

Hard-core carnivores will probably enjoy *Argentina* (☎ 551 9555), at Barónsstígur 11a, which specialises in large chunks of charcoal-grilled beef and lamb fit for a gaucho feast. It's all served up with Argentine wine and afterward you can even order a fine cigar. On Thursday, the special is prime rib, and there's live music on Sunday.

Vegetarian The excellent *Á Næstu Grösum*, the 'One Woman Vegetarian Restaurant' (☎ 552 8490), at the corner of Laugavegur and Klapparstígur, serves both macrobiotic and standard vegetarian fare. A substantial meal with coffee and cake costs under Ikr1000. It's open daily, except Saturday, from noon to 2 pm and 6 to 8 pm. Another choice is *Græni Kosturinn* (☎ 552 2028), Skólavörðustígur 8, which serves mild and spicy vegetarian dishes and sweets. Lunch specials are available for as little as Ikr350. It's open daily from 11.30 am to 9 pm (Sundays for dinner only).

Fine Dining Reykjavík has no shortage of upmarket wining and dining venues and, given the climate, a cosy fireplace-in-the-farmhouse or nautical sort of atmosphere gets a lot of mileage. Fine dining is generally expensive but some places do offer good value. For dinners out at finer restaurants, guests are generally expected to dress nicely. However, travellers who haven't packed their Sunday best will get away with smart casual dress.

Askur (☎ 553 8550) at Suðurlandsbraut 4 is an easy walk from the HI hostel and campground, and specialises in fish and lamb. In addition to the daily soup and salad bar, it puts on a lavish Sunday buffet.

Potturinn og Pannan (☎ 551 1690), at Brautarholt 22, has an all-day soup and salad buffet for Ikr790 and a daytime steak and potato special for Ikr990. It also does pizza and burger specialities for under Ikr900, and seafood, lamb, and beef dishes starting at Ikr1400.

Popular with visitors is *Fógetinn* (☎ 551 6323), which is housed in Skúli Magnússon's historical weaving shed, Reykjavík's oldest building. The restaurant specialises in lamb, ptarmigan, duck and seafood starting at about Ikr1300. With live music nightly, it's a pleasant way to enjoy fine cuisine.

One of the nicest seafood places is *Jónatan Livingston Mávur* (☎ 551 5520) at Tryggvagata 4-6 near the harbour, which specialises in fresh fish, lamb, wild game and French cuisine. On summer evenings, there's a seafood buffet. The indoor aquarium also merits a look, but you may begin to wonder whether the endearing faces are related to those on your plate.

Another fine seafood restaurant is the *Naust* (☎ 551 7759), which has a heavily nautical backdrop. It's housed in a former salt cellar at Vesturgata 6-8, near the harbour, and offers not only a vast range of seafood, but also Iceland's more bizarre traditional dishes. It's open for lunch from noon to 2 pm on weekdays and for dinner every day from 6 pm.

Another mainly seafood restaurant is *Við Tjörnina* (☎ 551 8666) at Templarasund 3, near the Tjörn, which is a recommended and moderately priced family place. The daily fish specials are good value at Ikr800, including soup and a bag of bread scraps for the ducks when you're finished. The cosy and personable *Skólabrú* (☎ 562 4455), just off Austurvöllur, is open for delicious fish specialities daily from 6 pm and for lunch on Monday to Friday from 11.30 am to 2.30 pm.

The upmarket *Lækjarbrekka* (☎ 551 4430), at Bankastræti 2, is housed in a building constructed in 1834 as the home of shipping merchant PC Knudtzon of Copenhagen and used alternately as a bakery and a private residence until 1980, when it was renovated as a restaurant. The quality varies, but it gets lots of mileage from its convenient location and popularity with tour groups. Every summer evening at 6 pm, it puts on a well-attended fish buffet. Around the corner at *Humarhúsið* (☎ 561 3303), Amtmannsstígur 1, the speciality is lobster. Lunch specials start at Ikr990 and dinners at Ikr1390. It's open every day and is increasingly a favourite with visitors.

Readers have also recommended *Gullni Haninn* (☎ 553 4780), or 'Golden Rooster', at Laugavegur 178, for traditional Icelandic food as well as international dishes.

One of the most unusual restaurants is *Perlan* (☎ 562 0200) the big pearly dome atop the Öskjuhlíð water tanks. The menu focuses on fish and meat dishes but the view, which changes as the restaurant revolves once every hour, doesn't come cheap; expect to spend around Ikr3000 per person without alcohol. There's also an artificial geyser which erupts occasionally and a walkway outside with recorded commentary about the view.

All of the big hotels prepare elegant but relatively ordinary seafood, lamb and beef dishes. The *Lónið* at Hótel Loftleiðir has a lunchtime buffet for Ikr1400. At *Hótel Holt*, a three-course set lunch costs Ikr1395. At *Café Ísland* in the Hótel Ísland, health food and salad bar lunches start at Ikr1000.

Entertainment

Cinemas The Reykjavík area has six main cinemas: *Bíóborgin* (☎ 551 1384), Snorrabraut 37 ; *Bíóhöllin* (☎ 557 8900), Mjódd

Centre, Álfabakki 8; *Háskólabíó* (☎ 552 2140), Hótel Saga, Hagatorg; *Laugarásbíó* (☎ 553 2075), Laugarás; *Regnboginn* (☎ 551 9000), Hverfisgata 54 and *Stjörnubíó* (☎ 551 6500), Laugavegur 94. Daily newspapers list shows and showtimes. Films are screened in their original language with Icelandic subtitles. Most features cost Ikr600.

The film *Iceland Experience*, in English and German, is shown at Tjarnarbíó hourly on Monday to Saturday from noon to 7 pm and Sunday from 2 to 9 pm. It deals with Icelandic culture and history from Settlement to modern times.

Cultural Activities Reykjavík has several theatre groups, an opera, a symphony orchestra and a dance company. Information on current events may be found in *What's on in Reykjavík*, in the daily papers or at the following box offices:

Alþýðuleikhúsið Theatre Group (☎ 551 5185), Vesturgata 3, book by phone
Icelandic Ballet (☎ 567 1988), book tickets by phone
Icelandic Opera (☎ 551 1475), Ingólfsstræti, open daily from 3 to 7 pm
Iceland Symphony Orchestra (☎ 562 2255), Hagatorg, box office at Gimli, Lækjargata, open Monday to Friday from 9 am to 5 pm
National Theatre (☎ 551 1200), Hverfisgata, open daily except Monday, 1 to 6 pm
Reykjavík Theatre Company (☎ 568 0680), Listabraut, Kringlan, open daily except Monday from 1 to 8 pm

Light Nights The show *Light Nights*, which is staged for tourists and performed in English, is an easily digested account of the sagas and the Settlement of Iceland. It focuses a bit heavily on the Vikings but that seems to be what tourists want.

The two-hour performances are held daily, except Sunday, at 9 pm through the summer (24 June to 29 August) at *Tjarnarbíó* (☎ 551 9181), Tjarnargata 10e. Tickets go on sale at 8 pm on the night of the performance, or may be purchased in advance at the Bankastræti tourist office and major hotels. Discounts are available for groups and holders of student cards.

Discos Discos provide the most frenetic excitement Reykjavík has to offer, but aren't for the timid or the destitute. All discos, as opposed to the pubs with dance floors, impose a cover charge of around Ikr1000. To drink yourself into any sort of credible stupor, you'll need an additional Ikr6000 per person.

Drinking and dancing establishments are open until 1 am weekdays and 3 am on Friday and Saturday nights. On weekends, you'll often find queues outside most of the popular clubs, especially during the 11 pm to 2 am rush hours. Generally, Friday is the night of choice with local youth, and rarely does anyone spend the entire evening in a single venue. Rather they circulate through various hot spots in search of the best action; this is known as *runtur*, the Icelandic pub crawl, which seems to be a sacred rite among 14 to 21 year olds. Older people are more likely to opt for pubs or less bacchanalian dance venues.

In many discos, it's an unwritten rule that men dress up a bit – even ties aren't out of line – but foreigners normally get away with more casual dress and women face no real dress restrictions. As for social restrictions, standards are pleasantly European and conservative foreigners may even feel uncomfortable with the typically unrestrained behaviour that surfaces when the action heats up.

Because discos pass into and out of fashion so quickly, it's difficult to make specific recommendations, but the most consistently popular and frantic place is still the huge *Tunglið* disco, at Austurstræti 22b. If you like it loud and trendy, start there and follow the crowds through the circuit. Their self-described ideal patron will be 'young, fashionable and skimpily clad'. Other popular spots include *Casablanca*, at Skúlagata 30; *Oðal*, on Austurvöllur; and *Rosenberg*, on Austurstræti.

A wilder, trendier and more superficial side of Reykjavík nightlife is found at *Ingólfskaffi*, at Hverfisgata 8-10. For a more elegant night out, try *Amma Lú* (☎ 568 9686) at the Kringlan Centre, but dress nicely or

ICELAND

you'll feel alien. It was named in honour of the owner's grandmother. Some areas are reserved for antiquarian bibliophiles (antiquarian books, that is) and others hope to conjure up Prohibition-era Chicago. The Erró paintings are a particular attraction.

Various clientele, from teenagers to pensioners, frequent Iceland's largest disco in the *Hótel Ísland* at Ármúli 9, where there is often live entertainment on weekends.

Dancing For old-fashioned dancing, the best options are *Ártún* at Vagnhöfði 11 and *Danshúsið Glæsibær* at Álfheimar 74. The latter caters especially for senior citizens.

Pubs Reykjavík's surprising variety of pubs offers a great night out and most serve meals as well as beer and booze. However, drinking a pint in Reykjavík is a major expenditure, and if you prefer spirits or cocktails... well, one tourist handout sums it up best: '... don't be surprised when you get a bill the size of a Third World country's defence budget'.

Reykjavík's oldest pub, the enduring *Gaukur á Stöng* (☎ 551 1556) at Tryggvagata 22, keeps on attracting crowds and mayhem with its live music and youthful atmosphere every night of the week. The action is naturally best on Friday and Saturday, but other nights also get lively. Nearby at Tryggvagata 20 is the louder and trendier *Glaumbar*, which caters to younger crowds who prefer music, drinking and dancing to conversation.

For heavy metal music and a crowded, smoky atmosphere where you can hang out with aspiring Hell's Angels, artists and spider women, try *22*, at Laugavegur 22. On weekends, there's a disco upstairs. It's known mainly as a gay venue, but heterosexuals are also welcome.

At *Berlín*, Austurstræti 22, you get live jazz performances on Thursday nights and a disco on weekends (Thursday 11 pm to 1 am and Friday 11 pm to 3 am). The friendly *Bítlaklubbarinn*, downstairs from the Kaffi Austurstræti, is a novel tribute to the Beatles. You can immerse yourself in Beatles' films, records and paraphernalia over coffee from

2 to 6 pm daily, or over beer from 6 pm to 1 am Thursday and Sunday and 6 pm to 3 am on weekends. Local guitarist Eiríkur Einarsson drops in occasionally for a live performance to commemorate the fab four.

The delightful Irish pub, *Dubliner* (☎ 511 3233), at Hafnarstræti 4, offers live music most nights; don't miss the house band, Papar, which plays hybrid Irish-Icelandic folk music. Another novel option is *Kaffi Brennslan* on Austurvöllur, which boasts 117 varieties of beer.

The best variety of high quality live music, including rock, blues, jazz, swing and so on, is at *Plúsinn* at Vitastígur 3. Performances are held Thursday to Sunday evenings from 8 pm to 3 am. Profits benefit the Icelandic Association of Pop Musicians.

The youth-oriented *Tveir Vinir* at Laugavegur 45 stages karaoke and live shows by Icelandic pop artists from Thursday to Sunday nights. Alternatively, try the immensely popular *Kringlukráin* in the Kringlan shopping centre.

If cost is a factor, check out *Svarta Kaffið* on Laugavegur during happy hour (from 6 to 9 pm), when a half litre costs only Ikr350; it's Iceland's cheapest draught beer. Alternatively, there's *Valtýr á Grænni Treyju* at Tryggvagata 26, which charges a reasonable Ikr390.

Spectator Sport
Football, Iceland's most popular spectator sport, is played on both local and international level at the Laugardalur Sports Centre. For information, see the sports sections of Reykjavík newspapers.

Getting There & Away
Air All domestic flights as well as most flights to Greenland and the Faroe Islands depart from Reykjavík city airport. International flights (including Greenland flights only when jets are used) depart from Keflavík international airport, 40 km west of the city. If you have a student card, you may be eligible for discounted airline tickets; check out Student Travel at the University

Bookshop on Hringbraut. Airline offices include:

Icelandair/Flugleiðir
Laugavegur 7 (☎ 569 0100, flight information ☎ 569 0300)
Hótel Esja, Suðurlandsbraut 2
Kringlan Centre shopping mall
Íslandsflug
Reykjavík city airport (☎ 561 6060)
Leiguflug
Hótel Loftleiðir (☎ 562 8011)

Bus Long-distance buses use the BSÍ terminal (☎ 552 2300; fax 552 9973) at Vatnsmýrarvegur 10. During the summer months there are daily services or connections between Reykjavík and Akureyri (Ikr3850), Mývatn (Ikr5150), Skaftafell (Ikr3000), Höfn (Ikr4300), Akranes (Ikr900), Borgarnes (Ikr1000), Reykholt (Ikr1300) and Reykjanes (Ikr450 to Ikr550). There are also services to Snæfellsnes – all north coast towns (Ikr2000 to Ikr2250) plus Búðir (Ikr2000), Arnarstapi (Ikr2000) and the West End – six times weekly, connecting with services to Ísafjörður (Ikr4930) via the *Baldur* ferry from Stykkishólmur. Some services to Þorlákshöfn (Ikr550) connect with the *Herjólfur* ferry to Vestmannaeyjar.

Travellers between Reykjavík and East Iceland must spend the night in Höfn, Akureyri or Reykjahlíð before they can make connections to their destination.

Ferry The car-ferry *Akraborg* (☎ 551 6420) makes at least four trips daily between Reykjavíkurhöfn harbour and Akranes, with extra sailings on Friday and Sunday evenings in summer. Once the new tunnel is completed between Mt Esja and Akranes, this service will be discontinued.

For information on the Viðey ferry, see Viðey in the Around Reykjavík section.

Getting Around
The Airport The Flybus (☎ 562 1011) to Keflavík international airport (which claims to be 'frequently on time') leaves the Hótel Loftleiðir exactly two hours prior to every international departure, stopping at Kópavogur and Hafnarfjörður if passengers are booked. Buses from Keflavík international airport to the Hótel Loftleiðir depart about 45 minutes after arrival of an international flight. The fare is Ikr600. From 15 June to 15 September, the airport bus which connects with early morning flight departures picks up passengers at the HI hostel/ campground, Grand Hótel Reykjavík, Hótel Esja and Hótel Loftleiðir between 4.30 and 5 am.

Bus Reykjavík's excellent SVR city bus system (☎ 551 2700) operates from 6.45 am (10 am on Sunday) until 1 am, although the last bus will pass a given stop anytime between 12.30 and 1 am. On weekdays, they run at 20-minute intervals until 7 pm. On weekends and evenings, buses run every half hour. They pick up and drop passengers only at designated stops which are marked with the letters SVR.

The two central terminals are at Hlemmur (which has an information desk) and Lækjartorg, both of which have several bus stops, so you may have to look around for the right one. The HI hostel/campground bus (No 5) stops on the north side of Laekjartorg. At Hlemmur, it stops near the south-west corner of Hverfisgata and Rauðarárstígur. Other main terminals are Grensás, at the corner of Grensásvegur and Miklabraut, and Mjódd shopping centre in the south-eastern suburb of Breiðholt (on the way to Mjódd, note the bizarre teepee-shaped church, Breiðholtskirkja).

The free Reykjavík maps from the tourist office also include a bus route map. The suburban timetable, entitled *Almenningsvagnar Leiðabók*, is available from the tourist office and bus terminals. During the day, suburban buses run about every half hour from the four major city bus terminals: Hlemmur, Grensás, Lækjartorg and Mjódd. For details, see under the individual suburbs.

The standard fare per ride on either city or suburban buses is Ikr120 and drivers are not permitted to give change. At bus terminals, you can buy a book of ten fares for Ikr1000, which is more convenient than grubbing around for exact change and of course it saves money. If you need to change buses, ask the driver for a *skiptimiði* (SKIFF-ti-midth-i), or transfer, which is valid for up to 45 minutes from the time of issue.

The museum bus, which circulates past the National Gallery of Iceland, National Museum, Árni Magnússon Institute, Nordic House, Ásgrímur Jónsson Museum, Einar Jónsson Museum, Kjarvalsstaðir, Electric Museum, Árbæjarsafn, Ásmundar Sveinsson Museum, and the Sigurjón Ólafsson Museum, operates daily between 21 June and 31 August from 1 to 5 pm.

Taxi Reykjavík is small enough to walk around, but taxis will be handy if you have a lot of luggage or you're catching an airport bus (most flights to/from Europe fly from Keflavík between 7 and 9 am). Since there's no tipping, taxi fares actually work out cheaper than in the USA or most of Europe. For example, between the Hótel Loftleiðir and the HI hostel or campground costs around Ikr600 for up to four people and luggage.

There are five taxi stations: Hreyfill (☎ 588 5522), Bæjarleiðir (☎ 553 3500), BSR (☎ 561 0000), Borgarbíll (☎ 552 2440) and BSH (☎ 565 0666).

Bicycle Because of Reykjavík's spread-out nature, the city lends itself to sightseeing by bicycle. Good quality bicycles may be hired from Borgarhjól (☎ 551 5653), Hverfisgata 50, as well as from the HI hostel on Sundlaugavegur and the campground in Laugardalur. All charge Ikr1000 per day.

Around Reykjavík

SELTJARNARNES
The small suburb of Seltjarnarnes occupies the western end of Reykjavík's peninsula. It offers nice sunset views when the weather is cooperating, and on clear days you can even see Snæfellsjökull. At the pond Bakkatjörn there's a small nature reserve with abundant bird life. The town swimming pool is one of the area's nicest (see Swimming under Reykjavík).

Nesstofa
Nesstofa, the National Medical Museum, is housed in an old stone building originally constructed for Iceland's first surgeon-general, Bjarni Pálsson, between 1761 and 1763. It houses a collection of old medical artefacts gathered by Reykjavík physician Jón Steffensen, who died in 1991. The oldest items date from the late 18th century. From June to September, it's open daily from 1 to 5 pm. Admission is Ikr200.

Rauða Ljónið
Seltjarnarnes may well be best known for *Rauða Ljónið*, a pub on Eiðistorg which claims to be the largest pub in the world. It's actually just a large glass-domed square which accommodates thousands as long as they don't want to sit on chairs. It's especially popular after sports matches.

Getting There & Away
To reach Seltjarnarnes, either walk 1.5 km west from Reykjavík centre or take bus No 3 from Lækjartorg.

VIÐEY ISLAND
Viðey (the 'wood island') lies one km north of Reykjavík's Sundahöfn harbour (near Laugardalur). Although it's only 700m from east to west and 1700m from north to south, it's the largest island in Kollafjörður and has figured prominently in the history of Reykjavík and Iceland.

History
Viðey is the remnant of a volcano that became extinct some two million years ago and eroded into little more than a low hill. The island was part of the estate claimed by Iceland's first settler Ingólfur Arnarson and there's evidence of habitation as early as the 10th century. It probably served as a minor religious centre in the 12th century, but its importance increased with the consecration

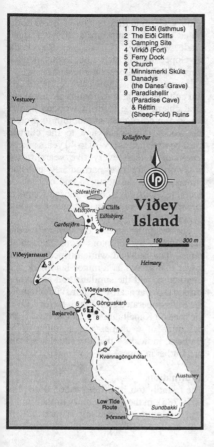

1 The Eiði (Isthmus)
2 The Eiði Cliffs
3 Camping Site
4 Virkið (Fort)
5 Ferry Dock
6 Church
7 Minnismerki Skúla
8 Danadys
  (the Danes' Grave)
9 Paradíshellir
  (Paradise Cave)
  & Réttin
  (Sheep-Fold) Ruins

Viðey Island

0 150 300 m

ICELAND

It was designed by Nicolai Eigtved (who also designed Amalienborg, the royal palace in Copenhagen) and built from local basalt and sandstone blocks. Completed in 1755, it is the oldest original building in Iceland. In 1774, the Viðey church was completed and consecrated. It is the second oldest church in Iceland and its interior furnishings are original. Skúli Magnússon died at Viðey in 1794.

In 1817, the island was bought by Supreme Court president Magnús Stephensen, who also brought Iceland's only printing press to Viðey. Until 1844, he operated it in a shed near Skúli Magnússon's old residence. Stephensen's descendants owned the property until 1901, when it was purchased by seminary instructor Eiríkur Briem who established a farm there. A fishing interest called the Million Company set up on the eastern side of the island and the community grew to about 100 people, but it was deserted before Icelandic independence in 1944. Subsequent owners donated the property to the city of Reykjavík on the 200th anniversary of its municipal charter in 1986.

Things to See & Do

You can walk wherever you'd like on the island but, with the encouragement of some very irritable nesting birds, you'll probably stick with the marked walking tracks. **Virkið** is about 300m west of the landing site. From there, follow the track south-east past the restaurant to the church and over the low pass Gönguskarð to reach **Danadys** (the Danes' grave) and Minnismerki Skúla (the Skúli Magnússon memorial). The next low hill to the south-east is called Kvennagönguhólar where you'll find the natural sheep-fold **Réttin** and the tiny grotto **Paradíshellir** ('paradise cave').

It's also worth continuing to the old **Sundbakki village site** where only an old schoolhouse still stands, or walk to the isthmus and see the ponds, the low cliffs of Eiðisbjarg and Vesturey's beautiful **basalt columns**. All around this peninsula are the **Áfangar** ('milestones'), twin basalt columns set up at intervals by local artist, R Serra.

of an Augustinian monastery in 1226 by Þorvaldur Gissurarson and the renowned Snorri Sturluson.

The monastery operated until 1539 when Dietrich van Minden, an aide of the Danish king, took over the island, drove the monks away and proclaimed Viðey a royal estate. It was restored in 1550 by Jón Árason, the last Catholic bishop of Iceland, and the fort Virkið was constructed as a defence against further aggression.

In 1751, the government presented Viðey to sheriff Skúli Magnússon and constructed the Viðeyjarstofa as his personal residence.

Places to Stay & Eat

The quaint and elegant upmarket restaurant *Viðeyjarstofa* (☎ 552 8470), in the farmhouse, serves coffee and cakes in the afternoon and is open for dinner from Thursday to Sunday evening. Reservations are essential.

Most visitors to Viðey just eat at the restaurant and return to Reykjavík, but there's also a campsite and barbecue facilities at Viðeyjarnaust, west of the ferry landing. Camping requires permission from the farmhouse.

Getting There & Away

The Viðey ferry (☎ 568 6199 or 852 0099) operates from 1 June to 20 September. On weekends, it leaves Sundahöfn every hour from 1 to 5 pm, returning from Viðey hourly from 1.30 to 5.30 pm. On Monday to Friday, it sails from Sundahöfn at 2 and 3 pm and from Viðey, at 3.30 and 4.30 pm. For restaurant patrons, there are evening sailings to Viðey at 7, 7.30 and 8 pm, returning at 10 and 11 pm and midnight. Special sailings can be arranged for groups. The trip from Sundahöfn to Viðey takes about five minutes and costs Ikr400 return.

LUNDEY

Tiny Lundey ('puffin island') is the only place near Reykjavík to see puffins. Cruises to Lundey leave from the Sundahöfn ferry dock on Tuesday, Thursday, Saturday and Sunday at 4 pm, summer only. The tours last 3½ hours, including a one-hour stop at Viðey island. They cost Ikr2800 per person and may be arranged through the Reykjavík tourist office or through BSÍ Travel.

HAFNARFJÖRÐUR

Although it's a suburb of Reykjavík, picturesque Hafnarfjörður, with 17,500 people, is one of Iceland's most pleasant and worthwhile towns to visit. Built on the cave-riddled 7000-year-old Búrfell lava formation, it arcs around a beautiful natural harbour formed by the Hamarinn cliffs. It was used in the early 15th century as an English trading centre, but in the early 16th century, German traders moved in and dominated until the imposition of the Danish Trade Monopoly in 1602. As Reykjavík developed during that tumultuous period, Hafnarfjörður relaxed into obscurity.

Hafnarfjörður is known as a centre for arts and culture, and also maintains old architectural charm in the form of wooden homes covered in corrugated aluminium to protect the wood (this concession to the climate must be replaced every 30 to 40 years and be repainted at least every five years). Also noteworthy are two particularly unusual homes; one at the northern end of town is decorated with lava chunk mosaics, and at the southern end sits a glimmering white pyramid.

The sculpture garden on Viðistaðir contains works by sculptors from Mexico to Japan. The red and white striped wooden tower that serves as a minor landmark is a lighthouse, and the similarly red and white striped tanks at nearby Straumsvík belong to the Swiss-operated aluminium factory. Over the road on Kapelluhraun ('chapel lava'), are the ruins of a chapel and a statue of St Barbara, indicating that the site dates from pre-Lutheran times.

Information

The friendly tourist office (☎ 565 0661; fax 565 4785), in the 19th-century timber building, Riddarinn, on Sögutorg, is open daily in summer from 1 to 5 pm.

Hafnarborg

When Hafnarfjörður celebrated its 75th anniversary in 1983, chemist Sverrir Magnússon and his wife, Ingibjörg Sigurjónsdóttir, donated their home as the Hafnarborg Institute of Culture & Fine Art. It opened in 1988 and is now used for concerts and exhibits by Icelandic artists. Visiting Icelandic artists working at the centre are provided with studio space and living quarters at Straumur, on Reyjanesbraut.

The centre, at Strandgata 34, is open from noon to 6 pm daily except Tuesday. The harbour-view coffee shop is open from 11 am to 6 pm Monday to Friday and from noon to 6 pm on weekends.

Víðistaðatún

Not far from the campground is Víðistaða-kirkja, a semi-circular church containing frescoes by the Spanish-Icelandic artist Baltasar, and a display of sculptures commissioned for the Hafnarfjörður art festivals of 1991 and 1993.

Post & Telecommunications Museum

This interesting collection of artefacts at Austurgata 11 tells the story of communications in Iceland from early Settlement days to the development of the postal and telephone systems. It's open Sunday and Tuesday from 3 to 6 pm or on other days by appointment (☎ 555 4321). Admission is free.

Maritime & Hafnarfjörður Folk Museums

The Maritime Museum (☎ 565 4242) at Vesturgata 8 is in a warehouse built around 1865. It contains nautical artefacts outlining Hafnarfjörður's history as a fishing and trading village, and is particularly strong on

exhibits about Leifur Eiríksson and his first voyage to Vinland.

The Hafnarfjörður Folk Museum, next door at Vesturgata 6, is in the town's oldest house, Sívertsens-Húsið, which was constructed between 1803 and 1805 by local trader and boat-builder Bjarni Riddari Sívertsen.

From 1 June to 30 September, the Maritime and Folk museums are open from 1 to 5 pm daily. In winter, they're open only on weekends. Admission to the Maritime Museum is Ikr200 (free for students and seniors) and the Folk museum costs Ikr100.

The restored historical home, Siggubær, on the corner of Hellisgata and Kirkjuvegur, is open weekends from 2 to 6 pm; at other times, phone curator Magnús Jónsson (☎ 555 4700) to arrange an opening. Another museum building, Smiðjan ('the smithy'), at Strandgata 50, is used for visiting exhibitions. Siggubær and Smiðjan may be visited on the Folk museum admission ticket.

Activities

Recommended horse-riding trips around Hafnarfjörður (and all over Iceland) are

---

Hidden Worlds

Once you've seen some of the lava fields and eerie natural formations that characterise much of the Icelandic landscape, it probably comes as no surprise that Icelanders believe their country is populated by hidden races of wee people – gnomes *(jarðvergar)*, elves *(álfar)*, fairies *(ljósálfar)*, dwarves *(dvergar)*, lovelings *(ljúflingar)*, mountain spirits *(tívar)*, angels *(englar)* and 'hidden people' *(huldufólk)*.

Because Hafnarfjörður lies in an enormous lava field at the confluence of several strong ley lines (natural energy lines known in China as 'dragon lines' and in Australia as 'song lines'), it seems to be particularly rife with these retiring creatures. In fact, construction of roads and homes in Hafnarfjörður is only permitted if it has been determined that the site in question is not already populated by little people.

A local seer, Erla Stefánsdóttir, is particularly attuned to their wavelength and has come up with a map, which is available from the Hafnarfjörður tourist office, showing all the best spots to catch a glimpse of these Hidden Worlds.

The beautiful Hellisgerði lava park and garden, near the town centre, is perhaps the best-known and most densely-populated Hidden Worlds outpost, and serves as a popular meditation spot with local humans. Here you may come into contact with several types of dwarves, gnomes, fairies and elves. Other particularly active sites include along Hraunbrun street; the hill Setberg and adjacent Setbergshamar cliffs; and the Hamarinn bluffs, behind the Flensborg school. If you need help locating and meeting these mostly friendly beings, guided tours of the Hidden Worlds are conducted weekly.

If you want to know even more about hidden Icelanders, four-hour courses are available on Monday, Wednesday and Friday between late May and early September. Contact the Elfschool (☎ 561 2080; fax 561 2014) at Vegmúli 2 in Reykjavík. ∎

available from Íshestar (☎ 565 3044). You can also go lava golfing at the 18-hole Hvaleyrarvöllur (☎ 565 3080).

Organised Tours

A novel option is the Blue Biking Tour from the AV bus terminal in Hafnarfjörður to the Bláa Lónið, via Reykjanesfólkvangur and Grindavík. It leaves daily at 9 am and costs Ikr4000 including bikes and equipment, a picnic lunch, vehicle escort, guide and transport back to Hafnarfjörður. An alternative tour, which costs Ikr800, leaves from the

same place at 7.30 pm and takes you around Bessastaðir and Álftanes.

More unique is Hafnarfjörður's Hidden Worlds Tour, which takes you through the domain of elves, leprechauns, fairies, gnomes and other wee people who inhabit the lava fields (see boxed aside). It runs every Thursday from mid June to late August; book through the tourist office.

The unashamedly tacky Longship Boat Tours (☎ 553 8100) give you a two-hour sightseeing buzz in 'modern Viking boats' – motorised zodiacs with a plastic dragon as a

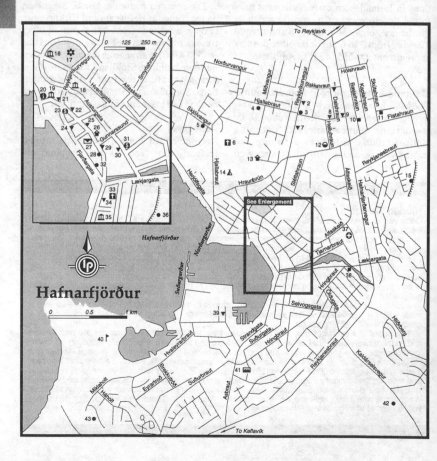

Hafnarfjörður

figurehead. They cost Ikr3300, including hotel pick-up from Reykjavík.

Special Events

In odd-numbered years in early July, Hafnarfjörður remembers its Viking past with an International Viking Festival. It attracts serious Nordic buffs from all over Europe and features parades, horse shows, Viking sports competitions and even marriages conducted according to pagan rites.

By some quirk of fate, Hafnarfjörður has become the proud butt of Icelandic humour and in 1996, it exploited that distinction with a well-attended Djók (pronounced 'Joke') festival, which may become an annual event.

Places to Stay

The Scouts' picturesque *Víðistaðatún Campground*, on Hjallabraut, is open from 1 June to 31 August and costs Ikr250 per tent and Ikr250 per person. The Scouts have also opened the 25-bed *Hraunbyrgi Youth Hostel* (☎ 565 0900; fax 555 1211) on Hrauntunga; hostel facilities are also available to campers. Beds cost Ikr1000/1250 for HI members/ non-members, including use of laundry facilities. Hafnarfjörður's second hostel, *Árahús* (☎ 555 0795; fax 555 3330), at

Strandgata 21, has a more central location and charges the same rates.

The popular and comfortable *Gistiheimilið Berg* (☎ 565 2220; fax 565 4520), at Bæjarhraun 4, charges Ikr4600/6500 for singles/doubles with a washbasin, including breakfast. Sleeping-bag accommodation costs Ikr1850.

Gistiheimilið Lækjarkinn (☎ 565 5132), which sits beside a small lake, charges Ikr3450/5100 for single/double rooms with breakfast and shared bath. Self-catering is available.

Places to Eat

Freshly caught fish and local vegetables are sold at the harbour market, *kænumarkaður*, which is held on Sunday from 11 am to 4 pm. At the *Kænan* (☎ 565 1550), at the small boat harbour, lunches start at Ikr750 with soup, a fish dish and coffee.

A down-to-earth place is *Gafl-Inn* (☎ 555 4477), serving snacks, fish and meat dishes and hot and cold sandwiches. Nearby are the *Hrói-Höttur Pizzeria* (☎ 565 2525) – the name means 'Robin Hood' – which does pizza, pitta sandwiches and burgers, and the always excellent *Pizza 67*. The *Singapore Restaurant & Takeaway* (☎ 555 4999), in the

ICELAND

PLACES TO STAY		21	A Hansen	19	Sívertsen's Húsið –
10	Gistiheimilið Berg	22	Súfistinn		Maritime & Folk
11	Gistiheimilið Hraun	24	Tilveran		Museums
13	Hraunbyrgi (Scouts)	25	Hamborgarahúsið	20	Tourist Office
	HI Hostel	29	Pattaya	23	Íslandsbanki
14	Víðistaðatún	30	Nönnakót	27	Post Office
	Campground	34	Fjörukráin	28	Hafnarborg
26	Árahús HI Hostel	39	Kænan	31	Landsbanki Íslands
38	Gistiheimilið			32	State Monopoly Shop
	Lækjarkinn	**OTHER**		33	Church
		3	Bókabuð Bodvars	35	Smiðjan
PLACES TO EAT			Bookshop	36	Hamarinn Cliffs &
1	Gafl-Inn	5	Lava House		View Disk
2	Singapore Restaurant	6	Víðistaðakirkja &	37	Hospital
	& Takeaway		Sculpture Garden	40	Golf Course
4	Samkaup	12	Bus Terminal	41	Swimming Pool
	Supermarket	15	Setbergshamar Cliffs	42	Íshestar
7	Pizza 67	16	Siggurbær	43	Pyramid House
8	Hrói-Höttur Pizzeria	17	Hellisgerði Park		
9	Kentucky Fried	18	Post & Telecommuni-		
	Chicken		cations Museum		

same area, serves South-East Asian cuisine from 6 pm. You'll find Thai dishes at the *Pattaya* (☎ 565 2978), on Strandgata in the centre. *Tilveran* (☎ 565 5250), open daily from noon to 11 pm, does beef, fish and lamb dishes with a slight gourmet twist.

For something lighter, the small *Súfistinn* (☎ 565 3740) café serves delicious fresh coffee roasted on site, and the non-smoking *Café Nönnakot* does memorable carrot cake á la mode. The name of the *Hamborgarahúsið* should be sufficient to reveal its speciality.

The cosy, upmarket restaurant *A Hansen* (☎ 565 1130) is housed in the 1880 home of Danish merchant PC Knudtzon. It's open for both lunch and dinner and features steak, seafood and Icelandic specialities. During happy hour from 9 to 11 pm, you get two beers for the price of one. Taxi transport is free from Reykjavík.

The equally expensive but novel *Fjörukráin* (☎ 565 1213), Strandgata 50, occupies an 1841 structure which features Viking-era architecture. One section resembles an English pub but specialises in fresh seafood. There's also a dining hall where the staff don Viking get-up and serve pagan feasts on rather earthy tableware. And yes, you can even sample mead. Upstairs is Freyjuhof, a pagan temple, which is used for banquets. Groups can also book hour-long cheese buffet cruises on the harbour aboard the restaurant's ship *Fjörunes*.

Getting There & Away
The bus terminal is about 1½ km from the centre, at the corner of Flatahraun and Helluhraun. From Reykjavík, take bus No 140 from Hlemmur or Lækjartorg; bus No 141 from Hlemmur or Grensás; or bus No 142 from Mjódd. In the wee hours of Saturday and Sunday mornings, there's a special service, No 149, which runs from Lækjartorg and Hlemmur. All buses pass Garðabær.

If passengers have booked, the Keflavík Flybus (☎ 552 2300) stops at the A Hansen and/or Fjörukráin restaurants.

Getting Around
Mountain bike rental is available to guests of the campground or the Hraunbyrgi HI Hostel. For a taxi, phone BSH (☎ 565 0666).

KÓPAVOGUR
With around 20,000 residents, Kópavogur is Iceland's second-largest community. The name means 'seal pup bay', but the only seals today are the stuffed ones in the Natural History Museum, Digranesvegur 12, which is open on Saturday from 1.30 to 4.30 pm.

Under threat of death, Icelandic leaders were forced to sign a decree pledging allegiance to Denmark in 1622. Today a small memorial stands at the western end of the inlet south of Kópavogur to recall this event.

In the distinctive church, Kópavogskirkja, which tops a small hill and could be mistaken for an opera hall, the stained-glass work is by Icelandic sculptor Gerður Helgadóttir. It likens the course of a human life to the passage of a single day from dawn to dusk. The view disc on the hill Víghóll identifies features of the surrounding panorama.

Places to Stay & Eat
Accommodation is available at the guesthouse of *Björg Traustadóttir* (☎ & fax 554 4228), Borgarholtsbraut 44, for Ikr3575/5000 for single/double rooms. *Kokkurinn við Kabyssuna* (☎ 567 7005), at Smiðjuvegur 6, is open every day for breakfast, lunch, dinner and drinks. You'll get sandwiches, fish & chips and pasta dishes, as well as full meals starting at Ikr650.

Getting There & Away
To get there, take bus No 140 from Hlemmur or Lækjartorg, bus No 141 from Grensás or Hlemmur, or bus No 160 from Hlemmur.

GARÐABÆR
Built on the lava from the Búrfell eruption of 7000 years ago, Garðabær contains numerous lava caves and formations. The original Garðabær consisted of a church and two farms, Skúlastaðir and Vífilsstaðir, which are mentioned in the *Landnámabók*, and as recently as the 1950s, it was still a rural

community. As Reykjavík grew, it became the city's most elite suburb, but given Iceland's nearly classless society, this isn't exactly obvious.

Accommodation is available at *Gistiheimilið Vefur* (☎ & fax 565 6474), at Hagaflöt 12. Single/double rooms with self-catering facilities cost Ikr3400/4700. Getting There & Away information is the same as for Hafnarfjörður.

MOSFELLSBÆR

Also known as Mosfellsveit, Mosfellsbær (population 4500) is one of Iceland's fastest growing towns. In the area are the hot springs which have provided Reykjavík with much of its hot water since 1933. The main tourist draw is the Álafoss Factory shop where Icelandic knitwear may be purchased at marginal discounts.

Farmer Þorarinn Jónasson (☎ 566 6179; fax 566 6797; mobile ☎ 985 29179) runs popular three-hour horse-riding tours from the farm Laxnes in Mossfellsveit for Ikr3000. The landscape is lovely and it makes an ideal introduction to riding, especially in preparation for a longer horse trek elsewhere in Iceland. BSÍ offers this tour for Ikr3200, including transport from Reykjavík.

The new *Reykjahvoll Youth Hostel* (☎ 566 7237; fax 566 7235), provides a quiet alternative to the one in Reykjavík. To get there from Reykjavík, take bus No 170 or 175 from the Grensás terminus and get off at the junction of Reykjavegur and route No 431 (Hafravatnsvegur). The hostel is just 200m further along Reykjavegur.

BESSASTAÐAHREPPUR

This town of just 1100 inhabitants on the windy Álftanes ('swan peninsula') was originally a manor farm. It was taken over by the Augustinian monastery at Viðey in the mid-13th century but in 1262 became crown property when Iceland surrendered to the king of Norway. During Norwegian and Danish rule, the estate served as the official residence of royal governors general. In the early 19th century, the parochial school at Skálholt moved briefly to Bessastaðahreppur before relocating permanently to Reykjavík in 1845. Today, the estate is the official residence of the Icelandic head of state. Although the home is closed to the public, the church is open to visitors.

BLÁFJÖLL SKI AREA

Iceland's premier ski area is in the 84 sq km Bláfjallafólkvangur reserve, just south-east of Reykjavík. It has two chair lifts, 10 rope lifts and three cross-country ski trails up to 10 km in length. It's normally open between mid-November and early May, when lifts operate from 10 am to 10 pm Friday to Monday and from 10 am to 6 pm Tuesday to Thursday. The service centre Bláfjallaskáli has a snack bar and a ski-hire shop. For a recorded message (in Icelandic) describing snow, weather and slope conditions, phone (☎ 558 0111).

Daytime and evening lift tickets cost a very reasonable Ikr600 each and a season pass is around Ikr6000 – not bad for a five-month season! In summer, Bláfjallafólkvangur offers lots of great hiking right in Reykjavík's backyard.

Getting There & Away

When the ski slopes are open, buses leave from BSÍ in Reykjavík on Monday and Friday at 2 pm; Tuesday, Wednesday and Thursday at 2, 4 and 6 pm; and on Saturday and Sunday at 1.30 pm, stopping at Garðabær, Hafnarfjörður and Kópavogur en route. For further information, phone BSÍ (☎ 552 2300). The adult one-way fare is Ikr450.

From mid-June to August, Reykjavík Excursions runs three-hour evening tours to Bláfjöll (and Heiðmörk) for Ikr2100. No other public transport serves the area in summer.

Reykjanes Peninsula

The Reykjanes peninsula is often the first bit – and sometimes the only bit – of Iceland that visitors see. On the way from the airport to Reykjavík, they're either intrigued by the stark but grand barrenness or cursing for committing themselves to a holiday in such a moonscape.

Old lava flows dominate the Reykjanes peninsula, particularly along the Reykjavík-Keflavík corridor. The southern half of the peninsula contains the geothermal fields of Svartsengi and Krísuvík, while the western end meets the Atlantic in low, wave-battered bluffs, and bird life is abundant all around the shoreline. Along the shore, note the many bleached driftwood logs lying on the beaches or standing in fences. Most of these were uprooted by spring ice break-ups along the north-flowing rivers of Siberia and washed into the Arctic Ocean currents to eventually be transported to these shores.

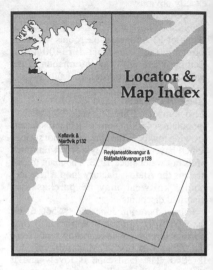

Locator & Map Index

REYKJANESFÓLKVANGUR

The 300 sq km Reykjanesfólkvangur was established in 1975 as a national reserve to protect the bizarre lava formations and other fabulous features, such as the lovely blue lake Kleifarvatn and the major geothermal zone at Krísuvík. For most of the week, the park is quiet and makes a wonderful escape from Reykjavík, especially when the weather is cooperating.

There are dozens of hiking tracks, the most popular of which include the 338m peak Helgafell, the loop past the remote Krísuvíkurberg cliffs and the walk from Krísuvík around the eastern side of Kleifarvatn. Selatangur, an abandoned fishing station at the park's south-western corner, is a two-km hike south of the Grindavík road. For serious hiking, pick up a copy of the park map at the Náttúruverndarráð office in Reykjavík (see National Parks in the Facts about Iceland chapter).

Kleifarvatn

This eerie 10 sq km lake reaches a depth of 97m. It was once considered 'dead', but recently it was stocked with trout which are now doing well. Some of the lava that flowed across Búrfellshraun and into Hafnarfjörður around the time of Settlement came from the craters around the pass Vatnsskarð, north of the lake. Local legends maintain that the lake is inhabited by an elusive monster.

Krísuvík (Austurengjar)

About two km south of Kleifarvatn is Austurengjar, which is more often called Krísuvík after the abandoned settlement further south. In the 1920s, this geothermal field of steaming vents, fumaroles, mud pots, clay and solfataras increased its activity after an earthquake. It can now be explored on a series of boardwalks but there's lots of steam and, when the wind blows from the west, visitors get a good drenching sauna. The geothermal borehole is the world's most

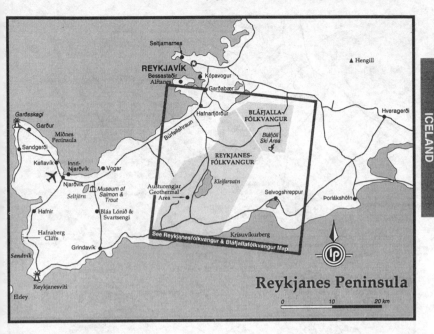

Reykjanes Peninsula

powerful. An impromptu snack kiosk is sometimes set up by the local equivalent of Alcoholics Anonymous to sell hverabrauð ('hot spring bread') baked in the geothermal heat.

South of Austurengjar, a few metres east of the road, you'll reach Grænavatn, a 44m deep crater lake coloured green by algae. Across the road is a smaller lake, Gestsstaðavatn, and beyond it, a well-isolated boarding school for troubled teenagers. Westward, along the Grindavík road, is the Krísuvík church, which was reconsecrated in 1964 and is now being restored by the National Museum.

The area is being considered for geothermal exploitation and several experimental bores have been drilled. East of Krísuvík are the craters Stóra and Lítla ('big' and 'little') Eldborg. From Stóra Eldborg, a rough 10 km hiking route leads to the cliffs of Krísuvíkurberg, where puffins, guillemots and other sea birds nest in the summer.

Continuing west from the church, the road passes some unearthly lava flows; fields of treacle, chocolate, caramel and rust-coloured scoria; and mounds of rainbow slag (also a type of scoria), which flashes sparkles of opalescent violet, green, yellow, red and orange.

Brennisteinsfjöll

This low range along the eastern boundary of the park spawned most of the lava that flowed through the reserve to the sea. It was first thought to be of pre-Settlement origin, but archaeology has revealed transport routes beneath the lava layers. The abandoned sulphur-mining operation at Brennisteinsnáma is accessible via an obscure walking route from either the Bláfjöll ski area or the longer track from the main road north of Kleifarvatn.

Organised Tours

Both BSÍ Travel and Reykjavík Excursions

ICELAND

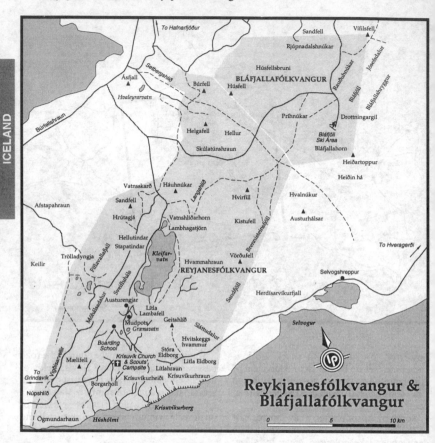

Reykjanesfólkvangur &
Bláfjallafólkvangur

offer six-hour tours through Reykjanes-fólkvangur, including fleeting visits to Grindavík and Bláa Lónið (the Blue Lagoon), for Ikr3400. Neither allows enough time to appreciate the magic of the place, but luckily you can leave the bus anywhere and continue with the tour on another day.

Places to Stay

Camping is available at the *scouts' campsite* beside the old Krísuvík church, but there is no other accommodation in the reserve. Wild campers (as well as hikers and hitchers) must be self-sufficient and carry water, since this porous volcanic area absorbs surface water and none is available between lakes.

Getting There & Away

Access is difficult and from Reykjavík or Hafnarfjörður, you can't visit the southern end of the park in one day without a vehicle unless you take a tour or get lucky with hitching. On public transport, you'll get only as far as Hafnarfjörður or Garðabær, then you'll have to walk or hitch. The quickest access to the trail system is south of Garðabær at the northern end of the park.

Route 42, the best access to Krísuvík, turns off the Reykjanes Highway (Route 41) immediately west of Hafnarfjörður.

GRINDAVÍK

With a population of 2100, Grindavík is a friendly and picturesque fishing village near the western end of Reykjanes. There are no must-see attractions, but you'll enjoy exploring the coastline and volcanic topography. Grindavík's heating comes exclusively from the Svartsengi geothermal power plant.

Horse rental (☎ 426 8303) is available from 11 am to 4 pm daily at the stables on Verbraut, near the western end of the village.

Things to See

Travelling north toward Svartsengi, note the wildly painted box which livens up the lava east of the road, and further along, the equally colourful water tank.

Instead of a seamen's monument engraved with names of those lost at sea, Grindavík has erected the moving sculpture, *Vonin* ('hope'), which unceremoniously depicts a seafarer's family gazing hopefully out to sea.

Places to Stay

At Hafnargata 17 is the relatively inexpensive *Gistiheimilið Fiskanes* (☎ 426 8280), which also has a lounge and cafeteria. It's open from 1 June to 31 August and charges Ikr1750 for a made-up bed and Ikr900 for sleeping-bag accommodation.

You'll find more upmarket accommodation five minutes away at Bláa Lónið. Free camping is available at the Austurvegur *campground*, east of the village.

Places to Eat

Grindavík's most popular eatery is the friendly *Sjómannastofan Vör* (☎ 426 8570), overlooking the harbour. Local fishing folk hang out there for light meals, snacks, desserts and coffee and the walls are adorned with old photos of fishing boats, shipwrecks and the wrath of the wind and waves being unleashed upon Grindavík. There are also several works of art.

The *Hafnarbjörninn* (☎ 426 8466) restau-

rant and pub at the bus terminal, Hafnargata 6, is open daily until 11 pm. It also sells general merchandise including souvenirs.

Getting There & Away

In the summer, buses run three times daily between Reykjavík and Grindavík (Ikr500), via Bláa Lónið; in winter, service is cut back to two daily. In July and August, a bus leaves Grindavík daily at 2.15 pm for Bláa Lónið and Keflavík international airport (Ikr400). To Keflavík town, Sérleyfisbifreiðir Keflavíkur (☎ 421 5551) runs four buses daily from Reykjavik, but they only go to Grindavík if passengers have booked.

AROUND GRINDAVÍK
Bláa Lónið (Blue Lagoon)

The Bláa Lónið, or 'Blue Lagoon', is actually a pale blue pool of effluent from the Svartsengi power plant (which is fuelled by seawater that has been heated after seeping beneath the lava). Algae thrives in the 70°C, 18% saline water that emerges from the pipes but, as the water cools in the air, the algae dies, leaving a sort of organic soup.

It may be known affectionately as the 'chemical waste dump' by visitors, but bathing in the lagoon really isn't dangerous. The chemical content of the silica mud combined with dead algae in the lagoon has been known to cure or relieve the effects of psoriasis. Patrons swear by its curative powers, which have now been officially sanctioned by the Icelandic surgeon-general, and a line of Blue Lagoon skin-care products is now available.

A swim in the lagoon can be an ethereal experience. Great clouds of vapour rise from the water, parting occasionally to reveal the immense stacks and buildings of the power plant and moss-covered lava formations in the background. The bottom is lined with chalky rocks and slimy white silica mud that feels just as disagreeable as it looks interesting. Bring enough shampoo to rinse your hair several times after leaving the lagoon, or it will be left a brick-like mass.

In summer, the bath house is open daily from 10 am to 10 pm. Off season, when an outdoor swim would be particularly appealing, it's open Monday to Friday from 2 to 9 pm and weekends from 10 am to 9 pm. Admission costs Ikr450.

Places to Stay & Eat The snack bar at the bath house sells soft drinks, chips and hot dogs. The *Gistihúsið Bláa Lónið* (☎ 426 8650; fax 426 8651) offers a sauna, jacuzzi, gym, restaurant and television. Single/double rooms with shower cost Ikr7150/10,075, including breakfast and transfers to Keflavík international airport. There's also a self-catering cottage which accommodates up to four people and costs Ikr6200 to Ikr14,000.

Camping is possible in the area but finding a suitable spot amid the lava fields is not an easy prospect.

Getting There & Away From Reykjavík, take the Grindavík bus from the BSÍ terminal. From 1 July to 31 August, it leaves at 10.30 am and 1.30 and 6 pm daily. From the lagoon back to Reykjavik, it passes at 12.35, 4.05 and 7.50 pm. The fare is Ikr500.

Many people catching afternoon flights from Keflavík stop at Bláa Lónið en route to the airport. The bus from Reykjavík to Bláa Lónið (Ikr500) leaves at 10.30 am and the one from there to the airport (Ikr350), at 2.15 pm. This allows about 2½ hours at Bláa Lónið.

Museum of Salmon & Trout

A worthwhile visit is the unique Museum of Salmon & Trout (☎ 421 2996), housed in an old icehouse at the lake Seltjörn, five km north of Bláa Lónið. If you're inspired by the fish displays, you can hire fishing equipment and have a go in the lake; they even offer courses in fly-fishing in the summer and ice-fishing in the winter. It's open daily from noon to 10 pm. Admission is Ikr150.

South-Western Reykjanes

West of Grindavík, the landscape steams with volcanic features – hot springs, solfataras and mud pots – especially around Gunnuhver at the peninsula's south-west

corner. There are also a couple of small shield volcanoes, Háleyjarbungar and Skálafell, and some fissures through the Stampahraun lava field. Eldvarpahraun, north-east of Stampahraun, has a row of active craters.

Reykjanesviti Offshore from the tuffaceous mountain Valahnúkur is a 50m pinnacle of rock called Karl ('man'). Beyond the chemical plant at the end of the Reykjanesviti road sits the oldest lighthouse in Iceland, built in 1878.

Eldey Icelanders claim that on Eldey island, 14 km off the western tip of Reykjanes, the last great auk was killed and eaten. This dubious honour is contested by the Faroe islanders, who claim the historic event took place on Stóra Dímun. Today Eldey is protected (a bit late for the auk, unfortunately) and contains the world's largest gannet (*Sula bassana*) colony.

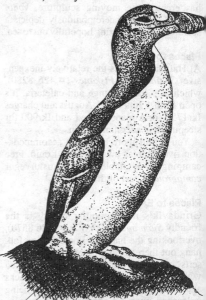

The last Great Auk was rumoured to have been killed on Eldey Island

From 1 June to 30 October, HI Tourist Service (☎ 421 3361), Tunguvegur 12, Njarðvík, organises morning or afternoon bird-watching, whale-watching and fishing tours to Eldey; three hours costs Ikr5300 and five hours, Ikr7670. Alternatively, book through BSÍ in Reykjavík (bus transfers are included in the price).

MIÐNES PENINSULA & HAFNIR

Miðnes, the sub-peninsula at the north-western tip of Reykjanes, is a flat green thumb fully exposed to the North Atlantic winds and waves. The peninsula was the subject of the first real estate deal made in Iceland. Steinunnur the Old, a widowed kinswoman of Ingólfur Arnarson, was offered all of Miðnes free of charge for her own use and insisted on trading a valuable embroidered cloak to secure the transaction. Over 1000 years later, this land would become the site of an international airport and controversial NATO base.

Since it has no mountains to trap incoming moisture, the worst weather actually by-passes it and comes ashore with full force at Reykjavík instead.

Garður & Sandgerði

Although the west coast of Miðnes is rugged and has historically proven hazardous to sea-farers, the villages of Garður (population 1100) and Sandgerði (population 1300) survive by fishing and fish processing. An interesting trip is to the abandoned fishing village and trading centre Bátsendar, which was destroyed by an unusually high tide on 9 January, 1798. The area offers good bird-watching, especially near Garðsskagi lighthouse, north of Garður.

On Garðvegur, north of the harbour in Sandgerði, there's a Nature Centre (☎ & fax 423 7551), where you can go beachcombing, poke around in tide pools, follow old hiking routes or watch sea, pond and marsh birds (170 species have been observed here). It makes a pleasant afternoon out. Sailing and whale-watching excursions are also offered. Admission is Ikr200.

Hafnir

The wooden houses of the picturesque halibut-farming village of Hafnir (population 100) cling to the rocky coastline just south of Miðnes. The halibut farm has an aquarium (☎ 421 6958) where you can see Icelandic fish and shellfish in their natural environment. It's open daily, May to September, from 1 to 5 pm. Smoked fish is available at reasonable prices.

A half-hour's walk west of the road, eight km south of Hafnir, will take you to the beautiful bird cliffs of Hafnaberg. Also, take a look at the anchor from the 'ghost ship' *Jamestown*, which drifted ashore mysteriously in 1870. The ship was loaded with a cargo of timber, but there was no one aboard.

Places to Stay & Eat

Both Garður and Sandgerði have snack bars, and Sandgerði boasts two other places: *Sjómannastofan Vitinn* (☎ 423 7755), a fish restaurant housed in an old fishing bothy, and a steak restaurant, *La Parilla* (☎ 423 7977). Camping is possible near the lighthouse on Garðsskagi, just outside Garður.

Getting There & Away

On weekdays, there are three or four daily buses from Reykjavík to Garður, Sandgerði and Hafnir, and less frequent service on weekends. On most runs, pick-up or drop-off in Garður, Sandgerði or Hafnir requires pre-booking through Sérleyfisbifreiðir Keflavíkur (☎ 421 5551). See also Tours under Keflavík & Njarðvík.

KEFLAVÍK & NJARÐVÍK

The sibling towns of Keflavík and Njarðvík lie about 40 km west of Reykjavík. Before the Danish Trade Monopoly of 1602, Keflavík, with 7500 people, was one of Iceland's largest trading centres. The English traded there as early as 1513, and in 1566, the first official trading licence was issued to the German merchant Jochim Thim of Hamburg. With the imposition of the trade monopoly, the Germans were ousted, but when it was lifted in 1855, Keflavík resumed its status as a trading centre. It also developed

ICELAND

ICELAND

PLACES TO STAY
15 Flug Hótel
16 Hótel Keflavík & Gistiheimilið Keflavík
23 Gisting
24 Campground
25 Laufás
27 Gisting Airport Youth Hostel
30 Gistiheimilið Kristína

PLACES TO EAT
1   Sparkaup Supermarket
4   Olsen, Olsen
5   Ráin
6   Bambúskófinn
7   Pizza 67 & Staðurinn Restaurant & Pub
8   Bakery
10 Strikið Pub & Disco
11 Kaffi Keflavík
12 Mamma Mía
18 Langbest
19 Glóðinn
20 Bogga-bar
22 Samkaup Supermarket
28 Pristurinn
29 Bakery & Fía-Kaup Supermarket

OTHER
2   Church
3   Bus Terminal & Tourist Information
9   Nyjabíó Cinema
13 Hospital
14 Íslandsbanki Bank
17 Byggðasafn Suðurnesi
21 Post Office
26 Triangular Church

into a fishing port and now boasts several fishing-related industries and a fleet of 50 boats. Currently, it's best-known as the service centre for the NATO base and Iceland's international airport (see boxed aside). Keflavík was granted municipal status in 1949.

Njarðvík, with 2500 inhabitants, is split by its bay into two parts, Ytri-Njarðvík and Innri-Njarðvík ('outer' and 'inner' Njarð-vík). It was first settled around 1300, but continued as a collection of rural farms until 1889, when it gained municipal status. It was united with Keflavík from 1908 to 1942,

then became a separate community until 1995, when the two municipalities amalgamated into a convenient entity called Reykjanesbær.

Information
The tourist information centre (☎ 521 5551) is at the Keflavík bus terminal at Hafnargata 12 . There's also an information desk at the international airport. The airport also has a restaurant, bar, duty-free shopping, airline offices and banking facilities.

Even if you have nothing to post, cast a glance at Keflavík's post office, which uncannily resembles a church.

Things to See
One of Keflavík's older homes is now the folk museum **Byggðasafn Suðurnesi**

The Keflavík NATO Base
When the 'protecting' British forces pulled out of Iceland in June 1941, American forces moved in and set up the base at Keflavík. Although they weren't particularly welcome after WWII, Iceland agreed to allow them use of the already constructed base at Keflavík as a refuelling and staging post for transport aircraft flying between North America and Europe. In true 'give an inch, take a mile' tradition, the US military used this and the creation of NATO in 1949 to weasel their way into permanent residence as custodians of the base. Since the end of the Cold War, operations have been scaled back, but arriving visitors at Keflavík are greeted by rows of camouflaged military jets and transport aircraft. There are now several political movements in Iceland aimed at disbanding the base and ousting what they see as a foreign occupying force. ∎

(☎ 421 3155), on Vatnsnesvegur. It's open on Sunday from 12.30 to 5 pm and at other times on request. The small **museum** and **stone church** at Innri-Njarðvík is open on Sunday in summer only from 2 to 5 pm.

In 1987, the new civilian air terminal **Flugstöð Leif Eiríksson** opened to handle increasing international passenger traffic. Of particular interest is the new sculpture, Magnús Tómasson's **Þotuhreiður** ('jet nest'), outside the terminal, which brings to light an unusual concept regarding large metal birds. It was selected for the site in a competition which attracted 52 entries. The runner-up was Rúrí's **Regnbogi** ('rainbow'), which stands nearby.

Activities
Both Keflavík and Njarðvík have **swimming pools** (with jacuzzis, saunas and solariums), open daily. Deep-sea fishing trips are available from Sjóstöng (☎ 421 1216); enquire at the Bogga-bar in Keflavík (see Places to Eat). Keflavík also has a golf course and two cinemas.

Places to Stay – bottom end
Near the Samkaup supermarket between Keflavík and Njarðvík is a beautifully laid-out *campground* (☎ & fax 421 1460). Sites cost Ikr250 per person and Ikr250 per tent.

A handful of guesthouses and hostels have also sprung up to accommodate Iceland's new arrivals or intending departees. One is *Laufás* (☎ 421 1786) at Þórustígur 10 in Njarðvík, where single/double rooms cost Ikr2300/3500 and sleeping-bag accommodation is Ikr1700/2500.

Nearby at Þórustígur 1, there's the *Gisting Airport Youth Hostel* (☎ 421 5662; fax 421 5316). HI members/non-members pay Ikr1000/1250. Alternatively, you have the *Youth Hostel Strönd* (☎ 421 6211), at Njarðvíkurbraut 48-50, near the church in Innri-Njarðvík. Sleeping-bag space costs Ikr1000 and made-up beds are Ikr1500, including airport pick-up. Airport transfers are also available, even early in the morning.

The friendly guesthouse *Gisting* (☎ 421 4372; fax 421 5887), Kjarrmói 1 in Ytri-Njarðvík, has single/double rooms with shared bath for Ikr2925/3965. It's open 1 June to 1 September.

Places to Stay – middle
The small and popular *Gistiheimilið Kristína* (☎ 421 5622; fax 421 5887), at Holtsgata 49 in Njarðvík, charges Ikr6175/7150 for a single/double, including breakfast. It offers free airport transfers.

Another option is the *Gistiheimilið Keflavík* (☎ 421 4377; fax 421 5590) at Vatnsnesvegur 9, which is affiliated with the hotel of the same name next door. Comfortable single/double rooms with shared bath cost Ikr6175/7800. Guests have access to the hotel's jacuzzis and fitness centre.

Places to Stay – top end
Two establishments vie for the title of *the* airport hotel. The larger is the *Flug Hótel* (☎ 421 5222; fax 421 5223), at Hafnargata 57 in Keflavík, where a single/double room with bath costs Ikr10,725/13,325.

Its main competitor is *Hótel Keflavík* (☎ 421 4377; fax 421 5590) at Vatnsnesvegur 12, which charges Ikr10,075/12,675 for singles/doubles with shower, including breakfast.

Places to Eat

Hafnargata, Keflavík's main street, has several snack bar and restaurant options. *Olsen, Olsen* (☎ 421 4457) transports you to the 1950s in small-town USA – if you can ignore that the 'period' juke box actually plays CDs. The rather daring menu (for Iceland, anyway) features chilli, corkscrew-shaped chips and a wide range of 'robust' hoagie sandwiches. It's open from 11 am to 11 pm Monday to Thursday and 11 am to 5 am on Friday and Saturday.

As always, the funky *Pizza 67* (☎ 421 4067), Hafnargata 30, is great value and on Friday and Saturday nights it's open until 5 am. Delivery is free anywhere in Keflavík or Njarðvík. Pizza is also the ticket at *Mamma Mia* (☎ 421 1544) on Hringbraut, and *Langbest* (☎ 421 4777), Hafnargata 62.

The well-appointed *Ráin* (☎ 421 4601), at Hafnargata 19a, features fish, lamb and beef dishes ranging from Ikr1500 to Ikr2500. Chinese and Thai takeaways are the speciality at *Bambúskófinn*, at the corner of Hafnargata and Tjarnargata.

A recommended spot, though it's nothing to look at from the outside, is *Bogga-bar*, at the harbour, which is one of the country's few drive-through fast food joints. It serves great cheap snacks and is a nice place to sit and enjoy them.

Glóðinn (☎ 421 1777), half a block from the Flug Hotel, offers fish and lamb dishes, as well as salads, pasta and snacks.

In Njarðvík, the choices are more limited: *Þristurinn*, at Hólagata 15, and the *Fitjagrill* on Fitjabraut, out of town near Route 41.

For self-catering, the *Hagkaup*, southwest of Njarðvík, has the best prices, but the *Samkaup* is ideally located beside the camp-ground. The convenient *Fía-Kaup* shop in Njarðvík stays open daily from 9 am to 10 pm.

Entertainment

Keflavík nightlife centres on the bar and disco at the *Strikið Café* (☎ 421 2012), which is open Sunday to Thursday until 1 am and on weekends until 3 am. An alternative is the *Staðurinn Pub* at the Pizza 67.

The restaurant and pub at the international airport serves arriving or departing passengers the least expensive alcoholic drinks in Iceland (although they're technically not in Iceland, which is why they're cheap). Get them while you can!

Getting There & Away

The Airport For their guests, hotels and guesthouses (and even the campground) in Keflavík & Njarðvík offer free or reasonably priced airport transfers. For information on the Flybus between the airport and Reykjavík, see Getting Around in the Reykjavík chapter.

Bus There are five to eight daily runs between the BSÍ terminal in Reykjavík and Keflavík/Njarðvík (Ikr450). There are also four daily buses between Grindavík and Keflavík (Ikr230), via Bláa Lónið.

Getting Around

Local buses between Keflavík and Njarðvík (Ikr120) operate, on average, every 45 minutes between 7 am and 6 pm. For a taxi, phone ☎ 421 4141 or 421 1515. Gistiheimilið Kristína and the Gisting Airport Youth Hostel hire out mountain bikes for Ikr1000 per day.

West Central Iceland

West Central Iceland extends from Reykjavík and its environs north to Laxárdalur and the Kolfningsnes peninsula at the base of the Westfjords. It includes the Akranes and Snæfellsnes peninsulas and the Borgarfjörður area. Historically, this is perhaps the richest area of Iceland, and many sites of interest relate to the sagas – particularly *Laxdæla Saga* and *Egils Saga*.

West Central Iceland also has its share of natural attractions, such as the famous Snæfellsjökull glacier and the caves and craters of Borgarfjörður. However, the weather funnel created by the Reykjanes, Snæfellsnes and Westfjords peninsulas often usher in westerly storm systems which may temper visitors' appreciation of the region.

BSÍ offers travellers a special three/five/seven-day West Iceland Passport for Ikr2500/3800/5000. It covers all scheduled bus routes in Borgarfjörður and Snæfellsnes, as well as admission to six museums and all swimming pools in the region. It also includes a one-way bus transfer from Reykjavík to Borgarnes, and a return via Akranes and the Akraborg ferry.

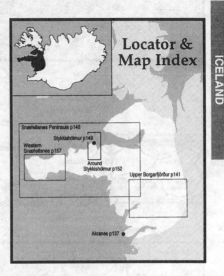

HVALFJÖRÐUR

Hvalfjörður ('whale fjord'), the long and beautiful fjord north of Mt Esja, has been known to host up to 17 whale species, especially in August. At its mouth is the Grundartangi ferro-silicon smelter, which produces a component used in steel. The raw iron ore is imported from Norway, then processed into ferro-silicon and exported.

Esja

Mt Esja, the landmark 918m peak north of Reykjavík, offers lots of wilderness hiking and climbing routes right in the capital's backyard. The most popular summit routes are from the river Mógilsá and the old farm Esjuberg, via the 850m spur Krehólakambur and 830m Kistufell.

Esjuberg was the site of Iceland's first church; the *Landnámabók* states that the first settler in the Kjalarnes region, Helgi Ketilsson (a son of Ketill Flatnose), received the land as a gift from Ingólfur Arnarson. When his Christian cousin Örlygur arrived in Iceland from the Hebrides, Helgi presented him with the Esjuberg estate, where he built a church in honour of St Columba. Although no church is in evidence today, the Esjuberg ruins are now a protected site.

Farms

Around Hvalfjörður are two farms called Saurbær, each with a church. The southern one, which was raided by English pirates in the 15th century, dates from Settlement times. Just south of it is the farm Hof, where one of the largest Settlement-era pagan temples is said to have existed, although excavations haven't revealed any evidence.

The church at Saurbær on the north shore, which is newer, contains beautiful stained-glass work and was built in memory of

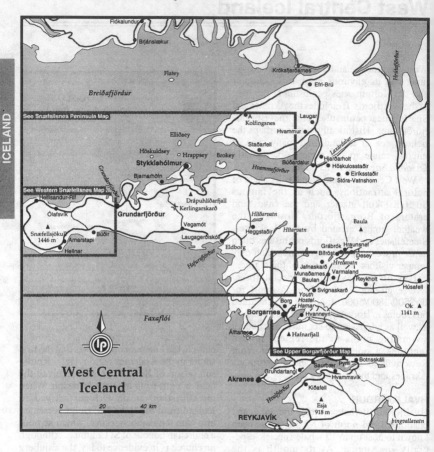

Hallgrímur Pétursson, who served there from 1651 to 1669. This poor leprous pastor composed Iceland's most widely known religious work, *50 Passion Hymns*, and Reykjavík's Hallgrímskirkja church is named after him.

Whaling Station

Iceland is quick to point out that it has followed all International Whaling Commission regulations since 1948, but it's now making noises about resuming commercial whaling. Iceland's four-boat whaling fleet once filled the country's annual 'scientific

whaling' quota of 400 cetaceans, which were processed for pet food, vitamins, chicken feed, bouillon cubes and lubricating oil at the Miðsandur NATO Fuel Depot on the northern shore of Hvalfjörður. Most of these whale products have cheap, easily produced substitutes, but like its neighbour, Norway, Iceland argues that the ban has produced an overpopulation of some whale species and that it's time for a 'harvest'.

In 1986, two Icelandic whaling vessels were sunk and the processing plant sabotaged by a Canadian protest vessel, but the industry seems unfazed. A brochure handed out to tourists blames Greenpeace for subversive activities and accuses the whales of consuming too much of Iceland's marine biomass, which they feel should be left to their sagging commercial fishery. For more on this issue, see the Facts about Iceland chapter.

Hvammsvík

The Hvammsvík (☎ 566 7023) recreation area, on the southern shore of the Hvalfjörður, offers camping, picnicking, horse rental, sport fishing and an inexpensive nine-hole golf course.

Places to Stay & Eat

Farmhouse accommodation is available at the recommended *Kiðafell* (☎ 566 6096). Sleeping-bag accommodation starts at Ikr850 with cooking facilities. For single/double rooms, the charge is Ikr3000/4030.

There are two petrol-station restaurants: *Þyrill* in the Esso petrol station on the northern shore and the simpler *Botnskáli*, near the head of the fjord.

Getting There & Away

From Reykjavík, all Akranes, Borgarnes, Snæfellsnes and Akureyri buses pass along Hvalfjörður. The impending construction of a tunnel across the mouth of Hvalfjörður in the next decade will cut off this 50 km detour.

AKRANES

Akranes ('field peninsula'), with a population of 5500, lies at the tip of the peninsula separating Hvalfjörður from Borgarfjörður. It's cut off from the mainland by the 555m mountain Akrafjall. The harbour, which faces Reykjavík across the water, has been a fishing centre since the Settlement era.

History

According to the *Landnámabók*, in around 880 the property Garðar, one km east of Akranes, was settled by the Celt Jörundur the

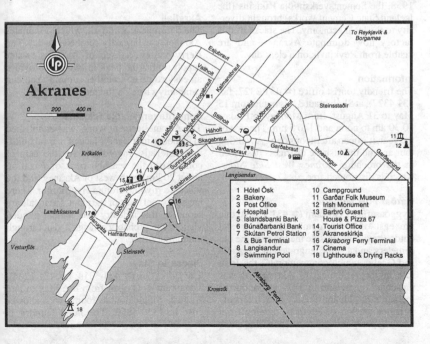

Akranes

0   200   400 m

To Reykjavík & Borgarnes

1   Hótel Ósk
2   Bakery
3   Post Office
4   Hospital
5   Íslandsbanki Bank
6   Búnaðarbanki Bank
7   Skútan Petrol Station & Bus Terminal
8   Langisandur
9   Swimming Pool
10 Campground
11 Garðar Folk Museum
12 Irish Monument
13 Barbró Guest House & Pizza 67
14 Tourist Office
15 Akraneskirkja
16 *Akraborg* Ferry Terminal
17 Cinema
18 Lighthouse & Drying Racks

Christian, and used as a hermitage. Ásólfur, a nephew of Jörundur, and 11 other Irish monks travelled together – after the manner of the 12 disciples – to Iceland. They first settled at Eyjafjöll on the south coast, but were driven away by neighbours who were envious of the ascetics' ability to attract fish to local streams. Ásólfur and company fled to Akranes and settled at Innrihólmur, just east of his uncle Jörundur's Garðar, where they lived as hermits and sages.

After his death, Ásólfur habitually appeared to friends and acquaintances in dreams, expressing discontent about their choice of his burial site at Innrihólmur. In order to mollify him, a church was built on the preferred site and his remains were placed inside.

Until the 17th century, when the fishing industry boomed and a town developed around the harbour, Akranes remained a rural farming and fishing region. It was granted municipal status in 1942 and in 1958, the Sementsverksmiðja Ríkisins (the Iceland State Cement Works) brought diversity to the local economy. The stacks of this factory now dominate Akranes, and are visible from Reykjavík on a clear day.

Information

The friendly tourist office (☎ 431 3327; fax 431 4327), at Skólabraut 31, is open from 15 May to 31 August, from Monday to Friday, 10.30 am to noon and 1 to 5 pm. The rest of the year, it's open afternoons only. A walking tour around the historic district is described in the brochure *Akranes West Side Story*, which is distributed free.

Garðar Folk Museum

Byggðasafnið í Görðum (☎ 431 1255), one km east of town, combines indoor and outdoor exhibits. Beside the tower is the old cemetery and a stone, engraved in Icelandic and Gaelic, which commemorates the Irish role in the settlement of Akranes. It was presented by Ireland in 1974 in honour of Iceland's 1100th anniversary of Settlement.

Inside are lots of artefacts, ranging from whaling paraphernalia to weapons and ships

used against the British in the cod wars. Its sailing days over, the 1885 cutter *Sigurfari* lies stranded in the sheep pastures near the museum.

From 1 May to 31 August, it's open daily from 10.30 am to noon and 1.30 to 4.30 pm. At other times, it's open Monday to Friday, 1.30 to 4.30 pm. Admission is Ikr250.

Langisandur

Langisandur, the one-km-long sandy beach, is probably the nicest in urban Iceland. When the sun shines, the sand catches the direct southern rays, and when the wind isn't screaming across the icy bay, it can be idyllic.

Akranes Church

The slightly seedy-looking Akraneskirkja was constructed in 1896. It attests to the wonders of corrugated aluminium, a common siding and roofing material in a treeless country.

Akrafjall

The 555m peak Akrafjall, which dominates Akranes, can be easily climbed in a day. The Berry valley, source of Akranes' water supply, splits the peak in two and provides an easy route up to either summit. You can camp anywhere on the mountain.

Sementsverksmiðja Ríkisins

The Akranes cement works was established in response to Iceland's lack of natural building materials. Ingredients for the cement come from the seashell beds of Faxaflói, about 20 km south-west of Akranes, and the volcanic rhyolite around Hvalfjörður. There are no formal tours of the plant, but locals are proud of this industry and cement-minded visitors can probably arrange a visit through the tourist office.

Places to Stay

The *Hótel Ösk* (☎ 431 3314; fax 431 1204), Vogabraut 4, is open from late May to late August. Single/double rooms with shower cost Ikr4350/5850. The hotel laundry is available to non-guests for a fee.

A second option is the new *Gistiheimilið Barbró* (☎ 431 4240; fax 431 4241) at Kirkjubraut 11. For single/double rooms without facilities, the charge is Ikr3000/4800. Rooms with showers cost Ikr4000/4900 and sleeping-bag accommodation is Ikr1250. Just off the Ring Road near Akranesvegamót is the *Hlaðir* (☎ 433 8970) community centre, which offers sleeping-bag accommodation for Ikr800.

Akranes' *campground* is on Víkurbraut, beside the school.

Places to Eat

A good choice for meals is the *Langisandur* (☎ 431 3191) at Garðabraut 2 near the beach. The guesthouse Barbró has an outlet of the acclaimed *Pizza 67* (☎ 431 4240). The usual hot dogs, soft drinks and other inexpensive snacks are served up at several petrol stations, including the popular *Skútan* (☎ 431 2061), at Þjóðbraut 9.

For self-caterers, there are two *bakeries* – one at Kirkjubraut 56 and the other at Skólabraut 14 – and a couple of *supermarkets* near the town centre. The State Monopoly shop is at Þjóðbraut 13.

Entertainment

Believe it or not, Akranes has a cinema, *Bíóhollin* (☎ 431 1100), at Vesturgata 27. Films are shown several nights weekly.

Getting There & Away

Bus The two or three daily buses between BSÍ in Reykjavík and Borgarnes pass by Akranesvegamót (*vegamót* means 'intersection'), to connect with short-haul buses into Akranes. The fare between Reykjavík and Akranes is Ikr900.

Ferry The ferry *Akraborg* (☎ 431 2275) sails at least four times daily between Reykjavíkurhöfn and Akranes. The walk-on fare is Ikr700.

Getting Around

You can hire bicycles at the Hotel Ösk for Ikr1000 per day.

BORGARNES

Borgarnes is different: it's the only Icelandic coastal town that isn't dependent upon fishing. Rather, it earns its keep as the trade and service centre for the Borgarfjörður district and as a transport link between southern, western and northern Iceland.

Strung out along a narrow two-km peninsula, Borgarnes enjoys a superb setting, but that also means that the weather can punish it from all directions.

Information

The tourist office (☎ 437 2108) is at Hyrnan, the Esso petrol station.

Things to See

The free **Borgarfjörður Museum** (☎ 437 2127), at Bjarnarbraut 4-6, is open daily in the summer from 2 to 6 pm. Displays include art, natural history and folk exhibits.

In the park near the centre is the **burial mound** of Skallagrímur Kveldúlfsson, the father of the skald Egill Skallagrímsson of the *Egils Saga*. The saga recounts that after his 17-year-old son, Böðvar, accidentally drowned, Egill carried his body to this mound and buried him beside his grandfather. The event is depicted on a lovely relief plaque, created by Danish artist, Annemarie Brodersen.

Organised Tours

The tourist office offers a 1½ hour walking tour around the town's saga sites for Ikr300.

Places to Stay & Eat

Borgarnes' only hotel is sterile-looking *Hótel Borgarnes* (☎ 437 1119; fax 437 1443), at Egilsgata 14, at the western end of the peninsula. Single/double rooms with bath cost Ikr7475/9100, including breakfast. The dining room is worthwhile.

The *Youth Hostel Hamar* (☎ 437 1663; fax 437 1041) may be inconvenient, but it's a real wonder. It's housed in a gabled farmhouse at the Hamar Golf Club, three km north of the centre on the Ring Road, and several travellers have nominated it as the world's best hostel! HI members/non-members pay Ikr1000/1250.

The *Summer Hotel Hvanneyri* (☎ 437 0000; fax 437 0048), lies 16 km from Borgarnes at the Hvanneyri agricultural college. It has a nice setting, but isn't on public transport routes. Single/double rooms without bath cost Ikr2730/3835; with shower they're Ikr3900/6050. Sleeping-bag accommodation starts at Ikr700. There's also a free agricultural museum on the site.

The *campground*, near the bridge opposite Hyrnan and the Esso complex, costs Ikr200 per person and Ikr200 per tent. The best sites are above the cliffs, over the water. Alternatively, you can wild camp along the beach across the bridge, which affords a wonderful evening view of the bright lights of Borgarnes.

Campers will appreciate the restaurant *Hyrnan*, which is a cut above other petrol-station restaurants and is a great spot to dry off. At the Brúarnesti Shell station is the universally recommended *Pizza 67*. The supermarket is opposite the Hótel Borgarnes in the 'progressive' shopping centre and the *Geira* bakery is diagonally opposite the campground.

Entertainment

The swimming pool, with a sauna, solarium and jacuzzis, can take the depression out of oppressive weather. Women's/men's saunas are available on Thursday/Friday from 5 to 9.30 pm. There's also a cinema screening films on Thursday and Sunday nights.

Getting There & Away

Borgarnes is the hub of all the bus routes linking Reykjavík, Akureyri, the Westfjords, Borgarfjörður and Snæfellsnes. BSÍ buses stop at Hyrnan (☎ 437 1200) or the Shell petrol station (☎ 437 1282). Siglufjörður buses stop at the Hotel Borgarnes (☎ 437 1219).

The first service from Reykjavík departs at 8 am daily except Sunday (or at 7 am on Monday, Wednesday, Friday and Saturday in high summer), and from Borgarnes at 10 am. There are also several Monday to Saturday

services to Reykholt (Upper Borgarfjörður) and Snæfellsnes. In the summer, the two daily Reykjavík-Akureyri services also pass through.

AROUND BORGARNES
Hafnarfjall

This crumbly scree mountain, along the Ring Road just south of Borgarnes, is beautiful to look at but unconsolidated and would prove difficult to climb. The grainy, light-coloured basalt composition is called *flyðrur*.

Borg á Mýrum

Iceland's most famous farm, Borg á Mýrum, 'rock in the marshes', is the historical equivalent of George Washington's Mt Vernon. The farmsite was chosen, in a fashion, by Egill Skallagrímsson's grandfather, Kveldúlfur, who got on the wrong side of King Harald Haarfager of Norway and fled to Iceland. As they approached land, Kveldúlfur fell ill and knew he would die. He instructed his son, Skallagrímur Kveldúlfsson, to make a coffin for him and throw it overboard, and to site the family farm wherever it washed ashore. This happened to be at Borg, and this is where Skallagrímur settled and reared his family.

During a hell-raising visit to England, Egill Skallagrímsson married his brother's widow, Ásgerður, but domestic life failed to tame him. Twenty years later, in 957, Egill finished wreaking his havoc in Europe and returned to Borg to settle down. Egill's son Þorsteinn built a church on the estate in 1003. His daughter Þorgerður married Ólafur Peacock, a hero of the *Laxdæla Saga*, and his other son Böðvar was, of course, buried in the mound in Borgarnes.

In 1197, the historian and descendant of the Borg dynasty, Snorri Sturluson, married the heiress of Borg and thereby acquired the property, but family responsibility ended there as far as Snorri was concerned. Leaving his wife at Borg, he moved further inland to Reykholt.

Today there's a small church at Borg, as well as the large rock that gave the place its name and a sculpture by Ásmundur Sveinsson. Icelanders maintain that an old grave discovered on the farm is that of Kjartan Ólafsson (who, according to *Laxdæla Saga*, was buried at Borg) but that's probably just wishful thinking.

Svignaskarð

The farm Svignaskarð, 20 km north-east of Borgarnes on the Ring Road, was once owned by Snorri Sturluson. On the hill Kastalinn above the farm is a view disc identifying features of the considerable panorama: cone-shaped Mt Baula, Hafnarfjall, Okjökull, Þorisjökull, Geitlandsjökull and Eiríksjökull. Nearby is a small stand of larch and dwarf birch.

Hítardalur

About 33 km north-west of Borgarnes, beyond the river Hítará, is Barnaborgarhraun, a lava field with a couple of impressive craters. Immediately to the east, at the 640m peak Fagraskógarfjall, the outlaw Grettir the Strong (of the *Grettis Saga*) hid from pursuers in a crack in the rock. The secluded mountain lake Hítarvatn at the upper end of the valley teems with trout. South of the lake is a region of lava

caves and to the north are some unusual rock formations.

Without a car, access to upper Hítardalur is difficult. You face a 20-km walk or an unlikely hitch from the main road along Route 539.

UPPER BORGARFJÖRÐUR

Varmaland

Varmaland is a possible base for exploring Upper Borgarfjörður. It was originally developed as an educational centre, but as it also lies in a geothermal area, it's now home to a summer guesthouse and is popular with Icelanders.

The waterfall Laxfoss, on the Norðurá, six km north-east of Varmaland, makes a pleasant day hike from the guesthouse. Fossilised plants are visible in the rocks near the falls.

Places to Stay & Eat The *Gistiheimilið Varmaland* (☎ 435 1303) is open from 15 June to 15 August. Made-up beds cost Ikr1890 and sleeping-bag accommodation is Ikr1170. Meals must be booked in advance. There's also a campground and a wonderful swimming pool.

Munaðarnes, not far from the Ring Road

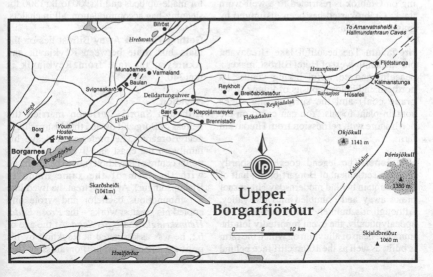

intersection with Route 50, is a summer camp for Icelandic government employees. Its restaurant (☎ 435 0021) has a lovely art collection and an excellent reputation. The coffee shop is open daily from 1 to 6 pm and the restaurant operates on Thursday, Friday and Saturday from 6 pm (specials from Ikr1280) and on Sunday from 11.30 am to 2 pm (specials for Ikr999). More down-to-earth cuisine is dished up at the nearby *Baulan* (☎ 435 1440) petrol station complex.

Getting There & Away Munaðarnes is accessible on the bus, but Varmaland is a five km walk from the Ring Road; get off at Baulan, at the Route 50 intersection. Buses between Borgarnes and Reykholt stop at Varmaland six times weekly in either direction.

Bifröst
Bifröst, on the Ring Road, is best known for its summer hotel and its geologically fascinating surroundings. The bizarre landscapes of the 3000-year-old lava field Grábrókarhraun are covered with moss, lichen and dwarf birch. The lava was originally spewed from the craters, Grábrók and Grábrókarfell, a km north-east of the Hótel Bifröst. Climbing on Grábrók is restricted to a well-worn track; Grábrókarfell has been disfigured by gravel extraction.

Hreðavatn The beautiful lake Hreðavatn, one km south-west of Hótel Bifröst, makes a peaceful and colourful hiking venue. Its northern end holds deposits of lignite (low-grade coal) and the surrounding rocks contain plant fossils. You can camp on the north shore with permission from Hreðavatn farm.

Hraunsnef The legend goes that shortly after the settlement of Borgarfjörður, half of the mountain behind modern-day Hraunsnef broke away and crumbled into the valley. Although it's unlikely that it happened so apocalyptically, the event reportedly left the immense heap of alluvium on which the farm is built, as well as the 100m cliff face behind it.

Desey Desey, the broad flood plain across the road from Hraunsnef, was created when the river Norðurá was dammed by lava from Grábrók and formed a lake across the valley. The dam subsequently broke, leaving the marshland seen today.

Baula The 935m grey rhyolite cone of Baula rises 11 km north-east of Bifröst. It consists mostly of scree but can be climbed in a day from the point where Route 60 passes its base. The base is a fairly easy hitch from Bifröst.

Places to Stay & Eat The *Hótel Bifröst* (☎ 435 0000) offers rooms, meals, petrol and a possible break in the trip between Reykjavík and Akureyri. Single/double rooms without bath cost Ikr3600/4650; with showers, they're Ikr5150/6900. Sleeping-bag accommodation costs from Ikr900 to Ikr1400.

The surrounding open countryside holds unlimited camping opportunities and despite its rugged volcanic nature, some surface water is available.

Hreðavatnskáli (☎ 435 0011), beside the Grábrók crater, charges Ikr2000 to Ikr3000 for made-up beds and Ikr900 to Ikr1300 for sleeping-bag accommodation, all in chalets.

Getting There & Away Bifröst lies on the main bus route between Reykjavík and Akureyri; the fare from Reykjavík is Ikr1340.

Reykholt
Although Snorri Sturluson married the heiress of Borg and owned that historic farm near Borgarnes, he preferred to leave his family on the coast and live at the educational centre of Reykholt (not to be confused with the farm of the same name in Biskupstungur). At this retreat, he lived like a rambunctious bachelor and wrote and copied his greatest works – the *Prose Edda*, *Heimskringla* and *Egils Saga*. At the age of 62, he was assassinated at Reykholt by his political enemy, Gissur Þorvaldsson (see boxed aside).

Reykholt is now just a farming hamlet set amid beautiful truncated hills and geothermal springs. In front of the present school is a statue of Snorri by Norwegian sculptor Gustav Vigeland. It was presented to Iceland in 1947 as a gift from Crown Prince Olaf of Norway, in gratitude for Snorri's *Heimskringla*, the collection of sagas about the kings of medieval Norway. A new church and cultural centre have recently been completed; displays include a small exhibit of Snorri's writings, a collection of written accounts about his life and copies of his works in numerous translations.

Snorri's Pool With the possible exception of Helgafell at Stykkishólmur, no saga site in Iceland is quite as haunting as Snorri's pool, a circular bath four metres in diameter. It is lined with stones and fed by a stone aqueduct from the Skrifla hot spring 100m away. Sheltered by the low hill Skáneyjarbunga to the north, the pool could be used for bathing all year round. The passage behind the pool is believed to lead to the cellar where Snorri Sturluson was murdered,

but most of it was destroyed when the school was built and only about 12m remain.

Places to Stay & Eat The *Edda Hotel* (☎ 435 1260; fax 435 1421) in Reykholt has a restaurant and pub, and charges Ikr3640/4750 for a single/double room with shared facilities. For Ikr975/1430, you get sleeping-bag accommodation in classrooms/double rooms. Other Reykholt services include a petrol station and general store.

There's farmhouse accommodation at *Breiðabólstaður* (☎ 435 1132; fax 435 1460), an old farm which is mentioned in the sagas. Single/double rooms cost Ikr3000/4030 and sleeping-bag accommodation starts at Ikr850.

At Kleppjárnsreykir on Route 50 about six km west of Reykholt is the *Runnar Hostel* (☎ 435 1262; fax 435 1437) which charges Ikr1000/1250 for HI members/non-members. The hostel reception is in the Blómaskáli petrol-station complex. Camping is also possible.

Getting There & Away The bus from Reykjavík to Upper Borgarfjörður does the

---

Snorri Sturluson

Snorri Sturluson, born in 1179, was the most renowned figure in medieval Icelandic literary history. His ancestry included the famous Snorri Goði of Helgafell, as well as the Sturlungs (who lent their name to the violent and chaotic period between 1200 and 1262) and the notorious Viking *skald* (court poet) Egill Skallagrímsson himself.

He was reared and educated at Oddi, in South Central Iceland and, as a young man, was conveniently married to the heiress of Borg, which was the estate of Egill Skallagrímsson. At the age of 36 he was appointed *lögsögumaður* (lawspeaker) of the Alþing and gained wealth and power travelling abroad. On one trip, he came into favour with Scandinavian royalty and made the unfortunate mistake of accepting a request to use his power to promote royal interests in Iceland.

Upon returning home to Reykholt, Snorri was again appointed lögsögumaður but found himself so busy writing he couldn't be bothered to turn up at the annual political conventions. During this period he was most prolific, turning out a large body of work which included the *Snorra Edda* and, it is presumed, *Egils Saga*.

It seems that Snorri had forgotten the deal he'd made with the Norwegian king, but as he'd unofficially given up his position of influence in the government, he wasn't able to keep his side of the bargain anyway. The king had not forgotten, however, and sent out a decree demanding Snorri's return to Norway – dead or alive. The ambitious *jarl* (noble) Gíssur Þorvaldsson, who aspired to the governorship of Iceland, visited Reykholt with a contingency of 70 armed men on the night of 23 September 1241. Aware of the danger, Snorri hid. A priest, who had been assured that no harm would come to the writer, revealed his whereabouts to the jarl. Unfortunately, honour wasn't one of Gissur's stronger virtues, and the priest later found Snorri hacked to death. ■

loop through Borgarnes, Varmaland, Reykholt and Hvanneyri once daily, Monday to Friday, in either direction. On Saturday, it does the loop only counter-clockwise and on Sunday, only clockwise. From Borgarnes, it leaves for Reykholt (Ikr400) at 10.30 am and 8.15 pm Monday to Friday, at 2.30 pm on Saturday and 2.45 pm on Sunday.

Flókadalur

Flókadalur, the valley of the Flókadalsá (a tributary of the Hvitá), upstream from Route 50, was named after disenchanted settler Hrafnaflóki Vilgerðarson (who gave Iceland its name). This broad grassy swathe slopes gently upward to the 1141m volcano Ok, which is capped by the Okjökull icefield. The name wasn't intended as an assessment of the place, but it's still appropriate. The best hiking access to Ok is from Húsafell or from Route F35, which passes its base.

The farm *Brennistaðir* (☎ 435 1193) has single/double rooms for Ikr3000/4030 and sleeping-bag space for Ikr1300.

Deildartunguhver

Iceland's most powerful and prolific hot spring, Deildartunguhver boils up at a temperature of 100°C and at a rate of 200 litres per second. A 60 km hot-water pipeline – Iceland's longest – has been installed to supply both Borgarnes and Akranes. A walkway allows public viewing. The spring is on Route 50 near the Reykjadalsá crossing, about 21 km from Reykholt. In the summer, vendors sell fresh greenhouse vegetables beside the spring.

Húsafell

Húsafell, formerly a sheep and cattle farm, is now Iceland's answer to the dude ranch. It sits in a picturesque geothermal area, surrounded by stands of birch along the turbulent river Kaldá, with good views of lava fields and distant glaciers. It appeals mainly to individuals and corporations who have summer homes there. Just west of Húsafell are the excavated ruins of a farm from the Settlement-era.

Places to Stay & Eat The small Húsafell service centre has hot springs, a snack bar, grocery kiosk, petrol station and geothermally heated swimming pool.

Self-catering *summer cottages* (☎ 435 1378; fax 435 1463) cost from Ikr26,000 to Ikr33,500 per week for up to five people. Sleeping-bag accommodation costs Ikr1300 per night and there are campsites scattered around the valley. You'll find made-up farmhouse beds and sleeping-bag accommodation, for standard rates, at nearby *Fljótstunga* (☎ 435 1198).

Getting There & Away A daily bus runs between Reykjavík and Húsafell (Ikr2250), via Þingvellir and Kaldidalur. From 1 July to 31 August, it leaves Reykjavík daily at 8 am and arrives in Húsafell at 3.15 pm, then returns to Reykjavík via Borgarnes. This can also be done as a return day trip from Reykjavík for Ikr4490 or with three Highland Pass vouchers. Sightseeing stops include Þingvellir, Surtshellir, Hraunfossar, Reykholt and Deildartunguhver, with an optional snowmobile tour on Langjökull. The highland portion of the trip isn't included in Omnibuspass.

Around Húsafell

Hraunfossar & Barnafoss Four km west of Húsafell is Hraunfossar, a water garden of falls and cascades where the river Hvitá emerges from beneath the lava flow. From there, a walking track leads upstream to the waterfall Barnafoss ('children's waterfall') where the constricted Hvítá roars through a narrow gorge. The name was derived from a legend that two children fell into the river from a natural bridge. To prevent similar accidents in the future, the main span was destroyed, but amid the rapids a second natural bridge is visible.

Hallmundarhraun Caves Most foreign visitors to Húsafell want to see the immense expanses of Hallmundarhraun, the lava flow created by craters beneath Eiríksjökull and north-western Langjökull. Four km long

Kalmanshellir, which was first investigated by a team of US and Icelandic spelunkers in 1993, is Iceland's longest known lava tube.

The second longest is the 3½ km long Surtshellir and Stefánshellir complex, north of the 4WD road, 14 km east of Húsafell, via the road which turns off at the farm Kalmanstunga. Two km south-east of the farm Fljótstunga, which lies 10 km north-east of Húsafell, is a third large cave, Viðgelmir. Both Viðgelmir and Surtshellir show signs of ancient occupation. Bring a torch.

All the lava tubes contain cave decorations, including grey stalactites and stalagmites, which are protected by law. Hitching will prove difficult on Hallmundarhraun, so prepare to walk the entire distance.

Kaldidalur

Although it's technically an interior route, Kaldidalur is more an extension of upper Borgarfjörður. It was used in ancient times as a short-cut between north-west Iceland and the annual parliaments at Þingvellir. In fine weather, the trip across affords glorious views across expanses of grey desert to the 1675m Eiríksjökull glacier, the 1355m Langjökull, the 1141m Okjökull and the 1350m Þórisjökull. At Langihryggur, the road crests at an altitude of 727m.

Organised Tours For details on the scheduled BSÍ sightseeing tour, see Getting There & Away under Húsafell. Reykjavík Excursions also operates day tours on this route for Ikr5400, with stops at Deildartunguhver, Reykholt and Hraunfossar.

Snowmobile excursions, sledding and summer skiing are available on the Langjökull Icecap with Langjökull Glacier Tours (☎ 567 1205 or 854 1433; fax 567 1707), Hesthamrar 22, Reykjavík. For a 10-hour guided tour from Reykjavík, with a short snowmobile ride on the glacier, the cost is Ikr8700. Less expensive options are also available.

Getting There & Away The daily bus from

Reykjavík to Húsafell (Ikr2250) follows the Kaldidalur route. For details, see Getting There & Away under Húsafell.

Arnarvatnsheiði

The lakes of Arnarvatnsheiði ('eagle lake moors'), along with the islands of Breiðafjörður and the hills of Vatnsdalur, make up Iceland's three legendary 'innumerables'. This vast lake-studded landscape, which extends for 80 km or so north of Húsafell, has long been a popular trout fishing venue, but its wild, lonely nature appeals to anyone seeking other-worldly solitude. It's most easily accessed on the 4WD track heading north-east from Surtshellir.

Popular horse tours over Arnarvatnsheiði are available from Arinbjörn Jóhannsson (☎ 451 2938; fax 451 2298) in Hvammstangi (see Around Hvammstangi in the North Central Iceland chapter). A nine-day wilderness riding and camping trip costs around Ikr65,000. He also organises shorter excursions.

LAXDÆLA SAGA COUNTRY

Laxárdalur, (salmon river valley) served as the setting for *Laxdæla Saga*, which is considered the most romantic and entertaining of all the Icelandic medieval sagas. The theme revolves around a love triangle involving 'the most beautiful woman in Iceland', Guðrun Ósvífursdóttir; Kjartan, the son of Ólafur Peacock (Ólafur was the illegitimate grandson of an Irish king) and a kinsman of the warrior-poet Egill Skallagrímsson; and Bolli Þorleiksson, the son of Ólafur Peacock's half-brother and foster-son of Ólafur himself.

You'd be hard-pressed to find an Icelander who hasn't read *Laxdæla Saga*, and its complex characters and genealogies are as familiar to Icelanders as soap opera plots are to modern-day TV addicts. Although the Laxárdalur landscape isn't Iceland's most exciting, those who know the tale may want to visit the settings that are so dear to Icelanders' hearts.

Búðardalur

Búðardalur, which means 'booth valley', is a village of 300 people on Hvammsfjörður, at the mouth of the Laxá. Here, Höskuldur Dalakollsson, great-grandson-in-law of Unnur the Deep-Minded (known elsewhere as Auður – more about her later), set up a boat shed and warehouse booths for his cargo enterprise.

Places to Stay & Eat You can camp at the official site (☎ 434 1132) or at the *Árblik Community Centre* (☎ 434 1366), which also has basic sleeping-bag accommodation for Ikr800. The guesthouse *Sjónarhóll* (☎ 434 1322), at Dalbraut 2, charges Ikr3200/4200 for single/double rooms. For meals, there's the *Dalabúð* petrol station snack bar, which is open Monday to Saturday, 8 am to 9.30 pm, and on Sunday from 10 am to 9.30 pm.

Getting There & Away In the summer, buses between Reykjavík and Króksfjarðarnes, via Búðardalur, run on Sunday, Tuesday, Thursday and Friday.

Eiríksstaðir

The abandoned farm Eiríksstaðir, across the Haukadalsá from Stóra-Vatnshorn church, was the home of Eiríkur Rauðe, before he was banished as an outlaw and left for Greenland. There his son Leifur the Lucky was born. Leifur Eiríksson, of course, went on to earn his place in history by 'discovering' North America. Some ruins are still visible but they're rather hard to discern.

The renovated farmhouse at *Stóra-Vatnshorn* (☎ 434 1342) offers singles/doubles for Ikr3000/4030, or sleeping-bag accommodation for Ikr1300. Fishing permits are available.

Höskuldsstaðir

Höskuldsstaðir farm, four km up the Laxá from Búðardalur, was the home of Höskuldur Dalakolísson and his wife Jórunn, whose progeny featured in several sagas. Their daughter was none other than Hallgerður Longlegs, wife of Gunnar of Hlíðarendi, who starred in *Njáls Saga*. Bolli Þorleiksson, of the *Laxdæla Saga* love triangle, was the son of Höskuldur's legitimate son Þorleikur. In addition, Höskuldur had an illegitimate son, Ólafur Peacock, by the Irish slave Melkorka (who was in turn the illegitimate daughter of an Irish king). Both Ólafur and his son, Kjartan, are key characters in the *Laxdæla Saga*.

Hjarðarholt

Across the river from Höskuldsstaðir is Hjarðarholt, the farm established by Ólafur Peacock in 960. There he built an elaborate residence and entertainment hall befitting his name. The feast he held for the funeral of his father, Höskuldur Dalakollson, reportedly catered for nearly 1100 guests. The farm is still inhabited and now includes a church.

Hvammur

A whole line of prominent Icelanders hail from the farm Hvammur in Skeggjadalur. It was originally settled by Auður the Deep-Minded around the year 895. From Norway, she had first moved with her father Ketill Flatnose to Britain, where she married Olaf the White, who became Olaf Godfraidh, King of Ireland. When he was killed in battle, she struck out for Iceland, where her brothers had already settled, and along the way, married off some of her children and grandchildren. In *Laxdæla Saga*, Auður is known as Unnur.

Auður's descendants, who remained at Hvammur, included Hvamm-Sturla, the forebear of the Sturlung clan. In 1179, her most famous descendant, Snorri Sturluson, was born there and a basalt sculpture now stands in his honour. More recently, Árni Magnússon, who rescued precious vellums from the 1728 fire in Copenhagen, was born and reared at Hvammur.

Krosshólar

Over the road, just a km from Hvammur, is the craggy hill Krosshólar. Although *Laxdæla Saga* maintains that Auður the Deep-Minded was a pagan, the *Landnámabók* claims that while in Britain she converted to Christianity, and was one of the first Christians to settle in Iceland. The hill now bears a stone cross inscribed with the *Landnámabók* passage:

She said her prayers at Krosshólar. She set up crosses there, for she had been baptised and was strong in her faith.

Laugar

Laugar, in Sælingsdalur, 15 minutes by road north of Búðardalur, is the birthplace of the *Laxdæla Saga* character Guðrun Ósvífursdóttir. The word *laugar*, a plural form of *laug*, means 'warm springs' and is attached to geothermal areas all over Iceland. A stone conduit, which was excavated beneath a rockfall at the farm, confirms that this spring was used for bathing and recreation at the time of Guðrun's birth around 973. By the stream at Sælingsdalur farm is Bollatóttir, the ruins of the shepherd's hut where Bolli Þorleiksson was killed to avenge the murder of Kjartan Ólafsson.

The small Dalir folk museum (☎ 434 1328) is open daily, 1 June to 31 August, from 10 am to 10 pm and costs Ikr200.

Places to Stay The Laugar resort has a campground and an *Edda Hotel* (☎ 434 1265; fax 434 1469), where single/double rooms with shared facilities cost Ikr3650/4750 and sleeping-bag accommodation costs Ikr900/1430 in mattresses/beds. There's also a licensed restaurant and a naturally heated swimming pool.

Getting There & Away

The only public access to the Laxárdalur area is by the twice-weekly Reykjavík-Króksfjarðarnes bus (from Reykjavík at 8 am on Tuesday and Thursday) and the weekly Reykjavík-Bjarkalundur bus (at 6 pm on Friday).

Snæfellsnes

Jutting into the Atlantic Ocean between Faxaflói and Breiðafjörður, the 100 km long Snæfellsnes peninsula is characterised by rugged mountains rising between a broad coastal plain on the south coast and a narrower one in the north.

The French science-fiction author Jules Verne noted that it was 'very like a thighbone in shape', but those with less sophisticated imaginations will probably look at the map and see something different. One of Iceland's best-known landmarks is the 1446m dormant volcano Snæfell. Its icecap, the glacier Snæfellsjökull, ushered Professor Hardwigg and his nephew to the centre of the earth in Jules Verne's classic, *A Journey to the Centre of the Earth*.

Most of Snæfellsnes inhabitants occupy the strip along the sheltered north coast, in the towns of Stykkishólmur, Grundarfjörður, Ólafsvík and Hellissandur-Rif. Due to the lack of natural harbours, the south coast population is dispersed on scattered farms.

The bird life in this worthwhile corner of Iceland is rich, the people are relaxed, the scenery is superb and the weather...well, that just has to be experienced.

SOUTH-EAST SNÆFELLSNES

The sparsely populated south-east coast of Snæfellsnes has some spectacular scenery. Unfortunately, all the weather systems moving in from the south-west come ashore on the broad coastal plain and run into the east-west mountain barrier, yielding predictably diluvian results.

Eldborg

The prominent crater, Eldborg, rises 100m above Eldborgarhraun. The *Landnámabók* mentions an eruption here during the early Settlement era.

The *Hótel Eldborg* (☎ 435 6602; fax 435 6603), in the Laugagerðiskóli school, west of the crater on Route 567, has a luscious hot swimming pool, kept that way by the warmest spring on Snæfellsnes. Single/double rooms cost Ikr3120/4200, sleeping-bag accommodation is Ikr900 and camping is Ikr350 per person. Book directly or through Úrval Útsyn in Reykjavík.

Three km from Eldborg is *Snorrastaðir*

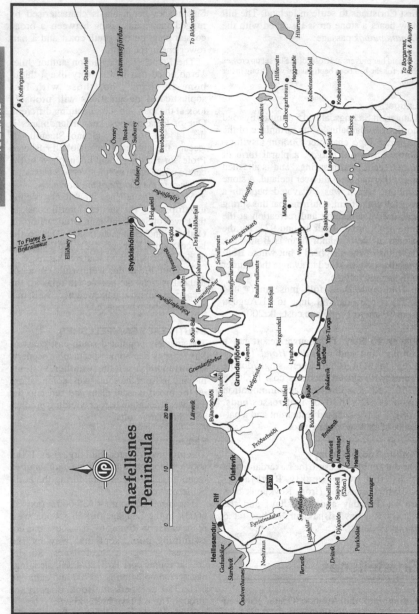

Snæfellsnes (☎ 435 6628), which has four six-person cabins and offers fishing trips and horse tours along nice broad beaches. Cabins start at Ikr36,100 per week.

There's no public transport to Laugagerði-skóli, but the crater is just a four-km walk from the farm Gerðuberg, which lies on the main road from Borgarnes to Ólafsvík.

Gullborgarhraun
The large lava field from the crater Gullborg, on Heggstaðir farm, is riddled with unusual lava caves but visitors need permission from the farmers. To get there, get off the Ólafsvík or Stykkishólmur bus at Kolbeinsstaðir and walk or hitch the nine km to Heggstaðir.

STYKKISHÓLMUR
The largest town on Snæfellsnes, Stykkis-hólmur, is named for the islet Stykki that partially shelters its harbour. It sits at the end of the complicated Þórsnes sub-peninsula which juts into Breiðafjörður.

For the past four centuries, Stykkis-hólmur, with its well-sheltered harbour, has been an important fishing, trading and administrative centre. In its more distant past, however, the area served as a religious centre for both pagans and Christians.

History
From the time of Settlement, the area has been significant to Þór worshippers. According to the *Eyrbyggja Saga*, the first settler Þórólfur Mostrarskeggi transplanted a wooden temple from his former home in Norway and named the farm Hofstaðir, 'temple stead'. The bay west of his farm he named Hofstaðavogur, 'temple bay'.

East of his property was a mountain that Þórólfur regarded as holy and so called it Helgafell ('holy mountain'). His son Þorsteinn Cod-Biter once reported seeing Helgafell open up in a vision of a fiery Valhalla, where he witnessed the dead feasting and enjoying themselves enormously. Thanks to an unfortunate fishing accident, Þorsteinn joined the after-life party at an early age.

Þórólfur gathered his relatives and organised the first Icelandic *þing*, or assembly, on the plain near his farm. Lest the holy land around there be defiled during these meetings, Þórólfur set up a toilet area on a small offshore islet which he called Dritsker,

ICELAND

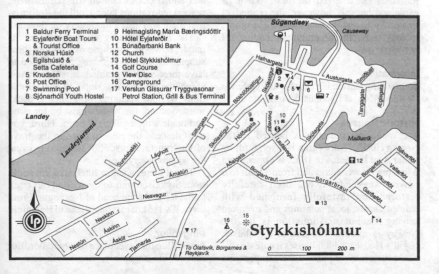

1	Baldur Ferry Terminal
2	Eyjaferðir Boat Tours & Tourist Office
3	Norska Húsið
4	Egilshúsið & Setta Cafeteria
5	Knudsen
6	Post Office
7	Swimming Pool
8	Sjónarhóll Youth Hostel
9	Heimagisting María Bæringsdóttir
10	Hótel Eyjaferðir
11	Búnaðarbanki Bank
12	Church
13	Hótel Stykkishólmur
14	Golf Course
15	View Disc
16	Campground
17	Verslun Gissurar Tryggvasonar Petrol Station, Grill & Bus Terminal

Stykkishólmur

or 'shitskerry'. (No one knows which islet this was, but many have surely gazed over Hofstaðavogur and wondered.)

When later settlers refused to comply with Þórólfur's toilet regulations, a long and bloody battle ensued, defiling the ground with blood as well. At this point, Þórólfur decided it was time to move the þing, and thereafter it met on the flat promontory Þingvöllur (which, incidentally, wasn't too holy for the purposes of relief).

The Christian church at Helgafell was built in the late 10th century by Snorri goði ('chieftain' or 'priest'), a Þór worshipper who converted to Christianity. Iceland experienced a rash of church-building at this time because the priests promised those who built them as many places in heaven as there were standing places in their churches.

Snorri was a central character in *Eyrbyggja Saga* and also makes guest appearances in *Laxdæla Saga* and *Njáls Saga*. Guðrun Ósvífursdóttir (of *Laxdæla Saga*) and Snorri exchanged their estates, Sælingsdalur and Helgafell, and Guðrun grew old at Helgafell. When her son Bolli came to ask which man she had loved the best during her lifetime, she understood him to ask which of her four husbands she'd loved the best. When he explained himself, however, she replied, 'I treated the worst the one I loved the most', thereby providing an enigmatic ending for her tragic tale.

Information

Tourist information is available at Eyjaferðir (☎ 438 1450), at Egilshúsið, Aðalgata 2.

Historic Houses

The municipal museum is housed in the Norska Húsið, 'Norwegian House', built by trader Árni Þorlacius in 1832. It's open from 3 to 6 pm on weekdays and from 11 am to 6 pm on weekends. It has been carefully restored and tastefully furnished with painted chests, local paintings and even old sewing machines. Admission is Ikr200. Nearby is another old house, Egilshúsið, 'Egill's House', which houses a cafeteria.

On the rocky hill above the campground

is a view disc identifying features around Breiðafjörður and the surrounding landscape.

Church

Stykkishólmur's new church is odd: it sits beautifully on a rocky knoll overlooking the village – some would even say it's a classic example of view enhancement. If you can avoid the notion that it's about to be shot into orbit, the architecture calls to mind the snow-capped Snæfellsnes peaks and the rounded icecap of Snæfellsjökull.

Súgandisey

The islet that shelters the harbour is accessible via a stone causeway from town. On top are some nice meadows for picnics and good views across Breiðafjörður. The whole islet is formed of interesting moss and lichen-covered basalt columns.

Helgafell

Helgafell, the holy mountain that was so prominent in Icelandic literature and history (see History earlier in this section) is actually just a 73m hillock. To the east is a grave believed to be that of Guðrun Ósvífursdóttir and Snorri Goði's church still stands there, several renovations later. Until the Reformation there was also a monastery on the site.

The hill apparently retains some of its magic, however, and those who follow some simple rules while climbing are entitled to have three wishes granted. First, you must climb the south-west slope to the temple ruins without speaking or glancing backward. Second, the wishes must be for good and made with a guileless heart. Third, you must descend the eastern slope to the grave of Guðrun Ósvífursdóttir and never reveal the wishes to anyone.

To get there, walk or hitch five km south from Stykkishólmur to the second dirt track to the left after the head of Nesvogur. From there, it's 1½ km east past a lake to Helgafell.

Þingvöllur

Þingvöllur, the level place to where Þórólfur moved his assembly, lies south-east of

Stykkishólmur. It contains the remains of some platforms and a block of blue basaltic stone containing deposits of red scoria that suggest blood. According to *Eyrbyggja Saga*, it was a site of human sacrifice to Þór, but historians generally agree that although rape, plunder, pillage and slaughter figured in pagan Icelandic tradition, human sacrifice didn't.

To visit Þingvöllur, walk or hitch to the intersection five km south of Stykkishólmur where a dirt track leads to the left near the head of Nesvogur. The site is near the water, five km north-east of the intersection.

Places to Stay

The *Hótel Stykkishólmur* (☎ 438 1330; fax 438 1579), with a posh dining room and a great view, charges Ikr6370/8650 for single/double rooms, with showers and breakfast. Off-season discounts are available.

Less sterile is the comfortable *Hótel Eyjaferðir* (☎ 438 1450; fax 438 1050), at Aðalgata 8. Single/double rooms with shared facilities cost Ikr4290/6630; with shower, they're Ikr5460/8000. All rates include breakfast.

A small private guesthouse, *Heimagisting María Bæringsdóttir* (☎ 438 1258), at Höfðagata 11, charges Ikr2550/3850 for single/double rooms with shared facilities. Sleeping-bag accommodation costs Ikr1300.

One of Iceland's finest hostels is the *Sjónarhóll Youth Hostel* (☎ 438 1095; fax 438 1579), at Höfðagata 1. Beds cost Ikr1000/1250 for HI members/non-members. Housed in one of the town's oldest buildings, it accommodates up to 50 people in two and four-bed dormitory rooms. It's open from 1 April to 30 September.

The *campground* (☎ 438 1136), near the sports complex, is very nice and offers full facilities, including a children's playground, barbecues and drying areas. For the first night, the charge is Ikr250 per person and Ikr250 per tent. For subsequent nights, the price drops to Ikr200 per person and per tent.

Further south, 10 km from Stykkishólmur near the intersection of Route 57, you'll find sleeping-bag accommodation at *Félagsheimilið Skjöldur* (☎ 438 1528). This community centre offers a dry space to crash for Ikr900.

Places to Eat

You'll find good snacks, chips, hot dogs and coffee at *Verslun Gissurar Tryggvasonar* (☎ 438 1254), the petrol station/snack bar near the campground. It's open every day from 8 am to 11 pm. The more upmarket cafeteria *Setta* (☎ 438 1428) at Egilshúsið, Aðalgata 2, is also good for meals. For pizza, burgers, sandwiches, fish or lamb specialities, try *Knudsen* (☎ 438 1600), on Aðalgata. The Hótel Stykkishólmur also has a fine bar and dining room. There's a *bakery* at Nesvegur 1, near the sports complex, and over the road is a full *supermarket*.

Getting There & Away

Bus Buses between Reykjavík, Stykkishólmur and other Snæfellsnes towns meet at an unassuming junction called Vegamót ('junction') and passengers sort themselves out according to destination.

The bus terminal is at the Verslun Gissurar Tryggvasonar petrol station. In summer, buses run from Reykjavík to Stykkishólmur (Ikr2000) daily except Saturday at 9 am. From Stykkishólmur to Reykjavík, they leave at 5.20 pm. On Monday, Wednesday, Friday and Saturday, another bus runs from Reykjavík at 7 am and from Stykkishólmur at 4 pm, to connect with the *Baldur* ferry to and from the Westfjords.

From Monday to Friday, 10 June to 8 August, there's a noon bus from Stykkishólmur to Hellissandur-Rif, via Grundarfjörður and Ólafsvík, which returns from Hellissandur-Rif at 3.50 pm. The around-the-glacier buses to or from Búðir or Arnarstapi connect at Hellissandur and Ólafsvík.

Ferry The ferry *Baldur* (☎ 438 1120; fax 438 1093) operates between Stykkishólmur, Flatey and Brjánslækur. The present car ferry, which replaces the former, smaller *Baldur*, has a vehicle ramp, so drivers no longer bite their nails to nubs wondering whether their vehicle will wind up in the drink. From 1 June to 31 August, there are two daily departures which connect with buses to/from Reykjavík in Stykkishólmur and with Westfjords buses at Brjánslækur. The fares to Flatey and Brjánslækur are Ikr1050 and Ikr1500 (with a 10% discount for Omnibuspass). Vehicles up to 4½ metres long cost Ikr3000.

Getting Around
You can hire mountain bikes from either of the hotels or at Egilshúsið for Ikr1000 per day.

AROUND STYKKISHÓLMUR
Breiðafjörður
A popular tourist activity in Stykkishólmur is a trip through the 'innumerable islands of Breiðafjörður' (for other 'innumerables', see Arnarvatnsheiði earlier in this chapter); estimates place the number at 2700. This maze of low, rocky and mostly flat islets is rich in bird life and, during nesting season, many are strewn with nests and eggs. In fact, the lighthouse island near Flatey is so densely populated that the guano makes it appear to be snow-covered. Expect to see kittiwakes, fulmars, gulls, guillemots, puffins and cormorants, among others. Seals are also abundant.

Island highlights include the basalt columns and 'pancake' rocks of Þórishólmur and Purkey; Dímonarklakkar, the highest island in the group; the old fishing station at Bjarney; and Flatey, the only inhabited island. With your own equipment, Breiðafjörður makes an ideal sea kayaking venue.

Flatey Flatey ('flat island') has a delightfully retro village, with lots of lovely historical buildings, including a recently-restored library. The church contains paintings by the Spanish-Icelandic artist, Baltasar. In the 11th century it was the site of a literary monastery,

Around Stykkishólmur

and in modern times it was the location of the film *Nonni & Manny*.

The farm *Krákuvör* (☎ 438 1451), 300m from the ferry dock, offers camping with all facilities. It's open from 15 June to 15 September. Sleeping-bag accommodation is available at the *Café Guesthouse Vogur* (☎ 438 1413; fax 438 1093), which also serves meals and coffee. Advance bookings are strongly recommended.

Organised Tours Boat tours of Breidafjörður are offered by Eyjaferdir (☎ 438 1450; fax 438 1050), at Egilshúsið in

Stykkishólmur. A 2½ hour trip, which winds through the southern islands, costs Ikr2300 per person. A four-hour tour, which is done only by group request, ventures further afield and includes Flatey, costs around Ikr3000. From Flatey, Tryggvi Gunnarsson (☎ 438 1216) offers boat tours.

BSÍ offers an 11-hour day tour from Reykjavík, including transport and a scallop-fishing (and tasting), birdwatching and sailing tour around the southern islands of Breiðafjörður, for Ikr6500 (Ikr4230 from Borgarnes). A three-day Flatey tour from Reykjavík, including transport, meals, a boat tour and sleeping-bag accommodation, costs Ikr17,700.

Drápuhlíðarfjall
This beautiful and colourful 527m mountain, south-west of Stykkishólmur, is composed of sulphur, basalt, jasper and rhyolite, as well as lignite containing fossilised plants and petrified wood. The best route up starts from about two km south of the intersection with Route 57.

Bjarnarhöfn
Looking for a stomach-turning experience? At the farm Bjarnarhöfn (☎ 438 1581), you can watch farmer Hildibrandur Bjarnason cure *hákarl* (putrid shark meat) in the traditional Icelandic way. You may even get to sample a freshly rotten bit. Bookings are essential.

Kerlingarskarð
Kerlingarskarð (witch pass) was named for a female troll, or witch, who was turned into the stone pillar at the north-western foot of Kerlingarfjall, the mountain east of the pass. Five km west of the southern slope of the pass was her fishing lake, Baulárvallavatn. In the 1800s, a local resident reported huge tracks leading into the lake, and four or five sightings of Nessie-style creatures have been reported there. When the clouds swirl down around the mountains and storms howl through Kerlingarskarð, it's easy to imagine how the strange tales surfaced.

All buses between Reykjavík and Stykkishólmur travel through the pass.

Berserkjahraun
The lava field Berserkjahraun ('berserks' lava') 15 km west of the intersection of the Stykkishólmur road and Route 57, was named after an unusual tale from *Eyrbyggja Saga*; see the boxed aside 'Gone Berserk'.

GRUNDARFJÖRÐUR
Formerly called Grafarnes, this village of 850 people was historically a trading centre but now relies on fishing and fish processing. Behind the town rise the forbidding 900m Helgrindur, the 'ridges of hell', and across the harbour is the prominent 463m landmark Kirkjufell, originally called Sukkertoppen ('sugarloaf') by Danish traders.

Places to Stay & Eat
The sleeping bag accommodation at *Grundarfjarðarskóli* (☎ 438 6866) is a bargain at just Ikr450.

A recommended accommodation choice is *Kverná* (☎ 438 6813), beside the river of the same name, one km east of town. Single/double rooms cost Ikr2930/3900 and sleeping-bag accommodation is Ikr1300. There are also six/nine-person self-catering cottages for Ikr30,350/37,120 per week. Meals are available and there's also a campground. This beautiful, friendly farm organises lots of activities, including fishing trips, horseback tours around Snæfellsjökull, sightseeing excursions, boat tours on Breiðafjörður, winter ski tours and walking tours to Kirkjufell, Helgrindur and Lysudalsskarð.

A similarly good-value alternative is *Suður-Bár* (☎ 438 6815), on the peninsula further east, which has made-up beds for Ikr1755, sleeping-bag accommodation for Ikr1170 and a five-person self-catering cottage for Ikr23,660 per week.

In addition to the petrol stations, you can eat at the bar, restaurant and coffee shop, *Ásakaffi* (☎ 438 6988), at the western end of town. There's also the restaurant *Krákan*

Gone Berserk

To visit each other, the settler Vígastyrr, at the farm Hraun, and his brother Vermundur at Bjarnarhöfn, had to take a long and circuitous route around an impassable lava flow. On one of Vermundur's Viking raids in Norway, he brought back two berserk brothers, Halli and Leiknir, who had been presented to him as a gift for good deeds done. Berserks – brawny, fighting thugs who were given to excessive, unrestrained and often disastrous tantrums – were valuable property in those days.

Much to Vígastyrr's dismay, one of the berserks, Halli, took a liking to Vígastyrr's daughter Ásdis. In desperation, Vígastyrr turned to Snorri Goði, the charismatic young chieftain whose power Vígastyrr had always envied and despised. Snorri advised him to offer his daughter in marriage only if the berserks could make a passage through the troublesome lava flow.

The berserks worked like mad, tearing a trench through the lava, and when it was completed, the berserks went to relax in the sauna recently constructed by the now-distraught Vígastyrr. At this point, the farmer saw his chance to wriggle out of the marriage agreement, and locked the berserks inside the sauna. Being berserks, they managed to escape, but they were soon cut down by Vermundur and buried in a deep pit in the lava. In the end, Ásdis married Vígastyrr's former enemy, Snorri.

The unusual – and clearly artificial – passage through the lava between Hraun and Bjarnarhöfn is still evident. The grave, which is marked by a memorial stone, was excavated in the 1800s to reveal the remains of two large men. ■

(☎ 438 6999), Sæbol 13. The *supermarket* is opposite the harbour.

Getting There & Away

In the summer, buses leave Stykkishólmur for Grundarfjörður (Ikr430) daily except Saturday at noon (these buses continue on to Hellissandur-Rif) and on Saturday at 4 pm. In the opposite direction, they leave Hellissandur-Rif at 3.50 pm daily except Saturday, and pass Grundarfjörður at 4.30 pm.

SNÆFELLSJÖKULL

The document that sent Jules Verne's adventurers into Snæfellsjökull, and on their way to the centre of the earth, read as follows:

Descend into the crater of Yocul of Sneffels,
Which the shade of Scartaris caresses,
Before the kalends of July, audacious traveller,
And you will reach the centre of the earth. I did it.
Arne Saknussemm

The 1446m, three-pronged peak of Snæfellsjökull was created when the volcano beneath the glacier exploded and collapsed into its magma chamber, forming a caldera. Although there are no reports of eruptions during the human history of Iceland, it's not yet considered extinct.

Prospective climbers can choose between

three routes to the summit: from Arnarstapi, past the north-east flank of Stapafell; from Route 54 about 1½ km east of Ólafsvík (see under Ólafsvík); and the longest and most interesting route, from the west side along Móðulækur. This last option passes near the red scoria craters of Rauðhólar, the waterfall Klukkufoss and through the scenic valley Eysteinsdalur.

On any of the routes, you should prepare for harsh weather conditions, and carry food and a stove to melt snow for water, as well as a map and compass. If you want to reach the summit, the ice conditions normally demand the use of crampons and ice axes. Don't hesitate to turn back if conditions worsen – it's hard to imagine how utterly nasty things can get up there.

With 4WD, you can drive in four km on the Móðulækur route and nearly three-quarters of the way to the summit on the other routes, snow conditions permitting. From either Ólafsvík or Arnarstapi (in good weather) allow at least four hours for the climb. The western approach takes considerably longer and will probably require an overnight on the icecap.

Organised Tours

Tours by snowmobile or snow-cat are operated by Tryggvi Konráðsson at Ferðaþjónustan Snjófell (☎ 435 6783; fax 435 6795), in Arnarstapi, and Gistiheimilið Höfði (☎ 436 1650; fax 436 1651), in Ólafsvík. From Reykjavík, day tours last 11 hours and cost Ikr8900, but glacier tours cost only Ikr3500 from Arnarstapi or Ólafsvík. Since darkness isn't an issue in the summer, some tours run at night because the snow is firmer and there is less recreational traffic on the glacier.

ÓLAFSVÍK

Ólafsvík (population 1250) began as a trading village and, in 1687, was the first place in Iceland to be issued a trading licence. The prominent ship, the *Swan of Ólafsvík*, called in there for 116 years until she ran onto an offshore reef in 1893.

Snæfellsjökull is considered one of the world's seven great 'power centres', giving Ólafsvík a sort of New Age following. There is power, certainly, but much of it seems to come in the form of wind and rain. Besides the obvious attraction of the glacier, there is a pretty waterfall, a nice arc of beach, an unusual triangle-themed church that was completed in 1967, and lots of mountain hiking routes. Near the campground, notice the beached fishing boat beside the road; one can almost imagine the sort of vile storm that heaved it out of the sea!

Information

The tourist office (☎ 436 1543) is in the Gamla Pakkhúsið. It's open daily from 15 June to 15 September, from 1 to 6 pm.

Gamla Pakkhúsið

Now the oldest building in town, Gamla Pakkhúsið, 'the old packing house', was constructed in 1841 by the Clausen family, which owned Ólafsvík's leading trading firm. It's now a folk museum (☎ 436 1543) open daily from 1 to 5 pm.

Snæfellsjökull Route

The route up Snæfellsjökull, which is normally taken too lightly by hikers, begins one km east of the campground. It's negotiable by 4WD part of the way, but on foot, it will take four hours to the edge of the ice. Beyond this point, you may need crampons and ice axes under some conditions, as well as expertise to recognise hidden crevasses.

Places to Stay

The *Gistiheimilið Höfði* (☎ 436 1650; fax 4361651), on the main road, offers comfortable singles/doubles for Ikr2800/3700 with shared facilities. Sleeping-bag accommodation costs Ikr1500. Alternatively, the *Gistiheimilið Ólafsvík* (☎ 436 1300; fax 436 1302), also on the main street, has single/double rooms for Ikr2925/3900, without bath.

The *campground*, north of the road one km east of town, occupies a lovely but exposed location. It costs Ikr250 per person plus Ikr250 per tent.

Places to Eat

Both guesthouses offer meals. The *Grillskálinn*, beside the Gistiheimilið Höfði, does burgers, hot dogs, chips and lunch specials, and there's a bakery in the same building. Alternatively, pick up a snack at the petrol station. There's a *supermarket* near the hotel, *Hvammur Supermarket* up the hill, and a kiosk by the swimming pool. The State Monopoly shop is on Mýrarholt, uphill from the main street.

Getting There & Away

Buses between Stykkishólmur and Hellissandur-Rif pass through Ólafsvík; see Grundarfjörður earlier in this chapter.

The clockwise around-the-glacier route to Búðir, Arnarstapi and Hellissandur – then back to Ólafsvík – leaves Ólafsvík at 11.45 am Monday to Friday. The counter-clockwise run leaves Ólafsvík at 3.20 pm on the same days. The entire circuit costs Ikr1300.

Getting Around

The Gistiheimilið Höfði hires bicycles for Ikr1000 per day.

HELLISSANDUR-RIF

Hellissandur-Rif, the westernmost village on

Snæfellsnes, is actually two communities just over two km apart, with a combined population of 630. The original fishing village of Hellissandur, or just Sandur, had no harbour and was exposed to the open sea. A new harbour was constructed at nearby Háarif (population 100), which was shortened to just Rif ('reef'). The venture was marginally successful and it now boasts a couple of fish-processing and freezing plants.

Perhaps the greatest appeal of this place is its front-row view of Snæfellsjökull and its convenience to the main sites of western Snæfellsnes.

The small Seamen's Cottage museum (☎ 436 6635), housed in an old fishing hut beside the main road, is open from June to August, from 1 to 6 pm daily except Monday. Admission is Ikr100. In the school in Rif is a free, informal natural history museum (☎ 436 6644), with collections of stones and sea birds. Between the two villages, a view disc identifies natural features.

Places to Stay & Eat

The recommended *Gistiheimilið Gimli* (☎ 436 6825; fax 436 6770), near the shore in Hellissandur, is the only formal accommodation. Sleeping-bag accommodation costs Ikr900 and single/double rooms with shared facilities cost Ikr2670/3700. With a shower, they're Ikr3050/4160. This place is especially good news for campers, because it also has cooking facilities and serves meals. Hellissandur also has a *campground*, which

occupies a sheltered hollow just off the main road.

There's a snack bar, the *Virkið*, at Hafnargata 9 in Rif, as well as a decent *grill* at the Esso petrol station in Hellissandur. The *supermarket* is in Hellissandur.

Getting There & Away

Buses to Grundarfjörður and Stykkishólmur leave at 4 pm Monday to Friday. To Reykjavík via Ólafsvík they leave at 5 pm Sunday to Friday and at 7.45 am on Saturday.

Getting Around

Bicycle hire is available from Gistiheimilið Gimli for Ikr1000 per day.

SNÆFELLSNES WEST END

The western end of Snæfellsnes, beneath the towering Snæfellsjökull icecap, may feel like the end of the world, but it has quite a few worthwhile sites.

Búðir

The former fishing village of Buðir, abandoned in the early 1800s, may seem an appropriate setting for a murder mystery somewhere in the Scottish Western Isles. The wide and lonely beach curves into the distance along Breiðavík, and west of the hotel is the leprechaun-infested Buðahraun lava field, and its 88m crater, Buðaklettur. The large lava tube beneath Buðahraun is said to be a gold-paved conduit to Surtshellir in Borgarfjörður.

Snæfellsnes West End Tour

If you're pressed for time, on summer weekdays you can do a circuit from Reykjavík around the West End of Snæfellsnes in just one day, using only scheduled public transport. It's one way to put an Omnibuspass or a West Iceland Passport to good use.

From Reykjavík, take the 9 am bus to the Buðir turnoff, and change to the West End bus. It stops for a two-hour lunch at Arnarstapi – allowing time for a cursory look around the sea cliffs – then continues clockwise around the glacier.

The next connection can be made at either Hellissandur-Rif at 3.50 pm or Ólafsvík at 4.30 pm. From Ólafsvík, you can either catch the 5 pm bus straight back to Reykjavík, or stay on the same bus to Stykkishólmur and take the 5.20 pm bus back to Reykjavík. The former option costs Ikr5300 for the entire trip and the latter, Ikr6000. Naturally, this journey can be broken anywhere en route. ∎

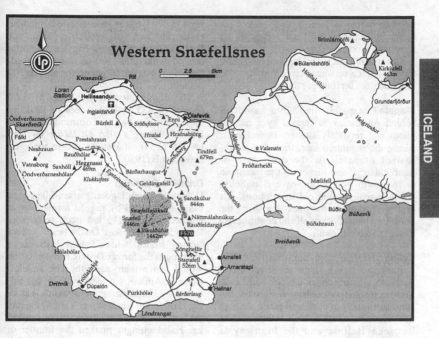

Places to Stay & Eat The lonely, romantic and elegant *Hótel Búðir* (☎ 435 6700; fax 435 6701), open from 5 May to 30 September, has a cosy licensed restaurant and a general store. Single/double rooms with shared facilities cost Ikr4485/5920; with shower, they're Ikr6050/7950 and sleeping-bag accommodation costs Ikr2100. All options include breakfast. The beautiful *campground*, in the middle of a lava field, offers basic facilities but is rather exposed, so bring a sturdy tent. The hotel restaurant serves up home-baked bread and homemade ice cream and unusual fish specialities – the fried plaice with bananas is recommended – but portions are small and prices a bit above average.

Gistiheimilið Lysuhóll (☎ 435 6716; fax 435 6816), five km east of Búðir and two km off the main road, has accommodation in single/double rooms for Ikr3000/4050 and sleeping-bag accommodation for Ikr1300. The naturally hot outdoor pool is open daily (except Tuesday) from 2 pm and the management can organise equestrian tours along the coast to Arnarstapi and inland to Snæfellsjökull.

In the same vicinity are a couple of farmhouse accommodation options: *Ytri-Tunga* (☎ 435 6698) and *Gistiheimilið Langaholt* (☎ 435 6719; fax 435 6789). Both have single/double rooms for Ikr3000/4050 and the latter has sleeping-bag accommodation for Ikr1300.

Arnarstapi

The former fishing village of Arnarstapi is a small service centre with farmhouse accommodation, a cafe-guesthouse, a campground and a small kiosk. Here the coastline is riddled with arches, caves, basalt cliffs and blow holes. The best-known feature is the circular arch, Gatklettur.

On a hill near the complex is the Arnarstapi landmark, a rough stone representation of demigod Barður Snæfellsás who, according to local legend, makes his home in Snæfellsjökull and serves as its appointed protector.

The area is great for hiking, but the Arctic terns can get a bit aggressive. You can also hire bikes for Ikr1000 per day.

Stapafell Stapafell, the 526m mountain behind Arnarstapi, is capped by a natural plinth and reputedly shelters leprechauns. Along the mountain face, three km north-east of Stapafell, is the deep gash of Rauðfeldargjá, and higher up the mountain to the north-west is the cave Sönghellir, which contains some old inscriptions. It's best reached along the track that skirts the north-east base of Stapafell and continues up towards Snæfellsjökull.

Hellnar Hellnar, 2½ km south-west of Arnarstapi, has a large sea-level cave, Baðstofa, which is chock-a-block with birds. You can reach it on foot from Arnarstapi, but approach quietly or panic will ensue. At high tide the cave emits a blue luminescence. Between Hellnar and the highway is Bárðarlaug, supposedly the bathing pool of Bárður Snæfellsás.

Lóndrangar The two rock pillars of Lóndrangar, the higher of which rises 75m above the sea, are remnants of an ancient basalt cinder-cone. They're a 15 minute walk from the main road, about five km west of the Hellnar turn-off.

Organised Tours For information on snowmobile tours, see under Snæfellsjökull, earlier in this chapter. A variety of boat tours are available from Nökkvj (☎ 435 6783 or 854 2832): a spin around the bay and through the sea caves (Ikr1200; with a barbecue at Hellnar, Ikr3900, or a run to Búðir, Ikr2900); a five hour whale-watching tour (Ikr6900); and a half-day of fishing, followed by a fish barbecue at Hellnar (Ikr27,000 for up to eight people).

Places to Stay & Eat The popular nine-room *Ferðaþjónustan Snjófell* (☎ 435 6783;

fax 435 6795) has an atmospheric farmhouse restaurant and single/double rooms for Ikr2100/3850. Sleeping-bag accommodation costs Ikr1000/1500 on a mattress/bed. Camping costs Ikr200 per person plus Ikr200 per tent.

The community centre, *Félagsheimilið Snæfell* (☎ 435 6750), has cooking facilities and sleeping-bag accommodation for Ikr975. There's also *Gíslabær Hellnar* (☎ 435 6757), at Hellnar, where made-up beds cost Ikr1950.

Dritvík & Djúpalón

Djúpalón ('deep lagoon') a sea-filled rock basin surrounded by rugged formations, is reached along a 1½ km track west from Route 574 to the coast. On the beach sit four 'lifting stones' where fishing boat crews working at the former Dritvík fishing station would prove their strength. The smallest stone is Amloði ('useless') at 23 kg; followed by Hálfdrættingur ('weakling') at 49 kg; Hálfsterkur ('half strong') at 140 kg; and the largest, Fullsterker ('fully strong'), at 155 kg. Hálfdrættingur marked the frontier of wimphood and any man who couldn't heft it was deemed unsuitable for the local version of polite society.

Just south of Dritvík is the crater Purkhólar, which has some unusual lava caves.

Hólahólar

The craters of Hólahólar, clustered about 100m west of the road, can be explored quickly. The main attraction is the crater Berudalur; a crack in the side issues into a natural amphitheatre.

Öndverðarnes

In fair weather, Öndverðarnes, the western-most cape of Snæfellsnes, is worth exploring on foot. It was once inhabited, but all that remains is a lighthouse and an abandoned stone well called Fálkí. Seals often laze on the pebble beach, and the bird cliffs of Svörtuloft, south of the cape, have been carved into sea arches and caves by the constant pounding of Atlantic breakers.

Skarðsvík, the bay east of the cape, has a nice sandy beach backed by a steep escarpment.

A walking track leads from Skarðsvík across the Neshraun lava flow to the crater Vatnsborg, between the road and the sea. The prominent crater, Saxhóll, may be climbed in a few minutes and offers a fine view over Neshraun and the sea beyond.

Gufuskálar

Gufuskálar boasts the highest structure in Iceland, the prominent 412m mast of the US Loran Station. The Írskibrunnur ('Irish well') south-west of the station, was built by Irish monks before the Norse settlement. The area is dotted with the ruins of hundreds of stone huts constructed by medieval Scandinavian settlers as fish-drying sheds, at a time when Iceland was supplying much of Europe with fish.

The small creek flowing through Gufuskálar is called Gufuskálamóða, which means 'steam basin river'. Its diminutive size would seem to more appropriately suggest the name Gufuskálalækur ('steam basin creek') but local legend has it that a huge underground river flows beneath its course.

ICELAND

South Central Iceland

South Central Iceland is known in the local tourist industry as the 'Golden Circle' or 'Golden Triangle', in reference to Gullfoss, Geysir and Þingvellir, the 'big three' destinations for Icelandair's stopover visitors. Whirlwind day tours packed with wide-eyed stopover tourists cruise out of Reykjavík in the morning, squeeze in all the main sights, and still leave time for a leisurely lunch, coffee and biscuits in the afternoon and a 45-minute shopping spree in Hveragerði's archetypal tourist trap, Eden. In the evening, the tourists wobble back into Reykjavík, heads spinning, wondering what happened!

But South Central Iceland isn't all tour buses, clicking cameras and whirring videos. Beyond the well-trampled Golden Circle are lots of worthwhile natural phenomena and historical sites. In addition to volcanoes, glaciers, geysers and hot springs, the region boasts broad sandy beaches, buried settlements, spectacular highlands and an archipelago of rugged new islands teeming with bird life.

The Interior

HVERAGERÐI

The first town east of Reykjavík on the Ring Road is Hveragerði ('hot springs garden'). It sits against the mountains in a valley bubbling and steaming with hot springs and fissures opened up by earthquakes and crustal shifting. Much of the resulting geothermal power is harnessed for heat and electricity and just below the church is a substantial urban geothermal field. Note the tiny geyser which spouts miniature eruptions every couple of seconds. Over 40% of Iceland's greenhouse agriculture exploits this geothermal heat, making Hveragerði Iceland's 'flower town' or 'greenhouse village'. Many of the town's 1600 people commute to the capital for work.

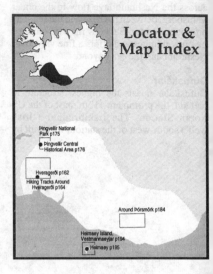

Locator &
Map Index

Þingvellir National Park p175
Þingvellir Central Historical Area p176
Hveragerði p162
Hiking Tracks Around Hveragerði p164
Around Þórsmörk p184
Heimaey Island, Vestmannaeyjar p194
Heimaey p195

Information

The tourist office Ferðaþjónusta Suðurlands (☎ 483 4280; fax 483 4287), at Breiðamörk 10, can help with tourist information and assist in planning hill walks. It's open 9 am to 6 pm Monday to Friday and from 9 am to 2 pm on weekends. It also serves as an Icelandair agency and car-hire office.

Laundry service is available at Reykjamörk 1.

Gufudalur Geothermal Area

Gufudalur, the 'steam valley', abounds with hot springs, geysers, mudpots, fumaroles and steaming vents. The best-known feature is Grýla, a 12m geyser which erupts several times daily. Tour groups sometimes coax a performance out of it by adding soap flakes, but this is certainly not recommended.

The original name was probably Grýta, which would refer to a gravel-throwing hot spring, but a misprint on a widely used map rendered it as Grýla, the name of an old witch

DEANNA SWANEY

DEANNA SWANEY

DEANNA SWANEY

Top: Leirhnjúkur solfataras, Krafla, North-East Iceland
Middle: Hiking near Landmannalaugar, Central Iceland
Bottom: Eerie formations at Núpsstaðarskógar, South-East Iceland

Top: Puffins, Látrabjarg, Westfjords, Iceland
Bottom: The 'haunted' Kerlingarfjöll mountains, Central Iceland

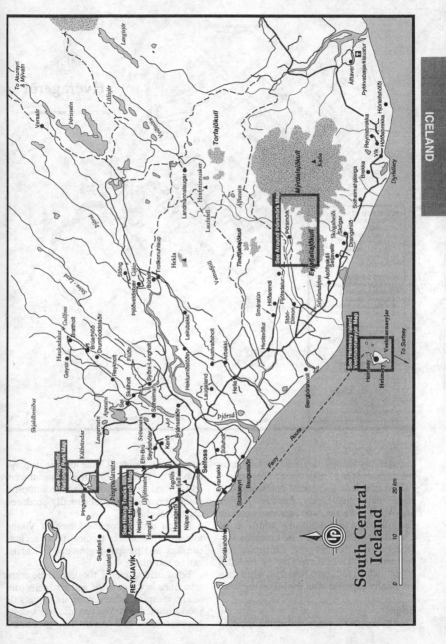

South Central Iceland

ICELAND

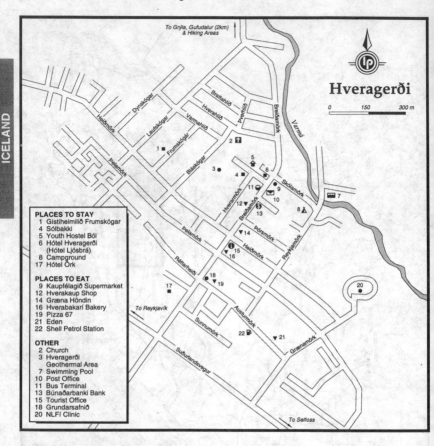

Hveragerði

0   150   300 m

PLACES TO STAY
1 Gistiheimilið Frumskógar
4 Sólbakki
5 Youth Hostel Ból
6 Hótel Hveragerði
   (Hótel Ljósbrá)
8 Campground
17 Hótel Örk

PLACES TO EAT
9 Kaupfélagið Supermarket
12 Hverakaup Shop
14 Græna Höndin
16 Hverabakarí Bakery
19 Pizza 67
21 Eden
22 Shell Petrol Station

OTHER
2 Church
3 Hveragerði
   Geothermal Area
7 Swimming Pool
10 Post Office
11 Bus Terminal
13 Búnaðarbanki Bank
15 Tourist Office
18 Grundarsafnið
20 NLFí Clinic

in pagan mythology. Grýla is best known as the mother of the 13 malevolent *jólasveinarn* ('Christmas lads'), vengeful hooligans with names like Ladle-Licker, Sausage-Grabber and Window-Peeper, who apparently remain despondent about Iceland's adoption of Christianity. One of these lads plagues Icelanders each day between Christmas and *Þrettandinn* ('Three Kings Day' or the '12th Night', which falls on 6 January), when they are finally expelled until the following year.

Eden

This rather tacky place makes the most of shop-happy Golden Circle tourists. It plays heavily on Hveragerði's greenhouse theme, and beyond the gift shop, a variety of tropical plants thrive in the geothermally-produced equatorial climate.

If you can ignore the kitsch (a Viking tomato!), the idea of tropical fruits such as bananas and pawpaws growing in Iceland can be intriguing.

Eden offers one of the largest postcard selections in the country, and also sells souvenir samples of the various vegetable produce and seeds. You can also buy woolly jumpers, meals and snacks. Tour groups are herded in here for about 45 minutes, so if you're not interested, bring a good book.

Grundarsafnið

The museum Grundarsafnið (☎ 483 4289) features puppets dressed up in antique clothing, performing skits from old Icelandic life. It's open daily from 2 to 6 pm on Tuesday, Thursday, Saturday and Sunday. Admission is Ikr100.

Research Centre for Geothermal Biology

This novel centre (☎ 567 4488), which runs from 20 June to 31 August, conducts research into the thermophilic (heat-loving) life in the Hveragerði hot springs. The idea is to use enzymes produced by these life forms for industrial and medical purposes. A two-hour lecture and field trip runs on Tuesdays at 1 pm and costs Ikr1600. Four-hour programmes, which include collecting and assessing samples, run on Thursdays at 1 pm and cost Ikr2600.

NLFÍ Clinic

The Náttúrulækningafélag Ísland (Naturopathic Health Association of Iceland) clinic (☎ 483 0300) is a centre for naturopathic treatment of rheumatism, stress, arthritis and orthopaedic problems. It may seem gimmicky, but many people swear by the curative powers of hot-spring water and mud. The strictly-controlled programme involves a lacto-vegetarian and seafood diet, massage, gymnastics and therapy in the hot springs. Double rooms, including meals and treatment, cost around Ikr7500 per person per night, with a week's minimum stay.

You can contact the clinic directly or write to the South Coast Travel Information Centre, Breiðamörk 10, Hveragerði.

Raufarhólshellir

The km-long cave Raufarhólshellir, the second largest lava tube system in Iceland, lies amid 5000 year old lava fields from the Leiti eruptions. The cave brims with officially protected formations but exploring it is dark and difficult going. Take a torch! To get there from Hveragerði, take a bus or hitch toward Reykjavík to the intersection of Route 39, then catch a Reykjavík-Þorlákshöfn bus 10 km south to the cave.

Kambar

Kambar, the ridge above Hveragerði (toward Reykjavík), offers a good view over the richest farmland in Iceland and on clear days you can see as far as Vestmannaeyjar and Eyjafjallajökull, which are identified by a view disc on the ridge. It's an eight km return trip from town or about 1½ km from the Ring Road. Skálafell, six km to the west, can also be climbed in a very long day.

Hiking

Hveragerði's appealing hill-walking opportunities merit a day or two of exploration. Unless you take the Gufudalur route, all walks begin by getting your feet wet crossing the stream Hengladalsá. From there, you can climb 497m high Selfjall in a couple of hours. Other trips include the walk along the river Grænadalsá up Grænadalur beyond Gufudalur. This route traverses pleasant mountain country, crossing warm streams and passing small lakes. You have a choice of several return routes, including one through Reykjadalur, another geothermal area.

A spectacular walk takes you to the hot stream in Klambragil. It begins by climbing the marked track up Rjúpnabrekkur and into lovely green Reykjadalur, with great views of the gorge Djúpagil and its impressive waterfall. Follow the track up Reykjadalur until you reach Klambragil, which contains an amazing hot stream. Many Icelanders use it for bathing but travellers may find it too hot. From Klambragil, numerous onward hiking possibilities present themselves, including Álftatjörn, Nesjavellir, Hengill and Ölfusvatn.

An eight-hour return day hike, beginning with the walk to Klambragil, will take you up 803m Hengill, a dormant volcano whose name means 'hanging over your head'. This colourful basalt and rhyolite area is thought to harbour the greatest geothermal potential

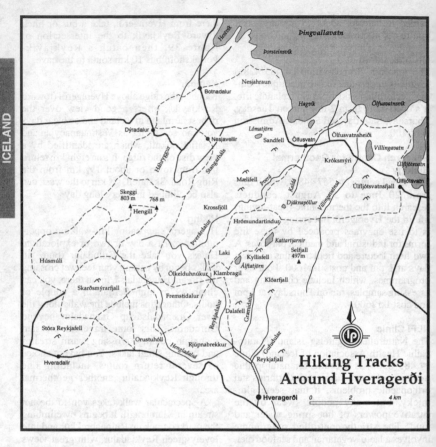

Hiking Tracks Around Hveragerði

0   2   4 km

● Hveragerði

in the world. Most of the route is marked, but it's still wise to carry the *Hengill* 1:100,000 (1988) topo sheet.

Organised Tours

Hestaleiga Reykjakot (☎ 483 4462) and Eld-Hestar (☎ 483 4884) hire out horses and offer two-hour to seven-day excursions into the scenic wilderness behind Hveragerði, as well as longer riding tours around Iceland. They're highly recommended.

Places to Stay

The guesthouse *Sólbakki* (☎ 483 4212),

Hveramörk 17, has single/double rooms for Ikr2990/4030 and sleeping-bag accommodation for Ikr1500. It also rents out a six-person cottage by the river Hvítá, 20 km from town, for Ikr36,000 per week.

The cosy and homely *Gistiheimilið Frumskógar* (☎ 483 4148; fax 483 4888) charges Ikr1625/2795 for single/double rooms, with breakfast and kitchen facilities. Sleeping-bag accommodation is Ikr1235 and three to eight-person self-catering flats cost from Ikr23,550 to Ikr46,400 per week.

The *Hótel Hvergerði* (☎ 483 4588; fax 483 4088) – also called Hótel Ljósbrá, at

Breiðamörk 25, offers good-value single/double rooms for Ikr3500/4550. It also operates the nearby *Youth Hostel Ból* (☎ 483 4198), which charges Ikr1000/1250 for members/non-members, or you can camp. Cooking facilities are available.

The *Hótel Örk* (☎ 483 4700; fax 483 4775), which offers tennis courts, saunas, golf, swimming pools and a large water fun park, charges Ikr9600/11,300 for a single/double room with shower and breakfast.

You'll find single/double farmhouse accommodation for Ikr3000/4000 at *Núpar III* (☎ 483 4388), along the road to Þorlákshöfn. Sleeping-bag accommodation starts at Ikr850.

The main *campground*, which may well be Iceland's least attractive, is on Skólamörk, near the swimming pool at the eastern end of town. It lacks hot water and showers, the facilities are dirty and it's replete with trash.

Places to Eat

Predictably, Hveragerði is the best place in Iceland for fresh vegetables. The bakery and coffee shop *Hverabakarí*, beside the tourist office, and the *Kjöris* ice-cream factory, on Austurmörk, are good for sweet snacks. The *Kaupfélagið* supermarket is on Breiðamörk, near Hótel Hveragerði. The garden centre *Græna Höndin*, the *Shell* petrol station opposite Eden and the *Esso* station on Breiðamörk all have decent snack cafeterias.

The best choice for a good meal is certainly *Pizza 67*, on Austurmörk. In addition to the *Eden* (☎ 483 4900) restaurant, there are also the dining rooms at *Hótel Örk* (☎ 483 4700) and *Hótel Hveragerði* (☎ 483 4588). The latter specialises in mountain lamb and various fish soups; in the summer, it's open daily from 8 am to 10 pm. The *Matstofa* (☎ 483 0300) at the NLFÍ Clinic serves exclusively vegetarian food, but reservations are required.

Getting There & Away

All buses between Reykjavík and Fjallabak, Þórsmörk, or Höfn pass through Hveragerði, and several daily buses between Reykjavík and Stokkseyri, Eyrarbakki and Þorlákshöfn also loop through Hveragerði. The first bus from Reykjavík leaves at 9 am and the last, at 11 pm. From Hveragerði, the first Reykjavík bus is at 9.50 am and the last, at 9.50 pm.

Most buses pick up or drop people on the main highway, near the Hotel Örk, but there's also a central bus terminal on Breiðamörk, roughly opposite the post office.

SELFOSS

Selfoss, ('barn falls'), with nearly 4000 people, is the largest town in southern Iceland. It lies on the banks of the Ölfusá in the midst of Iceland's richest farming district, and is the home of its largest dairy operations. Although there's little to draw tourists, it's quite a pleasant little town and its inexpensive accommodation and location in the heart of South Central Iceland make it increasingly popular with tour groups and a great a base for seeing the region.

Information

The tourist office (☎ 482 1704; fax 482 2764) is at Tryggvaskáli near the bridge in the heart of Selfoss. From 1 June to 15 September, it's open daily from 9 to 11.30 am and 12.30 to 8 pm.

Museum

The Selfoss Museum at Tryggvagata 23 is a sort of catch-all with folk, art and natural history exhibits. It's open daily from 2 to 5 pm between 6 June and 9 September. Admission is Ikr200.

Ingólfsfjall

According to legend, Iceland's first settler Ingólfur Arnarson is buried in Inghóll, a mound atop the 551m Ingólfsfjall. The peak is solid rock, however, so it's doubtful that anyone is actually buried there and more reliable sources place Ingólfur's grave in Reykjavík. If you're feeling restless, it's a nice day-hike to Inghóll. The best route up begins three km west of Selfoss along the Ring Road.

At the foot of the mountain, near the intersection of the Ring Road and the Biskupstungur road (Route 35), is the buried farm Fjallastún, which reputedly was Ingólfur Arnarson's first permanent winter home.

Places to Stay

As the name would suggest, the good-value *Gistiheimilið Home Away from Home* (☎ 482 1471; fax 482 1912), at Heiðmörk 2a, offers friendly hostel-style accommodation. Made-up beds cost Ikr1900 and sleeping-bag accommodation is Ikr1200. A large breakfast or packed lunch costs an additional Ikr650.

The hostel-style *Gistiþjónustan Selfoss* (☎ & fax 482 1675), in the school, charges Ikr1000 for sleeping-bag accommodation. Breakfast and dinner is available.

The *Hótel Selfoss* (☎ 482 2500; fax 482 2524), with an attached restaurant, cafeteria and bar, has singles/doubles with shower for Ikr6800/9400. Cheaper but also nice is the affiliated summer hotel *Þóristún* (☎ 482 2500; fax 482 2524), 100m away in a large but cosy house. Singles/doubles cost Ikr3650/5700 with shared facilities and Ikr4550/6990 with shower.

Selfoss also has a centrally located *campground* with grills, and laundry and cooking facilities for Ikr250 per person and Ikr250 per tent. On the same premises is the airy *Gesthús* (☎ 482 3585; fax 482 2973) chalet complex, with 11 eight-person cabins. Single/double rooms with shower and made-up beds cost Ikr4300/5800, while dormitory-style sleeping-bag accommodation is Ikr1400, including use of the swimming pool and jacuzzis. Campers pay extra to use the facilities. This place has a good reputation and is popular with budget travellers; it also hires out tents, horses and mountain bikes and organises hiking, riding and cycling tours.

On Route 30, 23 km from Selfoss, is the farmhouse *Brjánsstaðir* (☎ 486 5540; fax 486 5640). Single/double rooms with made-up beds, breakfast and use of the TV lounge cost Ikr3000/4050. Sleeping-bag accommodation starts at Ikr850.

Places to Eat

In addition to the *Betri-stofan* (☎ 482 2500), at Hótel Selfoss, a fine restaurant is *Inghóll* (☎ 482 2585), at the Fossnesti bus terminal, Austurvegur 46. For pizza, go to *Pizza 67* (☎ 482 2267), 400m down Tryggvagata. *Gjáin* (☎ 482 2555) on Austurvegur is good for pub meals and drinks. It's open weekdays from 8 pm to midnight and weekends from 6 pm to 3 am. At the Shell petrol station, just out of town toward Reykjavík, is a *Kentucky Fried Chicken* (☎ 482 3466) outlet. For coffee and snacks, try *HM Café*, on Eyrarvegur.

For self-catering, the good-value *supermarket* near the campground stays open until 10 pm daily.

Things to Buy

At Þingborg, on Route 1, 10 km east of Selfoss, you can buy quality hand-spun wool yarn or clippings for spinning and weaving yourself. It's open from 1 June to 1 September.

Getting There & Away

All buses between Reykjavík and Höfn, Skaftafell, Fjallabak, Þórsmörk, Flúðir, Gullfoss, Laugarvatn and Vík pass through Selfoss, so you'll have numerous options daily. The fare from Reykjavík is Ikr400.

HELLA

Hella was established in 1927 and developed from a single shop into a modest trading and agricultural village with 700 residents. The area is well-known to horse fans as Iceland's main horse-breeding centre and lies within close range of quite a few scenic attractions. On a clear day, there's a fine view of the volcano Hekla.

Information

The tourist office (☎ 487 5165; fax 487 5365), on the main drag, is open Monday to Friday from 9 am to 2 pm and 5 to 7 pm, and on weekends from 9.30 to 11 am.

Ægissíða

At the southern edge of Hella, on the western

bank of the Rangá, is the Ægissíða region. In the fields are ruins of 12 artificial caves believed to have been constructed by early Irish monks and hermits.

Oddi

The name of this farm and church, 10 km south of Hella, means 'triangle', in reference to the land between the angular confluence of the Þverá and the Ytri-Rangá rivers. Oddi once had a wealthy monastery and boarding school for children of the aristocracy. Of the priests who served as instructors at Oddi, six went on to become bishops.

Numerous scholarly works were written by Oddi residents. The *Prose Edda* was penned by Snorri Sturluson, who was reared there, and the poems of the *Elder Edda* were collected by Sæmundur Sigfússon, who was born there. Some believe the word 'Edda' itself is a corruption of 'Oddi'

To look at it now, you'd never suspect the early importance of this place, but the church does retain some relics of the Literary Era of the 1300s. To get there, take any bus east from Hella or west from Hvolsvöllur, get off at the intersection of Route 266 and walk or hitch the final four km to Oddi.

Árbakki Horse Farm

One of Iceland's largest horse farms, Árbakki (☎ 557 7556) lies on Route 271 five km north-east of Hella and if you like horses, it should be a requisite visit. Not only does it breed and sell horses, it also offers riding courses, organises tours of the farm and provides information for anyone interested in purchasing Icelandic horses.

Places to Stay & Eat

Hella's tourist centre is the *Gistiheimilið Mosfell* (☎ 487 5828; fax 487 5004) at Þrúðvangur 6, which has single/double rooms for Ikr3850/4950 and sleeping-bag accommodation for Ikr1100. It also administers the self-catering summerhouses over the road (Ikr4620 to Ikr9820) and a lovely riverside campground. Camping is also possible at the horse show grounds, south of the Ring Road.

Hellirinn (☎ 487 5104), in the Ægessíða area, offers sleeping-bag accommodation for Ikr780 to Ikr1500 and made-up beds for Ikr1500 to Ikr6000.

Near the Gistiheimilið Mosfell are the popular *Restaurant Laufafell* (☎ 487 5881), with good sit-down meals, and the attached *Grill-Skálinn* takeaway. In the next building to the east is a fairly well-stocked *supermarket*.

Getting There & Away

All buses between Reykjavík and Vík or Höfn make a brief stop at Hella. There are at least two scheduled buses daily. The fare from Reykjavík is Ikr900.

BISKUPSTUNGUR

Biskupstungur ('bishop's tongue') technically takes in the district between the river Hvítá to the east and Brúará to the west, split in two by the Tungufljót. For convenience, this section also includes the approaches to it along Route 35. This is the heart of Golden Circle country and thanks to lots of traffic, hitching is pretty good.

Kerið & Seyðishólar

Kerið, a 55m deep explosion crater harbouring a forbidding green lake, was formed 3000 years ago in a crater swarm known as Tjarnarhólar. About three km north-east across the road is the red-sided Seyðishólar crater group, which produced most of the surrounding lava field. There are lots of nice places to camp nearby and a surface stream west of the craters, but the wind can get fierce.

Svínavatn

On the small lake Svínavatn, seven km south of the Skálholt turn-off, is the Vatnasleða-og Skíðasleiga (☎ 486 4500), where you can hire water-skis, jet-skis and wetsuits for use on the lake. It also offers fishing and horse rental.

Sólheimar

At the tiny settlement of Sólheimar, you can stay at the comfortable *Gistiheimilið*

Brekkukot (☎ 486 4430), which charges Ikr2350/3000 for single/double rooms. Sólheimar also has a small shop, a swimming pool, a sports hall and a home for disabled people.

Skálholt

Between 1056 and the end of the 18th century, Skálholt served as one of the two bishoprics and theological centres in Iceland. Until the Reformation, when Catholic Christianity was ousted in favour of Danish Lutheranism as the official state religion, it saw a great deal of religious drama.

For five weeks each July and August, Skálholt hosts a classical music festival featuring composers and musicians from all over Iceland and Europe. For information, phone ☎ 565 0859.

History As a religious centre, Skálholt's importance began with Gissur the White, the lobbyist who railroaded the Christianisation of Iceland through the Alþing. Realising that Iceland's future lay with Christianity, he constructed a church at his Skálholt homestead and sent his son Ísleifur to Germany to study for the priesthood. Ísleifur returned in 1030 and established a parish on his late father's estate. In 1053, he was unanimously elected Bishop of Iceland.

Ísleifur Gissurarson was one of the best loved but least heeded religious figures in Icelandic church history. Though troubled by his ineffectiveness, he managed to win friends for Iceland in Rome and Germany and it was said that he performed miracles.

Ísleifur's son (clergic celibacy had been introduced in France during the previous century but hadn't yet become doctrine in Iceland) Gissur followed in his father's footsteps. To ease the church's financial difficulties, he introduced the tithe and divided the resulting revenues equally between the priests, the poor, the church building fund and the bishopric.

By this time, Skálholt had become the undisputed theological centre of Iceland. In the 12th century, an elaborate timber cathedral was constructed to replace Gissur's humble church and a seminary was organised, also establishing Skálholt as the nation's educational centre.

In 1550, during a spate of religious turmoil, Jón Arason, the best-known of the bishops, and two of his sons were executed at Skálholt for actively opposing the Danish Lutheran Reformation. The new Lutheran bishopric remained at Skálholt until 1797, when it was shifted to Reykjavík and the old timber church was dismantled.

In 1954, when the cornerstone was laid for the new commemorative church, crews discovered the coffin of another early bishop, Páll Jónsson, the nephew of St Þorlákur, who served from 1196 to 1211 and promoted both culture and learning within the church. According to his biography, *Páls Saga*, his death brought about great earthquakes and storms and he was universally mourned by his constituents. As the coffin was being opened, the heavens suddenly cut loose with such a deluge that excavators wondered whether they were doing the right thing. The coffin is now kept in the new church. When you're there, don't miss the beautiful modern mosaic by Nina Tryggvadóttir on the wall above the altar.

Places to Stay All Golden Circle tours stop at Skálholt for five minutes to see the mosaic. If you want more time, there's farmhouse accommodation at *Sel* (☎ 486 4441), three km from Skálholt, charging Ikr2990/4030 for single/double rooms; sleeping-bag accommodation starts at Ikr850. Six-person cottages are available for Ikr33,550 per week. The Reykholt HI hostel (see below) is only 10 minutes away by vehicle.

Getting There & Away In summer, daily buses leave BSÍ in Reykjavík at 11.30 am, pass Sel and the Skálholt turn-off (five km from Skálholt) northbound at about 1.45 pm, then continue to Geysir and Gullfoss before returning to Reykjavík. Southbound, they pass the Skálholt turn-off at around 2.45 pm.

Reykholt

This settlement of 100 people in the heart of

a geothermal area occupies itself with greenhouse agriculture and tourism. The main attraction is the geyser Reykjahver, which provides local energy. Services include a general shop, a petrol station and a naturally heated swimming pool.

Places to Stay Reykholt has both a *HI hostel* (☎ 486 8831; fax 486 8709) and a *campground* (☎ 486 8807). For the hostel, advance reservations are necessary. The price includes access to the swimming pool, jacuzzis and saunas. The homely guesthouse at nearby *Galtalækur* (☎ 486 8859) charges Ikr3380/4810 for single/double rooms with breakfast.

Getting There & Away The buses described under Skálholt also stop at Reykholt, which is on Route 35, less than 10 minutes north of the Skálholt turn-off.

Gullfoss

If Iceland has a star attraction, it's Gullfoss. Oddly enough, it only became known to foreigners in this century, having been overshadowed by the waterworks at nearby Geysir. Here the river Hvítá ('white river') drops a total of 32m in two falls and the canyon above and below them is 70m deep and 2.5 km long. When the sun is shining, you're likely to see a rainbow through the ample spray that forms.

The nearby farm Bratthold formerly included part of Gullfoss. In 1907, an Englishman made a bid to purchase the falls for Ikr50,000, but the farmer, Tómas Tómasson, refused to sell. Shortly thereafter, a law was passed preventing foreign interests from acquiring Icelandic waterfalls, but enforcement was lax and Gullfoss eventually fell into the hands of foreigners intent on hydroelectric development. Tómas Tómasson and his daughter Sigríður opposed the plan, and Sigríður walked all the way to Reykjavík to lobby her cause, and threatened to throw herself into the falls if they were to be destroyed. The government ruled against her, but in 1928, the lease on

the falls was not paid and the sales agreement was nullified anyway.

In 1939, Einar Guðmundsson, who had been reared as a foster son at Bratthold, purchased the farm from Sigríður and in 1975, offered it to the Icelandic government as a gift, to be turned into a nature reserve. Above the falls, there's now a monument and a small museum, *Sigríðarstofa*, in honour of Sigríður Tómasdóttir.

Places to Stay Farmhouse accommodation is now available at *Bratthold* (☎ 486 8941). Single/double rooms cost Ikr3000/4050, or you can camp, but there's no sleeping-bag accommodation. Horse rental is available and the farm organises riding excursions.

Getting There & Away The daily summer bus services to Gullfoss (Ikr1210) and Geysir (Ikr1140) from Reykjavík leave at 9 and 11.30 am daily (the former is via Laugardalur and the latter, via Skálholt and Reykholt) from 1 May to 30 September.

Haukadalur

Haukadalur ('hawk valley'), which lies upstream from the geothermal phenomena at Geysir, was originally established as one of the three great centres of learning in southern Iceland. Its most famous graduate was Ari the Learned (1067-1148), the author of the *Íslendingabók* and compiler of the *Landnámabók*.

Over the years, the land became eroded and the farm was abandoned. The church, originally built in 1842 (the ring on the church door is said to be from the staff of Bergþór, the troll of Bláfell), was renovated in 1939 after the site was purchased by Danish philanthropist Kristian Kirk. Kirk bequeathed the site to the Icelandic Forestry Commission (there really is one!), which curbed the erosion by planting over half a million trees. This area is not on the Golden Circle circuit, but it lies just a short walk up the Beiná valley from Geysir.

Day Tripping Through the Golden Circle

If you take the famous Golden Circle Tour, it's best to adopt a mellow attitude. So many daytrippers are processed through this region every summer day that groups find themselves falling over each other at the main stops, and so many sights are packed in that there's little time to absorb anything.

In fact, the main intent seems to be herding people into the coffee shops and restaurants and encouraging them to spend a bit more money. You get eight minutes at Geysir, for example, and 45 minutes at the hotel for cakes and coffee. Fortunately, you can leave the tour at any time and rejoin later (but let the guides know in advance when to pick you up).

The standard itinerary includes Eden in Hveragerði, the Kerið crater, the bishopric at Skálholt, lunch, Gullfoss, Geysir, a snack and, finally, a brief whirl through Þingvellir (just long enough to whet your appetite to return).

This tour is offered by both BSÍ and Reykjavík Excursions for around Ikr4600 per person without lunch. On the BSÍ tours, discounts are available for Omnibuspass holders. ∎

Geysir

All the world's spouting hot springs were named after this, the 'Great Geysir' (pronounced GAY-zeer), which first began erupting in the 14th century and ceased earlier this century after thousands of tourists tried to set it off by pouring in loads of rocks and dirt. When the water level inside the geyser was artificially lowered, it resumed activity for awhile, spouting up to 60m, but now it doesn't erupt at all.

Eruptions are caused when boiling water deep in the spring, trapped by cooler water on the surface, explodes and spews out everything above it. Up until a couple of years ago, as a celebration for Icelandic Independence Day every 17 June, tonnes of soap flakes were poured into the Great Geysir, sufficiently lowering the temperature and surface tension of the water to cause an eruption. This has now been deemed environmentally unsound and has been discontinued.

Fortunately for the tourist industry, the Great Geysir has a faithful stand-in: nearby Strokkur (the 'butter churn') spouts and sprays up to 20m every three minutes. Photographers must be quick or they'll miss the eruptions, which typically last only a couple of seconds.

In addition, the site includes lots of colourful hot springs, steaming vents, warm streams and psychedelic algae and mineral deposits. It's also worthwhile climbing up the hill Laugarfjall, which is topped by a view disc.

Places to Stay & Eat One of Iceland's great accommodation bargains is the *Hótel Geysir* (☎ 486 8915; fax 486 8715), with a beautiful dining room and single/double rooms for Ikr2200/3300; sleeping-bag accommodation is Ikr500 on the floor and Ikr1150 in a bed. The restaurant has a good reputation and the petrol station beside the hotel boasts a great snack bar.

The similarly good-value *Guesthouse Geysir* (☎ 486 8733) charges Ikr2000 per person for made-up beds and Ikr1050 for sleeping-bag accommodation.

The *campground* at Geysir is open from 1 May to 1 October. There are also plenty of wild campsites up in the hills and valleys, but be sure to get well away from the service centre.

Getting There & Away See the Gullfoss section for details on getting to Geysir by public transport.

Organised Tours

Between June and August, Björn Gíslason at Hvítárferðir (☎ 568 2504), Háagerði 41, 108 Reykjavík, offers a tame 5½ km raft tour through a scenic canyon on the Hvítá. The day tour costs Ikr4000 per person

This trip is also available through BSÍ for Ikr6500, with discounts for bus-pass holders.

It includes transport between Reykjavík and the put-in point Brúarhlöð, the raft trip, visits to Geysir and Gullfoss and a sampling of Icelandic refreshments at the farm Drumboddsstaðir.

FLÚÐIR

Flúðir is a town that has seemingly risen from nowhere in the past few years. It's set in the middle of a significant geothermal field and has developed into a greenhouse centre and holiday resort of sorts. In fact, it looks a lot like a planned community. For those with vehicles, it's centrally located for most sites of interest in South Central Iceland.

Information

For tourist information, see the Grund Tourist Centre (☎ 486 6756), beside the campground. It offers bicycle rental for Ikr750 per day and can arrange fishing permits. Horse rental and horse tours of up to three days are available from the farm Syðra-Langholt (☎ 486 6774).

Emil Áageirsson Agricultural Museum

This free museum (☎ 486 6635), housed in a couple of old outbuildings, displays a collection of old farming implements.

Places to Stay & Eat

The best accommodation is the *Edda Hótel Flúðir* (☎ 486 6630; fax 486 6530), which stays open year round. Single/double rooms with showers cost Ikr4680/6435, including use of the outdoor jacuzzis. Sleeping-bag accommodation at the affiliated *Skjólborg* costs Ikr900/1250 in the schoolrooms/dormitories. There's also a *campground* near the hotel.

Four km from Flúðir, beside the Hvítá, is *Gistiheimilið Nátthagi* (☎ 486 6737), a cottage accommodating groups of up to 12 for Ikr12,000 per day. It's used mostly by school classes, tours and hiking groups.

Budget farmhouse accommodation costs Ikr2100 per person at the horse farm *Syðra-Langholt* (☎ & fax 486 6674), 10 km south-west of Flúðir. Sleeping-bag accommodation is Ikr1300.

Full restaurant meals are served at the *Hótel Flúðir*. At the Grund Tourist Centre there's a *grocery*, *bakery*, camp shop and a small *cafeteria*.

Entertainment

Films are screened on Thursday at 9 pm in the community centre (☎ 486 6620). In the summer, the naturally heated outdoor pool, jacuzzis and solarium are open from 2 to 10 pm on weekdays and 10 am to 7 pm on weekends. There's also a nine-hole golf course at Efra-Sel, three km from Flúðir.

Getting There & Away

Buses from Reykjavík to Flúðir (Ikr780) leave on Sunday at 7.30 pm and on Monday, Tuesday, Thursday and Friday at 6.30 pm. From Flúðir, they leave at 7 pm on Sunday and 9.30 pm on Monday, Tuesday, Thursday and Friday.

ÞJÓRSÁRDALUR

The long, broad valley of the great Þjórsá ('bull river') winds its way south-west from the glacier Hofsjökull in the heart of Iceland to the Atlantic west of Hella. For the purposes of this book, Þjórsárdalur takes in the bit along Route 26 between Skarð and the intersection of Route F22.

Nearly all of Þjórsárdalur lies beneath lava deserts created by eruptions of Hekla, Iceland's best-known volcano. Around 8000 years ago, a river of lava swept over the landscape, covering 800 sq km on its way to the Atlantic. In 1104, the first Hekla eruption witnessed by settlers rendered nearly all of south central Iceland uninhabitable. Only two farms remain in the area, but the ruins of 20 have been excavated.

Hekla

Thanks to an almost perpetual bank of cloud that shrouds it, only lucky visitors will see the near perfect cone of Hekla ('the hooded'). Its present altitude is 1491m, over 40m higher than before its last big eruption in 1947. It erupted again in 1970 and most recently in 1991, when Reykjavík was practically emptied by hopeful spectators and photographers.

The account of St Brendan's voyages describes a great flaming mountain, which existed on the 'island of smiths' in Thule. Since it is visible from the sea, Hekla is probably the best candidate. Although it erupted in the early 9th century, just before Settlement, the settlers failed to recognise the danger it posed and established farms and homesteads in the inviting green valley. In 1104, however, disaster struck and everything within a radius of 50 km was destroyed, buried beneath a metre of solid ejecta, particularly tephra. Since that devastating eruption, the mountain has blown its top 14 times. In 1300 it split open, and over the next year it spewed ash across more than 83,000 sq km.

By the 1500s, mainland Europe had decided that vile Hekla was the entrance to hell, and literature of the day reported the skies around it were black with vultures and ravens, and that the moans of the condemned could be heard crying out from inside. The brush-off of the day in Europe was, 'Go to Hekla'.

In 1947, after over 100 years of inactivity, Hekla belched a mushroom cloud of ash that rose over 27 km into the air and spread as far as northern Russia. The eruption continued for 13 months and destroyed farms and fields before the mountain quietened down and lay dormant for 23 years. In 1970, nearly 50 million tonnes of ejecta spread out across the landscape and again destroyed crops. The most recent eruption occurred in January 1991, the day after the UN forces first attacked Baghdad.

Heklumiðstöðin The Hekla museum (☎ 487 6587), along Route 26 near Leirubakki, displays films, photos and artwork related to the volcano. From 1 June to 31 August, it's open daily from 10 am to 5 pm. Admission is Ikr200.

Climbing Hekla Hekla is a relatively easy climb but it is an active volcano and, as you

may suspect, it's not entirely safe. Wait for a day when the peak is clear of clouds (you may be waiting a long time!) and carry all the water you'll need.

There are three main routes to the peak, but the one from the north-east is the easiest. It begins along a well-marked walking track which turns off the Landmannaleið, about 10 km east of Route 26. Follow this track steadily uphill until you gain the ridge which forms the north-eastern flank of the mountain, and continue along this ridge south-west to the summit crater, keeping to the right of the prominent fissure. The round trip takes at least eight hours.

The other two routes begin on the mountain's western side, but they were greatly altered by flows from the 1991 lava, which have not yet been mapped. The new craters lie on the mountain's south-western and south-eastern flanks.

Here's an alternative route, as described by a reader:

Coming from Reykjavík on the Fjallabak bus, you pass the Leirubakki campsite and continue with the bus about 10 km, until the road passes south-east of Búrfell, a table-top mountain. Just before Búrfell, get off the bus. From there on, it's basically just walking straight toward the mountain peak.

About 300m from the road you cross a river – nothing to do but take off the boots and trousers and wade across. Remember to cross where the river is wide and therefore not too deep and powerful. This makes a convenient and easily remembered place to leave your backpacks while climbing the mountain; select a high spot in case of rain or crazy hot-weather melt-off situations.

After the river, you cross a couple of sandy hills. This is really pleasure walking compared to the lava fields to come. Next is crossing the lava fields which run right beside the pitch-black flow of lava from 1991. Walking on the older lava is easiest, since age has taken off some of the sharp edges.

When you reach the foot of Hekla, the snow begins and it's up to you to decide which is the easiest way up. It took me eight hours from the main road to the summit and back again and I never hurry while walking or climbing. Another advantage is that no jeeps or helicopters are necessary and backpackers can get there on public transport.

Jacob Hartmann, Denmark

Places to Stay Ten km from the mountain

is the popular *Gistihúsið/Youth Hostel Leirubakki* (☎ & fax 487 6591) on Route 26. This multi-storey 'mountain hut' accommodates up to 112 people (hope that it doesn't come to that!) with toilets, a sauna, cooking facilities and two outdoor jacuzzis with a front-row view of Hekla. Made-up beds cost Ikr2200 and sleeping-bag accommodation is Ikr1250 (Ikr1000 for youth hostel members). For space in the common dormitory, you'll pay Ikr900. There's also a campground with access to water and facilities for Ikr500 per person. Horse rental is also available.

An alternative is the *Laugaland* (☎ 487 6543) summer hotel, a half-hour drive from the mountain. Made-up beds cost Ikr1850 and sleeping-bag accommodation is Ikr900/1300 on a mattress/bed. Meals are available on request.

Getting There & Away The daily BSÍ Fjallabak 'tours' between Reykjavík and Skaftafell, which operate from early July to mid-September, leave from Reykjavík at 8.30 am and from Skaftafell at 8 am. The whole trip costs Ikr5265 (Ikr2200 with Omnibuspass) but you can stop anywhere along the way and resume the tour later. The BSÍ Sprengisandur tour and Reykjavík Excursions' Þjórsárdalur tour (see Organised Tours later in this section) also pass Leirubakki.

Tröllkonuhlaup
It was once believed that trolls inhabited the mountains around Hekla: a male troll in Búrfell and his sister in Bjólfell. They fancied a local farmer called Gissur of Lækjarbotnar for a meal, but the intended victim heard of the plot and escaped over the river. They followed him across the stepping stones at Tröllkonuhlaup ('troll woman's leap'), but never did get him into the stewpot.

This waterfall is probably best described as a picturesque cascade – that is unless the Burfellsvirkjun power station upstream has shut off the Þjórsá, as it did in 1996, leaving no sign of a river, let alone a waterfall. All passing tour buses stop for a brief look.

Stöng & Þjóðveldisbær
In 1104, the farm of Gaukur Trandilsson – the Reykjavík pub Gaukur á Stöng was named after him – was buried beneath a devastating eruption of Hekla. In 1939, Gaukur's holdings at Stöng were excavated by a team of Scandinavian archaeologists. Icelanders, using a strained comparison, refer to it as the 'Northern Pompeii'.

In 1974, to mark 1100 years of Settlement, the government decided to reconstruct an exact match a few km away at Búrfell (Þjóðveldisbær). The construction materials, layout, building techniques and indoor furnishings were meticulously selected to resemble a medieval Norse farmstead. Details of construction methods, materials and room plans are outlined in *The Reconstructed Medieval Farm in Þjórsárdalur*, available on the site or at the National Museum in Reykjavík. The reconstructed farm is highly worthwhile, but the original Stöng offers little but the outline of one foundation and a shelter which protects it from the weather. The reconstructed farm museum (☎ 487 7700) is open from 10 am to noon and 1 to 6 pm, 1 June to 15 September. Admission is Ikr150.

Several hours walk up the Fossá valley west of Stöng is Iceland's second highest waterfall, Háifoss, which plunges 122m from the escarpment above. You can camp anywhere in this valley. It's also worth visiting the gorge Gjáin, upstream along the Rauðá from the farm ruins, with its unusual rock formations and waterfalls. Near the Burfellsvirkjun power station is another beautiful falls called Hjálparfoss.

Other ancient farm ruins are found at Skeljastaðir, between Þjóðveldisbær and Stöng.

Getting There & Away Getting to Stöng without a car or bike is tricky, but hitching isn't impossible. By bus, the closest access is Búrfellsvirkjun power plant. From there, the reconstructed farm is only three km away, but Stöng is 12 km away by the shortest route. Buses to Búrfellsvirkjun leave Reykjavík at 7.30 pm on Sunday and at 6.30

pm on Tuesday and Friday; they return at 4.50 pm on Sunday and at 9.20 am Tuesday and Friday. See also Organised Tours below.

Organised Tours

Both Reykjavík Excursions and BSÍ run Þjórsárdalur tours, the former on Thursday and Saturday and the latter on Tuesday, Thursday, Saturday and Sunday, from June to August. They visit the Stöng ruins and the Búrfellsvirkjun power plant as well as the Gjáin gorge and Hjálparfoss, but not the reconstructed farm. The nine-hour tours cost Ikr6000.

Þingvellir

Since the Alþing was established there in 930, Þingvellir (the 'assembly plains') has been the most significant historical site in Iceland. Although it was selected for its topography, acoustics and proximity to most of Iceland's population, Þingvellir is more than a setting for historical drama. Nowhere else in Iceland is the rift between the European and North American plates more obvious. The broad, fissured and forested plain is dotted with a wealth of natural attractions – canyons, caves, streams, springs, waterfalls and ponds – and flanked by snow-covered peaks and the country's largest lake (nearly 84 sq km), Þingvallavatn. In autumn, the birch trees and tundra vegetation turn brilliant reds, oranges and yellows.

In 1928, the Icelandic government set part of Þingvellir aside as the country's first Þjóðarðurinn ('national park'). It thereby escaped becoming an enormous holiday camp, but to some extent is still used as a summer 'suburb' for weekenders from Reykjavík.

Most of the historical buildings are concentrated in one small area, having been moved there from around the park; the remainder is left pretty much to nature. A maze of hiking trails crisscrosses the plain and leads through the woods to points of interest or through scenic areas. The more adventurous can venture off into the surrounding mountains or around the lake shore. Walkers should pick up a copy of the topographic sheet Þingvellir 1:25,000 (1974), available from map shops in Reykjavík.

History

The descendants of Ingólfur Arnarson, Iceland's first settler, established the Alþing at Þingvellir, which was at the time the eastern edge of his property. This site was selected because the great fissure of Almannagjá above the surrounding plain provided the ideal open-air podium for the representatives and legislators who would arbitrate disputes and formulate laws for the young country.

Nearly everything that happened in Iceland until 1271 had some connection with the Alþing and the history of the country coincides for the most part with the history of Þingvellir. The annual summer convention of the Alþing was Iceland's event of the year and everyone who could attend did so. There, the courses of human lives were determined: legal disputes were settled, marriages arranged, business contracts drawn up, executions carried out and laws made.

It was at Þingvellir that Christianity was accepted as the national religion, Snorri Sturluson became lögsögumaður, and subsequent issues, such as the establishment of the bishoprics at Hólar and Skálholt and the introduction of tithes, were sanctioned. It was also there that Gunnar of Hlíðarendi met Hallgerður Long-Legs, who orchestrated the downfall of half of South Central Iceland (see the Njáls Saga aside).

In 1262, also at Þingvellir, Iceland surrendered itself to Norway, bringing about the Alþing's loss of power in 1271. In 1800 the body was dissolved completely, just after being moved to Austurvöllur in Reykjavík. When it reorganised and regained power in 1843, Iceland was already on its way to independence. At that stage, Þingvellir's importance as the seat of government

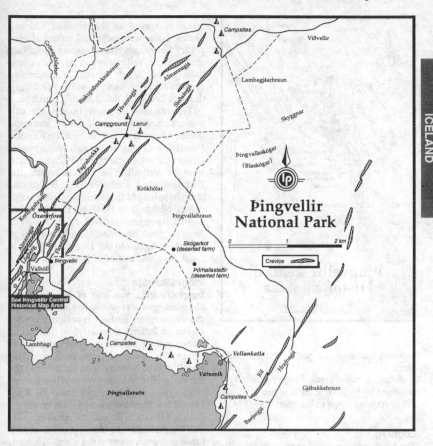

became little more than a novelty as Reykjavík took over both the business of government and Iceland itself.

On the 1000th anniversary of Settlement in 1874, Christian IX of Denmark became the first king to attend the assembly and many Icelanders gathered for the show. In 1930, Þingvellir hosted 30,000 guests – including King Christian X – in celebration of the 1000-year anniversary of the Alþing, and on 17 June 1944, 30,000 people witnessed the birth of the Icelandic republic. In 1974, in honour of Iceland's 1100th anniversary of Settlement, 60,000 Icelanders turned up at Þingvellir for the biggest party the country has ever known.

Almannagjá

The greatest rift at Þingvellir, Almannagjá formally includes the crack between Kárastaðastígur (the track leading in from the south), and Öxarárfoss (the 'axe river falls') where the Öxará flows into it from the north. Geologically, however, it runs all the way to Ármannsfell in the north and Þingvallavatn in the south. According to legend, the Öxarárfoss falls were created by artificially diverting the river's course in

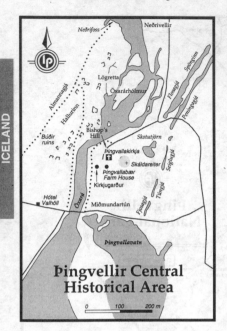

Þingvellir Central Historical Area

0   100   200 m

order to enhance the parliamentary backdrop.

Today, a broad track follows the gorge, bordered by high stone cliffs to the west and lower rock outcrops to the east.

Lögberg

The Lögberg ('law rock') served as the official podium during parliamentary sessions between 930 and 1271. There the lögsögumaður presided over the parliament and annually recited the law of the land. After Iceland's conversion to Christianity, the site was shifted from Spönginn, east of Flosagjá, to the slope east of Almannagjá. Active geological forces have caused the rock podium to subside into a grassy mound, but the site of its disappearance is marked by a flagpole.

Búðir

The Búðir ('booths') scattered around Þingvellir were owned by the goðar (chieftains) and used as shelters and meeting places. Some were large and served as temporary businesses where visitors could buy ale, writing vellum, weapons, shoes and meals. One dispute at such a concession reportedly resulted in someone being dumped head-first into a boiling cauldron.

The remains of many booths are still evident along Almannagjá. Snorri Sturluson owned a large one, Valhöll, near the Kastalar ('castle') rocks, as well as two smaller ones: Grýla near the Lögberg and Valhallardilkur west of Valhöll. The largest booth, the Biskupabúð at Bishop's Hill, beside the church, belonged to the bishops. One booth called Njálsbúð is believed to have been owned by representatives from the *Njáls Saga* region. Booth-building continued at Þingvellir right into the 18th century, when the Alþing was moved to Reykjavík.

Þingvallakirkja

Þingvallakirkja was one of Iceland's first churches, and was probably consecrated by the Norwegian Bishop Bjarnharður, who stayed in Iceland from 1016 to 1021. The timber and the bell for the original church at Þingvellir were gifts from King Ólaf Haraldsson of Norway, who ascended to the throne in 1015. Another royal bell and more Norwegian wood were presented by King Harald Hardraada in the mid-11th century.

When the royal church collapsed in 1118, the Þingvallabær farmer's private church came into general use. After it was enlarged, it became Þingvellir's main church, and was known as St Olaf's. The site was flood-prone, however, and in 1523 the building was moved to the site of the present church.

The present church, which was constructed in 1859, has three bells: one of the originals, one from 1698 and one cast on the occasion of Iceland's independence in 1944. The pulpit dates from 1683. Ófeigur Jónsson's *The Last Supper* was painted in 1834 and served as the altarpiece until it was sold in 1899 and replaced by a more modern painting of Christ healing the blind man.

The old work, purchased by an English-woman, Mrs Disney Leith, was installed in her family church on the Isle of Wight. It was ingeniously tracked down and returned to Iceland in time for the 1974 festivities.

If you find the church locked, contact the national park warden at the office in the Þingvallabær farmhouse.

Þingvallabær

The original Þingvöllur farm was owned by Þórir Kroppinskeggi, until the land was appropriated by the Alþing. Participants in the early annual sessions, which included nearly everyone in Iceland, were entitled to build booths, pitch tents, pasture their animals, gather wood and create whatever mess they wanted without compensating the farmer in any way. It is assumed, however, that he somehow profited from the intrusion.

The early farmhouse at Þingvallabær was large – over 25m long – in order to accommodate the numerous guests. The southern three gables of the new farmhouse, now a Þingvellir landmark, were built for the 1000th anniversary of the Alþing in 1930 by the state architect Guðjón Samúelsson; it's now used as a summer home by the Icelandic prime minister. The northern two gables were added in 1974 for the 1100th anniversary of Settlement; they now house the national park warden.

Drekkingarhylur

This pool in the Öxará above the bridge was called 'the drowning pool'. The Great Edict of 1564 declared that all women found guilty of infanticide, adultery, perjury or any other criminal act would be executed by drowning. The pool was much deeper then than it is today, having since been filled with materials leftover from bridge construction and renovation. Unruly men, incidentally, were generally executed by hanging or beheading.

Skáldareitur

The small cemetery behind the church was begun in 1939. It is commonly referred to as the Skáldareitur (the 'poets' graveyard') because the Independence-era poets Jónas Hallgrímsson and Einar Benediktsson are interred there.

Lögrétta

The exact meeting place of the Lögrétta ('law council') isn't known, but is thought to lie somewhere on the Neðrivellir ('low fields') east of the Lögberg. The text of the law book *Grágás* states that the Lögrétta would meet on three long benches, each accommodating 48 men. The middle bench was reserved for the voting members and the bishops and the other two were for their advisers.

Þingvallavatn

Originally known as Ölfusvatn, Iceland's largest lake, Þingvallavatn, sprawls over nearly 84 sq km south of Þingvellir National Park. On the north-eastern shore is Vellankatla ('the bubbling cauldron'), a spring that bubbles into the lake from beneath the lava field. Water enters the lake through this and several underground sources as well as from the river Öxará. The lake's main outlet is the river Sogið. Two volcanic craters, Sandey and Nesjaey, form islands in the west central part of the lake.

The Hótel Valhöll hires out rowing boats by the hour, but the winds across Þingvallavatn are normally too strong for comfortable human-powered boating.

Brennugjá

Brennugjá (the 'burning chasm') is the small rift to the west of Flosagjá. In the 17th century, nine men accused of sorcery were burned at the stake at the mouth of this chasm. Throughout the 1600s in Iceland, accusations and convictions of witchcraft were common and at least 22 people, including one woman, were convicted and executed.

Peningagjá

The Peningagjá fissure (the 'chasm of coins') is actually a part of the larger chasm, Nikulásargjá, near the Spönginn lava peninsula. Modern visitors have turned it into a kind of oracle, or more accurately, a wishing well. Petitioners pose a question that can be answered 'yes' or 'no', and a coin is dropped. If the coin can be seen hitting the bottom, the answer is 'yes'. Otherwise, it's 'no'. Even if that sounds dim-witted, the eerie depths of the sapphire-blue chasm glow with reflected light from the thousands of coins and it's worth a look.

Flosagjá

This chasm, west of Spönginn, is named for Flosi Þórðarson of *Njáls Saga*. In the clear water, the visibility is at least 70m.

Skógarkot

Most of the walking tracks through the Þingvellir plains converge at Skógarkot. This abandoned farm site below the small hill Sjógnarhóll was occupied until 1936. Just south-east lie the ruins of another farm, Þórhallastaðir. This was where ale was brewed and served to 13th-century Alþing participants.

Ármannsfell

Ármannsfell, the prominent mountain immediately north of Þingvellir, is named after the giant Ármann Dalmansson, whom folk legend identifies as the site's benevolent guardian spirit.

Skjaldbreiður

Although not inside the park, Skjaldbreiður is plainly seen from Almannagjá on a clear day. Its name, 'broad shield', has been extended to all the world's 'shield' volcanoes – the volcanoes of Hawaii, for example, are of this type. Its distinctly shield-like shape was created by oozing, slow-building lava. Once you've explored the park's level terrain, it makes a fascinating hike from Þingvellir. Allow at least three days and use the *Hengill* 1:100,000 topographic sheet.

Organised Tours

Many tours – particularly the Golden Circle tours – include Þingvellir, but they rarely allow more than an hour and include only a quick stroll along Almannagjá, past the lower waterfall and the Lögberg. Few people are satisfied with such a cursory treatment of this wonderful spot, and it's much more rewarding to visit on your own.

A great way to visit the lake is with Þingvellir Information Centre's (☎ 482 2660) cruise around Þingvallavatn on the boat *Himbrimi* (Icelandic for 'great northern diver', or 'loon'). The 1½ hour, Ikr1400, cruise embarks at Skálabrekka at 10 am on Tuesday, Thursday and Friday, and on Saturday and Sunday at 10 am and 1 and 3 pm. It visits the Þingvellir shoreline, as well as Sandey and Nesjaey islands.

Places to Stay & Eat

The most popular of the several national parks' campgrounds is *Leirur*, at the park headquarters. It also has a petrol station, shop and snack bar, and lies within walking range of the central historical area. Other campsites are found on the lake shore, east of Hvannagjá, and at the extreme northern end of the park.

The *Hótel Valhöll* (☎ 482 2622; fax 482 3622), across the Öxará from the historic church, offers fairly elegant single/double accommodation for Ikr6800/8500, with shower and breakfast. The architecture is reminiscent of an old gabled farmhouse and it's one of Iceland's nicer-looking hotels. The three hotel dining rooms serve meals for more sophisticated tastes than the petrol station can accommodate. Although the hotel also functions as a *HI hostel*, it lacks cooking facilities. Sleeping-bag accommodation in the eaves costs Ikr1000/1250 for HI members/non-members.

The nearest farmhouse option is *Efri-Brú* (☎ 482 2615; fax 482 2614), at Ulfljótsvatn south-east of the park. Single/double rooms cost Ikr3050/4030 and sleeping-bag accommodation is Ikr1300. Rates include use of cooking facilities. Fishing, horse hire and horseback tours can be arranged.

Getting There & Away

From 15 May to 15 September, BSÍ buses run from Reykjavík to Þingvellir daily at 1.30 pm, returning at 5 pm. From 1 July to 15 August, there's a run via Nesjavellir, leaving Reykjavík at 8.45 am and returning at 9.50 am. During the colourful autumn season, you're stuck with hitching or the Golden Circle tour.

AROUND ÞINGVELLIR
Mossfell

The farm and mountain Mossfell lie on the Þingvellir road, four km east of the Reykjavík suburb of Mosfellsbær. It was the last home of the poet Egill Skallagrímsson who, when he was old and slowing down, requested to be taken to the Alþing. His intent was to amuse himself by visiting the materialistically corrupt Alþing proceedings and flinging two chests of silver coins (which had been given to him by the king of England) from the Lögberg, to watch the violence and greed which would surely ensue.

His family refused to allow it, so one night when they were all at Þingvellir, he set out with some slaves, a horse and the two chests. The next day, he was found wandering senseless, but neither the slaves nor the coins were ever found. Legend speculates that Egill buried his treasure somewhere on the mountain, but somehow it seems unlikely.

Across Route 36 from Mossfell is Reykjahlíð, a geothermal area which provides some of Reykjavík's hot water.

Skálafell

Skálafell, between Reykjavík and Þingvellir, is a small and uncrowded ski area. The 770m mountain offers ski tow, cabins and good cross-country skiing. The season runs from mid-November to early May.

Nesjavellir

Near the foot of the mountain Hengill, immediately south-west of Þingvallavatn, bubbles a geothermal area and borehole field, which power the 190-megawatt Nesjavellir geothermal plant. It was formally opened on 29 September 1990, and is gradually increasing in capacity to its goal of 400 megawatts by 2010. These boreholes will give you some idea of the kind of power available here; the temperature in one of the 2000m deep holes approaches 400°C and the steam pouring out sounds like a jet engine. It now heats most of Reykjavík.

Organised Tours Reykjavík Excursions runs a day tour to Nesjavellir, taking in several 'clean-energy' sites – Krísuvík, Úlfljótsvatn, the Sog hydroelectric plant and Nesjavellir – and finishes with a boat trip on Þingvallavatn. It runs on Tuesday, Thursday and Sunday and costs Ikr6500.

Places to Stay The hotel and restaurant *Nesbúð* (☎ 482 3415; fax 482 3414) provides single/double rooms without bath for Ikr2175/3120 and sleeping-bag accommodation for Ikr1100. Boat hire and jacuzzis are available, and it's a good base for hikers. The owner offers transport from Reykjavík for Ikr1200.

Getting There & Away Buses run daily from Reykjavík (Ikr550) from 1 July to 15 August at 8.45 am and return at 9.30 am. It's also a straightforward walk from Hveragerði.

Laugarvatn

Laugarvatn, now an educational centre, was historically the site for Christian baptisms, which were performed in the hot spring Vígðalaug. On Friday nights, hundreds of Reykjavík families flee urban pressures and flock to this pretty lake for camping, barbecuing, sailboarding and enjoying the thermal springs.

The mountain backdrop offers lots of scope for hikers. Short day hikes will take you up the ravine Stóragil to several small caves; to the peak of Laugarvatnsfjall for a great lake panorama; through the forest on the Kóngsvegur bridle path; and up the Miðdalur valley to Gullkista. Pick up a free route map at the hotels or campground.

Information Today Laugarvatn serves as a major resort and offers sailboard rental, steam baths and naturally heated swimming pools. The farm Efstidalur (☎ 486 1186) offers horse rental and riding tours into the interior.

Places to Stay & Eat The are two Edda hotels, *Hótel Húsmæðraskóla* (☎ 486 1154; fax 486 1279) and *Gistiheimilið Menntaskóla* (☎ 486 1118). The former charges Ikr5200/7020 for single/double rooms and the latter, Ikr3650/4750. Both offer sleeping-bag accommodation in the schoolrooms for Ikr975 and in private rooms for Ikr1430. Both have restaurants, and there's also a small food shop at the *Esso station*. The grill-bar *Trítill* (☎ 486 1249) serves hamburgers, hot dogs and other snacks. The classier *Lindin* (☎ 486 1262), by the lake, specialises in pizza.

The *campground* is over the highway, about 400m north-east of the village. On summer weekends, this is a major Icelandic party venue – alcohol flows freely and duelling stereo systems become an integral part of the experience for everyone.

Getting There & Away Golden Circle tours pass Laugarvatn and will drop passengers there. Public buses on the Laugardalur route between Reykjavík and Gullfoss pass daily at 11 am (eastbound) and 5.45 pm (westbound). From Reykjavík, the fare is Ikr910.

Njáls Saga Country

Geographically, the valleys of Þórsmörk and Fljótsdalur form a transition zone between the country's richest agricultural area and the spectacular Fjallabak region. It encompasses green farmlands, scrubby forests, canyons and rugged glaciated peaks and valleys. To Icelanders, the region is known as Söguslóðum Njálu or *Njáls Saga* country. The plot and events of this saga are too complicated to describe in detail, but for a brief background for visiting the saga sites, see the boxed aside.

HVOLSVÖLLUR

This small service centre of 700 people is mainly a stop for tourists and travellers between Reykjavík and Þórsmörk or south-east Iceland. There's a swimming pool two blocks from the bus terminal. Horse rentals and tours through *Njáls Saga* country can be arranged with Saga-hestar (☎ 487 8138).

Bergþórshvoll

Bergþórshvoll ('Bergþór's knoll'), in the coastal region of low knolls and marshes known as Landeyjar ('land islands'), 20 km south of Hvolsvöllur, was the farm belonging to Njáll Þorgeirsson, hero of the *Njáls Saga*, and his wife, Bergþóra. It was, of course, the site where Njáll and his home and family were burned in the year 1011. The family was aware of the coming tragedy but, weary of the seemingly unending cycle of revenge killings, they submitted to their fate. Njáll, who didn't attempt to escape, asked his sons to remain indoors with him. Bergþóra stated that her husband's fate was also her own and some of the other women and children, whom the arsonists would have permitted to leave, also elected to remain.

The farm sits on a low hill above the surrounding fields. In 1951, archaeology revealed that a fire did destroy the building, and radio-carbon dating has since determined that it occurred in the 11th century. Unfortunately for saga fans, Bergþórshvoll isn't accessible by public transport, but there's not much to see anyway. Without a vehicle, the only access is by hitching or walking from Hvolsvöllur.

Places to Stay

The *Hótel Hvolsvöllur* (☎ 487 8187; fax 487 8391) charges Ikr3640/4745 for single/double rooms with shared facilities and Ikr7020 for doubles with shower. It also has a dining room and offers tourist information. Sleeping-bag accommodation is found at *Hvolsskóla* (☎ 487 8384) for Ikr900/1100 in eight/two-bed rooms. You can camp for Ikr450 per person.

Ásgarður (☎ 487 8367; fax 483 4467), just out of town, is made up as a tourist resort cum Viking-theme village. Made-up beds in double/dormitory rooms cost Ikr1900/1700 and sleeping-bag accommodation is Ikr1200. Four-person cottages are Ikr4900 per day and camping is Ikr400.

There's a camping available at the *Hlíðarendi Esso*.

Places to Eat

Most activity in Hvolsvöllur centres on the roadhouse-style *Hlíðarendi Esso*, which has a petrol station, grill, restaurant, supermarket, campground and bus terminal. Campers headed for Þórsmörk should pick up their last-minute supplies here. The *Shell* petrol station over the road also has a snack bar and is normally less chaotic.

Getting There & Away

Public transport to Hvolsvöllur is the same as to Selfoss or Hella. In the summer, the bus to Hvolsvöllur from Þórsmörk leaves the Húsadalur hut daily at 3.30 pm.

HVOLSVÖLLUR TO ÞÓRSMÖRK
Stóra Dimon

This monolithic mountain near the intersection of the old Ring Road and the Þórsmörk (Route 249) road was known in *Njáls Saga* as Rauðuskriður (the 'red scree'). It was the site of several events in the saga including reciprocal murdering of slaves by Bergþóra and Hallgerður and the ambush and murder of Þráinn Sigfússon by the sons of Njáll, including Skarpheðínn.

Gígjökull

The tortured mountains bordering the Markarfljót valley along Route 249 are characterised by rugged outcrops, deep gashes and high waterfalls. Along a small spur south of the main route, the steep glacier-tongue Gígjökull flows headlong into a small lagoon and fills it with calved icebergs. All eastbound Þórsmörk buses stop for about five minutes and the place resounds with creaking ice and clicking shutters.

Steinholtsjökull

Steinholtsjökull, which is a tongue of Eyjafjallajökull, flows into a small pond higher on the mountainside and is the source

of the short river Stakksholtsá, which has carved a sheer-sided 100m deep gorge, Stakksholtsgjá. From the road, the eastern fork of the canyon makes a spectacular two-hour return walk.

ÞÓRSMÖRK

The valley of Þórsmörk (the 'woods of Þór') is one of Iceland's most beautiful sites. Imagine a forested glacial valley full of flowers, braided rivers and clear streams surrounded by snowy peaks and glaciers and you'll have some idea of what awaits you. Since 1921, Þórsmörk has been protected by the Icelandic Forestry Department, but it certainly hasn't gone unnoticed.

On sunny summer weekends, Þórsmörk can be more crowded than central Reykjavík, most likely because a good proportion of central Reykjavík is in Þórsmörk. It's packed with tour buses, 4WD vehicles and hundreds of tents (on one weekend in 1996, the Reykjavík newspaper reported that 3000 people descended on the place). All-terrain vehicles play havoc with the landscape and no one goes walking in groups of less than 15. If you want to experience anything resembling solitude, go during the week or when it's raining.

Opportunities for hiking abound and one could easily spend a week exploring the area. There are lots of routes and tracks, but some of the most rewarding trips are cross-country, so carry topo sheets and a compass. The best maps are *Þórsmörk/Landmann-alaugar* 1:100,000 (1987) and the brochure entitled *Þórsmörk*, which is available from Ferðafélag Íslands for Ikr200 and shows most marked routes and tracks.

Valahnúkur

The summit of 458m high Valahnúkur, immediately west of Þórsmörk hut, is a popular climb from either Húsadalur or Þórsmörk hut. The view disc on top identifies all the mountains, valleys and glaciers within the far-ranging vista. At a leisurely pace, the round trip takes an hour from either side.

ICELAND

ICELAND

Húsadalur

Þórsmörk buses stop in Húsadalur, where there's a dormitory hut, a common hut and a kiosk operated by the Austurleið bus company. Access involves fording several large channels of the Markarfljót and should be done only in a 4WD vehicle.

On the hill behind the Húsadalur hut is the cave Sönghellir, from which a maze of walking tracks leads through scrubby birch forests to Þórsmörk hut, half an hour away.

The kiosk, which sells basic snacks, is open just a couple of hours a day. Campers are relegated to the designated site well away from the hut.

Goðaland

Goðaland ('land of the gods') encompasses the rugged area of eerie and bizarre hoodoo formations south and south-east of Básar, over the river Krossá from Þórsmörk.

There are lots of possible walking routes here, but the most popular leads from Básar hut to Fimmvörðuháls pass between

Njáls Saga

The story of Njáll has three parts. The first is the story of Gunnar Hámundarson of Hlíðarendi and his wife Hallgerður Longlegs, the daughter of Höskuldur Dalakollsson, a character in the *Laxdæla Saga*. The story began when Hallgerður had a quarrel with Bergþóra, the hot-tempered wife of saga hero Njáll Þorgeirsson of Bergþórshvoll, and the stage was set for the ultimate downfall of everyone involved.

Once the feud was well and truly under way, Hallgerður and Bergþóra took to murdering each other's slaves and employees. One of Hallgerður's victims was the foster-father of Njáll's three sons and one of those involved in the killing was Hallgerður's son-in-law, Þráinn Sigfússon. Moved to take revenge, Njáll's sons also became embroiled in the killing. Suspicion and ill-will escalated with the number of people involved and the killings became matters of vindictive malice rather than of family pride and honour.

After an emotional disagreement with a local farmer-merchant who refused to sell her produce, the obnoxious Hallgerður again flew into a rage and employed a slave to steal food from him. Trapped between his honour and his difficult wife, Gunnar grew angry and slapped her, then offered the farmer compensation for Hallgerður's foolishness.

The farmer eventually settled peaceably, but malcontents would not let the matter rest. Gunnar felt obliged to kill the farmer, an act which resulted in attempted revenge, further killing and Gunnar's being pronounced an outlaw. He planned to flee Iceland, but so great was his love of farm and country that he chose to remain and face his fate.

When a group led by the chieftain Gissur the White came looking for him at Hlíðarendi, Gunnar asked Hallgerður to give him a lock of her hair with which to repair his bow-string, so that he might have a chance against his attackers. She refused, recalling the time he'd insulted her by slapping her. Gunnar replied with one of the most oft-quoted lines in the sagas: 'To each his own way of earning renown...You shall not be asked again'. Although he fought bravely and wounded many, Gunnar finally fell.

The second part of the story is sometimes called *The Burning of Njáll*. Through all the turmoil, Njáll and Gunnar had managed to remain friends. Gunnar's death had been avenged by his son Högni and Skarphéðinn, Njáll's eldest and beefiest son. After a Viking spree on the mainland, two of Njáll's other sons, Grímur and Helgi, accompanied by Skarphéðinn and their brother-in-law Kári Sölmundarson, ambushed and murdered Þráinn Sigfússon, whom they held responsible for their foster-father's death and some incidents overseas that had endangered Grímur and Helgi.

In an effort to forestall further violence, Njáll fostered Þráinn's orphaned son, Höskuldur, taught him law and arranged a wife and a chieftaincy for him. The boy had a saintly disposition, however, and had no intention of joining the violence and bloodshed to avenge his father's death. But the evil Mörður Valgarðsson, who had incited trouble against Gunnar, now convinced Njáll's sons that Höskuldur would do just that. Of course, it wasn't long before Höskuldur was also dead.

Again Njáll was placed in a desperate situation but he chose to attempt a peaceable settlement. A chieftain of the widow's family, Flosi Þórðarson of Svínafell, was prepared to settle and be done with killing, but the settlement went wrong in a heated moment and Flosi himself was taunted into joining the violence. In a dramatic climax, Njáll and his sons, who were weary of all the craziness and bloodshed, allowed themselves to be burned to death in their home at Bergþórshvoll. The only survivor of the fire was Njáll's son-in-law Kári.

Eyjafjallajökull and Mýrdalsjökull. From Þórsmörk, the return walk to the pass can be done in a day. Alternatively, you can continue right over the pass and down past a series of superb waterfalls to the Ring Road at Skógar (see the following Skógar Hike section).

To reach Goðaland from the Þórsmörk hut, cross the pedestrian bridge, about one km downstream, then walk back upstream for two km along the southern bank of the Krossá. You can cross directly from

Þórsmörk to Básar in a high-clearance 4WD vehicle, but the water is fast and deep; exercise due caution and *never* try to cross on foot.

The travel agency Útivist (see Places to Stay), which owns the Básar and Fimmvörðuskáli huts, runs overnight hikes over the pass on weekends from 26 June to 9 October. Alternatively, it's wonderful to just spend a day wandering through the convoluted green peaks and valleys of Goðaland.

The anti-climactic third part of the saga involves an epic legal case, Kári's revenge for the Burning, the deaths of many of the arsonists and the ultimate reconciliation of Flosi and Kári. In the end, Kári was betrothed to Höskuldur's widow, Hildigunnur, to seal the settlement between the families. ■

Njáls Saga characters Gunnar & Hallgerður at the Alþing

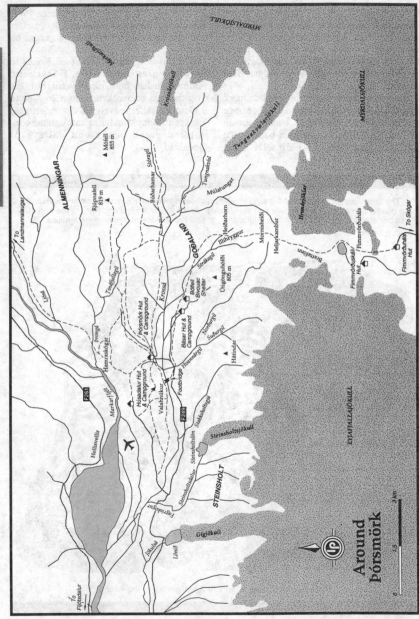

Around
Þórsmörk

Skógar Hike

Although the extraordinary hike over Fimmvörðuháls pass to Skógar can be done in a long day, most hikers prefer to break it up with a night in one of the two mountain huts near the pass.

The walk to Fimmvörðuháls begins about 1½ km east of the Básar hut (see under Goðaland). Look carefully; it starts climbing near a small bivouac hut, across a bridge to the left of the obvious road. From there, it climbs steadily to Mornisheiði, which affords great views of Mýrdalsjökull, Eyjafjallajökull and their attendant gorges and valley glaciers, as well as the rhyolite peaks of Landmannalaugar in the far distance!

At the southern end of Mornisheiði the track makes a small dip, then climbs steeply to the ridge Heljarkambar. You may appreciate a ski pole or some other aid for this climb. After that, the route levels out, crossing snowfields as it passes through Fimmvörðuháls pass with Mýrdalsjökull on the left and Eyjafjallajökull on the right. After passing to the right of a small lake, you'll see the Fimmvörðuskáli hut on the ridge ahead. For more on this hut and the smaller hut just beyond the pass, see Places to Stay later in this section.

From the pass, a rough track leads down to Skógar. Alternatively, you can turn right after crossing the footbridge (several km below the lower hut) and head downstream along the river. This scenic route, which eventually descends to the coastal plain at Skógafoss, passes numerous waterfalls and is much more interesting than following the road. This walk appears on the *Landmannalaugar-Þórsmörk* topographic sheet. Due to snow, the route is best from mid-July to early September, but you can ski at any time of year. For information on the popular Landmannalaugar-Þórsmörk trek, see the Fjallabak section of the Central Iceland chapter.

Places to Stay

Þórsmörk Area There are three huts in the Þórsmörk area – Þórsmörk, Básar and Húsadalur. For Icelanders, Þórsmörk is a place for partying and at weekends, staying at any of the huts becomes an exercise in endurance. They're normally packed to their ample capacities, and the alcohol and noise levels reach fever pitch.

All the huts have cooking facilities, but at weekends they're overtaxed, so it wouldn't hurt to bring your own stove. Guests must supply their own food and sleeping bags.

To book the *Þórsmörk hut* (and huts along the Landmannalaugar-Þórsmörk track), contact Ferðafélag Íslands (☎ 568 2533; fax 568 2535), at Mörkin 6, 108 Reykjavík. Club members/non-members pay Ikr750/1150 and hot showers are Ikr150/200.

To book *Básar hut* (or Fimmvörðuskáli hut – see the following section), contact Útivist (☎ 561 4330; fax 561 4606), Hallveigarstígur 1, Reykjavík. Básar costs Ikr600/1000 for members/non-members and hot showers are Ikr150/200.

For the *Húsadalur hut* or cabins, book through Austurleið (☎ 481 3717; fax 481 2710), in Hvolsvöllur. Beds cost Ikr1100 and the sauna is Ikr500 per half hour.

For environmental reasons, the grassy lawns and valleys around Þórsmörk are now closed to camping, but all three centres have designated *campsites* costing Ikr500 per person.

Fimmvörðuháls Pass The larger and more elegant of the two huts, *Fimmvörðuskáli* sits right on the crest with incredible views over both icecaps and down to the sea. Because it lies 600m west of the marked route, it's easy to miss in poor weather. Amenities include running water, cooking facilities, an indoor loo (although you'll wish it were outdoors!), an oil heater, blankets, comfy bunks and a large loft – shades of the Swiss Alps!

This 'palace in the wilderness' may be booked through Útivist. However, despite traditional mountain courtesies, they're happy to turn you away if a group is booked. For overnights, Útivist members pay Ikr550 and non-members pay Ikr1000, a bargain given the level of luxury. A stop for coffee or a warm-up costs Ikr100 per person.

About one km downhill on the Skógar side (at the end of the 4WD track), there's a dingy hut, used mainly by skiers, alpinists, 4WD motorists and tour groups visiting the icecaps in immense glacier buggies. It costs Ikr400 per person and no bookings are required.

Getting There & Away

Bus From 1 June to 15 September, the Þórsmörk bus leaves from BSÍ in Reykjavík daily at 8.30 am and arrives at Húsadalur around noon. It departs Húsadalur for Reykjavík at 3.30 pm. From Monday to Thursday, there's a second bus which departs from Þórsmörk at 8 am, and from Reykjavík at 5 pm arriving at 9 pm. The round-trip fare is Ikr4200 or three Highland Pass vouchers; with Omnibuspass, it's Ikr1500 or two Highland Pass vouchers.

Car & Motorcycle You may get to Básar with a normal car, but thanks to potentially hazardous river crossings, you need 4WD to reach Húsadalur or Þórsmörk huts.

Hiking You can walk from either Landmannalaugar (three or four days) or Skógar (one or two days). See under the Landmannalaugar to Þórsmörk Trek in the Central Iceland chapter.

FLJÓTSDALUR

Fljótsdalur, the heart of *Njáls Saga* country, is best known to travellers as the site of the cosy sod-farmhouse HI hostel (see Places to Stay).

Ten km north is 1462m Tindfjallajökull, a small icecap which can be reached on foot from the hostel.

Hlíðarendi

What remains of Hlíðarendi ('end of the slope'), the farm of Gunnar Hámundarson of *Njáls Saga* fame, lies 11 km west of Fljótsdalur. It's now abandoned and only some dilapidated ruins remain, but the setting is lovely and you can imagine the dismay Gunnar must have felt at the prospect of leaving it after being declared an outlaw.

Riding toward the river Markarfljót to leave his home forever, his horse stumbled and Gunnar turned to survey the scene:

How lovely are the hillsides, more lovely than they have ever seemed before, with their golden cornfields and new-mown hay. I am going home and will not go away.

It was, of course, a fatal decision for Gunnar, but he realised that and accepted his fate.

Places to Stay

The *HI hostel* (☎ 487 8498) offers a pristine setting for relaxation and the English warden keeps a library of books for guests who want to kick back. Advance booking is strongly advised, as this is the Iceland headquarters of Dick Phillips tours and is often occupied by groups. Other HI hostels in Iceland keep a listing of dates when Fljótsdalur is unavailable.

The nearby farm *Smáratún* (☎ 487 8471) provides single/double farmhouse accommodation for Ikr3000/4050 and sleeping-bag accommodation for Ikr1300.

Getting There & Away

Any bus between Reykjavík and South-East Iceland can drop you at Hvolsvöllur, from where you can either walk or hitch up Route 261 to Fljótsdalur. Buses from Reykjavík to Þórsmörk (Húsadalur) use Route 261 rather than the Ring Road and will stop at the Route 250 turn-off, nine km from Fljótsdalur hostel. Alternatively, you can get off at Hlíðarendi, have a look around, and walk the remaining 11 km to the hostel.

The only road route between Þórsmörk and Fljótsdalur is via the river Markarfljót bridges at Stóra Dimon.

The South Coast

ÞORLÁKSHÖFN

Þorlákshöfn, which has the only viable harbour facilities between Grindavík and Höfn, is an ordinary little fishing settlement of 1500 people in the Ölfus district southeast of Reykjavík. The town is named after its patron St Þorlákur who served as the bishop of Skálholt during the late 12th century. He was the only Icelander canonised by the Roman Catholic church and the new village church is named after him.

The small town museum and library (☎ 483 3990) is at Unubakki 4. As you enter the village, note the non-sculpture given a place of honour along the highway; it's a concrete jack used for shoring up wave-battered coastlines. Believe it or not, this thing actually features on the town crest.

Places to Stay & Eat

If you're lingering, Þorlákshöfn has a general store, bakery, supermarket and a *campground* (☎ 483 3631). The simple *Gistiheimilið Reykjabraut 19* (☎ 483 3630) offers single/double accommodation for Ikr2400/4030. The *Restaurant Duggan* (☎ 483 3915), Hafnarskeið 7, is open daily for breakfast, lunch and dinner. There's also a snack bar at the ferry terminal and a *Gallery Pizza* outlet.

Getting There & Away

Most visitors regard Þorlákshöfn as merely the ferry port for Vestmannaeyjar, and buses, which are all synchronised with the ferry timetable, connect it to Reykjavík and Hveragerði.

The three-hour sail between Þorlákshöfn and Vestmannaeyjar was once dreaded as a miserable corkscrew through sloppy seas, but the trip has been considerably improved by the new *Herjólfur*, which is three times bigger than the old one. The seas still get rough, however, and the queasy will want to take precautions.

The *Herjólfur* (☎ 483 3413; fax 483 3924) sails from Vestmannaeyjar (Heimaey) to the mainland at 8.15 am daily and from Þorlákshöfn at noon. On Friday and Sunday, there's a second departure at 3.30 pm from Heimaey and 7 pm from the mainland. In June and July, there's also a second ferry on Thursday. Passenger fares are Ikr1300, or

Ikr1100 with a student card or Omnibuspass. Vehicles under 4½ metres go for Ikr1300.

In early September, the *Herjólfur* sails to Norway for service and returns a month later (during its absence, it is replaced by a smaller vessel). See under Ferry in the introductory Getting There & Away chapter.

EYRARBAKKI

The wild, sandy coastline around Eyrarbakki is a beautiful place to observe bird life and the dramatic pounding of the surf on the broad beaches. Although its harbour is abysmal, Eyrarbakki was historically the greatest trading centre on the south coast, and some 530 people still make a living from the sea.

Things to See

Eyrarbakki's many old wooden buildings and quaint main street haven't changed much in the past century. The **church** dates back to 1890. **Húsið**, one of Iceland's oldest structures, was built in 1765 to house early Danish traders, and their clerks lived in the Assistentahús, just west of it. From 1917 to the early 1990s, it served as a friendly general store, run by Guðlaugur Pálsson. It now houses the **Árnes Regional Folk Museum** (☎ 482 2703), which is open daily, mid-June to late August, from 10 am to 6 pm. The seawall that shelters Húsið was originally constructed in 1799, in response to the same flood that ravaged Stokkseyri.

The museum **Sjóminjasafnið á Eyrarbakka** (☎ 483 1443) exhibits various nautical artefacts and the old Danish ship, the *Farsæll*. It's open from June to August, daily from 1 to 6 pm. A single Ikr200 ticket grants admission to both museums.

Other historical houses include the **bakery** (1884), the **blacksmith's forge** (1907), **Háeyri** (mid-19th century) and **Gunnar's House** (1913). The sculpture near the prison on the Lítli Hraun lava, east of town, is called *Krían* ('the Arctic tern').

Places to Stay & Eat

The *Ásheimar* (☎ 483 1120) guesthouse, housed in the historical guesthouse at

Eyrargata 36, charges Ikr3700/16,700 per night/week for a self-catering flat. There's also good beach camping but no official campground.

Kaffi Lefolii offers coffee, snacks and light meals in a pleasantly historical setting; it's open weekdays from 11 am to 11.30 pm and weekends from 11 am to 2 am. *Ás-Inn* at the Olís petrol station has a snack bar and is open later hours. Refreshments are also available at Háeyri, the old school.

Getting There & Away
All buses between Stokkseyri and Reykjavík pass through Eyrarbakki.

STOKKSEYRI
Stokkseyri, with 1500 people, occupies the 8000-year-old Þjórsá lava flow backed by a black driftwood-strewn beach. Despite its marginal harbour conditions, fishing is the economic mainstay. In response to the Básenda, or 'Great Flood' in 1799, a seawall was constructed west along the coast to the mouth of the Ölfusá lagoon.

An old fishing hut, Þuríðarbúð, which was named after Þuríður Einarsdóttir (1777-1863), the female captain of an old boat based there, has been converted into a small museum (☎ 483 1267). The village church dates from 1886.

Another museum is housed in an old creamery on the Baugsstaðir dairy farm (☎ 486 3369), at the Hróarholtslækur stream, 12 km east of town. It's open on weekends in July and August from 1 to 6 pm and at other times by appointment. Admission is Ikr100.

Places to Stay & Eat
For meals, the village has a general store, a *grill* at the Shell petrol station and there's the restaurant *Fjöruborðið* (☎ 483 1219). Accommodation is available at the self-catering guesthouse *Sæhvoll* (☎ 483 1284). There's no official campground but you can camp anywhere along the beach (above high-tide line).

Getting There & Away
Buses run between Reykjavík and Stokkseyri (Ikr680) at least three times daily in the summer.

SKÓGAR
Skógar, a small settlement just north of the Ring Road, is a summer resort that normally buzzes with tourism. Above the village are the white heights of the 1666m high glacier Eyjafjallajökull and its craggy green foothills. If you're lucky with the weather, Skógar is an ideal spot to relax and explore Iceland's extreme south.

The village has a bank, swimming pool and horse hire (☎ 487 8860).

Folk Museum
Don't miss the wonderful folk museum (☎ 487 8845), housed in several sod-roofed farmhouses as well as a modern building. It features extensive historical exhibits about life in southern Iceland. If you're lucky, the curator, Þórður Tómasson, will sing and play tunes on the farmhouse organ. It's open daily from 9 am to 6 pm from 1 May to 15 September and at other times by arrangement. Admission is Ikr200.

Skógafoss
About 500m west of Skógar thunders 60m Skógafoss, the lowest of over 20 waterfalls along the river route from Fimmvörðuháls. There's a legend that an early settler named Þrasi hid a chest of booty at Skógafoss, but it has never been found – and not for a lack of searching.

Fimmvörðuháls
Fimmvörðuháls, the broad pass between Eyjafjallajökull and Mýrdalsjökull (which was itself once covered in glacial ice) makes a great day-hike from Skógar. You can also continue north to Þórsmörk, a rewarding trip that is most comfortably made in two days, with a night at one of the two mountain huts at the pass. (see under Þórsmörk earlier in this chapter.)

The easiest but least interesting route to the pass is over the Skógarheiði 4WD road that leads to the lower hut. There's also a more scenic route up the east bank of the river, climbing from Skógafoss up past more than 20 impressive waterfalls. This track meets the 4WD road at a footbridge across the river; do not attempt to cross the river at any other point!

The round trip will take seven hours or so. A further hour of walking will take you to the edge of the Eyjafjallajökull icecap, but if you wish to explore further, prepare to stay at one of the huts or to camp. Keep in mind that there's snow year-round at the summit and visibility changes by the second. Don't venture onto the icecaps without a map, compass, supplies and some experience with glacier travel.

Places to Stay & Eat
The summer *Edda Hotel* (☎ 487 8870; fax 487 8858) has singles/doubles for Ikr3640/4745, as well as sleeping-bag accommodation in schoolrooms for Ikr975 and in rooms for Ikr1430. Nights at the *campground* are orchestrated by the calming roar of Skógafoss just 20m away. Camping at *Fossbúðin*, beside Skógafoss, costs Ikr350 per person and sleeping-bag accommodation is Ikr800/1300 on a mattress/bed. Meals are available at the hotel's licensed restaurant.

For information on huts, see Places to Stay under Þórsmörk.

Getting There & Away
All buses between Reykjavík and Höfn or Vík stop at the Edda Hotel in Skógar.

AROUND SKÓGAR
Drangshlíð
The farm *Drangshlíð* (☎ 487 8868; fax 487 8869), beneath the 478m mountain Drangshlíðarfjall, lies three km west of Skógar. The main interest is the large outcrop in the field (part of an extinct volcano) which contains caves now used as stables. Single/double farmhouse accommodation costs Ikr3000/4050 and sleeping-bag accommodation starts at Ikr850.

Seljavellir
Once a well-kept secret, the farm *Seljavellir* (☎ 487 8810) is a great place to settle in for hiking, mountain climbing or relaxing. There's a superb *campground* (Ikr200 per person), an outdoor swimming pool and a jacuzzi set in a rugged landscape beneath the 100 sq km Eyjafjallajökull icecap (beneath which lurks an active volcano which erupted in both 1612 and 1822). There's a natural hot pool about half an hour's walk up the valley from the campground.

Seljavellir lies three km north of the Ring Road. You can reach the turn-off on any bus between Reykjavík and Vík or Höfn. The farmers will pick up booked guests at the Ring Road.

Ásólfsskáli
The farm at Ásólfsskáli (☎ 487 8952) was originally settled by Ásólfur, the missionary who ended up resettling with his uncle at Akranes because he was driven out of the Eyjafjöll district. Wherever he went, the rivers filled with fish. His greedy neighbours were jealous and drove him away. Cosy six-person cottages start at Ikr37,000 per week.

Seljalandsfoss & Paradíshellir
The high and wispy falls, Seljalandsfoss, on the farm Seljaland is one of Iceland's most photographed images. Nearby to the north-west is unusual Gljúfurárfoss ('canyon river falls'), which tumbles from the same cliff into a wrap-around canyon; half of it is hidden from view. These two falls once lay along the Ring Road but a new causeway cuts off that bit of highway. Some scheduled Höfn-Reykjavík buses, however, turn off for a short photo stop at Seljalandsfoss while awaiting connections with the bus to/from Þórsmörk. Camping is available at the adjoining farm, Hamragarðar and there's self-catering sleeping-bag space at the community centre, *Heimaland* (☎ 487 8999).

West of Hamragarðar, near the farm Fit, is the cave Paradíshellir. Folk legends report that it was a hideout for the 16th-century outlaw Hjalti Magnússon. An easy track

ICELAND

leads from the sheep corral on the Ring Road.

Jökulsá á Sólheimassandur

This braided glacial river, flowing from the tongue of Sólheimajökull, is also known as Fúlilækur or 'stinking creek'. Due to the sulphur springs flowing into it, the water emits a rather unpleasant odour. It crosses the Ring Road 6½ km east of Skógar, from where the tongue of the glacier Sólheimajökull is plainly visible.

VÍK Í MÝRDAL

Although it's Iceland's rainiest spot, there's no denying that Vík, the country's southernmost village, is beautiful. The broad, sandy beaches of the south coast are punctuated by craggy cliffs and headlands teeming with bird life and pounded by high surf. Above the green hills rises the Mýrdalsjökull icecap, and beneath it snoozes Katla, one of Iceland's most notorious volcanoes. Its equally enchanting name means 'bay of the marshy valley'.

Vík began life as a fishing village. However, the poor harbour conditions meant that the fishing industry was abandoned early on, and in 1887, Vík received a trading charter. In 1906, a cooperative society was formed and remains the town's largest employer. It now has a population of around 500.

Information

The tourist office (☎ 487 1395) is at the Víkurskáli petrol station and bus stop. For souvenir shopping, check out the Katla Factory Outlet woollens shop.

Things to See

The lovely **church**, with its ideal setting, is normally locked up, but Vík's trademarks are offshore. The oft-photographed sea stacks of **Reynisdrangur** – Skessudrangar, Landdrangar and Langhamrar – dominate the view out to sea and their cliffs are squawking with avian activity. The highest rises 66m above the sea.

Organised Tours

Without a vehicle, seeing the sights around Vík will involve tours, long walks (mostly along roadways) or hitching.

BSÍ runs a 'South Shore Adventure' tour from Reykjavík that takes in Dyrhólaey and Sólheimajökull, as well as Eyrarbakki, Stokkseyri, Seljalandsfoss and Skógafoss. It operates on Monday, Wednesday, Friday and Sunday from June to September and costs Ikr5200 per person. The same tour is available on the same days from Reykjavík Excursions for Ikr5300.

Air sightseeing tours over the glaciers can be arranged through Reynisflug (☎ 487 1243; fax 487 1303), in Vík.

Places to Stay & Eat

The homely *Gistiheimilið Vík* (☎ 487 1230; fax 477 1418), Víkurbraut 24a, has single/double rooms for Ikr5200/7020. Sleeping-bag accommodation costs Ikr1200 and made-up beds in a separate cottage start at Ikr3965. Breakfast is Ikr720.

The more economical *Gistihús Ársalir* (☎ 487 1400) and coffee shop, Austurvegur 7, has single/double rooms for Ikr2665/3640 and sleeping-bag accommodation for Ikr1050.

The *Reynisbrekka Youth Hostel* (☎ 487 1106; fax 487 1303) is nine km out of town, but if you lack transport, the staff can fetch you from the bus stop. It's owned by south Iceland's only police officer, so don't be alarmed when you're picked up in the police car. The hostel charges the standard Ikr1000/1250 for HI members/non-members. Kerlingardalur ('witch valley') lies in the green hills above the hostel and provides super hiking opportunities; for routes, pick up the free map entitled *Gögukort – Höfdabrekka og Reynisbrekka*.

At the *Vík campground* (☎ 487 1210), in a pleasant location not far from the church, camping costs Ikr400 per person. Six-person farmhouse-style cottages rent for Ikr3650 per night and Ikr13,520 per week.

There are several farmhouse choices, all at standard farmhouse rates. Both *Sólheimahjáleiga* (☎ 487 1320; fax 487 1305), 23 km west of town, and *Brekka* (☎ 487 1420) offer single/double rooms and sleeping-bag accommodation, with cooking facilities.

Höfðabrekka (☎ 487 1208; fax 487 1218), five km east of Vík, has single/double rooms with shared facilities. It's reputedly haunted by Höfðabrekkujóka, the ghost of a former farmer's wife who came back to annoy the farmhand who got her daughter pregnant.

The *Víkurgrill* snack bar and *Ströndinn* restaurant are found at the Víkurskáli petrol station and bus terminal. The most excitement Vík ever sees unfolds here whenever a bus passes through. There's a *supermarket* on Víkurbraut.

Getting There & Away

Vík lies on the bus routes between Höfn and Reykjavík. Buses depart from Reykjavík at 8.30 am daily and Höfn at 9 am, passing eastbound through Vík at 12.15 pm and westbound at 3.15 pm. There's also another service which leaves Reykjavík at 5 pm from Monday to Friday, 1.30 pm Saturday and 8.30 pm Sunday; returning at 8 am Monday to Saturday. This bus does not travel east beyond Vík. The fare on either bus is Ikr1440.

Getting Around

Gistihùs Ársalir hires bicycles for Ikr1000 per day.

AROUND VÍK
Reynisfjall

When the weather cooperates, the abandoned Loran station atop 340m Reynisfjall, west of Vík, affords a magnificent view out to sea. The surrounding cliffs below provide nesting sites for thousands of sea birds, including puffins.

The long sandy peninsula west of Reynisfjall encloses a shallow lagoon, Dyrhólaós. When the waves aren't too high, the beach is great for camping (but there's no fresh water). Around Garðar, Iceland's southernmost farm, you'll find lots of caves, beaches and rock formations to explore.

Hjörleifshöfði

Prominent Hjörleifshöfði, rising from the sand flats south of the Ring Road, is named after Ingólfur Arnarson's blood brother, Hjörleifur. From Ingólfur's settlement at Reykjavík, Hjörleifur continued down the coast and established a farm near Vík. Shortly thereafter, however, he was murdered in a slave uprising. At the 221m summit stands a stone monument and some modern grave sites.

The headland once rose above the shore, but thanks to Katla jökulhlaups, three km of sandy beach and some rock pillars that were once sea stacks now stand between it and the water. South of Hjörleifshöfði is Kötlutangi, Iceland's southernmost point. Its cliffs are covered with nesting birds and behind the rescue hut on the seaward side is a large cave formed by wave action.

Dyrhólaey

This 120m spur of rock, cut into a natural arch by Atlantic breakers, stands in water deep enough to allow boats to pass through, hence the name ('door hill island'). In *Njáls Saga*, the hero's son-in-law Kári had his farm here. It's a prominent nesting site for eider ducks and Arctic terns, and a picturesque lighthouse stands on top. The offshore sea stacks are known as Háidrangur.

Without a vehicle or tour, you're in for a six km walk from Skeiðflötur farm on the Ring Road.

Laufskálavörður

The curious stone mounds along the rough desert stretch of Ring Road, from 35 to 45 km east of Vík, are cairns constructed by early travellers. They were intended not only to mark the track, but also to bring good luck, and by the looks of things, modern travellers have taken up the tradition. There should be lots of good luck floating around out there.

East of Laufskálavörður, note the contrast in vegetation between the grazed and ungrazed hillsides. Before the arrival of sheep, much of the non-forested landscape of Iceland looked like this.

Katla & Mýrdalsjökull

The 700 sq km glacier Mýrdalsjökull, Iceland's fourth largest icecap, rises to 1480m and reaches a thickness of over 1000m. The insidious volcano Katla ('cauldron'), which snoozes beneath Mýrdalsjökull just above the glacier spur Höfðabrekkujökull, is one of Iceland's most destructive volcanoes. When Katla boils over, as it has done 16 times since Settlement, it melts enough of the glacier above it to send a devastating wall of water, sand and tephra to wash away everything in its path. The liquid output of a Katla eruption has been estimated at a rate five times that of the Amazon – as much as 70 cubic km per second. The first recorded eruption was in 894, the last was in 1918 and another is expected this century.

For a close-up and personal view of Mýrdalsjökull, Geysir Snowmobile Expeditions operates one to six-hour summer glacier tours. The 12-hour tour from Reykjavík costs Ikr11,500, including six hours buzzing around the icecap. Contact Geysir Snjósleðaferðir (☎ 568 8888; fax 481 3102), Dugguvogur 10, 104 Reykjavík. BSÍ runs an abbreviated version of this tour for Ikr8500, including transport from Reykjavík and one hour on snowmobiles. It also runs winter and spring tours.

Hafursey & Mýrdalssandur

Like a green island, Hafursey rises 582m above the 700 sq km desert Mýrdalssandur. You can reach Hafursey via a 12 km jeep track leading north to its base from the Ring Road at Hjörleifshöfði.

The glacial sands of Mýrdalssandur were deposited by braided rivers and jökulhlaups generated by the volcano Katla beneath Mýrdalsjökull.

Álftaver

The Álftaver region lies between the Ring Road and the Kúðafljót river. Its 50 inhabitants have been able to remain because the Vellustrompur pseudocrater field shelters them from Katla's jökulhlaups. At the farm Þykkvabæjarklaustur, eight km east of the Ring Road on Route 211, a basalt monument commemorates the monastery which operated from 1168 until the Reformation in 1550. The current church was built in the 1800s.

This area is far from service centres, and can really only be explored in a private vehicle. You'll find basic accommodation at *Herjólfsstaðir* (☎ 487 1390), which has sleeping-bag accommodation for Ikr800.

Vestmannaeyjar

Vestmannaeyjar ('Westmen Islands') was named after the Irish slaves who unwittingly became their first inhabitants. Most of these islands were formed by submarine volcanoes between 10,000 and 5000 years ago, making them one of the world's youngest archipelagos. In 1963, the world witnessed the birth of its newest island, Surtsey, which kept spewing until 1967.

Most of the 16 islands are rocky and steep-sided affairs. Only Heimaey, the 'home island', with 5000 residents, supports a permanent human population. Other islands have only the temporary huts of puffin hunters and egg collectors.

The islands' economic mainstay is fishing, and although Heimaey accounts for less than 2% of Iceland's population, its fishing vessels supply 15% of the total national export. Both net boats and trawlers – 100 vessels in all – fish for halibut, cod, sole, haddock, ocean perch, lobster, herring, catfish and pollock in the islands' rich waters. Most of the catch is processed on Heimaey, but some is exported fresh to Europe.

History

The first Vestmannaeyjar volcanoes began erupting several hundred thousand years ago, but the new land didn't break the surface of the sea until perhaps 10,000 years ago. Heimaey was formed by the joining of several volcanoes about 5000 years ago in an eruption of Helgafell. Norðurklettur at the

Gullfoss waterfall, South Central Iceland

DEANNA SWANEY

DEANNA SWANEY

DEANNA SWANEY

Top: The móberg mountain Herðubreið, Central Iceland
Left: Jökulsárgljúfur canyon, North-East Iceland
Right: Jökultungur Ridge on Landmannalaugar-Þórsmörk trek, Central Iceland

Puffin Release

Puffin hunting is of major importance in Vestmannaeyjar, but an unwritten rule requires that only young or non-breeding puffins are to be taken. In the past, puffin down was used as a bedding material in the islands and the meat was a dietary staple, but it's now more of a delicacy.

In August, after the adult puffins have stopped feeding them, the juveniles, driven by hunger, leave their rocky nests in search of food. In Heimaey, thousands of the clumsy birds descend toward the lights of the town and land – sometimes, tragically, on the pavement or within range of ferocious cats. On such evenings, the children of Heimaey hurry around with cardboard boxes gathering up such unfortunate birds. They take them home and pamper them overnight, and next morning they carry them to the sea and fling them into the air. It's assumed the young birds are able to overcome the trauma of the whole experience and fend for themselves. ∎

north-western extreme of Heimaey is one, and east of it was a volcanic island comprised of Heimaklettur, Miðklettur and Ystiklettur. Another volcano, which erupted between 6000 and 5000 years ago, formed Stórhöfði.

According to the *Landnámabók*, Heimaey was first settled by five Irish slaves ('Westmen') belonging to Hjörleifur, blood-brother of Ingólfur Arnarson. After murdering their master near Vík, they fled to the rugged offshore islands, where they were certain no-one would pursue them. They were mistaken, however, and two weeks later they were tracked down and killed. The entire archipelago was named in their honour.

It is recorded that Vestmannaeyjar's first permanent settler was Herjólfur Barðursson, who settled in Herjólfsdalur on Heimaey. Although life was difficult on the rocky and

stormy island, it was more peaceful than on the feud-ridden mainland. A church was built in 1000 and the islands were placed under church jurisdiction. In 1413, however, an unscrupulous bishop presented the islands to the king of Norway as payment for outstanding debts.

In the following centuries, Heimaey became a sitting duck for any raiding party that happened by. First came the British privateers, who used Heimaey as their North Atlantic headquarters for over 100 years. They built fortifications and ruled by force until they were ousted by Danish traders in the mid-1500s.

In 1627, Heimaey was raided by Moroccan or Algerian pirates led by the Dutch renegade Jan Jantzen, who saw the undefended island as an easy target. Since there was little booty to be won, they murdered,

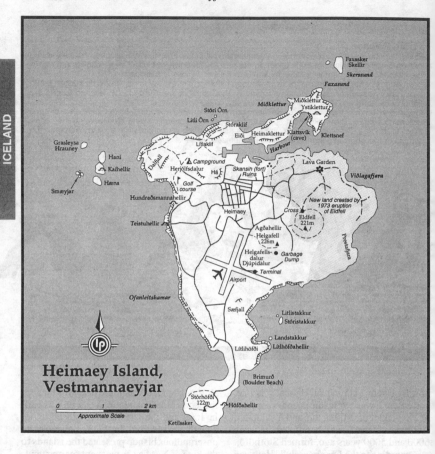

Heimaey Island,
Vestmannaeyjar

0   1   2 km
Approximate Scale

raped women and kidnapped 242 people, hoping to ransom them to the Danish king. Of those who didn't die from the strain, many women were sold as concubines and some of the men joined the pirate brigades. When the ransom was paid, only 13 people returned to Heimaey.

In the following years, disaster followed disaster. Heimaey experienced periodic shortages of fresh water, and that combined with the islanders' unbalanced diet of fish, eggs and sea birds brought on bouts of scurvy and dysentery. In 1783, a massive volcanic eruption on the mainland poisoned

the seawater and killed all the fish around Vestmannaeyjar.

At 2 am on 23 January 1973, the eastern slope of Helgafell exploded, and over the next five months, spewed out over 30 million tonnes of lava and tephra to create a new mountain, Eldfell. One third of the village was buried beneath the lava flow and the island grew by 15%. When you see Eldfell's proximity to the village, you can imagine how vulnerable residents must have felt. Overnight, Heimaey's 5000 inhabitants were evacuated to the mainland and, miraculously, there was only one fatality – a drug

ICELAND

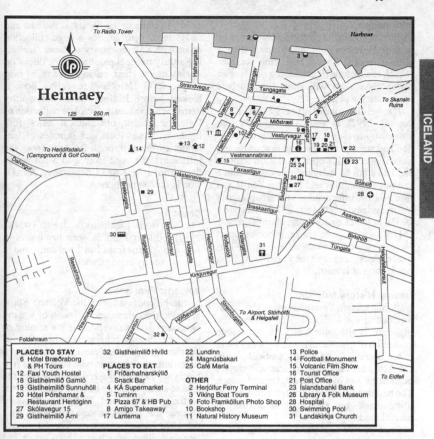

Heimaey

0   125   250 m

To Radio Tower

To Skansin Ruins

To Herjólfsdalur
(Campground & Golf Course)

To Airport, Stórhöfði
& Helgafell

To Eldfell

Harbour

PLACES TO STAY	PLACES TO EAT		OTHER		13 Police
6 Hótel Bræðraborg	32 Gistiheimilið Hvíld	22 Lundinn	2 Herjólfur Ferry Terminal		14 Football Monument
& PH Tours		24 Magnúsbakarí	3 Viking Boat Tours		15 Volcanic Film Show
12 Faxi Youth Hostel	PLACES TO EAT	25 Café María	9 Foto Framköllun Photo Shop		16 Tourist Office
18 Gistiheimilið Gamló	1 Friðarhafnarskýlíð		10 Bookshop		21 Post Office
19 Gistiheimilið Sunnuhóll	Snack Bar	OTHER	11 Natural History Museum		23 Íslandsbanki Bank
20 Hótel Þórshamar &	4 KÁ Supermarket				26 Library & Folk Museum
Restaurant Hertoginn	5 Turninn				28 Hospital
27 Skólavegur 15	7 Pizza 67 & HB Pub				30 Swimming Pool
29 Gistiheimilið Árni	8 Amigo Takeaway				31 Landakirkja Church
	17 Lantema				

addict who attempted to loot the pharmacy and died of smoke inhalation.

With the population safe, the most menacing problem was the lava's intrusion into the harbour – the steadily advancing flow threatened to seal it off and thereby devastate the island's economic mainstay. The hero of the day turned out to be the physicist Þórbjörn Sigurgeirsson, who suggested firefighters hose cold seawater onto the molten lava in order to slow its advance. No-one is certain whether the tactic worked or the lava, which halted just 175m short of closing off the harbour, simply ran out of steam. Whatever

the case, the harbour facilities were actually improved by the increased shelter gained from the flow.

HEIMAEY
The village of Heimaey, on the island of the same name, is characterised by brightly coloured roofs and spreads out across about a third of the island. It enjoys a spectacular setting, with the *klettur* (escarpments) rising abruptly behind the well-sheltered harbour on one side and the sibling hills – the steaming red Eldfell and the green Helgafell – on the other.

Information

Visitors normally allow themselves a day or two in Heimaey, but many wish they'd allowed more. If you have fine weather (which can include light rain, fog or overcast skies), three days will allow time to best appreciate the place.

The helpful tourist office (☎ 481 1271; fax 481 2792), at Vestmannabraut 38, can provide up-to-date accommodation information and steer you toward the best tours and sites of interest. It's open from 9 am to noon and 1 to 4 pm Monday to Friday, and from 1 to 4 pm on Saturday and Sunday. You'll also find tourist information at Ferðaþjónusta Vestmannaeyjar (☎ 481 2922; fax 481 2007), at Hotel Bræðraborg, Herjólfsgata 4.

Heimaey has two banks; a bookshop at Heiðarvegur 9, which sells English-language paperbacks; and the Foto Framköllun photo shop at Bárustígur 9.

Natural History Museum

Náttúrugripasafn Vestmannaeyja, which was founded in 1964, shouldn't be missed. The highlight is the aquarium with its unique collection of bizarre Icelandic fish; say hello to the friendly – and clearly sentient – jelly cat. Also check out the 'landscapes in stone', beautiful slices of polished agate and jasper. The best one has recently developed a disfiguring crack, but still suggests a magical natural landscape painting.

Once you've seen these items, the rest of the museum, which is one of the best in Iceland, seems anti-climactic – just the usual mineral samples and stuffed birds and fish. Note the bit of Surtsey lava on which Surtur apparently left his signature, and also the fossil clamshells from Tjörnes, which are encrusted with sugary orange crystals of silfurberg.

Admission, which keeps the fish in meals, is Ikr200. From 1 May to 15 September the museum is open daily from 11 am to 5 pm. The rest of the year it's open from 3 to 5 pm on weekends.

Folk Museum

The worthwhile Folk Museum (☎ 481 1194), upstairs in the library at the east end of Hásteinsvegur, houses a large collection of art with a Vestmannaeyjar theme, including a truly magical painting of the docks on a rainy night. There's also a nice relief map of pre-1973 Heimaey, revealing how it looked before Eldfell. Other noteworthy items include a nearly complete collection of Icelandic stamps, old nautical relics, folk implements and tools and samples of Icelandic currency through the ages (note the inflation!). It's open from 2 to 5 pm weekdays from 1 June to 15 September. Admission is Ikr200 per person.

Church

The old stone Landakirkja church (☎ 481 2916), built in 1780, is open to visitors in July and August from 1 to 2 pm daily, and at other times by arrangement.

Volcanic Film Show

Not to be confused with the Volcano Show in Reykjavík, Heimaey's version of steamy cinema provides diversion if it's raining or you've exhausted other possibilities. One of the two films, *Beyond the Limits*, is about a super-human fisherman who swam over five km in icy seas and walked barefoot over the lava to safety after his boat sank and the rest of the crew drowned. The other, *Days of Destruction*, covers salvage operations after the 1973 Eldfell eruptions. The 55-minute double feature, which is shown on an old 8mm projector, plays daily from 15 May to 30 September at 4 pm. In July and August there are additional showings at 1, 3 and 9 pm. Admission is Ikr500.

Eldfellshraun

The 1973 lava flow is now crisscrossed with a maze of hiking tracks. A particularly nice route will take you from the stairs on Kirkjuvegur, over the flow and down to the new black sand beach, past the restored Skansin fort. Continue east along the beach until you again hit the lava flow, then climb up to the harbour overlook. A walk along the road from here will take you to the unique lava garden, a lovely splash of flowery colour dotted with miniature buildings.

Eldfell & Helgafell

Look at a pre-1973 map or photograph of Heimaey and you'll scarcely recognise it. The island just wasn't the same without 221m Eldfell and its three sq km lava field, Eldfellshraun.

Eldfell is easily climbed by one of several routes; the easiest is through the northern entrance to the crater, where a cross was erected on 3 June 1993, to commemorate the 20th anniversary of the 1973 eruption. From there, a route leads up to the rim, and then east along the ridge. The summit bubbles with steaming vents and brilliantly coloured mineral deposits. In places, the ground is hot enough to melt the soles of your shoes! With difficulty, you can descend to the track which winds around the mountain's eastern slope, but it's extremely steep and crumbly; the best way down is the way you came.

The track down the west side of the crater ends at the foot of Helgafell (five metres higher than Eldfell), which was formed in an eruption 5000 years ago. On the southern slope of Helgafell is a foul-smelling garbage dump/landfill and the eastern slopes serve as a nesting site for irritable sea birds. To climb the mountain, the best route to the top is from the football pitch on the western slope.

Herjólfsdalur & the West Coast

The valley of Herjólfsdalur, the home of Vestmannaeyjar's first intentional settler, Herjólfur, is a green and grassy amphitheatre surrounded by the steep slopes of the extinct Norðurklettur volcano. Excavations have revealed remains of a 10th-century home assumed to have belonged to Herjólfur. Today, the valley is occupied by the campground and golf course. Between Heimaey village and Herjólfsdalur, don't miss the large football monument, which has no apparent purpose.

From Herjólfsdalur, you can follow the sheep tracks down the rugged west coast, which is indented with lava caves such as Hundraðsmannahellir and Teistuhellir.

Along the Ofanleitishamar cliffs, the sea makes so much noise that you can approach within three metres of puffins. The cliffs become increasingly higher as you move southward, then disappear at Stórhöfði, where islanders collect kelp.

Stórhöfði

Stórhöfði, the southernmost peninsula on Heimaey, appears to be an afterthought, tacked onto the main island by a low narrow isthmus. The lighthouse at the 122m summit affords a view across the island.

It's possible to scramble down to the boulder beach at Brimurð, on the east coast of the isthmus, and walk back towards Helgafell above the cliffs and the rolling surf that normally pounds that side of the island. From June to August, Lítlihöfði is a good place to see puffins.

Scrambles North of Heimaey

The nearly vertical slopes of the klettur escarpments can be negotiated with a bit of caution. It's a very challenging scramble from the *eiði* (isthmus) up to Heimaklettur and along the treacherous ridge to Miðklettur, but you can't reach Ystiklettur without technical equipment. What everyone wonders is how the sheep found their way to the top of Heimaklettur.

From the harbour, a steep track allows you to scramble to the Stóraklif radio tower on ropes, cables and ladders for the best view over the island. Looking down the rugged and inaccessible cliffs of the north-east coast, you'll see craggy sea stacks and thousands of nesting birds. (One spindly stack, which was once known as Cleopatra, has now been re-christened Marge Simpson!) On clear days, you can make out Surtsey to the south-west. Some maps show a route down the eastern slope of Stóraklif to the eiði, but it's only for the brave and nimble. From the radio tower, return to the large scree slope you climbed up and cross it. From there, with caution, it's possible to reach Dalfjall or even Stafsnses, but this isn't for the dizzy or faint-hearted.

ICELAND

Activities

Heimaey's swimming pool is open weekdays from 7 to 9 am and noon to 8.30 pm, and weekends from 9 am to 3.30 pm. The 18-hole golf course in Herjólfsdalur is reputedly one of the world's most unusual. A round costs just Ikr1500 and club hire is available.

Organised Tours

PH Tours (☎ 481 1515; fax 481 2007), at Hótel Bræðraborg, runs 1½ hour boat tours in the large boat *Viking* at 11 am and 4 pm. These tours take a novel approach, with a trumpet-tooting captain, some old seamen's rituals and exploration of bird cliffs and three sea caves. Trips cost Ikr1600. They may also be booked at Hótel Þórshamar. For full value, you may prefer the afternoon tours, since morning tours are constrained by the schedules of daytrippers from Reykjavík.

For sightseeing, sea-fishing and whale-watching from the boat *Lubba*, contact Ólafur Týr Guðjónsson (☎ 481 2333). Trips cost Ikr1200 per person for the first hour and Ikr800 for each additional hour (minimum four people), including fishing lines. Landings on some islands are possible.

Páll Helgason Travel (☎ 481 2922), Heiðarvegur 1, organises coach tours of Heimaey; there's normally at least one tour daily in the summer. Book directly or through Hótel Bræðraborg. Alternatively, phone Gisli Magnússon (☎ 481 1909), who operates good-value island tours.

Margo Renner (☎ & fax 481 2269) organises 2½ hour hiking tours through the lava, up the volcanoes and past the bird cliffs. Tours depart daily except Friday at 12.30 pm from the Vilberg bakery at Bárustígur 7. On Fridays in June and July, a midnight hike departs from the same place. Either tour costs Ikr700 per person, with a minimum of three people.

Special Events

The three-day Þjóðhátíð ('people's feast') is held over the first weekend in August to commemorate Iceland's first constitution, granted on 1 July 1874. Foul weather prevented Vestmannaeyjar people from joining the mainland celebration, so they held their own festival at home a month later. It has been an annual tradition ever since.

Festivities – an immense bonfire, music, singing, dancing and drinking – unwind in Herjólfsdalur, which fills with tents and barbecues, and even locals move outdoors for the event. It has been described as more a drunken orgy than a cultural festival, but if you're prepared for bacchanalian partying, it can be great fun. In recent years, however, admission has cost a rather formidable Ikr6500 per person.

Over Whitsunday weekend in May, the island hosts a three-day jazz festival and the Sjóstangaveiðimót, which is a deep-sea fishing competition.

On 3 June, the church organises a march up to the cross beneath the volcano Eldfell to pray and give thanks for being spared more damage in the 1973 eruptions. Everyone then retires to the Skansin to celebrate with music, singing and dancing.

Places to Stay

The popular Herjólfsdalur *campground* has hot showers and a warm-up hut with cooking facilities. Camping costs Ikr200 per tent with one person and Ikr200 for each additional person, including showers and use of laundry facilities.

The *Faxi Youth Hostel* (☎ 481 2915; fax 481 1497), Faxastígur 38, is open from 1 June to 15 September and costs Ikr1000/1250 for HI members/non-members. In July and August, it tends to fill up, so it's wise to book in advance.

Sleeping-bag accommodation with breakfast costs Ikr2000 at *Gistiheimilið Heimir* (☎ 481 1515; fax 481 2007), at Herjólfsgata 4 (look for the mural on the side). It also offers accommodation in private rooms for Ikr4700/6600 for single/double rooms with shared facilities or Ikr5900/8400 with bath, including breakfast. The associated *Hótel Bræðraborg*, in the same building, charges Ikr4290/6110 for single/double rooms with shared facilities and Ikr6300/8900 with a shower.

ICELAND

Wild Island Cuisine
In Vestmannaeyjar, puffins are considered a good feed, and gannets are also eaten, but outbreaks of psitticosis among the fulmars (and the birds' vile taste) exempts them from the stewpot. The eggs of sea birds, mostly guillemots and fulmars (both are larger than the eggs of domestic fowl), are gathered from the thousands of cliff-side nests with the help of practised rock-climbing and abseiling skills. Kelp, also prominent in the Vestmannaeyjar diet, is collected from the northern shore of the Stórhöfði peninsula on Heimaey. Rich in iron, the seaweed is a favourite of the islanders, who turn out at low tide to fill their net bags with slimy goodies. ■

The most upmarket choice is the *Hótel Þórshamar* (☎ 481 2900; fax 481 1696), Vestmannabraut 28, which charges Ikr5900/8400 for single/double rooms. Its subsidiary guesthouse, *Gistiheimilið Sunnuhöll* (☎ 481 2900; fax 481 1696), offers sleeping-bag accommodation for Ikr1300 and private single/double rooms for Ikr3100/4600 with shared facilities.

The recommended *Gistiheimilið Hvíld* (☎ 481 1230), Höfðavegur 16, offers good service and charges Ikr2000 per person for a room without bath. *Gistiheimilið Gamló* (☎ 481 1978) has a single room, a triple room, a house, and a holiday flat for up to five people. The charge is Ikr1500 per person, with a minimum of Ikr3000. *Gistiheimilið Árni*, near the swimming pool, charges Ikr2000 for made-up beds, with use of cooking facilities. You'll find sleeping-bag accommodation for just Ikr1000 at *Skólavegur 15* (☎ 481 2269).

The friendly *Gistiheimilið Einarshöfn* (☎ 481 3208), Kirkjuvegur 15, is run by Steina, an artist who spent many years in Australia. She offers made-up beds for Ikr1800.

Places to Eat
Heimaey now offers a wide choice of eateries. For quick snacks or early morning coffee, go to *Turninn* on Strandvegur. When

it opens at 7 am, it's the only light in town. At the harbour is the snack grill-bar *Fríðarhafnarskýlið*, whose name belies its size. The takeaway *Amigo* (☎ 481 2950) dishes up Chinese takeaways, as well as fast pizza, chicken and lamb dishes.

The informal *Café María* (☎ 481 3152), on Vestmannabraut, does coffee, snacks and light meals. It's open Monday to Thursday from noon to 11.30 pm and on Friday and Saturday from 10 am to 1 am.

The island's best pizzas are dished up at *Pizza 67* (☎ 481 1567), and the nearby *HB Pub* (☎ 481 1515) serves up pub meals featuring mainly good-value fish and meat dishes, but puffin (Ikr1600) is a speciality.

The pizzeria-pub *Lundinn* (☎ 481 1426), by the lava at Kirkjuvegur 21, serves up Vestmannaeyjar specialities including puffin – as the name would imply – as well as pizza, lamb and fresh fish. It's open until 10.30 pm. There are also dining rooms at the *Hótel Þórshamar* and *Hótel Bræðraborg*.

You'll find steaks and fish dishes at the more elegant *Hertoginn* (☎ 481 3317), on Vestmannabraut near the Hótel Þórshamar.

The town's most interesting and best value restaurant is the cosy Yugoslavian-run *Lanterna* (☎ 481 3393) at Bárustígur 11. Not only will you find pasta, pizza, salads, meat, fish, chicken, lobster and salmon dishes, you'll also get boscaiola, pleskavica, cevapi and other Balkan specialities. Meals cost from Ikr1000 to Ikr2500.

Heimaey's largest supermarket is the *KÁ*, on Strandvegur, and you'll find the peculiar-looking *Vöruval* supermarket on Vesturvegur, by the harbour. See *Magnúsbakarí*, Vestmannabraut 37, for baked goods, as well as coffee, tea and sweet snacks. Alcohol is sold at the State Monopoly shop at Strandvegur 50.

Entertainment
On weekends, the *HB Pub* and the *Lundinn* run popular live music programmes.

Getting There & Away
Air The Vestmannaeyjar airport is less than two km from Heimaey, so the Ikr300 airport

bus fare seems rather excessive and walking wouldn't be a bad idea. Even if you're not flying, it's worth peeking into the airport terminal to see the old photos and the antique plane hanging just above the floor.

The daily Flugleiðir (☎ 481 3300) and Íslandsflug (☎ 481 3050) flights from Reykjavík are quick and painless, and don't cost much more than twice the ferry fare (student card holders get a hefty discount). However, unpredictable weather may interrupt flight schedules, so phone the airline before traipsing out to the airport.

From 27 May to 1 September, Flugleiðir departs Reykjavík city airport at 7.20 am daily (8 am on Sunday). There are also daily flights at 1.30 and 6 pm (Saturday at noon and 4.30 pm). Daily except Saturday, there's a flight at 5 pm and on Tuesday, Thursday, Friday and Sunday, there's a late night flight at 10 pm. All flights return from Heimaey 45 minutes after departure from Reykjavík. Íslandsflug flies three times daily in the summer and is a bit cheaper than Flugleiðir.

More economical is Valur Andersen's friendly charter service, Flugfélag Vestmannaeyja (☎ 481 3255), in Hella. He offers charter flights to and from Vestmannaeyjar on request for Ikr2500 per person from Hella; Ikr2300 from Hvolsvöllur or Þórsmörk; Ikr2600 from Selfoss and Ikr1300 from Bakki airstrip, near the mouth of Markarfljót on the south coast. From any of these places, the flights work out cheaper than the bus/boat option via Þorlákshöfn.

Ferry The car ferry *Herjólfur* (☎ 481 2800; fax 481 2991) affords a spectacular arrival (if you aren't sick), sailing past the dramatic northern cliffs of the island and the sea caves just inside the harbour. For sailing times, see Þorlákshöfn earlier in this chapter.

Getting Around

Heimaey is small and the whole island can be comfortably visited on foot. Car hire is available from Bílaleiga Eyjabíll (☎ 481 1515), at Heiðarvegur 1. The rates are typically high, but the island is so small you won't build up much of a per-km charge. The Faxi HI Hostel hires mountain bikes for Ikr1000 per day. The local taxi service is Eyjataxi (☎ 481 2038).

SURTSEY

Surtsey, 18 km from Heimaey, was named for the Norse god Surtur, the one appointed to set fire to the earth the day the gods fall. Thanks to film, the world witnessed Surtsey's birth in 1963. Belching and spewing its way out of the sea, it sent a column of ash nearly 10,000m into the atmosphere – the plume could be seen as far away as Reykjavík.

Eruptions continued and, by 1967, Surtsey had reached a height of 150m and an area of three sq km. Although 30% of its area has eroded into the sea, the extremely high temperatures in the crater have fused the remaining material into more resistant rock. Scientists currently studying colonisation of volcanic islands have placed the island off-limits to visitors. You can get a vicarious view of Surtsey by watching the film *Birth of an Island* at the Volcano Show in Reykjavík.

Getting There & Away

Flugfélag Vestmannaeyja (see Getting There & Away under Heimaey) offers air sightseeing tours for Ikr2000 per person with a minimum of three people. From Reykjavík, two hour air tours are available from Leiguflug (☎ 552 8011) at the Reykjavík city airport.

The Westfjords

Extending claw-like toward Greenland and attached to the main island by a narrow isthmus, the Westfjords peninsula is Iceland's most rugged region. Geologically, it's also the oldest, a remnant of the basalt Thulean plateau heaved out of the sea 50 million years ago, forming a land bridge between Europe and Greenland. When it eroded and subsided, only small bits of land remained above sea level. One was this peninsula, which was subsequently flattened and carved by icecaps and glaciers into a convoluted coastline of 50 deep fjords and alternating steep headlands. The largest fjord, Ísafjarðardjúp, nearly splits the Westfjords into two unequal parts.

The central part of the peninsula consists of 700m-high rocky tundra plains, dotted with hundreds of ponds. The 176 sq km Drangajökull, the northernmost claw of the peninsula, is the region's only remaining icecap.

Most Westfjords people work in fishing and related industries. Thanks to the inhospitable landscape and the slackening fishing industry, the population is low and it's being further reduced by emigration. At present, the area has only 9700 inhabitants, 3500 of whom live in Ísafjörður. This represents the lowest population in the region since 1880, when Iceland had only 30% of its present population.

The Hornstrandir peninsula was abandoned in the 1950s and has now been set aside as a national monument. This wild and rugged area – with no formal accommodation – offers some challenging hiking routes, and several ferry pickups around its coastline. At the other end, Látrabjarg represents Iceland's westernmost point.

But travel in the Westfjords can be a convoluted affair. For the most part, the region's gravel highways follow the coast, winding energetically around fjords and headlands. In places, you must travel over 100 km to make 10 km of headway!

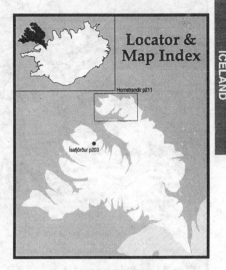

Locator & Map Index

Hornstrandir p211

Ísafjörður p203

ICELAND

Central Westfjords

ÍSAFJÖRÐUR

Ísafjörður, with 3500 people, is the commercial centre and largest settlement of the Westfjords. Formerly called 'Eyri' ('sandspit'), Ísafjörður gets my vote for the most impressively situated town in Iceland. It occupies a prominent spit surrounded on three sides by the calm waters of Skutulsfjörður ('harpoon fjord'), hemmed in by steep and towering peaks.

Despite Ísafjörður's growing reputation as a tourist destination, it probably won't see a real tourist invasion for some time. Access entails either a flight or a long bus ride over gravel roads through mountains.

History
The first inhabitants of the Skutulsfjörður

ICELAND

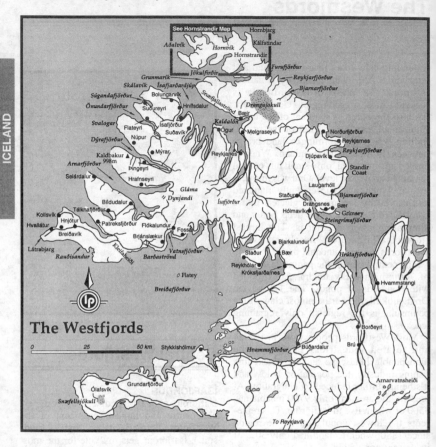

The Westfjords

0   25   50 km

area were Norwegian and Icelandic traders who set up temporary summer trading camps on the spit, transacted their business and moved on. In the 16th century, German and English firms established more permanent enterprises. There is mention of a Hanseatic League trading post on the spit as early as 1569. Under the Danish Trade Monopoly of 1602, the Danish usurped the old buildings and constructed new ones. Those still in existence are preserved at the Westfjords Maritime Museum.

In 1996, Isafjörður and the nearby villages of Suðureyri, Þingeyri and Flateyri amalga-mated into a single administrative unit called Ísafjarðarbær.

Information

Tourist Office The friendly Vesturfirðir tourist office (☎ 456 5121; fax 456 5122), housed in the restored 1781 building, Edinborgarhús, at Aðalstræti 7, is open Monday to Friday from 8 am to 2 pm and 4 to 6 pm and on weekends from 10 am to 2 pm. Plans for other rooms in Edinborgarhús include a café (with a view of Pöllin), a theatre and an arts complex.

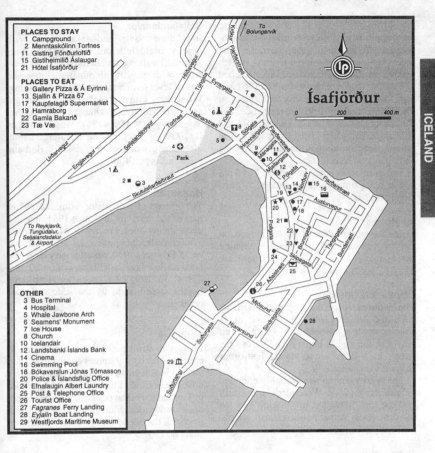

PLACES TO STAY
1 Campground
2 Menntaskólinn Torfnes
11 Gisting Fönðurloftið
15 Gistiheimilið Áslaugar
21 Hótel Ísafjörður

PLACES TO EAT
9 Gallery Pizza & Á Eyrinni
13 Sjallin & Pizza 67
17 Kaupfelagið Supermarket
19 Hamraborg
22 Gamla Bakarið
23 Tæ Væ

Ísafjörður

0   200   400 m

ICELAND

OTHER
3 Bus Terminal
4 Hospital
5 Whale Jawbone Arch
6 Seamens' Monument
7 Ice House
8 Church
10 Icelandair
12 Landsbanki Íslands Bank
14 Cinema
16 Swimming Pool
18 Bókaverslun Jónas Tómasson
20 Police & Íslandsflug Office
24 Efnalaugin Albert Laundry
25 Post & Telephone Office
26 Tourist Office
27 *Fagranes* Ferry Landing
28 *Eyjalin* Boat Landing
29 Westfjords Maritime Museum

Bookshops The Bókaverslun Jónas Tómasson on Hafnarstræti offers a wide and good-value selection of books and tourist publications – some in English or German – as well as maps, photocopies and Kodak film and processing. It's a good spot to pick up a couple of cheap reads.

Laundry For laundry services, go to Efnalaugin Albert at the corner of Póllgata and Skipagata. It's open Monday to Friday from 7 am to 6 pm. They need 24 hours to finish your washing.

Westfjords Maritime Museum
For rustic presentation, the Westfjords Maritime Museum (☎ 456 4418) is one of the finest in Iceland. It was originally suggested in 1939 by Barður G Tómasson, who thought the town should build a *sexæringar*, a six-oared sailing ship used for early transport. The ship *Ölver* was commissioned in the 1930s and completed in 1941 by retired boat builder and ship's captain Jóhann Bjarnason, who hailed from Bolungarvík. The rest of the museum grew up around it.

The museum originally occupied the swimming hall but, in 1988, it was shifted to the old trading houses at Neðstíkaupstaður, on the spit. It's full of wonderful old photographs and nautical paraphernalia. The oldest building is the log Tjöruhús, which was originally constructed in 1782. Attached to it is Krambuð, which was built in 1761 and used as a shop until early this century, when it was converted into a private residence. The Turnhús, originally used as a warehouse and fish-processing shed, dates from 1765. The other historic building is the Faktorshús, the shop manager's residence.

The museum is open daily from 1 to 5 pm and at other times by arrangement. Admission is Ikr200.

Ice House

Inside the eastern door of the Ice House, on Fjarðarstræti, are painted murals depicting the history of ice collection in Iceland. They're worth a quick look.

City Park & Church

The centrepiece of the city park, with its colourful flower garden, is an arch made from a whale's jawbone. It's getting a bit tatty, but the size is impressive. Across the street, in a large lawn, stands Ísafjörður seamen's memorial.

The nearby church was probably intended to call to mind a Westfjords mountain cascade, but it wound up looking like an old-time press camera with a flash attachment. It's definitely worth a look.

Tungudalur

The mouth of the Tungudalur valley begins about two km west of Ísafjörður. A further 30-minute walk from the highway will bring you to the Tunguskógar campground, a secluded retreat with waterfalls, birch trees and space for tents and caravans.

The peace, however, has been affected by the three-way tunnel, which now ushers traffic into Ísafjörður. Tungudalur also boasts a nine-hole golf course and two ski lifts, which were relocated from Seljalandsdalur after an especially bad avalanche season in 1995. The walk from town takes about an hour.

Seljalandsdalur

In summer, Seljalandsdalur, along with nearby Breiðafell and Heiðarfjall, offers super hill walking, and in the winter it's a ski resort with one lift, illuminated slopes and lots of level terrain for cross-country skiing. When there's no avalanche threat, overnight accommodation is available at the ski hut *Skíðheimar* (☎ 456 4136), which charges Ikr1000 for sleeping-bag accommodation, including use of cooking facilities. Bed and breakfast is Ikr1400.

Hnífsdalur

The village of Hnífsdalur, administered as part of the municipality since 1951, lies in a deep valley four km north of Ísafjörður. Winter avalanches pose a serious threat, and on 18 February 1910, a particularly large one crashed down on the village, killing 20 residents. In 1995, 13 precariously-placed homes were bought by the state and condemned.

Activities

Be sure to stroll past the swimming hall to check out the barmy statues out the front (and these things seem to be multiplying – there's now one in front of the museum and another in Tungudalur). The pool and its jacuzzis are open during odd and often-changing hours so check the notice on the door. Admission costs Ikr130.

Organised Tours

Vesturferðir (☎ 456 5111; fax 456 5185), or 'Westtours', offers a range of appealing excursions from Ísafjörður aboard the *Eyjalín*. Popular options include a four-hour cruise to Vigur (Ikr2900); three hours of sea-fishing (Ikr5500); town tours of Isafjörður and Bolungarvík (Ikr2800); a two-day Westfjords tour, including Látrabjarg (Ikr11,000); an amazing day tour to remote and spectacular Arnarfjörður (Ikr7500); and several one-day and multi-day excursions to Hornstrandir (see Hornstrandir later in this chapter).

Places to Stay

The *Hótel Ísafjörður* (☎ 456 4111; fax 456 4767), between Hafnarstræti and the shore, appropriately calls to mind a block of ice. Single/double rooms with bath and a buffet breakfast cost Ikr7700/9425. It also administers a subsidiary summer hotel, *Menntaskólinn Torfnes* (☎ 456 4485), at the school west of town. Singles/doubles with shared facilities cost Ikr4600/6600, including breakfast. Sleeping-bag accommodation in a schoolroom is Ikr900; in a room, it's Ikr1500. Fishing equipment is loaned free to guests.

Ísafjörður also has two guesthouses. At the generically-named *Gistiheimilið Áslaugar* (☎ 456 3868; fax 456 4075), Austurgata 7, single/double rooms without bath cost Ikr3200/4500 and sleeping-bag accommodation is Ikr1450/1900. The simpler *Gisting Fönðurloftið* (☎ 456 3659) at Mjallargata 5 charges Ikr1700 per person in made-up beds and Ikr1170 for sleeping-bag accommodation, with use of cooking facilities.

The town *campground* behind the summer hotel charges Ikr250 per person and Ikr250 per tent. Unfortunately, the toilet is inside the hotel, and at night, you must ring the bell and wait to be let in. The *Tunguskógar* campground, in Tungudalur, charges Ikr300/900 per tent/caravan and Ikr200 per person.

Places to Eat

The best quick eatery is *Pizza 67* (☎ 456 3367), which is attached to the *Sjallin* restaurant and café, at Hafnarstræti 12. Its direct competition is *Gallery Pizza* (☎ 456 5267), on the corner of Mánagata and Hafnarstræti, which serves up pizza, burgers, chicken and chips, spaghetti, sandwiches and other fast food in an 1884 house with a pleasant solarium. Around the corner is the more elegant *Á Eyrinni* (☎ 456 5267), serving complete meals in a formal dining room.

Believe it or not, Ísafjörður also boasts a new Thai restaurant, *Tæ Væ* (☎ 456 5499), at Aðalstræti 22b. It bills itself as the 'hungry man's friend', and is open Tuesday to Friday from 11.30 am to 8.30 pm and weekends from 2 to 8.30 pm (if you're hungry on Monday, you'll have to find another friend).

The *Hótel Ísafjörður* dining room is expensive but worth it, and the breakfast buffet is especially recommended. *Hamraborg* (☎ 456 3166), south of the hotel, is good for snacks and staples after hours.

The *Kaupfélagið Ísafirðinga* supermarket is at Austurvegur 2. *Gamla Bakariið*, on Hafnarstræti, opens early and does super pastries and baked goods. The State Monopoly shop at Aðalstræti 20 is open Monday to Friday from 10 am to 6 pm.

Entertainment

The cinema shows films several nights a week at 9 pm. Although Ísafjörður isn't known for its nightlife, on weekends you'd be hard-pressed to find someone who hasn't been participating in it. The pub *Krúsin* (☎ 456 3367), at Pizza 67, is open from Thursday to Saturday evenings. On Friday there's a disco and on Saturday there's live music until 3 am.

Getting There & Away

Air A flight into Ísafjörður's spectacularly-placed airport is unforgettable. Flugleiðir has three daily flights (two on Saturday) to and from Reykjavík, but they're dependent on the weather conditions. Íslandsflug flies at least once daily to and from Reykjavík and Flugfélag Norðurlands flies daily, except Saturday, to and from Akureyri.

Bus Iceland hasn't yet adopted tunnel-mania on a Faroese scale, but the dramatic – and slightly treacherous – mountain route into Ísafjörður from the south has now been replaced by a three-pronged tunnel which connects Ísafjörður with Önundarfjörður (Flateyri) and Súgandarfjörður (Suðureyri). The tunnel, which opened in late 1994, was closed for repairs in 1996, but will probably be operating by the time you read this.

Westfjords bus schedules are complicated because they're geared to coincide with bus tours and ferry schedules. The schedules described here apply in summer only.

From Reykjavík (Ikr4930), buses leave at

ICELAND

7 am on Monday, Wednesday, Friday and Saturday to connect with the 10 am *Baldur* ferry to Brjánslækur, which in turn connects with an Ísafjörður bus. From 6 July to 8 August, they leave Ísafjörður at 9 am daily, except Sunday, reaching Brjánslækur in time for the 1 pm ferry to Stykkishólmur, from where a Reykjavík bus leaves at 4 pm. From 14 June to 5 July and 9 to 31 August, that same service runs only on Tuesday, Thursday and Saturday. Ísafjörður-Brjánslækur buses (Ikr1630) also connect at 12.30 pm with a bus to Patreksfjörður and Breiðavík.

To avoid the Breiðafjörður ferry, you can take the bus from Reykjavík to Hólmavík (Ikr2900) on Sunday, Tuesday and Friday at 10 am, then continue to Ísafjörður (Ikr2600) along the serpentine Ísafjarðardjúp route. In the opposite direction, it leaves Ísafjörður on Sunday, Tuesday and Friday at 11.30 am and connects at Hólmavík with the Reykjavík bus at 4.30 pm.

To reach Akureyri from Ísafjörður (Ikr5570), you can either backtrack to Borgarnes or go to Hólmavík, connect with the Reykjavík bus to Brú, and there pick up the late bus to Akureyri. Miraculously, this also works in reverse.

Buses to Bolungarvík are described later in this chapter. Allrahanda Milli buses circulate several times daily along the route between Ísafjörður, Flateyri, Þingeyri and Suðureyri.

Getting Around

City buses operate Monday to Friday from 7 am to 7 pm and connect the town centre with the summer hotel, Tungudalur, Seljalandsdalur and – when there's a flight – the airport.

The Hótel Ísafjörður and the Summer Hotel hire out mountain bikes for Ikr200 per hour and Ikr1000 per day. This is ideal for trips to Bolungarvík or even toward Súðavík.

Taxis (☎ 456 3418) must be booked by phone.

BOLUNGARVÍK

Bolungarvík, only 15 km from Ísafjörður, is the Westfjords' second largest town with a population of 1500. With an impressive setting in a valley beneath high peaks, it's coming into its own as a day trip from Ísafjörður.

Ösvör

The *Landnámabók* records that Bolungarvík was originally settled by a woman named Þuríður Sundafyllir and her son Völusteinn. She earned her living by collecting a toll from fisherfolk who set out to sea from her farmstead, Ösvör. You can still see the boat landing and the ruins of a fishing station, which was restored in 1988 and turned into a free museum, Þuríðarbúð (☎ 456 7172). It conveys a good feeling for Westfjords life a century ago. From 1 June to 15 September, it's open weekdays from 8 am to 7 pm.

Hiking

The uninhabited coastal valley at Skálavík offers solitude and wilderness camping, 12 km from Bolungarvík along the jeep track leading north-west from the town. Alternatively, an eight km walk heads northwest from Bolungarvík along the Stígahlíð coast to a fine beach and picnic spot. This is a popular Sunday stroll.

The NATO Radar Base, on 636m Stigahlíð, makes a good day excursion and ends with a broad vista of both the sea and the highlands, but you enter this facility at your own risk.

Another possibility is the 16 km walk from Bolungarvík up the Syðridalur road to the Reiðhjallarvirkjun power plant, over Heiðarskarð pass, and down Hnífsdalur.

Several of these hikes appear on the brochure and map *Gönguleiðir í Nágrenni Bolungarvíkur*, which is distributed by the Ísafjörður tourist office.

Places to Stay & Eat

The good-value *Gistiheimilið Finnabær* (☎ 456 7254; fax 456 7234), at Vitastígur 1, has single/double rooms without bath for Ikr1500/2600, and sleeping-bag accommodation for Ikr900. The *Gestahúsið Jón Bakan* (☎ 456 7051), is in the centre of town at Aðalstræti 9. Single/double rooms with washbasins cost Ikr3000/4550 and sleeping-bag accommodation is Ikr650/1300 on a mattress/bed. Rates include use of the TV room and cooking facilities. The *campground* is between the Hólmá river and the swimming pool.

Fish & chips, pitta sandwiches, burgers, etc, are available at *Finnabær* (☎ 456 7254) on Vitastígur. There's also a snack bar and grill at the *Shell* petrol station.

Getting There & Away

In summer, buses leave Ísafjörður on weekdays at 10.30 am and 2 and 6 pm, and from Bolungarvík at 10 am and 1 and 5 pm, following a scenically precipitous route. The trip costs Ikr300.

SUÐUREYRI

The small and isolated fishing community of Suðureyri, on the 13km Súgandafjörður, developed in the 19th century around the farm Suðureyri at the foot of Mt Spillir. In 1899, when it counted only 11 inhabitants, it became a licensed trading place. The only site of interest in town is the grape-like monument to Icelandic 'poet from Pröm', Magnús Magnússon (no, not the Mastermind), who lived from 1873 to 1916.

At Staðardalur, near Mt Spillir, two km south-west of the village, is a church dating from 1886. At Botn, eight km up the fjord, several experimental salmon farms operate alongside a nature reserve with scrubby birch woods, fossilised plants and lignite deposits.

Places to Stay & Eat

The *Esso* (☎ 456 6262) petrol station has a snack bar and there's also a new *Gallery Pizza*. The *campground* is beside the football pitch.

Getting There & Away

From Ísafjörður, the Allrahanda Milli bus leaves at 8.45 am and 1.10 pm daily, arriving in Suðureyri at 12.30 and 5 pm. The trip to Ísafjörður takes only 40 minutes.

FLATEYRI

Flateyri, a fishing village of 400 people on Önundarfjörður, was licensed as a trading place in 1823, although trading had already ceased in the 18th century. In 1889, a Norwegian whaling station started operating at nearby Solbakki, but it burned down in 1901. At Hóll, at the head of the fjord, stands the chimney of another whaling enterprise from the same period, but this one never quite took off. There's a whale's pelvic bone in the town square and the church features some lovely stained glass work.

In late October 1995, as a prelude to a particularly harsh winter, a devastating avalanche rumbled into Flateyri, killing 20 people and destroying 17 homes. A small memorial museum (☎ 456 7773) in Hjarðardalur is open on request; admission is free.

Places to Stay & Eat

The *Vagninn Restaurant* (☎ 456 7751) and pub, Hafnarstræti 13, offers meals, snacks and mini-golf, while the *Esso* (☎ 456 7807) petrol station, at Ránargata 6, also has a snack bar. The six-person *Chalet Brynjukot* (☎ 456 7731), charges Ikr3320/16,700 per day/week. The *campground* is near the pool.

Getting There & Away

Íslandsflúg (☎ 456 7643) calls in at Flateyri daily, en route between Reykjavík and Ísafjörður.

The Allrahanda Milli bus (☎ 854 0085) leaves for Ísafjörður (Ikr440) at 8, 9.30 and 11 am, and 1.45 and 3.30 pm. From Ísafjörður, it runs at 8.45 am, and 1.20 and 4.30 pm. However, you need to book by phone or it may not stop.

ÞINGEYRI

This scenic village of 500 inhabitants was the first trading station in the Westfjords, and was the site of the local parliament mentioned in the *Gísla Saga*. Ruins are still visible at Valseyri, south of town. Þingeyri later became a service centre for Basque whalers and a fishing port for European and US boats. It's now dependent upon fishing.

Thanks to its dramatic peaks, the highlands of the Þingeyri peninsula in between Dýrafjörður and Arnarfjörður have been dubbed the 'North-Western Alps'. At the head of 39 km long Dýrafjörður is a nature reserve with fine campsites.

Sandfell

Sandfell, the 367m ridge behind Þingeyri, is accessible via a 4WD track which turns off Route 60 south of town. The steep climb makes a nice half-day hike directly from the village. Atop the ridge is a view disc and a radio tower.

Places to Stay

The official *campground*, with only basic facilities, is opposite the church. See also Núpur in the Around Þingeyri section.

Getting There & Away

Flugleiðir stops briefly at Þingeyri on Tuesdays, en route between Reykjavík and Ísafjörður.

Þingeyri lies just a km from the junction of Routes 60 and 622, along the Ísafjörður-Brjánslækur bus route. Allrahanda Milli buses from Ísafjörður (Ikr770) leave at 8.45 am and 1.10 pm, and return from Þingeyri at 10 am and 2.30 pm. This bus will continue to Núpur on request.

AROUND ÞINGEYRI

Haukadalur

Along Dýrafjörður, out along Route 622 from Þingeyri, is scenic Haukadalur, the site of events described in *Gísla Saga*. Beyond the end of the road, precarious tracks lead to the Ófæra bird cliffs and to the lighthouse at Svalvogar, 22 km from Þingeyri. There is no public transport.

Hrafnseyri

On Arnarfjörður across the pass from Þingeyri is Hrafnseyri, named for Hrafn Sveinsson, a local chieftain in the late 1100s and Iceland's first professional physician. The statesman Jón Sigurðsson, 'father of Icelandic independence', was born there on 17 June, 1811. Displays at the free museum (☎ 456 8260) at Hrafnseyri outline aspects

of his life. From 17 June to 1 September, it's open daily from 1 to 8 pm.

Gláma

The otherworldly Gláma moors, above the head of Dýrafjörður, were once covered in ice. If your destination is the summit of Sjónfrið, 920m above sea level, it's wise to camp at the head of the fjord. From there it's a long return day hike to the summit, for views across the entire Westfjords peninsula. A longer but easier route traverses the moors from the high pass between Hrafnseyri and Þingeyri. By either route, come prepared to camp in chilly and unpredictable weather.

Kaldbakur

The highest peak in the Westfjords, 998m Kaldbakur, lies in the rugged heart of the North-Western Alps and is best reached from the high pass between Hrafnseyri and Þingeyri. Prepare for a long and possibly snowy or rainy trek over rugged terrain. You'll need camping gear and footwear that can stand up to loose and unstable rock surfaces. Use the *Þingeyri* 1:100,000 (1989) topo sheet.

Núpur

At Mýrar, near Núpur, is the largest breeding ground for eider ducks in Iceland and possibly in the world. The *Edda Hotel* (☎ 456 8222; fax 456 8236) has a swimming pool and great hiking possibilities. Single/double rooms cost Ikr3640/4750 and sleeping-bag accommodation is Ikr1450.

On the remote northern shore of Dýrafjörður, 26 km by road from Þingeyri, is *Alviðra* (☎ 456 8229), with single/double rooms for Ikr3000/4030 and sleeping-bag accommodation for Ikr1300. Cooking facilities are available and six-person cottages start at Ikr33,550 per week.

On request, the Allrahanda Milli bus (☎ 854 0085) leaves Ísafjörður at 8.45 and 11.45 am and from the Edda Hotel at Núpur at 10.30 am and 3 pm.

Dynjandi

Sometimes known as Fjallfoss, the broad

waterfall Dynjandi plunges veil-like for 100m and below it, five smaller waterfalls carry the Dynjandi river into the sea at Arnarfjörður. They're protected in a nature reserve which lies just one km off Route 60. The easiest foot access to the top of the falls is downstream along the Dynjandi river from the highway, six km along Route 60 towards Flókalundur. Seen from across Borgarfjörður, Dynjandi is flanked by high rippled cliffs with the texture of a knitted jumper or a woven rug.

Buses between Brjánslækur and Ísafjörður take a 10 minute break at Dynjandi. For closer viewing, you can stay at the increasingly popular campground.

Nearby is the Mjólkárvirkjun ('milk river power plant') hydroelectric power station, named after the wild white water that drives it. Tours can be arranged on request.

ÍSAFJARÐARDJÚP

The largest of the Westfjords, 75-km-long Ísafjarðardjúp ('ice fjord deep') nearly bisects the Westfjords peninsula. The Ísafjörður tourist office operates daily boat tours along the fjord, including a visit to the island of Vigur.

Súðavík

The small fishing settlement of Súðavík, population 260, lies 22 km south-east of Ísafjörður by road. At Langeyri, two km to the south along Álftafjörður, is the remains of a Norwegian whaling station built in 1882 and operational until the 1900s.

On 16 January, 1995, a massive avalanche tumbled down the slopes, killing 14 people and destroying six homes. Many other homes were damaged and are now being replaced by quickly-constructed government housing.

There's an informal campsite near the swimming pool, and grill-snacks are available at the Shell petrol station. On Sunday, Tuesday and Friday, the Ísafjörður-Hólmavík buses pass through the village in either direction.

Vigur

The pretty little island of Vigur, at the mouth of Hestfjörður, is rich in bird life and contains a single farm. It boasts Iceland's only windmill as well as some antique farming paraphernalia. The Ísafjörður tourist office operates four-hour excursions to Vigur on the boat *Eyjalín* for Ikr2900, including refreshments. It leaves at 2 pm daily in the summer. Non-tour visitors need the farmer's permission to disembark or camp on the island – but the bird life is zealously guarded and permission is not readily granted.

Æðey

Æðey ('eider island'), east of Ísafjörður harbours one of Iceland's largest eider duck colonies. If you wish to disembark from the boat tour and camp or look around, ask the owner's permission through the Ísafjörður tourist office. It's generally easier to obtain permission to camp here than on Vigur.

Reykjanes

At the end of the brush-shaped peninsula between Reykjafjörður and Ísafjörður, 18 km off Route 60, is the friendly but well-weathered *Hótel Reykjanes* (☎ 456 4844; fax 456 4845). Housed in the district school, it offers meals and a naturally heated swimming pool. Single/double rooms cost Ikr3650/4750 and sleeping-bag accommodation costs Ikr1000/1450 in schoolrooms/private rooms. Camping is also available. From 1770 to 1790, salt was extracted from the hot springs here, but they're now used by the school to cultivate greenhouse vegetables.

Because Mjóifjörður is connected to Ísafjörður (not to be confused with the town of Ísafjörður) across its base by a mountain road, Reykjanes is not on public bus lines.

Ögur

The manor farm at Ögur, built around 1850, was once the largest farmhouse in Iceland. The church contains some ancient relics.

Vatnsfjörður

Vatnsfjörður, the site of a former church and

farm, was also the home of early saga-era chieftans. Later, it was converted into a residence and was inhabited alternately by church leaders and artists. Near the farm are sod ruins and some stone fish-drying racks built in the 1800s.

Snæfjallaströnd

The stretch of coast between Jökulfirðir and Kaldalón, Snæfjallaströnd ('snowy mountain coast'), was once inhabited as far as the cliffs of Bjarnarnúpur. In 1995, however, the last families left and it's now entirely abandoned. The beautiful green valley reaching inland from Bær, near the head of Kaldalón, allows straightforward access to a receding tongue of Drangajökull, the Westfjords' only icecap. With caution, you can explore its lower reaches, as well as the interesting exposed moraines.

If you're crossing to Hornstrandir on foot from Unaðsdalur, where there's a small church, be especially careful crossing the head of Leirufjörður. Inland, the six channels of the Jökulsá and Landá are dangerous, and the tidal flats can be very soggy.

Getting There & Away

Bus Buses between Ísafjörður and Hólmavík wind tryingly in and out of the fjords along Ísafjarðardjúp. Along this route, watch for the rare sea eagle, which occasionally makes an appearance.

Ferry The ferry *Fagranes* (☎ 456 3155; fax 456 4185) cruises through Ísafjarðardjúp at 8 am on Tuesday and Friday, stopping at Vigur and Æðey, and sometimes in Bær (Ikr850/1500 one-way/return to any of these). Other stops are by request only and are at the discretion of the captain. To Jökulfirðir, the fare is Ikr2000. For information on Hornstrandir trips, see Getting There & Away under Hornstrandir.

The ferry *Bliki* runs to Hesteyri, on Jökulfirðir, and to Grunnavík on request, from 15 June, on Sunday, Wednesday and Friday at 6 pm if there are at least four passengers. See the Ísafjörður tourist office for information and booking.

HORNSTRANDIR

The rugged 580 sq km wilderness peninsula of Hornstrandir, the northernmost bit of the Westfjords, was abandoned in the 1950s by its few residents because they found the isolation too trying. In 1975, the government created a national monument for recreation and the preservation of wildlife.

The Hornstrandir landscape takes in rugged headlands, sheer sea-cliffs, gently undulating uplands and glacial valleys. Vegetation is limited to grasses and small shrubs, but natural vegetation is gradually returning. Arctic foxes roam the highlands, seals lounge along the shorelines and whales are often observed offshore. Sea birds are abundant, predominantly along the northern coastal cliffs.

Hornstrandir's ominous location in the Greenland Sea, near the Arctic Circle, would suggest adverse weather conditions, and indeed, things can get nasty. However, most people visit the popular spots on the north coast, which are relatively sheltered from the prevailing south-westerly weather systems.

Access to the peninsula is by ferry or long walking routes from Norðurfjörður or Kaldalón, south-east of the reserve. From Norðurfjörður, allow at least a week to walk to the ferry pick-up at Hornvík. To reach Hornvík from Kaldalón, you'll need five or six days under optimum conditions. In years of heavy snow, some routes may not be passable.

Information

There are no tourist services anywhere on the peninsula. Farmstead remains are scattered around the valleys and there are 10 emergency huts dotted along the coast.

Hiking & Trekking

Although there has been discussion of building a hotel at Hornvík, there's not yet any formal accommodation in Hornstrandir and the area remains a wilderness. Warm, windproof and waterproof clothing is essential here at the doorstep of the Arctic and visitors

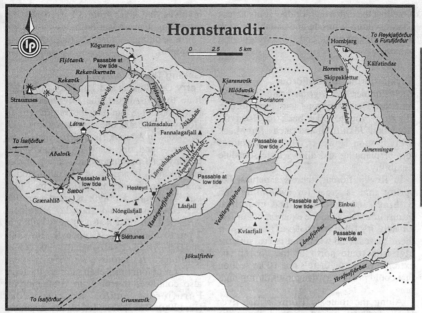

must be self-sufficient, with their own tent, sleeping bag, stove, fuel and food for their entire stay, taking unforeseen delays into consideration (should inclement weather delay the ferry pick-up, for example). Hikers also need a compass and Landmælingar Íslands' *Ramblers Map of Hornstrandir* 1:100,000. The map in this book offers some route suggestions, but is not sufficient for navigation.

Looking over the LÍ map, keen hikers are likely to be exhilarated by the number of possible routes it suggests. However, bear in mind that early in the season, many of the higher areas remain impassable or will prove very difficult due to deep snow. For extensive trips through the Hornstrandir interior, you'll need some experience with arduous snow conditions, even in mid-summer. Carrying a pair of crampons and an ice axe for negotiating steeper slopes is advisable.

Many of the Hornstrandir hiking routes cross tidal flats that are only negotiable at low tide. If your time is very limited, it may be handy to carry a tide table (available in Ísafjörður) and plan your trip accordingly.

Hornvík & Hornbjarg

At least 90% of Hornstrandir visitors go to Hornvík. The most popular walk is from the landing place and across the tidal flats to the lookout at Kálfatindar and on to the base of the famous horn of Hornbjarg. When you're crossing the high tide route at Skippaklettur, look for the rope placed there to help you across, and try to cross Hafnarós as far inland as possible.

Another good walk takes you west along the coast, past the basalt formations on Hornvík's western shore and up onto the cliffs for great views and a look at extensive sea-bird colonies. With more time, you can wander back towards Fljótavík or Aðalvík, where the ferry stops twice weekly, or cross over to Hesteyri in Jökulfirðir, along the easy routes from either Kjaransvík or Fljótavatn.

Note that the driftwood 'bridge' route across Kjaransvíkurá is unsafe and is liable to sink into the boggy muck under the weight of a person.

Reykjarfjörður & Furufjörður

Each summer, the *Fagranes* calls in several times at Reykjarfjörður and Furufjörður, allowing you to hike back to Hornvík, Aðalvík or Jökulfirðir and catch a ferry back to civilisation. However, this option requires lots of planning and allows little schedule flexibility.

In Reykjarfjörður, there's a natural hot spring that is great for swimming and bathing, and the abandoned church at Furufjörður has a unique exterior, but unfortunately, it's filled with bales of fibreglass. If there's a sea wind when you're crossing the high-tide route north of the church, be extremely careful; there's one 100m section that could prove very dangerous during high seas.

Along the route to Hornvík, the river Hrolleifsvíkurá is best climbed above the 200m level. Kyrskarð pass also has some steep sections, which are most comfortably done with an ice axe and crampons.

Organised Tours

If you're short of time, Vesturferðir in Ísafjörður runs quick day tours to Aðalvík, including a boat ride across Ísafjarðardjúp and a walk between Sæból and Hesteyri. The boat leaves at 9 am on Sunday and Wednesday from late June to early August and costs Ikr7500. For even more serious time constraints, there's a three-hour Jökulfirðir cruise (Ikr2500).

Longer hiking tours are also available. One is a four-day walk from Hornvík to Hesteyri which costs Ikr13,200 per person, including transport and guide. A three-day walk from Hesteyri to Aðalvík costs Ikr9900 per person. Both trips operate twice during the summer; neither includes meals. They also run hikers' transfers to Hesteyri by speedboat for Ikr2200 and five-day hiking tours to Reykjarfjörður (Ikr17,950), which

involves day hikes from a base camp and return flights from Ísafjörður.

For bookings, contact the tourist office in Ísafjörður.

Getting There & Away
Ferry On Monday and Thursday from mid-June to mid-August, the *Fagranes* leaves Ísafjörður at 8 am for the return trip to Hornvík (Ikr3500 one way or return) with two stops in Aðalvík (Ikr2250) – Sæbol and Látrar – and one each in Fljótavík and Hlöðuvík (if passengers are waiting or disembarking). It arrives at Hornvík around 2.30 pm and is back in Ísafjörður by 7 or 8 pm. Therefore, Hornvík is most crowded between Monday and Thursday afternoon. After 30 June, there's also a Friday sailing at 2 pm to Jökulfirðir – Grunnavík (Ikr2000) and Hesteyri (Ikr2000) – and Aðalvík, before returning to Ísafjörður.

Three or four times each summer, the ferry also continues overnight to Hrafnsfjörður, Furufjörður and/or Reykjarfjörður (Ikr4200). The latest details are available from the Ísafjörður tourist office.

If you're disembarking anywhere on Hornstrandir, let the captain know where and when you'll be re-embarking. Don't miss the boat, however; if you don't turn up at the specified time, authorities will be notified, causing an expensive search. If your schedule changes, pass a message through another (preferably trustworthy) hiker. If you prefer a more flexible itinerary, you'll have to finish your trip at an obligatory ferry stop, but you should still inform the tourist office of your intentions, so the alarm can be raised if you're not back in reasonable time. And don't forget to inform them when you do return safely!

South Coast

Not as scenic as the northern and western Westfjords, the south coast nevertheless gets a lot of tourist traffic. Thanks to complex bus schedules, nearly every Westfjords traveller passes through the bottlenecks at Brjáns-lækur and Flókalundur. There are no towns in the area.

The south coast fjords are typically shorter and shallower than their northern counter-parts, and the roads meander less. The landscape is also gentler, making for easier hiking, and timewise, it's much closer to Reykjavík.

Thanks to its south-westerly exposure, this side of the Westfjords catches much of the precipitation moving into the region. While the worst of it is normally blocked by Snæfellsnes, optimum conditions are rare.

REYKHÓLAR
The farming settlement of Reykhólar ('smoke hills') sits on a small peninsula encircled by hot springs. Historically, it was one of the Westfjords' richest farms. The Þörungaverksmiðja seaweed-processing factory operates near the shore and individ-uals can gather mussels and seaweed from the shore at low tide. Reykhólar has a geo-thermally heated swimming pool, Grettislaug, which is open from June to Sep-tember, 9 am to 10 pm.

Places to Stay & Eat
In the south-west corner of the peninsula, 10 km west of Reykhólar, is the farm *Staður* (☎ 456 7730), which has an old traditional church and views of Snæfellsnes across Breiðafjörður. Facilities are limited to a six-person cottage, which rents for Ikr37,100 per week. Phone from Reykhólar and someone will come to fetch you.

You can camp just about anywhere on the Reykhólar peninsula, but ask permission before camping on a farm.

Food services are limited to the restaurant, *Árnhóll* (☎ 434 7890), and a small shop.

Getting There & Away
In summer, buses run twice weekly between Reykjavík and Reykhólar (Ikr2950), via Króksfjarðarnes.

BJARKALUNDUR
The small service centre of Bjarkalundur offers rewarding hiking. The oddly-shaped and easily-climbed twin peaks of Vaðalfjöll rise six km to the north and make a great day hike, and rockhounds can poke around for quartz, jasper and zeolites. At the head of Djúpafjörður, west of Bjarkalundur, are the hot springs and steaming vents of the Djúpadalur geothermal field.

Places to Stay
The *Hótel Bjarkalundur* (☎ 434 7762; fax 434 7865) charges Ikr3380/4420 for single/double rooms and Ikr800/1250 for sleeping-bag accommodation on mat-tresses/beds. Camping is free. The rustic dining room serves up good country cooking.

Getting There & Away
In summer, there are buses from Reykjavík (Ikr2800) on Sunday, Tuesday and Thursday at 8 am. However, there's no bus between Bjarkalundur and Brjánslækur.

FLÓKALUNDUR
Around 860, Hrafnaflóki Vilgerðarson, for whom Flókalundur was named, climbed the mountain Lónfell and was clearly unim-pressed to gaze down on icebergs floating in the fjord. In that moment of disenchantment he named the country 'Iceland'. There's a monument to Hrafnaflóki beneath a small shelter on Route 62, one km from the inter-section with Route 63.

Flókalundur is a transport bottleneck between the *Baldur* ferry and buses to Breiðavík and Ísafjörður. If you're bored waiting for a bus, walk 200m to the intersec-tion of Routes 60 and 63 and see the curious stone pillar in the small gorge north of the bridge. Alternatively, diagonally opposite the hotel is a natural bathing pool and hot springs.

Inland, along the Ísafjörður road, is a mys-terious monument resembling a warrior from the New Guinea highlands. I first saw it in foggy drizzle and the appearance of a looming Melanesian face seemed rather incompatible with the Icelandic mist. In fact, it was constructed in 1947 by some bored

ICELAND

road workers with leftover materials and time on their hands!

Places to Stay & Eat

The summer *Hótel Flókalundur* (☎ 456 2011; fax 456 2050) on the abandoned farm Hella sits conveniently at the junction of the Patreksfjörður and Ísafjörður roads. The hotel is nice enough, but rather steep at Ikr5330/7540 for single/double rooms. The dining room offers palatable snacks, but is otherwise nothing special. The nearest camping is at Brjánslækur.

At *Fossá* (☎ 456 2000), 11 km east of Flókalundur, you can hire a six-person cottage for Ikr33,500 per week.

BRJÁNSLÆKUR

For travellers, the small farming centre of Brjánslækur is little more than a ferry terminal between Stykkishólmur, Flatey and the Westfjords. If you have some time there, look for Flókatóttir, the ruins of a hut believed to have been built by Hrafnaflóki Vilgerðarson in the 9th century. If that's the case, they're the oldest Norse ruins in Iceland. However, they're difficult to locate without a local guide.

Vatnsfjörður Reserve

The lake Vatnsdalsvatn, the centrepiece of Vatnsfjörður Nature Reserve, is a nesting site for harlequin ducks and both red-throated and great northern divers (loons). The cry of the diver is one of the most incredible sounds in nature, so it's worth listening for. It's a very pleasant eight km return hike along the eastern shore of the lake.

Surturbrandsgil

In the gorge Surturbrandsgil, above the Flókatóttir ruins, you can find fossilised plant leaves of species which are now found in lignite deposits in Florida and the Mediterranean area. To enter the gorge, you need a permit from the reserve office at Brjánslækur.

Places to Stay & Eat

The farm *Brjánslækur* (☎ 456 2011), on

Route 62, has a campground and sells trout-fishing permits for Vatnsdalsvatn and the Vatnsdalsá. The school *Birkimelur* (☎ 456 2006), west of Brjánslækur, has sleeping-bag accommodation for Ikr975. For meals, there's only the café and snack bar *Flakkarinn* (☎ 456 2020), opposite the ferry landing.

Getting There & Away

Bus schedules are timed to connect with the *Baldur* ferry, and few travellers linger in Brjánslækur. For ferry details, see Stykkishólmur in the West Central Iceland chapter.

From 14 June to 5 July and 9 to 31 August, buses run to Ísafjörður at 12.30 pm on Monday, Wednesday and Friday and to Breiðavík at the same time on Tuesday, Thursday and Saturday. From Ísafjörður to Brjánslækur, buses leave at 9 am on Tuesday, Thursday and Saturday; from Breiðavík, they depart at 9 am on Monday, Wednesday and Friday. From 6 July to 8 August, all these services run daily, except Sunday.

South-West Peninsula

The triton-shaped peninsula between Arnarfjörður and Breiðafjörður is rugged, wonderfully scenic and sparsely populated. Thanks to the guesthouse at Breiðavík, a growing number of travellers are visiting this westernmost bit of Europe and it's a high-light of many trips. The beaches are the finest in Iceland and, west of Patreksfjörður, off-shore sand deposits lend the water a lovely shade of 'Caribbean blue' – until you feel the water temperature, you'd swear this is a mis-placed corner of the tropics. This phenomenon continues all the way around the coast to Breiðavík.

The westernmost headlands are also dra-matic, with stunning cliffs, abundant bird and marine mammal life and fabulous hiking. It's also one of the best places to observe such rare species as the white-tailed sea eagle and the Icelandic gyrfalcon.

BÍLDUDALUR

Bíldudalur, a major supplier of shrimp and the home port of Iceland's first steam-powered fishing boat, has been a trading and fishing port since the 16th century.

Information

The tourist office (☎ 456 2165) at Hjartað, Dalbraut 13, is also a crafts shop specialising in natural materials, some by local artist Guðrún Einarsdóttir.

Selárdalur

North-west of Bíldudalur, on the Árnarfjörður road, is Selárdalur, the home of the fanatical 17th-century pastor Páll Björnsson. Although he was well educated, spoke many languages and was an accomplished mathematician, throughout his life he was convinced that the district was plagued by witches. When his wife complained that she was a victim of witchcraft, the good reverend had two neighbours burnt at the stake for alleged indiscretions.

Fossdalur Walk

A long but dramatic 15 km day hike will take you from the head of Fossfjörður and up Fossdalur across the plains of Fossheiði. You can either descend via the eastern slopes of Arnbýlisdalur to Tungamúli or further east, into Mórudalur along the Hóá and Mórá. A map of this hike is included in the brochure *Gönguleiðir á Barðaströnd*, which is available from the tourist office.

Places to Stay & Eat

The *Vegamót Guesthouse* (☎ 456 2232; fax 456 2144) has a petrol station, restaurant, snack bar and accommodation. Singles/doubles cost Ikr2470/4290 and sleeping-bag accommodation is Ikr1170. The village *supermarket* sells grocery staples and the *campground* is beside the football pitch. There's also a popular campsite 15 km away, at the Reykjafjörður swimming pool.

On the remotest shores of Árnarfjörður, 13 km west of Bíldudalur, the guesthouse *Grænahlíð* (☎ 456 2249) offers beds for Ikr1820, sleeping-bag accommodation for Ikr975 and a six-person house for Ikr3380/25,000 per day/week.

Getting There & Away

Íslandsflug (☎ 456 2151) flies daily to Bíldudalur, en route between Reykjavík and Ísafjörður.

There are daily buses from Patreksfjörður (Ikr600), via Talknafjörður. They run at 9.15 am on weekdays and 2 pm on weekends. From Bíldudalur, they leave at 10.45 am weekdays and 3.30 pm on weekends.

TÁLKNAFJÖRÐUR

Tálknafjörður, also known as Sveinseyri (population 360), has a great setting and offers a slice of remote, small-town Iceland. Five km north-west of Tálknafjörður is the Stóri-Laugardalur geothermal area.

Places to Stay & Eat

The small *Valhöll* (☎ 456 2599; fax 456 2666) guesthouse, by the shore, charges Ikr2150/2750 for a single/double with shared facilities and Ikr1170 for sleeping-bag accommodation. The *Skrúðhamar* (☎ 456 2631) charges Ikr2800/4150, for singles/doubles with breakfast. Sleeping-bag accommodation is also available at the *Grunnskólinn* (☎ 456 2649), just outside the village, for Ikr800. The *campground* (☎ 456 3639) is beside the swimming pool.

There's a snack bar at the *Esso Nesti* (☎ 456 2599) petrol station. The *Hópið* (☎ 456 2631) serves full meals and is recommended for its fish and steak specialities.

Entertainment

On weekends, the *Hópið* offers live music, dancing and drinking until 3 am. It's a great glimpse of nightlife in small-town Iceland.

Getting There & Away

On weekdays, the Patreksfjörður-Bíldudalur bus passes at 9.45 am northbound and 11.15 am southbound. On weekends, it passes at 2.30 pm/4 pm northbound/southbound. The fare to either place is Ikr300.

PATREKSFJÖRÐUR

Patreksfjörður, population 900, stands on a superb harbour formed by the two low sandy spits, Geirseyri and Vatneyri. The fjord – and subsequently the town – was named for St Patrick of Ireland, the spiritual guide of Örlygur Hrappson, the region's first settler. It has long been a trading place but only became a population centre this century. In 1983, a mudslide buried part of the town. The swimming pool is on Eyrargata and the cinema at Aðalstræti 27.

Information

The tourist information office (☎ 456 1411) is at the Vagga House, Aðalstræti 23. It's open daily from 1 to 6 pm.

Things to See

The **ancient walking route** that parallels the road over Kleifaheiði is well marked with cairns and yellow posts, and in clear weather it offers wonderful views. Above the town, on the Kleifaheiði road, you'll pass an odd **anthropomorphic monument**. It's similar to the one above Flókalundur, but has a stick through its nose and reportedly represents the foreman of the 1947 road crew that built it. Yes, it's another case of bored road workers with leftover time and materials.

On the southern shore of Patreksfjörður, a large **fishing boat** lies embedded in the beach sand. The accident that set it there involved the owner's desire for a new boat and an Icelandic regulation which limits fishing boats to one per person. The owner prefers to use it as a summer home rather than scrap metal, and keeps it in fine condition.

Places to Stay & Eat

At Aðalstræti 65 is the eight-bed *Youth Hostel Áfahús* (☎ 456 1280), in a nice old home by the shore. It charges Ikr1000/1250 for HI members/non-members. The boxy *Gistiheimilið Erla* (☎ 456 1227), at Urðargata 2, has made-up single/double rooms, with breakfast, for Ikr3200/5000 and sleeping-bag accommodation is Ikr1170.

For full meals, go to *Matborg* (☎ 456 1544), Eyrargata 6, which is open late and on weekends. At the reliable *Esso Patró* (☎ 456 1599) petrol station, you'll find brick-oven pizzas, as well as burgers, chicken, sandwiches and other light meals. *Nýja Bakariið* (☎ 456 1325) has a small coffee shop with outdoor seating.

Getting There & Away

The Patreksfjörður airstrip, across the fjord from the village, is set amid a beautiful field of sand dunes. Flugleiðir calls in here on Monday, Wednesday, Friday and Sunday, en route between Reykjavík and Ísafjörður.

From early July to early August, there are daily (except Sunday) buses to and from Brjánslækur (Ikr800), Breiðavík (Ikr500) and Ísafjörður (Ikr2200). From mid-June to early July and early to late August, they run on alternating days to/from Breiðavík and Ísafjörður.

LÁTRABJARG PENINSULA

Hnjótur

The worthwhile Egill Ólafsson Folk Museum (☎ 456 1590) is identified by the Norwegian Viking ship washed up outside. The ship was built in 1974 in Norway and presented to Iceland on the 1100th anniversary of Settlement. The other ship is the *Mummi*, Iceland's oldest steam-powered fishing boat, which was designed by the country's first maritime engineer, Bárður Tómasson. Other displays include examples and drawings of early implements and details of their function. Another section traces the history of aviation in Iceland.

The museum is open from 1 June to 15 September, 10 am to 7 pm daily and other times by arrangement. If it's locked, phone or ask around for the curator. Admission is Ikr200.

Places to Stay The *community centre* (☎ 456 1418) offers sleeping-bag accommodation for Ikr975.

Rauðisandur

Rauðisandur ('red sands'), a broad pink beach with pounding surf, lies south-west over the mountain from upper Patreks-fjörður. Access is difficult without a private vehicle and will probably entail a 15 km walk from the junction of Routes 612 and 614. But it's indisputably worth it, and on a fine day, it's absolutely idyllic.

If you read Icelandic, check out the novel *Svartfugl*, by Gunnar Gunnarson, which is based on a true tale of murder and deceit at Rauðisandur.

Places to Stay There are lots of great camp-sites and the farm *Melanes* (☎ 456 1594) has sleeping-bag accommodation for Ikr1050 and rooms for Ikr1365 per person. There's also a *campground* beside the lagoon, but with only basic facilities.

Breiðavík

Once a reform school, Breiðavík has now been converted into a fox farm and tourism complex. This remote restaurant and guest-house sits in a landscape of white sand, turquoise sea, crashing surf, green grass and dusky hills. If you can ignore the colour scheme and all the stuffed wildlife, the setting could hardly be better. Although the fox farm is a farm like any other, it's unsettling to realise that the baby foxes you're playing with are probably destined for dust collection in some wealthy closet.

Places to Stay & Eat The *Gistiheimilið Breiðavík* (☎ 456 1575; fax 456 1189) charges Ikr3000/4050 for single/double rooms and Ikr1300 for sleeping-bag accommodation, with use of cooking facilities. In the restaurant, you can get coffee at any time. Afternoon tea with coffee and pancakes is Ikr500, breakfast is Ikr700 and evening meals (normally fish) cost Ikr1300. On Sunday afternoon, the hostel offers a lavish all-you-can-eat buffet of puddings, cakes and snacks for Ikr850.

Kollsvík

To really escape the beaten path, spend a night or two at remote four-person guest-house *Stekkjamelar* (☎ 456 1573), on the lonely bay, Kollsvík. Beds cost Ikr1450 and

---

Déjà Vu

When the British trawler *Dhoon* foundered off Látrabjarg in 1947, the residents of nearby Hvallátur employed their expertise to haul 12 crew members to safety on the cliffs. So casual was the procedure that, halfway up, they fed the sailors warm soup to alleviate the chill before taking them to the top.

The following year a film crew, hoping to film a documentary about the rescue, set up a re-enactment of the scene. En route to Látrabjarg, however, they encountered a trawler that had run onto the rocks. Several of the crew had already perished and the others were in danger, so the villagers were obliged to repeat the previous year's rescue. It was captured on film and there was no need for a re-enactment! ■

---

sleeping-bag accommodation is Ikr975. Believe it or not, a tornado whirled through Kollsvík last century, smashing the buildings and killing their occupants. Access is only by private vehicle, but you can probably arrange to be picked up from Breiðavík.

Hvallátur

Between Breiðavík and Látrabjarg is the tiny farming settlement of Hvallátur which prides itself on being the westernmost inhabited place in Europe. On a sunny day, its golden, sandy beach is wonderful – and is sometimes used as an airstrip. Around the settlement are some old stone-and-sod ruins of buildings.

There's a small informal campsite on the beach, along the road, but you'll need to bring water, because surface water is normally unavailable.

Kóngshæð

The uplands north-east of Breiðavík are called Kóngshæð ('the king's head'), after the 'mountain king'. But don't look for Edvard Grieg's dancing cave-trolls; in the past, the name referred to the shepherd over-seeing the herding. This hill was the best vantage point for locating all the strays.

ICELAND

Látrabjarg

The Látrabjarg cliffs, which range from 40 to 511m high, extend for 12 km around the western end of the Westfjords. In fact, the Bjargtangi lighthouse is Europe's westernmost point.

On the cliffs are concentrated the densest population of bird life in Iceland, and historically, local people lowered themselves over the edge on ropes to retrieve sea birds' eggs right from the nests. Among the species that make up the screeching nesting colonies are razorbills (a third of the world's population), guillemots, cormorants, fulmars, ravens, gulls and kittiwakes. On calm days, you'll normally also see seals barking, lazing and flopping playfully on the rocks and in the waves around the lighthouse. Whales are often seen further out.

The puffins, however, are the main attraction. Like tuxedo-clad glitterati, they pose calmly for the paparazzi who edge ever closer to Europe's westernmost dropoff to capture their endearing little mugs on film. Visitors can often approach within a metre without so much as a flinch from the trusting little creatures.

Getting There & Away

From early July to early August, buses leave daily except Sunday from Ísafjörður (Ikr2650) and Brjánslækur (Ikr1630) for Breiðavík at 9 am and 12.30 pm, respectively. They leave from Breiðavík daily except Sunday at 9 am and connect with the *Baldur* ferry to Stykkishólmur and Ísafjörður buses at 12.30 pm. In June and most of August, buses run from Breiðavík on Tuesday, Thursday and Saturday, and from Ísafjörður on Monday, Wednesday and Friday.

From Breiðavík, the bus will continue to Látrabjarg (Ikr 220) on request, allowing two hours exploring on the cliffs before returning to Breiðavík. Otherwise, it's a 12 km walk from Breiðavík to the lighthouse at Látrabjarg. To see the highest cliffs, it's a 10 km walk from there to the southern shore, which requires an early start or overnight camping.

Strandir Coast

The east-facing Strandir coast, which extends over 150 km from Reykjarfjörður in the north to Brú in the south, is split into two equal parts by the 30 km long Steingríms-fjörður. South of the fjord, the land is characterised by low rolling hills and shallow grassy valleys. To the north, the coast grows steeper and more rugged, indented by deep fjords with a backdrop of snowy mountains.

The road and the bus lines only extend as far as Drangsnes, beyond which all exploration is by private vehicle or on foot. The country north of Hólmavík is one of the least visited parts of Iceland, and there are no tourist attractions to speak of and few amenities.

HÓLMAVÍK

The fishing village of Hólmavík (population 450), on the southern shore of Steingríms-fjörður, is the only Strandir settlement of any size. After it was established as a trading village in 1895, the population increased rapidly, but then began to decline, a trend which continues to the present day.

Things to See

Along the coast are lots of **fossils** in lignite. The church at **Staður**, 17 km north of Hólmavík, contains a pulpit dating back to 1731. If you have any doubts about Hólmavík's appeal as a tourist destination, note that the town is one of Iceland's greatest producers of **hákarl**; you can witness the process just south of the town.

A good short hike takes you about 1½ km north along the coast to Ós, then inland, across the Drangsnes road, up the hill Stakkar and down past the farm Kálfanes back to Hólmavík. A good four km hike leads from the Þverárvirkjun hydroelectric plant, up the Þverágljúfur and around the lake Þverávatn. At the Hótel Matthildur, you can pick up a copy of the hiking brochure

Gönguleiðir í Strandasýslu, which has maps of these and other hikes.

Places to Stay & Eat

The most popular accommodation is the *Hótel Matthildur* (☎ 451 3185; fax 451 3444), at Höfðagata 1, where single/double rooms cost Ikr2470/3900. Sleeping-bag accommodation is Ikr1170 and the dining room serves up acceptable meals. *Gistiheimilið Borgarbraut* (☎ 451 3136; fax 451 3403), at Borgarbraut 4, charges Ikr1700 per person and Ikr1100 for sleeping-bag accommodation. Cooking facilities are available. The official *campground* is beside the community centre.

At the *Félagsheimilið Broddanes* (☎ 451 3347), on Kollafjörður, 28 km south of Hólmavík, you'll find sleeping-bag accommodation in a delightful seaside setting for Ikr800.

There's a *cafeteria* and snack bar at the bus stop and petrol station in Hólmavík. The new *Café Riis* (☎ 451 3567), in a historic building dating from 1897, provides a town meeting place and is a welcome addition. What's more, the pizza and full meals are excellent.

Getting There & Away

Hólmavík is served by Íslandsflug (☎ 451 3167), Vitabraut 1, by air from Reykjavík on Monday and Thursday.

As for land transport, Hólmavík is a hub for connections between Ísafjörður and Reykjavík or Akureyri. In summer, buses run from Reykjavík (Ikr2900), via Brú, on Sunday, Tuesday and Friday, with continuing service to Drangsnes (Ikr400) on Friday only. From Hólmavík, they return to Reykjavík at 4.30 pm, and at Brú (Ikr1080), connect with the late bus to Akureyri (Ikr1820). All these services connect at Hólmavík with buses to and from Ísafjörður (Ikr2600).

DRANGSNES

Drangsnes, at the southern end of the Drangsnes peninsula, guards the northern entrance to Steingrímsfjörður. There's nothing to attract visitors but a sense of remoteness; there's not even a campground.

Places to Stay & Eat

Three km from Drangsnes is the farm *Bær* (☎ 451 3241; fax 451 3274), with single/double rooms for Ikr3000/4050 and sleeping-bag accommodation for Ikr1300. The uninhabited offshore island of Grímsey offers great hiking and a large puffin colony; the farm can arrange transport.

The geothermal resort *Laugarhóll* (☎ 451 3380) on Bjarnarfjörður, 19 km north of Drangsnes, includes a hotel with a dining room and sleeping-bag accommodation, a campground and a naturally heated pool. Rooms cost Ikr1820 per person and sleeping-bag accommodation is Ikr800/1100 on mattresses/beds. They can also organise hikes and boat trips.

You'll find supplies at the small *cooperative supermarket*.

Getting There & Away

The Friday buses from Reykjavík continue from Hólmavík to Drangsnes (Ikr400), returning at 7.45 am Saturday. No buses run north of Drangsnes, so you need a vehicle to reach Laugarhóll.

DJÚPAVÍK

The former herring-processing village of Djúpavík, which operated in the 1930s, is a quiet and rather unkempt place set beneath a rimrock ridge. It's now nearly abandoned and the annual number of foreign visitors could probably be counted on fingers and toes. If you like things that way, the *Hótel Djúpavík* (☎ 451 4037; fax 451 4035) offers single/double accommodation for Ikr3510/4550. The restaurant is recommended for hearty and down-to-earth meals.

At present, there's no public transport to Djúpavík.

NORÐURFJÖRÐUR

Norðurfjörður may enjoy a spectacular setting, but it's only visited as an access point for ambitious overland treks to Hornstrandir.

ICELAND

There's no specified campsite, but the village shop allows campers to use its public facilities. At Krossnes, east of Norðurfjörður, is a geothermally heated swimming pool. A lovely hike begins at the farm Árnes, on Norðurfjörður, and crosses the Reykjarnes peninsula, via Göngumannaskarð pass, to Naustavík, on Reykjarfjörður.

There's no public transport to Norðurfjörður.

North Central Iceland

North Central Iceland consists of three rugged peninsulas jutting into the Arctic Ocean, separated by bays and braided river deltas, and punctuated by rather unremarkable fjords. Most travellers between Reykjavík and Akureyri consider it a region to be passed through quickly. Since there's little of interest along the bus routes, and to reach the best of North Central Iceland requires time to abandon the main highways, those who are short on time may want to employ the same reasoning. However, tourists are refreshingly thin on the ground and the region is specked with some truly spectacular sites – from wildlife-rich Vatnsnes to historic Hólar, the lonely islands and headlands of Skagafjörður and especially, the enchanting town of Siglufjörður.

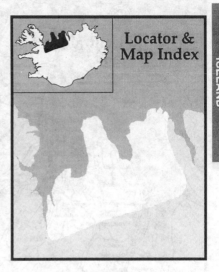

Locator & Map Index

Eastern Húnaflói

HRÚTAFJÖRÐUR

Hrútafjörður, the long narrow fjord extending south from Húnaflói ('bear bay' – after the many Greenland bears that have come ashore there), is surrounded by low, treeless hills. However, it's a nesting site for wild swans, ptarmigan, divers and golden plovers, and birdwatchers will be in their element.

Brú

This tiny junction, at the southern end of Hrútafjörður, acts mainly as a connection point for buses between Reykjavík, Akureyri and Hólmavík. Connections are generally good and you probably won't be kept waiting more than an hour.

The name means 'bridge' and that fairly sums up the extent of the place. There's the shiny new Brúarskáli petrol station restaurant and a post & telephone office (which

was shifted from dwindling Borðeyri in 1950), but scarcely anyone lives at Brú.

Staðarskáli

The motto of this snack bar-cum-restaurant, guesthouse, tourist office and petrol station used to be: 'Everyone stops at Staðarskáli'. But, since the nicer Brúarskáli opened at nearby Brú, the motto has now been commuted to: 'Most everyone drops in on Staðarskáli'. They no longer give away post cards of the petrol pumps, but it's still pretty tacky as Icelandic petrol stations go. All buses between Akureyri and Reykjavík stop here for half an hour, so lots of those dropping in don't really have much choice.

There are a couple of interesting things to do. One is a two-day return hike to Hrútafjarðarháls, the highlands south-east of Staðarskáli, to see Iceland's largest colony of great northern divers. The other is a two-day hike to Hveraborgir hot springs. In winter,

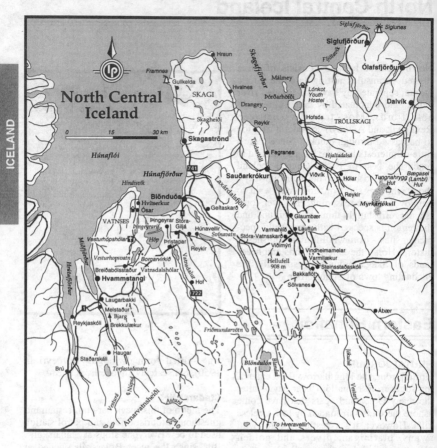

Staðarskáli organises two-day ice-fishing (Ikr6700) and snowmobile tours (Ikr8900).

Places to Stay *Staðarskáli* (☎ 451 1150; fax 451 1107) has a campground, a summer cottage, and a small guesthouse charging Ikr3185/4485 for single/double rooms without bath. The six-person summer cottage costs Ikr4355 per night. Bicycles are hired for Ikr1000 per day.

Reykjaskóli & Reykjatunga Museum
The district school on Hrútafjörður, which sits in an active geothermal field, has become

an unpretentious summer resort. The folk museum (☎ 451 0040) at Reykjaskóli displays an array of household and agricultural implements from early Iceland, with an emphasis on the local black magic practised in early medieval times. Note the well reconstructed interior of a 19th century homestead and the old shark-fishing boat *Ófeigur*. It's open daily, 1 June to 31 August, from 10 am to 7 pm, and other times by prior arrangement. Admission is Ikr200.

Places to Stay A stay at the *Sæberg Youth Hostel* (☎ 451 0015; fax 451 0034) will nicely break up the trip between Reykjavík and Akureyri, but bring your own groceries, as there's nothing available on site. Beds cost Ikr1000/1250 for HI member/non-members and camping costs Ikr325 per person.

The *Reykjaskóli Edda Hotel* (☎ 451 0004; fax 451 0044) has a geothermally heated pool and a licensed restaurant. Single/double rooms cost Ikr3650/4750, and sleeping-bag accommodation in the classrooms/rooms costs Ikr850/1300. However, there are no cooking facilities.

HVAMMSTANGI

Nondescript Hvammstangi (population 690), on the eastern shore of Miðfjörður, has been a licensed trading centre since 1895, but its current economy is based on shrimp and mollusc fishing. Unfortunately Hvammstangi lies six km off the Ring Road, so almost anything that could liven it up simply whizzes past. The area, however, does hold some interest.

Places to Stay & Eat

The *Hótel Selið* (☎ 451 2717) has singles/doubles for Ikr5400/7160, and guests receive a free pass to the swimming pool. Meal services are limited to the hotel restaurant and bar.

The *campground* is at Kirkjuhvammur, just north-east of town. The rocky hill Káraborg, just behind it, affords a wonderful view.

Farmhouse and sleeping-bag accommodation are available at *Melstaður* (☎ 451 2944; fax 451 2955), 13 km south of Hvammstangi. Single/double rooms cost Ikr3250/4550 and sleeping-bag accommodation is Ikr1300. Bicycles are available to guests. Also check out nearby Álfhóll, a hillock believed to be inhabited by elves.

Getting There & Away

Buses between Reykjavík and Akureyri will drive into Hvammstangi on request.

AROUND HVAMMSTANGI
Torfastaðavatn

Good trout fishing is relatively inexpensive at the lake Torfastaðavatn, west of Route 706 about 30 km south of Hvammstangi. Pick up permits from the farm Haugar (Ikr800/1300 per half-day/day), near the lake. Around the lake are plenty of decent campsites.

Bjarg

En route to Torfastaðavatn sits Bjarg, the farm that belonged to Ásdis, the mother of outlaw Grettir Ásmundarson ('Grettir the Strong') of *Grettis Saga* fame. Beneath a rock in the hayfield, Ásdis buried Grettir's head, which was presented to her by the killer. There's now a monument in her honour.

Laugarbakki

The *Edda Hotel Laugarbakki* (☎ 451 2904; fax 451 2801), near the junction of the Ring Road and the Hvammstangi road, has a geothermal pool and a licensed restaurant. Single/double rooms cost Ikr3650/4750 and sleeping-bag accommodation is Ikr1000/1430 in schoolrooms/rooms. The hotel can organise one-day bus and fishing tours to Arnarvatnsheiði for Ikr5000 per person, including fishing equipment hire. The trip must be booked one day in advance.

Brekkulækur

Brekkulækur (☎ 451 2938; fax 451 2998), 10 km south of Melstaður, has single/double rooms without bath for Ikr4225/5200. Here, Arinbjörn Jóhannsson organises adventurous and highly acclaimed eight to 14-day horse-riding and hiking tours around Arnarvatnsheiði and upper Borgarfjörður. A two-week, all-inclusive circuit starts at around Ikr168,000. He also runs bicycle tours.

On the gravel plain north of Brekkulækur is a field of fissure-eruption craters, known as Króksstaðakatlar, which make a pleasant day hike from the farm.

BLÖNDUÓS

With a population of about 1100, Blönduós is a trading centre and a shrimp and shellfishing community at the mouth of the river Blandaá. Its lack of harbour facilities inhibit

ICELAND

prosperity and population growth, but since the town is on the Ring Road, there is some activity in summer.

The first bridge over the Blandaá was constructed here in 1963. The river offers excellent salmon fishing but a one-day licence costs a staggering Ikr113,000, so don't forget your platinum hooks and 24-carat gold sinkers!

Information
The tourist office (☎ 452 4520; fax 452 4063), at the campground, is open daily, 1 June to 10 September, from 8.30 am to noon and 1 to 10 pm.

Hrutey
The islet of Hrutey, just upstream from the river bridge, is a nature reserve and the site of a reafforestation project. Access is via a footbridge from near the campground.

Handicraft Museum
The small Heimilisiðnaðarsafnið, or 'domestic craft museum' (☎ 452 4153), displays local textile work and handicrafts. It's open weekdays from 2 to 5 pm, and at other times by arrangement. Admission is Ikr200.

Church
The Blönduós church, which is consistent with the geological theme dominating modern Icelandic religious architecture, was unashamedly designed in the shape of a volcanic crater. With a telephoto lens and the right angle, you can actually photograph it against its source of inspiration.

Activities
The swimming pool, by the Ring Road north of the river, is open Tuesday to Friday from 10 am to noon and 2 to 9 pm and on Saturday and Sunday between 1 and 4 pm.

Short-term horse hire is available at Kúskerpi (☎ 452 4322), five km north of Blönduós, or Hestaleiga á Hamri (☎ 452 7134), 15 km from town. The latter offers free camping for riding guests.

Organised Tours
From 20 June to 20 August, Hallur Hilmarsson (☎ 452 4578) offers six-hour daily tours on the Skagi peninsula for Ikr5250. Stops include the cliffs at Króksbjarg; the Kálfhamarsvík basalt formations; the road at Digrimúli, which was built entirely by women; the seal colonies at Hafnir and Víkur; the bird cliffs at Ketubjörg; the Glaumbær museum; and the church at Viðimýri. Book directly, or through the tourist office.

Places to Stay
The *Hótel Sveitasetrið* (☎ 452 4126; fax 452 4989), at Aðalgata 6, has rooms for Ikr4300/6500 with shared facilities and Ikr5600/8400 with shower. All rates include breakfast.

More basic is the *Gistiheimilið Blönduból* (☎ & fax 452 4535), at Blöndubyggð10, 600m from the Ring Road. Made-up rooms cost Ikr1100 to Ikr1300, and sleeping-bag accommodation is Ikr780 to Ikr900, including use of cooking facilities.

The *campground* (☎ 452 4520) occupies a lovely setting near the river. If you prefer to settle in, *Glaðheimar* (☎ 452 4123; fax 452 4924), beside the campground, rents cottages for three/five/six/10 people for Ikr16,705/22,300/34,840/39,000 per week.

Four farms in the area offer farmhouse accommodation: *Dæli* (☎ 452 2566), *Hnausar* (☎ 452 4484), *Geitaskarð* (☎ 452 4341) and *Stóra Giljá* (☎ 452 4294). Dæli, Hnausar and Geitaskarð have private rooms; Hnausar and Geitaskarð have sleeping-bag accommodation; and Dæli and Stóra Giljá have cottages. At Hnausar and Geitaskarð, you can rent horses, and Hnausar has cooking facilities. Rates for single/double accommodation are Ikr3000/4050, sleeping-bag accommodation costs Ikr1300, and four/six-person cottages are Ikr19,570/37,100 per week.

Places to Eat
If you're not up to the relatively plush hotel dining room, your best bet is the recommended *Esso Skálinn* (☎ 452 4298), beside

the church. It also sells basic groceries. The other grill, *Blönduskálinn* (☎ 452 4350), at the Olís petrol station and bus terminal, could stand some improvement.

Getting There & Away
Air Íslandsflug flies between Reykjavík and Blönduós several times weekly. See the agent at Blönduskálinn (☎ 452 4289).

Bus All Reykjavík-Akureyri buses stop at the Blönduskálinn terminal. In summer, buses leave Reykjavík daily at 8 am and from Akureyri at 9.30 am. From 15 June to 15 September, afternoon buses leave from either end at 5 pm. Buses to Akureyri (Ikr1280) pass Blönduós at 12.30 and 9.25 pm; to Reykjavík (Ikr2570), they pass at 11.35 am and 7.10 pm. Reykjavík-Siglufjörður buses also stop at Blönduós.

AROUND HÚNAFJÖRÐUR
Upper Húnafjörður has a surprising array of natural features and historical sites, but unfortunately, very few are along the Ring Road bus routes.

Vatnsdalshólar
Another of Iceland's so-called 'innumerables', the grassy hills of Vatnsdalshólar, which cover about four sq km, were formed 10,000 years ago by the collapse of part of Vatnsdalsfjall. Here Vigdís, the wife of Ingimundur the Old of *Vatnsdæla Saga*, gave birth to their daughter Þórdís and thereby started the settlement of Vatnsdalur (see under Hof in this section). The birth is now commemorated by a small copse and plaque.

In October 1720, a great landslide dammed the river Vatnsdalsá south of the present Ring Road to form the lake Flóðið. Across the Ring Road from Vatnsdalshólar are the three smaller hills of Þrístapar, where the last execution in Iceland took place on 12 January 1830.

If you'd like to lose yourself in the innumerable hills of Vatnsdalshólar, take the bus between Reykjavík and Akureyri.

Hof
Hof (the 'temple') was the farm of the pagan Ingimundur, a hero of *Vatnsdæla Saga*, which was later condensed for inclusion in the *Landnámabók*. Ingimundur was the son of a Norwegian chieftain and was reared in a Viking household. As a supporter of King Harald Haarfager, he was awarded a silver charm depicting the Norse god Freyr.

Unfortunately, Ingimundur's charm went missing, and he was told by a medium that it would be found in the Icelandic grove where he and his family would settle and be happy. Although Ingimundur had no plans to emigrate, he accepted his fate and sailed to Iceland in search of the missing charm. He noted that the spot where his wife gave birth to their first child fit the medium's description. Further up the valley, as he was excavating a foundation for a temple to the Norse gods, he found the charm. His farm was thereafter named Hof.

At Hof, 20 km up Route 722 on the hill Goðhóll, you can still see remains of Ingimundur's temple, although it has never been excavated. Only keen saga buffs will fully appreciate the meagre ruins.

Hvítserkur & Ósar
Hvítserkur, a 15m-high sea stack just offshore near the northern end of the peninsula Vatnsnes, has been eroded by wave action into a bizarre and whimsical rock formation.

Legend recounts that Hvítserkur was a troll caught by the sunrise while attempting to destroy the Christian monastery at Þingeyrar. As with all trolls caught by the sunrise, he was turned to stone. Apparently, this troll can metamorphose at will into a grazing Brahman bull, an American bison, a dinosaur, an Asian elephant with a howdah on its back, and – most apparent of all – a large Alaskan moose dredging pond weeds from the bottom of a lake (as moose are known to do).

Places to Stay A short walk from Hvítserkur is Ósar and the *Sunset Youth Hostel* (☎ & fax 451 2678), which many travellers reckon is the best in Iceland, thanks to its friendly management, abundant hiking possibilities and nearby profusion of seals, ducks and sea birds. Fishing equipment and inexpensive permits are available to hostel guests. Rooms cost the standard Ikr1000/1250 for HI members/non-members. There are no buses to Ósar, but if you lack transport, ring the hostel and someone will pick you up at the Viðihlíð petrol station on the Ring Road.

In summer, sleeping-bag accommodation is available at *Vesturhópsskóli* (☎ 451 2683) school for Ikr650/900 on mattresses/beds. Guests also have access to the swimming pool.

Hindisvík

Hindisvík, at the northern tip of Vatnsnes, is the home of Iceland's largest readily accessible seal colony and breeding ground. There's no public transport, but the Sunset Youth Hostel is within easy striking distance.

Hóp

At high tide, Hóp is Iceland's fifth largest lake, at 44 sq km, but at low tide it shrinks to just 29 sq km. Whenever you see it, Hóp is a singularly uninteresting body of water except for the curious spit Þingeyraríf, which nearly bisects it. This 10 km-long sliver of land is just a few metres wide and if you're into unusual geographic phenomena, it would make a nice walk to the end and back.

One of Hóp's inflows, the Gljúfurá, crosses the Ring Road two km west of Vatnsdalshólar, where it passes through a scenic gorge before descending to the lake.

Þingeyrar

Þingeyrar, at the base of Þingeyraríf, is one of Iceland's greatest historical places. It was the site of a district assembly (*þing*), and where Jón Ögmundarson, the original Bishop of Hólar, founded Iceland's first monastery in 1112.

Hoping to alleviate some of the famine and crop failure that had plagued northern Iceland, the bishop vowed to build a church. With his own hands, he cleared the foundations and less than a week later, the soil regained its productivity. The bishop inter-

preted the miracle as a divine go-ahead for a Benedictine monastery. In the late 12th century, Þingeyrar became Iceland's greatest library, where monks wrote, compiled and copied histories and sagas. These included biographies of the Norwegian kings and the renowned *Jóns Saga Helga*, the posthumous biography of Bishop Jón himself.

The monastery no longer stands, but there's a wonderful stone church constructed by the Þingeyrar farmer between 1864 and 1877. The stones were dragged across Hóp on the ice. The pulpit, from Holland, dates from the 17th century, and the 15th century altarpiece was made in England and set with alabaster reliefs from the original monastery. Most impressive are the replica oak statuettes of Christ and the apostles. The originals were carved in the 16th century in Germany and stood in the church until earlier this century, when they were sold and later donated to the National Museum in Reykjavík.

Outside the church is the ovoid outline of an enclosure known locally as the Lögrétta. It is believed to be the remains of the meeting place of a district legislative body before the establishment of the monastery. Unfortunately, it's quite difficult to discern.

Getting There & Away Visiting Þingeyrar without a car is tricky, but worth the effort. Get off the southbound bus at the junction of the Ring Road and Route 721, then walk six km north to the site. Unfortunately, some travellers have found it closed, so before you traipse out there, check with the Blönduós tourist office.

Húnavellir

The *Edda Hotel* (☎ 452 4370; fax 452 4281) at Húnavellir ('bear plains') sits on the shores of Svínavatn ('pig lake'), 18 km from Blönduós. The lake was named after the swines of Ingimundur, from *Vatnsdæla Saga*. The hotel has a naturally heated swimming pool and a licensed restaurant. Single/double rooms cost Ikr3650/4750 and sleeping-bag accommodation costs Ikr1000/1450 in schoolrooms/rooms.

Borgarvirkið

On a 180m ridge near Vesturhópsvatn are the ruins of Borgarvirkið, a circular, fort-like stone enclosure rising above 10m basalt columns. Inside are the remains of a well and some dwellings. The site was renovated in 1950, but archaeologists still don't know its original purpose. Legend says that it was used as a lookout and defence post against attack from the south. On top is a view disc identifying features around upper Húnafjörður.

Getting There & Away To reach Borgarvirkið from the Ring Road, drive or walk west on Route 716. After six km, turn north at the junction with Route 717. Borgarvirkið lies five km further north, just west of the road.

Blönduvirkjun

The Blandaá begins in the Hofsjökull icecap, deep in the interior, and the residue it scours out clouds Húnafjörður several hundred metres from the river mouth. On the upper Blandaá is the new 1150-kilowatt-per-hour Blönduvirkjun hydroelectric plant, the fourth largest in Iceland.

Iceland doesn't really need the electricity, but it's hoped that Blönduvirkjun will provide power for new industry – including a mooted aluminium plant – which may provide jobs and stem emigration to urban centres. Long-term ecological impacts aren't yet known, but government compensation of farmers for flooded pastureland means that hitherto undeveloped land has been planted with non-native species as pasture for displaced sheep.

Organised Tours

From 1 July to 10 August, BSÍ offers a five-hour day tour of the Vatnsnes peninsula, departing from Staðarskáli on Monday, Wednesday and Friday at 1 pm. It first visits Gallery Bardursa in Hvammstangi, then heads north to Skarð hot springs and the Hindisvík seal colonies. Before returning to Hvammstangi, it stops at the outcrop Hvítserkur, the Kerfossar canyon, the ancient fort Borgarvirkið and the Reykjatunga museum. The tour costs Ikr2400 and must be pre-booked.

Skagafjörður

The Skagafjörður region includes the Skagi peninsula, the Skagafjörður islands and the Héraðsvötn delta, which measures 40 km long and 30 km wide at the mouth. The district is well known for its horse breeding.

SKAGASTRÖND

Also known as Höfðakaupstaður, Skagaströnd (population 700) is one of northern Iceland's oldest trading centres. It began as a German and English merchant town in the 1500s but is now mainly a fishing village. Of possible interest are the very unusual new church – another geological creation that looks a bit crystalline – and the winter ski slope on Spákonufjall east of the town.

Kyrpingsfjall

Kyrpingsfjall is actually a series of low gravel hills 25 km north of Skagaströnd. The southernmost is called Gullbrekka (the 'golden hillside'), below which is the bog Gullkelda. It's said that the farm Gullbrekka, which once existed on this site, sank into the bog Atlantis-style and neither the farm nor its inhabitants were ever seen again.

Places to Stay

The *Gistiheimilið Dagsbrún* (☎ 452 2730; fax 452 2882) charges Ikr4030/5200 for single/double rooms and Ikr1300 for sleeping-bag accommodation. You'll also find sleeping-bag accommodation for Ikr1000 in the *ski hut* (☎ 452 2272). The campground is just south of town.

Getting There & Away

No public transport serves Skagaströnd or anywhere on the Skagi peninsula.

VARMAHLÍÐ

Varmahlíð ('warm slope'), with a population

of 100, lies at the intersection of the Ring Road and the Sauðárkrókur highway. It's named after nearby geothermal sites, but there's also a convincing illusion that it's warmer than surrounding areas, probably because the slope faces the morning sun. Varmahlíð has recently developed into a service centre, and now boasts a bank, swimming pool, supermarket and tourist facilities.

The summit of 111m Reykjahóll affords a wide view over the town and surrounding green countryside.

Information
The tourist office (☎ 453 8860) is beside the Shell petrol station. From 15 June to 31 August, it's open daily from 10 am to 9 pm.

Natural History Museum
The school Varmahlíðarskóli contains a small natural history museum with displays on rocks, minerals, fossils and Icelandic flora. There's even a stuffed polar bear. It's open daily, 1 June to 31 August, from 9 am to 7 pm. Admission is Ikr200.

Places to Stay & Eat
Varmahlíð has a *supermarket*, *campground* and petrol station. The *Hótel Varmahlíð* (☎ 453 8170; fax 453 8870), which serves as the bus terminal, charges Ikr4800/6900 for single/double rooms without bath and Ikr6600/8950 with a shower. It also has a dining room, but your best bet for meals is the restaurant, snack bar and supermarket at the *Shell* station.

The summer hotel *Áning* (☎ 453 8130; fax 453 6087), in the village school, has basic single/double rooms for Ikr3700/4745 and sleeping-bag accommodation for Ikr900/1430 on mattresses/beds.

There are several farmhouse options to choose from, all of which charge standard farmhouse rates (Ikr3000/4700 for single/double rooms and Ikr1300 for sleeping-bag accommodation). On the Ring Road west of Varmahlíð is *Stóra Vatnsskarð* (☎ 453 8152), and 500m east of town is *Lauftún* (☎ 453 8133). South along Route 752, in Tungusveit, are *Varmilækur* (☎ 453

8021), *Steinsstaðaskóli* (☎ 453 8026), *Bakkaflöt* (☎ 453 8245; fax 453 8837), and *Sölvanes* (☎ 453 8068). All have sleeping-bag accommodation (Lauftún charges only Ikr1000), and Steinsstaðaskóli and Bakkaflöt have campsites. Bakkaflöt rents four/six-person cottages for Ikr29,000/40,250 per week.

Things to Buy
For an unusual souvenir, visit the workshop of Anna Hróðmarsdóttir (☎ 453 8031), who produces fine ceramics from volcanic ash.

Getting There & Away
All buses between Reykjavík and Akureyri stop at the terminal at the Hótel Varmahlíð.

AROUND VARMAHLÍÐ
Reynisstaður
Between 1295 and 1552, the church and farm at Reynisstaður, 14 km north of Varmahlíð, was the site of a monastery. The present church was built in the 1800s.

Vatnsskarð
At Vatnsskarð ('lake pass'), the Ring Road crosses from the Húnafjörður to the Skagafjörður watershed. At the eastern foot of the pass is the hill Arnarstapi, which bears a view disc and a monument to the Icelandic-Canadian poet Stephan G Stephansson, the 'Rocky Mountain Bard'.

At the western foot of the pass, the clearwater river Svartá ('black river') joins the milky white glacier-fed river Blandaá, creating an intriguing 'meeting of the waters'.

Víðimýri
West of Varmahlíð on the Ring Road is the old chieftain's residence, Víðimýri. The lovely turf-covered church, which is considered architecturally superior to other 19th century structures in Iceland, is open daily from 1 June to 31 August from 9 am to 6 pm, and at other times by arrangement (☎ 453 8167). Admission is Ikr100.

Glaumbær
The 18th century turf farm at Glaumbær

features some of the best remaining examples of early Icelandic building techniques. Snorri Þorfinnsson, the first European born in North America, is buried at Glaumbær, where he lived after his parents returned to their native Iceland. He was born in the year 1003 while his father, Þorfinnur Karlsefni, was involved in a winter expedition in Vinland. The farm now houses the Skagafjörður folk museum (☎ 453 6173), which is open from 9 am to 6 pm daily between 1 June and 1 September. Admission is Ikr200 per person.

The farm *Glaumbær* (☎ 453 8146) has a six-person cottage which rents for Ikr2800 per night. The only bus to pass Glaumbær is the one between Varmahlíð and Siglufjörður, which runs on Monday, Wednesday and Friday and returns on Sunday, Tuesday and Thursday. Fortunately, it's less than a two-hour walk from Varmahlíð.

Vindheimamelar

Hestasport, at the Vindheimamelar racing grounds 10 km south of Varmahlíð, runs 1½ hour tourist programs about the Icelandic horse. It begins with an audio-visual segment about the history and development of the breed, followed by a demonstration and horse show. Admission costs Ikr1600, including coffee and Icelandic refreshments. It begins at 2 pm (by reservation) from 15 June to 15 September. For bookings, or to organise riding tours, contact Hestasport (☎ 453 5066; fax 453 6004; email hestact@ks.is), Raftahlíð 20, 550 Sauðárkrókur.

Ábær

The farm Ábær, 65 km up the Jökulsá Austari from Varmahlíð and three km beyond the end of the road, has a lovely church which was once thought to be haunted. The parish is home to only one parishioner, and there's only one annual church service here, on the first Sunday in August. Over the nearby Merkagil gorge, between the neighbouring farms Merkagil and Gilsbakki, is an old cable car, which is still in working order.

SAUÐÁRKRÓKUR

With 2600 inhabitants, nondescript Sauðárkrókur is the second-largest town in northern Iceland, but since it's not on the Ring Road and gets only three buses a week from Reykjavík, it hasn't really seen much tourism.

The town obtained a trading licence on New Year's Day 1858, but its first settler didn't arrive until 1871 and its municipal charter had to wait until 1947. Economically, it's dependent on fishing, trading, wool tanning (at Loðskinn) and the tongue-torturing Gönguskarðsárvirkjun ('trail pass river hydroelectric station'). Sauðárkrókur also boasts a company which makes fibreglass with sand melted by geothermal heat.

Information

The tourist office is the front desk of Hótel Áning (☎ 453 6717). There's a nine-hole golf course on the hillside above town. Other services include banks, a laundry, swimming pool and horse rentals.

Things to See

Sauðárkrókur is not one of Iceland's more vibrant towns, but if you're stuck, you can have a look at the village **church**, which dates from 1892 and is open to visitors daily in summer. At the library on Faxatorg is a small local **art and folk museum** (☎ 453 5424). In July and August, it's open weekdays from 3 to 7 pm and also from 8 to 10 pm on Monday and Thursday.

A fine day hike will take you to the summit of 706m **Molduxi** for a broad view over all of Skagafjörður.

Organised Tours

For riding tours, Hestasport (☎ 453 5066; fax 453 6004) organises multi-day horse-riding tours and can also arrange visits to the September *réttir* (roundups). Eight or nine-day trips cost from Ikr95,000 to Ikr100,800. The réttir costs Ikr62,600.

The affiliated Activity Tours (☎ 453 5066; fax 453 6004; email hestact@ks.is), Raftahlíð 20, Sauðárkrókur, specialises in white-water rafting in North Central Iceland.

Day trips include the Hjaltadalsá (Ikr3400), Blandaá (Ikr3400), Jökulsá Vestari (Ikr3800) and the biggest of all, the Jökulsá Austari (Ikr7000). The Blandaá is a family sort of river while the Jökulsá Austari offers big white-water thrills, and is limited to participants over 18 years old. The Jökulsá Vestari trip is open to participants over 14 years old and includes a break at a hot spring and a novel opportunity to attempt cliff-diving.

Places to Stay

The hillside summer hotel, *Áning* (☎ 453 6717; fax 453 6087), charges Ikr5070/6825 for single/double rooms with bath, and Ikr1430 for sleeping-bag accommodation. Bicycles may be hired for Ikr1000 per day.

The *Hótel Mælifell* (☎ 453 5265; fax 453 5640), at Aðalgata 7 in the centre, charges Ikr3640/4745 for basic single/double rooms, and Ikr4200/7020 with shower. On weekends, there's a disco. The former Guesthouse Torg at Kaupvangstorg 1 has been taken over by the hotel and is now used as an annexe.

Guesthouse accommodation is available at *Fagranes* (☎ 453 6503), five km north of town. Made-up beds are good value at Ikr1560 and sleeping-bag accommodation is Ikr1100. The *campground* (☎ 453 6717) is beside the swimming pool.

Places to Eat

The *Kaffi Krókur* (☎ 453 6299), serves up full Icelandic and international meals. There's also the pub-style restaurant/snack bar *Pollinn* (☎ 453 6454), at Aðalgata 15, which serves pizza and other light meals. It's open Friday and Saturday until 3 am. A good value option is the enlarged snack bar and restaurant *Ábær* (☎ 453 5371), at the Esso petrol station. The State Monopoly shop is at Smáragrund 2.

Getting There & Away

Air In summer, Flugleiðir (☎ 453 5630) flies between Reykjavík and Sauðárkrókur daily except Saturday.

Bus Three buses a week connect Sauðár-krókur with Varmahlíð (Ikr250) and Siglufjörður (Ikr750). The bus runs southbound on Sunday, Tuesday and Thursday and northbound on Monday, Wednesday and Friday.

AROUND SKAGAFJÖRÐUR
Tindastóll

The 989m Tindastóll is a prominent Skagafjörður landmark, extending for 20 km along the coast north of Sauðárkrókur. The mountain and its caves are believed to be inhabited by an array of sea monsters, trolls and giants, one of which kidnapped the daughter of an early bishop of Hólar.

The summit affords a spectacular view across all of Skagafjörður. The easiest way to the top is from the high ground along Route 745 west of the mountain. At the mountain's northern end is a geothermal area, Reykir, which was mentioned in *Grettis Saga*. Grettir supposedly swam ashore from the island of Drangey in Skagafjörður and one of the hot springs at Reykir is named Grettislaug, or 'Grettir's bath'.

North of Reykir is the cove of Glerhallavík, where a beach is covered with surf-polished stones. There is also an old wishing-well, which contains a magic stone believed to float to the surface on Midsummer's Day.

From the farm Tunga, at the south-western foot of Tindastóll, it's an eight-km climb to the *Trölli mountain hut*. The hut has 18 beds but no cooking facilities. To book, contact Ferðafélags Skagafirðinga in Sauðárkrókur. Ferðafélag Íslands members use the hut at a discounted rate. Use the *Skagaströnd* 1:100,000 topographic sheet.

Drangey

The rocky island of Drangey in Skagafjörður is a flat-topped mass of tuff rising abruptly 200m above the water. The cliffs serve as nesting sites for thousands of sea birds and have been used throughout Iceland's history for egg collection and bird netting. *Grettis Saga* recounts that both Grettir and his brother Illugi lived on the island and were slain there.

From the landing place, a steep path leads to the summit. Icelanders maintain that a prayer is necessary before ascending, because only part of the island was blessed by the early priests, and the north-eastern section remains an abode of evil. Locals will only collect birds or eggs from the bits that have been stamped with the greater powers' official seal of approval.

Organised Tours Six-hour boat trips to the island, including a hike to the summit, can be arranged directly with the Fagranes farmer Jón Eiríksson (☎ 453 6503), or they may be booked through BSÍ or hotels in Sauðárkrókur. The trips cost Ikr3770 and depart daily at 10 am from the farm Fagranes, five km north of Sauðárkrókur. An abbreviated 2½ hour version, without the hiking, is available for Ikr2730.

Málmey
The 2½ sq km island Málmey, known mainly for its abundance of sea birds, isn't as foreboding as Drangey and rises to just over 150m. Nevertheless, it has been uninhabited since 1951. Boat tours to Málmey are conducted by the farmer at Vatn (☎ 453 7434) in Höfðaströnd.

Tröllskagi

Both the topography and climate of the Tröllskagi make it ideal hiking country. This rugged peninsula, which lies between Skagafjörður and northern Iceland's longest fjord, Eyjafjörður, is a maze of mountains, rivers and even a couple of miniature glaciers. This bit of Iceland enjoys relatively good weather and a mild summer climate.

The Tröllskagi's best-known attraction is Hólar, medieval Iceland's northern bishopric. Parts of the peninsula, especially around Ólafsfjörður and Siglufjörður, are reminiscent of the Westfjords. In its southern reaches, mountaineers will find some of Iceland's most challenging peaks and ridges within easy walking distance of the highway system.

HOFSÓS
Tiny Hofsós (population 200) has been a trading centre since the 1500s.

Things to See
The **Vesturfarasafnið** (☎ 453 7930) has a display on Icelandic emigration to North America, and is the office for the Icelandic-American Emigration Centre, which helps put North Americans of Icelandic extraction in touch with their roots; admission is Ikr300.

The affiliated **Pakkahúsið**, a log warehouse built in 1777 by the Danish Royal Greenland Company, is preserved *in situ* and contains an exhibit of implements used in hunting sea birds and gathering eggs on Drangey island. From June to September, it's open daily except Monday from 10 am to 6 pm. Admission is Ikr150.

South of town are some unusual **basalt formations** and near Grafarós, the mouth of the river Grafará, are the remains of a 19th century **trading post**. The farm Gröf, two km south of the river, has an old **turf church**, which was renovated and re-consecrated in 1953. You can pick up a key at the Sólvík coffee bar.

Places to Stay & Eat
Between 1 June and 31 August, the community centre *Höfðaborg* (☎ 453 7367) has sleeping-bag accommodation for Ikr850 and made-up beds for Ikr1690. The farm *Vatn* (☎ 453 7434), seven km north of town, has four four/six-person cottages for Ikr28,850/37,100 per week. The farm hires out horses and also organises excursions to Málmey island.

The *Youth Hostel Lónkot* (☎ 453 7432), further north, offers beds for Ikr1000/1250 for HI members/non-members. The sunken barbecue pit is probably worth writing home about and the super sea views include Málmey and the bizarre promontory Þórðarhöfði, which is tethered to the mainland by two delicate spits.

ICELAND

You'll find snacks at the *Esso* petrol station. At the *Sólvík* coffee bar (☎ 453 7939), opposite the Pakkahúsið, you can drink coffee and eat home-baked goods. In summer, it's open daily from 10 am to 10 pm.

Getting There & Away
The Siglufjörður bus (see under Sauðár-krókur) passes through Hofsós.

HÓLAR Í HJALTADALUR
The northern bishopric of Hólar was the ecumenical and educational capital of north-ern Iceland between 1106 and the Reformation, and continued as a religious centre and the home of the northern bishops until 1798.

The first bishop, Jón Ögmundarson, who served from 1106 to 1121, was nominated for sainthood by his Icelandic constituency. Although the canonisation was never recognised by Rome, a monk at the monas-tery of Þingeyrar (see Around Húnafjörður) entitled his biography *Jóns Saga Helga*, or the 'Saga of St John'.

The first timber cathedral at Hólar, which replaced a small turf church, was constructed by Bishop Jón using Norwegian wood. Until 1135, when the Skálholt cathedral was com-pleted, it was the world's largest wooden church.

Bishop Jón also established a successful school at Hólar, where church attendance and memorisation of sacred recitations were obligatory and the only books permitted were those the bishop himself judged to be edifying. He abolished all merriment and mischief, which he thought would detract from students' and parishioners' moral values. Public dances, love songs, celebra-tions and anything that could be construed as paganism or sorcery were forbidden within his jurisdiction. He even changed the names of weekdays named after Norse gods (those still used in English!) to the more mundane ones used in Icelandic today (see Language in the Facts about Iceland chapter). In short, Bishop Jón's word was law in northern Iceland.

After 1798, when the bishop's seat was abolished, Hólar became a vicarage and remained so until 1861, when the vicarage was shifted to Viðvík. In 1882, the present agricultural school was established, and in 1952 the vicarage was returned to Hólar. The agricultural college now offers two-year degrees in forestry, animal husbandry and fish farming.

Hólar Church
The red sandstone church, which has been recently renovated and whitewashed, was built in 1757 out of materials from Hólabyrða, the prominent mountain in Hólar's backdrop, after which the settlement was named. The church was financed by donations from Lutheran congregations all over Scandinavia. The altarpiece was donated by the last Catholic Bishop of Hólar, Jón Arason, in 1522. After he and his son were executed at Skálholt for opposition to the Danish Reformation, his remains were brought to Hólar and entombed in the bell tower, where there's now a mosaic of the good reverend.

The church is open daily from 2 to 6 pm. It's brimming with historical artwork, including a baptismal font carved from a piece of soapstone which washed in from Greenland on an ice floe. Guided tours cost Ikr100, and other Hólar sites are outlined in a brochure (Ikr150) from the information desk.

Viðvík
Near the junction of Route 76 and the two Hólar access roads (one on either side of the river Hjaltadalsá) are the farm and church at Viðvík, the home of Þórbjörn Öngull, who was responsible for Grettir's death in *Grettis Saga*. The church altarpiece dates from the early 18th century, but the church is normally locked.

Reykir
Hjaltardalur's uppermost farm is, as its name would suggest, a geothermal site. Its two hot springs, Vinnufólkslaug and Biskupslaug, served as the bathing place for the Hólar bishops and personnel.

Places to Stay & Eat

In summer, the *Hólar Agricultural College* (☎ 453 6300; fax 453 6301), opens its dormitories to travellers. Made-up beds cost Ikr2000 to Ikr3055 and sleeping-bag accommodation is Ikr850/1300 on mattresses/beds. There's also a *campsite* amid the trees, which costs Ikr250 per person and Ikr250 per tent.

For meals, there's only the *Hólar Primary School Restaurant*. Whatever the name may suggest, it offers adult lunches and dinners daily in summer, and a coffee-and-cake buffet on Sunday.

Getting There & Away

Nonni Travel offers day tours from Akureyri (see the Akureyri chapter). Otherwise, access to Hólar is difficult, as it lies 11 km from the intersection of Routes 76 and 769 (on the Varmahlíð-Siglufjörður bus route).

SIGLUFJÖRÐUR

Siglufjörður (population 1800), which may well be Iceland's loveliest town, enjoys a dramatic setting beside a small fjord at the northern tip of Tröllskagi. It's the sort of place that in any other country would probably develop into a trendy seaside art colony. The historic architecture, the colourful rooftops of upper town, the harbour and the inspiring backdrop are all delightful, and may call to mind an idyllic Hollywood fishing village. The modern sculpture near the shore – a gummi boat confronting monster waves – provides a feel for Siglufjörður's rugged past.

History

Siglufjörður was originally called Þormóðseyri, after the first settler, Þormóður Rammi, and the sandspit, or *eyri*. It gained municipal status in 1918 and soon prospered as the herring capital of Iceland. In the early 1940s, at the height of the fishery's activity, Siglufjörður was home to more than 3000 people. After the herring disappeared from Iceland's north coast, the town declined and has never fully recovered.

Síldarminjasafn

The friendly herring museum, Síldarminjasafn (☎ 417 1604), housed in a beautiful harbourside fishing hostel, contains nostalgic memorabilia from the boom days of the herring fishery. On Friday at noon and Saturday at 11 am, from 10 June to 9 September, you can watch herring-salting demonstrations, accompanied by lively traditional concertina music and song. It also runs films about the history of the town and its once predominant industry. It's open from 1 to 6 pm Sunday to Friday and 10 to 6 pm on Saturday. Admission is Ikr200 (Ikr400 for Friday and Saturday shows).

Bjarnarstofa

In the library is a small memorial museum, Bjarnarstofa (☎ 467 1272), dedicated to the priest and musician Bjarni Þorsteinsson. It's open weekdays from 2 to 5.30 pm (until 6 pm on Thursday).

Hiking

The old route over 630m Siglufjarðarskarð, between Siglufjörður and Fljótavík, was once thought to be haunted, but in 1735 it was consecrated by a Christian priest. In more recent years the greatest dangers have been from avalanches.

Since the opening of the 800m tunnel Strákagöng through the mountain Strákar, the road has been abandoned, but from early July to late August, it's open to foot traffic. The route up to the pass and north along the ridge to Strákar (above the tunnel) affords some wonderful views.

North along the western shore of Siglufjörður, it's a short walk to the abandoned herring factory, which was destroyed in an avalanche in 1919. Longer hikes will take you over the passes Hólskarð and Hestskarð to the uninhabited Héðinsfjörður, the next fjord to the east.

Other Activities

In winter, a ski lift operates in Skarðsdalur above the head of the fjord. From there, it's a lovely day-walk over Hólsfjall to the abandoned valley above Héðinsfjörður. In summer, you can opt for a nine-hole round of golf at the Hóll sports centre.

Special Events

Despite the utter demise of the herring industry, Siglufjörður still considers itself a herring fishery capital, and over the bank holiday in early August, the town stages a herring festival with much singing, dancing, drinking, feasting and fish cleaning. It's a lot of fun and may well be Iceland's most worthwhile annual festival.

Places to Stay

The *Hótel Lækur* (☎ 467 1514; fax 467 1721), the only formal accommodation in town, charges Ikr3420/5130 for single/double rooms with shared facilities, including breakfast. Sleeping-bag accommodation costs Ikr1105.

The *Gistiheimilið Hvanneyri* (☎ 467 1378), Aðalgata 10, is a cosier alternative which charges Ikr1950 per person with shared facilities and Ikr1000 for sleeping-bag accommodation.

The recently-renovated *Iþróttamiðstöðin Hóll* (☎ 467 1284) sports centre, near the ski slopes in Skarðsdalur, has sleeping-bag accommodation for Ikr900 per person. There's a five-person *summer cottage* (☎ 467 1919), at Suðurgata 86, which charges Ikr3705 per night. The main *campground* is 1½ km south-east of town but

there's also a small campsite near the harbour and town square.

Places to Eat

The cinema-inspired *Bíógrillið* (☎ 467 1790), in the centre, serves up snacks with a measure of history. Ask about the historical photos on the walls and you'll learn heaps about Siglufjörður's past. A nearby snack venue is *Bílinn* (☎ 467 1562), which does chicken and chips, burgers, hot dogs and sandwiches.

The licensed dining room at the *Hótel Lækur* (☎ 467 1514) is open all day, and on weekends there's music and dancing in the bar. There are also two *bakeries* which brew up superb coffee. The State Monopoly shop is at Eyrargata 25.

Getting There & Away

The precarious but lovely route into Siglufjörður, perched between the sea and the peaks, is one of Iceland's most scenic coastal routes. From 1 July to 31 August, buses run between Reykjavík and Siglufjörður (Ikr3500) daily except Saturday. From 20 May to 30 June and in September, they run three times a week in either direction.

Íslandsflug (☎ 467 1560) flies between Reykjavík and Siglufjörður daily except Saturday and Monday.

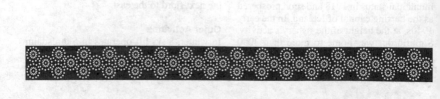

Akureyri

Akureyri (population 14,000), the 'meadow sand-spit', may well be the best of urban Iceland. Its setting is superb and sunny days are the norm in this small and tidy city planted beneath perpetually snow-capped peaks near the head of Eyjafjörður ('island fjord', after Hrísey island near its mouth).

Akureyri's climate supports diverse vegetation and locals put lots of effort into planting trees and gardens to maintain the town's lovely appearance. The results are exhilarating: along the streets, in flower boxes and in private gardens, grow some of the most beautiful and colourful blooms imaginable, and the clear air is saturated with the fresh scent of sticky birch sap. In the botanic gardens, species from Africa, the Mediterranean and China grow beside Alaskan, Greenlandic and indigenous specimens, all outdoors. You'd never guess you were just a stone's throw from the Arctic Circle. What's more, Akureyri's environs are undergoing some of Iceland's most enthusiastic reafforestation programmes.

The city's only aesthetic downfall lies in the high-density housing projects – reminiscent of the former Eastern Bloc – which characterise its growing outskirts.

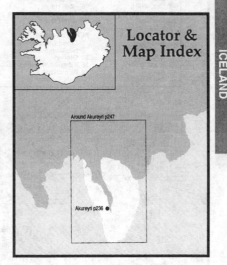

Locator & Map Index

ICELAND

Around Akureyri p247

Akureyri p236

History

The first permanent inhabitant of Eyjafjörður was Norse-Irish settler Helgi Magri (Helgi the Lean), so named because of an unfortunate nutritional deficiency during his youth in the Orkneys. Although Helgi worshipped Þór and tossed his high-seat pillars overboard to sanction his homestead site (they washed up seven km south of present-day Akureyri), he hedged his bets by naming his farm Kristnes ('Christ's peninsula').

Akureyri began as a trading centre just before the Danish Trade Monopoly of 1602 came into effect. Although the town was used for commercial enterprises, no-one actually lived there as all the settlers maintained rural farms and homesteads.

After business had boomed for a century and a half, Akureyri's first actual residence – that of the Danish trader Fridrik Lynge – was built in 1777. By the late 1700s, the town had accumulated a whopping 10 residents, all Danish traders. Population expansion didn't begin in earnest until Akureyri received its official municipal charter on 29 August 1862, when it had 286 people. The first cooperative society, Gránufélagsins, was established in 1870 at Oddeyri, the spit that juts into Eyjafjörður.

By the turn of the century, Akureyri numbered 1370 people. By this time, the original cooperative had begun to decline and, in 1906, was replaced by KEA (Kaupfélagið Eyjafirdinga Akureyrar, the Akureyri Cooperative Society), whose ubiquitous insignia still graces many Akureyri businesses.

The Akureyri Fishing Company is Iceland's largest and the city's shipyard is

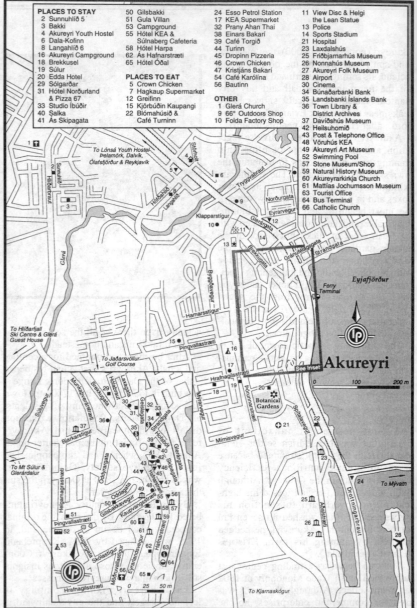

PLACES TO STAY
2 Sunnuhlíð 5
3 Bakki
4 Akureyri Youth Hostel
6 Dala-Kofinn
8 Langahlíð 6
16 Akureyri Campground
18 Brekkusel
19 Súlur
20 Edda Hotel
29 Sólgarðar
31 Hótel Norðurland
    & Pizza 67
33 Studio Íbúðir
40 Salka
41 Ás Skipagata

50 Gilsbakki
51 Gula Villan
53 Campground
55 Hótel KEA &
    Súlnaberg Cafeteria
58 Hótel Harpa
62 Ás Hafnarstræti
65 Hótel Óðal

PLACES TO EAT
5 Crown Chicken
7 Hagkaup Supermarket
12 Greifinn
15 Kjörbúðin Kaupangi
22 Blómahúsið &
    Café Turninn

24 Esso Petrol Station
17 KEA Supermarket
32 Prany Ahan Thai
39 Café Torgið
44 Turinn
45 Dropinn Pizzeria
46 Crown Chicken
47 Kristjáns Bakarí
54 Café Karólína
56 Bautinn

OTHER
1 Glerá Church
9 66° Outdoors Shop
10 Folda Factory Shop

11 View Disc & Helgi
    the Lean Statue
13 Police
14 Sports Stadium
21 Hospital
23 Laxdalshús
25 Friðbjarnarhús Museum
26 Nonnahús Museum
27 Akureyri Folk Museum
28 Airport
30 Cinema
34 Búnaðarbanki Bank
35 Landsbanki Íslands Bank
36 Town Library &
    District Archives
37 Davíðshús Museum
42 Heilsuhomið
43 Post & Telephone Office
48 Vöruhús KEA
49 Akureyri Art Museum
52 Swimming Pool
57 Stone Museum/Shop
59 Natural History Museum
60 Akureyrarkirkja Church
61 Mattías Jochumsson Museum
63 Tourist Office
64 Bus Terminal
66 Catholic Church

also the busiest in the country. Before the decline in herring stocks off northern Iceland, herring salting was the town's largest industry. Fishing remains important, but the emphasis is now on trawling, canning and freezing larger fish. At present, Akureyri's expanding industrial base includes such diverse enterprises as brewing, food processing and tourism.

Orientation

Akureyri is small and easy to see on foot. Most shops, restaurants and businesses are concentrated between the bus terminal and football stadium, and activity centres on the pedestrian shopping street of Hafnarstræti and the industrial area on the Oddeyri spit. The residential sections (as well as the campground, church, swimming pool, botanic gardens and medical centre) sprawl across the bluff above the city centre.

A walking tour around the museums and churches will easily occupy a day; add the botanic gardens and Kjarnaskógur wood and you'll need two days. Even if you're not into museums and churches, it's pleasant to stroll around and see the gardens and trees that make the city unique in Iceland.

Information

Tourist Office The tourist information office (☎ 462 7733; fax 462 7020), in the BSÍ bus terminal at Hafnarstræti 82, can book accommodation anywhere in Iceland and help with planning visits around the city, as well as tours to outlying areas. From June to August, it's open weekdays from 7.30 am to 7 pm and on weekends from 7.30 to 11.30 am and 1 to 6 pm. The rest of the year it's open weekdays from 8.30 am to 5 pm.

Money Akureyri has five banks, all of which do foreign exchange. The Landsbanki Ísland on Ráðhústorg provides free coffee while you're queuing. After hours, the tourist office changes money for a Ikr300 commission.

Post & Communications The post and telephone offices are on the Hafnarstræti mall.

The post office is open weekdays from 9 am to 4.30 pm and the telephone desk, from 9 am to 6 pm Monday to Friday, and on Saturday from 10 am to 3 pm.

Bookshops It's incredible that a town the size of Akureyri supports three bookshops. Two are on the pedestrian mall and the third is just around the corner on Skipagata. All sell a range of souvenir books in English, French and German as well as popular foreign language paperbacks and Icelandic titles. The Bókaverslunin Edda, on Hafnarstræti, specialises in periodicals.

Libraries The public library (☎ 462 4141), at Brekkugata 17, was first established in 1827 and houses more than 80,000 volumes, as well as the district historical archives. From 1 May to 1 October, it's open Monday to Friday, 1 to 7 pm.

Laundry In addition to the washing machines at the campground, there are laundry/dry-cleaning services at Þvottahúsið Höfði, at Hafnarstræti 34.

Medical Services The hospital (☎ 463 0100) is just south of the botanic gardens, on Spítalavegur. Doctors are on call 24 hours a day (☎ 852 3221). There's also a clinic, Heilsugæslustöðin (☎ 462 2311), at Hafnarstræti 99.

Emergency The fire brigade and ambulance services (☎ 112) and the Akureyri police (☎ 462 3222) are available 24 hours a day.

Film & Photography Two camera shops on the pedestrian mall sell and process film and repair cameras (all at typically shocking Icelandic prices). Kodak processing is available at Pedromyndir at Skipagata 16.

Outdoor Equipment For fishing and camping gear and sporting goods, try the Vöruhús KEA on Hafnarstræti, or the Hjólbarðaþjónusta 66° N outlet on Glerárgata, north of the centre.

ICELAND

Churches

Akureyrarkirkja The 'geological' theme common to new Icelandic church architecture has not been lost on Akureyrarkirkja. It's evident that it was designed by Gudjón Samúelsson, the architect who was also responsible for Reykjavík's Hallgrímskirkja, but Akureyrarkirkja is less blatantly 'basalt'. Few visitors are impressed with the exterior, but the interior certainly merits a look.

Built in 1940, Akureyrarkirkja contains a large and beautiful 3200-pipe organ and a series of rather untraditional reliefs of the life of Christ. There's also an unusual interpretation of the crucifixion and the centre window in the chancel originally graced the Coventry Cathedral in England (it miraculously survived the WWII bombing that destroyed the old cathedral).

The angel beside the altar was sculpted by the Dane Bertel Thorvaldsen, renowned for his intricacy with clothing detail. The ship hanging from the ceiling reflects an old Nordic tradition of votive offerings for the protection of loved ones at sea.

Akureyrarkirkja is open daily from 10 am to noon and 2 to 4 pm. In the summer, services are held at 11 am on Sunday.

Catholic Church The Catholic church in Akureyri is an attractive old house at Eyrarlandsvegur 26. It was built in 1912 and acquired by the church in 1952. On the nearby roundabout is Einar Jónsson's sculpture *Útlaginn* ('The Outlaw').

Glerá Church The new Glerá church, built in 1989 to replace the old parish church at Lögmannshlíð, rises amid drab housing blocks north of the river and adds a touch of character to an otherwise uninspiring scene. It was designed to resemble the outline of Mt Súlur, the prominent peak behind Akureyri, but the connection isn't exactly obvious.

Lögmannshlíð Church The former northern Akureyri parish church at Lögmannshlíð, built in 1861, sits high above the town near the river Lónsá. According to Settlement records, a religious structure has existed on this site since the 11th century, and the church contains artefacts dated as early as the 1600s. To get there, simply walk upstream from the Lónsá HI hostel, but it's wise to first phone the church caretaker (☎ 462 4637) to make sure it's open.

Museum Church The church at the Akureyri Folk Museum is constructed in typical 19th-century Icelandic style. It was originally built at Svalbarðseyri on the eastern shore of Eyjafjörður and moved to its present site in 1970. During WWII it was used as a storage shed by the British, but it has now been reconsecrated and is used for weddings and social functions. Its garden was begun as a nursery in 1898, and there has been some sort of garden there ever since.

It's open daily from 1 June to 15 September, from 11 am to 5 pm. Music performances are staged on Tuesday and Thursday at 9 pm. Admission is Ikr250.

Museums

Akureyri has quite a few museums, many of which are the homes of 'local boys made good'. It's to Iceland's credit that it remembers its artists, poets and authors rather than generals and politicians but, unless you're an Icelander or have a particular admiration for a particular artist's work, some museums may be of limited interest.

Matthías Jochumsson Memorial Museum Also known as Sigurhæðir, the Matthías Jochumsson Memorial Museum (☎ 462 4162), beside the Akureyrarkirkja stairs, honours the former Icelandic poet laureate and dramatist Matthías Jochumsson. Born in 1835, he wrote the noted play *The Outlaws* in 1861, and the Icelandic national anthem, *Iceland's 1000 Years*, in 1874. He also translated Byron, Shakespeare and German poetic works into Icelandic.

The house was built in 1902 and Jochumsson lived there until his death in 1920. The museum houses his collection of works and his personal property. It's open daily, 15 June to 31 August, from 2 to 4 pm.

Reverend Jón Sveinsson

Jón Sveinsson (nicknamed Nonni) was born in 1857 at Möðruvellir and moved south to Akureyri at the age of eight years. En route to Amiens, where a French noble had invited him to attend the Latin School, he visited Denmark and converted to Roman Catholicism. In 1878, he joined the Jesuit order and continued his theological education around Western Europe before accepting a teaching post in Ordrup, Denmark, in 1883. After several years, he went to England and was ordained a priest before returning to Denmark. There, he taught for 20 years until ill health forced him to retire to a more sedate literary life.

It was during his later years that Nonni wrote his best-known works, the *Nonni & Manni* children's adventures about his youth in Iceland and travels around the world. Originally written in German, the books have been translated into 40 languages, including Icelandic, and many of the original copies as well as numerous illustrations are now displayed in the Nónnahús museum. Nonni died in Germany in 1944. ∎

Nonnahús The most interesting of the artists' homes, Nonnahús (☎ 462 3555), Aðalstræti 45b, was the childhood home of Reverend Jón Sveinsson ('Nonni') who lived from 1857 to 1944 (see boxed aside). This cosy old house, built in 1850, is one of Iceland's best examples of early village dwellings. Perhaps its most interesting features are its cramped, lived-in atmosphere and simple furnishings, which reveal much about life in 19th-century Iceland. The house is open daily, 1 June to 15 September, from 10 am to 5 pm. Admission is Ikr200.

Laxdalshús At Hafnarstræti 11, near the bus terminal, is Akureyri's oldest building, Laxdalshús. It was constructed in 1795 as a Danish trading house, and now contains photos of historical Akureyri. From 1 June to 1 September, it's open daily from 11 am to 5 pm. There's a small café and video shows about the town's history.

Friðbjarnarhús Unless you're especially interested in the International Organisation of Good Templars (a remnant of the 11th to 13th-century Christian Crusades in the Middle East), Friðbjarnarhús (☎ 462 2035) may not be of much interest. It commemorates the founding of Iceland's first chapter

on 10 January 1884, and most of the items displayed relate to their activities. It occupies the 1856 home of the book merchant Friðbjörn Steinsson, at Aðalstræti 46. The museum is open weekends in July and August from 2 to 5 pm. Admission is free.

Akureyri Folk Museum (Minjasafn Akureyrar) At Aðalstræti 58, the Akureyri Folk Museum houses a large and interesting collection of art and practical items from the Settlement era to the present day. Particularly amusing are the collection of Icelandic milk cartons, the typewriters complete with Icelandic characters and the early television set. Admission is Ikr200. From 1 June to 15 September, it's open daily from 11 am to 5 pm.

Natural History Museum (Náttúrugripsafn) The rather ordinary Natural History Museum (☎ 462 2983), at Hafnarstræti 81, is worth a quick visit on a rainy day. It was founded in 1951 and boasts a complete collection of stuffed Icelandic birds and their eggs as well as stuffed fish and mammals and a variety of native shells, insects, fungi, lichen and flora.

The geological display is well-conceived, but the best exhibit is the stuffed 'great auk', (which has been extinct for 100 years). In fact, it isn't a great auk at all but a facsimile constructed from parts of other species. It's pretty well done, considering.

The museum is open from 10 am to 5 pm daily from 1 June to 10 September. Admission is Ikr100.

Davíðshús Tidy little Davíðshús (☎ 462 2874), Bjardarstígur 6, was built in 1944 by the poet, novelist and playwright Davíð Stefánsson, who became an Icelandic poet laureate. His most notable work was *Black Feathers*, published in 1919, and his most famous play was *The Golden Gate*. The latter is the tale of a woman who saved her worthless husband's rambunctious and unrepentant soul – after all other methods had failed – by packing it in a bag and smuggling it into heaven.

The museum was created upon the artist's death in 1964 and, as a respectful tribute, his books and belongings remain exactly as he left them. It certainly has a scholarly air, but it's a shame to see the poet's extensive library untouched and unavailable for use.

The museum is open daily, 15 June to 1 September, from 3 to 5 pm. Admission is Ikr100.

Art Museum (Listasafn) The Akureyri Art Museum (☎ 462 2610), Kaupvangsstræti 12, opened in 1993, gathers artworks which were previously scattered around town. The complex, known as Listagil, also holds studios, commercial galleries and an art school. It's open Tuesday to Friday, 2 to 6 pm; admission is free.

Stone Museum (Steinasafnið) The semi-interesting stone museum-cum-rock shop, beside the Bautinn restaurant on Hafnarstræti, is open daily from 1 July to 15 August, from 10 am to 5 pm. Admission is Ikr100.

Botanic Gardens
Akureyri is proud of its comfortable microclimate, and locals like to point out that plants from New Zealand, Spain and Tanzania can grow outdoors just a few km south of the Arctic Circle. Evidence of this is provided by the Lystigarður Akureyrar (☎ 462 7487), or botanic gardens. The gardens were first opened in 1912, two years after a local women's group founded the Akureyri Park Society to provide a green place for family recreation.

The society arranged to purchase the land, then set about planting and landscaping an old hay field. Subsequent donations of land increased the garden to its present 3½ hectares. The municipality took over management in 1955 and two years later, bought a private collection of Icelandic plants to create a botanical garden. It now boasts examples of every species native to Iceland, as well as an extensive collection of high-latitude and high-altitude plants from around the world, all meticulously labelled with scientific names and countries of origin.

The lawns are sheltered from the wind and make a nice place to crash in the sun. Around the gardens are statues of the poet Matthías Jochumsson, as well as Margrethe Schiöth, who voluntarily managed the gardens for 30 years. From 1 June to 31 October, they're open weekdays from 8 am to 10 pm, and on weekends from 9 am to 10 pm.

Helgi the Lean Statue
On the hill north-east of Klapparstígur, a five-minute walk from the city centre, is a statue of Helgi the Lean, the first settler in the Akureyri area. There is also a view disc.

Kjarnaskógur
An hour's walk south of town is Iceland's most visited 'forest', the Kjarnaskógur woods. This bushland area has a two km athletic course, walking tracks, picnic tables, an amusing children's playground and some novel fitness-testing devices. It's great for a few hours on a sunny day but there's no camping. The nursery and greenhouses at Grodvarstöð, east of the park, sell fresh vegetables and are open from 8 am to 6 pm on weekdays. Be sure to check out the amusing log sundial designed by Icelandic Scouts.

There's now a hotel, the Hótel Harpa

Kjarnalundur; see under Places to Stay later in this chapter.

Glerárdalur & Mt Súlur Hikes

A pleasant but demanding day hike is up the Glerá valley and to the summit of 1144m Mt Súlur. Begin by walking west on Þingvallastræti, and turn left just before the Glerá bridge (note the interesting cow statue at the dairy there). It's then an uninteresting but easy climb to the pungent landfill at the end of the Glerárdalur road, where you must descend a few metres to cross a small stream. From there, the route up Mt Súlur is fairly obvious. Climb over the style and follow the marked track. The yellow and red markers end above the vegetation line, but unless there's fog, the summit route is clear. It's about an hour from town to the garbage dump, then 2½ hours to the summit and a total of three hours back to town.

With two days, you can continue up the valley to the beautifully-situated Bægisel (Lambi) mountain hut, which accommodates up to six people. Around and beyond it are sites of ancient forests, and small quantities of petrified wood. This route also leaves from the landfill. To book the hut, contact *Ferðafélag Akureyrar* (☎ 462 2720; fax 7240), at Skipagata 12. Ferðafélag Íslands members pay Ikr450 and non-members, Ikr750.

From the Hlíðarfjall ski resort, there's a challenging but beautiful day hike up to the small glacier Vindheimajökull and the 1456m peak Strýta. Alternatively, from the Glerárdalur garbage dump, you can cross the river on the footbridge and follow the northern bank of the river upstream, then climb up to Bægisárjökull. From there, you can descend Bægisárdalur to the Ring Road in Öxárdalur. This is at least a three-day trip (see Öxnadalur under Around Akureyri).

For these walks, use the *Akureyri* 1:100,000 topo sheet.

Swimming

The swimming pool, beside the campground, is one of Iceland's best and is open long and convenient hours. In addition to saunas and jacuzzis, it offers tennis courts and a solarium. The solarium is open weekdays from 7 am to 9 pm and must be pre-booked (☎ 461 2532). Women's sauna sessions run on Tuesday, Thursday and Saturday and men's on Monday, Wednesday, Friday and Sunday. The pool is open Monday to Friday from 7 am to 9 pm, Saturdays from 8 am to 6 pm, and Sundays, 8 am to 5 pm.

Golf

Jaðarsvöllur, south-west of Akureyri, claims to be the world's northernmost 18-hole golf course (the one in Kangerlussuaq, Greenland, is further north) and during the perpetual summer daylight, you can play around the clock. Golfers may want to check out the annual 36-hole Arctic Open, which is played overnight in late June. Registration costs US$200 with a handicap limit of 28 for men and 36 for women. For information, contact the Akureyri Golf Club (☎ 462 2974; fax 461 1755), PO Box 896, Akureyri.

The miniature golf course beside the swimming pool is open daily from 10 am to 10 pm.

Skiing

Hlíðarfjall (☎ 462 2930), seven km up Glerárdalur, is probably Iceland's best downhill ski slope. The longest run is 2½ km long with a vertical drop of about 500m. The 20 km of cross-country ski routes are open whenever snow cover is sufficient.

Between January and May, the chair lift and three rope tows operate Monday and Friday, from 1 to 6.45 pm; Tuesday to Thursday from 1 to 8.45 pm; and on weekends from 10 am to 5 pm. On weekends, snacks are available at the Strýta warm-up hut. In the long hours of winter darkness, the downhill runs are floodlit. In season, buses connect the site with Akureyri three times daily.

Serious skiers can stay at the ski lodge (see Places to Stay – Hostels), which also has a restaurant. A ski school offers individual and group instruction and equipment hire.

Organised Tours

In the summer, BSÍ runs sightseeing tours around Mývatn, departing at 8.15 am daily, for Ikr4550 (half price with Omnibuspass). Nonni Travel (☎ 461 1841; fax 461 1843; email nonnitra@est.is), on Ráðhúsplads, runs two-hour town tours (Ikr1885) and day tours to Ólafsfjörður and Hólar (Ikr5395), Aldeyjarfoss and Laufás (Ikr6240), Hrísey (Ikr1820), Goðafoss, Mývatn and Krafla (Ikr4940), Grímsey by ferry (Ikr4745) or flight and ferry (Ikr7350), and others.

Horse tours and hire are available from outlying farms. The best known is Pólar Hestar (☎ 463 3179), at Grýtubakka (see Grenivík), which offers wilderness trips. Other operators include Lítla-Garður (☎ 462 2243), near the airport, and Alda (☎ 463 1267), at Melgerði south of town.

Special Events

The annual summer-long arts festival runs from 20 June to late August and attracts artists and musicians from around Iceland. For details on specific events and exhibitions, contact Gilfélagið (☎ 461 2609).

Places to Stay – bottom end

Camping The two-part *campground* (☎ 462 3379; fax 461 2030) is divided between a small lawn beside the swimming pool, which is mainly used by individuals, and the spacious grassy lawn across Þórunnarstræti, which accommodates caravans and tour groups.

Campsites cost Ikr250 per person and Ikr250 per tent, and the office provides free brewed coffee all day. Four-minute showers are available at the gym next door for Ikr50. The washer and dryer, which cost Ikr300 to wash and Ikr200 to dry, see a great deal of action. There's no city bus from the bus terminal, but there is a serpentine trail which climbs up onto the bluff from Hafnarstræti and makes quite a short-cut.

On the eastern shore of Eyjafjörður, six km away, is the quieter *Húsabrekka* (☎ 462 4921) campground, which has the same rates and services as the in-town site. Nine-person cottages cost Ikr27,820 per week. *Vaðlafell*

(☎ 452 4501) has a six-person cottage for Ikr4050 per night.

Hostels Akureyri has two HI hostels, one in town which is open all year and the other in the countryside, which opens from 1 June to 1 October. In either, mattresses/beds cost Ikr780/1365 and single/double rooms with made-up beds are Ikr2350/4095. Both offer cooking facilities and bicycle hire (Ikr1000 per day).

The friendly *Akureyri Youth Hostel* (☎ 462 3657), at Stórholt 1, is a 15 minute walk from the city centre. Unless you speak Icelandic, Danish or German, communication with the management may result in a good-natured comedy of errors. Advance bookings are essential in summer. The *Lónsá Youth Hostel* (☎ & fax 462 5037) is three km from the town centre near the river Lónsá. If you arrive after 5 pm, phone and the staff will fetch you in town. Akureyri town buses stop within several hundred metres of the hostel and the long-distance buses from Reykjavík will drop you within 500m of the hostel.

There's also the cosy *Skíðastaðir Hlíðarfjall* (☎ 462 2280), at the ski resort. No posh ski lodge, this – sleeping-bag accommodation is just Ikr975.

Places to Stay – middle

The number of accommodation choices in Akureyri has mushroomed in recent years, especially in the middle range.

Guesthouses All the middle-range accommodation in Akureyri is guesthouse-style. Some are small family homes, others are more commercial, and some have kitchen facilities. Rates are controlled by the municipality; the maximum for single/double rooms is Ikr2930/4225 in made-up beds and Ikr1950/2925 for sleeping-bag accommodation. Naturally, some charge less.

A popular guesthouse with made-up rooms or sleeping-bag accommodation is the centrally located *Salka* (☎ 461 2340), at Skipagata 1. Also convenient is the *Ás* (☎ 461 2248; fax 461 1073), with two locations. The one at Skipagata 4 has rooms only, while the other, at Hafnarstræti 77, also has sleeping-bag accommodation and cooking facilities. Both of these charge the maximum allowable rates.

A good deal is the leafy and conveniently located *Sólgarðar* (☎ 461 1133) at Brekkugata 6, which has single/double rooms for Ikr2535/3770 and sleeping-bag accommodation for Ikr1235. Cooking facilities are available.

The *Glerá* (☎ 462 5723) lies four km from town, halfway to the Hlíðarfjall ski area. It charges Ikr3000/4050 for single/double rooms. A solid mid-range option is *Gilsbakki* (☎ 461 2723) at Gilsbakkavegur 13, which charges Ikr2925/4225 for single/double rooms. Sleeping-bag accommodation costs Ikr1300. *Árgerði* (☎ 462 4849), at Tungusiða 2, has made-up rooms but no sleeping-bag accommodation or cooking facilities.

The following all have made-up rooms and sleeping-bag accommodation: *Bakki* (☎ 462 5774), at Bakkahlíð 18; the comfy *Brekkusel* (☎ 462 3961) at Hrafnagilsstræti 23; the low-key *Dala-Kofinn* (☎ 462 3035), at Lyngholt 20; the good-value *Súlur* (☎ 461 1160; fax 461 3077), at Þórunnarstræti 93; *Gula Villan* (☎ 461 2860), at Þingvallastræti 14; *Sunnuhlíð 5* (☎ 462 2236); and *Langahlíð 6* (☎ 462 3472). Brekkusel, Sunnuhlíð 5 and Langahlíð 6 lack cooking facilities.

Nearby farmhouse accommodation includes *Pétursborg* (☎ 461 1811; fax 461 1332), four km north of the town. Although rural, it's convenient, has a pleasant setting and offers cooking facilities and a boat for sea fishing. Made-up single/double rooms cost Ikr3055/4550.

Hotels The *Edda Hotel* (☎ 461 1434; fax 461 1423), at Eyrarlandsvegur 28, charges Ikr3650/4750 for single/double rooms and Ikr1000/1430 for sleeping-bag accommodation in schoolrooms/rooms. There's a second *Edda Hotel Þelamörk* (☎ 462 1772; fax 461 2337) at Þelamörk, 12 km north-west of Akureyri along the Ring Road. Prices are the same as in town.

Apartments The *Studio Íbúðir* (☎ 461 2035; fax 462 1227), at Strandgata 13, are actually self-catering flats accommodating up to four people. For two/four people, you'll pay Ikr6305/7280, but discounts are available if you stay more than one night. A similar deal is found at *Hotel Apartments* (☎ 892 9838; fax 462 2300), at Geislagata 10, where a self-catering flat for two to eight people rents for Ikr7410 per night.

Places to Stay – top end

Hotels Akureyri's most upmarket option is the *Hótel Kea* (☎ 462 2200; fax 461 2285) at Hafnarstræti 97, run by the KEA cooperative. It's plush enough, with a bar, cafeteria and dining room, but as with many Icelandic hotels, it feels a bit sterile. Single/double rooms with a shower start at Ikr10,000/ 12,350 and climb to Ikr16,575 for a double suite.

Slightly less expensive is the *Hótel Norðurland* (☎ 462 2600; fax 462 7962) at Geislagata 7. Singles/doubles cost 8700/ 10,300 with a shower and breakfast.

Moving down the scale, the peachy *Hótel Harpa* (☎ 461 1400; fax 462 7795) at Hafnarstræti 83 is rather more low-key than its neighbour, the Hótel Kea. It also has an annexe, the large new *Hótel Harpa Kjarnalundur* (☎ 461 1014; fax 461 2973), three km from town at the lovely Kjarnaskógar woods. At either place, singles/doubles without bath cost Ikr6400/ 8300; with bath, they're Ikr7400/8300.

The *Hótel Óðal* (☎ 461 1900; fax 461 1899) at Hafnarstræti 67 enjoys a quiet location near the bus terminal, but wouldn't look out of place in deepest Bavaria. It charges Ikr9295/11,375 for single/double rooms with shower and breakfast.

Places to Eat

Self-Catering Akureyri has a wealth of supermarkets and kiosks, all well stocked and convenient. There's a particularly good *KEA* supermarket at the campground, and it's open until 10 pm nightly. The *Hagkaup* at Norðurgata 62 on Oddeyri is good value but it's a bit of a walk from the centre. The

Kjörbúðin Kaupangi supermarket, on Þingvallastræti, is open from 9 am to 11 pm weekdays and 10 am to 11 pm on weekends.

Einars Bakarí sells fresh bread and cakes. The State Monopoly shop is at Hólabraut 16, near the cinema. Bread, cakes and pastries are available at *Kristjáns Bakarí*, in the Kaupangur shopping centre; it also has a range of fresh fruit and vegetables. For health food items, check out *Heilsuhornið* at Skipagata 6.

Snacks & Fast Food On the pedestrian shopping mall are several small kiosks selling hot dogs, chips, burgers, sandwiches and soft drinks. The *Turinn*, which appears to be a schoolhouse painted with a Coca-Cola motif, is actually an ice-cream shop.

The *Bíóbarinn*, at Geislagata 1 on Ráðhústorg, serves up hamburgers, hot dogs, chips and soft drinks to people on the run. On Friday and Saturday nights, it's open until 4 am.

For a more elegant class of snacks, there's the *Café Turninn* ice-cream bar at the Blómahúsið greenhouse, flower shop and gift shop, at Hafnarstræti 26.

Crown Chicken (☎ 462 1464), at Skipagata 12, does not only chicken but burgers, hot dogs and chips; a quick meal costs around Ikr600. It's open from 11 am to 11.30 pm daily in the summer. There's another outlet opposite the Akureyri Youth Hostel on Stórholt; this one is a genuine US-style drive-through.

At Hafnarstræti 89 is *Dropinn Pizzeria*, which is dearer than the chicken places, but you can drink a cold brew to the tune of the musical oldies in the background. It's open from 11.30 am to 1 am weekdays and until 3 am on Friday and Saturday.

Excellent afternoon coffees and snacks are found at the popular *Café Karólína* (☎ 461 2755), on Kaupvangsstræti, near the church. It's open Sunday to Thursday from 10 am to 1 am and on Friday and Saturday from 2 pm to 3 am. Alternatively, there's the *Við Pollinn* (☎ 461 2527) coffee shop and pub, at Strandgata 49, which is housed in a historic building near the water.

Restaurants If you can manage a splurge only once in Iceland, save it for Akureyri. As restaurants go, the *Bautinn* (☎ 462 1818), in the city centre, is one of Iceland's best bargains, and it serves the sort of fare that travellers are dreaming about by the time they get this far. The solarium atmosphere is cosy and doesn't cater specifically to tourists. You'll get all-you-can-eat soup and salad-bar meals with a variety of freshly baked bread for Ikr785. With a complete meal (main dish, potato dish and vegetable dish), which averages about Ikr1200, the soup and salad are included. Bottomless cups of coffee or soft drinks are just Ikr80. What's more, alcohol prices are lower than in most pubs. Daily specials, which are posted at the door, include creatively prepared fish, lamb, beef and vegetarian dishes as well as puffin and other Icelandic delicacies. In the afternoon, there's a coffee buffet and a range of desserts and ice-cream confections.

Competing directly with the Bautinn is the superb and equally economical *Greifinn* (☎ 461 2690), at Glerárgata 20, near the sports stadium. The soup-and-salad bar costs Ikr550 per trip as a meal and Ikr280 as an accompaniment to a main meal. Steak, lamb or fish dishes with potatoes, vegetables and trimmings cost from Ikr950 to Ikr2000. Other specialities include pizzas (Ikr500 to Ikr950), pasta (Ikr770), burgers (Ikr750) and hot sandwiches (Ikr900). It's open daily from 11.30 am to 11.30 pm. In the afternoon, it makes a good stop for an espresso or cappuccino. Draught/bottled beer costs just Ikr400/360 for 500 ml.

In the Hótel Norðurland is the ever-present but always laudable *Pizza 67* (☎ 461 2967). For fast Thai cuisine, the choice is the small *Prany Ahan Thai* (☎ 462 6430), in the Videoland shop on Geislagata. It also does takeaway meals. Nearby at Ráðhústorg is the more earthy *Café Torgið* with a grill and restaurant. It's open from 11.30 to 1 am daily, with live music most evenings and dancing on weekends.

Most of the big hotels have elegant and expensive dining rooms but they're typically high-budget places. One exception is the

Súlnaberg Cafeteria at Hótel Kea, which serves four or five different cafeteria meals daily. Immense portions of meat, salad, potatoes and vegetables cost around Ikr1100, while pasta and vegetarian dishes are around Ikr700. There is also a selection of salads and desserts. A snack of coffee and cake costs as little as Ikr175.

There are also two first-class restaurants. The atmospheric *Fiðlarinn* (☎ 462 7100), five storeys up at Skipagata 14, serves fine cuisine and enjoys a great fjord view. The *Höfðaberg* (☎ 462 2200), at the Hótel KEA, offers similarly top notch fare. The *Sjallinn* (☎ 462 2770) offers an international menu and fine nightlife (see Entertainment), and the *Hótel Óðal* also has a fine restaurant.

Entertainment

Pubs & Discos Several pubs and discos in the town centre are quite popular with youth, but Akureyri's nocturnal scene isn't quite as bacchanalian as Reykjavík's. The *Café Torgið* is probably the most popular night spot, with live music nearly every night until 1 am and dancing until 3 am on Friday and Saturday. The *Sjallinn* (☎ 462 2770), at Geislagata 14, has two pubs, the *Góði Dátinn* and the *Kjallarinn*. On weekends, it stages live music and dancing, which winds down at 3 am. For drinks, the *Dropinn Pizzeria* on Hafnarstræti is a good bet.

Cinema The cinema on Hólagata has two *salur*, each of which screens two films nightly. To find out what's playing and at what time, work it out from the advertising on the windows or enquire at the tourist office. Admission costs Ikr550.

Theatre Unfortunately for most tourists, Akureyri's theatre season runs from September to June. For information, contact the Leilfélag Akureyrar (☎ 462 1400).

Things to Buy

Akureyri has an Álafoss woollens factory outlet, Folda, where jumpers and other woollen goods may be purchased at factory prices. It's open from 9 am to 6 pm Monday

to Friday, on Saturday from 10 am to 4 pm and on Sunday from 1 to 4 pm. The shop is in the residential area about five blocks north of the campground.

On Hafnarstræti, several shops offer woollens and souvenirs on the nominally 'tax-free' scheme. The largest is Paris, which is open from 9 am to 7 pm on weekdays and 9 am to 1 pm on weekends.

Getting There & Away

Air In the summer, Flugleiðir (☎ 461 2200) has up to five flights daily between Akureyri and Reykjavík. The first departs from Reykjavík at 7.30 am and returns at 8.40 am, and the last leaves at 8.45 pm and returns at 9.55 pm.

Flugfélag Norðurlands (☎ 461 2100; fax 461 2106) has flights to/from Reykjavík on Monday, Thursday, Saturday and Sunday. It also flies between Akureyri and Keflavík (summer only), Egilsstaðir, Húsavík, Ísafjörður, Kópasker, Raufarhöfn, Vopnafjörður and Þórshöfn. From 14 June to 25 August, there's at least one daily flight to Grímsey.

Bus The bus terminal is in the tourist information office on Hafnarstræti. Between Akureyri and Reykjavík, buses depart daily at 9.30 am year-round, with additional departures at 5 pm from 15 June to 31 August.

From mid-July to 20 August, there's also a daily service over the Kjölar route, departing from Reykjavík at 9.30 am and from Akureyri at 8 am. Over the Sprengisandur route, buses run from Reykjavík to Akureyri on Monday and Thursday at 8 am, but they don't run in the opposite direction. The excursion trip costs Ikr4500 via Kjölur and Ikr9300 via Sprengisandur. Omnibuspass holders must pay a surcharge on these routes.

Buses to/from Egilsstaðir run daily from 17 May to 30 September. From 1 June to 31 August, there's an additional daily departure. All Egilsstaðir buses pass through Reykjahlíð and Skutustaðir, at Mývatn. In July and August, two additional buses run to Mývatn at 8.15 am and 8 pm. From 17 May to 30 September, buses from Mývatn to Akureyri depart at 8.15 am and 4.15 pm daily and, in July and August, there's another service from Mývatn at 7.30 pm.

To Húsavík, buses run at least once daily (except Saturday). From 15 June to 29 August, they run to Ásbyrgi from Akureyri Monday to Thursday at 8.15 am and Monday, Wednesday and Friday at 3.30 pm. From Ásbyrgi, at least one bus leaves daily (except Saturday). To Vopnafjörður, buses run daily from Sunday to Thursday, but some require connections in either Húsavík or Mývatn.

Buses to Dalvík, the Hrísey ferry and Ólafsfjörður leave Monday to Friday at 12.30 and 6.30 pm, with additional departures at 11.30 pm on Monday, Thursday and Saturday.

Ferry The ferry *Sæfari* sails to Grímsey on Monday and Thursday at 9 am (with stops at Hrísey and Dalvík) and leaves Grímsey for the return at 7 pm. The trip takes five hours each way and costs Ikr4160 return, and yes, that includes an Arctic Circle certificate. If you prefer a tour, contact Nonni Travel (see Organised Tours in this section).

Getting Around
Bus Akureyri has a regular town bus service that costs Ikr120. It runs daily from 7.30 am to 11 pm.

Car Hire Akureyri has several rental agencies; see Car Hire in the Iceland Getting Around chapter. Bear in mind that, for an extra charge, you can pick up a car in Akureyri and drop it off in Reykjavík or vice versa.

Taxi The BSO Taxi (☎ 461 1010) may be booked 24 hours a day.

Bicycle Once you've sweated up the steep slope onto the bluff, cycling around Akureyri is easy. The tourist office hires bicycles for around Ikr1100 per day.

Around Akureyri

ÓLAFSFJÖRÐUR
The fishing town of Ólafsfjörður is beautifully situated beneath snow-capped 1200m peaks. It makes an ideal day trip from Akureyri and, statistically, it enjoys excellent weather.

In the valley south of town is the large lake Ólafsfjarðarvatn, which is connected to the fjord Ólafsfjörður by a short tidal channel. The valley was an exclusively agricultural area until the 1890s, when a village grew up around the fishing port. Ólafsfjörður was granted trading rights in 1905 and became a municipality in 1944. It's now home to 1200 people.

Nátúrrugripsafnið
Ólafsfjörður's small natural history museum (☎ 466 2651) is open 1 June to 1 September from 2 to 5 pm and at other times on request. Admission is Ikr200.

Ólafsfjarðarmúli
For several weeks around the end of June, the beautiful 400m high headland, Ólafsfjarðarmúli, will allow you to see beyond the Arctic Circle and experience the real midnight sun. (Grímsey, which is right on the Arctic Circle, is visible in fine weather.) Unfortunately, there's no easy route up; the scree slopes are steep and rather hazardous climbing so most people do their viewing from the high point along the road.

A three km tunnel through Ólafsfjarðarmúli was opened in 1991, eliminating the drive around the headland to reach Ólafsfjörður from the south.

Drangarskarð
The old Drangarskarð hiking trail over the Drangar ridge is very steep and not easily negotiated. It leads uphill from Bustarbrekka (up the valley from Ólafsfjörður), then climbs precipitously over the ridge and ends up at Karlsá on Eyjafjörður. The indirect but exceptionally scenic route amounts to about

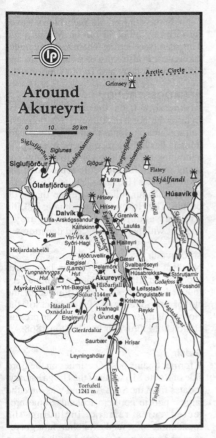

Around
Akureyri

10 km each way. From Karlsá, you can hitch or catch the bus back to Ólafsfjörður or Akureyri.

Places to Stay & Eat

The rather ordinary *Hótel Ólafsfjörður* (☎ 466 2400; fax 466 2660) has single/double rooms for Ikr3770/4615 with shower. The coffee shop/cafeteria serves reasonable lunch specials. The *supermarket* opens for a few hours on weekdays and the *Shell* petrol station has a grill and snack bar.

The basic *campground* is beside the swimming pool, just below the odd structure resembling an artificial ski jump. There's also a small ski lodge, *Skíðaskáli í Tindaöxl* (☎ 466 2207), charging Ikr900 for sleeping-bag accommodation.

Entertainment

The cinema in the centre shows films several times a week.

Getting There & Away

Between 1 June and 30 September, you can make a day visit to Ólafsfjörður from Akureyri (Ikr650) by taking the bus which leaves Akureyri on weekdays at 12.30 pm and returning on the 4.45 pm bus. There's also a bus from Ólafsfjörður at 8.45 am and from Akureyri at 7.30 am and 6.30 pm.

DALVÍK

Dalvík (population 1500), west of Hrísey island, has only become a population centre in the past century. Its excellent harbour has naturally meant that its economic emphasis is on fishing. In 1934, an earthquake measuring 6.3 destroyed or damaged 77 homes, leaving nearly half the inhabitants homeless. The unusual church contains a Bible published in 1584. The scenery around Dalvík is superb and offers some inviting hiking routes.

Hvoll Museum

The local museum (☎ 466 1497), which emphasises art and natural history exhibits, is open daily, 1 June to 15 September, from 1 to 5 pm. Admission is Ikr200.

Heljardalsheiði

A popular walk or horseback tour from Dalvík is over Heljardalsheiði. It begins at the end of Route 805, 20 km up Svarfaðárdalur, and traverses the Tröllskagi peninsula to Hólar. However, there's no public transport from Hólar.

This unmarked wilderness backpacking route passes through some of Iceland's best mountain scenery. Allow at least two days for the walk, and more if you'd like to explore the small glaciers Þverárjökull and

Tungnahryggsjökull. It's also wise to allow time for foul weather.

Another option between Hjaltadalur and Eyjafjörður is the route across Hjaltadals-heiði, a two to three-day moor walk between Hólar and the upper end of Route 814. You can also take the more difficult route up Kolbeinsdalur and via the Tungnahrygg and Bægisel (Lambi) huts through the pass between the glaciers. For hut information, contact Ferðafélags Akureyrar (see Glerárdalur & Mt Súlur Hikes, under Akureyri). Snow may be a concern before mid-July or after mid-September.

These routes are covered on the 1:100,000 topo sheets *Eyjafjörður*, *Akureyri* and parts of *Skagaströnd* and *Víðimýri*. Further information is available in the free brochure, *Introducing Svarfadardalur Nature Reserve*, distributed by the Akureyri tourist office.

Places to Stay & Eat

Dalvík has one summer hotel, *Sæluhúsið* (☎ 466 1488; fax 466 1661), with a restaurant. Single/double rooms cost Ikr3900/4875 with shared facilities and Ikr5200/6500 with shower. Sleeping-bag accommodation may also be arranged. The official *campground* (☎ 466 1600) is beside the school, but the valleys behind town offer unlimited wild campsites.

On Böggvisstaðafjall, the prominent ridge above Dalvík, is a small ski slope with lifts and a lodge, *Brekkusel Skíðaskáli* (☎ 466 1010). Rooms cost Ikr2200 per person and sleeping-bag accommodation on mattresses/beds is Ikr850/1200. There's also a snack bar selling light meals.

Dalvík has a well-stocked *supermarket* in its small shopping complex and, over the road near the harbour, there's a wonderful *bakery* and *coffee shop* with a patio for sunny days. At Skíðabraut 4 is the recommended *Pizza 67* (☎ 466 1587), which serves pizza, light meals and alcohol.

Getting There & Away

Buses from Akureyri (Ikr550) leave at 7.30 am and 12.30 and 6.30 pm on weekdays; from Dalvík, they run at 6.30 and 9 am, and

5 pm. In the summer, the *Sæfari* ferry leaves for Grímsey at 12.30 pm on Monday and Thursday (see Getting There & Away under Akureyri). It also sails between Dalvík and Hrísey on Monday and Tuesday mornings.

ÁRSKÓGSSTRÖND

Árskógsströnd, on the western shore of Eyjafjörður north of Akureyri, is a rich agricultural area. As far as tourism is concerned, it really has little to recommend it, except as a jumping-off point for visits to Hrísey. The string of tiny fishing settlements along the shore includes Hauganes, Hjalteyri and Lítla Árskógssandur, all with fewer than 100 people. The Hrísey ferry terminal is at Lítla Árskógssandur; buses from Akureyri connect with ferry arrivals and departures.

Möðruvellir

North of the Hörgá river is the large farm Möðruvellir. It was the site of a monastery founded in 1296 and the birthplace of the author Jón Sveinsson, the subject of the Nonnahús museum in Akureyri. The present church at Möðruvellir was built in 1868.

Gæsir

A former trading post, Gæsir lies on the fjord side of Route 816 south of the Hörgá estuary. It dates from the Saga Age and was once the largest port in northern Iceland. Some protected ruins remain, including the foundations of a medieval church, a graveyard and some grass-covered outlines where port trading offices once stood. To get there, head six km north from Akureyri along the Ring Road and turn east on Route 816, then continue another 5½ km to the site. It's just manageable as a day hike from the Lónsá youth hostel.

Places to Stay & Eat

Both *Syðri-Hagi* (☎ 466 1961) and *Ytri-vík/Kálfskinn* (☎ 466 1982; fax 466 1046) have farmhouse accommodation, summer cottages, sleeping-bag accommodation and meals (as well as horses for hire). Ytri-vík also has cooking facilities, hires horses, rowing boats and sailboards, and organises sea-fishing trips. Syðri-Hagi has a rowing boat for sea-fishing. Both charge Ikr3000/4700 for single/double rooms and Ikr1300 for sleeping-bag accommodation. Six-person cottages cost Ikr40,235 per week.

HRÍSEY

The low-lying island of Hrísey, in the middle of Eyjafjörður, measures about seven km long and 2½ km wide. It's the second largest island off the Icelandic coast, and has a population of around 260. During WWII, the island was a posting for five unarmed British army personnel whose job was to guard the entrance to Eyjafjörður and check passing trawlers for suspicious cargo or activities.

Information

The bank is open from 10 am to 4 pm Monday to Friday and there's also a supermarket, post office and swimming pool.

Things to See

The picturesque **village** at the island's southern end is a quiet spot with cobbled streets and few motor vehicles. The island's cliff-girt north-east coast is indented by **sea caves**, and the bush areas have reverted to a natural state, having been free of sheep for many years now.

The best vantage points for viewing the midnight sun are off limits, as most of Hrísey is a private ptarmigan and eider duck sanctuary. Visitors may not leave the road or marked nature trails without permission from the Hótel Brekka. The reserve hiking trails may be comfortably walked in two hours.

Places to Stay

The *Hótel Brekka* (☎ 466 1751; fax 466 3051) is a very popular spot during the summer. Single or double rooms with shared facilities cost Ikr4355. Sleeping-bag accommodation, with access to cooking facilities, is available at the *school* (☎ 466 1769) for Ikr1000/1300 on mattresses/beds. The hotel also hires bicycles for around Ikr1000 per day.

Eyland Chalets (☎ 466 6175) has an eight-person summerhouse for Ikr25,100 per week. Campers must stay at the official *campground* (☎ 466 1769), near the community centre.

Places to Eat

The speciality of Hótel Brekka's licensed dining room is 'Galloway Beef'. Originally imported from Scotland, it's now raised and sold in Iceland only on Hrísey. If you're not into expensive gourmet cow, the menu is replete with other possibilities. Otherwise, stop by the *Snekkjan* (☎ 466 1077) snack bar, or the *KEA* supermarket.

Getting There & Away

On weekdays, buses from Akureyri arrive at the ferry terminal at 1.05 and 7.05 pm. They leave for Akureyri at 9.15 am and 5.15 pm on weekdays.

From 1 May to 15 September, the ferry *Sævar* leaves Hrísey daily at 9 and 11 am and 1, 3, 5, 7, 9 and 11 pm, and returns from the mainland half an hour after each departure. The fare is Ikr375 each way. The ferry *Sæfari*, between Akureyri and Grímsey, stops at Hrísey en route. See Getting There & Away under Akureyri.

ÖXNADALUR

Through the valley Öxnadalur at the base of the Tröllskagi, Ring Road travellers are treated to the finest scenery between Reykjavík and Akureyri. The Ring Road follows a narrow valley for over 30 km and reaches its highest point at an altitude of 540m. It's excellent mountaineering country and the weather is as fine as you'll find anywhere in the Icelandic mountains.

Hraundrangi

The imposing 1075m spire of Hraundrangi and the surrounding peaks of Háafjall are probably the most dramatic in Iceland. Early settlers considered the summit of Hraundrangi inaccessible and perpetuated legends of a hidden cache of gold that awaited the first climber to reach the top. It was finally climbed in 1956, but the treasure seemed to have already gone missing.

ICELAND

Opposite the farm Steinsstaðir, near Hraundrangi, a view disc identifies rugged features of the surrounding ranges.

Bægisá

The beautiful Bægisá valley is accessible from between the farms Ytri-Bægisá and Syðri-Bægisá. At the head of the valley is a small remnant of the glacier Bægisájökull, surrounded by high peaks and steep rock walls. The area is ideal for advanced mountaineering techniques, but casual hikers and trekkers can also enjoy it.

Vindheimaöxl

Above the farm Neðri-Vindheimar, east of the Ring Road, is the steep and rocky Vindheimaöxl ridge, and higher up, the tiny remnant of the glacier Vindheimajökull. There's lots of loose scree, making for slow hiking in places. In fact, it's more easily reached from the Hlíðarfjall ski area in Akureyri.

Barkárdalur

For a pleasant wilderness trekking trip, leave the Ring Road and head west at the farm Ytri-Bægisá, which is a short walk across the river Hörgá. The second turning on your left is a small track leading five km up Barkárdalur to the six-bunk Bægisel (Lambi) hut. A further climb up the ridge will take you to the 12-bunk Tungnahryggur hut, in the second largest glacial area in northern Iceland. See also Heljardalsheiði, under Dalvík.

Places to Stay

Farmhouse and sleeping-bag accommodation is available at the beautifully located farm *Engimýri* (☎ 462 6838; fax 462 6938), which is run by the Jespersen family. The farmers offer trout fishing and a variety of riding tours. Seven and 10-day packages including accommodation and riding and sightseeing tours are available for between Ikr66,000 and Ikr88,000.

GRENIVÍK

Grenivík (population 300) got its start in

1910 and once the harbour and fish-freezing plant were opened, the population grew to its present level. The village has a supermarket, campground and petrol station. Most visitors are interested in the Laufás museum or one of the local horse tours.

Laufás Farm Museum

Laufás (☎ 463 3106), eight km south of Grenivík, originally served as a manor farm and vicarage. The turf farmhouse dates from 1850 and contains the usual household and agricultural implements used by the gentry during that period and earlier. The vicarage was home for not only the vicar, but also for his farm hands, and at any one time, up to 30 people occupied the building. The church, which accommodates 110 people in its 62 sq metres, was built in 1865 and dedicated to St Peter. From 1 June to 15 September, the museum is open daily, except Monday, from 10 am to 6 pm. Admission is Ikr150.

Organised Tours

Pólar Hestar runs five-day horseback tours from the farm Grýtubakki II (see Places to Stay), four km south of Grenivík, for Ikr17,000. The trip crosses the mountains to the Fjörður area at the northern end of the peninsula, deserted since WWII. There are departures every Tuesday from 7 June to 23 August, but they're popular and should be booked in advance. This may also be done as a walking tour. The company also organises 10-day trips to Mývatn and Krafla, and eight-day round-up tours.

BSÍ also offers this tour as part of a five-day package for Ikr56,900, including return flights from Reykjavík, three days riding, full board and a Mývatn tour.

Nonni Travel in Akureyri runs day tours to the Laufás farm museum.

Places to Stay

Grýtubakki II (☎ 463 3179; fax 463 3144) provides farmhouse accommodation.

Getting There & Away

There are no public Akureyri-Grenivík buses. Take the Mývatn or Egilsstaðir bus to

Grímsey's Check-Mate

Grímsey is known as the home of Iceland's most avid chess players, and historically, many a poor performance at this sacred pastime resulted in messy dives from the sea cliffs; on Grímsey, failure at chess was equated to failure in life. Enthusiasm for the game might have dampened in the past two generations, but everyone on the island knows the story of its rather unconventional American benefactor, Daniel Willard Fiske.

During the late 1870s, Fiske, a millionaire journalist and chess champion, set himself up as the island's protector after hearing about its passion for the game. He sent badly needed firewood (as well as chess supplies!), financed the island's tiny library and bequeathed part of his estate to the community without ever making a visit.

In the library at the community centre, you can see a portrait of Fiske and some of his donations. Grímsey celebrates his birthday on 11 November. For more on the amusing Fiske story, read Lawrence Millman's account of a visit to the island in his book *Last Places – A Journey in the North*. ■

the intersection of the Ring Road and Route 83, then hitch the remaining 22 km to Grenivík.

SVALBARÐSEYRI

The small settlement of Svalbarðseyri lies just 11 km by road from Akureyri on the eastern shore of Eyjafjörður. It's little more than a tiny harbour, a petrol station, swimming pool and the *Gistiheimilið Smáratún* (☎ 462 5043; fax 461 2643). Singles/doubles cost Ikr2340/3445 and sleeping-bag accommodation is Ikr1170. There's also a small snack bar and kiosk. Self-catering flats cost Ikr5070/32,300 per day/week.

GRÍMSEY

The northern tip of the 5.3 sq km island of Grímsey, 41 km north of the mainland, constitutes Iceland's only real bit of Arctic territory. Yes, Grímsey is dissected by the Arctic Circle, and only here will you see the real midnight sun in Iceland. Although the attention span of most tourists falters there, the island's 100m cliffs harbour extensive bird colonies, accommodating at least 60 different species. Of these, 36 nest on the island – kittiwakes, puffins, razorbills, fulmars, guillemots, Arctic terns etc. Historically, Grímsey provided an abundant supply of birds and fresh eggs, and its waters were some of Iceland's richest in fish.

Sandvík (population 120) is the island's only settlement. Services are limited to a church, swimming pool, guesthouse and community centre.

Organised Tours

Nonni Travel in Akureyri runs Grímsey tours daily. Flying both ways costs Ikr8125. On Monday and Thursday, you can take the ferry both ways for Ikr4745. If you opt to fly back, it's Ikr7350. Participants get a certificate stating that they've crossed the Arctic Circle. For longer stays, you can leave the tour on the island and return to Akureyri another day.

Places to Stay & Eat

You can camp nearly anywhere away from the village. Sleeping-bag accommodation costs Ikr750 in the *Múli* community centre (☎ 467 3138). Beside the airfield is the *Gistiheimilið Básar* (☎ 467 3103), which has rooms for Ikr2800 per person and sleeping-bag accommodation for Ikr1200. Meals are available here but they're not cheap.

Getting There & Away

Air In the summer, Flugfélag Norðurlands flies between Akureyri and Grímsey at least once daily (except Saturday). Discounted flights are available on Thursday and Sunday.

Ferry The ferry *Sæfari* sails to Grímsey from Akureyri on Monday and Thursday at 9 am, with stops at Hrísey and Dalvík, and returns from Grímsey at 7 pm. The trip takes five hours each way and costs Ikr4160 return.

KOLBEINSEY

The islet Kolbeinsey, 100 km from the mainland, is Iceland's most northerly scrap of land. Early records describe it as 200m long, but rough sea conditions and ice floes have eroded it down to a mere speck in the Arctic Ocean. It currently measures just 42 x 38 metres.

Because Kolbeinsey's existence adds 9400 sq km to Iceland's territorial fishing grounds, the cause of saving it sits high on the parliamentary agenda. A steel-reinforced concrete wall has been proposed to shelter the vulnerable shoreline, but Kolbeinsey's status is already in dispute, and once it is officially classed as just an offshore rock, the cause of saving it will become academic.

UPPER EYJAFJÖRÐUR
Kristnes

Kristnes, seven km south of Akureyri, was the original Eyjafjörður settlement. At Pollurinn ('the puddle') near the head of the fjord, Helgi the Lean found his high-seat temple pillars and hedged his bets religionwise by naming his farm 'Christ's peninsula'. The modern hospital on the site was the first large public building in Iceland to be heated geothermally.

Hrafnagil

Twelve km south of Akureyri is Hrafnagil ('raven's ravine') which was the historic home of Bishop Jón Arason of Hólar. Today, there's accommodation at *Hótel Vin* (☎ 463 1333; fax 463 1399), with a cafe, greenhouse and summer campground. Single/double rooms cost Ikr3640/4745 without bath, and sleeping-bag accommodation costs Ikr850/1560 on mattresses/beds. There's also a geothermally heated pool where you can soak to your heart's content.

Grund

The odd little onion-domed church at Grund was built by the farmer Magnús Sigurðsson in 1905. Its neo-Romanesque style seems anomalous in Iceland, but earlier this century it was one of the country's most impressive churches. For a peek inside, ask for a key at the farmhouse.

Saurbær

The farm Saurbær, 27 km south of Akureyri on Route 821, has an interesting turf-and-stone church which dates from 1838, which is now under national protection. It was constructed on the site of a church that had existed there since the 11th century.

Leyningshólar

Leyningshólar is a cluster of hillocks and moraines formed by landslides about 7500 years old. They provide nice campsites, but there are no facilities. The hills and their surrounding birch woods – which include the only original stand in the Eyjafjörður area – provide interesting hiking.

Torfufell

Torfufell, at the end of Route 821, offers good hiking, including a climb up Torfufell mountain and a walk up the Torfufellsá canyon.

Places to Stay

The farm *Öngulstaðir III* (☎ 463 1380; fax 463 1390), 12 km south of Akureyri on Route 829, has cooking and laundry facilities. Single/double rooms cost Ikr3000/4050 and sleeping-bag accommodation is Ikr1300.

Leafy *Leifsstaðir* (☎ & fax 462 1610), less than 10 km from Akureyri, has its own small woodland and charges Ikr3650/5850 for single/double rooms without bath.

Further south, on Route 826, is the lovely farm, *Hrísar* (☎ 463 1305; fax 463 1341), which offers pleasant four/six-person self-catering cottages for Ikr35,100/40,235, made-up beds for Ikr3000/4050, and sleeping-bag accommodation for Ikr1300. The fishing is fine and there's a small shop.

Getting There & Away

Apart from the Sprengisandur tours between Reykjavík and Akureyri, there's no public transport to Upper Eyjafjörður. The tours leave Reykjavík on Monday and Thursday at 8 am in July and August, but don't cover the southbound route, so the only access from Akureyri is by hitching or private vehicle.

GOÐAFOSS

One of Iceland's most recognisable and easily accessible major waterfalls is Goðafoss ('waterfall of the gods'). It was formed by the glacial waters of the river Skjálfandafljót, which cut through the 8000-year-old Bárðardalur lava field (from the Trölladyngja crater near Vatnajökull).

The falls' romantic name wasn't aesthetically derived. At the Alþing in the year 999 (possibly 1000), the lögsögumaður, Þorgeir, spent 24 hours meditating on the issue of a national religion. His cerebral pondering resulted in a public declaration that Iceland would thenceforth be a Christian nation, and would forbid the open practice of paganism. On his way home to Ljósavatn, he passed the familiar horseshoe-shaped waterfall near his farm Djúpá ('deep river') and tossed in his carvings of the Norse gods, thus bestowing the falls' present name.

Vaglaskógur

Vaglaskógur, a 300 hectare swathe of birch woods with trees up to 13m high, lies south of the Ring Road midway between Akureyri and Goðafoss. For some interaction with real trees, you can stay at the campground on the eastern bank of the lovely river Fnjóská. To get there, take the Akureyri-Mývatn bus to the intersection of the Ring Road and Route 832, then walk about three km south to Route 836.

Places to Stay & Eat

The *Fosshóll Youth Hostel* (☎ 464 3108; fax 464 3318) charges Ikr1000/1250 for HI members/non-members, and single/double rooms are Ikr3055/4560. Camping costs Ikr450 per person. The petrol station has a grocery shop and snack bar.

The name of the nearby Edda hotel *Stórutjarnir* (☎ 464 3240; fax 464 3224), nine km west of Goðafoss and flanked by scenic birch woods, means 'big ponds', after Ljósavatn, which is a short walk away. Singles/doubles cost Ikr3650/4750 without bath or Ikr5200/7020 with bath. Sleeping-bag accommodation costs Ikr1000/1430 on mattresses/beds. There's a geothermally heated outdoor pool and a licensed restaurant, but no inexpensive place to eat, so travellers may want to bring their own food.

Getting There & Away

Your best option for visiting Góðafoss is the morning Mývatn bus from Akureyri, which will drop you at Fosshóll. The return bus to Akureyri passes Fosshóll at 5.10 pm and the evening bus to Mývatn passes at 8.55 pm.

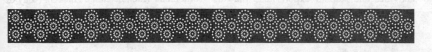

North-East Iceland

In North-East Iceland, the Ring Road takes a great short cut across the desert-like interior, neglecting a large area of practically uninhabited upland moors, wild coastal country and barren desert. Although it holds two of the country's most popular tourist attractions, Mývatn and Jökulsárgljúfur National Park, most of Iceland's north-eastern corner rarely sees visitors, and more visitors see the barren interior than venture up to Raufarhöfn or the Langanes peninsula. As a result, there are few facilities, and away from the Ring Road, traffic and public transport are scarce. If you venture off the worn routes, allow time for delays in out-of-the-way places.

At the other end of the spectrum, Mývatn is one of the natural wonders of the world. It's a highlight of any trip to Iceland and most visitors wish they'd allowed it more time. Also popular is the tongue-stifling Jökulsárgljúfur National Park, with its 'Grand Canyon' – the Jökulsá á Fjöllum – and myriad waterfalls. Other park attractions include the basalt sculptures of Vesturdalur and the striking cliffs of Ásbyrgi. Although Jökulsárgljúfur has only recently been discovered by non-Icelanders, it may catch up with Mývatn in popularity.

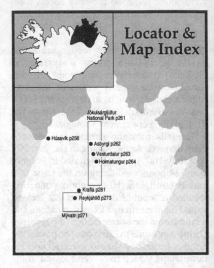

Húsavík Region

HÚSAVÍK

With a population of over 2500, Húsavík is the main town of North-East Iceland. Its picturesque harbour and snow-capped peaks would win it the title of 'most typical Icelandic town'. And no town could be typically Icelandic without an obvious dependence on fishing and fish processing. Mercantile activities and sulphur exports also play a role, as does tourism now that Húsavík is becoming known as a rewarding whale-watching venue.

The curious grass-roofed housing complex in the centre is a government-sponsored retirement community for senior citizens. Note also the fish-drying racks south of town and the wheels of dried fish at the harbour, both of which make fine photos.

History

Although the honours normally go to Reykjavík and Ingólfur Arnarson, Húsavík was the real site of the first Nordic settlement in Iceland. A Swedish Viking, Garðar Svavarsson, who set off around 850 for the mysterious Thule or Snæland ('snowland'), was actually responsible for the island's first permanent human settlement.

After a brief stop at Hornafjörður in the south, Garðar arrived at Skjálfandi ('shivering gulf') on the north coast and built a settlement which he called Húsavík ('bay of houses'). Modestly renaming the country Garðarshólmur ('Garðar's island'), he dug in for the winter. At the advent of spring, he

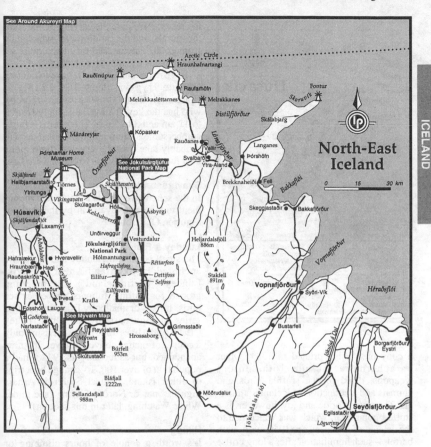

North-East Iceland

See Around Akureyri Map

See Jökulsárgljúfur National Park Map

See Myvatn Map

0   15   30 km

ICELAND

prepared to depart, but some of his slaves were inadvertently left behind. In effect, these castaways were Iceland's first settlers, but history hasn't credited them because their settlement was probably unintentional.

The historic Kaupfélag Þingeyinga was one of the first cooperatives in Iceland, and it still stands on the main street. Despite this town's early roots and economic importance, it only received municipal status in 1950.

Information

For tourist information, go to Ferðaskrifstofa Húsavíkur (☎ 464 2100), at Stórigarður 7. It's open weekdays from 9 am to 5 pm.

Húsavík has a car hire, banks and other facilities. Limited camping supplies and equipment are available at the Kaupfélag cooperative, and the bookshop opposite the church sells souvenir books and novels in both German and English.

Safnahúsið

The town museum, Safnahúsið Húsavíkur (☎ 464 1860), founded in 1980, exhibits folk, art and natural history and a wealth of photographs, paintings and books, including

ICELAND

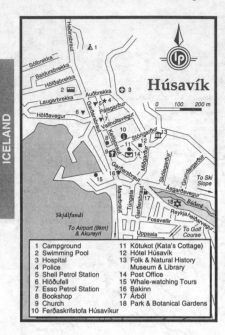

Húsavík

0   100   200 m

Skjálfandi

To Airport (9km)
& Akureyri

1 Campground	11 Kötukot (Kata's Cottage)
2 Swimming Pool	12 Hótel Húsavík
3 Hospital	13 Folk & Natural History
4 Police	Museum & Library
5 Shell Petrol Station	14 Post Office
6 Hlöðufell	15 Whale-watching Tours
7 Esso Petrol Station	16 Bakinn
8 Bookshop	17 Árból
9 Church	18 Park & Botanical Gardens
10 Ferðaskrifstofa Húsavíkur	

a copy of a Bible printed in 1584. Other paraphernalia include 16th-century weapons, dried plants, stuffed birds and animals and a collection of Icelandic minerals. The town's pride and joy, however, is a stuffed polar bear, which was welcomed to the island of Grímsey in 1969 with both barrels – such humiliation after a long cruise from Greenland on an ice floe.

It's open weekdays, from 1 June to 31 August, from 10 am to noon and 1 to 5 pm. Admission costs Ikr200.

Húsavíkurkirkja
The cross-shaped church in Húsavík is unique in Iceland. Constructed in 1907 from Norwegian timber, it's a bit like a gingerbread house. The altarpiece depicts the resurrection of Lazarus, but the Middle Eastern architecture sits in a lovely, green Icelandic backdrop. Húsavík residents served as models for the characters in the painting, but not everyone was happy with

the result. Also note the carving on the font, the murals, and the candlesticks, which date from 1600. The unusual bit of sculpture on the lawn has a distinctly industrial feel.

To visit the interior, you'll have to hunt up Hjörtur Tryggvason (☎ 464 1238), at Hjarðarhóli 20 (500m east of the church), who has the key. It's available daily from 9 to 11 am and 3 to 5 pm. This seems a fairly cumbersome system and the bookshop will probably take over the key sometime in the near future, so it may pay to check there first.

Svavarsson Monument
In the school grounds is a statue and monument to Garðar Svavarsson by the sculptor Sigurjón Ólafsson.

Lundey & Flatey
The small islands of Lundey and Flatey lie anchored in Skjálfandi, near Húsavík. Lundey ('puffin island') is a breeding ground for puffins, fulmars and other sea birds. It rises dramatically from the sea in a series of high nest-covered cliffs. Flatey ('flat island') lives up to its name, rising only a couple of metres above sea level. It's now abandoned, but as recently as 1942 it had a population of over 100. To arrange boat trips to either island, contact Sjóferðir Arnars Sigurðssonar or Norður Sigling (see under Whale Watching, later in this section).

Hiking
It's worth a couple of hours climbing or driving to the top of 417m Húsavíkurfjall. If you see any islands not identified on the view disc, you're probably not going mad. On clear, hot and sunny days, you may witness the Fata Morgana effect (see Arctic Phenomena in the Facts about the Region chapter), which is common along Iceland's Arctic Ocean coast. On exceptionally clear days, you can see the Vatnajökull icecap.

Another walk takes you to lake Botnsvatn, in a hollow behind the village, where re-afforestation projects are greening the landscape. Campers are welcome around the lake but there are no facilities. From the lake, you can walk up the jeep track to another lake, Höskuldsvatn, high in the moors about 12 km from town.

Whale Watching

Húsavík is known as Iceland's foremost whale-watching venue. The area is a veritable cetacean paradise and you'll almost certainly see whales. In June 1996, boats observed minke whales, humpback whales, fin whales, sei whales, orcas, white-beaked dolphins and harbour porpoises. Minke whales were seen on 93% of the trips and humpbacks showed up 63% of the time.

The boat *Whalewatcher* (☎ 464 1748) does up to four trips a day and charges Ikr3300 for 2 to 2½ hours. It also runs bird-watching and sea-fishing tours to Lundey (two hours, Ikr1700) and Flatey (six hours, rates depend on the number of passengers). Contact Sjóferðir Arnars Sigurðsonnar (☎ 894 2948; fax 464 2369), Litlagerði 8, 640 Húsavík.

The larger *Knörrinn*, a 20-tonne oak fishing boat, runs whale-watching trips twice daily and charges Ikr4200 for 3½ hours. It's operated by Norður Sigling (☎ 854 5351; fax 464 2350), Langabrekka 21, 640 Húsavík. The same company also runs daily combination whale and puffin-watching tours to Lundey.

Other Activities

North-east of town, two ski lifts operate during winter. There is also a swimming pool and a golf course in town.

Organised Tours

Monday to Friday at 10.30 am, 18 June to 31 August, BSÍ runs 8½ hour tours to Dettifoss and Jökulsárgljúfur National Park. The cost is Ikr4100.

You can also arrange three-day tours to Kverkfjöll and Askja with Ice & Fire Expeditions (☎ 464 2200; fax 464 2201). From 28 June to 1 September, tours depart from the Shell petrol station on Monday and Friday at 10 am. The price (not including food) is Ikr12,220 but discounts are available to Omnibuspass holders. Accommodation is in huts (Ikr2300 extra) or camping (Ikr900);

participants must bring their own sleeping bags and tents.

From Kverkfjöll, you can also continue across Vatnajökull by snowmobile or snow buggy to Jöklasel, on the icecap near Höfn. Contact Ice & Fire Expeditions in Húsavík or Jöklaferðir (☎ 478 1701; fax 478 1901), PO Box 66, 780 Höfn. See also Southern Vatnajökull in the South-East Iceland chapter.

Places to Stay

The *campground*, near the swimming pool, is lovingly run by the dedicated Gunnar, who has single-handedly provided campers with heated lavatories and laundry and cooking facilities. Drop by and give this friendly guy a vote of thanks! Campsites cost Ikr450 per person.

The basic, streamside *Gistiheimilið Árból* (☎ 464 2220; fax 464 1463), housed in a 1903 building at Ásgarðsvegur 2, charges Ikr4095/6045 for single/double rooms with shared facilities and Ikr1200 for sleeping-bag accommodation. *Kötukot* (☎ & fax 464 2323), or 'Kata's Cottage', a pinkish house at Ketilsbraut 20, has airy and comfortable single/double B&B accommodation for Ikr3500/4500. Just out of town at *Saltvík* (☎ 464 2062), there's basic sleeping-bag accommodation for Ikr1300.

The *Hótel Húsavík* (☎ 464 1220; fax 464 2161) charges Ikr8125/8840 for single/ double rooms with shower and breakfast. Sleeping-bag accommodation costs Ikr1300, without breakfast.

Places to Eat

The *Setberg* dining room at the Hótel Húsavík does standard fish, beef and lamb fare, and the lower-key licensed restaurant *Bakinn* (☎ 464 1215) does grill meals and pizza. Both the *Esso* and *Shell* petrol stations have snack bars and coffee shops selling ice cream, hot dogs, burgers, sandwiches, cakes, coffee and pizza. When the sun shines, tables are set up outside.

Self-catering is a joy in Húsavík. In addition to the cooperative *supermarket*, there's a *fish market* at the harbour. Locally grown vegies and Iceland's cheapest hardfiskur (haddock) are sold at the *flea market* opposite the church, and 18 km down the road at Hveravellir are greenhouses selling fresh local produce. The State Monopoly shop is at Túngata 1.

Getting There & Away

Air From 27 May to 1 September, Flugleiðir (☎ 464 1080) has services to and from Reykjavík on Monday, Wednesday, Friday and Sunday. Flugfélag Norðurlands (☎ 464 1080) flies between Húsavík and Akureyri on Saturday and Sunday, and to and from Reykjavík on Tuesday, Thursday, Saturday and Sunday. There's a local bus service run by Björn Sigurðsson between the airport and the town (Ikr400).

Bus The bus terminal is at Garðarsbraut 7, near the harbour. From 18 June to 31 August, there's at least one daily service between Akureyri and Húsavík (Ikr1100), and daily connections, except Sunday, from Húsavík to Ásbyrgi (Ikr800) at 10.30 am. On Monday, Wednesday and Friday from 20 June to 27 August, they continue from Húsavík to Raufarhöfn (Ikr1700) and Vopnafjörður (Ikr3100). From Vopnafjörður, the bus leaves for Húsavík at 8 am the same days. Between Húsavík and Mývatn (Ikr880), from 15 June to 31 August, there are three daily services on weekdays and one on weekends.

TJÖRNES

The stubby peninsula Tjörnes, north of Húsavík, separates Skjálfandi from Öxarfjörður. Colonies of puffins and other sea birds nest on the 50m cliffs along the eastern coast, and near the northern end is a lighthouse, from which clear weather allows a good view of Grímsey on the Arctic Circle.

For most visitors, Tjörnes is just a quick puffin-viewing stop on Jökulsárgljúfur National Park tours from Mývatn or Húsavík.

Ytritunga Fossils

From Ytritunga farm, a track leads down the coastal cliffs on either side of the Hallbjarnarstaðaá river mouth, which contains alternating layers of fossil shells and lignite. The oldest layers, which were laid down about two million years ago, are at about the 12m level. The present water temperature along Iceland's Arctic Ocean coast is around 4°C, yet the creatures that inhabited the shells are now found only in waters of 12°C or warmer, an indication that the sea has cooled over the past two to three million years. Newer layers at Ytritunga contain fossils of cold-water molluscs still living around Iceland.

At the farm Hallbjarnarstaðir, 12 km north of Húsavík on Route 85, is the Steingervingasafn fossil museum (☎ 464 1968), which displays interesting finds from this area, including plant and animal fossils from the Pleistocene era. It's open daily, 1 June to 15 September, from 9 am to 8 pm.

Þórshamar Home Museum

Near the river Máná, on Route 85, is the worthwhile Þórshamar Home Museum (☎ 464 1957), which contains objects dating all the way back to the Settlement era. It's open daily, 10 am to 6 pm, from 1 June to 31 August. Admission is Ikr100.

Mánáreyjar

Háey and Lágey, two small islands 10 km off the Tjörnes north coast, are called Mánáreyjar ('moon river islands'). They are remnants of old volcanic plugs.

Hiking

From the farm Syðritunga, an old 20 km track crosses the mountains and moors of the Tjörnes' interior to Fjöll on Öxarfjörður. It can be walked in a long day but is more pleasant if spread over two days.

Getting There & Away

Buses between Húsavík and Ásbyrgi follow the route around the Tjörnes peninsula.

KELDUHVERFI

Like Þingvellir, low-lying Kelduhverfi reveals some of the most visible evidence that Iceland is spreading from the centre. Beside the drowned estuary of the Jökulsá á Fjöllum, the Mid-Atlantic Ridge enters the Arctic Ocean in a series of odd cracks, fissures and grabens up to six or seven metres deep. Most of those in evidence today were formed by earthquakes and dramatic fissuring and subsidence during the Krafla eruption of 1977. The locals were literally rattled, but you can imagine their surprise to discover that their farms had actually increased in size overnight!

Kelduhverfi Lakes
Near the estuarine lake Víkingavatn, north of the highway at Kelduhverfi, is a farm of the same name which has been occupied by the descendants of the original farmer for nearly four centuries. Between Víkingavatn and Lón, the lagoon to the west, look out for a large and interesting tree. Anything relating to a large tree would be notable in Iceland, but this one appears to be devouring a house.

East of Víkingavatn is Skjálftavatn ('shivering lake') so newly formed by surface subsidence that it hasn't yet made it onto most maps. It's now used for freshwater fish farming. Continued spreading may eventually result in the invasion of the entire area by seawater (similar to the process occurring in Eritrea, where Africa's Great Rift enters the Red Sea).

Places to Stay & Eat
Four area farms, *Hóll* (☎ 465 2270), *Skúlagarður* (☎ 465 2280; fax 465 2279), *Víkingavatn* (☎ 465 2293), and *Unðirveggur* (☎ 465 2261) offer accommodation. All but Unðirveggur, which has only summer cottages (Ikr37,100 per week), have made-up rooms (Ikr3000/4050 for singles/doubles), and sleeping-bag accommodation (Ikr1300) is available at Víkingavatn. Hostel-style Skúlagarður, which occupies an old school, offers both sleeping-bag accommodation (Ikr1300) and camping. Skúlagarður and Hóll are especially handy for visits to Ásbyrgi and Jökulsárgljúfur National Park. Hóll also hires out horses and all but Unðirveggur offer meals.

REYKJADALUR & AÐALDALUR
The gentle, grassy valleys of the Laxá and Skjálfandafljót, south of Húsavík, are separated by green moors that belie the area's substantial geothermal activity. Reykjadalur ('smoky valley') is one of several parallel valleys separated by low hills.

Aðaldalshraun
The distinctive birch-and-scrub-covered lava field, Aðaldalshraun, takes in nearly 100 sq km. Near the farm Knútsstaðir, between Route 85 and the river Laxá, are some strange caves and hollow hills formed when steam lifted the surface of the lava into bubbles that hardened before breaking. The driver of the bus from Húsavík to Akureyri will point them out for you.

As you head south from Mývatn, notice the farm Laxámýrar ('salmon river marshes'), near the intersection of Routes 87 and 85, which is the family farm of British television personality Magnús Magnússon. There, the relatively wealthy can enjoy salmon fishing for a paltry Ikr40,000 per day. With an experienced fishing guide, it costs up to Ikr100,000 per day.

Hveravellir
The geothermal site, Hveravellir, in Reykjadalur, provides some of Húsavík's hot water supply. The most active of its three geysers, Ystihver, 300m east of the road, spouts up to three metres every two to three minutes. The farm sells fresh vegies from its geothermally heated greenhouses. All buses between Mývatn and Húsavík pass it.

Laugar
Laugar ('hot springs'), north-east of the Ring Road on Route 846, is often referred to as Laugar í Þingeyjarsýsla to distinguish it from the host of other 'Laugars' in Iceland. The school was built in 1924 and the following year received Iceland's first indoor swimming pool. Between 10 June and 26 August it operates as a summer hotel. Other facilities include a snack bar, kiosk, petrol station and campground. Buses between Akureyri and Mývatn pass within one km of the hotel.

Grenjaðarstaður

The wealthy old farm, Grenjaðarstaður, beside the Laxá, served as a church and vicarage during the last century, but in the churchyard is a stone with runes dating from medieval times. The turf farmhouse, constructed in 1876, now houses a low-profile folk museum (☎ 464 3545). It's open daily from 1 June to 31 August from 10 am to 6 pm. Admission is Ikr200.

Grenjaðarstaður lies five km from public transport routes. Get off the Húsavík-Mývatn bus at the intersection of Routes 87 and 853. Walk two km west, turn left on Route 854, then walk the remaining three km to the farm.

Þverá

The stone church at the farm Þverá dates from 1878 and the accompanying turf farmhouse was the original home of Iceland's first cooperative organisation, Kaupfélag Þingeyinga, founded in 1882. Þverá now belongs to the National Museum in Reykjavík and may be opened for display in the future. It's at the confluence of the Laxá and Þverá rivers, seven km upstream from the Route 856 Laxá bridge.

Places to Stay & Eat

Between 10 June and 26 August, the Laugar school operates as the *Hótel Laugar* (☎ 464 3120; fax 464 3163). Singles/doubles cost Ikr3650/4750 and sleeping-bag accommodation in the classrooms is Ikr1000/1430 on mattresses/beds. As the name would imply, it boasts a fine hot pool.

Several Reykjadalur and Aðaldalur farms offer accommodation. In Reykjadalur, there's *Narfastaðir* (☎ 464 3102; fax 464 3319), with single/double rooms for Ikr3000/4050. A copper bell which was dug up here in 1995 is thought to date from the early 13th century. *Heiðarbær* (☎ 464 3903; fax 464 3950), is a potential backpackers' resort, with sleeping-bag accommodation (Ikr975), as well as a swimming pool, campground, restaurant and jacuzzis.

In Aðaldalur, there are several choices. *Hagi* (☎ 464 3526) and *Hafralækur* (☎ 464 3561) both have beds, cottages and sleeping-bag accommodation. *Rauðaskriða* (☎ 464 3504; fax 464 3644), just off Route 85, has beds, a lovely dining room and a fine country view. *Hraunbær* (☎ 464 3595), with beds and cooking facilities, is also recommended. *Grímshús* (☎ 464 3551) has only sleeping-bag accommodation (Ikr1235).

JÖKULSÁRGLJÚFUR NATIONAL PARK

The formidable name of this fabulous national park means 'glacial river canyon', and in tourist literature it's referred to as 'Iceland's Grand Canyon', perhaps to lure visitors with a sense of the familiar. However, the park is also known for its diverse birch forests, striking rock formations and the canyon Ásbyrgi, created by a natural catastrophe 200 km away. At the park's southern end is Dettifoss, Europe's greatest waterfall, which is predictably touted as the 'Niagara of Europe'. Fortunately, you won't find any kitsch wax museums or coloured floodlights here – just nature at its finest.

At the heart of the park is the 30 km Jökulsárgljúfur, which averages 100m deep and 500m wide. In its uppermost reaches is a series of waterfalls: Selfoss, Dettifoss, Hafragilsfoss, Réttarfoss and Vígabjargsfoss (which nearly disappeared when the Jökulsá á Fjöllum changed course in 1940).

Most of the land now protected within Jökulsárgljúfur historically belonged to the Ás estate, one of Iceland's largest private holdings, which extended from Dettifoss to Öxarfjörður. Until the early 1800s, there was a church at Ás, near the highway on the northern end, but it's now gone and only remnants of the cemetery are visible. The deserted Svínadalur area in the upper park served as a farm and a summer dairying enterprise as recently as 1946.

Ásbyrgi has long been considered prime farmland, and in medieval times the living was good due to the anomalous profusion of trees. However, conditions deteriorated after it was ravaged by *jökulhlaup* floods in the 17th and 18th centuries.

The national park was established in 1973,

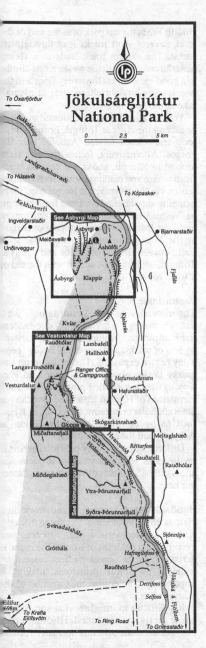

Jökulsárgljúfur
National Park

0   2.5   5 km

To Öxarfjörður

Bakkahlaup

Landgræðslusvæði

To Húsavík

Kelduhverfi

Ingveldarstaðir

See Ásbyrgi Map

Meiðavellir

Ásbyrgi

Ásshöfði

Unðirveggur

To Kópasker

Bjarnarstaðir

Fjalllið

Ásbyrgi   Klappir

Kvíar

Kjalarás

See Vesturdalur Map

Rauðhólar   Lambafell

Hallhöfð

Langavatnshöfði

Ranger Office
& Campground

Hafursstaðavatn

Vesturdalur

Hafursstaðir

Gloppa

Skógarkinnshæð

Miðaftansfjall

Meltaglshæð

Hvannstaði   Réttarfoss

Hólmatungur   Sauðafell

Miðdegishæ

Rauðhólar

See Hólmatungur Map

Ytra-Þórunnarfjall

Syðra-Þórunnarfjall

Svínadalshás

Sjónnípa

Gróthás

Hafragilsfoss

Rauðhóll

Dettifoss

Selfoss

Eilífur
698m

To Krafla
Eilífsvötn

Jökulsá á Fjöllum

To Ring Road

To Grímsstaðir

ICELAND

initially including only the farm Svínadalur, part of Vesturdalur and a small portion of Ásheiði. In 1974, the huge Ás estate was added and in 1978, Ásbyrgi came under national park protection. Jökulsárgljúfur now contains 150 sq km and extends 35 km from south to north.

Orientation

The park's southern anchor is Dettifoss, and eight km to the north are the springs and luxuriant vegetation of Hólmatungur. Right in the heart of the park is Vesturdalur, with lots of caves and Iceland's most interesting basalt formations. Near the northern end is Ásbyrgi, a verdant forested plain enclosed by ruddy canyon walls. The northernmost thumb of Jökulsárgljúfur, Landgræðslus- væði, is part of the alluvial delta of the Jökulsá á Fjöllum.

Maps Jökulsárgljúfur offers excellent hiking and trekking. The best walking map is the *Dettifoss* 1:100,000 sheet, but if you also want to hike at Mývatn, it's worth purchasing the thematic *Húsavík-Mývatn* 1:100,000 map, which includes both areas. The park brochure, sold for Ikr100 at visitors centres and some tourist offices, shows the main hiking routes and is adequate for most hikes.

Information

Park information is available at the ranger stations in Ásbyrgi and Vesturdalur.

Jökulsá á Fjöllum

Iceland's second longest river, the Jökulsá á Fjöllum ('glacial river from the mountains') starts in the Vatnajökull icecap and flows 206 km to the Arctic Ocean at Öxarfjörður. Its 30 km canyon through Jökulsárgljúfur National Park was formed by jökulhlaups – minor ones on an average of every 10 years and a major one once or twice in a century.

Ásbyrgi

Just south of Route 85 is the lush horseshoe-shaped Ásbyrgi canyon, which extends 3½ km from north to south, averages one km in

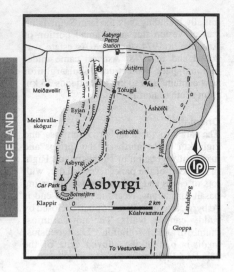

Hiking From the car park near the end of the road, several short tracks lead through the forest. The eastern track leads to a spring near the canyon wall, the western one climbs to a good view across the valley floor and the one leading straight ahead ends at a small lake at the head of Ásbyrgi.

You can also climb to the summit of Eyjan or ascend the cliffs at Tófugjá. From there, a loop track leads around Áshöfði past the gorges. Alternatively, follow the rim right around to Klappir, above the canyon head, from where you can head south to Kvíar and return via the river. For a longer trip, carry camping supplies and continue from Klappir to Vesturdalur (four hours), Hólmatungur and Dettifoss in two days, staying overnight at the Vesturdalur campground. The only trail between the canyon floor and rim is at Tófugjá, which can be scaled with the aid of a fixed rope.

Vesturdalur

The diversity of the Vesturdalur ('west valley') makes it a favourite off-the-beaten-track attraction. Vesturdalur is crisscrossed by lots of tracks, and you could easily spend a day or two exploring. The bushy scrub and grassy lawns around the campground give way to the cave-riddled pinnacles and rock formations of Hljóðaklettar, and you can see the Rauðhólar crater row, the ponds of Eyjan (not to be confused with the Eyjan at Ásbyrgi) and the canyon itself.

Unfortunately, the only public transport is on the tours, which move about in packs and allow only 45 minutes of breathless sightseeing here.

Hljóðaklettar A surprising and rewarding visit is to Hljóðaklettar ('echoing rocks'), with its unique swirls, spirals, rosettes, honeycombs and columns of basalt. The name is derived from an acoustic effect created by some of the spiral formations, making it impossible to determine the direction of the roaring river.

It's difficult to imagine what sort of volcanic activity produced Hljóðaklettar. Polygonal basalt columns normally form in

width and reaches 100m in depth at its head. Near the centre of the canyon is the prominent outcrop Eyjan (the 'island'). Thanks to protection from grazing sheep and the windbreak provided by the canyon walls, Ásbyrgi is well forested, with birch trees up to eight metres high.

There are two stories about the creation of Ásbyrgi. The early Norse settlers believed that Óðinn's normally airborne horse, Slættur (known in literature as Sleipnir), accidentally touched down on earth and left one hell of a hoofprint to prove it. Given Ásbyrgi's shape, it's not difficult to imagine how this explanation surfaced.

The other theory, though more scientific, is equally incredible. Geologists believe that the canyon was created apocalyptically by an eruption of the Grímsvötn caldera beneath distant Vatnajökull. It released an immense jökulhlaup, which ploughed northward down the Jökulsá á Fjöllum and gouged out the canyon in three days or less. After flowing through Ásbyrgi for 100 years or so, the river shifted eastward to its present course. There is evidence that sometime in its history, Ásbyrgi was flooded with sea water.

Vesturdalur

0   1   2 km

To Ásbyrgi
Lambafell
Kirkjan
Hallhöfði
Langavatnshöfði
Rauðhólar
Jökulsá á Fjöllum
Hljóðaklettar
Kastali
Langahlíð
Jaxlinn
Car Park
Tröllahellir
Bægisstaðamýri
Vesturdalsá
Eyjan
Karl og Kerling
Kallbjörg
Svínadalur
Miðaftansfjall
To Hólmatungur
Gloppa

instantaneously cooled lava perpendicular to the direction of flow. Because they were formed in vertically oriented volcanic plugs, the Hljóðaklettar columns lie horizontally. This explanation notwithstanding, there are formations for which there seems to be no rhyme or reason.

The best formations, which are also riddled with lava caves, are found along the river, north-east of the parking area. The largest cave, Kirkjan ('the church'), is west of the river in a grassy pit, about 15 minutes walk from the parking area.

Rauðhólar The Rauðhólar ('red hills'), crater row, immediately north of Vesturdalur, was responsible for the Hljóðaklettar basalt. The craters can be explored on foot, but they're a two-hour return walk from the parking area, so tour participants can't reach them in the allotted time.

Karl og Kerling Karl og Kerling ('the man and the witch') on the west bank of the river, can be accessed in an hour from the Vesturdalur car park. Across the river is Tröllahellir, the largest cave in the gorge, but it's only reached on a five-km cross-country

trek from Route 864. Follow the jeep track to the abandoned site of Hafursstaðir farm, then strike out toward the canyon. The descent to the cave requires extremely careful route selection.

Eyjan From Karl og Kerling, you can return to Vesturdalur by walking around Eyjan, the mesa-like 'island' covered with low scrubby forests and small ponds. Follow the river south to Kjalbjarg then turn west along the track to the abandoned site of Svínadalur, where the canyon widens into a broad valley, and follow the western base of the Eyjan cliffs back to the Vesturdalur parking area. Under ideal conditions, the circuit takes about three hours. A shorter walk is from the campground up onto the Eyjan plateau, which can be easily explored, even away from the established path.

Hólmatungur

The real attraction of the lush Hólmatungur area is its peaceful greenery and, in fine weather, it's surely one of Iceland's most beautiful spots. At the mouth of the spring-fed Holmá, the harsh lines of the canyon soften and produce several nice waterfalls – Hólmáfoss on the Hólmá, and Víga-bjargsfoss and Réttarfoss on the Jökulsá á Fjöllum. The best overall view of Hólma-tungur is from the hill Ytra-Þórunnarfjall, a km south of the car park.

The most popular walking route is the three-km loop from the parking area to the Jökulsá á Fjöllum, north to Hólmáfoss and then back along the Hólmá toward the Hólmatungur parking area.

Super Dettifoss tours from Mývatn stop briefly at Hólmatungur, otherwise (unless you have a private vehicle) Hólmatungur is four hours on foot north of Dettifoss and three hours south of Vesturdalur. Since camping is prohibited, it must be visited on a day hike from either place. It's a great spot for a picnic lunch on the first day of the Dettifoss to Ásbyrgi hike (see later in this section).

ICELAND

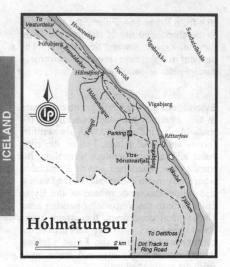

Hólmatungur

0   1   2 km

Dirt Track to Ring Road

To Dettifoss

Eilífur

Eilífur, the 698m peak at the south-western corner of the park, is a *móberg*, or what geologists would call a hyaloclastite mountain. It was formed when lava flowed into the glacier, melted a cavity inside it and filled it with igneous material. When the glacier melted, a moulded mountain remained. However, Eilífur is now so eroded that its origins aren't as clear as those of other móberg formations.

The area can be explored on foot from the jeep track, which connects Krafla with Dettifoss. Fresh water is available at lake Eilífsvatn, two km south of the peak outside the park. This road is closed to private vehicles, but foot access is permitted.

Dettifoss

Dettifoss, with the greatest volume of any waterfall in Europe, is a real powerhouse. It's only 44m high, but 500 cubic metres of water per second sends up a plume of spray that can be seen a km away and forms brilliant double rainbows above the canyon. All Jökulsárgljúfur tours stop at Dettifoss for about an hour.

The Super Dettifoss Tours from Mývatn visit the western bank, while other tours stop at the more heavily visited eastern bank. It's difficult to determine which is the better vantage point; most people who've seen the western bank cast a vote in its favour because the entire face of Dettifoss is visible, as opposed to just a side view. The car park on the western bank is a 20 minute walk from the viewpoints.

Hafragilsfoss

In one of the deepest parts of the canyon, two km downstream from Dettifoss, the 27m-high Hafragilsfoss cuts through the Raudhólar crater row to expose the volcanic dyke that formed them. From the eastern bank, the best view is down the canyon from the small hill just north of the Hafragilsfoss parking area. In the same area are numerous red scoria cones and craters.

The overlook on the western bank affords a marginal view of the falls, but the view down Jökulsárgljúfur canyon is one of the best available. You can climb down to the river from the vantage point, but near the bottom, you must lower yourself down a vertical wall on fixed ropes. It can be challenging for the inexperienced – and you have to climb back up!

Selfoss

Only 11m high, Selfoss is a broad but striking waterfall about 30 minutes walk above Dettifoss. A short way further upstream tumbles a brand new waterfall which has so far reached a height of three metres.

Dettifoss to Ásbyrgi Hike

The most popular hike in the park – and rightfully so – is the two-day trip from the western side of Dettifoss to Ásbyrgi. Public transport to the start of the hike is limited to the Super Dettifoss Tour from Mývatn, but you can rejoin the tour at Ásbyrgi after the hike or continue on public transport.

From Dettifoss, head north along Sandadalur (the gash-like valley between the parking area and the canyon) until you begin seeing yellow trail markers. If you go left up the hill, it will lead you around the rim of

Hafragil. Go right and you'll descend steeply into the canyon, to re-emerge on the rim beyond Hafragilsfoss. With a heavy pack, this will be extremely tricky as it involves some serious scrambling and climbing.

From Hafragilsfoss, the route leads north along the rim to beautiful Hólmatungur. You'll cross the Hólmá on two bridges, then descend past Hólmáfoss. The trail then joins a lateral moraine beneath towering basalt cliffs and crumbled basalt columns, and follows the yazoo (parallel) river Brandslækur, which eventually must be forded. After the ford, the trail climbs back to the canyon rim for a beautiful walk over the moors, punctuated by views down to bizarre basalt formations in the canyon below. One formation looks like a V8 engine that has lost oil and self-destructed!

At unassuming Kallbjörg, it's a 100m detour to an overlook perched on a column of rock with sheer drops on three sides. You don't realise the drama until you're right on top of it. Another short detour will take you to Gloppa, a basalt amphitheatre which ominously resembles the maw of a hellishly large shark. Here you can view the river through a natural window. A longer two-km return side trip winds down into the canyon to the foot of the rock formations Karl og Kerling. The requisite first night campsite is at the *Vesturdalur campground*, which costs Ikr500 per person, including a park map. Don't be tempted to camp at the parking area picnic site, however inviting, as you'll be chased out and possibly fined.

The next day, the trail winds through beautiful Hljódaklettar and Rauðahólar to the Kvíar trail junction, where you must decide whether to shoot across the moorland to the incredible view from the head of Ásbyrgi or continue following the canyon rim. Both are equally worthwhile, although the former gets a bit soggy in places. The two options rejoin at the head of Tófugjá, a challenging descent (with a pack, anyway) into Ásbyrgi with the aid of a fixed rope.

Organised Tours
Several companies offer tours of Jökul-

sárgljúfur; see Organised Tours under Mývatn, later in this chapter. From Akureyri and Húsavík, Ice & Fire Expeditions conducts tours Monday to Friday at 10 am for Ikr4100. They take in all the same sights as the Sigfússon tour from Mývatn, but in the reverse order. Note that participants may leave any of these tours at any time and rejoin later, with advance arrangements.

Places to Stay
Camping inside the park boundaries is limited to the official *campgrounds* at Ásbyrgi and Vesturdalur. Ásbyrgi has two campgrounds, one near the mouth of the canyon and the other at the upper end. The latter has tourist information and is nearer the long-distance trailheads and the facilities at the Ásbyrgi petrol station. Both sites cost Ikr500 per person. Five-minute hot showers cost Ikr150.

The upper campground looks promising from the parking area, but the enticing path into the trees leads to an immense shaved lawn that probably represents Iceland's greatest example of deforestation in modern times. It also reveals something about the nature of Icelandic camping, which is not a family outing but rather a group activity and an excuse to party hard.

As the only campground in the park south of Ásbyrgi, Vesturdalur is the overnight stop for hikers walking from Dettifoss to Ásbyrgi. The facilities don't really merit Ikr500, but the setting is pleasant. Too bad those inviting picnic tables and benches are in the parking lot and nowhere near the campground!

The nearest formal accommodation is the summer *Hótel Lundur* (☎ 465 5224), eight km north-east of Ásbyrgi on Route 85, with a swimming pool, campground and restaurant. For single/double rooms, the charge is Ikr3650/4750. Sleeping-bag accommodation is Ikr850/1300 on mattresses/beds. See also the farmhouse options under Kelduhverfi, earlier in this chapter.

Places to Eat
The snack bar, supermarket and petrol station at the *Ásbyrgi* farmstead on Route 85,

one km from the main Ásbyrgi campground, is the only place to purchase supplies. Prices are rather high, but the staff are friendly and ready to help with questions.

Getting There & Away

Bus There are buses between Húsavík and Ásbyrgi, which is the logical jumping-off point for self-guided visits in the park.

Hitching Hitching isn't recommended along the lightly travelled route between the Ring Road and Dettifoss unless you're prepared for a 20 km road walk before you get onto the park trail system.

North-Eastern Circuit

KÓPASKER

Kópasker, a tiny village of 150 people on the eastern shore of Öxarfjörður, became an official international trading port in 1879. Today it's involved in agricultural trade and the shrimp industry. There's little to see in the immediate area, but the village is an ideal entry point into the wilds of Iceland's far north-east.

On 13 January, 1976, Kópasker suffered a severe earthquake which destroyed several buildings and cracked the harbour wall. Rockslides and fissuring were violent and evidence of the seismic activity can still be seen at Hraunhólar near Presthólar, about five km south of town.

You may also want to have a look at Snartarstaðir, an early district assembly site just east of Route 85. The church beside it was built in 1928.

Folk Museum

At the original schoolhouse is a small library and folk museum (☎ 465 2171). It's open from 15 June to 30 August, on Tuesday, Thursday and Saturday from 1 to 5 pm.

Rauðinúpur

The Melrakkaslétturnes peninsula, between Öxarfjörður and Þistilfjörður, is character-

ised by low-lying flatlands, ponds and marshes. In its far north-western corner is the extinct 73m crater Rauðinúpur and a cliff-girt headland occupied by nesting sea birds. A rough five km track turns off to Rauðinúpur from Route 85, 18 km north of Kópasker. It's a remote and scarcely visited place and can only be reached on foot or in a private vehicle.

Places to Stay & Eat

The *Esso* (☎ 465 2183) petrol station has a kiosk, a snack bar and automobile services, and beside it is the official *campground*. Diagonally opposite is the *Gistihúsið Kópasker* (☎ 465 2121), which has single/double rooms for Ikr3315/4290 and sleeping-bag accommodation for Ikr1500. The village also has a new supermarket, the *Verslunin Bakki*.

Getting There & Away

Buses run to and from Húsavík (Ikr1150) and Vopnafjörður (Ikr1950) on Monday, Wednesday and Friday. Flugfélag Norðurlands flies between Akureyri and Kópasker four times weekly, with cheap deals on Monday and Wednesday.

RAUFARHÖFN

The port of Raufarhöfn (population 450), perhaps the finest in north-eastern Iceland, has functioned since the Saga Age. It's formed not by a sheltered fjord, but by the small Ásmundarstaða islands, just offshore. The town's economic high point came early this century during the herring boom. The land surrounding the village is flat and relatively uninspiring, but wide driftwood-covered beaches and profuse bird life add interest.

Between Raufarhöfn and the farm Blikalón, we turned north down to the shore, a windswept bay where the waves have thrown up a huge wall of big rocks. We camped here and the next morning was perfect – sunny, no wind and lots of bird life: eider ducks, whooper swans, thousands of greylag geese, gannets fishing in the bay, divers, cormorants, oystercatchers, skuas, plovers etc.
Mats Reimer & Camilla Ingebretsen, Sweden

If you take this route, be warned that during the nesting season the birds can be positively paranoid. You may be confined to your tent by dive-bombing hordes!

Hraunhafnartangi

The remote peninsula Hraunhafnartangi is the northernmost point of the Icelandic mainland, but if it were just 2½ km further north, it would lie within the Arctic Circle and its tourist novelty value would increase immeasurably. Even so, the latitudinal hype can't be avoided, and guests at the Hótel Norðurljós still receive a certificate stating they've approached the magic line!

Even without the Arctic Circle looming out to sea, Hraunhafnartangi wouldn't lack interest. There's not only a lonely lighthouse, but also a Saga Age landing site and the burial mound of saga character Þorgeir Hávarsson, who killed 14 enemies before being struck down in battle. Camping is possible anywhere on this remote headland.

Rauðanes

South of Viðarfjall, midway between Raufarhöfn and Þórshöfn, a jeep track heads north from Route 85 to Rauðanes. This small and scenic peninsula is endowed with steep cliffs full of nesting birds, caves, offshore sea stacks and an exposed rock face, Stakkatorfa, where a great chunk of land collapsed into the sea. To get there, walk or drive four km to the bridge before the farm Vellir; from there, it's three km north-east to the cape.

Places to Stay & Eat

The *Hótel Norðurljós* (☎ 465 1233; fax 465 1383) charges Ikr3770/5525 for single/double rooms and Ikr1235 for sleeping-bag accommodation. Alternatively, there's the *Guesthouse VR* (☎ 465 1201), at slightly lower rates. The *campground* (☎ 465 1151) is beside the swimming pool.

Meals are available at the Hotel Norðurljós or the *Esso* (☎ 465 1256) petrol station. Groceries are available at the *Verslunarfélag Raufarhafnar*.

Getting There & Away

Buses to and from Húsavík (Ikr1700) and Vopnafjörður (Ikr1400) pass Raufarhöfn on Monday, Wednesday and Friday. Flugfélag Norðurlands flights between Akureyri and Kópasker continue to Raufarhöfn. Discounted flights are on Wednesday and Friday.

LANGANES

Shaped like a goose with a very large head, the foggy Langanes peninsula is one of the loneliest corners of Iceland. Route 869 ends only 17 km along the 50 km peninsula and access to Fontur at the tip of the goose's beak is along a 4WD track.

Most of flat or undulating Langanes, which is riddled with abandoned farms, is rich in marshland as well as Arctic and alpine flora. The tallest peak of mountainous Southern Langanes, Gunnólfsvíkurfjall, rises to 719m and the easternmost coasts are characterised by cliffs up to 130m high.

For camping, hiking and exploring off the beaten track, this is as wild as coastal Iceland gets. Drinking water is plentiful but there are no facilities beyond Þórshöfn, so carry everything you'll need. Hikers should allow a week for the return trip from Þórshöfn to Fontur.

Brekknaheiði

The moors at the base of Langanes form a tundra plain of lakes, marshes and low hills. It's pleasant and unchallenging walking country.

Fontur

The fogbound cliffs at the north-eastern tip of Langanes have long proved dangerous to passing ships. There's a lighthouse at the cape which dates from 1910 and a monument to the shipwrecked English sailors who died of hypothermia after ascending the ravine there. It's now called Engelskagjá ('English gorge').

Skoruvík

The area along the bay Skoruvík, between the head and the beak of Langanes, is a major breeding ground of the peripatetic Arctic tern. The beach below the lighthouse is littered with driftwood.

Skálabjarg

The Látrabjarg of the east, Skálabjarg is a long and formidable bird cliff on the wild south coast of Langanes. At the turn of the century, the ruined farm of Skálar, north-east of the cliff, was a prosperous fishing village.

Þórshöfn

Although it has served as a busy port since saga times, most of the growth in Þórshöfn (population 430) has occurred in the past century. It became a recognised trading site in 1846, but had no permanent residents until 1875. In the early 20th century, a herring-salting station was established and, although the herring fishery has all but disappeared, the village still relies on fishing.

Places to Stay & Eat

The *campground* is north of town, near the sports ground, and the *Hótel Jórvík* (☎ 468 1149; fax 468 1399) opposite, provides formal accommodation and meals. Single/double rooms cost Ikr3250/4160. Snacks are available at the *Olís* petrol station and the *Esso-skálinn*, which also serves as the bus terminal.

You'll find two farmhouse accommodation options on Þistilfjörður, west of town: *Ytra-Aland* (☎ 468 1290) and *Svalbarð* (☎ 468 1385). Both offer single/double rooms for Ikr3000/4050 and sleeping-bag accommodation for Ikr1300. There's also the farm *Fell* (☎ 473 1696), at the western end of Bakkafjörður, 15 km south-east of Þórshöfn, which charges the same rates, with cooking facilities. Camping and fishing are also possible.

Getting There & Away

Buses from Húsavík (Ikr2400) and Vopnafjörður (Ikr900) pass on Monday, Wednesday and Friday.

BAKKAFJÖRÐUR

Bakkafjörður is a fishing settlement of 130 people, with a half-decent harbour. It lies on the southern shore of Bakkaflói with a view to Gunnólfvíkurfjall, the highest point on Langanes.

Skeggjastaðir

The church at the estate farm, Skeggjastaðir, six km from Bakkafjörður, was originally built of wood in 1845, but has since been radically renovated. The pulpit, which was crafted in Denmark, dates from the early 1700s. With permission from the proprietor, you can camp at Skeggjastaðir and visit the church. A km north-west of the farm towers the unusual sea stack Stapi.

Places to Stay & Eat

Bakkafjörður's only accommodation is the *Bakkafjörður Youth Hostel* (☎ 473 1686; fax 1668), which is open from 1 June to 31 August and charges Ikr1000/1250 for HI members/non-members.

The unofficial *campground* is beside the school. Groceries are sold at the *KL cooperative shop*.

VOPNAFJÖRÐUR

Vopnafjörður can claim the dubious honours of being the home town of a former Miss Universe and the site of some of Prince Charles' angling holidays. Icelanders also claim that Father Christmas makes his home on 1251m Smjörfjöll ('butter mountain'), south of town.

The population of this fishing village and former trading centre on the Kolbeinstangi peninsula is around 700, and another 220 people live around the district.

Bustarfell

The farm Bustarfell, at the foot of the mountain of the same name, lies 23 km west of Vopnafjörður. The folk museum (☎ 473 1466), in an 18th-century gabled turf farmhouse, is one of Iceland's finest. It's open daily, 15 June to 15 September, from 10 am to 7 pm. Admission is Ikr200.

West of the farm, the road climbs the mountain and passes two lakes. There's a view disc across the highway from the first lake, Nýkurvatn.

Places to Stay & Eat

Apart from the *campground* (☎ 473 1122), the only town accommodation is *Hótel Tangi* (☎ 473 1224; fax 473 1146). From 1 June to 10 October, single/double private rooms cost Ikr3445/4550 and sleeping-bag accommodation is Ikr1365. It also runs cruising, fishing and whale and seal-watching excursions on the fjord. The private guesthouse *Skjól* (☎ & fax 473 1332), in Vatnsdalsgerði, four km from town at the head of Vopnafjörður, offers simple accommodation for Ikr1500.

Eight km south of Vopnafjörður on Route 917, *Syðri-Vík* (☎ 473 1199) has single/double farmhouse accommodation for Ikr3000/4050 and sleeping-bag accommodation for Ikr1300. Six-person cottages rent for Ikr37,120 per week. Peripherals include cooking facilities and horse hire.

The only *restaurant* is the hotel dining room, but there are snack bars at the *Esso* (☎ 473 1200) and *Shell* (☎ 473 1204) petrol stations. The *Kauptún* supermarket has groceries.

Getting There & Away

Buses leave Húsavík for Vopnafjörður (Ikr3100) at 1.30 pm on Monday, Wednesday and Friday, and from Vopnajörður on the same days at 11.30 am. To/from Egilsstaðir (Ikr1200), they leave on the same days at 6.45 pm/9.45 am.

Flugfélag Norðurlands flies between Akureyri and Vopnafjörður daily except Saturday, with discounted flights on Monday and Thursday. On Monday, Wednesday, Thursday and Friday, Flugfélag Austurlands connects Vopnafjörður with Egilsstaðir.

NORTH-EAST INTERIOR

Heading north from Egilsstaðir, the major transport hub south of Vopnafjöðdur, the Ring Road takes a drastic short-cut inland across the stark and barren highlands of the north-east interior. There's little to lure travellers off the Egilsstaðir-Mývatn bus, but the loneliness can be an attraction in itself in this eerie and otherworldly place of endless vistas.

If you won't be travelling into the interior, you'll catch a glimpse of it here. The land is dotted with small lakes caused by melting snowfields; streams and rivers wander aimlessly and disappear into gravel beds. In summer, the grey landscape seems unimaginably dull, where even a sprig of grass would considerably liven the scene, but in spring, the land is spattered with clumps of tiny purple blooms which somehow gain root in the gravelly volcanic surface.

Jökuldalsheiði

The vast Jökuldalsheiði moorland, along the Ring Road between Jökuldalur and Möðrudalur, is quite verdant and was farmed until 1875, when the cataclysmic explosion of the Askja caldera displaced its inhabitants. Although the former greenery has since returned, the area remains abandoned.

Möðrudalur

An oasis in the barrens amid an entanglement of streams, isolated Möðrudalur is the highest farm in Iceland at 470m. The bus between Egilsstaðir and Mývatn stops for half an hour. You can avoid the high prices at the *Fjalla-kaffi* snack bar by wandering over the road to see the church and its interesting altarpiece. This nontraditional interpretation of the Sermon on the Mount is the work of Jón Stefánsson, the local farmer who constructed the church in 1949.

Biskupsháls

Folktales say that early bishops from Skálholt in the south and Hólar in the north habitually met atop this tuffaceous ridge, which is perpendicular to the Ring Road about 10 km south of Grímsstaðir. They constructed a cairn there to mark the boundary between their two dioceses.

Grímsstaðir

Grímsstaðir is a remote farm near the intersection of the Ring Road and Route 864 near the Jökulsá á Fjöllum, and on a clear day, the distinctive form of Herðubreið deep in the interior is plainly visible. Before the river was spanned, it was crossed by ferry. The old ferryman's hut, built in 1880, can still be seen on the western bank, two km downstream from the Ring Road bridge. It's reputedly haunted.

Grímsstaðir is the best starting point for hitching from the Ring Road to Dettifoss and Jökulsárgljúfur National Park. Minimal supplies are sold at the petrol station.

Hrossaborg

The 40m high and 500m long crater Hrossaborg means 'horse fortress', and is used as a corral by horses seeking shelter from fierce winds. It's situated at the intersection of the Ring Road and the dirt track Route F88 to Herðubreið.

Places to Stay

The rather aloof farm *Grímstunga* (☎ 464 4294) offers basic single/double accommodation for Ikr3000/4050, sleeping-bag accommodation for Ikr1300 and trout fishing licences for Ikr1200 per day. There's also a *campground*, but the charge seems high for a desert site with only basic toilets and cold water taps.

Wild camping is strictly prohibited around Grimsstaðir, and the farmers (who are also the campground operators) have erected lots of 'No Camping' signs. Wild campers should walk at least five km north along Route 864 and camp well out of sight. The best sites are west of the road towards the Jökulsá á Fjöllum. Hitchers have also been hassled in this area.

Mývatn

In 1974, Mývatn ('midge lake') was set aside as the Mývatn-Laxá special conservation area, and the pseudocrater field at Skútustaðir, at the southern end of the lake, is preserved as a national natural monument. Mývatn is a place to savour, where travellers can settle in for a week of sightseeing,

touring and relaxing and never become bored.

The Mývatn basin sits squarely on the Mid-Atlantic Ridge. Although most of the interesting sights are volcanic or geothermal features, the centrepiece is the 37 sq km lake Mývatn itself, which averages a depth of only 2½ metres. The lake is nearly bisected by the peninsula Neslandatangi, which separates Ytriflói or 'outer gulf' from the larger Syðriflói or 'southern gulf'. The lake contains over 50 islands and islets, most of which are pseudocraters formed by gas explosions caused when molten lava flowed into the water.

Thanks to its location in the rain shadow of the Vatnajökull icecap, Mývatn is statistically the driest spot in Iceland and in summer you can expect at least some fine weather. The frequently icy winds may seem uncomfortable, but you'll be thankful for the relief they offer from the swarms of midges for which the lake is named. Campers will appreciate a tent with a good insect screen.

Geology

At the close of the ice age 10,000 years ago, the Mývatn basin was covered by an icecap, and it was volcanic eruptions beneath this ice that moulded the symmetrical móberg peaks south of the modern lake. Near Reykjahlíð, spur glaciers pushed up terminal moraines, but many of these were later buried beneath lava flows. One of these moraines became the earth dam that formed Mývatn from the meltwater of retreating glaciers.

Immediately after the ice disappeared, so did the lake. Volcanic activity to the east formed the Lúdent tephra complex and, over 6000 years later, another cycle of activity created the Ketildyngja volcano, 25 km south-east of Mývatn. The lava from that crater flowed north-west, nearly to the sea, along the Laxá valley, and created a lava dam and a new, improved Mývatn. After another millennium or so, a volcanic explosion along the same fissure spewed out Hverfell, the classic tephra cone that dominates the modern lake landscape. Over the next 200

ICELAND

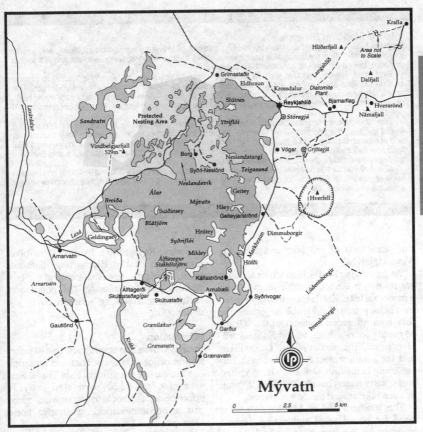

Mývatn

0   2.5   5 km

years, activity escalated along the eastern shore and craters were thrown up across a wide region, providing a steady stream of molten material flowing toward Öxarfjörður. The lava dam formed during the end of this cycle created the present Mývatn shoreline.

Between 1724 and 1729, the Mývatnseldar ('Mývatn fires') eruptions began at Krafla, north-east of the lake. This dramatic and sporadically active fissure erupted as recently as 1984. In the early 1990s, subsurface rumblings were on the increase and the magma chamber had filled; experts believed that another big eruption was

imminent but as yet, there has been no major activity.

Orientation

There's a lot to see at Mývatn and it's also used for access to Jökulsárgljúfur National Park, the Kverkfjöll ice caves and the Askja caldera.

A good day hike from Reykjahlíð would include climbing Hverfell crater and a few hours exploring Dimmuborgir. Another could take in the Námaskarð geothermal area and a climb up Námafjall. A third day might be spent cycling to the waterfowl conserva-

ICELAND

Into the Madding Swarms

If you're being driven to distraction by swirling swarms of Mývatn's eponymous midges, and you're wondering why nice creatures like pandas are going extinct when species like this are left to run rampant, take a moment to consider the adversary.

First of all, Mývatn has two species of midges, both of which are apparently attracted to carbon dioxide (emitted when people exhale), hence the clouds of them that gather around your face. The small, skinny mosquito-like ones are called *mýflugur*, or *rikmý*. Although they invade your eyes, ears, nose and mouth – and occasionally make a kamikaze dive for your lungs – they're chironomids and don't bite.

The other species is the fatter and even more pesky *bitmý*, or blackfly, and as the Icelandic name would suggest, they do bite. They seem to be particularly fond of thick hair, where they can curl up and imitate chainsaws – it's a real buzz, but not a particularly pleasant one. They are, however, a vital food source for wildlife. Their larvae are eaten by brown trout and both the harlequin duck and Barrow's goldeneye subsist on them during the nesting season.

About all you can do for relief is wear a head net, which you can buy for around Ikr400 at any Mývatn hotel or guesthouse, or pray for a good wind, which will send the nasty little buggers diving for shelter amid the vegetation. ∎

---

tion area west of the lake and climbing Vindbelgjarfjall.

As for visiting Krafla, high winds and dust storms may make access difficult, even with a mountain bike. Krafla is most easily visited by hitching from Reykjahlíð or joining the four-hour afternoon segment of the 'Grand Mývatn' tour, which visits Námaskarð, Hverarönd, Bjarnarflag, Viti, Leirhnjúkur and the southernmost Krafla fissures. You can camp in the hills well away from visited areas (carry water) but it's forbidden to camp or even hike around the power station.

The southern end of Mývatn, which is good for two days of sightseeing, is best explored on foot from Skútustaðir. Hikes to more distant mountains and lava fields such as Lúdent, Þrengslaborgir or Búrfell require more time.

REYKJAHLÍÐ

According to the *Landnámabók*, the first settler in Mývatn's main population and service centre, Reykjahlíð, was the farmer Arnór Þorgrímsson. The earliest residents of Mývatnsveit – as the area is known – found a lush landscape of birch woods and grasslands. However, overcutting and grazing diminished the greenery and subsequent lava flows finished off the defoliation.

Today, Reykjahlíð's livelihood revolves around the nearby Bjarnarflag diatomite plant, the Krafla power station and the burgeoning tourism industry. The population, including surrounding farmsteads, is just under 600.

Information

Tourist Office The helpful new tourist information office is in the school and museum, one km east of the village. Eldá Travel Services (☎ 464 4220) can also provide information and book tours, onward transport or accommodation, or arrange horse tours.

Money The Sparisjóður Mývetninga, down the side street between the swimming pool and the eastbound highway, is open for currency exchange between 9 am and 4 pm on weekdays. When the Gamli Bærinn opened next door, the Hótel Reynihlíð turned its bar into an Íslandsbanki, which offers foreign exchange. From 15 May to 15 September, it's open weekdays, 9.15 am to 4 pm.

Fishing Permits Fishing permits for Mývatn are available from Ferðaþjónustan Eldá. For trout fishing in the Skógartjörn ponds, licences may be purchased at Hella, three km north of Reykjahlíð.

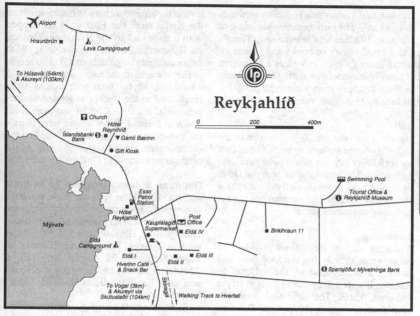

Reykjahlíð

Church

During the Krafla eruption of 1727, the Leirhnjúkur crater, 10 km north-east of Reykjahlíð, kicked off a two-year period of volcanic activity, sending streams of lava along old glacial moraines and past Reykjahlíð to the lake shore. On 27 August, 1729, the flow ploughed through the village, destroying farms and buildings, but amazingly the well-placed wooden church, which sat on a low rise, was spared – some say miraculously – when the flow parted and missed it by only a few metres; it was renovated on its original foundation in 1876. You can still see remnants of the original Reykjahlíð farm, which was destroyed by the lava.

Past miracles notwithstanding, it couldn't escape modern sensibilities, and in 1972 the original church was demolished and reconstructed on the same site. The interior of the present church is filled with carvings, paintings and batik-style art. The wooden carving

on the pulpit is a representation of the church that survived the lava.

Reykjahlíð Museum

The exceptional natural history museum at the tourist information office presents the Mývatn story with the help of a cute little

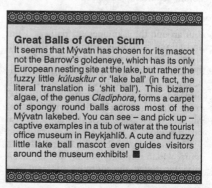

Great Balls of Green Scum
It seems that Mývatn has chosen for its mascot not the Barrow's goldeneye, which has its only European nesting site at the lake, but rather the fuzzy little *kúluskítur* or 'lake ball' (in fact, the literal translation is 'shit ball'). This bizarre algae, of the genus *Cladiphora*, forms a carpet of spongy round balls across most of the Mývatn lakebed. You can see – and pick up – captive examples in a tub of water at the tourist office museum in Reykjahlíð. A cute and fuzzy little lake ball mascot even guides visitors around the museum exhibits! ∎

lake ball and a refreshing economy of words and pictures. The bird dioramas are some of the most life-like you'll ever see. There's also a small library of books and videos on nature-related topics, as well as a collection of historic snowmobiles, dating from as early as 1942. It's open from 9 am to 10 pm daily, 10 June to 25 August. Admission is free.

Golf

There's a six-hole par 20 golf course in the valley above the swimming pool. Green fees are Ikr500 per day, but you'll need your own equipment. The petrol station near the Hótel Reynihlíð has a tiny mini-golf course, where you'll pay Ikr200 per person per game, including equipment rental.

Swimming

A stormy day in Reykjahlíð couldn't be better spent than at the outdoor pool and jacuzzi, one km east of the village. In summer, it's open daily from 10 am to 10 pm and costs Ikr160. The *gufubaðið* (sauna) is open from 10 am to 10 pm on Tuesday, Thursday and Saturday.

Organised Tours

Tourism with a capital 'T' reigns at Reykjahlíð, and numerous Mývatn-area tours are run by Jón Árni Sigfússon (☎ 464 4196; fax 464 4380) and Ferðaþjónustan Eldá (☎ 464 4220; fax 464 4321). Tours can get extremely crowded, so book at least a day before departure.

Mývatn & Krafla A three-hour whirlwind tour around the lake operates daily at 1 pm and allows a fleeting glimpse of the main sights. The Eldá version features the known sites, plus the turf-roofed cottage at Ytrineslönd, where char is smoked, and a small bird and egg museum. The tours cost Ikr1600 from Eldá and Ikr2275 from Jón Árni Sigfússon. Pick-ups at Skútustaðir can also be arranged.

The more comprehensive Grand Mývatn tours, which run daily at 8.30 am, are actually two tours: the morning segment is a four-hour version of the around-the-lake tour

and, in the afternoon, it visits Námaskarð and the Krafla area. The Eldá tours are capped with a tasty visit to the Hverabrauð bakery on Bjarnarflag, and a surprise treat. With either company, segments cost Ikr1800 each.

For something different, you can take a 45-minute Mýfar boat tour across from Reykjahlíð to the thickly vegetated Slútnes peninsula. It's like a bit of the tropics set down in Iceland. For a longer tour, there's the two-hour trip to Geiteyjarströnd and the pseudocraters on the southern shore. Make arrangements through Ferðaþjónustan Eldá.

Dettifoss & Jökulsárgljúfur To Dettifoss and Jökulsárgljúfur National Park, you have two options. Tours run by Jón Árni Sigfússon take in the eastern side of Dettifoss, Hafragilsfoss, Hljóðaklettar and Ásbyrgi, as well as Tjörnes, Húsavík and Hveravellir. From 20 June to 31 August, they run on Tuesday, Thursday and Saturday at 8.30 am and cost Ikr3700 (discounts with Omnibuspass).

Eldá offers the highly recommended Super Dettifoss Tour, which follows the western bank of the Jökulsá á Fjöllum to Selfoss, Dettifoss and Hafragilsfoss. It then makes stops at Hólmatungur, Hljóðaklettur, Ásbyrgi, Tjörnes and Húsavík. This tour costs Ikr4160. It's also the best access to use for the Dettifoss to Ásbyrgi hike in Jökulsárgljúfur National Park; it will drop you at the Dettifoss parking area and pick you up at the Ásbyrgi petrol station.

Gjástykki Eldá's exciting new Gjástykki option takes you into the heart of the Krafla central volcano, where the landscape still steams with heat from the 1981 to 1984 eruptions. Before entering the lava, you'll climb the ridge Hrafntinnuhryggur, which is littered with sparkling shards of obsidian (volcanic glass). You'll then follow the rift zone north to Gjástykki to spend several hours wandering on foot through steaming craters, fissures, lava domes and deposits of rainbow-coloured slag.

The finale is a close-up view of the brilliant red ridge that has become synonymous with Gjástykki. This landscape may be fresh from the centre of the earth, but in places, it certainly doesn't feel terrestrial! The last stop is a quick spin past Sjálfskapar Viti (see the aside Homemade Hell, later in this chapter.) Tours leave daily at 8.45 am, from 15 July to 20 August, and cost Ikr3600.

Lúdentsborgir Jón Árni Sigfússon now offers a new five-hour tour to the Lúdentsborgir craters and the Selljahjallagil gorge. It departs daily at 9 am from 1 July to 25 August, and costs Ikr2790.

Herðubreið & Askja Long but rewarding day tours run to Herðubreið and the Askja caldera, deep in the interior, from 20 June to 14 July and 16 August to 31 August at 8.30 am on Monday, Wednesday and Friday (snow conditions permitting); from 15 July to 15 August, they leave daily at 8.30 am. These tours last from 12 to 14 hours and cost a well-spent Ikr5265. Many people opt to stay at the Þórsteinsskáli or Dreki huts and catch another tour back.

Kverkfjöll Another worthwhile trip is the three-day tour to the ice caves at Kverkfjöll, which is the source of the Jökulsá á Fjöllum, and the Askja caldera. It departs weekly on Monday and Friday in July and August and costs Ikr12,220, excluding food and camping or hut fees. For more information, see under Húsavík earlier in this chapter.

Air Sightseeing Mýflug Air Service (☎ 464 4400; fax 464 4341) operates charter and sightseeing tours in and out of Reykjahlíð airfield, including 'flightseeing' tours over Mývatn, Krafla, Herðubreið, Askja, Kverkfjöll, Jökulsárgljúfur National Park and the island of Grímsey (or any combination of these). See Mýflug Air Service at the Reykjahlíð airstrip or Ferðaþjónustan Eldá. You'll pay about Ikr8500 per person per hour of flying time.

Special Events
In early July, there's an annual Mývatn marathon which follows a circuit around the lake, as well as three and 10 km fun runs. For information, contact the organisers via email (myvatn@mmedia.is).

Places to Stay
The following accommodation is in the Reykjahlíð area. Further options are listed under Skútustaðir later in this section.

Camping Camping outside the reserve is difficult due to the lack of surface water, and wild camping inside the reserve is prohibited and may attract a fine. However, Reykjahlíð has three official campgrounds. The largest is the so-called *Lava Campground* which lies about 300m uphill from the church and is surrounded by lava. It has showers, drying sheds and flush toilets, but no cooking facilities. Camping costs Ikr450 per person, including showers. Laundry service is available for Ikr300 to wash and Ikr300 to dry.

The other campground, *Eldá* (☎ 464 4220), has a better location, right on the lake shore, and also charges Ikr450 per person. There's a separate section for cars and caravans. Free hot showers are available and cooking facilities are planned.

The third campground is at *Vogar* (☎ 464 4399; fax 464 4341), three km south of Reykjahlíð. It accommodates recreational vehicles and caravans, and tent campers may park vehicles beside their tents. Camping costs Ikr400 per person, including use of cooking facilities.

Guesthouses The friendly and highly recommended guesthouse, *Eldá* (☎ 464 4220; fax 464 4321), has four locations around Reykjahlíð, but all guests should check in at Eldá I ('Bjarg'), at the Eldá campground. Single/double rooms cost Ikr3300/4350 and sleeping-bag accommodation on a mattress/bed costs Ikr900/1250. All four houses are very nice, but Eldá IV, near the post office, offers cooking facilities and a TV lounge.

Vogar (see above listing under Camping), has single/double accommodation with shared facilities for Ikr2210 per person, and sleeping-bag accommodation for Ikr1365.

Fishing permits are sold and there are cooking facilities and a lounge.

In the village is *Gistiheimilið Birkihraun* (☎ 464 4196; fax 464 4380), at Birkihraun 11, with basic single/double rooms for Ikr3700/5400. Affiliated with the Lava Campground is *Hraunbrún* (☎ 464 4305), which has sleeping-bag accommodation for Ikr1200 and made-up beds for Ikr2000. Sleeping-bag accommodation in simple cottages at the Lava Campground also costs Ikr1200, and self-catering *summer houses* for up to 15 people cost Ikr6000 per night.

Hotels The main upmarket tourist lodging is *Hótel Reynihlíð* (☎ 464 4710; fax 464 4371) which charges Ikr8900/10,600 for singles/doubles with a shower; budget rooms cost Ikr4400/5400. Prices include a continental buffet breakfast.

The *Hótel Reykjahlíð* (☎ 464 4142; fax 464 4336) is a small 12-room hotel on the lake shore charging Ikr5000/7475 for a single/double room with shower. It's much less lively than the Hótel Reynihlíð but has superb lake views.

Places to Eat

The best place in town for a meal – and it's a real treat – is the cosy and popular *Gamli Bærinn* (☎ 464 4170), beside the Hótel Reynihlíð. It serves not only as a licensed pub and restaurant, but also as a sort of community centre. A good budget option is the goulash soup, which costs Ikr480 and comes with delicious homemade bread. The grilled Arctic char (Ikr1090) and the vegetable crepe (Ikr540), are indescribably good. There's also a choice of salads, sandwiches and sweet desserts.

The *Hverinn* (☎ 464 4155) is a sort of glorified snack bar and a place for drenched campers to dry out and munch on chicken and chips, burgers, hot dogs, and other light meals, or down light beer and soft drinks. It's open from 10 am to 11 pm daily.

The *Hótel Reykjahlíð* has a low-key dining room and the *Hótel Reynihlíð* has a large restaurant with a diverse menu. These days everyone is welcome, even if they only

want coffee and chips (about Ikr350)! Buffet breakfasts cost Ikr800.

There's also a snack bar at the *Esso* petrol station, and apart from the Hótel Reynihlíð dining room, it's the only place for a morning cup of coffee. The *Kaupfélagið* supermarket is open Monday to Saturday from 8 am to 7 pm and on Sunday from 10 am to 6 pm. Don't miss the gooey cake-like *hverabrauð* ('hot spring bread'); it's full of molasses and is slow-baked underground on the Bjarnarflag flats geothermal area east of town. Once you've started with a loaf and a stick of butter, it's difficult to stop. If the supermarket runs out, you'll also find it at the gift kiosk near the Hótel Reynihlíð, but it's at least twice the supermarket price.

For fresh smoked salmon and Arctic char at reasonable prices, go to *Reykhúsið Geiteyjarströnd*, near Dimmuborgir about six km south of Reykjahlíð. You'll pay around Ikr1400 per kg for char and Ikr1800 per kg for salmon.

Getting There & Away

Air In summer, Íslandsflug flies daily between Reykjavík and Mývatn. Flights are aimed at day-trippers, who depart from Reykjavík at 7.40 am, do the Grand Mývatn tour, and fly out of Mývatn at 5 pm. The whole package – return flights from Reykjavík and the guided tour – costs Ikr17,050.

Bus The Hótel Reynihlíð is Mývatn's main long-distance bus terminal, although buses to/from Akureyri also stop at Skútustaðir. Buses between Akureyri and Mývatn take less than 1½ hours. From 1 May to 30 June and 1 September to 30 September, there are daily departures from Akureyri at 8.15 am and from Reykjahlíð at 4.15 pm. From 1 July to 31 August, there are additional daily departures at 8 pm from Akureyri and at 8 am and 7.30 pm from Reykjahlíð.

To Egilsstaðir, buses depart from Mývatn at 8.15 pm daily and return at 4 pm daily. These services connect with buses to/from Höfn in the south-east. From Húsavík, buses run two or three times daily in either direction during summer months.

To travel between Reykjahlíð and Skútustaðir at the southern end of the lake, use the Akureyri buses.

Getting Around

Without a car or bicycle, you may find getting around Mývatn a bit frustrating. At present, your only options are walking, hiring a bike or joining tours that spend just a few crowded photo moments at the main attractions. Many people try to hitch around to the sights and invariably find themselves walking anyway. Most of the vehicles travelling around the lake belong to tourists and tour companies, neither of which are disposed to picking up dust-beaten hitchers!

There are a few hiking trails, but they won't take you to all the points of interest, so you must sometimes walk along the road. Watch out for high-speed vehicles which scatter gravel all over the place. Allow about three hours to walk between Reykjahlíð and Skútustaðir.

Bicycle If you have calm wind and weather, the best option is to hire a mountain bike. The Lava Campground and the Hótel Reynihlíð petrol station both charge Ikr1000/1500 for six/12 hours for 21-speed mountain bikes. Eldá hires 18-speed mountain bikes for Ikr700/1100 for six/12 hours. The 37 km ride around the lake can be easily done in a day, allowing time for sightseeing at all the major stops. Cyclists must contend with tour buses and caravans on often rough unsurfaced roads, so exercise due caution.

AROUND THE LAKE

By car or bicycle, Mývatn is 37 km around by the shortest route. There are walks and side-trips away from the main roads so, even with a motor vehicle, allow at least a day to explore the sites, and two days if you want to hike the Hverfell-Dimmuborgir trail system.

Hverfell & Dimmuborgir Trail

In a day, you can walk the track from Reykjahlíð to Dimmuborgir and back, and explore the sites of interest along the way. Start by walking south-east from the intersection of the Ring Road and the round-the-lake route. After a few minutes, the trail reaches a dead end at a pipeline. Here, you should turn right and walk a few metres to the point where the track continues south toward Hverfell. It meanders a bit through an overgrown lava field before reaching Grjótagjá, but it's well marked and easy to follow.

Stóragjá This rather eerie, hidden fissure is found just 100m south-east of the Reykjahlíð intersection of the Ring Road and the round-the-lake route. It contains a 28°C hot spring, which is reached by a ladder from the footpath. A few metres south of the ladder, you'll see a pool hidden in a crack between boulders. Bathers must lower themselves into the spring on an attached rope.

Unfortunately, Stóragjá is cooling down and the water temperature fosters the growth of potentially harmful algae, so check that you haven't got any cuts and shower when you've finished bathing. Note that it's much cleaner in the spring than later in the season when – as locals like to point out – only tourists and drunken Icelanders take advantage of its charms.

Grjótagjá In a gaping fissure, along the walking track between Reykjahlíð and Hverfell, is the beautiful hot spring, Grjótagjá.

Grjótagjá is divided into sections for men and women. Although it was once popular with local bathers and party-makers, in the late 1980s it heated up to 60°C and was too hot to be bearable. Over the past several years, however, the men's section (accessible through the main northern entrance) has cooled down to 48°C, while the women's section (around the corner from the men's) stands at a more tolerable 47°C. Records show that the cooling continues at about 1° per year. Unlike Stóragjá, the well-circulating water quickly filters out impurities.

Even if you can't take the heat, Grjótagjá

ICELAND

is worth a visit. Especially when the sun is shining, the steam, underground pools and light filtering through cracks in the roof create a mesmerising otherworldly effect. It's accessible via the Hverfell footpath or on the driveable track that turns off the Ring Road about one km east of Reykjahlíð.

Hverfell The classic tephra ring Hverfell stands prominently, 163m above the lava fields east of the lake. It appeared 2500 years ago in a cataclysmic eruption of the existing Lúdent complex. The 1040m-wide crater serves as a Mývatn landmark and is surely one of Iceland's most interesting mountains.

The crater is comprised of loose tephra gravel, and close-up, resembles a mound of ball-bearings. If you want to hike to the top, follow the ready-made tracks, where you're least likely to damage the feature. The track ascends the northern slope, then circles around the western rim of the crater to a lookout at the southern end before descending steeply towards Dimmuborgir.

In the past, the crater floor, which is connected to the rim by several footpaths, served as the hikers' message billboard, with pictures and slogans written in light-coloured stone patterns. Some messages remain, but because of damage to the formation, the crater floor is now closed to hikers.

Dimmuborgir The convoluted 'black castles' of Dimmuborgir are good for hours of imagination-invoking exploration. It's believed that the oddly shaped pillars and crags were created 2000 years ago by lava from the Þrengslaborgir and Lúdentsborgir crater rows (which originally erupted 9000 years ago). The lava flowed across older Hverfell lava fields and was dammed into a fiery lake in the Dimmuborgir basin. When the surface of this lake cooled, a domed roof formed over the still-molten material below. It was supported by pillars of older igneous material welded by the heat of the lava lake. When the dam finally broke, the molten lava drained in stages and the odd pillars of Dimmuborgir remained marked with terraces at various surface levels.

The remaining formations contain natural arches, caves and zoomorphic features. Perhaps the most interesting is a large lava cave known as Kirkjan ('the church'), because its interior resembles a vaulted Gothic cathedral.

To prevent erosion, vandalism and injury – and to protect the nascent lava field vegetation from the armies of feet trampling through (up to 1000 visitors per day!) – the tourist association has roped off specific walking routes. It's not as much fun as before, when you could explore (and become lost) at will, but it does ensure that Dimmuborgir remains worthwhile for future visitors. Especially if you're walking with children, beware of the small and innocent-looking cracks that run throughout the area. Many are deep and dangerous fissures with no bottom in sight.

Markhraun The lava flow between Dimmuborgir and the lake shore is called Markhraun. It was originally formed in the Hverfell eruption and was later covered by lava from Lúdentsborgir and Þrengslaborgir.

Höfði
The forested lava headland Höfði is covered with wildflowers and birch and spruce trees. In the spring, the fresh scent of the vegetation is very pleasant and its rambling footpaths can be easily covered in an hour. It's also excellent for picnics and relaxing. Listen to the wild and chilling cries of the great northern divers on the lake and observe the many small caves and *klasar* (lava pillars) along the shore. In summer, it's open from 9 am to 7 pm and there's an admission charge of Ikr150.

Kálfaströnd The Kálfaströnd coastline, on the southern shore of the Höfði peninsula, has some of the most interesting klasar formations on the lake. It is also a nesting site for great northern divers.

Syðrivogar
Syðrivogar is a small lava-rimmed inlet at the extreme south-eastern corner of lake

Mývatn. It contains prolific underwater springs, which supply most of the fresh water entering the lake.

Pseudocraters

The pseudocrater 'swarms' that formed most of Mývatn's islands, as well as the small hills around the southern, western and south-eastern shores, were formed as molten lava from the craters east of the lake flowed across existing lava fields and into the water. Trapped subsurface water boiled and exploded in steam eruptions through the lava surface, forming small scoria cones and craters. The largest of these, which measure more than 300m across, are east of Vindbelgjarfjall on the western shore of Mývatn. The smallest ones – the islets and those south of the lake – are just a couple of metres wide.

Arnarbæli The unusual hollow pseudocrater Arnarbæli lies south of the lake, just off the road near Skútustaðir. Access is thwarted by marshy ground; the most direct route is along the track that turns off just west of the farm Garður.

Skútustaðagígar The most accessible pseudocrater swarm is the Skútustaðagígar, near Skútustaðir on the southern lake shore. This field, which surrounds the lovely pond Stakhólstjörn, was designated a national natural monument in 1973, and the pond and surrounding boggy marshland are havens for nesting waterfowl. Hiking trails wander through and over the craters; a complete circuit of Stakhólstjörn takes about an hour at a leisurely pace. The features are rather delicate, so hikers must remain on the marked tracks.

Skútustaðir

The settlement of Skútustaðir serves as Mývatn's secondary service centre. During saga times, it was owned by the notorious Vigaskúta ('Killer Skúta'), who was known for his ruthlessness and was marked for assassination by his neighbours. He was clever though, and more often than not turned the tables on those who threatened him.

One point of interest is the church, east of the village, which contains a painting of the Last Supper and makes a quiet and shady vantage point.

Horse Riding Safari Horses (☎ 464 4279) hires horses for trips along the river Kraká or through the pseudocraters. The charges are Ikr1200/2100/3000 for one/two/three hours.

Places to Stay & Eat Sleeping-bag accommodation is available at the community centre *Skjólbrekka* (☎ 464 4202) for Ikr850. The *campground* costs Ikr450 per person.

The farm *Skútustaðir* (☎ 464 4212) has single/double rooms for Ikr3000/4050 and sleeping-bag accommodation for Ikr1300, including the use of cooking facilities. *Garður III* (☎ 464 4314; fax 464 4324), about 3½ km east of Skútustaðir, offers beds for Ikr1820 and sleeping-bag accommodation for Ikr1105, with use of kitchen facilities. The farm *Grænavatn* (☎ 464 4194), two km south of Garður III, has a campground with a nice view of the lake Grænavatn. It's popular with anglers. Skútustaðir also has a swimming pool, general store, *cafeteria* and a petrol station and *snack bar*.

Laxá

One of the many Icelandic rivers called 'salmon river', the beautiful Laxá flows toward Öxarfjörður from the western end of Mývatn, and is one of the best – and most expensive – salmon-fishing venues in the country. The clear and turbulent stream rolls across the tundra and past numerous mid-channel islets. More affordable brown trout fishing is also available. Permits may be purchased at the farm Arnarvatn and at Ferðaþjónustan Eldá in Reykjahlíð. Even for non-anglers, this is one of the best places to see harlequin ducks, which are only around in the spring until early July.

Vindbelgjarfjall

The easy climb up 529m Vindbelgjarfjall

('the windbag'), west of the lake, takes about half an hour up and 15 minutes down. Because it's so near the lake, the summit offers one of the best views across the water, pseudocraters and protected wetlands along the north-western shore. As with most peaks near the lake, it's composed of unconsolidated volcanic slag.

Protected Nesting Area

The bogs, marshes, ponds and wet tundra along the north-western shore of Mývatn are a high-density waterfowl nesting zone. Off-road entry is restricted between 15 May and 20 July (when the chicks hatch), but overland travel on this soggy ground would be challenging at any time.

Most species of waterfowl present in Iceland are found here in great numbers – including nearly 10,000 breeding pairs of ducks, representing 15 species – and the area is world-famous among birdwatchers. Three duck species, the scoter, the gadwall, and Barrow's goldeneye, breed nowhere else in Iceland. Also present are incredible numbers of eider ducks, harlequin ducks, red-breasted mergansers, mallards, long-tailed ducks, pintail ducks, tufted ducks, wigeons, goosanders, teals, shovellers, whooper swans, horned grebes, great northern divers (loons), red-throated divers, black-headed gulls, ptarmigans, Arctic terns, great skuas, several species of geese, ravens, gyrfalcons, golden plovers, snipe, whimbrels, wheatears, and lots of other species.

Harlequin ducks are common around Mývatn

Mink and Arctic fox, which take advantage of the abundant avian prey, are also occasionally observed.

Eldhraun

The lava field along the northern lake shore, unimaginatively called Eldhraun ('fire lava'), includes the flow that nearly engulfed the Reykjahlíð church. It was belched out of Leirhnjúkur during the Mývatnseldar in 1729 and flowed down the channel Eldá ('fire river'). With some slow scrambling, it can be explored on foot from Reykjahlíð.

Hlíðarfjall

The prominent 771m rhyolite mountain Hlíðarfjall, four km north of Reykjahlíð, is sometimes called Reykjahlíðarfjall. It makes a pleasant day hike from the village, affording spectacular views over the lake on one side and over the Krafla lava fields on the other.

BJARNARFLAG

The Bjarnarflag flats, three km east of Reykjahlíð, overlie an active geothermal area, and during this century they have been the site of several economic ventures. Early on, farmers tried growing potatoes, but unfortunately, they often emerged from the ground already boiled (silly, but true!) and only a couple of potato fields remain. In 1938, a sulphur mine was opened, but it closed down shortly after a massive boiler explosion. In the early 1950s, attempts to extract sulphur from the solfataras (volcanic vents) that dot the area proved uneconomical and were also abandoned.

A cinder-brick factory has been set up to manufacture building materials from the volcanic ash deposits, and nearby is the underground bread oven where hverabrauð is packed into milk cartons and slowly baked for 22 hours into delicious cake-like loaves. Look for the small, round glass doors that open into the ground, but don't disturb the bread.

In the late 1960s, 25 test holes were bored at Bjarnarflag to ascertain the feasibility of a proposed geothermal power station. One, which lies just south-east of the 'bakery', is 2300m deep and the steam roars out of the pipe at 200°C.

Kísilgúrverksmiðja

The most prominent and unusual Bjarnarflag enterprise is the geothermal diatomite plant. Diatoms are tiny microfossils, the skeletal remains of a type of single-celled algae. Although they are only about one twenty-thousandth the size of a sand grain, the 15m-thick deposits on the floor of Mývatn are thickening at a rate of one mm annually. Near the northern end of the lake, a barge gathers sediment from the lake bed and pipes it to the shore, where it is strained and channelled in holding ponds to settle. It is then transported to the plant and treated with fire and steam to remove further impurities before it's exported. Diatomite is used as a filler in fertilisers, paints, toothpaste and plastics and as a filtering agent for oil, pharmaceuticals, aviation fuel, beer and wine.

In September 1977, a series of earthquakes resulted in the destruction of the diatomite holding ponds. The plant itself was damaged and the bore holes, which served as its power source, were blocked with new lava. Repairs were made but the operation didn't re-open until 1980.

Unfortunately, the environmental impact of diatomite extraction isn't fully known. The collection barge may infringe on the waterfowl breeding grounds, increasing the water's depth and preventing some bird and fish species obtaining food from the lake bed. Furthermore, if the extraction of diatomite continues at its present annual rate of 25,000 tonnes, supplies from the northern lake bed will be exhausted within a decade and operations will have to move into unspoilt areas to supply the plant.

Námafjall

Produced by a fissure eruption, the pastel-coloured Námafjall ridge lies south of the Ring Road, six km east of Reykjahlíð. It sits squarely on the spreading zone of the Mid-Atlantic Rift and is dotted with steaming vents. A trail leads from the highway at Namaskarð pass to a view disc at the summit. This 30 minute climb provides a grand vista over the steamy surroundings. North of the pass is another ridge, Dalfjall, which sports a large and growing notch – dramatic evidence that the mountain is being split in two by tectonic spreading.

Hverarönd

Hverarönd, the geothermal field immediately east of Námafjall, is full of mudpots, steam vents, sulphur deposits, boiling springs and fumeroles, some of which are real dynamos. Visitors may roam freely, but to avoid risk of serious injury and damage to the natural features, avoid the lighter coloured soil and don't venture beyond the ropes placed around the more enticing (or intimidating, depending on your disposition) features.

KRAFLA

Technically, Krafla is just a mountain seven km north of the Ring Road, but the name is now used for the entire volcanic region as well as a geothermal power station and the series of eruptions that created Iceland's most awesome lava field.

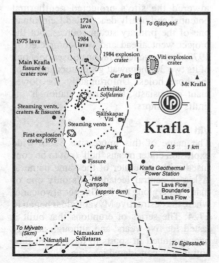

The heart of volcanic activity is known as the Krafla central volcano, but it bears little resemblance to the popular image of a volcano. Rather than a cone-shaped peak, Krafla is a largely level system of north-south trending fissures underlain by a great magma chamber. Activity is normally characterised by fissuring and gradual surface swells followed by abrupt subsidence, which triggers eruptions. At present, the ground surface is rising, indicating possible activity in the near future.

If you can melt deep into the hills, you'll find some viable campsites, but note that camping is prohibited anywhere around the power station.

Kröflustöð

The idea of constructing a geothermal power station at Krafla was conceived in 1973 and preliminary work commenced with the drilling of 24 test holes to determine project feasibility and provide steam sources should the plan be given the green light.

On 20 December, 1975, however, after a rest of several hundred years, the Krafla fissure burst into activity with the first in a series of nine eruptions and 20 cases of surface subsidence. This considerably lowered the site's projected geothermal potential and nearly deactivated Leirbotnar, one of the primary steam sources, but the project went ahead and was completed in 1978. The present operation utilises only one of its two 30-megawatt generators and 17 of the bore holes. Unfortunately for power plant enthusiasts, the Krafla station is off limits to visitors.

Viti

The name of this impressive 320m-wide explosion crater means 'hell' (not to be confused with the crater of the same name at Askja in central Iceland). It's only one of many vents along the Krafla central volcano, where the destructive Mývatnseldar began in 1724. The series of eruptions that built it lasted for five years, and although activity has continued in spurts to the present day, Viti is now considered inactive.

Behind the crater are the 'twin lakes', boiling mud springs which aren't included in the guided tours. During the Mývatnseldar, they spurted mud up to 10m into the air, but they're now down to a mere simmer.

Homemade Hell

The impressive crater known as Sjálfskapar Viti, or 'homemade hell', near the Krafla car park, isn't like other craters in the area. When teams were drilling the Krafla boreholes, one was so powerful that when they hit the steam chamber it exploded. A huge crater was created and bits of the drilling rig were discovered up to three km away. Miraculously, no-one was killed. Had the project been successful, this one borehole would have been sufficient to power the entire Krafla power station. Now, the same work is done by 17 boreholes! The Eldá Gjástykki tour is the only one to stop here. ■

Leirhnjúkur & Kröfluöskjunni

The horrendous red warning sign that once forbade visitors entering the Leirhnjúkur and Kröfluöskjunni area has now been removed, so tourists can no longer photograph it with a backdrop of tour groups, cyclists, grandparents and young children streaming in as if it were a fun fair! This is one of Iceland's most impressive – albeit potentially risky – attractions and no-one is going to keep the tourists out!

To be safe, avoid the lighter coloured soil around the mudpots, snowfields that may overlie hidden fissures, sharp lava chunks and scoria slopes. As Krafla is expected to erupt again within the next few years, a visit will naturally involve some risk. (At the first sign of an eruption, you can expect half the population of Iceland to descend on the place rather than follow official advice and clear out!)

Leirhnjúkur The big attraction at Krafla is the colourful Leirhnjúkur crater, which originally appeared in August 1727. It started out as a lava fountain, and spouted molten material for two years before subsiding. After a minor burp in 1746, it became the menacing sulphur-encrusted mudhole that tourists love today. In fact, it was Leirhnjúkur lava that flowed through Reykjahlíð, destroying farms and threatening the church.

A well-defined track leads north-west to Leirhnúkur from the Krafla parking area. Along the way, note the steaming vents on the pastel coloured rhyolite mountain to the west. The Leirhnjúkur crater lies just north of this mountain.

Kröfluöskjunni The source of the lava layers at Kröfluöskjunni is the north-south tending fissure that bisects the Krafla caldera. From the rim above Leirhnjúkur, you can look out across flows from the original Mývatnseldar, as well as from the 1975 eruptions, which are all overlain in places by the still-steaming 1984 lava. Some areas west of Leirhnjúkur remain so hot that they feel like a natural sauna. In 1975, the small grass-filled crater on the western slope of the rhyolite mountain, south of Leirhnjúkur, set off a series of explosive eruptions known as the Kröflueldar ('Krafla fires'), which were a continuation of the Mývatnseldar of the early 18th century.

Gjástykki
Gjástykki, the remote 'fissured area' at the northernmost end of the Krafla fissure swarm, was the source of the first 1724 eruptions, and was also activated when Leirhnúkur went off in the 1975 eruptions. However, the current Gjástykki lava fields were created by the Krafla central volcano between 1981 and 1984. The best-known Gjástykki landmark is a beautiful red mountain which protrudes from the steaming 1984 lava.

Organised Tours
The second segment of the daily Grand Mývatn tour from Reykjahlíð takes in the most interesting Krafla sites, but the Gjástykki tour offers the most revealing perspective on the area's geological drama. For more details, see Organised Tours under Reykjahlíð.

Getting There & Away
The best way to reach Krafla is on the daily bus, which leaves at 1 pm from the Hótel Reynihlíð and costs Ikr400 each way (this is also the bus used for second half of the Grand Mývatn tour). While cycling to Krafla is also feasible, most people find the high winds, sandstorms and steep hills make it less than appealing. With all the summer tourist traffic, hitching isn't too difficult.

From Reykjahlíð, it's also a wonderful day hike to Leirhnúkur. The marked footpath strikes off to the north-east from near the airport, along Langahlíð. Another walking route leads from Namaskarð along the Dalfjall ridge to Leirhnúkur. Together, they make a long but viable return day hike.

SOUTH-EAST OF MÝVATN
With lots of time and an inclination to walk long distances over rugged terrain, you'll enjoy exploring the scattered mountains and geological features in the deserts south and east of the main lake area.

Lúdentsborgir & Þrengslaborgir
The Lúdentsborgir crater row, east of Mývatn, is part of the eight-km Þrengslaborgir fissure, which lies five km due east of southern lake Mývatn. The craters, which were formed in eruptions between 9000 and 6000 years ago, rise an average of 100m above the surrounding lava desert. The largest, Lúdent, measures nearly one km in diameter and 70m deep. In fact, this landscape was considered uncannily lunar, and in 1968 the Lúdent crater area was used as a training ground for the moon-bound astronaut Neil Armstrong.

To get to Lúdent, follow the light track rounding the southern base of Hverfell, then continue five more km south-eastward through the Lúdentsborgir row to Lúdent itself. Þrengslaborgir lies a couple of km further south-east. For tour information, see Organised Tours under Reykjahlíð.

ICELAND

Bláfjall

About 15 km south-east of Grænavatn, near the southern shore of Mývatn, is the 1222m table mountain Bláfjall ('blue mountain'). Like other Icelandic table mountains, it was formed in a sub-glacial volcanic eruption during the last ice age.

There are no marked routes in the area and getting there from Grænavatn is tough going, through marshes and across ropy, chunky lava flows. A longer but easier route is around the lava field from the farm Baldursheimur, south of Skútustaðir. Surface water is available in some places, but not on the lava field.

Búrfell

Another table mountain, which is accessible across formidable lava fields, is 953m Búrfell, which lies 12 km south of the Ring Road and 15 km east of Mývatn. It's a beautiful, symmetrical peak, but unless you're a masochist, it's probably not worth the effort of getting there.

Búrfellsheiði, between the mountain and the Ring Road, is popular with Icelandic ptarmigan hunters, who come to procure the main course of their traditional Christmas Eve dinner.

Sellandafjall

The third big table mountain visible from Mývatn is the 988m Sellandafjall, which is a manageable 12km hike south of Baldursheimur farm (itself eight km south of the Ring Road). It's the most eroded of the three and is therefore the most easily climbed. From the intersection of the Ring Road and Route 849, allow at least three days for the return trip to the summit. Although it's a relatively easy walk, this cross-country wilderness trek requires careful preparation and good maps.

East Iceland

Because it's away from the spreading zone along the Mid-Atlantic Ridge, the east is one of Iceland's oldest and most geologically stable regions. A big attraction here is the good chance of sunshine; in summer it's often cool but clear. The region also boasts the country's largest forest and longest lake, as well as some fine waterfalls and a wealth of rugged and remote peaks and headlands.

Those who prefer quiet and unstructured travel will probably appreciate eastern Iceland's lack of organised tourism and those arriving on the ferry at Seyðisfjörður are normally knocked over by East Iceland's typically steep snow-topped peaks, rugged coastline, deep fjords and lightly populated farmlands. Still, many travellers seem to shoot quickly off to Mývatn or Skaftafell without having appreciated the appeal of this largely tourist-free corner of the country.

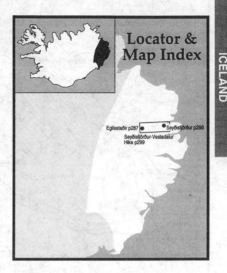

Locator & Map Index

Egilsstaðir p287　　　●Seyðisfjörður p298
Seyðisfjörður-Vestadalur
Hike p299

The Interior

EGILSSTAÐIR
Egilsstaðir, which started out as a large farm in the late 1800s, is now eastern Iceland's transport and commercial hub. It sits in the Lagarfljót valley farming district beside the lake Lögurinn (the 'smooth one'). Although it's small and rather sterile-looking, many travellers arriving on the Seyðisfjörður ferry spend a night here.

Information
The tourist complex, with a petrol station, cafeteria, bus terminal, bank, supermarket and campground, contains everything of interest to travellers (except perhaps the post office, which is just up the hill). The tourist office, Ferðamiðstöð Austurlands (☎ 471 2320; fax 471 2035), is at the campground. From 15 June to 31 August, it's open daily

from 7 am to 11 pm. From 1 to 15 June and 1 to 15 September, it's open 9 am to 5 pm.

Things to See & Do
Egilsstaðir's monotonous box-like architecture is broken only by the **church**, which dominates the town and attempts to emulate its mountain backdrop. It's actually one of Iceland's nicer geological-theme churches.

East of the campground, a rocky hill and a **view disc** provide a good excuse to laze in the sun, and east of town is a pleasant green park with jogging tracks. The new and worthwhile cultural museum, **Minjasafn Austurlands** (☎ 471 1412), outlines the history of the Eastfjords from Settlement to the present day. Features include a restored farmhouse and displays of pagan relics and traditions, including a grave. On weekends, you can watch spinning and weaving demonstrations and ride in a horse-drawn carriage. It's open daily from 28 May to 1

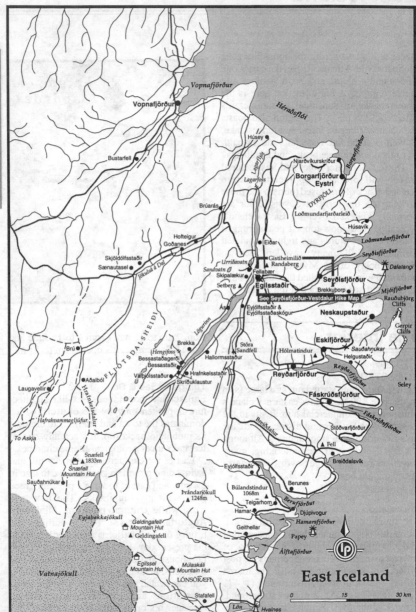

East Iceland

0   15   30 km

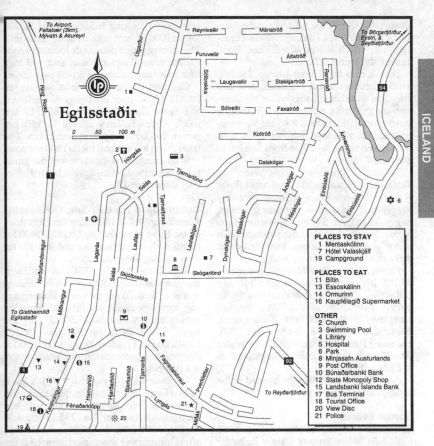

Egilsstaðir

```
0    50    100 m
```

PLACES TO STAY
1 Mentaskólinn
7 Hótel Valaskjálf
19 Campground

PLACES TO EAT
11 Bítin
13 Essoskálinn
14 Ormurinn
16 Kaupfélagið Supermarket

OTHER
2 Church
3 Swimming Pool
4 Library
5 Hospital
6 Park
8 Minjasafn Austurlands
9 Post Office
10 Búnaðarbanki Bank
12 State Monopoly Shop
15 Landsbanki Íslands Bank
17 Bus Terminal
18 Tourist Office
20 View Disc
21 Police

September, 11 am to 5 pm. Admission is Ikr200.

Swimming

Egilsstaðir's amazing new swimming pool is open Monday to Friday from 7 am to 9.30 pm and on weekends from 10 am to 7 pm. Admission costs Ikr180.

Horse Riding

For horse tours through the spectacular Eastfjords, contact Lomma Hestar (☎ & fax 471 1727), at Útnyrðingsstaðir, which runs five and six-day trips.

Organised Tours

On Monday and Tuesday, Tanni Travel (☎ 476 1399; fax 476 1599), runs tours to Borgarfjörður Eystri for Ikr3120. On Wednesday, it visits Hallormsstaður and Hengifoss (Ikr2925). The Thursday tour (Ikr2210), is an abbreviated version of the Wednesday Hengifoss tour, and is designed for people leaving on the *Nörrona* ferry. On Friday, 10-hour tours run to remote Hafrahvammagljúfur and the hot waterfall at

Laugavellir (Ikr3850). All tours leave from the campground at 10 am, except the Thursday tour, which leaves at 9.30 am. Book through the tourist office.

There's also an 11 hour tour to Snæfell, which includes stops at Hallormsstaður and the warm waterfall at Laugarvellir, reindeer-viewing and hikes around Snæfell itself. It leaves from Egilsstaðir at 9.45 am on weekends and costs Ikr3640, without lunch. This is an option to use for hikes from Snæfell to Lónsöræfi.

To really come to grips with the Vatnajökull icecap, Tanni Travel runs offbeat – and slow-motion – one to five-day Vatnajökull tours in a lumbering glacier buggy. The driver, Sveinn Sigurbjarnarnson (who is quite a character), has participated in many glacier expeditions and conducted these tours for nearly two decades.

Finally, you can do a three-day excursion, which includes nights at Snæfell and Dalakaffi, a hike to Hafrahvammagljúfur gorge, and stops at the hot waterfall Laugarvellir, the turf farm Sænautarsel, Askja and Herðubreið. It costs Ikr17,000, excluding food. Book through Philip Vogler (☎ 471 1673; fax 471 2190), Skógarlöndum 3, Egilsstaðir.

Any of these tours may be booked at the campground in Egilsstaðir.

Special Events

Egilsstaðir's annual jazz festival, Djasshátíð Egilsstaða, which attracts mainly Icelandic musicians, takes place at the Hótel Valaskjálf around the last week in June.

Places to Stay

Camping Oddly, Egilsstaðir has no hostel, so most budget travellers wind up at the *campground*, which is one of Iceland's nicest. It has the tourist office, bus terminal, a children's play area, hot showers and a common room where you can eat or spend rainy days chatting, reading or writing letters. Tent sites are well sheltered, but caravans are relegated to the large common area. Camping costs Ikr450 per person and dormitory sleeping-bag accommodation,

with use of cooking facilities, costs Ikr900 (or Ikr1000 in huts with en suite facilities). The most negative point is its location opposite the town slaughterhouse, and you may hear some unpleasant goings-on over there.

Camping is also available at *Skipalækur* (☎ 471 1324), over the bridge in Fellabær, and *Stóra Sandfell* (☎ 471 1785), 17 km south of town. They charge Ikr350 per person and Ikr350 per tent or caravan. The latter offers horse rental for Ikr1200 per hour.

Wild camping is possible on the small rocky outcrops outside of town, but it's officially discouraged.

Guesthouses The cosy little *Gistiheimilið Randaberg* (☎ 471 1288), five km from town on the Eiðar road, charges Ikr1820/2990 for rooms with shared facilities and Ikr1000 for sleeping-bag accommodation.

Skipalækur (☎ 471 1324), in Fellabær, has smart lakeside chalets as well as standard rooms at Ikr2020 per person, and sleeping-bag accommodation for Ikr1300. Four/six person chalets cost Ikr29,300/37,115 per week. The *Gólfskálinn Ekkufelli* (☎ 471 1344), also in Fellabær, charges Ikr1200 for sleeping-bag accommodation. Yes, it really is a golf hut.

Gistiheimilið Helgafell (☎ 471 1322), right beside the bridge in Fellabær, has made-up beds for Ikr1950 and sleeping-bag accommodation for Ikr1235. *Fellaskóli* (☎ 471 2264), the Fellabær school, also offers inexpensive accommodation; beds are Ikr2000 and sleeping-bag accommodation is Ikr1350.

The farm *Stóra Sandfell* (☎ 471 1785), 17 km south of town, charges standard farmhouse rates: single/double rooms for Ikr3000/4050 and sleeping-bag accommodation for Ikr1300. At *Setberg* (☎ 471 1929), on the lake shore five km south of Fellabær, there's a four-person self-catering cottage for Ikr32,500 per week.

Hotels The large and bland *Hótel Valaskjálf* (☎ 471 1500; fax 471 1501) costs Ikr5655 /7540 for singles/doubles with shared facilities and Ikr7540/9425 with bath. However,

DEANNA SWANEY

DEANNA SWANEY   DEANNA SWANEY   DEANNA SWANEY

DEANNA SWANEY

A: Colourful slopes of Brennisteinsalda
B: Svartifoss, Skaftafell National Park
C: Historic turf church dating from 1200,
   Núpsstaður farm

D: Lómagnúpur cliffs & Núpsá
   River, Núpsstaður
E: Crevasses on Skaftafellsjökull
   glacier, Skaftafell National Park

Top: Álftavatn Lake on Landmannalaugar-Þórsmörk trek, Central Iceland
Bottom: Hrafntinnusker on Landmannalaugar-Þórsmörk trek, Central Iceland

its cinema may offer a welcome respite from a rainy day. From 1 June to 1 September, the hotel also runs the summer hotel *Mentaskólinn* (☎ 471 1505), with single/double rooms for Ikr6500/8450, with breakfast. Sleeping-bag accommodation is Ikr1500.

Places to Eat

Although the *Hótel Valaskjálf* dining room seems as bland as its architecture, each summer Thursday there's a 'Feast in the East', featuring such goodies as hákarl, brennivín and other traditional treats. The meal is accompanied by live accordion music, folk songs and dancing.

There's also an excellent new formal restaurant *Ormurinn*, which does fish, chicken and pasta dishes for very good prices. Even lobster starts at only Ikr1290. It's open weekdays from 11.30 am to midnight and on Friday and Saturday until 3 am.

Over the bridge in Fellabær is the friendly and cosy *Pizza 67* (☎ 471 2270), where the view takes in both the lake and the mountains. On summer weekdays, it's open from 11.30 am to midnight; on Friday and Saturday, there are live bands which normally play until 3 am.

For lesser budgets, the green and leafy *Essoskálinn* petrol station serves up hearty daily specials as well as the old standbys: burgers, hot dogs, pitta sandwiches, fish & chips and surprisingly good pizzas. There's good variety, it's good value, and if it's raining, the television offers a bit of diversion. Alternatively, try the *Bítinn*, at the Shell petrol station, which competes admirably with a range of main meals as well as the standard chicken, burgers, chips and pizzas.

Except on Sunday, self-caterers can rely on the well-stocked *supermarket* in the tourist complex. In season, a *farm market* sells produce, smoked salmon and snacks in the grassy area north-east of the bank. The State Monopoly shop is opposite the tourist complex in the oddly-coloured shopping centre .

Getting There & Away

Air Flugleiðir (☎ 471 1210) flies at least once daily to and from Reykjavík, and Flugfélag Austurlands (☎ 471 1122) does the route on Monday and Saturday. The latter also flies to and from Höfn four times weekly. Flugfélag Norðurlands (☎ 471 1210) flies between Egilsstaðir and Akureyri daily except Wednesday and Saturday, with discount flights on Tuesday and Thursday. Íslandsflug (☎ 471 1122) flies daily to and from Reykjavík.

Bus The Egilsstaðir bus terminal, one of the four Ring Road cornerstones, is at the campground, but some services, such as to Breiðdalsvík and Höfn, also stop at the airport.

From 1 June to 31 August, buses to Höfn (Ikr3300) depart daily at 3.30 pm; coming from Höfn, they leave at 8.30 am. These connect with buses to/from Akureyri (Ikr3300) and Mývatn (Ikr2100). This means that you can now travel between Akureyri/Mývatn and Höfn in a single day.

In summer, buses run to and from Eiðar (Ikr260) at 2 pm on Monday and Thursday, and to and from Hallormsstaður (Ikr500) on Monday and Thursday. To Reyðarfjörður (Ikr650), Eskifjörður (Ikr900) and Neskaupstaður (Ikr1200), they run daily except Sunday; and to Fáskrúðsfjörður (Ikr1200), Stöðvarfjörður (Ikr1100) and Breiðdalsvík (Ikr1400), they go daily, Monday to Friday.

From 1 June to 31 August, buses travel each way between Seyðisfjörður (Ikr800) and Egilsstaðir on weekday mornings. On Wednesday, to accommodate *Nörrona* ferry passengers, there are two additional runs in either direction. On Thursday, there's an additional afternoon departure in either direction, and on weekends, there's one daily bus each way.

To and from Vopnafjörður (Ikr1200) and Húsavík (Ikr4050), buses run on Monday, Wednesday and Friday.

Excursions run to Borgarfjörður Eystri, Snæfell and Mjóifjörður. See Organised Tours earlier in this section.

ICELAND

Getting Around

You can hire bicycles at the tourist office for Ikr200/500/800 per hour/half-day/day, plus a deposit of Ikr1000. For car hire information, see the Iceland Getting Around chapter.

LAGARFLJÓT

The 'smooth river', Lagarfljót, begins in the Vatnajökull icecap and flows north to the Arctic Ocean. For much of its length, it isn't a river at all but rather a long narrow lake, Lögurinn. Like long narrow lakes elsewhere, Lögurinn is reputed to harbour a resident monster, Lagarfljótsormurinn, which is said to put in an occasional appearance.

The lake is 24 km long and under two km wide at its widest point, and reaches a depth of 112m. South of Hallormsstaður on the eastern shore and Fellabær on the west, access is a challenge but it's ideal for cycling; the mostly flat terrain welcomes even inexperienced cyclists. Hitching is easiest at weekends but to do a circuit of the lake shore, plan on walking many of the 56 km between those two places.

Eyjólfsstaðaskógur

This small but lovely forested area lies east of the Ring Road, 11 km south of Egilsstaðir. There's a picnic site and 3½ km of leafy walking tracks to a couple of nice waterfalls.

Accommodation is available at Eyjólfsstaðir farm (☎ 471 1732; fax 471 2271), on the lake side of the road. Single/double rooms cost Ikr2925/4225 and sleeping-bag accommodation is Ikr1170.

Hallormsstaður

Believe it or not, Iceland has a forestry commission, and Hallormsstaður, on the eastern shore of Lögurinn, is its showcase. In addition to protecting the native dwarf birch and mountain ash, it is planting spruce, Alaskan poplar and Siberian larch. Much of the forest is laid out in neatly ordered rows, but tree-starved Icelanders still flock to it and everyone appreciates the leafy reprieve. Don't miss Iceland's oldest tree, Guttormslundur, 2½ km south of the Edda Hotel, which was planted in 1938 and has now attained the whopping height of 15m!

Formerly a large farm, Hallormsstaður takes in 800 hectares. It was the home of Guðmundur Magnússon, Iceland's prominent 18th century publisher and translator.

From 10 am to 10 pm daily, you can hire pedal boats, rowboats or canoes or arrange horse-riding tours from Fljótsbátar (☎ 471 1765), at Atlavík.

Places to Stay & Eat Hallormsstaður has an *Edda Hotel* (☎ 471 1705; fax 471 2197),

Wood carving on the church door, Valþjófsstaður

with a restaurant and sleeping-bag accommodation but no pool. Single/double rooms cost Ikr3650/4750 and sleeping-bag accommodation is Ikr850/1300 on mattresses/beds. Alternatively, there's the *Hústjörnarskóli* (☎ 471 1761) school, which charges the same rates. Down the hill, near the lake shore at Atlavík, is a beautiful *campground*, which on summer weekends attracts particularly raucous parties.

Getting There & Away There are buses from Egilsstaðir on Tuesday and Thursday at 9.45 am, returning the same days at 6.30 pm. See also Organised Tours under Egilsstaðir.

Hrafnkelsstaðir
The farm Hrafnkelsstaðir, 10 km south-west of Hallormsstaður, lies near the head of Lögurinn. It was here that the reformed Hrafnkell Hallfreðarson Freysgoði of *Hrafnkels Saga* fame fled after being tortured and forced to leave his ancestral farm Aðalból in Hrafnkelsdalur. For more history, see Hrafnkelsdalur, later in this chapter.

Valþjófsstaður
The unassuming church at Valþjófsstaður, at the head of Lögurinn, is worth a look. The door, which depicts an ancient battle scene, is a replica of the famous original, which was carved at Valþjófsstaður around 1200 and is displayed at the National Museum in Reykjavík. The farm Valþjófsstaður also dates back to the 13th century.

Skriðuklaustur
A couple of km along the road north of Valþjófsstaður is Skriðuklaustur, which was the site of a monastery from 1493 until the Reformation, when it was demolished by order of the Danish king, and a church until 1792. The unusual stone building you see now was built in 1939 by Icelandic writer Gunnar Gunnarsson. It's currently used as an agricultural and sheep research institute. If there's someone there, visitors are welcome to have a look around.

Hengifoss
While the Icelanders love Hallormsstaður, the big Lögurinn attraction for foreigners is Iceland's third highest waterfall, Hengifoss ('hanging falls'). This unforgettable dynamo sounds like a Boeing 747 taking off as the water plummets 120m into a brown and red-striped gorge.

Hengifoss is reached on a well-defined sheep track. Turn west from the southern end of the first bridge south of the farm Brekka (or north of Bessastaðagerði) on the western shore of Lögurinn. Allow an hour to climb up and a half hour down. Halfway up is a smaller waterfall, Lítlanesfoss, which is surrounded by spectacular basalt columns.

BSÍ Tours to Hallormsstaður and Hengifoss run from Egilsstaðir on Wednesday and Thursday; see Organised Tours under Egilsstaðir.

Lagarfoss
The Lagarfoss falls are actually a long, turbulent chute along a small tributary of Lagarfljót, where a power plant is fed by a six-metre drop in one small channel. The main interest is the fish ladder, where jumping salmon may be seen from late July to late August.

Access is difficult without a car, but you can take the excursion bus from Egilsstaðir toward Borgarfjörður Eystri to the junction of Routes 94 and 944, then walk south-westward on 944 for 10 km to the falls. The return trip will probably involve hitching but at this point, you'll have realised that Lagarfoss isn't worth the effort.

Urriðavatn
The lake Urriðavatn, two km along the Ring Road west of the Lagarfljót bridge, contains the only hot springs used for heating east of Iceland's main volcanic zone. It's also a source of water for Egilsstaðir.

Eiðar
Eiðar, 15 km north of Egilsstaðir, was the farm of Helgi Ásbjarnarson, grandson of Hrafnkell Freysgoði. The church, built in 1887, contains an interesting statue of Christ

which washed up on the shore at Héraðssandur, north of Eiðar. Its location beside a popular trout lake, Eiðavatn, makes it especially appealing for anglers. There are also several forest hiking tracks and birdwatchers can observe great northern divers, greylag geese and whooper swans.

At 8 pm on Wednesday, from 25 June to 15 August, the Edda Hotel stages outdoor theatre performances of *Here in East Iceland*. Tickets plus camping fees cost Ikr1200 (Ikr1000 if booked at the Egilsstaðir tourist office). Programmes on other nights cost Ikr600 and include traditional music and folk dancing.

Places to Stay & Eat Eiðar has an *Edda Hotel* (☎ 471 3803; fax 471 3870), with a swimming pool and licensed restaurant. Single/double rooms cost Ikr3650/4750 and sleeping-bag accommodation is Ikr1000/1450 in schoolrooms/rooms. Alternatively, there's the more intimate *Gistiheimilið Eiðar* (☎ 471 3846; fax 471 3856), at the farm Þrándarstaðir, which has single/double rooms for Ikr3120/4485 and sleeping-bag accommodation for Ikr1100.

Getting There & Away In summer, scheduled buses run between Egilsstaðir and Eiðar on Monday and Thursday afternoons. For the plays, bus transport is provided from Egilsstaðir for Ikr260 each way.

Héraðsflói

The shores of the bight Héraðsflói form an intriguing landscape of sand dunes, basalt outcrops and marshes at the deltas of Lagarfljót and Jökulsá á Dal (marked Jökulsá á Brú on the Landmælingar Íslands' *Ferðakort* 1:500,000). This is also one of the best places in Iceland to observe the Fata Morgana effect which, on bright sunny days, augments the view out to sea with beautiful (but fictitious!) rocky islets.

Húsey

The friendly farm at Húsey, near the shores of Heraðsflói, doubles as the isolated *Húsey Youth Hostel* (☎ 471 3010; fax 471 3009).

Over 30 bird species breed at Húsey and it's a great spot to observe geese, wading birds and seals (the farmers hunt, tan and eat them). Beds cost Ikr1000/1250 for HI members/non-members, and camping is possible.

Recommended horse-riding tours, including an eight-day tour around Borgarfjörður, may be arranged. Contact the hostel owner Örn Þorleifsson, Húsey, Hroarstunga, 701 Egilsstaðir.

Getting There & Away On your own, you'll need a car or bicycle to reach Húsey. However, the wardens may also fetch booked guests from Egilsstaðir or the Brúarás bridge, which is cheaper. Take the Mývatn bus from Egilsstaðir and meet them at the eastern side of the bridge, 20 km north-west of Egilsstaðir.

SNÆFELL

Fljótsdalsheiði ('river valley moors'), an expanse of spongy tussocks of wet tundra, boulder fields, perennial snow patches and alpine lakes, stretch westward from Lögurinn into the bleak interior. The 1833m extinct volcano Snæfell ('snow mountain'), at the southern end of Fljótsdalsheiði, is the country's highest outside the Vatnajökull massif and is popular with hikers and mountaineers. Although it's not a difficult climb, weather can be a concern and technical equipment is required.

Access to Snæfell is by 4WD, and only for two months at the height of summer. You can also walk the 60 km from the end of Lögurinn, along the road heading steeply uphill from Bessastaðir farm, near the bridge across Bessastaðaá. It winds upward for about eight km onto the tundra moors. When you see a mound of stones to your right known as Klausturshæð Þerfall Teigsberg (identified by an odd structure that looks like a cross or an antenna, but is actually neither and serves no apparent purpose), climb up for an amazing view nearly halfway across Iceland. On a clear day you can see Askja, Herðubreið, Vatnajökull and Snæfell.

If you continue along this road, you'll

eventually reach Snæfell. Along the way, watch for wild – albeit introduced – reindeer. At the base of the peak, at 800m elevation is the *Snæfell mountain hut* accommodating up to 60 people. Beds and use of cooking facilities cost Ikr750/1150 for Ferðafélag Íslands members/non-members.

Snæfell-Lónsöræfi Hike

One of Iceland's most challenging and rewarding treks takes you from Snæfell to the Lónsöræfi district in South-East Iceland. The five-day route begins at the Snæfell hut and heads across the glacier Eyjabakkajökull (an arm of Vatnajökull) to Geldingafell, Egilssel and Kollamúli huts before dropping down to the coast at Stafafell.

This route should not be taken lightly, and is for experienced trekkers only. You'll need good route-finding skills, and for the glacier crossing you must be able to use a compass and have crampons and an ice axe. If you're unsure of your skills, you'd probably be happier doing the trip commercially with Ferðafélag Íslands.

Maps You'll need the following topo sheets for walking in this region: *Hornafjörður* 1:100,000 (1986), *Hamarsfjörður* 1:100,000 (1987) and *Snæfell* 1:100,000 (1988).

Access To get started, you can take the Austurleið Snæfell tour from Egilsstaðir on Tuesday or Thursday. Alternatively, take Tanni Travel bus to Snæfell hut (weekends only); for information contact Tanni Travel Service (☎ 471 2499), Sólvellir 4, in Egilsstaðir, or Jeppaferðir (☎ 471 2189), Bjarkarhlíð, also in Egilsstaðir. Weather conditions permitting, it will drop you at Sauðhnúkur, or possibly Bjálfafell, near the base of Eyjabakkajökull.

At the southern end, pick-up can be arranged from the Illikambur parking area or from the Skyndidalsá river crossing (which can't be forded on foot). Contact the Lónsöræfaferðir Ferðaþjónusta (☎ 478 1717), at the Stafafell Youth Hostel. (See also Lónsöræfi in the South-East Iceland chapter.)

The Route The first day is to Geldingafell Hut, which is 32 km from Snæfell Hut, but only 22 km from Bjálfafell. A compass and a good map are essential for the five-km glacier crossing. At the glacier snout is a large ice cave containing an impressive river, so you need to climb fairly high up to avoid the crevasses and cave roof. Assuming that 0/360° is corrected north, follow a compass bearing of 130°. Once you're off the glacier, cross the stream Bergkvísl and traverse north-east around the hills; it's easiest to stay as low as possible. The 16-bed *Geldingafell Hut* lies on the north-western slope of Geldingafell, at the confluence of two rivers. (Doing the hike in the opposite direction – that is, from Stafafell to Snæfell – aim for the northern slope of the prominent double-pronged peak). Beds cost Ikr550/800 for Ferðafélag Íslands members/non-members.

From Geldingafell Hut to 16-bed *Egilssel Hut*, it's 18 km, mostly over snowfields. From Egilssel, it's an easy three to four-hour hike down to the lovely 25-bed *Múlaskáli Hut*, in the heart of idyllic Lónsöræfi. The richly-coloured rhyolite area around Múlaskáli is full of interesting day hikes.

Both Egilssel and Múlaskáli huts cost Ikr550/800 for club members/non-members. Múlaskáli Hut lies just 40 minutes from the Illikambur parking area; the Jökulsá í Lóni is crossed on a footbridge. You can either arrange to be picked up at Illikambur or continue along the road over beautiful Eskifell and down to the Skyndidalsá river crossing.

Advance hut reservations are recommended for July and August. Contact Ferðafélag Íslands in Reykjavík.

Organised Tours

BSÍ runs a 10-hour tour from Egilsstaðir to Snæfell each Wednesday from 1 July to 15 August, for Ikr3200 per person or three Highland Pass vouchers (with or without Omnibuspass).

It also runs three-day excursions from Egilsstaðir on Thursday, from 8 July to 8 August. These tours include a night at the Snæfell mountain hut; a hike to the gorge

ICELAND

Hafrahvammagljúfur; visits to the hot springs at Laugarvellir and the turf farm Sænautarsel; and stops at Askja and Herðubreið before finishing up at Mývatn. During the same period, there are Sunday departures from Reykjahlíð (Mývatn). Tours cost Ikr15,200, without food. Book through BSÍ or directly through the operator, Philip Vogler (☎ 471 1673; fax 471 2190), Dalskógar 12, Egilsstaðir.

Ferðafélag Íslands leads Snæfell to Lónsöræfi hikes several times in the summer.

JÖKULSÁ Á DAL

The name of this 150 km long river means 'glacial river of the valley', but it's also known as Jökulsá á Brú, as it was originally spanned by a natural bridge (which has since collapsed) at the farm Brú, 28 km upstream from the Ring Road. Each hour, this silty and turbulent watercourse deposits in Héraðsflói nearly one tonne of Icelandic real estate for each km of its length.

Brúarás

The farm Brúarás (☎ 471 1046), near the Ring Road bridge, resembles a concrete hotel more than a farm, but it offers comfortable single/double rooms for Ikr3000/4050 and sleeping-bag accommodation for Ikr1300.

The first bridge was built here by Hanseatic League traders in the 16th century. Folktales record that in the 16th century, one of those Nessie-style monsters was observed in the river near the present-day Ring Road bridge.

Goðanes

The stretch of the Jökulsá á Dal along the present Ring Road is said to be haunted not only by monsters but also by mischievous leprechauns and bloodthirsty Norse deities. The outcrop called Goðanes lies about three km west of the farm Hofteigur and was the site of an ancient pagan temple where some ruins are still visible. The iron-stained spring, Blóðkelda ('blood spring'), carries an apocryphal legend that the blood of both

human and animal sacrifices once flowed into it.

Accommodation is available at *Dalakaffi* (☎ & fax 471 1057), at Skjöldólfsstaðir, which has somehow become a cult favourite. Made-up beds cost Ikr1500 and sleeping-bag accommodation on mattresses/beds is Ikr800/1000. Camping costs Ikr300 per person. It's on the Ring Road about 60 km north-west of Egilsstaðir. There's also a well-known *café* serving up breakfast, coffee, homemade bread and cakes, and other snacks.

Sænautasel

Beside the lake Sænautavatn, 20 km west of Dalakaffi, is the reconstructed turf farmhouse, Sænautasel (☎ 472 1287), which was abandoned in the 1940s. It's now open to the public.

Hafrahvammagljúfur

In its upper reaches, the Jökulsá á Dal flows through the gorge Hafrahvammagljúfur, flanked by 160m cliffs. It's accessible on the 4WD track which leads toward Snæfell from the farm Brú. Several tours stop here; see Organised Tours under Egilsstaðir.

HRAFNKELSDALUR

The tributary valley of Hrafnkelsdalur, south of the Jökulsá á Dal, is bursting with Saga Age ruins. The farm Aðalból was the home of Hrafnkell Hallfreðarson Freysgoði, the priest of Freyr and hero of the popular *Hrafnkels Saga*.

From the farm Brú, beside the Jökulsá á Dal, a 4WD track continues up the valley and connects with the Bessastaðir track. This offers an alternative route to Snæfell, but otherwise, there's little in the valley to justify the considerable effort of getting there. However, saga buffs may take exception to that assessment.

Getting There & Away

No public transport (in fact, scarcely anything mobile) finds its way into Hrafnkelsdalur. Without a sturdy vehicle or mountain bike, you'll have to follow literally

Hrafnkels Saga

The saga of Hrafnkell, a priest of the god Freyr, is one of Iceland's most popular sagas and has been translated into English. The story is particularly interesting because its premises seem to derail any modern notions of right, wrong and justice served.

The main character, Hrafnkell, was a religious fanatic who built a temple to Freyr on the farm Aðalból in Hrafnkelsdalur. There he held animal sacrifices and offered up half his wealth in veneration of Freyr.

Hrafnkell's prized stallion, Freyfaxi ('the mane of Freyr'), was his treasured possession, and he swore to the gods to strike down anyone who dared ride him without permission. As might be expected, someone did. It seems the stallion himself tempted one of Hrafnkell's shepherds into riding him to find a herd of lost sheep. He returned from the excursion exhausted and covered with mud. Hrafnkell, of course, knew what had happened and wasted no time taking his axe to the errant youth.

In a moment of belated conscience, he offered the boy's father, Þorbjörn, compensation for the loss of his son in the form of foodstuffs and financial help. Proudly, the man refused, and the characters were launched into a court battle that ultimately led to Hrafnkell being declared an outlaw. Responding with a decidedly wait-and-see attitude, he chose to ignore the sentence and return home.

He didn't have long to wait before Þorbjörn's nephew Sámur Bjarnason took the matter into his own hands. Hrafnkell was summarily subjected to the particularly painful and humiliating Norse custom of stringing enemies up by their Achilles tendons until they were prepared to make enough concessions to their torturers.

Hrafnkell had given up his estates and his priestly authority as a result of the experience. His temple was destroyed and the hapless Freyfaxi was weighted with stones, thrown over a cliff and drowned in the water below. Hrafnkell, by now convinced that his favourite god didn't give two hoots about his predicament, renounced his beliefs and relocated to a new farm beside Lagarfljót, which he called Hrafnkelsstaðir. He vowed to reform his naturally vengeful character and become a kind and simple farmer. So great was his success with the new farm, however, that he gained even more wealth and power than he'd had at Aðalból and it appeared as though history was fated to repeat itself.

One day, Sámur's brother Eyvindur came by en route to Aðalból. As he passed Hrafnkelsstaðir, Hrafnkell's maid saw him and reminded her employer of his responsibility to take his revenge. Something snapped in Hrafnkell. Abandoning his vow to reform, he set out in pursuit of the troublesome brothers and made quick work of dispatching Eyvindur before tackling Sámur and forcing him to flee the ill-gotten Aðalból. Hrafnkell thereby regained his former estates and, as far as anyone knows, lived there happily ever after. ∎

in Hrafnkell's footsteps and walk the 73 km from the Ring Road to Snæfell! Prepare for wintry conditions at any time of year.

The Eastfjords

Although not as large nor as rugged as their counterparts in north-west Iceland, the Eastfjords nonetheless provide lots of scenic value. Villages are small and quiet and everywhere you'll find lots of opportunities to hike and explore.

Most trekking here entails route-finding, and topo sheets and navigational skills are important for off-track forays. With careful planning, you can follow old riding and walking routes through the mountains from Borgarfjörður Eystri in the north to Breiðdalsvík in the south, passing through Seyðisfjörður and Reyðarfjörður en route. However, it does require a measure of scree-sliding, snow-walking, boulder-hopping and bog-slogging. Parts of this route are currently being marked and in the next few years, it should become much easier to follow.

BORGARFJÖRÐUR EYSTRI

The village of Borgarfjörður Eystri, also known as Bakkagerði, probably receives less attention than it should. Beneath a stunning backdrop of rugged rhyolite peaks on one side and the spectacular Dyrfjöll mountains on the other, it enjoys the best setting in eastern Iceland.

Iceland's best-known artist, Jóhannes S

Kjarval, who lived at the nearby farm Geitavík, took much of his inspiration from the place and most of its few visitors are also delighted by it.

Information
The tourist information office (☎ 472 9977; fax 472 9877) is at the Álfasteinn rock shop.

Church
The pride of the village seems to be the beautiful altarpiece in its church – a Kjarval painting depicting the Sermon on the Mount with Dyrfjöll in the background and a typically Icelandic sky above. If you wish to see more of Kjarval's work, there's a free exhibition in the Fjarðarborg community centre.

Sod Home
In the village is the historic and well maintained sod-covered home, Lindarbakki, but it's inhabited and not open to visitors.

Álfasteinn
The rock shop Álfasteinn ('elf stone') is strictly for tourists and it does a booming business collecting semiprecious stones, polishing them up, gluing them into kitsch shapes and selling them at premium prices. They do have some high quality items, but many of the best have been imported from Brazil. From 1 June to 8 September, it's open daily from 10 am to 6 pm.

Álfaborg
The name of this small mound and nature reserve near the campground means 'elf rock' and is the 'borg' that gave Borgarfjörður Eystri its name. From the view disc on top, there's a fabulous vista of the surrounding fields which in summer turn white with blooming Arctic cotton.

Horse Riding
Short horse-riding excursions and longer trips over the Loðmundarfjarðarleið can be arranged with Guðmundur Sveinsson at the farm Bakki (☎ 472 9987), south-west of the village.

Rockhounding
Borgarfjörður Eystri is popular with rockhounds, who come to search for jasper, zeolite, obsidian, basalt and agate. Some of the best hunting grounds are near the beach east of town, but note that collecting stones in Iceland is technically prohibited (apparently, the rule doesn't apply to those who collect and sell the rocks to tourists). While you're poking around, note the sandy spit across the estuary, which is a nesting and roosting site for thousands of gulls; the slightest disturbance results in a panicked explosion of flapping wings and feathers!

Places to Stay & Eat
In summer, sleeping-bag accommodation is found at *Fjarðarborg* (☎ 472 9920), in the centre, for Ikr700. At the farm *Stapi* (☎ 472 9983), on the coast 500m south of town, there's a cosy mountain-hut style guesthouse where single/double made-up rooms cost Ikr3000/4050 and sleeping-bag accommodation is Ikr1300. Stapi also offers cooking facilities and camping.

The *campground* beside the church has sinks and flush toilets. Meals are available at *Fjarðarborg* in the community centre.

Getting There & Away
Flugfélag Austurlands has five weekly flights to and from Egilsstaðir. Otherwise, the only public transport is the seven-hour BSÍ tour from Egilsstaðir on Monday and Tuesday, which runs from 1 June to 31 August. In fact, it's not so much a tour as an escorted visit to the Álfasteinn rock shop. It costs Ikr3120. Hitching from Egilsstaðir rates from poor to medium.

AROUND BORGARFJÖRÐUR EYSTRI
There are lots of mountain walks within easy reach. For a short scramble amid rhyolite peaks, walk around the estuary to Geitfell and Svartfell. However, in non-vegetated areas, note that the unconsolidated material makes for an experience akin to walking on thousands of tiny ball-bearings.

Staðarfjall

The colourful 621m rhyolite peak, Staðarfjall, rises eight km south-east of Borgarfjörður Eystri and makes a nice day walk. The best access is up the ridge from Desjamýri farm, across the estuary from Borgarfjörður Eystri. Legend has it that a troll is buried in the gravel near the mountain's base.

Dyrfjöll

One of Iceland's most dramatic ranges, the Dyrfjöll mountains rise precipitously to an altitude of 1136m between the Lagarfljót valley and Borgarfjörður Eystri. The name means 'door mountain' due to the large and conspicuous notch in the highest peak – an Icelandic counterpart to Sweden's famous Lapporten. The range is composed of heavily glaciated basalt, tuff and rhyolite. There are no actual walking tracks, but day hikes and longer routes may be taken from Borgarfjörður Eystri.

Njarðvíkurskriður

Njarðvíkurskriður, a dangerous scree-slope along Route 94 near Njarðvík, was a habitual site of accidents in ancient times. All the tragedies were blamed on a nuisance ghost, Naddi, who dwelt in a sea-level cave beneath the slope.

In the early 1300s, Naddi was exorcised by the proper religious authorities and in 1306, a cross was erected on the site bearing the inscription *Effigiem Christi qui transis pronus honora – Anno MCCCVI –* 'You who are hurrying past, honour the image of Christ – 1306 AD'. The idea was that travellers would repeat a prayer when passing the danger zone and therefore be protected from malevolent powers. The cross has been replaced several times since, but the current one still bears the original prayer.

LOÐMUNDARFJARÐARLEIÐ

The relatively little-known mountain route between Borgarfjörður Eystri and Loðmundarfjörður is sure to increase in popularity in coming years. It follows a 4WD track up over the pass and opens up lots of opportunities to explore in the pristine surroundings. The required topo sheet is *Dyrfjöll* 1:100,000 (1986).

The route begins at the farm Hvannstöð, nine km south of Borgarfjörður Eystri, and continues for 30 km over Húsavíkurheiði. You can either descend along the side track to the small bay of Húsavík or continue down to the deserted fjord, Loðmundarfjörður. From there, the route follows the historic 30 km bridle path up Hjálmárdalur and across Hjalmardalsheiði to Seyðisfjörður.

Note that visitor facilities are available only at the farm Stakkahlíð.

Hvítserkur

One of Iceland's most unusual mountains, Hvítserkur rises to an altitude of 775m above Húsavíkurheiði. Hvítserkur is composed of rose-coloured rhyolite shot through with complicated basalt dykes.

Húsavík

This small bay and deserted farm site is a six km return side trip from the main route. It isn't particularly interesting, but in fine weather, it's a pleasant trip down to the shore.

Nesháls

At the Nesháls pass, between Víkurá and Loðmundarfjörður, the track reaches an altitude of 435m. Just west is the 830m peak Skælingur, sometimes called the 'Chinese temple', which would be more accurately described as the 'Tibetan lamasery'.

Loðmundarfjörður

This short but beautiful fjord was once well-settled, and at least 10 farms occupied the upper basin. However, after the coastal supply boats stopped running, construction of all-season roads into such sparsely populated domains seemed uneconomical and the region was abandoned.

The entire valley is now deserted except for the friendly farm *Stakkahlíð* (☎ 472 1510; fax 472 1578), at the head of Loðmundarfjörður, where sleeping-bag accommodation costs Ikr1365, including showers and cooking facilities. There's also a *campground*. Stakkahlíð lies near the foot of Hraunið, an enormous rhyolite scree, which eroded from the hill Flatafjall.

The symmetrical 925m peak, Karlfell, stands prominently above Loðmundarfjörður and dominates the view from the head of the fjord. Reindeer roam the area and petrified wood deposits indicate that this was once forested country. On the inlet Álftavík is a small natural harbour, Lotna, which was formed by volcanic dykes.

Organised Tours

A jeep tour along the Loðmundarfjarðarleið leaves from Egilsstaðir daily at 10 am, from mid-July (or whenever the road opens) to 31 August. It also stops in Borgarfjörður Eystri. The return trip costs Ikr5000, but if you wish to arrange onward boat transport to Seyðisfjörður (see under Seyðisfjörður), the jeep portion costs only Ikr3000. This trip is also available with four Highland Pass vouchers. Book through the campground in Egilsstaðir. A minimum of five passengers is required.

SEYÐISFJÖRÐUR

Seyðisfjörður (population 890), the terminal for the ferry from the European mainland, is many travellers' first view of Iceland. This architecturally interesting town, surrounded on three sides by mountains and on the other by a deep, 16 km long fjord, makes a suitably pleasant introduction.

History

Seyðisfjörður started in 1834 as a trading centre and herring fishery and, thanks to its sheltering fjord, grew over the following decades into eastern Iceland's largest settlement. During this period of prosperity, most of its beautiful and unique wooden buildings were constructed by Norwegian settlers, who came for fishing opportunities. Seyðisfjörður attained municipal status in 1895.

During WWII, Seyðisfjörður was used as a base for British and American forces, but the only attack was upon the oil tanker *Grillo*, which was bombed by three German warplanes. The bombs missed their target, but one exploded so near that the ship sank to the bottom, where it remains to this day.

Information

Tourist Office The Austfar tourist informa-

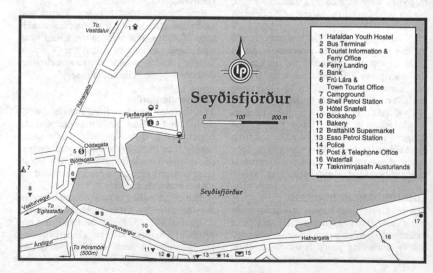

1	Hafaldan Youth Hostel
2	Bus Terminal
3	Tourist Information & Ferry Office
4	Ferry Landing
5	Bank
6	Frú Lára & Town Tourist Office
7	Campground
8	Shell Petrol Station
9	Hótel Snæfell
10	Bookshop
11	Bakery
12	Brattahlíð Supermarket
13	Esso Petrol Station
14	Police
15	Post & Telephone Office
16	Waterfall
17	Tækniminjasafn Austurlands

ICELAND

tion centre (☎ 472 1111) is in the Smyril Line building at the ferry dock. For the benefit of arriving ferry passengers, it stocks brochures on activities, attractions and accommodation around Iceland. The desk also sells bus passes and books onward accommodation. It's open weekdays until 5 pm. The new town tourist information office is in the Frú Lára (☎ 472 1551).

Money Perhaps because travellers expect to feel a budgetary pinch in Iceland, Seyðisfjörður greets them with some of the country's highest prices. You may want to hold off on non-essential purchases until Egilsstaðir or beyond.

On Thursday, when the ferry arrives, the bank opens early, but not early enough for arriving passengers to change money and catch the first bus to Egilsstaðir. It can also become a crowd scene, so try to pick up enough Icelandic currency in Europe or the Faroes to get you through to Egilsstaðir (note that 'enough' is probably twice what you expect to need!)

Post & Communications The post and telephone office is on the eastern shore of the fjord, opposite the ferry dock towards the small boat harbour.

Fishing Permits Fishing permits for the Fjarðará are available at the Shell petrol station. They cost Ikr1200/1800 for a half/full day. Sea fishing is free to anyone.

Tækniminjasafn Austurlands

The Tækniminjasafn Austurlands (☎ 472 1596), Hafnargata 44, is a town historical museum honouring Seyðisfjörður's centenary in 1995. It's housed in the 1894 home of ship owner Otto Wathne. From 28 May to 1 September, it's open Tuesday to Sunday from 2 to 5 pm. Admission costs Ikr200.

Seyðisfjörður-Vestdalur Hike

A wonderful introduction to hiking in Iceland will take you up Vestdalur through the new nature reserve and around Mt Bjólfur to the Seyðisfjörður-Egilsstaðir road. It makes an ideal day hike, but early in the season, it may be impassable due to snow.

Start by walking up the road past the HI hostel and the fish plant, to where a rough jeep track takes off up the glacial valley to your left. The track peters out after a few hundred metres, but keep walking uphill, along the left side of the Vestdalsá river. After a couple of hours and several tiers of glorious waterfalls, you'll arrive at a small lake, Vestdalsvatn, which remains frozen most of the year. Here, you'll see Mt Bjólfur to your left. Tradition has it that it was once capped by a pagan temple. Avalanches from this mountain caused fatalities in Seyðisfjörður in 1895 and 1950.

From the lake, bear left and make your way westward over the tundra, through the snowfields and past a small ski hut to the highway. From there, you can hitch to either Seyðisfjörður or Egilsstaðir. The trip can also be done in the opposite direction – and more easily because it's mostly downhill.

Fjarðarsel

Upriver from the centre, 15 minutes on foot, is the Fjarðarsel hydroelectric power station. This remnant of modern technology 1913-style is one of the oldest in the world still in use.

Loðmundarfjörður Hike

The six to eight-hour walk north to Loðmundarfjörður begins from Sunnuholt, on the northern shore of Seyðisfjörður beside a heap of decrepit cars and scrap metal. First, climb up the mountain Grýta, following a route marked by wooden stakes, and into the valley Kólstaðadalur, where you'll have a view over Seyðisfjörður and beyond.

After climbing to the head of the valley and up to the ridge Hallið, you're ushered onto the Hjalmardalsheiði heath, which should be crossed keeping the Gunnhildur ridge to your left. The route down the valley to Loðmundarfjörður is clear and well-marked. The farm Stakkahlíð is at the head of the fjord (see Loðmundarfjarðarleið earlier in this chapter). A bridge is currently being built over the river Fjarðará.

Organised Tours

In July and August, two-hour fishing and sightseeing trips around the fjord are conducted on Thursday afternoons at 2 pm. The cost is Ikr1800, including refreshments.

Three-hour tours to Loðmundarfjörður run on Friday and Sunday from June to August at 1 pm and cost Ikr3000; on other days, there's a minimum total charter fee of Ikr20,000. You can arrange to be dropped at Loðmundarfjörður and either walk back to Seyðisfjörður or arrange to be picked up by jeep to return to Egilsstaðir (minimum five people). These trips depart from the Þórshamarsbrygjan pier near the cooperative supermarket.

Six-hour charter fishing trips to the sea cliffs at Skálanes cost Ikr30,000 for groups of up to 10 anglers.

Book any of these trips through the Hótel Snæfell.

Places to Stay

Many ferry travellers wind up at the clean and cosy *Hafaldan Youth Hostel* (☎ 472 1410; fax 472 1486), which is a great place to stay before or after a long boat ride. What's more, they have the entire Twin Peaks series on video. Due to the ferry schedules, advance bookings are advised for Wednesday and Thursday. Beds cost Ikr1000/1250 for HI members/non-members.

If the hostel is full, there's farmhouse accommodation at *Þórsmörk* (☎ 472 1324), on Route 93 just out of town. Single/double made-up rooms cost Ikr3000/4050 and sleeping-bag accommodation costs Ikr1300.

The pleasant and well-located *Hótel Snæfell* (☎ 472 1460; fax 472 1570) costs Ikr5135/7150 for singles/doubles with showers and Ikr1000 for sleeping-bag accommodation. This isn't bad considering the charge is nearly half the room rate for a meal in the dining room!

The *campground* is beside the Shell petrol station. Note that camping is no longer permitted in Vestdalur or anywhere along the road, but there is an alternative campground at Vestdalseyri, near the mouth of the Vestdalsá. It's away from the worst of the fishy odour that pervades Seyðisfjörður.

Places to Eat

The only fully fledged restaurant is the *Hótel Snæfell* dining room, where the food is nothing special and seems inordinately expensive.

The cooperative gift shop *Frú Lára* (☎ 472 1551) serves coffee, tea, cakes and snacks, and on Sunday, it puts on a coffee and cake buffet. You'll also find snack bars at the *Shell* (☎ 472 1386) and *Esso* (☎ 472 1240) petrol stations. In hopes of attracting overnight stays in Seyðisfjörður, on Wednesday all of the above establishments offer free coffee to departing ferry passengers.

Seyðisfjörður has two supermarkets, *KHB* and *Brattahlíð*, both of which close for lunch from 12.30 to 1.30 pm. However, the kiosk is open for lunch, and coffee and snacks are available at the Smyril Line office, near the ferry dock.

Entertainment

The hotel bar hosts live music shows every Wednesday evening.

Things to Buy

Obligingly for ferry passengers, local residents hold an art & craft market on Wednesday afternoon and Thursday morning.

Getting There & Away

Bus There's at least one bus to and from Egilsstaðir (Ikr800) every day, but the schedule isn't as convenient as one might expect. From 1 June to 31 August, buses in either direction run twice daily on Monday and Tuesday, three times on Thursday, four times on Wednesday and once on other days. Fortunately, hitching to Egilsstaðir around the ferry schedule is quite easy.

Ferry In summer, the Smyril Line ferry *Norröna* arrives from Esbjerg (Denmark), Tórshavn (the Faroe Islands) and Bergen (Norway) on Thursday at 7 am and departs for Tórshavn and Esbjerg at 11 am. For more information concerning travel to or from the Faroes, Britain and Denmark, see the Getting There & Away chapter.

MJÓIFJÖRÐUR

The next fjord south of Seyðisfjörður, Mjóifjörður, ('narrow fjord'), lies well off the worn tourist circuits. In fact, the district, with a population of just 35, is well off anyone's circuit!

Things to See & Do

Mjóifjörður is flanked on both sides by spectacular **cliffs**. The several abandoned **turf farmsteads**, the early 20th century **Norwegian whaling station** at Asknes and the 19th century **wooden church** at Brekkuþorp are worth visiting, but the best known attraction is the ruin of the **Dalatangi light**, Iceland's first lighthouse. The new lighthouse and the nearby vegetable and flower gardens are also of interest.

Thanks to the dearth of sheep in Mjóifjörður, parts of the district are covered with blueberries, which are ripe for the picking in late August.

Places to Stay & Eat

Sólbrekka (☎ 476 0007), at Brekkuþorp, is open from 1 July to 25 August. The charge for single/double rooms is Ikr3000/4050 and sleeping-bag accommodation is Ikr1300. There's also a campsite out the back, but you can camp almost anywhere along the fjord. Coffee and refreshments are available and basic supplies may be purchased in the *shop* at Brekkuþorp.

Getting There & Away

Bus At the moment, there's no bus transport to Mjóifjörður or Dalatangi, not even a tour bus, and it lies 47 km from the nearest scheduled bus route.

Hitching Hitching into Mjóifjörður is as near to hopeless as you're likely to get.

Hiking In two days, you can walk from Neskaupstaður. Follow the fjord to Kirkjuból, eight km west of Neskaupstaður, then cross 1100m Goðaborg and descend through the Reykjaá valley to the southern shore of Mjóifjörður.

Ferry Your best option to Mjóifjörður is the ferry *Anný* (☎ 477 1321), which sails daily from Neskaupstaður to Brekkuþorp at 2 pm, and also at 8 pm on Wednesday and Thursday.

REYÐARFJÖRÐUR

Reyðarfjörður, formerly called Búðareyri, sits at the head of the largest fjord on the east coast. It's a relatively new settlement, having become a trading place early this century. During WWII, it was one of several Allied bases in Iceland.

Things to See & Do

Above the fjord, two km east of town, is a **view disc** accompanied by a commanding vista. The very energetic can make the 985m climb up **Hólmatindur** which rises behind the town. It's an easier proposition from this side than from Eskifjörður. The most unusual attraction is the 27°C **warm spring** at the head of the fjord, which has been converted into a hot pot for bathing by diverting the water into a decrepit vehicle.

The town also has a small **WWII museum** (☎ 474 1245), which holds relics from the war era. It's open 1 June to 31 August from 1 to 5 pm. Admission is Ikr200.

Places to Stay & Eat
The *Hótel Búðareyri* (☎ 474 1378; fax 474 1187), on Búðargata, has ordinary single/double rooms with shared facilities for Ikr33575/5000. There's also a *Youth Hostel* (☎ 474 1447; fax 474 1454), at Búðargata 4 in the centre. It charges the standard Ikr1000/1250 for HI members/non-members.

Campers can resort to the *campground* at the west end of town. It costs Ikr350 per person; the adjoining pond is popular with salmon anglers.

For meals, you can choose between the *Hótel Búðareyri* dining room or the *Shell* or *Olís* petrol stations.

Getting There & Away
In summer, buses run Monday to Saturday at 8.15 am from Neskaupstaður (Ikr600) and at 9.50 am from Egilsstaðir (Ikr650). There are also afternoon or evening buses on weekdays, and a morning bus on weekends. On Monday, Wednesday and Friday, buses between Egilsstaðir and Höfn also stop in Reyðarfjörður.

ESKIFJÖRÐUR
Stretched along a short side-fjord of Reyðarfjörður, the friendly village of Eskifjörður (population 1060) looks over the water to the majestic 985m peak of Hólmatindur. If you're the sort who likes to discover and experience things for yourself, it may well be the nicest of all the Eastfjords towns.

Eskifjörður was a recognised trading centre as early as the late 1700s and its herring fishery reached its height in the late 19th century, but the village didn't receive municipal status until 1974.

Information
For tourist information, phone the town offices (☎ 476 1170). Eskifjörður is one of the least expensive places to fish for salmon in Iceland. A one-day licence costs Ikr400, plus an additional Ikr350 per kg of fish taken.

Freezing Plant
Be sure to have a look inside the freezing plant (Australians may assume it's the source of the town's name!), whose walls are graced with murals by the Spanish-Icelandic artist, Baltasar.

Sjóminjasafn Austurlands
The Maritime Museum (☎ 476 1179) is housed in a warehouse dating from the early 1800s. There you'll see two centuries of the east coast's historic herring and shark fisheries and whaling industry. It's open daily, 15 June to 31 August, from 2 to 5 pm. Admission costs Ikr200.

Helgustaðir
At Helgustaðir, nine km south-east of Eskifjörður, are the remains of the world's largest Iceland spar (silfurberg) mine. It began operating in the 1600s but is now abandoned. The largest specimen taken from Helgustaðir weighed 230 kg and is now on display in the British Museum. Geology buffs may want to have a look, but note that the mines are a national preserve, so absconding with anything of interest is officially not allowed.

Hólmatindur & Hólmanes
The peak of Hólmatindur is beautiful, residents agree, but it's also a nuisance, as it cuts out all sunlight to the village from September to April. The four rivers tumbling down its slopes also pose avalanche threats. The southern shore of the Hólmanes peninsula, below Hólmatindur, has recently been designated a nature reserve. Hiking in the area offers superb maritime views, as well as the chance to observe the protected vegetation and bird life.

Hiking

In addition to Hólmanes, you'll find longer hiking routes: Oddsskarð, Helgustaðarsveit, Hellisfjörður, Vindháls and the mountain areas around the end of the peninsula, where you may even see reindeer. Transport is difficult, but access is easier from Eskifjörður than Neskaupstaður. For guided hiking tours, contact Sigurgeir Jóhannsson (☎ 476 1524).

Places to Stay & Eat

The simple *Hótel Askja* (☎ 476 1261; fax 476 1561) charges Ikr2795/4615 for single/double rooms with shared facilities. The dining room serves meals and light snacks. The free *campground* is near the river at the western end of town, but good wild camping is possible just up the valley, or you can camp at the abandoned farm Byggdarholt, one km outside the town. Oddsskarð, the pass leading over to Neskaupstaður, has a ski slope and a basic ski hut, *Skíðaskáli* (☎ 476 1465), which is used as a mountain hut in summer.

The *Shell* and *Esso* petrol stations, along the main drag, have grills and snack bars. For coffee and snacks, the *Sel* coffee house, at Strandgata 34, is open daily from 2 to 6 pm.

Getting There & Away

Access from Egilsstaðir (Ikr900) or Neskaupstaður (Ikr400) is via the buses described under Reyðarfjörður.

NESKAUPSTAÐUR

Sometimes called Norðfjörður, Neskaupstaður (population 1640) is the largest settlement in the Eastfjords. As with most coastal towns, it began as a trading centre. The first merchants arrived in 1882, and by 1900 the town had attracted 100 permanent residents. It prospered during the herring boom around the turn of the century, but then lapsed into obscurity.

The highway approach to Neskaupstaður crosses 632m Oddsskarð, the highest highway pass in Iceland, via a narrow 626m tunnel. Its lovely position does have drawbacks; backed by steep slopes, it's prone to avalanches, and in 1974 a large one tumbled down and killed 12 residents.

Natural History Museum

In the village centre is a free natural history museum, Náttúrugripasafnið í Neskaupstað (☎ 477 1606), with lots of stones, some pinned insects and stuffed birds and fish. It's open daily, 15 June to 31 August, from 1 to 5 pm.

Hiking

A rewarding hike will take you up 1100m Goðaborg from the farm Kirkjuból, eight km west of town. From the summit, you can also descend into Mjóifjörður, the next fjord to the north; allow two days and due to late snows at higher altitudes, only attempt it at the height of summer.

Another walk is from Oddsskarð along the ridges eastward to the deserted fjords, Hellisfjörður and Viðfjörður. For route-finding, use the *Gerpir* 1:100,000 (1986) topo sheet. The dramatic Gerpir cliffs, Iceland's easternmost point, may only be reached with difficulty. The easiest way to visit this beautiful place is on the Saturday hiking tours organised by Fjarðaferðir, at Hótel Egilsbúð. You travel by boat to Barðsnes, then visit the Rauðubjörg cliffs and climb up to the Skollaskarð pass for a view of Gerpir. The trip takes 5½ hours and costs Ikr1800. Fjarðaferðir also runs other hiking tours. If you read Icelandic, pick up the handy Rotary Club pamphlet describing hikes around Neskaupstaður.

Organised Tours

The Fjarðaferðir (☎ 477 1321) boat charter operates two-hour cruises around Norðfjörður for a look at sea level caves, raucous bird colonies and impressive seacliffs (including Iceland's highest, Norðurfjarðarnípa). They depart daily at 2 pm and Wednesday to Friday at 8 pm from the pier opposite the hotel and cost Ikr1850 per person. Book through the Hótel Egilsbúð. For less formal cruising, jet-skis may be hired at Hafnarbraut 25.

Places to Stay & Eat

The *Hótel Egilsbúð* (☎ 477 1321; fax 477 1322), near the harbour, charges Ikr3600/4500 for single/double rooms without bath and Ikr6110/8900 with showers. All rates include breakfast. The free *campground* lies at the eastern edge of town, two km from the harbour.

The hotel restaurant, *Stúka Egils Rauða* (☎ 477 1321) serves up pizza, pitta sandwiches, burgers and full steak and seafood meals, and on weekends, you get a dose of karaoke. For a real treat, try the recommended *Pizza 67* (☎ 477 1867), on Egilsbraut. If a snack will suffice, there's the *Café Króki* (☎ 477 1169) or the *Olís* petrol station (☎ 477 1476), both on Hafnarbraut.

Getting There & Away

Air Íslandsflug (☎ 477 1800) flies daily, except Saturday, between Reykjavík and Neskaupstaður.

Bus On weekdays from 27 May to 1 September, there are morning and evening buses from Egilsstaðir to Neskaupstaður (Ikr1200), via Reyðarfjörður and Eskifjörður. In the opposite direction, they run in the morning and afternoon. There is also one Saturday departure in either direction.

FÁSKRÚÐSFJÖRÐUR

The village of Fáskrúðsfjörður was originally settled by French fisherfolk during the late 1800s. It is sometimes known as Búðir, meaning 'booths'. The French left in 1914 and the current population of 720 continues to decline.

Things to See & Do

From Dalir, above the head of the fjord, you can hike the old route up over Stuðlaheiði to Reyðarfjörður. Near the mouth of the fjord are two islets. **Andey** ('duck island') has a large colony of eider ducks, and the green island **Skrúður** is home to a colony of gannets and a large cave which is believed to shelter a giant. Skrúður is reached by boat from the farm Vattarnes (☎ 475 1397).

Above the southern shore of Fáskrúðs-fjörður is the laccolithic mountain **Sandfell**, part of the volcanic system that dominated the Eastfjords during the Tertiary geological period. It's one of the world's best visible examples of this sort of igneous intrusion.

Places to Stay & Eat

The pleasant looking *Hótel Bjarg* (☎ 475 1466; fax 475 1476) charges Ikr3510/4875 for singles/doubles without bath and Ikr4485/5915 with bath. The alternative is the *campground*, west of the village. Fáskrúðsfjörður's only eatery is the *Hótel Bjarg* dining room.

Getting There & Away

On weekdays from 1 May to 31 October, buses run between Fáskrúðsfjörður and Egilsstaðir (Ikr1200), leaving the former at 8.20 am and the latter at 10 am. The same buses also service Stöðvarfjörður and Breiðdalsvík. On Monday, Wednesday and Friday, buses between Egilsstaðir and Höfn stop in Fáskrúðsfjörður, Stöðvarfjörður and Breiðdalsvík.

STÖÐVARFJÖRÐUR

This small village of 350 inhabitants, on the fjord of the same name, is sometimes called Kirkjuból (not to be confused with the farm Kirkjuból near Neskaupstaður). It derives most of its income from fishing.

Steinasafn Petru

The best thing in Stöðvarfjörður is Steinasafn Petru (☎ 475 8834), at Fjarðarbraut 21. This diverse exhibit of stones and minerals has been assembled as a labour of love by resident Petra Sveinsdóttir. The stones are collected not because they're especially rare or valuable, but for their beauty or interest. The most interesting pieces are inside, but it's also worth looking around the garden, which is a mish-mash of interesting beach junk – buoys, bits of machinery from ships, spare washing machine parts, garden gnomes etc. If you want to support Petra's laudable enthusiasm, some of the rocks are for sale. Phone in advance to arrange a visit. Admission is Ikr150.

ICELAND

Places to Stay & Eat

The simple *Gistiheimilið Hanna* (☎ 475 8960; fax 475 8961) charges Ikr2500/3000 for single/double rooms. Alternatively, there's the *campground*, east of the village. Meals and snacks are available from the *Bóðinn* restaurant on Fjarðarbraut.

Getting There & Away

See under Fáskrúðsfjörður earlier in this chapter.

BREIÐDALSVÍK

The young village of Breiðdalsvík (population 260) is beautifully situated, but its main claim to fame is that it was attacked by a German bomber in 1942. Coincidentally, the nearby farm Snæhvammur also suffered war damage when a mine exploded on the beach in 1940. A challenging walking route leads from Snæhvammur across the scree slopes to Stöðvarfjörður fjord.

Places to Stay & Eat

Accommodation and meals are available at the welcoming *Hótel Bláfell* (☎ 475 6770; fax 475 6668). Single/double rooms cost Ikr3640/4750 without bath and Ikr5200/7020 with showers. The hotel also maintains self-catering cottages in Norðurdalsur, 15 km from town, and its highly acclaimed restaurant is worth checking out. The *campground* is behind the hotel.

Rooms, meals and laundry services are found at the farm *Fell* (☎ 475 6679), six km up the fjord from the village. The charge is Ikr3000/4050 for single/double rooms and Ikr1300 for sleeping-bag accommodation.

Getting There & Away

For bus information, see under Fáskrúðsfjörður earlier in this chapter. The fare to Egilsstaðir is Ikr1400 and to Höfn, Ikr2000.

AROUND BREIÐDALSVÍK
Breiðdalur

As the Ring Road returns to the coast from its inland jaunt through the north-eastern deserts, it passes through the lovely Breiðdalur valley, nestled beneath colourful

rhyolite peaks. Near the head of the valley you may see reindeer, and at Þorgrímsstaðir, further downstream, there's a 250m waterfall harnessed for electricity. At the abandoned farm Jörvík, a forestry reserve harbours native birch and aspen.

The beautifully situated private guesthouse *Innri-Kleif* (☎ 475 6789) charges Ikr1170 for hostel-style sleeping-bag accommodation.

Berunes & Berufjörður

South of Breiðdalur along the Ring Road is Berufjörður, a longish steep-sided fjord flanked by rhyolite peaks. The southwestern shore is dominated by the mountain Búlandstindur, which rises 1069m above the water.

Around Berufjörður are several historical walking routes through the steeply rugged terrain. The best known of these climbs from Berufjörður, the farm at the head of the fjord, and crosses the 700m Berufjarðarskarð into Breiðdalur. Either accommodation option can recommend other hiking routes.

Places to Stay The *Berunes Youth Hostel* (☎ & fax 478 8988), with 20 bunks and a campground, makes a good staging point for trips in this area. The building dates from 1907 and the neighbouring church was used in the 1800s. Beds cost Ikr1000/1250 for HI members/non-members, including use of cooking facilities, but there's no local shop. Breakfast costs an additional Ikr550. It's open from 15 May to 15 September.

The farm *Eyjólfsstaðir* (☎ 478 8137), on the south-western shore of Berufjörður, offers camping for Ikr400 per person or sleeping-bag accommodation starting at Ikr1300. The nearby river Fossá is riddled with cascading waterfalls.

Getting There & Away All buses between Egilsstaðir and Höfn pass Berunes.

DJÚPIVOGUR

Djúpivogur (population 590), a quiet fishing village at the mouth of Berufjörður, is the oldest trading centre in the Eastfjords. It has served as a commercial port since the 16th century and thrived through the inception and heyday of the Danish Trade Monopoly.

Historic Buildings
Some of the town's lovely wooden buildings date from the late 19th century; the trading house and the Hótel Framtíð are among the finest examples, but the church, and the historical homes called Sólhóll, Dalir and Hraun are all worth a look.

Hiking
The Djúpivogur peninsula is compact and ideal for short hikes from town. A particularly nice walk is to **Álfkirkja** ('elf church') on the rock formation Rakkaberg, north of town and just west of the official campground.

Organised Tours
For information on recommended tours to Papey Island, see Papey under Around Djúpivogur, later in this chapter.

Places to Stay & Eat
As Icelandic hotels go, the nine-room *Hótel Framtíð* (☎ 478 8887; fax 478 8187) is both pleasant and comfortable. Singles/doubles cost Ikr3650/4750 with shared facilities, but if the hotel isn't full, sleeping-bag accommodation is available for Ikr1450. Guests have access to the sauna, and may also arrange bike rental, sea fishing and cruises to Papey. The small dining room specialises in locally caught fish and other fresh seafood.

The official *campground* is at Hermannastekkur, near the junction of the Ring Road and Route 98, but it's exposed to fjord winds. You can also camp beside the Hótel Framtíð.

For farmhouse accommodation, see the farm *Hamar* (☎ 478 8958; fax 478 8968), 10 km west of town. It's quite nice, with a nine hole golf course, horse hire, hiking, and fishing in the river Hamarsá. It's open from 1 June to 15 September and charges Ikr1690 per person for beds and Ikr1100 for sleeping-bag accommodation.

Getting There & Away
Djúpivogur lies on the Ring Road, so all buses between Egilsstaðir and Höfn stop there. The fare to Höfn is Ikr1150 and to Egilsstaðir, Ikr2000.

AROUND DJÚPIVOGUR
Búlandstindur
This obtrusive pyramid-shaped peak rises 1068m above the south-western shore of Berufjörður. The westernmost ridge is known as Goðaborg or 'God's rock'. When Iceland officially converted to Christianity in either 999 or 1000, locals supposedly carried their pagan images to the top of this mountain and threw them over the cliff. The tourist literature says that it's an easy climb to the top, but that may be a bit optimistic; you be the judge.

Teigarhorn
On the farm Teigarhorn, four km from Djúpivogur, is the historic Weyvadts House. It was constructed in the early 1880s, and the trading office has been preserved just as it was left in 1883. The farm also has the finest deposits of zeolite in Iceland. Don't get any ideas about collecting, however, as the geology is officially protected. If you'd like to visit, enquire at the Hótel Framtíð in Djúpivogur.

Djáknadys
The odd heap of stones, Djáknadys, lies beside the Ring Road, 12 km west of Djúpivogur on the northern shore of Hamarsfjörður. It's believed to be the result of a battle between two early ecumenical authorities who fought and killed each other on this spot. It's said that travellers who toss three stones on the pile will avoid misfortune on their journey.

At the farm Bragðavellir, five km to the west at the head of Hamarsfjörður, two Roman coins were unearthed in 1952. This led to speculation that a lost Roman ship might have stopped by in the dim and distant past. It's far more likely, however, that the coins were merely plundered souvenirs from

Britain or other former Roman lands ravaged by the Vikings.

Papey

The name of the lovely offshore island of Papey ('friars' island') indicates it was once a hermitage for the Irish monks who inhabited Iceland before the arrival of the Norse. It's thought that they fled in the face of Nordic settlement. This small and tranquil island was once a farm, but is now inhabited only by seals and nesting sea birds. In the early summer, the dramatic 45m cliffs are crowded with nests. Other highlights include the monks' ruins from the pre-Norse era; the Hellisbjarg lighthouse, which dates from 1922; Iceland's oldest and smallest wooden church (it holds three people), built in 1805;

and the remains of an apartment house from the early 1900s.

Places to Stay There's no formal accommodation, but there is a toilet hut and water, and camping is allowed by prior arrangement.

Organised Tours From 1 June to 15 September, five-hour tours to Papey leave from Djúpivogur daily at 1 pm and cost Ikr2750. They visit the natural sites, as well as the historic buildings. No one who's done this tour has regretted it, and in fine weather, it's truly magical. Bring good footwear, as a visit involves a climb up a rope ladder and quite a lot of hiking. For bookings, contact Papeyjarferðir (☎ & fax 478 8183), or book through the Hótel Framtið, both in Djúpivogur.

South-East Iceland

The topography of Iceland's south-eastern quarter is dominated by the vast Vatnajökull icecap, which is the world's third largest after those of Antarctica and Greenland. Most of the region's population lives in Höfn, Kirkjubæjarklaustur, or on farms strung out along Vatnajökull's southern flank.

Here, nature reigns supreme, as is evident in the 30 km long Lakagígar (Laki) fissure, Iceland's most destructive volcano, which caused famine and destruction across the country in the late 18th century. Similarly, beneath the Vatnajökull system lie Grímsvötn and Öræfi, volcanoes which cause more damage locked beneath the ice than they would if allowed to spout. Eruptions cause glacial melting and pressure from the heat and steam actually lifts the icecap, releasing devastating floods (the most recent of which occurred in late 1996) that spread out across surrounding lowlands. The residue from these jökulhlaups, combined with the scouring action of ice against rock, has formed the great deserts of glacial detritus known as the *sandur*. They are characterised by sandy plains, long empty beaches and shallow lagoons enclosed by sandspits and barrier islands.

Few travellers in South-East Iceland miss Skaftafell National Park, a pristine enclave between Vatnajökull's southernmost extremes. Although it's a popular holiday spot, you can easily escape the crowds by striking out on foot. Also an obvious attraction, the Vatnajökull icecap is popular with skiers and climbers as well as casual visitors, many of whom join guided tours from Höfn.

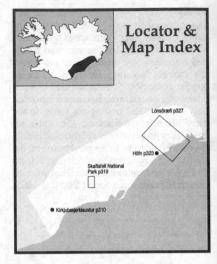

Locator & Map Index

Lónsöræfi p327

Höfn p323

Skaftafell National Park p319

Kirkjubæjarklaustur p310

smaller valley glaciers slide down from the central icecap in crevasse-ridden rivers of sculpturing ice. The best known of these is probably Skaftafellsjökull, a relatively small glacier that ends within 1½ km of the Skaftafell campground. Two much larger valley glaciers, Skeiðarárjökull (the normal outlet for Grímsvötn jökulhlaups) and Breiðamerkurjökull, flow down to the sandur plains in broad, spreading sheets and are plainly visible from the Ring Road.

KIRKJUBÆJARKLAUSTUR

Many a foreign tongue has been tied in knots trying to wrap itself around Kirkjubæjarklaustur (population 300), but it really isn't so difficult – at least there aren't any accented letters. Try breaking it into bits: *Kirkju* meaning 'church', *bæjar* meaning 'farm' and *klaustur*, meaning 'convent'. If it's still a problem, just do as the locals do and call it 'Klausturs' (pronounced more or less like 'Cloisters').

Southern Vatnajökull

Vatnajökull ('water glacier'), far and away Iceland's greatest icecap, rests on top of 8400 sq km of otherwise rugged territory and approaches one km thick in places. Scores of

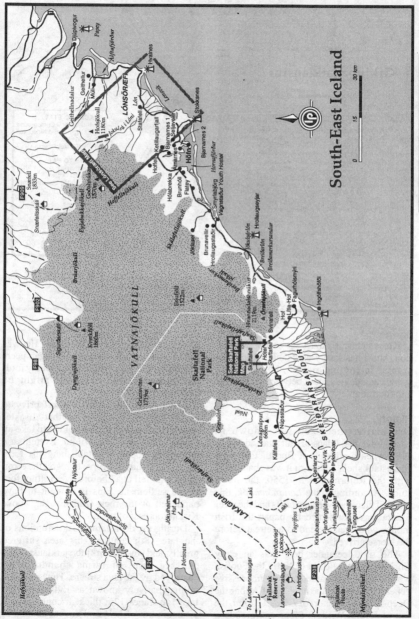

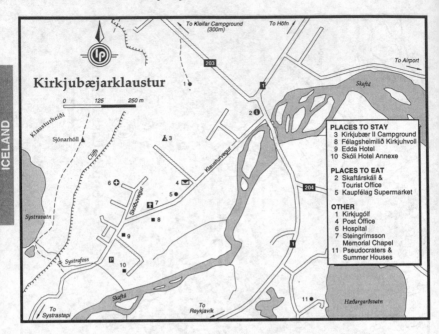

Kirkjubæjarklaustur

0   125   250 m

Klausturheiði

Sjónarhóll

Cliffs

Systravatn

Systrafoss

Systrastapi

Skaftá

To Kleifar Campground (300m)

To Höfn

To Airport

Skaftá

To Reykjavík

Klausturvegur

Skólavegur

To Systrastapi

Hæðargarðsvatn

PLACES TO STAY
3 Kirkjubær II Campground
8 Félagsheimilið Kirkjuhvoll
9 Edda Hotel
10 Skóli Hotel Annexe

PLACES TO EAT
2 Skaftárskáli &
   Tourist Office
5 Kaupfélag Supermarket

OTHER
1 Kirkjugólf
4 Post Office
6 Hospital
7 Steingrímsson
   Memorial Chapel
11 Pseudocraters &
   Summer Houses

Klausturs isn't a must-see sort of destination, but it has a very agreeable setting and several interesting sights, and it's worth spending a day en route between Reykjavík and Skaftafell.

History

Originally, the place was known as Kirkjubær; the 'klaustur' bit was added in 1186 when a convent of Benedictine nuns was established. Although it was abandoned with the Reformation in 1550, the name stuck. According to the *Landnámabók*, this tranquil place between the cliffs and the river Skaftá was first settled by papar, the Irish monks who used Iceland as a retreat before the Norse arrived.

The first Icelander here was an early Christian, Ketill Fíflski or Ketill the Foolish who, despite his name, had an impressive genealogy. He was the nephew of Auður the Deep-Minded (Unnur) of *Laxdæla Saga*, the son of Jórunn Wisdom-Slope and grandson

of the renowned Ketill Flatnose. He was called 'the Foolish' because his pagan peers saw his religious deviation as decidedly foolhardy, given that the gods might be displeased.

Ketill, who considered himself privy to divine favour, prophesised that disaster would befall any pagan so bold as to take up residence there. One Hildur Eysteinsson arrived in hopes of establishing his farm there but he didn't survive to regret the error. In fact, he fell dead before ever setting foot in the settlement. This is thought to have happened at the rock Hildishaugar, above Kirkjugólf east of town.

During the devastating Laki eruptions of the late 18th century, this area suffered greatly, and west of Kirkjubæjarklaustur you can see ruins of farms abandoned or destroyed by the lava stream. The lava field, unimaginatively known as Eldhraun ('fire lava') averages 12m thick. It contains over 12 cubic km of lava and covers an area of

565 sq km, making it the largest recorded lava flow from a single eruption.

Information

Tourist Office The tourist information office (☎ 487 4620), at the Skaftárskáli petrol station, is open daily, 1 June to 31 August, from 9 am to noon and 1 to 5 pm. Staff can help with information about anywhere in the south-eastern region.

Money The Landsbanki Íslands is open Monday to Friday from 9.15 am to 4 pm.

Steingrímsson Memorial Chapel

The modern and distinctly atypical wood and stone chapel was consecrated in 1974. It commemorates Jón Steingrímsson's Eldmessa (fire sermon), which saved the town from the lava on 20 July, 1783. (See the boxed aside Hellfire & Brimstone.)

Hellfire & Brimstone

The eruptions of the volcano Laki, in the late 18th century, brought death and devastation to much of south-eastern Iceland, especially to nearby Kirkjubæjarklaustur. On 20 July 1783, a particularly insidious flow of chunk-ridden lava bore down on the town, and residents feared for their lives and property. As the stream threatened to engulf the town, the pastor Jón Steingrímsson gathered his parishioners into the church and delivered a passionate hellfire and brimstone sermon while some appropriate special effects smoked and steamed just outside. By the time the oratory ended, the flow had stopped at a rock promontory (now called Eldmessutangi, 'fire sermon point') just short of the town, and the grateful residents credited their good reverend with some particularly effective string-pulling on their behalf. ■

Kirkjugólf

Although it's as natural as whole wheat and muesli, it's easy to see why early settlers assumed that this 80 sq metre honeycombed surface once served as the floor of a church. It is actually the smoothed surface of vertical

basalt columns. It lies in a field about 400m north of the Skaftárskáli petrol station.

Systrastapi

Things religious pervade this area and the prominent rock pillar Systrastapi ('sisters' pillar'), near the line of cliffs west of town, provides a good example. The story goes that two unruly nuns were executed and buried atop the rock. One was allegedly guilty of slandering the pope and the other was accused of all sorts of heinous crimes, including fraternising with the devil, sleeping with parishioners and desecrating the communion host. After the Reformation, it was said that flowers bloomed for the first time on Systrastapi.

Just west of here is the site of the original church, which was reportedly saved by Jón Steingrímsson's Eldmessa.

Systrafoss & Systravatn

The prominent waterfall that tumbles down the cliffs, through the ravine Bæjargil, is known as Systrafoss, which tumbles out of the lake Systravatn (Iceland gets a lot of mileage out of geographic nomenclature!). The latter was reputedly a bathing place for the nuns. Legend has it that during one bath, two nuns were dragged down to their doom after greedily reaching for a gold ring that appeared on a mysterious hand there. The lake is a short and pleasant walk up the cliffs from the village.

Landbrot

This vast pseudocrater field south of the Ring Road was formed during the Laki eruptions of 1783, by steam explosions in the lava-heated marshes. It's now a repository for Icelandic summer homes.

Foss á Síðu

On the farm Foss á Síðu, 12 km east of Klausturs, is a nice waterfall which normally tumbles down from the cliffs. During especially strong sea winds, however, it actually tumbles up! Take a look as you pass on the bus.

Opposite Foss á Síðu is the outcrop

Dverghamrar, which contains some classic basalt columns. Four km east of Foss is Brunahraun, the easternmost flow of the Skaftáreldar lava, which poured out of Lakagígar in 1783.

Organised Tours
For information on tours to the Lakagígar craters, see Lakagígar, later in this chapter.

Places to Stay
The *Kleifar campground*, a km north-west of the Skafárskáli petrol station, may be a good walk from the bus stop, but campers are rewarded with a serene lawn beside a beautiful waterfall. It costs Ikr200 per person and Ikr200 per tent. The more popular *Kirkjubær II campground* (☎ & fax 487 4612) charges the same rates, but is right in town. It also offers hot showers and both cooking and laundry facilities.

Klaustur's centre of activity is the *Edda Hotel* (☎ 487 4799; fax 487 4614) and the *Skóli* hotel annexe. Single/double rooms without bath are Ikr3650/4750, and with a shower they're Ikr5200/7020. Sleeping-bag accommodation costs Ikr1300. The hotel has a restaurant and coffee shop as well as a nice swimming pool.

You'll also find sleeping-bag accommodation at the *Félagsheimilið Kirkjuhvoll* (☎ 487 4840; fax 487 4842), which is open from 1 May to 1 October and costs Ikr1000. The *Félagsheimilið Tungusel* (☎ 487 1358), 28 km south-west of town, charges Ikr700 for sleeping-bag accommodation, but it caters mainly for groups.

There's also a glut of farmhouse accommodation. One which caters for budget travellers is *Nýibær* (☎ 487 4678), across the river west of town, where sleeping-bag accommodation costs Ikr850/1300 on mattresses/beds. *Hunkubakkar* (☎ 487 4681) on the Laki road, *Efri-Vík* (☎ 487 4694), which features a superb nine-hole golf course, six km from town on Route 204, and *Geirland* (☎ 487 4677), out past Kleifar, all offer single/double rooms for Ikr3000/4050. Hunkubakkar and Efri-Vík also have sleep-ing-bag accommodation for Ikr1300, and Efri-Vík has fishing and horse rentals.

Places to Eat
You'll find grill snacks and groceries at the *Skaftárskáli* (☎ 487 4628) petrol station. The *supermarket* is just east of the chapel.

Entertainment
The Félagsheimilið Kirkjuhvoll sometimes hosts dances on weekends.

Getting There & Away
The bus terminal is at the Edda Hotel. All buses between Reykjavík and Höfn pass through Kirkjubæjarklaustur. In summer they run daily from Reykjavík (Ikr2500) at 8.30 am and arrive in Kirkjubæjarklaustur at 1.30 pm. Westbound buses depart from Höfn (Ikr1800) at 9 am and arrive at 12.45 pm, then continue on to Reykjavík.

The Fjallabak bus between Reykjavík and Skaftafell passes around 6.30 pm eastbound and 9 am westbound daily from early July to 8 September. The entire route costs Ikr5265, but holders of the Full-Circle Pass – provided they haven't yet used the bit of the Ring Road being cut off with the tour – or Omnibuspass pay about half price.

LAKAGÍGAR
The Laki eruptions of 1783 were among the most catastrophic volcanic events in human history, and were by far the most devastating Iceland has yet known. Although Laki is extinct and hasn't erupted at all in modern times, it has loaned its name to the volatile 25 km Lakagígar crater row which stretches south-westward from its base. The main period of activity, which started in the spring of 1783 and lasted for 10 months, was known as the Skaftáreldar ('shaft river fires'). It's suspected that the Lakagígar fissure is somehow connected with the Grímsvötn volcano beneath Vatnajökull.

Of all the misfortunes to befall Iceland during the Norwegian and Danish regimes, the Skaftáreldar brought the most suffering. During the Skaftáreldar, the Laki fissure spewed more than 30 billion tonnes of lava and 90 million tonnes of sulphuric acid. Across Iceland, farms and fields were devastated and well over half the livestock succumbed to starvation and poisoning. Some 9000 people – 20% of Iceland's population – were killed and the remainder faced the *Moðuharðindi* ('haze famine') that followed. Traces of ash from the Laki eruptions have been found around the world.

Lakagígar Crater Row

The Lakagígar crater row is fascinating to explore, particularly the crater nearest Laki itself, which contains a nice lava cave. Another cave, two hours walk south of the parking area, shelters a mysterious lake. The area is also riddled with black sand dunes and lava tubes, many of which contain tiny stalactites. Nowadays, the lava field belies the apocalypse that spawned it just over 200 years ago and the sharp, black boulders are overgrown with soft and spongy moss. This appealing natural cushion is ideal for a nap in the sun!

Laki

Laki itself can be climbed in less than an hour from the parking area, and yields a fantastic view of the active fissure. The easiest route lies to the left of the crest leading up to the first plateau.

Lakagígar Road

In most years, the 4WD road from just west of Kirkjubæjarklaustur to the Lakagígar crater row is passable after early July. There are still lots of puddles and some rivers to ford so, after rain, the route may forestall low-clearance vehicles.

Fjarðrárgljúfur This peculiar and picturesque canyon, carved by the river Fjarðrá, is lined with steep rock walls and chunky promontories. It lies on the Laki road, 3½ km north of the Ring Road. A walking track begins at the mouth of the canyon and follows the southern rim for a couple of km to some wonderful views into the depths.

Around the nearby farm Holt is the small Holtsborg nature reserve. This is the only

place in Iceland where wild roses grow naturally.

Fagrifoss These surprising and relatively little-known falls on the Geirlandsá lie just east of the Laki road, hidden from view by a low rise. Their name means 'beautiful falls'; decide for yourself whether they're appropriately named! Look for the turn-off about 20 km north of the Ring Road.

The Hole Not far from Fagrifoss is a very deep hole in a small slump crater just east of the Laki road. It doesn't seem to have a particular name – it's just called 'the hole'. Locals will tell you it's the back door to hell (Hekla is the front door). In 1989, an impromptu French expedition, the Groupe Speleo Gaillard, descended into the hole and ran out of rope at 45m with lots of hole left beneath them.

The entrance to this unassuming cavern is just 35 cm across and hidden in a cleft in the rocks, so it's unlikely you'll find it without a guide. It's just a couple of metres east of the Laki road about midway between the craters and the Ring Road. The Laki tours stop briefly to toss in a few rocks.

Organised Tours

The best access to the Lakagígar area is with the worthwhile BSÍ tour from Skaftafell or Kirkjubæjarklaustur. It departs daily, 1 July to 31 August, at 8 am from Skaftafell (Ikr4355) and at 9 am from Kirkjubæjarklaustur (Ikr3055). Omnibuspass holders get a discount, or you can pay with two Highland Pass vouchers. The tour allows plenty of time at points of interest, and most participants reckon it's exceptionally good value. Stops include attractions along the Laki road and three hours to explore the craters area. You can also camp at Laki and return with the tour on another day.

Tours start at the Edda Hotel (☎ 487 4799) in Kirkjubæjarklaustur. If you're staying at the campground or one of the farmhouses, ring in advance so they'll know to fetch you.

ICELAND

Getting There & Away

After rain, the Laki road gets very muddy and becomes difficult even for 4WD vehicles. It sees very little traffic in any case, so hitching is also difficult.

THE SANDUR

The broad desert expanse that sprawls along Iceland's south-eastern coast is known as sandur, which is another Icelandic word come into general international usage to describe a topographic phenomenon. In this case, it's the deposits of silt, sand and gravel scraped from the high peaks by glaciers and carried down in jökulhlaups (glacial bursts) and braided glacial rivers.

Meðallandssandur

Meðallandssandur spreads across the Meðalland district south of Eldhraun and east of the river Kuðafljót. This sandy desert is so flat and featureless that a number of ships have run aground on its coast, apparently unaware they were nearing land. There's now a lighthouse in case someone still hasn't learned their lesson.

Lómagnúpur

The immense landmark Lómagnúpur ('loon peak') rises like an island 668m above the sandur. It's plainly visible from Kirkjubæjarklaustur, 35 km to the west, and from the Öræfi far to the east. It's most impressive when seen from the Núpsá valley.

Núpsstaður

Beneath the western cliffs of Lómagnúpur sits the farm Núpsstaður ('peak stead'), which is overlooked by bizarrely eroded cliffs and pinnacles. The farm buildings date back as far as the early 19th century and the small turf church, which is dedicated to St Nicholas, was mentioned in church records as early as 1200. It was renovated in 1657 by Einar Jónsson and has recently been restored again by the National Museum. This is one of the last turf churches in Iceland to remain in general use.

Inland from Lómagnúpur is Núpsstaðarskógar, a beautiful woodland area on the

> ### True Grit
> When driving on the sandur in high winds, you won't be able to avoid the sandblasting a vehicle will suffer, but it will help to rinse the car with water (don't wipe it) once you're across. Car-wash hoses may be used free of charge at most Icelandic petrol stations. To avoid fouling the engine, it also helps to place a strip of cardboard between the radiator and the grille.
>
> For cyclists, the sandur becomes a nightmare when the wind is blowing. The fine sand and talcum-like glacial flour whip up into abrasive clouds, drift across the road and reduce visibility. Cyclists tell tales of literally being blown off the road and into sand drifts with no shelter from the stinging clouds. Be prepared to put up a tent in the bleakest of surroundings and wait out the weather! ∎

slopes of the mountain Eystrafjall. Along the western flank of Skeiðarárjökull are the dramatic peaks of Súlutindar.

Grænalón

From the southern end of Núpsstaðarskógar, a good two or three-day hike will take you over the ridges and valleys west of immense Skeiðarárjökull to Grænalón ('green lagoon'). This ice-dammed lake is best-known for its ability to drain like a bathtub. The 'plug' is the western edge of Skeiðarárjökull, and when the water pressure builds to breaking point, the glacier is lifted and the lake lets go. It has been known to release up to 2.7 million cubic metres of water at 5000 cubic metres per second in a single burst.

To get started, you'll have to join the Núpsstaðarskógar tour (see Organised Tours later in this section), as it's impossible to cross the Núpsá and Súlaá on foot. Leave the tour at the Réttarlækur toilet block, at the southern foot of Súlutindar, where there's a decent campsite, and pick your way up the ridge. You should then head north toward the hill Eystrafjall and along Sléttur to Eggjar, which lies immediately south of Grænalón.

The topo sheet to use is *Lómagnúpur* 1:100,000 (1986). For guidelines, see the map *Kirkjubæjarklaustur Skaftárhreppur*, which is distributed free by the tourist office in Kirkjubæjarklaustur .

Organised Tours One of Iceland's most rewarding day tours – especially when the sun is shining – is the eight hour Núpsstaðar-skógar tour run by Hannes Jónsson (☎ 487 4785; fax 487 4890) at Núpsstaður.

After a short ride to the eastern slopes of Lómagnúpur, you travel on foot to the river Núpsá, where you're pulled across on a raft and then driven to Núpsstaðarskógar. From there, a couple of hours walk brings you to the confluence of the Núpsá and Hvitá, which spill over two spectacular turquoise-coloured waterfalls to converge in a dramatic canyon. For the best view, you must climb a vertical cliff with the aid of a rope and a bit of adrenalin. On the way back, you'll have amazing close-up views of the face of Skeiðarárjökull.

The tours run daily from 1 July to 31 August from 9 am to 6 pm, and cost Ikr3050 (Ikr2000 with Omnibuspass) or two Highland Pass vouchers. They leave from the farm Nússtaður and connect with scheduled buses between Kirkjubæjarklaustur and Skaftafell. This tour is the access to use for the hike to Grænalón, but you must arrange in advance when and where you want to be picked up. The Núpsstaðarskógar tour passes around 5 pm on its way back to the Ring Road. (See also Organised Tours under Skaftafell National Park.)

Skeiðarársandur

Impressive Skeiðarárjökull, 'the wandering river glacier', is Iceland's (and Europe's) largest valley glacier and covers an area of 1600 sq km. Its relentless scouring action combined with the many Grímsvötn jökulhlaups is responsible for this 600 sq km glacial delta, the largest of Iceland's sandur.

Since Settlement, Skeiðarársandur has swallowed a considerable amount of farmland and it continues to grow. The area was once relatively well-populated (for Iceland, anyway), but in 1362 the volcano Öræfi beneath Öræfajökull erupted and the subse-

quent jökulhlaup laid waste to the entire district.

The Ring Road across Skeiðarársandur, built in 1974, was the last bit of the National Highway to be constructed. Long gravel dykes have been strategically positioned to channel floodwaters away from this highly susceptible artery. They did little good, however, when in late 1996, three Ring Road bridges were destroyed by the massive *jökulhlaup* released by the Loki eruption. They were immediately replaced by temporary structures until permanent repairs could be made the following spring.

Ingólfshöfði

The promontory Ingólfshöfði rises 76m above a sandy barrier island, about eight km across a shallow tidal lagoon from the mainland coast. Access to the headland is up a sandy ramp on the northern slope of the promontory.

It was here that Ingólfur Arnarson, Iceland's first settler, stayed over the winter on his original foray in Iceland and on the cape stands a monument to that effect. It was probably greener and more inviting in Ingólfur's day, but in the summer, it's still rife with nesting puffins and other sea birds, and you'll often see seals and whales offshore.

Organised Tours A 4WD track connects Ingólfshöfði to the farm Fagurhólsmýri, but even on foot or with a 4WD, it's a rough route across wet tidal flats, and it's easy to bog in the muck. Fortunately, daily from 1 June to 30 August, farmer Sigurður Bjarnason runs tractor-and-haywagon tours for Ikr500 per person (minimum Ikr3000) from Fagurhólsmýri. Book through Öræfaferðir (☎ & fax 478 1682)

You can also visit Ingólfshöfði on horseback. See Svínafell & Svínafellsjökull, later in this chapter.

Hof

At the farm Hof ('temple') is a peat-brick and wooden church on the 14th-century foundation of a temple dedicated to Þór. It was reconstructed in 1884 and now sits pleasantly in a thicket of birch and ash with flowers growing on the grassy roof. Nearby are the ruins of Gröf, a farm which was destroyed in the jökulhlaup caused by the 1362 Öræfi eruption.

Places to Stay & Eat There are rooms and sleeping-bag accommodation at *Hof I* (☎ 478 1669; fax 478 1638); meals are also available. Nearby is another farm, *Lítla-Hof* (☎ 478 1670), with rooms for Ikr1800 per person. At either, single/double rooms cost Ikr3000/4050 and sleeping-bag accommodation is Ikr1300. The nearest shop and *snack bar* is at the Fagurhólsmýri airstrip, five km away.

Breiðamerkursandur

The easternmost of the big sandurs, Breiðamerkursandur is the home and main breeding ground of Iceland's largest colony of great skuas, the original dive-bombers, which nest in grassy tufts atop low mounds. Thanks to this rich, easy-to-catch bounty, there's also a growing population of Arctic foxes. If you want to see the birds, you can avoid painful aerial attacks by wearing a hat or carrying a stick or other item above head level.

Breiðamerkursandur also figures in *Njáls Saga*, which ends with the remaining protagonist, Kári Sölmundarson, arriving in this idyllic spot to 'live happily ever after':

Flosi gave to Kári in marriage his niece Hildigunn, the widow of Höskuld Hvitanesgóði. To begin with, they lived at Breiða.

Kári's farm Breiða was destroyed by the glacier in the 17th century, but that was long after Kári and Hildigunn would have had any use for it.

Above the sandur nowadays, you'll see an expansive panorama of glacier-capped mountains fronted by deep lagoons. The 742m Breiðamerkur was once a *nunatak* enclosed by Breiðamerkurjökull and Fjallsjökull, but the glaciers have since retreated and freed it. At the foot of the peak

is the glacial lagoon Breiðárlón, which is crowded with icebergs calved from the glacier. Though similar to nearby Jökulsárlón, it's less touristy and is worth the short walk to see it.

JÖKULSÁRLÓN

The 100m deep Jökulsárlón ('glacial river lagoon') is more or less an obligatory stop for travellers between Skaftafell and Höfn. It's full of large icebergs calved from the glacier Breiðamerkurjökull and taken out of context, it makes a classic Arctic scene. In fact, it was interesting enough to some locations coordinators that parts of the James Bond film *A View to a Kill* were shot there.

Breiðamerkurjökull seems to advance and retreat with some frequency, and in the small restaurant near the lagoon hang aerial photos taken in 1945, 1982 and 1990. It has retreated considerably even since 1990 – much of the tongue shown in the photo is now gone and, over the past few years, the lagoon appears to have nearly doubled in size.

Speaking of changes, the growing lagoon on one side and the battering from wind and waves out to sea are rapidly eroding the gravel bar that supports the Ring Road and creates the abbreviated river Jökulsá. Both the Jökulsá bridge and Iceland's main road link are under threat and engineers are frantically looking for a remedy before the whole thing collapses.

Boat Trips

For Ikr1500, you can take a 30 minute spin past the icebergs in a novel wheeled boat. Cruises leave from the dock whenever a willing boatload is waiting.

Places to Stay & Eat

The *Hali Restaurant* beside the lagoon sells coffee, fast food and sticky snacks daily in the summer from 9 am to 8 pm. The current Jökulsárlón *campsite* is on a minuscule bit of turf appended to the restaurant. However, you can also pitch a tent just about anywhere in the area.

Getting There & Away

Assuming that most passengers will be chafing at the bit to snap a few photos of Jökulsárlón, all public buses stop for 10 to 20 minutes. Glacier tours from Höfn stop long enough for a lagoon cruise.

ÖRÆFAJÖKULL & HVANNADALSHNÚKUR

Öræfajökull, the southernmost spur of Vatnajökull, isn't a glacier but actually a separate icecap over the immense Öræfi caldera. The nunatak protruding above Öræfi's crater rim is known as Hvannadalshnúkur, which at 2119m is the highest point in Iceland.

Hvannadalshnúkur

The best access for climbing Hvannadalshnúkur is from Sandfellsheiði, above the abandoned farm Sandfell, about 12 km south-east of Skaftafell. You'll reach the tricky crevasse-laden edge of the glacier at about 1300m and climb another 400m before it levels off and smooths out. From there, it's a technical climb to the peak of Hvannadalshnúkur, which rises 200m above the icefield four km away. Expeditions must be well-versed in glacier travel, and although most guided expeditions manage the trip in a very long and taxing day (see Organised Tours in this section), independent climbers should carry enough supplies and gear for several days.

Organised Tours

The company Öræfaferðir (☎ fax 478 1682) runs guided 13-hour ascents of Hvannadalshnúkur. They provide transport up to the snow line, where you transfer to nordic skis for the ascent to the 1820m crater rim. After skiing across the crater, you'll make the final summit ascent with technical climbing gear. The day trip costs Ikr5000 per person, with a minimum of two people, or Ikr7500 with just one person, including transport, guide and use of skiing and climbing equipment. This is certainly one of the best and most remarkable deals in Iceland.

If you're not up to climbing the mountain, you can opt for five hours of nordic skiing on Öræfajökull for Ikr2000, including use of ski equipment. Non-skiers may hike to the top and sled down for only Ikr1000.

In the winter, they'll take you to the top of Hvannadalshnúkur by glacier buggy and you can ski down 2000m of virgin snow. Tours run from January to May and cost Ikr14,950 per person; participants must provide their own ski equipment. Due to crevasses, no skiing is possible in the summer.

SVÍNAFELL & SVÍNAFELLSJÖKULL

The farm Svínafell, eight km south-east of Skaftafell, was the home of Flosi Þórðarson, the character who burned out Njáll and his family in *Njáls Saga*. It was also the site where Flosi and Njáll's family were finally reconciled, and thus ended one of the bloodiest feuds in Icelandic history:

It was snowing furiously... They walked to Svínafell through the snowstorm. Flosi was sitting in the main room. He recognised Kári at once and jumped up to welcome him, embraced him and sat him on the high-seat beside him. He invited Kári to stay the winter and Kári accepted.

In the 1600s, the glacier Svínafellsjökull nearly engulfed the farm, but it has since retreated. From the road it's a short walk over the prominent terminal moraine to the snout of the glacier. From Skaftafell, it's five km along the side roads.

Swimming

The Flosalaug at Svínafell is a swimming complex with a pool, jacuzzis and showers. It's open daily, 1 to 10 pm.

Organised Tours

Öræfaferðir (☎ & fax 478 1682) offers four-hour guided walks on Svínafellsjökull for just Ikr1000 per person, and tours run with even one person. For an additional Ikr500, you can attempt a technical ice climb; the price includes equipment and instruction. This makes a great-value day trip from Skaftafell.

Horse-riding tours to Ingólfshöfði and

other places may be organised at the farm Svínafell (☎ 478 1661), but you need five people.

Places to Stay & Eat

The *Hótel Skaftafell* (☎ 478 1945; fax 478 1846), at Freysnes at the foot of Svína-fellsjökull, charges Ikr3380/4420 for single/double rooms with shared facilities and Ikr4680/6435 with shower. Breakfast costs Ikr720. Meals are available at the petrol station.

SKAFTAFELL NATIONAL PARK

Skaftafell is Iceland's second largest and best-loved national park, and its stunning yet accessible scenery may well be unmatched in Iceland. Nowhere else can you so easily approach a glacier, see such lovely natural vegetation, enjoy such stunning panoramas of ice and ice-scoured rock, or gaze across a tangled web of braided rivers as they slice across the sandur.

Yes, Skaftafell merits its reputation and few travellers fail to at least put in an appearance. In fact, few Icelanders can resist it either, and on long summer weekends you're looking at a mob scene, with tent-fly-to-caravan-door camping conditions, a cacophony of boom-box stereo systems, raucous all-night parties and hour-long queues at the toilets. It can be lots of fun but may prove disappointing if you've come to camp and commune with nature, so time your visit accordingly. Having said that, if you're prepared to get out on the more remote trails and take advantage of the fabulous day hiking on the heath and beyond, you'll leave the crowds far behind.

History

The historical Skaftafell was a large farm at the foot of the hills west of the present campground, but a build-up of the sandur forced the farm to shift to a more suitable site, on the heath 100m above the sandur. Shortly afterwards, three other farms were established on the heath, and there are records that another farm and church existed in the early 1300s, near the foot of Jökulfell, on the other side of Morsárdalur.

The district came to be known as Hérað Milli Sandur ('land between the sands'), but after all the farms were annihilated by the Öræfi eruptions of 1362, the district became the 'land under the sands' and was renamed Öræfi ('waste land'). Once the vegetation returned, however, the farm Skaftafell was rebuilt in its former location on the moor.

The modern park was jointly founded in 1967 by the Icelandic government and the World Wildlife Fund for Nature). It originally contained only the area cradled between Skeiðarárjökull and Skaftafellsjökull, and included Skaftafellsheiði ('shaft mountain heath'), the Morsárdalur valley and the Skaftafellsfjöll range. In June 1984, the park was expanded to include about 20% of the Vatnajökull icecap. Sheltered as it is by mountains, Skaftafell enjoys decidedly better weather conditions than its surroundings.

Maps

The map on the old national park brochure was considerably better than the new one (Ikr100), which is scarcely adequate. If you do find an old one (the photo on the old one has blue sky, while the new one has grey sky), snap it up.

Landmælingar Íslands publishes a thematic map of Skaftafell National Park showing the non-glacial area of the park at 1:25,000 and the Öræfi district at 1:100,000. It's available in Reykjavík (see Maps in the Iceland Facts for the Visitor chapter) and at the Skaftafell service centre shop. You can also use the *Öræfajökull* 1:100,000 (1986) topo sheet.

Information

The Skaftafell service area has an information office, coffee shop, cafeteria, supermarket and toilet block. At the shop, you can change cash for a commission of Ikr100 and travellers' cheques for Ikr165. To phone overseas from Skaftafell, dial ☎ 90 (rather than 00).

All flora, fauna and natural features of the

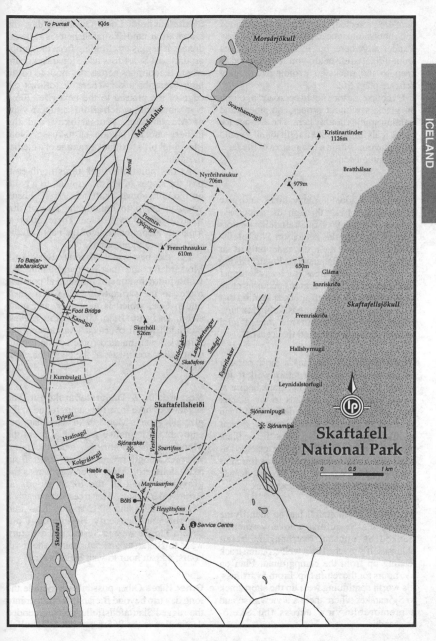

To Þumall   Kjós

Morsárjökull

Morsárdalur

Morsá

Svarthamragil

Kristínartinder
1126m

Bratthálsar

Nyrðrihnaukur
706m

Fremra-
Djúpagil

979m

Fremrihnaukur
610m

650m

Gláma

Innriskriða

Skaftafellsjökull

Fremriskriða

To Bæjar-
staðarskógur

Foot Bridge

Kambsgil

Skerhóll
526m

Storilækur

Langibarrungur

Smágil

Skaðafoss

Eystrilækur

Hallshyrnugil

Kumbulgil

Skaftafellsheiði

Leynidalstorfugil

Eyjagil

Sjónarnípugil

Sjónarnípa

Hrafnagil

Sjónarsker

Vestrilækur

Svartifoss

Kolgráfargil

Hæðir   Sel

Magnúsarfoss

Bölti

Heygötufoss

Skeiðará

Service Centre

Skaftafell
National Park

0   0.5   1 km

park are protected, open fires are prohibited and rubbish must be carried out. Hikers may wander anywhere, but in the high-use area around Skaftafellsheiði, you're requested to keep to the tracks to avoiding damaging delicate plant life.

Of course, advice not to approach or climb on glaciers without proper equipment and training applies doubly here. The average ice block calving off Skaftafellsjökull would crush anyone within a few metres of the face. Use common sense!

Hiking

Skaftafell is ideal for day hikes and also offers longer treks through its wilderness regions. At least 90% of Skaftafell's visitors keep to the popular routes on Skaftafellsheiði and most of the rest wander only as far as the springs at Bæjarstaðarskógur. Hiking in other accessible areas, such as the upper Morsárdalur and Kjós regions, requires more time, motivation and effort. Bear in mind that without a permit, camping is forbidden anywhere in the park outside the official campground, including on the icecap!

Skaftafellsjökull The park's most popular trail is the easy two hour return walk to the glacier Skaftafellsjökull. The track begins at the service centre and leads to the glacier face where you can experience first-hand evidence of glacial activity – bumps, groans and flowing water – as well as the brilliant blue hues of the ice itself. The glacier has been receding in recent years – as much as one metre per day – and over the past decade has lost nearly one km of its length.

Svartifoss If Skaftafell has an identifying feature, it's Svartifoss, a lovely waterfall flanked by unusual overhanging basalt columns. It's reached by a well-trodden track leading up from the campground. Plan on 1½ hours for the return trip. From Svartifoss, it's worth continuing west up the short track to Sjónarsker where there's a view disc and a memorable view across the Skeiðarársandur.

Skaftafellsheiði Loop On a fine day, the loop walk around Skaftafellsheiði is a hikers' dream. It begins by climbing from the campground past Svartifoss and Sjónarsker, from where it continues across the moor to 610m high Fremrihnaukur. There, it follows the edge of the plateau to the next rise, 706m Nyrðrihnaukur, which affords a superb view of Morsárdalur, Morsárjökull and the iceberg-choked lagoon at its base. Note Morsárjökull's textbook example of a medial moraine.

At this point, the track turns north-east, past the slopes of Kristínartindar, to a point on the cliff above Skaftafellsjökull. There, you can begin to fathom the size of this relatively small river of ice! There are great lookouts along the edge of the heath all the way down to Sjónarnípa.

For the best view of Skaftafellsjökull, Morsárdalur and the Skeiðarársandur, it's worth following one of the several possible routes to the summit of 1126m Kristínartindar. One, which is unmarked and quite steep, leads up from Gláma, the highest Skaftafellsjökull overlook. An easier route follows a well-marked route up the prominent valley south-east of the Nyrðrihnaukur lookout.

Morsárdalur & Bæjarstaðarskógur The seven-hour hike from the campground to the glacial lagoon in Morsárdalur is ordinary but enjoyable. Alternatively, you can cross the Morsá on the footbridge, near the point where Kambgil ravine comes down from Skaftafellsheiði. Make your way across the gravel riverbed to the birch woods at Bæjarstaðarskógur. The trees here reach a whopping 12m and 80°C springs flow into the tiny but heavenly Heitulækir ('hot stream') to the west in Vestragil. The return walk to Bæjarstaðarskógur takes about six hours; add an hour to visit Heitulækir.

Other Hikes Other possibilities include the long day trip beyond Bæjarstaðarskógur into the rugged Skaftafellsfjöll. A recommended destination is the 965m summit of Jökulfell

Icebergs at Jökulsárlón, South-East Iceland

Top: Rhyolite formations at Landmannalaugar, Central Iceland
Bottom: Natural bridge on Virkisfell, Kverkfjöll area, Central Iceland

ICELAND

Jökulhlaup!

On the morning of 29 September 1996, a 5.0 earthquake shook Vatnajökull icecap. By that evening, continuing seismic activity had made it clear that molten magma from a new volcano, in the Grímsvötn region beneath Vatnajökull, had made its way through the earth's crust and into the ice. By Tuesday, 1 October, two cauldrons, each over 1½ km wide, had appeared on the icecap between Grímsvötn and the Bárdarbunga volcano, indicating the eruption of a four-km long subsurface fissure, dubbed 'Loki' (this was the name used by the press, anyway). The following day, the eruption burst through the surface, ejecting a column of steam that rose 10,000m into the sky and inspired impressive aerial photography which was televised worldwide. Over the next few days, the activity intensified and the fissure, which had now grown to nine km in length, began ejecting black clouds of ash and fountains of molten rock along with the steam.

Scientists' concerns lay not so much with the ejecta itself, but with the fact that the sub-glacial lake in the Grímsvötn caldera was filling with water from ice melted by the heat of the eruption. Initial predictions on 3 October were that the ice would lift and the lake would give way within 48 hours and spill out across Skeiðarársandur, threatening the Ring Road and its vulnerable bridges, which serve as vital links between eastern and western Iceland. In hopes of diverting floodwaters away from the bridges, massive dike-building projects were organised on Skeiðarársandur.

The eruption continued almost constantly, but on its 14th day, it fizzled out, leaving an ash-caked ice canyon 3½ km long and 350m wide on the surface of Vatnajökull, a new mountain peak protruding from the ice 200m below the old surface, and a menacingly pregnant Grímsvötn.

After several weeks without activity, now-complacent local farmers optimistically predicted that the jökulhlaup would wait until spring. On 5 November, however, nearly a month after the eruption had begun, the ice lifted and the Grímsvötn reservoir drained in a massive jökulhlaup, releasing up to 3000 billion cubic litres of water within several hours. Despite the dike-building efforts, the floodwaters destroyed the 375m Gigja bridge and the 900m Skeiðarár bridge, both on the Skeiðarársandur, as well as another 50m bridge nearby. The warden at Skaftafell reported seeing enormous multi-tonne blocks of ice being hurled across Skeiðarársandur.

It's thought that the 'Loki' eruption will turn out to be Iceland's fourth largest of the 20th century, after those of Katla in 1918, Hekla in 1947 and Surtsey in 1963. ■

ridge, which affords a commanding view of the vast expanses of Skeiðarárjökull. Even better is a three-day excursion into the **Kjós** region. When you reach Kjós, a very difficult hike is up Þumall ('the thumb'), then west along the glacier edge, around the valley rim, and northward down to your starting point.

Another possibility is to ascend along the eastern flank of **Skaftafellsjökull**. At the first big ravine on your right, cross the stream and ascend along the north bank to the ridge. From there, turn left and follow the ridge to the 1174m summit of Hafrafell. You can actually descend the ridge as far as **Efrimenn**, where there's a spectacular view of Skaftafellsjökull and Svínafellsjökull.

Wilderness camping permits are available from the visitors centre for Ikr500 per person per night. Also enquire about river crossings along your intended route. On hot days and after heavy rains, the rivers can become swollen and uncrossable.

Grímsvötn

Historically, Grímsvötn has been known to blow its top and release apocalyptic jökulhlaups, and in fact, it was Grímsvötn which caused the cataclysmic flood that carved out the Ásbyrgi canyon in just a few days (see the North-East Iceland chapter). In 1934, it had a fit of temper which released a 40,000-cubic-metre-per-second jökulhlaup, which swelled the river Skeiðará to nine km in width, and large areas of farmland were laid waste. Until October 1996, it remained deceptively inconspicuous, quietly rumbling away beneath a mantle of Vatnajökull ice. (For details, see the Jökulhlaup boxed aside.)

Organised Tours

The difficult hike up to Þumall may be done with Icelandic Mountain Guides (☎ 854 2959; fax 551 1392). For two to four people, the two-day trip costs Ikr20,000.

Alternatively, you can follow the more challenging four-day route from Skaftafell, over Skeiðarárjökull to Grænalón and down the canyon of the Núpsá to Núpsstaðar-skógar. This one costs Ikr19,000 for four to 12 people.

Perhaps the most ambitious option is the incredible 12-day trek up the Eldgjá fissure (see the Central Iceland chapter) to the Lakagígar crater row, Núpsstaðarskógar, Grænalón and over Skeiðarárjökull to Skaftafell. This takes you through one of Iceland's wildest regions and exceptional stamina is required; guide prices depend on the number of participants.

In the summer, Jórvík Aviation (☎ 854 2300) runs flightseeing trips over the national park and Vatnajökull for Ikr4500 per person.

Places to Stay & Eat

Most visitors wind up in the *campground* at park headquarters, which is a spacious grassy field broken only by hedges and bar-becue spits. It costs Ikr500 per person in a tent or caravan. The tepid showers are prob-ably the most expensive in Iceland at Ikr180 for five minutes and there are only two stalls – one each for men and women; despite the requirement that people shower two at a time, queues do back up. As for meals, if you avoid the alcohol, the service centre cafeteria is reasonably good value. The curried fish is especially nice.

An alternative is the farm *Bölti* (☎ 478 1626), on Skaftafellsheiði above the western end of the campground. Private single/double rooms cost Ikr3450/5000 and sleep-ing-bag accommodation in five-bed dorms is Ikr1300. The house is a bit of a museum; note the Persian carpet on the bathroom floor!

The nearest farmhouse sleeping-bag accommodation is at the farms Hof and Lítla-Hof (see under Hof earlier in this chapter), 23 km away. There's also a hotel at nearby Svínafell (see Svínafell & Svínafellsjökull, earlier in this chapter).

Getting There & Away

From 1 June to 15 September, buses run daily between Reykjavík and Höfn, leaving each end at 8.30 am and passing Skaftafell at 2.45 pm eastbound and 11.15 am westbound. The Fjallabak bus, which runs from early July to 8 September, follows the scenic inland route through Landmannalaugar and Eldgjá. It leaves Skaftafell at 8 am and Reykjavík at 8.30 am daily and costs Ikr5265, with dis-counts for holders of bus passes.

HÖFN

The name of this town, which means 'harbour', is pronounced like an unexpected hiccup; if you're not prone to hiccups, just say 'hup' while inhaling. Sprawling across a sandy spit in the lagoon Hornafjörður, Höfn is a rather characterless farming, fishing and fish-processing town set amidst stunning surroundings. Since the completion of the Ring Road brought it within a day's drive of Reykjavík (until 1974, Höfn-ites had to drive to Reykjavík via Akureyri), the population has swollen to 1750 and is still growing.

Höfn is one of the cornerstones of the Ring Road and bus schedules force travellers to stay overnight there. If you're not taking a Vatnajökull glacier tour, at least try not to arrive on a Saturday or Sunday. Höfn may have a hiccup name, but its demeanour is definitely a yawn.

Information

In summer, the private tourist office (☎ 478 1701; fax 478 1901), at the campground, is open daily from 7.30 am to midnight. It handles foreign exchange from 8 to 9 am and 6 to 7 pm. On weekdays, the swimming pool is open from 7 am to 1 pm and 2.30 to 9 pm and on weekends from 10 am to 4 pm.

Regional Museum

The regional museum (☎ 478 1833), housed in an 1864 trade warehouse, which was moved to Höfn from Papaós, further east, has both nautical and agricultural displays as well as small natural history and marine life exhibits. From 1 June to 31 August, it's open daily from 10 am to noon and 2 to 5 pm. Admission is Ikr200.

ICELAND

Höfn

0   200   400 m

To Airport, Edda Hotel,
Reykjavik & Egilsstaðir

Silfurbraut

Smáratún

Austurbraut

Þjóðvegur

Vesturbraut

Silfurbraut

Kirkjubraut

Júlíatún

Vikurbraut

Kirkjubraut

Skarðsfjörður

Þykkvibær

Lyngeyjarvegur

Silkuvegur

Vikurtún

Sandaskæreyjar

Hafnarbraut

Svalbarð

Alaugareyjarvegur

Höfðavegur

Ránarslóð

Hafnarbraut

Króseyjarvegur

Hornafjörður

Óslandsvegur

Ósland

PLACES TO STAY
3 Campground
7 Hótel Höfn
13 Nýibær Youth Hostel
15 Ásgarður Hotel Annexe
16 Gistiheimilið Hvammur

PLACES TO EAT
5 Esso Petrol Station
6 KASK Supermarket
9 Ósinn & Shell Petrol Station
10 KASK Supermarket
12 Hornabær Shop
17 Hafnarbúðin Snack Bar

OTHER
1 Regional Museum
2 Bus Terminal
4 Tourist Information & Jöklaferðir Tours
8 Hospital
11 Post Office
14 Swimming Pool
18 Landsbanki Íslands Bank

Special Events

In 1993, hoping to attract attention (and tourists), Höfn kicked off a new annual festival, Hátið á Höfn ('party in Höfn'), in honour of the lowly lobster. It takes place around the first or second week in July with a fun fair, flea markets, dancing, music, ice sculpture competitions (yes, in July!), special tours, lots of alcohol and even a few lobsters.

Organised Tours

For information on Vatnajökull tours, see under Vatnajökull Icecap later in this chapter.

Places to Stay

Lots of travellers stay at Höfn's hilly *campground* on Þjóðvegur, at the north end of town. This is also the tourist office and bus terminal, but it's a 10 minute walk from the centre. Camping costs Ikr400 per person, not including use of showers or washing machines.

If you'd prefer a roof over your head, try the *Youth Hostel Nýibær* (☎ & fax 478 1736), at Hafnarbraut 8, near the harbour. It's friendly and cosy, and charges Ikr1000/1250 for HI members/non-members.

The *Hótel Höfn* (☎ 478 1240; fax 478 1996), another of those uninspired Icelandic hotels, has single/double rooms with shared facilities for Ikr5000/7800. With a shower, they're Ikr7605/9620. The hotel annexe, *Ásgarður*, has single/double rooms with bath for Ikr6305/8515 and sleeping-bag accommodation for Ikr1560.

The *Gistiheimilið Hvammur* (☎ 478 1503), near the harbour, charges Ikr3900/5000 for single/double rooms with shared facilities. Sleeping-bag accommodation is Ikr1300. All rooms have satellite television.

There's an *Edda Hotel* (☎ 478 1470; fax 478 1496), at the school Nesjaskóli, seven km from Höfn, where you'll get private single/double rooms for Ikr3650/4750 and sleeping-bag accommodation for Ikr1000/1430 on mattresses/beds.

One km from the airport is the new farmhouse accommodation *Seljavellir* (☎ 478 1797; fax 478 1434), which has single/double rooms with television for Ikr3000/4050 and sleeping-bag accommodation for Ikr1000. Nearby is the small and rustic *Gistihúsið Árnanes* (☎ 478 1550; fax 478 1810; email arnanes@eldhorn.is), which charges Ikr3050/4680 for single/double rooms and Ikr1430 for sleeping-bag accommodation.

There's also lots of farmhouse accommodation around Höfn; see under Mýrar District later in this chapter.

Places to Eat

The *Hótel Höfn* dining room is good for coffee but the food is nothing special unless there's a seafood buffet. The inexpensive *Ósinn* (☎ 478 2200) restaurant, in the Shell petrol station, is open daily from 9 am to 10 pm. As *the* hangout in Höfn, this is about as exciting as it gets. It offers a range of tasty meals, including salads, pizza, burgers, grill snacks, soup and steak and lamb dishes. Daily specials cost around Ikr1000 for a complete meal.

For lesser snacks, try the *Hafnarbúðin* (☎ 478 1095), a snack bar on Ránarslóð near the harbour. It's open from 7.30 am to 11.30 pm daily except Saturday, when they keep the lights burning until 4 am. On Sunday, they lie in until 9 am. The *Esso* station near the campground also has a grill bar which stays open until 11.30 pm nightly.

There are *KASK* cooperative supermarkets on Hafnarbraut, and on Vesturbraut near the campground. The latter is open from 9 am to 7.30 pm daily in the summer. The *Hornabær* shop, near the HI hostel, is open from 9 am to 11.30 pm daily.

Things to Buy

You can pick up locally-made handicrafts, including Icelandic jumpers, at Handraðinn

Hornafirði, in the historical Pakkhúsið, near the harbour.

Getting There & Away

The Höfn bus terminal is at the campground. From 1 June to 15 September, there are daily buses between Reykjavík and Höfn (Ikr4300), leaving either place at 8.30 am and arriving at 5 pm.

To Egilsstaðir (Ikr3300), buses leave daily at 8.30 am; from Egilsstaðir, they leave at 3 pm. There's an additional bus as far as Djúpivogur (Ikr1150) at 9.35 am on Sunday and from Tuesday to Friday.

Getting Around

Mountain bikes may be hired at the campground for Ikr350 per hour, Ikr1000 for a half day and Ikr1500 for a full day. A recommended bike tour is to Stokksnes, about two hours each way.

AROUND HÖFN
Bjarnarnes

The ownership of this historical farm had been so disputed over the centuries prior to the Reformation that it was placed in the care of the bishop of Skálholt. The bishop would certainly have been amused by the present church at Bjarnarnes, which inexplicably strays from the prevailing geologic theme in Iceland. Perhaps the architect mistakenly heard 'geometric', as the building appears to be the result of a high-speed collision between a pyramid and a cylinder.

Ketillaugarfjall

This prominent and colourful mountain rises 670m above the Hornafjarðarfljót delta near Bjarnarnes. Its name derives from a legend about a woman named Ketillaug, who carried a pot of gold into the mountain and never returned. A brilliantly coloured alluvial fan at its base is visible from the road.

Hoffell & Goðaborg

Another tale of gold, this time found rather than lost, revolves around the beautiful 1420m mountain Goðaborg ('god's rock'), behind the farm Hoffell.

It seems that a shepherd stumbled across an odd door in the mountainside and found a heap of stones guarded by an unfriendly bull. Not interested in a confrontation he'd surely lose, the shepherd returned to his flock on the moors only to discover that his shoes were full of leaves which he later discovered were made of gold. It's believed the mountain does contain gold deposits but it's also rich in Iceland spar (silfurberg), jasper and marble.

Mýrar District

Mýrar is the lovely region of wetlands surrounding the deltas of Hornafjarðarfljót and Kolgrímaá. Rising above are some formidable glaciers, and the area is home to lots of water birds.

Places to Stay Mýrar has several farmhouse accommodation options. *Brunhóll* (☎ 478 1029; fax 478 1079) and *Flatey* (☎ 478 1036; fax 478 1598) have sleeping-bag accommodation for Ikr1300, cooking facilities, and single/double made-up rooms for Ikr3000/4050. Flatey also organises unique summer and winter horse tours.

In the same district is *Hólabrekka* (☎ 478 1022), and a bit further west are *Brunavellir* (☎ 478 1055) and the traditional-looking *Smyrlabjörg* (☎ 478 1074; fax 478 2043), all of which offer private rooms and charge the same rates. Smyrlabjörg also has sleeping-bag accommodation and kitchen facilities, and serves up home-baked bread for breakfast. It's only 19 km from Jöklasel and also offers trout fishing.

About two-thirds of the way between Höfn and Jökulsárlón is *Hrollaugsstaðir* (☎ 478 1057) with cooking facilities, made-up rooms, sleeping-bag accommodation and horse rental.

A rural hostel experience is available at the *Vagnstaður Youth Hostel* (☎ 478 1567; fax 478 2167), along the Ring Road, 50 km west of Höfn. It's accessible on any Reykjavík bus. Rates are Ikr1000/1250 for HI members/non-members.

VATNAJÖKULL ICECAP

There are many routes onto the Vatnajökull icecap, but the easiest is up the road to the broad glacial spur, Skálafellsjökull. Once you're there, Vatnajökull presents a clean white slate, but unless you're set up for a real polar-style expedition, travel on Vatnajökull is limited to commercial tours.

Organised Tours

Independent expeditions on Vatnajökull require experience in glacier travel, orientation, equipment and rescue procedures. If you have enough cash, however, Jöklaferðir, in Höfn, can take care of the logistics and take you on skiing, snowmobiling and glacier buggy trips on the icecap. Before deciding between snowmobiles or glacier buggies, consider the words of journalist Kevin Pilley: 'Going on a skidoo safari is like driving solidly for 16 hours over a never-ending series of sleeping policemen. You have to believe in your buttocks'.

These tours require at least six participants and most are booked from overseas, but if they have extra space or need passengers to make up a group, casual travellers may be able to join at a discounted rate. For information, contact Tryggvi Árnason (☎ 478 1503; fax 478 1901), Jöklaferðir, PO Box 66, 780 Höfn, or call up www.eldhorn.is/glaciert on the Internet.

Jöklasel Day Tour A quick and painless (except for the price) way to get above the valley glaciers and onto the icecap is with the daily Vatnajökull tour from Höfn or Skaftafell. The tour takes you past the Smyrlabjargarárvirkjun power plant and then 16 km up a twisting 4WD road to the Jöklasel glacier lodge and restaurant at the edge of Skálafellsjökull. There's also a mountain hut and a parking area full of glacier travel paraphernalia.

From 20 June to 4 September, tours depart from the Höfn campground daily at 9 am. The price of Ikr9165 includes one hour walking; a two-hour skidoo or glacier buggy *(thiokol)* excursion to 1128m Miðfellsegg and 1250m Birnudalstindar; and a cruise on

Jökulsárlón. For transport only, the cost is Ikr3100 from Höfn and Ikr1600 from Smyrlabjargarárvirkjun. With a 2½ hour snowmobile trip to Brókarjökull, the cost is Ikr10,200.

Without a guide, or technical gear and expertise, hikers must not wander past the red poles planted in the ice about a km from the hut. Beyond here are lots of snow-bridged crevasses and the danger is extreme. Even lower down, avoid any linear depressions in the snow. White-out conditions may also be a problem.

For more time on the icecap, you can stay at Jöklasel and rejoin the tour on another day.

Day Trips from Jöklasel From Jöklasel, you can also arrange day excursions by glacier buggy to Brókarjökull (2½ hours, Ikr8300), Hvannadalshnúkur (8-11 hours, Ikr17,000), Kverkfjöll (7-10 hours, Ikr15,000), Grímsvötn (7-10 hours, Ikr15,000) or Goðahnúkur (7-10 hours, Ikr15,000). The last three can be done as two-day excursions for double the price, including a stay overnight in mountain huts. Snowmobile excursions from Jöklasel cost Ikr4700 for the first hour and Ikr3200 for each additional hour.

Winter Glacier Buggy Tour Another possibility is the five-day glacier buggy tour conducted from 1 March to 31 May and 8 September to 15 October. It begins at Jöklasel and makes a circuit of the huts at Goðahnúkur, Snæfell, Kverkfjöll, Grímsvötn and Esjufjöll before returning to Jöklasel. This grand Vatnajökull circuit costs Ikr63,700, but console yourself in the fact that meals and hut fees are included.

Icecap Crossing A new option for mid-July to mid-August is to travel across the glacier by skidoo or glacier buggy to Kverkfjöll and meet up with the Ice & Fire Expeditions tours from Mývatn or Húsavík. After crossing the icecap, you stay overnight at Sigurðarskáli hut (Kverkfjöll) and continue to northern Iceland with the bus tour. These trips can also be run in the opposite direction. The

Vatnajökull portion of this tour operates on Tuesday and Saturday and costs Ikr15,000 per person. If you prefer your own steam, four-day guided nordic ski trips between Jöklasel and Kverkfjöll can also be arranged.

Other Options For other Vatnajökull options, see under Egilsstaðir and Snæfell in the East Iceland chapter; Skaftafell National Park, earlier in this chapter; or the Kverkfjöll Route in the Central Iceland chapter.

Places to Stay & Eat
The *Jöklasel mountain hut* (☎ 478 1503) has a beautifully situated restaurant and charges Ikr1500 for sleeping-bag accommodation. There are also basic Iceland Glacialogical Society *huts* at Grímsvötn and Goðahnúkur, right on the ice; at Esjufjöll on a nunatak in the south-eastern part of the icecap; at Kverkfjöll in the north; and at Jökulheimar (accessible by 4WD track from Veiðivötn), in the west. Any of these huts costs Ikr750 per person.

Lónsöræfi

Lónsöræfi ('lagoon wilderness') is a private nature reserve belonging to the vast farm Stafafell. The spectacularly colourful rhyolite scenery and countless hiking options will keep you occupied for days, but it's also a friendly and relaxing spot to settle in and enjoy the facilities and hospitality.

STAFAFELL
Stafafell is nestled between the rainbow-hued Lónsöræfi peaks and Lónssandur, the delta of Jökulsá í Lóni. It functioned as a remote parsonage until 1920 and the present church contains some lovely artefacts, including an original altarpiece. Because it's in a rain shadow of sorts, it's better protected than coastal areas to the west or north-east.

Lón
The name 'Lón', which is pronounced 'lone' and means 'lagoon', fairly sums up the

ICELAND

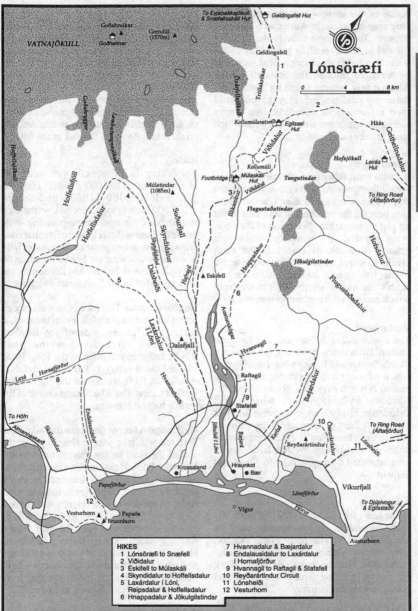

HIKES

1 Lónsöræfi to Snæfell
2 Viðidalur
3 Eskifell to Múlaskáli
4 Skyndidalur to Hoffellsdalur
5 Laxárdalur í Lóni,
  Reipsdalur & Hoffellsdalur
6 Hnappadalur & Jökulgilstindar
7 Hvannadalur & Bæjardalur
8 Endalausidalur to Laxárdalur
  í Hornafjörður
9 Hvannagil to Raftagil & Stafafell
10 Reyðarártindur Circuit
11 Lónsheiði
12 Vesturhorn

nature of this shallow bay enclosed by two long spits between the Austurhorn and Vesturhorn. To the north-west is the delta of Jökulsá í Lóni, a breeding ground for swans – and there are lots of them. Boat tours can be arranged through the Stafafell hostel. Alternatively, you can amble for hours along the empty sandspits and enjoy the loneliness (pun more or less intended). Don't miss seeing the enormous colony of swans which nests at the eastern end of Lón.

Austurhorn

As with most other peaks in the region, the batholithic peak Austurhorn, at the eastern end of Lón, was formed as an igneous intrusion beneath the surface and was then thrust up and revealed through erosion of the overlying material. It's composed mainly of granite. Beneath its slopes is the farm Hvalnes, where there's a lighthouse and a former fishing-boat landing. This is the best access for strolls on the Fjörur sandspit, which encloses the eastern portion of Lón.

Vesturhorn

The commanding 575m peak and its companion Brunnhorn form a cape between Skarðsfjörður and Papafjörður. Papafjörður, which was once a fishing station and trading centre, is worth exploring. Ruins of the settlement Syðri-Fjörður, which was abandoned in 1899, are still visible and just south of it are the more intriguing ruins of Papatóttir. There you'll find remnants of buildings constructed by the Irish monks who inhabited the region prior to Norse settlement.

Þórisdalur

In the late 17th and early 18th centuries, the farm Þórisdalur, on the western bank of Jökulsá í Lóni, was the home of the Skálholt clergyman, physician and naturalist Þórður Þorkelsson. Here he wrote a definitive work on glacial geology which was published posthumously in Germany.

All sorts of supernatural skills were attributed to Þórður, including the ability to detect and intercept the spirits of *utilegumenn* ('outlaws') as they passed into the district over Almannaskarð. He somehow always managed to send them packing back to where they'd come from.

Geithellur

The farm Geithellur was the site where famous first settler Ingólfur Arnarson and his chum Hjörleifur spent their winter holiday on their initial visit to Iceland in the 860s.

Hiking

For hiking in Lónsöræfi, you need the *Hornafjörður* 1:100,000 (1986), *Hamarsfjörður* 1:100,000 (1987) and *Snæfell* 1:100,000 (1988) topo sheets. Use the map in this book for basic route-planning only. Some of these walks require substantial river crossings, so use extreme caution, especially in warm or wet weather. For information on the walk between Snæfell and Lónsöræfi, see under Snæfell in the East Iceland chapter.

Reyðarártindur This four-hour walk begins seven km east of Stafafell. From the road, it ascends the eastern side of the Reyðará valley and circumscribes the peak Reyðarártindur, returning to the Ring Road via the Ossurá valley, 11 km east of Stafafell. Across the Ring Road near the start of this walk is a view disc which names some of the visible natural features.

Hvannagil A four or five-hour day hike from Stafafell will take you to Hvannagil, at the end of the road on the eastern bank of the Jökulsá í Lóni. Head up this dramatic rhyolite valley, and after less than one km, you'll see a sheep track climbing the ridge on your right. At the top of this ridge, you'll have a view down Seldalur. Keep to the left side of this valley until you pass the side valley, Raftagil, which descends back to the Jökulsá í Lóni. You can pick your way down Raftagil or follow the ridge above the eastern side of Seldalur. Aim for the radio antenna, from where a road descends back to Stafafell.

Tröllakrókur This trip begins at the

Illikambur parking area. From there, it's five to six hours to Egilssel hut at Tröllakrókur ('trolls' hooks'), an area of bizarre wind-eroded pinnacles. Above, you can see the tongue of Öxarfellsjökull, the eastern extreme of the Vatnajökull icecap. Allow two days for the return trip from Illikambur.

As a six-hour return side trip, you can cross the ridge north of Kollumúli into Viðidalur, along the Viðidalsá. Many of its feeder streams flow from beneath the small quadruplet icecaps: Tungutindar, Hofsjökull, Flugustaðatindur and Jökulgilstindar.

Geldingafell For some serious trekking, tackle the six-day return trip to Geldingafell hut, which sits beneath the north-eastern edge of Vatnajökull between the Lónsöræfi and Fljótsdalur headwaters. The trip begins along the Tröllakrókur route and continues up the same valley onto the lonely moors south-east of the mountain, Snæfell. The hut, at 820m elevation, accommodates 10 people. From Geldingafell, you can continue on to Snæfell in a couple of days (see Snæfell in the East Iceland chapter).

Vesturhorn It's possible to walk around Vesturhorn on a day hike. The Vesturhorn route follows the west bank of the Fjarðará, until it empties into Papafjörður. From there, follow the shore (which is indistinct in places) to the cape at Papaós and on to the Stokksnes 4WD track. There you can either return to the Ring Road, just below Almannaskarð, or continue to the lighthouse and NATO radar station on Stokksnes spit.

Although actual walking time is just a few hours, allow an entire day, as there are lots of side routes and you may have trouble hitching to and from Stafafell. All surface water here percolates into the sand, so no water is available on the spit.

Jökulgilstindar This two-day trip climbs up to the 1313m-high icecap Jökulgilstindar. Begin by walking from Stafafell up the 4WD track along the eastern bank of Jökulsá í Lóni then continue up the valley through the Austurskógar woods toward Hnappadalur.

You can either continue up to the headwaters of Hnappadalur or climb Jökulgilstindar to the base of the glacier.

Other Routes Another hike is the one or two-day trip up Endalausidalur, from the western foot of Almannaskarð, and down the eastern bank of Laxárdalur í Hornafjörður. Other possibilities include the two day trip up Laxárdalur í Lóni, through Reipsdalur and down Hoffellsdalur back to the Ring Road. Or you can ascend Skyndidalur and skirt the glacier tongue of Lambatungnajökull then descend along Hoffellsdalur. The Stafafell hostel can provide information and directions for these and other hikes and routes.

Organised Tours
Lónsöræfaferðir (☎ 478 1717), at the Stafafell Youth Hostel, arranges 'recommended horse tours and 4WD excursions into Lónsöræfi. Hikers' jeep transfers to Illikambur cost Ikr1500 one way and Ikr2700 return (including about three hours at Illikambur). Transfers to Austurskógar, over the Skyndidalsá river crossing, cost Ikr700 one way. Short horseback tours cost Ikr1200 per hour; rates for longer trips depend on the length of the trip and number of people. Fishing trips and permits can be arranged on request.

From 20 June to 7 September at 9 am, one-day jeep and hiking tours run from Höfn and include 4WD transport up the Jökulsá í Lóni and a three-hour guided hike from Illikambur, through a loop past Múlaskáli hut, Kollumúli and Viðidalur. This trip costs Ikr5135 or four Highland Pass vouchers. Contact Guðbrandur Jóhannssoon (☎ 478 1799), in Höfn.

Places to Stay & Eat
The friendly and cosy *Stafafell Youth Hostel* (☎ 478 1717; fax 478 1785) ranks among the nicest in Iceland, and you'll never forget the hospitality here, thanks to the efforts of Mr Bergsveinn Ólafsson. Accommodation is in either the 19th-century farmhouse or two new summerhouses, all with access to

cooking facilities. The hostel costs Ikr1000/1200 for HI members/non-members, camping is Ikr300 per person and single/double farmhouse accommodation is available for Ikr2500/3600. Eight-bed self-catering cabins with shower and television cost Ikr4000. A full breakfast is Ikr600 and dinners range from Ikr700 to Ikr1300.

On Álftafjörður, at the mouth of Geithellnadalur, is the farm *Múli* (☎ 478 8949), which has simple sleeping-bag accommoda-tion, with cooking facilities, for Ikr1300. The speciality is horse-riding, and it can arrange one or two-day horseback tours through Geithellnadalur.

Getting There & Away
All buses between Höfn and Djúpivogur or Egilsstaðir pass Stafafell. To board the bus there, either flag it down at the gate or ask the Stafafell warden to book it for you.

Central Iceland

Iceland's vast, barren interior comprises one of Europe's greatest wilderness areas, and although it isn't a true desert – it receives far too much precipitation for that – it's as close as you'll get anywhere in Europe. Historically, interior routes were used during summer months as short cuts between the northern and southern coasts. It was a region which existed only as a barrier between where one was and where one wanted to go, and early travellers put it behind them as quickly as possible.

Even today, travelling in Iceland's uninhabited centre isn't like travelling anywhere else in the country. There are practically no services, accommodation, bridges or guarantees should something go awry. In some cases, there isn't even a road. Gazing across the expanses, you could imagine yourself in Tibet, Mongolia or, as many people have noted, on the moon. The Apollo astronauts even held exercises here in preparation for their lunar landing.

Weather is always a concern. Conditions can be fickle and snow isn't uncommon even in the summer months of July and August. I've experienced whiteout blizzards at Kverkfjöll; simultaneous sand and snowstorms driven by 50 knot winds at Askja; and a horizontal rain of ice cubes in Kaldidalur – and those were all in July! Good warm clothing and protection for the face and eyes from gritty, wind-driven sand are particularly important.

Notwithstanding the elements, this area features some of Iceland's best trekking routes, most notably the Landmannalauggar to Þórsmörk trek.

If you're driving, it's recommended that vehicles travel in pairs, so if one gets bogged, the other can drag it out or fetch help. Carry lots of supplies, especially if you can scarcely afford to take one vehicle, let alone two! For more on driving in the interior, see Car & Motorcycle in the Iceland Getting Around chapter.

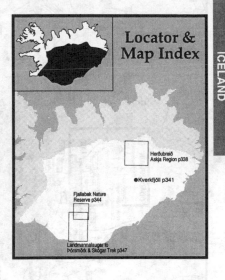

Locator &
Map Index

Interior Routes

KJÖLUR ROUTE

The name of the Kjölur Route, which crosses the central highland desert, means 'keel' and refers to the perceived shape of the topography. At its highest point, the track reaches 700m as it passes through the 30-km-wide valley between the Langjökull and Hofsjökull icecaps. The Kjölur Route is greener and more interesting – and passes through less inhospitable territory – than its counterpart, the Sprengisandur. However, it was historically the less popular of the two, thanks to the general belief that it was infested by particularly fearsome outlaws.

Hveravellir

Hveravellir, the 'hub' of the Kjölur Route, is a geothermal area of fumaroles and multi-coloured hot pools. Among them are

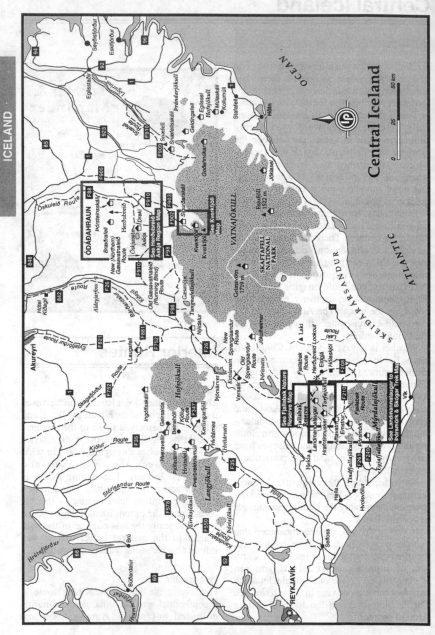

Central Iceland

Bláhver, a brilliant blue pool; Öskurhólhver, Hveravellir's largest hot spring; and Eyvindarhver, named after the outlaw Fjalla-Eyvindar. Hveravellir is reputedly one of the many hideouts of this ubiquitous character who spent much of his life outdistancing pursuers across the Icelandic interior. On a small mound near the geothermal area are the ruins of a shelter where he is believed to have holed up with his wife, Halla, and their family during one 18th century winter.

Services at Hveravellir include a petrol pump and a new Ferðafélag Íslands *hut*, which accommodates 40 people. The hut has cooking facilities and there's a hot pool just a few metres away. This makes an excellent break on a Kjölur crossing and is the end of the Kjölur Trek (see later in this section).

Hofsjökull

The 995 sq km Hofsjökull icecap, east of the Kjölur pass, is the third largest icecap in the country. A caldera, or collapsed magma chamber, has been recently discovered beneath it.

Geirsalda

Near the highest point on the Kjölur Route, at 670m, is a view disc and a monument to Geir Zoëga who died in 1959. He served as president of Ferðafélag Íslands for over 20 years. The site is known as Geirsalda ('Geir's Crest').

Beinahóll

The rather spooky name of this hill at the edge of the Kjalhraun lava flow, near Geirsalda, means 'bone hill'. The story goes that in October 1780, a party of four men and a flock of sheep set out to cross Kjölur from Skagafjörður. They realised it would be difficult so late in the year, but decided to have a go anyway. When bad weather set in, they decided to hole up until the weather system passed, but it was three weeks before there was any change and by then, all had perished.

Icelanders believe that Beinahóll is haunted by the victims of this unfortunate incident (this presumably includes the sheep), and that to remove any of the bones or disturb the site is to invite permanent bad luck. If you should hear ominous bleating in the night ...

Kerlingarfjöll

Kerlingarfjöll ('witch mountains') are considered the most 'alpine' of all Iceland's ranges, and the highest peak Snækollur rises to 1482m. Until 150 years ago, Icelanders believed that these peaks harboured the vilest sort of outlaws, and that in the heart of the range existed a deep and isolated Shangri-la type valley where these loathsome characters operated a clandestine outlaw society. People were so frightened by the prospect of encountering them that Kerlingarfjöll wasn't explored until the mid-19th century.

Skíðaskólinn í Kerlingarfjöllum The summer ski school (☎ 852 4223), at Ásgarður, near the base of imposing rhyolite peaks, has seven rope-tows from 200 to 700m long, a campground, mountain hut, petrol station, swimming pool and jacuzzis. One km from the ski slopes is a long valley full of roaring hot vents and billowing steam, which are quite beautiful amid the ice and snow. The skiing may not be world class, but it's a beautiful spot and has a unique off-season appeal.

The slopes open as soon as the Kjölur Route becomes passable and don't close until the snow is gone, which is normally in early August or later. Ásgarður lies seven km from the slopes, so skiers must catch the morning bus (Ikr350).

Ski equipment rental costs Ikr1150 per day (Ikr700 for skis and poles and Ikr450 for boots). Full/half-day lift tickets are Ikr900/600 and Ikr1500 for an entire weekend (Friday afternoon to Sunday afternoon). Group ski lessons cost Ikr700/1200 for half/full-day or Ikr2000 for an entire weekend. Private lessons cost Ikr1500 per hour. You can use the jacuzzis for Ikr300 per session and snowmobile transfers to the slopes are Ikr500.

ICELAND

Places to Stay & Eat At the *ski hut* (☎ 852 4223), there's a snack bar that has light meals and basic accommodation. Sleeping-bag accommodation with breakfast is Ikr2000. For guests, set breakfast and lunch menus are Ikr800 and Ikr600 respectively, and dinner ranges from Ikr800 to Ikr1200. Camping costs Ikr350 per person. Two-day packages, including transport from Reykjavík, meals and sleeping-bag accommodation cost Ikr10,000. Book through BSÍ in Reykjavík.

Hrútafell

The relatively tiny 10 sq km icecap, atop the *móberg* peak Hrútafell ('ram's mountain') rises over 700m above the surrounding landscape. From the Kjölur Route, as soon as Hrútafell comes into view, look on the eastern side of the road for a cairn shaped exactly like a Hershey's Kiss!

Hvítárvatn

The pale blue lake Hvítárvatn ('white river lake') is the source of the glacial river Hvítá. A glacier tongue of Iceland's second largest icecap, Langjökull, calves into the lake and fills it with icebergs.

In the marshy grasslands north-east of Hvítárvatn is *Hvítárnes hut*. Built in 1930, it was Ferðafélag Íslands' first hut. Oddly, the hut is another Kjölur site believed to be haunted, this time by the innocuous spirit of a young woman. If a female camper sleeps in one particular bed, it is said she will dream of the ghost carrying two pails of water. Still, don't be put off breaking your trip in this idyllic and isolated setting. The hut has space for 30 people but no cooking facilities. From the Kjölur road, where the bus will drop you, it's an eight km walk along the 4WD track to the hut.

For information on snowmobile and skiing trips on Langjökull, see Kaldidalur in the West Central Iceland chapter.

Kjölurvegur Trek

The easy and scenic Kjölurvegur trek, which follows much of the historic Kjölur Route (west of the present route), runs from Hvítárvatn to Hveravellir, via the Hvítárnes,

Þverbrekknamúli and Þjófadalir *huts*. From the Hvítárvatn turn-off, it's eight km along the 4WD track to Hvítárnes hut. The marked route is easy to follow and huts are three to five hours apart.

The route can be done in three days at a leisurely pace. Access is via the Kjölur bus, but remember to reserve a seat for the day you want to be picked up. This trek can also be organised by BSÍ for Ikr10,920 per person, including transport from Reykjavík or Akureyri, hut fees and a map.

Organised Tours

There's a fine line between scheduled buses and organised tours on this route, but technically, the daily Kjölur buses between Reykjavík and Akureyri are scheduled, and include rest stops, but no sightseeing or photo stops. However, the Kjölur Route is also done as a guided tour from Akureyri on Wednesday and Saturday at 8.30 am. This costs Ikr7410, or three/six Highland Pass vouchers with/without Omnibuspass.

Places to Stay

Ferðafélag Íslands maintains *mountain huts* at Hvítárnes; Hveravellir; Þverbrekknamúli, eight km west of Innri-Skúti hill; Þjófadalir, 10 km south-west of Hveravellir; and Hagavatn, near the southern end of Langjökull and about 15 km off the Kjölur Route by 4WD track. All these huts have outdoor pit toilets but no running water or cooking facilities. At the Hagavatn hut, the surface water situation is unpredictable, so you may have to carry water or melt snow.

Getting There & Away

Most travellers opt for the scheduled BSÍ buses, which leave Reykjavík and Akureyri daily at 9 am. The one from Reykjavík stops briefly at Gullfoss and Geysir, makes a 30 minute lunch stop at Kerlingarfjöll and a 10 minute break at Hveravellir before continuing to Akureyri. The bus from Akureyri makes the same stops, but in reverse.

The normal fare is Ikr5265 or four Highland Pass vouchers; with Omnibuspass, you'll pay just Ikr1200 or one Highland Pass voucher. With the Hringmiði (ring pass), you can replace the Akureyri-Reykjavík portion of the Ring Road with the Kjölur Route and pay only the Omnibuspass fare. Since the stretch between Reykjavík and Akureyri isn't the Ring Road's most interesting section, this isn't a bad option.

Of all the interior routes, the Kjölur is probably the best suited to cycling and hiking.

SPRENGISANDUR ROUTE

The Sprengisandur Route (F28), crosses the pass between Tungnafellsjökull and Hofsjökull at over 800m elevation. The name 'Sprengisandur' refers to the desert moors that lie around the northern end of this 20 km saddle. It may be less interesting than Kjölur, but does offer some wonderful views of Vatnajökull, Tungnafellsjökull and Hofsjökull, as well as Askja and Herðubreið from the western perspective.

Sprengisandur is to Icelanders what the Santa Fe Trail is to Americans, and the name conjures up cowboy images of outlaws and long sheep drives across the barren wastes. The historical route, which is now abandoned, actually lies a few km west of the current route.

Skagafjörður Approach

The 81 km Skagafjörður access (F72) to the Sprengisandur Route connects southern Skagafjörður with the F28, near the lake Fjórðungsvatn 20 km east of Hofsjökull.

Its main site of interest is Laugafell, an 890m mountain with some nice hot springs bubbling on its north-west slope. There's a 15-bunk Ferðafélag Íslands hut and a beautiful geothermally heated pool. The hut is open in summer but there are no cooking facilities. Some stone ruins near the springs are reputed to be from an old dwelling.

Eyjafjörður Approach

The road from southern Eyjafjörður (F82) connects up with the Skagafjörður road at Laugafell. For information on sites of interest along this route, see Upper Eyjafjörður in the Akureyri chapter.

Bárðardalur Approach

The route through Bárðardalur follows Route 842, which turns into F48 and carries on across Sprengisandur through 240 km of inhospitable territory all the way to Þjórsárdalur (it meets up with the other two approaches about halfway through). It was used historically by the clergy from the southern bishopric at Skálholt when travelling to visit their flock in eastern Iceland. This is the route used by the BSÍ Sprengisandur tours.

In upper Bárðardalur, halfway between Goðafoss and Aldeyjarfoss, is the remote Hótel Kiðagil (☎ 464 3290). Rooms cost Ikr2470/3900 for singles/doubles and sleeping-bag accommodation is Ikr1170. It's open 20 June to 1 September.

Aldeyjarfoss

One of Iceland's most photogenic waterfalls, Aldeyjarfoss, flows over a layer of intriguing basalt columns on the Skjálfandafljót (the 'shivering river') in upper Bárðardalur. More basalt patterns can be seen in the shallow canyon above the falls. Sprengisandur bus tours between Mývatn and Reykjavík (but not those terminating in Akureyri) make a photo stop here.

Nýidalur & Tungnafellsjökull

Nýidalur, sometimes known as Jökuldalur, was only discovered in 1845. With a campground, two Ferðafélag Íslands huts and lots of hiking possibilities, it makes a great break in a Sprengisandur journey. The huts, which accommodate up to 160 people, both have kitchen facilities and cooking implements, and are open from 1 July to 31 August. Nights are particularly chilly hereabouts – it has something to do with the 800m elevation – so bring good warm gear.

Although there aren't any hiking tracks per se, the hiking is great. Soft options include strolling up the relatively lush Nýidalur valley or wandering up the 150m hill east of the huts for a wide view across the desert expanses. A more challenging day hike will take you up to the colourful Vonarskarð pass, a broad 1000m-high saddle between Vatnajökull, Tungnafellsjökull, and the green Ógöngur hills. This route also passes some active geothermal fields. Other possibilities include day walks to the base of Tungnafellsjökull or across the vast desert landscape east of Nýidalur.

Innra-hreysi

Innra-hreysi, a lonely spot north of the Þjórsárver nature reserve along the Old Sprengisandur Route, harbours another of the outlaw Fjalla-Eyvindar's ruined shelters; this one is thought to date from 1772. They're certainly not worth the 23 km hike from Nýidalur but if you're walking or cycling the 48 km Old Sprengisandur Route between Nýidalur and Versalir, you'll go right past them.

Versalir

Iceland's most remote farm, *Versalir* (☎ 487 5078; fax 487 5278), is open from 1 July to 31 August. It lies on a bleak gravel plain along the Sprengisandur Road, north of Þórisvatn. Although farming isn't really viable here, there is a restaurant, petrol pump and accommodation. Made-up beds cost Ikr3650 and sleeping-bag accommodation is Ikr1365. Six-person cottages cost Ikr7800 per night. If you're arriving with a tour, be sure to ask the driver to drop you at the right place.

With a 4WD vehicle or enough energy to walk up the Old Sprengisandur Route, you can visit the worthwhile Þjórsárver nature reserve, in the grassy wetlands 25 km north of Versalir.

Þórisvatn

Before water was diverted from Kaldakvísl into Þórisvatn from the Tungnaá hydro-electric scheme, it had a surface area of only 70 sq km. Now it's Iceland's second largest lake at 82 sq km. It lies 11 km north-east of the junction between Route 26 and the Fjallabak Route. Sprengisandur tours pause here briefly to explain the hydroelectric configuration.

Hrauneyjar

In the Hrauneyjar region, west of Þórisvatn, is the *Hrauneyjar* (☎ 487 7782; fax 487 5278) guesthouse and restaurant, which sits in the bleakest position imaginable, but is readily accessible to many interior attractions. Single/double rooms cost Ikr2400/3850 and sleeping-bag accommodation is Ikr1700. They'll also arrange excursions to sites of interest, including the beautiful Dynkur waterfall.

Dynkur

A worthwhile 4WD excursion (or two to three-day hike) from Hrauneyjar will take you to the intriguing waterfall Dynkur, on the upper Þjórsá. It's a sort of Gullfoss-in-the-desert, but without the crowds and tour buses.

Veiðivötn

This beautiful area just north-east of Landmannalaugar (see under the Fjallabak Route) is an entanglement of small desert lakes in a volcanic basin, a continuation of the same fissure that produced Laugahraun in the Fjaliabak Reserve. This is a wonderful area for wandering and you can spend quite a lot of time following 4WD tracks which wind across the tephra sands between the numerous lakes. On the hill to the north-east is a view disc pointing out the various lakes and peaks.

Veiðivötn lies 27 km off the southern end of the Sprengisandur Road south of Þórisvatn. Unfortunately, the tours don't stop there and access from Landmanna-laugar is thwarted by the substantial river Tungnaá, so you'll need private transport to get there. At Tjaldvatn (the 'camping lake'), below 650m Miðmorgunsalda, is a *campground* with huts, but no meals are available. The area appears on the Landmælingar Íslands' map *Þórsmörk/Landmannalaugar* 1:100,000 (1986).

Organised Tours

There are a couple of variations on the Sprengisandur tour, which is operated by Guðmundur Jónasson Travel (☎ 511 1515;

fax 511 1511) in Reykjavík. From south to north, buses travel from Reykjavík to Akureyri on Monday and Thursday at 8 am. On Wednesday and Saturday, they end instead at Mývatn, a slightly shorter trip. From north to south, they depart only from Mývatn on Thursday and Sunday at 8.30 am.

Any of these tours costs Ikr7450, or six Highland Pass vouchers. With Omnibuspass, they're Ikr4500 or four Highland Pass vouchers. With the Full-Circle Pass, discounts are available only if you replace the Ring Road between Reykjavík and Akureyri with the Sprengisandur Route.

There also are three-day Highland Special tours, which travel from Reykjavík to Mývatn on the Sprengisandur Route, then continue to Akureyri and return to Reykjavík via the Kjölur Route. For five days sleeping-bag accommodation, including guide and full board, the charge is Ikr39,150. Alternatively, there's the three-day hotel-based Heartbreaker tours which follow the same route and cost Ikr29,180, including a guide, accommodation and half-board.

ÖSKJULEIÐ ROUTE

The Öskjuleið Route (the name means 'Askja way') leads to Herðubreið and Askja, the most popular wonders of the Icelandic desert. For much of the way, it follows the western bank of the Jökulsá á Fjöllum, meandering across tephra wasteland and winding circuitously through rough, tyre-abusing encounters with the 6000 sq km lava flow, Ódáðahraun ('evil deeds lava'). It then passes the oasis Herðubreiðarlindir, which presents a superb close-up view of Iceland's most distinctive mountain, Herðubreið (unless, of course, you're greeted by a wall of blowing sand, as is often the case).

From Herðubreið, the Öskjuleið wanders southward through dunes and lava flows past Dreki hut and up the hill toward Askja, where vehicles may be halted by deep snowdrifts short of the road's end.

As with all interior routes, the Öskjuleið is open only to 4WD vehicles, but it's still touch and go; sometimes you touch the pedal and only go deeper into the sand. Even the Askja Lunar tour has been known to get bogged!

Grafarlandaá
This tributary of the Jökulsá á Fjöllum is the first major stream to be forded on the southbound journey to Herðubreið and Askja. It has a reputation as the best tasting stream in all of Iceland – try it and see if you agree! The banks also make a nice picnic spot.

Herðubreiðarlindir
The grassy oasis of Herðubreiðarlindir was created by springs flowing from beneath the Ódáðahraun lava. This mini tourist complex six km from Herðubreið has a nature reserve information office, a *campground* and the Ferðafélag Íslands' *Þorsteinsskáli hut*. The hut, which accommodates 40 people, is open from June to August and has cooking facilities but no cooking utensils.

Behind the hut is another Fjalla-Eyvindar shelter; this one is scarcely large enough to breathe inside. It was renovated in 1922 on the remains of the original, which had long since collapsed. Eyvindar is believed to have occupied it during the hard winter of 1774-75, when he subsisted on angelica root and raw horse meat stored on top of the hideout to retain heat inside.

Four km downstream from Herðubreiðarlindir, the Jökulsá á Fjöllum is dramatically beginning to carve a brand new gorge. It's worth seeing and most tours stop for a quick photo session.

Travellers on the BSÍ Askja tours may get off at Herðubreiðarlindir and rejoin the tour on another day. Southbound, the bus passes at lunchtime and northbound, around 6 pm en route back to Mývatn. Kverkfjöll tours also pass, but only on their northbound leg.

Herðubreið
It has been described as a birthday cake, a cooking pot, a lampshade and other things, but the more sophisticated tourist industry likes to call it the 'Queen of the Icelandic desert'. Whatever you see in Herðubreið's oddly symmetrical shape, it's certainly a

ICELAND

ICELAND

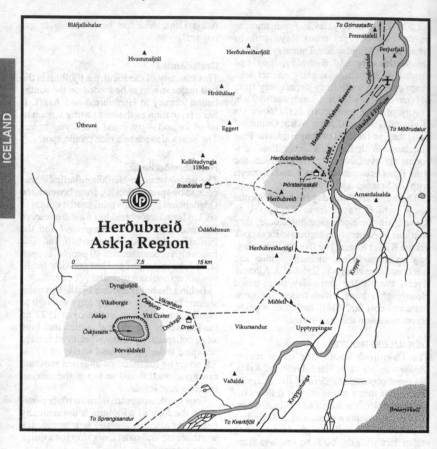

Herðubreið Askja Region

0   7.5   15 km

welcome view after all those kilometres of desert you've crossed to reach it.

If 1682m Herðubreið appears to have been made in a jelly mould, that's not far off base. It's another of the móberg mountains, the result of sub-glacial volcanic eruptions. In fact, if Vatnajökull was to suddenly be stripped of ice, Grímsvötn, Öræfi and Kverkfjöll would probably emerge looking more or less like Herðubreið.

Hiking The Landmælingar Íslands topo sheet for this area is Sheet 84, *Herðubreið* 1:100,000 (1986). If you don't require such

great detail, use sheet 8, *Mid-Austurland* 1:250,000.

From Þorsteinsskáli hut, a trail runs all the way around Herðubreið and can be hiked in a day. The mountain looks the same from all sides, so disorientation is a possibility, but if you remember that Kollótadyngja is west-north-west and Herðubreiðarlindir is east, orientation won't be difficult.

Under optimum conditions, Herðubreið can be climbed from Herðubreiðarlindir in a long day, but only because daylight isn't an issue in the Icelandic summer. The route to the top ascends the western slope, but it's

ICELAND

quite steep and snow or bad weather may render it impossible without mountaineering gear. It's best to climb in the morning, before the snow becomes slushy in the relative warmth of afternoon. From the base to the top takes three to 3½ hours each way. Note the two cairns on the rim, which are there to show you the start of the route back down. Don't go alone, prepare for the foulest weather imaginable, and you'll probably be fine. Also, remember to inform the attendant at Herðubreiðarlindir of your intentions.

Kollótadyngja

The 1180m peak Kollótadyngja, 10 km north-west of Herðubreið, is a textbook example of a shield volcano. Its broad shield-like cone oozed lava gently rather than exploded violently. At its base is the Ferðafélag Íslands' *Bræðrafell mountain hut*, which accommodates 16 people and has a coal stove but no running water. The best access is the trail leading west from the Herðubreið circuit.

Drekagil

The name of the gorge Drekagil, 35 km south-west of Herðubreið, means 'dragon ravine', after the form of a dragon in the craggy rock formations that tower over it. The canyon behind the Ferðafélag Íslands *Dreki hut* resembles something out of Arizona or the Sinai; bitter winds and freezing temperatures just don't suit this desert landscape!

The Dreki hut, which accommodates 20 people, is an ideal base for a day or two of exploring the area. Not only does the dramatic Drekagil ravine offer an easy stroll up to an impressive waterfall, you can also walk eight km up the road to Askja. There are no cooking facilities but it does have a stove for heating, and water is available from the river. Members/non-members of Ferðafélag Íslands pay Ikr450/750. Camping is also permitted, but the wind and cold can become oppressive.

At Dreki, the Gæsavatnaleið (F910) Route turns off the Öskjuleið to cross some intimidating expanses and connect with the Sprengisandur Route at Nýidalur. See under Gæsavatnaleið later in this chapter.

Dyngjufjöll

The stark Dyngjufjöll range, which shelters the Askja caldera and the Drekagil gorge, is what remains of a volcanic system that collapsed in on its magma chamber. Þórvaldsfell, the highest point along its southern rim, rises to an altitude of over 1500m.

This inhospitable territory may be intriguing but it isn't terribly inviting to the casual hiker. If you come to explore beyond the tracks and footpaths, make careful preparations and take due precautions.

You'll find overnight accommodation at the remote and basic *Dyngjufell hut*, west of the caldera. No running water is available. The charge is Ikr450/750 for members/nonmembers of Ferðafélag Íslands.

Askja

Askja shouldn't be missed. It's difficult to imagine what sort of forces created this immense 50 sq km caldera, but this cold, windy and forbidding place sets one to thinking about the power of nature and who's in charge and all that.

The cataclysm that formed the original Askja caldera happened not so long ago – in 1875 to be exact – when two cubic km of tephra was ejected from the volcano, making a mess as far away as mainland Europe. Activity continued over the next 30 years, culminating in another massive collapse of surface material, this time over an area of 11 sq km and 300m below the rim of the original. This new depression subsequently filled with water and became Öskjuvatn. What's most daunting is to realise that such cataclysmic events could be replayed at any time.

The deepest part of the collapsed magma chamber contains the sapphire blue lake Öskjuvatn, the deepest in Iceland at 217m. It's thought to have some hazardous quirks, possibly odd currents or whirlpools, as suggested by the 1907 disappearance of the two German researchers, Max Rudloff and Walther von Knebel, who'd taken a rowing boat onto the lake.

In the 1875 eruption, one active vent, near the north-eastern corner of the lake, exploded and formed the tephra crater Viti, which still contains a hot lake. Viti is an ideal temperature for swimming, but the route down is rather slippery.

Askja has erupted frequently over the last century and as recently as 1961 the vents at

Öskjuop near the road entrance to the caldera exploded and formed the Vikraborgir crater row.

Organised Tours

The most practical way to reach Askja is with the BSÍ Askja Lunar tour, which departs from Reykjahlíð (Mývatn) on Monday, Wednesday and Friday from 30 June to 14 July and 16 August to 31 August, and daily from 15 July to 15 August. The 15-hour tour is fairly gruelling by Icelandic standards and requires from 1½ to three hours walking, depending on the snow and road conditions. Carry strong footwear and lots of good warm clothing. At Viti, most people just strip off and jump in, but if you're shy, you may want to bring a swimming costume.

The price of Ikr5265 or four Highland Pass vouchers includes transport and guide only, so bring a lunch. Omnibuspass holders receive a 10% discount.

As always, you can leave the tour at Herðubreiðarlindir or Drekagil and rejoin it later. Tell the driver when and where you want to be picked up so you'll have a seat going back to Mývatn.

Öskjuvegurinn Hike Ferðafélag Akureyrar (☎ & fax 462 2720) organises hut-based hiking tours from Þorsteinsskáli hut at Herðubreiðarlindir, along the Öskjuvegurinn Route to Svartárkot, in upper Barðárdalur. The route runs via the huts at Brædrafell, Dreki, Dyngjufell and Stóraflesja. It takes you over the heart of the vast Ódáðahraun lava flow. With proper planning, this five-day trip may also be done independently.

GÆSAVATNALEIÐ

The 120 km Gæsavatnaleið (the F910), also known as the Austurleið (it doesn't pass anywhere near its namesake Gæsavötn), connects the Sprengisandur Route and the Öskuleið. It's not nearly as treacherous as it once was, as a new road has been built north of the old one and the largest river is now bridged. There's little traffic – maybe three to five cars daily in summer – but the scenery is tops. The road crosses vast lava fields and sandy stretches, and there are always high icecaps in the backdrop.

The bits over the lava fields are naturally slow going, so plan on 1½ days to drive it. If you report to the warden in Askja that you're going this way, the main concern will be that you don't camp along the way, as much of the route lies inside a nature reserve.

Old Gæsavatnaleið

If anyone tells you the Gæsavatnaleið is impossible, they're speaking of the old southern route, which is best known as the road followed by the escaping hero, Alan Stewart, in the thriller *Running Blind*, by Desmond Bagley. In fact, it's not really impossible, but as yet, no tour companies are willing to brave it and with the opening of the new Gæsavatnaleið, the route isn't even being maintained by use. As a result, this is one of Iceland's roughest journeys and should only be tackled in a hardy 4WD by those who know what they're doing.

Coming from the west, the track begins at Tómasarhagi, north of Nýidalur, then crosses maze-like lava fields, perennial snow patches and unbridged rivers to reach the welcome green oasis, Gæsavötn ('goose lakes').

Unfortunately, things don't get any easier. From Gæsavötn, the track climbs through deep sand and lava to the icy 1000m boulder-studded Trölladyngjuháls pass, with the black Dyngjujökull icecap (a spur of Vatnajökull encrusted with black volcanic sand) looming to the south and the dormant volcano Trölladyngja to the north. Glacial meltwater, snowfields, wind, snow and blowing sand are all possible hazards.

At this stage, the road turns north and levels out on the sandy and often soggy outwash plain of Vatnajökull. When the surface is not too warm, wet or dry, it's possible to proceed across this desert to Dreki hut on the Öskjuleið.

KVERKFJÖLL ROUTE

The 108 km Kverkfjöll Route (F98) connects Mödrudalur on the Ring Road with the Sigurðarskáli hut, five km from the Kverkfjöll ice cave. Along the way are several sites of interest, including the twin pyramid-shaped Upptyppingar hills near the Jökulsá a Fjöllum bridge and the Hvannalindir oasis where there is – you guessed it – another of good ol' Fjalla-Eyvindar's winter hideouts! He even constructed a rather high-tech (for those days) sheepfold at this one, so the sheep could visit the stream without having to face the elements. Hvannalindir lies about 30 km north of the Sigurðarskáli hut.

Kverkfjöll

Kverkfjöll is actually a mountain spur capped by the ice of Kverkjökull, a northern tongue of Vatnajökull. Through common usage, however, it has also come to refer to the hot spring-filled ice caves which often form beneath the western margin of the Dyngjujökull ice.

For hiking in this area, be sure to carry

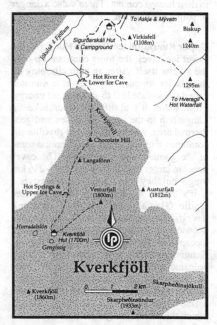

Kverkfjöll

plenty of water, as only silty glacier water is available higher up.

Lower Kverkfjöll Ice Caves

Besides being the source of the roiling Jökulsá á Fjöllum, central Iceland's greatest river, Kverkfjöll is also one of the world's largest geothermal areas. The 1½ km lower Kverkfjöll ice caves lie five km from Sigurðarskáli hut, a half-hour walk from the end of the 4WD track which turns off the Ring Road near Möðrudalur.

Here the hot river flows beneath the cold glacier ice, clouds of steam swirl over the river and melt shimmering patterns on the ice walls, and there you have it – a tourist attraction. Perhaps this was the source of the overworked fire and ice cliché that pervades almost everything ever written about Iceland. However, as we all know, fire and ice don't mix well, and huge blocks of ice frequently crash down from the roof. Don't enter the ice caves or you risk being caught in their heated combat. There's also a danger of sulphur inhalation.

Upper Kverkfjöll Ice Cave & Hut

From the lower ice caves, the tours continue up onto the glacier itself. After an hour climbing up the glacier tongue, they stop at a *nunatak* called Chocolate Hill to stoke up on energy. From there, it's a stiff 1½ hour hike up Langafönn to the upper ice caves and geothermal area, where sulphur and rhyolite silt combines with the steam heat to create some of the gooiest mud imaginable. The caves here are larger than the lower ones – 2½ km long – but they aren't quite as impressive.

It's then a 40-minute climb to the Icelandic Glacialogical Society's six-bunk *Kverkfjöll mountain hut*, at 1720m. There's no water or heating but it makes a viable icecap base. Nearby is the beautiful lagoon Gengissig, which was formed in a small volcanic eruption in 1961. Another hour beyond the hut will take you to the highest peak of western Kverkfjöll, at 1850m, with a fine view over the *kverk* (gap) through which the Kverkfjöll glacier passes.

Virkisfell

A one-hour marked hike from behind Sigurðarskáli hut will take you up Virkisfell ('fortress mountain'). At the top is an amazing natural bridge and a spectacular view over Kverkfjöll and the headwaters of the Jökulsá á Fjöllum. Follow the red sticks from the hut.

Biskupsfell

From Sigurðarskáli hut, a 3½-hour hike marked with yellow sticks leads to the peak of Biskupsfell ('bishop's mountain'). It's so called for the prominent spire on the top, which is said to resemble a bishop in full regalia.

Hveragil

There's a five-hour return hike from Sigurðarskáli hut to the 30°C hot river in Hveragil, where you can strip down and bath in a hot waterfall. The wardens at the hut can provide specific directions.

Organised Tours

Without a robust 4WD vehicle, the only way to visit Kverkfjöll is on a tour, and the most popular and easiest to join is the Ice & Fire Expeditions (☎ 464 2101) tour. The tours last three days from Akureyri, Húsavík or Mývatn. You must bring your own food, warm clothing and sleeping bag, and if you're camping, a sturdy tent. Hiking boots or other strong footwear are essential.

Tours run on Monday and Friday in July and August, departing Akureyri at 8.15 am, Húsavík at 10 am and Mývatn at 11 am. The tour costs Ikr12,500 (10% less with Omnibuspass), not including hut or camping fees, or it eats up nine Highland Pass vouchers (with or without Omnibuspass).

From Kverkfjöll, you can travel right across Vatnajökull to or from Jöklasel, near Höfn. Travel on the ice is by snowmobile or glacier buggy. This extension operates twice weekly from mid-July to mid-August and costs Ikr15,000. These trips are coordinated between Ice & Fire Expeditions and Jöklaferðir (☎ 478 1503; fax 478 1901), in Höfn. See under Vatnajökull Icecap in the South-East Iceland chapter.

Places to Stay

At Kverkfjöll, you can choose between the 70-bunk Ferðafélag Íslands' *Sigurðarskáli hut* or the *campground*, which consists of a few strips of turf laid on the gravel. The hut costs Ikr750/1150 for members/non-members of Ferðafélag Íslands and camping costs Ikr450 per person. A three hours walk up the Kverkjökull glacier is the more basic *Kverkfjöll hut*, which costs Ikr400/750.

Fjallabak Reserve & the Fjallabak Routes

The Fjallabak ('behind the mountains') Route (F208), north of the Mýrdalsjökull massif, is a spectacular alternative to the coastal route between Hella and Kirkjubæjarklaustur. It begins near the Sigölduvirkjun power plant on the Tungnaá and passes through the scenically diverse Fjallabak nature reserve to Landmannalaugar. From there, it continues east past the Kirkjufell marshes and enters Jökuldalur, then follows a riverbed for 10 km or so before climbing to the Herðubreið lookout and descending to Eldgjá.

For the next 40 km the road is fairly good but there are a couple of river fords, so conventional vehicles going to Eldgjá from the east may have difficulties during high water. At Búland, the route joins the F208 and emerges at the Ring Road south-west of Kirkjubæjarklaustur.

Organised Tours

The only public transport is the loosely defined BSÍ tour. This popular option runs daily from 1 July to 8 September (river conditions permitting). It departs from Reykjavík at 8.30 am and Skaftafell at 8 am, and makes short stops at points of interest along the way. The longest is an hour at Eldgjá for a walk to the fallen attraction, Ófærufoss. Both buses arrive at Landmannalaugar around 1 pm and leave at 2.30 pm.

Most travellers break this trip at Land-mannalaugar, which is advisable. The normal one-way fare, regardless of the number of stops, is Ikr5265 or four Highland Pass vouchers, and it's unquestionably worth the money. Holders of Omnibuspass (and Full-Circle Pass, provided the route takes the place of the Ring Road stretch) pay half price or two Highland Pass vouchers.

LANDMANNALAUGAR

If you're tempted to do the BSÍ Fjallabak tour from Reykjavík to Skaftafell in a single day, think again. Once you've seen Land-mannalaugar, you'll regret not allocating more time. The time allotted by the bus tour isn't enough for even a fleeting glimpse of what's there. Its magnificent rhyolite peaks, rambling lava flows, blue mountain lakes and soothing hot springs will hold anyone captive for several days!

Landmannalaugar lies 600m above sea level and comprises the largest geothermal field in Iceland outside the Grímsvötn caldera in Vatnajökull. The trademark varie-gated peaks of Landmannalaugar are composed of rhyolite, a combination of minerals metamorphosed by geothermal and volcanic activity. This activity is believed to have been centred on the Torfajökull caldera, 10 km south-east of the Landmannalaugar hut, but the most recent volcanic eruption occurred at the Veiðivötn fissure in 1480. In fact, this north-east to south-west tending crater row was the source of all activity between the Laugahraun and Ljótipollur craters.

Although Landmannalaugar gets quite chilly, the weather is generally more stable than in coastal areas, and when it does rain, it's more of a wind-driven horizontal mist than a drenching downpour. However annoying, it doesn't curtail outdoor activi-ties, and conditions can change literally from moment to moment.

Information

The Landmannalaugar hut wardens can help with specific questions, including directions and advice on hiking routes. There's a tourist information office at the junction of the F208

ICELAND

ICELAND

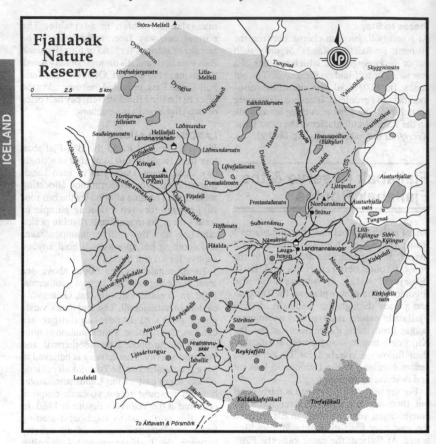

Fjallabak Nature Reserve

0   2.5   5 km

Stóra-Melfell ▲

Dyngjuhorn

Tungnaá

Skyggnisvatn

Vatnaöldur

Hrafnabjargavatn

Litla-Melfell

Dyngjur

Dyngjuskarð

Eskihlíðarvatn

Fjallabak Route

Herbjarnar-fellsvatn

Saúðaleysuvatn

Hellisfjall
Landmannahellir

Lóðmundur

Lóðmundarvatn

Hnausar

Hnausapollur
(Bláhylur)

Tjörvafell

Svartikrókur

Krókslljáhraun

Helliskvísl

Kringla

Langasáta
(792m)

Lifrafjallavatn

Dómadalshraun

Ljótipollur

Austurbjallar

Landmannaleið

Fitjafell

Khaldaklofsfjöll

Domadalsvatn

Frostastaðavatn

Norðurnámur
● Stútur

Austurbjalla-vatn

Tungnaá

Höfðavatn

Suðurnámur

Námskvísl

Lítli-Kýlingur Stóri-Kýlingur

Háalda

Laúga-hraun

Landmannalaugar

Norður Barmur

Kirkjufell

Vestur-Reykjadalir

Dalamót

⊚

Jökulgil

(Suður) Barmur

Kirkjufells vatn

Svartikambur

⊚ ⊚

Reykjadalir

⊚
⊚ ⊚
⊚

Störihver

Austur

Hrafntinnu-sker
⊚

Reykjafjöll

Ljósártungur

Íshellir

▲
Laufafell

Jökulgil

Jökultungur

Kaldaklofsjökull

Torfajökull

To Álftavatn & Þórsmörk

---

and the Landmannalaugar turn-off, but in numerous visits, I've never found it attended.

There's no petrol at Landmannalaugar, despite some maps which indicate that there is. If you're coming from the west, you'll need enough fuel to get you back to Hella should the road between Landmannalaugar and Eldgjá be closed by flooding.

Hot Springs

Just 200m from the Landmannalaugar hut, both hot and cold water flow out from beneath Laugahraun and combine in a

natural pool to form the most ideal hot bath imaginable. Don't miss it!

Landmannahellir & Lóðmundur

Before the religious community constructed a proper hut, the Landmannahellir cave served as an early travellers' shelter. The cave lies at the end of a turn-off from the Landmannaleið, which intersects with F208 (formerly F22) just north of the lake Frostastaðavatn. It's accessible only with 4WD or on foot.

The striking 1070m móberg peak Lóðmundur, near Landmannahellir, rises from rugged and colourful wilderness country. Like all móberg peaks, it was formed in a volcanic eruption beneath an earlier icecap. On foot, it's a hard going seven km south-west of the F208.

Hiking
Laugahraun & Brennisteinsalda
Laugahraun, the convoluted lava field behind Landmannalaugar hut, offers vast scope for exploration. Across it, the slopes of the rainbow-streaked mountain Brennisteinsalda ('burning stones crest') are punctuated by steaming vents and sulphur deposits. It's possible to climb to the summit for a good view across the rugged and variegated landscape.

If you're fit, the day tour across the Fjallabak Route allows just enough time to dash across Laugahraun and up to Brennisteinsalda, but you'll regret having to see it that way. There are many variations on this walk, and the rhyolite landscapes, hot vents and the peak itself are worth more than a glance. From Brennisteinsalda, it's another 90 minutes along the Landmannalaugar to Þórsmörk route to the impressive Stórihver geothermal field.

Frostastaðavatn The blue lake Frostastaðavatn lies behind the rhyolite ridge immediately north of the Landmannalaugar hut. A walk over the ridge will be rewarded with far ranging views as well as close-ups of the interesting rock formations and moss-covered lava flows flanking the lake. If you walk at least one way on the road and spend some time exploring around the lake, the return trip takes two to three hours. It's also possible to walk right around the lake; watch for divers and ducks around the shore.

Bláhnúkur The name of this big blue peak immediately south of Laugahraun means, strangely enough, 'blue peak'. If you like scrambling on ball bearings, you can climb right to the 943m summit, but the scree does get steep and slippery so watch your footing. The route is up the north-eastern ridge, across Grænagil from the Landmannalaugar

hut. Don't try to ford the river; there's a plank bridge just downstream from the mouth of the ravine. The easiest route back down passes below Brennisteinsalda and returns to the Landmannalaugar hut via Laugahraun.

Ljótipollur The incredible red crater lake Ljótipollur ('ugly pond') makes a fine day hike from Landmannalaugar and affords vistas of many types of terrain, from tephra desert and lava flow to marsh and braided glacial valley. Technically, Ljótipollur is a *maar* lake, or one which has been created in a volcanic explosion. Oddly enough, it's rich in trout.

Start by following the road from Landmannalaugar hut back to the T-junction and turn left. Here you can either cross the lava field and climb up the prominent south-pointing ridge of Norðurnámur or continue past the crater Stútur, where a walking track turns right and heads north-east along the southern slopes of a low ridge. The lake shore is best accessed along a walking track leading down from the northern rim.

After about one km, you'll reach an indistinct saddle, from where you can climb over the 786m peak Norðurnámur (which is worthwhile) or just traverse along its western base to emerge on the Ljótipollur road. A number of routes ascend to the crater rim, but the most interesting is probably the footpath which climbs its southernmost slope.

If you walk all the way around the crater rim, it's an 18 km hike which takes the better part of a day.

Tjörvafell & Hnausapollur Another good day walk from Landmannalaugar is around the peak Tjörvafell and the crater lake, Hnausapollur (also known as Bláhylur). Tjörvafell is a gravelly peak rising about 200m above the tephra desert and can be easily climbed for a good view.

Places to Stay
The Ferðafélag Íslands *hut* at Landmannalaugar accommodates 115 people on a first-come first-served basis, but in July and

August it's often booked out by tour groups and club members.

The once soggy and gravelly *campground* has been improved with a layer of turf to make it more amenable to tents. Because the hut and campground share facilities, on July and August mornings the toilet block resembles the London Underground. In case of emergencies, there are primitive toilets on the perimeter of the campground.

South-east of Torfajökull, at Strútslaug hot springs, Dick Phillips (the British tour company) has a *mountain hut* which is open to the public. However, apart from taking one of his tours, there's no easy access, and getting there involves walking along Hólmsárlón from the 4WD track, across the *sandur* north of Mýrdalsjökull or cross-country from Álftavatn. For details, contact Dick Phillips at the address under Organised Tours in the Getting There & Away chapter.

Getting There & Away

For information on tours, see Organised Tours at the beginning of this section.

Car & Motorcycle A non-4WD vehicle wouldn't have a hope of completing this route. If the rivers are low, a conventional vehicle could possibly reach Landmannalaugar from the west and Eldgjá from the east, but the route between the two would be impassable under any conditions.

Bicycle Because much of the Fjallabak Route is along rivers (or rather *in* rivers!), it's not ideally suited to mountain bikes. Lots of people do attempt it, but it's not casual cycling by any stretch. In places, the only way through is to wade across (or along) icy rivers carrying your gear and the bike on your back. If the weather has been dry it may not come to that – but don't count on it.

Hiking For details on hiking to Landmannalaugar, see the following section on the Landmannalaugar to Þórsmörk Trek.

LANDMANNALAUGAR TO ÞÓRSMÖRK TREK

The trek from Landmannalaugar to Þórsmörk is the premier walk in Iceland. In fact, it seems destined to someday join the Milford Track and the Inca Trail as one of the great walks of the world, so if you want to do it while it's still relatively unknown outside Iceland, you'd best hurry. The best map of the route is Landmælingar Íslands' *Þórsmörk/Landmannalaugar* 1:100,000 (1986). Trail information is available from the hut wardens at Landmannalaugar, Þórsmörk or Álftavatn, or at Ferðafélag Íslands in Reykjavík.

In the high season, the trek can be completed in three or four days by anyone in reasonable physical condition. Many people do it independently, but the tour companies Útivist and Ferðafélag Íslands both offer organised trips (see Organised Tours in the Iceland Getting Around chapter).

In most years, the track is passable for casual trekkers from mid-July to mid-September, although it can also be done on skis in the winter. Early in the season (early to mid-July), there is normally lots of snow and you may need crampons or ski poles to help with control on the steeper slopes. It positively bustles in July and August so, to avoid the crowds, consider walking it in early September when you'll have crisp weather and the chance to watch the northern lights from near-empty huts. This late in the year, however, some of the snow bridges across ravines may have collapsed, necessitating detours.

Most hikers walk from north to south to take advantage of the net altitude loss and the shower at the Þórsmörk hut. Many hikers don't stop at Þórsmörk – or stop just long enough for a shower – but continue along the Þórsmörk to Skógar track and make a five or six day trip of it.

Landmannalaugar to Hrafntinnusker

The route begins behind the hut at Landmannalaugar and crosses the Laugahraun lava flow before climbing into the rhyolite peaks and steaming vents at

ICELAND

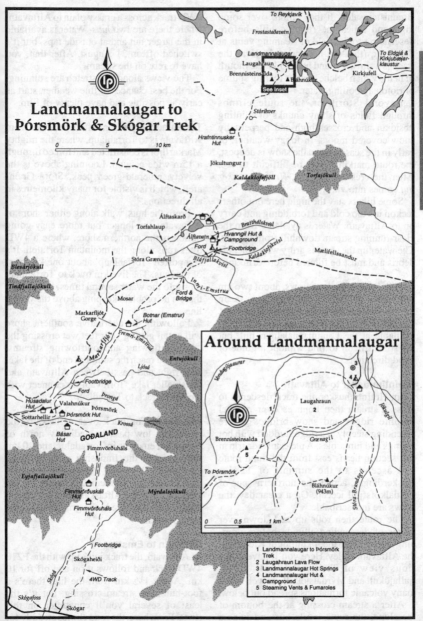

Landmannalaugar to Þórsmörk & Skógar Trek

0   5   10 km

To Reykjavík

Frostastaðavatn

Landmannalaugar
Laugahraun
Brennisteinsalda   Bláhnúkur

See Inset

To Eldgjá &
Kirkjubæjar-
klaustur

Kirkjufell

Störihver

Hrafntinnusker
Hut

Jökultungur

Kaldaklofsfjöll

Torfajökull

Álftaskarð

Torfahlaup

Bratthálskvísl

Álftavatn
Ford

Hvanngil Hut &
Campground

Footbridge

Stóra Grænafell

Bláfjallakvísl

Kaldaklofskvísl

Mælifellssandur

Blesárjökull

Tindafjallajökull

Mosar

Markarfljót
Gorge

Botnar (Emstrur)
Hut

Inni-Emstrúa

Ford &
Bridge

Fremri-Emstrúa

Markarfljót

Entujökull

Ljósá

Footbridge

Ford

Prongá

Húsadalur
Hut

Valahnúkur

Þórsmörk Hut

Þórsmörk

Sottarhellir

Krossá

Básar
Hut

GOÐALAND

Fimmvörðuháls

Eyjafjallajökull

Fimmvörðuskáli
Hut

Fimmvörðuháls
Hut

Mýrdalsjökull

Footbridge

Skógaheiði

4WD Track

Skógá

Skógafoss

Skógar

Around Landmannalaugar

Vondugljáaurar

Laugahraun

Jökulgil

Brennisteinsalda

Grænagil

Stóra-Brandsgil

To Þórsmörk

Bláhnúkur
(943m)

0   0.5   1 km

1 Landmannalaugar to Þórsmörk
   Trek
2 Laugahraun Lava Flow
3 Landmannalaugar Hot Springs
4 Landmannalaugar Hut &
   Campground
5 Steaming Vents & Fumaroles

Brennisteinsalda. It then climbs over some high and lonesome rhyolite hills before descending to the field of steaming vents at Stórihver, (the 'big hot springs'). Near the track is a sinister round hole – like the mouth of hell – which belches forth a roaring spume of riotously boiling water.

Beyond Stórihver, the route climbs through fields of shiny chunks of glinting obsidian and crosses high and perpetually snow-covered moors. In foggy weather, or early in the season when the snow is deepest, the route markings may be difficult to see. After the crest of the pass, *Hrafntinnusker hut* comes into view.

Some hikers stay the night here but others reckon it's too cold and forbidding and carry on to Álftavatn. Water is available from the clear-running stream downhill from the hut. The water up the slope is gritty with volcanic debris and must be filtered before drinking.

Íshellir Across the lava flows, about two km due west of Hrafntinnusker hut, is an impressive ice cave with geothermal activity. It's marked on the Fjallabak Reserve map available at the Landmannalaugar hut, but it's still difficult to find without a guide or good directions.

Hrafntinnusker to Álftavatn

From Hrafntinnusker, the track descends to cross a stream then bounces over parallel rhyolite ridges and snow bridges before ascending steeply to a ridge studded with hot springs and fumaroles. A pleasant side trip in this section heads east from the main route and ascends to the summit of 1281m Húskerðingur, across the northern spur of Kaldalkofsfjöll icecap. On a clear day, the views are indescribable.

The route then rolls up and down over ridges of descending altitude before dropping steeply from the Jökultungur Ridge into the Álftavatn valley. Here you'll have a glorious view of Tindfjallajökull, Eyjafjallajökull and Mýrdalsjökull, as well as the many volcanic formations spread out below.

After a stream crossing at the bottom of the slope, the route levels out and joins a

4WD track across a grassy plain to Álftavatn, where there are two *huts*. Water is available in the larger hut and at outside taps, but it's switched off on 31 August. After that, you have to rely on the stream.

The views along this stretch are stunning. For the best chances of fine weather, start as early as possible and have plenty of film.

Torfahlaup A pleasant afternoon hike from Álftavatn is to Torfahlaup, where the mighty Markarfljót is constricted and forced through a 15m-wide canyon. Looming above is the velvety, emerald-green peak, Stóra Grænafell, which is visible for many kilometres in all directions.

From the huts, walk along either shore of Álftavatn; the longer but more easy-going option is the northern shore, where a 4WD track runs along the mountain Torfafell. It's signposted 'Torfahlaup' about one km west of the huts. The five km track to Torfahlaup dips into the water several times, but on foot there's no problem keeping above the waterline.

Following the alternative southern shore will entail getting your feet wet crossing the lake's inflowing and outflowing streams. When you reach the southern end of the lake, bear right and pass between Álftavatn and the smaller lake, Torfavatn, to connect with the 4WD track to Torfahlaup.

Álftaskarð The track over Álftaskarð, the prominent low pass immediately north of Álftavatn, emerges in Torfadalur, and 20 km later reaches the imposing móberg peak, Laufafell. This road eventually connects with Route 26. Immediately south of the intersection of the Álftaskarð and Torfahlaup tracks, note the cave in the gruesome pinnacle just uphill.

Álftavatn to Emstrur

At Álftavatn, the track joins up with the F210 4WD track and follows it on and off for 10 km. About 1½ km from the hut, there's a foot-numbing stream crossing, but it's the least of several you'll encounter on this stage. From here, the road climbs steadily for several kilometres before dropping into the pleasant oasis Hvanngil where you cross a stream on two small footbridges.

Here there's a rather crude *sheep hut* with pit toilets and sleeping-bag accommodation in the loft (the sheep occupy the lower floor!) for Ikr650. Several hundred metres away is a *campground* with running water and flush toilets. Sites cost Ikr350 per person. From the toilet block, a short cut through the lava cuts about 500m off the road.

After rejoining the road, you cross the raging Kaldaklofskvísl on a footbridge. At the intersection on the southern bank, follow the route posted 'Emstrur/Fljótshlíð'. The left turning, which is the Fjallabak Syðra Route, goes to Mælifellssanður. Several hundred metres south of the intersection, you'll have to ford the knee-deep Blá-fjallakvísl.

The track then enters a lonely and surreal five km stretch of black sand and pumice desert, skirting the obtrusive pyramid-shaped peak, Stórasúla. The next barrier is the murky river Innri-Emstruá. The glacial torrent portion is bridged, but at times of high water – after rains or warm sunny periods – you'll still have to ford a knee-deep side channel.

Across the bridge, continue up the other side of the gully and at the crest, watch on your left for the signpost which reads 'FÍ Skáli'. Here, the track strikes off across the desert through some Sahara-like passes and desolate hills. After 1½ to two hours, you'll reach the *Emstrur hut* (also called Botnar, Skáli or Botnskáli).

Markarfljótsgljúfur A rewarding and requisite two km side trip from the Emstrur hut will take you to the Markarfljót canyon. Just as impressive as better known Jökul-sárgljúfur in North-East Iceland, this gaping green gorge will take your breath away. To get there, follow a direct south-west bearing from the hut. After one km, you'll see the canyon.

Emstrur to Þórsmörk
From Emstrur hut, the track crosses a small heath then drops steeply to cross the roiling Fremri-Emstruá on a small footbridge, just below the Entujökull glacier tongue. It then climbs slowly to a plateau that levels out and occasionally offers views of the Markar-fljótsgljúfur, just a few hundred metres west of the route. After dropping briefly to cross Slyppagil, a large, intimidating gorge containing an unexpectedly diminutive stream, the route levels off for several km of flat, easy walking.

The next landmark is the Ljósá ('river of light'), which is crossed on a footbridge at a point where the river squeezes through a two-metre-wide fissure. The view down to the water can be quite mesmerising.

Over the next hill is the unbridged river Þrongá, which must be forded. Unfortunately, the marked route doesn't cross at the easiest point so you may want to head upstream over the small hill and look for a better spot. If you're alone, be especially cautious and use a ski pole or other means of support when crossing – and don't look down!

The onward route on the opposite bank isn't obvious; look for a V-shaped ravine just west of the marked crossing point. There, the track enters the grassy birch and mushroom studded Þórsmörk woodland and, at this point, you're less than an hour from trail's end. When you reach a junction, the right fork leads to Húsadalur and the left fork to the Ferðafélag Íslands' *Þórsmörk hut*. Camping is restricted to a site near the hut.

For more on Þórsmörk or the continuing route to Skógar, see the South Central Iceland chapter.

Mountain Huts
Ferðafélag Íslands owns and maintains several *huts* along the route: at Landmanna-laugar, Hrafntinnusker, Álftavatn (two huts), Emstrur and Þórsmörk. The huts at Landmannalaugar and Þórsmörk, and the larger of the two Álftavatn huts, cost Ikr750/1150 for members/non-members of Ferðafélag Íslands. Hrafntinnusker, the smaller Álftavatn hut and Emstrur hut cost Ikr450/750. Only the more expensive huts

ICELAND

have running water and kitchen facilities (and Þórsmörk has hot showers!).

Due to the hike's popularity, it's wise to pay hut fees and pick up keys in advance through the wardens in Landmannalaugar or Þórsmörk, or through Ferðafélag Íslands in Reykjavík. Otherwise, you can take your chances on space availability and just turn up; there are wardens at Landmannalaugar from June to September, at Álftavatn in July and August and at Þórsmörk from May to September. However, Hrafntinnusker hut is unattended, so you'll need a key to get in.

Camping is permitted around any of the huts but wilderness camping inside the Fjallabak Reserve requires a permit costing Ikr400 per night. These may be purchased from the hut wardens at Landmannalaugar or Þórsmörk. The wardens at Álftavatn, which is outside the reserve, may also try to charge Ikr400 per person to camp around the lake, but unless you use the hut facilities, they have no right to charge and you're under no obligation to pay.

Other Treks

If you need more solitude than this trip can offer, there are lots of other routes through Fjallabak and around Landmannalaugar, Torfajökull and Eldgjá.

Unless your route-finding skills are particularly well honed, you may wish to join one of the popular Dick Phillips group treks; see Organised Tours in the regional Getting There & Away chapter. Ferðafélag Íslands and Útivist also run guided excursions in the region.

Getting There & Away

For access information, see under Fjallabak Route, earlier in this section. Access to Þórsmörk is described in the South Central Iceland chapter.

LANDMANNALAUGAR TO ELDGJÁ

East of Landmannalaugar, the F208 leaves Fjallabak Reserve and skirts the river Tungnaá as it flows past Norðurnámshraun. Although the Icelandic highlands are home to relatively few bird species, you'll often spot great northern divers, ducks and other water birds in the marshes and lakes around the foot of the 964m rhyolite peak Kirkjufell.

After dropping into Jökuldalir, the road deteriorates into a valley route along a riverbed and effectively becomes a 10 km long ford interspersed with jaunts across the odd sandbar or late snowfield. When it climbs out of the valley, it ascends the tuff mountain Herðubreið (not to be confused with the better known Herðubreið on the Öskjuleið), which affords a far ranging vista across the lowlands to the south.

ELDGJÁ

Geologically, Eldgjá (ELD-gyow; the 'fire gorge') is a volcanic rift stretching 40 km from Mýrdalsjökull to the peak Gjátindur. At its north-eastern end, Eldgjá is 200m deep and 600m across, with odd reddish walls that recall the fire for which it's named. The rift has erupted numerous times, most notably around the time of Settlement.

Although it's not as outwardly spectacular as you may expect, Eldgjá is quite intriguing and the name alone conjures up images of a malevolently mysterious and powerful place.

Ofærufoss

Until January 1993, the two-segment waterfall, Ofærufoss, was spanned in the middle by a natural stone bridge that appeared to have been lifted straight from the English countryside and plopped down in a most unlikely setting. Unfortunately, flooding and a particularly heavy load of snow that winter cost Iceland one of its most picturesque tourist attractions. If you want to see how it once looked, there are still lots of pre-1993 postcards and tourist brochures floating around out there.

The falls are on a tributary stream dropping from the northern rim of Eldgjá, an easy two km walk from the parking area. The track follows the southern bank but it's normally easy to wade across the river to the falls.

Hánípufit

In the green and fertile Hánípufit area, eight km south of the Eldgjá turn-off, the river Skaftá widens into an entanglement of cascades and waterfalls measuring 500m across in places. It's unusual and quite beautiful.

Places to Stay

At Lambaskarðshólar, west of the road near the Syðrifærá, is the mountain hut *Hólaskjól* (☎ 854 6011 or 487 4840; fax 487 4842). Here you'll find sleeping-bag accommodation for Ikr850 per person, hot showers and a campground. It's a great place to hole up for a couple of days.

Nearer the Ring Road is the farm *Flaga II* (☎ 487 1368), which has single/double accommodation for Ikr3000/4050.

Getting There & Away

See the description of the Fjallabak tour, earlier in this chapter.

FJALLABAK SYÐRA

The Fjallabak Syðra Route runs roughly parallel to the Fjallabak route. It begins at Fljótsdalur and passes north of the glaciers Eyjafjallajökull and Mýrdalsjökull to connect with the main Fjallabak Route at the river Kúðafljót. It allows access to the Landmannalaugar to Þórsmörk trek, and actually follows the route for 10 km, between Álftavatn and the river Innri-Emstruá.

There's no public transport along this route. It may appear tempting to walk or cycle from Fljótsdalur, but several substantial unbridged rivers would preclude that.

ICELAND

Facts about Greenland

It's said that once a traveller has seen the world, there's always Greenland, the big white island which dominates the top of the world map. Beyond Ilulissat and Kulusuk (the world's most unusual daytripper's dream) and the Disko Bay area, travellers will still find a bit of space between rucksacks. However, as a growing number of visitors are discovering this vast wilderness, anyone who's saving Greenland for last may not beat the crowds.

Greenland's rugged and dramatic landscape can be at times forbidding, and the country's diversity is expressed in subtle variations on Arctic conditions: rocky, treeless mountains; dry or boggy tundra; long, sinuous fjords; and expansive sheets and tortured rivers of ice. But what Greenland lacks in range, it makes up for in quality.

It's a challenge to describe this country. One can only repeat the words 'beautiful', 'spectacular', 'magnificent' so many times before they begin to sound flat and meaningless. Much of coastal Greenland meets the sea in towering cliffs, walls of glacial ice and ancient rock – the oldest on the planet. Away from the coast, the land lies locked beneath the original deep freeze, a 3000m thick blanket of ice. The seas, near which all the population is found, are just a couple of degrees above freezing, and are infested with mountains of floating ice.

Despite its small population of 55,000, Greenlanders call their home *Kalaallit Nunaat* (KHLAKH-let NOO-naht), the 'land of the people'. Greenlanders are proud of their country – or more accurately, enamoured with it. Travellers will find them both friendly and welcoming, and perhaps even a bit sympathetic – after all, foreigners didn't have the good fortune to inherit the place as a birthright. Travelling by boat between villages, you need only watch your fellow passengers to see their fascination with their surroundings. They gaze at the shore with the sort of reverence normally reserved for a wise and respected elder. As one Greenlandic poet put it, 'I get dizzy of all this beauty and shiver with happiness'.

Historically, the land never allowed the human population to grow larger than it was capable of supporting and the concept of cities and towns is a very recent one in Greenland. The capital and largest settlement, Nuuk, boasts a population of 14,000 and the next largest city, if plopped down in somewhere like Germany, wouldn't even merit inclusion on a road map.

The ancient Inuit culture left little evidence – no pyramids, palaces or temples – that it has been around for millennia. The greatest achievement of the Inuit people is that they have survived thousands of Arctic winters and thrived in a country that casual observers might regard as uninhabitable wasteland. That's unfortunately more than can be said for Greenland's Norse colonies, which lasted only a few centuries before mysteriously disappearing from the face of the earth.

Nowadays, little remains for polar explorers to discover, and Greenland, as a part of the Kingdom of Denmark, is facing the transition from a resourceful and independent past to a modern European present. Today it's a country of far-flung towns and villages, virtually none connected by road. Even so, people visit their neighbours by Mercedes in the summer and dogsled in the winter. In the supermarkets they buy pineapples from Hawaii, tomatoes from Mexico and frozen seal steaks from the nearest fjord. They live in 100-unit blocks of flats or in brightly painted Scandinavian bungalows, and for a living, they practise anything from law or word processing to fishing or seal hunting.

HISTORY
Inuit History
The Inuit (pronounced 'INN-ooit') people, sometimes called Eskimos ('eaters of raw meat' in Native American languages – this

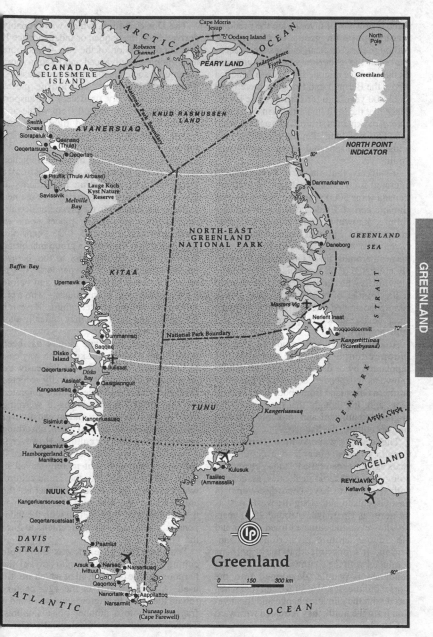

GREENLAND

name is now out of favour), are the predominant population group in Greenland. Although the American Indians are descendants of the Siberian peoples who are thought to have migrated into North America across the Bering Land Bridge some 25,000 to 23,000 years ago (or earlier) there is evidence that the Inuit first arrived in Alaska by *umiaq*, or skin boat, from 7000 to 8000 years ago. This was long after the presumed land bridge had disappeared beneath the Bering Strait.

It's likely that the first Greenlanders migrated from Ellesmere Island in northern Canada some 5000 years ago during a warm climatic period. Evidence of this Stone Age culture, known as Independence I (after Independence Fjord in Peary Land, north Greenland), has been uncovered only around the northernmost tip of Greenland. It probably consisted of no more than 500 nomadic individuals who eked out a meagre existence at the frontier of human endurance. These people sustained themselves by hunting polar bears, musk oxen, Arctic hares and other animals.

At this stage, there's evidence that the Independence I people were either supplanted by or developed into the culture known as Independence II, which inhabited northern Greenland from about 3400 to 2600 years ago. It's thought that they eventually migrated southward and probably replaced another culture, the Saqqaq.

The second wave, which came from Canada to west Greenland around 3800 years ago, has been called Saqqaq by anthropologists. Archaeological sites associated with the Saqqaq have been discovered in East Greenland and along the west coast as far north as Upernavik. Around 2500 years ago, however, the climate turned colder and the Saqqaq culture mysteriously disappeared. It's possible that they, perhaps combined with the southward-moving Independence II people, developed into the Dorset culture. It's also suggested that when faced with the climatic change and the invasion from the north, they retreated westward to Canada.

The Dorset culture, which was probably derived from the Saqqaq or Independence II – or a combination of the two – was more technologically advanced and lived in more communal societies than their predecessors. They carved weapons and artistic pieces from bone and ivory, used sleds to transport belongings and burned oil from whale and seal blubber for heat and light. For that reason, perhaps, this group thrived during the cooler climatic period.

However, recent finds of wooden kitchen tools, sewn garments and artistically ornamented bone hunting implements at Qeqertasussuk in the Disko Bay area seemed to throw a spanner into the preceding scenarios. Radio-carbon dating places some of these artefacts at around 4000 years old, suggesting that there was a group inhabiting the west coast slightly prior to the Saqqaq period – that is, before Independence II was thought to have migrated south and before the Saqqaq arrived from Canada – who were as advanced as the Dorset culture. Research is ongoing and the results may radically alter long-held theories.

Evidence of the Thule culture has been found from western Alaska all the way east to Greenland, indicating that the eastward migration was rapid. The generally accepted theory is that the Thule culture migrated directly from Canada during a warming trend in the 10th century and spread all over Greenland in less than 150 years, absorbing or supplanting all other cultures. However, it has also been suggested that Independence II didn't migrate south but merely stayed in place and developed into the Thule culture, which eventually moved south across the entire island. An alternative suggestion is that the Dorset culture met up with the Independence II in north-west Greenland to form the Thule culture.

Whatever the case, it was the Thule culture that developed the *qajaq* (kayak), the harpoon and the dogsled, all of which are still used. A climatic shift in the 12th century forced the Thule to migrate southward and it fragmented into a number of subcultures. There's conclusive archaeological evidence that the modern-day Greenlandic Inuit – known as the Inussuk culture – have descended from the Thule.

The Norse

The two main accounts of Norse history in Greenland are the *Grænlendinga Saga* or *Tale of the Greenlanders* and the *Saga of Eiríkur Rauðe*. Because they were written well after the fact, neither can be relied upon to tell the whole story. In some cases they even contradict each other but the sagas, combined with archaeological evidence, have allowed researchers to piece together much of the tale of the Greenland Norse.

According to the sagas, the first European discovery of Greenland was in 900 when an Iceland-bound Norwegian, Gunnbjörn Ulfsson, was blown off course. He came ashore at Gunnbjarnar Skerries near present-day Ammassalik on the east coast, then did an about-turn and returned to Iceland.

Early Icelanders had a tendency to get caught up in vicious family feuds involving generations of revenge killings. One so embroiled was Snæbjörn Galti, who avenged the death of a family member and, then, to avoid the court system and being declared an outlaw, decided to escape from Iceland and head for the western land reported by Gunnbjörn 78 years earlier. He gathered some companions and prepared to set off. Before they could leave, one member of their party recounted a dream he'd had of their intended venture, which is recorded in a passage that is one of the most poignant in the sagas:

I can see death in a dread place, yours and mine. North-west over the waves, with ice and cold and countless wonders...

Undaunted by the ominous warning, Snæbjörn and his companions set sail and landed at the icy fjord Bláserk, near Ammassalik. They built a hut just before the snows began to fall, intent on holing up for the winter. Snæbjörn, a fairly disagreeable character, took to quarrelling with his companions in their confined winter quarters,

and the predictable happened. The dream's prophecy came true, and only a couple of the party returned home alive.

Nearly a century later, Norwegian Eiríkur Rauðe Þorvaldsson, now known as Eric the Red, and his father were exiled from Norway after a rather bloody revenge killing. They fled to Iceland where they settled in the Laxdæla country of the north-west, but Eiríkur was again convicted of outlawry in 982 when he avenged the killing of two of his slaves, who had vandalised a neighbour's property. Rather than remain *persona non grata*, he left Iceland for Gunnbjörn's and Snæbjörn's land over the western horizon.

Like the others, Eiríkur first came ashore at Bláserk but considered the place unlucky after Snæbjörn's fiasco so he continued further down the coast. After rounding Cape Farewell, he landed on a small island, modestly naming it Eiríksey ('Eiríkur's isle'), and settled in for the winter. The following summer, he continued further up the nearest fjord, Eiríkur's fjord, and found some tolerable country reminiscent of north-west Iceland. Eiríkur took the best plot of land for himself, naming it Brattahlíð ('steep hillside') and built his farm.

In 986, Eiríkur returned to Iceland to share the news of his success and report that the new country, *Grænaland*, was rich, fruitful and ripe for settlement. This was, of course, a bit of an overblown assessment, but as the *Saga of Eiríkur Rauðe* puts it:

The land he discovered he called Greenland because he said it would attract people if the country had a beautiful name...

'Green' may not be the first word that springs to mind when one arrives there, but the ploy worked and Eiríkur left Iceland with 25 ships loaded with prospective colonists, 14 of which actually survived storm, doubts and trepidation to land and settle. People continued to arrive and when all the amenable land had been settled in the Østerbygd or 'eastern settlement', as Eiríkur's colony was later known, people moved several hundred km up the coast to near the site of present-day

Nuuk, establishing the Vesterbygd or 'western settlement'.

Eiríkur's wife Þjóðhildur had converted to Christianity and, in her enthusiasm for her new religion, she had a church built at their farm. Eiríkur's refusal to convert outraged Þjóðhildur, who refused to sleep with a pagan husband. It was fortunate for Leif Eiríksson, who introduced his mother to Christianity, that he had already been born, because Eiríkur never converted and Þjóðhildur never relented. Perhaps that's the source of his nickname, 'Leif the Lucky'.

At their peak, the Greenland colonies included some 300 farms with around 5000 inhabitants who, though not exactly thriving, successfully ran sheep, cattle and hogs, and hunted seals, caribou, walrus and polar bears.

In 1261, Greenland was annexed by Norway (a year before the same thing happened to Iceland) and a trade monopoly, which limited the colonies to trade only with Norway, was summarily imposed. The agreement was that two ships would visit annually with supplies and carry locally-made goods back to Europe. Unfortunately, a notable cooling trend in the late 13th century caused glaciers to advance. Animals died, the seas choked with ice and shipping became impossible. To compound matters, the port of Bergen – where Greenland-bound cargo was loaded – was destroyed by the Hanseatic League in 1392, preventing traffic from leaving Norway in any case.

By the 15th century, the Greenland colonies were left with no link to the outside world and a century later, they'd disappeared without a trace. The last report from the Østerbygd is from 14 September 1408, when a wedding took place at the Hvalsey church between a Greenland colonist and an Icelander whose ship had gone astray. Once married, they returned to Iceland to provide a detailed account of the event.

About what happened to the colonies, there are several hypotheses, but few clues. Based on a 1379 report of a skræling attack on the Vesterbygd, some believe the colonies were destroyed by the Inuit, who may have felt threatened by the newcomers. It's unlikely, however, that they had the means or the demeanour to totally obliterate the colonies, and this theory hasn't gained much of a following. Other suggestions include a devastating climatic change, a scourge of caterpillars which destroyed the grazing lands, a massive epidemic, inbreeding, emigration to North America, absorption into the Inuit community and kidnapping by English pirates.

Several inconclusive shreds of evidence seem to support this last theory. In 1448, Pope Nicholas sent an epistle to Irish bishops recounting that the Greenland colonies were plagued by heathen barbarians and that around 1418, some church properties had been destroyed and many inhabitants taken as slaves. It was fairly clear, however, that only a portion of the colonies had been affected.

Furthermore, in his diary, Poul Egede, the son of Greenland apostle Hans Egede, reported an Inuit legend about repeated raids by pirate ships. Although the Inuit and the colonists together resisted the onslaught, many people and much property were lost. It is unlikely, however, that the entire population could have been obliterated in this manner, and the disappearance of the Greenland colonies remains one of the great mysteries of history.

The North-West Passage

In the late 16th century, speculation about a possible North-West Passage, linking Europe with the far East, was reaching fever pitch. In 1575, Martin Frobisher, outfitted by entrepreneur Michael Lok, sailed from London, across the Atlantic, up the west coast of Greenland and into the Canadian archipelago. Believing that he had found the gateway to Asia on Baffin Island, he picked up a stone and returned home.

This set off the second great scam in North Atlantic history. Lok, hoping to attract investments, decided that his souvenir contained gold-bearing ore. A second expedition resulted in three shiploads of worthless mica,

Wrong-Way Bjarni & the Norse Discovery of America

The first Norse seafarer to sight the North American coast was Bjarni Herjólfsson, an Icelander who'd set off to visit family in Greenland and was blown off course. Instead, he came upon a hilly and wooded land. Disgusted at having missed Greenland, he turned about and left without disembarking. (Had he gone ashore, perhaps a statue of Bjarni Herjólfsson might now grace the lawn of Hallgrímskirkja in Reykjavík.)

As it happened, Leif Eiríksson, the son of Eiríkur Rauðe, was overcome with curiosity about this new land – and the description 'wooded' sounded particularly alluring in treeless Greenland. He set off on an expedition and managed to visit places he called Helluland (the 'land of flat stones', probably Baffin Island), Markland (the 'land of woods', or Labrador) and Vinland (the 'land of wine').

The whereabouts of Vinland has never been conclusively determined, but it became the site of the only known Norse colony in North America. This rather half-hearted attempt at colonisation didn't mesh well with the American natives, who were dubbed *skrælings* ('those wrinkled by the sun') and the project was abandoned.

According to the solar reckoning described in the sagas, Vinland would have been roughly between the latitudes of Boston and Washington in the present-day USA. However, modern archaeological research has revealed that the Vinland colony was probably further north at L'Anse aux Meadows (originally L'Anse aux Meduses, 'jellyfish cove'), Newfoundland, which has now been named a UNESCO world heritage site. ■

which were assayed in Britain by the unscrupulous Lok as high-value ore. The fraud wasn't discovered until after a third voyage, which resulted in the loss of a ship and 40 sailors.

Despite that, Greenland suddenly became the flavour of the month. In 1585, John Davis, a humble but skilled navigator, set off toward the Greenland coast in two small ships, the *Sunneshine* and the *Mooneshine*. On this and his two subsequent voyages, he managed to establish a rapport with and gain the esteem of the Greenlandic Inuit. He closely observed their customs, and wrote the first ethnographic study of the Arctic peoples. He also took prodigious notes on Greenland's topographic features, currents, vegetation and wildlife.

Thanks to the search for the elusive North-West Passage, later voyagers augmented the growing store of North Atlantic knowledge in Europe. In 1607, Henry Hudson explored the east coast of Greenland and went on to discover Jan Mayen Island. On his third voyage, in 1610, he discovered the vast Canadian bay which is named after him (assuming it was the Pacific Ocean), but as a result of mutiny he was set adrift, never to be seen again.

After Thomas Sutton in 1612 and William Baffin in 1615 unsuccessfully searched for the North-West Passage, the British Admiralty decided to offer a £20,000 reward for its discovery. Although the race heated up, the following 200 years saw little headway toward the prize.

In 1818, however, Lieutenant William Parry embarked on a three-year voyage which took him as far as McClure Strait, further west than anyone had been before, but he was turned back by impenetrable pack ice. Other explorers made their bids for the prize, but in 1854, Robert McClure finally succeeded by doing the route from west to east. He entered the Arctic from the Bering Sea, spent two years beset by ice at Banks Island, walked to Dealy Island near Parry's 'furthest west' and sailed home to England with Sir Edward Belcher, who was attempting the route from east to west.

Christianity & Trade Monopoly

After the Danish absorption of Norway in 1380 and the disappearance of the original Norse colonies, it was 300 years before Europeans again attempted to colonise Greenland. In fact, after Norway's trade monopoly had failed so miserably, European awareness of the island had dwindled to practically nil. In the late 16th century, encouraged by speculation about a North-West Passage to the East Indies, interest in the place was revived.

Whaling has historically been an important economic venture in Greenlandic waters. During the late 16th century, with the first rumblings about a North-West Passage, whaling nations discovered the rich waters of Davis Strait between Greenland and Baffin Island. For two centuries, up to 10,000 men arrived annually on Danish, Norwegian, British, Dutch, German and Basque whaling vessels to hunt in the Arctic waters. Many of them came ashore, leading to interbreeding with the Greenlandic people.

In 1605, the Danish king Christian IV sent an expedition to Greenland and claimed it for Denmark. The first renewed attempt at permanent European colonisation, however, came in 1721 when the Danish granted Hans Egede permission to establish a trading post and Lutheran mission. Egede's original plan was to find the Norse colonies, which he was sure had reverted to paganism during the intervening years, but having no luck, he decided that Inuit souls were also valuable.

His first mission, on the island of Håbets Ø, established what Denmark considered colonial 'grandfather' rights to Greenland. The mission was relocated to the present site of Nuuk (formerly Godthåb, 'good hope') in 1728. Five years later, a Moravian mission was also set up in Godthåb. Both were successful at converting the native Greenlanders to Christianity, and overturning local notions that hell was a cold place and that seals, rocks, shrubs and icebergs all had immortal souls of their own.

By 1776, Denmark decided to play its hand with Greenland and impose a trade monopoly, administered by the Royal Greenland Trade Department, as it had done earlier in both Iceland and the Faroes. While other monopolies failed in the 19th century, Greenland remained closed to non-Danish shipping and trade until 1950.

Further Exploration

With the North-West Passage conquered, Arctic exploration turned towards new goals: reaching the North Pole and exploring the icy Greenlandic interior. In the late 1800s, the goal of every Arctic expedition was to reach a 'furthest north' which was further north than any previous expedition had reached, especially those that had been sponsored by other nations. The USA, it seemed, was the most enthusiastic pursuer of this issue.

In 1883, the USA sent Adolphus Greeley to Ellesmere Island (Canada) to set up a base at Fort Conger and carry out scientific research. Greeley, not content with such a mundane task, sent an expedition led by Lieutenant James Lockwood up the west coast of Greenland to beat the previous furthest north record held by the British. Although they surpassed it by four nautical miles, it was deemed a negligible victory. Unfortunately, the supply ships sent to provision Lockwood didn't appear for two years and 16 of his 25 men died of starvation on Ellesmere Island.

Perhaps the most renowned Arctic explorer was American Robert Peary, who 'discovered' the fictitious Peary Channel in north Greenland in 1900 and reached the North Pole in 1909. A confused and insecure man, he believed that respect and self-worth came only with success and renown. He went alone to the Pole, he said, because no other person he knew deserved to share in the acclaim. It was later suggested that he went alone because he never really went at all, but this issue has been fairly conclusively settled in his favour.

In fact, Peary was bothered more that Frederick Cook (who was known to have faked several claims, most notably the first ascent of Alaska's Mt McKinley) claimed to have reached the pole 12 months before himself than by his error about Peary Channel. Unfortunately, Peary's mistake was only corrected at the cost of the 1907 Mylius-Erichsen expedition, a Danish-Greenlandic mapping and surveying crew, which had been counting on his reckoning.

A Greenlander from Ilulissat, Jørgen Brønlund, aged 29, made his mark in history by leaving the famous note which revealed the party's fate:

Perished 79 fjord after attempting to return across inland ice in November. I arrived here in waning moonlight and could go no further due to frost-bitten feet and darkness. The others' bodies will be found mid-fjord off glacier (about 2½ leagues). Hagen died 15 November, Mylius about 10 days later. Jørgen Brønlund.

A different sort of explorer was the Norwegian Fridtjof Nansen, known as the first European to cross Greenland's inland ice. Apparently not overly confident of his capabilities, Nansen decided to begin on the barren east coast and travel towards the populated west, thereby preventing himself turning back. The trip across Greenland began on 15 August 1888 and was successfully completed on 26 September. Nansen was also known for his theory of ice drift in the Arctic which he proved by constructing a ship, the *Fram*, allowing it to freeze into the drift ice, and following its path through the Arctic Ocean. In 1922, he was awarded the Nobel Peace Prize for his work with prisoners of war and refugees after WWI.

The most beloved of the Greenland explorers was Knud Rasmussen, who was born in Ilulissat in 1879. He combined his explorations of Greenland and the North American Arctic with ethnological studies of all the Inuit tribes in the region, collecting their literature, songs and mythology. He crossed the icecap by dogsled in 1912 and, in 1921, embarked on his crowning achievement – an expedition from Upernavik (Greenland) to the Bering Strait (Alaska) – tracing in reverse the ancient Inuit migration routes and comparing the various cultures he encountered along the way. This expedition was described in the journal *Across Arctic America*, published in 1927. Greenlanders now refer to Knud Rasmussen as 'Kununnguaq' (little Knud).

Recent History
Although Denmark had officially claimed

The Greenlandic Flag
The Greenlandic flag was designed by local artist Thue Christiansen, who intended it to represent the sun, the sea, the inland ice and the icebergs. It consists of a half-red and half-white circle on a rectangular half-white and half-red background and is the first Scandinavian flag to stray from the Nordic cross motif. It is used interchangeably with the Danish and Faroese flags and may also be flown in Denmark or the Faroes. ∎

Greenland in the 1600s, the issue of Danish sovereignty over the island was dredged up by Norway in 1924. Norway felt that the discovery of East Greenland by Icelanders prior to the Danish-Norwegian union entitled them to it, especially since the issue hadn't been broached at the time of confederation. The matter was taken before the international court in The Hague in the early 1930s, which resulted in the granting of Danish sovereignty over the entire island.

In 1940 Hitler occupied Denmark and in early 1941, before the US had officially entered the war, the US military moved into Greenland and set up bases at Søndre Strømfjord (Kangerlussuaq), or 'Bluie West Eight', and Narsarsuaq, or 'Bluie West One', as well as a number of meteorological, reconnaissance and refuelling stations around the island. Søndre Strømfjord was not only a meteorological station, as claimed, but also operated as a way station for trans-Atlantic bombers and cargo shipments.

The Narsarsuaq base was originally a supply base for Greenland and later served as a way station for Allied aircraft crossing the Atlantic. According to the Danish/American agreement, it should have been run down after WWII, but due to a perceived Communist threat, it remained operational well into the Cold War. In 1958, after its usefulness expired, all the military surplus was sold to Norway and the site destroyed and abandoned.

In 1953, Greenland became a county of

GREENLAND

Denmark and Greenlanders acquired full Danish citizenship. After 20 years, however, they were ready for more autonomy and pressed for increased responsibility in domestic affairs. On 1 May 1979, the county council was replaced by the Landsting (parliament) and the Landstyre (Home Rule government), but Greenland also retained two representatives in the Danish parliament. The Royal Greenland Trade Department (KGH), which had been responsible for trade and mercantile activities, was replaced by Kalaallit Niuerfiat (the ubiquitous KNI) to handle all trade matters and the government infrastructure.

In late 1990, Premier Jonathan Motzfeldt responded to allegations of misuse of public funds by calling an election for March 1991. As a result, Siumut retained power by Motzfeldt was successfully challenged for the party leadership by Lars Emil Johansen.

GEOGRAPHY & GEOLOGY

When most people think of a typically Danish scene, they don't normally imagine towering peaks, glaciers and icebergs – but then, few realise that Greenland comprises 98% of the land area in the Kingdom of Denmark. With an area of 2,175,600 sq km and a 40,000 km coastline, Greenland is the world's largest island – over 2½ times the size of the second-largest island, New Guinea, and 52 times the size of mainland Denmark.

Greenland is the northernmost country in the world. Its southernmost point, Cape Farewell (Nunaap Isua), lies at 59° 45' north latitude while the northernmost point of the mainland, Cape Morris Jesup, is at 83° 20' north. Oodaaq Island, a tiny scrap of rock off the north coast, is the world's most northerly land at 83° 40' north.

Although Greenland is vast, 1.8 million sq km (that's all but 375,600 sq km of the total area) lies beneath a sheet of ice up to 3000m thick – a burden so great that the island's interior has sunk beneath its weight into an immense concave basin which reaches a depth of 360m below sea level. This vast ice sheet, which can often be seen from trans-

Atlantic flights, measures 2500 km from north to south and up to 1000 km from east to west. It contains over four million cubic km of ice, which amounts to one billion litres of water for every person on earth.

Around its edges, the icecap spills down in thousands of valley glaciers, which have sculpted the coast into deep fjords and dramatic landscapes. The largest, the Humboldt Glacier in the north-west, measures 120m high and 80m wide. If Greenland were to melt, global sea level would rise an estimated six metres and many of the world's coastal cities might look more like Venice.

All but the southern quarter of Greenland lies north of the Arctic Circle. In the far north, the sun is visible for nearly three months during the summer but nowhere on the island is there darkness between late May and mid-July. During mid-winter, southern Greenland experiences several hours of real daylight. On the Arctic Circle, which passes just south of Kangerlussuaq, the sun doesn't rise at all on 21 December. The far north experiences true polar night with several

How the Greenland ice Cap was formed

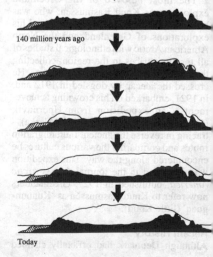

140 million years ago

Today

weeks of constant darkness and two months of little more than a hazy twilight before the sun returns and builds up to its summer marathon.

Greenland's nearest neighbour is Canada, whose Ellesmere Island lies only 26 km away across Kennedy Channel from the north-west coast. At its nearest point, Iceland is about 300 km away across Denmark Strait and Svalbard (Norway) lies about 500 km east of the north-east coast.

Geologically, Greenland and Iceland could scarcely be further apart. While Iceland's landscape is the world's youngest and most dynamic, Greenland's is the oldest yet discovered – you need not be a geologist to wonder at its compressed, scraped, ground and tortured surface. The Illua formation near Nuuk dates back at least 3.7 billion years (the earth itself is thought to be around 4.6 billion years old!) and when the airport was constructed at Nuuk, the tarmac was blasted out of metamorphic rock that had been around for over three billion years.

CLIMATE

As you'd expect, Greenland isn't as warm as most places. Fortunately, the continental effect gives it a more stable and extreme climate than Iceland and the Faroes have. In summer, maximum daytime temperatures average between 10 and 18°C in the south and between 5 and 10°C in the north but with the normally windy conditions, you'll prob-ably need a jacket or pullover even on the warmest days.

In winter in the far south, temperatures of -20°C can be expected but, further north and on the ice, the legendary bitter temperatures of the Arctic become reality. It's not unusual for the thermometer to hover at a chilling -40°C for weeks. The good news is that the coldest days are also the clearest and calmest, and the seemingly unearthly beauty of such an Arctic winter day (or night!) is indescribable.

At times, the south-western coast blocks warm air masses moving up from North America and captures storm systems which seem to hang on for days before raining themselves out. This is especially true around the Nuuk area, which experiences Greenland's foulest weather. Occasionally, south Greenland also sees enduring bouts of wet and windy conditions. Even on calm summer days, fog is common around all the coasts, especially in the far south, but it frequently lifts before noon, or doesn't roll in until late afternoon.

In short, bear in mind that Greenland is an Arctic country and the weather could do anything at any time; in July, you may see anything from snow to 25°C in the shade.

FLORA & FAUNA
Flora

Arctic vegetation is fairly limited and typi-cally stunted. In sheltered areas around

GREENLAND

A Summer Night's Dream

On my second day in Upernavik, it started to snow, and it wasn't just a friendly flurry. In fact, it snowed for two days, and at night it got cold enough for the snow to build up and remain on the ground and the roofs. I had to convince myself that it really was the 25th of July.

I put on my warmest sweater and went outside; the Friday night seemed almost surreal. It was nearly midnight and local people were walking up and down the main street, apparently aimlessly. Some were carrying plastic bags containing bottles bought at one of the three kiosks (small evening shops that thrive on selling beer). Others were sheltering in porticoes, try to chase away the boredom with beer and shouts. Believe it or not, they were even drinking in the entrance to the police station. Meanwhile, all the dogs in town were howling – perhaps the weather had reminded them of the hard labour of the winter season. The light of the midnight sun was being filtered by snow clouds and gave the sky an ethereal yellowish grey luminescence. Just another Upernavik summer night...

Frank Smits, Netherlands

Qaqortoq and Narsarsuaq, there are stands of dwarf birch, alder, juniper and willow. In late summer, the lowland areas of the south are carpeted with the beautiful national flower, the rosebay or *niviarsiat*, which means 'young maidens' (also known as broad-leaf willow herb or dwarf fireweed). Other flowering plants that splash their colours across the landscape include chamomile, dandelion, harebell, buttercup, gentian, saxifrage, Arctic cotton (whose Greenlandic name means 'like a hare'), Arctic poppy and many more.

Boggy tundra and dry tundra vegetation are also found in abundance: huckleberries, crowberries and lowbush cranberries, as well as miniature flowering plants, mosses, sedges, lichens and grasses.

Fauna

Due to the harsh conditions, Greenland's fabulous Arctic wildlife is necessarily sparse, and you may see larger land mammals only at Kangerlussuaq, where caribou and musk oxen are abundant.

Musk ox

Other prominent mammal species include polar bears, lemmings, Arctic hares, Arctic wolves and Arctic foxes. The foxes come in two colours: those on the inland ice are white, while coastal dwellers have blue-grey coats.

The musk ox populations are concentrated at Kangerlussuaq, in South-West Greenland, and in the North-East Greenland National Park. Musk oxen resemble American bison but their nearest relatives are actually the Rocky Mountain goat and the European chamois. The barren ground caribou *(Rangifer tarandus)*, often called 'reindeer', are smaller than but taxonomically identical to the caribou of north-western Canada and Alaska. In Canada, they've been known to breed with domestic European reindeer, which are considered a subspecies.

Although polar bears wander throughout Greenland and often make appearances in Nanortalik ('the place of bears') and Ammassalik, they're always welcomed to the human realm with both barrels. The North-East Greenland National Park is now open to the public, but access is difficult and expensive, and you'd probably have more successful polar bear spotting in either Svalbard or Churchill, Manitoba (Canada).

Numerous marine mammals inhabit Greenlandic waters. Among them are many species of whales. Common cetaceans include the pilot whale, fin whale, sei whale, minke whale, orca (killer whale) and humpback whale, and visitors see them regularly from coastal ferries.

There are also several species of porpoise, as well as the beautiful and unusual beluga, or white whale, and the narwhal, which is known for the spiral tusk that protrudes from its upper jaw. The tusk is normally unique to the male but has also been noted in females on rare occasions.

Common pinnipeds include walrus, ringed seals, hooded seals, bearded seals, spotted seals and harp seals. The harp seal, whose Latin name *Pagophilus groenlandicus* means 'ice-lover from Greenland', is one of the mainstays of the Inuit diet, and is of increasing value to the Greenlandic fur

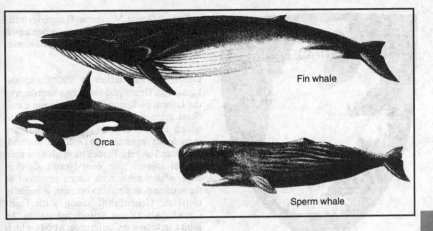

Fin whale

Orca

Sperm whale

industry. In many cases, harp seal hunters take the meat and sell the skins to the Qaqortoq tannery.

Fish are abundant in both fresh water and salt water. The lakes and streams abound with trout and Arctic char. Although Greenland has only one salmon stream (Kapisillit, near Nuuk), the seas are rich in Atlantic salmon, as well as over 100 other fish and shellfish species, making Greenlandic waters some of the world's richest.

Although Greenland is not considered a prime birdwatching destination, 52 bird species breed on or near the shores. Among them are cormorants, puffins, guillemots, murres, eider ducks, sea eagles, dovekies, buntings, skuas, kittiwakes, ptarmigans and swans. There are also four birds of prey: the snowy owl, sea eagle, peregrine falcon and gyrfalcon.

As for insects, mosquitoes, midges, no-see-ums and other annoyances are most prominent, but there's also the odd butterfly to brighten the scene.

National Parks

Greenland has only one national park – but it's the world's biggest! The remote North-East Greenland National Park is home to musk oxen, polar bears, caribou, Arctic wolves, foxes, hares and a variety of delicate plant life. For more information, see the East Greenland chapter.

GOVERNMENT & POLITICS
Government

Until 1953, Greenland was a colony of Denmark, but a constitutional change in that year gave it county status, with the same relationship to Denmark that Alaska has to the USA. Greenlanders were given full Danish citizenship and all the rights and privileges of Danes on the mainland.

The Faroe Islands received Home Rule in 1948 and in the 1970s, Greenland began rumbling about the possibilities of a similar set-up at home. In 1978-79, the Greenland Home Rule Act of the Danish parliament, confirmed by a referendum in Greenland, turned it into a self-governing overseas administrative division of the Danish realm. After a further referendum in 1982 and negotiations until 1985, Greenland, though part of Denmark, opted out of the European Union.

Currently the Landstyre or Home Rule administration has jurisdiction over such matters as organisation of home rule and local government, culture, telecommunications, housing, taxation, education, foreign trade, transport, public works, renewable resources, conservation and environmental

GREENLAND

Greenland Coat of Arms

Danish Queen Margrethe II remains official head of state, and has been represented in Greenland since 1993 by High Commissioner Bjarne Pedersen.

Other Representation In addition to the Landsting, Greenland elects two members to the Danish Folketing. It also sends an unofficial delegation to the Nordic Council, in which both it and the Faroe Islands are regarded as separate from Denmark. Iceland, Greenland and the Faroes have also set up a special alliance, the West Nordic Conference, which deals with issues pertinent to these three Scandinavian outliers, especially tourism. Greenland, along with Inuit Canada, Alaska and Russia, belongs to the Inuit Circumpolar Conference, a body which deals with Inuit interests in the respective countries.

Judicial System

Greenland's judicial system includes only lower courts and travelling judges. Higher-level cases must be heard in Denmark. Greenland is not, however, subject to the Danish criminal code and has a unique penal system which avoids imprisonment or other negative punishment of criminal offenders. It instead subjects them to fines, counselling sessions and, in the most severe or repeated cases, reform centres. This system is based on the traditional Inuit method of child-rearing and has thus far proven relatively successful. The most serious offenders are sent to zero-security reform centres, but go about their business pretty much as usual. It is not uncommon, for example, for several convicted criminals, including murderers (while Greenland has only 80 burglaries a year, there are 10 to 12 cases of manslaughter annually) to be permitted to go hunting (armed!) with an unarmed guard.

protection, public health, hunting, agriculture and religion. These responsibilities are divided between seven branches, each of which is headed by an elected member. One branch could be loosely defined as an executive body whose director, Lars Emil Johansen, serves as the head of the Home Rule government.

All other responsibilities – foreign relations, defence, security, currency and most of the judicial system, are left to the Danish government, policy and law.

Greenland is divided into 18 *kommuner* or municipalities; in addition to the main towns, there are 80 smaller district villages which range in population from 60 to 600.

Legislative & Executive Branches Legislative responsibility belongs to the parliament, or Landsting, which meets three times annually and is comprised of 31 seats, which are elected every four years by residents of individual legislative districts. After the general vote, the Landsting elects the premier, or head of government, and the cabinet (Landstyre), which is comprised of six ministries.

Politics

Political Parties After the March 1995 elections, members of five parties were elected to the Landsting by 70% of the 38,500 registered voters.

The strongest party, with 38.5% of the

vote and 12 seats, is Siumut ('Forward'), a moderate socialist or centre-left party that favours Greenlandic autonomy while remaining within the Kingdom of Denmark. Atassut ('Solidarity') promotes closer ties with Denmark and has 10 seats, with 29.7%. Inuit Ataqatigiit (the 'Inuit Brotherhood') is a Marxist-Leninist party that advocates giving up home rule for complete independence; it has 6 seats and 20.3% of the vote. The Issittrup Partii ('Polar party') promotes minimalisation of both Danish and Home Rule government economic controls and increased privatisation of business. After the 1991 election, the conservative Centre Party won two seats and was represented for the first time.

Currently, Greenland is ruled by a centre-right coalition of the Siumut and Atassut parties, and the current premier is Siumut's Lars Emil Johansen, a former teacher.

Political Issues The main political issues in Greenland are its relationship with Denmark, fishing rights and international relations. Some 500 Greenlanders per year study in Denmark, most in engineering, medicine, and psychology – and most return to Greenland after their studies.

Currently, 8000 Danes live in Greenland, providing most of the high-school teachers and 75 of the country's 85 doctors. In 1995, in response to a budget surplus (due mainly to a 20% rise in shrimp prices), Denmark threatened to cut its annual budget subsidy by 97% (approximately US$500 million). Premier Lars Emil Johansen retorted with 'one has to be prepared that Greenland will one day cut its ties with Denmark'. He added that 'we do not exclude a modification of the Danish constitution governing our relations. Each time I meet young educated Greenlanders, I think we are nearer to independence, but independence is a sensitive issue.'

Fishing rights are a perennial issue of dispute between Greenland, Canada, Iceland and the European Union. In 1995, Greenland agreed to allow EU vessels to fish Greenlandic waters for an annual fee of US$50 million. Iceland prevents Danish vessels fishing in the waters between Greenland and Iceland and has even forced Danish trawlers out of the area. Each year, halibut quotas are agreed upon between Greenland and Canada but inevitably, allegations of cheating frequently arise from one side or the other.

ECONOMY

Since the 1960s, Greenland – with Danish collaboration – has developed into a modern welfare state, in which traditional hunting, weapons, navigational technology and communications have been replaced by Western technology. Nearly all manufactured and consumer goods, machinery, food, animals and petroleum products are imported from Denmark and subsidised to keep prices more or less on a par with those on the mainland.

Nowadays, Greenland's living standards are comparable to those of mainland Europe, and although the economy has been in decline since 1989, Greenland's annual gross national product is about US$1 billion (half provided by Danish subsidies). In spite of its protectionist approach toward its fisheries, Greenland's largest trading partners are Denmark, Norway and the USA, in that order. Official unemployment figures are currently below 10% and the ultimate goal of all financial policy is economic independence from Denmark.

Fishing

While the public sector accounts for two thirds of employment, Greenland's real economy is predictably based on fishing and related industries, and approximately 200,000 tonnes of fish are taken annually in Greenlandic waters, about 25% by foreign vessels. Currently, the most lucrative catch is shrimp, followed by prawns, halibut and redfish. The greatest fishery is off the west coast, inside the 200-mile zone awarded in 1977. Processing is increasingly done aboard ship or on shore prior to export.

Other significant fisheries include salmon, capelin, haddock and cod, but in the past four decades, cod stocks have virtually disappeared. This is partly due to a 2°C drop in sea temperatures, but also to overfishing.

GREENLAND

The Home Rule administration owns about a third of the trawlers operating in Greenland but most fishing is done from private trawlers. To ensure future stocks, each species is regulated by a quota. Since three quarters of Greenland's fishery income is dependent upon shrimp, the Greenlandic economy got a considerable boost in 1995 when shrimp prices rose by 20%.

Subsistence Hunting

Special dispensations have been allowed by the International Whaling Commission (IWC) regarding what it calls 'aboriginal subsistence whaling', which it defines as 'whaling for purposes of local consumption carried out by or on behalf of aboriginal, indigenous or native peoples who share strong community, familial, social, and cultural ties related to a continuing and traditional dependence on whaling and the use of whales.' In northern and eastern Greenland, 80% of the economy is based on subsistence hunting and fishing, but moving south, the proportion drops until it reaches about 20% in far southern Greenland.

The most recent annual quotas, for 1995 to 1998, allow Alaskan Natives 51 bowhead whales; the Russian Inuit, 140 grey whales; and Greenlanders, 19 fin whales and 115 minke whales off West Greenland and 12 minke whales off East Greenland.

In fact, whaling and sealing are perennial points of contention between Greenland and other countries. Foreign environmental groups, particularly Greenpeace, have effectively destroyed the sealskin market in Europe and North America. Greenpeace has now admitted that it made a mistake in the case of Greenland and has withdrawn objections to subsistence hunting (except in the case of endangered species), suggesting that Greenland cultivate new markets in Asia and South America. However, many Greenlanders still react bitterly towards the organisation and its sympathisers.

Agriculture & Mining

Fishing will always be an economic mainstay, but Premier Lars Emil Johansen hopes for Greenland to develop economic diversity based on other raw materials and tourism. The former is dominated by sheep farming (South Greenland has 60 sheep farms supplying both local and export markets), agriculture and mining – specifically oil, gas, zinc, and gold (in 1996, the *Mining Journal* devoted an entire supplement to Greenland).

The recently discovered Fylla offshore oil and gas fields, 160 km from Nuuk, may compare to Norway's North Sea fields. Exploration rights are now being sorted out, but it will be five to 20 years before they're on line. Canadian companies have discovered zinc and gold reserves around Nanortalik, but the profitability of extraction doesn't look good.

Tourism

In 1995, Greenland attracted around 15,000 tourists, and this is projected to rise to 35,000 by 2002. Infrastructure is being improved, but most ventures seem to concentrate on low volume, high cost tourism while Greenland's wilderness and natural attractions are crying out to active lower-budget travellers. Cruises are actively courted, particularly for Nanortalik, Disko Bay and Uummannaq, and among other new tourism projects is a US$90 million ski resort at Apussuit, near Maniitsoq.

POPULATION & PEOPLE

Greenland's population currently stands at around 55,000. Of these, 80% are Inuit or mixed Danish and Inuit, and the remaining 20% are of European extraction, mainly Danish. Most Greenlanders live on the west coast, although there are isolated communities on the east coast and in the far north. The capital and largest city, Nuuk, has around 14,000 people.

EDUCATION

Greenland has the same educational standards as the rest of the Kingdom of Denmark: education is free and compulsory for nine years from the age of seven. Primary school children attend school in their home towns and villages, while secondary education is

The Greenlandic National Dress

The beautiful Greenlandic women's national dress is fairly consistent from region to region, but some details do vary. A standard feature is a light red, long-sleeved cotton or silk anorak – flower-patterned for younger women and plain for older women – with decorated sleeves, beaded black skin wristbands and a colourfully striped or checked silk waistband. The collar is made of black skin on the outside and embroidered cloth on the inside. This is topped off with a multicoloured beaded cape draped across the shoulders, back and chest. The designs of these capes are left to individual taste.

The trousers are made of fine skin from the harbour seal (formerly, they were made of dogskin). Around the waist is a band of black skin with the hair removed and on the front of the thighs are two decorative appliquéd stripes. This appliqué technique, known as *avittat*, involves attaching small coloured strips of skin.

The lovely oversized boots, or *kamiks*, are of sealskin with the hair removed. The kamiks worn by older women are dark blue or yellow. Those of younger married women are red, and young unmarried girls wear white ones, normally decorated with appliquéd bands and topped with broad strips of lace. This colour differentiation is attributed to the Moravian missionaries, who encouraged women to wear hairbands coloured according to their age and marital status.

This dress is worn only on special occasions, but is bright and colourful enough to enliven any occasion. To my knowledge, it is the world's only women's national dress which includes trousers rather than a skirt.

The men's dress is also smart, but less colourful, consisting simply of dark blue cloth trousers and a white or black cotton anorak with a hood and breast pocket. Their kamiks are shorter than women's, with a wide appliquéd border at the top. ■

typically provided at boarding schools in district towns.

Nuuk is the educational centre of the country, with the University of Greenland (with 100 full-time students), a Business College and training colleges for teachers and nurses.

ARTS & CULTURE
Qajaq & Umiaq

The *qajaq*, or kayak, the long, narrow boat which is now used recreationally around the world, was originally developed by the Inuit as a hunting boat. It was designed without a keel and was propelled and steered with a double-bladed paddle. The traditional Greenlandic qajaq was constructed with a driftwood or whalebone frame, covered with a tightly-stretched sealskin and waterproofed with animal fat. It was ideal for hunting walrus, seals, polar bears and whales, as it could be rolled over and then righted by the occupant without taking on water.

GREENLAND

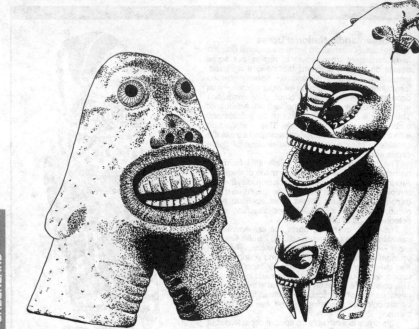

Greenlandic carvings, called tupilak, were originally used to cast misfortune on enemies

The original Greenlandic qajaqs were longer and considerably narrower than their modern recreational counterparts. Some measured of up to seven metres, yet the narrow hull allowed very little space for the occupant's legs.

A similar skin-covered boat, which was used by women, was called an *umiaq*, or 'women's boat'. It was open and not specifically designed for hunting, although it was sometimes used to take whales. Its purpose was the transport of women, children, older people and cargo.

Although the hunting qajaq is occasionally used around Avanersuaq and on the east coast, skin boats haven't been in common use since the 1950s. However, several towns now have qajaq clubs, which attempt to preserve construction and handling skills and promote qajaq skills among younger people,

thereby reviving a bit of Greenland's traditional heritage.

Tupilak

Greenlandic *tupilak*, small carvings which had their origins in East Greenland around Ammassalik, were made from bone, skin and chunks of peat, and were used to cast misfortune and even death on enemies. One had to use extreme caution, for if the victim's power were greater than the maker's, the spell would backfire and harm would boomerang back to its maker instead.

Modern tupilak, which are produced and sold as art and souvenirs, are carved from caribou antler, soapstone, driftwood, narwhal tusk, walrus ivory and bone. These carvings are small and meant to be held in the hand. Some represent polar bears, birds or marine mammals but most are just hideous imaginary beings. They are no longer intended to project misfortune – only to satisfy artistic urges and stimulate financial good fortune for their makers.

Literature

Oral Tradition Historically, Greenlandic storytellers were esteemed and were believed to have particularly astute insights into other realms. Stories were carefully passed down through generations and, amazingly, they emerged little altered by embellishment or lapse of memory as so frequently occurs with oral traditions.

Collections of Inuit stories, myths and songs reveal a great deal about the people's everyday life, the balance of the universe, their relationship with nature and the animals they hunted. Much like Aesop's fables, Greenlandic stories often conveyed a lesson or suggested an appropriate code of behaviour in the communities. In 1919, explorer Knud Rasmussen went to Ammassalik, east Greenland, to compile a collection of these stories.

Written Literature Although written litera-

ture is a recent addition to Greenlandic culture, writing is a popular pastime, and the Greenlandic Society of Authors already has 100 members.

The best information on written west Greenlandic literature – and the only Greenlandic works available in English translation – are in Michael Fortescue's bilingual work *From the Writings of the Greenlanders/Kalaallit Atuakkiaanit* (University of Alaska Press, 1990). Of the 245 pages, only 71 are actual text, but they'll certainly whet your appetite for Greenlandic literature.

The volume offers a selection of eleven texts in English and Greenlandic written or recorded between 1922 and 1982, three essays or parts of essays, two folk tales/legends and excerpts from six novels. It also contains introductions to Greenlandic writers and illustrations by Greenlandic artist Aka Høegh.

The folk tales are probably the most satisfying, mainly because they're complete stories and don't leave loose ends. In *Igimarasussuaq*, for example, a wife outwits her spouse-eating husband with magic spells.

Most interesting, however, are the novel excerpts, which range from Augo Lynge's science fiction novel, *The 300th Anniversary* (1931), which was the second novel ever written in Greenlandic, to Hans Anthon Lynge's more recent comic novel *Just Before the Ship Came In* (1982). The excerpt from the latter includes hilarious accounts of life in a North-West Greenlandic fishing village, and observations of a Danish fishing boat by Greenlandic characters going about their usual business.

The only other novel set in the present is Hans Hendrik's *The Kid* (1971), in which the protagonist, a young Greenlander in Denmark, gets mixed up in a conflict between two women. Other featured novels include Otto Rosing's *Taseralik* (1955); Frederik Nielsen's *This Land Shall Be Yours* (1970); and Hans Lynge's *The Will of the Invisible* (1976), which are all set in the distant past.

· The book concludes with an extensive 50-page glossary, which is too detailed for the casual reader and too limited for serious language students. You can use it to work out that *Nunatoqqami*, 'in the old land,' is comprised of the noun *nuna* (land), the suffix *toqqat* (old), and the locative inflection *-mi*, but more complicated phrases remain impenetrable.

SOCIETY & CONDUCT

On the whole, visitors find Greenlanders friendly and welcoming. The Inuit seem to enjoy life and appreciate social interaction. Often, however, they're not particularly open or talkative, which seems to cause communications breakdowns between European and Inuit people all around the Arctic.

The Inuit don't place a lot of emphasis on talk. Even at parties and on festive occasions, there may be a marked lack of conversation. Europeans often take this as shyness, rudeness or standoffishness. In return, Inuit people often consider Europeans too loud, brash, boisterous and chatty. A possible explanation is offered in *The Last Kings of Thule* by Jean Malaurie, who writes that 'the Inuit are still afraid that they will paralyse the forces of nature with the spoken word'.

Perlerorneq

One factor common to high latitudes in the long dark winters is a high incidence of depression, which the Inuit recognise and call *perlerorneq* ('the burden'). Violent or other abnormal behaviour is often blamed on it but people don't try to explain it away or make excuses. Rather, they accept it as part of life.

It's interesting that winter depression is common in polar regions, among people of all cultures. It was long believed that this stemmed from restlessness through being forced into long periods of inactivity. It has now been determined that the condition stems from a lack of vitamin D (obtained from natural sunlight) during the long, dark winters. In many places, this is treated with daily doses of artificial sunlight and the results have been very good.

Relation to Nature

Although the Inuit culture is rapidly adopting many European values, gadgets and customs, its traditional philosophy is more Eastern than Western. There's an overall concern with harmony and balance with the environment and its inhabitants, including rocks, fish, vegetation, animals and even abstracts such as moods and misfortunes. The maintenance of this balance is essential for happiness and stability.

The traditional Inuit love the land and are comfortable with it on its own terms. They don't want to change or conquer it but rather to get along with it, fearing and respecting it, and accepting its kindness as well as its wrath. They aren't sentimental about the death of animals or the relationship between animals and humans, and they feel it's natural that animals give up their lives to sustain human life, much as humans have historically sacrificed their own lives to the harsh elements and at times, to the animals themselves.

This interdependence is again part of the ideal balance. If the more traditional people sometimes convey reservations about their dealings with outsiders, much of it may stem from a fear of the power Europeans seem to wield over the land and the environment: power that can permanently upset the balance so important to the traditional Inuit.

Children

Greenlanders believe their children are born with complete personalities and are endowed as a birthright with the wisdom, survival instinct, magic and intelligence of their ancestors. It is believed that a child who has lost contact with its ancestors cannot survive. Therefore, Greenlandic children are neither punished nor chastised, because to do so would be construed by the ancients as a message of dissatisfaction with their gifts and may place the child in danger of losing his or her heritage.

Modern Changes

It must be noted though that modern Greenland is a developed country with a Western

European culture and outlook, and few modern Greenlanders would subscribe to or wish to return entirely to traditional ways.

While most Greenlanders have adapted to European values, some still aren't comfortable with the new way of life. The land and the seasons are predictable but 'success', as Westerners define it, is anything but certain, and people may not be able to reconcile the veneration of money and the power it gives with reverence for the land and the spiritual nature of all things. This is certainly one of the main causes of the high incidence of alcoholism, suicide and feelings of inadequacy that pervade Arctic societies today.

On the other hand, most Greenlanders would admit that they've been fortunate to have had the Danes in control of their country. Denmark's relatively enlightened attitude toward traditional native cultures has spared them much of the outright exploitation, plunder, military bases and outside immigration that Inuit in other countries have inherited. Instead, it has provided schools, hospitals and housing (which unfortunately sacrifices aesthetics for sheer bulk, with frightening results).

When murmurings about Home Rule first surfaced in the 1970s, the Danes didn't fight it. It's also to their credit that they've held on for so long; to my knowledge, there's never been a European colony that's provided so little wealth and so much liability as Greenland has for Denmark. Yet the Danes sense a responsibility to Greenland and, if they do let it go, the transition will happen slowly, and only when Greenland is ready to manage on its own.

LANGUAGE

The official language of Greenland is Greenlandic, one of many Inuit dialects spoken in the Arctic, which is related and similar to dialects spoken in northern Canada and Alaska. Regional variations do occur, inspiring amusement among Greenlanders from different areas, but essentially, all West Greenlanders can understand each other. East Greenlanders, however, speak a separate dialect and although some words are related, east and west Greenlandic aren't mutually intelligible.

The second language is Danish, which is spoken by nearly everyone. Although Greenlanders who have been reared in Denmark will speak English and many young people are learning it at school or from television, only a small percentage of Greenlanders speak any language other than Greenlandic and Danish.

Greenlandic

Greenlandic is a polysynthetic language, in which entire ideas are expressed in a single word by addition of prefixes and suffixes to a root subject; hence the impossible-looking mega-syllabic words which intimidate foreigners with their sheer length when written on a page. Some English speakers have noted that written Greenlandic, to them, resembles the result of a small child banging on a typewriter. For example, a newspaper headline announcing a harpoon-throwing competition would read: *Unammineq naakkiarneqqortusaanneq toraajuneqqussaanneq*. If that looks formidable, it is, and some outsiders who've lived for years in Greenland still don't have a grasp of the language.

One barrier to communication in Greenlandic for non-native speakers is spontaneous abbreviation of words. When translated into English in its purest form, Greenlandic may seem stilted and formal. For example, a word which visitors will notice at the airport is *aallariartartorfik*, or 'departures', which means literally 'the place for the one who has the intention of going somewhere'. In everyday speech, Greenlanders are more likely to say just *aallafik*, 'the place for going'.

Your only option to learn more than a few snippets of Greenlandic is to go to Greenland and find a native speaker as a tutor. One publication for self-teaching is *Grønlandsk for Begyndere* by Karl-Peter Anderson but you'll have to speak Danish first to get anything out of it. More highly regarded is *Qaagit* by Birgitte Hertling. The best phrasebook is *Greenlandic for Travelers*

GREENLAND

GREENLAND

Greenlandic Towns & Villages

Most Greenlandic towns and villages are known by two names, one Danish and one Greenlandic. In this book, I have used mainly the Greenlandic names.

The following table contains the alternative names of major towns and villages:

Greenlandic	Danish/European
Aasiaat	Egedesminde
Alluitsoq	Lichtenau
Alluitsup Paa	Sydprøven
Appat	Ritenbenk
Igaliku	Igaliko or Garðar
Igaliku Kujalleq	Søndre Igaliko or Undir Høfdi
Iqaluit	Frobisher Bay (Canada)
Ilimanaq	Claushavn
Ilulissat	Jakobshavn
Ittoqqoortoormiit	Scoresbysund
Kangerluk	Diskofjord
Kangerlussuaq	Søndre Strømfjord
Kangerluarsoruseq	Færingehavn
Kangilinnguit	Grønnedal
Kulusuk	Kap Dan
Maniitsoq	Sukkertoppen
Narsarmiit	Frederiksdal
Nerlerit Inaat	Constable Pynt
Nuuk	Godthåb
Oqaatsut	Rodebay
Paamiut	Frederikshåb
Pituffik	Thule Airbase
Qaanaaq	Thule
Qassiarsuk	Brattahlid
Qaqortoq	Julianehåb
Qasigiannguit	Christianshåb
Qeqertarsuaq	Godhavn
Qeqertarsuatsiaat	Fiskenæsset
Sisimiut	Holsteinsborg

(Attuakiorfik, Nuuk, 1993), also by Birgitte Hertling, which costs Dkr98 and is sold at tourist offices and bookshops.

The best available work on East Greenlandic is *Vocabulaire du Groenlandais de l'Est* by Robert Gessain, Louis-Jacques Dorais and Catherine Enel, with translations into West Greenlandic, Danish, French and English. It's most readily available from the bookshop in Ammassalik.

Pronunciation & Spelling I have the utmost respect for any foreigner who has learned to speak Greenlandic, and so do the Greenlanders. Pronunciation is challenging and is difficult to demonstrate in a pronunciation guide. Consonants come from deep in the throat and some vowels are scarcely pronounced. You'll just have to listen to get the hang of it.

Although a standardised orthography has been introduced in recent years, the spelling of Greenlandic words is still not consistent (and the spoken language may provide some clues as to why). Keep in mind that regional variations occur, so take the following vocabulary as a rough guide only. After you've spent some time in Greenland, things may become clearer.

Courses If you'd like to study basic Greenlandic, the Knud Rasmussen Højskoliat (☎ 14032; fax 14907), PO Box 1008, DK-3911 Sisimiut, offers intensive two-week introductory courses each September. They're normally conducted in Danish, but teachers typically also speak English.

Words & Phrases Here are a few West Greenlandic words and phrases which may be useful to travellers. Note that superlatives are constructed by adding *suaq* to the end of the root word and diminutives by adding *nnguaq*. Therefore, the word for 'ship' is *umiarsuaq*, the superlative of *umiaq*, the name of the traditional-sized boat. The word for 'house', on the other hand, is *illu*. Therefore, a small hut or cottage would be called *illunnguaq* while a mansion would be *illorssuaq*.

Basics

Hello.	*Inuugujoq, kutaa/ Haluu.*
Goodbye, best wishes. (long-term parting)	*Ajunnginniarnat/ Inuulluarit.*
Goodbye, see you later. (short-term)	*Takuss.*
Thank you (very much).	*Qujanaq (qujanarssuaq).*
Cheers!	*Kasuuta!*
Welcome!	*Tikilluarit!*
Yes.	*Aap.*

No.	Naagga/Naamik.
Maybe.	Immaqa (uupa in East Greenland)
That's fine/good.	Ajunngilaq.
Where is ...?	... sumiipa?
How much is it?	Qanoq akeqarpa?
What time is it?	Qassinngorpa?
When? (for an event)	Qanga?
When? (for a meeting)	Qaqugu?
Help!	Ikiunnga!

Small Talk

What is your name?	Qanoq ateqarpit?
My name is ...	...-imik ataqarpunga.
Where do you come from?	Suminngaaneerpit?
What is your job?	Sulerisuuvit?
I am tired.	Qasivunga.
I am happy. (short term)	Nuannaarpunga.
I am happy. (long term)	Pilluarpunga.
I am angry.	Qamappunga.
I am disappointed.	Pakatsisimavunga.
I'll take this.	Pisiarerusuppara.
It is dangerous.	Navianarpoq.
Mush, you huskies!	Gamma, gamma!/ Ingerlagit!

very funny	nuann
very good	torrak/ajunngeqaaq
stranger	takornartaq
visitor	tikeraaq

Transport

reservation (for one)	inimik pissarsiniarneq
reservation (for a group)	inissanik pissarsiniarneq
ticket	billettit
ship	umiarsuaq
plane	timmisartoq
helicopter	helikopterit/ qulimiguulik
boat	umiaq
open motorboat	pujortuleeraq
small cabin boat	angallak sukkasooq
large motorboat/ fishing boat	sukasuuliaq
dogsled	qimusseq

travel	angalaneq
expensive	akisuvoq
north	avannaa
south	kujataa
east	kangia
west	kitaa

Around Town

tourist office	allaffianut
museum	katersugaasivik
post office	allakkerivik
shop	pisiniarfik
church	oqaluffik
toilet	anartarfik
bath	uffarfik
school	atuarfik
accommodation	akunnittarfik
tent	tupeq

Useful Words

today	ullumi
tomorrow	aqagu
winter	ukioq
summer	aasaq
water	imeq
man	angut
woman	arnaq
father	ataata
mother	anaana
son/daughter	qitornaq
child	meeraq
house	illu
party (for a birthday or holiday)	onalliuttorsiorneq
party (for fun)	unnussiuaarneq/ nuannaaratiginneq
home-brew	immiaq
weather	sila
rain	sialuk
sun	seqineq
fog/cloud	pujoq
snow	aput
ice	siku
wind	anori

Animals

Animals play a major role in Greenlandic life and frequently come up in conversation. The

GREENLAND

following are some of the ones more commonly referred to:

polar bear	*nanoq*
capelin	*ammassak*
caribou	*tuttu*
cod	*saarullik*
diver (loon)	*tuullik*
dog	*qimmeq*
eagle	*nattoralik*
fjord cod	*uugaq*
fox	*terrianiaq*
guillemot	*serfaq*
halibut	*nataarnaq/qaleralik*
hare	*ukaleq*
mosquito	*ippernaq*
musk ox	*ummimaq*
ptarmigan	*aqisseq*
seal	*puisi*
ringed seal	*natseq*
harp seal	*aataaq*
bearded seal	*ussuk*
hooded seal	*natsersuaq*
shark	*eqalussuaq*
sheep	*sava*
sea trout or char	*eqaluk*
walrus	*aareq*
whale	*arfeq*
narwhal	*qilaluaq qernertaq*
beluga	*qilaluaq qaqortaq*
minke whale	*tikagullik*
fin whale	*tikagulliusaaq*
wolf	*amaqqeq*

Days

Monday	*Ataasinngorneq*
Tuesday	*Marlunngorneq*
Wednesday	*Pingasunngorneq*
Thursday	*Sisamanngorneq*
Friday	*Tallimanngorneq*
Saturday	*Arfininngorneq*
Sunday	*Sapaat*

Months

January	*Januari*
February	*Februari*
March	*Martsi*
April	*Apriili*
May	*Maaji*
June	*Juuni*
July	*Juuli*
August	*Augusti*
September	*Septembari*
October	*Oktobari*
November	*Novembari*
December	*Decembari*

Geographical Features & Place Names

Geographic names in Greenland are by no means exclusive to one particular place, and a glance at a large-scale map may reveal five or six places called *Qeqertarsuaq*, a couple called *Narsaq*, a few *Nuussuaq*s, the odd *Kangerlussuaq* and at least one *Tasersuaq*. Names in Greenlandic were not given to features or areas to simply endow a name or to honour some famous person or thing. Since maps weren't in use among the earlier hunting cultures, the names in effect *were* the map.

In order, the five previously mentioned names, which belong to commonly-visited villages and towns as well as scores of other places, mean 'big island', 'plain', 'big promontory', 'big fjord' and 'big lake'. Some other useful geographical terms include:

fjord	*kangerluk*
hot spring	*puilasoq*
iceberg/icebergs	*iluliaq/ilulissat*
inland ice	*sermerssuaq*
island	*qeqertaq*
lake	*taseq*
land	*nuna*
mountain	*qaqaq*
mountain glacier	*sermertaq*
peninsula	*qeqertaaminerssua*
promontory	*nuuk*
river	*kuuk*
sea	*imaq*
valley	*qooroq*
valley glacier	*sermeq*

Numbers

Numbers in Greenlandic only go up to 12. After that you have to use Danish numbers because after 12 there is only *passuit*, 'many'.

1	ataaseq	11	elleve
2	marluk	12	tolv
3	pingasut	13	tretten
4	sisamat	14	fjorten
5	tallimat	15	femten
6	arfinillit	16	seksten
7	arfineq marluk	17	sytten
8	arfineq pingasut	18	atten
9	qulingiluat	19	nitten
10	qulit	20	tyve
11	arqanillit	21	en og tyve
12	arqaneq marluk	22	to og tyve
		30	tredive
		31	en og tredive

Danish Numbers

1	en	40	fyrre
2	to	50	halvtreds
3	tre	60	tres
4	fire	70	halvfjerds
5	fem	80	firs
6	seks	90	halvfems
7	syv	100	et hundrede
8	otte	101	et hundrede een
9	ni	120	et hundrede tyve
10	ti	1000	et tusind

GREENLAND

Facts for the Visitor

PLANNING
What Kind of Trip?
Your style of travel will derive from your budget, curiosity and adventurous spirit. Tour operators can concoct cruising, kayaking, hiking, dogsledding and sightseeing packages, but package tours leave little time for the independent exploration and discovery that Greenland so intriguingly invites.

On the other hand, tour packages obviate the headaches independent travellers face when sorting out timetables and booking ferries and flights. Book flights and ferries as far in advance as possible. Although the summer KNI ferry schedules and Grønlandsfly timetables may not be finalised and published until May, Greenland Travel in Copenhagen (see Organised Tours in the Getting There & Away chapter) can provide preliminary schedules as early as December or January.

When to Go
Greenland's tourist season begins in early July and continues to the first week in September. In May, the winter snows haven't yet melted and new snow is possible until early June. Spring doesn't really begin to take off until mid to late July and spring wildflowers bloom from mid-July to mid-August. Berries normally ripen in mid-August and last until mid-September, when the tundra explodes with brilliant autumn colours. In late August, you can expect freezing temperatures at night and increasingly cooler days. Mid-September brings new snow and genuinely cold weather.

The mosquito season runs from late June to early August, but stragglers hang around until late August, especially around Disko Bay. Their nuisance value cannot be overstated, and anyone attached to their sanity should wear long clothing, invest in a head net (sold at some hotels, hostels and tourist offices) and load up on repellent, or the Greenlandic equivalent, *piteraq* – vodka flavoured with pepper – which may not ward off the mosquitoes, but will at least help you ignore them (it's named after a hurricane-force wind which occurs in East Greenland).

December, January and February are incredible in the Arctic, with long black nights and normally clear but bitterly cold days, with a brief period of pale red light as far north as Disko Bay. 'Winter' dogsledding and skiing tours, however, normally occur between late March and early May, thereby avoiding the extreme hours of darkness and low temperatures of deep winter.

The best times to view the aurora borealis in southern Greenland are from late August to early November and mid-February to

---

Greenland on a Shoestring
Budget travel in Greenland can be a challenge, but here are a few tips to help keep costs down:

- Bring a tent – you can camp for free anywhere outside villages and although facilities are few, water is normally plentiful. Illulissat, Narsarsuaq and Kangerlussuaq have organised campgrounds.
- Self-cater at supermarkets and harbour markets or gather your own food (see Fishing & Hunting and Food for more tips).
- Organise you own accommodation, boat charters and dogsled trips, but be aware that your travel insurance company may not cover you if something goes wrong.
- Walk or use your own sea kayak to get around.
- Fly into one region and explore it fully (such as the area covered by one chapter of this book). The Thule area and anywhere in East Greenland will be tough for budget travellers.

early April. (In 1996, they appeared in Nanortalik the first week in August!) Greenland's northernmost regions are actually too far north to experience the best auroral displays.

Maps

Greenland's coastal areas are covered in 1:250,000 series topo sheets by the Dansk Geodætisk Institut, now known as Kort og Matrikelstyrelsen (KOM). The scale makes them of limited use to trekkers, but for much of Greenland, they're the only available mapping. To order maps or catalogues, contact Kort og Matrikelstyrelsen (☎ 45-35 87 53 10; fax 45-35 87 50 51), Kortsalget, Rentemestervej 8, DK-2400 Copenhagen NV, Denmark.

Greenland Tourism has produced an excellent series of hiking maps at a scale of 1:100,000. The best is the two-part *Hiking Routes – East Greenland: Ammassalik/ Tasiilaq*, which comes with an elaborate hiking guide and costs Dkr250. The folder *Hiking in South Greenland* includes three maps: *Narsarsuaq*, *Narsaq* and *Qaqortoq*, and a cursory information booklet. Other maps in the series are *Tasermiut Fjorden – Nanortalik*, *Ivittuut*, *Nuuk*, the three-part *Kangerlussuaq-Sisimiut* and the soon-to-be-published *Ilulissat* and *Maniitsoq*. They depict hiking routes of varying difficulty, fords, fishing streams, sheep farms and mountain huts, among other things. Some include hiking information on the back.

Saga Maps has taken the KOM mapping and patched contiguous sheets into 20 regional maps which cover all populated areas of Greenland. They're not only cheaper than the KOM sheets, but also eliminate the need to purchase several sheets for trips in one region. They're sold folded/flat for Dkr58/78 and as plastic laminated sheets for Dkr98. Folders of four sheets (divided into South Greenland, South-West Greenland, Disko Bay, and North-West Greenland & Thule/East Coast) cost Dkr185; a complete set of 20 maps costs Dkr775. They also publish historic maps/guides to the Western Settlement, Sisimiut/Kangerlussuaq, Disko

Bay and Ammassalik (Dkr58 each). To order, contact Tage Schjött (☎ & fax 33-628 35848), La Coma del Colat 22, La Massana, Andorra.

Greenland Travel, formerly the backpackers' travel agency, DVL Rejser, distributes four DVL-Rejser walking maps of popular hiking areas at a scale of 1:100,000; these include Kangerlussuaq (Dkr115), Sisimiut (Dkr115), Nuuk (Dkr160) and Narsarsuaq-Narsaq-Qaqortoq (Dkr160). They're sold at the youth hostels in Narsarsuaq and Ilulissat. Otherwise, contact Greenland Travel, Gammel Mønt 12, DK-1175 Copenhagen, Denmark. Note that these maps are not without error and cannot be relied upon for serious exploration off the main routes.

Atuakkiorfik, in Nuuk, publishes the detailed and well-presented *Kalaallit Nunaat Atlas*, with internationally intelligible maps and text in Danish, Greenlandic and English. It costs US$50 from Atuakkiorfik, PO Box 840, DK-3900 Nuuk, or at Atuagkat in Nuuk, Greenland Tourism in Ilulissat, the bookshop in Sisimiut and occasionally in other shops.

International Distributors The following places are recommended distributors, have catalogues and do mail order:

Denmark
   Nordisk Korthandel, Studiestræde 26-30, DK-1455, Copenhagen.
Germany
   Internationales Landartenhaus, Geocenter, Postfach 800830, Schockenriederstr 40-A, D-7000 Stuttgart 80.
USA
   Maplink (☎ 805-965 4402), 25 E Mason St, Dept G, Santa Barbara, CA 93101.
UK
   Stanfords (☎ 0171-836 1321), 12-14 Long Acre, London WC2E 9L.

HIGHLIGHTS

When it comes to highlights, Greenland presents a special case. There are few 'sights', and the biggest appeal is the country itself, with its awe-inspiring landscapes and overpowering silences. The following list (in no particular order) includes interesting and accessible spots to begin your discovery, but don't limit your exploration to these sites or you'll miss the many surprises Greenland can offer:

1. Tasermiut Fjord – the soaring granite ramparts of Uiluit Qaaqa and Ulamertorsuaq.
2. Ferry trip to Aappilattoq – deep sapphire-blue waters and towering granite spires.
3. Nanortalik – a relaxed and friendly town amid scenic country.
4. Uummannaq – the best of Arctic Greenland, with a dramatic setting.
5. Disko Island – geologically, Greenland's newest addition; good hiking, summer dogsledding and bizarre landscapes.
6. Ammassalik – a superb setting, a fine network of hiking routes and some of Greenland's most interesting individualists.
7. Narsarsuaq to Kiattuut Sermiat hike – an easy day hike to a beautiful mountain lake and a spur of the inland ice.
8. Unartoq Hot Springs – From these lovely 40°C waters you can watch icebergs floating past in the fjord.
9. Hvalsey ruins – Hvalsey contains the best-preserved Norse ruins in Greenland.
10. Ilulissat Kangerlua – the world's most prolific glacier outside Antarctica fills Disko Bay with immense icebergs.

Other highlights include hiking and wildlife-viewing in Kangerlussuaq; hiking on the relatively green Narsaq peninsula; Igaliku, the former ecumenical centre of the Norse colonies; the unique Stone & Man sculpture project in Qaqortoq; and the old Kolonihavnen district of Nuuk.

TOURIST OFFICES

Greenland Tourism (☎ 45-33 13 69 75; fax 45-33 93 38 83; email greenfo@inet.unic.dk), Pilestræde 52, PO Box 1139, DK-1010 Copenhagen K, Denmark, is the Home Rule Administration's tourism and tourist information agency. It's still trying to sort out its role, how much control it will exert over tourism and how much it will compete with private enterprise. Currently, all tour operators, hotels and boat charter operators as well as airlines and ferries must hold shares in this agency.

One publication worth looking for before you leave home is the booklet *Facts About Greenland*, published by Greenland Tourism. It contains useful titbits for independent travellers.

Local Tourist Offices

Tourist information offices in Greenland are now officially tied to and overseen by Greenland Tourism (☎ 22988; fax 22877; email tourism@greennet.gl), Hans Egedesvej 29, PO Box 1552, DK-3900 Nuuk. Most offices provide maps and brochures, and organise day tours and activities. In Aasiaat, Paamiut, Upernavik, Qeqertarsuaq, Maniitsoq, Kangaatsiaq, Ivittuut, Qaanaaq and Ittoqqoortoormiit, tourist enquiries are handled by town offices or just dedicated individuals. Hotels, seamen's homes and youth hostels also provide tourist information.

All the offices are helpful, but note that some are run by private tour companies or hotels, which may result in monopoly prices and a tendency to discourage budget or non-package travellers. The most objective offices are at Nuuk, Nanortalik, Narsaq, Ammassalik and Sisimiut; these welcome independent travellers and actively encourage and provide information on hiking and other non-organised activities, while still offering reasonably-priced tours and activities.

Other fully-fledged tourist offices are generally helpful, but would, for example, sell you a helicopter tour before they'd help you plan a hike. Take a helicopter tour by all means – it will be a fabulous experience – but don't let anyone discourage you from setting out under your own steam, or you may well miss the best that Greenland has to offer.

Tourist Offices Abroad

In addition to Greenland Tourism, Danish Tourism Boards dispense limited Greenland information and provide commercial investment guidelines. Greenland Travel in Copenhagen is also an invaluable source of pre-trip assistance.

Canada
     Danish Tourism Board, PO Box 115, Station N, Toronto, Ontario M8V 3S4
Denmark
     Danish Tourism Board, HC Andersens Boulevard 22, DK-1553 Copenhagen
     Grønlands Rejsebureau, Gammel Mønt 12, PO Box 130, DK-1004 Copenhagen
France
     Office National de Tourisme de Danemark, 142 Champs Elysées, F-75008 Paris
UK
     Danish Tourism Board, Sceptre House, 169-173 Regent St, London W1R 8PY
USA
     Danish Tourism Board, 655 Third Avenue, 18th floor, New York, NY 10017

VISAS & DOCUMENTS
Visas

Citizens of Nordic countries – Norway, Sweden, Finland (including Åland), Iceland, the Faroes and Denmark – need only a valid identification card to enter Greenland. Citizens of countries not requiring visas, including Australia, New Zealand, Canada, Japan, the US and EU countries, need only a valid passport for stays of up to three months in Denmark, the Faroes, Greenland, Iceland, Finland, Norway or Sweden.

Countries requiring visas for Denmark, the Faroes and Greenland include most northern and central African countries, Yugoslavia, Bulgaria, Romania, Turkey, China, all former Soviet republics, India, South Africa and a handful of others. For specifics, see the nearest Danish embassy.

Technically, tourists must show sufficient funds for their intended length of stay, but customs and immigration formalities are normally rudimentary, especially for those entering Greenland from Denmark or Iceland.

Thule Airbase Permits

Visitors to the US base in Thule (Pituffik) require a permit to enter the base area. Danish citizens must apply to the Ministry for Foreign Affairs, Asiatisk Plads 2, DK-1402, Copenhagen K. Others should contact Danish embassies or the US Air Attaché, 24 Dag Hammarskjölds Alle, DK-2100, Copenhagen Ø, Denmark. Currently, permits are required even by transit passengers.

EMBASSIES
Greenland is represented abroad by Danish embassies and consulates:

Australia
     Royal Danish Embassy, 15 Hunter St, Yarralumla, ACT 2600 (☎ 06-9273 2195)
Canada
     Royal Danish Embassy, 85 Range Road, Apt 702, Ottawa, Ontario K1N 8J6 (☎ 613-234 0704)
Germany
     Königliche Dänische Botschaft, Pfälzerstrasse 13, 5300 Bonn 1 (☎ 0228-72 99 10)
New Zealand
     Contact the embassy in Australia
UK
     Royal Danish Embassy, 55 Sloane St, London SW1X 9SR (☎ 0171-235 1255)
USA
     Royal Danish Embassy, 3200 Whitehaven St NW, Washington, DC (☎ 202-234 4300)

CUSTOMS
Travellers over 18 may import duty-free one litre of spirits and one litre of wine. Anyone over 15 can bring in 250 grams of tobacco and 200 cigarette papers or 200 pre-rolled cigarettes. Although hunting rifles can be brought in with airline permission, revolvers and automatic weapons are not allowed. Live animals of any kind are also prohibited. These regulations apply to Danish citizens as well as to foreigners.

MONEY
Costs
Thanks to Danish subsidies, food and consumer goods costs are surprisingly lower than in Iceland and many are on a par with those in Copenhagen. However, accommodation, restaurant and transport costs remain high. Greenland has no highways, and population centres are linked only by ferries, charter boat or air.

Except for Narsarsuaq, Nerlerit Inaat, Kangerlussuaq, Pituffik, Nuuk, Kulusuk and Ilulissat, air travel is by helicopter, which makes the cost of flying prohibitive. The flight between Nuuk and Narsarsuaq – less

GREENLAND

than an hour– costs Dkr2250. The 10 minute flight between Narsarsuaq and Qaqortoq costs Dkr680 and from Nanortalik to Upernavik, it's Dkr9960. Children travel at 40% to 90% discount.

Currency

The Danish krone (Dkr) and Faroese króna (Fkr) are used interchangeably throughout the Kingdom of Denmark – that is, on the mainland and in the Faroes and Greenland. One krone is equal to 100 øre. Notes come in denominations of 50, 100, 500 and 1000 kroner. Coins are available in 25 and 50 øre and 1, 2, 5, 10 and 20 kroner denominations.

Currency Exchange

All brands of travellers' cheques and all Scandinavian and other major currencies may be exchanged for Dkr in any bank or KNI office. Eurocheques are also negotiable as are cheques drawn on Danish or Faroese banks.

The approximate exchange rates at the time of publication were:

Australia	A$1	=	4.78
Canada	C$1	=	4.56
France	FF1	=	1.13
Germany	DM1	=	3.82
Iceland	Ikr	=	0.09
Japan	¥100	=	5.20
New Zealand	NZ$1	=	4.31
Norway	Nkr1	=	0.97
UK	£1	=	10.26
USA	US$1	=	6.28

Changing Money

Greenland has two banks, Nuna Bank and Grønlandsbanken, both with branches around the country. To change travellers' cheques, banks charge from Dkr30 per transaction in Nanortalik to Dkr75 in Ilulissat. In villages without banks, KNI performs bank functions and handles foreign exchange, but exchange rates may be up to 10% lower than in banks.

Credit Cards

Major credit cards are accepted at tourist restaurants and hotels in larger towns (including Narsarsuaq and Kangerlussuaq), and Visa or MasterCard cash advances are available at Nuna Bank and Grønlandsbanken. As yet, ATMs may only be used for cash advances on credit cards issued by Danish banks, but that's certain to change in the near future.

POST & COMMUNICATIONS
Post

All Greenlandic towns have a post office, Kalaallit Allakkeriviat, offering the usual gamut of postal services as well as fax and telephone facilities. Most Greenland post offices are open Monday to Friday from 9 am to noon and 1 to 3 pm. Some post offices distribute free postcards with photographs or drawings of Greenlandic scenes and indigenous birds and wildlife.

Postal Rates Postal rates for airmail postcards and letters weighing less than 20 grams are Dkr4.50 within Greenland and Europe, and Dkr5.50 to other countries. Airmail letters from 20g to 100g go for Dkr7.50 within Greenland, Dkr9.50 within Scandinavia, Dkr18 to Europe and Dkr23 to other places.

Receiving Mail To receive mail, have correspondence addressed to you care of Poste Restante in the main town of the area you're visiting. For South Greenland, use DK-3920 Qaqortoq; for the South-West, use DK-3900 Nuuk; for Disko Bay, use DK-3952 Ilulissat; for East Greenland, DK-3913 Tasiilaq. To speed things along, it helps to add 'Greenland via Denmark' after the postal code.

Telephone

Telephone offices are associated with post offices and you can phone or fax to anywhere in the world. However, reverse-charge calls are not accepted.

Greenland's country code is ☎ 299. To access an international line, dial ☎ 009, then the desired country code, area code and phone number. To phone Denmark, just dial ☎ 9 followed by the eight-digit number.

Keeping in Touch

Cellular phones are all the rage in Greenland and they've already replaced two-way radios for short-range contact between boaters, hunters, dogsled drivers and their families at home. While hiking alone on the Sermilikvejen, in a remote area of Ammassalik island, I stopped to dry off after crossing a stream. When I turned around, I was surprised to see a Greenlandic hunter – the first person I'd seen all day – who was approaching, sipping Coca-Cola (which incidentally is as scarce in Greenland as air-conditioning). Noting that he appeared to be speaking, I stood to greet him, only to realise that he was pre-occupied in conversation on a cellular phone. He went striding past without glancing up and disappeared over the next hill.

Deanna Swaney

Fax

Fax services are available at post offices and cost Dkr40/30 for the first page/subsequent pages within Greenland, Dkr65/55 to Denmark and Dkr100/80 to elsewhere in Scandinavia. Rates to other countries average Dkr120/100.

BOOKS

Publishing in Greenlandic is subsidised by Denmark, and all towns have free public libraries. Several towns also have shops selling Greenlandic or Danish-language school texts and novels, but few sell foreign-language books. Hotels may offer pulp novels and some tourist offices sell souvenir books, but the best selection is at Atuagkat in Nuuk, which has German and English-language books on Greenland and Arctic themes, history books, souvenir books and a very limited selection of novels.

Guidebooks

Apart from this book, the only English-language Greenland guide is *Trekking in Greenland* (Skarv Guides, 1990) by Torbjørn Ydegaard, which is requisite for serious hikers. It's available from Grønlands

Rejsebureau in Copenhagen (for a publisher address, see Trekking later in this chapter). The same author has also written the more esoteric *Slæderejser i Grønland* (Skarv Guides, 1989) – available only in Danish – which has all you need to know about dog-sledding tours.

The small *Grønland Natur Guide* (Forlaget Komma, 1990), by Jon Feilberg, is a handy little pocket book with colour photos and references on Greenland's flora, fauna and geology. It's useful even if you can't read the Danish text.

Travel

The Arctic has inspired some of the best travel literature ever written and the journals of explorers like Robert Peary, Fridtjof Nansen and Knud Rasmussen provide insight into the region and its traditions. Some of the best are *Across Arctic America* by Knud Rasmussen, *The Friendly Arctic* by Vilhjalmar Stefansson and *Arctic Adventure* by Peter Freuchen, but these are becoming increasingly difficult to find. Biographies of these explorers are also available in several languages.

Arctic Dreams (Charles Scribner's Sons, 1986; Bantam, 1987) by Barry Lopez, draws you into the spell of the Arctic, and the author clearly conveys his deep feelings for the place. Much of this book deals with Greenland, but he also wanders through Canada, Alaska, Siberia and northern Scandinavia.

The Last Kings of Thule (University of Chicago Press, 1985), by Jean Malaurie, a professor at the Sorbonne in Paris, is a classic which should be read as an entertaining account of the author's two years among the polar Inuit rather than as a serious anthropological study.

The Noose of Laurels (Grafton Books, 1991) by Wally Herbert traces the bitter rivalry between Robert Peary and Dr Frederik Cook in their quest to be first to the North Pole.

The entertainingly written *Last Places – A Journey in the North* (Houghton Mifflin Co, 1990), by Lawrence Millman, recounts a series of improbable but true experiences in

GREENLAND

Greenland. Especially amusing are his accounts of being sexually harassed by Greenlandic women – finally a man learns what women travellers deal with all over the world!

For the last word on the Arctic explorers and the race for the North-West Passage, see the superb book, *The Arctic Grail* (Viking Penguin, 1988), by Pierre Berton.

N by E, by illustrator Rockwell Kent (University Press of New England, Hanover, NH, 1996), is a journal of a 1920s sailing trip from Nova Scotia to Illorsuit (near Uummannaq), where he was shipwrecked. Later books, *Salamina* (after his Greenlandic mistress in Illorsuit) and *Rockwell Kent's Greenland Journal*, describe his Greenlandic exploits in the 1930s, providing a vivid portrayal of European entry into Inuit culture. Kent's quirky politics – including sympathy for everything from German WWI imperialism to Leninism, Stalinism and the Viet Cong – irked both US and Canadian authorities, and add a further dimension.

Land Under the Pole Star, by Helge Ingstad, is an exhaustive compilation of information on the Norse movements and North Atlantic colonies. It deals in depth with the connection between Greenland and North America.

The witty *Sea, Ice & Rock* (Hodder & Stoughton, 1992), by Sir Robin Knox-Johnston & Chris Bonnington, traces a joint sailors' and mountaineers' holiday in East Greenland. The expedition sailed from Scotland to the ice-filled fjord Kangerlussuaq (one of several Kangerlussuaqs on the east coast), and attempted to climb the Cathedral, one of Greenland's highest peaks.

Another intrepid sailor book is *Ice!* (Avon Books, 1978), by Tristan Jones, whose forays into Arctic waters make entertaining reading. His journey includes a sail into Scoresbysund and up Greenland's east coast before heading for Svalbard.

The cult favourite, *An African in Greenland* (Ulverscroft, UK), by Tete-Michele Kpomassie, tells the tale of a Togolese man who travels to Greenland and draws parallels between the Inuit and his own people.

Fiction

The most famous novel ever written about Greenland is *Miss Smilla's Feeling for Snow*, by Peter Høeg (published in the USA as *Smilla's Sense of Snow*). It follows the eponymous Miss Smilla Jaspersen, a Greenlander from Thule, in her search for clues to support her suspicions of murder in the death of a young Greenlandic boy in Copenhagen. Her uncanny familiarity with ice and snow leads her back to Greenland. It's now being made into a film which Greenland Tourism hopes will put the country on the tourist map.

The Greenlanders (Collins, 1988), by Jane Smiley, is a fictionalised account of the lost Norse settlements in Greenland, told in a haunting saga form. You could imagine you're reading a translated bit of ancient literature. It's highly entertaining, but doesn't purport to be anything but a novel of how things could have happened.

General

The Arctic World (Century Publishing, 1985) by Fred Bruemmer, was intended to be a coffee-table book, but it contains one of the best descriptions of the transition of the Inuit people from hunting culture to European culture. The photos, taken in Greenland, Canada, Alaska, Siberia and Scandinavia, convey well the character of the Arctic landscape and people.

The coffee-table book *Grönland* (Pawlek Verlag, Hersching, Germany, 1990), by Max Schmidt, is packed with ethereal photos by one of the world's best photographers. It's available for DM49.80 from the publisher, Pawlek Verlag, Gachemanstrasse 29, D-8036, Hersching, Germany.

Another worthwhile German coffee-table publication is *Grönland* (Bucher, 1994), which consists of three parts. Journalist Hans Joachim Kürtz has written a background essay and Norbert Schürer provides information on Greenlandic travel, history, flora and fauna. Photographer Hubert Stadler contributes stunning photos which capture Greenland's icebergs, inland ice, culture, wildlife and Arctic light.

In *Arctic Wars, Animal Rights, Endan-*

gered Peoples (University Press of New England, 1992), author Finn Lynge passionately argues for Inuit rights to hunt Arctic animals, and suggests that Western conservationists' notions of whaling and seal-hunting are uninformed and border on the hysterical. However, he fails to note that few people – even diehard conservationists – dispute that the Inuit should have subsistence hunting rights, and leaves untouched the stickier and more relevant issue of the commercial hunting that is the focus of most environmental campaigns.

The Frozen Echo: Greenland and the Exploration of North America, ca AD 1000-1500 (Stanford University Press, 1996), by Kirsten Seaver, is the best and most thorough available investigation of the Greenlandic Norse. The main thesis is that visits from Greenland to the American continent continued through the 14th century, but it encompasses masses of theoretical, archaeological and literary background, and still manages to be lucid and entertaining. It's highly recommended.

A lovely new publication is the superb *Frozen Horizons – The World's Largest National Park* (Atuakkiorfik, Nuuk, 1996), by Ivars Silis, which is a natural history and photo book about the magnificent North-East Greenland National Park. The Latvian author, who lives in Greenland, has travelled through the park photographing and studying the environment. You can order it (Dkr177) from Atuakkiorfik (☎ 22122; fax 22500), PO Box 840, DK-3900 Nuuk.

The excellent section on Greenland in the Smithsonian Institution's *Handbook of North American Indians, Volume 5, Arctic* (1984) includes chapters on the prehistory of Greenland as well as the history of the Greenlandic Eskimos, Norse and colonials. It's available in most public libraries in North Americ For information on natural history books and field guides, see Books in the Iceland Facts for the Visitor chapter.

ONLINE SERVICES

The most comprehensive site is the Greenland Guide (www.greenland-guide.dk),

which includes tourist information – Greenland Tourism, Greenlandair, Greenland Travel, Arctic Adventures, travel agents, hostels etc – as well as information on philately and Santa Claus.

GO!, or Greenland Online! (www.go.gl), has nearly as many links, and Greenland Homerule (www.gh.gl) has an excellent page with links to ministries, parliament, press releases, history, etc. Nuuk (www.greennet.gl/nuukcity) has its own page, and although most of it is in Danish, it includes some amazing photos.

There's also a Greenland email directory at (www.greennet.gl//./mailregister/maileng.html), and last but not least, the CIA's home page on Greenland (www.odci.gov/cia/publications/95fact/gl.html), which contains surprisingly up-to-date information on population, government, economy, etc.

Greenland's first Internet magazine *Atagu* (atagu.ki.gl) contains essays in English and Danish. The Thule Greenland Field Project (www.peregrinefund.org/Greenlnd.html) has been surveying the North-West Greenland peregrine falcon (and other bird) populations since 1993. The Mining Journal (www.rfg.dk/mining journal/index.html) also has a Greenland supplement. Robert Petersen has an excellent article *Colonialism as Seen from a Former Colonized Area* at (spirit.lib.uconn.edu/ArcticCircle/Cultural Viability/petersen.html).

Two sites devoted to marine mammal awareness are the High North Alliance (www.highnorth.no/) and the Tirpitz (tirpitz.ibg.uit.no/wwww/ss.html) site of the University of Tromsø, Norway.

NEWSPAPERS & MAGAZINES

The Greenlandic press is limited to two weekly papers in Danish and Greenlandic and several small local periodicals. Larger tourist hotels can provide foreign language newspapers, however late they may arrive.

For a good range of Greenland-related topics in Danish, English and Greenlandic see *SULUK*, the semi-annual Grønlandsfly in-flight magazine, which is distributed free on aircraft, and in airline and tourist offices.

Annual subscriptions cost US$28 from Atuagassivik/Eskimo Press, PO Box 939, 3900 Nuuk.

RADIO & TV

Both television and radio are operated by Radio Greenland. Television, however, is only available in towns. Programmes are in Danish or have Danish subtitles (there isn't enough room on the screen for the Greenlandic words!). In addition, US and Canadian news broadcasts and programming are available via satellite. On a recent visit, I was greeted at the Narsarsuaq airport lounge by a news broadcast from Whitehorse in Canada's Yukon Territory!

Radio programmes are broadcast in Danish and Greenlandic and are received everywhere in the country with the aid of relays.

LAUNDRY

The big hotels all have expensive laundry services; more realistically priced services are limited to the seamen's homes and youth hostels.

LEGAL MATTERS

The export of artefacts – by definition anything made prior to 1940 – is prohibited without an export licence from the National Museum in Nuuk. It's also forbidden to disturb any historic or prehistoric sites or remove souvenir stones from ruins. If you discover anything that appears significant, contact the Grønlands Nationalmuseum & Arkiv (☎ 22611), PO Box 145, DK-3900 Nuuk.

PUBLIC HOLIDAYS & SPECIAL EVENTS
Public Holidays

Greenland observes the following public holidays:

1 January
   New Year's Day
6 January
   Epiphany
March or April
   Maundy Thursday, Good Friday, Easter Sunday, Easter Monday

1 May
   Labour Day
May
   Common Prayer's Day
May
   Ascension Day
June
   Whitsunday, Whitmonday
21 June
   National Day, Ullortuneq (Longest Day)
1 November
   All Saints' Day
24 December
   Christmas Eve
25 December
   Christmas Day
26 December
   Boxing Day
31 December (afternoon only)
   New Year's Eve

Special Events

Several local festivals are staged around the country. In northern Greenland, a celebration – and a sigh of relief – marks the end of the polar night, when the sun returns after its sojourn below the horizon. In Ilulissat, this occurs in mid-January; in Upernavik, in early February; and in Qaanaaq, late February. Around Easter, villages north of the Arctic Circle hold dogsled races which are accompanied by festivities.

In summer, some South Greenland towns and villages hold a sort of 'sheep rodeo' which includes shearing, herding and other ovine-related competitions. A new event in Qaqortoq is the Festival of Art and Music, which takes place in late June and early July. The Nuuk marathon is held in July or August. In late August or early September, the Grønlandsmesterskab national football tournament is held in changing venues. It includes a week of play-offs and stirs up lots of excitement.

Every three to four years, Greenland hosts the Inuit Circumpolar Conference, a week-long cultural meeting where Inuit from Greenland, Canada, Alaska and Russia gather and discuss Arctic issues which affect them all. The official proceedings are accompanied by cultural exhibitions, and visitors are welcome.

In mid to late August, don't miss the first

day of school, when parents and kindergar-ten-age children dress in national costume. The new scholars are formally introduced to academic life by their families, who parade them through the school grounds and throw fistfuls of coins into the crowd. Other children scramble to scoop up as many coins as they can.

Aasivik, a two-week cultural and political gathering, was first held in 1976 as a forum for musical, artistic, traditional and political expression, and subsequently became an annual event. It always features presenta-tions of traditional theatre, drum dances and folk music but, in recent years, the scope has been extended to electronically synthesised Greenlandic rock music! It starts around 15 July and is held in a different location each year. For details, contact Niels E Høegh (fax 25983), PO Box 312, 3800 Nuuk.

In general, Greenlanders aren't unduly concerned with the future, and are happy to have fun today. Parties, which the Danes like to refer to as *mik*, happen anytime someone takes a notion to provide food, sweets, coffee and alcohol. They aren't normally earth-shaking affairs, but do offer a glimpse into modern Greenlandic society. Most town tourist offices can arrange a coffee-mik in a local home for around Dkr40.

ACTIVITIES
Hiking & Trekking
Trekking in Greenland isn't much like trek-king anywhere else. Apart from the odd sheep track in South Greenland and a few tracks around Narsarsuaq and Ammassalik, trails are essentially nonexistent and all run cross-country or along dogsled routes. In short, you need to be better prepared for trekking in Greenland than in most other places; you'll need to be good at reading a compass – including knowing the compass deviations for the applicable latitude – and at finding your way in some of the most diffi-cult non-technical country around.

In places, the terrain (even along popular routes) can become suddenly impassable, requiring long detours. Thick low-lying veg-etation hides fields of ankle-cracking boulders. Mossy bogs and hidden waterholes abound and walkers must make their way along steep, rocky and slippery mountain-sides, climbing and descending often to avoid the rough bits. At times, detours will take them over lofty mountains or up boulder-choked valleys to avoid dangerous stream crossings.

In short, Greenland isn't an ideal country for casual or amateur trekkers but it does provide some of the world's most magnifi-cent and rewarding walks and some of its most profound silence. Best of all, it's rela-tively undiscovered and you're not likely to run into another party, even on the more popular multi-day trips in South Greenland, which at the time of writing were attracting 20 to 30 groups per year.

Despite the low numbers, being lost or injured while trekking is a real possibility and the need for caution and precautions can't be overstated. Greenlandic weather can be horrendous, even in summer, with fog and freezing rain that can obscure the terrain for days on end. Under such conditions, even the best map and compass won't help you. In recent years, several trekkers have gone missing in Greenland and have never been found. This isn't to put you off trekking – there is no better way to appreciate the wil-derness – but outdoor skills and careful preparation are of utmost importance.

In this book, I'll only discuss the most popular routes. There are plenty of others but don't set off without carefully seeking out local advice. If trekking is your main empha-sis in Greenland, you're strongly advised to pick up a copy of the Skarv Guide *Trekking in Greenland* (1990) by Torbjørn Ydegaard. It provides up-to-date information on routes, access and practicalities. If you can't find it in a local travel bookshop, it can be ordered from Munksgård International Publishers (☎ 45-33 12 70 30; fax 45-33 12 93 87), Nørre Søgade 35, DK-1370 Copenhagen K, Denmark.

Trekkers, even day hikers, should tell someone about their plans and estimated time of return – and remember to inform them when the trip is complete. Rescue helicopters cost around Dkr40,000 per hour and it's the missing hiker who pays. If you advise someone of your itinerary and change it without notifying them, you could very quickly end up poor.

More serious adventurers should note that it is illegal to set off on an expedition to the inland ice without first obtaining a permit and purchasing search-and-rescue insurance covering up to Dkr900,000 (see the following Mountaineering section).

For further trekking guidelines, see the Fishing & Hunting, Books, Maps and Wild Foods sections of this chapter.

Mountaineering

For mountaineers who dream of doing a first ascent, Greenland offers plenty of scope, but for serious expeditions outside inhabited areas, the previously mentioned insurance keeps cropping up like a bad dream. Officials just don't like the idea of people risking their lives for the thrill of the experience.

There are four major climbing areas in Greenland: the Stauning Alps in North-East Greenland; around Ammassalik in East Greenland; around Kap Farvel and Nanortalik in South Greenland; and the Kangerlussuatsiaq (Evighedsfjord) in South-West Greenland. Of these, Ammassalik and Nanortalik are the most accessible. Greenland's highest peak, 3708m Gunnbjørns Fjeld, lies between Ammassalik and Ittoqqoortoormiit; and Uummannaq, in North-West Greenland, has an intriguing technical peak.

For rock climbers, Greenland's southern tip offers myriad challenging – and in many cases unclimbed – walls and spires which rival those of Yosemite, Patagonia and the Karakoram. Two of the world's highest and most impressive granite faces, 2012m Uiluit Qaaqa and 1830m Ulamertorssuaq, rise above Tasermiut Fjord near Nanortalik. Best of all, access is straightforward and no official insurance policy is required.

For specifics on organising a mountaineering expedition in Greenland, contact the Dansk Polarcenter (☎ 45-32 88 01 00; fax 45-32 88 01 01; email: dpc@dpc.dk), Stra-

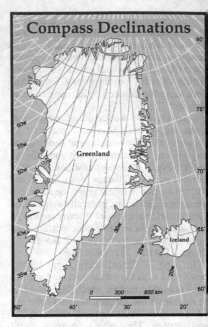

ndgade 100H, 1401 Copenhagen K Denmark.

Kayaking

Although it was developed in Greenland, the days of the practical hunting qajaq – the sealskin-covered one-person craft that made Greenland famous – are probably numbered as they've been replaced by the buzzing Mariner-powered speedboats (which pursue passenger ferries like barking hounds chasing cars!)

Thanks to qajaq clubs, however, whose efforts are aimed at a revival of the Greenlandic qajaq for practical, competitive and recreational purposes, it is now making a comeback. In Nuuk, the motto of the local Qajak Klubben is *Qajaq, Atoqqilerparput* o 'Qajaq, we are beginning to use it again'.

Avid sea kayakers will probably drool a they cruise the coastline. Recreationa kayaking (with a 'k', the word refers to the wider canvas or fibreglass varieties) has only recently been introduced, but recreational kayaks and equipment can now be hired in several towns. These are fine for short trips, but for longer expeditions it's best to bring your own equipment. The most convenient are the folding Klepper or Feathercraft models.

Taking into consideration the wind, weather, technical difficulty, exposure, landscapes and accessibility, the most suitable areas for kayaking are Tasermiut Fjord, near Nanortalik; Kangerlussuaq; the Narsarsuaq-Narsaq-Qaqortoq region; Nuup Kangerlua (Godthåbsfjord); and around Uummannaq. The Ilulissat area is also superb, but the icebergs do present dangers, and stories of capsize and death by rolling iceberg follow kayakers around Greenland like tales of bears in Canada.

Fishing & Hunting

Greenlandic lakes, particularly in the south, are rich in Arctic char and salmon, while the fjords teem with cod that seem to snap at anything, so it makes sense for trekkers to carry a fishing rod and lures. You'll need to buy a non-resident licence from a police station, tourist office or hotel; a one/three-month non-commercial fishing licence costs Dkr200/500. Ask for a list of regulations when purchasing a licence.

For hunting larger animals, which are probably best left to the locals anyway, many regulations apply, and polar bear, musk ox, snowy owl, gyrfalcons and sea eagles may not be taken by foreigners under any circumstances. Many other species are protected over large areas and some may not be removed from the country.

Before you rush off and buy a caribou hunting licence (Dkr3000), consider that there are no roads, and aircraft may not be used in hunting areas. This means hunters must carry all their gear on foot and – if they bag something – carry out the carcass afterwards.

If you can't be dissuaded – and are not content to just photograph the wildlife – you can get a rundown on seasons and regulations from Greenland Home Rule, Denmark

Office, Pilestræde 52, DK-1112 Copenhagen K, Denmark.

Skiing

Skiing in Greenland becomes more popular every year. Cross-country skiing is possible nearly anywhere in the winter, but there are also several summer skifields. The most organised are Kangerluarsunnguaq, near Nuuk; Apussuit, near Maniitsoq; and on Disko Island.

The largest alpine ski area is Nuuk's Kangerluarsunnguaq summer ski centre, with a one km run and 300m vertical variation. Apussuit, near Maniitsoq, offers excellent summer skiing and a vast new facility is now being developed on the glacier north of Sisimiut.

There are also small winter-only ski lifts at Sisimiut and Ammassalik, and two on the slopes of Quassussuaq behind the Nuuk airport.

WORK

As yet, few Greenlanders are qualified for technical positions, and skilled Danes are often needed for job-training or to fill positions for which no qualified Greenlanders can be found – but Greenlanders take hiring precedence. Most Danes work on three-year contracts, and although some get caught by Greenland's spell and stay on, most return to Denmark. Some contracts may include cushy fringe benefits – high wages, subsidised living quarters and regular trips home – but they're available only to persons relocating from Denmark (including those of Greenlandic heritage) and are becoming increasingly rare.

Because Greenland has opted out of the EU, non-Danish citizens may not work there, and there's no shortage of unskilled labour, so few foreign job seekers have luck finding work. Even fishing and fish-processing jobs almost invariably go to locals.

However, if you have a marketable skill and are keen to work in Greenland, contact a Danish consulate and see what sort of advice they can offer. Those who speak

Danish and/or an Inuit dialect have the best chances of success.

Scientific Research

For advice and permission to pursue scientific research or stage expeditions in Greenland, see the Dansk Polarcenter (☎ 45-32 88 01 00; fax 45-32 88 01 01), Strandgade 100H, DK-1401 Copenhagen K. For information, advice and resources, you may want to get in touch with the Scott Polar Research Institute (☎ 01223-337733; fax 01223-336549), Lenofield Rd, Cambridge CB2 1ER, UK.

Business & Investment

Prospective business investors in Greenland should contact the Grønlands Baseselskab A/S, Kristianiagade 1, PO Box 2669, DK-2100 Copenhagen Ø. They produce an English-language publication entitled *This is Greenland*, which paints the rosiest possible picture of the country's trade, industry and economic potential.

ACCOMMODATION
Camping

Narsarsuaq, Ilulissat and Kangerlussuaq have organised campgrounds, while most other towns have set aside camping areas, but without facilities or charges.

There are no restrictions on wilderness camping, and you can simply strike out into the bush and camp quite literally wherever you'd like. In the interests of the fragile Arctic ecosystems, you should practice minimal impact camping. For recommendations, see the Iceland Facts for the Visitor chapter.

If you're using a mountain stove, the local name for Coleman fuel (white gas, Shellite) is *rense bensin* or *lampeolie*. It's available from many youth hostels, tourist offices, shops and even petrol stations.

Youth Hostels

Most budget and mid-range travellers wind up staying in the pleasant youth hostels, or *vandrehjemmene*. They're maintained independently by villages, tourist offices, travel agencies or private individuals, and nearly every city and town has one.

Most hostels have hot showers and cooking facilities, some offer laundry facilities, and they aren't overly concerned with rules, regulations and curfews. You'll normally need your own sleeping bag, although some hostels provide bedding for an additional Dkr50 per night.

The least expensive hostels charge around Dkr120, but the average is Dkr150 and the most expensive hostel, one of several in Nuuk, charges Dkr250. The hostels in Narsarsuaq, Narsaq and Ilulissat are loosely affiliated with the Danish Youth Hostel Association, but there's no discount for hostel association members.

STI (formerly Nuna-Tek) Hostels

The hostels formerly owned by Nuna-Tek, an institution of the Greenland Home Rule government responsible for public works, are in the process of being transferred to another Home Rule entity, *Sanaartortitsiviit* (STI for short), or 'building services'. They provide housing for STI students.

During the summer holidays, some of these hostels are open to travellers. Some STI hostels serve officially as summer youth hostels while in others, accommodation may only be arranged through local tourism authorities. Prices are roughly the same as for youth hostels and some even offer meals and laundry service.

Seamen's Homes

A semi-budget alternative in Greenland and the Faroes are seamen's missions or seamen's homes (*sømandshjemmene* in Danish; *umiartortuq angerlarsimaffii* in Greenlandic; and *sjómansheimið* in Faroese).

Their historical purpose, as missions of the Danish Lutheran church, was to provide clean, safe lodging for sailors and fisherfolk while they were in port. As they're Christian-oriented, the staff begins the day with formal prayers and hymn-singing. If you can accept this – and the regulations against alcohol and

GREENLAND

carousing – they're a viable alternative to hotels.

All seamen's homes have a cafeteria which serves snacks and *smørrebrød* (open-face sandwiches) all day, and set menus at mealtimes. Some rooms have private baths and hot showers; there's also a common TV room open to guests. Double rooms without/ with bath cost around Dkr475/600.

Mountain Huts
In South Greenland, sheep stations in the Narsaq, Qaqortoq and Nanortalik districts make hostel-like huts available to hikers (in fact, they're locally known as 'youth hostels'). For basic dormitory-style accommodation, they average Dkr125 per person.

These relatively opulent huts normally offer comfortable accommodation, including cooking facilities (some even have video players!), and should not be confused with the more spartan shepherds' huts, which are basic little shelters where herders sleep during roundup and patrol. These are found scattered around sheep-grazing areas of South Greenland and can be used by walkers as emergency shelters. In any case, Greenlandic weather can be vile, so never set off walking there without a tent.

The Ammassalik and Sisimiut districts have also established several mountain huts and base camps for hikers, and other areas may follow suit in the near future. Hut accommodation is also available in several abandoned villages, which are typically used as summer camps for hunters or school-children.

Hotels
Most Greenlandic towns have at least one upmarket hotel and, as with most North Atlantic hotels, they're typically rather drab. However, they are very comfortable and their restaurants and pubs may even serve as a town social centre.

The cheapest double rooms start at around Dkr600, while tourist-class hotels may cost over Dkr1000. Normally, rates include a continental breakfast, if that's any consolation.

FOOD
Self-Catering
Economy-conscious travellers will want to buy supermarket food and prepare it themselves on a camping stove or in hostels. You'll find an amazing variety of groceries, although you may sometimes find several shelves of sundry pasta products but nothing, for example, that can be used to make a sauce. Or a supermarket may offer pineapples and mangoes, but there's not an onion in sight. Generally, prices are comparable to those in Copenhagen, and compared with Iceland, they may seem quite economical.

Greenland has two major supermarket chains: the government KNI and the Brugsen cooperative. Brugsen has shops in Sisimiut, Maniitsoq, Nuuk, Paamiut, Qaqortoq and Nanortalik, but KNI (pronounced KOH-enee) is represented in all major towns. In larger towns, both chains may also have smaller kiosks which stay open longer hours – normally until 7 or 8 pm – but prices may be higher and the selection of goods more limited. Smaller villages often rely on just a small KNI shop or kiosk. Most shops are open weekdays from 9 or 10 am to 5 pm, but in smaller places, they may close for lunch. They're also open from 9 or 10 am until midday on Saturday, and kiosks may open on Sunday as well.

Every town also has a bakery which supplies fresh bread, cakes, doughnuts and biscuits daily except Sunday. In some towns, the bakery is associated with the Brugsen or KNI supermarket.

Restaurants
Apart from the tourist hotels, Greenland has only a few restaurants. Hotel fare is predictably expensive but normally quite good. A typical meal consists of a fish, mutton or beef dish, accompanied by those boiled potatoes and soggy frozen vegies that are ubiquitous in the North Atlantic. Salads may be available, but aren't included in meal prices.

Seamen's homes do acceptable cafeteria meals, and there's a growing number of smaller cafés serving up popular dishes – several even offer Thai cuisine! For a quick snack, you can resort to the *grill-baren*, found in most towns. They specialise in hot dogs, chips and burgers for people on the run, and are commonly used as hangouts by the under-18 crowd.

Traditional Foods

Although visitors may be put off traditional Greenlandic fare for sentimental or ideological reasons, remember that whales and seals have dominated the Inuit subsistence hunting culture for thousands of years with no adverse effects on the populations, and that the current declines in cetacean numbers were brought about by European commercial whalers.

Traditional Inuit practice neither commercial nor recreational whaling or sealing, and animals are only hunted on a small scale for subsistence purposes. When an animal is killed, every bit of it is used, including the blubber, oil, skin and bones. While some may assume that the meat-rich Greenlandic diet is unhealthy, the country in fact has one of the world's lowest rates of cardiovascular disease, due to the consumption of unsaturated fatty acids found in marine mammals.

Each district has an annual whale quota (see Economy in the Facts about Greenland chapter), and whenever a whale is taken, people clamour to buy the blubber and the choice cuts. Traditionally, whales are respected beings, and people are grateful to whales that willingly give up their lives for human sustenance. Traditional hunters wouldn't decimate the population of any species, lest they deplete their children's inheritance, and if a person is accidentally injured or killed during the hunt, it's considered a fair balance.

Fresh whale steaks, which cost around Dkr30 per kg, are rich and filling fare. Whale blubber, or *mattak*, which is relatively tasteless and difficult to chew, is rich in vitamins and fats which the body uses efficiently to retain heat. Even a thin slice will provide several hours of jaw work!

There's no quota on seal hunting, apart from the tradition that people take no more than they can use, but the tannery in Qaqortoq, which buys sealskins from hunters, has inspired liberal interpretations of the tradition. Frozen seal meat is sold in supermarkets, but you'll also find fresh seal at the *kalaaliaraq* or *brædtet* (harbour market). Seal is tougher than whale and tastes more fishy. It can be cooked by cutting it into chunks and boiling it for an hour; it's popular to prepare the resulting stock as *suaassat* (seal broth soup with rice and onions).

In addition to marine mammals, harbour markets also sell a range of fish, including sea trout (*eqaluk*), salmon (*kapisillit*) and capelin (*ammassat*), as well as sea birds, caribou (*tuttu*) and occasionally musk ox (*ummimaq*). Meat and fish, particularly capelin, are dried for the winter and salmon is salted and smoked.

People also pick, collect and preserve wild foods – berries, mushrooms and greens – which appear during the short summers. A favourite is angelica, which may be eaten raw with sugar or boiled cod liver; it's also used in jams or as a salad accompaniment to game dishes.

Having said that, the Greenlanders' increasingly European outlook has brought changes. Modern young Greenlanders may well shoot at birds and seals for fun rather than food, and for the most part, only older people keep to traditional foods. In fact, the youngsters consume at least as much ice cream, sweets, hamburgers and junk food as the rest of the Western world, and respect for hunting traditions seems to be fading quickly.

Wild Foods

In the summer, you can supplement your diet with some of Greenland's abundant wild foods. From August to early September, the bush is carpeted with huckleberries (small blueberries). The tundra also offers a bounty of bitter black crowberries, which improve greatly with the addition of sugar. Occasionally, you'll also find bright red lowbush cranberries growing alongside them.

Angelica grows all over South Greenland and wild chamomile is abundant on the

Narsaq peninsula and surrounding areas. In the same area, wild thyme makes an excellent tea, as well as seasoning for European freeze-dried fare. In late summer, common harebells *(Campanula greseckiana)*, known locally as Grønlandsk blåklokke, grow everywhere and the sweet, slightly fragrant flower is delicious.

Several types of edible mushrooms grow in Greenland but the most delicious is the large, chocolate-coloured one with the spongy centre (called slippery jack in English and *steinpilz* in German) which reaches its peak in early August. It's found all over South Greenland.

Fishing also provides nourishment, and in the fjords, you don't even need a rod – just a lure, hook and line will do, as the cod snap at anything that moves. In the lakes, use a small hook to catch pan-sized Arctic char. For fishing licence information, see Fishing & Hunting under Activities in this chapter.

At low tide, you can collect blue mussels in sheltered areas which aren't exposed to direct sunlight. They're excellent steamed or fried with butter and garlic. However, avoid collecting near towns where they may be tainted by sewage or other pollution. Many varieties of Arctic seaweed are delicious as well, especially the slimy species known as 'sea lettuce'.

DRINKS
Non-Alcoholic Drinks
Greenland may well be the last place in the world where you can't get Coca-Cola (except at Pituffik, of course, and occasionally around Ammassalik). The choice of fizzy soft drinks is limited to the locally-produced Faxe Kondi brand, which is palatable but unmemorable. Coffee is a national institution and may be served up at any time of day.

Alcohol
Visitors arriving from Iceland may well be delighted with Greenland's relatively low alcohol prices, which are still higher than anywhere outside Scandinavia.

Although alcoholism isn't more prevalent in Greenland than in Iceland or the Faroes, it's more apparent, and on weekends or after payday, heavy partying can get out of hand. Many outsiders deride Greenland for its pervasive alcohol problems, but many other countries have similar – albeit better-hidden – ones. In Greenland's case, several causes have been cited: seasonally-affected depression (or 'SAD syndrome'); a sense of hopelessness from being 'caught between cultures'; and a genetic intolerance of alcohol which is seen in many people of Central Asian origin (it's related to low supplies of the amino acid which breaks down alcohol). In fact, it's probably a combination of those and other factors.

As a result, the Home Rule Administration attempts to limit the problem by restricting the hours in which alcohol may be sold. Patrons over 18 years of age may buy full-strength beer, wine and spirits in kiosks and supermarkets from noon to 6 pm on weekdays and from 11 am to 1 pm on Saturdays, or in licenced pubs and bars in the afternoon and evening. At other times, you can buy only 3.5% beer. Outside alcohol cannot be consumed on ferries (many people clearly feel this regulation was made to be broken), but beer and wine are available at mealtimes from ships' cafeterias.

The most popular brews are Danish Carlsberg and Tuborg, which are sold in 350 ml bottles for Dkr16 to Dkr20 in shops and Dkr25 to Dkr45 in bars and restaurants. In shops, the 3.5% beer costs from Dkr6 to Dkr8 per 350 ml bottle.

Most of the wine is French or Spanish, but Californian, Chilean, Italian and Australian wines are also available. A 750 ml bottle of table wine costs from Dkr65 to Dkr130. The wine cooler known as Nuuk Imeq (Nuuk water), which is bottled and sold in Greenland, isn't bad, but may be too sweet for some tastes. It takes more gumption to sample the local home-brew called *imiaq*.

THINGS TO BUY
Most Greenlandic towns have hotels or craft shops where visitors can buy soapstone, caribou antler and walrus and narwhal-ivory

carved to make jewellery or tupilak. Paamiut, with a reputation for fine tupilak carvings, offers good prices and high quality.

Greenlandic music, which is exceptionally good, may be a surprise for visitors. Two of the most popular rock recordings are *Miki Goes to Nuussuaq* by the band Zikasa and *Utaqqivunga* ('I'm waiting') by the powerful female singer Mariina Band. For Danish-influenced folk music, look for something by Rasmus Lyberth. Strong political protest music was the forté of the band Sume. They've now disbanded, but recordings are still available.

For light pop music, the Ole Kristiansen band is popular. Anguigaq, a group from Qaanaaq, specialises in rock music reflecting more traditional influences. These recordings are available at music shops in larger towns, including Nuuk, Qaqortoq, Ilulissat and Sisimiut.

Greenland's fabulous geology also has souvenir value, and shops in Narsaq and Ilulissat specialise in local gemstones – particularly *tuttupit*, which is unique to Greenland's Narsaq peninsula and Russia's Kola peninsula (see the boxed aside under Narsaq in the South Greenland chapter). The Greenlandic variety has an exquisite pink colour which intensifies in sunlight, and is thought by some to have spiritual powers. Other fabulous stones include garnets, amazonite, moonstone and several types of quartz and granite.

In Qaqortoq, which has a tannery, and Narsaq, which has a fashion fur workshop, you can purchase seal and fox furs – but naturally, purchases should reflect consideration of home-country import regulations and environmental impact.

Note that the export of artefacts – by definition anything made prior to 1940 – is prohibited without an export licence. See Legal Matters for more information.

Getting Around

Getting around in Greenland will probably be your biggest expense and greatest source of uncertainty. The best advice anyone can give is to remember the word *immaqa* ('maybe'), which seems to have been invented specifically for the Greenlandic transport system. In fact, Greenlanders will tell you the name of their national airline isn't Grønlandsfly, but Immaqa Air!

AIR

Given the climate, Greenland is well-served by its national airline, Grønlandsfly (Greenlandair), but the inordinately high cost of flying means that budget-conscious travellers will want to do as little of it as possible.

Grønlandsfly links most settlements by scheduled air routes with a fleet of Sikorsky S-61N and Bell helicopters, as well as several De Havilland Twin Otters and Dash-7 fixed-wing aircraft. Kangerlussuaq, Nuuk, Ilulissat, Narsarsuaq, Pituffik (Thule), Nerlerit Inaat and Kulusuk are served by fixed-wing aircraft. As yet, other major towns have only helicopter service, but new airports are currently under construction at Aasiaat, Maniitsoq and Sisimiut, and are planned for Uummannaq (Qaarsut), Upernavik and Paamiut. There's also discussion of building an airport at Qaanaaq.

As previously mentioned, *immaqa* has become ubiquitous, thanks to the fickle Greenlandic weather, which obviates rigid interpretation of flight schedules. Timetables exist mainly for convenience, but to rely on them may well amount to inconvenience; allow plenty of leeway when booking connecting flights.

The fares and flight frequencies described in this book apply only between mid-June and early September. In the winter, flights are less frequent and *immaqa* really comes into its own, so it's wise to contact Grønlandsfly directly.

Special Fares

Around Disko Bay and South Greenland, several seats on each flight are reserved as 'Green Seats' and are offered at about 30% lower than the normal fare. Naturally, they fill up quickly, so book early. Also ask about 'harpoon' or *tuukkaq* fares, which must be purchased 14 days in advance and offer good value subject to certain restrictions.

Grønlandsfly also has a special Max-2940 fare, which allows travel between any two towns in Greenland – regardless of the distance or number of connections involved – for a maximum of Dkr2940 each way. If that seems too good to be true, as it would if you're looking at a trip from, say, Nanortalik to Qaanaaq, it may well be. In order to qualify for the fare, you must have confirmed advance bookings for each leg of your intended flight, which with Grønlandsfly is nigh unto impossible even at the best of times.

Air Charter

In addition to its scheduled routes, Greenlandair runs a charter service, GLACE (☎ 27788; fax 29388), which charters five-seater planes. Sample rates include: Nuuk-Kangerlussuaq (Dkr17,600); Nuuk-Narsarsuaq (Dkr24,800); Ilulissat-Pituffik (Dkr44,400); Kangerlussuaq-Pituffik (Dkr55,900); Kangerlussuaq-Nerlerit Inaat (Dkr54,000); Nuuk-Kulusuk (Dkr33,600); and Narsarsuaq-Kulusuk (Dkr30,800). They charge an additional Dkr5000 for each night the pilot must wait.

Airline Offices

The main Grønlandsfly office (☎ 24488; fax 23788) is in Nuuk; the postal address is PO Box 1012, DK-3900 Nuuk, Greenland. All airports have small subsidiary offices but in smaller towns, tickets and bookings are normally handled by KNI offices. In Denmark, Contact the Grønlands Rejsebureau (☎ 45-33 13 10 11; fax 45-33 13 85 92) at Gammel

Mønt 12, PO Box 192, DK-1004 Copenhagen.

BOAT
Ferry

KNI owns a fleet of coastal ferries used to transport passengers up and down the west coast between Aappilattoq (near Cape Farewell) in the south and Upernavik in the north, and for soft sightseeing and meeting Greenlanders, you can't beat them. They're not cruise ships by any description, but they're safe, comfortable and take you past soaring peaks and through seas choked with mountainous icebergs and ice floes.

Unfortunately, KNI's finest ship, the *M/S Disko*, has recently been renovated and pressed into service as a tourist cruise ship (see later in this section). Regular passenger routes are handled by the three smaller boats, the *Sarpik Ittuk*, *Sarfaq Ittuk* and *Saqqit Ittuk*. These three are pretty much a mix 'n match bunch, so they may be juggled around from year to year, but typically, each one handles roughly one third of the distance between Qaqortoq and Upernavik (Qaqortoq to Nuuk; Nuuk to Ilulissat; and Ilulissat to Upernavik). On some runs, however, their routes overlap; for example, several times during the summer, the boat between Nuuk and Ilulissat continues north to Uummannaq or Upernavik.

Each ferry has couchettes, cabins (more like dormitories with space for four people and no locks on the doors), showers, and cafeterias where you can eat, socialise or watch videos (yes, you get the worst of American cinema several times a day, complete with Danish subtitles). They're too large to dock at smaller villages, requiring a tender to take people ashore. They're certainly adequate for the job and, especially if you've never sailed on the *Disko* (which is a magic old boat brimming with personality), you'll probably be quite impressed.

There are also smaller short-haul ferries. The tiny but comfortable *Aleqa Ittuk* runs between Narsaq and Aappilattoq. The *Taterak*, which handles routes between Narsarsuaq and Nanortalik, is the least comfortable boat, mainly because the non-smoking section is deep in the claustrophobic hull and the more comfortable saloon quickly fills with thick clouds of smoke. The *Tugdlik* and *Aviaq Ittuk* serve towns and villages around Disko Bay and the Kangaatisiaq district.

The larger ferries and some smaller ferries book out early and ship-capacity regulations are strictly adhered to, so if you're on a rigid schedule, purchase your tickets at least six months in advance; otherwise, you may have to take your chances on the waiting list. Grønlands Rejsebureau in Copenhagen can book summer itineraries as early as January, even before the timetable is available to the public.

In this book, summer deck class fares only are given; to work out cabin fares, add approximately 120%. Students, pensioners and children aged four to 13 years pay half-fare. Children under four ride free.

For a copy of the latest timetable, bookings or updates on vessels and routes, contact KNI Trafikkontoret (☎ 25211; fax 24431), Aqqusinersuaq 4, PO Box 608, DK-3900 Nuuk, Greenland, or better, the Grønlands Rejsebureau (☎ 45-33 13 10 14; fax 45-33 13 85 92) at Gammel Mønt 12, P O Box 130, DK-1004 Copenhagen, Denmark.

KNI Cargo Boat

KNI also has a fleet of cargo boats which are based in district towns and used to supply district villages once or twice weekly. They're permitted to carry a maximum of 12 paying passengers each, but they fill up quickly, so book early. Children and senior citizens pay half fare.

Greenland Tourism Cruises

The wonderful old *M/S Disko*, a character of a ship with private cabins, a large cafeteria, a kiosk, hot showers and a video hall, has been purchased by Greenland Tourism, renovated, and converted into a tourist cruise ship. Greenland Tourism has also acquired the summer services of the Russian-registered *M/S Ioffe* (also called the *Marine Adventurer*). These ships ply two main routes.

The *Disko* offers several itineraries. The five-day option sails from Kangerlussuaq, out through the stunning fjord of the same name, to Sisimiut, Kangerluk, Qeqertarsuaq, Qullissat and Uummannaq (Dkr7490). The four-day tour begins in Uummannaq and sails to Ilulissat via Saqqaq and Eqip Sermia (Dkr6490). The eight-day cruise combines these two options (Dkr10,990). Once each September, the *Disko* does an eight-day run between Kangerlussuaq, Ilulissat and Qaanaaq, also calling in at Siorapaluk and Qeqertaq (Dkr13,200 from Kangerlussuaq and Dkr10,300 from Ilulissat). These connect with flights between Pituffik, Kangerlussuaq and Copenhagen.

The *Ioffe* does three-day programmes from Narsarsuaq to Qalerallit Sermia and Eqalugaarsuit (Dkr2200); six-day return cruises from Narsarsuaq to fabulous Lindenows Fjord, via Alluitsup Paa, Nanortalik, Prins Christians Sund, and returning via Aappilattoq and Hvalsey (Dkr5500); and eight-day cruises combining these two options (Dkr7800).

Rates given are for the most basic available accommodation, and include transfers between airports and harbours, full board and guided tours in each port of call. For information and bookings, contact Greenland Tourism (☎ 45-33 13 69 75; fax 45-33 93 38 83), attn: Birgitte Skovsgård.

Charter Boat

Villages and sites that can't be reached by ferry or KNI cargo boat are normally accessible by charter boat. Nearly every Greenlandic family owns a powerboat of some description and finding someone to take you to an out-of-the-way place generally isn't too difficult.

The Home Rule government has devised a complex set fee schedule for boat charter. As a general guideline, a small, open boat under 2.8 metres in length costs Dkr120 per hour and a nine to 10.5 metre boat is Dkr280 per hour. Overnight waiting hours are half-price. Officially, however, you must pay for a minimum of six hours whether you use them or not, and there's a 50% surcharge for the first eight hours.

Anything up to six hours' charter in an open boat holding up to four or five people, including the pilot, is Dkr1080. Larger boats holding up to 12 or so people cost Dkr2520. In practice, however, few people follow the official guidelines. For short hauls, such as between Narsarsuaq and Qassiarsuk or between Nanortalik and Tasermiut Fjord in South Greenland, you'll pay only several hundred Dkr and for short trips of up to three or four hours, you'll probably pay 50% to 75% of the official rate.

CAR & MOTORCYCLE

Thanks to valley glaciers and impossibly rugged terrain, only two Greenlandic settlements – Ivittuut and Kangilinnguit – are connected by road. The longest drives in Greenland include the 70 km of roads around Kangerlussuaq, the five km between the Narsarsuaq harbour and Hospital Valley, the eight km route from Qassiarsuk to Tasiusaq,

GREENLAND

The Fate of the *Kununguak*

Most Greenland buffs are probably familiar with the *Disko*'s sister ship, the *M/S Kununguak* (named for Knud Rasmussen), which was taken off Greenland service in 1992. The idea was to turn it into a sort of floating bar travelling between Sweden and Finland. Unfortunately, it was discovered too late that it lacked a regulation fire sprinkling system. Installation would have cost around Dkr20 million – which was deemed uneconomic – and the dear old *Kununguak* is now unhappily languishing in some Scandinavian port awaiting a renovation that will probably never happen. Anyone who has further information on the fate of the *Kununguak*, please get in touch; I'd love to track it down!

Deanna Swaney

and the short routes around Arsuk and Kangillinguit.

Even so, Greenlanders do a fair bit of driving. In fact, the city of Nuuk, with just 14,000 people and 5.2 km of road, has 15,000 vehicles (90% of which are unregistered!). Even in smaller towns that can be crossed on foot in five minutes, everyone seems to own a vehicle and people take the car whenever they set foot out the door.

Car hire is available in Nuuk and Kangerlussuaq, but otherwise, local drivers have the streets to themselves (pedestrians take the hint). In most towns, visitors rely on taxis, buses or their own two feet.

DOGSLED

In the long months of continuous snow and frozen seas in Arctic and east Greenland, most people get around by dogsled. Greenlandic mushers harness the dogs in a fan formation, as opposed to the more complicated and tangle-prone in-line formation used by their Alaskan and Canadian counterparts.

For visitors, a 'winter tour' can be both exciting and memorable. The high season is from March to May when days are longer and temperatures not as extreme as in midwinter. As yet, summer visitors can only sample dogsledding on Disko Island, but a summer programme is also being developed for Sisimiut.

In many Arctic towns and villages, the dogs spend their days snoozing on the rocks, but Greenlandic sled dogs bear little resemblance to the drooling, tail-wagging pooches most visitors associate with the husky breed. In fact, many seem only a generation or two removed from wolves and their penchant for snarling, howling and ill-tempered demeanour must be taken seriously. Puppies are normally relaxed, but to approach or pat adult dogs would be to court disaster.

Except around Ammassalik, Greenlanders are not permitted to keep sled dogs south of the Arctic Circle, nor can they keep other dogs north of the Circle. This means that dogsledding is not available in Nuuk, Qaqortoq or elsewhere in southern Greenland.

Popular tourist dogsledding venues include Tasiilaq, Uummannaq, Ilulissat, Sisimiut, Qasigiannguit and smaller places. Most dogsled trips are arranged by hotels, but individuals may also speak directly with the dogsled owners and drivers.

Tourist dogsled trips range from one-day samplers to two-week expeditions, and include accommodation in villages or hunting camps. They're offered mainly by hotels in Arctic and East Coast towns. Informal dogsled trips may also be arranged with local hunters; expect to pay around Dkr475 per person per day for a realistic taste of traditional Arctic life. Note, however, that winter visitors face difficult or expensive transport logistics.

ORGANISED TOURS

Getting around Greenland isn't always convenient, and even independent visitors often participate in organised excursions. Of course, you can book an all-inclusive tour through the sights of South Greenland, Nuuk and Disko Bay, but most packages cost a small fortune and you'll lose the flexibility that Greenland invites. If you're going this route, you'll find some suggestions in the Getting There & Away chapter at the beginning of the book. In addition, several Icelandic companies offer programmes in Greenland. Recommended choices include Guðmundur Jónasson in Reykjavík and Nonni Travel in Akureyri.

For independent travellers, a good option is to join à la carte day tours. In many towns, tourist offices and private operators run day tours to points of interest for Dkr400 to Dkr900 per person. The two main operators are Grønlands Rejsebureau (Greenland Travel) and Arctic Adventure (see Organised Tours in the Getting There & Away chapter). These offer a range of hotel-based packages and day tours, mainly around South Greenland and Disko Bay, and also run dogsledding tours in both East and West Greenland. For something really different, ask about a seven-day Polar Night package tour to Ilulissat sometime between 20 November and 13 January, when the sun isn't visible at all.

Greenland Outfitters

A group of specially-trained guides and tour organisers known as Greenland Outfitters provide customised itineraries, including hiking, mountaineering, kayaking, sailing, dogsledding, snowmobiling, fishing and hunting. All speak some English and are licenced and insured to guide travellers. For a complete list of Greenland Outfitters, contact Greenland Tourism, PO Box 1552, DK-3900 Nuuk.

South Greenland

In Greenlandic, South Greenland is sometimes known affectionately as 'Sineriak Banaaneqarfik' ('banana coast'), but don't be fooled – it was also the source of the island's verdant-sounding name. Okay, it isn't Ecuador or Bali, but it is a less harsh variation on the Arctic than places further north.

Many visitors to Greenland get their first taste of the country here in the south, and it's an overwhelming introduction. In fair weather, the planes approach Narsarsuaq airport just a few hundred metres above the stark white icecap before descending the Qooroq or Kiattut Sermiat (labelled Kuusuup Sermia on the hiking map) glaciers between towering peaks, and passengers are treated to vistas of fjords, ice and snowy mountains. Confronted by this visual overload, you'll realise what a fabulous place this is, and nestled amid all the spectacular scenery are hundreds of Norse and Eskimo ruins, colourful towns, tiny villages, sheep farms and even a hot spring where you can bathe while watching the icebergs drift past in the fjord.

NARSARSUAQ

The name of this settlement of 180 people means 'the big plain', which may be an apt description by Greenlandic standards, but we're not talking about the Ukraine here. In fact, it's just a small flat area – just big enough for the international airport – combined with a braided river delta.

Narsarsuaq's magnificent setting makes a beautiful introduction to Greenland, and there's plenty to see and do, but bear in mind that Narsarsuaq owes its existence to the international airport, and does not offer a representative view of the country.

History

In April 1941, after the invasion of Denmark by Nazi forces, the USA and Denmark signed a treaty calling for temporary US

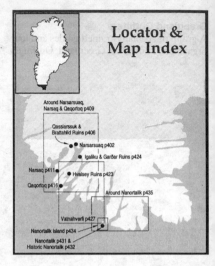

supply bases in Greenland. The original US plan was to construct a base on the isthmus above Igaliku, but locals resisted and the uninhabited Narsarsuaq delta became the nearest logical alternative.

The base, known as 'Bluie West One', was constructed practically overnight in July 1941, five months before the US had officially entered WWII. During the war, it was used as a way-station for bombers crossing the Atlantic, and by 1945 it had become Greenland's largest settlement, with a population of 12,000 and all the trappings of a small US town. From 1943 to 1944, a hospital was constructed on the site, which subsequently became the focus of much controversy and rumour (see boxed aside).

Although the original agreement with Denmark stipulated that the bases would be decommissioned when the war ended, during the Cold War the Americans actually increased their presence in Greenland. In fact, at one stage, they intended to construct

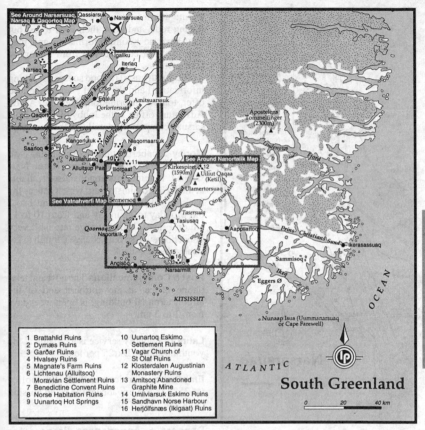

1 Brattahlid Ruins
2 Dyrnæs Ruins
3 Garðar Ruins
4 Hvalsey Ruins
5 Magnate's Farm Ruins
6 Lichtenau (Alluitsoq) Moravian Settlement Ruins
7 Benedictine Convent Ruins
8 Norse Habitation Ruins
9 Uunartoq Hot Springs
10 Uunartoq Eskimo Settlement Ruins
11 Vagar Church of St Olaf Ruins
12 Klosterdalen Augustinian Monastery Ruins
13 Amitsoq Abandoned Graphite Mine
14 Umiiviarsuk Eskimo Ruins
15 Sandhavn Norse Harbour
16 Herjólfsnæs (Ikigaat) Ruins

South Greenland

0   20   40 km

ATLANTIC OCEAN

a road over the icecap from Narsarsuaq to Kangerlussuaq, but when they realised the costs involved the project was abandoned.

On 11 November 1958, the US closed the Narsarsuaq hospital and offered what remained of the base to Denmark free of charge. However, the Danes didn't want it and when Norway offered to pay nearly US$250,000 for salvage rights, the offer was accepted and the Norwegians took out four times their investment's worth in equipment. The following year, Denmark established a civilian airfield on the site and on 1 January 1987, the airfield came under the jurisdiction of the Greenland Home Rule Administration.

In 1959, the Danish passenger ship *Hans Hedtoft* ran foul of an iceberg off Nunaap Isua (Cape Farewell) on its maiden voyage and went down with no survivors. To prevent similar disasters in the future, the Ice Patrol was established at Narsarsuaq. Its task is to monitor and track drift ice in Greenlandic waters using reconnaissance planes and helicopters.

Today, Narsarsuaq is an odd sort of place which revolves around the international airport. Although it's considered a village in

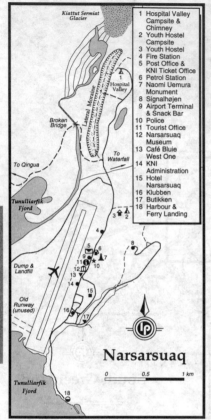

1 Hospital Valley
   Campsite &
   Chimney
2 Youth Hostel
   Campsite
3 Youth Hostel
4 Fire Station
5 Post Office &
   KNI Ticket Office
6 Petrol Station
7 Naomi Uemura
   Monument
8 Signalhøjen
9 Airport Terminal
   & Snack Bar
10 Police
11 Tourist Office
12 Narsarsuaq
   Museum
13 Café Bluie
   West One
14 KNI
   Administration
15 Hotel
   Narsarsuaq
16 Klubben
17 Butikken
18 Harbour &
   Ferry Landing

Narsarsuaq

0   0.5   1 km

the Narsaq district, only people who are employed in Narsarsuaq may live there.

Orientation
Maps Hikers should pick up the *Hikers' Guide – South Greenland*, which includes three detailed hiking maps and a descriptive booklet. It's sold at the youth hostel for Dkr200.

Information
Tourist Offices The private tourist office, South Greenland Tourism, is open from 10 am to 6 pm daily in the summer. They dis-

tribute leaflets, rent bicycles, tents and fishing rods, and book their own tours, but they have no hiking information and may well try to discourage you from hiking on your own.

The youth hostel (a good source for hiking information) and the Hotel Narsarsuaq also offer tourist information, and the Arctic Adventure office in the lobby of Hotel Narsarsuaq can provide details on their tours.

Money Your best option for exchanging cash or travellers' cheques is the Hotel Narsarsuaq. Foreign exchange is also available at the KNI Administration, which acts as the bank. It's open from 10 to 11 am and 1 to 2 pm Monday to Thursday and from 10 to 11 am on Friday. The exchange rate isn't very good, however, so only change enough to get you to the next bank.

Post & Communications The post and telephone office, at the northern end of the airport terminal building, is open weekdays from 1 to 3 pm.

Laundry Laundry service is available at the youth hostel for Dkr25 per load.

Emergency Services include the police (☎ 35222), fire brigade (☎ 000) and nursing clinic (☎ 35253).

Dangers & Annoyances Prepare for encounters with the legendary Arctic mosquito with a repellent containing lots of that bug bane, DEET. If that isn't sufficient to keep them at bay, pick up a head net from the Hotel Narsarsuaq.

Naomi Uemura Monument
The monument in the tiny park, opposite the airport terminal, honours Naomi Uemura, the Japanese national hero who went solo to the North Pole, crossing Greenland's inland ice from south to north. This most recent great Arctic explorer met his end in 1985 during an attempt at a first solo winter ascent of Alaska's Denali (Mt McKinley).

The Hospital at Bluie West One

During WWII, an immense 250-bed hospital was constructed in Hospital Valley, north of Narsarsuaq, and the purposes of this installation remain a matter of hot contention. Rumour has it that during the Korean War, the Narsarsuaq hospital received the US military's hopeless casualties – those so badly injured they would have dampened public war enthusiasm had they gone home. Families received bottles of ashes and were told their soldiers had been killed in action.

Recent Danish research has determined to its own satisfaction that this is all rumour, and maintains that the hospital was used only for US personnel and as a way-station for Greenlandic tuberculosis patients. To support these findings, the museum in Narsarsuaq displays photos of the hospital in action and contains letters from personnel who vouch that there was no activity there during the Korean War.

However, the hospital remained well-guarded and off limits to civilians during the Korean War, and although US Defense Department documents about the base have now been declassified, anything relating to the hospital remains classified. The official US line is that the facility was intended for rehabilitation purposes and as a medical unit for base personnel, and that it was completed but never opened. ■

Narsarsuaq Museum

The worthwhile Narsarsuaq Museum, south of the airport terminal, includes a variety of historical exhibits on the Norse, sheep farming and the US presence in South Greenland. From 15 May to 15 October, it's open Monday to Saturday from 10 am to 3 pm. Admission is Dkr10.

Signalhøjen

The climb to the radio tower atop 240m Signalhøjen, or Signal Hill, makes a short scenic hike from the village. There are two routes; one heads uphill from behind the youth hostel (past the off-limits reservoir area), and the other, up the gravel track behind the Butikken. Immediately west of Signal Hill is a lower peak, which is also capped by a bit of abandoned machinery, and from the saddle between the two, a rough track descends steeply to the Butikken route. It's best used for the descent, as the lower trailhead is very hard to find.

Hospital Valley

Over the moraine from Narsarsuaq is Hospital Valley, which contains lots of detritus left behind after the USA pulled out – bits of planes, machinery, and unidentified scraps interspersed with chunks of concrete, springs and debris from ruined military buildings. The museum has several photos of the valley at the height of operations, but the only remaining structure is a lone chimney and fireplace. Two species of orchid, *Platanthera hyperborea* and *Leuchorchis albida*, bloom in Hospital Valley from early to late August.

Horse Riding

The tourist office can arrange horse rental for around Dkr100 per hour, except during the sheep round-up, when the horses are all busy with other things. You can't take the horses too far from the settlement, but they're great for rides to Hospital Valley.

Organised Tours

Jacky Simoud (☎ & fax 72571; VHF radio 10, 'Puttut'), who is based across the fjord in Qassiarsuk, runs transfers to Qassiarsuk for Dkr80/150 one-way/return aboard the old wooden boat, *M/B Puttut*. He also runs Blue Ice Camp, at the mouth of Qooroq Fjord, which makes an ideal base for hikes to Motzfeldt Sø (see Around Igaliku later in this chapter). Other tours include Qooroq Fjord (Dkr320), fishing at Qingua, at the head of the Narsaq peninsula (Dkr320, plus Dkr50 equipment hire), and a Qassiarsuk coffee mik (Dkr200, with transfers from Narsarsuaq).

Arctic Adventure (☎ 35240) runs guided day-cruises to Narsaq (Dkr700), Qooroq

GREENLAND

Fjord (Dkr400), Itilleq and Igaliku (Dkr650) and Qassiarsuk (Dkr225); walks to Tasiusaq (Dkr450) and Kiattut Sermiat (Dkr200); and helicopter flights to the inland ice at Nordbosø (Dkr750). The office is in the lobby of Hotel Narsarsuaq.

South Greenland Tourism runs bus tours around Narsarsuaq (Dkr50), and can also book other tours.

Places to Stay

The most pleasant accommodation is the sparkling *Youth Hostel* (☎ 35221), which is beautifully situated on a gravel plain covered with blooming harebells and willow herb. It's steep at Dkr165 for beds and Dkr85 per person for camping, but the quality justifies it and the kitchen facilities are the best you'll ever see in a hostel. Meals are available if booked in advance: breakfasts cost Dkr30, breakfast and a lunchpack made from leftovers are Dkr65, and dinner is Dkr75. Non-guests may use the shower or the kitchen for Dkr25 each and laundry costs Dkr25 per load. Hiking maps are sold for Dkr250. Unfortunately, it closes around 31 August and doesn't re-open until mid-June.

The most convenient *camping* is beside the youth hostel, and costs Dkr85 per person, including use of hostel facilities. For wild camping, head out to Hospital Valley, three km north of the hostel. White gas for camping stoves is available at the youth hostel and on weekdays at the petrol station.

Hotel Narsarsuaq (☎ 35253; fax 35370) may look like just another block of flats in the cluster, but the interior is very nice and, as the only hotel in Narsarsuaq, it's often packed with tour groups. Single/double rooms with bath cost Dkr850/1040, and extra beds may be added for Dkr200. Rooms with shared baths cost Dkr550/700 and Dkr150 for extra beds. All rooms include breakfast. Amenities include a restaurant, cafeteria, bar and laundry service, and guests may use the small gym and sauna. After the youth hostel closes in late August or early September, you may be able to organise less expensive beds, but don't count on it.

Places to Eat

The Hotel Narsarsuaq *cafeteria* serves a limited menu of surprisingly good food between 7 and 9 am, noon and 2 pm, and 7 and 9.30 pm. A buffet breakfast, including cereal, fruit, yoghurt, rolls and trimmings – and perhaps the world's worst coffee – costs Dkr45. Superb buffet lunches and dinners cost Dkr75.

For more extravagant meals, you can resort to the hotel *dining room*, where excellent à la carte meals cost from Dkr175 to Dkr200. Look on the menu board near the stairway for the daily special, which costs Dkr135. When it's requested by tour groups, the special is replaced by a Greenland buffet, featuring seafood, reindeer, whale and other local specialities for Dkr135 for hotel guests and Dkr150 for outsiders. Meals are also available at the *Youth Hostel*, but you must book in advance. For prices, see under Places to Stay.

The new *Café Bluie West One*, beside the museum, serves up coffee, sandwiches, cakes and alcoholic drinks, and the outdoor seating is especially appealing on sunny days (as long as there's a breath of wind to keep the bugs away!).

When the airport terminal is open, the *Grill-baren* in the lounge serves hot dogs and plastic-wrapped microwave versions of other things. You can also get coffee, soft drinks and packaged snacks.

The supermarket, marked *Butikken*, in a block of flats south of the hotel, sells everything from groceries to socks to rifle ammunition. There's a good selection of frozen and freeze-dried food as well as alcohol and limited fresh produce. It's open from 8 am to 5.30 pm Monday to Friday and from 9 am to 1 pm on Saturday.

Entertainment

Apart from the popular bar at the *Hotel Narsarsuaq*, Narsarsuaq has little nightlife. However, every second Saturday in the summer, Narsarsuaq throws a party at *Klubben* ('the club'), which attracts nearly everyone in the village as well as people from Qassiarsuk and surrounds. It's a great opportunity for dancing, drinking, chatting and meeting locals of all generations. It's lots of fun and visitors are welcome as long as they realise this is a local gathering and not a tourist programme.

At 8.30 pm nightly, the hotel shows educational videos about Greenland upstairs in the conference room. Admission is Dkr35 (or Dkr45 with tea or coffee). Afterwards, there's someone on hand to answer questions.

Getting There & Away

Air In summer, weather permitting, SAS flies nonstop to and from Copenhagen on Tuesday and Saturday, and Icelandair flies to and from Keflavík, Iceland, on Monday and Thursday. Grønlandsfly (☎ 35288) has at least three daily helicopter connections to Paamiut (Dkr2520), Qaqortoq (Dkr680), Narsaq (Dkr490) and Nanortalik (Dkr1120); and twice weekly flights to Kangilinnguit (Dkr1360) and Kangerlussuaq (Dkr3730). They also fly to Nuuk (Dkr2250) three times weekly in DeHavilland Dash 7 aircraft.

Ferry The *Taterak* calls into Narsarsuaq at least once weekly in the summer, with service to Qassiarsuk (Dkr55), Itilleq (Dkr80), Narsaq (Dkr130), Qaqortoq (Dkr195) and Nanortalik (Dkr370). Tickets are available at the KNI office in the airport terminal, which is open Monday to Saturday from 8 am to 3 pm.

Getting Around

Narsarsuaq stretches for several km, but you can easily walk anywhere. It's a half-hour walk from the hotel to the harbour with luggage, and 10 minutes longer from the youth hostel. The free Hotel Narsarsuaq bus meets incoming flights and ferries, and shuttles guests to the hotel. Transfers in the white youth hostel van cost Dkr5 per person to or from the harbour, airport or Hospital Valley.

The tourist office rents mountain bikes for Dkr35 per hour, Dkr50 for three hours and Dkr100 per day, plus a Dkr100 deposit. For a week, you'll pay Dkr500 plus a Dkr600 deposit.

AROUND NARSARSUAQ
Narsarsuaq Valley Hike & Inland Ice

The walk through Hospital Valley and into Narsarsuaq Valley (also called Flower Valley), which follows a proper walking track, is one the easiest and most pleasant in Greenland.

From the rubbish tip, at the northern end of Hospital Valley, it climbs a small rise for a spectacular view before descending into Flower Valley. At the foot of the hill, a farmer is attempting to cultivate crops in the pleasant micro-climate.

The track continues up the valley through relatively luxuriant vegetation, with trees up to three metres high in some sheltered enclaves. Near the head of the valley, the route crosses glacier-scoured boulders and patches of glacial silt to arrive at the foot of a 300m cascade.

Casual walkers may turn back at this point, but it's worth carrying on up the winding 300m ascent to a haunting prehistoric-looking lake flanked by tundra and glacier-scraped boulders. From the lake, the trail makes a 1½-km descent to the tortured geology at the flank of the Kiattut Sermiat glacier, which is a spur of the inland ice. Hikers traditionally carry a bottle of whisky or vodka and drink a toast to the 10,000-year-old ice cubes they can chisel off and place in the drinks.

The return walk can be completed quickly in about six hours, but it's more pleasant to take a picnic and allow an entire day. Arctic Adventure offers this as a guided day hike for Dkr200, including lunch.

Mellemlandet

A longer trip for experienced trekkers will take you to Mellemlandet, the 'middle land'. From the lake above the head of Flower Valley, climb the ridge to the east and into the 500m to 900m hills, which are dotted with some lovely lakes. You can continue north-east for 12 rugged km through Mellemlandet to the promontory that overlooks the split of the vast glaciers Kiattut Sermiat and Qoorqut Sermiat. Allow at least

GREENLAND

three days for the return trip from Narsarsuaq.

Greenland Travel offers this hike as an escorted expedition.

Qooroq Fjord

Most of the icebergs around Narsarsuaq were born in the glacier Qoorqut Sermiat and calved into ice-choked Qooroq Fjord. Arctic Adventure runs four-hour cruises on Tuesday and Friday for Dkr400. Make arrangements at office in Narsarsuaq.

For information on the Blue Ice Camp, at the mouth of the fjord, see Around Igaliku, later in this chapter.

Nordbosø

The spectacular lake Nordbosø lies at an altitude of 800m, surrounded by mountains and ice. On Fridays, Arctic Adventure operates one-hour helicopter tours for Dkr750. Very experienced hikers can reach Nordbosø via Qassiarsuk or Qingua, but would require excellent compass and map-reading skills. From the lake, it's a three-day return climb to the summit of 1650m Valhalla.

QASSIARSUK (BRATTAHLID)

Across Tunulliarfik (Eiríks Fjord), a half-hour by boat from Narsarsuaq, is Qassiarsuk, with around 125 people. Qassiarsuk was Eiríkur Rauðe's Brattahlid (originally Brattahlíð), which he considered the richest and best site in Greenland when he arrived in 982.

In addition to a wealth of Norse ruins, there's a 1982 memorial to Eiríkur Rauðe by Greenlandic artist Hans Lynge, and a statue of the area's first modern sheep breeder, Otto Frederiksen, who set up a farm in 1924 and thereby created an economic base for the community. Both monuments are partially constructed of the beautiful red and white Igaliku sandstone, which is found only in this part of Greenland. It appears vaguely edible, something like a cherry vanilla marble cake.

Visitors should beware of the pack of mad ATV's (All Terrain Vehicles) which terrorises the street and everything in it!

Qassiarsuk & Brattahlid Ruins

0   50   100 m

1 Havsteen-Mikkelsen Bronze Sculpture
2 Otto Frederiksen Monument
3 Frederiksen Museum
4 Coffee Mik Home (Laura Frederiksen)
5 Café Brattahlid
6 Youth Hostel
7 1000-year Anniversary Monument
8 KNI Shop, Post & Telephone Office
9 Harbour & Ferry Landing

Ruins

The tiny square foundation beside the current church is all that's left of Þjóðhildur's Church, the first Christian church in the New World. It was built by Eiríkur Rauðe's wife, Þjóðhildur, a zealous convert to Christianity, sometime around the year 1000.

Among the other ruins are foundations of a later church and the hall of a great manor house, which was the home of Eiríkur and Þjóðhildur themselves. All that remains of the latter is a bit of a fireplace and a running water system. Beside it is the ruin of a cattle and sheep byre, and evidence of a *þing*, or political assembly area. Nearer the water are remains of Eskimo dwellings which used an ingenious system of heat conservation.

The fanciful bronze sculpture on the rock is by artist Sven Havsteen-Mikkelsen. According to Rie Oldenburg of the Narsaq Museum, a portion of it is a map of the settlement at its height. The stars, moon and sun are symbols of navigation; the cross represents *den Hvide Kristus*, the 'White Christ'; and the persons on the left are probably Eiríkur and Þjóðhildur. The 'ghost' is actually a figure head from a Viking ship – probably a dragon – and the rider with his long hat is from later times. The 'U' beneath the sun indicates the location of Þjóðhildur's church in relation to the other homes.

Church

The current village church was financed and built by the local residents in the 1930s, after the Danish government repeatedly refused to appropriate funds for a church. Each year, they sold their best sheep to the slaughterhouse in Narsaq to add to the fund. When the government recognised their commitment to the project, it put up half the finances, and the church was constructed in 1936.

Through WWII, the church was used by Americans from the Narsarsuaq base, who donated the hymn board which is still used. The interior colour scheme is said to include white for snow and ice, blue for the sky and sea, yellow for the sun and red for the warmth of fire.

Frederiksen Museum

The 1924 home of the first Greenland sheep breeder, Otto Frederiksen, has been turned into a memorial museum containing photos of life in Qassiarsuk and of the 1952 royal visit by King Frederik and Queen Ingrid. It's open Monday from 2 to 5 pm, Tuesday from 10 to 11.30 am and Thursday from 10 to 11.30 am and 2 to 3 pm. If you're there at another time, contact Hans Christian Motzfeldt (☎ 35077) to arrange an opening.

Organised Tours

Qassiarsuk tour operator, Jacky Simoud (☎ & fax 72571), knows the village well and offers transfers and day tours from Narsarsuaq. He can also arrange a coffee mik (Dkr35) with a local woman, Laura Frederiksen (☎ 35090), and barbecues and stays at his lovely and remote Blue Ice Camp, across the fjord.

The Arctic Adventure day tour from Narsarsuaq (Dkr225) offers a brief introduction to the Norse in Greenland. For Dkr450, you can add a guided 16 km return hike to Tasiusaq (see later in this chapter). It's possible to stay in Qassiarsuk or Tasiusaq and return to Narsarsuaq on a later tour.

Places to Stay & Eat

The *Youth Hostel* (☎ 72555), the yellow building near the KNI shop, is run by Poul and Amalie Frederiksen and offers basic beds for Dkr125. It contains a looselydefined cafeteria which serves coffee, tea and sweet treats from 10 am to 4 pm daily. Lunches (Dkr75) must be ordered in advance. From 1 to 8 pm, beer costs Dkr25, but from 8 pm to midnight – when you really want it – the price climbs to Dkr30. No English is spoken.

The *Brattahlid Café*, run by Ellen and Dorthe, does coffee, snacks, sandwiches and meals (sometimes). It's currently housed in a tent, but they're looking for a permanent location. It's open from 2 to 5 pm daily except Sunday.

The small *KNI shop*, which packs in a surprising range of groceries, is open 9 am to 4 pm Monday to Friday and 9 am to 1 pm on Saturday.

Getting There & Away

In summer, the ferry *Taterak* sails between Narsarsuaq and Qassiarsuk weekly (Dkr53). The best and most reliable access is with Qassiarsuk tour operator Jacky Simoud (☎ & fax 72571; VHF radio 10, 'Puttut'), who runs transfers from Narsarsuaq several times daily for Dkr80/150 one-way/return. You can book directly or through the Narsarsuaq Youth Hostel. Informal boat charters from

GREENLAND

Narsarsuaq harbour cost from Dkr50 to Dkr150.

AROUND QASSIARSUK
Tasiusaq

The sheep station Tasiusaq huddles beside the Tasiusaq, an inlet of ice-filled Nordre Sermilik Fjord, and presents remarkably pastoral scenes complete with tractors, balers and hayfields.

Places to Stay When you reach the farm, bear left over a small rise and you'll see the comfy and friendly *Youth Hostel*, run by Otto and Jørgine Frederiksen. It has a great sunny porch and basic cooking facilities. Beds cost Dkr125.

Getting There & Away It's an easy and rewarding eight km walk across the peninsula from Qassiarsuk. The route follows a clear tractor track and you're rewarded with lovely vistas all the way. For an alternative route back to Qassiarsuk, head north along the shore to the next big valley and cross the Qorlortup Itinnera pass, where there's a superb waterfall. This circuit is about 22 km, but the relatively hospitable terrain makes it an easy day hike.

Alternatively, follow the northern shore of Tasiusaq across the first major stream, then turn inland and parallel the tractor track back to Qassiarsuk. This route also has a lovely waterfall and the easy walk crosses gentle, sheep-grazed moorland.

Poul and Jørgine Frederiksen can provide transport from Qassiarsuk for Dkr60/100 one-way/return. Arrange it through the youth hostel in Qassiarsuk.

Qingua & Eqalorussit Kangillit

A 10 km shore walk north of Qassiarsuk is the Qingua sheep farm, at the head of Qingua Fjord. From there, you can walk up the western bank of the river past several waterfalls and back down to the head of the spectacular Eqalorussit Kangillit icefjord. Alternatively, from the farm Qorlortoq, you can follow the Paaratiisip River up past the lake Ivianguissanguit to connect with this

route at the Natinguaq Pass. Together, these routes make an excellent two to three-day loop from Qassiarsuk.

If you want to reach Narsarsuaq, you'll have to organise boat transport from Qingua or a tractor from Kiattut, as the river which flows from Kiattut Sermiat cannot be crossed on foot (the footbridge has been broken for years).

QASSIARSUK TO NARSAQ TREK

Thanks to its four youth hostels, Qassiarsuk to Narsaq may well be the best-trodden trek in Greenland. The sheep farms on the northern half of the peninsula are mostly linked by tractor tracks, so walking is relatively easy, but the southern half of the walk is more challenging. Although you can stay in youth hostels (all Dkr125) for three or four nights, you'll need a tent for the last two nights (unless you arrange boat transport to Narsaq from Ipiutaq).

Most people walk this route from north to south. Peak elevations mentioned here are based on the *Hiker's Guide – South Greenland* (see Maps under Narsarsuaq), which is requisite for all hikers. There was a half-hearted attempt to mark this route with red and white blazes, but as yet, only small sections are marked and they invariably disappear when the going gets rough. It's safest to ignore them and rely on your map and compass.

Stage 1: Qassiarsuk to Tasiusaq or Nunataaq

The first day of this hike is a gift: an easy eight km amble over the pass from Qassiarsuk to the *Tasiusaq Youth Hostel* where you can relax in the sun or just explore the area, or you can continue to the youth hostel at Nunataaq (see stage 2).

Stage 2: Tasiusaq to Sillisit

The second day takes you south-west along the head of the Tasiusaq Bay to the farm Nunataaq, where there's a new *Youth Hostel* (Dkr125) run by friendly Enooraq Frederiksen. Follow the tractor track inland for about

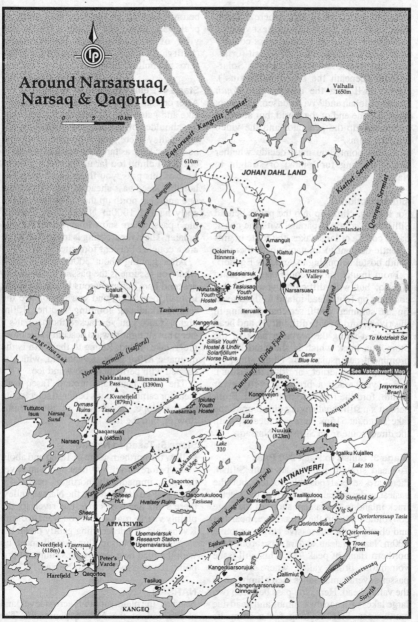

three km, past a small lake, where a sheep track leads over a pass into the next valley.

It's then an up and down cross-country route past numerous lakes to Sillisit (originally the Norse settlement, Unðir Solarfjöllum, 'beneath the sunny mountains'). Here you'll find the comfortable *Youth Hostel* of Johan and Vivi Knudsen. This may seem like the end of the world, but at night, they crank up the generator and the video machine hums.

At this point, you must decide whether you're heading for Ipiutaq or straight to Narsaq.

Ipiutaq Option
For Ipiutaq, climb up into the peaks behind Sillisit and continue parallel with the coast; past a couple of large lakes, the route begins a gentle descent to Ipiutaq, where there's a youth hostel belonging to Aqqaluk Egede.

From Ipiutaq most people take a boat to Narsaq, but with difficulty, you can also continue on foot. Head inland to the stream (in late summer, you'll see char jumping in this river), ford it (with difficulty!), and head south-west along the northern bank of the Store Ilua inlet, which is sheltered by the prominent peninsular peak Nunasarnaq (in Danish, Strygejernet, or 'the flat iron'). When you reach a broad gravelly river mouth, ford the river and turn inland. From here, it's a stiff, challenging climb up to the lake Taseq, at 515m. Here you meet up with the direct route from Sillisit to Narsaq.

Stage 3: Sillisit to Peak 936 Pass
To head straight for Narsaq from Sillisit, there are several possible routes, but the easiest is described here. Follow the tractor track inland to the eastern shore of the large convoluted lake in the pass. Here, bear left and climb up the successive ridges onto the 600m Naajat plateau, and traverse around the northern flank of peak 786. This will issue you into a broad valley, where the route passes several small lakes then climbs up to the valley head. Here, you pass between two large lakes on a narrow isthmus and head due south-west. Start looking for a campsite

before climbing up the easy pass north of peak 936. There you'll have a spectacular view of the saw-toothed Redekammen (Killivaat) ridge, which rises to 1210m across Tunulliarfik Fjord.

Stage 4: Peak 936 Pass to Taseq
After crossing the pass, descend past a small lake and gain some altitude to take you over the shoulder of the hill and down into the next valley. Here, you'll be able to see the next pass; keep as far to the north as possible, but don't climb too far up the slope. Southwest of this pass, you'll see an obvious but horribly steep pass ahead of you. Avoid this one and bear north up the valley toward the aptly-named 1000m Nakkaalaaq ('crumble') pass, where snow lingers until August or later. The river crossing is tricky, but there are a couple of decent ford sites.

After gaining about 300m, you'll reach what you assume is the pass. It's not, and to descend here is treacherous to say the least. Instead, bear north and you'll soon see the real Nakkaalaaq, looming another 150m higher. Once you've cracked the pass, it's a steep but straightforward descent to the blue-green lake, Taseq. Rising to the north is the dramatic 879m peak, Kvanefjeld, which is capped with permanent snow and ice.

The stark landscape around Taseq isn't ideal for camping, so it's better to select a site up the slope, beside one of the streams flowing into the lake.

Stage 5: Taseq to Narsaq
Follow the northern shore of Taseq and about 750m before its outflow, bear uphill and over the pass immediately north of peak 643. Once you've dropped into the Narsaq valley, there's no need to cross the river to the plainly visible road unless you want to climb Kvanefjeld. By descending gently down the slope toward Narsap Ilua, you'll meet up with the road near the Dyrnæs ruins. At this point, it's an easy hour into Narsaq.

NARSAQ
Narsaq ('the plain') sprawls across level land at the end of the Narsaq peninsula. The

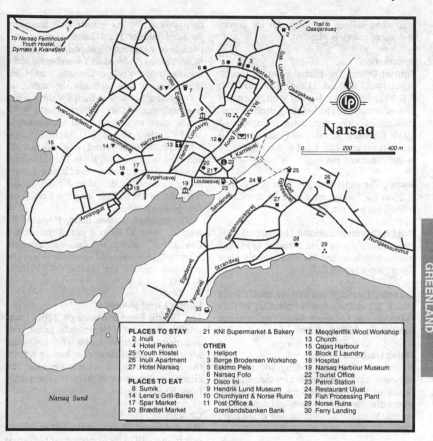

Narsaq

0   200   400 m

PLACES TO STAY	21 KNI Supermarket & Bakery	12 Meqqileriffik Wool Workshop
2 Inuili		13 Church
4 Hotel Perlen	**OTHER**	15 Qajaq Harbour
25 Youth Hostel	1 Heliport	16 Block E Laundry
26 Inuili Apartment	3 Børge Brodersen Workshop	18 Hospital
27 Hotel Narsaq	5 Eskimo Pels	19 Narsaq Harbour Museum
	6 Narsaq Foto	22 Tourist Office
PLACES TO EAT	7 Disco Ini	23 Petrol Station
8 Sumik	9 Hendrik Lund Museum	24 Restaurant Ujuat
14 Lene's Grill-Baren	10 Churchyard & Norse Ruins	28 Fish Processing Plant
17 Spar Market	11 Post Office &	29 Norse Ruins
20 Brædtet Market	Grønlandsbanken Bank	30 Ferry Landing

GREENLAND

current population is around 1800, but it seems larger because it's so spread out. It's as if the developers realised they had surplus space and planned the settlement with gaps to fill in later. Interestingly, Narsaq buildings reflect the widest colour range in Greenland, with several shades in between the standard red, blue, yellow and green.

History

This invitingly flat space couldn't have been ignored by the 10th-century Norse colonists and indeed, it's dotted with their ruins. The present town was founded in 1830 and

thanks to its deep-water harbour, it became a Royal Greenland Trade Department station in 1833, gaining town status in 1959.

If Greenland has an industrial centre, Narsaq is it. In 1953, a shrimp-processing and fish-freezing plant was opened and the Danish government supplied labour by forcibly evacuating the village of Niaqornaq, on the northern shore of Nordre Sermilik Fjord. The facility now doubles as a slaughter-house, which means D-Day for 15,000 tender new lambs each season. There's also a small woollens and fur factory, a bone-carving shop and a mineral-polishing and craft shop selling jewellery. An ice cream and juice factory is planned.

Information

Tourist Office The friendly Narsaq tourist office (☎ 31325; fax 31394), PO Box 148, DK-3921 Narsaq, is helpful with brochures and information. The building itself is constructed of stone and dates from around 1930. It's open Monday to Friday from 10 am to noon and 1 to 4 pm and on Saturday from 10 am to 1 pm.

Money The bank, which is at the post office, is open for foreign exchange on weekdays from 9 am to 3 pm.

Post & Communications The post office is open from 9 am to 3 pm Monday to Friday. but the telephone and fax office is only open from 9 am to noon.

Laundry Laundry services are available in Block 'E', in the colourful complex of flats at the west end of town. Laundry tickets are available at the INI office.

Qajaq Harbour

Historically, Narsaq's sealing and whaling activities have been centred on the old peninsula at the north-western end of town, where the hunters moored and hung their qajaqs. You may still see the odd qajaq here, especially when tour groups are about.

Narsaq Harbour Museum

The Narsaq Harbour Museum (☎ 31666) takes in the old 1883 Nordprøven trading station buildings beside the picturesque old harbour: a cooperage/blubber storage house, stable, chapel, shop, Frederik Høegh's printworks, several stone houses and a recent replica of a traditional sod hut. On sunny days, you'll also appreciate the harbour-view picnic tables.

The oldest building, the Farés printing office, was built in 1830 of clay and grey stone as the residence of the Royal Greenland Trading Company manager. It was considered a model for the community and

in payment for his efforts, the company awarded builder Hans Jakob Hansen four pounds of sugar and eight pounds of coffee. In later years it served as a warehouse and a trading company office. The small turf building behind it was probably the stable. In 1908, a new house was built for the trading post manager, and was inhabited until 1953.

The main exhibition building, known as 'A-34', after the WWII identification number painted on its roof, was built in 1928 and used as a shop until 1960. The subsidiary rooms were used for storage. It now houses a large collection of cultural exhibits and artefacts. In the blubber house is a small but fine geology exhibit.

The museum is open daily, 1 June to 31 August, from 12.30 to 4 pm. Admission is Dkr10, but students and senior citizens are admitted free. Special openings may be arranged through the curator (☎ 31616 or 31233).

Henrik Lund Museum

The Henrik Lund Museum (☎ 31616) was actually the home of Greenlandic priest, poet and painter Henrik Lund and his wife, Malene. He's best known for having written the song *Nunarput* which became the Greenlandic national anthem. It's open daily from 10 am to noon.

Church

The prominent church on the hill in Narsaq was built in 1926 by Qaqortoq architect and builder Pavia Høegh.

Cemetery

Recently, a team of gravediggers discovered the ruins of a Norse settlement in the cemetery. A visitor to the town in 1894 noted that many of the trading buildings in early Narsaq had been constructed of stones from this site. So far, a fireplace, cooking pot and several stone tools have been uncovered, but the sensitive nature of the location prevents further excavation.

Fish Plant Ruins

Narsaq's third major ruin lies east of town,

in the meadow beyond the fish-processing plant. They consist of an excavation eight metres long, half a metre wide and half to four-fifths of a metre deep. Around it is a stone and turf wall. During the excavation, more houses were uncovered but this is the best-preserved.

Surprisingly, these ruins are thought to date from 982, and it has been mooted that Eiríkur Rauðe stayed here before continuing up the fjord to Brattahlid. Based on this, Narsaq celebrated its 1000th anniversary in 1982, and you may still find the commemorative posters showing an artist's conception of the Norse settlement.

To get there, walk through the plant yard and cross the fence; the visible part of the excavation is in the far north-eastern corner of this meadow.

Organised Tours

Arctic Adventure runs several tours, which may be booked through the youth hostel or Hotel Perlen. On Tuesday, Wednesday and Saturday, there's a five-hour town tour (Dkr185, with lunch) which visits the qajaq harbour, museum, church, Eskimo Pels and the brædtet. It can also be done as a day trip from Narsarsuaq (Dkr700), including return boat transport.

On Wednesday or Saturday, you can cruise to Tuttutoq Isua (Dkr400), which reveals the most extensive Eskimo ruins in South Greenland. The tour includes lunch and a brief stop at Niaqornaq, which was abandoned in the 1950s to provide labour for new industries in Narsaq.

A popular seven-hour cruise (Dkr650) crosses Ikersuaq (Bredefjord) to visit the twin tidewater glaciers spilling down from the inland ice. The tour stops between the glaciers for a picnic, visits waterfalls and bird cliffs and also stops briefly at an abandoned Inuit settlement. It operates on Monday and Thursday.

The tourist office also arranges a geological hike on Kvanefjeld and Illimmaasaq (Dkr300); a walking tour of Narsaq (Dkr100); a hike to Dyrnæs Norse ruins (Dkr100); a visit to local artists and artesans

(Dkr100); a Greenlandic buffet or barbecue (Dkr150); and a botanical walk learning about Arctic flora (Dkr100) and other hiking tours of varying length (Dkr150 to Dkr300).

Places to Stay

Independent travellers love the cosy old *Youth Hostel* (☎ 31665), which sits on a ridge with a great view of town. The Dkr125 charge gives you rooms with only one set of bunk beds in each, and access to the hot showers and cooking facilities. It's open from 15 June to 5 September and is popular with groups, so advance booking is advised. There are lots of *campsites* out toward Dyrnæs and in the Narsaq valley, but the most convenient site is beside Inuili.

Alternatively, you can stay at the 20-bed *Narsaq Farm Youth Hostel* (☎ 31049 or 72072; fax 31064), north of town toward the Narsaq valley. Beds cost Dkr130. There is also a summerhouse which rents for Dkr2000 per week. Transport from town costs Dkr50 per person and to Kvanefjeld, Dkr100 per person. Fishing equipment can be hired for Dkr50 per day.

The *Hotel Perlen* (☎ 31675), Narsaq's main hotel, is run by Arctic Adventure for their tour groups, but it's open to anyone if there's space available. Single/double rooms with shower and toilet cost Dkr650/900, including breakfast. During the summer, Arctic Adventure takes over the *Inuili* vocational school and uses its flats as single/double rooms with bath for Dkr650/900. The *Inuili apartment*, at Savaasit Qaqqaat B247, offers a bath, kitchen and TV for Dkr250/500 with one/two people.

The more basic *Hotel Narsaq* (☎ 31325; fax 31394) charges Dkr300/700 for single/double rooms with bath.

A unique option is *Kuutsiaq Reindeer Glacier Lodge* (☎ 31620; fax 31634), PO Box 12, Narsaq. This wilderness outpost across Bredefjord emphasises reindeer hunting on a private concession.

Places to Eat

Despite its size and importance, Narsaq is short of eateries. For snacks, try the fast food

GREENLAND

at *Lene's Grill-baren* near the qajaq harbour. The *Hotel Narsaq* restaurant is pretty good, but meals must be booked in advance. Occasionally they put on a Greenland buffet featuring local delicacies. The *Hotel Perlen* serves breakfast only.

The well-stocked *KNI supermarket* sells everything you need for self-catering. There's also a small *Spar* near the hospital, and the *Sumik* kiosk is open daily from 7 am to 10 pm. The *bakery*, which specialises in fiberbrød and delicious pascokerne, also sells pastries and other sweets.

For fish, go as early as possible to the *brædtet*, where the catch is sold as soon as it's brought in.

Entertainment
The best place for relaxed dancing, drinking and socialising is the *Hotel Narsaq*, which is good fun and has live bands on weekends. The misleadingly named *Restaurant Ujuat*, near the youth hostel, is actually just a bar. *Disco Ini*, near the sports hall, is more welcoming to outsiders, but take a reading of the mood before barging in. Both are open on weekdays until midnight for drinking and dancing (with the emphasis on the former), but on weekends, they stay open until 1 am.

Things to Buy
The lapidary shop of Børge Brodersen (☎ 31062) specialises in jewellery produced from the local gemstone, tuttupit, as well as jewellery made from bone and local stones.

The wool workshop Meqqileriffik (☎ 31477) produces socks, gloves, hats, bags and jumpers of Greenlandic wool. Eskimo Pels (☎ 31001) designs, creates and sells mainly seal and fox furs, but they also stock quality carvings and jewellery.

The clay workshop Marriorfik (☎ 35454), near the heliport, produces handmade pottery with Greenlandic motifs. At Narsaq Foto, local photographer John Rasmussen (☎ 31135) sells his black and white images of Greenlandic life.

Getting There & Away
Air In summer, the Grønlandsfly (☎ 31488) chopper does the five-minute buzz over to Qaqortoq (Dkr280) at least three times daily except Sunday. You can also fly to and from Narsarsuaq (Dkr490) or Nanortalik (Dkr1150) at least twice daily (except Sunday).

Ferry One of the large ferries calls in at least weekly, en route between Qaqortoq

The Greenland Tuttupit
In 1957, the beautiful soft mineral *tuttupit* was discovered by the West almost simultaneously in two sites: the Ilimmaasaq intrusion, a uranium-bearing geological formation near Narsaq, and on the Kola peninsula in Arctic Russia. It's found nowhere else.

Most stones from the Narsaq deposit, which is the larger of the two, have a deep red colour, but may also appear in pink, blue or white forms. They're often infused with dark green ægirne, white albite and analcime, and yellow pyrochlore and zincblende.

Due to microscopic impurities within the crystal structure, tuttupit may become faded when stored in the dark, but when exposed to sunlight, the colour is revived. If the stone is boiled, however, the colour may be lost forever. The Russian variety, which is often violet in colour, may be brightened by exposure to x-rays.

The Inuit name, which means 'reindeer blood', is derived from a legend of a girl called Tuttu, or 'reindeer', who fled to the mountains to give birth to her child in solitude. When the blood and placenta fell upon the ground, it seeped into the earth and turned to tuttupit stone. Oddly, the same legend appears among the Saami of the Kola peninsula. Among New Age cultures in the USA and Europe, the tuttupit crystal is thought to hold spiritual powers and is highly sought after.

Technically, it's illegal to remove tuttupit from Greenland, but locals have noted the tourist market for this beautiful stone and either sell it outright or produce unique tuttupit jewellery. So far, the government hasn't attempted to control the trade. ■

(Dkr135) and Nuuk (Dkr865); the *Aleqa Ittuk* runs between Qaqortoq, Narsaq and Itilleq (Dkr100) twice weekly; and the *Taterak* does weekly runs between Narsarsuaq (Dkr130) and Qaqortoq, via Narsaq.

Getting Around

You can hire mountain bikes from Helgi Jónasson (☎ 72072 or 31049; fax 31064) for Dkr50/75/400 per half-day/day/week from the blue house beside the Hotel Perlen. He also has a vehicle to hire for Dkr250 per day. Narsaq also has a taxi service (☎ 72050 or 72020).

AROUND NARSAQ
Qaaqarsuaq

Qaaqarsuaq ('big mountain') is the prominent 685m peak behind the town. The summit makes a popular day hike, or you can just climb up to the 400m-high saddle for great views of the town. The track to the saddle leads up from behind the Inuili complex; from there, you can continue south to the summit, east to Taseq, or drop into the Narsaq Valley for a nice loop walk.

Dyrnæs

The ruins at Dyrnæs, an hour north of town on foot, feature the ruins of a cruciform Norse church and a hall which probably belonged to an early noble. It was described by Icelander Ivar Bardsson in his 14th-century account as the largest parish in Greenland. The ruins haven't been fully excavated and what's left isn't overly impressive, but the setting is nice and it's a convenient trip from town, especially if you're walking to Kvanefjeld.

From 1956 to 1984 Dyrnæs was used as the headquarters for geological studies on the uranium-bearing Illimmaasaq intrusion, which contains some 200 different minerals.

Kvanefjeld (Kuannersuit) & Illimmaasaq

The 879m peak of Kvanefjeld, eight km from Narsaq, is the site of uranium deposits too remote for commercial exploitation, and some old exploratory diggings. Some skewed reasoning regarding these deposits led Narsaq to accord Danish nuclear physicist Niels Bohr honorary residency. The neighbouring peak, 1390m Illimmaasaq, is known for its tuttupit deposits (see boxed aside). The altitude and geological makeup of this peak combine to inhibit vegetation, making it a rather weird and barren place.

Either mountain makes a tough but beautiful hike. Follow the road toward Dyrnæs but after the bridge, keep following the road. Kvanefjeld is the obvious peak at the head of the valley. Late in the summer, you can continue up to Illimmaasaq, which has a small glacier on its north-eastern slope.

Organised Tours The tourist office organises eight-hour geological hikes up Kvanefjeld and Illimmaasaq for Dkr300, including transport to the base of Kvanefjeld. This is a great way to learn about the unusual geology of the Illimmaasaq intrusion.

Getting There & Away If you want a head start, Helgi Jónasson (☎ 31049; fax 31064) will take you to the end of the road at the base of Kvanefjeld for Dkr100 per person, with a minimum charge of Dkr200.

Tuttutoq Isua

Tuttutoq Isua ('reindeer promontory'), also called Stephensen's Harbour, lies across Nordre Sermilik Fjord from Narsaq. The site, which is South Greenland's largest and best preserved Eskimo ruin, was inhabited between 1350 and 1650 and had at least 24 winter houses, two tent foundations and lots of meat caches and graves. It was first mentioned in a geological survey carried out by K Stephensen in 1912. The best access is on a day tour from Narsaq.

QAQORTOQ (JULIANEHÅB)

With a population of 3500, Qaqortoq (pronounced like a very throaty *KRA-kror-tok*), the 'white place', is the big city and hub of South Greenland. Many visitors find it the cleanest and tidiest of all Greenlandic towns, and in mid-summer it explodes with wildflowers.

GREENLAND

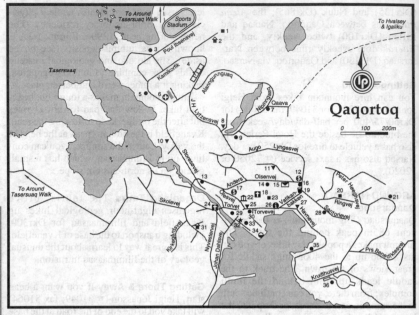

Qaqortoq

0   100   200m

History

The original Qaqortoq was founded by Norwegian trader Anders Olsen in 1775 and named Julianehåb after Queen Juliane Marie of Denmark. Among other things, it was a convenient base for Hans Egede's missionaries' futile search for the 'lost' Norse colony of Østerbygd, which they assumed was on the east coast of Greenland. It wasn't until 1779, after a survey of Norse ruins and identification of sites mentioned in the sagas, that it was postulated and proven that the elusive Østerbygd was actually beneath their feet. The search for the colonists themselves, however, carried on into the early 1800s.

Over the following decades, Qaqortoq developed into a trading station between the Danes and increasing numbers of Greenlanders, who were fascinated by European trade goodies. Modern Qaqortoq is an active port town and trade remains its mainstay. It's also home to Greenland's only tannery.

Information

Tourist Office The tourist office (☎ 38444; fax 38495) is worth visiting to book the youth hostel, pick up brochures or cruise through the well-stocked shop selling T-shirts, carvings, maps and books. They also organise excursions (see Organised Tours later in this section). If the Qaqortoq Turistforening again takes over the operations, as is mooted, it will also be useful for tourist information. The office is open Monday to Friday from 10 am to 5 pm, Saturday from 10 am to 1 pm and Sunday from 1 to 4 pm.

Money Grønlandsbanken and Nuna Bank are open Monday to Friday from 10 am to 3 pm and on Thursday until 5 pm.

Bookshops The Qaqortoq bookshop, upstairs in the Pilivik KNI shop, has a few items of interest in Danish and Greenlandic, but for tourist publications, you'll have

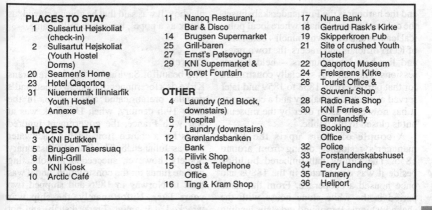

PLACES TO STAY
1   Sulisartut Højskoliat
    (check-in)
2   Sulisartut Højskoliat
    (Youth Hostel
    Dorms)
20 Seamen's Home
23 Hotel Qaqortoq
31 Niuernermik Ilinniarfik
    Youth Hostel
    Annexe

PLACES TO EAT
3   KNI Butikken
5   Brugsen Tasersuaq
8   Mini-Grill
9   KNI Kiosk
10 Arctic Café

11 Nanoq Restaurant,
    Bar & Disco
14 Brugsen Supermarket
25 Grill-baren
27 Ernst's Pølsevogn
29 KNI Supermarket &
    Torvet Fountain

OTHER
4   Laundry (2nd Block,
    downstairs)
6   Hospital
7   Laundry (downstairs)
12 Grønlandsbanken
    Bank
13 Pilivik Shop
15 Post & Telephone
    Office
16 Ting & Kram Shop

17 Nuna Bank
18 Gertrud Rask's Kirke
19 Skipperkroen Pub
21 Site of crushed Youth
    Hostel
22 Qaqortoq Museum
24 Frelserens Kirke
26 Tourist Office &
    Souvenir Shop
28 Radio Ras Shop
30 KNI Ferries &
    Grønlandsfly
    Booking
    Office
32 Police
33 Forstanderskabshuset
34 Ferry Landing
35 Tannery
36 Heliport

better luck at the tourist office. The museum also sells historical publications.

Film & Photography Fuji and Kodak print and slide film is available at Radio Ras near the seamen's home.

Laundry Qaqortoq has two laundry services, one downstairs in the block of flats on the corner of Nipinngaaq and Qaava Sts and the other downstairs in block 2, on Lytzensvej near the intersection with Alanngunnguaq.

Fountain
No discussion of Qaqortoq would be complete without a mention of the Torvet (town square) fountain which, the locals are proud to point out, dates from 1928 and is the only one in Greenland. The names of prominent Greenlanders are engraved in brass letters on its Igaliku-sandstone base, but many of the letters have been nicked by souvenir hunters and working out the names from the remaining letters is a bit like playing Wheel of Fortune.

Harbour
At the busy harbour, you'll find everything from trawlers and cargo ships to derelicts and ambitious cruising yachts. Even the odd iceberg finds its way in, and it's great for lots of bright and colourful photos.

Qaqortoq Museum
Thanks to the efforts of archaeologist and former curator Joel Berglund, Qaqortoq has one of Greenland's finest museums. The building was constructed as a blacksmith's shop in 1871 and behind it is a traditionally furnished sod hut, built around 1905. On the front lawn is a big gun from an ill-fated whaling vessel which foundered off Greenland's east coast in the 1700s and was brought to Qaqortoq in 1933 by Knud Rasmussen.

Exhibits include drawings and photos of early Qaqortoq, indigenous sealskin qajaqs and other ingenious hunting and fishing implements, as well as artefacts from the Dorset, Thule, Norse and Greenlandic cultures.

From June to September, it's open weekdays from 10 am to noon and 1 to 3 pm, and on Saturday from 10 am to 2 pm. Admission is free.

Historic Buildings
The wonderful black-tarred log building on the harbourfront was designed by the Danish Royal Architect Kirkerup. Prefabricated in Denmark, it was broken down log by log, shipped to Greenland and reassembled on site in 1797 as the residence of the colonial overseer. It is now used as the KNI office.

The small red house between this building

GREENLAND

and the harbour is the Forstanderskabshuset, the colonial assembly hall, where local political leaders and the town council – consisting of KGH officials and traders, the town priest and the best local hunters – held hot-air sessions. The hall was specially constructed for that purpose from 1858 to 1859 and later served as a school, a bakery and a carpentry. It has now been taken over by the museum but is closed to the public.

A couple of doors up is the KGH manager's residence dating from around 1855. The yellow half-timbered building beside it was constructed in the 1880s and once housed a cooperage. From the same period is the white stone house with the shaked (shingled) roof and red steps leading up one side. This was the colonial bakery and brewery. The yellow stone house which now houses the Qaqortoq Museum was built in 1871 as a blacksmith shop.

West of the old church is a yellow wooden building which was built as a school in 1909. It now contains the town library and the monument in front commemorates the 1952 royal visit.

Near the Pilivik shop is a little Igaliku sandstone building which was built in 1929 as the public bathhouse. It was later used as a taxi office, but is now abandoned.

Stone & Man

The brilliant *Stone & Man* project, the brainchild of Greenlandic artist Aka Høegh, attempts to turn amphitheatre-shaped Qaqortoq into a sculpture gallery which will never be completed. She has commissioned artists from around Scandinavia and beyond, who have already used their inspiration to create shapes and reliefs from natural stone formations all over town. As a result, there's a sense of discovery around every corner. A map and directory to the sculptures is sold at the tourist office shop for Dkr10.

Vatican Hill

The prominent red house atop Vatican Hill, overlooking the harbour, was once occupied by a KGH trader who was something of a playboy. It was said that he always stayed 'as drunk as a pope', hence the hill's name.

Church

The beautiful Saviour's Church, Frelserens Kirke, is a forerunner of modern Greenland's popular prefabricated architecture. In the early 19th century, when Denmark was at war with France, the government ignored pleas for a church from such a backwater post as Julianehåb. The Danish Missionary Society, however, succeeded in collecting private funds for the construction, and it was built in Norway in 1826 and shipped two years later. Unfortunately, the ship was wrecked at Paamiut (Frederikshåb) and not until 1832 was the salvaged timber erected on its current site.

Inside is a life preserver from the ship *Hans Hedtoft*, which struck an iceberg off Cape Farewell on 30 January 1959 and sank with no survivors. A monument on the flower-filled lawn between the church and the bridge commemorates Greenland Apostle, Hans Egede, and his wife Gertrude Rask, who established Greenland's first Christian mission near Nuuk in 1721.

The tourist office has a key to the church and can take you on a quick guided tour.

Tannery

The Kalaallit Nunaata Ammerivia tannery, between the harbour and the heliport, turns seals into fur coats and is one of Qaqortoq's economic mainstays. Whether you approve of it or not (in Qaqortoq, you'd best appear to approve), the finished product can be lovely, and most of the skins are sold to the tannery by local people who shoot the seals themselves for food. (However, items produced from Arctic foxes, musk oxen and polar bears may not be so defensible.) Finished products are sold at the tourist office or crafted into designer garments at the Eskimo Pels workshop in Narsaq.

You can learn all about the tanning process in 1½ hour tours (Dkr35), which can be arranged through the tourist office.

Activities

The Sulisartut Højskoliat, or Workers' Folk High School, runs cultural workshops on lapidary work, soapstone carving or fur-sewing for Dkr150 per afternoon session. Make arrangements through the tourist office.

Organised Tours

The tourist office and Arctic Adventure (see the Hotel Qaqortoq) run boat tours to the hunting and fishing village of Eqalugaarsuit (population 120) and the abandoned site of Nugatsiaq (Dkr650), and will run with even one person. Tours include seal and whale-watching and the chance to meet local hunters and fisherfolk. On the return, they stop at the abandoned village of Kanger-miutsiaat.

All-day guided charters to Hvalsey and Upernaviarsuk (Dkr400) operate with a minimum four participants. Arctic Adventure runs the same tour (Dkr300) on Wednesdays, without Upernaviarsuk, regardless of the number of passengers.

The tidewater glacier tour (Dkr700), described under Narsaq, also runs from Qaqortoq with a minimum of 10 people. Every second Monday in summer, the tourist office does excursions to Uunartoq hot springs (Dkr700). They need a minimum of 10 people, and include lunch and a guide.

Town tours (Dkr75) feature a three-hour stroll through old Qaqortoq, a visit to the museum, a tour of the tannery and a circuit around the most prominent Stone & Man sculptures. They need a minimum of four people. On Wednesdays, Arctic Adventure runs a five-hour version of this tour for Dkr185, with lunch.

The tourist office can also organise six-hour fishing or hunting trips with locals for Dkr425. If you're willing to help with the work, you can arrange such trips informally for less. Just head to the harbour and ask around for someone who'll take you along on their day's fishing.

Places to Stay

The *Youth Hostel* once occupied a wonderful site beneath a lulling waterfall at the mountain ridge, but in February 1993 its location proved its undoing when it was utterly crushed in an avalanche. The hostel now consists of dormitory rooms at the Sulisartut Højskoliat (see below) with beds for Dkr165. Amenities include cooking facilities and a video lounge. It also opens up six luxury student houses at the business college, *Niuernermik Ilinniarfik*. Each house accommodates seven people and has a bath, kitchen and washing facilities, and costs Dkr175 per person. Neither complex has a permanent attendant, but if you arrive during the day, you can check in at the Sulisartut Højskoliat. For the student flats, book through the tourist office and ask them to meet your boat or helicopter.

The *Sulisartut Højskoliat* (☎ 38466; fax 28873) has single/double rooms with bath for Dkr575/1000 and made-up single rooms without bath for Dkr325 to Dkr480. It's used mainly by tour groups and delegations, but is also open to individuals.

The friendly *Seamen's Home* (☎ 38239; fax 38678) is the green building midway up the hill from the harbour. For small but clean single/double rooms, you'll pay Dkr495/645 without bath or Dkr595/795 with a bath and toilet. There's also one tiny single room which costs only Dkr250. Guests can use the comfy sitting room with a library of books in several languages. As with all seamen's homes, it emphasises Christian religious values, and alcohol is prohibited.

The sparkling *Hotel Qaqortoq* (☎ 38282; fax 37234), perched on the hill overlooking the harbour, is one of Greenland's more architecturally interesting hotels. Singles/doubles with bathroom, TV and telephone cost Dkr795/1050 with breakfast.

Places to Eat

Self-Catering Of Qaqortoq's two supermarkets, the larger is the immense and well-stocked *Brugsen*, which also has a good-value bottle shop. The *bakery*, near the fountain, sells a variety of bread, doughnuts and pastries; it's open Monday to Friday from 7 am to 4 pm, Saturday from 7 am to

GREENLAND

noon and Sunday from 8 am to noon. Fresh fish, whale and seal are sold at the *brædtet* near the harbour. The *KNI supermarket*, near the fountain, opens weekdays from 10 am to 5 pm and on Saturday from 10 am to 2 pm. There's also a *KNI Kiosk* on Nipinngaaq, which is open until 8 pm nightly. The small *Brugsen Tasersuaq* outlet and the *KNI Butikken* are open Monday to Saturday from 7.30 am to 6 pm and on Sunday from 9 am to 6 pm.

Fast Food The stand-by *Grill-baren*, near the fountain, serves up hamburgers, chips, ice cream and the like. *Ernst's Pølsevogn* dishes up hot dogs from a mobile outlet beside the harbour. There's also a *Mini-Grill* beside the lake on JH Lytzensvej and the sports centre has a small cafeteria.

Cafés & Restaurants The best general eatery is the friendly *Arctic Café* (☎ 38027), which is open daily from 8.30 am to 9 pm. You'll find full English breakfasts (Dkr30), eggs and bacon (Dkr22), salads (Dkr20), omelettes (Dkr45), pizzas (Dkr90) and full meals of lamb, beef or whale (Dkr75 to Dkr105). In the afternoon, you can stop by for coffee, tea or ice cream.

For an elegant splurge, the *Hotel Qaqortoq* restaurant (☎ 38282) offers fine dining accompanied by a broad glassy vista of the harbour, icebergs and distant peaks. It's open for lunch from 11.30 am to 2 pm and for dinner from 5 to 8.30 pm. From 2 to 4 pm daily they serve coffee and snacks. Set lunches are Dkr70 and dinners start at Dkr130 (without drinks or salad). It's great for coffee and dessert (Dkr65) on summer evenings, when the harbour colours are brightest. Non-hotel guests need a reservation and patrons must dress smartly. The cosy candle-lit pub, which strives for elegance, is open nightly except Monday.

The *Seamen's Home* cafeteria is open Monday to Saturday from 7 am to 9 pm and on Sunday from 8 am to 10 pm. Hot meals are available only from 11.30 am to 1 pm and 5 to 7 pm daily. Prices are quite reasonable: from Monday to Saturday, a small/large

portion of the daily special costs Dkr36/42. On Sunday it's Dkr42/50. Salad or bread is extra. The popular restaurant *Nanoq* serves meals from 5 to 9 pm, but is best known for its pub. It's open daily except Tuesday.

Entertainment
The *Nanoq bar* is open daily except Tuesday, with dancing on pay-days and weekends. The *Skipperkroen Bar & Disco Qaava* (☎ 38373), known as a venue for dancing, drunkenness and fighting, is open Monday to Thursday from 7 pm to 1 am and on Friday and Saturday from 7 pm to 3 am. The disco operates on Fridays from 11 pm to 3 am. Happy hour, with cheaper drinks, runs from 7 to 9 pm.

Getting There & Away
Airline and ferry tickets can be purchased from the helpful KNI ticket office (☎ 38240), in the historical centre.

Air Grønlandsfly (☎ 38188) has scheduled helicopter flights to and from Nanortalik (Dkr860) three or four times weekly. Flights between Qaqortoq and Narsaq (Dkr280) operate several times daily except Sunday and services to and from Narsarsuaq (Dkr680) run two or three times daily except Sunday.

Ferry The *Aleqa Ittuk* runs twice weekly between Qaqortoq and Narsaq (Dkr115), Alluitsup Paa (Dkr150) and Nanortalik (Dkr255); and weekly to Igaliku (Dkr135), Narsarmiit (Dkr315) and Aappilattoq (Dkr375). The *Taterak* sails weekly between Qaqortoq and Narsarsuaq (Dkr195), via Qassiarsuk (Dkr180) and Itilleq (Dkr170). It also sails weekly to Nanortalik (Dkr255), via Eqalugaarsuit (Dkr105), Saarloq (Dkr100), Ammassivik (Dkr180) and Alluitsup Paa. The big ferries sail between Qaqortoq and Nuuk (Dkr845) once weekly.

KNI's cargo boats *Anguteq Ittuk* and *Ujarak* carry supplies and passengers to remote settlements in the Qaqortoq, Narsaq and Ivittuut districts. On Monday, the *Anguteq Ittuk* sails to Kangilinnguit (Dkr500) and on Tuesday, returns to Qaqortoq via Arsuk (Dkr435). On Wednesday, it sails to Nanortalik via Ammassivik and Alluitsup Paa, returning by the same route on Thursday. The *Ujarak* does a return trip to Qasimiut (Dkr245) on Monday; to Igaliku and back on Tuesday; to Eqalugaarsuit, Saarloq, and back on Wednesday; to Narsaq, Qassiarsuk and Narsarsuaq on Thursday, and back by the same route on Friday. Each boat may carry a maximum of 12 passengers. Fares are from Qaqortoq.

Getting Around

Qaqortoq's city bus system consists of a passenger van which runs across town approximately every half-hour. It costs Dkr10 per ride and basically takes you wherever you'd like to go. Taxis (☎ 37233, 38233 or 37777) charge Dkr35 to anywhere around town.

Bicycle hire is available from the Ting & Kram shop (the name means 'Odds & Ends'). The tourist office rents double kayaks for Dkr250 per day and Dkr1100 per week.

The 40-passenger boat *M/B Polarmoon* and 17-passenger *M/B Polarfox* may be chartered from Rederianpartsselskabet (☎ 38400; fax 28600), and they're economical if you can divide the cost among a large group. The tourist office also arranges charters for smaller groups.

AROUND QAQORTOQ

Hiking

Qaqortoq offers lots of great day hikes. The map in this book is for route-planning only; for navigation, the *Qaqortoq* sheet of the *Hiking Map – South Greenland* is essential.

A quick jaunt will take you up 220m Peters Varde ('Peter's Cairn'), which is best accessed via the waterfall ravine behind the former youth hostel.

Other day walks include the three to four-hour circuit of the 'big lake', Tasersuaq, where locals swim on sunny days. Begin by heading west from town past yards of industrial detritus and following the track along the lakeshore. The marked route along the western shore keeps to high, dry ground, but the route back, along the eastern shore, gets pretty soggy. The inflowing river at the lake head is most easily crossed above the obvious waterfall about 150m from the shore. From this point, you can extend the hike by crossing the scenic pass to Eqaluit ('sea trout'), on Kangerlluarsuk Fjord. You must return by the same route. This option takes two hours each way.

Other hikes include the three-hour return climb to 412m Storefjeld and the two-hour return climb to the parabolic dish on Harefjeld. From Harefjeld, you can descend the northern slope and continue west along the southern shore of Tasersuaq, then over the pass to Munkebugten (Monk's Bay). It's then three km west along the shore to the sea level cave, Uglspils Hule.

A longer hike will take you along the shore of Munkebugten to its north-western end, then follow the stream up the steep ravine to its source in a small pond, at the base of 418m Nordfjeld. A climb over the peak and a descent of its steep north-eastern slope eventually brings you to the western shore of Tasersuaq, near Qaqortoq. Allow at least six hours return.

Qaqortoq to Igaliku Trek

The four or five-day trek from Qaqortoq to Igaliku, one of Greenland's premier walks, offers a combination of Norse history and wonderful scenery. The route, which is now marked, begins at the end of Qaava street in Qaqortoq, crosses a low pass, and then follows an arm of Qaqortoq Fjord (Julianehåbs Fjord). Beyond a grotty sheep hut, you'll reach a narrow isthmus with a lovely lake in the middle. This is a common first-night campsite, and is about as far as one could go in a day hike from Qaqortoq – allow 10 to 12 hours for the return trip.

Unless you're a real roadrunner, don't believe anyone who says it's possible to reach Hvalsey from Qaqortoq in a single day. Although the long hours of daylight would make it logistically possible, it would be a miserably long slog.

From the isthmus, follow Tartoq, a lovely

bay surrounded by peaks with a waterfall at its northern end. The route along Tartoq is steep, bouldery and plagued by entangling vegetation. It's slow going and you'll be relieved to get into the low pass, which allows relatively easy walking. Unfortunately, the route deteriorates here and continuing to Hvalsey involves a traverse along a steep coast, or a trying climb through boulders and bushes over a 350m pass followed by a long and tedious descent to the mouth of a river that will get you wet. From the river, it's an hour along a steep coastal stretch to the ruins. Camping at Hvalsey (see later in this section) is permitted only outside the fence.

The rest of the route to Igaliku is fairly straightforward, but still involves several climbs and some problematic boulder fields. Follow the shore past the Qaqortoq sheep farm and into the valley at the head of Tasiusaq Bay, where you should keep to the western bank.

From there, it's a matter of picking your way through hills and valleys to Igaliku. There are two main routes: one continues up the broad valley above Tasiusaq and another bears east about two km above the head of Tasiusaq and continues north-east past Lake 380 and Lake 410. The objective is the northern shore of the largish Lake 400, beneath Qalilingmiut Qaaqa. From here, you can descend the stream to the shore four km south-west of Itilleq. Suggested *campsites* are marked on the map in this book.

A more challenging alternative is to follow the first major stream west of Hvalsey uphill to Lake 470, then descend the outflowing stream to the mouth of Lakseelv. Following the river up the valley, you'll have views of the spectacular saw-toothed Redekammen Ridge. Across the pass at the valley head, you'll reach Lake 230, from where you should bear due east to meet up with the marked route at Lake 400.

Coming from Igaliku, begin by walking south-west over the low hills – or along the shore south-west of Itilleq – and climb up the stream which flows down from Lake 400. There's a good *campsite* on the north-eastern

shore of this lake and another one beside Lake 310, around the ridge to the south.

Hvalsey

Known to Greenlanders as Qaqortukulooq, the Hvalsey ruins are the most extensive and best preserved Norse ruins in Greenland. They occupy a level coastal strip beneath Qaqortoq peak, at the head of Hvalsey Fjord, which was named after the 'whale island' in its middle. Alone and abandoned in the wilderness, they elicit a sense of timeless awe.

Hvalsey was first inhabited in the late 10th century and first mentioned around 1390 in the Icelandic annals, *Flateyjarbók*. Its church, which was one of the last built during the Norse era, measures 16 by eight metres at the base and was constructed of hewn granite and lime mortar. The nearby manor farm oversaw about 30 smaller farms in the district, and a great hall, a dwelling, several barns and byres and burial sites have all been excavated nearby. Although district tithes would have been paid to the Hvalsey church, there's no evidence of a warehouse for storing agricultural produce.

In the early 15th century, two notable events were recorded. The first was the 1407 execution of a resident called Kolgrim, who was burned at the stake after being convicted of using sorcery to seduce Steinum, the wife of Thorgrim Søløveson and daughter of the sheriff, Hrafn. According to the *Flateyjarbók*, Steinum went mad and died at an early age.

The second event, which is the last reference to the Greenlandic Norse colony before it vanished, was on 14 September 1408 when the prominent Icelander Þórstein Ólafsson of Skagafjörður married Greenland colonist, Sigrid Björnsdóttir. The ecumenical records explain that the ceremony took place over three Sundays with two priests officiating. Wedding guests included a large number of Greenland colonists as well as outsiders.

For the complete scoop on Hvalsey, see *Hvalsø – the Church and the Magnate's Farm* by Joel Berglund, which is available in English, Danish and Greenlandic editions at

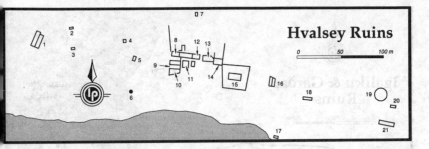

Hvalsey Ruins

0   50   100 m

1	Byre & Barn
2	Outbuilding
3	Sheep Shed*
4	Sheep Shed*
5	Outbuilding
6	Well
7	Storehouse
8	Great Hall
9	Pantry
10	Kitchen
11	Bedroom
12	Storeroom
13	The Old Hall
14	Byre & Barn
15	Church
16	Sheep Shed
17	Storehouse
18	Livestock Building*
19	Horse Fold
20	Gravesite*
21	Livestock Building*

* Possible Functions

the Qaqortoq tourist office souvenir shop for Dkr58.

Organised Tours The Qaqortoq tourist office runs half-day boat tours to Hvalsey and Upernaviarsuk; see Organised Tours under Qaqortoq earlier in this chapter. The walking route from Qaqortoq to Hvalsey is described in this chapter under the Qaqortoq to Igaliku Trek.

Upernaviarsuk Research Station
For farmers and agriculture fans, Uperna-viarsuk is a must-see. This experimental research station is dedicated to coaxing the Arctic into agricultural productivity. A range of tenderly tended temperate vegetables happily grow outdoors, and the greenhouses shelter tomatoes, cucumbers and the spindly shrub that represents Greenland's only apple tree. Researchers also hope to develop a hybrid sheep that can withstand the harshest climatic conditions.

ITILLEQ
Tiny Itilleq, (the 'crossing place'), is mainly an access for Igaliku, to which it is connected by a three km tractor track known as Kongevejen, or 'the king's way'. It's Greenland's largest sheep farm, with good pasturelands as well as extensive haymaking to keep the sheep in winter fodder.

Near the landing site are the recently excavated ruins of an Eskimo dwelling and several winter storage houses with sealskin roofs. They were probably inhabited between 1750 and 1850.

Getting There & Away
The *Taterak* calls into Itilleq weekly, or you can charter a boat from Narsarsuaq (see Organised Tours under Narsarsuaq). You can also walk from Qaqortoq (see under Qaqortoq to Igaliku Trek).

IGALIKU (GARÐAR)
Igaliku (roughly pronounced 'ee-GOLLY-co'), the 'deserted cooking site', is a tiny village of 52 people near the head of Igaliku

GREENLAND

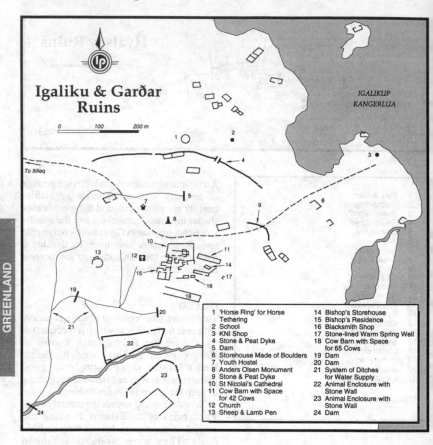

Igaliku & Garðar Ruins

IGALIKUP KANGERLUA

To Itilleq

1 'Horse Ring' for Horse Tethering	14 Bishop's Storehouse
2 School	15 Bishop's Residence
3 KNI Shop	16 Blacksmith Shop
4 Stone & Peat Dyke	17 Stone-lined Warm Spring Well
5 Dam	18 Cow Barn with Space for 65 Cows
6 Storehouse Made of Boulders	19 Dam
7 Youth Hostel	20 Dam
8 Anders Olsen Monument	21 System of Ditches for Water Supply
9 Stone & Peat Dyke	22 Animal Enclosure with Stone Wall
10 St Nicolai's Cathedral	23 Animal Enclosure with Stone Wall
11 Cow Barn with Space for 42 Cows	24 Dam
12 Church	
13 Sheep & Lamb Pen	

Fjord. The Norse called it Garðar, and in the early 12th century, it was the episcopal seat of Norse Greenland.

The village is dotted with Norse ruins and is also interesting for its productive vegetable gardens and colourful laundry lines. The modern church, which is constructed of edible-looking Igaliku sandstone, is also worthwhile. Beneath a blue house near the cathedral ruin is a protected warm spring which reaches a scalding 4°C and serves as storage for fish and a perpetually liquid source of water. Igaliku's present economy is dominated by sheep breeding.

History

Feeling cut off from the European religious community, the 12th century Greenland Norse made a formal request to the Norwegian king, Sigurd Jorsalafare, to establish their own bishopric. Their methods, which included accompanying the petition with lavish gifts – walrus tusks, whalebone and two polar bear cubs – apparently worked, because the king granted their wish and set about searching for a suitable bishop. The lucky nominee turned out to be a Swedish monk called Bishop Arnald.

In 1124, when the bishop's seat was

announced, the colonists enthusiastically set about building a cathedral at Garðar, as the Norse called the site of modern Igaliku. Meanwhile, in 1125, Bishop Arnald travelled to Iceland, where he stayed through the winter, posing as a commoner. The following year he sailed to Greenland and took up his post just after the cathedral was completed.

Modern Igaliku was founded in 1783 by Norwegian colonist Anders Olsen, who also founded Fiskenæsset (Qeqertarsuatsiaat), Qaqortoq and Maniitsoq. He retired to this quiet and secluded spot in 1782. Most of Igaliku's current residents are in some way descended from him, and today there's a family graveyard and a monument dedicated to him.

St Nicolai's Cathedral

Although it was once an imposing structure, to call this ruin a cathedral stretches the word well beyond its intent. All that remains of the foundation, which measures 16 by 27m, are a few sandstone boulders which appear to be vaguely artificial, the result of dismantling the structure for more practical uses such as homes and sheds. Without a guide, you'll find little to indicate that this was once a bishop's seat.

The cathedral, constructed between 1124 and 1126, was dedicated to St Nicolai, the patron saint of seafarers, and by Greenlandic standards it was elaborate. Its windows were of rough glass rather than stretched animal stomachs, the interior was decorated with soapstone carvings of religious themes and a large bell called the faithful to worship. Beneath the building were found 25 walrus skulls and the chancel hid five narwhal skulls, which may have been held over from pre-Christian times.

Farm & Storehouse Ruins

The church perimeter is dotted with evidence of the wealthy church farms: large byres and storehouses, a great hall for social and ecumenical events and an elaborate irrigation system. One of the most prominent ruins is the tithe barn, which was used for the colonists' tithes to the church and also their

taxes, which awaited shipment to Iceland, Denmark and, ultimately, Norway. In fact, records show that by 1261, the church owned just about everything in Norse Greenland.

A grave excavated in 1926 contained the skeleton of Bishop Jan Smyril, the third bishop of Garðar, still wearing a blue sapphire episcopal ring and holding a walrus-tusk crosier. The skeleton was found with a hole in the skull and the left foot broken, which appeared to be evidence of foul play.

Organised Tours

Arctic Adventure in Narsarsuaq runs tours to Igaliku (Dkr650), including transport, a smørrebrød lunch and a guided walk over Kongevejen.

Places to Stay & Eat

The cosy *Youth Hostel* (☎ 35151; fax 38510), run by Abel and Johanne Lynge, charges Dkr150 with use of cooking facilities. It's open from 1 May to 1 September. Meals are available at the cafeteria, and groceries are sold at the *KNI Butikken* near the shore. The best campsite is on the northern shore of the lake immediately north of Igaliku.

Getting There & Away

The *Aleqa Ittuk* runs weekly between Qaqortoq and Igaliku (Dkr135), but most visitors arrive by ferry or charter boat at Itilleq and walk the three km Kongevejen (the 'king's way') over the peninsula to Igaliku. There are even benches for relaxing along the way. The less energetic can arrange rides with a local farmer.

On the other end of the motivation spectrum, you can walk from Qaqortoq to Igaliku in four or five days (see Qaqortoq to Igaliku, earlier in this chapter).

AROUND IGALIKU
Nuuluk & Lake 380

A stiff and challenging slog will take you to the summit of the 823m Nuuluk, south of Igaliku. The most amenable ascent is up the north-western ridge; it's hard going at first

GREENLAND

but gets easier as you reach the more solid rock near the summit. To extend the trip, continue west from the summit to Lake 380, which is drained to the west by a stream which has cut a steep-sided ravine down toward the shore of Tunulliarfik. The ravine contains a series of scenic waterfalls.

Blue Ice Camp

At the mouth of Qooroq Fjord is the Blue Ice Camp, run by Jacky Simoud (☎ & fax 72571) in Qassiarsuk. It provides simple accommodation in a wilderness setting, and makes a useful base for hikes to Motzfeldt Sø. Accommodation in four dome tents, with four beds each, costs Dkr150 per person, including use of kitchen facilities. Transfers from Narsarsuaq cost Dkr150 per person. You can also make evening excursions from Narsarsuaq for Dkr450, including return transfers, a barbecue dinner and one drink.

Motzfeldt Sø

Strong hikers will love the challenging but rewarding trek from Igaliku to the incredible mountain lake, Motzfeldt Sø. This long elbow-shaped lake is constricted by towering 1600m peaks and fed by two glaciers which calve into the water. You'll need six days for the return trip from Igaliku or Camp Blue Ice.

First head east along the shore from Igaliku. After rains, it may be difficult crossing the river mouth at the northern tip of Igalikup Kangerlua. Five km from Igaliku, you'll reach the mouth of the dramatic valley Qoororssuaq, a deep gash between the 1752m Illerfissalik and 1680m Suussugutaussa. Turn inland here and continue northward. After crossing the pass at the head of this valley, you'll descend to the Qoorqup Kuua, the river which drains Motzfeldt Sø. Scree, gravel, and boulder moraines here provide evidence of heavy glaciation, and make for very heavy going. Niobium has been discovered in the area and there has been discussion of setting up a mining operation, but nothing has yet come of it.

The southern end of this hike is included on the *Narsaq* sheet of the *Hiking Map – South Greenland*. As yet, Motzfeldt Sø itself doesn't appear on any hiking map, but it is included on the Saga Maps *Eastern Settlement* map.

VATNAHVERFI

Vatnahverfi is a remote peninsula of lakes, moors and fells between Igalikup Kangerlua and Alluitsup Kangerlua (Lichtenau Fjord or Hrafns Fjord). It was heavily settled by the early Norse and is now dotted with unexcavated ruins of sheep farms and dwellings. The lakes are full of Arctic char and numerous possible routes, and the gentle landscape invites wandering. Some people spend as much as two weeks exploring it on foot.

The map in this book is for route-planning only. The best maps are the Narsaq and Qaqortoq sheets of the 1:100,000 *Hiking Map – South Greenland*. The DVL-Rejser *Narsarsuaq-Narsaq-Qaqortoq* map includes only the northernmost end of the peninsula. The Saga Maps divide Vatnahverfi between the *Ivittuut/Narsarsuaq/Qaqortoq* and *Nanortalik* sheets.

The most popular trek runs between the tiny sheep station, Igaliku Kujalleq (the Norse Unðir Høfði, also called Søndre Igaliko), and Alluitsup Paa (Sydprøven), at the southern tip of the peninsula. Several other Vatnahverfi walks are outlined in *Trekking in Greenland* (see Books in the Greenland Facts for the Visitor chapter).

Igaliku Kujalleq to Alluitsup Paa

Access Because reaching Igaliku Kujalleq is more tricky than Alluitsup Paa, most people do this walk from north to south. From Igaliku, the recommended access is via Iterlaq. Start out by heading east along the shore of Igalikup Kangerlua eastward. You'll have to wade a couple of large streams; the one coming down from Qoororssuaq should be crossed as near its mouth as possible. From there, cross the 150m pass north of Akuliaruseq to Iterlaq.

It's impossible to cross the glacial river flowing out of Jespersen's Brae, so you'll have to radio from Igaliku in advance to

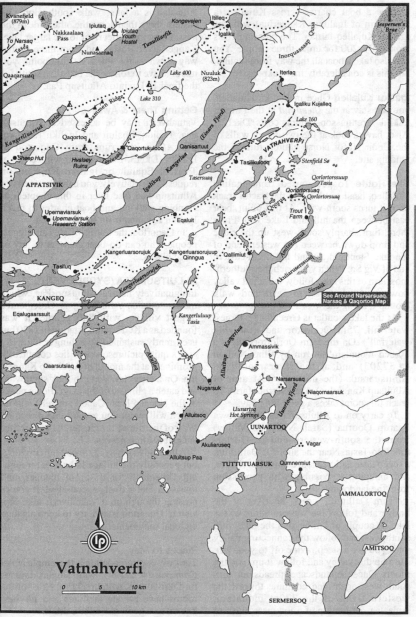

GREENLAND

Vatnahverfi

0   5   10 km

arrange a boat charter across Kujalleq (a small arm of Igalikup Kangerlua) with the Igaliku Kujalleq farmer. The crossing costs around Dkr200 for up to three people. You can also take a boat all the way from Igaliku, but this is considerably more expensive.

Igaliku Kujalleq Once in Igaliku Kujalleq, you can stay at the *sheep hut* at the farm of Eskild Jeremiasson, which costs Dkr125. Also, have a look at the two-metre walls of the Unðir Höfði Norse church ruin at the landing site.

The Route To get started from Igaliku Kujalleq, head south along the tractor track until it turns south-west. At this point, bear east between the hill and Lake 160. From there, turn sharply south-west up the ridge and drop down between the western end of the lake Stenfjeld Sø and the north-eastern end of Vig Sø. When you reach the southern-most arm of this lake, follow the small valley down to Qorlortorssuup Tasia and walk around it along the western shore.

At the lake's outlet is Greenland's largest waterfall, 75m Qorlortorsuaq, (the 'big waterfall'). On the farm Qorlortorsuaq is a 10-bed mountain hut run by Elias Nielsen (☎ 37203) and at the river mouth on Amitsuarsuk (the northernmost arm of Alluitsup Kangerlua), a failed trout farm. To reach this point takes a good long day.

To carry on to Alluitsup Paa, head down Saarup Qoorua (Sarah Nielsen's Valley) from the south-western end of Qorlortorssuup Tasia. Near the shore at Qallimiut, a sheep farm and a school camp offer shelter, and camping is possible with permission from the landowner.

From Qallimiut, cross the river at the bridge and follow the western shore of the lake. A couple of km beyond the lake, turn south-west and follow the connecting valley until you see a steep ravine off to your left. Turn up this valley and follow it up onto the moors. Once the landscape spreads out, turn south-west again and continue toward the western flank of the 770m mountain, Amaataa. At the top of a low pass north of

Amaataa is a lake; walk south along its eastern shore then down the other side of the pass, along the outlet river to the larger lake, Kangerluluup Tasia, and from there all the way down to the fjord. At this point, you merely have to follow the coastline south for the final 10 km into Alluitsup Paa.

Getting There & Away
Vatnahverfi may be accessed at Alluitsup Paa, Tasiluq, Eqaluit and Igaliku Kujalleq. The *Aleqa Ittuk* runs from Qaqortoq to Igaliku (Dkr135) weekly and will call in at Tasiluq, Eqaluit or Igaliku Kujalleq on request. Alternatively, you can take a ferry to Alluitsup Paa (see later in this chapter) or combine walking and boat charter to reach Igaliku Kujalleq from Igaliku/Itilleq.

In Qaqortoq, the tourist office can suggest people who can do boat charters to any of these places.

ALLUITSUP PAA (SYDPRØVEN)
Imaginatively-named Alluitsup Paa, which means 'outside Alluitsoq', is Greenland's largest village, with 800 people. It was founded as a KGH trading station in 1830 but is currently sustained by fishing activities.

It's quite picturesque and lies colourfully prominent at the mouth of Alluitsup Kanger-lua. On a clear day, you can look southward and catch a glimpse of the magnificent peaks of the Nunaap Isua (Cape Farewell) region, which will tempt you toward that direction. West of the village is a cluster of three or four ancient Eskimo graves.

Alluitsup Paa may at times seem inviting, but generally the village is known through-out Greenland for its aloof manner, and tourism is not actively encouraged. If you're passing through on a Vatnahverfi hike or a visit to Uunartoq island, try to keep a gauge on local sentiments.

Places to Stay
The only accommodation is the simple *Hotel Qannivik* (☎ 39199), with singles/doubles for Dkr650/865, with breakfast. None of the rooms have private facilities and it's best known as a good place for a drink.

Getting There & Away
In summer, the *Taterak* calls in twice weekly, en route between Qaqortoq (Dkr150) and Nanortalik (Dkr145).

AROUND ALLUITSUP PAA
Alluitsoq (Lichtenau)
Alluitsoq (the 'place with few breathing holes for seals') was originally called Lichtenau or 'meadow of light'. Founded in 1774 as a Moravian Mission, in 1814 it was the birthplace of Samuel Petrus Kleinschmidt, who worked at a similar mission at Nuuk and produced the first Greenlandic translation of the Bible. In 1900, the buildings were handed over to the Danish government and now house a YMCA camp and a home for people with alcohol and social problems.

Alluitsoq is a pleasant five km walk north along the coast from Alluitsup Paa, and lies along the main Vatnahverfi hike from Igaliku Kujalleq.

Uunartoq Island
Uunartoq Island not only has Greenland's best and most accessible hot springs, it also offers excellent campsites and a large collection of Eskimo ruins. The hot springs were known during the Norse days and are mentioned in the sagas. Visitors still come to swim and laze in the 37°C to 40°C natural pools amid fields of delightful wildflowers while gazing out at the mountainous icebergs in Uunartoq Fjord.

There are actually three hot springs in a small area of the island's west coast, and their temperatures remain consistent year-round. During the Norse period, they reputedly had medicinal value and were placed in the care of the church.

The extensive Qerrortuut Eskimo ruins, 26 houses which were inhabited in the late 18th and early 19th centuries, lie on the island's south-east coast. In 1930, a set of mummies was discovered amid remains of carved wooden toys and personal artefacts.

Organised Tours
When there's sufficient interest, the Qaqortoq tourist office organises day tours (Dkr700) to Uunartoq Island. The Nanortalik tourist office can offer suggestions for boat charters which, with a group, can be quite economical.

Getting There & Away From Alluitsup Paa, you can charter motorboats to drop you at Uunartoq Island and pick you up at a pre-specified time. Allow Dkr250 to Dkr300 for the return trip. On its scheduled run between Qaqortoq and Nanortalik, the *Aleqa Ittuk* will stop if at least five people wish to disembark.

Uunartoq Fjord
At Niaqornaarsuk, up the eastern shore of Uunartoq Fjord, are ruins of a Norse sheep farm and a manor house measuring nearly 60m in length. At Narsarsuaq (yes, another one!), directly opposite on the western shore, stood a medieval Benedictine convent and immediately to the west, a church from the same era. Scattered around are the remains of 25 other structures as well as evidence of quite extensive farming activities.

At Vagar, near the mouth of Uunartoq Fjord, are the ruins of another large farm and a Norse church dedicated to St Olav of Norway. It was discussed in the Icelandic *Flateyarbók*.

NANORTALIK
If you have only a short holiday in Greenland, you may want to consider spending it in Nanortalik (population 1550), which has some of Greenland's friendliest people and most spectacular surroundings. Although it's Greenland's southernmost community, this hunting and fishing town has more in common with the traditional hunting districts of the far North than it does with other towns in South or South-West Greenland.

Nanortalik may lack a tourist-class hotel, but it is attracting a growing number of cruise ships and has gained a reputation as a mecca for hikers, trekkers, rock climbers, mountaineers and other independent travellers. The main draws are the imposing granite peaks and spires of the Nunaap Isua (Cape Farewell) and Tasermiut Fjord regions,

GREENLAND

where the scenery is comparable to that of Patagonia or Yosemite. Comparisons may fall short, however; you'll just have to see it for yourself!

Unbearable

Loosely translated, the name Nanortalik means 'bear country', and although bears do occasionally float in on ice floes from East Greenland, they're most emphatically unwelcome in their namesake town. In fact, any bear that inadvertently wanders into this otherwise friendly community won't be tolerated longer than it takes someone to grab a rifle! ■

History

The Norse name for Nanortalik Island was Hrakbjarnarey ('bear hunt island') and historically it was probably a hunting ground for both Norse and Eskimo people. The first permanent human population probably arrived in 1778, when an informal whale blubber and sealskin trading post was established by Julianehåb traders.

In 1797, a permanent trading and supply depot was set up at Sissaritoq to serve Cape Farewell communities, as well as much of East Greenland. In 1830, it was shifted south-west to its current location, which had better harbour facilities.

Early this century, the steady growth in the district population was halted by a decline in seal stocks. This resulted in the abandonment of outlying settlements and a period of decline until the changeover was made from a hunting to a fishing-based economy. In 1950, the region bounced back and although smaller settlements never got back on their feet, Nanortalik gained town status. Fishing remains the economic mainstay.

In August 1997, Nanortalik celebrates its 200th anniversary with a big bash and a royal visit from Queen Margrethe II. Celebrations are scheduled through the entire month.

Information

Tourist Office The friendly Nanortalik Tourist Service (☎ 33441; fax 33442), PO Box 160, DK-3922 Nanortalik, in the historic part of town, is competently run by René and Dorthe Nielsen. It's one of Greenland's most active tourist offices; they love independent travellers and always have time to help. If there's no-one in, go next door to the two-storey blue house (a former church) that overlooks the shore, and someone will assist you. Inside the tourist office is a small shop selling carvings, T-shirts, books and limited outdoor and mountaineering equipment.

Money Grølandsbanken, inside the post office building, is open from 9 am to 3 pm, Monday to Friday. This is the cheapest place in Greenland to change travellers' cheques, at just Dkr30 commission per transaction.

Post & Communications The post and telephone office, opposite the Brugsen supermarket, is open Monday to Friday from 9 am to 3 pm.

Laundry If you've just returned from a two-week trek or kayak trip around the never-never and your clothes are becoming a social problem, just buy a laundry ticket at the Brugsen or KNI supermarkets and use the laundrette at B480 Chemnitzip Aqq.

Old Harbour

Nanortalik's historical harbour area seems too picturesque to be real, and looks like a New England fishing village that has been reconstructed as a film-set, complete with a painted backdrop. Most of the historical buildings are constructed from stone and heavy timber and date from the 19th century. Strolling around at different times of day, you'll see the hour-to-hour changes in the tide and the odd northern light.

Nanortalik Museum

The excellent and worthwhile town museum, beside the old harbour, is housed in historical buildings of the KGH (Royal

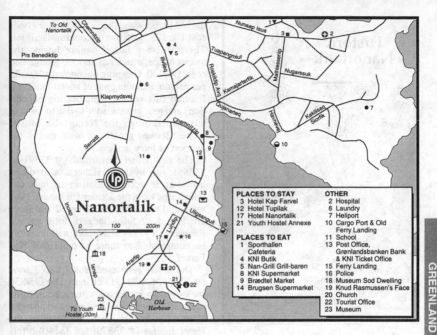

PLACES TO STAY
3 Hotel Kap Farvel
12 Hotel Tupilak
17 Hotel Nanortalik
21 Youth Hostel Annexe

PLACES TO EAT
1 Sporthallen Cafeteria
4 KNI Butik
5 Nan-Grill Grill-baren
8 KNI Supermarket
9 Brædtet Market
14 Brugsen Supermarket

OTHER
2 Hospital
6 Laundry
7 Heliport
10 Cargo Port & Old Ferry Landing
11 School
13 Post Office, Grønlandsbanken Bank & KNI Ticket Office
15 Ferry Landing
16 Police
18 Museum Sod Dwelling
19 Knud Rasmussen's Face
20 Church
22 Tourist Office
23 Museum

Greenland Trade Department). There are lots of photos of historic Nanortalik, qajaqs, tupilaks and other relics from Greenland's past. Allow at least a couple of hours to do it justice. It's open Sunday to Thursday from 1 to 4 pm; admission is free.

Sod House

Just west of the old harbour, a traditional Greenlandic sod house has been reconstructed to show visitors how Greenlanders lived before the Danes imported modern European housing. Someone from the museum or the tourist office will unlock it and explain things for you.

Knud Rasmussen's Face

This large boulder near the church was once called simply 'The Face' but, since Knud Rasmussen became a national hero, the locals decided it looked an awful lot like him.

Activities

Nanortalik Island and Tasermiut Fjord are ideal for sea kayaking, and the tourist office hires out kayaks and equipment for spins around the harbour, around the island or longer trips into Tasermiut or Sarqaa fjords. Single kayaks rent for Dkr250/900/3000 per day/week/month and doubles are Dkr300/1000/3500, plus a deposit of Dkr2500 per kayak. Rental fees include life jackets, paddles, dry suits and ANNA emergency kits. When hiring kayaks, you must show proof of travel insurance which does not exclude sea kayaking.

You can also hire fishing equipment for Dkr75/200 per day/week.

Organised Tours

The Nanortalik tourist office can suggest affordable boat charters to places such as Jakobinerhuen, Tasiusaq, Kuusuaq, Ulamertorsuaq, Klosterdalen, the Tasermiut glacier face Cape Farewell and Lindenows

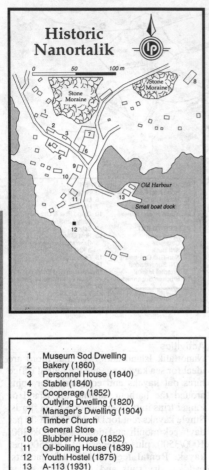

Historic Nanortalik

0   50   100 m

Stone Moraine

Stone Moraine

Old Harbour

Small boat dock

1   Museum Sod Dwelling
2   Bakery (1860)
3   Personnel House (1840)
4   Stable (1840)
5   Cooperage (1852)
6   Outlying Dwelling (1820)
7   Manager's Dwelling (1904)
8   Timber Church
9   General Store
10 Blubber House (1852)
11 Oil-boiling House (1839)
12 Youth Hostel (1875)
13 A-113 (1931)

Fjord. Speedboats for up to five passengers cost Dkr1800 per day. With up to 12 people, or if you have a lot of gear, you can charter the 12-passenger *Colo* for Dkr4400 per day.

Places to Stay

Nanortalik's best accommodation – and an ideal retreat – is the cosy and historic little *Youth Hostel* (☎ 33441; fax 33442), between the old harbour and the sea. Dormitory beds cost Dkr125, with use of cooking facilities. There's also a *hostel annexe* beside the tourist office, which has a video lounge and costs Dkr150. Camping outside costs Dkr35 per person, including use of hostel facilities. It often fills with mountaineering expeditions and tour groups, so it's wise to book in advance through the Nanortalik tourist office. Booked guests are often met at the heliport or ferry landing.

The new *Hotel Nanortalik* (☎ 33391 or 33386), run by Niko Hansen, also offers hostel-style accommodation in barracks transferred from the former US base at Narsarsuaq. Dorm beds cost Dkr150 and there are also four fully-fledged hotel rooms. Rates aren't yet available, but will probably be comparable to those at the Hotel Kap Farvel.

The newly renovated *Hotel Kap Farvel* (☎ 33294; fax 33131) charges Dkr575/850 for single/double rooms without bath. Book in advance or you may find it locked up tight. If you can handle the ambient noise, the *Hotel Tupilak* (☎ 33379; fax 33140) offers single/double rooms with communal facilities for Dkr400/550, with breakfast. There are no private baths, but guests have access to the sauna. True to its name, it also sells tupilak.

Note that the tourist office can also arrange hostel-style accommodation for Dkr125 in all Nanortalik district villages except Alluitsup Paa.

Places to Eat

Eating at the *Hotel Kap Farvel* (☎ 33294) bar-cum-dining room is always an unconventional experience, and often involves chasing up the chef (who incidentally does an excellent job). The more dependable *Hotel Tupilak* (☎ 33379) also serves meals, but it's still wise to book in advance.

The third option is the *Nan-Grill Grill-baren* which serves snacks, hot dogs, sandwiches and soft drinks until 9 pm nightly. The *Sporthallen Cafeteria* does basic burgers, hot dogs, chips, coffee and soft drinks in the afternoon and evening, but

GREENLAND

closes for four weeks in summer. The *brædtet* harbour market sells whale, seal and whatever else may appear in the catch of the day.

Nanortalik has both *KNI* and *Brugsen* supermarkets, which are open from 9 am to 5.30 pm Monday to Thursday, 9 am to 6 pm on Friday and 9 am to 1.30 pm on Saturday. The *bakery* is inside the Brugsen supermarket; from Monday to Thursday, it opens at 7 am. After hours shopping is available at the *KNI Butikken*, which is open from 7 am to 9 pm every day.

Entertainment
The Hotel Tupilak disco and other impromptu festivities boom from Monday to Thursday from 6 pm to midnight and on Friday and Saturday from 6 pm to 1 am. The hotel also has a TV/video machine and a sauna. A step down the entertainment scale is the bar at the Hotel Kap Farvel, where the objective is simply getting blotto as quickly as possible.

Getting There & Away
Book and purchase airline and ferry tickets at the Grønlandsbanken counter in the post and telephone office.

Air Nanortalik often experiences fog, which rolls in to engulf the town in cream of mushroom soup and causes delays in helicopter schedules. When the elements are smiling on Nanortalik, Grønlandsfly (☎ 33288) flies three times weekly to or from Narsarsuaq (Dkr1120), Narsaq (Dkr1150) and Qaqortoq (Dkr860).

Ferry The *Taterak* sails weekly from Nanortalik to Qaqortoq (Dkr255), via Ammassivik (Dkr170), Saarloq (Dkr190) and Eqalugaarsuit (Dkr205), while the *Aleqa Ittuk* does a weekly run between Qaqortoq, Nanortalik, Narsarmiit (Dkr120) and Aappilattoq (Dkr160), ice conditions permitting. The trip from Qaqortoq takes 10 to 12 hours, but it can be fabulous in fine weather. Conditions permitting, the ferries travel via the Sermersuup Sarqaa Sound.

Otherwise, they pass west of Sermersoq Island, affording dramatic views of the island's high granite cliffs. Fares are from Nanortalik.

Getting Around
An Avon rubber dinghy with a 40 hp outboard motor may be hired from the tourist office for Dkr500/800/2500 per half-day/day/week. Rental rates include life jackets, floating survival suits and a VHF radio. The tourist office requires anyone hiring an Avon to show proof of travel insurance.

AROUND NANORTALIK ISLAND
Sissaritoq (Old Nanortalik)
West across the bay from Nanortalik is the relatively extensive Eskimo site of Sissaritoq, or Old Nanortalik, which once had a shop, manager's residence and blubber storage facilities as well as lots of old stone and peat dwellings. It's recognisable by the large white cross crowning a knoll there. Between the ruins and Qaqaarssuasik (Storefjeldet) is a bizarre 'mosaic' formation, a field of gravel pebbles which is clearly artificial. These mosaics have been found around the Arctic, but as yet, there's no solid explanation of their purpose.

En route, hikers will cross the outlet of a dammed lake which serves as Nanortalik's water supply. Along the way, watch for an odd upright basalt pillar standing beside a tiny knoll about 150m from the shore. This is known as the Bear Stone, an old lintel from one of the ruins which was once used by a spoilt Inuit boy to tie up his pet polar bear cub.

Quassuk (Ravnefjeldet)
A good, clear trail will take you to the summit of intriguing 308m Quassuk, or Ravnefjeldet ('ravens mountain'), immediately north-west of Nanortalik

From Nanortalik, turn north on the gravel road just west of the KNI Butikken, follow it out past the last subdivision and take the left fork through the gravel excavations, keeping to the left of several small ponds.

GREENLAND

Nanortalik Island

0   1   2 km
Approximate Scale

Quassuk
(Ravnefjeldet)
308 m

NANORTALIK
ISLAND

Kunnguaq
River

Vandsø

Qaqaarssuasik
(Storefjeldet)
559m

Reservoir

Nanortalik

OQQUITSOQ

1   Good Fishing Beach
2   Nassifik (Eskimo Ruins & Graves)
3   Winter Provisions Cache
4   Bear Stone
5   Numerous Eskimo Graves & Dwellings
6   Sissaritoq (Old Nanortalik)
7   Mosaic Formation
8   Crater Lake
9   Pukitsit (Small Hut Ruins & Winter Provi-
    sioning Grounds)
10 Erliva Beach (Good Fishing)

Northern Peninsula

For an excellent day hike, cross the low pass between Qaqaarssuasik and Ravnefjeldet and follow the eastern coast of the long peninsula at the northern end of Nanortalik Island. You can make a loop walk out of it by following the coastline back to Nanortalik, around the eastern slopes of Ravnefjeldet. There are a few bogs along the way so wear good hiking boots.

QOORNOQ & SARQAA

The Qoornoq and Sarqaa sounds, the southernmost extensions of Søndre Sermilik Fjord, are readily accessible from Nanortalik by motorboat or kayak, and make interesting day excursions or longer trips. Near the eastern shore of Qoornoq Sound is the island of Umiiviarsuk, which has been an Eskimo hunting camp for many generations and is still used by modern Inuit hunters. Strewn about are the ruins of several nicely intact Eskimo dwellings and there's also a pleasant pebble beach and appealing places for a picnic.

As you head north along Qoornoq, you'll catch views of the granite hulk of Ulamertorsuaq, which rises above Tasermiut Fjord further east. At the southern tip of Amitsoq Island are the ruins of an abandoned graphite mine, where the rocks shimmer with an iridescent film of graphite grease. Several mine tunnels remain, but they're in a hazardous state of repair, and scraps of equipment lie rusting around what was once a plant which crushed and extracted the graphite.

Further north, on Sarqaa Sound, you'll

Continue to the end of the road and look for the trail, which heads north-west along the base of Ravnefjeldet. After 200m, it begins a slow and easy climb. At the summit, there's lots of scope for exploring and great views of Søndre Sermilik Fjord, Amitsoq Island and the remotest parts of Nanortalik Island.

Qaqaarssuasik (Storefjeldet)

The lovely 559m Qaqaarssuasik (Storefjeldet, or 'big mountain') is the island's highest peak, and its summit presents quite a surprise. After you've slogged up the rockfields, you're met by several cairns and a breathtaking drop-off into the sea. About 175m below the summit is a crater-like formation which contains a rather mysterious Greenland-shaped lake.

There are no tracks, but it's most easily climbed from the head of the bay west of Nanortalik. You can also take the steeper route up its southern face, from behind the Sissaritoq ruins.

GREENLAND

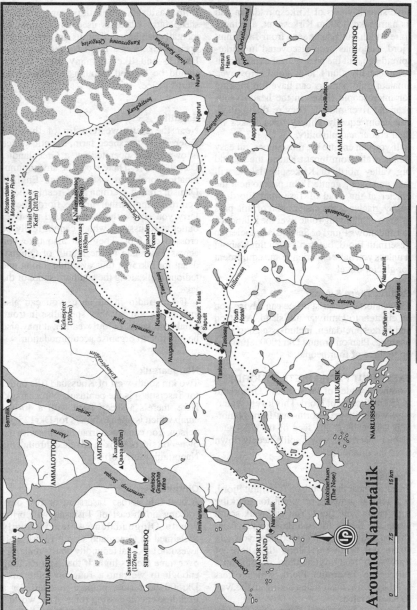

Around Nanortalik

GREENLAND

have superb views of Kirkespiretdalen and its namesake, 1590m Kirkespiret, a spindly spire which can also be seen from Tasermiut Fjord. Gold has been discovered in Kirkespiretdalen, but the prospects of exploiting it commercially don't look good. However, amateur gold-panners can have fun looking for microscopic flakes in the beach sands near the river mouth. They're distinguishable from equally glittery mica flakes by their colour and pliability.

If you can endure the mosquitoes, an easy 12 km walk from Ippatit Kuuat, the second big valley north of Kirkespiretdalen, will take you over a gentle 182m pass to near the glacier at the head of Tasermiut Fjord. A valley glacier at the eastern end of this pass offers a challenging route over the inland ice to Lindenows Fjord or Sermitsiaq glacier on Tasermiut Fjord, but don't even think about it unless you have experience and equipment for glacier travel.

Getting There & Away
The Nanortalik tourist office can advise you on charters to Umiiviarsuk Island, Amitsoq and Kirkespiretdalen, including a go at gold panning. Plan on around Dkr1000 return for up to three or four people.

TASERMIUT FJORD (KETILS FJORD)
Another wonder of far southern Greenland is 75 km Tasermiut Fjord. This lovely waterway winds its way north-east from Nanortalik and ends at the face of the tidewater glacier Tasermiut, which spills steeply down from the inland ice.

Tasiusaq
Tasiusaq, near the mouth of Tasermiut Fjord, is a logical jumping-off point for trekking trips around the fjord. You can walk south along the ridges for two days to the face-shaped mountain, Jakobinerhuen; you can strike out north-east along the shore of Tasersuaq to Qinguadalen; or continue further up Tasermiut Fjord, which offers level but slow, bush-laden hiking all the way to Klosterdalen.

North of Sisoorartut Kuua, over the bay from Tasiusaq, Nanortalik town owns a sheep farm which is used as a retreat by mentally handicapped adults. In summer, it's open to hikers as a *Youth Hostel*. Beds cost Dkr125 and like so many other things, should be booked through the Nanortalik tourist office.

Saputit
Near the south-western tip of the lake Tasersuaq is the sheep farm, Saputit, which is owned and operated by a Greenlandic/Danish couple. There won't be any communication problems – they speak English, Danish, French, German and Greenlandic! If you're hiking further up the fjord, they'll ferry you across the lake beyond the river outlet at Kuussuaq, which cannot really be crossed on foot. They can also take you across Tasersuaq to the mouth of Qinguadalen for Dkr500, thus avoiding a long and tedious walk along the southern shore of the lake.

If you radio in advance, you can also arrange for a meal; they specialise in trout, whale and lamb. In foul weather, it may also be possible to organise accommodation.

Nuugaarsuk
Two km south-west of Kuussuaq (the outlet for Tasersuaq) is the peninsula Nuugaarsuk. Here, there's a sheep farm with a 40-bed *camp* which is open to hikers for Dkr125 per person. You can make arrangements with the owner on site or book in advance through the Nanortalik tourist office.

Qinguadalen
A boat ride across Tasersuaq or two days walking north-east of Tasiusaq will bring you to Qinguadalen, which is loudly acclaimed as Greenland's only forest. This awesome arboreal fecundity boasts real *trees* over three metres high. If that isn't exciting enough to warrant a four-day hike or a Dkr500 boat ride, prepare yourself for a backdrop encompassing some of the world's most stunning vertical granite formations.

Ulamertorsuaq

When seen from below, the hulking granite mass of 1830m Ulamertorsuaq doesn't seem to belong to this planet. Hikers will find interest around the base, but for world-class rock climbers, its sheer 1000m walls and the bizarre columnar turret appended to its western face represent a sort of Nirvana; it's currently the most popular climbing destination in South Greenland. Behind it rise the sheer faces of 2045m Nalumaasortoq and other spectacular granite peaks, offering further challenges.

Klosterdalen & Uiluit Qaaqa

Klosterdalen, also known as Uiluit Kuua, lies 14 km south of the Tasermiut glacier face, and many of those brochure scenes of campers beneath soaring granite pinnacles were photographed here. The river that gushes out of Klosterdalen drops over a waterfall into the fjord, and the broad valley is green and inviting – albeit choked with bushes which stifle all but the most determined hikers.

Keen hikers can bash the bushes upstream for six km, then branch off up a steep side valley to the north, which climbs above the bush line and eventually leads over a 1000m pass and down to the fjord Kangikitsoq, which is near – but not accessible on foot to – Aappilattoq. This is part of the 14-day circuit described under Hiking, later in this section.

Near the valley mouth, north of the river, are the ruins of an Augustinian monastery dating from the mid-14th century. You can imagine the sort of inspiration the ascetics could derive in such a setting, but one can only wonder how they endured the mosquitoes and midges without the odd uncharitable thought.

South of the river are several inviting campsites, which are sheltered by bushes one to two metres high. Unfortunately, the river cannot normally be forded, and the only way between the campsite and the ruins is by boat past the river mouth.

The 2012m massif Uiluit Qaaqa, or 'Ketil', as the Norse knew it, rises above the landing site. Its sheer 1400m wall is one of the world's highest cliff faces, and is inspiring increasing interest as one of the world's ultimate climbing thrills. (If Ketil isn't enough of a rush, there's always 2300m Apostelens Tommelfinger on Lindenows Fjord!) Even for non-climbers, this hulking granite mass is a sight to behold.

Hiking

Tasermiut Fjord offers loads of hiking possibilities, but all require time and stamina. Tasermiut Fjord's greatest curse, which cannot be taken lightly, is the profusion of bushes and shrubs which proliferate up to 150m elevation. At low tide you can follow the beach, but at other times you'll need sterling patience, a real will to succeed – and perhaps even a machete. In places, you won't manage more than about one km per hour.

The 37 km walk from Tasiusaq into Klosterdalen is a popular choice, as is the three to five-day return walk into Qinguadalen. Note, however, that periods of high water may make the hike along Tasersuaq impassable.

Serious trekkers can tackle the 14-day circuit which begins at Tasiusaq and heads north along the fjord to Klosterdalen. It then ascends the river and crosses the high pass over to Kangikitsoq Fjord. There, it turns into the next valley to the south and returns to Tasermiut Fjord via a steep and challenging route over another pass into Qinguadalen. The route then follows the southern shore of Tasersuaq back to Tasiusaq. However, the passes may be closed by snow for much of the summer, so seek local advice before attempting it.

An even more ambitious route will take you from the snout of the tidewater glacier Sermitsiaq, near the head of Tasermiut Fjord, up to the icecap and across the ice to the head of Lindenows Fjord on the east coast. In fact, from here, you can cross the icecap between Greenland's east and west coasts in just 30 km! This hike is only for those with technical gear and experience in glacier travel.

GREENLAND

Organised Tours

The Nanortalik tourist office organises trout fishing expeditions to Tasermiut Fjord. They can also help you arrange boat charters to the hot springs on Uunartoq Island (Dkr570). In season, whale-watching tours are conducted around Nanortalik Island for Dkr200 per person and sightings are guaranteed – if you don't see a whale, the trip is free!

Getting There & Away

On Monday at 9 am and Thursday at 10 am, you can go to Tasiusaq on the KNI cargo boat *Klapmydsen* (Dkr90); it returns to Nanortalik at 1 pm. There are only 12 passenger places available, so book as far in advance as possible. This can be done through the Nanortalik tourist office, which can also suggest charters to Tasiusaq for around Dkr1000 for up to five people. To Klosterdalen, you'll pay around Dkr1800 and to Jakobinerhuen, Dkr500. If a boat is already going to drop or pick up another party, you may be able to take the unused portion of their one-way charter for a reduced rate. Remember that informal charters don't include insurance so use discretion when selecting a boat.

NUNAAP ISUA (CAPE FAREWELL)

The Nunaap Isua area is quite simply one of the most beautiful places on earth – the Cape Horn of Greenland's Patagonia. While access to the cape itself is difficult, the wonderful villages of Aappilattoq and Narsarmiit and their stunning backdrops are readily accessible from Nanortalik.

Narsarmiit (Frederiksdal)

Narsarmiit (formerly Narsaq Kujalleq), Greenland's southernmost settlement, has a population of about 190. It was founded by Moravian missionary Konrad Kleinschmidt in 1824 and named Frederiksdal after King Frederik VI. Materials for its lovely Moravian church, which dates from 1826, were transported from Qaqortoq in skin boats, or *umiaq*. During WWII, the US military built a radio navigation station which provided an economic base for the village.

Herjolfsnæs & Sandhavn

Herjolfsnæs, which lies across the fjord Narsap Sarqaa from Narsarmiit, was one of the major Norse settlements in the Østerbygd. The large parish church on the site, which was excavated by the Danish National Museum in 1921, dates back to the beginning of the 13th century. Examples of Norse clothing, which fit the fashion around the beginning of the 16th century, were found in permafrost beneath the churchyard (replicas are on display at the Qaqortoq museum).

Sandhavn, which was probably the first trading post in Greenland, lies beside a sandy bay less than an hour's walk across the peninsula from Herjolfsnæs. It was established by Icelandic merchant Herjólfur and served as a sort of entry and exit point for the country before the end of the 10th century.

There's not much left of either Herjolfsnæs or Sandhavn, but Norse history buffs will still find interest. Access is by boat charter only. From Nanortalik, official prices range from Dkr3000 for up to eight people to Dkr4100 for up to 14, but you'll probably find something for less. Better still, make informal arrangements with a private boat owner in Narsarmiit.

Norse costumes excavated at Herjolfsnaes

Aappilattoq

Frequently ice-choked and sheltered by a high mountain wall to the west, Aappilattoq enjoys a striking setting at the end of Torsukaataq Sound. Behind the church, which merits a look inside if it's open, rises a rock dome which affords a good view of the settlement and the surrounding peaks and waterways.

Organised Tours

In early August, the tourist office conducts eight-day polar bear and whale-watching tours which round Nunaap Isua, continue up the east coast into Lindenows Fjord (see below) and return through Prins Christians Sund. The self-contained charter boat, *Colo*, accommodates up to eight passengers. The Dkr7000 price may seem extravagant, but it includes a Greenlandic feast in Aappilattoq and you'll never regret making the trip.

Individual bookings are accepted and departures are guaranteed, regardless of the number of participants. For information, contact the Nanortalik tourist office.

Places to Stay

In Narsarmiit or Aappilattoq, camping is permitted anywhere outside the populated area. There's an especially nice *campsite* facing the water near the summit of the prominent rock immediately east of Aappilattoq.

Basic accommodation is available at the *Service House* in Aappilattoq for Dkr125, and may be booked through the Nanortalik tourist office. They can also arrange hostel-style accommodation at Narsarmiit.

Getting There & Away

Ferry The ferry *Aleqa Ittuk* sails between Nanortalik, Narsarmiit and Aappilattoq weekly from mid to late summer, ice conditions permitting. Torsukaataq Sound, which is lined with towering granite peaks, may well be the most spectacular waterway on the Greenland ferry system.

The KNI cargo boat *Klapmydsen* sails from Nanortalik to Narsarmiit (Dkr180) and Aappilattoq (Dkr220) on Monday, Tuesday, Thursday and Friday.

Boat Charter For groups of eight to 12 people, the Nanortalik tourist office can help you organise weekend boat charters, and once they're booked, additional people may join in. Boats normally anchor overnight at Kangia Fjord on Eggers Ø and in amenable weather, may even make a landing on Nunaap Isua itself. The price is Dkr1500 per person.

LINDENOW'S FJORD

Lindenow's Fjord, which is technically on the East Coast, has attracted polar bear hunters and mineral investigations, but as yet, the area remains uninhabited. This 65 km ice-choked fjord exemplifies the dramatically rugged east coast landscape and it's worth the effort and expense of getting there. Near its head rises the mass of 2300m Apostelens Tommelfinger ('the apostle's thumb'), one of the world's most spectacular granite faces. From one side, it's a sheer rock wall, but from another perspective, it recalls a soaring European cathedral.

Getting There & Away

Greenland Tourism runs summer cruises on the icebreaker *M/S Ioffe* between Narsarsuaq and Lindenow's Fjord, via Prins Christians Sund; see under Boat in the Greenland Getting Around chapter. See also under Getting There & Away for Nunaap Isua, earlier in this chapter.

GREENLAND

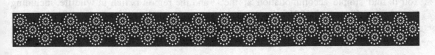

South-West Greenland

The south-western coast of Greenland stretches from Ivittuut in the south to beyond the Arctic Circle, which crosses between Maniitsoq and Sisimiut. The latter is not only the southernmost town permitting sled dogs, but also the first one heading north which experiences the true midnight sun in late June. Many people catch their first glimpse of Greenland at the international airport at Kangerlussuaq, which has direct connections with Denmark.

The coastal regions of South-West Greenland catch the brunt of dismal weather fronts from the south-west, but the meteorological tendencies improve greatly further north, and Kangerlussuaq is known for the warmest and most stable summer weather in Greenland. Sisimiut's climate is generally as good as that of the Disko Bay area further north.

Greenland's capital and largest metropolis, Nuuk (population 14,000), is swelling with migrants attracted from Greenland's towns and villages by economic opportunity. Historically, the region is known as the site of the Norse Vesterbygd, the 'western settlement', which disappeared even before the Osterbygd in South Greenland. The Nuuk area later served as headquarters for Greenland's first two Christian missions.

ARSUK

Arsuk was originally established as a trading station and survived on hunting. When fishing became Greenland's economic mainstay, some small villages were doomed, but Arsuk survived by shifting its economy accordingly. Arsuk also boasts one of Greenland's longest roads, which leads five km to the town dump.

Places to Stay

You'll find simple accommodation at the *Guesthouse Kialaaq* (☎ 10016; fax 10133), owned by Jakunnguaq Hansen. Beds cost Dkr300, with breakfast.

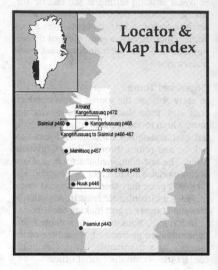

Locator & Map Index

Around Kangerlussuaq p472
Sisimiut p460 ● ● Kangerlussuaq p468
Kangerlussuaq to Sisimiut p466-467

● Maniitsoq p457

Around Nuuk p455

Nuuk p446

Paamiut p443

Getting There & Away

Ferries call in at Arsuk both northbound toward Nuuk (Dkr1290) and southbound toward Qaqortoq (Dkr715). The KNI cargo boat *Aqaluk Ittuk* sails weekly between Paamiut, Arsuk and Kangilinnguit (see under Ivittuut and Paamiut). The stretch between Narsaq and Arsuk is known for the worst ice conditions on the west coast and delays aren't uncommon. (One year, we were stuck in pack ice for two days near the mouth of Arsuk Fjord.)

IVITTUUT & KANGILINNGUIT

Lightly populated and little-visited Ivittuut ('the grassland') lies midway between Qaqortoq and Paamiut. It's ideal for wilderness excursions – hiking, sea kayaking, mineralogy, fishing and whale-watching – and the region is rich in wildlife, including musk oxen, Arctic foxes and eagles.

Until the past decade, a cryolite mine operated here. Cryolite, which was extracted

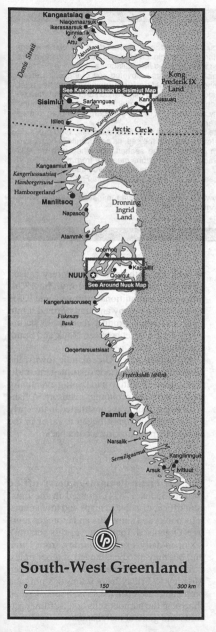

South-West Greenland

0   150   300 km

for use by the Allied war effort during WWII, is a unique form of sodium crystal used in the production of aluminium. However, commercial quantities played out and the abandoned 30,000 sq metre quarry has now filled with water.

Ivittuut's ample hiking possibilities are outlined on Greenland Tourism's *Ivittuut* 1:75,000 hiking map. The district is also known for the unusual pillar formations beneath the upper reaches of Ikka Fjord (see boxed aside). The fjord is accessible on foot via an easy pass over from Kangilinnguit, but currently, access to the formations is limited to divers involved in ongoing scientific investigations.

Although Ivittuut is the district town, most of the people live in nearby **Kangilinnguit** (Grønnedal), to which it is joined by the only road in Greenland linking two populated places. Originally the site of a Norse nobleman's estate, Kangilinnguit was used in WWII as a supply depot and a US naval station. It's now the Danish Greenlandic naval headquarters.

There are virtually no tourist services, but the area is rich in excellent hikes and the few visitors are still likely to have it all to themselves.

Information
Tourist information is provided by the Ivittuut Kommunia (☎ 10177; fax 10173), DK-3930, Kangilinnguit.

Place to Stay
The *Ivittuut Youth Hostel* (☎ 10177; fax 10173), which charges Dkr250 for beds, is the only accommodation. Facilities include communal baths, lounges and cooking facilities. Check in through the Ivittuut Kommunia office.

There are no restaurants or shops – not even a KNI kiosk – so bring all your supplies from elsewhere.

Getting There & Away
Air In the summer, Grønlandsfly flies four times weekly between Kangilinnguit and

The Petrified Warriors of Ikka

Ikka Fjord, across the peninsula from Kangilinnguit, is known in Inuit legend as the place where invading warriors – presumably Norse – crashed through the thin ice to their deaths in the frigid sea water. It's said they descended to the sea floor and were petrified into stalagmite-like stone pillars.

In 1963, Danish geologist Hans Pauly and Danish Navy divers recovered one of these 'invaders' from the sea bed. They dubbed it *ikaite* and left it lying on their boat deck, but when they returned after a lunch break, the pillar had disintegrated into a puddle of water and loose white sand. Information on the phenomenon was published in Danish, but didn't receive outside attention until 1995, when the Imperial College, London, along with the University and Museum of Copenhagen, attempted to map the ikaite formations using sonar, GPS and diving apparatus.

Ikaite, it turns out, is a form of calcium carbonate that is stable only under extremely high pressure – such as at the multiple atmospheres of pressure found beneath the sea. Its occurrence in Ikka Fjord is due to the presence of calcium springs, which issue from the seabed, combined with the 2°C temperature and pressure of the fjord water. In places, the formations measure from two to 20m in height. Due to the temperature imperative, researchers are fairly certain they developed since the end of the last ice age, 10,000 years ago. Currently, there are moves to preserve Ikka Fjord as a national marine park and nature reserve.

Although ikaite pillars haven't been found anywhere else in the world, minerals with the same chemical composition exist in Japan, Alaska and Antarctica. ■

Narsarsuaq (Dkr1360) and once or twice weekly to and from Paamiut (Dkr1160).

Ferry Every second weekend in summer, KNI's *Anguteq Ittuk* sails from Qaqortoq to Kangilinnguit (Dkr500). The Paamiut district KNI boat *Aqaluk Ittuk* does a weekly run from Paamiut to Arsuk (Dkr235) and Kangilinnguit (Dkr315). The fare between Arsuk and Kangilinnguit is Dkr80. There's no boat service to Ivittuut, which is accessible by road from Kangilinnguit.

PAAMIUT (FREDERIKSHÅB)

Paamiut, or 'those at the mouth', in reference to its position at the mouth of Kuannersooq (Kvanefjord), has a population of around 2800. It's informally known as Greenland's 'artists' colony', for its quality tupilak and other carvings. It's also the site of a maritime training school.

History

The original colony of Frederikshåb was established by Jakob Severin in 1742 around the mouth of Præstevigen creek. It was originally intended as a trading station but management problems and a heavy build-up of pack ice in the mid-18th century caused difficult times in the colony. In 1774, however, ice conditions improved, and KGH took over the colony and transformed it into a fur and whale-product mercantile station serving the district between Nuuk and South Greenland.

As with so many Greenlandic towns, the preoccupation with trade disrupted the traditional hunting culture and fishing eventually took over as the economic mainstay. A fish-processing plant was constructed in the early 1970s and although it began to falter in the 1980s, it's now making a comeback.

Information

The efficient Paamiut tourist office (☎ 17673; fax 17854), housed in the museum office, distributes maps and town plans, sells books and souvenirs and arranges tours (see Organised Tours later in this section). It's open daily, except Saturday, from 1 to 3 pm, but may also be attended at other times.

The post, telephone and fax office is open Monday to Friday from 9 am to 3 pm, and both banks are open the same hours. A small shop near the harbour sells books, film, postcards and general merchandise.

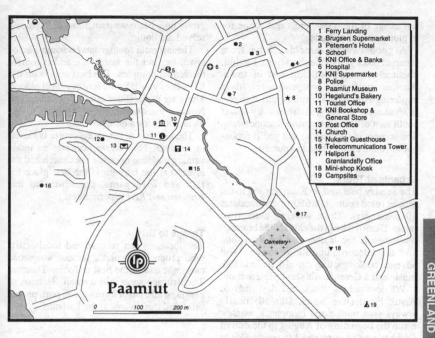

1 Ferry Landing
2 Brugsen Supermarket
3 Petersen's Hotel
4 School
5 KNI Office & Banks
6 Hospital
7 KNI Supermarket
8 Police
9 Paamiut Museum
10 Hegelund's Bakery
11 Tourist Office
12 KNI Bookshop &
   General Store
13 Post Office
14 Church
15 Nukariit Guesthouse
16 Telecommunications Tower
17 Heliport &
   Grønlandsfly Office
18 Mini-shop Kiosk
19 Campsites

Paamiut

0   100   200 m

GREENLAND

Paamiut Museum

The recently expanded Paamiut Museum, which is housed in the old trading company buildings, displays Eskimo and Inuit artefacts, qajaqs and historical photos, and has a historical exhibit, a 'whaling in Paamiut' room and a geology section with one of the best stone collections in Greenland. Another room accommodates exhibitions. It's open on Wednesday from 3 to 5 pm, Thursday from 10 am to noon and Sunday from 1 to 4 pm. At other times, check with the tourist office and you'll probably be allowed to look around. Admission is free.

Church

Paamiut's colourful and unusual church appears to be a veritable collection of afterthoughts. The typically Greenlandic churchyard is very colourfully decorated with bright plastic blooms, while a larger cemetery further inland takes the concept to even greater extremes. To have a look

around, you may have to chase up the attendant; the tourist office can help.

Telecommunications Tower

Even if you have only a short time in Paamiut, be sure to hike up to the telecommunications tower on the hill south of town, which affords a great, colourful view over the town and harbour, and right out to sea.

Kuannersooq (Kvanefjord)

Paamiut sits at the mouth of Kuannersooq, commonly called Kvanefjord, the long multi-armed fjord which reaches inland toward several dramatic tidewater glaciers. Locals enjoy sailing up the fjord for family outings, and on summer Sundays, the tourist office runs nine-hour boat tours right to the glacier face (see Organised Tours).

Hiking

The Paamiut area offers myriad hiking opportunities, but very few foreigners take advantage of them so there's real scope for exploration and solitude.

A good two or three-day hike from Paamiut takes you to the short fjord, Eqaluit, about eight hours walking east of town. Another great place to spend a few days exploring is around the mini-fjord Kangerluarsukasik, about 1½ hours by boat south-east of Paamiut, across Kuannersooq. The scenery is spectacular and you'll probably have the entire place to yourself.

Organised Tours

The Sunday boat tour up Kuannersooq to the glacier (nine hours, Dkr650) accommodates 10 passengers. Town walking tours (two hours, Dkr50) take in the church, the brædtet, the museum, the leather and fur workshop and the telecommunications tower. With advance bookings, they can also include folk music and a Greenlandic choir presentation.

Whale-watching tours and day trips to Arsuk Fjord (five hours, Dkr450) nearly always spot minke and humpback whales. From the beginning of August to the end of October, you're guaranteed to see whales or you pay nothing for the tour (or you get another tour free).

The 20 km wide Frederikshåbs Isblink glacier is probably Paamiut's best hope of attracting package tours. The tourist office can help you arrange boat charters to its massive face.

Places to Stay & Eat

The best accommodation option is the new guesthouse *Nukariit* (☎ & fax 17798), which is housed in the former Nuna-Tek hostel and offers cooking facilities. Single/double rooms cost Dkr450/600 with communal bathroom and toilet. It also has the best restaurant in town. Through the tourist office, you may be able to organise informal hostel-style accommodation at the *school*.

Seedy *Petersen's Hotel* (☎ 17299) charges Dkr325/500 for single/double rooms with communal facilities, but rooms are most frequently rented by the hour and lone travellers may feel uncomfortable. In its

grotty little bar/restaurant, most of the meals served are liquid.

The informal *campground* is south-east of town, beyond the last kiosk and colourful residential complex. The best area is on the hill where you'll find a few dry level places. There are no facilities but lots of space. The Nukariit guesthouse allows campers to use its facilities for a nominal fee.

The *grill bar* at the sports centre is closed in summer. The *bakery* occupies an unassuming building opposite the church and the *brædtet* at the harbour is the best place for fish and wild game. Paamiut also has *Brugsen* and *KNI* supermarkets.

Things to Buy

The museum can recommend local artists who produce Paamiut's famous soapstone carvings; one of the best is Tobias Thorsen. The Brugsen shop sells a small selection of carvings, and when ferries are in port, people often sell their wares at the harbour.

Getting There & Away

Air Grønlandsfly (☎ 17288) has two weekly helicopter services between Paamiut and Narsarsuaq (Dkr2250) and flies two or three times weekly between Paamiut and Nuuk (Dkr2250).

Ferry The big ferries call in on their weekly cycle between Qaqortoq and Nuuk. It's normally 16 hours between Paamiut and Nuuk (Dkr955) and 19 hours to Qaqortoq (Dkr995). As you sail into Paamiut, note the shipwreck, the *Greenland Star* (home port 'Manitzoq'), which is moored on the rocks just outside the harbour entrance. It's now a real rust-bucket, but in Nuuk you may find old postcards which portray it in its former glory.

The Paamiut district KNI boat has space for 10 passengers and runs weekly between Paamiut, Arsuk (Dkr235) and Kangilinnguit (Dkr315), travelling south one day and returning the next.

QEQERTARSUATSIAAT (FISKENÆSSET)

This village, 150 km south of Nuuk, sits on a small, flat peninsula near the open waters of Davis Strait. It was founded as Fiskenæsset by Anders Olsen, who determined a settlement was needed between Paamiut and Nuuk. It turned out to be a rich fishing ground, and at one time the salmon were so thick in the bay that the light reflecting from their bodies was thought to be supernatural. Just offshore, the Fiskenæs Banke was discovered to be teeming with cod.

Today, Qeqertarsuatsiaat is a village of seal hunters and its few visitors come mainly to buy Qeqertarsuatsiaat bags, which are handmade by local women.

Akunaat (Lichtenfels)

South-east of Qeqertarsuatsiaat is the ghost village of Akunaat, founded by German missionaries, which had a church and mission station known as Lichtenfels ('rock of light'). When the settlement was abandoned, Qeqertarsuatsiaat decided to expand its own church, and the Akunaat church was dismantled for materials. The churchyard contains graves of Greenlanders and Germans with inspiring epitaphs in German.

Places to Stay & Eat

There are a couple of bed & breakfast possibilities, but they must be arranged through the Nuuk tourist office. Otherwise, carry a tent. The *KNI shop* offers basic supplies.

Getting There & Away

The big ferries call in weekly en route between Nuuk (Dkr580) and Qaqortoq (Dkr1455), but only stop long enough to drop off or take on passengers and cargo. The local KNI boat, *Aqaluk Ittuk*, sails weekly to and from Nuuk (Dkr320).

KANGERLUARSORUSEQ (FÆRINGEHAVN)

The Danish name of tiny Kangerluarsoruseq, 52 km south of Nuuk, means 'Faroese harbour'. Last century, Denmark was struggling to shelter Greenlanders from encroaching modern society by limiting trading rights to a government monopoly. At the same time, Faroese fisherfolk working in Davis Strait felt that, as citizens of the Danish realm, they were as entitled to exploit this fishery as any other Danish concern. The government refused them access to Greenlandic settlements but in 1900 offered them this bit of land on which to set up an operations base. In its heyday, Færingehavn thrived on the prawn and cod fisheries, justifying a large Danish fish-processing plant.

Nowadays, few residents remain in Kangerluarsoruseq, but it claims the dubious honour of having Greenland's largest petrol tank complex. The old town, Gamla Færingehavn, remains quite picturesque.

There's no accommodation, so visitors need their own tents.

Getting There & Away

In summer, KNI's *Aqaluk Ittuk* runs weekly to and from Nuuk (Dkr150). The Nuuk tourist office occasionally runs day tours to the settlement.

NUUK (GODTHÅB)

Nuuk, which proudly claims to be the world's smallest capital city, means 'the promontory' and is pronounced 'nuke' (and invites a measure of ribbing from English-speakers).

Nuuk's founder, Hans Egede, originally named the town Godthåb ('good hope') but sadly, his optimistic vision has been dashed by sometimes overwhelming social problems. Modern Nuuk houses 15% of Greenland's population in monumentally ugly housing projects and the current sprawl spawned by urban drift has lent it an impersonal, non-Greenlandic air.

Nuuk may be fascinating for politicians, businesspeople and social anthropologists – and hikers will find plenty of interest – but otherwise, the worthwhile sights can be covered in one day.

History

Once the Norse had settled all the favourable lands in South Greenland, they sailed up the

GREENLAND

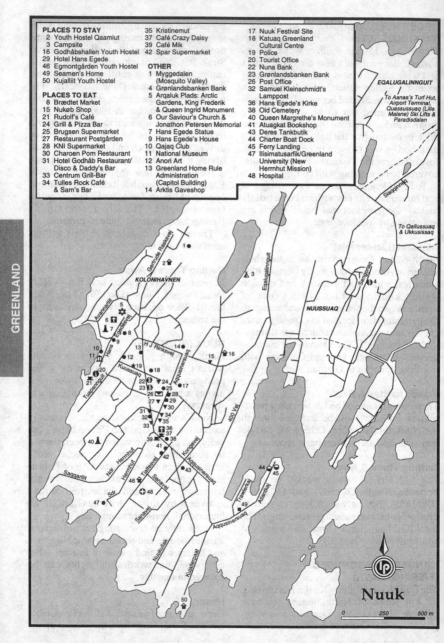

PLACES TO STAY
2 Youth Hostel Qaamiut
3 Campsite
16 Godhåbshallen Youth Hostel
29 Hotel Hans Egede
46 Egmontgården Youth Hostel
49 Seamen's Home
50 Kujalliit Youth Hostel

PLACES TO EAT
8 Brædtet Market
15 Nukøb Shop
21 Rudolf's Café
24 Grill & Pizza Bar
25 Brugsen Supermarket
27 Restaurant Postgården
28 KNI Supermarket
30 Charoen Pom Restaurant
31 Hotel Godhåb Restaurant/
   Disco & Daddy's Bar
33 Centrum Grill-Bar
34 Tulles Rock Café
   & Sam's Bar

35 Kristinemut
37 Café Crazy Daisy
39 Café Mik
42 Spar Supermarket

OTHER
1 Myggedalen
   (Mosquito Valley)
4 Grønlandsbanken Bank
5 Arqaluk Plads: Arctic
   Gardens, King Frederik
   & Queen Ingrid Monument
6 Our Saviour's Church &
   Jonathon Petersen Memorial
7 Hans Egede Statue
9 Hans Egede's House
10 Qajaq Club
11 National Museum
12 Anori Art
13 Greenland Home Rule
   Administration
   (Capitol Building)
14 Arktis Gaveshop

17 Nuuk Festival Site
18 Katuaq Greenland
   Cultural Centre
19 Police
20 Tourist Office
22 Nuna Bank
23 Grønlandsbanken Bank
26 Post Office
32 Samuel Kleinschmidt's
   Lamppost
36 Hans Egede's Kirke
38 Old Cemetery
40 Queen Margrethe's Monument
41 Atuagkat Bookshop
43 Deres Tankbutik
44 Charter Boat Dock
45 Ferry Landing
47 Ilisimatusarfik/Greenland
   University (New
   Herrnhut Mission)
48 Hospital

KOLONIHAVNEN

EQALUGALINNGUIT

To Aanaa's Turf Hut,
Airport Terminal,
Quassussuaq (Lille
Malene) Ski Lifts &
Paradisdalen

To Qallussuaq
& Ukkusissaq

NUUSSUAQ

Nuuk

0   250   500 m

Nuuk (Godthåb) coat of arms

west coast in search of green pastures. Ameralik Fjord, which they called Lysefjord (the 'light fjord'), seemed as good a site as any, and to the east, they found pockets of land with grass suitable for grazing sheep.

This was the Norse Vesterbygd ('western settlement'). Compared to its eastern counterpart, little is known of the Vesterbygd. It's believed that the Eskimos, called *skrælings* by the Norse, repeatedly attacked the settlement and eventually caused it to fall, but there's little evidence to support this.

The missionary Hans Egede first landed at Håbets Ø, about 18 km west of present-day Nuuk. Subsequent reconnaissance led him to establish his mission on a peninsula where he found meadows, nesting ducks and 12 families of Greenlandic souls.

The mission and trading company were officially founded on 29 August, 1728, and the locals, who weren't pleased with the intrusion, headed for less congested lands. Danish king Christian IV became dismayed at the cost of Hans Egede's religious and trading enterprises and considered withdrawing support of the project. However, Egede convinced him to reconsider, and in 1733 the king sent three German Moravian missionaries to assist in the Christianisation of Greenland. Predictably, tensions and rivalries arose between the two missions, and the Moravians set up a new mission, New Herrnhut, on the other side of the peninsula.

Although both missions had noble intentions, they introduced new problems to the local populace. One Greenlandic leader, Ulaajuk, became dismayed at the growing materialism and dependence among his people and moved them away. What he didn't anticipate was the 1736 smallpox epidemic which decimated both the European and Inuit populations and killed Hans Egede's wife, Gertrude Rask. Hans, who later became known as the 'Greenland Apostle', returned to Denmark and left his sons to carry on his work.

In the mid-19th century, Moravian missionary Samuel Kleinschmidt became proficient with the Greenlandic language and in the following years conducted the first philological study, produced a grammar and orthography, and translated the Bible into Greenlandic.

The missions and trading companies continued to attract people to Godthåb, and during WWII the town became the administrative centre of Greenland. In the 1950s, when Greenland became a full county of Denmark, the city boomed. A new reservoir brought running water, a new harbour was constructed and the promise of high wages attracted a wave of Danish immigration and technical expertise.

Despite a tragic tuberculosis epidemic, the population continued to grow and the immense apartment blocks began springing up (the largest of these, Blok P, houses 1% of Greenland's population under one roof!). Between 1950 and the present, Nuuk gained 13,000 of its current 14,000 inhabitants and in the 1970s, an airport was constructed at the foot of Quassussuaq (Lille Malene). The growth has now spawned two suburbs: Nuussuaq, which is now Greenland's second largest town with 5000 people, and a brand new development, Eqalugalinnguit. The resulting rampant construction is currently spreading out along the airport road.

GREENLAND

Orientation

Maps The tourist office distributes free city maps with information in English, Danish, German and Greenlandic. An essential map for hikers is the 1:75,000 *Hiking Map West Greenland – Nuuk*, which is sold at the tourist office and several shops around town.

Information

Tourist Office The Nuuk Tikilluarit tourist office (☎ 22700; fax 22710), in the Santa Claus house at Hans Egedesvej 29, Kolonihavnen, distributes maps, brochures and city tour programmes. From 15 June to 15 September, it's open Monday to Friday from 10 am to 5 pm and on weekends from noon to 4 pm.

Money There are branches of both Nuna Bank and Grønlandsbanken in the centre and in Nuussuaq. They're open Monday to Friday from 10 am to 3 pm (until 5 pm on Thursday). They charge Dkr50 to change travellers' cheques.

Post & Communications The main post office is open Monday to Wednesday from 10 am to 3 pm, on Thursday from 9 am to 5 pm, and on Friday from 9 am to 3.30 pm. The Santa Claus House also has a post office.

The telephone exchange, at the main post office, is open Monday to Friday from 10 am to 5 pm and on weekends from noon to 4 pm. To book overseas calls from other telephones, dial ☎ 0012. Directory assistance is ☎ 0019.

Bookshops Atuagkat (☎ 21337; fax 23378), Greenland's largest bookshop, is on Aqqusinersuaq between the new harbour and the city centre. It publishes and distributes the *Kalaallit Nunaat Atlas*, and also stocks scholarly works, field guides and souvenir books dealing with Greenlandic history, culture, economy, politics and natural history.

You'll also find postcards, maps, guidebooks and novels, mainly in Danish or Greenlandic. The airport kiosk sells the news magazines *Time* and *Newsweek*.

Emergency Services Emergency services in Nuuk include the police (☎ 21448), Sana hospital (☎ 21101), fire brigade (☎ 000) and ambulance (☎ 25552).

Katuaq Greenland Cultural Centre

The huge new triangular cultural centre, Kulturip Illorsua Katuaq, which now dominates a large area of central Nuuk, takes in over 4000 sq metres of airy open space for art exhibitions, conferences, concerts and other cultural performances. The architect's idea was to emulate the individual houses and open spaces in Greenlandic towns and villages. The windows are placed to emphasise the Arctic light, and suggest the northern lights, icebergs and rock.

It houses the Greenland Art School, the Groenlandica library of Arctic literature and NAPA Nordic Institute. It's open daily for exhibitions and in the evening for cultural events. There's also a small café serving coffee, tea and snacks, and a reading library with Nordic and Arctic newspapers, books and magazines.

Samuel Kleinschmidt's Lamppost

For some reason, this nondescript red post capped by an old lantern has a strange appeal. In the mid-1800s, Moravian missionary Samuel Kleinschmidt walked between

Samuel Kleinschmidt

his home and his mission at New Herrnhut. In order to light his way on dark winter mornings, he hung a lantern on this post at the mid-point of his journey and picked it up on his way home at night.

New Herrnhut Mission

New Herrnhut, built in 1747, was the early headquarters of the Greenland Moravian Mission which was dispatched by King Christian IV and instructed to assist Hans Egede's efforts. This arrangement didn't work out, and the Moravians established their own mission on the other side of the peninsula. The building has housed the National Museum and the National Theological Seminary, but is now home to the University of Greenland, which has several faculties and 100 full-time students.

Hans Egede's Church

Although it was named after Greenland's first Christian missionary, Hans Egede's church was consecrated on the 250th anniversary of the founding of his mission and is a singularly uninteresting building.

Greenland Seminary

The building which houses the Greenland Seminary or Illiniarfissuaq, which was founded in 1845, was constructed in 1907. It now features on Nuuk's coat of arms. In front is a monument to Greenlandic teacher Jørgen Brønlund who perished in Peary Land with the Mylius-Erichsen expedition.

Kolonihavnen

Quiet and picturesque Kolonihavnen ('colony harbour') sits juxtaposed against the apartment blocks looming on the hill above and provides a quiet and picturesque alternative to modern Nuuk.

Most of the buildings date from the 18th and 19th centuries and form the heart of old Nuuk, and one can still imagine it as the heart of the settlement before the new industrial harbour was constructed. From here the hunters set out in their qajaqs, it was the central business district, and the place that whalers brought their victims for flensing.

On weekends, you may catch a qajaq demonstration at the headquarters of the Nuuk qajaq club, beside the National Museum.

Arctic Gardens If you thought Samuel Kleinschmidt's lamppost strained the margins of tourist interest, check out the so-called Arctic Gardens, on Arqaluk Plads, where meticulously laid-out garden boxes feature the same grassy vegetation as the square itself. Fortunately, the city has recognised the failure of this project and is attempting to rectify it with a bit of imagination and tending.

Towards the church from the gardens is a statue commemorating the 1952 visit of King Frederik and Queen Ingrid to Nuuk.

Church of Our Saviour & Monuments The lovely Frelserens Kirke ('Church of Our Saviour'), was consecrated on 6 April 1849, with several renovations since. If it's unlocked, take a look inside. The chalices date from 1722 and bear the initials of King Christian IV, and the altar has the mark of King Frederik VII. You'll also find artistic marble reliefs depicting Hans Egede and Gertrude Rask.

On the stony hill beside the church is a statue of Hans Egede, which enjoys a great view of the contrasting old and new parts of Nuuk. In front of the church is a bust of the down-to-earth-looking hymnist and organist, Jonathon Petersen, by sculptor Hans Lynge.

Hans Egede's House The yellow house where Hans Egede lived while overseeing his Nuuk mission was built in 1728, making it the oldest useful structure in Greenland. It's now the home of Greenland's premier, Lars Emil Johansen.

Greenland National Museum The National Museum, which occupies three buildings in Kolonihavnen, depicts 4500 years of Greenlandic culture. One hall is filled with historical dogsleds, qajaq and umiaq. Another room is devoted to the cultures of East Greenland, and other exhibits include artefacts from the earliest Greenlandic cultures: traditional hunting tools and methods, historical and modern Greenlandic dress, geology, Eskimo and Inuit art, and Norse history.

However, the best known pieces are the 15th century Qilaqitsoq mummies, from near the north-western town of Uummannaq. They came to the attention of the modern world in 1972, when two brothers uncovered them while hunting, but were content to let them rest in peace. In 1977, when the director of the National Museum got wind of the brothers' discovery, Qilaqitsoq was suddenly on the map. The mummies made the cover of *National Geographic* and were considered world-class archaeological finds.

The museum is open daily, except Monday, from 1 to 4 pm. Groups may enquire about special openings by phoning ☎ 22611.

Santa Claus House In 1992, Nuuk attempted to create a tourist attraction by constructing a Santa-theme cafeteria and souvenir shop. The building now houses the tourist office, but there's still a Christmas-theme cafeteria and post office. It's also worth seeing Greenland's 'largest tree', which is planted in concrete out the front. You can also see a column full of pacifiers (dummies) from children who've outgrown these symbols of childhood and to prove it, have consigned them to Father Christmas.

Hiking
Nuuk's hinterlands offer some fabulous day hikes. The best will take you up the peaks Quassussuaq (Lille Malene), Ukkusissaq (Store Malene) or around Quassussuaq through Paradisdalen. The map to use is the reverse side of the *Hiking Map West Greenland – Nuuk*, which is sold at the tourist office and several shops in town.

On weekdays, bus No 3 runs hourly to Aanaa's turf hut and the airport; wait at the bus stop opposite the Hotel Hans Egede, beside Greenland's only traffic light. On weekends, you'll have to walk or take a taxi.

Bus No 2 runs to Nuussuaq half-hourly (hourly on weekends).

Quassussuaq From the airport or Nuussuaq, it's an easy climb up 443m Quassussuaq. The most direct route is straight up the ski-lift behind the airport terminal. Alternatively, walk east along the shore of Malene Bay (Malenebugten) from Nuussuaq and ascend Quassussuaq's south-western ridge.

Paradisdalen Loop Paradisdalen ('paradise valley'), which lies east of Quassusuaq offers another route to the summit and a fabulous 16 km four to six-hour loop hike around Quassussuaq.

This well marked and well trodden route, which roughly follows a winter ski trail, is normally done clockwise from the Aanaa's turf hut parking area, about one km south-west of the airport. The track parallels the coast north-eastward to the mouth of Paradisdalen, between Quassussuaq and 472m Kuanninguit. It then cuts back over a low pass between Quassussuaq and Ukkusissaq to follow the power lines along the southern shore of the lovely lake Qallussuaq (Cirkusøen).

To return to Nuuk from the outflow of Qallussuaq, simply follow the ski trail and power pylons toward the shore of Malenebugten and cut west toward Nuussuaq. Naturally, this route can also be done in reverse.

Ukkusissaq From the Qallussuaq lake on the Paradisdalen loop, energetic hikers can climb to the twin 761m and 772m peaks of Ukkusissaq. You'll have fabulous views over Nuuk, its landmark peak 1210m Sermitsiaq, the vast Akia (Nordlandet) peninsula and the fjord Kangerluarsunnguaq. In the saddle between the peaks is a lovely blue-green mountain lake.

Kangerluarsunnguaq (Kobbefjorden) Summer Ski Centre
The Kangerluarsunnguaq summer ski centre, on the Teqqiinngallip Sermiat glacier,

offers year-round skiing within fairly easy reach of Nuuk. Accommodation is provided in three mountain huts in the Iluliumanersuaq valley and another at the glacier. The surrounding peninsula also offers lots of dramatic hiking, including a climb up 1184m Hjortetakken ('antler peak').

From March to November, the tourist office runs one-day and weekend tours which begin with a cruise from Nuuk, followed by a hike to the ski centre for lunch, then on to the mountain huts higher up. On the weekend trip, you can also opt to climb to the summit of 855m Aajuitsoq (Chappas) peak, then descend to the small hut at Amiitsoq for the cruise back to Nuuk. The one-day/weekend options cost Dkr495/800, including transport, guide and hut accommodation; meals and skiing are extra.

The four-day hike to the ski centre from Nuuk is mostly easy, but does include several challenging stretches and river crossings. In winter, you can cut off two days by skiing right across the fjord. The essential Nuuk area hiking map is described under Orientation earlier in this section.

Organised Tours

The tourist office organises numerous day tours and hikes, but it's best to book ahead, as all tours have minimum group sizes and organising something on the spot can be hit or miss.

Popular options include a hike to Ukkusissaq (Tuesday, six hours, Dkr250); an evening cruise around the Nuuk peninsula (three hours, Dkr295); a city sights tour (Wednesday, two hours, Dkr160); a Greenlandic picnic at the Aanaa's turf hut (Wednesday, four hours, Dkr250); a coffee mik (one hour, Dkr60); a midnight sun whale-watching cruise (daily, four hours, Dkr430); a whale-watching cruise to the abandoned settlement of Kangeq (Friday and Saturday, four hours, Dkr475); and a cruise to Sermitsiaq island and beyond to the Bjørneøen Eskimo ruins (Saturday, eight hours, Dkr750). Individual flightseeing tours by helicopter or seaplane can also be arranged (30 minutes, Dkr740) and in May

and June, they organise one to two-hour snowmobile tours to Quassussuaq or Ukkusissaq for Dkr250 to Dkr450.

The arts and handicrafts tour (Monday, two hours, Dkr150) visits a qajaq-builders' workshop, the leather-tanning shop, Kittat and a local artist, and finishes with a spin through the Landsting Hall, where the corridors are lined with Greenlandic art. The Home Rule tour (Thursday, 1½ hours, Dkr100) takes you through the Home Rule Administration offices and explains government workings.

For other possibilities, see under Kangerluarsunnguaq Summer Ski Centre, earlier in this section, and under Nuup Kangerlua, later in the chapter.

Special Events

For an exhausting tour of Nuuk, you can compete in the Nuuk Marathon, which is run in late July or early August. For details, call up the organising committee's Internet site (www.qdata.gl/uk/hotel/naape/mrt/honen/htm). In 1996, 30 runners completed the race.

In March, the city hosts a snow sculpture festival which is open to artists from around the world. The Nuuk Festival, in early August, features several weeks of live music, art exhibitions, food stalls and even a crane for bungee jumping. The action revolves around a Big Top tent erected near the corner of Kongevejen and Aqqusinersuaq. In the open programme, which takes place one Saturday evening, people in the audience are invited to dance, sing, play music, recite poetry and speak their mind.

Places to Stay

Nuuk was the last city in Greenland to get a youth hostel, and now it has four! The most basic is the *Godhåbshallen Youth Hostel* (☎ & fax 21654), in the sports hall at Vandsøvej 2, which is frequently used by visiting sports teams. It's the cheapest place in town at just Dkr95, but isn't terribly clean and can get quite noisy and disorganised.

A better choice is the *Kujalliit Youth Hostel*, which must be booked through the

GREENLAND

tourist office (☎ 22700; fax 22710). It sits magically on a quiet promontory jutting into the sea, and although it's an easy walk from the centre, there's no bustle. Rooms with access to cooking facilities cost Dkr150, plus Dkr50 if you need bedding.

A step up is the *Egmontgården Youth Hostel*, Tjalfesvej 8, which also must be booked through the tourist office. Dorm rooms with shared bath and kitchen facilities cost Dkr150. At the *Youth Hostel Qaamiut*, at CE Jansensvej 25, self-catering student apartments cost Dkr250 for one or two people.

The mid-range place to stay is the *Seamen's Home* (☎ 21029; fax 22104), near the new (Atlantic) Harbour. Single/double rooms with communal facilities cost Dkr395/620. With private facilities, they're Dkr595/860. Guests have access to the TV lounge and laundry facilities.

Luxury has arrived in Nuuk. The *Hotel Hans Egede* (☎ 24222; fax 24487) has single/ double rooms with private bath, TV/video, radio, mini-bar and telephone for Dkr1045/Dkr1295. For 'business class' (ie expense account) accommodation, they're Dkr1290/1590. Family rooms for three or more people cost Dkr495 per person. A bare bones 'economy' room costs Dkr695/995.

The recommended *campsite* is on the eastern shore of the lake at the end of Børnehjemsvej, north of the centre. It's a nice quiet area just a few minutes walk from the centre. You can buy camping stove fuel at Deres Tankbutik; ask for *rense bensin*, which costs Dkr9.95 for 500ml.

Places to Eat

The *Hotel Hans Egede* has the elegant restaurant *Sky Top* (☎ 24222), which serves international cuisine and gourmet versions of Greenlandic specialities including reindeer steaks (Dkr180), salmon (Dkr150), whale (Dkr140) and beef dishes (Dkr145 to Dkr190). Portions are small but the price and quality are high – add alcohol and the bill doubles.

For trendy but tasty cafeteria-style snacks and meals, try *Rudolf's Café* (☎ 24724) in Kolonihavnen. Especially recommended are the coffee, the cheese and walnut salad and the variety of cakes, pastries and pies.

More down-to-earth is the *Kristinemut* (☎ 25040), which has adopted an odd cowboy theme and serves up large portions and simple but good value specials. A buffet breakfast costs Dkr39, lunches are around Dkr35, and a spare rib special is just Dkr49.

Attached is the pub-style *Tulles Rock Café* (☎ 21240), which emulates a Hard Rock Café but unfortunately the MTV music videos on the screens don't correspond with the music piped through the audio system. It does a bacon and egg breakfast (Dkr25), as well as a wide range of meals and snacks, including steaks, salads, burgers, ribs and even 'surf & turf' (steak and lobster). The filling 'buffalo wings' are a good value choice at Dkr45, and on Saturday, there's a fish buffet for Dkr59. In the afternoon, coffee and cake costs just Dkr27. It's open Monday to Thursday from 8 am to midnight, Saturdays from 8 am to 3 am and Sundays from 10 am to midnight.

The unassuming family-oriented *Café Crazy Daisy* (☎ 23636), opposite the Atuagkat bookshop, shelters a menu ranging from hot dogs, burgers and chips to full meals: fish, steaks, pasta, pizza, chicken and Chinese and Thai cuisine. It opens at 9 am and English is spoken. More formal Thai dining is found at the unfortunately-named *Charoen Porn* (☎ 25759), beside the Hotel Hans Egede. It's open daily, except Monday, from 6 to 11 pm.

The *Restaurant Postgården* (☎ 24041), opposite the Hotel Hans Egede, has a relaxed atmosphere and daily specials starting at Dkr50. It's open daily from noon to 9 pm.

The *Hotel Godthåb* (☎ 21105) has a fine restaurant, bar and disco, but the dining is least peaceful on Wednesday and Saturday nights, when the disco is in force. On Saturday from 2 to 4 pm, there's a free mini-buffet for Daddy's bar patrons.

The *Seamen's Home* (☎ 21029) cafeteria dishes up basic but tasty hot meals. Lunch on Monday to Saturday costs Dkr40/45 for small/large portions. On Sunday, the price increases to Dkr50/55. Dinners are Dkr35/40 and between meals there are snacks, salads, sandwiches, desserts and hot and cold drinks.

A trio of places in the centre grill up a range of snacks and fast food. The *Centrum Grill-Bar* is mainly a hot dog stand; the *Grill & Pizza Bar* (☎ 25901), at the petrol station on H J Rinkesvej, offers basic snacks from 11 am to 10 pm daily; and the *Café Mik* serves light meals from 9 am to 6 pm daily, but is best known as a good drinking establishment.

For self-catering, you can choose between the well stocked *Brugsen* store, which has an attached bakery open from 6.30 am to 8 pm daily, or the extensive *KNI* supermarket, on the ground floor of the Hotel Hans Egede. The *brædtet* is down the hill in Kolonihavnen. The *Spar* market, near the Atuagkat bookshop, is open until 7 pm and on weekends and the *Nukøb* is open seven days a week from 11 am to midnight.

Entertainment
The *Moby Dick*, in the Hotel Hans Egede, offers quiet drinks, pool tables and billiards. It's open weekdays until midnight and on Friday and Saturday until 3 am, but don't bring a jacket or you'll pay Dkr25 to check it at the door! More upmarket is the quiet *Sky Top*, which attracts businesspeople with a view over the bright lights of Nuuk, low-key dancing and little drunken mayhem.

The *Hotel Godthåb*, which has cleaned up its image, offers disco dancing on Friday and Saturday until 3 am. In the same building is *Daddy's*, a quiet bar which is more of a serious drinking, darts and billiards venue. It's open Monday to Thursday from noon to midnight and Friday and Saturday till 3 am. For live music performances, there's a cover charge of Dkr50.

Gone are the days when patrons risked life, limb and reputation venturing into the *Kristinemut*, affectionately called 'Mutten'; it's now a respectable western-theme night spot with a disco, billiards and pool. Lone women may still feel uncomfortable, but any attention is unlikely to amount to anything.

It's open from Monday to Thursday until midnight and on Friday and Saturday until 3 am. The disco blares nightly from 6 pm to closing, but whenever there's live music (normally on Saturday), there's a Dkr50 cover charge. *Sam's Bar* in the attached Tulles Rock Café offers music nightly, with live bands at weekends.

The *community assembly hall* near Samuel Kleinschmidt's lamppost is used for films, dances and especially bingo – a winning combination to be sure. Information on scheduled events is available from the tourist office.

Things to Buy
Nuuk is good for buying high quality art and craftwork: carvings, books, artwork and furs. The Arktis Gaveshop, on the hill north of the centre, offers a good selection. Another recommended art shop is the friendly Anori Art (☎ 27874), at Indaleeqqap Aqqutaa 14. Atuagkat and the seamen's home stock limited supplies of souvenirs and film.

Getting There & Away
Air Grønlandsfly (☎ 28888) has direct flights between Nuuk and Ilulissat (Dkr2780), Maniitsoq (Dkr1119), Kangerlussuaq (Dkr1480), Narsarsuaq (Dkr2250), Paamiut (Dkr2250) and Kulusuk (Dkr2720). There are also weekly flights to and from Keflavík, Iceland, via Kulusuk and in summer, First Air flies between Nuuk, Kangerlussuaq and Iqaluit, Nunavut, Canada (Dkr1840), with connections to Ottawa.

Ferry The southern and central Greenland ferry routes meet in Nuuk, and on some runs travellers between South Greenland and Disko Bay must break their journey here.

At least once weekly, the big ferries connect the capital with Qaqortoq (Dkr845), via Qeqertarsuatsiaat (Dkr270), Paamiut (Dkr435), Arsuk (Dkr590) and Narsaq (Dkr865), and with Ilulissat (Dkr945), via Maniitsoq (Dkr285), Kangaamiut (Dkr370), Sisimiut (Dkr535), Aasiaat (Dkr820),

Qasigiannguit (Dkr910) and sometimes Kangaatsiaq (Dkr775) and Qeqertarsuaq (Dkr865). To Qaqortoq takes about 36 hours and to Ilulissat, 43 to 49 hours (depending on whether they detour to Qeqertarsuaq).

The weekly KNI supply boat *Aqaluk Ittuk* sails between Nuuk, Kapisillit (Dkr200), Kangerluarsoruseq (Dkr150) and Qeqertarsuatsiaat (Dkr320).

Getting Around
The Airport The Nuuk airport lies seven km north-east of town. Airport transport is fairly good, with an efficient taxi service (Dkr100 for up to three people) and hourly buses (weekdays only), which cost Dkr10. The tourist office runs transfers to and from the airport for Dkr70 per person, which is only economical if you're alone.

Bus Drivers on Nuup Bussii, Nuuk's city bus system, would make a worthy showing in any aggressive driving competition, so pedestrians should take due precautions. Bus No 3, which connects the seamen's home, the city centre, Nuusuaq and the airport, is probably the most useful to travellers. It runs hourly on weekdays from 5.30 am to 5.30 pm. Bus Nos 1 and 2 run every 15 minutes between 6.25 am and 11.30 pm on weekdays and hourly or so on weekends. Buses cost Dkr10 per ride.

Taxi For taxi services, ring Taxa Taxi (☎ 22222 in Nuuk or 22202 in Nuussuaq) or Mini Taxi (☎ 21818). The tourist office does transfers from the harbour or airport to hotels and hostels for Dkr70 per person.

Bicycle The bicycle shop Polarcykler (☎ 27202), at Kiqutaarnat 38, hires mountain bikes for Dkr100 per day. By the time you read this, the tourist office should also be hiring bicycles for the same rate.

NUUP KANGERLUA (GODTHÅBSFJORD)
An excursion up 120 km-long Nuup Kangerlua provides insights into village life and glimpses of some remains of the Norse Vesterbygd. Access into the fjord is via charter boat, the tourist office helicopter tour or the weekly KNI boat from Nuuk to Kapisillit.

Qoorqut
Qoorqut, about 56 km from Nuuk on a small sub-fjord, lies in an excellent freshwater fishing area. The geological base of the area, Qoorqut granite, is over three billion years old and was formed perhaps 25 km beneath the surface. The quirky Qoorqut Mountain Hotel burned down a few years ago and won't re-open, but it does make a challenging hiking destination from Nuuk.

Kapisillit
The village of Kapisillit ('salmon') lies 101 km north-east of Nuuk. It was once a reindeer-farming centre, but is best known for Greenland's only salmon stream, two km north-east of the village. In August you may see the fish making their way upstream to spawn. A hotel is planned for Kapisillit, and may be open by the time you read this.

The 470m ascent up Pingo, behind the village, is fairly easy, as is the four km walk across a narrow isthmus for a view of the Kangersuneq Icefjord (Nuuk Isfjorden). It's a long and difficult day trip up 924m Nikku, which affords a view to the glacier and the Kangersuneq Icefjord.

South from Kapisillit and nearby Itinnera (the former reindeer farm), is superb trekking country, with deep valleys and pleasant highlands punctuated by large lakes – Nattoralinnguit Tasia, Illorssuit Tasia and Qajaqtariorssuaq. Across the peninsula, on a north-eastern extension of Ameralla Fjord, are the ruins of the Vesterbygd Norse settlement, Sandnæs (Kilaersarfik), which includes church ruins.

At the head of Ameralla Fjord, is Austmannadalen ('east man valley'). It was named by Norwegian explorer Fridtjof Nansen, who crossed Greenland from east to west in 1888. Here he descended from the icecap to the west coast and broke up his sled and other equipment to build a rowing boat

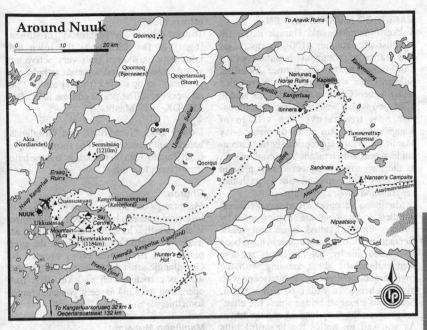

Around Nuuk

0   10   20 km

To Anavik Ruins

Qoomoq

Qoornoq (Bjørneøen)

Qeqertarsuaq (Storø)

Nerlunaq Norse Ruins

Kapisillit

Kapisillit   Kangerluaq

Qingaq

Itinnera

Tummerattup Tasersua

Akia (Nordlandet)

Sermitsiaq (1210m)

Qoorqut

Sandnæs

Nansen's Campsite

Austmannadalen

Ersaq Ruins

Quassussuaq

Kangerluarsunnguaq (Kobbefjord)

Ameralla

NUUK

Ski Centre

Nipaatsoq

Ukkusissaq

Mountain Huts

Hjortetakken (1184m)

Ameralik Kangerlua (Lysefjord)

Hunter's Hut

Præste Fjord

To Kangerluarsoruseq 32 km & Qeqertarsuatsiaat 132 km

GREENLAND

to take him back to Nuuk. Austmannadalen leads right to the inland ice at a lake appropriately called Isvand ('ice water').

Hiking

You can also travel on foot. The walking route from Nuuk to Qoorqut is one of Greenland's most challenging popular routes. It passes through extremely remote and rugged country, but the inland portion of the hike offers gentler terrain. All but about 10 km of this route is shown on the 1:75,000 *Hiking Map West Greenland – Nuuk*.

If you'd like to attempt the 14-day route all the way from Nuuk to Kapisillit and Austmannadalen, via Qoorqut, then you'll also need the DVL-Rejser 1:100,000 *Nuuk-Godthåbsfjorden* walking map. Detailed route descriptions are provided in the book *Trekking in Greenland*.

Organised Tours

The Nuuk tourist office offers a 4½ hour helicopter tour of the fjord (Dkr1595) which stops for about 45 minutes each at the Nipaatsoq Norse ruins (which date from around 1300); the icecap at the head of the glacier Kangaussarsuup Sermia; Kapisillit village; and the abandoned settlement of Qoornoq on Qoornoq island. It also runs weekend boat tours to Kapisillit (Dkr1195), including meals and basic accommodation.

Getting There & Away

Ferry The weekly KNI supply boat *Aqaluk Ittuk* sails between Nuuk and Kapisillit for Dkr200. It takes only 12 passengers, so book early.

Boat Charter Boat charters for up to 12 passengers may be arranged through the Nuuk tourist office or Nukik Charter (☎ 20035). For first class amenities and prices, groups of up to 16 people can charter the *M/S Maya* (☎ 26450), PO Box 162, DK-3900 Nuuk.

MANIITSOQ (SUKKERTOPPEN)

Sukkertoppen, the old Danish name for Maniitsoq (population 4100), means 'sugar loaf', after a prominent mountain which dominated the town's former location. Sukkertoppen was founded by Norwegian trader Anders Olsen in 1755 and relocated in 1781, and with it went the name. The mountain now towers over the village of Kangaamiut, 65 km north of present-day Maniitsoq. More appropriate is the Greenlandic name, which means 'the rough place', as the new town is squeezed into a basin backed by cliff walls and split by gash-like canyons and low, rugged hills.

Maniitsoq's economic mainstay is fishing, but diets and incomes are supplemented by hunting caribou, musk oxen and seals. Deposits of niobium and uranium have been discovered nearby, but the locals are less than enthusiastic about messing with the environment or blighting the landscape with big machines in order to mine them. Greenland's longest bridge spans the channel between the ferry landing and the town. As you sail in, notice the beautiful hills around the harbour, which resemble a miniature from a classical Chinese painting.

Maniitsoq coat of arms

Information

Tourist Office The Maniitsoq Turistforening (☎ & fax 13899) at the town hall nominally exists, but isn't very active and you'd be lucky to find someone to help you. It's meant to be staffed from 11 am to 2 pm on weekdays. The postal address is PO Box 319, DK-3912 Maniitsoq.

Money Both Nuna Bank and Grønlandsbanken are represented. The former is open from 9 am to 3 pm on weekdays and the latter from 10 am to 3 pm.

Church

Maniitsoq's old church, built in 1864, is of historical interest, but its 1981 replacement is also worth a look. The altar and font are made of beautiful rough-cut stone, the altarpiece is a driftwood cross created by Greenlandic artist Aka Høegh, and the altar itself is carpeted with sealskin. If it isn't open, ring ☎ 13284 to see if you can arrange something.

Maniitsoq Museum

The Maniitsoq Museum (☎ 13277) lies in a valley one km north-east of the centre. Its buildings, originally constructed in 1874 at the harbour, were used as a work shed, bakery and blacksmith's shop. They were dismantled and reassembled at their current location to make way for the fish-processing plant.

Archaeological digs indicate that Maniitsoq was first inhabited 3200 years ago by the caribou-hunting Saqqaq culture. The museum displays artefacts dating from Saqqaq times right up to the early 1900s. Another section is devoted to local art and features the work of Kangaamiut artist, Jens Kreutzmann.

The museum is open Monday, Tuesday, Thursday and Friday from 10 am to 3 pm and on Sunday from 1 to 3 pm. Admission is Dkr5.

Hiking

Mâniitsoq island offers good hiking opportunities through its labyrinth of narrow

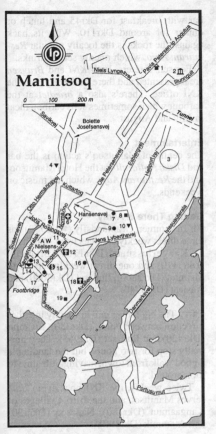

Maniitsoq

0   100   200 m

GREENLAND

gorges, and although it looks small on the map, it's a two or three day hike to the northern tip of the island. Most of the valley floors are rather soggy, claustrophobic and plagued by mosquitoes, but the landscape of criss-crossing gorges, which is probably unique in the world, makes it worthwhile.

A good destination is 570m Pattefjeld, which is about three hours each way, but it's hard to resist exploring several of the beautiful valleys and gorges en route. The most direct route is via Blomsterdalen, then over Kig Pass, and down Langedal and the going is pretty easy. The southern slope of

Pattefjeld is a nearly vertical granite wall. To reach the summit, cross Borgmester pass and keep bearing right; the way to the top will be clear, although there's a lot of scree near the summit.

You may be able to pick up a hand-drawn map at the seamen's home, and a *Hiking Map West Greenland – Maniitsoq* is being published in 1997.

Skiing
For winter skiing, Maniitsoq island has 100 km of cross-country ski track and 500 sq km of cross-country terrain. See also Apussuit, under Around Maniitsoq later in this chapter.

Organised Tours
The Kommunia has formulated several guided tours, including a city tour (Dkr50); a hike and a Greenlandic picnic (Dkr90); and a visit to a local artist – soapstone carver Nuka Lybert, painter Marianne Jensen or sealskin seamstress Marta Bilmann (Dkr125). In May and June, there are also three-hour snowmobile tours to Pattefjeldet (Dkr250).

Also available are charter possibilities to magnificent Kangerlussuatsiaq (Evigheds-fjord or 'Eternity Fjord'), which is one of Greenland's finest mountain-climbing areas. You can also be put in touch with the Maniitsoq Kayak Association, which hires kayaks and can organise guided kayaking trips around the island, Kangerlussuatsiaq or Hamborgersund.

Places to Stay

The summer-only *Youth Hostel* (☎ 3999; fax 3839) is at the only six-storey building in town, the ATI (Aalisakkanik Tunusassior-nermik Ilinniarfik) school on Pavia Petersen -ip Aqqutaa near the museum. Beds in single rooms with shared facilities cost Dkr210.

The *Hotel Maniitsoq* (☎ 13035; fax 13377), which overlooks the harbour, offers private baths, telephones and TVs in every room. In summer, single/double rooms with bath cost Dkr790/1140, including breakfast. With shared facilities, they're Dkr740/1090. Groups get a break on the price.

The friendly and helpful *Seamen's Home* (☎ 13535; fax 13553) has single rooms with shared facilities for Dkr395. With private bathroom, single/double rooms are Dkr550/750. Unfortunately, there's a 9 pm curfew; after that, you must ring the bell to be let in.

Because the town is so cramped for space, camping is difficult. It's no longer possible to camp near the reservoir at the end of Imeqvej – it's now cordoned off by a fence and lots of *Adgang Forbudt* (Entry Forbidden) signs. Currently, the best place to camp is about three km from town, just beyond Kig pass, which connects Blomsterdalen and Langedalen.

Places to Eat

The *Seamen's Home* cafeteria is a decent choice, but probably the nicest inexpensive place to eat is *Café Puisi*, which serves up the usual burgers, chips and sandwiches as well as a good selection of Thai dishes. It's open Monday to Saturday from 10 am to midnight and on Sunday from 10 am to 10 pm.

The *Hotel Maniitsoq* has a restaurant and

bar with breakfast for Dkr45 and lunch or dinner for around Dkr110. With its back against the rocks is the locally popular *Restaurant Aajo*, which mainly serves drinks.

For self-caterers, both *KNI* and *Brugsen* are represented and there's a *bakery* near the KNI office. There's also a *brædtet* at the harbour which sometimes sells caribou meat in July and August.

Entertainment

The centre of Maniitsoq's action is the bar and *Disko Nattoralik* at the Hotel Maniitsoq, and the *Restaurant Aajo*, which has music on weekends.

Getting There & Away

Air In summer, Grønlandsfly (☎ 13759) has three direct weekly services from Maniitsoq to Kangerlussuaq (Dkr1760) or Nuuk (Dkr1110) and one direct weekly service to Sisimiut (Dkr2800), Ilulissat (Dkr3060) and Aasiaat (Dkr3740).

Ferry The big ferries call in weekly in either direction between Nuuk (Dkr380), Sisimiut (Dkr420) and Ilulissat (Dkr965). They normally stop for two hours, but the landing is a good walk from town, leaving little time to look around.

Twice weekly, the KNI boat *Aviaq Ittuk* serves Maniitsoq and the district villages of Kangaamiut (Dkr180), Napasoq (Dkr130) and Atammik (Dkr190).

AROUND MANIITSOQ
Apussuit

Skiing has been popular in Maniitsoq since the 1970s and the town supports two ski clubs which actively promote the sport. From April to July, alpine skiing is possible on the glacier which covers the 1000m high icefield of Apussuit, on the mainland 30 km from Maniitsoq. It's accessible by taking a boat to Tasiusaq bay, about 20 km from Maniitsoq. It's 10 km from there to base camp, which is accessible on skis or snow-mobiles early in the season and by jeep or on foot later in summer.

The *base camp*, 270m above sea level,

accommodates 16 people and has cooking facilities, toilets, showers and a sauna. From base camp, you travel by snowmobile to the *upper hut* at 930m, which has cooking facilities and space for up to 12 people. Accommodation at either will cost Dkr250 per day, including three meals; day visits cost Dkr200 per person, including two meals; ski rental is Dkr150 per day; and lift tickets cost Dkr80 per day, including four hours on the three lifts and two hours of wilderness skiing using snowmobiles.

The main downhill run measures 1600m with a vertical drop of 320m. The more difficult run down the southern slope of Apussuit drops 800m in 8000m. Currently, there are plans for a fully fledged international summer ski resort at Apussuit by the year 2000, including a 300 room tourist-class hotel, chalets, restaurants and a ski school.

Getting There & Away The Maniitsoq tourist office can provide information on boat charters or addresses of ski clubs, which run weekend tours for Dkr900, with a minimum of eight participants.

Kangaamiut

The isolated and beautifully situated village of Kangaamiut was the original Sukker-toppen, and it has the sugar-loaf mountain to prove it. However, the only boat landing site lies several km up a rocky channel and the village itself occupies a hillside facing the open sea, with only a small rock harbour to shelter it from the waves. As a result, in 1781 the greater powers decided to shift the village – and the name – to the present site of Maniitsoq. As yet, there are no tourist facilities.

Getting There & Away The KNI cargo boat from Maniitsoq calls in twice weekly (Dkr180) in summer, and the big ferries between Nuuk (Dkr490) and Ilulissat (Dkr860) anchor once or twice weekly and provide tender service to the shore.

Hamborgerland

Don't look for McDonald's here; the island of Hamborgerland, or Sermersuut, north of Maniitsoq, has nothing to do with fast food. It's simply one of the most spectacular sights on the west coast of Greenland: an island of sheer and jagged granite spires, tangled glaciers and utterly forbidding terrain. Hamborgersund, the channel between the island and the mainland, is surprisingly well sheltered and normally remains calm.

Getting There & Away In fine weather, the big ferries pass through Hamborgersund between Maniitsoq and Sisimiut, allowing excellent viewing. Don't miss it! To actually land on the island, you must charter a boat from Maniitsoq.

SISIMIUT (HOLSTEINSBORG)

Sisimiut ('the fox hole burrowers') lies 75 km north of the Arctic Circle and is Greenland's northernmost ice-free port. With 4400 residents, it's the country's third largest town, after Nuuk and Nuussuaq. The harbour is bright and colourful and the weather is better than most other parts of the west coast.

Sisimiut (Holsteinsborg) coat of arms

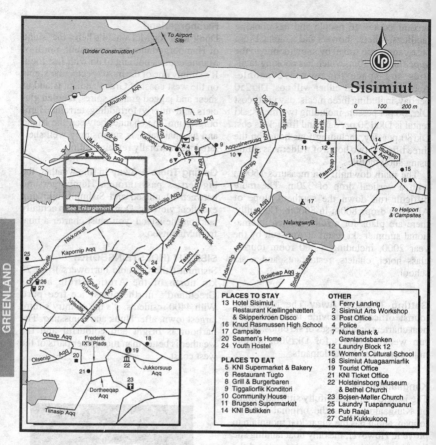

PLACES TO STAY
13 Hotel Sisimiut,
   Restaurant Kællingehætten
   & Skipperkroen Disco
16 Knud Rasmussen High School
17 Campsite
20 Seamen's Home
24 Youth Hostel

PLACES TO EAT
5 KNI Supermarket & Bakery
6 Restaurant Tugto
8 Grill & Burgerbaren
9 Tiggaliorfik Konditori
10 Community House
11 Brugsen Supermarket
14 KNI Butikken

OTHER
1 Ferry Landing
2 Sisimiut Arts Workshop
3 Post Office
4 Police
7 Nuna Bank &
   Grønlandsbanken
12 Laundry Block 12
15 Women's Cultural School
18 Sisimiut Atuagaamiarfik
19 Tourist Office
21 KNI Ticket Office
22 Holsteinsborg Museum
   & Bethel Church
23 Bojsen-Møller Church
25 Laundry Tuapannguanut
26 Pub Raaja
27 Café Kukkukooq

History

Sisimiut lies amid once rich whaling grounds and is also the southernmost extent of walrus habitat, factors which historically attracted a relatively large population to the district. When the Dutch whalers and traders arrived in the 17th century, the Sisimiut area had already established itself as a trading centre between the people of northern and southern Greenland.

After setting up his mission at Nuuk, Hans Egede came to Nipisat in the Sisimiut district to form a joint mission and whaling station. Twice he established his project and twice it

was burned out by the Dutch whalers, who claimed the missionaries were invading their whaling grounds.

It wasn't until 1756 that the Danish successfully set up a mission, Ukiivik, on the northern side of Ulkebugt near present-day Sisimiut. They named it Holsteinsborg after the Danish count Johan Ludwig von Holstein, the president of the missionary college and a mission patron back in Copenhagen, and in 1764, the settlement and some of its original buildings were shifted to its present site. In 1775 the blue Bethel church was constructed.

Niels Egede, son of Hans, stayed on there until 1782.

Although civil construction continued, the 19th century was characterised by plagues which decimated the local population. In 1800, 222 people succumbed to influenza and in 1850 the purely Greenlandic population was wiped out by smallpox.

Late last century, the whaling industry began to decline and by the early 20th century, it was replaced by fishing and shrimping. Population growth resumed and by the mid-1950s, Sisimiut had transformed from a traditional hunting and fishing community into the shrimping centre of Greenland. It now processes nearly 10,000 tonnes of shrimp annually.

Information

Tourist Office From 15 June to 31 August, the friendly Sisimiut Tourism (☎ 14848; fax 15622), PO Box 65, Jukkorsuup 6, DK-3911 Sisimiut, actively tries to develop the area's adventure tourism potential, and does a fine job. It's open Monday to Friday from 9 am to 6 pm and on Saturday from 10 am to 1 pm. The staff speak English, German, Danish and Greenlandic.

Bookshop A range of books is available at the Sisimiut Atuagaarniarfik (☎ 15590; fax 15690), including souvenir books, a few English language books on Greenlandic topics and the *Kalaallit Nunaat Atlas*. It's open Monday to Friday from 9 am to 5.30 pm and on Saturday from 9 am until 1 pm.

Laundry Sisimiut has two laundry services, Blok 12 and Tuapannguanut, at opposite ends of town. They're open weekdays and Saturday from 8 am to 8 pm and on Sunday from 8 am to 4 pm. Blok 12 closes on Monday and Tuapannguanut closes on Tuesday.

Emergency Services Emergency numbers include the police (☎ 14222) and medical services (☎ 14211)

Old Town & Holsteinsborg Museum

Sisimiut's old town dates from the mid-18th to mid-19th centuries, and you enter it beneath a whale-jawbone arch. The Gammelhuset ('old house') which houses most of the town museum, was originally prefabricated in Norway and erected at Isortoq around 1756. It was moved to its present location eight years later and has been recently restored. Other exhibits are housed in the Gamla Materialhandel (the 'old general shop'), which was built in 1846.

The kindergarten building beside it was built at Assimmiut in 1759 and moved to Sisimiut eight years later, where it served as the vicarage. Behind it are two stone buildings; one was a blacksmith and the other a laundry, post office and jail. The blue Bethel Church, Greenland's oldest church, was consecrated in 1775. The red church further up the hill, which looks slightly oriental with its upturned eaves, was built by Bojsen-Møller in 1926 and extended to its present size in 1984.

Other historical buildings from the old colony include the Halvvejshuset ('half-way house'), a half-timbered warehouse which was built in 1844, and the two-storey timber construction manager's residence, which dates from 1846. Beside the harbour are several stone warehouses built in the 1860s and extended to two storeys in the present century – the bottom storeys are made of stone and the upper floors of timber. One originally housed a cooperage and the others were used for the extraction and storage of fish oil and whale oil.

The museum currently displays the usual Greenlandic gamut of Settlement history, hunting and fishing tools and relics, and local art and clothing. From 21 June to 1 September, it's open daily, except Tuesday and Friday from 2 to 5 pm. The Bethel Church opens on Monday from 11 am to noon and Thursday from 3 to 4 pm.

Hiking

There are a number of possible walks from Sisimiut; the following are two of the most popular but the tourist office can help you

GREENLAND

with other suggestions. The best map to use is the DVL-Rejser *Sisimiut 1:100,000* walking map, or the westernmost sheet of the *Hiking Map West Greenland – Kangerlussuaq-Sisimiut*.

To explore the Saqqaq Eskimo ruins on the island of Teleøen, a detailed map and guide in French or Danish is available from the tourist office.

Nasaassaq (Kællingehætten) This 775m peak, whose Danish name means 'the witch's cowl', dominates the view inland from Sisimiut. The climb to the top is quite steep and will take an entire day. Route-finding on this mountain isn't particularly easy and the weather is changeable, so inexperienced trekkers may want to engage the services of a local guide.

Begin by heading east past the heliport and the lake east of town, then head up the ravine north of the massif, bearing right at the top onto the level area beneath the summit. From there, turn east and follow the clear route directly up to the summit; at one very steep bit, there are ropes to assist you. The summit is marked with a large cairn.

Assaqutaq A long day hike will take you to a view of the abandoned village of Assaqutaq, which lies on an offshore island. The route is well marked with cairns and orange blazes, but visibility is often poor. It begins at Nalunguarfik (Spejdersøen, or 'scout lake') in town and heads south to the shore of Amerloq Fjord, following the bizarrely eroded and marshy southern slopes of Nasaassaq.

Halfway along is a deposit of garnet-bearing rock, known as Sisimit, and beyond, a couple of abandoned Eskimo whaling settlements. Return the way you came or, if your orientation skills are exceptional, you can return the other way around Nasaassaq.

Skiing
In winter, a ski-lift supported by the local ski club operates at the foot of Nasaassaq. It is open from 1 February to 30 April and lift tickets cost Dkr75.

For information on Sisimiut's new all-season ski resort on Aqqutikitsoq glacier, see Organised Tours later in this section. Note that this glacier is also accessible on foot from Sisimiut in three or four days.

Swimming
Sisimiut's amazing and popular open-air swimming pool is open during summer.

Organised Tours
The number of tours organised by the tourist office is mind-boggling. They're too numerous to describe here in detail, but this section should give some idea of the range available. Best of all, prices average about 25% lower than comparable tours elsewhere in Greenland, making them exceptionally good value. Most tours have minimum participation numbers and operate weekly or even less frequently, so pre-booking is necessary.

Town tours include city sightseeing on foot (Dkr120); a visit to the Natseq leather and fur workroom (Dkr120) to see local women making kamiks, the traditional boots that are part of the Greenlandic national costume; a visit to Knud Rasmussen's High School to see arts and crafts displays and learn about the school's unique programmes (Dkr75); a Greenlandic barbecue at the campsite (Dkr250); and a four-hour hike to Teleøen (Dkr120), the island immediately west of Sisimiut, to see the telegraph station and Saqqaq culture ruins, and learn about Sisimiut's economic background.

In summer, there are weekly nine-hour cruises on the *Polarstar* to the mountain hut on the fjord, Kangerluarsuk Ungalleq, also known as Two-Fjorden (Dkr495); a four-hour cruise to the district's abandoned settlements (Dkr350); and day cruises to the 18th century whaling station at Nipisat and the abandoned villages of Uummannaarsuk and Assaqutaq, also visiting ruins from the Saqqaq culture (Dkr495).

Dogsled tours operate from February to early June and range from a two-hour spin near town (Dkr395) to a three-day run to Kangerlussuaq (Dkr3800, including food and camping gear); a four-day circuit around enormous lake Tasersuaq (Dkr4890); and a five-day expedition to Isortuarsuk on Nordre Isortoq Fjord. In between are a four-hour ascent of Qiterlinnguaq peak (Dkr595); an eight-hour mush up Naqinnersuaq (Dkr1025); an eight-hour tour on Kangerluarsuk Tulleq Fjord (Dkr1025); a two-day hunting trip (Dkr2180) to the settlement of Narsaq; a two-day tour to the mountain hut on Kangerluarsuk Ungalleq (Dkr2180); and an overnight trip to Sarfannguaq (Dkr2180). For overnight trips, participants must bring their own warm clothing and polarguard sleeping bags, but the tourist office provides equipment and can hire out warm fur clothing.

Hiking and mountain-biking tour possibilities include a six-hour climb up Nasaassaq (Dkr250); a nine-hour hike or mountain-bike trip to Assaqutaq settlement (Dkr250); a boat tour and hike to the summit of Sisimiut's landmark peak, Præstefjeldet (Dkr250); and a mountain-bike ride to the Kisaq mountain hut behind Nasaassaq. Guided hikes from Sisimiut to Kangerlussuaq last anywhere from nine to 13 days; the cost depends on the length of the trip. Trips can also be arranged at the canoe centre on lake Amitsorsuaq.

Other adventures will take you to Sisimiut's new all-season ski resort on the Aqqutikitsoq glacier ski fields, above the head of Kangerluarsuk Ungalleq Fjord. It offers everything from gentle cross-country terrain to extreme skiing. Boat transfers are available to the head of the fjord (Dkr395), from where you can continue on foot, or you can just spend a weekend in the mountain hut (Dkr995). Two-day ski trips include a boat transfer to the mountain hut, hiking and snowmobiling to the glacier, and skiing or dogsledding at the resort (Dkr4495); alternatively, you can use a helicopter transfer (Dkr4995).

Places to Stay
South of the centre is the comfortable *Youth Hostel* (☎ 14848), which operates from 14 June to 15 August. Beds cost Dkr190, including use of cooking facilities. There's no

attendant; guests should book in through the tourist office.

The *Hotel Sisimiut* (☎ 14840; fax 15615), which is an adequate mid-range hotel, charges Dkr750/1150 for single/double rooms with bath. Two/three-room self-catering flats cost Dkr1530/1650. Half-board and full-board meal plans are also available. The entrance isn't on the main street, but around the corner on Piitarsuup.

Another option is the *Seamen's Home* (☎ 14150; fax 15791), which charges Dkr415/615 for singles/doubles without bath and Dkr595/795 with private facilities. Family rooms with facilities cost Dkr830 for three people and Dkr200 for extra beds.

Accommodation is also available at the *Knud Rasmussen High School* (☎ 14032; fax 14907), where beds cost Dkr150 in the dormitory area and single/double rooms in the new section are Dkr200/350, including linen.

The recommended *campsite* is at the lake Nalunguarfik (Spejdersøen), one km east of town. There are several *mountain huts* on Kangerluarsuk Ungalleq and along the Kangerlussuaq to Sisimiut Trek, as well as a *Youth Hostel* in Sarfannguaq village, which charges Dkr150 for beds.

Places to Eat
The *Restaurant Kællingehætten* at the Hotel Sisimiut serves typical Danish fare: continental breakfast, cold buffet and smørrebrød, in addition to simple hot meals. It also has an attached bar and lounge.

The *Seamen's Home cafeteria* serves breakfast (Dkr45) from 6 to 10.30 am, set lunches (Dkr60) from 11.30 am to 1.30 pm, and dinners (Dkr60) from 5.30 to 7.30 pm. You can buy snacks and soft drinks throughout the day. As with all seamen's homes, alcohol is forbidden.

Over the road from the old town is the basic *Restaurant Tugto*, which serves full, good value meals. It's open Sunday and Tuesday to Friday from noon to 2 pm and 6 pm to midnight (until 3 am on Friday) and Saturday from 6 pm to 3 am. For inexpensive snacks, try the *Grill & Burgerbaren* on the main road.

Daily from noon to 1.30 pm, the *Community Centre* dishes up real Greenlandic fare – including whale, seal, musk ox, caribou and fish – for down-to-earth prices. It's all locally oriented and if you're tired of the touristy Greenland buffets, this is a super choice.

Sisimiut also has a *brædtet*, *Brugsen* and *KNI* supermarkets and a *KNI bakery*. Off the main road is *Tiggaliorfik Konditori*, a wonderful independent bakery and pastry shop.

Entertainment

The *Restaurant Tugto* has dancing and disco music every night except Monday. The *Pub Raaja* is open daily except Monday for drinking and dancing. For drinking and dancing with the emphasis on the former, check out the *Café Kukkukooq* (yes, the name is Greenlandic for cockerel!). There's also weekend action at the Hotel Sisimiut's *Skipperkroen* disco.

More sophisticated entertainment is occasionally available from the local folk dance troupe, the amateur theatre group Pakkutat, and the Erinaq choral society.

Things to Buy

Sisimiut, the home of ULO Music (☎ 14811; fax 14812), is a good place to buy Greenlandic music recordings, including ethnic music, drum-dances, choral music, Inuit rock and even Arctic reggae!

Getting There & Away

Air A new airport is being built across the fjord from town, to be connected by a bridge at the narrowest point. As yet, however, all air service is by helicopter.

Grønlandsfly has at least one daily (except Sunday) flight between Sisimiut and Kangerlussuaq (Dkr1040) and weekly flights to Maniitsoq (Dkr2800) and Ilulissat (Dkr2340). Connections to anywhere else in Greenland must be made through Kangerlussuaq.

Ferry The big ferries call in at least weekly in either direction, and during late July and

early August, there are twice as many services. Sample deck-class fares include: Maniitsoq (Dkr420), Aasiaat (Dkr490), Qasigianguit (Dkr615), Ilulissat (Dkr655), Maniitsoq (Dkr420) and Nuuk (Dkr710).

The KNI cargo boat *Finhvalen* sails to Sarfannguaq (Dkr120) on Wednesday and Friday and to Itilleq on Tuesday and Thursday (Dkr145). To get those fares, book directly through the KNI office (the tourist office tacks on a commission). Both trips depart at 9.30 am and return to Sisimiut by 5.30 pm.

Getting Around

There are two charter boats, *M/S Karl Thygesen II* and the *M/S Polarstar*, which are available for day trips or longer excursions to outlying areas. The former carries up to 12 people and may be chartered for Dkr650 per hour or Dkr5000 per day and the latter carries up to 30 passengers and charters for Dkr1100/10,000 per hour/day (9 am to 4 pm).

The tourist office hires mountain bikes for Dkr100 per day.

KANGERLUSSUAQ TO SISIMIUT TREK

The 150 km walk between Kangerlussuaq and Sisimiut is one of the most popular treks in Greenland and, as with Iceland's Landmannalaugar to Þórsmörk trek, it's destined to become one of the great walks of the world. This is due mainly to its relative accessibility; the route begins at Greenland's largest international airport and ends at a lovely town which is well served by coastal ferries.

The trek takes from 10 to 14 days and requires careful planning, but anyone who is reasonably au fait with route finding and is not daunted by the prospect of at least 10 days walking can probably handle it. The trip normally begins in Kangerlussuaq. This way, the easier section is covered when your rucksack is heaviest; by the time you reach the more rugged country around Sisimiut, your supplies will have run down.

The walk description and the map in this book are intended as a rough guide only. All hikers need the essential three-part 1:100,000 *Hiking Map West Greenland – Kangerlussuaq to Sisimiut*, which shows the route in detail, or the old DVL-Rejser walking maps *Søndre Strømfjord* 1:100,000 and *Sisimiut* 1:100,000. However, the latter maps use the old Greenlandic orthography for place names, so spellings may not match those in this book.

Note that the compass deviation in this area is approximately 41.8° W.

The Routes

Essentially, there are two routes – a High Route and a Low Route. The former is more challenging and its use is discouraged by hunters, who fear that hikers may spook the caribou that provide their bread and butter. Therefore, Greenland Tourism promotes the increasingly popular Low Route, which has now been marked.

The Low Route The Low Route begins two km east of the Kangerlussuaq harbour. Turn north onto the gravel track which climbs past the Kellyville radar facility and issues onto the tundra. Pass around the southern shore of Hundesø (marked Limnæsø on the new hiking map) and south along the north-western shore of the large elongated lake immediately to the south. There, it bears west past a chain of lakes and south along the arc-like southern shore of the large lake Qarlissuit to the eastern end of the vast lake Amitsorsuaq (marked Amitsuaq on the DVL-Rejser map). At the eastern tip of the lake is a small hut which may be used by hikers free of charge.

From this point, it's at least 1½ days along the southern shore of Amitsorsuaq to the canoe centre near the western end of the lake. There's a big 14-person hut where beds cost Dkr100, and a small shop where you can stock up on supplies, which are ferried in by helicopter. Canoes can be hired (Dkr200 per day) for paddling around the lake.

From Amitsorsuaq, the route follows the lake's outlet stream to the bay Kanger-luatsiarsuaq, which is an arm of an even

larger lake, Tasersuaq. From the western end of Tasersuaq, the route again follows the outflowing stream through the marshy valley Itinneq. Several km short of Maligiaq Bay, it cuts north and climbs to the 400m level on the slopes of Iluliumanersuup Portornga, which is the highest point on the trek, to the western end of Lake 290. This is part of a chain of lakes, which you should follow westward along their southern shores. On a hillock at the eastern end of the Hut lake is a small hunters' hut, which may be used by hikers.

Traverse along the northern shore of Hut Lake, keeping to the hillside rather than the lakeshore, and follow the inflowing stream to its head at a 250m pass, north of peak 427. From this pass, the route heads down valley, straight to the head of the fjord Kanger-luarsuk Tulleq. Midway between Hut Lake and the fjord is a new mountain hut which is also open to hikers.

Follow the hillside above the southern shore of the fjord to connect with the dogsled track over the Qerrottusup Majoria pass. Ascend along the eastern bank of the river, cross the pass, and follow the southern bank of the river flowing down the other side. This leads you into the valley immediately north of Nasaassaq (Kællingehætten), which will take you into Sisimiut.

The High Route A detailed description of the High Route appears in the hiking guide *Trekking in Greenland*. See Books in the Greenland Facts for the Visitor chapter.

Sarfannguaq

The village of Sarfannguaq ('the small channel') can be easily reached on foot from the High Route of the Kangerlussuaq to Sisimiut Trek, or on a rather long detour from the Low Route. It's also often used as a starting or ending point for the Kangerlus-suaq to Sisimiut trek, as it allows you to cut off the section between the Nerumaaq Valley and Sisimiut, which is the most difficult bit of the hike.

Sarfannguaq, which is dotted with ancient

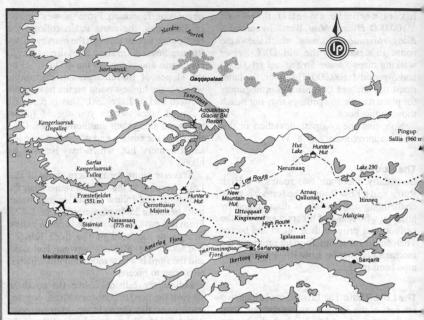

Eskimo ruins, has a post office; a *youth hostel*, with beds for Dkr150; and a *KNI Butikken*, where you can restock with basic supplies for the onward journey. Locals operate a free ferry service across Sarfannguaq channel.

The village can also be reached by charter boat or organised tour from Sisimiut (see earlier in this chapter).

KANGERLUSSUAQ (SØNDRE STRØMFJORD)

Kangerlussuaq ('the big fjord') lies just north of the Arctic Circle in Greenland's widest ice-free zone (200 km) at the head of its third longest fjord. Thanks to its inland position, the continental effect provides a stable climate and some of the island's most extreme temperatures, which range from minus 50°C in winter to 28°C in the 24 hour summer daylight. It's also the best place in Greenland to observe native wildlife.

History

Prior to the US occupation, there was no actual settlement at Kangerlussuaq, but it was a prime caribou-hunting and camping ground. The nearest major habitation was 90 km away at Arnangarnup Qoorua, or Paradisdalen, where extensive ruins have been found. It's now a protected historical site and nature reserve.

On 9 April 1941, after the German occupation of Denmark, a defence treaty between the USA, the Greenland governor Eske Brun and the Danish ambassador Henrik Kaufmann handed the security of Greenland over to the US military. The long and narrow Søndre Strømfjord was considered an ideal location for the US base Bluie West Eight, because the climate was much more stable than at Narsarsuaq in South Greenland.

The Sondrestrom airbase was officially founded on 7 October 1941, and overnight a military airfield and a host of personnel barracks were constructed. During the war, it

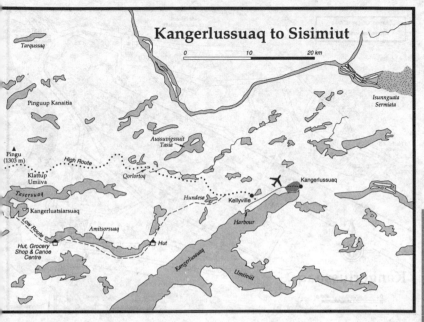

Kangerlussuaq to Sisimiut

became the main way-station for bombers and cargo carriers flying between North America and Europe. At the height of WWII, over 8000 military personnel were stationed there.

In 1950, the defence treaty expired and the base was handed back to Denmark. However, the continuing cold war threat prompted a renewed agreement and Bluie West Eight again became Sondrestrom airbase and was returned to US military operations on 27 April 1951. Three years later, Scandinavian Air Systems (SAS) was granted permission to use Sondrestrom as a stopover on its transatlantic flights between Copenhagen and Los Angeles. The Transit Hotel (now Hotel Kangerlussuaq) was built in 1960.

From 1958, the Americans set up four DEW-line (Distant Early Warning) radar bases in Greenland – two on the icecap and one each in Sisimiut and Kulusuk – to provide early warning of a possible Soviet attack. The main activity at Sondrestrom airbase was to supply these stations.

After the Soviet Union collapsed and the 'communist threat' dematerialised, both the DEW-line and the airbase became redundant. The DEW stations were closed in 1990 and 1991, and on 30 September 1992 the base was closed and the 14 remaining personnel sent elsewhere. The following day, the base came under the control of Greenland Home Rule. It was officially renamed Kangerlussuaq and the administration was assumed by Mittarfeqarfiit, or MIT, the Home Rule agency for airports in Greenland. In the summer of 1993, it hosted the International Scouts Jamboree around Lake Helen, at Kellyville.

Orientation

Most items of interest to tourists are at the airport terminal, including the post and telephone offices, the Hotel Kangerlussuaq, the

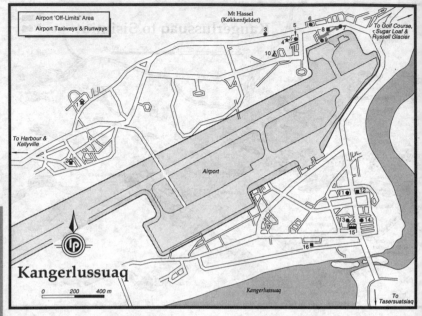

To Harbour &
Kellyville

Airport

Kangerlussuaq

0   200   400 m

Kangerlussuaq

To
Tasersuatsiaq

Mt Hassel
(Køkkenfjeldet)

To Golf Course,
Sugar Loaf &
Russell Glacier

Airport 'Off-Limits' Area
Airport Taxiways & Runways

SAS and Grønlandsfly desks, the giftshop and the restaurant, bar and cafeteria.

Information

Tourist Office Under the enthusiastic guidance of Johanne Eriksen, the Greenland Tourism information office (☎ 11098, fax 11498), in the airport terminal, is one of Greenland's most efficient. It not only provides tourist information and organises a wide range of tours, but also hires out vehicles and camping gear. It's open Monday to Friday from 8 am to 4 pm.

Money There's no bank, but you can change money at the desk of the Hotel Kangerlussuaq, which offers a fair rate and takes no commission.

Laundry You'll find automatic washing machines in Corridor C, the eastern extension of the airport terminal. Laundry services are also available to hotel guests.

Left Luggage The tourist office has a left luggage facility for Dkr50 per week.

Electricity Because Kangerlussuaq was originally constructed by and for Americans, the power supply emerges at 110V rather than the usual 220V.

Art Exhibit

At the community centre, the Municipal Council holds a variety of exhibitions of local arts & crafts. Information is posted on notice boards around the town. It's open from 1 to 9 pm every day; admission is free.

Bluie West Eight Museum

In the former base commander's office on the old Sondrestrom US airbase is a museum dedicated to the history of Søndre Strømfjord/Kangerlussuaq. Admission is Dkr10.

1	Team Arctic Youth Hostel
2	Youth Hostel
3	Stone Designs by Alibak Johansen
4	Police
5	Library
6	Butikken
7	Corridor C Laundrette
8	Hotel Kangerlussuaq, Airport Terminal, Cafeteria, Den Grønne Bar, Restaurant, Tourist Office, Post & Telephone Office, SAS Euro-Class Lounge
9	Directional Sign
10	Campground
11	Tennis Courts
12	Tuttu Inn
13	Bowling Alley
14	Conference Centre
15	Swimming Pool & Gymnasium
16	Ummimmaq Inn

Kellyville

Kellyville, inland from the harbour and overlooking Lake Helen, is home to the Sondrestrom Incoherent Scatter Radar Research Centre. It is run jointly by the Danish Meteorological Institute and the private American company SRI International, with additional funding from the US National Science Foundation. It's currently conducting ionosphere research, with emphasis on the aurora borealis. The tourist office organises guided tours of the site.

Activities

Kangerlussuaq is the Arctic equivalent of a Club Med, thanks to the American military,

which left behind a host of recreational facilities – including a gymnasium, a bowling alley, an indoor swimming pool and an 18 hole golf course!

For a round at the Sondie Arctic Desert Golf Club, you'll pay Dkr50 per person plus Dkr50 to hire clubs and Dkr15 for golf balls. The indoor swimming pool and gymnasium – complete with body-building equipment – is open Tuesday to Friday from 4 to 8 pm, Saturday from 1 to 5 pm and Sunday from 10 am to 2 pm. Admission is Dkr15.

The bowling alley is open Monday to Thursday from 5 to 10 pm and on Saturday and Sunday from 12.30 to 6 pm. On Saturday, there's an open bowling tournament for anyone interested. The community centre, which is open from 1 to 9 pm daily, offers billiards tables, chess sets and dart boards.

There are also several local clubs, which are involved in a range of recreational pursuits. From May to September, the Søndrestrøm Rowing Club operates on Tasersuatsiaq (Lake Ferguson), south of the fjord. The tourist office hires canoes for Dkr150/200 per half/full day. The Rifle Club stages shooting competitions on weekends; the Diving Club (yes, they dive in the fjord!) is a wealth of information on Arctic diving; and the Sondie Aero Club, which owns its own plane, organises expeditions in the air.

Organised Tours

Kangerlussuaq has one of Greenland's busiest tourist offices, which has come up

The Core of the Matter in Kangerlussuaq

As a former military installation, Kangerlussuaq is a natural site for scientific research. The Polar Ice Coring Office (PICO), a department of the University of Alaska Fairbanks, has overseen all US scientific concerns in Greenland. One project was concerned with the study and breeding of gyrfalcons; another was the office's namesake project – core drilling on the inland ice to extract data about the earth's climatic history.

A similar project was the Greenland Icecore Programme, or GRIP, sponsored by a consortium of eight European countries, which set up a core-drilling operation at the thickest point on the inland ice, 800 km north-east of Kangerlussuaq. In mid-1992, after four years work, the operation finally reached bedrock at a depth of 3028.8m. The 5799 icecores extracted, each measuring 55 cm, represent a historical record reaching back a quarter of a million years. The results are undergoing analysis in Belgium. ∎

Kangerlussuaq Wildlife

Kangerlussuaq is the best place to see and photograph Greenlandic wildlife. In the early 1960s, 27 musk oxen were introduced to Kangerlussuaq from north-east Greenland. This herd, the first in west Greenland, thrived and there are now 3500 musk oxen in the Kangerlussuaq area. In 1986, several musk oxen were transplanted from Kangerlussuaq to Pituffik, and there is talk of establishing another herd around Narsarmiit in South Greenland. In 1992, subsistence hunters were permitted to take a quota of 650 musk oxen while 10 went to trophy hunters.

Late September is the season for love on the musk ox calendar, and it's awesome to watch and hear amorous and headstrong males doing horn-to-horn combat for eligible females. The calves are born early in summer.

The best viewing is east and south-east of the airport. If you want good photos, a telephoto lens will be essential. Although they appear to be harmless, a cornered or irritated musk ox can become extremely unpleasant, so don't approach within about 35m or there could be problems. If the animal begins to snort or brush the hair from its face, you're too close and it's preparing an attack.

There are also 3000 caribou in the Kangerlussuaq area, which is down from an all-time high of 40,000 in the 1970s. The decline has been attributed to a shortage of their favourite meal, reindeer moss. The best viewing is from north-east of the airport.

You'll also have the chance to see other animals and birds, including Arctic fox, Arctic hare, ptarmigan, gyrfalcon and smaller birds. ■

with enough tour possibilities to keep you occupied for days and – it hopes – prevent you rushing off to Sisimiut or Ilulissat immediately after landing.

The hottest tour is the 'Musk Ox Photo Safari' (Dkr150), which takes you into the hinterlands on a quest for photogenic musk oxen and caribou; a variation adds coffee and cake at the Restaurant Roklubben (Dkr200).

Some recommended adventures include a jeep tour up Sandflugtdalen and a barbecue at Russell Glacier (Dkr550); a week-long camping and fishing trip on the fjord (Dkr4095); a mountain-bike ride to Russell Glacier (Dkr250, including bike hire); an all-day Sunday rockhounding trek to Granatfjeldet, 'garnet mountain' (Dkr225); and one-hour helicopter tours to the inland ice (Dkr450 on weekdays and Dkr600 on Sundays).

Other possibilities include the Greenlandic flora tour (Dkr150), which seeks out Arctic wildflowers; a bus tour around Kangerlussuaq (Dkr150); introduction to the Greenlandic national costume (Dkr75); a tour of the old Sondrestrom airbase and museum (Dkr100); midnight sun tour to Kellyville (Dkr150, or Dkr200 with local alcohol tea); a seal barbecue (Dkr150); seal flensing (Dkr100); a Greenlandic buffet in a mountain hut (Dkr325); and a course in rapelling, or abseiling (Dkr325).

Lots of dogsled tours run between March and May: a two/four-hour introductory tour (Dkr575/750); an all day tour to a mountain hut (Dkr1375); a two day run down the fjord (Dkr2600); and a three day trip all the way to Sisimiut (Dkr3900). Other winter tours include northern lights viewing (Dkr150) and drives on the fjord (Dkr250) or Tasersuatsiaq (Dkr500).

Special Events

A new event is the Arctic Circle Race, in which a slate of intrepid cross-country skiers complete the Kangerlussuaq to Sisimiut route in just three days. Eight-day all inclusive race packages are available from Copenhagen, Oslo or Stockholm (Dkr8900), Ottawa (C$2800) and Reykjavík (Dkr9500). For details, contact the Greenland Ski Federation (☎ 71412; fax 25465), PO Box 84, DK-3900 Nuuk or Team Arctic (☎ 45-32 52 30 66; fax 45-32 52 30 86), Amager Landevej 171C, DK-2770 Kastrup, Denmark.

Places to Stay

The *Team Arctic Youth Hostel* (☎ & fax

11433), at Old Camp, two km west of the airport terminal, offers beds and use of communal facilities for Dkr150. Bedding is an additional Dkr25. Check in at Kangerlussuaq Tourism at the airport terminal, which can arrange pick-up from the airport.

Down the main road from the airport terminal is *Hotel Kangerlussuaq* (☎ 11180; fax 11284). With three buildings – Hotel Kangerlussuaq, Ummimaq (musk ox) and Tuttu (caribou) – it accommodates up to 400 guests in varying degrees of comfort. Single/double rooms without bath cost Dkr520/580, including breakfast. With private facilities, they're Dkr850/1050. Dormitory/hostel accommodation costs Dkr235/150. The reception desk is actually at the airport terminal.

At the organised *campground*, west of the airport terminal, camping costs Dkr40 per person and allows access to the barbecues, picnic tables, toilets and washing facilities; showers are available at Hotel Kangerlussuaq. Book in at the hotel reception. You can hire tents and camping equipment from the tourist office in the airport terminal. Tents cost Dkr75/200 per day/week. Sleeping bags, backpacks and fishing gear are each Dkr50/150 and cooking equipment is Dkr25/75.

The tourist office also keeps a list of remote private *cabins* which may be rented by hikers, and there are also several *mountain huts* along the Kangerlussuaq to Sisimiut trek.

Places to Eat

For meals, your main choice is the airport restaurant and cafeteria. The *Hotel Kangerlussuaq Restaurant* (☎ 11300 ext 1105) is open from Monday to Saturday from 6 to 9 pm. The *Cafeteria* (☎ 11300 ext 1104) is open daily from 7 am to 9 pm, serving breakfast, sandwiches and hot lunches and dinners. Because Kangerlussuaq enjoys special liberal alcohol regulations, beer, wine and spirits are available with meals from 10 am to 8.45 pm. Alternatively, you can check out the new *Restaurant Roklubben*

(☎ 11300 ext 1144), at the Søndrestrøm Rowing Club on the shore of Tasersuatsiaq.

Groceries may be purchased at the *Butikken* opposite the airport terminal. It's open Monday to Friday from 10 am to 5 pm and on Saturday from 9 am to noon.

Entertainment

Although Kangerlussuaq once catered for US service personnel, there's only one public bar, *Den Grønne Bar*, at the airport terminal. It's open a bizarre range of hours: Monday and Wednesday from 10 am to 1 pm and 5 to 10 pm; Tuesday and Thursday from 5 to 10 pm; and Friday from 10 am to 1 pm and 5 to 7 pm. During happy hour, from 5 to 7 pm, the drinks are half price.

In the evening, the *SAS Euro-Class lounge* is open to Hotel Kangerlussuaq guests for drinking and dancing. You can also buy alcohol at the *bowling alley* and the *Søndrestrøm Rowing Club*; the latter occasionally runs bingo games.

Getting There & Away

Air SAS uses Kangerlussuaq as its main terminal in Greenland and virtually everyone passing through is transiting between SAS and Grønlandsfly flights. For more information, see the Getting There & Away chapter at the beginning of the book.

Grønlandsfly has direct flights between Kangerlussuaq and Ilulissat (Dkr1270), Maniitsoq (Dkr1720), Nuuk (Dkr1440), Sisimiut (Dkr1010), Pituffik (Dkr1910) and Kulusuk (Dkr2320).

Ferry Kangerlussuaq is well off the regular ferry lines, but ferries occasionally do call in and if you have the opportunity to sail, don't miss it. Its outermost 50 km, constricted between high glacier-ravaged peaks, are nothing short of awesome. The harbour must be dredged regularly, but is still too shallow for ships to berth and passengers and cargo must be ferried ashore on landing barges.

Kangerlussuaq is also a terminal for tourist cruises on the *M/S Disko*.

GREENLAND

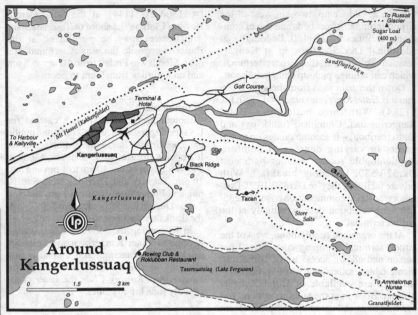

Around
Kangerlussuaq

Getting Around

Bus Orange town buses cover the road between the youth hostel and the Ummimaq building approximately hourly from 5 am to midnight, Monday to Friday. They'll also go to the rowing club and the golf course, but not to the harbour. For timetable information, phone ☎ 11300 ext 3000).

Minibus taxis run transfers to Sugar Loaf (Dkr250), Tasersuatsiaq (Dkr250) and the harbour/Kellyville (Dkr300).

Car & Motorcycle The tourist office can arrange car hire for Dkr700 per day, including one tank of fuel. Motorcycles can be hired for Dkr450 per day, including fuel.

Bicycle The tourist office hires mountain bikes for Dkr50/75/100 for one/four/eight hours, plus Dkr100 deposit. For a weekend/week, they're Dkr150/400 plus a Dkr300 deposit. They're excellent for rides out to the

harbour or Kellyville, or along tracks further inland.

AROUND KANGERLUSSUAQ
Hiking

Although the Kangerlussuaq to Sisimiut trek is the star hiking venue, Kangerlussuaq offers numerous other hikes and if that's your emphasis, you could spend an entire holiday exploring this area. The following are just several of the many possibilities.

Sugar Loaf Sugar Loaf, east of the golf course, is marked as point 400 on the DVL-Rejser and Saga maps and makes an easy 20 km return hike from the settlement. A gravel road leads up to the former radio installation, providing a great view of the airport and the glaciers spilling down from the inland ice.

Russell Glacier The easy and straightforward three or four day return trip to Russell

Glacier is a good – if misleading – introduction to hiking in Greenland. In fact, there's a motorable track all the way up the Sandflugtdalen valley to the glacier face. Hikers who would rather avoid doing it the easy way with jeep tours (see Organised Tours under Kangerlussuaq) should leave the road and follow the dry silt riverbed. Don't approach the ice face too closely; this broken and active glacier frequently gives birth to some whopping big ice cubes.

Ammalortup Nunaa From the rowing club (Roklubben) on Tasersuatsiaq, better known as Lake Ferguson, walk east along the north-ern lake shore, then ascend the ravine beneath the southern slopes of 630m Tasersuatsiaap Kinginnera and over the lake-studded pass down to Orsuarnissarajuttoq.

Continue in a south-easterly direction along the lake's southern shore. From the south-eastern end, head south-east over a minor pass before descending steeply down to the beautiful large lake, Ammalortoq, with deposits of glacial silt on its north-western and south-western shores.

If you use the lake shore as your base camp, this area is good for a couple of days of exploring. From Kangerlussuaq, allow two or three days for this hike.

Disko Bay

The largest and newest island off the Greenland coast shelters Disko Bay (Qeqertarsuup Tunua in Greenlandic), an iceberg-studded expanse 300 km north of the Arctic Circle. The five main towns of Disko Bay – Kangaatsiaq, Ilulissat, Qeqertarsuaq, Qasigiannguit and Aasiaat – have a combined population of about 12,000. Visitors heading north up the coast normally feel they're getting their first real taste of the high Arctic here. During winter, Disko Bay is normally the southern extent of the pack ice. In summer, the northern hemisphere's most prolific tidewater glacier advances up to 30m a day and calves formidable bergs – some weighing up to seven million tonnes – filling the Ilulissat Kangerlua (Jakobshavn Icefjord) and spilling them into Disko Bay to wander for centuries around the Arctic.

If you visit Disko Bay between late May and mid-July, you'll experience the true midnight sun. For a month, there's no hint of twilight and visitors may sleep restlessly as the sun circles day after day without setting.

KANGAATSIAQ

Kangaatsiaq (population 450), the 'little headland', is Greenland's newest town. It was founded in January 1985 and serves a vast district of 80,000 sq km with just 1300 people spread over four villages.

Locator & Map Index

Disko Island Walking Routes p495
Qeqertarsuaq p494
Ilulissat p483
Hiking Around Ilulissat p487
Aasiaat p477
Qasigiannguit p479

Information

There are few facilities but tourist information (☎ 40077; fax 40030) is available through the Kangaatsiaq Kommunia, PO Box 551, DK-3955 Kangaatsiaq. They organise 12 to 18-day kayaking, dogsledding, camping and hunting tours around this vast untouristed district, and currently hope to establish a series of guided walking tours.

Places to Stay & Eat

The only accommodation is a municipally-owned *hostel* with space for six people. Groceries are available at the *KNI Butikken*.

Getting There & Away

The big ferries stop briefly at Kangaatsiaq en route between Nuuk (Dkr1030) and Ilulissat (Dkr280), and the small *Aviaq Ittuk* sails at least three times weekly between Kangaatsiaq, Aasiaat and other southern Disko Bay villages.

Frozen Assets

Most visitors to Disko Bay come to see its world-famous icebergs, but did you know that 'bergy bits' of Disko Bay ice – that is, semi-trailer-sized chunks – are towed into harbours, chipped into cubes and exported to Japan and Europe to chill drinks? That scotch you order in a Tokyo pub may contain 25,000-year-old cubes from the frozen heart of Greenland's icecap, and the air that fizzes out as they melt has been trapped since long before anyone ever heard of smog alerts. ∎

GREENLAND

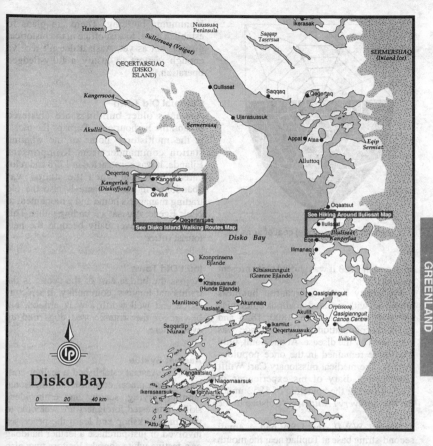

QEQERTARSUAQ
(DISKO
ISLAND)

Hareøen

Nuussuaq
Peninsula

Sullorsuaq (Vaigat)

Saqqap
Tasersua

Ikerasak

SERMERSUAQ
(Inland Ice)

Kangersooq

Qullissat

Saqqaq

Qeqertaq

Akullit

Sermersuaq

Ujarasussuk

Appat Ataa

Eqip
Sermiat

Alluttoq

Qeqertaq

Kangerluk
(Diskofjord)

Kangerluk

Qivitut

Oqaatsut

See Hiking Around Ilulissat Map

Qeqertarsuaq

Ilulissat

See Disko Island Walking Routes Map

Eqe

Ilulissat
Kangerlua

Disko Bay

Ilimanaq

Kronprinsens
Ejlande

Kitsissunnguit
(Grønne Ejlande)

Qasigiannguit

Kitsissuarsuit
(Hunde Ejlande)

Akunnaaq

Akullit

Orpissooq
Qasigiannguit
Canoe Centre

Maniitsoq

Aasiaat

Saqqarlip
Nunaa

Ikamiut

Qeqertasussuk

Ilulialik

Kangaatsiaq

Niaqornaarsuk

Ikerasaarsuk

Iginniarfik

Attu

Disko Bay

0   20   40 km

GREENLAND

AASIAAT (EGEDESMINDE)

Aasiaat, Greenland's fifth-largest community and one of its friendliest settlements, sits amid low, stark and rocky islets near the southern entrance to Disko Bay. The area is short on rugged peaks, but its relative flatness makes a pleasant change.

The name Aasiaat means 'the spiders', but was probably originally intended to be 'Aasiat' or 'the gathering place', which has the same root as the name of the annual Greenlandic cultural festival, 'Aasivik'. Although the town's coat of arms depicts a spider web, Aasiaat spiders don't spin webs,

but instead contend with the Arctic climate by burrowing underground.

The district is now home to 4700 people, 3200 of whom live in Aasiaat proper.

History

The original site of Aasiaat, immediately south of the present town, had long been locally called Eqaluksuit ('sea trout') but when Niels Egede founded a settlement there in 1759, he renamed it 'Egedesminde' in honour of his father, Hans Egede. It was a fertile site but out of the way as a trading

Aasiaat (Egedesminde) coat of arms

post, and in 1763 it was shifted to its present location.

Prosperity in the mercantile business alternated with repeated smallpox epidemics and four times (in 1776, 1800, 1825 and 1852) the population of Egedesminde was decimated by the disease. At one point, only 21 people remained in the once populous district. The medical missionary Carl Wulff published a diary of his experiences in Aasiaat during the epidemic of 1852 under the title *Solhverv i Natten*, or 'Solstice in the Night'.

During WWII, the USA had a small second-string base at Tupilaq near the mouth of Aasiaat harbour. When the base shut down the local economy stagnated and for years, primitive methods of fish salting and shrimp processing carried the meagre economy. In the mid-1980s, however, an efficient fish and shrimp-processing plant was established, and today Aasiaat prospers once again.

Information
The friendly tourist information service (☎ 42277; fax 42287), PO Box 220, DK-3950 Aasiaat, in this little-visited town remains informal. For information, look up Knud Aborg, in the school near the footbridge, or Arne Astrud at the Aasiaat Kommunia building. There are plans to establish a real tourist office in the historical district, but as yet, Aasiaat doesn't receive enough visitors to justify a fully-fledged operation.

Colonial Old Town
Aasiaat's older buildings are clustered around the harbour area. Perhaps the nicest is the multistorey home of the whaling station commander from Kronprinsens Ejlande. It was constructed in 1778 and relocated to Aasiaat when the station was abandoned in 1826. There is also the old trading manager's home and a monument to Niels Egede, Aasiaat's founding father. This building may eventually become the new tourist office.

Inuit Old Town
Across the bridge east of the centre is the traditional hunters' community. It's picturesque and well worth a walk around, but beware of the irritable sled dogs tied up everywhere.

Aasiaat Systue
In 1982, Aasiaat established a leather-craft shop which places emphasis on traditional tanning, drying, sewing and embroidery skills. Interested foreigners are welcome to visit the workshop and learn the processes involved or just purchase a leather handbag or a festive white anorak. Visitors may also commission custom-made pieces for reasonable prices, including bits of the beautiful Greenlandic national costume.

Aasiaat Museum
The Aasiaat Museum is small but well presented and very much worth visiting. It is in the residence of the poet, merchant and parliamentarian Frederik Lynge. There's an array of things from the area's history as well as an assortment of decomposing historical machinery lying around outside. It's open Wednesday from 1 to 5 pm and on Sunday from 11 am to 3 pm. Admission is Dkr10.

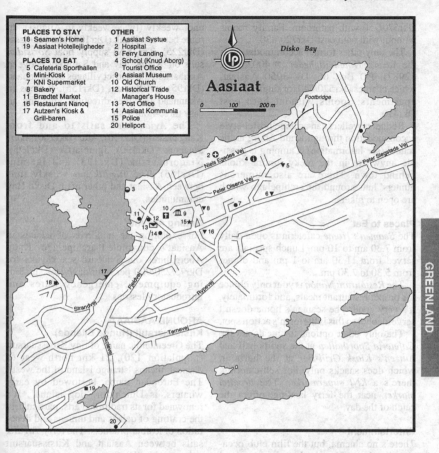

PLACES TO STAY
18 Seamen's Home
19 Aasiaat Hotellejligheder

PLACES TO EAT
5   Cafeteria Sporthallen
6   Mini-Kiosk
7   KNI Supermarket
8   Bakery
11 Brædtet Market
16 Restaurant Nanoq
17 Autzen's Kiosk &
    Grill-baren

OTHER
1   Aasiaat Systue
2   Hospital
3   Ferry Landing
4   School (Knud Aborg)
    Tourist Office
9   Aasiaat Museum
10 Old Church
12 Historical Trade
    Manager's House
13 Post Office
14 Aasiaat Kommunia
15 Police
20 Heliport

Disko Bay

Aasiaat

0   100   200 m

Footbridge

Niels Egedes Vej

Peter Siegstads Vej

Peter Olsens Vej

Fjeldvej

Rypevej

Strandvej

Sletvej

Ternevej

GREENLAND

Hiking

The terrain around Aasiaat is relatively flat and ordinary, but walkers who prefer strolling rather than puffing up and slipping down mountains will find it unchallengingly perfect. In any case, the low hills behind town offer some fine views across the archipelago, and the 10 sq km island is readily manageable.

Organised Tours

The Kommunia offers several day tours, but you'll need a group to make them worthwhile. These include day tours by boat to

small villages and abandoned settlements in southern Disko Bay (Dkr500); two-hour whale-watching cruises (Dkr250); a four-hour boat tour to the hot springs on Saqqarllip Nunaa island (Dkr500); and four-hour fishing trips for cod, catfish or capelin (Dkr500), including rods and/or nets.

Places to Stay

Aasiaat lacks a hotel but there's a comfortable *Seamen's Home* (☎ 42175; fax 42910) near the harbour tanks. Single/double rooms cost Dkr410/620 without bathroom and

Dkr570/750 with bathroom. Family rooms without/with bath cost Dkr720/830.

The only other formal accommodation is the *Aasiaat Hotellejligheder* (☎ 40035; fax 42987), PO Box 66, DK-3950 Aasiaat, which charges Dkr520/640 for single/double apartments; rooms without bath cost Dkr410.

Budget travellers can arrange hostel-style accommodation through Knud Aborg at the school (see Information). Camping is possible anywhere in the rocky tundra knolls behind town. There are also numerous hunters' huts around the archipelago which are open to hikers.

Places to Eat
The *Seamen's Home* cafeteria is open daily from 7.30 am to 10 pm. Lunch specials are served from 11.30 am to 1 pm and dinner from 5.30 to 7.30 pm.

The *Restaurant Nanoq* is your only choice for proper restaurant meals, and fortunately, it's very good. The seamen's home doesn't serve alcohol so this is the town's action spot.

The only other options for meals are the *Cafeteria Sporthallen* at the sports hall and *Autzen's Kiosk Grill-Bar* at the harbour, which does snacks only. For self-catering, there's a *KNI supermarket*. The *brædtet market*, near the ferry landing, offers the catch of the day.

Entertainment
There's no cinema, but the film club occasionally shows films in the primary school auditorium. On Friday and Saturday nights, the *Restaurant Nanoq* puts on a disco.

Getting There & Away
Air A new airport is being built in Aasiaat, but currently only helicopter services are available. Grønlandsfly (☎ 42288) flies daily except Sunday between Aasiaat, Ilulissat, Qasigiannguit and Qeqertarsuaq (all Dkr680). There are also weekly services to Sisimiut (Dkr3020) and Maniitsoq (Dkr3740).

Ferry The big ferries call in at Aasiaat at least

once weekly (twice weekly in August), en route between Nuuk (Dkr1085) and Ilulissat (Dkr225). The KNI supply boat *Sortsiden* sails on Wednesday and Saturday between Aasiaat and the district villages of Akunnaaq (Dkr95) and Ikamiut (Dkr155). It stops in Akunnaaq in either direction, allowing an easy three-hour visit.

The *Aviaq Ittuk* sails to and from Kangaatsiaq (Dkr130), Attu (Dkr200), Iker-asaarsuk (Dkr190), Iginniarfik (Dkr195), Niaqornaarsuk (Dkr195) and Ikamiut (Dkr155). The *Tugdlik* has weekly runs between Aasiaat and other main Disko Bay communities.

Getting Around
For exploring the hundreds of islands in Aasiaat's convoluted archipelago, Knud Aborg hires out Svalbard sea kayaks for Dkr75/250/900 per hour/day/week, including equipment, emergency flares and introductory lessons.

AROUND AASIAAT
Kitsissuarsuit (Hunde Ejlande)
The Greenlandic name of tiny Kitsissuarsuit (population 120), 21 km north-west of Aasiaat, means 'strange island of the west'. The European name, bestowed by early whalers, is Dutch for 'dog island'. It's renowned for its traditional arts, particularly the crafting of qajaqs and umiaqs and decoration of leather products. The ferry *Tugdlik* sails between Aasiaat and Kitsissuarsuit twice weekly (Dkr85).

Akunnaaq
The other district village, Akunnaaq (population 200), lies 23 km east of town. The KNI supply boat does a return trip from Aasiaat (Dkr95) in a single day, so it's a convenient place for a glimpse into village life on Disko Bay.

QASIGIANNGUIT (CHRISTIANSHÅB)
Qasigiannguit ('small spotted seals') sits at the foot of a long escarpment which rises almost vertically above its well-sheltered small-boat harbour.

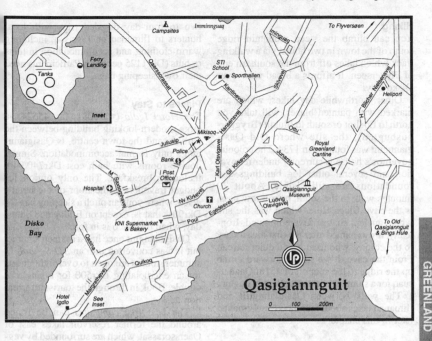

Qasigiannguit

0   100   200m

History

The Qasigiannguit area has been inhabited for over 4000 years, and remnants of the Saqqaq, Thule and Dorset cultures have been found here. The earliest evidence yet discovered of habitation in Greenland is the skeleton of a Saqqaq woman who lived 4000 years ago on the island of Qeqertasussuk.

The town was founded in 1734 by Poul Egede, son of Hans Egede, and set up as a trading station by Jakob Severin, who also founded Ilulissat. The Danish name, Christianshåb ('Christian's hope') refers to King Christian IV of Denmark. Flooding and icy winds from the east made the original site unfavourable, and in 1764 the town was moved across the bay.

Qasigiannguit was used briefly as a military post to protect Danish whaling interests from Dutch 'intruders' and experienced a minor trade war between Denmark and Holland in the mid-1700s. However, nothing took off economically for over two centuries.

When the rich offshore shrimping grounds were discovered in the early 1950s, the town numbered just 245 people. However, once the shrimp-processing plant was built in 1952, Qasigiannguit began to grow and it now has around 1800 residents.

Information

The small tourist office (☎ & fax 45656) is at the Hotel Igdlo, PO Box 1555, DK-3951 Qasigiannguit. It's open weekdays from 8 am to 5 pm, Saturday from 9 am to 7 pm and Sunday from 1 to 4 pm.

Qasigiannguit Museum

The Qasigiannguit Museum (☎ 45477) has an excellent collection of relics from the Saqqaq through to the present Inuit culture. It's open Tuesday, Thursday and Sunday from 2 to 4 pm. At other times, you can arrange private openings.

Hiking

You can climb the steep mountain ridge south of the town in two hours, via a walking track which takes off from the southern end of Flyversøen. It affords a broad view over Disko Bay.

Other worthwhile day hikes, which are marked with painted blazes, will take you north to Eqaluit or south to Illukut (Bryggerhusbugten), the site where Old Qasigiannguit was founded in 1734. The colonial governor's house is currently under renovation and several other log buildings and foundations are still visible. About 20 minutes walk to the south, over a low pass, is the cave Bings Hule, which was the site where ancient shamans were initiated. Ironically, it was named after the first missionary to the colony, who used it as a quiet retreat. From the cave, it's a straightforward climb up the ridge to the summit of 451m Qaaqarsuaq for a stunning view over Paradisbugten.

The walk between Qasigiannguit and Ilimanaq takes about four days (see Ilimanaq later in this chapter).

Organised Tours

The tourist office runs eight-hour boat tours to Ikannuit (Dkr850), where there's a small fish processing plant and a view of rural life in the district. They also do boat tours to Akullit and Granatbugten, which is rich in natural garnets (Dkr850), and five-hour midnight sun cruises (Dkr800).

Organised hikes include a fishing expedition to Strømstedet and a climb up the ridge west of Flyversøen (Dkr300); hikes to Old Qasigiannguit and Bings Hule (Dkr200); a five-hour return climb up 451m Qaaqarssuaq (Dkr200); and a guided town tour (Dkr125).

From March to May, they run alpine and cross-country ski tours, and dogsled trips may be arranged on your own or through the Hotel Igdlo. The hotel/tourist office offers the easiest but not the cheapest options: you can choose from half/full day trips with a Greenlandic hunter to Mågefjeldet/Akullit (Dkr450/925); a day of ice fishing by dogsled (Dkr500); half-day snowmobile tours to Ilimanaq or Ikamiut (Dkr1450); and

two to four-day dogsled trips with local hunters to Ilimanaq or Tasiusaq, including warm clothing and accommodation in tents or huts (Dkr1125 per day). Participants need their own sleeping bags.

Places to Stay

The *Hotel Igdlo* (☎ 45081; fax 45524), a large modern-looking building between the harbour and the town centre, is Qasigiannguit's only formal accommodation. Single/double rooms with bath cost Dkr740/940, including breakfast. The only option for budget travellers is the floor of the hotel's disco, where you can pitch a sleeping bag for Dkr90 – that is, except on Friday and Saturday, when the disco is in force.

Qasigiannguit once had a seamen's home, but it was converted into an *STI School*. In summer, rooms are open to overnight guests for an excruciating Dkr500 for a single or double. Book in through the tourist information desk.

The best free *campsites* can be found around the former reservoir lakes east of Qaerssorassat, which are surrounded by vegetation and low hills. The Hotel Igdlo also has *campsites* for Dkr35 per person, and the hotel showers are open to campers for Dkr30/150 per day/week. You can also set up camp at Flyversøen, a tidal lake north of the inlet. The tourist office hires three-person tents for Dkr50/150 per day/week and sleeping bags for Dkr25/100.

Places to Eat

The *Hotel Igdlo* has both a cafeteria and an upmarket restaurant. The only alternatives for meals are the grill bar *Mikisoq* in the centre and the *Royal Greenland Cantine*, near the museum. The *KNI supermarket* has a good selection of groceries and an excellent *bakery*.

Entertainment

The heart of the action is the *Hotel Igdlo* disco, which operates on Friday and Saturday nights from 11 pm to 2 am, and occasionally features live music. When the

DEANNA SWANEY

Tundra in autumn colours and the Ilulissat Icefjord near Ilulissat, Disko Bay, Greenland

DEANNA SWANEY

DEANNA SWANEY

DEANNA SWANEY

DEANNA SWANEY

A	B
C	D

A: Late sun and luminescent icebergs, Tasiilaq (Ammassalik), East Greenland
B: Kong Oscars Havn, Tasiilaq from summit of Sømandsfjeldet
C: Peaks near mouth of Kangerlussuaq, Greenland
D: Cutting the ice through Torssuqaatoq Sound, southern Greenland

hotel is fully booked, they also invite a live band to play in the restaurant in the evening.

Getting There & Away

Air In summer, you can fly to or from Ilulissat at least once daily, except Sunday (Dkr680, but a few discounted Dkr440 'Green Fare' seats are also available). You can also fly to Qeqertarsuaq (Dkr680) five times weekly.

Ferry The big ferries sail in at least once a week on their runs between Nuuk (Dkr1210) and Ilulissat (Dkr135) or Upernavik (Dkr795). The *Tugdlik* and *Aviaq Ittuk* also call in once or twice weekly; the former serves main Disko Bay communities – Aasiaat (Dkr170), Ilulissat, Saqqaq (Dkr265) and Qeqertarsuaq (Dkr220) – and the latter connects with mostly smaller places around southern Disko Bay – Aasiaat, Kangaatsiaq (Dkr245), Akunnaq (Dkr130), Attu (Dkr315) and other villages.

Getting Around

In winter, the tourist office rents out snow-mobiles, with a driver, for Dkr250 per hour.

AROUND QASIGIANNGUIT

Qeqertasussuk

On the island of Qeqertasussuk, at the eastern end of Sydostbugten, archaeologists have excavated some fascinating discoveries. Organic material uncovered here has been dated to as early as 4000 years ago, and artefacts from the site provide evidence that society of that period was far more advanced than previously assumed. The best access is by charter boat from Qasigiannguit.

Akullit

The village of Akullit, which was abandoned in the early 1960s, is now used as a hunting camp and a summer holiday camp for school children. The tourist office in Qasigiannguit offers worthwhile boat tours and dogsled trips.

Orpissooq & Lake Ilulialik

In 1989, near the head of the bay Orpissooq,

the remains of an ancient Saqqaq autumn campsite were excavated by the Qasigiann-guit museum. They uncovered not only several fireplaces and tent foundations, but also a wealth of stone and bone tools and artefacts. Several so-called 'boiling stones' – artificially-worked fist-sized cobbles – were found alongside the cooking areas, leading to speculation that they were heated and dropped into skin bags of soup to add or preserve heat (a practice common among Native Americans). Orpissooq is accessible by charter boat from Qasigiannguit.

At the western end of the lake Ilulialik, just up the valley from the head of Orpis-sooq, is the Qasigiannguit Canoe Centre (☎ 45539), Kirkevej 19, Dk-3951 Qasigia-nnguit, where you can hire canoes to explore the lake and get good close-up views of the glacier flowing into its eastern end. A 5½ metre Canadian canoe for three or four people costs Dkr100/350 for two hours/one day. For Dkr2950 per person, you get boat transfers from Qasigiannguit, three days of canoe hire, a guide, a hiking map, camping and cooking gear and half board.

ILIMANAQ (CLAUSHAVN)

The Danish name for the tiny community of Ilimanaq (population 70) probably honours Dutch whaling captain, Klæs Pieterz Thop, who operated in Disko Bay from 1719 to 1732. Its more beautiful Greenlandic name means 'hopeful place for hunting'.

Ilulissat Kangerlua Hike

For a look at the ice-choked Ilulissat Kanger-lua (Jakobshavn Icefjord) from the southern perspective, make a day hike north along the coast to Aappaluttuarssuk. En route, you can visit the three ancient ruined settlements of Iglumiut, Avannarliit (Nordre Huse) and Eqe.

If you have more time and don't want to return the way you came, walk east along the shore for a couple of km (with great views of the fjord all the way!) and turn inland over the pass to Tasersuaq Qalleq. Follow the western shore of the lake south to the next lake, Tasersuaq Alleq, then turn due west and return to Ilimanaq by climbing directly over the mountain.

You can also walk between the two Tasersuaq lakes and cross over to the convoluted bay Tasiusaq, which is cut off from Disko Bay by the icefjord itself.

Ilimanaq to Qasigiannguit Trek

A relatively easy four-day trek connects Ilimanaq with Qasigiannguit. The landscape may not be overwhelming, but the hike isn't difficult and is accessible to anyone who's reasonably fit. The best available map is Saga Maps' *Disko Bugt-Qeqertarsuup Tunua* 1:250,000.

Start off by walking south along the coast to meet up with the marked dogsled track. From the broad open area marked Narsarsuaq, you can continue south along the uninteresting dogsled route or head east, toward hill 320. Skirt this hill to the north and east, then turn south and climb up onto the pass. When you're immediately west of hill 430, turn south-west and keep going until you reach the small lake immediately west of hill 420. Follow its outlet river down to the western shore of Qinguata Tasia and cross the isthmus.

After climbing partially up the other side, you'll reach the head of a long narrow lake. Follow its eastern shore to the end, then bear east and then south around the eastern slope of Salleq (marked 'Sagdleq'). Near the southern end of Salleq, follow the western shoreline of Sallup Tasia. At the end of this lake, strike west toward the outflow of lake 90, which may only be crossed at low tide! Once you're safely across, follow the western shore of this lake down the valley into Qasigiannguit.

Getting There & Away

You can walk between Ilimanaq and Qasigiannguit in four days, but thanks to the icefjord, you'll need a boat to/from Ilulissat. The KNI boat *Narhvalen* stops at Ilimanaq twice weekly on its run between Ilulissat (Dkr80) and small Disko Bay villages.

ILULISSAT (JAKOBSHAVN)

However scruffy and unkempt, Ilulissat ('the icebergs') is the Arctic you came to see – cold, mirror-like seas crowded with icebergs and floes, an often unrelenting grey sky and a disorderly spirit noticeably missing from the tidier towns further south. Not surprisingly, it's now Greenland's most popular tourist destination, and attracts not only summer visitors on the ferries and flights, but also a swelling number of cruise ships and spring dogsled tourists.

Ilulissat is also the home town of Arctic explorer Knud Rasmussen and of Jørgen Brønlund, who wrote the note that described the awful fate of the Mylius-Erichsen expedition in north-east Greenland (see the History section in Facts about Greenland for more detail).

History

From 4000 to 3500 years ago, the Ilulissat area was inhabited by the Saqqaq and Dorset cultures. The abandoned village of Sermermiut, beside the icefjord, dates back perhaps 3500 years and is one of over 120 archaeological sites in the Ilulissat district. When the Norwegian missionary Poul Egede arrived in 1737, Sermermiut was the largest

Ilulissat (Jakobshavn) coat of arms

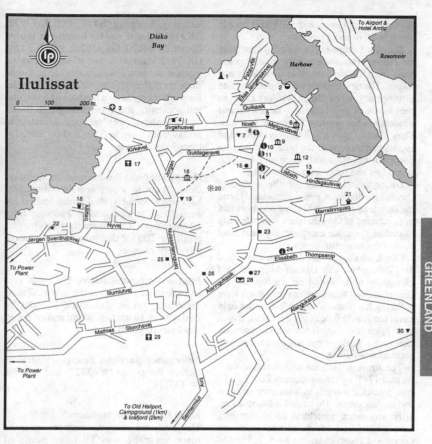

Ilulissat

Disko Bay

Harbour

Reservoir

To Airport &
Hotel Arctic

To Power
Plant

To Power
Plant

To Old Heliport,
Campground (1km)
& Icefjord (2km)

GREENLAND

PLACES TO STAY
4 Hotel Hvide Falk
21 Youth Hostel
23 Hotel & Cafeteria
    Naaleraq
25 Skolehjemmet
26 Sporthallen & Cafeteria

PLACES TO EAT
5 KNI Shop & Bakery
7 Grill-baren Centrum &
   Ilulissat Centre
   Marked
15 Brædtet Market
19 Ristorante Pizzeria
    Panorama

27 KNI Supermarket
30 KNI Kiosk

OTHER
1 Knud Rasmussen
   Memorial
2 Ferry Landing
3 Hospital
6 Cold Museum
8 Nuna Bank
9 Hunting & Fishing
   Museum
10 Tourist Nature
11 Grønlandsbanken Bank
    & Airport Bus Stop

12 Emanuel A Petersen
    Art Museum
13 Greenland Stone Shop
14 Ilulissat Tourist Service
16 Knud Rasmussen
    Museum
17 Zion's Church
18 Hotel
    Jakobshavn/Disco
    Kununnguaq
20 Viewpoint
22 Police
24 Greenland Travel
28 Post Office
29 Naalakkatta Illua

Inuit village in Greenland, with 200 people living in 20 or more houses.

The first Europeans to visit Ilulissat were the Norse, who undoubtedly sailed up the coast from the Vesterbygd to hunt seals and walrus. The next contact wasn't until the late 17th century, when Dutch whalers came to hunt for whale products (such astrain oil and whalebone) for growing European markets. They named the place Maklykkout and established trade with the Inuit, exchanging European beads, wood, guns and iron for skins, furs and other animal products.

Unfortunately, some of the outsiders cheated the locals at every opportunity, and the Dutch government became so upset that mistreatment of Greenlanders was officially placed in the same category as piracy, and carried the same stiff penalties!

Dutch whaling around Ilulissat was halted in 1780, when the Danish king decided monopoly trade would be appropriate for Greenland and that the nuisance Dutch were blocking his plans. The result was the only naval battle ever fought in Greenland, which took place just outside the present harbour. Denmark was victorious and the Dutch competition was ousted.

The town of Ilulissat was founded on 3 August 1741, by the missionary Poul Egede, who intended using it as a summer mission and trading centre. He named it Jakobshavn, after influential merchant Jakob Severin, who controlled much of the trade on Greenland's west coast.

Due to the success of the religious mission, local Inuit were attracted to the European settlement and by 1782, Ilulissat had grown into a colony and later became the metropolis and service centre of Disko Bay. In addition to tourism, its present economy is bolstered by its 70-boat fishing fleet and several shrimp and halibut-processing plants. It's now Greenland's fourth largest town, with a population of 4570.

Information
Tourist Office Ilulissat actually has two competing tourist offices – the Ilulissat Tourist Service (☎ 44322; fax 43933),

Kussangajannguaq B447, PO Box 272, DK3952 Ilulissat, and the Italian-run Tourist Nature (☎ 44420; fax 44624), PO Box 169, DK-3952 Ilulissat – but it seems they've reached an amicable agreement, and now share the different facets of the tourist trade. Both offices organise a plethora of tours, and sell souvenirs and foreign-language books on Greenland; they're open Monday to Friday from 9 am to 5 pm and on Saturday from 9 am to 1 pm.

Money The Nuna Bank is open on weekdays from 10 am to 3 pm, and the Grønlandsbanken, on Monday, Wednesday and Friday from 10 am to 3 pm and on Thursday from 10 am to 5 pm. Unfortunately, they charge a punitive Dkr75 commission to change travellers' cheques.

Post & Communications The main post and telephone office is in the new KNI shop on Alanngukasik. It's open Monday to Friday from 10 am to 4.30 pm and on Saturday from 10 am to 1 pm.

Emergency Services Emergency services include the police (☎ 43222) and hospital (☎ 43211).

Knud Rasmussen Museum
The lovely red house that once served as the town vicarage was also the home of Greenland's favourite son, Arctic explorer, anthropologist and author Knud Rasmussen, who was born there on 7 July 1879. It now houses the town museum and is dedicated to Kununnguaq or 'little Knud', whose typically Greenlandic philosophy of life was summed up in his oft-quoted utterance 'Give me winter, give me dogs, and you can have the rest'.

One room is devoted to his expeditions and his anthropological and linguistic studies across the North American Arctic. Other exhibits deal with Greenlandic traditions, early Danish life in Greenland and ancient Inuit artefacts and history. Upstairs

Knud Rasmussen

If Greenland has a favourite son, it's Arctic explorer Knud Rasmussen, who was born in Ilulissat on 7 June 1879. The son of local pastor Christian Rasmussen and his wife Sophie, his ancestry was Danish, Norwegian and Greenlandic, and the people of Ilulissat came to know him as Kununnguaq, 'little Knud'.

Knud hadn't made any career plans early on and after completing school in Copenhagen, he began looking around for something that suited him. Among his attempts were opera singing and medicine, both of which were quickly abandoned. His talent as a writer was discovered in accounts of his journeys to Lapland and Iceland. In 1902, he joined the Danish Literary Expedition to north-west Greenland, led by Ludvig Mylius-Erichsen. This resulted in his first book, *The New People*, about the traditional polar Eskimos of the Melville Bay area.

From 1906 to 1908, Knud was invited to join the Ethnographical Expedition to North-West Greenland, which attempted to find the route travelled by early migrants to Greenland from Canada's Ellesmere Island.

By 1910, Knud had clearly found his calling in life and, together with fellow Arctic enthusiast Peter Freuchen (who later wrote the book *Arctic Adventure*, which details many of their exploits together), he established a trading company in Qaanaaq (Thule), with the objective of funding subsequent expeditions. Freuchen wrote: 'Rasmussen was something of a dandy and always carried a pair of scissors for cutting his hair and beard. Even in the most biting cold, he washed his face every day with walrus blubber, and his footwear was the most beautiful in the Arctic.'

Their joint business was successful, and between 1912 and 1919 Knud conducted four more expeditions to Greenland. The objectives of these trips were, among other things, to ascertain the existence of the Peary Channel, search for missing explorers, chart the northern coastline of Greenland and perform an ethnographical study in east Greenland.

It was the experience gained from these trips that led to what he hoped would be the fulfillment of his dreams – to trace the migration of the Inuit peoples from Siberia all the way to Greenland.

The 5th Thule Expedition set out in 1921 to gather ethnographical, archaeological, geographical and natural history data from Greenland right across the North American Arctic. He visited all the Inuit communities in Arctic Canada and Alaska, collecting myths, legends and linguistic studies, and would have continued across to Arctic Russia, but was denied permission by the Soviet authorities.

The result of this expedition was *The 5th Thule Expedition – The Danish Ethnographical Expedition to Arctic America*, which detailed linguistic and cultural differences between the Inuit groups across the region. It was also the basis for Rasmussen's best-known book, *Across Arctic America*. These projects earned him an honorary doctorate from Copenhagen University.

Two subsequent expeditions, the 6th and 7th Thule Expeditions, involved surveying, aerial photography and geological, zoological, ethnographic, botanical and glaciological studies on the east coast of Greenland. Knud also tried his hand at film direction with the making of *Palos Brudefærd* (Palo's Wedding) in the summer of 1933 in Ammassalik. Sadly, during the filming he contracted food poisoning from pickled auks and died shortly afterwards, on 21 December 1933. ∎

is a small reference library on Arctic exploration and outside are a whale jawbone arch, an umiaq and a small turf hut.

The museum is open Tuesday to Friday from 9 am to 4 pm and on Sunday from 1 to 4 pm; admission is Dkr25.

Emanuel A Petersen Art Museum

Most of the works in this museum are by Danish artist Emanuel A Petersen, who was born 18 February 1894 in Frederiksberg, Denmark. During his career, he made several trips to Greenland to paint its extraordinary landscape and light. Through numerous exhibitions around Europe and his illustrations in the book *Greenland in Pictures*, published in 1928, he introduced the European continent to the magic of the Arctic. When he died on 27 December 1948 in Farum, Denmark, he left an extraordinary collection of paintings of early 20th century Greenland, many of which are exhibited here.

The collection is housed in a building constructed in 1923 by architect Helge Boysen-Møller for use as a residence by trade commissioners. Among its 14 commissioners was portrait and landscape artist, Hans Jacobi.

It's open Monday to Friday from 11 am to 3 pm and on Sunday from 1 to 4 pm. Admission is a rather steep Dkr25.

Hunting & Fishing Museum

This new museum emphasises the hunting and fishing traditions of the polar Inuit, and contains both traditional and modern tools, implements and conveyances. There are no set opening hours; for a look around, ask for the key at the Knud Rasmussen Museum.

Cold Museum

The Cold Museum (☎ 43643) is housed in Ilulissat's oldest building, the tarred 'black warehouse', above the harbour, which dates from Ilulissat's commercial whaling days. It's called 'cold' not because it once served as an icehouse, which would have been redundant in Greenland, but because it doesn't require heat to preserve its contents. It's now a repository for tools and machinery from the old trading settlement – including a collection of fire extinguishers, bakery machinery and scales – as well as a wooden dory called *Dory*, and a recreated cooperage. You can arrange a visit by phoning in advance.

Zion's Church

The pleasant-looking Zion's Church was constructed around 1782 from heavy timbers. The missionary Jørgen Jørgensen Sverdrup had instilled such religious fervour in the community that it decided Ilulissat needed its own church. From 1777 to 1779, the Greenlandic residents of Ilulissat and nearby Oqaatsut collected 59 whales and 157 barrels of whale oil. The Danish inhabitants collected 52 barrels of oil and 25 whales which, all told, covered the cost of the church.

Around the start of the 20th century, the western end was used as a hospital. In 1907, the building was restored, and in 1929, it was expanded and moved 50m inland.

The church is open only on Sundays; at other times, visits must be arranged through the Ilulissat Tourist Service. Above the altar is a copy of the famous *Christus* by Bertel Thorvaldsen. The chalice dates from 1840, the candlesticks from 1789, and the font and christening dish from 1779. Note the portraits of Hans Egede and Jørgen Jørgensen Sverdrup, and the lovely votive ship which hangs from the ceiling.

Naalakkatta Illua

The name of this small church near the Sporthallen means simply 'the house of Our Lord'. It was originally constructed at the coal mining village of Qullissat on Disko Island, but when the coal ran out in 1972, the settlement was abandoned and the following year the church was moved to Ilulissat. Whoever did the job apparently took quite literally Christ's admonition that his church be built upon a rock.

Ilulissat Kangerlua

The main tourist attraction of Ilulissat is the Ilulissat Kangerlua (Ilulissat Icefjord). The glacier face of the Sermeq Kujalleq, or Jakobshavns Isbræ, measures five km wide and 1100m thick. At the glacier face, the sea is about 1500m deep, but only 80m rises above the surface. It flows an average of 25m daily and is the world's most prolific glacier outside Antarctica. The Sermeq Kujalleq is the source of a tenth of the icebergs floating in Greenlandic waters, amounting to 20 cubic km annually or about 20 million tonnes per day – enough to supply New York with water for a year.

The fjord is so choked with floating ice, however, that liquid water is not in evidence at all. The largest bergs, nine-tenths of which typically float beneath the surface, actually rest on the bottom, and many settle on the 260m-deep underwater moraine across the mouth of the fjord, until they break up or enough pressure builds up behind them to shove them out to sea. It's a scene out of a *National Geographic* Arctic documentary, and it's unique in the northern hemisphere.

The icefjord is most easily reached from the old heliport, 1½ km from Ilulissat, where a well-trodden 15 minute track leads to the

shore (see the following Hiking section). From there, you can continue east along the shoreline to Seqinniarfik or all the way to Inussussuaq, or return via the partially-marked coastal route.

Hiking

Local hiking clubs have now marked a series of walking routes with blazed cairns. At the time of writing, your map options are the rough but surprisingly adequate tourist office sketch map (Dkr5), the 1:250,000 Saga Map *Qeqertarsuup Tunua*, or its base map, Kort & Matrikelstyrelsen's 1:250,000

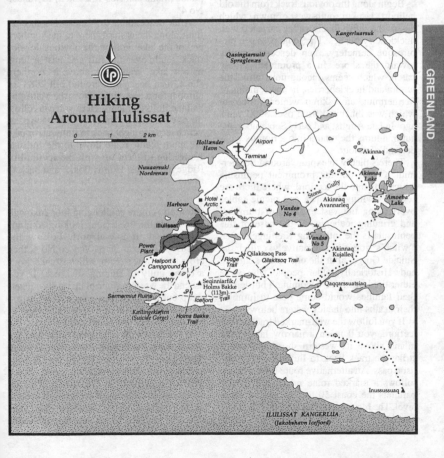

Hiking Around Ilulissat

Jakobshavn. However, the new 1:75,000 *Hiking Map West Greenland – Ilulissat* should be available by the time you read this.

The compass declination in this region is about 43°W.

Sermermiut

The easiest and most popular walk from Ilulissat will take you to the ruins of Sermermiut, the Ilulissat Kangerlua, and 113m Seqinniarfik (Holms Bakke), where the entire town of Ilulissat gathers on 13 January to welcome the sun back after its six-week sojourn below the horizon.

Begin along the obvious track from the old heliport, 1½ km south-west of town, which passes through a lovely valley carpeted with huckleberry bushes. The route passes a picturesque cemetery, then descends gently toward the shore. In a prominent grassy patch, which seems incongruous amid the tundra and huckleberries, lie the remains of Sermermiut, an Eskimo winter settlement which was inhabited from over 3500 years ago. In late August and early September, the autumn turns the tundra into a riotous wonderland of colour.

There's plenty to explore around Sermermiut. Check out the prominent peninsula which juts into the icefjord, where there are several inviting benches and picnic tables overlooking the vast expanse of bumping and grinding icebergs. At the base of this peninsula is the intriguing Kællingekløften ('witch's gorge'), alternatively called the Suicide Gorge, after the cliff at its southern end. Historically, older people who were either tired of life or becoming a burden on their families would come here to jump to their deaths into the icy waters below.

If you follow the well-marked track up the icefjord, you'll reach a narrow lake; head inland above its western shore and you'll strike the track back to Ilulissat via Qilaqitsoq pass. An alternative route back to town follows a marked route northward, which parallels the coast 50 to 75m above water level. The blazes peter out after less than one km, but if you keep following the coast, you'll inevitably wind up at the power station (look for the tastefully-painted stacks) immediately west of Ilulissat.

Vandsøen

The five-hour circuit across the Ilulissat plain, past the five Vandsøen lakes, makes a pleasant and easy day hike, but the ground does get soggy in places. Begin by crossing the bridge above the harbour and continue on to the reservoir, where you turn east and follow its southern shore. Cross the river connecting the reservoir with the next lake upstream, then bear east and follow the highest ground available past three small ponds (Vandsøen Nos 1, 2 and 3) to Vandsø No 4.

After descending to Vandsø No 5, continue along the eastern shore to the southern end of the lake. Follow the obvious dogsled track south over the hill and past a long, narrow lake. Walk west, above its northern shore, then bear north around hill 208 – or climb it for a nice view across the Vandsøen and the Ilulissat plains. Here you can follow the obvious trail up and over Qilakitsoq pass, which leads straight back to Ilulissat, or take the more scenic route down to the Ilulissat Kangerlua to meet up with the Icefjord or Ridge tracks past Holms Bakke and back to town.

Akinnaq

A more challenging loop hike will take you to the mysterious-looking Akinnaq region east of the airport. Follow the Vandsøen route as far as Vandsø No 4, then cross the inflow stream, which streaks down a broad gully of shining slickrock. If you ascend the western slope of this gully – it gets steep but the stone provides a good grip – you'll reach a wild and eerie landscape of boulders, peaks and small lakes.

If you follow the prominent ridge due east, you'll reach the largish crater-like Akinnaq lake; from its western shore, it's an easy scramble up 395m Akinnaq peak, which offers a view north to Oqaatsut and southwest back to Ilulissat. Keep to high ground as you pass south of Akinnaq lake, then descend slightly to an amoeba-like lake immediately to the south-east, and cross its outflow stream, which tumbles over a series of miniature, terrace-like waterfalls.

Here the going gets a bit tougher, as you must traverse the slope southward against the lay of the land, which means constant ascents and descents over steep humpback rocks; in places you'll probably have to backtrack to find a passable route. If you're tempted downhill toward the west, you'll reach the eastern bank of Vandsø No 5, and there rejoin the Vandsøen route. However, if you keep to the high ground, you'll eventually descend into the deep gash-like valley between Aqinnaq Kujalleq and the area's most prominent peak, Qaaqarssuatsiaq. This valley is dominated by a long, narrow and haunting lake. If you follow the low ridge above its northern shore, you'll eventually meet the Qilakitsoq track.

Organised Tours

The Ilulissat Tourist Service (☎ 44322; fax 43933), Tourist Nature (☎ 44420; fax 44624); Arctic Adventure (☎ & fax 35240) and Greenland Tours' Elke Messner (☎ 44411; mobile ☎ 74174; fax 44511) run a range of tours through Ilulissat's dramatic surroundings. (Elke Messner and her partner Dieter Zillmann, based in Oqaatsut, offer very good value.)

On offer are two-hour excursions by boat to the icefjord by day (Dkr325) or in the midnight sun (Dkr375); day boat-charters to the hunting and fishing villages of Ilimanaq or Oqaatsut (Dkr625 – add a barbecue in Oqaatsut and it's Dkr825); or a five-day boat tour to the tidewater glacier Eqip Sermiat. Helicopter tours range from short hops to the inland ice (Dkr975) or Ilulissat glacier (Dkr1200) to five-hour tours with stops at Ilulissat glacier and Alluttoq (Arveprinsens Ejlande), and fishing in Boye's lake (Dkr1595).

You can also choose from several guided hiking tours: a two-day hike to Oqaatsut (Dkr1575), with food, basic accommodation and return boat transport; three days to Bredebugten and Ujup Kua (Dkr1995); and a fabulous 10-day route from Ilulissat to Uummannaq (Dkr11,975), with meals, camping, boat transfer to Qoororsuaq, a taxing but stunning hike across the hulking Nuussuaq peninsula and boat trip from Kuusuup Nuua, south-east of Ikerasak, to Uummannaq. The trip includes village visits in Appat (abandoned), Qeqertaq and Ikerasak.

Dogsled tours, most of which run from March to May, are extremely popular. They can be individually organised, but those on a tight schedule may prefer package trips, which range from a quick spin around town to transfers to Camp Ice Cap and longer hunting and fishing trips on the sea ice. Most tours are organised by the tour agencies and conducted by the local dogsledding organisation. They last from one hour to 12 days, with overnight stays in hunting huts, and cost from Dkr450/1000 for one/six hours to Dkr3000/5800/8600 for two/four/six days. The 12-day tour (Dkr13,750), which runs from Ilulissat over the Nuussuaq peninsula's 800m Majoriaarsuaqsiaq pass to Uummannaq, is only for those who can handle a bit of discomfort in exchange for a truly breathtaking experience.

Fishing trips throughout the district are available in summer or winter. They range from two to nine days and average Dkr800 per day, including transport, meals, fishing equipment and camping or hut accommodation. The nine-day option (Dkr6975) amounts to a magical commune with nature on beautiful Alluttoq island, and includes a guide, meals and camping.

Shorter options include two-hour town tours (Dkr150); two/three-hour guided hikes around Sermermiut (Dkr150/225); and a Greenlandic barbecue (Dkr325).

Places to Stay

Ilulissat is packed with tourists from mid-July to mid-August, and last-minute accommodation may be hard to find; book in advance or bring a tent.

Camping Toilets, showers and washing facilities have been set up for campers at the old heliport. Pay the Dkr35 per day fee and pick up keys to the facilities from the Ilulissat

Tourist Service. They also sell Dkr5 shower tokens, which yield three minutes of hot water. Unfortunately, there have been quite a few thefts from tents at this site; don't leave valuables unattended.

It's also possible to hike out of town and find a suitable spot just about anywhere, but note that camping is prohibited anywhere in the Sermermiut valley.

The Ilulissat Tourist Service hires tents (Dkr150 per day), sleeping bags rated to -40°C (Dkr100), cooking pots (Dkr15) and fishing equipment (Dkr100). Discounts are available on longer term rental.

Hostels The large, friendly and popular *Ilulissat Youth Hostel* (☎ 43377; fax 44577) offers showers, cooking facilities, washing machines and a TV room. However, individuals attempting to use the kitchen may find themselves at odds with large tour groups. From June to September, bunk beds in a double room cost Dkr175. From October to May, the price climbs to Dkr250.

The *Ilulissat Sporthallen* (☎ 43459; fax 44342), PO Box 105, DK-3752 Ilulissat, has four 12-bed rooms, cooking facilities and a TV lounge. Made-up dormitory beds cost Dkr190 and sleeping-bag accommodation is Dkr100, with discounts available to groups. Sleeping-bag accommodation at the school dormitories, *Skolehjemmet*, costs Dkr150.

The tourist office can also arrange B&B accommodation in private homes in town or in outlying villages for Dkr200.

Hotels The *Hotel Arctic* (☎ 44153; fax 43924), which is well removed from traffic and noise, occupies an isolated promontory with a view over the bay and icebergs and features conference facilities, a dining room, a bar with live music and dancing, a souvenir shop and a billiard room. For tourists who must have igloos in Greenland, several tacky-looking aluminium igloos have been anchored to the rock as annexe accommodation. For this 'luxury in the Arctic', you'll pay Dkr875/1245 for single/double rooms, with breakfast. Family rooms for three are

Dkr1500. The hotel operates a shuttle service to the harbour or airport (Dkr30).

More central is the less pretentious *Hotel Hvide Falk* (☎ 43343; fax 43508), although it's nearly as expensive. There's a bar with live music on weekends, a dining room overlooking Disko Bay and a small souvenir shop. Singles/doubles cost Dkr820/1120, with breakfast, and family rooms are Dkr1440. Harbour or airport transfers are included in the room price.

The *Hotel Naaleraq* (☎ 44040; fax 44360), at the cafeteria and restaurant of the same name, is a small and cosy place with character. Without a meal plan, single/double rooms without bath cost Dkr450/550; doubles with bath are Dkr750 and full-board costs an additional Dkr175.

Places to Eat
Self-Catering The best-stocked supermarkets are the *Ilulissat Centre Marked* and the *KNI* complex on Alanngukasik. The former is open from 9 am to 6 pm on weekdays, 9 am to 5 pm on Saturday and noon to 5 pm on Sunday, and the latter, from 10 am to 4.30 pm Monday to Saturday. The *brædtet market* is in the centre, oddly distant from the harbour area, and three small *KNI shops* are scattered around town. The one on Noah Mølgårdsvej has an attached *bakery* serving coffee or tea for Dkr4.

Fast Food For hot dogs, snacks or coffee, try the *Grill-baren Centrum* or the more down-to-earth *Cafeteria Sporthallen*.

Cafés & Restaurants Fine dining is found at the *Arctic* and *Hvide Falk* hotels, both of which offer fine views; the latter has an especially ice-choked vista.

For good cafeteria meals and reasonably priced restaurant fare, nothing beats the homely *Naaleraq Cafeteria & Restaurant*. It's open from 7 to 10.30 am for breakfast, noon to 1.30 pm for lunch and 5 to 9 pm for dinner.

A great new place is the Italian-oriented *Ristorante Pizzeria Panorama*, which is open Monday to Friday from 4 pm to midnight and on weekends from noon to midnight. They not only do excellent pizza, but also recommended pasta dishes and salads.

Entertainment

The *Naaleraq Cafeteria* engages Greenlandic bands and offers either disco or live music and dancing nightly.

A more typical local experience awaits you at the *Disco Kununnguaq*, at the former Hotel Jakobshavn, where Ilulissat youth go to dance, drink and take in the sounds of local musicians. It's open nightly except Monday. Bouncers keep things running smoothly, but unaccompanied visitors should still prepare for attention. There's no cover charge at either place but it costs Dkr10 to check in your coat and bags.

Things to Buy

Greenland Stone (☎ 43372) is owned by Ms Kaja Mørup, who creates lovely jewellery from Greenland's intriguing ancient geology, and every piece comes with a written description of the stone and its properties. But this is more than a rockshop – it's also a museum of fabulous gem and mineral specimens from around the country. Don't miss it.

Getting There & Away

Air Ilulissat is the transport hub of northern Greenland and since 1984, has had an 800m runway equipped to handle fixed-wing aircraft as large as Dash-7s. There has been talk of extending it to accommodate big jets, but the Dkr200 million price tag to blast through the rock has proven an obstacle.

Grønlandsfly (☎ 43246) also has direct flights to and from all major Disko Bay towns (Dkr680) as well as Kangerlussuaq (Dkr1300), Nuuk (Dkr2780), Sisimiut (Dkr2340), Uummannaq (Dkr1540) and Upernavik (Dkr3800).

Ferry As a major ferry terminal, Ilulissat is served two or three times weekly to and from Nuuk (Dkr1255), and in the high season, twice weekly from Uummannaq (Dkr590) and Upernavik (Dkr715). It's also a base for

the smaller ferry *Tugdlik*, which plies the main routes around Disko Bay, connecting Ilulissat with Qeqertarsuaq (Dkr235), Qullissat (Dkr250), Saqqaq (Dkr190), Qasigiannguit (Dkr135), Kitsissuarsuit (Dkr190) and Aasiaat (Dkr200).

The KNI cargo boat, *Narhvalen*, sails at least weekly to Ilimanaq (Dkr80), Qeqertaq (Dkr195), Saqqaq and Oqaatsut (Dkr80).

Getting Around

The streets of Ilulissat are named after prominent Greenlanders who were born in or lived in Ilulissat. If you happen to be driving around Ilulissat in winter, bear in mind that dogsleds have the right of way!

The Airport The airport bus (Dkr20) leaves from in front of the shop Tøj og Sko, near the Grønlandsbanken, 1¼ hours before flight departures.

Bus The Ilulissat town bus (☎ 43402) has no fixed route or timetable, but circulates according to the wishes of the passengers – a bit like a communal taxi. It runs on weekdays from 7.30 am to 10 pm and costs Dkr10 per ride.

Taxi Taxi services (☎ 43181 or 44044) can be booked or flagged down on the street. No taxis circulate between midnight and 6 am; trips during these hours must be pre-booked.

Boat Charter Boat charter for 12/14 passengers (Dkr5750/6750 per day) may be arranged through the Ilulissat Tourist Service.

AROUND ILULISSAT
Oqaatsut (Rodebay)

About 20 km north of Ilulissat is the lethargic village of Oqaatsut ('the cormorants'), named after the bird colony which inhabits the nearby cliffs. It first operated as a trading post for 18th century Dutch whalers, who bestowed its Dutch name, which means 'bay of rest'. There's little to see but the remains of the plant used for processing and pressing whale blubber into train oil.

The village now has a population of around 60 and is known for its friendly inhabitants and lack of cars.

Organised Tours Several Ilulissat travel agencies offer day tours aboard the *Niga* (Dkr775), a lovely wooden ship once used to transport the local doctor around the Uummannaq district.

The Oqaatsut-based Elke Messner tour agency (☎ 44111; fax 44511) offers a week's accommodation in the guesthouse for Dkr1900, including transfers from Ilulissat on the *M/B Smilla*. A day-trip from Ilulissat, including transfers and full board in a private home, is Dkr650.

Places to Stay The *Oqaatsut Guesthouse* occupies a recently renovated colonial building and features kitchen facilities, a living area and a choice of bed or sleeping-bag accommodation. Book through Elke Messner (see Organised Tours earlier in this section).

Getting There & Away Oqaatsut makes a convenient destination for a two-day return hike from Ilulissat. Follow the dogsled track north from the airport to Bredebugt. Here, the sled route heads straight across the bay, but in summer, following it could prove problematic. A better idea would be to turn east and follow the shoreline right around the bay to the lake Kangerluarsup Tasia Qalleq. Bear north-west to the northern end of the Qarajaq cove to re-connect with the sled track into Oqaatsut.

Otherwise, the KNI cargo boat *Narhvalen* runs twice weekly from Ilulissat (Dkr80).

Ataa
At the tumbledown remains of Ataa on Alluttoq (Arveprinsens Ejlande), abandoned in 1946, are the new *Smilla Camp* cabins, which were used in the film *Miss Smilla's Feeling for Snow*. These are run by local guide Uno Fleischer, who led a 4000 km dogsled journey from Thule to Alaska in 1992, in the tracks of Knud Rasmussen. For comfortable wilderness accommodation,

you'll pay Dkr495 per person, including meals. Boat transfers from Ilulissat cost Dkr975; by helicopter, they're Dkr2800.

Appat (Ritenbenk)
In 1781, the town of Ritenbenk, which had been situated at the site of present-day Saqqaq, was shifted to Alluttoq. In the 1930s, this prosperous fishing village counted more residents than Ilullisat, but during WWII, it was abandoned for unspecified military reasons. The former shop and the residences of the colony governor and vicar are now protected historical buildings and are used as children's summer camps and hunters' camps. Basic sleeping-bag accommodation in the former colonial governors' residence costs Dkr150.

Camp Ice Cap
Camp Ice Cap, just a few hundred metres from the inland ice, has tent accommodation for Dkr100 or Dkr300 with full board. Transfers from Ilulissat by boat cost Dkr1550 and by helicopter, Dkr1850. From the camp, you can make short dogsled tours on the inland ice (Dkr500). It may be booked through the Ilulissat Tourist Service.

SAQQAQ
Set in relatively lush surroundings on the southern coast of the vast Nuussuaq peninsula, Saqqaq is one of the nicest villages on Disko Bay. The name means 'sunny side' – and who could resist a place called Sunny Side, Greenland? The village survives mainly on income from its meat and fish-processing plant. The church, which was built in 1908, is particularly photogenic.

Archaeological excavations west of the settlement have revealed the existence of an Eskimo culture which inhabited this area between 2900 and 4400 years ago. Saqqaq later gave its name to this culture.

Hannibal's House
Saqqaq is known for the greenhouses and gardens of its modern benefactor Danish Greenlander Hannibal Fencker, who served as the trading station manager and was ded-

icated to improving local living conditions. He supplied Saqqaq's electrical generator, grew vegetables in the 24-hour Arctic daylight without chemical fertilisers, reared village orphans and promoted secondary education for village folk.

Although he died in 1986, the big red house at the eastern end of the village is still known as 'Hannibal's house' and his greenhouse garden – the world's most northerly – remains a tourist attraction of sorts. The house is now owned by a couple of Danish doctors and is rented out as a summer house.

Hiking

There's plenty of hiking on the great Nuussuap peninsula. To warm up, make the taxing day hike to the summit of 1150m Livets Top, immediately north-east of Saqqaq.

Undoubtedly, the finest destination is the unforgettable emerald-coloured lake, Saqqap Tasersua, which slices through the heart of the peninsula. It's a five-day return walk. Saqqaq is also a common starting or finishing point for the demanding 10-day trek across the peninsula to Kuusuup Nuua, near Uummannaq. It's better to do the trip from north to south, as transport is easier from Saqqaq than from Kuusuup Nuua. The Ilulissat Tourist Service offers this hike as an organised trip.

Getting There & Away

The *Tugdlik* calls in at Saqqaq weekly on its rounds through Disko Bay. The fare from Ilulissat is Dkr190.

Disko Island

Most visitors comment that the landscape, particularly Qeqertarsuaq's backdrop, resembles something you'd expect in a warmer desert clime. The main attraction here is hiking through the island's high, striated, mesa-like mountains. Geologically, Disko Island (along with the adjacent Nuussuaq peninsula) is the newest land in

Greenland – only 50 million years old – and is comprised of the same igneous basalt formations typical of the Faroe Islands and Iceland's Westfjords.

The flora is also of interest, especially around the several 'warm' springs (3 to 10°C), which contain high concentrations of radioactive fluoride. Around the Englishmen's Harbour spring grow three species of orchid as well as the carnivorous plant, peningula. Populations of these rare plants are small but tenuously stable, so please leave them alone to propagate.

QEQERTARSUAQ (GODHAVN)

The Greenlandic name of both Disko Island and its town means 'big island'; the Danish name of the town means simply 'good harbour'. The town itself is of limited interest, but it's a good staging point for hikes around Disko Island.

History

Qeqertarsuaq was a European whaling port long before the town was actually founded in 1773. From then, it gradually grew into the trading centre of northern Greenland and remained the most important town north of Nuuk up until 1950. However, as other Disko Bay communities began to prosper, Qeqertarsuaq sank quickly into its present obscure position as a scientific base. The Arctic Research Station outside town carries out environmental studies while the Meteorological Institute Ionosphere Station does meteorological and climatic observations.

Qeqertarsuaq, with 1100 people, is the island's only permanent habitation apart from tiny Kangerluk (Diskofjord), 30 km to the north-west on the fjord of the same name.

Information

The Qeqertarsuaq Tourist Service (☎ 47196; fax 47198), at the town museum, is open Monday to Friday from 1 pm to 4 pm.

Qeqertarsuaq Museum

The Qeqertarsuaq museum is open the same hours as the tourist office. Admission is free. Opposite the village bakery is a traditional

GREENLAND

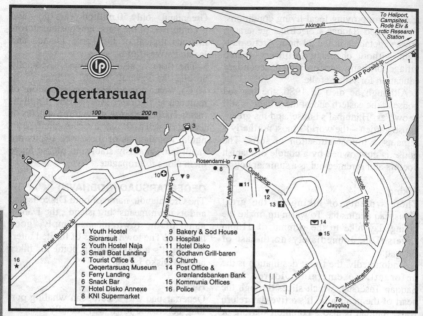

Qeqertarsuaq

0   100   200 m

To Heliport,
Campsites,
Rode Elv &
Arctic Research
Station

Akinguit

M P Porsild-ip

Siorarsuit

Rosendarni-ip

Oqaluffiup

Jacob - Danielsen-ip

Peter Broberg-ip

Adam Meiløard-ip

Arqaluatip

Televel

Avguisinertaq

To
Qaqqaliaq

1	Youth Hostel	9	Bakery & Sod House
	Siorarsuit	10	Hospital
2	Youth Hostel Naja	11	Hotel Disko
3	Small Boat Landing	12	Godhavn Grill-baren
4	Tourist Office &	13	Church
	Qeqertarsuaq Museum	14	Post Office &
5	Ferry Landing		Grønlandsbanken Bank
6	Snack Bar	15	Kommunia Offices
7	Hotel Disko Annexe	16	Police
8	KNI Supermarket		

sod house which has been left intact but is uninhabited.

Church

Qeqertarsuaq's unique and odd-looking church dates from 1915. Ostensibly, Danish architect Bojsen-Møller designed it to emulate the Viborg church in Denmark, but you'd be forgiven for seeing it as a squared-off version of something you'd find in Bangkok. Local people like to call it 'God's inkhouse', and the bell tower resembles a storybook wishing well.

Arctic Research Station

The Arctic Research Station was founded by Morten Porsild of the University of Copenhagen in 1906 for scientific investigation of Arctic ecosystems. Today, it carries out field work and holds classes. The technical library, opened in 1966, contains the largest collection of Arctic studies in Greenland.

Visits must be organised in advance; the tourist office runs hour-long tours of the facility for Dkr100.

Qaqqaliaq

At the southernmost tip of Disko Island, Qaqqaliaq or Udkiggen (the 'lookout'), stands a tower which was used by early whalers as a lookout. Its frame was constructed of four whale jawbones, but the finished product resembles an American football planted in the headland. Whenever a whale was spotted, a cannon was fired to alert the fleet and set the hunt in action. Qaqqaliaq is about a 30 minute walk from the town and is still a good spot for whale-watching.

Organised Tours

The most worthwhile tours – which would be difficult to organise on your own – are the two to seven-day trips to Disko Island's 1500

GREENLAND

sq km icecap, Sermersuaq. From Qeqertarsuaq, you travel by boat around the southern peninsula and into the big fjord Kangerluk. Beyond the hunters' hut at Qiviitut, you continue up the small fjord Kangikerlllak, then climb up the valley on foot to the base camp at about 700m elevation.

Two-day tours start at Dkr1700, while a week on the ice plus a village visit in Kangerluk is Dkr5950. Rates include transport, meals, mountain hut accommodation, skis, snowmobiles and dogsled travel. For details and bookings, contact Johanne Olsen at Qimussiussisoq (☎ 47383; fax 47385), PO Box 35, DK-3953 Qeqertarsuaq. (The name of the agency means 'dogsled driver'.)

The tourist office organises midnight sun boat tours (Dkr450); a three-hour town tour (Dkr200); and two-day boat tours to Kangerluk (Dkr1840).

Places to Stay

This tiny town manages to support three youth hostels, which attract lots of tour groups and are good value all around. The *Siorarsuit, Napasunnguit* and *Naja* youth hostels offer comfortable dormitory accommodation, showers and cooking facilities for Dkr175. The Youth Hostel Naja also has two double rooms. Guests must book in through the tourist office. Free camping is available at any of the hostels, but campers pay Dkr20 to use the hostel showers.

The renovated *Hotel Disko* (☎ 47310; fax 47313) – formerly the grotty Hotel Puisi – still looks more like a grill bar (which it also is) than a hotel. Single/double rooms with shared facilities cost a rather extortionate Dkr800/1100.

Otherwise, there's always wild camping, which is very pleasant in this area. You'll find lots of dry level campsites across the bridge over the Rode Elv ('red river') and northward along its banks. The Arctic Research Station offers accommodation only to invited researchers and students of Copenhagen University.

Places to Eat

Meals are available at the *Hotel Disko* and the *Godhavn Grill-baren*. There's also a *bakery*, a *snack bar*, a small *KNI supermarket* and of course, the *brædtet* at the harbour. Trekkers may want to bring supplies from the mainland.

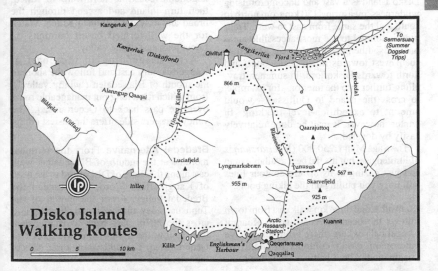

Disko Island Walking Routes

Getting There & Away

Air In summer, Grønlandsfly flies between Ilulissat and Qeqertarsuaq (Dkr680) at least four times weekly. A couple of discounted Green Seats (Dkr450) are available on each flight. You can also fly to Aasiaat for the same fare.

Ferry One of the big ferries serves Qeqertarsuaq weekly, offering direct connections to Ilulissat (Dkr235) and Qasigiannguit (Dkr245). More convenient is the *Tugdlik*, which sails in three times weekly from Ilulissat, Aasiaat (Dkr180) and Qasigiannguit.

AROUND DISKO ISLAND
Qullissat

From the 1930s, a profitable coal mine operated at Qullissat on the north-east coast of Disko Island, but it shut down in 1969 and the village – once home to 1500 people – was abandoned in 1972. It's now used as a hunting camp and summer retreat, and is accessible weekly from Ilulissat on the ferry *Tugdlik* (Dkr250).

Hiking

Disko Island is a vast and uncompromising wilderness, measuring 120 km from north to south and the same from east to west. Trekking is limited to the most accessible areas on the southern peninsula near Qeqertarsuaq: west towards Itilleq (Laksebugt) and north towards Diskofjord. In summer, travelling further into the interior – for example, to cross the island to Qullissat – would amount to expedition-level trekking. In winter, however, it may be done relatively easily by dogsled.

The Saga Map 1:250,000 *Qeqertarsuaq* is of limited use, but it's the best available map and just gazing at its bizarre contour lines will have you pulling on the hiking boots.

Kuannit A fine three km walk east from town follows the beautiful coastline to Kuannit ('angelica') where there's an impressive outcrop of basalt columns to spark the imagination. About halfway along the route is the formation known as Elephant Rock – looking west, you can see the ears, head and trunk of an elephant on the shore. From Kuannit, it's impossible to continue further east because the cliffs drop right into the sea. Nor can you travel further east by walking around Skarvefjeld, as the route is blocked by a gaping ravine that cannot be crossed on foot.

Skarvefjeld From Qeqertarsuaq, it's a straightforward climb to the summit of Skarvefjeld ('cormorant peak') which is visible from Blæsedalen. Follow the south-western ridge up the mountain to the truncated summit. It's important to go in clear weather, as parts of the route are frequently obscured by fog.

Itilleq & Kangerluk Loop This is another good walk, which requires five days or more. The coastline west of Qeqertarsuaq is relatively easy walking but at times you'll have to divert up the slope and away from the shore. From the pleasant beach at Killit (Fortune Bay), which was once the site of a Dutch whaling station, follow the steep but negotiable coastline northward to Itilleq, then turn inland and ascend through the broad and easy pass, Itinneq Killeq. Watch for the well-formed basalt columns on Luciafjeld, east of the valley.

After descending to the coast at Kangerluk, turn east and follow the shore to the mouth of Blæsedalen ('windy valley'), from which it's a long but manageable route over the pass back to Qeqertarsuaq. The valley's eastern side offers the easiest going.

Brededal Alternative From the terminal moraine at the mouth of Blæsedalen, walk east along the shore of Diskofjord to the head of Kangikerllak Fjord, then ascend the Brededal valley. From the mouth of the Tunusua valley, turn west and climb up it to cross the 567m pass back to Blæsedalen, then follow the valley southward back to Qeqertarsuaq. This adds about three days to the total hike.

North-West Greenland

Currently, North-West Greenland is finding its way onto more and more tourist itineraries. Uummannaq is now a standard cruise and tour group destination; lots of independent travellers ride the boat to Upernavik, Greenland's northernmost ferry terminal; and the increasing access to the Avanersuaq (Thule) district is helping to satisfy longstanding outside interest in the region.

However, it's worth noting that the traditional Arctic cultures described by Knud Rasmussen and other polar explorers and researchers are changing fast. Only 40 years ago, this society still lived and hunted as it had for thousands of years, but in the intervening period, the Danes introduced formal education, Western health care, the Danish language, new social values and economic dissatisfaction. The US base at Pituffik brought demands for concession to the typically culturally oblivious US military. Although the traditional hunting culture has by no means disappeared, particularly in the Avanersuaq and Upernavik districts, it has now been extended to include junk food, alcohol, videos, snowmobiles, cellular phones, speedboats and prefab housing.

UUMMANNAQ

If the far south is Greenland's 'banana coast', Uummannaq (population 1300) with its 1175m red gneiss peak, Uummannaq Mountain, is its Rio de Janeiro. Uummannaq, meaning 'heart-shaped' (more like a seal heart than a Valentine greeting), sits at 70° north latitude, the same as North Cape, Norway, and Prudhoe Bay, Alaska, yet nearly half of Greenland is still north of it. It's also known as Greenland's sunniest spot, and the dry climate does wonders keeping the summer mosquitoes at bay.

The way Uummannaq rambles over striated gneiss hills, anchored to the rocks with pipes and cables, one wonders whether a big wind might not send the town tumbling into the sea. In fact, it's one of only a couple of

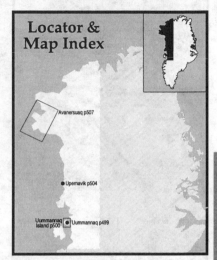

Greenlandic towns where everyone lives in single family dwellings; there's too little level space and too much solid rock to anchor those monstrous blocks of flats.

History

This district has been a seasonally inhabited hunting ground for several millennia, and Dutch whalers found joy there in the 17th century. The first permanent settlement, however, was founded on the Nuussuaq peninsula in 1758 and shifted to the present site of Uummannaq in 1763. It developed over the years into a sealing district and service centre for the mines around outlying Maarmorilik and Qaarsut.

In the 1960s, a shrimp-processing plant was built at Uummannaq and the town gradually transformed from a hunting to a halibut fishing district.

Information

The Uummannaq Tourist Service (☎ 48518;

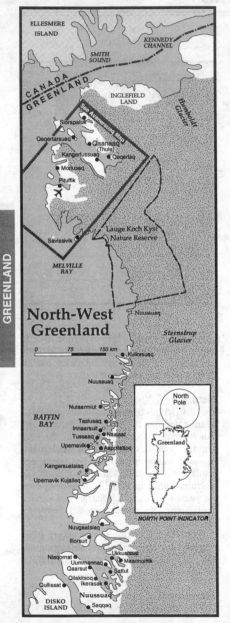

North-West Greenland

fax 48262), PO Box 202, DK-3961, at the Hotel Uummannaq, monopolises the local tourist scene. However, it's still a good source of tourist information and is open from 9 am to 5 pm on weekdays.

The Kommunia office is also friendly, and may be able to help you informally organise dogsled trips with local hunters.

The banks, KNI ticket office and the post and telephone offices share the same building 100m from the harbour. They're all open Monday to Friday from 9 am to 3 pm. For books, try the museum shop. Postcards, shoes, clothing and sports equipment are available at the KNI shop. You'll find an especially good selection of postcards at the Rema shop up the hill.

Church & Sod Huts

The unique Uummannaq church, consecrated in 1935, was constructed of granite boulders chipped from the nearby hillside. Climb up to the bell tower for a nice harbour view.

The three traditional sod huts on the church lawn are preserved as national historical buildings. The largest was constructed in 1925 and once housed two families. Another, also built in 1925, was inhabited until 1982. The third dates from 1949, when it served as a potato storage shed.

Uummannaq Museum

The Uummannaq Museum (☎ 48104) is one of Greenland's better town museums. The northern end of the main building was constructed in 1880 as a home for the Royal Greenland Trade Department clerk. It was enlarged nine years later and converted into a hospital, with further additions in 1921. In 1988, it became the town museum. The nearby yellow houses were built in 1907, one as the vicarage and the other as the doctor's residence. (Note that the doctor's home is larger than the old hospital!)

An entire room is devoted to the ill-fated 1930 inland ice expedition of German scientist Alfred Wegener. There's also background information on the Maarmorilik mine, Greenlandic archaeology and history,

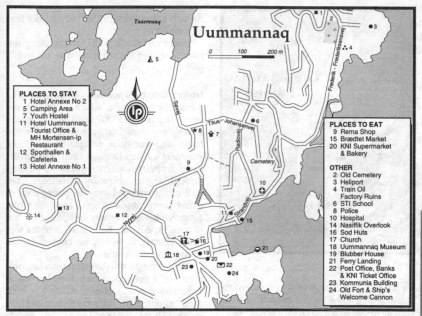

PLACES TO STAY
1 Hotel Annexe No 2
5 Camping Area
7 Youth Hostel
11 Hotel Uummannaq,
  Tourist Office &
  MH Mortensen-ip
  Restaurant
12 Sporthallen &
  Cafeteria
13 Hotel Annexe No 1

PLACES TO EAT
9 Rema Shop
15 Brædtet Market
20 KNI Supermarket
  & Bakery

OTHER
2 Old Cemetery
3 Heliport
4 Train Oil
  Factory Ruins
6 STI School
8 Police
10 Hospital
14 Nasiffik Overlook
16 Sod Huts
17 Church
18 Uummannaq Museum
19 Blubber House
21 Ferry Landing
22 Post Office, Banks
  & KNI Ticket Office
23 Kommunia Building
24 Old Fort & Ship's
  Welcome Cannon

GREENLAND

the Qilaqitsoq mummies, the whaling era, the history of the museum itself and a library of Arctic-interest books.

It's open 10 am to 3 pm Monday to Friday and on Sunday from 11 am to 3 pm. At other times, phone to arrange a visit.

Blubber House

The yellow-washed boulder house opposite the sod huts was built in 1860 and served as a whale-oil warehouse. The blubber wasn't actually boiled down there, as the smell would have driven everyone out of town.

Train Oil Factory Ruins

Near the heliport are the ruins of the old train oil factory, where whale blubber was boiled down into lamp oil. The smell required that it be located well away from the centre. Nearby are the town's first petrol tanks, which were used during WWII.

Around Uummannaq Island

Uummannaq sits on a small, precipitous island, with limited walking opportunities. You can, however, hike into the hills above the reservoir and up to the shoulder of Uummannaq Mountain; with extreme caution, some people make it as far as the uppermost black stripe, but it's wise to aim

Ship's Welcome

It's an Uummannaq tradition to heartily welcome the first ship to sail into the harbour each spring. Lookouts are posted on Nasiffik hill, west of town, and when they call out 'Umiarssuaq!' ('Ship!'), the entire village gathers on the hill to await the arrival. From the fort hill, south of the harbour, three old cannons are fired in welcome not only to the ship but also to the springtime. The cannons are fired again for the departure of the season's last ship, but with considerably less fanfare. ∎

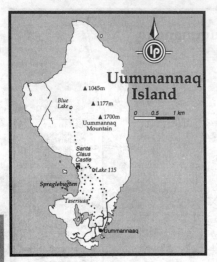

for a lesser goal. The geology on this island is fascinating and it's a safe bet you've never seen anything like it anywhere else.

Santa Claus' Castle It's apparent that Santa Claus is wealthy enough to maintain homes all around the Arctic, but there seems to be some dispute about his official residence (for tax purposes, perhaps?). The Finns have him living in Rovaniemi, Icelanders say he's resident in Hveragerði and Vopnafjörður, and the Swedes have him somewhere around Kiruna. Even the Turks have a claim on him, maintaining that St Nicholas was a native of their fair land. Well, I've always been told he was a fellow Alaskan, from the village of North Pole near Fairbanks. It comes as no surprise then that Danes and Greenlanders cite his official address as Spraglebugten, DK-3961 Uummannaq.

In fact, his 'royal castle' is a traditional sod hut which was built near the shore at Spraglebugten for a Danish children's TV programme, *The Christmas Calendar*; Santa liked the place so much that he took over the payments. From town, it's a leisurely two-hour return walk. Be aware, however, that Santa is a very busy guy, so you may not find anyone home.

Under an hour's walk further along the coast is a cave known locally as 'the troll's grotto'.

Uummannaq Mountain Wonderful Uummannaq Mountain, which is one of the most unusual and colourful sights in the Arctic, provides both a backdrop for the town and constant entertainment. Like Australia's Ayers Rock, it changes dramatically from moment to moment, passing through any combination of colours from dull cloud-wrapped grey to pastel rose to carrot orange, back to sepia and pale violet to grey. It may appear unclimbable, but several expeditions have made it to the top. Most visitors, however, are content to just tramp around the base.

The mountain and the entire island is composed of a geological formation known as basement gneiss – granite which has been metamorphosed by intense pressure and heat into wild black, white and rose swirls, whorls and stripes.

From Santa's Castle, it's a leisurely three or four-hour walk to the northern tip of the island, and mostly uphill. At one moment, I came eye-to-eye with an Arctic hare, who only noticed me when I was about three metres away. Lucky for the poor animal that I wasn't a hunter! On the lower shoulder of Uummannaq Mountain are several small but deep mountain lakes which vary in colour from emerald to azure. The views of the mountain and the snow caps of the Nuussuaq peninsula are magnificent all the way.

Frank Smits, Netherlands

Dogsledding
Uummannaq is among the best places for traditional dogsled trips with local seal hunters, who guide tourists during the slack hunting period from March to May. The seas, which are permanently-frozen in winter, provide a level sledding surface between the far-flung villages of the district. These villages hire out their community halls to sledding parties for around Dkr500 per night and the driver's fee normally works out to about Dkr400 to Dkr500 per person per day.

In the sledding season, dogsled races are held around the district and provide a festive atmosphere. If you prefer something more structured, see Organised Tours below.

Organised Tours

Popular Uummannaq Tourist Service trips include nine-hour boat tours to the prolific Store Qarajaq glacier (Dkr1160), which advances 7½ km per year; popular excursions to the Eskimo ruins and mummy cave at Qilaqitsoq (Dkr320); whale-watching by boat around Qaarsut (Dkr535), where you can also find handmade clothing and Inuit art; midnight sun whale-watching cruises (Dkr310); three-hour guided hikes to Santa's Castle (Dkr95); and a full-day tour to Qilaqitsoq, the abandoned settlement of Uummannatsiaq and the fishing and hunting village of Ikerasak (Dkr965). Any of these tours require a minimum of eight people.

The hotel also arranges dogsledding tours: seven-hour ice-fishing trips by dogsled (Dkr1200); seven-hour tours to district villages (Dkr1200); or a three-hour tour around the island (Dkr700).

Places to Stay

Uummannaq finally has a *Youth Hostel*, where basic accommodation with cooking facilities costs Dkr175. The *Sporthallen* offers youth hostel-style accommodation with a kitchen, but charges Dkr525 per person. Either place must be booked through the Hotel Uummannaq.

The *Hotel Uummannaq* (☎ 48518; fax 48262), which prides itself on being Greenland's most northerly tourist-class hotel, has a superb position overlooking the harbour. Single/double rooms in the main building cost Dkr800/1010 and, in one of the two annexes, Dkr575/725, all including breakfast. All rooms have private bath, colour TV, radio and telephone, and group discounts are available. For full board, add Dkr250.

Camping can be problematic, mainly because the island is made of solid rock. There are a few level, grassy spots around the reservoir and there are also acceptable sites around the Santa Claus' Castle at Spraglebugten, where the valley floor is level and grassy, and a small mountain stream flows through.

Places to Eat

For a great meal and an iceberg-studded view, go to the *MH Mortensen-ip Restaurant* at the Hotel Uummannaq, which frequently puts on Greenland buffets. Otherwise, try the *grill-baren* at the harbour or the *Sporthallen* cafeteria.

The *brædtet* is opposite the ferry landing, near the hotel. Just inland from the harbour area is the *KNI supermarket*, which is open 9 am to 5.30 pm weekdays and on Saturday mornings, and the same building also houses an exceptional bakery. The *Rema shop* also sells groceries.

Getting There & Away

Air Grønlandsfly (☎ 48246) has four to five weekly helicopter departures between Ilulissat and Uummannaq (Dkr1540), and two or three weekly flights to and from Upernavik (Dkr2260).

Ferry The big ferries serve Uummannaq at

A Meeting of Old & New

The ferry trip between Ilulissat and Uummannaq may well be the most geologically fascinating in Greenland, thanks to the region's bizarre make-up. Here the new basalt formations of Disko Island and the amazing Nuussuaq Peninsula collide with the multi-billion-year-old rocks of the Greenlandic mainland, and nowhere else is the contrast more pronounced.

Disko Island and the Nuussuaq Peninsula are composed of striated and eroded basalt layers which lie perfectly horizontally, like a well-executed *millefeuilles* topped with icecap frosting! On the approach to Uummannaq, however, look to the east and you'll see the vertical and more weather-resistant metamorphosed rock of the ancient mainland, which towers over the sea in sheer, colourful and contorted cliffs. ■

GREENLAND

Qilaqitsoq mummy

least weekly in each direction (in August, twice weekly) on their runs between Ilulissat (Dkr590) and Upernavik (Dkr605). En route between Ilulissat and Uummannaq, watch for the abandoned village of Qullissat on Disko Island and the enormous Arctic Energy oil-drilling rig on the north-western shore of the Nuussuaq peninsula.

In summer, the district KNI boats *Hvalfisken* or *Hvidfisken* connect Uummannaq with its outlying settlements at least once weekly: Ukkusissat (Dkr135), Saattut (Dkr95), Illorsuit (Dkr180), Ikerasak (Dkr110) and Qaarsut (Dkr85).

Uummannaq is also the destination of most of Greenland Tourism's summer *Disko*

cruises. For details, see under Boat in the Greenland Getting Around chapter.

Getting Around
You can arrange charter boat excursions to any of the district's seven villages, Kuusuup Nuua (for the trek to Saqqaq) and other sites of interest (Dkr450 to Dkr1000 per person, or Dkr875 per hour for the boat).

AROUND UUMMANNAQ
Qilaqitsoq
Qilaqitsoq ('where the sky is low') was cat-apulted to international fame in 1977 when the National Museum in Nuuk – and through it, the archaeological world – learned of the 1972 discovery of eight mummies in a cave there. *National Geographic* did a cover story on the find and suddenly, people everywhere were captivated by the haunting face of the six-month-old boy who had lived and died in 15th century Greenland.

The mummies were originally discovered by ptarmigan hunters Hans and Jokum Grønvold from Uummannaq, who photographed the site and reported their find to government authorities. However, nothing more was said about the discovery until 1977, when Claus Andreasen took over the director's post at the National Museum.

In addition to the well-known six-month-old baby, there was a four-year-old boy, apparently with Down's Syndrome, and one of the six adults (all women) suffered from a debilitating disease. According to Greenlandic custom, the bodies were dressed in heavy clothing suitable for the long, cold journey to the land of the dead. There was no evidence of violence, famine, accident or epidemic which may have caused their deaths. Food poisoning is postulated, as are drowning and hypothermia. It is most probable, however, that they were considered burdens on the society of the day and were sent off to die of exposure.

Several of the mummies are displayed in the National Museum in Nuuk, and you can read more about the discovery and subsequent research in the February 1985 issue of *National Geographic*. The museum in Nuuk also sells the booklet *Qilakitsoq – the Mummy Cave*, available in English, Danish or Greenlandic for Dkr10.

The Hotel Uummannaq organises three-hour boat tours to Qilaqitsoq and the nearby Qilaqitsoq Eskimo ruins. See Organised Tours in the Uummannaq section.

Qaarsut

Qaarsut ('naked mountain'), with a population of 200, sits in a broad, level valley on the Nuussuaq peninsula, 21 km west of Uummannaq. It subsists on seal hunting, fishing and seal-leather working at the Neriunaq Cooperative, and will be the site of Uummannaq's new airport.

Until 1924, the first coal mine in Greenland operated in Qaarsut and supplied the district with inexpensive fuel. This mine was the site of the country's first labour strike, which forced the foremen and the village priest to work as miners!

The Hotel Uummannaq runs charter trips for visits to Qaarsut's sandy beach and for climbing or hiking around the distinct cone-shaped peak, 1900m Qilertinnguit. The KNI boats *Hvalfisken* or *Hvidfisken* call at least in weekly (Dkr85).

Ikerasak

Ikerasak ('the sound') occupies an island of the same name, 40 km south-east of Uummannaq. It has several traditional peat dwellings still in use and at the nearby abandoned village of Uummannnatsiaq is a school camp for Uummannaq district students. It's an easy day walk from Ikerasak. The Hotel Uummannaq arranges transfers and day tours to the island, or you can go with the KNI boat (Dkr110).

Maarmorilik

The former mining village of Maarmorilik (the 'place of marble'), 30 km north of Uummannaq, was once an enormous quarry which supplied marble to Europe. It was first operated by the Danish and Canadian venture Greenex and later by the Swedish firm Boliden which employed 300 workers. The 1000m mountain known as 'the black angel' (owing to a dark ore deposit on one rock wall) also yielded lead, zinc and silver ore. This ore was transported from the rock face at 600m elevation to the processing area on a 1½ km suspension cable, then processed on site and exported to Europe in powder form.

Eight million tonnes of ore were extracted from the time mining began in 1972 until the early 1990s, when decreasing production made it unprofitable. When activities ceased, the mine closed and the buildings were either removed or burned.

Maarmorilik has long been – and still is – closed to outsiders; in fact, when it was operating, the miners couldn't even bring their families for visits. That may change in the future but, currently, there's little to see.

UPERNAVIK

Upernavik ('the spring place') is the most northerly ferry terminal in Greenland, and many travellers sail up just for curiosity value. A 13th-century rune stone found on the island, which bears record of a visit by three Norse, provides evidence that Norse hunters ventured at least this far north.

Here, you're nearly 800 km north of the Arctic Circle at a latitude of 72° 50' north, and the average summer temperature is 5°C.

Upernavik coat of arms

GREENLAND

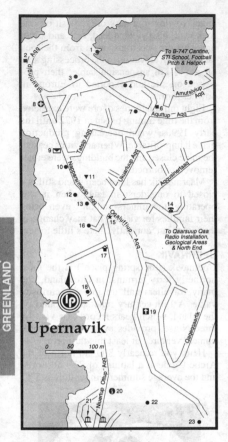

PLACES TO STAY
2 Kuunut Municipal Hostel & Amerivik Skin Workshop
6 Municipal Hostel B-540
17 Kolligiet Hostel

PLACES TO EAT
1 Brædtet Market
3 KNI Supermarket & Bakery
11 Pølsebaren
12 Kiosk Olearaq
13 Nellie's Kiosk
16 Kiosk Kaarup

OTHER
4 1929 Jorgensen Warehouse
5 KNI Ticket Office
7 Historic 1936 KNI Office
8 Hospital
9 Post Office & Grønlandsbanken Bank
10 Kommunia Building
14 Telephone Office
15 Police
18 1912 Blubber House
19 New Church
20 Tourist & Museum Office
21 Old Town Museum
22 Old Cemetery (Grave of Navarana)
23 Cemetery

With a population 1100, or 2600 in the district, the economy is based on fishing, and several Upernavik district settlements have fish-processing plants, but many people still rely on sealing and polar bear hunting.

Not only is Upernavik village a fascinating introduction to Greenland's more traditional side, the fabulous geology of Upernavik Island also merits exploration.

Information
The Upernavik Tourist Service (☎ & fax 51700), at the museum, is headed by the friendly tourist officer and museum curator, Ms Pauline Knudsen. The banks, and the KNI, post and telephone offices are open from 10 am to 3 pm Monday to Friday.

Old Town Museum
Upernavik's Old Town Museum, which is Greenland's oldest, is a real surprise, and the new visitors' book, which was started in 1980, is still only half full. The previous one, which remains on display, lasted over 60 years and contains inscriptions from numerous Arctic explorers and scientists.

The museum is currently being renovated and, as a result, will probably lose its formerly cosy and disorganised character, but the exhibits remain worthwhile. Most interesting is the original qajaq ensemble complete with harpoon, throwing stick, bird skewer, knife, seal-stomach float (to prevent seals diving after being hit or sinking after being killed) and line made of leather thong. Other assorted historical paraphernalia includes a collection of Greenlandic money which was in use until the Danish notes became the standard currency in the 1950s. Some specimens date back to 1911.

There are currently plans to incorporate the entire historical district into the museum. The former bakery and cooperage is being developed into a workshop and the old general shop will contain exhibits on traditional hunting and fishing methods.

From 1 June to 31 August, it's open daily from 9 am to 5 pm; the rest of the year, it's open from 2 to 5 pm daily.

Amerivik

At Amerivik, the skin house, near the harbour, you can watch local women making skin clothing and purchase handmade pillows, skin bags and boots.

Church

The new church, which dates from 1926, was renovated in 1990. Take a look at the crucifix, which was taken from the old (museum) church, and the pulpit and kneeling altar, which are decorated with pearl and embroidered sealskin. The altarpiece of the *Madonna and Child* was done by Danish artist Mathias Fersløv Dalager (1770-1842).

Cemetery

Due to the permanently frozen ground, the graves in Upernavik's cemetery are raised and covered with rock and concrete, and the plastic flowers that cover them provide just about the only splash of colour in this rather drab, untidy town. Downhill from the main cemetery, near the museum church, is the grave of Navarana Freuchen, the wife of Peter Freuchen; she died on the fifth Thule expedition with polar explorer Knud Rasmussen.

Around Upernavik Island

Once you've seen the cemetery and the museum, it's worth exploring Upernavik island. Sadly, its small size means that the new airport, which should be operating by 2000, will dramatically alter its intriguing landscapes.

South of Upernavik is sheltered **Eqalugaarsuit** ('sea trout bay'), where dwarf willows can grow even in the high Arctic. It's also pleasant to climb to the island's highest point, 150m **Inuusuussuaq** ('the summit of life') for a view over the town to the west and 130m Umiasuussuk to the east.

The three-hour return walk to the island's northern tip, **Naajarsuit**, takes you through magical ancient landscapes. From the cemetery, head north-east along the broad ridge and past the radio tower (the hundreds of guy wires are difficult to see). After 30 minutes, you'll reach a gash-like valley, which slices across the island and contains the Qataarmiut Eskimo ruins and a couple of nice lakes. The acoustics in this valley permit you to hear a whisper from several hundred metres away, and its steep northern slopes reveal some brilliantly coloured mineral deposits, including veins of natural graphite and streaks of red, violet, orange, green and yellow rock. At the northern tip of the island are twisting bands of folded granite, feldspar and gneiss inlaid with garnets.

Places to Stay

All accommodation in Upernavik must be booked through the Kommunia office. From 1 to 31 July, you can stay at the *Kolligiet*, opposite the KNI shop. The clean and spacious rooms cost just Dkr150 per person, but the hostel lacks cooking facilities. Rooms at the *STI School* (☎ 51099; fax 51478) are available in summer for Dkr350 per person, including use of cooking facilities and the TV lounge.

There are also two small hostels, *Kunuut* and *B-540* (the 'Blue Hostel'), but they're almost always full of seasonal workers. If there is space, they charge Dkr375 to Dkr410 for made-up beds, and Dkr150 for sleeping-bag accommodation. The latter has cooking facilities. The tourist office can arrange accommodation in *private homes* for around Dkr200 per person, but you must book in advance.

The hills and valleys north of town offer lots of scenic *campsites*, but many level areas can be quite soggy.

GREENLAND

Places to Eat

The only meal choices are the basic *Pølsebaren*, which does the usual hot dogs, and the *B-747 Cantíne*, which serves set lunches and dinners comprised of a greasy meat dish, boiled potatoes and once-frozen vegetables for Dkr40.

If those dubious options fail to appeal, you'll have to rely on the *KNI supermarket* and *bakery*, which are open Monday to Thursday, 10 am to 5.30 pm, on Friday from 10 am to 6 pm, and Saturdays from 9.30 am to 1 pm. The *brædtet* is near the harbour, and there are several smaller kiosks – *Olearaq*, *Kaarup* and *Nellie's* – which stay open after hours and on weekends.

Getting There & Away

The ticket office for KNI boats and Grønlandsfly flights is now at the harbour.

Air There are three weekly helicopter flights between Ilulissat (Dkr3800) and Upernavik, via Uummannaq (Dkr2260). The cost of chartering a helicopter to Pituffik or Qaanaaq has now dropped to around Dkr11,000 per hour.

Ferry Upernavik is the northernmost terminus on the West Greenland ferry lines. Ferries from Ilulissat (Dkr715) and Uummannaq (Dkr605) stay in port for just an hour, but on several August runs, the schedules allow you to disembark in Upernavik and catch another ferry south 24 hours later.

To visit the beautiful northern reaches of Upernavik district – for example, the marvellous Apparsuit bird colonies or the rock pinnacle Kullorsuaq (the 'devil's thumb'), you can charter a boat or connect with the KNI supply boats *Angaju Ittuk* and *Hvalen*, which take 12 passengers. They run weekly between Upernavik and Upernavik Kujalleq (Dkr190), Kangersuatsiaaq (Dkr135), Aappilattoq (Dkr90), Innaarsuit (Dkr120), Tasiusaq (Dkr180), Nuussuaq (Dkr300) and Kullorsuaq (Dkr435).

Getting Around

With lots of time, you can charter a boat up through icy Melville Bay to Savissivik and Qaanaaq. A recommended charter operation is run by Hans Weyhe and Marlene Myrup (☎ & fax 51500), Upernavik.

Avanersuaq (Thule District)

Named after the 4th-century geographer Pytheas' land of Ultima Thule (the 'furthest north'), the Avanersuaq ('the great north') or Thule district is an enigma. It was the first part of Greenland to be colonised by Eskimo people from the west, and modern Thule Inuit refer to themselves not as just Inuit, but Inukuit, the 'great people'.

Avanersuaq, which is among the northernmost inhabited places on earth, encompasses 297,000 sq km and has a population of just 850. It's also the last bastion of the US military in Greenland. Artistic talent runs especially high and it's an excellent place to look for traditional Inuit art.

Visits to Avanersuaq are logistically and

Avanersuaq coat of arms

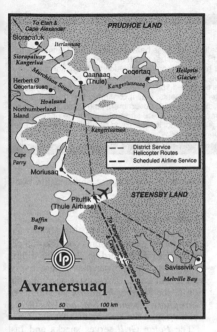

Avanersuaq

District Service
Helicopter Routes
Scheduled Airline Service

0   50   100 km

financially challenging, and ongoing changes mean that visitors will no longer find the utopia described by Knud Rasmussen and other Arctic explorers and anthropologists, so think carefully before sorting out a trip here. For travellers who only want to attain a new 'furthest north', parts of Svalbard are actually further north and are cheaper and easier to visit!

Note that foreigners currently may not enter the Avanersuaq district between 15 September and 15 April. However, as dog-sledding and hunting tourism increase in popularity, this may change.

PITUFFIK (THULE AIRBASE)

The US military airport at Pituffik serves as a transportation link to the communities of the Avanersuaq district, but you'd be hard-pressed to find a less inspiring place. All visitors and transit passengers visiting Thule Airbase require a visitors' permit issued by

the US Air Attaché, the Danish Ministry of Foreign Affairs or Danish embassies. For details, see Visas in the Greenland Facts for the Visitor chapter.

Places to Stay

Accommodation is available only to holders of visitors' permits, and anyone classed as a tourist is confined to the *Transit Guesthouse*, and may not walk around outside. Business visitors and others are housed at the *Base Hotel/Hostel* and are allowed a bit more freedom of movement.

Getting There & Away

On Tuesday from 15 June to 15 August, SAS flies between Copenhagen, Kangerlussuaq and Pituffik. A maximum of 14 seats per flight may be occupied by tourists.

QAANAAQ (THULE)

Qaanaaq, the world's most northerly palindrome, was moved 200 km north to its

---

The Shortest Distance Between Two Points?

So you think the Avanersuaq district is remote? So do its inhabitants. A woman from Savisivvik, the southernmost village of Avanersuaq district, explained that a visit to relatives in Kullorsuaq, the northernmost village of Upernavik district – a total distance of about 200 km – actually amounts to a rather serious journey. This is especially relevant, because there have been lots of marriages between these two communities. For the fewest headaches, people can choose between a hazardous eight-hour private boat charter through ice-choked seas or an equally treacherous four-day winter dogsled trip over the sea ice.

To make the trip on public transport – and people do take this route – involves a helicopter flight to Pituffik, a plane from Pituffik to Kangerlussuaq, another plane to Ilulissat, a two-day ferry trip to Upernavik and another day on the KNI boat to Kullorsuaq. Since none of these transport services connect, the trip can take well over a week. What's more, the distance covered is equal to a flight to New York and the cost involved would probably have flown them around the world twice! ■

GREENLAND

Plutonium Peril in Pituffik

The Thule Airbase is a bone of contention in international relations between Greenland, Denmark and the USA. The greatest controversy involves the US B-52 bomber which crashed near Thule in 1968 and was later revealed to have been carrying four hydrogen bombs with nuclear detonation devices.

Of the 1000 individuals who worked on the two-month clean-up operation, 118 have since died, half of them from cancer. In 1988, health problems prompted 166 workers to file a joint complaint, but only in 1995, with the US declassification of related documents, was it confirmed that the plane did indeed carry six kg of plutonium. Upon this revelation, the Danish government paid US$9000 tax-free compensation to each of the 1500 Danish and Greenlandic workers and residents of the base area.

In 1996, the US Air Force awarded a US$268 million contract to Greenland Contractors of Denmark to maintain the Thule Air Base for the following five years. ■

present location in 1953 after being displaced by the US airbase at Pituffik. Its population stands at around 400.

Information

Tourist information is available from the Avanersuup Kommunia (☎ 50077; fax 50073), PO Box 95, DK-3971 Qaanaaq. It's open weekdays from 9 am to 3 pm. There are no banks, but you can change money at the KNI office from 10 am to 3 pm weekdays.

Museum

Qaanaaq's town museum is dedicated to Knud Rasmussen, who spent much of his career researching and exploring in the district. Displays include items relating to his work and archaeological finds from around the district. The attached handicraft centre sells locally-produced items.

Organised Tours

Several spring dogsled trips with local hunters may be arranged through Greenland Travel in Copenhagen – see Organised Tours in the Getting There & Away chapter – and provide an intimate glimpse into traditional Greenlandic life. Eight-day trips between Qaanaaq and Siorapaluk (Dkr8995) include meals, seal and walrus-hunting, and accommodation in cabins and igloos. However, the most challenging possibility is an incredible 15-day hunting trip (Dkr18,950) over the sea ice to several Avanersuaq district villages.

For warmth on these trips, the Kommunia office hires out traditional fur-lined anoraks, polar bear-skin trousers, and sealskin boots for Dkr150 per day.

Places to Stay & Eat

Hotel Qaanaaq (☎ 50234; fax 50064) has space for 10 guests. Rooms cost Dkr425 per person and full board in the hotel dining room costs Dkr225 per day. Alternatively, you'll find basic, inexpensive accommodation at the *Telegraph Station* (☎ 50055) or *Ionosphere Research Station* (☎ 50027); book through the Kommunia offices.

The *Polar Grill* serves snacks and fast food and the *KNI supermarket* is stocked whenever the flight comes in. Note that visitors may not bring alcohol into the Avanersuaq district.

Things to Buy

The Ultima Thule shop (☎ 50077; fax 50073) markets genuine and original artwork and crafts typical of the Avanersuaq district.

Getting There & Away

Air From 1 April to 29 September, Grønlandsfly has weekly flights on Wednesday from Kangerlussuaq (Dkr3080), via Pituffik. They use fixed-wing aircraft as far as Pituffik, where they change to helicopters to complete the journey. Other Avanersuaq district villages are also accessible by helicopter.

Ferry Although KNI is unlikely to ever start a regular ferry service to Avanersuaq, in answer to a growing market demand, the *M/S*

Disko now does one annual run from Kangerlussuaq and Ilulissat to Qaanaaq, normally in the first week of September, when ice conditions are most favourable. The return trip is organised by Greenland Tourism and starts at Dkr10,300/13,200 from Ilulissat/Kangerlussuaq, including full board. For details, see Boat in the Greenland Getting Around chapter.

You can also charter boats from Upernavik to Qaanaaq; see Getting There & Away under Upernavik. From Qaanaaq, you can charter private boats in the summer or dog-sleds in the spring to the other Avanersuaq district villages of Savissivik, Siorapaluk, Qeqertaq and Moriusaq.

SIORAPALUK

Siorapaluk, the third most northerly civilian settlement in the world, after Longyearbyen and Ny Ålesund in Svalbard (Alert on Canada's Ellesmere Island is a military post), has neither electricity nor running water. In winter, temperatures reach -50°C and lower, and water is made by melting ice.

The locals survive by hunting seals, narwhals, walrus, birds and polar bears and fishing for halibut. The area is known for its agate deposits.

You can reach Siorapaluk from Qaanaaq by private boat or helicopter charter. Accommodation is in a cabin which may be booked through the Kommunia in Qaanaaq.

GREENLAND

East Greenland

Culturally and linguistically, the isolated eastern coast of Greenland, known to Greenlanders as Tunu or Tunua (the 'back side'), differs greatly from West Greenland. Noticeably more laid-back than the more populous west coast, it remains dependent on subsistence hunting and fishing, and families may spend over half the year at remote hunting camps. Although tourism is big business around Tasiilaq (Ammassalik), the people seem well equipped to handle it, and it will be a while before radical changes come to this beautiful area.

History
It's believed that the Independence I culture migrated to East Greenland via Peary Land in the extreme north, and the Saqqaq culture came from the west coast. They met somewhere around the present site of Ittoqqoortoormiit, but their settlement there lasted only briefly. In the 15th and 16th centuries, a second wave migrated from the Thule area to several sites on the coast, but by 1800, all but Ammassalik had been abandoned.

The first European settler to East Greenland was Gunnbjörn, the lost sailor from Iceland, who washed up in 875 and named the offshore islets he'd found Gunnbjörn's Skerries before moving on posthaste. After the settlement of the Norse Østerbygd, however, Europeans most likely sailed up the east coast on hunting or exploratory expeditions.

Until the late 19th century, historians mistakenly assumed that the Østerbygd was on the east coast, but several hundred years of searching proved fruitless. In 1884, when the Danish Umiaq expedition, led by Gustav Holm, returned empty-handed, it was decided the Østerbygd was actually Eiríkur Rauðe's settlement on the west coast. The expedition wasn't entirely in vain, however, as it ran across a community of 416 Inuit near the site of present-day Tasiilaq, and took home some 500 artefacts (which have now

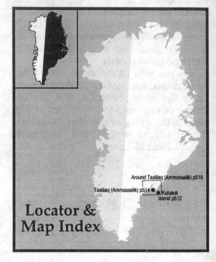

Locator &
Map Index

Around Tasiilaq (Ammassalik) p518

Tasiilaq (Ammassalik) p514 ● Kulusuk
Island p512

been returned to Greenland for display). Ten years later, the first Royal Greenland Trade Department trading post was established on Ammassalik Island.

KULUSUK (KAP DAN)
For many years, tourism in Greenland was well-contained, and over 30% of the country's annual tourist count visited only the small island village of Kulusuk. Although it's now being overshadowed by Ilulissat as the main tourist draw, Kulusuk remains a popular destination, mainly due to the international airport, which was built in 1958 to service the US DEW-line radar station. At one point, 2000 US military personnel – more than the entire east Greenlandic population – were stationed there.

The ease of access is increased by the fact that Kulusuk is just a 1½ hour flight from Reykjavík, and that several Icelandic airlines offer day tours. Most visitors spend only four hours in Greenland, and rarely does anyone

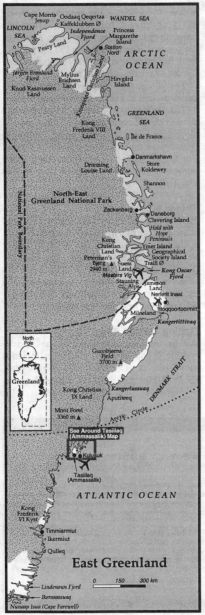

linger more than five days in the Ammassalik district. These short-term visits mean that Kulusuk hasn't been overwhelmingly affected by easy access from the outside world (it also means that the outside world hasn't been significantly affected by Kulusuk).

Fortunately, daytrippers get a splendid impression of Greenland, as Kulusuk is a textbook village – a tiny isolated settlement clinging to a rocky island planted in an icy bay and backed by dramatic peaks. The church, built in the 1920s, was a gift from the crew of a shipwreck, and the residents still survive largely by hunting seals and polar bears, and travel by dogsled in the winter. And of course they make carvings and beadwork for the tourists...

Cemetery

Don't miss the beautiful, haunting cemetery in Kulusuk, which is festooned with plastic flowers and set against a stark and icy Arctic backdrop. Taking photos is no problem, but on a day tour, it may involve some jostling!

Icelandair Qajaq & Dance Demonstration

Icelandair organises an informal qajaq demonstration and drum dance performance for day tours. It is lots of fun, but if the performers decide they'd rather spend a day hunting, the show may be pre-empted. They take place on the bluff behind the church and all visitors are welcome to attend.

Hiking

The most popular walk is the 40 minute stroll between the airport and Kulusuk village. You can either follow the road or strike out across the tundra, where you'll see some lovely miniature Arctic flowers, including glacier buttercups.

Alternatively, follow the gravel track over to the site of the old DEW-line radar station, which lay across the low pass from the airport. When the Americans left, they removed the installation lock, stock and barrel, and only a few scraps of unsightly rubbish remain. Another great walk will take

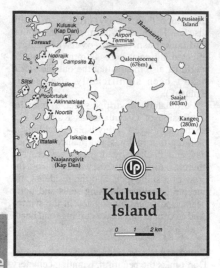

Kulusuk Island

0   1   2 km

you straight up the hill, south of the airport, to an eerie mountain lake.

Places to Stay & Eat

The tourist office in Tasiilaq can arrange hostel-style accommodation at the *Kulusuk Youth Club* for around Dkr200 per person. It's open from late June to early August.

The facetiously-named six-room *Hotel Hilton* (☎ 18488), at the airport, was originally intended for weather-stranded passengers, but it's open to anyone, whatever the weather. Rooms cost Dkr450 per person. With full board, they're Dkr700, or you can opt for à la carte cafeteria meals.

The village *KNI shop* has a range of groceries as well as souvenir books and curios.

The Tasiilaq tourist office has established a small *tented camp* about 1½ km from the airport, in hopes of encouraging visitors to spend more time exploring Kulusuk Island. For details and bookings, contact them at the address given under Tasiilaq, later in this chapter.

Things to Buy

East Greenlandic carvings, beadwork and other gifts are of consistently high quality. In Kulusuk, most curios are sold by street vendors when tour groups pass through. You'll normally pick up something for less than you would in Tasiilaq, and the lack of a set price structure results in delightfully informal and low-pressure sales practices.

Getting There & Away

Air In summer, Grønlandsfly has twice-weekly flights between Keflavík (Iceland) and Kulusuk (Dkr2260). On Wednesday, these flights continue to Kangerlussuaq

---

Daytripping in Kulusuk

In summer, tiny Kulusuk may see 50 or more foreign visitors daily, at least five days a week. While the village welcomes the income this provides, few daytrippers have had previous exposure to Greenland or its culture, and misunderstandings do occur.

Tourists' most common misconception is that they are dropping from the sky into a Third World country. This is simply not the case. Although some Greenlanders choose to follow traditional ways, Greenland is a developed, modern country with political and economic ties to modern Europe – as well as lots of the nasty trappings of Western society – and economically, Greenlanders are better off than many Europeans or North Americans.

Unfortunately, some well-meaning Santa Claus figures have taken to distributing token gifts of sweets, money, balloons and pens to Greenlandic children. Not only does this patronising behaviour upset the parents, it also demeans the children by inspiring the more enterprising ones to petition subsequent visitors for more of the same. Please resist the temptation to try to change what you see, however different it may be from your home environment, and open your mind to new experiences and ways of life. Isn't that why you're travelling in the first place? ■

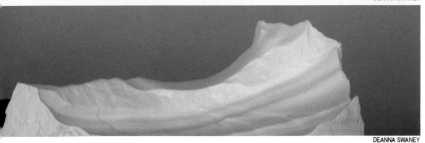

Top: Iceberg in the midnight sun, near Upernavik, North-West Greenland
Middle: Unusual iceberg, near Uummannaq, North-West Greenland
Bottom: Iceberg in Disko Bay, Greenland

Top: Harbour at Klaksvík, Borðoy, Faroe Islands
Middle: Sumba, Suðuroy, Faroe Islands
Bottom: Tórshavn, the eastern harbour, Faroe Islands

(Dkr2380), and on Saturday to Nuuk (Dkr2720). They return on the same days.

Most visitors to Kulusuk are on day tours from Reykjavík with Icelandair, Íslandsflug or Flugfélag Norðurlands. These tours, which are described in brochures as 'one-day jaunts to another planet', provide unsuspecting day-trippers with an overwhelming introduction to the tip of the Greenlandic iceberg; no-one ever comes away unaffected. (For airline contact details, see Air in the Iceland Getting Around chapter.)

The popular Icelandair tours (Dkr2270) run daily except Sunday and include return transport from Reykjavík, a packed lunch, a guided tour of Kulusuk village and the aforementioned dance and qajaq demonstrations. If you're lucky with the weather, the tour finale will exceed your wildest expectations.

To extend the tour to Tasiilaq, which may not be visited on a day tour, the price increases to Dkr3330/4260/4750 for two/three/five days, including helicopter transfers between Kulusuk and Tasiilaq, and accommodation and full board at the Hotel Angmagssalik. Because Icelandair cannot carry passengers in transit to West Greenland, Kulusuk passengers cannot officially leave the Ammassalik district, or remain in Greenland more than five days. When a plane arrives at Kulusuk, either Grønlandsfly or Alpha Air helicopter flights shuttle passengers between Kulusuk and Tasiilaq (Dkr400). Technically, the Alpha Air flights are available only to passengers on scheduled airlines (Grønlandsfly and Flugfélag Norðurlands), but at the time of writing, charter airline passengers (Icelandair and Íslandsflug) were also accepted. If you're not on an organised tour, shuttle transfers must be pre-booked.

Greenlandic authorities don't stamp passports; if you want a souvenir stamp, try the police station in Tasiilaq or Icelandair, who are happy to oblige.

Ferry Ice conditions permitting, the KNI cargo boat connects Tasiilaq to Kulusuk (Dkr90) at least weekly.

TASIILAQ (AMMASSALIK)

Tasiilaq, on Ammassalik Island, is the largest community on Greenland's east coast and the administrative centre for Ammassalik district (population 3000). As with Kulusuk, it enjoys stunning surroundings, and most of its 1600 people still hunt and fish for personal food supplies.

Its official name is Tasiilaq ('like a still lake'), but the more commonly-used name, Ammassalik, means 'capelins', which are small, delicious fish which inhabit these waters. The name change ostensibly came about after the death of a man whose name was Ammassalik, as it's considered disrespectful to speak the names of the dead. The fish were locally renamed *kersaqat* and the town was renamed after the lake-like bay (normally called Kong Oscars Havn) which is almost enclosed by the island.

Information
Tourist Office For tourist information, speak with Gerda Vilholm at the bookshop Neriussaq (☎ 18018), from 2 to 6 pm daily. The tourist office (☎ 18277; fax 18077), PO Box 120, DK-3913 Tasiilaq, at the Kommunia building, can arrange hire of two/four-person tents, sleeping bags, backpacks and stoves/cooking pots. Methylated spirits and Coleman fuel for mountain stoves are sold at the bookshop for Dkr25 per litre.

Money Grønlandsbanken, in the post office, is open Monday to Thursday from 10 am to 2.30 pm, and on Friday from 10 am to 3 pm.

Post & Communications The post and telephone office is in the bank and is open the same hours. The Neriussaq bookshop also has a pay phone and public fax service.

Bookshop The friendly Neriussaq bookshop (☎ 18018; fax 18009), run by Gerda Vilholm, has souvenir books, maps and English-language reading material. While browsing, you can eat a snack or have a cup of coffee or tea. It's open from 9 am to 6 pm daily.

GREENLAND

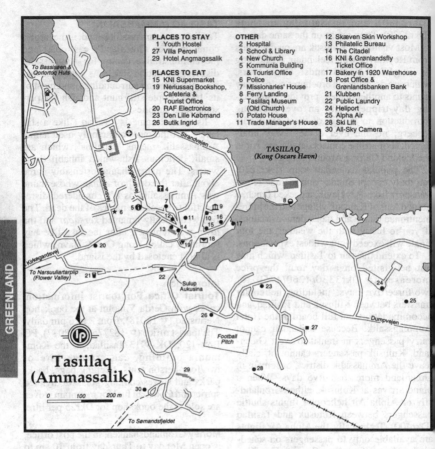

PLACES TO STAY
1. Youth Hostel
27. Villa Peroni
29. Hotel Angmagssalik

PLACES TO EAT
15. KNI Supermarket
19. Neriussaq Bookshop, Cafeteria & Tourist Office
20. RAF Electronics
23. Den Lille Købmand
26. Butik Ingrid

OTHER
2. Hospital
3. School & Library
4. New Church
5. Kommunia Building & Tourist Office
6. Police
7. Missionaries' House
8. Ferry Landing
9. Tasiilaq Museum (Old Church)
10. Potato House
11. Trade Manager's House
12. Skæven Skin Workshop
13. Philatelic Bureau
14. The Citadel
16. KNI & Grønlandsfly Ticket Office
17. Bakery in 1920 Warehouse
18. Post Office & Grønlandsbanken Bank
21. Klubben
22. Public Laundry
24. Heliport
25. Alpha Air
28. Ski Lift
30. All-Sky Camera

TASIILAQ
(Kong Oscars Havn)

Tasiilaq (Ammassalik)

0   100   200 m

To Bassisøen & Qorlortoq Huts

To Narssuuliartarpilip (Flower Valley)

To Sømandsfjeldet

Strandvejen

Sulup Aukusina

Football Pitch

Dumpvejen

Kirkegardsvej

Church

The new pentagonal church, built in 1985, has an unusual steeple which uncannily resembles the nose of an intercontinental ballistic missile. The interior décor blends appealing traditional and modern Greenlandic art, and the votive ship is a model umiaq, a sealskin-covered women's boat. For a look inside, pick up the key from the Kommunia tourist office.

Tasiilaq Museum

The Tasiilaq Museum (☎ 18311; fax 18711) is housed in the old church, which was con-structed between 1903 and 1908 and expanded in the 1950s. For a while, it even served as the town school. The new museum contains a wealth of information pertaining to the history and culture of east Greenland, including an early hunting tent, several qajaqs and lots of old photographs. In July and August it's open Tuesday to Wednesday and Friday to Sunday from 1 to 4 pm and on Thursday from 10 am to noon and 1 to 4 pm.

Other Historical Buildings

Tasiilaq's oldest building, the Citadel, was constructed in 1894 as the home of the first

Danish missionary and his wife, who shared it with a trade manager, a carpenter and a sailor. The next oldest building is the Missionaries' House, built in 1895 as a home for Danish missionaries. In that capacity, it also served as an impromptu church, school and hospital.

The original of the imposing Trade Manager's Home dates from the 1920s, but it was destroyed by fire in the late 1950s. It was rebuilt shortly afterwards and is still the residence of the KNI trade manager. In 1932 and 1933, Knud Rasmussen occupied the attic while filming *Palos Brudefærd* ('Palo's Wedding').

Near the harbour are two former warehouses. One is the post-war replacement of a 1920's structure, which is now a bakery. Beside it is another 1920s-era building which served as a warehouse and ironmongery, and is now used as a carpentry.

Not so old but still interesting is the turf-roofed building known as the Potato House. It was originally built in the mid-1900s for dry storage of vegetables and is still used to store potatoes.

Narsuuliartarpiip

Upstream along the river, beyond the cemetery, is Narsuuliartarpiip (the 'flower plain'), which is also called Blomsterdalen (Danish for 'flower valley'), in reference to its variety of Arctic flora. On sunny days, locals use the shallow lakes and streams as swimming holes. The easy walk up the valley is on most tourist agendas, and in an hour or two you'll see some wonderful lakes and waterfalls, and will want to just keep exploring.

Qeqqartivagajik (Sømandsfjeldet)

From the radio tower near the hotel, it's a stiff but straightforward climb up 679m Qeqqartivagajik (Sømandsfjeldet). Fit hikers can do the return trip in three hours, but lesser mortals need more time. On clear days, the summit view encompasses Tasiilaq, Kong Oscars Havn, the inland ice and the wild iceberg and floe-studded coastline, and may well be the most spectacular sight you've ever seen. Don't just take my word for it!

Skiing

In the winter, a small ski lift operates just south of town, above the prominent football pitch. The Narsuuliartarpiip valley offers excellent cross-country skiing; you can hire nordic skis from the Hotel Angmagssalik for Dkr55 per day.

Kayaking

The tourist office hires kayaks for day paddles in the immediate area, but they're increasingly concerned about safety and may ask you to demonstrate an Eskimo roll before they'll send you off on a longer paddle. They cost is Dkr150 per day, including equipment.

Mountaineering

The dramatic Tasiilaq-area landscape is a natural attraction for mountaineers. Local mountain guide Hans Christian Florian runs Mount Forel Expedition Support (☎ 18320), a professional guiding service which assists in organising mountain expeditions, and can handle permits, fuel and insurance logistics, and organise helicopter and dogsled transport. He can also organise Stauning Alps expeditions; climbs on Greenland's second highest peak, 3360m Mt Forel in Schweizerland; a number of unnamed first ascents; and the popular inland ice crossing between Isortoq and Kangerlussuaq.

Guided day climbs of prominent Polham's Fjeld, across Kong Oscars Havn from Tasiilaq, cost Dkr500 for one or two people, plus Dkr250 for each additional person, including charter boat, guide and equipment. These relatively easy technical climbs offer an ideal introduction to climbing in East Greenland. Climbs of Greenland's highest peak, 3730m Gunnbjörns Fjeld, including a chartered ski-plane from Akureyri (Iceland), a guide, equipment, food and fuel, cost US$5000 per person (minimum five people). You can also add climbs of nearby peaks, 3700m Qaaqaq Kershaw (the Dome) or 3700m Qaaqaq Johnson (the Cone).

Organised Tours

The tourist office can help arrange informal

GREENLAND

tours with local hiking, fishing, dogsled and snowmobile guides. There are no set rates, but dogsled trips average Dkr435/885 for four/eight hours and Dkr950 per 24 hours. Snowmobile trips cost Dkr595/795 for four/eight hours.

From 1 March to 15 May, the Hotel Angmagssalik runs half-day dogsled trips to Sarfakkajik Fjord across the island (Dkr435); one-day trips to Ikateq (Dkr885); full-day snowmobile tours to Tiniteqilaaq (Dkr985); and half-day snowmobile tours to Asingaleq mountain (Dkr595). Nordic ski trips with dogsled support are around Dkr500, including equipment hire.

In summer, the hotel offers à la carte day tours: a walk in Narsuuliartarpiip (Dkr75); an iceberg cruise (Dkr245); and five-hour cruises to Ikateq village or the remote Qernertivartivit hunting camp (Dkr435). In heavy ice, these are replaced with cruises on Kong Oscars Havn (Dkr150). Helicopter tours to 1200m Mittivakkat glacier (Dkr695) take 10 minutes each way, but allow 30 minutes on the icecap.

Places to Stay

The *Hotel Angmagssalik* (☎ 18293; fax 18393) charges Dkr495/695 for single/double rooms without bathroom and Dkr755/955 with private facilities. It's not a five-star affair but the management is friendly, the rooms are comfortable and it offers the best view of any hotel in Greenland. The glass-covered dome mounted on metal legs on the nearby hill is an all-sky camera used for photographing the aurora borealis during periods of high activity.

The *Youth Hostel*, at the secondary school, is open from the last week in June to the first week in August. For a bed and basic facilities, including a kitchen, you'll pay Dkr150. Bring your own sleeping bag. Book and check in through the tourist office.

The third option is the red house, *Villa Peroni* (☎ 18394; fax 18143), owned by Italian tour operator Robert Peroni. If he's between tour groups, the house rents for Dkr200 per person. There's no running water but it's comfy and sits in a hunters'

neighbourhood with lots of kids and opportunities for contact with locals. It accommodates four to six people. Bookings or enquiries should be directed to Bo Thalund.

For visits to Kuummiut and other settlements, the tourist office can arrange hostel-style accommodation in village schools for Dkr100 to Dkr200. There's also a small cabin hostel for visitors to Tiniteqilaaq.

The best *campsites* are in Narsuuliartarpiip, one to two km upstream from the Klubben.

Places to Eat

The *Hotel Angmagssalik* dining room offers breakfast and lunch buffets and set dinners for guests, but non-guests pay Dkr115 for lunch or dinner.

The *Neriussaq bookshop* runs a small microwave snack kiosk serving sandwiches, hot dogs, burgers and other simple snacks. They also sell coffee, tea and ice cream, and do a continental breakfast and sack lunches for prospective day-hikers. It's open from 9 am to 6 pm daily.

Self-caterers can resort to the *bakery*, the *KNI supermarket* and the after-hours kiosks *Den Lille Købmand* and *Butik Ingrid*, which are open 8 am to 9 pm. *RAF Electronic* also sells grocery staples.

Entertainment

The best drinking spot is the lively *Hotel Angmagssalik* public bar, but the local action spot is the pub and disco, *Klubben*. Visitors may attend only if invited by a local at least 24 hours in advance, and there's a Dkr25 cover charge. It's open from 8 to 11 pm on Wednesday and from 8 pm to 1 am on Friday and Saturday.

At the town meeting house there's a non-alcoholic *disco* for local youth which operates on Wednesday, Friday and Saturday. However, foreigners would certainly be the centre of attention and may not feel entirely comfortable.

A local rule prohibits photography inside pubs and discos.

Things to Buy

Greenland's philatelic centre (☎ 18044), which is based in Tasiilaq, is open for sales and tours Monday to Friday from 9 am to 3 pm. Tasiilaq also has a skin workshop, Skæven, open Monday to Friday from 8 am to 5 pm. The turn of the century building originally served as the home of the assistant colonial trade manager. In subsequent years, it housed Tasiilaq's first nurse as well as four members of Poul Emile Victor's expedition and Danish painter Gitz Johansen.

Getting There & Away

Grønlandsfly and KNI boat tickets may be booked and purchased at the KNI ticket office from 9 am to 2.30 pm Monday to Friday.

Air All air access to Tasiilaq is via Kulusuk; the 15 minute Grønlandsfly (☎ 18388; fax 18242) or Alpha Air (☎ 18663) shuttle between Kulusuk and Tasiilaq costs Dkr400. When ice conditions prevent the KNI supply boats from getting through, helicopter transport is available to Isortoq (Dkr600), Tiniteqilaaq (Dkr450), Sermiligaaq (Dkr600) and Kuummiut (Dkr500).

Helicopters may be chartered through Grønlandsfly or Alpha Air for Dkr20,100 per hour.

Ferry The two KNI supply boats, the *Anders Olsen* and the *Netside*, carry 12 passengers each and circulate between Tasiilaq and Kuummiut (Dkr135), Kulusuk (Dkr90), Isortoq (Dkr175), Ikateq (Dkr100), Sermiligaaq (Dkr190) and Tiniteqilaaq (Dkr145), stopping for an hour in each village. They hit Kuummiut and Kulusuk twice weekly, and other settlements only once. Ice conditions normally permit them to start running in late July or early August and service continues until routes are no longer passable.

Once a year, normally in August, the *Anders Olsen* carries hunters north to Kangerlussuaq (don't confuse it with the one on the west coast) and other places for their winter sojourn. This beautiful fjord, a 48-hour sail up the coast, is the main access route to Greenland's highest mountain, 3700m Gunnbjørns Fjeld. There's room for 24 people, but it's normally booked far in advance and locals take first priority.

Getting Around

Taxi To summon a taxi, phone (☎ 18252 or 18470).

Boat Charter The KNI boat *Anders Olsen* and *Netside* charter for Dkr15,000 and Dkr7500 per day, respectively. The hotel boat *Timmik* costs Dkr7200 per day.

Several local people offer informal boat charters; for the best rates, provide details well in advance about exactly what you want to do and how much time you want to spend. The Kommunia tourist office can provide suggestions.

AROUND TASIILAQ
Tasiilap Kuua

The mountain hut at Tasiilap Kuua, perched dramatically at the edge of a glacier tongue, makes an ideal retreat and a base for ice and mountain hiking. Beds cost Dkr100, with access to cooking facilities, but you must bring your own food and sleeping bag.

It's accessible by speedboat charter from Tasiilaq for Dkr500 per person. Alternatively, you can take the KNI cargo boat to Kuummiut and arrange a charter from there. It can also be reached by helicopter, obviating the uphill walk to the hut, or by dogsled in winter. For arrangements, contact Hans Christian Florian (☎ 18320) in Tasiilaq.

Hiking

This region presents numerous adventurous routes and is truly one of the planet's most spectacular places. The Tasiilaq tourist office, which promotes the area's hiking potential with some zeal, has produced an incredible double map and booklet, the 1:100,000 *Hiking Map – East Greenland*, which describes the many possibilities. It sells for Dkr250 at the Neriussaq bookshop. As there's a slight chance of encountering bears, seek local advice before striking out on a longer hike.

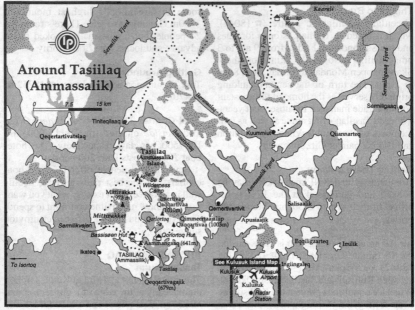

Around Tasiilaq (Ammassalik)

0   7.5   15 km

Sermilik Fjord

Tiniteqilaaq

Qeqertartivatsiaq

Tasiilaq
(Ammassalik)
Island

Sø 5
Sø 5
Wilderness
Camp

Mittivakkat
(973 m)

Mittivakkat

Imertivap
Qaqqartivaa
(1010m)

Qorlortoq

Qimmeertaajallip
Qaqqartivaa (1003m)

Sermilikvejen

Basissøen Hut

Qorlortoq Hut
Aammangaaq (641m)

Ikateq

TASIILAQ
(Ammassilik)

To Isortoq

Tasiilaq

Qeqqartivagajik
(679m)

Kuummiut

Qeqertivartivit

Apusiaajik

Salisaalik

Eqqiligaarteq

Imilik

See Kulusuk Island Map

Kulusuk
Kulusuk
Airport
Kulusuk
Radar
Station

Ingiingaleq

Ammassalik Fjord

Kaarali

Tasiilap
Kuua

Qinngerivartivit Fjord

Tasiilaq Fjord

Hormangat Fjord

Sermiligaaq Fjord

Sermiligaaq

Qiiannarteq

Basissøen & Aammangaaq Loop For a
longer hike, there's a compact four-person
mountain hut near the shore of Basissøen,
north-west of Tasiilaq. Follow the shore
north-west from town and cross the footbridge over the large stream which defines
the first major valley. Basissøen lies in the
next valley, north of the 641m peak,
Aammangaaq (Præstefjeldet). To reach the
small hut, you must ford the river. This can
either be done at the mouth or at the deeper
but easier marked ford at the outlet of
Basissøen. You're now on the route known
as the Sermilikvejen, the quickest and most
direct route between Tasiilaq and Sermilik
Fjord, and a prominent dogsled route to the
village of Ikateq ('dark water'). The hut,
which isn't exactly obvious, is embedded in
the hillside about 20m above the lake.

From the hut, continue past a smaller lake,
then up and over an obvious but low pass to
lake 168 (Icy Lake). You must cross the river,
but at several spots you can just step across

on rock bridges. If you follow the often
boggy and rocky lakeshore eastward, you'll
reach an abrupt drop where Icy Lake drains
into a convoluted tangle of turquoise lakes in
a dramatic waterfall, which can be heard as
a roar even from several km away. From
here, it's easy going down the slope back to
the aforementioned footbridge. This loop
takes about seven hours from Tasiilaq.

Aammaqqaaq & the Søen Begin as you
would for the Aammangaaq Loop, but
instead of heading up past Basissøen, keep
following the shore. Again, the river which
flows out of Basissøen must be forded. After
rounding the northern head of Tasiilaq bay,
cross the base of the Aammaqqaaq peninsula; the free Qorlortoq hut lies over a largish
river on the eastern side of the peninsula.

If you continue upstream past the waterfall, you'll reach the enormous Sø 1, or
Qorlortoq Sø. Follow the western shore right
around to the inflowing stream at its northern

end, then turn north and keep climbing up the same valley, always keeping to the western side, past three more lakes, Sø 2, Sø 3 and Sø 4. At the south-eastern corner of the fifth lake, Sø 5, is a new wilderness camp established by the Tasiilaq tourist office. It consists of three mountain huts and a tented camp; beds cost from Dkr150 to Dkr250.

Although the one-way hike from Tasiilaq can be done in a day, it's more comfortable allowing two days each way.

Longer Hikes Longer hiking possibilities include the challenging but classic hike across Dødemandsdalen to Sermilik Fjord. This and a range of other routes are depicted and described in the booklet and two-part 1:100,000 *Hiking Map – East Greenland*, which is available from the Neriussaq bookshop in Tasiilaq.

ITTOQQOORTOORMIIT (SCORESBYSUND)

Ittoqqoortoormiit ('the people with much peat') occupies one of the finest districts for local hunters in the country and musk oxen, seals and polar bears are plentiful. It sits at the mouth of Kangertittivaq, or Scoresbysund, which is by far the world's longest and widest fjord.

The Danish name honours Captain William Scoresby, a Scottish whaler who arrived in 1822. As far as anyone knows, he was the first European to set foot in North-East Greenland. The current residents of Ittoqqoortoormiit are mostly descended from Ammassalik emigrants who sailed north in September 1925 on the vessel *Gustav Holm*.

The town of 480 residents holds little interest, but Ittoqqoortoormiit is a logical launch point for wilderness expeditions, and the nearby Stauning Alps attract an increasing number of climbers seeking challenging new terrain. However, the shortage of visitor facilities, supplies and transport cannot be overstressed.

Information

For information, contact the Ittoqqoortoor-miit Kommunia (☎ 55077; fax 55074), PO Box 505, DK-3980 Ittoqqoortoormiit.

Dangers & Annoyances Rumours about occasional drunken violence in Ittoqqoor-toormiit are unfortunately well-founded; during times of unrest, visitors should keep a low profile.

Organised Tours

Nonni Travel (☎ 461 1841; fax 461 1843), Brekkugata 5, PO Box 336, 602 Akureyri, Iceland, offers adventurous 10-day trips by dogsled (US$3050), kayak (US$3500) or inflatable boat (US$3300) through the wilderness of Liverpool Land, Jameson Land and Milne Land.

Places to Stay & Eat

There are no hotels or restaurants, but the electric company does have a *Guest Hostel* (☎ 55066) with five rooms and kitchen facilities. Rooms cost Dkr500 per person. You may also be able to find a place to crash at the school or the TV station (of all places), but if you're on a budget, bring a tent. Supplies are available at the *KNI Shop*.

Meals are available daily at the *hostel* in Nerlerit Inaat, but accommodation is open only to airport workers.

Getting There & Away

Access to Ittoqqoortoormiit is via the Nerlerit Inaat (Constable Pynt) airfield, which was constructed by ARCO in 1985 to provide an access and service base for oil-drilling crews. When discoveries proved disappointing, ARCO pulled out and handed the airport over to the municipality.

Grønlandsfly has weekly services to Nerlerit Inaat from Keflavík, Iceland, (Dkr5160), and services to and from other parts of Greenland all use this international link, making flights incredibly expensive. From Nuuk, you'll pay Dkr6140 and from Kangerlussuaq, it's Dkr6160. From Uummannaq, the nearest west-coast town, it's Dkr9000! Helicopter shuttles between Ittoqqoortoormiit and Nerlerit Inaat cost Dkr610. Most charter flights for expeditions

GREENLAND

The Sirius Sledge Patrol

During WWII, it became apparent that the long and uninhabited coastline of north-east Greenland required some sort of military protection. From a military sledge patrol which had operated during the war evolved the Sirius Sledge Patrol, which was officially established at Daneborg in 1950.

Its task is to patrol 160,000 sq km along the entire north-east Greenland coastline – in summer by boat and plane, and in winter by dogsled. After the creation of the North-East Greenland National Park on 22 May 1974, the patrol members inherited the job of park rangers.

Patrol members, who are selected from the officers' ranks of the Danish army, do two-year stints on the patrol. They work in pairs, often moving through some of the planet's most remote wilderness for several months at a time. Their only company is a team of sled dogs and the only contact with the outside world is by radio. It may sound romantic, but combine tent camping and draughty abandoned hunting camps with temperatures of -50°C and you begin to wonder what motivates some people! ■

to the Stauning Alps originate in Akureyri, Iceland.

NORTH-EAST GREENLAND NATIONAL PARK

The world's largest national park, established in 1974 and expanded in 1988 to encompass a total of 972,000 sq km, takes in the entire north-eastern quarter of Greenland and extends 1400 km from south-east to north-west. UNESCO has recently named it a Man and the Biosphere Reserve.

Described as an 'Arctic Riviera' or 'Arctic Shangri-La', the park's vast tundra expanses provide a haven for musk oxen, polar bears, caribou, Arctic wolves, foxes, hares and a variety of delicate plant life, while the fjords shelter seals, walruses and whales. Most of the park, however, lies on the icecap.

The park was long closed to all but scientific research teams, but it's now open to private expeditions. However, there are no facilities and the difficulty of access means that most visitors are still professional botanists, biologists, geologists and other Arctic researchers.

In the far north-east, at Danmarkshavn and Daneborg respectively, are a weather station and a Danish military installation where the Sirius Sledge Patrol rescue rangers are stationed.

Information

Your best source of information on park ecology is the magical *Frozen Horizons – The World's Largest National Park*, by Ivar Silis (see Books in the Greenland Facts for the Visitor chapter).

Oodaap Qeqertaa – the Furthest North

For years, geography books told us the northernmost point of land in the world was Greenland's Cape Morris Jesup, at 83° 20' north latitude. Then, a small island was discovered off the north coast – a speck of land way up north of Peary Land called Kaffeklubben Ø, 'coffee club island'. It was named by Danish geologist Dr Lauge Koch after the afternoon coffee club at the Geological Museum in Copenhagen, where Dr Koch enjoyed the company and professional discussions of his colleagues.

Kaffeklubben Ø's day in the sun was not to last, however. Further north, amid the ice floes, a scrap of gravel less than 100m across was discovered peeping out of the sea. It was named Oodaap Qeqertaa or Oodaaq Island, and at 83° 40' north, it usurped the title of the world's northernmost land.

The island is now protected inside the North-East Greenland National Park. The very wealthy may be able to reach it by charter helicopter, but Oodaaq is scarcely large enough for a heliport, and is unlikely to ever become a tourist destination. ■

Traditional hunters and officials on public business are allowed unlimited park access, but other visitors require permits issued by the Dansk Polarcenter (☎ 45-32 88 01 00; fax 45-32 88 01 01; email dpc@dpc.dk), Strandgade 100H, DK-1401 Copenhagen K. Applications must be made by December of the year prior to the intended visit, in plenty of time for the Polarcenter's annual meeting which determines who gets the year's permits.

Organised Tours

The recommended tour organiser is Arcturus, in the UK (see Organised Tours in the Getting There & Away chapter), which runs adventure expeditions every year to far-flung areas of the park, including the Stauning Alps, Dronning Louise Land and even Peary Land!

Getting There & Away

Most park visits begin at Mesters Vig airport. Expeditions can charter five-passenger Piper Navajos from Flugfélag Norðurlands in Akureyri, Iceland, for as little as Dkr25,000. A 15-passenger jet charter costs around Dkr37,800. For details, contact Flugfélag Norðurlands (☎ 354-461 2100; fax 354-461 2106), Akureyri Airport, Akureyri, Iceland.

GREENLAND

Facts about the Faroe Islands

An old Faroese legend says that when the earth was created, the foreman in charge cleaned his nails and what he discarded plopped into the North Atlantic to become the Faroe Islands. Those are romantic beginnings, to say the least!

This is one of those mysteriously remote sorts of places, akin to the Aleutians or the Falklands, that most would be hard-pressed to find on a map, let alone aspire to visit. These 18 spots of land in the North Atlantic seem to get very little press and, although they're a stone's throw from mainland Europe, few Europeans ever think much about them.

Therefore, visitors are normally not prepared for the undeniable beauty of the Faroese landscape. From the sea on a fine day (which, in the Faroes, includes anything from patchy cloud right down to a medium drizzle), the first view of the towering cliffs, layer-cake mountains, crashing surf, and millions of circling, squawking sea birds dive-bombing the colourful Faroese fishing boats is likely to produce an aesthetic jolt. It's just as you'd imagine the 'stormy North Atlantic' to look. Add the odd lighthouse on a craggy headland and you've got the stuff of paintings.

Even under scrutiny, the scene remains inspiring. The Faroes are islands of green grass and grey gravel, splashes of white or yellow flowers, patches of snow at high altitudes, herds of ratty-tatty sheep grazing on the hillsides, cascading waterfalls and villages of colourful modern homes.

Apart from the many Danish visitors who specifically visit the islands, most travellers going independently to the Faroes don't arrive there by choice. They are usually on an obligatory two-day stopover imposed by the Smyril Line company while the ferry travelling between Denmark and Iceland collects passengers in Bergen, Norway. Consequently, a proportion of these travellers arrive in the Faroes without knowing what there is to do, where to go or what the place is all about.

Fortunately, the islands are quite easy to get around. The road system is well maintained and the Faroese have tunnelled like moles through the roughest bits (this is a matter of some resentment in Denmark, which has picked up the tab for some non-essential tunnels). In addition, there's an excellent transport network with bus, ferry and helicopter routes connecting all parts of the country with the capital, Tórshavn.

Two-day stopover passengers are generally happy to learn that some of the Faroes' most magnificent landscapes lie within a couple of hours by bus from the capital. If you have more time, you'll want to venture out to some of the more remote islands, each of which offers something unique and more of those inspiring scenes that send your senses into overload.

HISTORY
The Monks

Like Iceland, the Faroes were uninhabited when Europeans first stumbled upon them. It's possible that these islands were discovered as early as the 6th century, when St Brendan and his monks passed by on their seven-year cruise through unknown parts. However, there's no evidence or tradition that they made a stop there. They did, however, run across two islands several days' sailing from Scotland, one of which they named the Island of Sheep and the other the Paradise of Birds. Some modern-day historians speculate that the Island of Sheep is somewhere in the Faroes (*Føroyar*, pronounced 'FER-ya', is derived from *faar oy* meaning 'the islands of sheep') and that the Paradise of Birds is in fact Mykines, the westernmost island of the Faroes. Mykines has an unusually dense bird population, and a voyager trying to avoid the narrow and potentially hazardous channels between the islands would most likely have passed it.

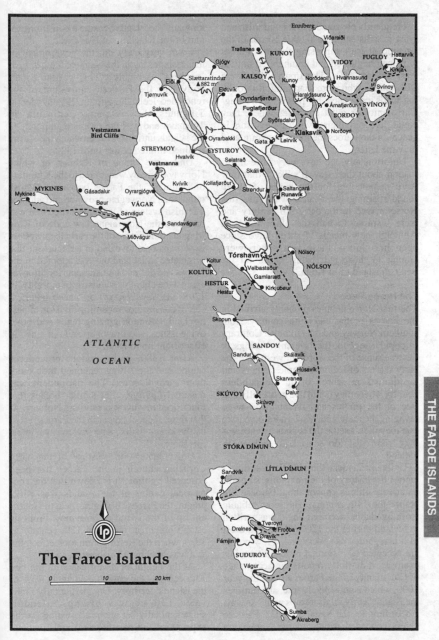

The Faroe Islands

0   10   20 km

Frequently obscured by rain and mist, and lying in a distant, inhospitable corner of the Atlantic, it isn't surprising that the Faroes remained neglected and uninhabited until at least the late 600s. The first settlers were Irish monks who were searching, no doubt, for lands populated by pagans 'awaiting' Christianity or quiet countries where they could live out their lives of devotion in peace. In the Faroes the monks encountered only the latter.

Unfortunately, we have very little information about their stay. It's likely that they were responsible for the herds of sheep found roaming the islands when the first Norse arrived in the early 9th century and were inspired to call the place Føroyar. Although new breeds of sheep have since been introduced, these first sheep were similar to those still being raised on the Scottish island of St Kilda.

The Norse Period

The first Norse peoples probably arrived in the Faroes in the early 9th century from southern Norway and the Orkneys. Contrary to popular legend, they weren't Vikings in the true sense of the word but were, like the early settlers of Iceland, simple farmers and pastoralists in search of an independent country where they could live peacefully and free of the pirates and tyrants who were ravaging the mainland. Modern Faroese joke that they didn't settle the islands by choice – they were just too seasick to sail on to Iceland.

Unlike Icelanders, the early Faroese didn't record the history of their exploits, so comparatively little is known about Faroese life before the 14th century. The most reliable work available, *Færinga Saga*, was written in Iceland during the 1200s. Although most of it is regarded as apocryphal, a few points are accepted as historical probabilities. For example, it dutifully reports the acceptance of Christianity in the Faroes around the year 1000, which is most likely true, and outlines the islands' early relationships with Norway. According to the saga, in 1035 Faroese chiefs conceded tribute to the Norwegian

king and the islands became a constitutional part of the Kingdom of Norway.

From very early on, the government of these islands lay in the hands of the *Alting* or 'peoples' assembly'. This parliamentary body was the Faroese equivalent of the renowned Icelandic Alþing. It convened at Tinganes, the 'assembly peninsula' in Tórshavn and was the ultimate authority in the islands until 1035, after which the Alting retained limited power until 1380.

Under the Union of Kalmar, in which Norway formally was joined to the Kingdom of Denmark, the Faroes became a Danish rather than Norwegian province and adopted a Danish system of law and justice that was based on the Norwegian law code of King Magnus. The nature of the early legal system is perhaps best revealed in a document that originated in Iceland but was adopted in the Faroes and defined punishments for offences against the church's standards of morality. In 1298, the *Seyðabrævið* or 'sheep letter', a sort of constitution regarding division of pastureland, common grazing lands and other ovine issues, was drawn up and remained in effect right up to 1866.

After 1380, parliamentary procedures ceased and the Alting remained little more than a royal court. The parliament was renamed *Løgting*, after similar bodies that functioned in what was southern Norway. At that time, the real power in the Faroes rested on the king's bailiff, who saw to royal interests there.

Unfortunately, the history of the early Christian church in the Faroes has been obscured by time. It is known that the ecumenical centre of the islands was Kirkjubøur, the Faroese bishopric, near the southern tip of the island of Streymoy. From its establishment in the early 12th century to 1535, when the Reformation took effect, the seat was held by 33 bishops.

At the height of its influence in the late 13th century, the church held about 40% of the islands' territory. One particularly motivated 13th-century bishop, Erlendur, singlehandedly set about alleviating (at the expense of the parishioners) any financial worries the church might have had. As a result, several of the church buildings at Kirkjubøur were torched and the grand 'unfinished cathedral' remains roofless as a monument to skirmishes between supporters and detractors of this unpopular church leader.

Reformation & Trade Monopoly

Early trade regulations required that all commerce between the European mainland and the Faroe Islands passed through Bergen in Norway, where customs taxes would be collected. In the middle of the 13th century, however, a group of northern German cities were forming the Hanseatic League, a mercantile association destined over the next century to take effective control of commerce throughout the continent.

At the time, Norwegian regulations forbade the league's entry into Scandinavia (including Iceland and the Faroes), but in 1361 Norway, whose population had been decimated by the Black Death, realised it was powerless to resist economic encroachment from the south. The competition meant a predominantly healthy and consistent mercantile atmosphere for nearly 200 years.

During the civil war launched by King Christian III of Denmark to wrest power from Christian II, the powerful German trading companies in Lübeck supported the soon-to-be-deposed king. Having backed the loser, they were expelled from the Scandinavian commercial scene. In 1535, King Christian III granted Thomas Köppen of Hamburg exclusive trading rights in the Faroe Islands, a pattern of arrangement that would remain in effect for the next 300 years.

Also in 1535, Denmark decided to introduce religious enlightenment in the form of the Protestant Lutheran church and release the provinces from the 'yoke of Catholicism'. The Reformation process, which lasted five years, effected the transfer of church properties into state hands and replaced Latin with Danish as the language used in ecclesiastical matters. These events tightened Denmark's grip on the Faroes and its other overseas provinces.

After Köppen, the monopoly passed through various hands, but it didn't have such devastating effects on the Faroes as the similar Danish Trade Monopoly of 1602 had on Iceland. Ironically, the Icelandic Company, which was responsible for so much suffering in that country, probably served the Faroes better than any other establishment had or would. The worst moments came during the mid-1600s when Denmark was fighting with Sweden and wartime prices forced the Icelandic Company out of the Faroese markets.

The stipulations laid out for Köppen (and subsequent monopolists) included requirements that only quality goods could be supplied and only in quantities commensurate with the market. They also required that prices reflect the true market value of the goods delivered and that traders conduct themselves in a friendly and honest manner in all their dealings with the islanders.

Most of the goods exported from the Faroes – wool stockings, meat, sheepskins and fish – were sent to Holland and, under the terms of the monopoly agreement, traders were obligated to purchase at predetermined prices as many of these items as the Faroese could produce for sale. In theory, it seemed an equitable deal for everyone, but in practice, greed and dishonesty often meant the guidelines were ignored and the Faroese faced shortages and delays, while both they and the traders found themselves forced to accept inferior goods. Occasionally, the market for Faroese goods (which the trading company was required to accept) declined and the monopolists often lost money on the deal. Smuggling and piracy grew rampant and the system began to collapse.

Trying another tack, in 1655 the Danish government presented the Faroes to Christoffer von Gabel (and subsequently to his son, Frederick) as a personal feudal estate. Their oppressive reign brought little more than hardship to the islanders, who were harshly exploited by the overlords. In 1709, the 54-year-old von Gabel dynasty was nipped in the bud by the Danish government, which seized control of both the

Faroes and the trade monopoly. Like governments everywhere, however, it proved hopelessly inept at market economics. Throughout the 18th century, they and the merchants operated at a loss and, on 1 January 1856, the monopoly was finally abandoned as a failure.

Modern History

During the 19th century, Denmark's association with the Faroes was characterised by its increasing domination over the islands and their conversely decreasing autonomy. Through the early part of the century, the Løgting had remained a psychological link with the Faroes' long-lost independence, though it had been stripped of its power. In 1816, however, it was officially abolished and replaced by a Danish judiciary. The use of the Faroese language was discouraged and Danish became the language of official proceedings. In 1849, the Danish legislature (Rigsdag) officially incorporated the Faroes into Denmark, allowing the islands two Rigsdag seats.

In 1852, the obstinate Faroese re-established their Løgting as a county council, initially as an advisory body but with hopes of gaining momentum towards independence. The next major step came in the 1890s, when, thanks to a period of economic prosperity, many islanders were becoming increasingly obsessed with the idea of home rule. Only the wealthy opposed the proposal, fearing it would result in their being taxed to support local government.

Early in the 20th century, Faroese viewpoints polarised. The Unionist Party promoted full association with Denmark and the Home Rule Party advocated gradual independence under the guidance of Faroese statesman Jóannes Patursson.

Concurrent to these developments was another spurt of growth in the Faroese economy. As time passed the population grew and, of necessity, the economy expanded to include fishing as well as the traditional shepherding and agriculture. By right of their Danish citizenship, the Faroese

were granted fishing rights throughout the Danish-controlled North Atlantic region. In 1872 they replaced their low, open fishing boats with more seaworthy English wooden ships. In turn, these were replaced later by steam trawlers. The fishery developed rapidly into a thriving enterprise.

During WWII, the British occupied the Faroes in order to secure the strategic North Atlantic shipping lanes and prevent the islands following the rest of Denmark into German occupation. This political separation from Denmark resulted in the upgrading of the Løgting to a legislative body, although the Danish prefect retained executive power. Some factions were prepared to take advantage of Denmark's extreme vulnerability and declare complete independence at this stage, but others expressed reservations.

On 23 March 1948, the *Act on Faroese Home Rule*, a variation on a proposal made by the Danish government immediately following the war, was passed. The Faroes' official status had been changed from 'county of Denmark' to 'self-governing community within the Kingdom of Denmark'. When Denmark joined the European Community, the Faroes refused to follow. Over the locally hot issue of fishing rights, the Faroe Islands maintain their claim to a 200-mile exclusion limit.

The islands have created an official flag and they are issuing their own stamps. Faroese banknotes are issued by the National Bank of Denmark. The Faroese oversee their own affairs insofar as Denmark is not affected by their decisions. Føroyskt has been declared the official language of Home Rule *(Landsstýri)* proceedings, but Faroese children must learn Danish at school.

Denmark retains control of and financial responsibility for insurance, banking (to a lesser extent), defence, foreign relations and justice. The Landsstýri is entirely responsible for communications, economic and cultural issues as well as administering health, education and social programmes. For its part, Denmark provides an annual grant of Dkr1.2 billion (1995) to pay for it all.

Economic Turmoil

In the late 1980s, rampant government spending resulted in the Faroes' enjoying the world's highest standard of living. Low taxes and seemingly endless credit led to a Faroese consumption rate 10 times greater than that of mainland Denmark. Many people were deluded into believing all was well; the 'success story' seemed likely to allow the Faroes to follow the same road as Iceland, towards complete independence.

But there were complications. In the early 1990s, a decline in North Atlantic fish stocks, representing 96% of the Faroese export economy, reached a crisis state. Thanks primarily to the application of high-tech fishing equipment and heavy overfishing in territorial waters between 1986 and 1993, the annual catch in the once-abundant waters dropped from about 150,000 tonnes in 1990 to just 110,000 tonnes in 1994. The economic mainstay of the debt-ridden populace was languishing, so the national bank Sjóvinnubankin, overburdened with defaulted loans and supporting a national debt of Dkr9.4 billion, was forced to call in the receivers in October 1992.

The Faroese government had to borrow Dkr500 million from Denmark in an effort to lift its economy out of the shambles. The figure grew to Dkr1.8 billion, in addition to the annual grant of Dkr1 billion. The deal was that the administration of Sjóvinnubankin would be handled by the Danish national bank until the loan was repaid. The Danes insisted on austerity measures. A tough budget slashed public spending, increased taxation and introduced a 10% wage cut for public employees.

There was talk of cutting the fishing fleet of 200 trawlers by as much as half and closing all but six of the country's 22 fish processing plants. Unemployment increased in a country where 6% of the population had already emigrated (mainly to Denmark) to find work. Most of those leaving were educated younger people who were taking their children with them. Others stayed at home and claimed Danish unemployment benefits.

Late in 1993, unemployment hung at around 20% in Tórshavn (higher in outlying islands) and nearly all of the fish-processing plants and trawlers were in receivership.

The Faroes had effectively returned to colonial status. In September 1993 a delegation went to Copenhagen in hopes of negotiating the fourth emergency aid package of the year. This time they asked for between Dkr3 billion and Dkr4 billion to prevent banks from closing and to reduce the 1994 budget deficit, but the Danes came up with just Dkr1.3 billion and encouragement to further cut spending. Sjóvinnubankin was amalgamated with Føroya Banki in late 1993, after Føroya Banki was bailed out. A third bank went bankrupt and was closed down entirely. In the face of all these pressures, a growing international boycott on Faroese products in response to the islands' continued practice of *grindadráp* (see the boxed aside later in this chapter) was merely another thorn in the side.

The austerity programme worked. There was no need to sell off much of the fishing fleet, so it survived virtually intact. Unemployment peaked at 26% in January 1994 then it fell steadily to about 10% by mid-1996. With such high unemployment rates, annual inflation stayed low at between 2 and 3% (after the 7% increase in 1993 due to the introduction of 25% VAT on almost all goods and services). By 1995 the economy was definitely recovering, helped by a resurgence in fish stocks, particularly cod and herring. That year the annual catch in Faroese waters rose to nearly 170,000 tonnes and similar figures are expected for 1996. Eight fish processing plants had re-opened by mid-1996. The population stabilised too, with the decrease (emigration-immigration) slowing from 4% in 1993 to 1% in 1995, and possibly changing to a net increase in 1996.

However, economic problems persisted in the form of a Dkr1 billion debt which the Faroese acquired when their government took control of Føroya Banki from the Danish Den Dansk Bank in 1994. The scandal associated with this debt, which the Faroese claim they were unaware of before the bank was acquired, is threatening the current Danish government.

One bright spot on the economic horizon is the discovery of oil in the sea between the Faroes and Shetland Islands, but it hasn't yet been determined whether the bulk of the field lies in Faroese or British waters. In 1996 various vessels were exploring the seabed offshore, and drilling of a very deep test-bore took place at Lopra on the island of Suðuroy. Even if it does offer some hope, any benefits wouldn't be felt for quite a number of years.

The Faroese relationship to the European Union, of which Denmark is a member, is a less pressing issue compared to the recent economic and population problems. Understandably, Denmark sees the EU as a potential source of funds to shore up the Faroese economy and take some of the strain off the Danish taxpayers. The Faroese want neither to jeopardise their position in the kingdom as regards fishing rights, nor to open their own territorial waters to European interests and competition. With the fisheries having made a comeback and the Faroes still outside the EU, such traditional markets as Germany and Britain being obligated to buy fish from EU countries cuts the Faroes out of the competition. It seems a no-win situation unless the Faroese can somehow convince the EU to admit them to the fold without requiring them to relinquish their territorial waters. However, increasing requirements for fish within the EU may lead to access improvements for Faroese fish products in the near future.

GEOGRAPHY

The 18 islands of the Faroes cover a land area of 1399 sq km. The compact archipelago is shaped like a southward pointing arrow that appears to be threatening Scotland 280 km away. The islands lie 600 km west of Norway and about 400 km south-east of Iceland. The greatest distance from east to west is about 80 km, from north to south 115 km.

The islands can be divided roughly into four geographical areas. At the heart of the country are Streymoy and Eysturoy, the two most populated islands. The capital city of Tórshavn lies near the southern tip of Streymoy in one of the country's most climatically vulnerable situations. Also clustered around the southern tip of Streymoy are the small but beautiful islands of Koltur, Hestur and Nólsoy.

West of Streymoy are Vágar (the only island with enough level land suitable for an airport) and magnificent Mykines, the westernmost island in the group, renowned for its diverse bird life.

North-east of Eysturoy are the rugged, finger-like northern islands Kalsoy, Kunoy, Borðoy and Viðoy, as well as the rounder Svínoy and Fugloy. Apart from Klaksvík on Borðoy, the Faroes' second-largest community, these islands are well off the tourist track, but they offer the most spectacular walking and the most dramatic scenery in the country.

Finally, the southern group of islands, Suðuroy, Sandoy, Skúvoy, Stóra Dímun and Lítla Dímun, form the tip of the Faroese arrow. The climate here is generally the best in the archipelago. Lítla Dímun is the only one of the 18 main islands that is not inhabited – and once you've seen it, you'll probably be able to work out why.

GEOLOGY

Geologically, the Faroe Islands are eroded remnants of the Thulean plateau, a mid-Atlantic continent built up volcanically after North America, Greenland and Europe, tectonically speaking, went their separate ways. Other bits of this long-disappeared Atlantis include the Westfjords of Iceland, County Antrim in Northern Ireland, bits of southern Greenland and parts of Western Scotland.

The rock strata of the Faroes are quite interesting. Their terraced 'layer-cake' appearance is derived from four stages of basalt-building vulcanism separated by substantial periods of geological inactivity. Small seams of coal between two of the basalt layers provide evidence that life had time to take hold between those stages. The final volcanic stage was one of intrusion in which molten material forced its way into vertical and horizontal cracks in the existing rock, forming erosion-resistant dykes and sills.

During the Great Ice Age, the Faroes and all of what is now their continental shelf were blanketed with ice. Towards the end of that era, after the icecap had begun to melt, its remnants gouged out the cirques, valleys, sounds and fjords that characterise the islands today. The resulting landscape is primarily a series of mountain ridges and arêtes separated by textbook cirques. The best examples can be found on the north-eastern islands of Kalsoy, Kunoy, and Borðoy.

The strata of the Faroes dip slightly toward the south-east. Therefore, the northern and western coasts, whose layers are more resistant to the onslaught of the waves, meet the sea in steep cliffs that reach up to 750m at Enniberg on the island of Viðoy. The southern and eastern shores, which are far more susceptible to wave erosion, have more gently sloping coastlines and less dramatic drop-offs.

CLIMATE

The climate of the Faroes is similar to Iceland's, only a bit warmer and – if you can believe it – stormier. Precipitation in some form – drizzle, mist, downpour, snow, etc – can be expected about 280 days of the year. Fortunately, weather is somewhat localised – it could be bucketing down in Tórshavn while Suðuroy basks in the sun. If you're interested in timing excursions to take advantage of the best weather, tune in to Útvarp Føroya radio (89.8 MHz FM, 531 kHz MW), which broadcasts weather information in English at 8.45 am on weekdays.

Thanks to the tropical current of the Gulf Stream, which sweeps past the islands, the water temperatures remain about 10°C all year, moderating the climate and providing an ideal environment for fish and plankton. The annual average temperature range is only 8°C (from 3°C in January to 11°C in July).

ECOLOGY & ENVIRONMENT

The Faroese pride themselves on having the cleanest marine environment in the North Atlantic. Although water and air pollution are minimal, fish farming has caused localised pollution problems. Despite fairly large numbers of sheep, giardia has not been reported. With relatively low numbers of tourists, the impact of tourism on the environment is imperceptible.

Wild camping is frowned upon by the authorities, ostensibly for environmental reasons. Since many streams and rivers in the islands are used by towns and villages for drinking water, take care not to pollute them.

FLORA & FAUNA
Flora

Despite an absence of trees, the entire landscape seems to be cast out of some uniformly green material. In fact, there are 1600 species of plants growing in the Faroes, most of these being grasses, sedges, mosses, lichens and fungi. More complex vegetation (flowering species and ferns) usually grows in sheltered ravines where the sheep can't reach. Tree growth is inhibited by salt spray, wind and sheep.

Historically, driftwood was a valuable commodity with collection strictly controlled. Any tree or bit of uncut wood that drifted ashore automatically belonged to the farmer on whose property it landed. If the wood were cut or altered by humans in any way, it would revert to the Crown and be put up for auction by the local authorities. The finder would receive a third of the auction price.

Fauna

Although the Faroes are home to several species of introduced pests – rats, mice and rabbits – the bird life is most prolific. Thanks to the profusion of plankton and therefore fish and other sea life, the bird population is possibly the densest in the world. Whether or not this is true, it isn't difficult to believe when you see the high nest-covered cliffs.

Forty-nine species of birds breed regularly in the Faroes and nearly 30 others do so occasionally. Among them are the comical puffins, which are netted and eaten in large

THE FAROE ISLANDS

The oystercatcher – avian mascot of the Faroes

quantities. Other common species include guillemots, fulmars, great skuas (these become health hazards if you imprudently wander too close to their eggs!), razorbills, gannets, cormorants and kittiwakes. Most of these feast on herring, crayfish and small eels, although the larger birds sometimes eat larger fish as well.

Inland you'll find great colonies of eider ducks, golden plovers, snipe, rock doves and the avian mascot of the Faroes, the oystercatcher or *tjaldur*. In addition, about 200 more species are occasional visitors to the islands. The only bird of prey in residence is the merlin, a small, dark-plumed falcon.

The best time to observe the birds is in the summer, roughly between April and August. All Faroese species are protected and tourists aren't permitted to net them or collect eggs. In addition, fulmar chicks may be afflicted with psittacosis (also known as 'parrot fever'), a contagious pneumonia-like disease that can also affect humans, so it's best to leave them well alone.

In the sea around the Faroes swim large pods of pilot whales or *grind* (pronounced 'grint'), victims of the *grindadráp*, bloody massacres of 1500 to 2000 of these creatures

Pilot whale – victim of the *grindadráp*

annually. (For details, see the boxed aside later in this chapter.) Other cetaceans that inhabit the Faroes (unaffected by grindadráp) include bottlenose whales, fin whales, killer whales (orcas), dolphins and porpoises. The only pinniped that breeds along the Faroese coast is the grey seal, which inhabits sea-level caves and is rarely seen.

There are only five species of freshwater fish found in the Faroes: the Arctic char, salmon, eel, river trout and stickleback. Saltwater fish and shellfish species, many of which are in decline from overfishing, include Atlantic halibut, sand eel, redfish, haddock, lemon sole, blue whiting, lobster and scallops. Cod is also present, but not in the quantities encountered further north and west.

Domestic animals include cattle and sheep, sheep, and more sheep. There are nearly twice as many Faroese sheep as there are people.

GOVERNMENT & POLITICS

Although many Danes maintain that the islands are as much a part of their country as is Copenhagen, the Faroese like to believe that they're actually an independent nation under the protection of mother Denmark. The truth is, the Faroes remain in a sort of autonomous limbo between Danish control and independence. Although they receive much of their annual budget from Denmark, some of the functions of the Home Rule government are supported by locally collected taxes including VAT. The Faroes have their own flag, stamps and currency, but defence and foreign relations are handled by Denmark. Faroese citizens, however, don't pay taxes to the Kingdom of Denmark and refuse to join the motherland in the European Union.

Until 1948 the Faroes, like Greenland, were a county of Denmark. In a referendum held in 1946, however, the islands voted for a Home Rule government, one which provided for an independently functioning government within the Kingdom of Denmark.

The seal of the leader of the Faroe Islands Government

The Home Rule government or Landsstýri is headed by a *Løgmaður* ('lawman'), with three to six subordinates, and a bureaucratic jumble of committees, boards and councils. Danish interests in joint affairs are overseen by a representative known as the *Rigs-ombudsmand*. Conversely, the Faroese elect two representatives to the Danish Parliament, or Folketing.

The legislative duties are covered by the Løgting, a 32-member parliament which opens its annual session on the Faroese national holiday, Ólavsøka, on 29 July. Elections to the Løgting are held every four years. The seats are occupied by five major and three smaller political parties. The five major parties are: the Peoples' (Conservative) Party or Fólkaflokkurin; the Unionist Party or Sambandsflokurin; the Republicans or Tjóðveldisflokkurin; the Home Rule (Liberal) party or Sjálvstýrisflokkurin; and the Social Democrats or Javnaðarflokkurin. These five represent both liberal and conservative views as well as both Unionist (pro-Danish) and nationalist leanings. The Prime Minister is the Unionist Edmund Joensen who was elected in 1994 and now leads a coalition of Conservatives, Unionists, Liberals and Trade Unionists.

The 1994 elections to the Løgting led to 14 new members of parliament and a total of eight parties represented, a consequence of the recent economic and political upheaval. The crisis has put a strain on the relationship between the Faroese and Danish governments; in fact, Faroese politicians are now more accountable to the public and the entire home rule set-up is under scrutiny.

In theory, the Faroese finance their own government (responsible for domestic issues), while the Danish government handles matters relating to foreign relations, banking and defence. Until the recent emergency banking measures came into play (see the History section earlier), legislation concerning matters of insurance and banking regulations originating on the Danish mainland had to be passed through the Faroese Løgting before it could be put into effect in the Faroe Islands. Legislation relating to penal codes and civil laws must still be subjected to local approval.

Although Faroese defence is technically the responsibility of Denmark, it seems to rest primarily on NATO in the form of an American-controlled NATO base north of Tórshavn.

Individual communities often have their own government authorities in charge of local issues such as education. Due to the remote nature of many communities, these officials actually have a great deal of control over local affairs.

ECONOMY

You probably won't be surprised to learn that the economy of the Faroe Islands is now based almost entirely upon fishing and fish processing. However, it hasn't always been so. Up until the mid-1800s, subsistence farming was the primary economic activity and householders raised sheep for wool, milk and mutton; they also cultivated potatoes and some even kept cattle for beef and chickens for eggs. When the population began to increase, the economy had to diversify. Fishing, already a significant economic factor elsewhere in the North Atlantic, seemed the obvious answer.

Initially, most fishing took place far offshore around Greenland, Canada, Svalbard

Grindadráp

Although many foreigners consider the grindadráp an abomination rather than anything remotely resembling culture, to most Faroese it's as much a part of life as Christmas.

Here's how it works. Upon sighting a pod of migrating pilot whales ('grind'), a fishing boat sounds the alarm by sending a radio message to the shore and hoisting a flag as a signal that whales are present and the hunt is to begin. Someone on shore yells the war cry 'grind!' and mayhem ensues. That area of the island effectively shuts down as everyone runs to their motorboats to join in.

The pod is surrounded by the boats. In earlier times, the last whale in the pod would be speared, causing it to surge ahead and lead the rest of the whales toward the shore. Today, the whales are merely herded towards a beach using motorboats. Once they're too close to shore to escape by sounding, people attack them in the shallow water with knives, hooks and harpoons and struggle to get them onto the beach, turning the water red with blood.

Historically, if the whales were trapped but failed to beach, the boats would move in and people would attack the whales with spears. This practice has now been officially banned and the use of gaffs has been made illegal in waters over one metre deep. However, it's reported that both spears and gaffs are still being used, despite the law.

Often 100 or more whales are taken within 15 minutes. The largest whale goes to the boat which first sighted the pod and the rest are divided among registered residents of the participating district. After the bodies are carved up and distributed, everyone marches off to a party singing the *Grindevise*, a multiplicity of verses extolling Faroese humankind's conquest over the hapless cetaceans that unwisely passed too close to the islands for their own good. The gist goes something like 'We are strong men and killing whales is our greatest joy...'

In order to justify the hunt, the Faroese maintain that they aren't breaking any International Whaling Commission regulations because it's a 'traditional, communal and non-commercial hunt', and that they are not severely depleting the whale population. Whale meat accounts for about one quarter of all meat consumption in the Faroes, and there is a limit to catches to avoid waste. The Faroese claim to

(Spitsbergen) and Iceland. Most of these had waters rich in shrimp and cod, while Iceland offered coalfish and haddock as well. From the nearby North Sea, the Faroese took mackerel and whiting. Although a small proportion of the Faroese annual catch still comes from foreign or international waters, domestic fishing (since the extension of the exclusion limit to 200 miles in 1977) has increased to become more important, and increasingly high technology has been employed to make the most of the resource.

By the late 1980s, the Faroes' standard of living ranked as the world's highest, but a combination of factors sent the economy into a nosedive. Before the fishing industry crashed in the early 1990s, nearly 58% of the islands' annual catch came from Faroese waters. Dried, chilled, frozen or salted fish and fish meal comprised 96% of Faroese exports and nearly 25% of all employment in the Faroes was in some way related to fishing or fish processing. Another 10% involved manufacturing equipment for the fishing industry. Unemployment was negli-

gible; the Faroes actually suffered from a labour shortage and foreign labour was imported in order to satisfy the market. Most foreigners working in the Faroes were, of course, involved in the fishing industry.

A recent economic venture is fish farming and, at the time of writing, there were 36 fish farms in the Faroe Islands raising primarily roe and small fry as well as trout and salmon. Outside Tórshavn, many people supplement other incomes with agriculture, raising a few sheep and cultivating potatoes for personal consumption.

In addition to fishing, there's a small woollens industry and tourism is on the increase. After the recent economic crisis the Faroese are looking to boosting tourism as a source of income. The Faroes, along with Iceland and Greenland, have formed the West Nordic Tourist Board, a body for promoting the region as a whole in hopes of attracting international visitors and their money.

Currently, however, the Faroese economy is recovering from the crisis. The unemploy adhere to regulations specifying that the whales, once beached, must be killed as quickly as possible and not permitted to suffer unnecessarily. However, in the heat of the action, regulations may be forgotten and it's not clear whether the minimum standards for humane killing stipulated by the International Whaling Commission are being met.

Although drive hunts of small whales are prohibited throughout Europe by the European Convention for the Conservation of Wildlife, Denmark has been able to exempt the Faroe Islands from the legal requirements of the convention. Over the past few years, the Faroese have come under extreme pressure from international environmental organisations to abandon what some would call an anachronistic tradition. Predictably, T-shirts advocating the equivalent of a 'greenie-*dráp*' have appeared and the Faroese have complained that boycotts of Faroese products and other foreign efforts to curtail the hunt were violations of the United Nations Covenants of 1966. In 1989, an article was published in the West Norden Tourism Conference newspaper under the headline: 'The Faroese will not stop their Pilot Whale Hunt'. Full stop.

Even more recently, the government issued a pithy 28-page defence of the practice, which they distribute to tourists for Dkr30. To get hold of a copy, contact the Department of Fisheries (☎ 11080, fax 14942), PO Box 64, FR-110 Tórshavn, Faroe Islands. If you're interested in international efforts to halt the practice, contact The Whale & Dolphin Conservation Society (☎ 01225-334511; fax 01225-480097), Alexander House, James St West, Bath, BA1 2BT, UK.

The grindadráps normally take place in the summer when the pilot whales are migrating past the islands (during my recent visit in June 1996, nearly 1000 whales were beached within a few days of each other at Miðvágur and Vestmanna/Leynar), but a successful hunt isn't broadcast internationally. Due to the local distaste for international campaigns against the practice, tourists aren't particularly welcome to watch and it's been reported that cameras have been smashed by defensive participants.

In any case, anyone who does witness a grindadráp will need a strong stomach and to keep reminding themselves that it's a tradition carried over from the Viking days. It may well be the most graphic remaining example of what that culture must have been like. ■

ment problem has diminished and people who emigrated to Denmark and other EU countries in search of better conditions are beginning to return home. (For more information, see Economic Turmoil in the History section of this chapter).

POPULATION & PEOPLE

At the end of 1995, about 43,400 people lived in the Faroes, 13,800 of them in the capital, Tórshavn, and 4500 more in the second-largest town, Klaksvík. There are approximately 100 other communities of varying size. Up to now, migration into Tórshavn from the countryside hasn't caused any significant decline in the rural population but, between 1990 and 1995, economic migration to Denmark and the EU resulted in a population loss of over 14,000. This has been partially offset by immigration, a birth rate of 1.5% and a natural annual increase of 0.6%, which is one of the highest in Western Europe.

The majority of Faroese are of Nordic origin, descended from early Norwegian set-tlers who arrived during the Viking era. There are also a few Danes, most of whom live in the capital.

ARTS

Many of the elements that characterise Western European arts and culture have never been important in the Faroes. Individual artistic expression has only really emerged during this century. As for poetry and literature, much of this trend may be attributed to the former status of the Faroese language, which was regarded as a 'peasant' dialect with no written form. Lack of musical tradition or classical composition is largely due to the absence of musical instruments, other than the human voice, until the end of the 1800s.

Artistic endeavours, at least as far as a national heritage was concerned, were thwarted by a general lack of time in the subsistence households. The visual arts didn't mature on the Faroese scene until fishing replaced agriculture as the economic mainstay.

THE FAROE ISLANDS

Music & Dance

The earliest Faroese music would be considered rather bland by modern standards. The historical music was designed to accompany the Faroese chain dance and the *kvæði*, a large body of late medieval ballads. Danish songs, poems and ballads were also set to music and danced to, as were humorous and teasing anecdotes about everyday life.

The music was nearly always written in 6/4 time, primarily in order to best accompany the chain dance. Melodies, commonly sung in a minor key, were very simple and repetitive. Accompaniment was with voice only, since no musical instruments were present in the Faroese tradition. Nowadays, rather than receiving everyday air-play, dancing takes place mostly on special or festive occasions that emphasise traditional events or national identity.

The very simple chain dance was once popular all over Scandinavia, but has survived intact only in the Faroes. It's a fairly slow and repetitive series of steps, mimicking perfectly the music that accompanies it. The dancers are expected to take the feelings behind the words and interpret them in their dancing. Although the steps remain the same, a sad text is danced in one way and a gleeful text in another. When everyone reaches the same wavelength, so to speak, conveying the emotion behind the song, then the effort is considered a success.

The dances are led by a choir leader, who sets the mood for the occasion. It begins with a circle on the dance floor formed by the leader and several dancers with hands and elbows joined. At this point, everyone present is welcome and expected to participate. As more people join in, the circle grows, and when they can no longer be contained in the room, they develop into serpentine rows that wind their way through the room and allow everyone to dance near everyone else sometime during the song.

As for modern music, Steintór Rasmussen and his pop group Frændur are probably best known, mainly in the Faroes and Denmark. Their disco dance-music is accompanied with Faroese lyrics.

Literature

The first Faroese story traditions were passed on orally, for there was no written language to record them. During the Middle Ages, people occupied themselves through long winter nights with recitations of stories and poetry that had been handed down for generations. Those stories purporting to be historical were called *sagnir*, but it's not difficult to imagine that after several generations of retelling, they lost some of their original credibility. Fictitious stories, those that become more interesting over years of retelling, were known as *ævintýr*. The ballads, presented in verse and often set to music and dance, were called the *kvæði*. All these forms were carried over into the 19th

Faroese National Costume

The Faroese national costume is worn only on special occasions, including religious functions and high school graduations – young men and women consider it important to acquire this get-up for use at festivities.

Although the costume is distinctive in style, there's a lot of room for individual variation, and a festive group of Faroese so dressed can really be quite colourful. The men's costume includes a lavishly embroidered vest over a white shirt. Over this they wear a dark-coloured, embroidered woollen waistcoat with closely spaced silver buttons and matching calf-length homespun trousers with decorative buttons on the knees. This is topped off with a reddish cap with black stripes for young men and dark blue ones for older men.

Women's dress includes an ankle-length red skirt with a uniquely patterned red and black bodice, gathered in front with a laced silver chain. Over the top, they wear a patterned apron and a beautiful cape which is embroidered with the family's own unique design. This is often accompanied by a large ribbon around the neck. Both men and women wear the same Welsh-style black shoes. ∎

entury, when what remained of them was collected and written down lest they be lost forever.

In the early 1800s, the first modern aroese poet, Nólsoyar-Poul Poulson, composed brilliant politically-inspired ballads lealing with the corruption and troubled ecoomics of the day. His most famous work is he 229-verse *Fuglakvæði*, which compared olitical leaders and monopolistic traders to irds of prey. Poul himself was portrayed as he oystercatcher, whose job was to warn the rdinary citizens – the smaller, weaker birds to beware of those in power.

In the short history of Faroese literature, he best-known writer is Heðin Brú whose ooks are extremely popular in the Faroes nd have gained acceptance abroad as well. ike many eminent authors in small nations, is work deals primarily with the struggle etween forces that would modernise and omogenise the world and those which value reserving the uniqueness of the smaller ocieties. His most renowned work is *The ld Man and his Sons* published during WWII.

Other Faroese authors include Jørgen-rantz Jacobsen and William Heinesen who oth got around the lack of a written lanuage by using Danish rather than Faroese. hey are fairly well known outside the slands but aren't as popular in their homeand due to their unusual humour and their ealing with uncomfortable topics disconertingly close to home.

oetry The first Faroese poetry (for reading, s opposed to singing) wasn't written until he early 20th century when J Djurhuus pubshed a collection of his work, thereby xposing the need for some sort of standrdised written language. His brother, Hans, ook up poetry as well, much of his work xtolling the grandeur of the Faroese landcape.

Rói Patursson, a more recent poet, has rned to modern lyrical constructions and inimalist language. He is now becoming cognised throughout Scandinavia as a litary force.

Visual Arts

Again, the visual arts are very young in the Faroes and haven't yet had time to develop into any sort of national tradition. Several painters have come forth during this century with some interesting interpretations of the inspiring landscape and harsh environment. Up to now, the most renowned has been Sámal Joensen Mikines (Faroese sometimes tack the name of their home island onto their surname as a patronymic of sorts) who was inspired to surrealism by the gloomy magnificence of Mykines.

Somewhat more faithful to reality is Ingálvur Reyni, who emphasised colour as a means of expressing a more positive aspect of the landscape than Joensen Mikines had. Another landscape painter, Ruth Smith, was particularly adept at conveying the overall mood of the country by capturing the clear and unusual light that characterises the higher latitudes.

The best of Faroese art is displayed in an annual national exhibition during the Ólavsøka or St Olav's Day festivities in Tórshavn in late July. Those visiting at other times can see the permanent exhibition at the National Gallery, also in Tórshavn.

LANGUAGE

It may be surprising to learn that the national language is not Danish but Faroese, locally called Føroyskt (pronounced 'FOOR-isht'). Although nearly every Faroese learns Danish at school and many go on to learn English and German, the people have successfully resisted, wherever possible, the encroachment of foreign languages into everyday life.

Faroese is a Germanic language derived from Old Norse, significantly influenced by Gaelic, and is related most closely to Icelandic and some Norwegian dialects.

The original language of all Scandinavia (except Finland) was Old Norse, and only after the period of migration and settlement did individual areas begin to develop their own linguistic characteristics. Although some medieval Faroese manuscripts exist, when Norway was absorbed by Denmark the

THE FAROE ISLANDS

Faroese dialect ceased to be a written language and was replaced by Danish as the written language of the islands.

In 1781, the scholar Jens Christian Svabo travelled to the Faroes to research and preserve what remained of the Faroese language. He collected stories, songs, and as much vocabulary as he could muster, then set about creating an orthography so he could record it all.

Subsequent researchers followed his example and before long Faroese had many orthographies, but none stood out as a feasible standard. Disputes arose and it wasn't until 1890 that a standard written version of Faroese was adopted. It wasn't long before the first Faroese literature began to appear, and in 1948 the language Føroyskt was made official and given equal status with Danish in public and government affairs.

As in Icelandic, new words to describe new ideas and inventions are not merely borrowed from Danish or English, but are either taken directly from the local language or created from existing words.

Pronunciation

In most cases, Faroese words are stressed on the first syllable. Grammar is quite similar to that of Icelandic but pronunciation is another matter entirely. A lot of Icelandic, Danish and even Gaelic influences come in to play. For example, the name of the Eysturoy's village Eiði is inexplicably pronounced 'OY-yeh'. The nearby village of Gjógv is referred to as 'Jagv'. The name of the capital, Tórshavn, gets the more or less Danish pronunciation, 'TORSH-hown'. As you can see, it can get a bit complicated and unusual.

Unless you're one of those lucky people who can pick up the general tone and pronunciation of a language just by listening, it may be a good idea to show the text in the following vocabulary section to a local and ask for the correct pronunciation before attempting or slaughtering it.

If you still have problems, quite a few Faroese speak at least some English. Everyone speaks Danish and therefore they can handle Norwegian and Swedish as well.

Basic Vocabulary

The Faroese will be surprised but proud if foreigner attempts to struggle through word or two of their language. After years o struggle trying to preserve the language, it successful restoration as an official languag is a matter of national pride. That an outside would recognise it as unique, let alone bothe to use it, will inspire them even more.

Basics

Hello.	Hey/Góðan dag.
Good morning.	Góðan morgun.
Good evening.	Gott kvøld.
Good night.	Góða nátt.
Good-bye.	Farvæl.
Please.	Ger so væl.
Thank you.	Takk fyri.
Thank you very much.	Túsund takk.
Welcome.	Vælkomin.
Excuse me.	Orsaka.

Useful Words & Phrases

How's it going?
  Hvussu gongst?
What's your name?
  Hvussu eitur tú?
Do you speak English?
  Tosar tú enskt?
Where is the ...?
  Hvar er ...?
What would you like?
  Hvat vilt tú hava?
What time is it?
  Hvat er klokkan?
How much is this?
  Hvussu nógv kostar tað?

bus	*bussur*
boat	*bátur*
plane	*flogfar*
bank	*banki*
post office	*posthús*
youth hostel	*ferðamannaheim*
supermarket	*keypsamtøka*
restaurant	*matstova*
cafe	*kaffistova*
tourist office	*ferðaskrivstova*
road	*vegur*
street	*gøta*

village	bygd
map	vegakort or kort
rucksack	ryggsekkur

Geographical Features

bay	vágur
bird cliffs	fuglaberg
coast	strond
harbour	havn
island	oy or oyggj
lake	vatn
mountain	fjall
mountain pass	fjallaskarð
ravine	gjógv
river or stream	á
slope	brekka
valley	dalur

Food & Drink

bread	breyð
butter	smør
cheese	ostur
chocolate	sukurláta
egg	egg
fish	fiskur
fruit	frukt
lamb	lamb
meat	kjøt
milk	mjólk
mutton	seyðakjøt
pork	grísur
potato	epli
salmon	laksur
sausage	pylsa
sugar	sukur

Days

Sunday	sunnudagur
Monday	mánadagur
Tuesday	týsdagur
Wednesday	mikudagur
Thursday	hósdagur
Friday	fríggjadagur
Saturday	leygardagur

Numbers

1	eitt
2	tvey
3	trý
4	fýra
5	fimm
6	seks
7	sjey
8	átta
9	níggju
10	tíggju
11	ellivu
12	tólv
13	trettan
14	fjúrtan
15	fimtan
16	sekstan
17	seytjan
18	átjan
19	nítjan
20	tjúgu ('CHEW-wah')
21	ein og tjúgu
30	tredivu
40	fjøriti
50	hálvtrýs
60	trýs
70	hálvfjers
80	fýrs
90	hálvfems
100	hundrað
101	hundrað og eitt
121	hundrað ein og tjúgu
200	tvey hundrað
1000	túsund

Facts for the Visitor

PLANNING

When to Go

Most of the islands' tourism takes place between 1 June and 1 September, but even at the height of the season there's no need to worry about overcrowding. The Faroes are still well off the beaten track.

Off-season travel can be lovely, with the layer-cake mountains looking especially magical when frosted with snow, but for visitor facilities and climate the only practical time to visit is in the summer, when hotels, youth hostels and transport are operating. Particularly interesting times to be in the islands are around mid-summer and at the end of July (for the Ólavsøka festivities).

Maps

A handy booklet of topographic maps covering the Faroes at 1:100,000 scale (last updated in 1994) is available at tourist offices and bookshops in the Faroes for Dkr115, or directly from the publishers Kort og Matrikelstyrelsen (☎ 35 87 50 50; fax 35 87 50 51), Rentemestervej 8, DK-2400 Copenhagen, Denmark. In Danish the Faroes are called Færøerne. They also cover the islands with two separate topographic sheets at the same scale. The northern section includes Streymoy, Eysturoy, the north-eastern islands and the western islands as well as Koltur, Hestur and Nólsoy. The southern section includes Suðuroy, Sandoy, Skúvoy, Stóra Dímun and Lítla Dímun.

There's also a 1:20,000 series of 53 topographic sheets covering the whole archipelago. The base mapping for this series dates back to the 1930s but it's being updated; Vágar, Hestur, Koltur and most of Streymoy, Eysturoy and the north-eastern islands have already been covered. If you're planning any serious walking, these are by far the most useful and detailed maps available. If you'd like to study the maps before you go, write for a catalogue and order

directly from Kort og Matrikelstyrelsen. Some of the more popular sheets are sold by the Faroe Islands Tourist Board and bookshops in Tórshavn for Dkr70 each.

The tourist board also sells the 1:200,000 scale *Faroe Islands Map & Travel Guide* for Dkr20. It includes street plans of all the larger settlements plus accommodation, service, bus and ferry information.

A map of Tórshavn is found in the tourist board handout *Around the Faroe Islands*, but they have a clearer map called *Tórshavn City* with information on the back. Alternatively, there's the *Tórshavnar Býarkort*, a detailed large-scale map available from bookshops and tourist offices for Dkr10.

SUGGESTED ITINERARIES

Depending on the length of your stay, you might like to see and do the following:

Two days
　　Tórshavn and the Vestmanna Bird Cliffs tour or a visit to a village such as Gjógv, Kirkjubøur, Oyndarfjørður or Tjørnuvík
One week
　　As above plus Klaksvík, the islands of Viðoy (for the tough walk to the Enniberg cliffs) and Fugloy and perhaps a day excursion to Nólsoy or Kalsoy
Two weeks
　　As above plus the islands of Vágar and Mykines

HIGHLIGHTS

It's naturally up to every traveller to discover their own highlights, but some of the best sights and experiences in the Faroes are:

1. Vestmanna Bird Cliffs tour
2. A walk to the Enniberg Cliffs on Viðoy
3. The cliffs on Fugloy
4. Mykines
5. Hiking on Vágar
6. A walk to the lighthouse at Kallur on Kalsoy
7. The village of Fámjin on Suðuroy
8. The village of Saksun and the Dúvugarður museum
9. Tinganes peninsula in Tórshavn
10. The village of Gjógv on Eysturoy

TOURIST OFFICES
Local Tourist Offices

National tourist information is available at the Faroe Islands Tourist Board on Gongin in central Tórshavn. The Tórshavn city tourist office handles enquiries about the city and environs but can also help with queries regarding sites of interest outside the city. There are also smaller tourist offices at the Vágar airport, in Klaksvík, Tvøroyri on Suðuroy island, and Fuglafjørður and Saltangará on Eysturoy island.

The tourist board publishes an informative series of free leaflets giving details of walks in the Faroe Islands, ranging from easy to fairly difficult. Many other free leaflets and brochures are available, including *Around the Faroe Islands* and *Where to Stay*.

The following are the addresses of the various offices and private bureaux:

Faroe Islands Tourist Board, PO Box 118, Gongin, FR-100 Tórshavn (☎ 16055; fax 10858)

Kunningarstovan City Tourist Office, PO Box 379, Niels Finsensgøta 13, FR-100 Tórshavn (☎ 15788; fax 16831)

Tora Tourist Traffic (private agency), Niels Finsensgøta 21, FR-100 Tórshavn (☎ 15505; fax 15667)

Kunningardiskurin Tourist Information Desk, Vágar Airport, FR-380 Sørvágur (☎ 33200; fax 33100)

Norðoya Kunningarstova Tourist Office, Nólsoyar Pálsgøta, FR-700 Klaksvík (☎ 56939; fax 56586)

Kunningarstovan Suðuroy Tourist Office, FR-800 Tvøroyri (☎ 72480; fax 72380)

Tourist Offices Abroad

The Faroes and Denmark have several offices which offer tourist information and guidelines for commercial ventures. There is also a new source of information in the USA which is independent of the tourist board.

If you have any questions about the Faroes, contact one of the following offices. For addresses of Danish tourism boards, see the Greenland Facts for the Visitor chapter.

Denmark
Færøernes Repræsentationskontor, Højbroplads 7, DK-1200 Copenhagen K (☎ 33 14 08 66); Danish Tourist Board, Vesterbrogade 6D, DK-1620 Copenhagen V (☎ 33 11 14 15)

UK
Faroese Commercial Attaché, 150 Market St, Aberdeen, AB1 2PP, Scotland (☎ 01224-592777)

USA
Faroe Islands Tourist Information Office, c/- John Gasbarre, PO Box 823, Vineyard Haven, Maine 04863-0823 (☎ 1-207 863 9987; fax 1-207 863 9916; email islandman@island man.com).

VISAS & DOCUMENTS
Visas

For information on who needs a visa to enter Denmark (including the Faroes and Greenland) see Visas & Documents in the Greenland Facts for the Visitor chapter. Technically, visitors to the Faroes must be able to show sufficient funds for their intended stay, but formalities are normally cursory, especially if you're entering from another Nordic country. What officials are really looking for is alcohol, which they're quite touchy about.

Other Documents

HI hostel cards, student identity cards and proof of age over 65 (for seniors) will all yield some discounts in the Faroes. If you're intending to hire a vehicle, don't forget your driving licence.

EMBASSIES
Faroese Embassies Abroad

The Faroes are represented abroad by Danish embassies and consulates which are found in the capital cities of most countries, as well as many smaller Scandinavian cities. For a listing, see Embassies in the Greenland Facts for the Visitor chapter.

Foreign Embassies in the Faroes

Most consular representation in the Faroes is of the honorary variety, although there are some official representatives based in Tórshavn. Some of the most useful are:

France
Valdemar Lützen (☎ 11020)
Germany
Ása á Dul Jacobsen (☎ 14949)

THE FAROE ISLANDS

Italy
    Renate Simonsen (☎ 12600)
UK
    Johan Mortensen (☎ 13510)

CUSTOMS

Visitors over 18 years of age may import three kg of chocolate, 50 grams of perfume and a quarter of a litre of *eau de toilette*. They may also import 200 cigarettes, 50 cigars or 250 grams of tobacco.

Alcohol is strictly and puritanically controlled in the Faroes. Those over 18 years of age may bring in one litre of wine (less than 22% alcohol content), one litre of spirits (from 22% to 60% alcohol) and two litres of beer (less than 5.8% alcohol) in long-necked bottles only (the import of cans or non-returnable containers is prohibited). Under normal circumstances, two additional litres of spirits may be imported upon payment of duties.

Animals may not be brought into the Faroes under any circumstances. Those who wish to bring in firearms must have an export licence from the country of origin and written permission from the Faroese government and police. Otherwise, transit passengers must leave firearms in the care of customs and collect them upon their departure from the Faroes.

To import recreational fishing equipment you need a veterinarian's certificate stating that the equipment has been disinfected by immersion for at least 10 minutes in a solution of 2% formaldehyde. Alternatively, it can be disinfected upon arrival in the Faroes (which is free of charge) or left with customs until your departure. This is to prevent contamination of Faroese inland waters by foreign fish diseases.

MONEY
Costs

The minimum price for a single hotel room is about Dkr500, but there are also guest-houses, youth hostels and campgrounds offering more economical options. Eating out, supermarket food and bus travel are expensive compared to most other Western European countries. Tipping is not required. For further information on costs, see the Regional Facts for the Visitor chapter.

Currency

Although the Faroes issues its own currency the Faroese króna (Fkr) is tied to the Danish krone; the two are used interchangeably throughout the Kingdom of Denmark, that is on mainland Denmark and in the Faroes and Greenland. The Faroes don't mint coins, so all coins in use are Danish. One króna is equal to 100 øre.

Notes come in denominations of 50, 100, 500 and 1000 krónur, and coins (Danish only) in use are 25 and 50 øre, one krone and two, five, 10 and 20 kroner.

Currency Exchange

The Faroese króna is always equal and interchangeable with the Danish krone (Dkr). However, prices given in this section are in Dkr. Exchange rates at the time of going to press were:

Australia	A$1	=	4.78
Canada	C$1	=	4.65
Germany	DM1	=	3.82
France	FF1	=	1.13
Iceland	Ikr1	=	0.09
Japan	¥100	=	5.20
New Zealand	NZ$1	=	4.31
Norway	Nkr1	=	0.97
UK	UK£1	=	10.20
USA	US$1	=	6.28

Changing Money

Foreign currency may be exchanged at any Faroese bank during regular hours, from 9 am to 4 pm Monday to Friday and until 6 pm on Thursday. The exchange bank at Vágar airport is open between 10 am and 2 pm and for arriving and departing international flights. Normally a small commission is charged for exchange services. After hours hotels will also normally exchange money (as will tourist information offices and travel agencies). All brands of travellers' cheques and all major currencies are accepted.

Post offices in Tórshavn, Runavík, Vestmanna, Vágur, Tvøroyri, Klaksvík and Saltangará will exchange postal cheques from France, the Netherlands, Luxembourg and the UK, and postal savings-bank cheques from Norway, Finland, Sweden and Germany.

Major credit cards such as Eurocard, MasterCard, Visa and American Express are widely accepted in the Faroes, particularly by tourism-oriented establishments. Banks will issue cash advances on credit cards and also cash Eurocheques. Visa, Plus, Eurocard, MasterCard, Cirrus and JCB are accepted by the Føroya Banki ATM at Niels Finsensgøta 15, Tórshavn.

Tipping & Bargaining

Tipping is not required in the Faroes and bargaining is not acceptable, since all prices are fixed.

Taxes & Refunds

Travellers can now get a partial refund of the 25% VAT when they leave the country. If Dkr300 or more is spent in any one shop which displays the 'Tax-free for Tourists' sign, you will be given a refund cheque for about 15% of the value of the goods. Obtain your refund from either the Farstøðin transport terminal or Vágar airport (at the Flogfelag Føroya office) on departure. The goods will have to be shown to customs.

POST & COMMUNICATIONS

The postal service in the Faroes is called Postverk Føroya. Post offices are found in most towns and villages around the islands but opening hours vary widely. The central post office in Tórshavn is open Monday to Friday from 9 am to 5 pm. Photocopying is available there for Dkr1 per A4 page.

The Faroes became a separate postal zone on 30 January 1975, and have since issued a variety of interesting and collectable stamps. Philatelists interested in obtaining a catalogue of Faroese stamps should write to Postverk Føroya, Frimerkjadeildin, FR-159 Tórshavn, Faroe Islands. See also the Things to Buy section at the end of this chapter.

Postal Rates

The postal rate for letters and postcards weighing less than 20 grams to destinations within the Kingdom of Denmark and the rest of Europe is Dkr4.50 priority (A) and Dkr4 economy (B). To other countries, it's Dkr7.50 (A) and Dkr5.50 (B). The A/B rates for letters and cards between 20 and 100 grams are Dkr6.50/6 to Scandinavian countries, Dkr13/11 to the rest of Europe and Dkr18/15 to the rest of the world.

Express Mail services are available from Tórshavn. Rates vary greatly but, to give you some idea, to Europe (outside Iceland and Denmark) the charge is Dkr300 for the first kg and Dkr20 for each additional kg. To North America, it's Dkr300 for the first kg and Dkr50 for each additional kg.

Receiving Mail

Reliable poste restante services are available in Tórshavn. To receive mail, have it addressed to you at Poste Restante, Central Post Office (miðbynum), FR-100 Tórshavn, Faroe Islands. It will help with filing if the surname is capitalised or underlined.

Telephone

International telephone calls can be made from the telephone office at Tinghúsvegur 3, Tórshavn, open daily from 8 am to 9 pm. The telephone office and the post offices sell telephone cards with denominations of Dkr20, 50 and 100.

From public phones, local calls cost Dkr2 for up to five minutes. However, it can be difficult to find a public phone in the Faroes. Apart from the telephone offices in Tórshavn and Klaksvík, try inside the Farstøðin transport terminal, some of the places to stay in Tórshavn and the youth hostel in Klaksvík. The phone in the hostel in Klaksvík and the one on the island of Mykines only accept phone cards.

For reverse-charge (collect) calls, you must first ascertain whether Denmark (and therefore the Faroes) has a reciprocal agreement with the destination country. You can book operator-assisted calls of any kind by dialling ☎ 0013. For telephone information and directory assistance ring ☎ 0033.

The Faroes' international country code is ☎ 298. To make an international call, first dial the international access code ☎ 009 and then the country code, area or city code and phone number (to ring Denmark, use just 0 rather than 009). For calls within the Faroes, just dial the telephone number – there are no area codes to worry about.

Fax

Fax services are available from telephone offices and the post offices in Tórshavn, Klaksvík and Tvøroyri. The charge is Dkr20 for the first page (then Dkr10 for each subsequent page) to mainland Denmark and Iceland; Dkr30 (then Dkr15) to anywhere else in Europe; and Dkr50 (then Dkr25) elsewhere. For incoming faxes, the public fax number at the telephone office in Tórshavn is 298-16498.

BOOKS

Central Tórshavn has two very good bookshops in the city centre, and there's another in Klaksvík. Although most publications are in Danish or Faroese, some foreign-language titles are available in HN Jacobsens Bókahandil on Vaglið, near the town hall in Tórshavn. Another bookshop, Bókasølan, has some tourist publications and English-language paperbacks; it's upstairs in the SMS Shopping Centre.

Guidebooks

Apart from this book and a few pages of coverage in several Scandinavia guides, there are no practical English-language general guidebooks dealing with the Faroe Islands. For interesting background reading and tour suggestions, take a look at *The Faroes – the Faraway Islands* by Anthony Jackson (Robert Hale, London, 1991). Although it purports to be a guidebook, it's short on practical information and the hardback format makes it less than conveniently portable. It's best used for planning before you leave home.

A new series of four walking guides will be published in English. The first, *Streymoy and Eysturoy – a walkers guide* by Andrew Jennings, Fríðunn Hansen and Tom Todd (Bókadeildin, Tórshavn) should be available by spring 1997. These guides will detail the nature, history and culture along traditional and other walking routes in the islands.

In German, there are two guidebooks. *Färöer Reisehandbuch* by Ulrich Kreuzenbeck and Hans Klüche, published by Nordis Verlag of Düsseldorf, is a bit dry and extremely outdated but most of the information is useful. For Danes, this book has been translated into Danish and marketed as a *Skarv Guide*.

Alternatively, if you read German and have Dkr175, practically everything you'd ever want to know about the Faroes – and more – is found in the well-presented German publication *Die Färöer – Inselwelt im Nordatlantik* by Sabine Gorsemann (DuMont Verlag, Köln, 1990). It's available from HN Jacobsens Bókahandil in Tórshavn.

Literature & Fiction

A few works of modern Faroese literature have found their way into English translation, most prominently the works of William Heinesen *(Neils Peter*, *Tower at the Edge of the World*, *The Black Cauldron)* and Heðin Brú *(The Old Man and his Sons)*, which can be found at the two main bookshops in Tórshavn.

Although it was written in Iceland, you may want to read the English translation of the *Færinga Saga* (sometimes spelt *Færeyinga Saga)*, which outlines the settlement of the Faroes and the misadventures of their early characters. The English version, *The Faroese Saga*, was translated by GVC Young and Cynthia Clewer and published in Belfast in 1973.

If you're interested in the Faroese pilot whale issue, look for the anti-grindadráp novel, *The Faroes Venture* by Jeremy Lucas (Jonathan Cape, London, 1987). It isn't particularly well written, but one supposes his heart is in the right place.

General

There's the usual gamut of coffee-table publications extolling the Faroese landscape in brilliant glossy colour (primarily green). These are available in several languages at the previously mentioned shops. You can also purchase Faroese-English dictionaries including the basic *Zijo's English-Faroese* phrasebook available for Dkr25 at HN Jacobsens Bókahandil.

A brief but wonderfully clever account of travelling in the Faroes is included in the North Atlantic travelogue *Last Places – A Journey in the North* by Lawrence Millman, published by Houghton-Mifflin (Boston, 1990). Another light and positive account of life in the Faroes is *The Atlantic Islands* (1970) by Kenneth Williamson, who was there during WWII.

The best and most thorough historical treatise on the islands is *Faroe – the Emergence of a Nation* by John F West, published by C Hurst & Co (London, 1972).

For a good general description of Faroese history, economy and culture, look for *The Faroe Islands* by Liv Kjørsvik Schei and Gunnie Moberg (John Murray, London, 1991). It contains lots of information as well as some nice drawings and colour photos, but the text is mercilessly dry.

ONLINE SERVICES

There's lots of tourist and general information on the Faroese University Internet home page (www.sleipnir.fo/).

NEWSPAPERS & MAGAZINES

The five local newspapers, all in Faroese, are published one to five times weekly. Copenhagen, Frankfurt, London and New York papers are flown in, but they're often several days old when they hit the stands. International news magazines, including *Time*, *Newsweek* and *Der Spiegel*, are sold in the airport kiosk and the sweet-shop/newsagent in the SMS Shopping Centre in Tórshavn.

RADIO & TV

Útvarp Føroya, the local radio station (89.8 MHz FM, 531 kHz MW), broadcasts on weekdays from 7.15 am to 2 pm and 5 to 8 pm, Saturday from 7.15 am to 10 pm, and Sunday from 10 am to 7 pm. The English-language weather report is broadcast at 8.45 am on weekdays.

Sjónvarp Føroya, the Faroes' television station, broadcasts daily except Monday. It first hit the scene in 1984 and, now that the initial bugs have been worked out, the Faroese are fairly happy with the result. Films are screened in the original language with Danish or Faroese subtitles. Foreign television programming is available by satellite.

LAUNDRY

The Faroes isn't flush with laundrettes, but Tórshavn has two and there's also one in Klaksvík. Dry cleaning is also available in Tórshavn. See the relevant chapters for details.

WOMEN TRAVELLERS

Women are unlikely to have any special problems while travelling in the Faroe Islands.

GAY & LESBIAN TRAVELLERS

Perhaps due to the strength of the Christian Lutheran church, gay issues receive little attention. Although Faroese people are by no means intolerant, gay couples are advised to be discreet to avoid upsetting some of the more traditional locals. There are no specifically gay bars or clubs on the islands.

DISABLED TRAVELLERS

Most public transport in the Faroes can take at least one passenger in a wheelchair and some hotels and hostels have wheelchair access. For further details, see the Faroese Tourist Board leaflet *Where to Stay*, or contact the Faroese Association for the Handicapped (☎ 17373), Íslandsvegur 10c, FR-100 Tórshavn, open on weekdays from 9 am to 4 pm. Effata (☎ 16929) at Íslandsvegur 10 can give help and advice to the deaf and hard-of-hearing. There's also a Society for the Blind at the same address (☎ 18222).

THE FAROE ISLANDS

SENIOR TRAVELLERS

Senior travellers with proof of age over 65 get 50% discount on bus and passenger ferry single fares. There are few other discounts available, but it doesn't hurt to ask anyway.

TRAVEL WITH CHILDREN

Unless your kids are extremely mellow and can entertain themselves for hours on end, the Faroes' penchant for unpleasant weather conditions may make camping with children less than pleasant. Children aged seven to 13 get 50% discount on bus and passenger ferry single fares, and discounts are usually available on tours; enquire when booking. Museum entrance fees are either reduced or free for children.

USEFUL ORGANISATIONS

Several European countries have Faroese friendship societies which coordinate activities and keep up with the latest news and information on island happenings. They shouldn't be used as tourist information offices, but if you have a particular interest you may want to contact one of the following:

Færøsk-Dansk Forening – Tove Danielsen, Tórugata 2, FR-100 Tórshavn, Faroe Islands
Deutsch-Färöischer Freundeskreis – Holger Andersen, Jütlandring 180, D-24109 Kiel, Germany
The Scottish-Faroese Society – Tony Jackson, 37 Grange Road, Edinburgh, EH9 1UG, Scotland

PUBLIC HOLIDAYS & SPECIAL EVENTS

The Faroes recognise an unusually large number of public holidays, including:

1 January
    New Year's Day
6 January
    Epiphany
March
    Gregorius' Day
March or April
    Maundy Thursday, Good Friday, Easter Sunday, Easter Monday
25 April
    Flag Day
1 May
    Labour Day
11 May
    Common Prayers Day
May
    Ascension Day
June
    Whitsunday, Whitmonday
5 June
    Constitution Day
28 & 29 July
    Ólavsøka (Faroese National Day)
1 November
    All Saints' Day
24 December
    Christmas Eve
25 December
    Christmas Day
26 December
    Boxing Day
31 December (afternoon only)
    New Year's Eve

Special Events

Ólavsøka, the Faroese National Day, is the main festival of the year in the islands. It conveniently takes place at the height of summer, on 28 and 29 July, and the normally reserved Faroese cut loose and celebrate, some assisted with copious quantities of alcohol. The festival is named in honour of St Olav, or Olav II Haraldsson, patron saint of Norway, who pressed for acceptance of Christianity in Scandinavia and devised Norway's religious code in the year 1024. It is likely, however, that the festival actually dates back to pagan times and adopted St Olav's name as a convenient way of lending it Christian sanction.

Festivities actually begin on 27 July with an open-air rock concert which lasts for over eight hours. One of the highlights of this two day (often dragging on into three) festival is the rowing competition in which villages compete against each other. The locals practice throughout the year for this event in their traditional craft which are shaped like miniature Viking ships. These are still in everyday use in the Faroes, primarily for fishing. Other Ólavsøka events include horse races, art exhibitions, chain-dancing, a variety of sporting competitions and the obligatory religious services.

In mid-July, the western Faroes hold the annual two-day Vestanstevna, which alter-ates on four-year cycles between Sørvágur (1997), Miðvágur (1998), Sandavágur (1999) and Vestmanna (2000). Many other small towns and villages also stage local festivals at various times of the year, and some can get pretty exciting. They all follow basically the same agenda as Ólavsøka, with rowing competitions, sports matches, both chain and modern dances, religious meetings, feasting and alcohol. Approximate dates and locations are outlined in the sections on the separate towns.

ACTIVITIES

Hiking & Trekking

For those with webbed feet or a high tolerance for wet and stormy conditions, the Faroes offer some superb hiking opportunities. Before the road system existed, routes between villages followed the shortest distances along ridges and over passes. They crisscrossed the country and were marked by cairns placed closely enough to be seen from one to the next in the typical weather conditions such as moderate fog or misty drizzle.

Although they're little used today and many of the cairns have long been destroyed, these routes still provide excellent opportunities for visitors to get out and travel on foot through the astonishing vertical scenery that is the Faroes' trademark.

As throughout the North Atlantic, weather is changeable. A warm sunny day may quickly turn cold and wet or blustery, so be prepared with a range of suitable clothing for all eventualities. A waterproof and windproof outer layer will be of utmost importance to prevent hypothermia. Although the temperature may be well above freezing, wet and/or windy weather can rob the body of heat faster than it can be produced, and without proper protection, the results can be life-threatening.

In addition to appropriate clothing, trekkers should carry a compass and, if possible, 1:20,000 scale topographic sheets for the area being explored. The 1:100,000 maps will be sufficient for experienced trekkers but if you have any doubts about your ability to pick your route through rugged and often fog-bound mountains, you're better off with larger scale maps. Although it's best to travel in groups (or at least in pairs), those with wilderness common sense who prefer the hermit experience shouldn't encounter any serious problems. Remember to tell someone where you're going and report your safe return.

All the old buildings, stone fences, cairns and relics which dot the landscape are officially protected and it's against the law to damage them. Pile a nearby rock on the cairn if you'd like, but don't remove any.

For information on camping in the bush, see Accommodation later in this chapter.

Fishing

In the Faroes, fishing is less restricted and more reasonably priced than in Iceland. If you're doing a lot of camping and walking through the highlands, you may want to bring along a rod and reel to help supplement your diet.

Salmon and sea trout inhabit the lakes Saksunarvatn and Leynavatn on Streymoy. Although you can get a licence for Saksunarvatn – enquire at the Dúvugarður museum (☎ 22303) in Saksun – the best fishing spot is the last pool before the sea, where no licence is required. A full-year licence for Leynavatn costs Dkr800 and a one-day licence is Dkr200, available from the Kunningarstovan tourist office in Tórshavn or the Statoil petrol station in Kollafjørður.

In the case of other lakes and streams, fishing is permitted upon payment of a fee to the landowner. Sea trout, brown trout, Arctic char and salmon are all available in Faroese lakes. Fishing for saltwater species from the shore is free and you don't need a licence. Stream fishing is permitted only between 1 May and 31 August, but lake fishing continues year round. It's best to try for salmon towards the end of the season. Fishing around stream mouths and fish farms is subject to special regulations. Specifications are updated annually and can be obtained from the tourist offices. Although no fishing permits are required for sea angling,

THE FAROE ISLANDS

organised transport is likely to be quite expensive.

Freshwater fishing trips, as well as deep-sea fishing for cod, haddock, halibut and herring, can be arranged through the tourist offices and private tour companies; for some ideas, see under Tours in the Faroes Getting Around chapter and Diving, below. Tourist offices can also help you arrange boat hire or charter from individuals in outlying villages.

Diving

Certified scuba divers can get advice on conditions etc from Harald Petersen (☎ & fax 2057555), Klaksvík Diving Service, Kjalarvegur 31, FR-700 Klaksvík, or Áki Dimon (☎ 71180), FR-800 Tvøroyri. Four-hour diving trips for experienced divers, including spear fishing and shipwreck exploration with a qualified instructor, are available for Dkr605: contact Kunningarstovan Suðuroy (☎ 72480; fax 72380), FR-800 Tvøroyri. Air tanks can be filled as required.

WORK

In the late 1980s, quite a few foreigners came to the Faroes to supplement the short labour force and earn fairly high wages in the fishing industry. Nearly every town had its cannery or processing plant and at the very least a harbour full of fishing boats, and there were normally job vacancies during the summer season to be filled by temporary overseas labour.

However, the days of easy and lucrative summer employment in the Faroes are over. With the current economic situation, a foreigner's chances of finding work are negligible. The situation may change, however, so here's a rundown on how to find work:

Citizens of Scandinavian countries need only turn up at the fish plant and if work is available, they can start immediately. Although Denmark is in the EU, the Faroes are not, and citizens of the EU and other countries must obtain official permission to work in the islands. First you must find a prospective employer – a cannery, fishing boat, construction company or whatever –

then apply to the police in Tórshavn for a work permit. Unless the potential employer can convey a sense of urgency to the powers that be, you may have to wait several months before a decision is forthcoming. Those who choose to work illegally are beyond protection of the law and may be taken advantage of by unscrupulous employers – so use good judgement.

Note that most canneries don't provide accommodation for workers and housing must be arranged individually. In Tórshavn this normally means the campground or renting a flat. In other villages, you'll have to convince youth-hostel management to waive the stay limits or rent a room from a local family. Employers may be able to provide suggestions.

If you want to work on a fishing boat, lucrative employment may be hard to come by, but if you'd just like a cultural experience, ask around the villages and see what turns up. You may be able to find unpaid work on one of the small family boats that fish for personal supplies.

ACCOMMODATION
Camping

If you're on a strict budget, camping will offer some relief from the Faroes' high accommodation prices. The Faroese word for campground is *campingpláss*, and you'll find a few organised campsites around the country. In the best-organised sites, you'll pay around Dkr40 to Dkr50 per person.

Wild camping is possible throughout the islands, but you'll need permission to camp on farms or private property and there's a law restricting camping to sites with running water and toilet facilities. (Note that this does not apply to uninhabited mountain regions well away from the road system.) When hiking or camping on private farms, take care not to trample fields planted for hay and remember to leave gates as you find them open or closed.

If you're doing your own cooking, carry a stove and sufficient fuel for the duration of your intended hike. Open fires are forbidden but there isn't any wood anyway. The only ludicrous rules for buying methylated spirits have been scrapped; now you'll just be asked what it's for.

Surface water is potable anywhere outside settled areas and there's no problem drinking it directly from streams. If there are sheep on the slopes higher up (as there invariably will be) and you're concerned about giardia, you may want to purify the water (see Health in the Regional Facts for the Visitor chapter at the start of this book). To ensure continuing cleanliness of streams and rivers, toilet areas, soap and dishwashing must be kept well clear of running water. See the Minimum Impact Camping section under Accommodation in the Iceland Facts for the Visitor chapter.

HI Hostels

Faroese hostels, *ferðamannaheim*, belong to the Danish Youth Hostels Association, the YMCA and other organisations. Most of these offer hot water, cooking facilities, luggage storage and opportunities to meet other travellers. Sleeping bags are normally welcome and guests need not provide or rent sleeping sheets; in fact, some hostels require guests to provide their own sleeping bag, because no blankets are available.

If you're planning a lot of hostel stays, it's worth joining Hostelling International to take advantage of the lower rates available to members. Dormitory rates range from Dkr70 to Dkr100 for members and from Dkr70 to Dkr150 for non-members.

Seamens' Homes

For information on seamens' homes (*sjómansheimið*), see Accommodation in the Greenland Facts for the Visitor chapter.

Guesthouses & Self-Catering

Most guesthouses are only open seasonally. Typically, rates range from Dkr300 to Dkr500 for a double.

Nordica (☎ 10809; fax 10886), Handilskjarnin, Postbox 1159, FR-110 Tórshavn, takes bookings for self-catering flats and apartments throughout the Faroes. High season rates (1 July to 18 August) range from Dkr300/1800 to Dkr833/4500 (daily/weekly). The minimum let is two days. Contact Nordica and ask for a copy of their brochure.

In the Faroes, the tour agency Tora Tourist Traffic keeps lists of families offering B&B for tourists. Most of these are clean and pleasant and offer an excellent introduction to the Faroese lifestyle. Prices are Dkr280/430 for a single/double, all including breakfast and most including use of cooking facilities. Alternatively, groups may rent entire houses or flats accommodating from two to 16 people at daily rates between Dkr480 and Dkr660 or at weekly rates between Dkr2880 and Dkr3960, in the high season (19 June to 21 August). Bookings should be made through Tora Tourist Traffic (☎ 15505; fax 15667), Postbox 3012, FR-110 Tórshavn, Faroe Islands, or at the tourist offices.

Hotels

Hotel accommodation in the Faroes is limited to Tórshavn and a handful of smaller towns. Most places are fairly characterless and desperately expensive, but they are comfortable and feature all the expected amenities: restaurants, pubs, private baths, telephones and television.

In Tórshavn, the price of a double hotel room is around Dkr800. Smaller hotels are a bit cheaper but may lack some of the amenities.

FOOD
Self-Catering

Supermarkets and cooperatives in Tórshavn are, on the whole, as well stocked as their counterparts in Copenhagen. Most towns and villages have at least a kiosk (similar to a US convenience store or an Aussie milk bar) selling basic groceries, normally open until 11 pm on weeknights and for varying hours on Saturday and Sunday.

You'll also find bakeries and butcher shops open during normal shopping hours. For details about fish, see Traditional Foods later in this section.

THE FAROE ISLANDS

Restaurants & Cafeterias

If you're coming from Europe, Faroese restaurants will seem quite expensive. Plan on Dkr30 to Dkr60 for a continental buffet breakfast and between Dkr135 and Dkr220 for lunch or dinner. Meals typically consist of some sort of meat or fish and potatoes accompanied by a small and precious pile of steamed frozen vegies and possibly even soup and salad.

Hot-dog stands and cafeterias offer the closest thing to fast food available in the Faroes. The latter serve varieties of small and decorative salads and Danish-style smyrjubreyð (smørrebrød or open-face sandwiches) sporting fish, lunch meat and colourful vegetables plastered together with butter and mayonnaise or tartar sauce. There'll also be a selection of cold desserts and cakes and a hot-meal counter where you can get hot dogs, fish and chips, chicken and possibly some sort of daily special. Specials typically cost from Dkr40 to Dkr55.

In a country dependent on fish, it's disappointing to find that cafeterias seem to serve only frozen reconstituted fish patties imported from Denmark. Even if they're not cold when they hit the display case, after a couple of hours they become downright disagreeable. Even less appealing are the burgers (from Dkr35 to Dkr40), which normally consist of a few grams of beef mince padded out with other ingredients.

Petrol stations in the countryside often have snack bars and there are a couple of coffee shops in Tórshavn and Klaksvík.

Traditional Foods

The first thing visitors notice about the traditional Faroese diet is the marked lack of green vegetables to accompany the ubiquitous meat and potatoes. Travellers from more fertile countries with more agriculturally amenable climates may even find some of it rather unappealing.

Meat in one form or another is the basis of every meal. One of the most popular treats is skerpikjøt, well-aged, wind-dried mutton which requires a hefty knife and powerful jaws to appreciate. New batches of skerpikjøt are prepared at Christmas time and are intended to last through to the following Christmas. Things may begin to get a bit green around November, but I don't think that has much effect on the taste and this is one Faroese delicacy that grows on you. In addition to mutton, fish and puffin meat are also dried. The drying shed, a standard feature of many Faroese households, is known as a hjallur.

Another meat variation is rast kjót or boiled mutton. Similarly boiled fish is called rastan fisk. After a grindadráp, a popular meal with the locals will consist of grind og spik or 'whale and blubber'. Whale meat isn't fishy and tastes like a very rich cut of beef.

Several varieties of sausage are also common. The one made of offal, trimmings and spices is called Føroyskt rollipylsa. A more interesting variety is called blóð pylsa and you can probably work out what its main ingredient would be.

The Faroese version of the Icelandic svið is called seyðar høvd and that's just what it is – a sheep's head. You'll find these peering at you from inside plastic bags in supermarket freezers.

Of course, fresh fish figures prominently in the diet but commercially caught fish all end up on the export market and supermarkets only sell it dried and frozen. If the Faroese want to enjoy freshly caught fish, they must arrange it themselves. If you feel like enjoying a meal straight from the North Atlantic, ask around the harbour in any village and see who has extra fish to sell. Alternatively, see Fishing under Activities later in this chapter.

The Faroese are also fond of sea birds and sea-bird eggs, and go to great lengths to collect them. Birds are normally collected in long-handled nets known as fleygustong, which resemble long-handled lacrosse rackets. The trusting and clumsy little puffins are the most vulnerable, and are sometimes eaten stuffed with sweet dough and baked or roasted. Gannets and guillemots are also netted and eaten in large quantities. Oily fulmars were once eaten as meals of last resort but many now carry psittacosis or 'parrot fever' and are mostly left alone.

The Faroese are permitted to gather seabird eggs for nine days each June, allowing the birds to produce another egg before the end of the mating season. Egg collectors lower themselves over cliffs to reach the nests of the prospective parents, who assumed their precariously placed homes were inaccessible to such dangers.

DRINKS
Alcohol
Until 1992, the Faroese government's attitude toward alcohol bordered on the paranoid. Things have since mellowed and it's now possible to get a drink in licensed restaurants, clubs and pubs, but for travellers it's still a topic of amusement. For example, Café Natúr in Tórshavn serves beer in a pleasant atmosphere, but you can expect to fork out Dkr50 for half a litre.

If you enjoy a spot of alcohol, drink up on the plane flying in or in one of the Faroesbound ferry's three bars – and stock up with the maximum allowance at the duty-free bottle shop before arriving in the Faroes. The only cheap and readily accessible alcoholic beverage is the 2.8% brew called *ljóst pilsnar*, available in shops and kiosks for about Dkr7, but it tastes more like fizzy mountain spring water than anything else.

It's pleasant but doesn't pack much of a punch.

Despite the efforts of Christians and the temperance societies, the Faroes suffer a high rate of alcoholism. However, there aren't as many drunks around as before the rules were relaxed, which may provide some sort of commentary on the effectiveness of prohibition.

Pubs & Clubs Now that alcohol laws have been relaxed, you can get a casual drink in a pub. Some restaurants are licensed to serve alcohol with meals, but there are also places in Tórshavn and Klaksvík where you can just sit and enjoy a drink.

Tórshavn has several private clubs which are open to members and their guests only (Faroese residents must pay steep membership fees to join). For details, see under Entertainment in the Tórshavn chapter.

State Alcohol Stores Wine and spirits are available at state alcohol stores in Tórshavn, Klaksvík and most other towns. They're open Monday to Thursday from 2 to 5.30 pm and Friday from 2 to 7 pm. In Tórshavn, the store opens at 10 am on Thursday and Friday. Beer may be purchased at Föroya Bjór depots and at Restorffs Bryggjarí (Brewery) outlets around the country. Addresses in Tórshavn and Klaksvík are:

Prohibition in the Faroes
The alcohol paranoia in the Faroes all began back in the darkest 1800s when destitute farmers habitually bartered bits of land with grocers in exchange for foodstuffs. You can imagine what happened when the grocers realised they could stock alcohol as well. Farmers would awaken from a euphoric stupor to find themselves former farmers, and shopkeepers found themselves suddenly in the real-estate business. At that stage, alcohol was banned as an undesirable influence.

The total ban was later lifted, but local religious forces kept control in the form of rationing. Until 1992, through a long and tedious process, prospective imbibers were required to provide proof that they were up-to-date on their tax payments before being eligible for the quarterly distribution of alcohol allotments which had to be ordered from Copenhagen. You can imagine the condition of the country immediately following the arrival of these anxiously awaited supplies!

Travellers in the late 80s remember with fond amusement the page of steps necessary to simply buy a beer - prefaced with the words 'Here is the troublesome way you have to go...'. It first involved getting themselves into the rationing scheme, which was in itself a time-consuming process, and then having to wait a week before they could get hold of the goods and begin chug-a-lugging. ■

Rúsdrekkasøla Landsins
   State Alcohol Store, Hoyvíksvegur 51, Tórshavn
   (☎ 14277)
Föroya Bjór
   Akranesgøta 10, Tórshavn (☎ 13434)
Restorffs Bryggjari
   Landavegur 32, Tórshavn (☎ 14728)
Rúsdrekkasøla Landsins
   State Alcohol Store, Bøgøta 38, Klaksvík
   (☎ 56477)
Föroya Bjór
   Klaksvíkvegur, Klaksvík (☎ 55454)

ENTERTAINMENT

The Faroese stage several annual music festivals. Summartónar, the Faroe Islands Festival of Classical and Contemporary Music, takes place during the two weeks after mid-summer. The Faroese Folk Music Festival lasts for a week in mid-July and there's also a Jazz, Folk and Blues Festival during August, arranged by the Nordic House.

In Tórshavn, you'll find a cinema, a night club/disco, a swimming pool and a sports complex. Klaksvík is quieter, but it does have a disco for young people, a sports hall and a swimming pool. Toftir has a sports stadium where international football matches are occasionally held. Weekly Faroese evenings in Tórshavn, Klaksvík and Vágar feature food, singing and dancing. For details, see the relevant chapters.

THINGS TO BUY

As in Iceland, the most popular souvenirs are locally knitted woollens, but Faroese designs are slightly different to the Icelandic ones.

There are two woollens factories on Eysturoy: Tötingarvirkið at Gøta and Snældan at Strendur.

Locally handknitted garments can be purchased at the outlets Føroyskt Heimavirki at Kongabrúgvin in Tórshavn or Norðoya Heimavirki at the head of the harbour in Klaksvík. Prices of woollens are comparable to those in Iceland at around Dkr650 for a traditional handmade pullover.

Faroese stamps are also an interesting commodity. Since the islands stopped using Danish stamps and began printing their own in January 1975, more Faroese stamps seem to be ending up in collections than stuck on envelopes and postcards. Collectors should visit the Frímerkjadeildin (☎ 15557; fax 10576), or 'philatelic bureau', at Traðargøta 38 in Argir, just a km down the coast from Tórshavn. Limited philatelic services are also available at the central post office in Tórshavn.

For those whose tastes run a bit higher, the Faroes offer what is undoubtedly one of the world's great kitsch finds – stuffed birds. Yes, some Faroese spend their lives netting and skinning puffins, filling them with sawdust and selling them to discerning tourists who want to take a bit of that island charm home with them. Before you buy one, however, consider the sort of industry you're supporting and check the import restrictions in your home country (or in those countries you'll be passing through en route). Understandably, quite a few don't yet appreciate such things.

THE FAROE ISLANDS

Getting Around

The Faroese transport system is superb, easily the equal of that in any other northern European country. Roads are surfaced and the difficult or twisting sections have been bypassed by tunnelling through the mountains. The only inhabited place not yet connected to the highway or ferry system is Gásadalur on the island of Vágar. (Plans to bore a tunnel to Gásadalur were shelved during the recent economic crisis.) Streymoy and Eysturoy are connected across Sundini, the channel that separates them, by a 226m-long bridge. Hvannasund between Borðoy and Viðoy and Haraldssund between Borðoy and Kunoy are both crossed by earth-dam causeways.

All but three of the islands, one uninhabited, are connected to the ferry system, and many have helicopter services as well. Frequent buses run to most accessible parts of the islands and travellers in a hurry can always join a tour for easy excursions from the capital. If you're on just a brief visit, you may want to remember the word *kanska* ('maybe'). The Faroes' nickname, 'the islands of maybe', was coined by occupying British soldiers during WWII in reference to the weather's final say in just about everything. Don't wander off to Mykines or Fugloy, for example, if you must catch the Iceland ferry the following day – or you could become the next victim of kanska.

AIR
Since there is only one airport on the Faroes, the international terminal on Vágar, all inter-island air travel is by helicopter (*tyrlan*, pronounced 'TOOR-lan') – and it's a surprisingly inexpensive way to get around. Several times a week, helicopters connect Vágar airport with Tórshavn, Klaksvík, Skúvoy, Froðba (on Suðuroy) and Stóra Dímun (the only access to this island). There are also routes from Vágar airport to Mykines and Gásadalur and from Klaksvík to Svínoy and Fugloy.

Flights are normally booked out – especially flights to Mykines – so it's wise to book several weeks in advance. Helicopter services are operated by Atlantic Airways (☎ 33410; fax 33380), Vágar Airport, FR-380 Sørvágur. The maximum baggage allowance on the helicopters is 20 kg per person. The Tórshavn heliport lies about 500m north of the campground.

Some sample one-way fares include the following (children between two and 11 years of age fly half-price and younger children get 90% discount):

Tórshavn to Skúvoy or Stóra Dímun – Dkr130
Tórshavn to Klaksvík – Dkr215
Vágar to Gásadalur or Mykines – Dkr145
Klaksvík to Svínoy or Fugloy – Dkr110

BUS
The Bygdaleiðir long-distance bus service is excellent. It follows a strict and convenient schedule and, when combined with the ferry services, links virtually every corner of the country, including some fairly remote outposts like Trøllanes on Kalsoy, Dalur on Sandoy, and Bøur on Vágar.

Some long-distance buses only go to certain destinations on request. When you board the bus, tell the driver where you want to go so he or she will know when to stop or radio ahead for a connecting bus to meet you at the appropriate junction.

The bus and ferry timetable and map *Ferðaætlan* is issued annually. It can be bought on board ferries, from bus drivers, from the Farstøðin (harbour) transport terminal in Tórshavn and from tourist offices for Dkr20, but Travelcard purchasers receive one free upon request.

Travel Passes
Bus fares are fairly steep and add up quickly if you're doing a lot of running around. If you're staying awhile and doing lots of excursions into remoter areas, you may want

to buy a transportation pass. The Strand-faraskip Landsins Visitor Travelcard costs Dkr385/600/900 for four/seven/14 days of unlimited travel on both buses and inter-island ferries. Passes are sold at travel agencies, the Farstøðin transportation termi-nal at Tórshavn harbour and the information desk at Vágar airport.

Airport Bus

The Faroes' international air terminal is on Vágar – a bus ride, a ferry ride and another bus ride away from Tórshavn. There are two daily direct buses from the capital (the bus crosses on the ferry). These buses (Dkr100) depart about three hours before flight depar-tures.

CAR & MOTORCYCLE

Driving or riding a motorcycle in the Faroes is easy. There are few unsurfaced roads and most of the islands which have roads are connected to Tórshavn by car-ferry. The greatest hazards while driving are fog, sheep and precipitous drop-offs which become even more significant in the presence of the typically distracting Faroese scenery. It's possible to bring a vehicle from Europe on one of several ferries: the *Nörrona* from Esbjerg (Denmark), Seyðisfjörður (Iceland) or Bergen (Norway) and the *Smyril* from Aberdeen (Scotland). For details, see under Ferry in the regional Getting There & Away chapter at the beginning of the book.

Car Rental

You must be at least 18 years old to rent a car in the Faroes. It's expensive but a better deal than in Iceland because there's no per-km charge and the daily rate decreases the longer you keep the car. For a compact or a sedan, the first six days will cost from Dkr440 per day while weekly rental starts at Dkr2464. Insurance will cost an additional Dkr100 to Dkr130 per day. A deposit of around Dkr1200 may be required against liability; the 25% VAT and petrol are not included. Some companies have special weekend rates. Car rental outlets include:

Avis Bílutleigan, Vágar Airport, FR-380 Sørvágur (☎ 32765; fax 33155)
Avis Føroyar v/Johs Berg, Staravegur 1, FR-110 Tórshavn (☎ 13535; fax 17735)
Eyðbjørn Hansen, Varðagøta 75, FR-100 Tórshavn (☎ 13375; fax 11495)
Hertz, Svend Aage Ellefsen, FR-360 Sandavágur (☎ 32583)

Driving Regulations

For those hiring a vehicle or driving their own vehicle, third party insurance is compul-sory. Rental agencies will normally tack it onto the hire costs but, if you're travelling with your own vehicle on the ferry, you'll need proof of third party insurance or you'll be required to purchase very expensive Tryggingarsambandið Føroyar insurance from the customs department. Front and rear seat belt use is compulsory in the Faroes. The speed limit on open highways is 80 km/h and 50 km/h through villages. As with the rest of the Danish kingdom, the Faroese keep to the right.

It's also important to note that the country is mostly open-range and animals may wander onto the road just about anywhere. Be particularly alert in heavy fog because motorists must take financial responsibility for anything they hit, be it accidental or not.

In Tórshavn, drivers must place a parking disc in the front window, set to the time when the car was parked. These discs are available free at the tourist office and at local banks. Legal parking spaces are marked with a 'P' followed by a number and the word 'tíma', indicating the number of hours you're per-mitted to park there (Saturday times in brackets).

Tunnels

The Faroe Islands look as if very large rabbits have been busy at work; I wouldn't be surprised if they had the densest concen-tration of highway tunnels anywhere outside the Alps. Given the impossibly steep and rugged landscape, however, many villages would be utterly cut off from the outside world were it not for tunnel technology. The latest tunnel (between Lopra and Sumba on

THE FAROE ISLANDS

Suðuroy) is being constructed to cut out an awkward section of mountain road.

Several tunnels, especially in the north-eastern islands, are wide enough for only one vehicle, but passing bays are set at intervals of about 300m. If you see a 'V' in your direction, you have to pull in and allow oncoming vehicles to pass. If they're marked with an 'M', the other driver must give way.

Drivers of large vehicles should be aware of tunnel dimensions. The tunnel between Hvalba and Tvøroyri on Suðuroy is only 3.2 metres high. Both of the Borðoy tunnels are 3.3 metres high.

The longest tunnel in use (3500m) is between Kollafjørður and Kaldbaksfjørður on Streymoy. It bypasses the high mountain road between Tórshavn and Kollafjørður and has made the trip from Tórshavn to Eysturoy safer but considerably less interesting. The next longest, at 3310m, connects Haraldssund and Kunoy on Kunoy island.

Fuel Availability & Costs

Leaded petrol, unleaded petrol and diesel are all available in the Faroes, costing Dkr7.68, Dkr7.55 and Dkr3.66 per litre respectively.

BICYCLE

Although in the Faroes you'll have lots of steep hills, tunnels, wind and rain to contend with, cycling is still better than in Iceland, as the highways are generally wide and sur-faced and cyclists don't have to endure the sandstorms and gravel-tearing motorists from hell that plague Iceland's basic roads.

Still, cycling in the Faroes shouldn't be taken lightly. Suitable windproof and water-proof clothing is essential and you'll need more than just a light jacket on all but the few finest days of the year. On most days, warm gloves, a muffler and a good warm hat will also be appreciated. When the weather becomes really insufferably wretched, remember that if there's space available (and there nearly always is), buses will accept bicycles as luggage for Dkr10 per ride, regardless of the distance involved.

The biggest obstacle for cyclists is the tunnels, which should be avoided if at all possible. Under certain conditions, toxic gases can be trapped in the more congested tunnels, and some, such as the Kollafjørður-Kaldbaksfjørður tunnel and the one from Oyrarbakki to Vesturdalur, should be consid-ered unsafe for cycling. The others should be passed through as quickly as possible. You'll need a good bicycle light both front and back, visible from several km away in a dark tunnel. It's also a good idea to be sure your brakes are in excellent working order, since the hills are quite steep, highways are nor-mally wet, and the drop-offs are severe.

Hire

Bicycle hire is available from The Faroe Islands Tourist Board (☎ 16055), Gongin, Tórshavn (mountain bikes for Dkr100 per day or Dkr560 per week); Erling Midjord (☎ 16756), Hetlandsvegur 8, Tórshavn (Dkr80 per day); and John W Thomsen (☎ 55858), Nólsoyar Pálsgøta, Klaksvík (Dkr50 per day; discount for further days).

Repairs

Repairs can be done by Hilmar Danielsen (☎ 12897), Bøkjarabrekka, Tórshavn.

HITCHING

If you can cope with the weather, hitching is a great way to get around in the Faroes and an excellent way to meet the people. What's more, unless you're very unlucky, you'll never wait long for a lift. British reader Inge Tribe writes: 'I found hitching in the Faroe Islands to be excellent and the best way to meet locals who are normally friendly but quite reserved.'

Although hitching in the Faroes is proba-bly safer than anywhere else in Europe, it is not a totally safe way of getting around. Just because we mention it doesn't mean we rec-ommend it. Women should exercise the usual precautions when accepting rides, and everyone should beware of drunken drivers.

BOAT

Ferry

All the islands in the Faroes except Koltur, Stóra Dímun and Lítla Dímun are connected

THE FAROE ISLANDS

Boat Travel around the Faroes			
Route	Frequency	One-way fares (in Dkr)	
	(w – weekly, d – daily)	Passenger	Car (with driver)
Tórshavn-Tvøroyri (Suðuroy)	1-2 d	80	130
Gamlarætt-Skopun (Sandoy)	5-7 d	30	80
Tórshavn-Vágur (Suðuroy)	2 w	70	130
Tórshavn-Strendur	15 w	30	80
Vestmanna-Oyrargjógv (Vágar)	10 d	30	80
Leirvík (Eysturoy)-Klaksvík	6-10 d	30	80
Sørvágur (Vágur)-Mykines	1-2 d	60	N/A
Sandur-Skúvoy	1-3 d	30	"
Hvannasund-Svínoy	1-2 d	30	"
Hvannasund-Fugloy	1-2 d	30	"
Klaksvík-Húsar (Kalsoy)	2-3 d	30	"
Tórshavn-Nólsoy	2-4 d	30	"
Gamlarætt-Hestur	2-3 d	30	"

by the ferry or bus system. Some routes are served by car-ferries but others carry passengers only. The table above is a rough guide to routes, approximate frequency of sailings and one-way fares for passengers and for passenger cars (with driver). Students (who hold valid student cards), children between seven and 13, and people over 65 receive up to 50% discounts. Sailings operating to or from the Gamlarætt ferry terminal north of Kirkjubøur connect with buses to and from Tórshavn.

Some ferry trips, especially those to Mykines and Svínoy or Fugloy, require navigation through open seas in small boats and are frequently cancelled in rough weather. If you're planning any of these trips, remain as flexible as possible.

Yacht Charter

The yacht Norðlýsið, originally constructed at Tórshavn in 1945 as a ketch-rigged fishing vessel, was rebuilt and re-rigged in the late 1980s as a schooner. It's now chartered out for trips around the islands. On day trips, it will accommodate up to 40 passengers; for longer overnight trips, it has a capacity of 17. For more information phone ☎ 17500, in Tórshavn.

The touring boat Amadeus, which accommodates 40 passengers, may also be chartered for day trips. They charge Dkr900 per hour for the first five hours and Dkr500 for each subsequent hour. For more informa-

tion contact Óðin (☎ 12499; fax 19124), or see the Internet site at www. ozemail. com.au/skuvadal/amadeus.html.

ORGANISED TOURS

The Faroe Islands are ideal for leisurely independent exploration on the public transport system, but if you're pressed for time or would like to reach out-of-the-way places you may want to join a tour.

Compared to making your own arrangements, tours are fairly expensive. More importantly, scheduled tours are frequently cancelled due to lack of interest and/or foul weather, two very real possibilities in the Faroes. If you haven't reserved your tour abroad and paid in advance, the chances of cancellation are quite high unless you can muster enough interest to keep it going; your best chances will be while the Norröna is away in Norway and the islands are crawling with Iceland-bound ferry passengers. Naturally, as the Faroes grow in tourist popularity, these problems will become less common.

Some of the more prominent agencies specialising in North Atlantic travel include:

Atlantic Adventure, í Grønulág 2, FR-100 Tórshavn (☎ 17059; fax 17108) – This agency offers perhaps the widest variety of packages available in the islands, including guided mountain hikes and fishing excursions. All tours must be booked from abroad and prices include flights. Prices range from Dkr3250/4790 (hostel/hotel B&B) for a six-day independent trip around the Faroes (planned itinerary) to Dkr4895/5520 (full board, hostel/guesthouse) for a seven-day guided walking tour around Vágar, Streymoy and Eysturoy (including Slættaratindur) and Dkr4290/5870 (hostel/hotel B&B) for a seven-day fishing tour, including fishing licences.

Gunnar Skúvadal, FR-350 Vestmanna (☎ 24305; fax 24292) – This exceptionally friendly operation conducts boat tours to the Vestmanna Bird Cliffs for Dkr150 per person, with price reductions for larger groups.

Jóan Petur Clementsen, FR-210 Sandur (☎ 86119) – This operator runs daily tours on his boat *Hvíthamrar* around the coasts of Sandoy or Skúvoy for Dkr150 per person.

Kunningardiskurin, Vágar airport, FR-380 Sørvágur (☎ 33200; fax 33100) – The airport tourist office takes bookings for several hiking and trekking tours, with prices from Dkr60 to Dkr500 per person. There's also a horse-riding trek (Dkr150 per person) and a bus tour (Dkr130 per person, minimum 10 participants).

Kunningarstovan, Niels Finsensgøta 13, FR-100 Tórshavn (☎ 15788; fax 16831) – The city tourist office can book the following: trips to the storm petrel colony on Nólsoy Island; hiking trips on Streymoy, Eysturoy and Sandoy; and sea-angling trips on request. The Nólsoy trips are operated by the ornithologist Jens-Kjeld Jensen and the price of Dkr300 per person includes transport, tour and overnight sleeping-bag accommodation on the island. Four-day hiking trips for more than two people cost Dkr3800 (including dinner, B&B in hotels and guesthouses).

Kunningarstovan Suðuroy, FR-800 Tvøroyri (☎ 72480; fax 72380) – Day tours offered by this office include guided hikes (Dkr165 and Dkr195), sailing and sea-angling (Dkr275) and bus tours (to Sandvík for Dkr165 or to Sumba for Dkr319).

Norðoya Kunningarstova, Nólsoyar Pálsgøta, FR-700 Klaksvík (☎ 56939; fax 56586) – This tourist office offers a variety of day trips including hiking, bus trips, sea-angling and sight-seeing by boat or on foot. These tours cost from Dkr120 to Dkr150 per person (minimum four participants required for most tours).

Palli Lamhauge, FR350 Vestmanna (☎ 24155; fax 24383) – Palli operates boat tours to the Vestmanna Bird Cliffs (Dkr150 per person) and Eiði via Risin and Kellingin (Dkr200 one way). He also runs tours to Mykines, Gjógv and Saksun. An overnight stay at Slættanes and a guided walk on Vágar can be added to the basic bird cliff tour.

Smyril Line Tours, Postbox 370, J Broncksgøta 37, FR-110 Tórshavn (☎ 15900; fax 15707) – The ferry company offers bus and boat tours around the islands with prices ranging from Dkr85 for a tour to Kvívík to Dkr235 for a morning sail on the schooner *Norðlýsið* and Dkr475 for a whole-day tour (on Friday) to the Northern islands, as far as Viðareiði.

Strandfaraskip Landsins, Postbox 88, Yviri við Strond 4, FR-110 Tórshavn (☎ 16660; fax 16000) – The state shipping company operates various boat and fishing day trips. Prices range from Dkr100 per person for the boat tours to Kunoyarnakkur (from Klaksvík) and Enniberg (from Hvannasund, minimum 10 participants) to Dkr150/200 for fishing trips/Mykines tours from Sørvágur.

Tora Tourist Traffic, Niels Finsensgøta 21, FR-100 Tórshavn (☎ 15505; fax 15667) – This agency provides tours for individuals and groups, mainly by bus but also by boat. Trips range from Dkr140 for a tour around Kirkjubøur to Dkr370 for the Vestmanna Bird Cliffs tour (including transport from Tórshavn) and Dkr475 for the new Sunday tour to Sandoy. They'll also provide guides for individual mountain hiking for Dkr195 per hour.

Tórshavnar Ríðiskúli, Marknagilsvegur 81a, FR-100 Tórshavn (☎ 16896) – The riding school runs tours to various destinations around Tórshavn. Evening tours, with a minimum of four people, cost from Dkr150 (one to two hours) to Dkr300 (three hours); six-hour tours, with a minimum of four people, cost Dkr550 (including lunch); and an overnight tour to Kvívík, with a minimum of six people, costs Dkr1250 (including accommodation and meals).

Viking Adventures, Postbox 1371, Tinghúsvegar 42, FR-110, Tórshavn (☎ 16005; fax 19124) – Offer sea-angling trips with fixed departures in summer. Prices start at Dkr250 per person (three hours) with rod rental from Dkr75. A minimum of five people is required. Day charter of the boat costs Dkr5500 (for 12 hours).

Óðin, Postbox 1371, FR-110 Tórshavn (☎ 12499; fax 19124) – Óðin run charters and tours on their boat *Amadeus* between Tórshavn and Nólsoy, Hestur, Koltur and Sandoy. The tours cost Dkr150, Dkr200, Dkr250 and Dkr250 respectively; book directly or with Kunningarstovan in Tórshavn. Landings are possible on the islands and you may be able to hike on Koltur. For all trips, a minimum of seven people is required.

Further details on day trips can be found in the relevant sections of this book. Abroad, you'll find assistance at offices of the Danish Tourism Board. Addresses are listed in the Tourist Information section of the Greenland Facts for the Visitor chapter.

THE FAROE ISLANDS

Tórshavn

Although it's the capital and by far the largest community of the Faroes, Tórshavn, like Reykjavík, isn't your typically vibrant European capital. If you thrive on round-the-clock action (or action of any kind) you'll shrivel up and fade away here.

Whatever it lacks in thrills, however, Tórshavn makes up in picturesque charm. Just a stroll around Tinganes, the small peninsular headland where the town began nearly a thousand years ago, is enough to endear this quiet and rainy little place to just about anyone.

The rest of Tórshavn, a mixture of quiet but pleasant harbour areas, colourfully painted residential sections and even a city park boasting proudly that forests have finally made their debut in the Faroes, all hold a peculiar appeal. The Faroese writer William Heinesen states that Tórshavn was for him, as Cuzco was for the Incas, the 'navel of the universe'. Few Faroese would argue, but visitors will come to their own conclusions about this intriguing place.

History

The name of the Faroese capital means 'Thor's harbour' after the slow-witted and

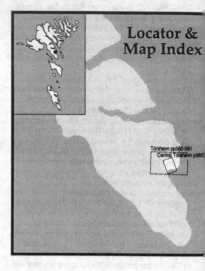

Tórshavn city seal

relatively innocuous god Þór, best liked by the settlers who fled the wrath and tyranny of Oðinn's gang on the Scandinavian mainland.

For the early settlers, the setting of Tórshavn was far from ideal. It was far from the best harbour in the Faroes (the present harbour was constructed in 1927) and its position on an exposed headland did nothing to shelter it from the weather. Furthermore, it had poor soil and no cliffs teeming with edible birds and their eggs. In short, it was not conducive to traditional settlement. However, it was central and, for that reason, it became the site of the early parliament, the Alting.

The Alting was organised in the early 9th century, around the time of Settlement, and was first mentioned in the 13th century Icelandic work *Færinga Saga*. Around the year 1000, this parliamentary body accepted Christianity as the official religion of the islands. Although the Alting was dissolved by the Faroes' incorporation into Norway in 1035, it was re-formed as the Løgting in 1380, when Norway was absorbed into the Kingdom of Denmark. At that time, however, it was almost completely deprived of power and remained little more than a council until modern times. The Løgting continued to function, nonetheless, and official records of its annual conventions on Tinganes each 29 July, Ólavsøka or St Olav's Day, have been preserved since 1615.

With Tórshavn as an official meeting place, a market soon sprang up to accommodate the parliamentary representatives and visitors. It seemed to follow naturally that foreign monopoly traders would also eventually establish businesses. To fortify the trading area and construct amenities, debtors and poor islanders were impressed into service.

When monopoly trading was finally abolished for economic reasons in 1856, the Faroese took to fishing and bought up larger sea-going British fishing boats so they could fish further offshore than their own tiny open boats would allow. Tórshavn, although it was the capital, had very marginal harbour facilities and was being left behind the rest of the country economically. In 1927, the harbour was upgraded; now it's the centre of the fishing industry, commerce, transport and trade in the islands.

Tórshavn, having grown by 1000% since the early 19th century, had a population of 5600 by 1950. Since then, the population has tripled and migrants continue to arrive from the countryside to this, the Faroes' closest approximation to a big city.

Orientation

Tórshavn is a small city and is easily negotiated on foot. The older section surrounds the two harbours, which are separated by Tinganes, the original site of the Løgting and the trading settlement. The Farstøðin transport terminal at the eastern harbour serves inter-island and international ferries and long-distance buses. The western harbour is used mainly for commerce.

The modern town centre focuses on the

area between Tinganes and Winthersgøta, just up the hill from the harbours. There you'll find most of the shops, restaurants and services. The SMS Shopping Centre on RC Effersøesgøta is an indoor shopping mall with a supermarket, cafeteria, bookshop, snack bar, newsagent and several other shops. Outlying areas are primarily residential with the exception of Gundadalur, where you'll find the city park, the sports complex, the youth hostel and a few businesses. The central industrial zone is on the hill between Gundadalur and the campground.

Information

Tourist Offices The Faroe Islands Tourist Board (Postbox 118, FR-110 Tórshavn; ☎ 16055; fax 10858), is on Gongin (Tinganes). It's open Monday to Friday from 8 am to 5 pm and on weekends from 2 to 5 pm. In addition to being very friendly and helpful with information and brochures, they also hire out mountain bikes, book tours and accommodation and sell topographic maps, a variety of tourist publications and literature about the Faroe Islands.

The Kunningarstovan city tourist office (☎ 15788; fax 16831) is at Niels Finsensgøta 13, and is open Monday to Friday from 8 am to 5.30 pm, and Saturday from 9 am to 2 pm. They have many useful brochures, handle enquiries, book tours and hotels and sell topographic maps and postcards. Weather information and forecasts for 10 villages are posted daily on the notice board outside the office.

Both offices distribute the useful free publication, *Around the Faroe Islands*, with details on sights and tourist facilities around the islands.

Money Banks are open on weekdays from 9 am to 4 pm; on Thursday they remain open until 6 pm. All banks handle foreign exchange. Outside banking hours, the tourist office will exchange money and, in a pinch, so will the Hotel Hafnia. They both charge a higher commission, but the hotel is open in the evenings and on Sunday.

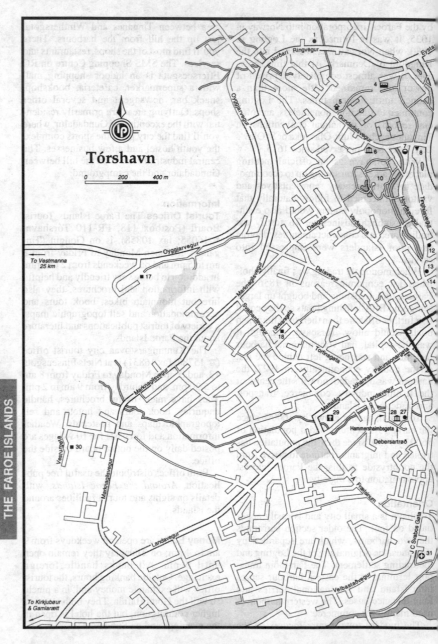

Tórshavn

0   200   400 m

To Vestmanna
25 km

To Kirkjubøur
& Gamlarætt

PLACES TO STAY
5 Youth Hostel
9 Camping Ground
17 Hotel Føroyar
18 Skrivaragøta 3
22 Guesthouse Skansin
30 Guesthouse Undir Fjalli
& Atlantic Adventure

PLACES TO EAT
8 Statoil Grocery Shop
& Petrol Station
15 Pizzaria
24 Pylsuvognurin Snack Bar

OTHER
1 Nordic House
2 Post Office
3 Heliport
4 Swimming Pool
6 Listaskálin Art Museum
7 Bíl Taxi Stop
10 Viðarlund Park
11 SMS Shopping Mall
12 YMCA & Scout Shop
13 Sjónleikarhúsið Theatre
14 Auto Taxi Stop
16 Kongaminnið Obelisk
19 Police
20 Myntvask Laundrette
21 Smyril Line Office
23 Strandfaraskip Landsins
(Ferry Service Office)
25 Farstøðin Bus & Ferry Terminal
26 Skansin Fort
27 National Library
28 Náttúrugripasavn Museum
29 Vesturkirkjan
31 Hospital

Post & Communications The central post office is on Vaglið behind the Ráðhús or town hall. It's open Monday to Friday only, from 9 am to 5 pm. Photocopying, telephone cards and fax and philatelic services are also available there.

At the telephone office, Tinghúsvegur 3, you can send and receive faxes, purchase telephone cards and make both local and international calls. The office is open daily from 8 am to 9 pm.

Bookshops For foreign language publications, the best bookshop is HN Jacobsens Bókahandil at Húsagarður on the town square. It's in a beautiful old wooden house which was constructed in 1860 and used as a secondary school until 1918, when the bookshop took over. It's worth a look even if you're not buying reading material.

Other bookshops in town, all of which carry some English and German titles, include one upstairs at the SMS Shopping Centre and Hjalmar Jacobsens Bókahandil at Niels Finsensgøta 14.

Libraries The Faroese National Library (☎ 11626; fax 18895), Føroya Landsbókasavn, is at JC Svabosgøta 16. It's open Monday to Wednesday from 10 am to 8 pm and Thursday and Friday from 10 am to 5 pm. They have a wide selection of books about the Faroes and they also stock foreign newspapers. Their Internet homepage is found at www.sleipnir.fo/flb/ flbheim.htm.

The Tórshavn city library is at Niels Finsensgøta 7.

Laundry The Myntvask automatic laundrette on J Broncksgøta is open Monday to Saturday from 6 am to 9 pm and Sunday from 3 to 9 pm. It costs Dkr30 to wash and Dkr1 per minute to dry.

If you'd rather have someone else do your laundry, try Seytjan on Áarvegur 12, open Monday to Friday 9 am to 5.30 pm, Saturday 9 am to 2 pm.

Medical Services For the casualty ward at the Landssjúkrahúsið (National Hospital)

dial ☎ 13540. It's on JC Svabosgøta. There's a pharmacy on the ground floor of the SMS Shopping Centre.

Emergency To phone the police, ambulance or fire brigade, dial ☎ 000 and indicate which service you require. Emergency calls are free from public telephones.

Film & Photography If you're out of film and heading for Iceland, you may want to stock up here. Three shops in Tórshavn sell film (including Kodachrome) and camera supplies. Two recommended places are SMS Foto in the SMS Shopping Centre and Fotobúðin at Niels Finsensgøta 8, both of which do one hour print processing.

Video film for cameras is available from Radiohandilin on the 3rd floor of the same building as Fotobúðin. A VHS-C 30 minute cassette will cost Dkr95.

Left Luggage The youth hostel will store guests' luggage for a nominal fee. There are lockers primarily for Smyril Line stopover passengers at the Farstøðin transport terminal at the harbour; the charge is Dkr5. Steinatún Kiosk, at the intersection of Winthersgøta and Niels Finsensgøta, will also store luggage. It's open Monday to Friday from 7.30 am to 8 pm, Saturday from 9 am to 8 pm and Sunday from 2 to 6 pm. The charge is Dkr10 per day for a maximum of three days.

Camping Equipment Outdoor equipment including fishing tackle, stove fuel (gas) and stove alcohol can be found at Valdemar Lützen, down the hill from the town hall, just west of the seamen's home, or at their other outlet on Skálatroð, by the western harbour. You can also try Skótabúðin (the Scout shop) at Hoydalsvegur 6. Paraffin (kerosene) is available from Katrina Christiansen on Bringsnagøta.

Tinganes
Until the early 1900s, the small peninsula of Tinganes was all there was to Tórshavn. This was where early settlers first set up the Alting

in 825 and here the Alting (and later Løgting) continued to meet. Christianity was introduced to the Faroes here in 999 and it was also here that all the early traders met, conducted their business and had their warehouses. In fact, apart from a tiny station on Suðuroy, it was the only place in the Faroes where it was legal to carry out trading. Unfortunately, in 1673, a devastating fire on Tinganes destroyed many of the historical buildings; only Munkastovan and Leigubúðin were spared.

Tinganes still gives the impression of being a trading place and a stroll through the narrow streets will conjure up some romantic images of what 'wonderful Copenhagen' must have been like several centuries ago during the good old days of maritime trade. Though small, Tinganes is genuine and, as yet, there haven't been any historical gimmicks aimed at tourists. Currently, the only building which looks out of place is the modern Faroese Tourist Board which was built to house the now defunct Sjóvinnubankin.

Munkastovan It's assumed that the heavy stone-walled Munkastovan dates from at least the 15th century. The building apparently once served some sort of religious role since its construction technique closely matches that of the stone cathedral at Kirkjubøur. The name Munkastovan means 'monks' living quarters'. After the 1673 fire, only this building and nearby Leigubúðin survived.

Leigubúðin The Leigubúðin served as the king's storehouse where agricultural goods paid as taxes were kept until they could be transported to the mainland. No one is sure exactly how old it is, but it dates at least to the 16th century.

Reynagarður Reynagarður, constructed in 1630, well illustrates typical Faroese architectural design of the early 1600s, with four wings arranged around a central courtyard. The original southern wing retains its Faroese architectural character, but the restored western wing reflects strong Danish influences. It originally served as a vicarage.

Portugalið Just south of Reynagarður is the stone Portugalið or Myrkastovan ('dark house'), which was constructed in 1693. It served as a guard house during the reign of the Danish-sanctioned feudal lord Frederik von Gabel. The basement was used as a dungeon of whim for those who fell foul of him. On the wall is an inscription with the date (1693), the Danish royal insignia of Christian V and von Gabel's name.

Skansapakkhúsið Out at the far end of Tinganes, the Skansapakkhúsið ('fort warehouse') was constructed in 1750 and served as an artillery cache. During the war against Britain in 1808, it was emptied of supplies by Captain Baugh of the British naval brig Clio, which threatened to destroy Tórshavn if the town did not surrender all means of resistance. The Faroes were thus disarmed and vulnerable to privateers and opportunists. Several other warehouses around the end of the peninsula date back to the era immediately following the fire of 1673. They now function as government offices.

Krákusteinur Despite St Brendan's alleged assessment that the Faroes were 'the paradise of birds', Faroese birds haven't fared particularly well since humans showed up. In the interest of protecting domestic sheep from nuisance birds such as eagles, crows and ravens, from the 17th to 19th centuries all male residents of rural districts were annually required to pay a 'beak tax'. The minimum was one raven's beak or two crow's beaks per man. The beak of a sea eagle allowed life exemption from the tax, which probably explains why sea eagles no longer inhabit the Faroes. Fortunately, this tax didn't bring about the complete extinction of the species; there are still a few left in Norway, Iceland and Greenland.

The beaks were turned over to district sheriffs, who in turn submitted them to the Løgting. The flat rock, Krákusteinur ('crow rock'), lies on the eastern shore of Tinganes near Skansapakkhúsið. One of the Løgting's annual orders of business was to assemble at this stone and burn all the beaks that had been collected that year.

Gongin The narrow lane Gongin was the main street in old Tórshavn. It's lined with some lovely 19th century wooden houses.

Museums

Smiðjan í Lítluvík This rather low-profile gallery is housed in an old iron forge on Grím Kambansgøta not far from the western harbour. It has no set opening hours, but visiting exhibitions are advertised at the Kunningarstovan tourist office. For adults, admission costs Dkr20.

Listaskálin Listaskálin, the Faroese Museum of Art, on the northern edge of Viðarlund park, is an airy museum with a fine collection of works by Faroese artists including painters Ruth Smith, Sámal Joensen Mikines and Ingálvur av Reyni, and sculptors Fridtjof Joensen and Janus Kamban. The museum also opens for musical and theatrical performances and special exhibitions. It's open between 3 June and 1 September on weekdays from 11 am to 5 pm, and Saturday and Sunday, 2 to 6 pm. Admission is Dkr20 per adult. During the winter, opening hours are shorter.

Nordic House The architecturally interesting turf-roofed Nordic House, designed by the Norwegian architect Ola Steen and the Icelander Kolbrún Ragnardóttir, was completed in 1983. It is one of several in the Nordic countries. The spacious interior is used as a theatre and a conference, concert and exhibition hall. It functions as a venue for visiting exhibitions by artists from around Scandinavia, including Iceland and Greenland. For information about what's on, pick up a brochure at the tourist offices or phone ☎ 17900.

The library, halls and cafeteria are open Monday to Saturday from 10 am to 6 pm and Sunday from 2 to 6 pm. On Tuesday evenings during summer, a 'Faroese evening' is

staged for tourists, costing Dkr200 if booked through Tora Tourist Traffic.

Historical Museum The new historical museum at Hoyvík, Fornminnisavn, is a must for anyone interested in Faroese history. The new building also houses the previously separate Bátasavn (maritime museum). It contains religious and maritime artefacts, boats, early artwork and practical household, fishing, navigation and farming implements from the Viking Age through to the medieval period. Many of the items excavated from archaeological sites at Sandur, Tjørnuvík and Kirkjubøur are on display here. The most interesting maritime exhibit is the 150-year-old *fýramannafar* or 'four-man conveyance' from Hvalvík, whose design is believed to have evolved from the early Viking ships. There are also several more modern exhibits.

In the summer (from 19 June to 31 August), it's open Monday to Friday from 10 am to 4 pm and on weekends from 1 to 5 pm. At other times of the year it's only open on weekends from 1 to 5 pm. Admission for adults is Dkr20. English descriptions are provided on the exhibits and there's also a free general leaflet in English.

Bus Nos 3 and 4 pass near the museum, on Hvítanesvegur. Alternatively, walk the two km from the campsite, turning right just beyond the heliport and following the path through Hoyvík. This route passes an old farmhouse and outbuildings which were recently restored by the historical museum as an open air museum.

Natural History Museum The exhibits at the Natural History Museum, Náttúrugripasavn, revolve mainly around the Faroese fascination with marine mammals. There are skeletons of a grey seal, a pilot whale, a bottle-nosed whale and a killer whale. And, of course, this wouldn't be complete without all the implements of destruction that reduced them to skeleton form.

There's also a comprehensive collection of stuffed Faroese birds and a display on North Atlantic geology. Another section

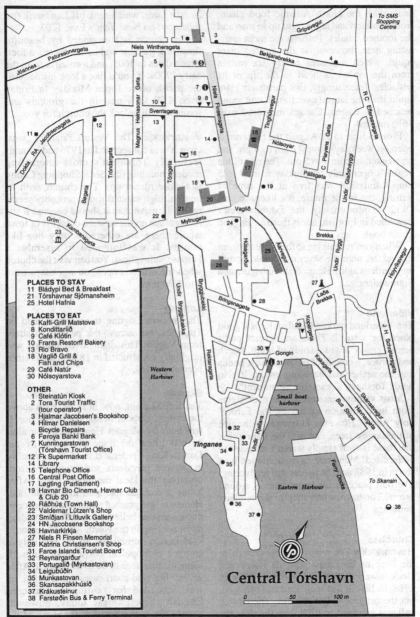

To SMS Shopping Centre

Gripsvegur

Niels Winthersgøta

Jóhannes Paturssonargøta

Bøkjarabrekka

R C Effersøesvegur

Magnus Heinasonar Gøta

Niels Finsensgøta

Sverrisgøta

Tinghúsvegur

Nólsoyar

C Pløyens Gøta

Pálsgøta

Undir Gladsheyggi

Dokta R A Jacobsensgøta

Tróndargøta

Tórsgøta

Vaglið

Brekka

Undir Ryggi

Hoyvíksvegur

Grím Kambansgøta

Myllnugøta

Húsagøtur

Ánvegur

Brekka

Brynjúlvsgøta

Bringsnagøta

Laða Brekka

J H Schrøtersvegur

Undir Bryggjubakka

Bryggjubakki

Rektaragøta

Kongagøta

Gongin

Skansavegur

Havnargøta

Bus Stops

Western Harbour

Small boat harbour

Undir Kjallara

Tinganes

Reynargarður

Eastern Harbour

Ferry Docks

To Skansin

PLACES TO STAY
11 Bládýpi Bed & Breakfast
21 Tórshavnar Sjómansheim
25 Hotel Hafnia

PLACES TO EAT
5 Kaffi-Grill Matstova
8 Kondittaríið
9 Café Klótin
10 Frants Restorff Bakery
13 Rio Bravo
18 Vaglið Grill & Fish and Chips
29 Café Natúr
30 Nólsoyarstova

OTHER
1 Steinatún Kiosk
2 Tora Tourist Traffic (tour operator)
3 Hjalmar Jacobsen's Bookshop
4 Hilmar Danielsen Bicycle Repairs
6 Føroya Banki Bank
7 Kunningarstovan (Tórshavn Tourist Office)
12 Fk Supermarket
14 Library
15 Telephone Office
16 Central Post Office
17 Løgting (Parliament)
19 Havnar Bio Cinema, Havnar Club & Club 20
20 Ráðhús (Town Hall)
22 Valdemar Lützen's Shop
23 Smiðjan í Litluvík Gallery
24 HN Jacobsens Bookshop
26 Havnarkirkja
27 Niels R Finsen Memorial
28 Katrina Christiansen's Shop
31 Faroe Islands Tourist Board
32 Reynargarður
33 Portugalið (Myrkastovan)
34 Leigubúðin
35 Munkastovan
36 Skansapakkhúsið
37 Krákusteinur
38 Farstøðin Bus & Ferry Terminal

Central Tórshavn

0   50   100 m

deals with the North Atlantic food chain, from plankton and algae right up to man and the toothed whales. Perhaps the most interesting item, however, is the stuffed giant squid, which measures nearly six metres from the top of its head to the tip of its tentacles. Interestingly, this particular giant squid isn't the largest ever found; one found beached in eastern Canada measured over 16½ metres!

From 3 June to 31 August the museum is open on weekdays from 11 am to 4 pm and on weekends from 3 to 5 pm. The rest of the year it's open only on Sunday from 3 to 5 pm. Admission was free at the time of writing, but in the future, it's likely to cost Dkr20. Unfortunately, the exhibits aren't described in English, nor is there an English guide book.

When you're walking to the museum from the centre, note the several nice old homes and gardens along Hammershaimbsgøta and Sigmundargøta.

Viðarlund

The Viðarlund park in Gundadalur is a good place for a stroll. There are several paths across grassy lawns, stands of birch, beech and spruce, a couple of pleasant duck ponds and the archetypal babbling brook. It also holds Tórshavn's seamen's monument.

Most visitors' interest in the park stems from its distinction as having the Faroes' only 'forest'. However, judging from the size of the largest trees, one gets the impression that these islands simply weren't intended to be forested! Many trees were destroyed by a storm in 1988 and the park is still recovering. The best place to see larger trees is around central Tórshavn, where they're sheltered by buildings.

Churches

Havnarkirkja The white 'harbour church' at the base of Tinganes, with its interesting clock-tower, was consecrated way back in 1788. In 1865 it was renovated and enlarged, but the original pulpit remains. The church bell was salvaged in 1708 from the ship, the

Norske Løve, which sank off Lambavík (on Eysturoy) on New Year's Eve, 1707.

The church is surrounded by beautiful flowering gardens and inside there's a font, which dates to 1601, and a crucifix from the early 1700s. If you'd like a look inside, visit the parish office (open Monday to Friday from 4.30 to 6 pm) in the grounds and someone will unlock the church for you.

Vesturkirkjan The Vesturkirkjan or 'west church' was consecrated in 1975 and is architecturally Tórshavn's most interesting modern building (the SMS Shopping Centre is a close runner-up). The church, with its unusual high vaulted roofs, probably seems more obtrusive than it should because it sits rather alone on the western outskirts of town where there are otherwise only box-like houses. It was intended to resemble a Faroese sailing boat. You can visit the church when the office is open, on weekdays from 4 to 5.30 pm.

Løgting

The modern Løgting is no longer held on Tinganes, but across the pedestrian street from Vaglið. This distinctive building was originally constructed in 1856 and has since been expanded.

Skansin

The fort Skansin, now in ruins, rises above the eastern harbour beside the lighthouse. It was built by Magnus Heinason a year after he was given the trade monopoly by the Danish King Frederik II in 1579, ostensibly to prevent privateers and smugglers from upsetting the local monopoly trade. After losing a considerable sum in a pirate raid, Heinason was granted a ship and a licence to pursue anyone believed to be illicitly trading or plundering in the North Atlantic region.

Heinason turned out to be not only a crooked monopolist, but a pirate himself, using his privilege to do as he pleased. After several bungled court cases against him, he was beheaded for raiding an innocent English ship. Faroese today, however, believe the conviction was the work of his enemies and lately he has been elevated to the status of martyr and national hero.

In 1677, Tórshavn was attacked and sacked by the French, with whom Denmark was at war, and Skansin was destroyed and not rebuilt until 1780. During the British occupation of the Faroes in WWII, it was used as the Allied naval headquarters.

You can still see several old bronze guns from 1782 and two British guns from WWII, and this is one of the pleasant spots to relax in Tórshavn. There's a fine view out to sea and it's a perfect vantage point for watching goings-on in the harbour.

Ráðhús
The imposing stone Ráðhús building on Vaglið was constructed of basalt in 1894. It served as a school until 1955, but 20 years later it was renovated and converted into the town hall.

Statues & Monuments
Niels R Finsen Memorial Niels R Finsen was the Faroese physician who won the Nobel Prize for medicine around the turn of the century and is now considered the father of radiology. As a child, he carved his initials into a rock in what is now a tiny city park. A plaque reads 'On this rock Niels R Finsen carved his name as a youth. His achievement has etched it into the hearts of all'.

Kamban Sculptures Beside the bank on Niels Finsensgøta is a sculpture by the Faroese artist Janus Kamban, who was born in 1913 and studied at the Copenhagen Academy of Art. His favourite subjects deal with everyday life in the Faroes; this one portrays a Faroese couple. There are two more: one in the grassy square along Undir Ryggi, uphill from the city centre, and the other on Dokta RA Jacobsensgøta.

Kongaminnið This basalt obelisk in the park, just above the intersection of Hoyvíks-vegur and RC Effersøesgøta, commemorates the 1874 visit of King Christian IX of Denmark to the Faroe Islands. There are some other surprisingly interesting sculptures in this park.

RC Effersøe Monument In front of the Løgting building is a bust of the poet Rasmus Cristoffer Effersøe, who lived from 1857 to 1916. A newspaper professional who worked actively for the revival of the Faroese language, he was also an early advocate of strict controls on alcohol. The monument was completed in 1933.

Sport
The large city sports centre in Gundadalur has a football pitch, badminton courts and a swimming pool. The swimming pool is open weekdays from 6.45 to 9 am and 3 to 8 pm, except Wednesday when it's open only in the morning. On Saturday and Sunday it's open from 8 to 10 am and 2 to 5 pm.

For information on scheduled sporting activities, contact the Faroese Sports Association (%y12606) at the Gundadalur centre. International sporting matches can't be held in Tórshavn because of the astroturf surface. Instead, they're played in Toftir on Eysturoy island.

Organised Tours
Tora Tourist Traffic (☎ 15505) offers a 'World's Smallest Capital' tour around Tórshavn, which includes a guided walk around the old town, visits to the Nordic House and the Hoyvík open air museum and coffee at the Hotel Föroyar. It leaves on Monday at 1 pm, lasts four hours and costs Dkr230 per person.

Tórshavnar Ríðiskúli (☎ 16896) runs horse-riding tours to various destinations around Tórshavn. The evening tours on Monday, Tuesday and Friday (summer only), require a minimum of four people. Prices are Dkr150 for one to two-hour tours or Dkr300 for three-hour tours. Six-hour tours (Tuesday, Saturday and Sunday, or by arrangement), need a minimum of four people and cost Dkr550, including lunch.

Special Events
Each summer, Tórshavn stages three annual

THE FAROE ISLANDS

music festivals. Summartónar, the Faroe Islands Festival of Classical and Contemporary Music (☎ 14815; fax 14825), takes place during the two weeks after midsummer. About 50 concerts are held in Tórshavn and in towns and villages throughout the islands. Venues in Tórshavn are the Nordic House, the Listaskálin art museum and churches.

The Faroese Folk Music Festival (☎ 14815; fax 14825) lasts for a week in the middle of July. For four days in mid-August, Tórshavn hosts the Tórshavn Jazz, Folk and Blues Festival (☎ 15121; fax 10221). These festivals attract artists from all over Scandinavia, as well as quite a few from around Europe and other places.

Places to Stay – bottom end

Many budget travellers in Tórshavn wind up at the *campground* (☎ 17661, evenings only), which lies 1½ km north along the coast from the centre. It costs Dkr40 per person for tent or caravan camping. For this you get a wet spot on the grass and use of the kitchen, toilet and shower facilities. Beware, however, that parts of the site are flood-prone. On one occasion, most of the campers woke to find themselves surrounded by water and there was an evacuation to the toilet block. Pitch your tent on the highest ground available, and try to avoid the hard ground in the central area near the kitchen and toilets.

Up beyond Viðarlund Park in Gundadalur is the official HI hostel, *Tórshavn* (☎ 18900; fax 15707). Accommodation is in two to eight-bed dormitories set off by partitions inside a sports hall. Cooking facilities are available and you can catch up on the latest BBC news on the television in the dining area. HI members/non-members pay Dkr85/95. Breakfast costs an additional Dkr35. Cooking facilities are available but there's a dire shortage of utensils. The hostel is open 5 June to 6 September.

A local couple at Skrivaragøta 3 have turned part of their home into dormitory-style accommodation unofficially known as *Bill's Bed & Breakfast* (☎ 11686). For sleep-ing-bag accommodation in the dormitory, they charge Dkr80 per person, with discounts to groups of over 10 people. Single/double rooms cost Dkr180/280. Breakfast is an additional Dkr40 but cooking facilities are available.

The house is at the western end of town about 1½ km from the centre. From the northern end of the pedestrian mall (Niels Finsensgøta), turn left and continue five blocks to Torfinsgøta. There, turn right and climb until you see Skrivaragøta, which is the fourth street on the left.

Places to Stay – middle

The *Guesthouse Undir Fjalli* (☎ 17059; fax 17108) at Vesturgøta 15, at the extreme south-western end of Tórshavn, is operated by the tour company Atlantic Adventure. During the school year it's a student dormitory, but from 28 June to 10 August it's used as a guesthouse. Single/double rooms with shower cost Dkr360/430 and extra beds may be added for Dkr90 each (all prices include breakfast). Guests have access to the coin-operated laundry machines.

At Tórsgøta 4 in the centre, just downhill from Vaglið square, is the popular *Tórsh-avnar Sjómansheim* (☎ 13515; fax 13286) or seamen's home. Like all seamen's homes, it subscribes to a fairly strict code of behaviour, although the alcohol restrictions aren't as apparent in the Faroes as in Greenland. Single/double rooms without bath cost Dkr275/395; with bath, a double costs Dkr495. Extra beds cost Dkr100 each. All prices include breakfast.

Near the harbour at Jekaragøta 8 is the clean *Guesthouse Skansin* (☎ 12242; fax 10657), which charges Dkr360/490 for single/double rooms with shared facilities, including a lavish breakfast and use of cooking facilities. Slightly less expensive is *Bládýpi Bed & Breakfast* (☎ 11951; fax 19451) in a nice part of town at Dokta Jacobsensgøta 14-16. Single/double rooms with shared facilities cost Dkr210/320, including a buffet breakfast.

Tora Tourist Traffic (☎ 15505; fax 15667) keeps lists of people who have *B&Bs* and bookings should be made through the company or the tourist offices. Prices are Dkr280/430 for a single/double, all including breakfast and most including use of cooking facilities. Alternatively, groups may rent entire *houses* or *flats* accommodating from three to six people at a daily rate of Dkr520 or a weekly rate of Dkr3120, in the high season (19 June to 21 August).

The company Nordica (☎ 10809; fax 10886) has a booklet listing five *holiday houses* in Tórshavn, suitable for two to eight people, with high season (1 July to 18 August) rates ranging from Dkr533/3200 to Dkr667/4000 (daily/weekly). Bookings should be made directly with Nordica.

Places to Stay – top end
Tórshavn has two upmarket hotels. The more popular with tourists seems to be the *Hotel Hafnia* (☎ 11270; fax 15250), just up the street from the harbour. It's central, clean and pleasant but not pretentious. Single/double rooms with private bath begin at Dkr670/830, including a continental buffet breakfast. Extra beds are available for Dkr155 each.

The *Hotel Föroyar* (☎ 17500; fax 16019), which serves mainly as a convention centre, occupies a beautiful location on the hillside above Tórshavn. However, it's an expensive view, with rooms starting at Dkr630/780 single/double.

Just a few years ago, the convention hall was the only place in the Faroes licensed to sell alcohol. Business people attending conventions were permitted to wash down their lunches with a half-litre glass of lager in the conference room. The price? A mere Dkr75. Long live alcohol reform!

Places to Eat
Self-Catering The largest and best-stocked supermarket is *Miklagarður*, in the SMS Shopping Centre on RC Effersøesgøta. There's also an Fk supermarket on Dokta Jacobsensgøta. When these aren't open, you'll find plenty of kiosks that sell basic groceries. They're slightly more expensive than the supermarkets, but stay open evenings and weekends.

For groceries and freshly baked goods (including excellent pastries), try the *Frants Restorff* bakery outlet on Tórsgøta, open daily from 7 am to 11 pm.

If you're looking for alcohol, refer to the list of outlets under Drink in the Faroes Facts for the Visitor chapter.

Snacks & Light Meals The nicest – but not the cheapest – place for a snack is the cosy *Kondittaríið* at Niels Finsensgøta 11 on the pedestrian mall. It's open weekdays from 9 am to 6 pm (7 pm on Friday) and Saturday between 9 am and 2 pm.

For hot dogs, burgers and chips, try the *Pylsuvognurin* opposite the Farstøðin transport terminal or *Kaffi-Grill Matstova* at Tórsgøta 17, open daily from 11 am (2 pm on Sunday) to 11 pm. There's also a grill on Vaglið, beside the Raðhús, which is open on weekdays (11.30 am to 1 pm and 5 to 11 pm) and on Saturday from 5pm to midnight. Takeaway fish and chips costs Dkr45.

More pleasant and popular is the refurbished *Café Nátur* in old Tórshavn, near the harbour. You won't get anything startling, but the atmosphere is great for a baked potato, a cup of coffee or a glass of draught beer. It's open Monday to Friday from 9 am to midnight, on Saturday from 9 am to 1 am and Sunday from noon to midnight.

The *Pizzaria* (☎ 18866) on upper Niels Finsensgøta is open daily from 5 to 11 pm (midnight on Friday and Saturday) and it's licensed to sell alcohol. The menu has a wide selection of pizzas, including vegetarian, with prices between Dkr60 and Dkr75 for medium sized pizzas. Home delivery is available for Dkr30.

The new *Café Klótin* is open Monday to Thursday from 7 pm to midnight and on Friday and Saturday from 10 pm to 4 am. It's on Sverrisgøta, next to Kondittaríið.

Cafeterias *Perlan* in the SMS Shopping Centre serves a variety of salads, smørrebrød, desserts and hot snacks, as well as a daily special, all for reasonable prices. The special costs Dkr39 and consists of a meat dish, boiled potatoes and vegetables. It's open from 9 am to 5.30 pm weekdays (on Friday until 7 pm) and from 9 am to 2 pm on Saturday.

The *Sjómansheimið* cafeteria (in the seamen's home) offers à la carte, smørrebrød and set specials. A continental breakfast (7 to 10 am) costs Dkr30, lunch (11.30 am to 2 pm) costs Dkr45 and dinner (5.30 to 9.30 pm) costs Dkr55. On Sunday, breakfast is available from 8 am. Sunday lunch costs Dkr85. The food is consistently pretty good.

There's also a cafeteria in the Nordic House and another in the swim hall at the Gundadalur Sports Centre, which is open the same hours as the centre itself.

Fine Dining Both top-end hotels have relatively elegant licensed dining rooms which offer à la carte lunch and dinner menus. At the *Hotel Hafnia* you can get a buffet breakfast including coffee, juice, cereal, fruit, bread and cold meats and cheeses for Dkr60. For other meals, watch what you order. There's a story about a group who went in for a blow-out meal, but it turned out to include the worst, toughest Dkr135 steak imaginable, accompanied by chips, one sprig of broccoli, two miniature corn cobs and a bit of watercress – a real rip-off. Timing is also important; the dining room is open all day, but, outside regular meal hours, the menu is very limited.

The *Hotel Föroyar* is a bit more sophisticated, but still isn't anything to write home about. Two-course lunches cost from Dkr160 to Dkr190 and dinners, which may include such Faroese specialities as puffin or lamb, are Dkr170 to Dkr260. The dinner menu includes soup, vegetarian dishes, main courses with salads, and desserts.

You could also try the licensed restaurant *Rio Bravo* at Tórsgøta 11, just a couple of blocks uphill from the city centre. The emphasis is on steaks, which cost around Dkr160. Starters average Dkr65 and desserts Dkr40. It's open for dinner from 5 to 11 pm nightly except Friday and Saturday, when it closes at 1 am.

Alternatively, there's the relatively new and rather cheaper licensed restaurant

Nólsoyarstova, on Gongin just opposite the Faroe Islands Tourist Board. Starters cost Dkr50 to Dkr70; fish dishes, Dkr140 to Dkr155; steaks from Dkr112 to Dkr157; puffin from Dkr175; and desserts, Dkr40 to Dkr45. The restaurant is open on weekdays from noon to 2 pm and 5 to 11 pm and on weekends from 5 pm to midnight.

Entertainment

Bars & Clubs Tórshavn now has six licensed restaurants and cafés (some of which may only serve alcohol with meals), including *Café Natúr* which occasionally stages live music on Friday and Saturday nights.

Most Tórshavn clubs are only open to members and their guests. However, at *Club 20*, you need not be a member to get in. This night club and disco is in the same building as the Havnar Club and cinema; between 10 pm and 4 am on Friday and Saturday it attracts locals in the 18 to 25 age group. Sometimes there's live music. On Thursday the cover charge is Dkr20, while on Friday and Saturday it's Dkr70 (on other nights admission is free). It also has a café, which is open Monday to Thursday from 7 pm to midnight and Friday to Sunday from 5 pm to midnight.

If you want to drink in the classier *Havnar Club* while enjoying a great view of the harbour, you'll have to wangle an invitation from a club member.

Theatre The Tórshavn theatre company is called *Leikarafelag Føroya*, but performances are mainly in Faroese and staged in the winter so few visitors will be able to catch a production. They use the Sjónleikarhúsið at Hoydalsvegur 2. Visiting theatre groups perform from time to time either there or at the Nordic House. Contact the Kunningarstovan tourist office for tickets and programme information.

Cinema The two-screen *Havnar Bio* screens three or four films nightly, seven days a week. Admission is Dkr50 to Dkr55 per film.

Getting There & Away

For a concise schedule and fare listing of long-distance buses and inter-island ferries, pick up a copy of the booklet *Ferðaætlan* for Dkr20 from Strandfaraskip Landsins at the Farstøðin transport terminal.

Air See the Regional Getting There & Away chapter for details on flights to/from Vágar airport, the nearest airport for Tórshavn.

Helicopter The Tórshavn heliport lies north of the campground along the coast road. For information and booking, contact Atlantic Airways (☎ 33410; fax 33380), Vágar Airport, FR-380 Sørvágur. For a rundown on flights and fares, see the Faroes Getting Around chapter.

Bus All long-distance buses depart from the bus stops in front of the Farstøðin transport terminal.

Bus services to and from Tórshavn include the following:

Bus No	destination	daily services	fare (Dkr)
100	Vestmanna	4-10	40
101	Gamlarætt	3-8	20
104	Kaldbak	3-5	10
400	Leirvík	6-9	50

From these terminals, you'll find connecting buses to all corners of Streymoy and Eysturoy, as well as ferries to many of the outer islands.

To Vágar airport (1½ hours; Dkr100) and Mykines (3¾ hours; Dkr160), take the Vestmanna bus No 100 and connect with the ferry to Oyrargjógv, then take bus No 300.

To reach Klaksvík (Dkr80; two hours) and the north-eastern islands, take bus No 400 to Leirvík and connect with the ferry from there. It continues from Leirvík to Fuglafjørður (Dkr 50; 1¾ hours).

To Hestur (one hour; Dkr50), Sandoy (70 minutes; Dkr50) or Skúvoy (three hours; Dkr100), take bus No 100 to Gamlarætt and connect with the appropriate ferries.

For Gjógv (two hours; Dkr50), Eiði (two hours; Dkr50), Tjørnuvík (1¼ hours; Dkr50), and Saksun (1½ hours; Dkr50), take bus No 400 to Oyrarbakki and connect with bus Nos 205, 200, 202 and 204, respectively. For Oyndarfjørður (1½ hours; Dkr50) and Strendur, on the western shore of Skálafjøður (1¼ hours; Dkr50), take bus No 400 and change at Skálabotnur to bus Nos 481 and 480, respectively.

For the eastern shore of Skálafjørður (1½ hours; Dkr50), take bus No 400 and change to bus No 440 at Søldarfjørður.

Ferry Both international and inter-island ferries leave from the ferry dock at the eastern harbour. For information on international routes, see the Getting There & Away chapter at the beginning of the book. Inter-island routes to/from Tórshavn and applicable fares are outlined in the Faroes Getting Around chapter.

There's a marina for private yachts, with full facilities, at Argir two km south of Tórshavn. For information, contact Argja Marina Club (☎ 10028), FR-160 Argir.

Getting Around

The Airport The airport for Tórshavn and the rest of the Faroes is in a windy pass on Vágar Island. The airport bus (No 100/300) leaves from the Farstøðin transport terminal approximately three hours before the international flight departures. For bookings, contact the tourist office or phone ☎ 12626.

Bus The red Bussleiðin city buses operate daily and run to just about any place you'd like to go in tiny Tórshavn. On weekdays they run on half-hourly cycles during the day and hourly in the evening.

On Saturday there's an hourly service, while on Sunday and on holidays they run 1½ hourly services. The single ride fare is Dkr10. Monthly bus passes are available for Dkr200 from the Steinatún kiosk on Niels Winthersgøta. Passes for 10 trips cost Dkr80. Timetables are available at the Farstøðin transport terminal and the tourist office.

Taxi Taxis can be found at the Auto and Bíl

stands and at the Ráðhús. You can also call a taxi at the Tórshavn taxi service (☎ 11234 or 11444).

Bicycle Tórshavn is pretty good for cycling due to its relatively sparse traffic, but it's small enough for you to go anywhere on foot as well. For information on bike hire, see under Bicycle in the Faroes Getting Around chapter.

Streymoy & Eysturoy

The two largest islands of the Faroese archipelago, Streymoy and Eysturoy, are the geographical and economic heart of the country. The island of Streymoy, which covers 373 sq km, comprises 25% of the land area and has over 40% of the Faroes' population. The name means 'island of currents', in reference to both the ocean waters around it and the numerous streams and waterfalls that cascade from its peaks.

Less evocative is the name of Eysturoy ('eastern island'), which refers only to its position relative to Streymoy. It's oddly shaped and divided into two parts by the fjords Funningsfjørður and Skálafjørður. The western part is a long dagger-shaped chunk, while the eastern side is a rambling series of fjords and headlands. Eysturoy covers 286 sq km and has around 9000 inhabitants in its 30 villages, many of which are monotonously strung out along southern Skálafjørður.

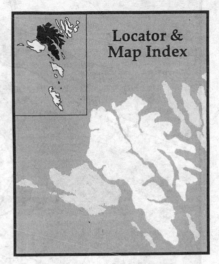

Locator & Map Index

Streymoy

KIRKJUBØUR

Kirkjubøur was the largest and wealthiest farm in the Faroes and the episcopal centre of the country during medieval times. At that time, the islet Kirkjubøhólmur was once connected to Streymoy and formed part of the settlement. Excavations have revealed that the settlement once supported several hundred inhabitants.

Kirkjubøur's position was probably selected due to the driftwood and seaweed beds deposited there by the Gulf Stream. Driftwood was important for fuel and construction in the treeless Faroes and the seaweed was dried to make fertiliser, which allowed grain to grow in the poor climate and scanty soil.

There's also speculation that the site was first occupied by Irish monks even before the Norse colonisation. The small bay just south of the settlement is known as Brandansvík, after St Brendan, who reputedly sailed across the North Atlantic in the 6th century. Ruins of small stone houses and fireplaces have been discovered just south of the farmhouse and, although they haven't been excavated, it's presumed they were once occupied by Irish friars. However, it's just as possible that the bay was named for St Brendan's church, the ruins of which are also locally known as the 'Mary Church' or 'the mortuary'.

Magnus Cathedral

The largest and most striking ruin at Kirkjubøur is the 'unfinished cathedral', a grand Gothic church originally intended to be dedicated to St Magnus, Earl of Orkney. Construction was begun by Bishop Erlendur of the Faroes, who served from 1269 to 1308 and employed some ruthless methods of fund collection for this pet project. However, disputes ensued among his constituents

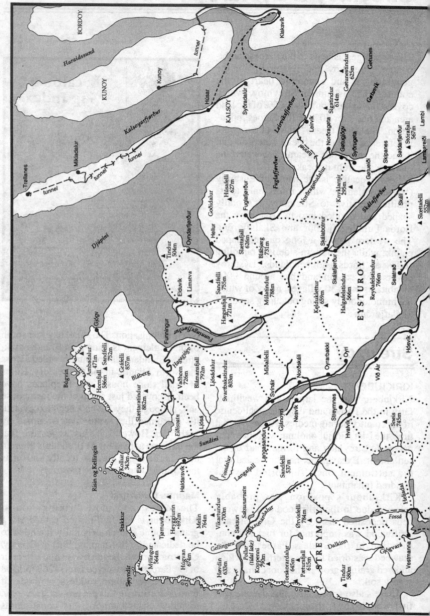

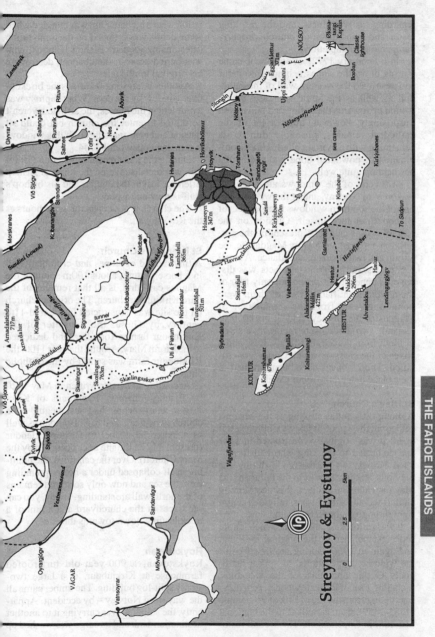

Streymoy & Eysturoy

0   2.5   5km

regarding his worthiness, and the resulting arson and vandalism of church property hampered its completion.

On 6 February 1772, an avalanche came roaring down the slopes behind Kirkjubøur and destroyed the western wall of the cathedral as well as the spiral staircase, which wound up towards the unfinished bell tower. Surprisingly, however, quite a lot of the cathedral remains, probably due to its cementing with a mortar called *skilp*, a combination of powdered bone and shells that has held up quite well.

At several of the windows are reliefs of Håkon V of Norway, and at the western end one of the southern windows bears reliefs of Bishop Erlendur himself. Outside on the eastern wall is another representing the crucifixion of Christ, with Mary Magdalene, the Virgin and two angels in attendance. A small cache of seven religious artefacts was discovered beneath this panel, but only four of them were identifiable. Two of them were bone fragments from the remains of St Magnus of the Orkneys and St Þorlákur of Iceland. Two others were reputedly a shred of cloth from the Virgin Mary's dress and a sliver of the cross on which Christ was crucified. These objects have been returned to their place behind the relief panel.

St Olav's Church

Although it's not as striking as the Magnus cathedral, the age of St Olav's Church sets it apart. It was originally constructed in 1111 and dedicated to the king who had formulated Norway's Christian code during the previous century. Thanks to the failure of the Magnus cathedral project, this unassuming church served as the Faroes' religious centre right through to the Reformation.

It was restored in 1874, after which it bore little resemblance to the original building, and again in 1966. During the first facelift the windows were altered to appear artificially Gothic and most of the valuables, including a set of intricate wooden pew carvings dating from the life of Erik of Pomerania (1385-1459), were carted off to the National Museum in Copenhagen. The second resto-

ration went a bit better but was bungled when some debris was dropped on the tomb of the (presumably jocular) Bishop Hilarius, who was buried beneath the chancel, destroying his original tombstone.

Another interesting feature is the bricked-over window by the door. When leprosy was a problem in the Faroes, the afflicted weren't permitted to enter the church but could sit outside and hear mass through this window. It remained open until 1744.

During the most recent renovation (1989-90), workers discovered the tomb of Bishop Erlendur inside the church and his bishop's staff is now on display.

The church is now open the same hours as the Roykstovan.

St Brendan's Church

A tiny mound of stones and crumbled wall in a horse pasture, about 100m south of the Magnus cathedral, is all that remains of the third Kirkjubøur church. The original church on the site was constructed in the mid-11th century by Gæsa, the daughter of the Kirkjubøur farmer Tórhallur, and dedicated to the Virgin Mary. Around the year 1100, the Kirkjubøur farm was seized by the Catholic church.

According to a letter written in May 1420 by Bishop Johannes Teutonicus of Kirkjubøur, construction had just begun on a church to be dedicated to St Brendan as well as a memorial chapel to Bishop Erlendur (presumably on the site once occupied by the Mary Church). Over the centuries, the building itself collapsed under a heavy pounding from the sea and now only scattered remains of the north wall are standing. Today, you can see traces of the churchyard and a hint of a track leading down towards the islet.

Roykstovan

Roykstovan, a 900-year-old turf-roofed farmhouse at Kirkjubøur, is a large two-storey split-log building. The timber came all the way from Norway – by accident. Apparently, the ship that was carrying it to another destination sank and its cargo was washed up at this natural collection point by the obliging Gulf Stream.

The interior of the building is laid out to reflect the Faroese lifestyle during medieval times. There's a dungeon in the basement. On the main floor above it is the large *roykstova* (all-purpose room) that served as the eating, sleeping, entertaining and living area. In the small attic on the top floor, you can see the room where King Sverri received his education way back when the building was new. The beautifully painted doors, however, were carved in 1907. This building has been occupied by 18 generations of the same Faroese family.

The farmhouse museum is open daily in the summer. Admission is fairly steep at Dkr20. The dungeon may be visited free – entry is from the back of the house – but it's just a big room used to store junk. The house is open from 10 am to 5.30 pm Monday to Saturday and from 2 to 5.30 pm on Sunday.

Gamlarætt

Gamlarætt is a purpose-built ferry terminal just over 1½ km north of Kirkjubøur. From here, ferries connect Streymoy with Sandoy and Hestur.

Velbastaður

The small and very average Faroese community of Velbastaður, five km up the coast from Kirkjubøur, enjoys a particularly good view out across the strait Hestsfjørður to the beautifully shaped islands of Koltur and loaf-shaped Hestur.

Syðradalur

The tiny seaside village of Syðradalur lies 12 km north of Kirkjubøur. It's the best vantage point for the odd profile view of Koltur Island, and behind it there's also a nice cirque valley.

Buses no longer run from Syðradalur to Tórshavn, but hitching is possible. Alternatively, in fine weather, it's a pleasant hike. The walking route takes off from the western side of Route 10, less than one km above the Hotel Føroyar in Tórshavn, and climbs over the moors to the dam on the river Sand before descending in two steep steps to Syðradalur. From the Hotel Føroyar, it's about eight km each way.

Hiking

Since Kirkjubøur is only eight km as the crow flies from Tórshavn, you may want to consider walking one way if you have a fine day.

There are actually three routes, of which two are described in a Faroese Tourist Board walks leaflet. The easiest leads southward from the Kirkjubøur road, about 2½ km west of central Tórshavn. It begins opposite the end of Landavegur and heads straight up the hill, climbing up and along the slopes of Kirkjubøreyn before descending to the shore just outside Kirkjubøur. It's cairned all the

---

Sverri Sigurdsson

Perhaps Kirkjubøur's most renowned resident was Sverri Sigurdsson, the illegitimate son of King Sigurd of Norway, whose mother was a Norwegian milkmaid named Gunnhild. The child Sverri was born in the Faroes in 1149 and, in 1151, was brought to Kirkjubøur. The religious community of the day wouldn't have taken kindly to a young unmarried mother, so she hid the child in a cave above the village and cared for him there.

One day a Faroese man whom she'd known in Norway arrived and before long they were married, agreeing to rear the boy as their own. After the wedding they went to Norway but stayed only a couple of years. On their return to the Faroes, they placed Sverri in the care of the Kirkjubøur Bishop, Hrói, who saw to it that the heir to the Norwegian throne received a proper education.

In 1174, after his mother had disclosed his royal lineage, Sverri again left the Faroes, this time to claim his father's throne. The entire account of his interesting life is related in *Sverri's Saga*, which was recorded in Iceland shortly after his death in 1202. ∎

way. To return via this route, walk north of Kirkjubøur until you reach the sheep grid, then climb 50m up the hill to connect with the track.

The second route leaves from the street Heiðatún in the suburb of Argir (south of Tórshavn) and climbs 245m to the small lake Porkerisvatn before descending to Kirkjubøur. The final km of this route drops very steeply and you may prefer scrambling up it back to Tórshavn, rather than struggling in an out-of-control descent. This route isn't clearly marked, so don't attempt it in bad weather.

For a change of scenery, a third option is to follow the coast right around the southern tip of Streymoy, but stay well back from cliff edges and rocks where waves are crashing. This route will require at least three hours one way.

Organised Tours

Tora Tourist Traffic in Tórshavn conducts a guided tour of Kirkjubøur and nearby Velbastaður for Dkr140 per adult, including transport, guide and museum admission. It departs Tórshavn on Wednesday at 9 am and returns at noon. On Monday afternoons between 2 and 6 pm, Smyril Line runs a tour around Tórshavn which continues (by bus) to Kirkjubøur. The cost is Dkr165 per adult. Book as far in advance as possible either directly with the agencies or through the tourist offices.

Getting There & Away

Between Tórshavn and Gamlarætt, bus No 101 runs three to seven times daily (30 minutes; Dkr20). The same bus goes to Kirkjubøur two to five times daily (35 minutes; Dkr20). If your bus terminates at Gamlarætt, you'll have to walk almost two km south to Kirkjubøur. Unless the day is particularly fine and you want to hike around the area, two hours is more than sufficient to visit the site.

KALDBAK

The small village of Kaldbak lies on the northern shore of the magnificent fjord

Kaldbaksfjørður with its numerous wispy waterfalls and impossibly steep cliffs. When the wind is howling up the fjord – a common occurrence – the waterfalls actually go upwards!

The only item of interest in the village itself is the cosy wooden turf-roofed church, which was built in 1835. It has a small wooden steeple and is surrounded by a rambling stone wall. The carvings in the choir screen (hearts, fiddles and shamrocks) are unique in the Faroes. However, you may have problems visiting on any day but Sunday.

Getting There & Away

Bus No 104 does the quick run back and forth from Tórshavn five times daily on weekdays, four times on Saturday and three times on Sunday.

KVÍVÍK

Kvívík on Vestmannasund is one of the lushest parts of the Faroes. On a fine day its fields glow a brilliant green and there are fine views across the strait to Vágar Island and southward to Koltur. Kvívík is the site of the ruins of an 11th-century farm which has been studied recently.

Farm Ruins

The farm house apparently belonged to a family of high social standing because by Faroese standards it is immense – 22m long and 5.75 metres wide. The walls were constructed of double rows of stone, which were insulated with a layer of mud and gravel between, together forming a 1½ metre-thick obstacle to the wind and cold.

In traditional Faroese style, the quarters consisted of the large roykstova where the occupants cooked, ate, slept and entertained. In the centre of the room is a large fireplace, seven metres long and one metre wide, which was used for both heating and cooking. The clay floor around it was pounded solid over a base of flat stones and is reminiscent of modern linoleum on cement.

Outside the great house is a cow byre, as

yet the only ruin of its kind in the Faroes. It measures 10 metres by 3½ metres and it was apparently more luxurious than many early Faroese commoners' dwellings.

There isn't really very much to look at, but archaeologists and other ruin buffs may be interested in a visit. Across the bridge from the ruins, near the village church, is an old turf-roofed vicarage constructed in the traditional Faroese manner.

Leynar

If you're interested in woodcraft, visit the shop of Ole Jakob Nielsen at the village of Leynar two km from Kvívík. He's been interested in woodturning since the early 1960s and creates splendid and utilitarian works of art from scraps of wood that otherwise would be discarded. Leynar also has a very nice beach.

Getting There & Away

To reach Kvívík from Tórshavn, take the Vestmanna bus which departs six to nine times daily (Dkr30; 25 minutes). The two airport buses bypass Kvívík but the others go through the village.

VESTMANNA

Although it's the second-largest town on Streymoy, Vestmanna itself is of little interest. Most visitors come for the spectacular Vestmanna Bird Cliffs tours, but for those with more time, there are several pleasant walks in the area. This is also the departure point for the Vágar ferry.

Vestmanna Bird Cliffs

The superb boat tours to the wild Vestmanna Bird Cliffs of north-western Streymoy are probably the highlight of the Faroe Islands. When the weather is cooperating, you sail from Vestmanna out onto the open sea and up the west coast of Streymoy to towering cliffs and sea stacks which teem with fulmars, kittiwakes, guillemots, razorbills and even, occasionally, puffins. When the seas are calm enough, the boats pass through some beautiful sea caves beneath the cliffs.

The recommended tour is with Gunnar Skúvadal (☎ 24305; fax 24292) in his eight-metre Faroese launch *Urðardrangur* or his more modern speedboat *Barbara*. He speaks English, Danish and German and is well-versed in the natural and human history of the region – and his enthusiasm never wanes! If his tours are full, there's also Palli Lamhauge (☎ 24155; fax 24383) in his boats *Fríðgerð* or *Silja*.

Either tour costs Dkr150 per person and, weather permitting, departures are four times daily (connecting with buses from Tórshavn) at 9.40 am and 2.25, 5 and 8 pm. Tora Tourist Traffic does the same trip on Wednesday and Saturday for Dkr370; the extra Dkr220 buys you a Dkr40 bus trip from Tórshavn. Smyril Line offers a similar tour on Tuesday for Dkr305 from Tórshavn.

Hiking

From Vestmanna, there are separate roads leading up through the valleys of Fossdal and Heljadal, which may double as hiking routes. In each valley there's a hydroelectric power plant and two reservoirs to provide them with water. In Fossdal, the road passes between two dammed lakes, wanders over a low pass and disappears. From this road, there are several walking routes over to Saksunardalur, any of which can be easily done in a day.

Another option is to walk up the river Gjógvar from the top of the village. This route will lead to the Dalkinn ridge and around its eastern slope, past the upper Fossdal reservoir, before dropping down into Saksunardalur. This trip takes about five hours each way.

From the head of the lower reservoir on the Heljadal side, the road makes a loop up to the dam on the second lake and then returns. This is about a four-hour return trip from Vestmanna.

Places to Stay & Eat

If you have a hankering to stay in Vestmanna, the *Guesthouse/Youth Hostel La Carreta* (☎ 24610; fax 24708) will be happy to accommodate you. Single/double guesthouse rooms with shared facilities cost

Dkr250/350. Hostel accommodation costs Dkr90 per person. The attached licensed restaurant serves traditionally prepared lamb and fish dishes; specialities include fiskefrikadeller (Faroese fishcakes) for Dkr55 and lamb cutlets for Dkr130. It's open from 7.30 am to 10 pm.

Alternatively, a *holiday home* accommodating six people may be booked through Tora Tourist Traffic in Tórshavn for Dkr520 per night. Nordica also has two *holiday homes* accommodating five to seven people for Dkr386 or Dkr600 per night.

Kaffistovan at the ferry dock serves quick microwave snacks and it's a warm place to wait for the ferry to Oyrargjógv. There's also a snack bar at the Shell petrol station diagonally opposite the harbour parking area.

Getting There & Away
Buses travel to/from Tórshavn four to 10 times daily (50 minutes; Dkr40) and the ferry to Oyrargjógv on Vágar island leaves the harbour 13 to 15 times a day. On weekdays, the first daily departure is at 6.30 am and the last trip back is at 7.25 pm (8.25 pm in winter).

KOLLAFJØRÐUR
The village of Kollafjørður, at the southern entrance to Sundini (the sound between Streymoy and Eysturoy), is of little interest except for its turf-roofed church, which was described by a German scientist in 1828 as 'the most miserable house of God in the whole of Christendom'. Well, it's not all that bad now – it was thoroughly renovated in 1837 – although several years ago a drunk driver went off the road and wound up inside the church. The considerable damage has now been completely repaired.

The interior is wooden, typical of 19th-century Faroese churches, and the roof is covered with turf. Unfortunately, for a look inside you'll either have to peer through the windows or turn up on a Sunday, when it may be unlocked. On the door are some unique carvings.

Kollafjarðardalur
Beyond the head of the fjord from Kollafjørður is the deep and lovely valley of Kollfjarðardalur, where the new tunnel from Kaldbaksfjørður emerges from the mountain.

Places to Stay & Eat
Accommodation and meals are available at the *Hotel Geyti* (☎ 21021; fax 21366), a funky little place beside the road in the village of Kollafjørður. Rooms cost Dkr200/400 for a single/double without breakfast.

Tora Tourist Traffic and Nordica take bookings for two *holiday homes* in Signabøur, on the opposite side of the fjord, which accommodate five to six people for Dkr520 per night.

In upper Kollafjarðardalur there's a *Statoil* petrol station with a tourist office, a pretty good snack bar and a coffee shop. It's open daily from 7.30 am (8 am on Saturday and 1 pm on Sunday) to 8.30 pm.

Getting There & Away
All buses running between Tórshavn and Leirvík pass through the Kollafjørður area (Dkr30; 20 minutes).

VIÐ ÁIR
Við Áir, on the Streymoy shore of Sundini, was the last commercial whaling station in the Faroes. Its main quarry was the blue whale, and in the first two decades of this century 178 were harpooned and boiled down. Over the next 20 years, only a third of that number was taken, which was evidence that stocks were being depleted rather than any sudden penchant for conservation. The whalers then turned their attentions to the more plentiful (and therefore more profitable) fin whales. Commercial whaling from Við Áir was abandoned in 1959, but was resumed in 1962 and then closed for good in 1966.

At Hvalvík, near the bridge just north of Við Áir, is another of those old turf-roofed churches, this one reconstructed in 1829 after being destroyed by a storm. It is presumed that the original was built during the 18th century.

SAKSUN

Saksun's unusual setting makes it somewhat of a tourist destination. The hillside village of typical farmhouses is divided into two parts by the river Dalsá . Downstream from the village is the beautiful and almost perfectly round tidal lake Pollur ('pond'), which offers good fishing. It's a wonderful walk above its southern bank to Ósin ('mouth'), which is its outlet to the sea. The Saksun church, which overlooks Pollur, was moved to its present position from Tjørnuvík in 1858. Today, the village is home to 32 people.

Saksunardalur

One km along the Dalsá ('valley river') above the village is the lake Saksunarvatn – also good for trout and salmon fishing. The valley once offered excellent camping, but congestion and careless campers polluted the stream and valley, and camping is now forbidden.

Dúvugarður Museum

At the end of the northern road in Saksun is the 19th-century turf farmhouse Dúvugarður. It has been converted into a folk museum which attempts to convey the rigours of Faroese life from the medieval era to the 1800s. The museum building contains the usual roykstova, a guest bedroom, a bedroom for visiting clergy and a cow byre. It was inhabited as recently as WWII. The museum is open daily in the summer from 2 to 5 pm. Admission is Dkr15.

Hiking

There are several good walking routes around Saksun, any of which can be completed in a day. The easiest one merely follows the river up Saksunardalur. It's also possible to walk across to Vestmanna, from south of the Heljardalsá river mouth in Saksunardalur via the Foss hydroelectric project. The route begins by traversing the eastern ridge of Ørvisfelli.

Another option is to walk from Saksun village up the very steep hillside above the river Gellingará, over the narrow pass between the cirques and down into Tjørnuvík. The path is not easy to find.

For a bit more of a challenge, climb from Saksunardalur up to the 676m Borgin ridge and follow it up to the 790m Koppenni and beyond to the 777m Malaknúkur. From there, you'll have astounding views both north and south along the coast, the same stretch seen on the Vestmanna Bird Cliffs tours. Alternatively, head north from Saksun to Kambsmúli; along the way are several small lakes with profuse bird life.

Organised Tours

On Friday at 1 pm, there's a five-hour Tora Tourist Traffic tour from Tórshavn which visits the city historical museum, the ruins at Kvívík near Vestmanna, then Saksun. At Dkr275 per person it's pretty steep, considering that it includes only a guide, transport and museum admission.

Smyril Line does a four-hour tour on Wednesday from Tórshavn to Saksun, starting at 3 pm. The charge is only Dkr155.

Getting There & Away

On weekdays there are two daily buses (No 204) to/from Oyrarbakki (on Eysturoy) connecting with buses (No 400) to/from Tórshavn (confirm with the driver). The fare from Tórshavn is Dkr50 and the journey time is 1¼ hours.

TJØRNUVÍK

Like Saksun, Tjørnuvík enjoys a super location, tightly wedged between two headlands with a wide sandy beach. In bright and calm weather (of which there is precious little), it's a good place to sit and watch the surf or read a book. More likely, you'll be huddled in the chilly wind for just as long as it takes to snap a photo. The view out to sea includes the photogenic sea stacks, Risin og Kellingin, the remnants of a bungled attempt to tow the Faroes to Iceland (see under Eiði). One of the most spectacular Faroese cliffs, the 564m Mýlingur, lies only four km west of the village, but you'll have to walk up to Skoradalsheggjur to see it.

Medieval Farm

Tjørnuvík's most interesting attraction is the excavated medieval farm and grave site near the eastern end of the town. Like the farmhouse at Kvívík, this building also had thick stone walls but rather than one large all-purpose room, there were two major rooms, one for sitting and one for sleeping. The building also sported a gabled roof and a wooden floor which rested on joists. Wood was scarce, so any damage to this floor was repaired with the more traditional stamped clay.

During medieval times hazelnuts were a common folk cure for hangovers and a great many hazelnut shells were found in the boards and clay near one of the sitting benches that line the walls of the living room. One can only imagine the rollicking parties that must have taken place there!

Haldarsvík

Haldarsvík, four km along the road southeast of Tjørnuvík, is notable for its unusual octagonal stone church, which dates back to 1856. Just uphill from the church is an odd futuristic seafarers memorial by Faroese sculptor Janus Kamban.

Fossdalur

About six km south-east of Tjørnuvík along Sundini, the road crosses the Foss or 'falls river'. The waterfall in question is generically known as Foss, which means 'falls'. It's the highest in the Faroes, falling 140m in several steps. The best view is available down the slope from the road.

Places to Stay

Contact Nordica regarding booking the two *holiday homes* in Tjørnuvík and the one in Haldarsvík. All three accommodate five people. Charges are Dkr480, Dkr600 and Dkr309 per night, respectively.

Tora Tourist Traffic can book *B&B* accommodation in Langasandur. Single/

double rooms with shared facilities cost Dkr280/430.

There's also the hostel-style 'camp and conference centre' *Leguhúsið í Nesvík* (☎ 22533; fax 22544) which is only open to groups of 10 or more people. However, it's not available from mid-June to mid-August. A dormitory bed costs Dkr70.

Getting There & Away

Coming from Tórshavn (1½ hours; Dkr50), first take bus No 400 to Oyrarbakki, from where bus No 202 does two to four daily runs to Tjørnuvík.

Eysturoy

OYRARBAKKI

Nearly everyone using the bus system around the Faroes winds up spending some time at the Oyrarbakki Shell petrol station since all the buses stop here and exchange passengers before continuing on their merry ways. This is thanks mainly to the bottleneck caused by the Sundini bridge between Streymoy and Eysturoy.

Places to Stay

At Oyri, south of Oyrarbakki, there's the new *Hotel Oyri* (☎ 22144; fax 22527). It's just a small place with rooms costing Dkr250/400 for a single/double and Dkr100 for an extra bed.

EIÐI

Eiði (pronounced 'OY-yeh') sits on a pass between the Eysturoy mainland and the hulking Kollur peninsula, which makes up in sheer bulk what it's lacking in area. The word eiði refers to just this sort of pass, a low windy isthmus lying between highlands. The village church, built in 1881, is one of the nicest in the Faroes. As in most Faroese churches, model sailing ships hang from the ceiling as a petition for the safety of sailors far from home. The small lake north of the village is stocked with fish.

Things to do in Oyrarbakki

In the first edition of this book, we wrote that there was absolutely nothing to see or do here while waiting for a bus, save going for a bite in the petrol station snack bar or changing money at the bank next door. The comment elicited the following letter from a reader, which may be of use to anyone who is bored at Oyrarbakki:

If you're stuck waiting for the bus, it's either for 10 minutes or two hours for more obscure destinations. There are a few things you can do. The post office is beside the bank. Across the road is a lane down to a landlocked fish farm and you can go down and dream about fresh protein as it jumps before your eyes. The tidal currents can make impressive eddies around the bridge foundations.

If you have the two hours, wander across the bridge and turn right, past the fertile (read smelly) shallows on the west bank. These attract waterfowl and are perfect for fish farms. Forty minutes (two km) up the road are the mouths of Norðaragjógv and Sunnaragjógv, both gorgeous gorges with waterfalls (you can see one cutting into the slope from the Oyrarbakki petrol station). The lucky can arrange to flag down the Tjørnuvík bus and avoid walking the road back, since it is scheduled to meet up with the Leirvík and Tórshavn buses at the Oyrarbakki petrol station.

Tom, Australia

Folk Museum

The village folk museum, *Eiðibygdasavn*, is a collection of several traditional turf-roofed houses with box beds etc. It's open on Monday, Wednesday and Sunday, and on other days by arrangement with Anna Ellingsgaard (☎ 23014). Admission costs Dkr20.

Eiðisvatn

The lake Eiðisvatn sits on the plateau about 130m higher than its namesake village. It's quite beautiful and merits a day-hike. The lake is reputed to offer fairly good trout fishing.

Risin og Kellingin

These two sea stacks, whose names mean 'the giant and the witch', feature on nearly every tourist brochure about the Faroes and probably merit a photo or two of your own.

The story goes that an Icelandic giant thought he'd like to drag the Faroes a bit closer to home, so he took a heavy rope and secured it around the most solid thing he could find which turned out to be the rock Kollur. He and his wife (who happened to be a witch or a hag, depending on your transla-

tion) also splashed into the sea and began to tug, but it still failed to budge.

They struggled all through the night (everyone knows giants and witches are only permitted to be abroad at night) and scarcely noticed the time passing. When the sun appeared, they attempted to flee underground, where supernatural beings are obligated to remain by day, but it was too late and they were turned to stone on the spot.

For the best view of the stacks, follow the road to the northern end of the small lake at Eiði, then turn east and head out to the coast. Follow the low cliffs for a few hundred metres and they should come into view. Other good but distant views are available from the village of Tjørnuvík on the island of Streymoy, and from the road that enters Eiði from the east. If you're interested in getting closer for a photograph, see the Hiking and Organised Tours sections.

Hiking

A very pleasant and easy two-hour walk leads from Hotel Eiði up to the 343m top of Kollur. It's grassy slopes and great views all the way; you'll be able to see down to Risin og Kellingin from near the top. The summit ruin was a WWII watch tower. Beware of skua attacks on this route!

THE FAROE ISLANDS

Organised Tours

On Saturday at 10 am, Tora Tourist Traffic run a seven-hour bus tour to Eysturoy (including Eiði) for Dkr365 per person.

To see the Risin og Kellingin stacks by boat, make arrangements with Palli Lamhauge (☎ 24155; fax 24383) in Vestmanna. On request, he'll take groups to Eiði via the Vestmanna Bird Cliffs and Mýlingur for Dkr200 per person (each way).

Places to Stay & Eat

The *Hotel Eiði* (☎ 23456; fax 23200), with a wonderful lake view, seems a rather sterile and impersonal place from the outside, but it's quite nice inside and the staff are friendly. Singles/doubles with attached bath cost Dkr485/585, including a continental breakfast. A buffet lunch or three-course dinner in the dining room costs Dkr135 or Dkr150 per person. The hotel also allows camping; campers may use their showers, toilets and kitchen for Dkr50 per person.

Tora Tourist Traffic can arrange accommodation in a *holiday house* for six people, for Dkr480 per night.

A *supermarket* in the village sells a full range of groceries.

Getting There & Away

To reach Eiði (1¼ hours; Dkr50) from Tórshavn, you must first take bus No 400 to Oyrarbakki. From there, bus No 200 goes to and from Eiði three to five times daily.

GJÓGV

The village of Gjógv (pronounced 'jagv') is named after its harbour, which is an unusual sea-filled gorge. Although it's one of the Faroes' most pleasant villages, there really isn't anything of specific or overwhelming interest. In the village are two rustic old general stores which date from the late 1800s, but neither still operates. However, the post office still functions.

You can wander about on the beach, visit the churchyard with the local seamen's memorial or walk through the old, narrow streets. Otherwise, relax on the grassy hillside above the harbour's northern precipice and enjoy the view of Kalsoy.

Also, notice the geological oddity along the shore where the horizontal strata of the waterfront is broken by an intrusion of basalt 'posts' lying stacked on their sides. They've resisted erosion better than the surrounding materials and form a natural staircase from the sea up to the grassy bluffs.

Slættaratindur

Gjógv is a good base for climbing Slættaratindur or Gráfelli. From the road, which reaches an altitude of about 400m at the pass between Eiði and Funningur, the climb up 882m Slættaratindur isn't too difficult and the view is wonderful. One route ascends the southern flank of the mountain to the east ridge, where it turns west for the summit. Definitely try for a nice day, since finding the way can be difficult in heavy cloud cover (which becomes fog at this altitude). Be especially wary of the *hamar*, or horizontal bands of cliff.

The mountain immediately north of Slættaratindur is 857m Gráfelli, another dramatic peak which may be climbed up its south-east pointing ridge.

Ambadalur

Another great day walk from Gjógv is over the pass immediately west of town and down into Ambadalur on the other side. From there you'll see the pinnacle Búgvin. At 188m, it's the highest sea stack in the Faroes.

Organised Tours

On Saturday at 10 am, Tora Tourist Traffic runs a seven-hour bus tour to Eiði, Gjógv, Funningur and Oyndarfjørður for Dkr365 per person, including lunch in Gjógv.

Places to Stay & Eat

The *Gjáargarður Youth Hostel* (☎ 23175; fax 23505) is a pleasant grass-roofed building with balconies on all four floors, originally intended to resemble a traditional Faroese farmhouse (it wound up looking like a Swiss chalet). The top floor is arranged like an old Faroese roykstova.

Family rooms with six beds and a kitchen, bath and toilet are available for Dkr500 per night. Single/double private rooms are Dkr300/400. Dorm beds cost Dkr80/100 for youth-hostel members/non-members. It's wise to book in advance, as the hostel is often used by school trips and other groups. As a result, the management sometimes goes a bit over the top with rules and regulations. Camping is permitted in the hostel grounds for Dkr50 per person in a tent or caravan.

Meals and supplies are available at the hostel but, since the closure of the village stores, prices have climbed beyond reasonable limits, so it's wise to take groceries from elsewhere. Cooking facilities are available but they're short on equipment, so you may want to supply your own cooking implements as well.

Alternatively, there's a *holiday house* in the village which accommodates eight people for Dkr600 per night. Contact Nordica for bookings.

Getting There & Away

To reach Gjógv from Tórshavn (two hours; Dkr50), first take bus No 400 to Oyrarbakki. From there, connect with bus No 205 which runs twice on weekdays and once on Saturday. Note that there is no bus to or from Gjógv on Sunday.

FUNNINGUR

Funningur provides the best view of the rugged, serrated ridges and cliffs of Kalsoy Island across the strait Djúpini and the road leading down into the village makes a serpentine descent of 300m in only three km – with magnificent views all the way. In the backdrop rises Slættaratindur, the Faroes' highest point.

In the *Færinga Saga*, Funningur is described as the place where the first Viking settler, Grímur Kamban, built his house in 825 AD. The village church has a traditional turf roof, and the current building was consecrated in 1847. The old wooden figure of Christ inside is battered and showing some age, but it's quite beautiful.

With some struggle, the surrounding mountains are climbable. There's also a fairly hazardous hike across to the west coast, which takes off from the village, heads south along the coastline, then climbs above the road and wanders inland and over the pass Kvígandalsskarð before descending quickly to Svínáir on the shore of Sundini. It's less than 10 km and could be negotiated in a full day, but two days would be more pleasant.

Getting There & Away

From Monday to Saturday, bus No 205 runs between Oyrarbakki and Gjógv, stopping in both Funningsfjørður and Funningur (1¾ hours; Dkr50). Once or twice a day, it makes a side trip out to Elduvík en route.

ELDUVÍK

Elduvík, another village at the end of a road, has a lovely setting, surrounded by green fields and peaks. It's known for its colourfully painted houses, which are great for photos on a fine day. Elduvík is especially popular with the Faroese who visit on special occasions to eat at the country restaurant Lónin, which serves nice but expensive fare.

Hiking

A good hike from Elduvík is across the low pass to Oyndarfjørður (however, for a short section, the path has disappeared). Another option is to take the six-km mountain route to Funningsfjørður. Make your way up the Stór river valley behind the town and over the moors to the pass from where it's a quick, steep descent through layers of cliffs to Funningsfjørður. A third option is to ascend the north-east ridge of 721m Hægstafjall, but it will require a bit of climbing and scrambling. The summit affords spectacular views across to Kalsoy island.

Places to Stay & Eat

The guesthouse and hostel, *Lónin í Elduvík* (☎ 44944), has a double room for Dkr350 and dormitory accommodation for Dkr125. The attached restaurant serves snacks and traditional Faroese fare all day. In the summer, it's open daily from 10 am to 10 pm.

There are also two *holiday homes* in the village which can accommodate eight or nine people for around Dkr750 per night each. Contact Nordica for bookings.

Getting There & Away

To reach Elduvík (1¼ hours; Dkr50) from Tórshavn, take bus No 200 to Oyrarbakki, then connect with bus No 205 which runs twice on weekdays, once on Saturday. Note that the only southbound bus which stops in Elduvík calls at 1.40 pm (weekdays only). Heading toward Gjógv, they stop at 8.05 am (Saturday only), 8.25 am and 2.50 pm.

OYNDARFJØRÐUR

Oyndarfjørður is prime walking country and, because of its pleasant hostel, many people on the two-day Smyril Line stopover rush straight up here from the ferry dock in Tórshavn. Although the village itself lacks the charm of Gjógv or Elduvík, its hostel is more casual and sees fewer groups than the one at Gjógv, making it generally more pleasant for adult travellers.

The appealing little church in Oyndarfjørður, with a shabby turf roof and an unkempt churchyard, seems not to have seen much attention since it was built in 1838.

However, the real 'attraction' in this tiny village is the mildly entertaining Rinkusteinar or 'rocking stone'. On the shoreline below the entrance to the village is an immense underwater boulder (about eight by six by three metres) that moves back and forth with the wave action. A small stone attached to a rope, which is in turn attached to the boulder, bobs up and down as the big rock rocks. How this bizarre phenomenon was ever discovered is a complete mystery.

Hiking

The most popular day hike from Oyndarfjørður is up the track to the north-west, past the great swampy cirque of Vatnsdalur, through the low pass between the 500m peaks of Limstúgva and Tindur, and down along the coastline to the village of Elduvík on Funningsfjørður. From there, you can

return to Oyndarfjørður by bus (with great difficulty) or walk back the way you came.

Another super walk is up the winding road past the Hellur intersection to the highest hairpin bend, then diagonally up the slopes to the boggy pass between Hellur and Fuglafjørður. If you scramble up to the ridge east of the pass, you'll have a fine view across to the finger-like north-eastern islands. From the pass, you can continue down to the village of Fuglafjørður and work out the rather involved bus schedule back to Oyndarfjørður (it's 33 km by bus with a change at Skálabotnur). It's easier to just return the way you came.

Places to Stay & Eat

The *Fjalsgarður Youth Hostel* (☎ 44522; fax 44570), on a rise at the far end of the village, has private single/double rooms for Dkr200/300 and two six-bed apartments for Dkr360 per day. Dormitory accommodation costs Dkr90. To visit during the ferry stopover en route to Iceland, it's wise to book in advance. Camping on the hostel grounds, including use of their facilities, costs Dkr50 per person.

Breakfast or lunch is available at the hostel for Dkr35 to Dkr45 and dinner for Dkr50 to Dkr100, but they must be ordered in advance – on the previous day, if possible. Alternatively, you can use the kitchen facilities and rustle up your own grub.

Nordica can also arrange *holiday homes*, which accommodate five or six people for Dkr480 per night each.

You can buy basic groceries at the village *shop* or *kiosk*, but the range is limited so it's probably better to bring your own supplies.

Getting There & Away

Bus No 400 between Tórshavn and Skálabotnur connects with bus No 481 to/from Oyndarfjørður (25 minutes; Dkr20). The latter runs four times on weekdays and twice on weekends. The entire trip from Tórshavn takes 1½ hours and costs Dkr50.

SKÁLAFJØRÐUR

Skálafjørður is the name given to both the long, sheltered fjord enclosed by the south-

THE FAROE ISLANDS

ernmost peninsulas of Eysturoy, and also to the village at its head. Because Skálafjørður is the Faroes' best harbour, in the mid 1800s Governor Carl Emil Dahlerup worked towards shifting the commercial and political centre of the country from Tórshavn to Toftir or Strendur – a good idea which never actually took hold.

During the German occupation of Denmark in WWII, Skálafjørður served as a British naval base. Today, it's one of the most populated – and least interesting – areas of the country. The western shore villages of Strendur, Við Sjógv, Innan Glyvur and Skáli; and on the eastern shore, Nes, Toftir, Saltnes, Runavík, Saltangar , Glyvrar, Lambareiði, Søldarfjørður, Skipanes and Gøtueiði, are combining into an increasingly congested conurbation – a sort of Faroese megalopolis.

Glyvrar

If you're passing through Glyvrar, don't miss glancing at the church, originally built in 1927. It was once just an average-looking building, but to accommodate rapid population growth in the Skálafjørður area, it had to be expanded in 1981. The result is bizarre.

It's also worth looking at the folk museum Bygdasavnið Forni, which is furnished as a 19th-century Faroese home. In the summer, it's open Monday, Wednesday and Sunday from 4 to 7 pm and admission costs Dkr30 per person.

Høganes

A group of musicians and other interested people got together and formed the group Tónasjón, which is a contraction of the Faroese words for 'Music and Drama'. The idea was to create an environment where esoteric (or spontaneous) music and drama could be staged and appreciated. Somehow, they came up with the sloop Høganes, which is moored at the quay in Runavík. If you're interested in attending a performance (or performing yourself), contact the group at ☎ 47744.

Toftir Windmill

The huge modern windmill on the hilltop above Toftir is a feasibility study regarding electricity production.

Toftavatn

A pleasant half-hour walk leads from Runavík or Toftir up to the mountain lake Toftavatn, where fishing is possible. To walk all the way around the lake will take over an hour.

Nes

Just a hop south of Toftir is the tiny community of Nes, which has an interesting old-style church with a slate roof and natural wood inside. If you walk further south along the coast, you'll have a view across to Tórshavn five km away.

Strendur

Just up from the old ferry terminal in Strendur is the wool-spinning factory, Snældan, which also has an outlet for reasonably priced woollen goods. It's housed in a concrete building with a corrugated aluminium roof.

Special Events

The annual local festival, Skálafjarðarstevna, takes place in Runavík sometime around mid-June. Expect the athletic contests and chain-dance-till-you-drop sort of entertainment that always accompanies Faroese festivals.

Places to Stay & Eat

See Tora Tourist Traffic about B&B accommodation in Toftir, which costs Dkr280/430 for single/double rooms with shared facilities. There's a cafeteria and grill-bar on Toftir quay, open daily from 5 pm (7 pm at weekends) to midnight.

In Runavík there's Runavíkar Sjómansheim (☎ 47420; fax 48830), which charges Dkr265/370 for single/double rooms with shared facilities (including breakfast). With private bath, they're Dkr365/460. Extra beds cost Dkr130. The attached cafeteria has an à la carte menu but also serves set meals and snacks. A continental breakfast costs Dkr42

THE FAROE ISLANDS

while lunch and dinner are Dkr51 to Dkr85 each.

In the summer, meals are also available from 9 am to 7 pm at the *Ólastova* in Salt-angar. Alternatively, there's the *Statoil* petrol station at the Skálabotnur road junction, which has a cafeteria selling tasty toasties, pastries and coffee. It's open Monday to Saturday from 9 am to 10.30 pm and Sunday from 2 to 11 pm.

Rather out of the way, in Selatrað, is the Scout Centre, *Skótadepilin* (☎ 48950) which offers hostel-style accommodation in a quiet setting. Dormitory beds cost Dkr90 per person while camping costs Dkr40. For bookings, contact the YMCA (☎ 11075; fax 10775) in Tórshavn.

Getting There & Away

Since the ferry stopped running frequently between Tórshavn and Skálafjørður, more buses were laid on and there are now up to eight bus connections daily (1½ hours; Dkr50). To the eastern shore of Skálafjørður, take bus No 400 to Søldarfjørður and change to bus No 440, which continues on to Toftir. For the western shore of Skálafjørður (1¼ hours; Dkr50), take bus No 400 to Skála-botnur, then change to bus No 480, which continues to Strendur. On weekdays, three buses continue from Strendur to Selatrað.

Ferries from Tórshavn to Toftir and Strendur operate three times daily on week-days.

GØTA

Gøta is actually divided into the villages of Norðragøta, Gøtugjógv and Syðrugøta. The area enjoys a wonderfully scenic and dra-matic setting, and on both shores of the broad fjord Gøtuvík the mountains rise steeply from the sea. The northern shore ascends to 625m and the southern, to 516m. It's a nice walk up the chasm Gøtugjógv, behind the village. You can also continue up to the relatively easy 295m summit of Knyklarnir, which affords a great view over the magnif-icent surroundings.

Norðragøta was the home village of Tróndur Gøtuskegg, a hero of the *Færinga Saga*, and part of the tale takes place there.

Tötingavirkið

In Syðrugøta is the spinning and woollens mill Tötingavirkið, where Faroese wool becomes Faroese yarn and pullovers. Visi-tors can have a look around the place, or visit the outlet where wool, yarn and knitwear are sold. There's also a café which is open on weekdays from 9 am to 5 pm and on Saturday from 10 am to 2 pm.

Syðrugøta Ruins

The ruins at Syðrugøta reveal the early Faroese settlement patterns. Five small and simple farmhouses have been excavated, as well as a central churchyard and cemetery. It's expected that a large central landowner's home will be discovered somewhere near the church to complete the *bygd* or settlement. Interestingly, the current parish church, which was rebuilt in 1833, isn't anywhere near this medieval site, but in Norðragøta.

Blásastova

The character-filled old farmhouse called Blásastova, at Norðragøta, serves as a local museum. Visits must be pre-arranged through the tourist office in Tórshavn or with Frants Jacobsen (☎ 41724).

Getting There & Away

Bus No 400 between Tórshavn and Leirvík/Fuglafjørður passes through Gøta six to nine times daily (1¼ hours; Dkr50).

FUGLAFJØRÐUR

With around 1400 inhabitants and a magnif-icent setting, Fuglafjørður ('bird fjord') is the sixth-largest town in the Faroes. It has little interest in its own right, but does boast one of the most active fish-processing centres in the Faroes and the harbour is par-ticularly colourful. It's also worthwhile visiting for the walk over the pass to Oyndarfjørður (see under Oyndarfjørður), or up the steeper route to the 731m peak Bl bjørg. From the top there are good views that encompass most of Eysturoy and several other islands – weather permitting, of course.

Varmakelda
Midway between the town of Fuglafjørður and Leirvík is Varmakelda, the Faroes' only warm spring. Unfortunately, at a chilly 18°C, it's only 'warm' relative to the sub-Arctic seawater a few metres away. It lies near the shore of Fuglafjørður fjord, about 700m north-east of the turnoff for the coastal route (as opposed to the tunnel route) to Leirvík.

Places to Stay & Eat
The *Scout Cottage* (☎ 44860; fax 45180) offers dormitory sleeping-bag accommodation for groups. Group dormitories are also available three km from Fuglafjørður at the *Skótahúsið Kambur* (☎ 44437), in the Kambsdalur sports centre, which also has a cafeteria. For bookings, contact the YMCA in Tórshavn (☎ 11075; fax 10775). Both places charge Dkr80 per person. In the village, there's a licensed restaurant, *Muntra*, and a *grill-bar*.

With Nordica, you can book accommodation in a three-person *apartment* for Dkr373 per night, or in a five to eight-person *house* for Dkr467 or Dkr560 per night.

Getting There & Away
Bus No 400 from Tórshavn terminates in Fuglafjørður (1¾ hours; Dkr50), with six to nine services daily. Bus No 440 goes from Fuglafjørður to Toftir (30 to 50 minutes; Dkr30) four or five times on weekdays.

LEIRVÍK
Leirvík, which lies through the tunnel from Norðragøta, faces the southern ends of the rugged islands of Kalsoy and Borðoy. Most travellers who visit Leirvík are on their way to Klaksvík.

Places to Stay & Eat
The petrol station across the highway from the ferry landing has a basic *snack bar* and coffee shop. In the centre, there's a *supermarket* near the church and a kiosk-cum-youth hangout which serves snacks; it's open until 11 pm nightly (10 pm on Sunday).

Leirvík has six *holiday homes* for three to nine people which can be booked with Nordica. Charges range from Dkr467 to Dkr700 per night. Tora Tourist Traffic books *houses* holding eight people for Dkr660 per night.

Getting There & Away
Bus Between Tórshavn and Leirvík (1½ hours; Dkr50), bus No 400 makes six to nine trips daily. The bus and ferry coordinate quite well, making a convenient connection to Klaksvík, where it's presumed everyone is headed anyway.

Ferry The ferry trip between Leirvík and Klaksvík must be one of the loveliest 30 minute rides on earth. It passes beneath the towering peaks of southern Kalsoy, and between the beautiful headlands of Kunoy and south-western Borðoy, before chugging into Klaksvík's well-sheltered harbour.

The ferry *Dúgvan* makes six to 10 trips daily between Klaksvík and Leirvík, starting at 5.50 am (westbound) and 6.45 am (eastbound). The last crossing of the day is at 8.05 pm (westbound) and 8.45 pm (eastbound). Amazingly, this ferry connects like clockwork with the bus system, which in turn connects Leirvík with Tórshavn and Klaksvík with other parts of the north-eastern islands.

THE FAROE ISLANDS

Outer Islands

Visitors with more time than the two-day ferry stopover affords may want to explore beyond the main islands. The dramatically rugged north-eastern islands are comprised of narrow finger-like ridges protruding above the surface of the water. At their heart is Klaksvík, the Faroes' second-largest town. The Faroes' southernmost island, Suðuroy, enjoys a combination of precipitous cliffs and gentle hills, as well as a tendency towards the finest weather in the country. The smaller islands of Sandoy, Vágar and Nólsoy show what village life is like on the more isolated outer islands.

Mykines, Skúvoy, Hestur, Koltur and Stóra Dímun, all of which are inhabited for at least part of the year, are both isolated and entirely rural. Each has only a handful of people living in a single village or settlement. Lítla Dímun, the smallest of the main islands, is uninhabited and practically inaccessible.

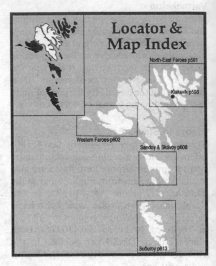

Locator & Map Index

North-East Faroes p591

Klaksvík p593

Western Faroes p602

Sandoy & Skúvoy p608

Suðuroy p613

North-East Faroes

The six islands that comprise the sparsely-settled north-eastern Faroes, Borðoy, Viðoy, Svínoy, Fugloy, Kunoy and Kalsoy, are among the most beautiful in the North Atlantic. Outside of Klaksvík, the lack of harbours and exposure to harsh, cold and windy conditions can make life here difficult.

Level (or relatively level) land is highly valued and, for the most part, the islands' few villages cling to steep hillsides which threaten to heave them into the sea. All the villages are now connected by tunnel or ferry but, instead of encouraging residents to remain in their no longer isolated homes, the new infrastructure has inspired many to use them as escape routes. One-way trips to Tórshavn or Klaksvík are growing more common and some villages like Skálatoftir

and Múli on Borðoy have been abandoned altogether.

BORÐOY
Klaksvík

Klaksvík, on the island of Borðoy, has around 4500 inhabitants. Like most Faroese towns, its economy is based on fishing and fish processing. The harbour itself is interesting – it boasts just about every type of high-tech fishing craft ever conceived.

Klaksvík was given municipality status in 1908, when it had only 700 residents. As fishing replaced farming as the primary economic venture in the islands, Klaksvík, which makes a perfect U-turn around one of the finest natural harbours in the country, grew in both importance and population. During the 1950s, fishing-related industries and supporting businesses were established, including the country's only brewery, Föroya Bjór. Today, 13% of the Faroes' fishing exports comes from Klaksvík.

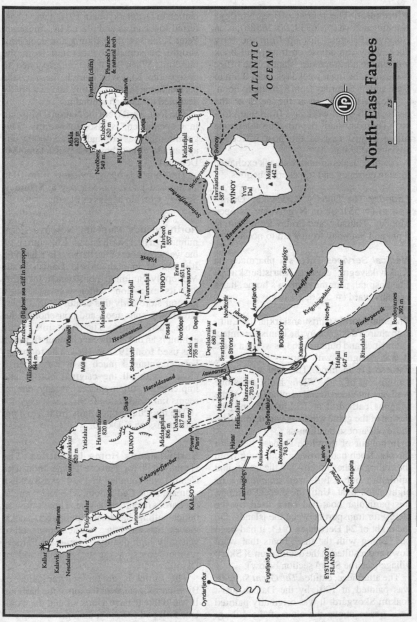

North-East Faroes

Information The tourist office, Norðoya Kunningarstova (☎ 56939; fax 56586), is on Nólsoyar Pálsgøta, just up from the ferry dock. They can advise on travel and book tours in the north-eastern islands. The office is meant to be open weekdays from 8 am to 6 pm and on Saturday from 8.30 am to noon.

The post office is at the head of the harbour. It's open weekdays from 9 am to 4 pm (Thursday until 5 pm). The telephone office is just east of the post office on Biskupsstøðgøta.

All three banks around Klaksvík exchange foreign currency and travellers' cheques.

Laundry The laundry Klaksvíkar Dampvaskarí (☎ 55160), on Nýggivegur, is open Monday, Thursday and Friday from 9 am to 5 pm and Saturday from 9 am to noon.

Medical Services There's a pharmacy on Klaksvíksvegur, close to Christianskirkja. The hospital, near the seamen's home, has a casualty ward (☎ 55463).

Christianskirkja Christianskirkja, the Lutheran church designed by the Danish architect Peter Koch and built in 1963, is worth a visit. It was designed with various elements of Faroese life in mind. The roof gables are reminiscent of early Viking halls, the stone walls are intended to call to mind those of the Magnus cathedral at Kirkjubøur and the design of the gable windows was inspired by those of Faroese boathouses.

In honour of the close Faroese ties with the sea, Koch had a rowing boat hung from the ceiling of the church – not the traditional miniature but a full-sized *áttamanfar* or eight-oared boat. Until the present century, this particular boat had been used by the clergy for transport between the islands. On the night of 24 December 1913, it had been out fishing with the three boats that went down and resulted in the decimation of Skarð village (see the Skarð section below).

The altarpiece, entitled *The Great Supper*, was painted in 1901 by the Danish artist Joakim Skovgård. It was originally painted as a fresco above the altar of the Viborg church in Denmark, but in 1910 it was transferred to a canvas and placed in a museum. Peter Koch saw the painting and decided it should be somehow liberated from the museum. When he was commissioned to design the Klaksvík church, he saw the perfect home for the painting and essentially designed the church around it.

The font, a gift from the National Museum in Copenhagen, is also noteworthy. This granite relic was originally used 4000 years ago as a sacrificial bowl in a pagan temple in Denmark.

The church is open to visitors from 10 to 11 am and 1 to 4 pm Monday to Saturday. Sunday worship begins at 11 am.

North Islands Museum Norðoya Fornminnasavn (the North Islands Museum) is on the western shore of the harbour in Klaksvík. It's housed in both an old Danish Trade Monopoly building, constructed in 1838, and its extension, which was used as a general store early this century. On display are photographs, tools and household relics from earlier days. The most interesting exhibit is an old apothecary (chemist), which was used from 1932 to 1961. The room has been maintained much as it was when it closed, with all the original bottles and implements still in place. At any rate, it seems fairly rustic for 1961.

The museum is open daily from 2 to 4 pm and admission is Dkr20.

North Islands Home Industries The Heimavirkið (or Faroese Home Industries Centre) was founded in 1934 by a Swedish woman, Anie Cederblom, who had come to the Faroes the previous year. There's now an outlet selling handmade pullovers, socks, gloves, hats and other woollen goods, all of generally high quality. A top-class Faroese jumper costs in the neighbourhood of Dkr500.

The outlet is on the seaward side of Biskupsstøðgøta, near the top of the harbour. If you'd like to have a look around the woollens mill and see the spinning, washing and

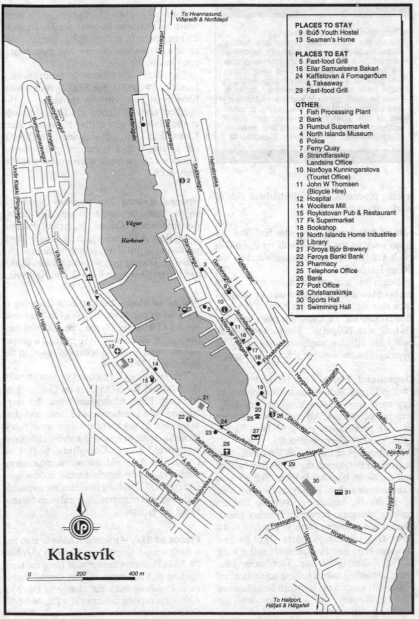

PLACES TO STAY
9 Ibúð Youth Hostel
13 Seamen's Home

PLACES TO EAT
5 Fast-food Grill
16 Eilar Samuelsens Bakari
24 Kaffistovan á Fornagørðum
    & Takeaway
29 Fast-food Grill

OTHER
1 Fish Processing Plant
2 Bank
3 Rumbul Supermarket
4 North Islands Museum
6 Police
7 Ferry Quay
8 Strandfaraskip
    Landsins Office
10 Norðoya Kunningarstova
    (Tourist Office)
11 John W Thomsen
    (Bicycle Hire)
12 Hospital
14 Woollens Mill
15 Roykstovan Pub & Restaurant
17 Fk Supermarket
18 Bookshop
19 North Islands Home Industries
20 Library
21 Føroya Bjór Brewery
22 Føroya Banki Bank
23 Pharmacy
25 Telephone Office
26 Bank
27 Post Office
28 Christianskirkja
30 Sports Hall
31 Swimming Hall

Klaksvík

0   200   400 m

THE FAROE ISLANDS

Climate-Controlled Klaksvík

During the boom days of the late 1980s, Klaksvík was planning to construct an architectural oddity, a kind of see-through shelter over the harbour that would connect both shores and provide a sort of greenhouse effect (it might have improved the weather, as well). Plans had been drawn up and financial backing was being sought when the bottom dropped out of the already over-extended credit economy – and that was the last anyone heard of environmental engineering in Klaksvík. ■

---

dyeing processes, it's on the harbour side of Klaksvíksvegur.

Háfjall & Hálgafell A popular half-day trip from town is the steep climb up the 647m peak Háfjall ('high mountain') and/or the 503m Hálgafell.

Begin by walking from the end of the harbour towards the heliport on Uppsalagøta then turn right towards the base of the pass Brúnaskarð and walk up to the point between Háfjall and Hálgafell. Then choose your peak; the difficult horizontal cliffs may be bypassed on the western side of the ridge.

Organised Tours The tourist office (☎ 56939; fax 56586) can book a variety of day tours from Klaksvík, which run daily, weather permitting. All require a minimum of four participants and cost Dkr150 per adult, unless otherwise stated.

The three-hour bus tour to Viðareiði stops at Árnafjørður, Depil, the Kósin fish factory and the North Islands Museum. There's also a three-hour tour to Kunoy and a town tour of Klaksvík, including visits to the art gallery, museum, brewery (Tuesday only), church and woollens factory. The five to 12 hour trip to Kalsoy costs Dkr120 and includes ferry and bus transport and a walk to the Kallur lighthouse. Three-hour boat tours, including use of fishing equipment en route, sail around the northern headlands of Kunoy, Borðoy and Viðoy to view the Enniberg cliff from below.

Four-hour scuba diving trips, with dives down to 30m, can be arranged for Dkr300/ 150 per person, including equipment, with groups of two/four people. The minimum is one person, the maximum 10.

The ferry company, Strandfaraskip Landsins (☎ 56006; fax 57275), runs a four-hour boat tour on the *Barsskor* to the northern ends of Kunoy and Kalsoy to look at the Kalsvík bird cliffs. It departs from Klaksvík at 1 pm on Friday and costs Dkr100 per person, with a minimum of 10 people. Bookings can be made at their office near the ferry dock.

Special Events The two-day Norðoyastevna festivities are held annually during the first week of June. In typical Faroese style, they're characterised by rowing competitions, sports matches, dancing and feasting. During that weekend, extra ferries are rostered between Leirvík and Klaksvík.

Places to Stay – bottom end Camping is allowed by the swimming pool in Klaksvík, but it's a bit public. By the time you read this, the tourist office may have opened a proper campground on the outskirts of town, in the direction of Norðoyri.

The very nice (if a bit quirky) youth hostel, *Ibúð* (☎ and fax 57555), is on Garðavegur. It's only three blocks up from the ferry landing by a combination of lanes and passages, but to get there the first time you'll probably have to follow the more circuitous signposted route. Dormitory beds cost Dkr80/100 for youth hostel members/non-members, while single/double rooms cost Dkr195/300. Cooking facilities are available and, with advance notice, meals can be provided for groups.

Places to Stay – middle Klaksvík also has a large and imposing *Seamen's Home* (☎ 55333), across the harbour from the ferry landing at Víkavegur 39. For single/double rooms without bath the charge is Dkr270/ 420; with private facilities it's Dkr460/640. Cafeteria meals are available and, even if you're staying elsewhere, this is a good option for meals in Klaksvík.

There's a *B&B* with single/double rooms for Dkr280/430 and an *apartment* accommodating eight people costing Dkr520 per night. For bookings, contact Tora Tourist Traffic in Tórshavn.

Places to Eat *Kaffistovan á Fornagørðum* is popular with local youths and it's open daily from 9 am (3 pm on Sunday) to midnight. It serves lunch specials as well as fish, chicken, chips and such fast fare all day. There's also a takeaway next door with fish and chips for Dkr35. There's a small *grill-bar* on Gerðagøta and another more popular one near the museum.

The *Seamen's Home cafeteria* has a buffet breakfast for Dkr55, while two-course lunches and dinners with vast portions cost Dkr80 and Dkr70 respectively. Nearby, on Klaksvíksvegur, there's an easily recognised restaurant and bar called the *Roykstovan*; there's a painted Faroese scene on the gable-end. Fast food is available at the bar, but full meals are only available to groups who order in advance.

You'll find excellent gooey concoctions at *Eilar Samuelsens Bakari* on the eastern side of the harbour. The two main supermarkets, *Fk* and *Rumbul*, are on the same road. There's also a state liquor store at Bøgøta 38.

Entertainment If you think the action is thin in Tórshavn, you haven't seen Klaksvík, where there's not even a cinema and the theatre is locked up tight and gathering dust most of the time. However, things are changing and the *Roykstovan* now boasts a smoky bar serving real draught beer. Other nightlife is aimed at younger clientele; there's a weekend disco in the sports hall for those aged 15 to 20.

However, as well as the sports hall, there's also Svimjið, the swimming hall, both at the head of the harbour. Svimjið has a pool, sauna, swim jets and showers. Admission costs Dkr15.

When at least 15 people are interested, some locals get together and run a traditional

Faroese evening on Tuesday from 7.30 pm. Crafts are displayed and entertainment includes chain dancing. The Dkr175 price includes food. Make reservations where you're staying or with the tourist office.

Getting There & Away On weekdays, bus No 500 makes seven daily runs to and from Viðareiði on Viðoy Island (45 minutes; Dkr30), stopping at Norðdepil and Hvannasund (20 minutes; Dkr20) en route. There are three runs on Saturday and two on Sunday. To Haraldssund (15 minutes; Dkr10) and Kunoy (30 minutes; Dkr20) on Kunoy Island, bus No 504 runs four times daily and twice on Saturday. Wait for buses at the bus shelter adjacent to the ferry quay.

The car-ferry *Dúgvan* makes six to 10 trips daily between Klaksvík and Leirvík (on Eysturoy island). The first crossings depart at 5.50 am (westbound) and 6.45 am (eastbound). The final trips of the day depart at 8.05 pm (westbound) and 8.45 pm (eastbound).

To reach Kalsoy Island, take the passenger ferry *Barsskor*, which runs two or three times daily to Syðradalur and Húsar. From Húsar, bus No 506 offers connections north to Mikladalur and Trøllanes (one hour from Klaksvík; Dkr50). Upon arriving in Húsar, the ferry turns around and returns to Klaksvík.

Getting Around For taxi service, ring HA Johannesen (☎ 55225), Bil (☎ 55555) or Ásmundur Poulsen (☎ 56222).

Bicycles may be rented from John W Thomsen (☎ 55858), on Nólsoyar Pálsgøta, for Dkr50 per day.

Around Borðoy

Outside of Klaksvík, the island of Borðoy has all the standard stunning scenery associated with the north-eastern islands: steep cliffs, sharp ridges and a couple of diminutive villages clinging to the steep hills above the shores.

Árnafjørður Árnafjørður ('eagle fjord') is

THE FAROE ISLANDS

the village between the two Borðoy tunnels. Despite the fish farm, it's a scenic and secluded little place but, between the time your bus emerges from one tunnel and delves into the next, you won't catch much more than a fleeting glimpse of it. During WWII a sea-mine washed ashore here and blew up several houses.

Norðdepil This tiny settlement at the western end of the Borðoy-Viðoy causeway dates back to 1866. For many years it was known to travellers as the site of the quirky and colourful Hotel Bella (you can't miss it – the buildings are painted a shade of yellow not found in nature) and its wonderful restaurant. In 1990, however, the owner closed it and left for Denmark.

Fossá The abandoned village of Fossá, north of Norðdepil, was bought in 1969 by the museum society of Klaksvík, with the intention of transforming it into a typical medieval Faroese village. More than 25 years later, however, nothing has been forthcoming. The place is now used as a campground for scouts and school groups.

Múli Múli, occupying the bluffs near the northern tip of Borðoy, lies at the end of an unsurfaced road from Norðdepil. It's one of the most remote spots in the country and is subject to the fierce winds that howl through the *eiði* of Viðoy. Until the road was completed in 1989, residents had to rely on helicopter connections and the small ferry service across the sound to Leiti on Viðoy.

A few years ago, Múli liked to claim that it had 154 all-year-round inhabitants, 150 of whom were sheep. Sadly, only the sheep remain, as the last people left in 1994, although a few houses are occupied during summer holidays. Múli lies only seven km from Norðdepil, so it would be an easy day walk out and back.

KALSOY

Kalsoy has the most enigmatically rugged form of any of the Faroe Islands. The western coast consists only of steep cliffs, while on the eastern slopes there are four tiny settlements – Syðradalur, Húsar, Mikladalur and Trøllanes, whose combined populations add up to 136. They're connected along a partly unpaved road by four dark tunnels. Thanks to its shape – and because so many holes have been drilled in it – the island is whimsically known as 'the flute'.

Hiking

Ridge-walking on the southern end of Kalsoy isn't too difficult, but it becomes more daunting as you move north; the easiest route up to the crest is from Húsar, where there's a prominent notch in the island's skyline. It's also possible to climb up the 743m Botnstindur from Syðradalur.

Some visitors simply choose to walk from the ferry landings at Syðradalur or Húsar up to Trøllanes. There are four unlit tunnels along the way, but none of these sees enough traffic to pose problems with noxious gas (you will need a torch). The last tunnel, which is over two km long, seems to be the narrowest and darkest and, since it serves a village with only 20 inhabitants, it's rarely used by vehicles. Walking through it is quite an eerie experience; the cold, damp darkness in the heart of the mountain is really quite extraordinary. The precipitous and dangerous path between Mikladalur and Trøllanes isn't recommended.

A wonderful walk from Trøllanes will take you to the lighthouse at Kallur, on the island's northern tip. Begin by climbing the hill north of the village, then bear north-west across the boggy hillside. After about one km you'll see the lighthouse perched on a hill in the distance. From the lighthouse, you can cross the short isthmus to Kalsoy's northern cape, where there's a good chance of seeing puffins. There's a natural sea-arch underneath this northern tip of the island, and it affords a great view of the cliffs and a sapphire-coloured cove hidden in the rocks below. On a clear day, you can see all the way to the Risin og Kellingin sea stacks at the northern end of Eysturoy.

Places to Stay & Eat

The only accommodation is in Mikladalur where there are two large and comfortable *holiday homes*. They accommodate up to 11 people and cost Dkr600 and Dkr720 per night. Bookings should be made with Nordica in Tórshavn.

The *Kaffistovan* coffee shop in Mikladalur opens whenever there are enough tourists around. A small *shop* in Húsar sells basic provisions.

Getting There & Away

From Klaksvík, the ferry *Barsskor* sails to Syðradalur and Húsar twice daily on Monday, Wednesday, Saturday and Sunday and three times on Tuesday, Thursday and Friday. Upon arriving in Húsar, it returns immediately to Klaksvík. Along the way, the channel is marked by buoys made from five-gallon plastic petrol containers!

The Kalsoy ferries are met by bus No 506, which runs between Húsar and Trøllanes. If you just want a quick visit to the island, the best connections are available on Tuesday and Thursday, when you can sail from Klaksvík at 12.50 pm to catch the 1.20 pm bus to Trøllanes. You can then walk out to the lighthouse and be back in time to catch the 5.15 pm bus back to Húsar and the ferry back to Klaksvík.

From Klaksvík to Trøllanes by boat and bus takes an hour and costs Dkr50.

KUNOY

The cigar-shaped island of Kunoy, with only 36 sq km, has a total of 126 residents in its two villages, Haraldssund and Kunoy. Since the construction of an earth-dam causeway between Strond (Borðoy) and Haraldssund, and a three-km tunnel through the heart of the island, both of Kunoy's once remote villages now enjoy road access from Klaksvík. There's now a café in Kunoy.

Skarð

This remote field on north-eastern Kunoy was once a village. It was abandoned in 1913 after seven men, the entire male population of the village (save for one man of 70 and a boy of 14) perished in a Christmas Eve fishing accident. The women couldn't make a go of it alone and everyone decided to move down to Haraldssund.

Although nothing of interest remains at Skarð, it's a nice seven km walk out from Haraldssund. Allow four hours for the return trip, and an additional three hours if you're walking all the way from Klaksvík.

Ridge Walk

The ridge walk along Kunoy's spine is difficult in places, but can be negotiated on foot as far north as the 806m Middagsfjall, where an immense gunsight notch will abruptly halt your progress. To get past it, technical climbing expertise would be required.

Probably the best access to the ridge is up the Glyvursá stream, from Haraldssund to the 703m peak above Kunoyarnes, but it's extremely steep. From there, follow the ridge northwards for over six km to Middagsfjall and the notch. The most difficult and dangerous part is the descent from the ridge to the shore. The least precipitous routes are back the way you came or down Myllá to the village of Kunoy.

This is quite a long hike over difficult terrain, so either allow a long day or camp somewhere on the way. Weather is an important consideration because the ridge is completely exposed and there's no shelter if it gets unpleasant.

Getting There & Away

Bus No 504 runs between Klaksvík, Haraldssund (15 minutes; Dkr10) and Kunoy (30 minutes; Dkr20) four times daily on weekdays and twice on Saturday. Alternatively, Haraldssund is a walkable seven km from Klaksvík.

VIÐOY

Viðoy ('wood island'), shaped like a smoker's pipe (or an upright vacuum cleaner, depending on the state of your imagination), is the northernmost of the Faroe Islands. Although it has never supported a single tree, lots of driftwood floats in from Siberia and North America, hence the name. Although it's accessible by bus from Klaksvík, Viðoy seems a world apart.

Viðoy is separated from northern Borðoy by the Hvannasund sound, which is constricted at Norðdepil-Hvannasund. It once experienced tidal bores of over half a metre, but the causeway at the narrowest point has put a stop to that. The same thing still happens to a lesser extent in Svínoyarfjørður, south of Viðoy, and boating through the pools and eddies can be tricky.

Hvannasund

The only reason to visit Hvannasund would be to catch the ferry *Másin* ('gull') to the islands of Svínoy and Fugloy. Beyond the previously mentioned tidal quirks, this is normally a rough ride. If you stay below, you're more likely to get sick, but if you stay out in the fresh air on deck, you'll have to hang on tightly to avoid being catapulted into the sea!

In theory, the ferry calls in at either or both sides of the Svínoy eiði, as well as at Hattarvík and Kirkja on Fugloy. In practice, this is rarely possible. Neither island has a harbour and landing entails pulling alongside the concrete wharfs, loading and unloading passengers and freight, while avoiding being smashed to bits or washed away by the surf.

If the situation appears hazardous, the ferry won't dock. The obvious corollary is that, once there, visitors may not be able to leave as quickly as they'd planned. If you go, be prepared for this eventuality or bring enough money for the helicopter flight back (see Getting There & Away under Svínoy).

Viðareiði

The Faroes' northernmost village, Viðareiði, lies in a low and windy pass between the Enniberg headland and the main body of Viðoy. Looking west from the village, there's a spectacular view to the northern precipices of Borðoy, Kunoy and Kalsoy.

The church in Viðareiði is noteworthy for its silver altar, which was presented to the village by the British government in thanks for assistance given to the crew of the British brigantine *Marwood*, which foundered there in 1847. Note also the silver crucifix donated by the Hamburg monopoly merchant Thomas Köppen in 1551. You may have to hunt up someone to let you in for a look – try at the hotel. The rectory is reputedly haunted.

Hiking

Enniberg Although many tourist brochures claim that the 750m high Enniberg is the highest sea cliff in the world, I suspect it is, more accurately, the highest in Europe (even the 820m Kunoyarnakkar on neighbouring Kunoy is higher, but it's not considered a sheer cliff.) That doesn't mean you won't be overwhelmed by Enniberg. From below it looms formidably, but from the top it defies description; it will be one of the most memorable sights you'll ever see.

To get there, take the road leading northwest from Viðareiði and when it ends, head directly up the southern ridge following a prominent trail of cairns. The route is steep and loose and requires some scrambling. Once on the 844m summit of Villingadalsfjall, continue westwards down an easy ridge until it swings to the north. On this northern spur, there's a notch which you can descend into from the left-hand (western) side of the ridge. Keep going to what appears to be the end of the world at Enniberg. Return the same way you came.

If you stop to appreciate all the incredible views along the way, you'll need six or seven hours for the walk. Otherwise, it can be managed in five. Try to avoid this walk in poor weather; not only would the spectacular views be irrelevant, poor visibility and exposed conditions would make for difficult navigation and potentially hazardous hiking.

See also Organised Tours later in this section.

Dalar From Vidareiði, a driveable track leads three km down the exposed eastern coastline to Dalar, where there are some fish farms. They are fed by the stream Dalá, which tumbles down from a high cirque. It makes a nice short walk from Viðareiði.

Ridge Walk Another trip from Viðareiði begins with a climb up the ridge south of the village to the summit of 751m Malinsfjall. From there, continue south along the obvious ridge for a further six km until you're level with Hvannasund. Then there's a steep and difficult descent to the village. If this sounds daunting, you can make the trip in the opposite direction, although the Malinsfjall descent is not to be taken lightly either due to the horizontal cliff-bands. Some worthwhile side trips along this route are up 687m Mýrnafjall and 651m Enni, above Hvannasund. This trip can be done in a full day (it would be better appreciated in two), but watch the weather because the ridge is quite exposed.

Organised Tours

On Tuesday at 7.30 am, Tora Tourist Traffic operates a 9½ hour tour from Tórshavn to Viðareiði and Klaksvík. The tour costs Dkr510 per person, including transport, guide and lunch at the Hotel Norð.

If you have at least four people, Norðoya Kunningarstova (☎ 56939; fax 56586) in Klaksvík can arrange walking tours to Enniberg, with a guide. The trip costs Dkr150 per person, including a packed lunch.

Places to Stay & Eat

The *Hotel Norð* (☎ 51244; fax 51245) in Viðareiði is an ideal remote retreat, especially if you want to hike through the spectacular surroundings and return to a hot shower and restaurant meal afterwards. A single/double room costs Dkr390/485 with private bath, including a continental breakfast. À la carte lunches and dinners cost between Dkr130 and Dkr150 each. The hotel has a bar serving beer and wine.

The hotel is open from 1 June to 1 October, and other times on request. For accommodation or meals, be sure to book in advance. Otherwise, you're liable to find the place deserted.

Tora Tourist Traffic can arrange stays in a nine-bed *holiday house* in Viðareiði for Dkr660 per night.

Basic foods are available at the small *supermarket* near Hotel Norð.

Getting There & Away

Bus From the causeway at Hvannasund an eight-km one-lane road hugs the western coastline to Viðareiði. On weekdays, bus No 500 makes seven daily runs between Klaksvík and Viðareiði (45 minutes; Dkr30), stopping in Norðdepil and Hvannasund (20 minutes; Dkr20) en route. On Saturday there are three runs, on Sunday there are two.

Ferry From Monday to Saturday, the ferry leaves Hvannasund at 9.10 am and calls in at Svínoy, Fugloy and Svínoy again before returning to Hvannasund in the afternoon. On Sunday at 1.30 and 4.30 pm (26 May to 18 August), there are return trips to Fugloy and Svínoy. On Monday at 2.50 pm (3 June to 26 August only), and Friday at 6 pm, there's an additional sailing to both islands.

There is no real arrival timetable for these boats, as their movements are dependent upon the direction of the wind and waves, which stops are possible, and which way the boat travels around Svínoy.

SVÍNOY

Svínoy could well be the least visited of the easily accessible islands. Wherever it's described, it's always referred to as relatively flat (when you see this island, 'flat' is certainly not the first word that springs to mind!) and uninteresting. If you're the sort who appreciates places that the tourism industry pans as flat and uninteresting, here's your opportunity. Personally, I think they just want to put visitors off and keep it for themselves!

With the exception of a couple of broad valleys and the eiði, which divides the island into two unequal parts, Svínoy's coastline is surrounded by cliffs which reach a height of 587m at Havnartindur on the west coast. On the northern peninsula, which resembles a profile of Opus the Penguin, is one of the Faroes' sheerest precipices, Eysturhøvdi. The best view of this is from the ferry to or from Fugloy.

THE FAROE ISLANDS

Hiking

From Svínoy village, where all of the island's 64 residents live, there are several good walking routes. One is up the 461m peak Keldufjall, above the cliffs on the north-western coast, which provides a fine view of Fugloy and of Viðoy's entire remote eastern coast.

Another walk will take you to the end of the jeep track and east up the slope to the 345m high Eysturhøvdi (the tip of the penguin's beak). You can walk up one of these routes and down the other in a single day.

The third option is to walk south from Svínoy village up the valley of the Stórá, and from its headwaters across the moors and down the steep valley Yvir í Dal to the shore. At this stage, the only realistic route back to the village is the way you came.

Lastly, from the western end of the eiði you can walk up the track going off to the south until it peters out on the cliffs. Again, the easiest return route is the way you came.

Places to Stay & Eat

Svínoy now has a hostel, *Vallaraheimið Svínoy* (☎ 51105), which is open from 25 June to 15 August and costs Dkr100/150 for HI members/non-members. Cooking facilities are available. Alternatively, you can arrange a *holiday home* for up to six people for Dkr600 per night; book through Nordica. You can buy supplies at the small village *shop*, which is usually open when the ferry arrives.

Getting There & Away

Air On Wednesday morning, Friday afternoon and Sunday afternoon, the helicopter *Snípan* flies from Klaksvík to Svínoy, then continues to both Kirkja and Hattarvík on Fugloy before returning to Klaksvík. The fare between Klaksvík and either Svínoy or Fugloy is Dkr110.

Ferry The ferry between Hvannasund and Svínoy only stops at Svínoy if weather and surf conditions permit. Stops may be made at either or both ends of the eiði. If you're

waiting to be collected here, you might have to run the 1½ km over the eiði to catch the boat wherever it docks.

For information about the ferry to/from Svínoy, see the Hvannasund and Getting There & Away entries in the Viðoy section.

FUGLOY

Fugloy ('bird island') has some breathtaking nest-covered cliffs, complete with residents – and the island itself is shaped like a small, fat bird.

Hiking

If you don't dawdle, you can explore most of Fugloy in a day trip from Hvannasund. This includes walks up to the 448m cliffs at Eystfelli (which forms the bird's head), the 620m cliffs at Klubbin (the bird's tail) and both of the island's villages, Hattarvík and Kirkja (the bird's neck and feet, respectively).

Since one never really knows at which village the boat will land, there's no recommended itinerary. Just try not to miss either of the cliffs, because they're both spectacular and the wild vistas across all the other northern islands are equally outstanding.

The Klubbin cliffs descend from a plateau-like ridge, which is high enough to be covered with tundra tussocks and boreal vegetation rather than grass. Across the island at Eystfelli, a broad natural amphitheatre seems to sweep upward towards oblivion before cresting and wholeheartedly dropping into it. Near the lighthouse there's a natural stone arch in the rock and, not far away, the profile of an ancient Egyptian head (it's only logical that one should find a Pharaoh somewhere in the Faroes, and it seems he's turned up on Fugloy).

Places to Stay & Eat

There's really no formal accommodation on Fugloy, but, in a pinch, you can camp near Kirkja, with permission. If you'd rather have a roof over your head, there are two *holiday houses* in Kirkja. Each accommodates six to nine people and costs Dkr520 per night.

Book through Tora Tourist Traffic in Tórshavn.

For self-catering, Kirkja has a tiny *general store* which opens for a while on weekday and Saturday mornings and from 4 to 5 pm on weekday afternoons.

Getting There & Away

For information on the ferry to/from Fugloy, see under Hvannasund or Getting There & Away under Viðoy. For details on helicopter transport, see Getting There & Away under Svínoy.

Western Faroes

West of Streymoy is the island of Vágar, which is shaped like some nondescript carnivore threatening to eat a smaller island, Mykines. The two islands lie in the path of most weather systems sweeping in from the south-west and have a reputation for disagreeable weather.

It's unfortunate that inclement Vágar is the only island with enough level land for the international airport, which traverses a windswept valley between Miðvágur and Sørvágur. Naturally, international flight schedules frequently fall victim to good old Faroese kanska!

Kanska also determines access to Mykines. Since the strait between Vágar and Mykines isn't well protected, the wrath of the wind and sea can cut the smaller island off for days. So great is Mykines' appeal, however, that many visitors risk being marooned for a while rather than miss it.

VÁGAR

Apart from the airport and the Mykines ferry, Vágar's main attractions for visitors are its lakes, its precipitous western and southern coasts, and its mountain country. The island is quite hilly and crisscrossed by walking routes that will take you up and down valleys, past lakes, and to steep cliffs that plunge hundreds of metres to the sea.

If you'd like to spend time wandering away from civilisation and aren't overly-concerned with weather, Vágar is the best place to do it. Thanks to the airport, bus connections are good. However, the entire northern half of the island is wild, roadless country. There were once two villages, Víkar and Slættanes, on the northern coast, but both have been abandoned. The latter is now used as a holiday retreat.

Vágar is also known for some of the largest and bloodiest *grindadráps* in the Faroes. The village of Miðvágur seems especially adept at ambushing the pilot whales that migrate past the southern coast of the island.

Information

The Kunningardiskurin tourist office on Vágar is at the airport (☎ 33200; fax 33100). It's open daily from 9 am to 5 pm.

The Føroya Banki at the airport opens for arriving and departing international flights.

Sandavágur

The most prominent building in Sandavágur is the church, which was built in 1917. Inside, there's an interesting 13th-century runic stone, which was found soon after the church was consecrated. An inscription dedicated the church to the town's Norwegian founder, Torkil Onundarson.

Just south-east of Sandavágur is the prominent rock pinnacle Trøllkonufingur ('troll woman's finger'), also known as Kongsspiret ('king's spire') in honour of the 1844 visit of Crown Prince Fredrik of Denmark. To catch a glimpse of it, follow the highest road in the village two km to its end, around the eastern headland. A further 10 minute walk will take you to a better view of Trøllkonufingur as well as some high cliffs and the southern islands.

Miðvágur

Miðvágur, the grindadráp capital of the Faroes, was also the site of the first kindling of Faroese as a written language. During the 1770s, Jens Christian Svabo, who was born in Miðvágur in 1746, prepared a Faroese-Latin-Danish dictionary, basing his phonetic

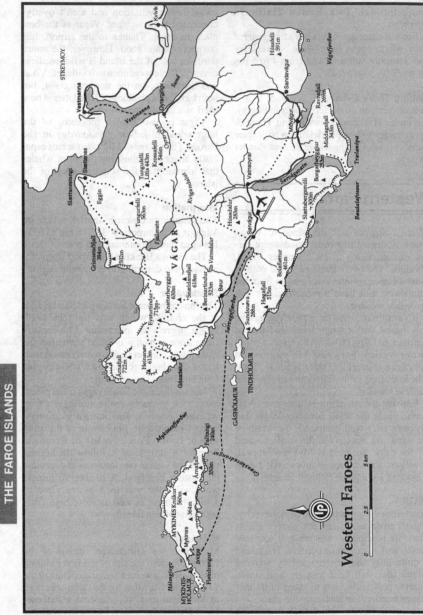

Western Faroes

spellings on the Vágar dialect of Faroese. Although his orthography was subsequently replaced by Hammershaimb's, which was based on Old Norse and is still in use, Svabo's dictionary remained in print until 1966.

Kálvalíð Kálvalíð, the medieval farmhouse and folk museum on the hillside above Miðvágur, once served as a home for widows of the local clergy. This turf-roofed building of stone and wood houses old farming and household implements used during earlier times and provides insight into medieval Faroese life. Here lived the heroine in the novel *Barbara*, which was written by the Faroese author Jørgen-Frantz Jacobsen and is available in translation. The story is based on the Faroese myth of Beinta, a twice-widowed clergyman's wife, who could neither resign nor reconcile herself to the sullen life she was expected to lead. In the future, another building owned by Vága Dansifelag – the childhood home of local poet Mikkjal á Ryggi – will become a local writers' museum.

To arrange a visit, contact Rigmor Heinesen (☎ 33319), who is available on weekdays from 10 am to 7 pm. Admission is Dkr30.

Fjallavatn
The name of this beautiful and rather haunting body of water in north-west Vágar means 'mountain lake' (such imagination goes into naming Faroese features). It's a pleasant and relatively easy 10 km day walk from the road. There's a route in from Sørvágur and another from Vatnsoyrar, where a small road leads about halfway up to the lake. The lake shore can get boggy so appropriate footwear is recommended.

Sørvágsvatn
The sausage-shaped lake on southern Vágar (its name literally means 'south Vágar lake') is the Faroes' largest inland body of water. During the summer months it's popular for brown trout fishing.

The 146m high promontory Trælanípa,

just east of the narrow strip of land separating the lake from the sea, towers over the outlet for Sørvágsvatn. This was once used for the disposal of slaves (mostly from the British Isles) who were deemed no longer useful around the farms.

The lake is drained by what may be the world's shortest river (about 30m), which plunges into the sea over the substantial waterfall Bøsdalafossur. To get there from the road, walk south along the eastern shore of the lake. It takes about an hour each way to the waterfall. You won't see anything of the falls without climbing out onto the furthest rocks but under no circumstances should this be attempted during high seas when there's a risk from rogue waves.

Sørvágur
The village of Sørvágur, at the head of Sørvágsfjørður, is interesting mainly for its fish farms. The fjord seems to be a prime spot for pisciculture and several circular farms are strung along its length. The local folk museum is open on Sunday from 3 to 4 pm, or by arrangement with Herálvur Jakobsen (☎ 32893). Adult admission costs Dkr20. Otherwise, there's little of interest.

Sørvágur is also the departure point for the Mykines ferry.

Drangarnir & Tindhólmur
Vágar has some of the most dramatic sea-stack formations in the Faroes, including the towering pinnacles of Drangarnir, just off the island's south-western tip. They are best viewed from the Mykines ferry, but the land-bound can see them from Bøur across Sørvágsfjørður. They first come into view about one km west of Sørvágur.

Also worthy of note is the steep and serrated islet of Tindhólmur, and to the west its chunky little sidekick Gáshólmur. Tindhólmur rises almost vertically 262m above the sea and is home to clouds of sea birds. An oft-repeated tale recounts that the islet was once also inhabited by a single family. They are said to have abandoned their rocky outpost after their young son was carried off by an eagle.

THE FAROE ISLANDS

There's an easy and excellent walk from Sørvágur to Lambadalur, following a path along the southern shore of the fjord. From Lambadalur, easy grassy slopes lead up to the back of the 288m sheer precipice called Sundsnøva. The views of the islets from there are magnificent. Allow three to four hours return.

Gásadalur

Gásadalur, which sits high on a bluff above the sea, is the island's westernmost village and the last in the Faroes without road or ferry connections. The plan to make a tunnel to the village has now been shelved indefinitely. Unless that situation changes, the 15 residents only have access to the rest of the country by helicopter, foot or private boat.

For hikers, Gásadalur makes a great destination for a day hike. The trip begins in Bøur, four km west of Sørvágur, and follows a beautiful but steep and marginally treacherous route to Gásadalur. The well-marked way climbs to nearly 500m before dropping down into the village.

Organised Tours

The airport tourist office (☎ 33200; fax 33100) can arrange day and overnight tours by horse, boat, bus or on foot. A minimum of five participants is required, unless otherwise specified.

On Monday and Saturday, there's a six-hour guided walk from Bøur to Gásadalur for Dkr130 and on Wednesday, a six-hour tour from the airport to the Sørvágur Bird Cliffs for Dkr150. On Friday, you can take a four-hour guided walk to Bøsdalafossur from Miðvágur for Dkr60. On Sunday afternoon there's a bus tour around Vágar for Dkr130 (with a minimum of 10 participants), including a museum and church visit.

Four-hour horse-riding tours to Bøsdalafossur depart on Thursday and Friday and cost Dkr150 per person. Other riding tours can also be arranged.

An overnight tour which includes the Vestmanna Bird Cliffs with Palli Lamhauge, an overnight stay at Slættanes and a walk to Vatnsoyrar, departs from Oyrargjógv on Monday at 7 pm and costs Dkr500 per person.

Two to three-hour boat trips depart from Sørvágur on Monday and Wednesday at 2 pm. The Monday tour either follows the southern shore of Vágar or visits the gannet colony on Mykines. It costs Dkr200 per person. On Wednesday, there's a fishing tour to Tindhólmur for Dkr150 per person.

Places to Stay

The most popular option with travellers is the *Youth Hostel Ferðamannaheimið á Giljanesi* (☎ 33465; fax 32901) in Sandavágur. This very odd little prefabricated building lies squashed between the road and the sea about 700m west of the town. Dormitory rooms cost Dkr90, including use of cooking facilities. Meals can be ordered in advance; breakfast costs Dkr40, while lunch and dinner are Dkr60 each. Camping is available outside the hostel for Dkr50 per person.

In the village of Bøur, four km from Sørvágur, there's the nice chunky *Gistingarhúsið í Bø* (☎ 33052; fax 33488), which is open from 15 May to 1 September. They charge Dkr275/350 for single/double rooms, including breakfast. Lunch and dinner are available if ordered in advance.

Another option is the *Hotel Vágar* (☎ 32955; fax 32310) at the airport. Its rather stark appearance (reminiscent of an overfunded polar research station) perfectly matches its surroundings. Single/double rooms with private bath cost Dkr510/680, including a continental breakfast. The restaurant is open from 7 am to 9 pm daily.

Through Tora Tourist Traffic, you can arrange *B&B* accommodation in Miðvágur, with single/double rooms for Dkr280/430.

The island also has five four-to-eight-person *holiday homes*; three in Sandavágur, one in Miðvágur and one in Sørvágur. They charge Dkr467 per night, except for the one in Sandavágur, which charges Dkr560. Contact Nordica for bookings.

Places to Eat

In addition to the licensed dining room at the *Hotel Vágar*, there's the airport *cafeteria*, which serves snacks and light meals. However, it caters to a captive clientele and probably wouldn't be most people's first choice. It's open from 9 am to only 6 pm daily.

Near the ferry landing down in Sørvágur is the *Kaffistova Grill*, a combination coffee shop and grill-bar where you'll get coffee and snacks from 2 to 11 pm daily in the summer. Grill meals are available after 6 pm only. In Miðvágur, your only option is *Miðvágs Grill*, a scruffy shack beside a factory, which is open daily from 6 to 11 pm.

Sørvágur has a good *supermarket* which also sells paraffin and stove alcohol. For drinks, visit the state alcohol store in Miðvágur.

Getting There & Away
Air The international airport has a helicopter service to Gásadalur, Mykines and Tórshavn on Wednesday, Friday and Sunday, with connections to the southern and north-eastern islands. For information on international flights to/from Reykjavík, Glasgow and Copenhagen, see the Getting There & Away chapter at the beginning of the book.

Bus The most convenient way to reach Vágar from Tórshavn or Klaksvík is on the airport bus (1½ hours; Dkr100), which crosses on the Vestmanna-Oyrargjógv ferry. Alternatively, take bus No 100 to Vestmanna, cross on the ferry and continue on bus No 300 to Sandavágur, Miðvágur, the airport and Sørvágur. From there, the bus continues out to Bøur, 10 minutes from Sørvágur, once or twice daily.

MYKINES
Mykines, the Faroes' westernmost island, isn't like the rest, and it's no wonder it's a favourite with visitors. It's the greenest, friendliest, most independent and among the most beautiful of the islands.

Mykines' moods are manifold. Seen from Vágar, different atmospheric effects can turn it into Michener's Bali Hai or Rachmaninoff's Island of the Dead. Perhaps it's nicest to believe, however, that Mykines really is the 'paradise of birds' described by St Brendan in the 6th century.

The island's star attractions are the little puffins which are present in delightfully overwhelming numbers. Everyone, it seems, likes puffins in one way or another: the Faroese like them stuffed with sweet dough and baked, Icelanders like them roasted and doused in gravy, and visitors normally just like them on film. In German their name means 'diving parrots', and in Spanish, 'little friars' – both are apt descriptions of these endearingly comical characters.

As for the weather, Mykines, like Vágar, sits in the path of North Atlantic weather systems, and seems to catch and delay quite a few passing storms. If you want to see the island at its best, bring a few good books and settle in somewhere until the sun emerges. It will be worth it.

Information
Tourist information in Mykines is handled by Katrina Johannesen (☎ 18432) at Kristianshús.

Mykines Village
Lying up 135 concrete steps from the ferry landing site, Mykines' single village is magical, with earthen streets and bright turf-roofed houses. Up on the hill is the white turf-roofed church.

With only 18 inhabitants, the village is a quiet place and in fact, the village school has only one pupil. The teacher commutes weekly by helicopter between this school and the one at Stóra Dímun, which also has a single pupil. Therefore, the two students attend school on alternating weeks.

Mykineshólmur
Mykines is ideal walking country. Because of the ferry schedule, however, day visitors only have time for a quick visit to Lundaland (the 'land of puffins') on Mykineshólmur, an islet connected to Mykines by a footbridge over a 35m deep gorge, Hólmgjógv. Nevertheless, the walk is certainly one of the most beautiful in the Faroes. The lighthouse on the westernmost cape one km beyond the bridge

Bird Hunting on Mykines

On the islet of Mykineshólmur, attached to Mykines by a small footbridge, is the home of the only gannet colony in the Faroes, with around 1400 breeding pairs. Annually, the villagers catch and consume 300 to 500 birds. Only Mykines landowners are permitted to participate in the hunt, which takes place for only one day a year between 20 and 25 August. Because the collection of birds entails dangling on the cliffs from 100m ropes, calm weather is essential for a successful hunt. Only larger young birds may be taken.

The puffin hunt on Mykines begins on 7 July and continues until 10 August, at which time the remaining puffins fly out to sea. During that time, you may have the opportunity to see locals on the cliffs catching puffins in a *fleygustong*, the bird net resembling a large lacrosse racket. Some of the puffins are eaten locally and others are sold to restaurants and private individuals for Dkr20 per bird.

Guillemots, on the other hand, are shot only in the month of January. However absurd it sounds, Mykines residents maintain that Faroese guillemots are left alone and that they shoot 'only Icelandic guillemots' that have come to winter in the Faroes. One can imagine them checking passports before they pull the trigger! ∎

has a magnificent location and is surrounded by some of the world's densest bird colonies.

Guided walks to Mykineshólmur are available from the guesthouse for Dkr50 per person.

Knúkur

If you have more than a few hours, it's worthwhile climbing up to the island's summit, 560m Knúkur. It's only three km from the village but is still a hefty climb and it would be difficult to do both the Mykineshólmur and Knúkur walks in a single day (ie between ferries). An excellent side trip would be to Steinskógurin ('the stone forest') at Korkadalur, near the northern coast. This trip can be done as a four-hour guided hike with a local farmer for Dkr600 per group.

East of Knúkur, things become more precipitous and the walk to the eastern end of the island is more challenging. Try walking down the steep north-east ridge of Knúkur.

Places to Stay

The village guesthouse is signposted *Kristianshús* (☎ 18432; fax 10985). It's certainly not the most attractive building in the village, but it's warm and dry. A bed costs Dkr195 per person (including breakfast) or Dkr100 for sleeping-bag accommodation.

There are also other private households offering informal guesthouse accommodation. If you're interested, contact Kunningardiskurin (☎ 33200; fax 33100) at Vágar airport, which keeps a current list of homestay accommodation.

Another option is, of course, to bring a tent. The weather can be unpleasant but the surroundings are idyllic. If you intend to camp anywhere around the village, you'll need permission from the villagers as well as access to toilet facilities and running water. For advice on where to camp, see the village plan above the ferry landing.

Places to Eat

The only place to eat is the guesthouse, which has a *cafeteria*. It's housed in the former studio of the Faroes' most celebrated painter, Sámal Elias Joensen Mikines (1906-79), who hailed from Mykines (hence his name). With advance warning, they can serve up snack meals of chips, hot dogs or whatever happens to be available. Lunch (Dkr50) and dinner (Dkr70) should be ordered the day before. It's open from 4 to 6 pm and 8 to 10 pm, or whenever there's a little sign in the window.

The guesthouse also has a small *general store*, but grocery availability is as unpredictable as the weather. If you're bringing food from elsewhere, bear in mind that it's not unusual to be marooned on the island for longer than you'd bargained.

Getting There & Away

Air From the international airport on Vágar, there's return helicopter service to Gásadalur (also on Vágar) and Mykines at 9 am on Wednesday; 9.30 am and 3.39 pm on Friday; and 4.09 pm on Sunday. Naturally, most visitors take the Friday option so they can return to Vágar on the same day. These trips are also popular with Faroese so they should be booked well in advance. The fare from Vágar is Dkr145 each way.

Ferry During summer, the passenger ferry *Súlan* sails from Sørvágur to Mykines and back daily at 11 am, weather permitting (the Sunday morning sailing only operates from 25 May to 1 September). On Tuesday, Saturday and Sunday, it also runs at 3.05 pm, and on Friday, at 5.15 pm. Friday is the most popular day for travellers since they can travel out on the morning ferry and return in the evening, allowing over six hours on the island. After dropping and collecting passengers, the ferry returns immediately to Sørvágur. This schedule is valid only between 1 May and 1 September; at other times, sailings are by arrangement. Advance reservations must be made with Kunningardiskurin (☎ 33200; fax 33100), 9 am to 5 pm daily.

Southern Faroes

The southern islands form the point of the Faroese 'arrow' and include the relatively large islands of Suðuroy and Sandoy as well as the three smaller islands of Skúvoy, Stóra Dímun, and Lítla Dímun. Suðuroy is the most visited of the southern islands, and has a youth hostel, three hotels and other accommodation.

The scenery is fine and what's more, the weather is reputedly the clearest and warmest in the islands. (In fact, Suðuroy fish farms do better than those around other islands due to the comparative warmth of the waters.) A trip to the southern islands probably won't warrant sun-block or a swimming costume, but if you've been rained out of Tórshavn, Mykines, and the north-east, you can always resort to Sandoy or Suðuroy and hope for the best.

SANDOY

Although Sandoy is the least rugged of the Faroes – the highest peak, Tindur, rises just 479m – it's not without interest. It boasts the country's only sand dunes, hence the name 'sand island', and some dramatic cliffs along the western coast. The roadless north-eastern half of the island is excellent hiking country. Sandoy covers an area of 112 sq km and has a population of 1400, divided among five villages.

Information

The tourist information service on Sandoy is at the Shell petrol station (☎ 61046) in Sandur.

Skopun

The ferry from Gamlarætt goes to Skopun, a village of 525 people which was founded in 1833. It's the site of a fish processing plant and little else, but the surroundings are quite pleasant. On the pass above town are two beautiful lakes, Norðara Hálsavatn and Heimara Hálsavatn, which are popular with trout anglers. Access is along the Faroes' oldest road, which crosses the pass connecting Skopun and Sandur.

From Skopun, it's a wonderful walk past the end of the track west of town to the 269m cliffs of Djúpaberg. For a longer day hike, pick your way south along the rough five km of coastal cliffs to Søltuvík, then follow the road into Sandur.

Sandur

Sandur sits on a small peninsula between two lakes, Sandsvatn and Gróthúsvatn, and two bays, Sandsvágur and Grótvík. At the head at Sandsvágur, between the village and the mountain, is an area of incongruous sand dunes and a beach of black basalt sands. On the hill between Sandur and Grótvík is an area of greenhouse agriculture.

An easy two to three-hour walk from the

village will take you around the lake Sandsvatn. Alternatively, walk over to the beautiful bay Søltuvík on the west coast. From there, you can continue north along the wild and scenic cliffs which extend to the island's north-western tip.

Church The history of the Sandur church is one of the most interesting in the Faroes. The site has been used as the parish centre since the 11th century and archaeology has revealed that at least six consecutive churches have existed there since.

The first building was constructed in the 11th century, most likely very soon after the introduction of Christianity. It was a stave (wooden) structure about nine metres long and probably not too comfortable during poor weather. The second church was built less than 200 years later, this time enclosed in heavy stone masonry, and was much stronger and resisted the climate better than its predecessor. The third and fourth churches were built in the mid and late 17th century, the fifth in 1711, and the sixth church was constructed on the site in 1762. The current building, a typical black wood structure with a turf-roof and small white steeple, was built in 1839. If you manage to get inside, notice the lathe-turned columns in the choir screen which are unique in the Faroes.

Although the site is open to anyone, its layered history is neither evident nor interpreted for visitors – so don't go expecting a Faroese version of Troy. Perhaps it's better to appreciate the fact that they haven't bothered to make a fuss about such things anywhere in the country.

Trøllkonufingur

The 'troll woman's finger' or Trøllkonufingur (not to be confused with the pinnacle of the same name on Vágar) is a much-photographed sea stack north of the tiny settlement of Skarvanès. There's no public transport to the rock but it's an easy four km walk each way along the coastal track from the Skálavík road. Alternatively, you can return to Sandur by walking the four km from Skarvanes across the 300m high moor to Dalur on the east coast, and take bus No 601 back from there.

Skálavík

Skálavík is known only as the home town of the Faroes' most renowned writer, Heðin Brú. For visitors, it's the start of a scenic walk over the mountain Heiðafjall to Húsavík.

At Skálhøvdi point, east of Skálavík, there's a great natural rock arch at sea level, but it is only visible from offshore. If you're travelling on the ferry between Sandur or Suðuroy and Tórshavn, take notice of it as you pass. Between Húsavík and Dalur are some large sea-caves which are also worth a look.

Húsavík

Húsavík, one of the Faroes' most charming villages with many traditional turf-roofed homes, certainly merits a visit. The name of this village of 167 people means 'bay of houses'. It was settled very early in Faroese history but, after the pestilence that ravaged all of Europe in the 14th century, its population was drastically reduced. There are a

couple of interesting sights, not least of which is its lovely dark sandy beach.

Longhouse Ruins Just north of the main road through the village is the ruin of an ancient longhouse belonging to the farm Heimi á Garði. It was built around the same time as the first 11th-century stave church in Sandur and is believed to have been owned during the 14th century by the wealthy and influential Guðrun Sjúrðardóttir of Norway and Shetland.

This manor house was similar in layout to the farmhouses excavated at Kvívík and Tjørnuvík, but was a much more sophisticated structure. Rather than the stamped mud floors typical in these longhouses, the floor of this one consisted of flagstone mosaics. It had a wooden roof overlain by the usual insulating layer of turf.

Folk Museum One old Húsavík farmhouse, Jógvans Breyt, with an ancient chimney and fireplace, has been converted into a folk museum (☎ 61744). Between 1 June and 31 August, it's open on Wednesday from 3 to 5 pm and Sunday from 4 to 6 pm and other times by prior arrangement. Admission costs Dkr20 per adult.

Organised Tours

Páll í Dalsgarði (☎ or fax 61549) in Skálavík runs overnight walking tours to a remote mountain hut for Dkr200 per person, including meals.

Jóan Petur Clementsen (☎ 86119) in Sandur runs daily wildlife tours on his homebuilt boat *Hvíthamrar*. The three-hour tours depart at 10.30 am, 2.30 and 7.30 pm and cost Dkr150 per person. The route takes you around the coasts of Sandoy or Skúvoy.

The occasional six-hour tour from Tórshavn to Sandoy with the *Amadeus* (☎ 12499; fax 19124) includes a visit to Skopun and costs Dkr250. Also from Tórshavn, Smyril Line runs a 5½ hour Thursday tour to Sandoy which costs Dkr235 per person. On Sunday from 9 am to 5 pm, Tora Tourist Traffic runs a similar tour for Dkr475 per person, including lunch. Transport on Sandoy is by bus.

Places to Stay & Eat

Tora Tourist Traffic lists five *holiday homes* on Sandoy: one in Sandur, Skopun and Skálavík and two in Húsavík. Prices are Dkr520 per night, except the house in Skálavík, which is Dkr660 per night. Nordica also books *holiday homes*, one in each of the four main villages, for Dkr300 to Dkr750. Talk to the tourist office at the Shell petrol station or Thorstein Holm (☎ 61758) for advice on *B&B* accommodation, averaging Dkr205/310 for singles/doubles.

There's a new café and guesthouse in Húsavík called *Café 31* (☎ 61116), open daily from 10 am to 10 pm. Single/double rooms cost Dkr180/270 and camping costs Dkr40. Dinner is available if you reserve in advance. Each of the four main villages has a small *grocery kiosk* where you can purchase basic supplies.

Getting There & Away

The most popular way to visit Sandoy is with the ferry *Tróndur* between Gamlarætt and Skopun, on the northern end of the island. The 30 minute trip is normally a relatively smooth crossing. It operates six or seven times daily on weekdays and five at weekends. Some of these stop at Hestur en route.

On Saturday between 4 May and 5 October the ferry *Sildberin* has a return sailing between Sandur and Hvalba (Suðuroy), via Skúvoy.

Getting Around

From Skópun, bus No 600 travels to Sandur (30 minutes; Dkr20) and Skálavík three to five times daily, connecting with the ferries to/from Gamlarætt. Two to five times daily, this bus connects with bus No 601 at the Lítlavatn intersection and continues to Húsavík and Dalur. The trip from Skópun to Húsavík takes 45 minutes and costs Dkr30.

SKÚVOY

Skúvoy, a tiny island of only 10 sq km and 90 residents, is named after the ubiquitous great skua. These raucous gull-like birds have a habit of attacking (à la Hitchcock's *The Birds*) intruders on their territory. The island has several sites of interest but thanks to incidents involving illegal collection of birds' eggs by foreign 'birdwatchers', islanders have developed an ambivalent attitude toward tourism.

This small and compact island can easily be explored on foot in one day. Climb to the summit of 392m Knútur for a far-ranging view down the magnificent line of cliffs along the west coast. You can walk along them as well.

Skúvoy Village

From the harbour, a set of steps climbs up to the island's single village. According to the *Færinga Saga*, the entire island could never be captured as long as it had 10 men to defend these steps.

To visit the graves of Sigmund Bresterson and his friend Thorer (see boxed aside), climb up through the town to the cemetery.

Places to Stay & Eat

There are no restaurants or accommodation on Skúvoy, and overnight guests may not receive the warmest reception anyway. If you're keen on staying, ask in the village for permission to camp.

Getting There & Away

Air Helicopter services between Tórshavn, Skúvoy, Stóra Dímun and Froðba (Suðuroy) operate once on Wednesday, Friday and Sunday (not to Froðba on Sunday). The return services on Wednesday and Friday operate about an hour after the outward service, allowing precious little time for a look around Skúvoy. On Sunday, you only get 10 minutes! The fare between Tórshavn and Skúvoy is Dkr130.

Ferry The ferry *Sildberin* operates between Sandur and Skúvoy one to three times daily, taking about 35 minutes each way. It's best to visit on a Tuesday or Thursday, when you can cross from Sandur at 8.20 am and return at 4.25 pm.

Sigmund Bresterson

Skúvoy was the adopted home of Sigmund Bresterson, the hero of the *Færinga Saga*. While in Norway he was coerced into accepting Christianity by the tyrant king Olaf Tryggvason, and sent to the Faroes to convert the locals from paganism. At some time around the year 1000, he proclaimed the islands a Christian nation and settled down to a peaceful life on Skúvoy.

However, things didn't turn out to be so peaceful. Sigmund proceeded to get himself into all sorts of local religious scrapes, the last of which resulted in a swim for his life from Skúvoy to Suðuroy. To make matters worse, he had to carry his friend Thorer, who had, in mid-channel, weakened to the point of exhaustion. Unfortunately, Thorer drowned before they reached shore.

Upon arriving in Suðuroy, Sigmund was welcomed and then promptly murdered by greedy Thórgrim the Evil, who fancied some of the trinkets Sigmund was carrying. Thorer's body washed up beside Sigmund's, and Thórgrim hid them both on his farm near Sandvík. Years later, Sigmund's relatives discovered the bodies and carried them home to Skúvoy where they were buried in the churchyard above the village. ■

STÓRA DÍMUN

Stóra Dímun has an area of 2½ sq km and reaches an altitude of 395m. Today it's inhabited by a single family who stay for part of the year. During the Viking Age, this steep and rather inhospitable island was home to several prominent characters in the *Færinga Saga*. Until 1920, the ruins of a wretched church from the earlier days of Faroese Christianity still stood on the island.

Getting There & Away

By sea, Stóra Dímun can only be reached in clear and calm weather, but there are no scheduled ferries in any case.

Egg Collection on Skúvoy

Egg collection has always been an important activity on Skúvoy island. On the 300 to 400m cliffs of the west coast, there's an immense guillemot colony and visitors to Skúvoy during early June may be lucky enough to witness the collection of the eggs. Collectors are lowered over the cliff's edge in slings on a 150m length of rope, and use a bag attached to a long pole to pluck the eggs from the nests. This is done only during the first week or so of the mating season to allow the birds time to produce another egg and perpetuate the colony. Of course, the procedure isn't entirely safe, but the collectors who survive do receive a great deal of respect. ■

Helicopter services operate from Tórshavn, Skúvoy and Froðba (Suðuroy) on Wednesday, Friday and Sunday (not from Froðba on Sunday). To visit this remote island, however, you must first secure permission from the farmer. Contact the Tórshavn tourist offices for details.

LÍTLA DÍMUN

Lampshade-shaped Lítla Dímun is the smallest of the Faroes' 18 main islands, with an area of less than one sq km. The lower third of the island is sheer cliff while the 413m summit looms dauntingly above the sea.

The island is reputed to have been inhabited at some time in the dim and distant past. When the first Norse people arrived, they discovered a strain of dark brown Soay sheep from St Kilda island, west of the Hebrides. It's suspected they were introduced by the Irish monks who arrived in the Faroes during the late 7th century (although in the early 6th century, St Brendan passed through and described a place he called the 'island of sheep'). In the summer, Lítla Dímun is still inhabited by sheep (the white variety) which happily nibble on its grassy summit, but there are no permanent human inhabitants.

In the *Færinga Saga*, Lítla Dímun is the site of a battle between saga hero, Sigmund Bresterson, and Thrand of Gøta and his men. Two of Thrand's men were killed before Sigmund managed to escape on his ship.

Getting There & Away
There are no regular transport connections to the island but in any case, you'd need a particularly good reason to go (and some particularly good connections to get you there). The island is accessible only by helicopter or a very rough boat landing and an intimidating cliff climb up to the steep grassy slopes above. You can have a good look at it, however, from the ferry between Tórshavn and Suðuroy.

SUÐUROY
Suðuroy, the southernmost of the Faroes Islands, is marginally drier and warmer than the others. It likes to boast that it has all the amenities of Tórshavn but none of the traffic.

Tvøroyri
Although Tvøroyri has the largest population on Suðuroy, this overgrown village is really of little interest except as a transit point between the northern and southern halves of the island. If you find yourself pacing up and down the main street looking for something to do between bus connections, all I can suggest is a walk around the harbour and fish-processing area. Failing that, try a good book or splurge on a meal at the hotel.

With a bit more time, you can walk from Trongisvágur (at the head of the fjord) north over the ridge to a popular camping and fishing lake in Vatnsdalur. From Trongisvágur, the walk takes one to two hours each way.

From the southern end of the tunnel between Trongisvágur and Hvalba there's a short but lovely walk to the cliffs and a commanding view of the roiling cove Trongisvágsbotnur. The walk from Tvøroyri to Fámjin is described under Fámjin, later in this chapter.

Information The tourist information office, Kunningarstovan Suðuroy (☎ 72480; fax 72380), is one block uphill from the main road, near the harbour.

The post office is open Monday to Friday from 9 am to 4 pm. There's a casualty ward

at the hospital (☎ 71133), just uphill from the hotel.

Sandvík
Situated on a peninsula that on a map looks like Pac-Man hellbent on gobbling up the Dímuns, Sandvík is Suðuroy's northernmost village. It is also the place where, the *Færinga Saga* tells us, Sigmund Bresterson swam ashore and was murdered by Thórgrim the Evil (see the boxed aside under Skúvoy).

In the centre of Sandvík, just below the church, is a traditional Faroese house dating from 1860, and behind the village, a road leads up the valley to some of Suðuroy's many sea cliffs. Halfway along this road, an old route turns south and steeply climbs to the summit of 373m Skálafjall before descending into Hvalba.

Hvalba
From the first available records of the Faroese Løgting, we learn that Hvalba was ravaged in 1629 by three shiploads of Barbary pirates and 30 of its inhabitants were kidnapped. Although a ransom was demanded for their return, the town couldn't raise the money and the poor victims were carried away to slavery in North Africa.

Near Hvalba is the only Faroese coal mine (still in operation), and west of the town, through the eiði, is a rugged old landing site which is fortunately no longer in use.

Froðba
Froðba was Suðuroy's original settlement

A Whale in Every Pot
During the first Faroese election of representatives to the Danish parliament in 1851, Hvalba was the polling headquarters for Suðuroy island. Just as voting was about to begin, the cry of 'grind!' went up, signalling pilot whales off the coast, and all interest in the election was summarily abandoned in favour of the grindadráp. Voting was resumed later, on the spot where the kill took place. ■

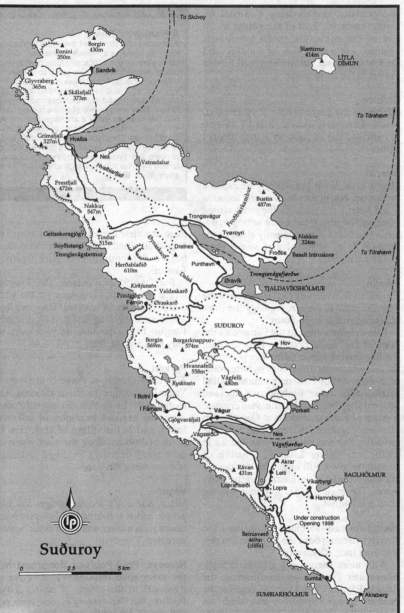

THE FAROE ISLANDS

Suðuroy

0   2.5   5 km

and predates neighbouring Tvøroyri by several centuries. East of the village at the end of the peninsula you'll see basalt columns. For a good view of the cliffs and the fjord, walk up the winding road behind Froðba to the radio tower.

Drelnes

Drelnes is the purpose-built ferry terminal across Trongisvágsfjørður from Tvøroyri. It's also the site of Suðuroy's state alcohol store.

Øravík

Øravík is so tiny it can scarcely be called a settlement, but, thanks to its central location – and hotel – it's probably the most visited place on Suðuroy. It has a nice setting opposite a beach and is conveniently close to the Drelnes ferry terminal and some good walking country.

Fámjin

From Øravík, a winding road leads across the pass Øraskarð to Fámjin, arguably the most charming village on Suðuroy.

Fámjin is important to the Faroese as the home of the Faroes' first flag. Prior to 1920, the flag used at public gatherings portrayed the ram and tjaldur (the cheeky oystercatcher of Nólsoyar-Poul Poulson's famous ballad *Fuglakvæði*). After Finland and Iceland adopted flags bearing Scandinavian crosses, a group of Faroese students at Copenhagen University designed the red, white, and blue cross flag that was adopted by the Faroes in 1920. Jens Oliver Lisberg, a native of Fámjin, is given full credit for the design because he died of influenza shortly afterwards. The original flag is now housed in the church at Fámjin.

Hiking An easy 15 minute walk from the church will take you to the lovely and excellent trout lake, Kirkjuvatn.

With more energy, it's a pleasant walk from either Tvøroyri or Øravík across the ridge to Fámjin. From Tvøroyri, begin at the head of Trongisvágsfjørður and climb the slope up the 330m pass Oyrnaskarð. From

---

A Fishwives' Tale

According to a story from the trade monopoly days, Fámjin has a French connection. Once upon a time in the 1700s, two local men rowed out to sell part of their fish catch to a French merchant ship anchored offshore. Two discerning women on board demanded they be permitted to inspect the catch before agreeing to buy. They were lowered into the rowing boat and the men, aware of a shortage of females on shore, decided this was an opportunity too good to miss. They kidnapped the women and, realising that an impending storm would prevent the French from taking any action, forced them back to the village where they were all married. ∎

---

there, the view improves as you traverse the Dalsá valley and cross the 249m Valdaskarð before descending past Kirkjuvatn to Fámjin.

For Dkr195 per person, the Tvøroyri tourist office offers four-hour guided walks every Thursday in summer. They run from Vágur up Botnsdalur and past Ryskivatn to Fámjin. This is possible on your own, but only with a good map.

Porkeri

The 1847 church at Porkeri, just east of Vágur, is another in the traditional turf-roofed style. In the hillsides around Porkeri are some exposed examples of columnar basalt, and at the village of Hov, five km north of Porkeri along the road, there are more basalt intrusions forming a procession of posts along the slopes.

Vágur

Vágur, Suðuroy's second village, has 1400 people and is a fishing and fish-processing centre with a nicer and more rustic appearance than Tvøroyri.

Nólsoyar-Poul Poulson Monument Near the main road through Vágur, there's a memorial to the efforts of Nólsoyar-Poul Poulson, the 19th-century Faroese hero, poet and genius. He led the earliest opposition to

the trade monopolies which he believed were crippling the economic potential of the Faroe Islands and the ingenuity of the people. For more on this historic figure, see the boxed asideunder Nólsoy.

Hiking It's an easy walk from Vágur through the eiði to the west coast, where you'll find a good view along some relatively low cliffs. Only slightly more challenging is the walk up the Fámara road north-west of the village. Take the left fork and descend to the lighthouse on the beautiful coast at Fámara. Another option is to take the right fork and follow the track for 1½ km to Ryskivatn, the lake which feeds the small Botni power plant 250m below.

Lopra
Lopra, at the terminus of the rather expensive tunnel to Sumba, has little to offer except accommodation (see the following Places to Stay section).

Sumba
There's nothing special to see or do in Sumba except gaze at the view from the cliffs to the north, and appreciate that the next landfall to the south is Scotland.

The 469m cliffs of Beinisvørð lie only a few hundred metres walk from the mountain road between Lopra and Sumba. They provide a magnificent and easily accessible view up and down Suðuroy's incredible western coast. From Beinisvørð, it's possible to walk down the steep slope into Sumba. The road passes close to the cliffs at Lopranseiði, two km above Lopra, Suðuroy's narrowest point, where there's a large puffin colony.

Organised Tours
The tourist office in Tvøroyri can organise several tours around Suðuroy. Four-hour fishing trips run to Lítla Dímun on Tuesday and cost Dkr275. Two-hour bus tours to Sandvík (Dkr165) run on Tuesday and four-hour tours to Sumba (Dkr319) run on Thursday. Three or four-hour hiking tours to Hvannhagi (Dkr165) or Fámjin (Dkr195)

run on Wednesday and Thursday, respectively. All tours start at 9 am and must be booked at least one day in advance; the tourist office can advise on the minimum participation factor.

Special Events
Suðuroy's big annual festival, Jóansøka (St John's Day) or Midsummerfest, is held on the weekend nearest to 24 June in Vágur.

Places to Stay
The *Hotel Tvøroyri* (☎ 71171; fax 72171) lies uphill from the main street near the eastern end of Tvøroyri. It's clean and comfortable and has single/double rooms with shared bath for Dkr300/400, including breakfast. The attached dining room, open from 7 am to 10 pm, is the only restaurant in town. Lunch or dinner will cost around Dkr85.

In Øravík, the *Hotel Øravík* (☎ 71302; fax 72057), with attached dining room, has single/double rooms for Dkr500/750 with private facilities or Dkr300/450 without. In the same building is the *Áargarður Youth Hostel* (☎ 71302; fax 72057), with dorm beds for Dkr100 and breakfast for an extra Dkr50. Camping costs Dkr50 per person.

Travellers in Vágur can stay at the *Scouts' Centre* (☎ 73060), which offers sleeping-bag accommodation for Dkr70 per person and camping for Dkr40 per person. Reserve through the YMCA (☎ 11075; fax 10775) in Tórshavn. There's also a pleasant *campground* (☎ 73216) near the end of the lake in Vágaseiði where camping costs Dkr40 per person.

In Vágur, the hotel accommodation choice is simple – there's only one. The *Hotel Bakkin* (☎ 73961) looks a bit seedy from the outside, but isn't too bad inside. They charge Dkr250/350 for singles/doubles with shared bath, including breakfast. Other meals will run between Dkr80 and Dkr120.

Frítíðhúsið í Lopra (☎ 73910), in Lopra, is a small block of flats, each with four beds, television, attached bath and phone costing Dkr475 per day.

For *B&B* accommodation in Tvøroyri,

contact Tora Tourist Traffic in Tórshavn. Single/double rooms cost Dkr280/430. They can also organise *holiday homes* in Froðba for Dkr520, Hvalba for Dkr520 and Akrar for Dkr660 per night. *Holiday homes* are available in Tvøroyri, Froðba, Fámjin, Hvalba (three properties), Vágur and Nes, at prices ranging from Dkr309 to Dkr720. Contact Nordica for bookings.

Places to Eat

Tvøroyri has a bakery, two supermarkets and two *grill-bars* on the main street. In Trongisvágur, there's a *Brugsen* supermarket and a *cafeteria* in the sports hall. The supermarket in Vágur is tucked away near the harbour just off the main road and there's a grill-bar, *Grillbarin Báran*, near the head of the fjord. Sumba also has a grill-bar, the *Aldan*. There's a grill-bar and a shop selling groceries in Hvalba, as well as small grocery shops in Fámjin and Lopra.

Getting There & Away

Air There's a helicopter service between Tórshavn and Froðba (near Tvøroyri) on Wednesday and Friday, stopping en route at Skúvoy and Stóra Dímun. The fare from Tórshavn is Dkr215.

Ferry During the summer, ferries sail from Drelnes to Tórshavn at 6.10 am on Monday and Friday; at 7 am daily on other days; and at 5.15 pm on Sunday. In the opposite direction, they leave Tórshavn at 5.30 pm from Monday to Friday, except Wednesday; at 8 pm on Wednesday and weekends; and at 9.30 am on Sunday. The trip takes about two hours. On Wednesday and Friday, there's a sailing from Tórshavn to Vágur and back.

The *Smyril* sails between Tórshavn and Drelnes on Friday at 10.30 am and Tuesday at 4 pm (passengers only).

Getting Around

Tvøroyri is the transport hub of Suðuroy. From there, buses head south to Øravík, Vágur and Sumba and north to Hvalba and Sandvík. The heliport is at nearby Froðba

and the main ferry terminal is across the fjord at Drelnes.

Bus No 700 runs from Tvøroyri and Drelnes to Øravík and Vágur (45 minutes; Dkr30) four to 10 times daily. From Tvøroyri and/or Drelnes, bus No 702 runs to Hvalba and Sandvík (35 minutes; Dkr20) three to eight times daily. Bus No 703 runs between Froðba and Fámjin (40 minutes; Dkr20), via Tvøroyi, Drelnes and Øravík, three to six times daily.

Bus No 704 runs between Vágur and Sumba (40 minutes; Dkr30) three to six times daily. When the new tunnel opens in 1998, the trip will become shorter and considerably less interesting than the current route over the mountain.

Bicycles may be hired from the camping shop DJ Enni in Tvøroyri. It's open weekdays from 8 am to 5 pm.

Other Islands

The three small islands of Nólsoy, Koltur and Hestur lie clustered around the southern tip of Streymoy. They offer easy day excursions from Tórshavn or off-the-beaten-track hiking destinations.

NÓLSOY

Just a 20 minute ferry ride from Tórshavn, Nólsoy makes an excellent day trip.

Nólsoy's picturesque little village and harbour lie just north of the island's isthmus, which is just a few metres wide. It has the dubious honour of having the Faroes' largest collection of stuffed birds, and visitors can also see the rowing boat *Diana Victoria*, in which Ove Joensen rowed for 42 days between Nólsoy and Langelinje in Denmark.

From the village, cairns mark the seven km route southwards around 371m Eggjar-klettur, the island's highest point, and along the slopes to Øksnatangi. Here on Nólsoy's beautiful south-eastern cape, you'll find a classic lighthouse perched above the sea. From there, you can also visit the southwestern cape, Borðan, which has a less

Nólsoyar-Poul Poulson

During the early 1800s, the Faroese genius Nólsoyar-Poul Poulson (who, as his name would suggest, hailed from the island of Nólsoy) attempted to rid the Faroes of what he perceived as its greatest inequity and threat to prosperity, the monopoly trading scheme (see the History section of the Faroes Facts about the Country chapter). Smuggling and piracy had proliferated in Tórshavn and officials had become hopelessly corrupt. He felt that something should be done about it before the system collapsed and left the islands destitute.

After purchasing the remains of a wrecked ship from the Hvalba (Suðuroy) district auction, Poul went to Vágur and set about refurbishing it. From the efforts of Poul and his brothers emerged the *Royndin Fríða*, the only ocean-going schooner in the Faroes.

After the ship was launched on 6 August 1804, Poul and his crew plied the waters between the Faroes and the mainland carrying much-needed food and vaccines to the Faroese people, working all the while to muster resistance to the trade monopolies and pleading his case in Denmark. On one sailing trip to plead his case in Denmark (which had, incidentally, just engaged itself in a war with the British who had cut off Faroes-bound ships by blockading the North Sea), Poul managed to carry a bit of grain back to Tórshavn. Unfortunately, his greater cause was stalled and he only found himself embroiled in litigation and becoming unpopular in high and powerful places. To make matters worse, the *Royndin Fríða* was seized in a naval confrontation with a British warship off Denmark in 1808 and was inadvertently destroyed while being towed into harbour.

Although unsuccessful in his struggle to abolish the monopolies, Poul aroused a bit of healthy speculation about their centuries old economic system. The monopoly trading was finally abolished for economic reasons in 1856, and today Nólsoyar-Poul Poulson is regarded as a Faroese national hero and Nólsoy's favourite son. Nearly every town and village has a street named in his honour. ∎

---

interesting lighthouse. These lighthouses were originally built in the late 1700s to aid smugglers running goods into Tórshavn during the days of the trade monopoly.

Organised Tours

A boat tour on the *Amadeus* (☎ 12499), which includes circumnavigation of Nólsoy, sails on Tuesday, Wednesday and Thursday at 9 am, in summer. The four-hour tour costs Dkr150 per person with a minimum of seven people.

There's also a tour with local ornithologist and guide Jens-Kjeld Jensen to the world's largest storm petrel colony. The tour includes the ferry between Tórshavn and Nólsoy, a night walk to view the colony and overnight stay at the Kaffistovan guesthouse. It costs Dkr300 per person for sleeping-bag accommodation and Dkr350 for made-up rooms. It operates on Tuesday and Friday, or by arrangement. You can book through Kunningarstovan in Tórshavn.

Places to Stay & Eat

The only formal accommodation on Nólsoy is the *Kaffistovan Guesthouse* (☎ 27175) which also has a restaurant. The cost is Dkr200/300 for a single/double in made-up rooms and Dkr80 for sleeping-bag accommodation. The restaurant serves up hot drinks and a variety of snack foods. It's open daily from 8 am (10 am on Sunday) to 11 pm. Tora Tourist Traffic can arrange overnight accommodation in a seven-bed *holiday house* for Dkr520 per night. The village also has a well-stocked *supermarket*.

Getting There & Away

The ferry *Ritan* sails between Tórshavn and Nólsoy two to four times daily. From Monday to Friday, the first sailing from Tórshavn is at 7 am and the last at 6 pm, with a varying number of runs in between. On Saturday it sails from Tórshavn at 9.15 am and 3 pm, and on Sunday at 10 am and 7.30 pm. It returns from Nólsoy 20 minutes after leaving Tórshavn.

HESTUR

The island of Hestur ('the horse') lies about three km off the south-west coast of

THE FAROE ISLANDS

Streymoy, 20 minutes by ferry from Gamlarætt (or an hour via Sandoy). Its single village, also called Hestur, with 43 inhabitants, clings to the island's eastern shore.

The seas around Hestur are particularly rich in fish and seals and the west coast harbours a large guillemot colony. Life has never been particularly easy there, however. In 1919, two fishing boats were sunk in a storm and a third of the island's men were drowned. The island has never fully recovered its liveliness.

Hiking

Near the northern end of the island are Hestur's two highest points – Múlin and Eggjarrók – both of which rise to 421m and can be reached by climbing the very steep valley headwall behind the village. After the ground levels out, bear north to reach the peaks or south to a lovely moorland dotted with four smallish lakes. The largest is Fagradalsvatn ('beautiful valley lake').

On the formidable west coast, about 1½ km north of the lighthouse and below the cliffs immediately south-west of Fagradalsvatn, is the unusually shaped pinnacle Álvastakkur ('elf stack'). It can be viewed from the cliffs above or from the sea, but it's impossible to climb down to it without technical equipment. From the village, there's a much easier three km walk south along the coast road to the lighthouse at Hælur, on Hestur's southern tip.

Places to Stay & Eat

The opulent *community centre* (☎ 28027) in Hestur village has rooms which it rents to groups or individuals for Dkr120 per person, including use of the kitchen facilities and swimming pool. The pool is open to the public from 8 am to 10 pm daily.

The village has a small *shop*, but supplies are limited, so it's wise to carry groceries from Tórshavn.

Getting There & Away

From Monday to Saturday the ferry *Tróndur* runs between Gamlarætt and Hestur two or three times daily, with some trips running via Skopun on Sandoy. If you wish to just do a day trip to Hestur, you can travel on Saturday or Sunday at 8.45 am – unfortunately via Skopun – and return to Gamlarætt at 5.20 pm on Saturday, or 5.40 pm on Sunday.

KOLTUR

The meaning of the name of this uniquely-shaped island isn't clear, but it probably isn't 'the colt', despite the fact that it appears to be trotting along just behind Hestur. From the relatively flat plateau of the southern end, Koltur sweeps magnificently skyward, ending at the 478m Kolturshamar. This conical mountain is quite steep and, although it's possible to climb, it wouldn't be easy.

In the last decade, Koltur was abandoned by the sheep farmers whose animals used to graze on its southern half. However, people have now moved back to the island and parts of the old village are about to be restored.

If you wish to visit Koltur on your own, you must secure permission from the tenant, Bjørn Patursson (☎ 86026; fax 28091).

Getting There & Away

At the moment, the only access to Koltur is the eight-hour Sunday tour aboard *Amadeus*, which departs from Tórshavn at 10 am and costs Dkr250 per person. The tour spends several hours walking around the island, and visits the bird colonies on the western cliffs. The boat returns to Tórshavn via the Hestur bird cliffs. Bookings may be made through the Kunningarstovan tourist office in Tórshavn or directly with Óðin Tours (☎ 12499; fax 19124).

Index

LOCAL ALPHABETS

The Icelandic-Faroese characters á, í, ó, ú and ý are all ordered among the a, i, o and y listings, as is the practice in the local alphabets. The characters ö and æ appear among the o and a listings respectively. The Icelandic characters ð and þ follow the z in this listing (in Iceland ð follows d and þ follows z or is found among or after the t listings). The Danish character ø comes last of all.

MAPS

TEXT

Thanks

At Lonely Planet we appreciate the efforts of the many people who take the time to write in and tell us of their experiences. The following is a list of travellers and others (apologies if we've missplet your name) who wrote in about their travels to Iceland, Greenland & the Faroe Islands. Their names are listed below:

Lars Arvidsson, Hayden Banks, Christoph Beiglboeck, Ray Bell, Rita Bertol, Delbert Blake, Isabelle Bocken, James Bohannon, G Bolton, Tracy Bonham, Ingrid Bremer, Stephen Brown, Peggy Cami, Salvatore Campeggio, James Cowling, Trevor Cox, C Crowder, Johnathon Culp, Margaret Davies, Nigel & Anne deGay, Craig Faanes, JP Fjallsbak, Andrew Ganner, Sabine Gilcher, J Gordalla, Gordon Gore, Lars Grosse Wortmann, Naomi Grove, Shaun Hampton, Trevor Hartley, Tim Hewson, PG & RM Hurst, Chuck Hutton, Jurgen Jacoby, Pamela Judson-Rhodes, Myra Kirchen, Bruce Kleinman, Evangelos Kotsopoulos, Bill Lamp, A Lascurain, Melvyn Lawes, Anke Lind, Jozef Maes, Luis Ignacio Marchesi, Ian McManus, A Monaco, Christopher Morden, Karin & Richard Morgan, John & Ann Murray, Olafur P Olafsson, Edmond Paulussen, Michael Pearson, David Peeters, Giancarlo Perlo, Lasse Petersen, Rob Porges, Stephen Reid, Ian Richards, Mathias Schluter, Kevin Sheard, T Sidey, Scott Slotterbeck, Heriette Snyder, Vivienne Steiniger, Matti Straub, Mark Tanner, David & Rhoda Wilson, K W Wood.

LONELY PLANET PHRASEBOOKS

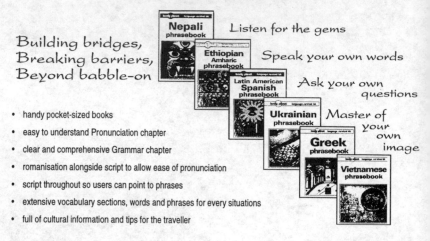

Building bridges,
Breaking barriers,
Beyond babble-on

Listen for the gems

Speak your own words

Ask your own
questions

Master of
your
own
image

- handy pocket-sized books
- easy to understand Pronunciation chapter
- clear and comprehensive Grammar chapter
- romanisation alongside script to allow ease of pronunciation
- script throughout so users can point to phrases
- extensive vocabulary sections, words and phrases for every situations
- full of cultural information and tips for the traveller

'...vital for a real DIY spirit and attitude in language learning' – Backpacker

'the phrasebooks have good cultural backgrounders and offer solid advice for challenging situations in remote locations' – San Francisco Examiner

'...they are unbeatable for their coverage of the world's more obscure languages' – The Geographical Magazine

---

Arabic (Egyptian)
Arabic (Moroccan)
Australia
  Australian English, Aboriginal and
  Torres Strait languages
Baltic States
  Estonian, Latvian, Lithuanian
Bengali
Burmese
Brazilian
Cantonese
Central Europe
  Czech, French, German, Hungarian,
  Italian and Slovak
Eastern Europe
  Bulgarian, Czech, Hungarian, Polish,
  Romanian and Slovak
Egyptian Arabic
Ethiopian (Amharic)
Fijian
Greek
Hindi/Urdu

Indonesian
Japanese
Korean
Lao
Latin American Spanish
Malay
Mandarin
Mediterranean Europe
  Albanian, Croatian, Greek, Italian,
  Macedonian, Maltese, Serbian,
  Slovene
Mongolian
Moroccan Arabic
Nepali
Papua New Guinea
Pilipino (Tagalog)
Quechua
Russian
Scandinavian Europe
  Danish, Finnish, Icelandic, Norwegian
  and Swedish

South-East Asia
  Burmese, Indonersian, Khmer, Lao,
  Malay, Tagalog (Pilipino), Thai and
  Vietnamese
Sri Lanka
Swahili
Thai
Thai Hill Tribes
Tibetan
Turkish
Ukrainian
USA
  US English, Vernacular Talk,
  Native American languages and
  Hawaiian
Vietnamese
Western Europe
  Basque, Catalan, Dutch, French,
  German, Irish, Italian, Portuguese,
  Scottish Gaelic, Spanish (Castilian)
  and Welsh

LONELY PLANET JOURNEYS

JOURNEYS is a unique collection of travel writing – published by the company that understands travel better than anyone else. It is a series for anyone who has ever experienced – or dreamed of – the magical moment when they encountered a strange culture or saw a place for the first time. They are tales to read while you're planning a trip, while you're on the road or while you're in an armchair, in front of a fire.

JOURNEYS books catch the spirit of a place, illuminate a culture, recount a crazy adventure, or introduce a fascinating way of life. They always entertain, and always enrich the experience of travel.

THE GATES OF DAMASCUS
Lieve Joris
Translated by Sam Garrett

This best-selling book is a beautifully drawn portrait of day-to-day life in modern Syria. Through her intimate contact with local people, Lieve Joris draws us into the fascinating world that lies behind the gates of Damascus. Hala's husband is a political prisoner, jailed for his opposition to the Assad regime; through the author's friendship with Hala we see how Syrian politics impacts on the lives of ordinary people.

Lieve Joris, who was born in Belgium, is one of Europe's leading travel writers. In addition to an award-winning book on Hungary, she has published widely acclaimed accounts of her journeys to the Middle East and Africa. *The Gates of Damascus* is her fifth book.

'Expands the boundaries of travel writing' – Times Literary Supplement

KINGDOM OF THE FILM STARS
Journey into Jordan
Annie Caulfield

Kingdom of the Film Stars is a travel book and a love story. With honesty and humour, Annie Caulfield writes of travelling in Jordan and falling in love with a Bedouin. Her book offers fascinating insights into the country – from the traditional tent life of nomadic tribes to the first woman MP's battle with fundamentalist colleagues. *Kingdom of the Film Stars* unpicks some of the tight-woven Western myths about the Arab world, presenting cultural and political issues within the intimate framework of a compelling love story.

Annie Caulfield, who was born in Ireland and currently lives in London, is an award-winning playwright and journalist. She has travelled widely in the Middle East.

'Annie Caulfield is a remarkable traveller. Her story is fresh, courageous, moving, witty and sexy!' – Dawn French

LONELY PLANET TRAVEL ATLASES

Lonely Planet has long been famous for the number and quality of its guidebook maps. Now we've gone one step further and in conjunction with Steinhart Katzir Publishers produced a handy companion series: Lonely Planet travel atlases – maps of a country produced in book form.

Unlike other maps, which look good but lead travellers astray, our travel atlases have been researched on the road by Lonely Planet's experienced team of writers. All details are carefully checked to ensure the atlas corresponds with the equivalent Lonely Planet guidebook.

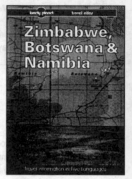

The handy atlas format means no holes, wrinkles, torn sections or constant folding and unfolding. These atlases can survive long periods on the road, unlike cumbersome fold-out maps. The comprehensive index ensures easy reference.

- full-colour throughout
- maps researched and checked by Lonely Planet authors
- place names correspond with Lonely Planet guidebooks
  – no confusing spelling differences
- legend and travelling information in English, French, German, Japanese and Spanish
- size: 230 x 160 mm

Available now:
Chile & Easter Island • Egypt • India & Bangladesh • Israel & the Palestinian Territories • Jordan, Syria & Lebanon • Kenya • Laos • Thailand • Vietnam • Zimbabwe, Botswana & Namibia

---

LONELY PLANET TV SERIES & VIDEOS

Lonely Planet travel guides have been brought to life on television screens around the world. Like our guides, the programmes are based on the joy of independent travel, and look honestly at some of the most exciting, picturesque and frustrating places in the world. Each show is presented by one of three travellers from Australia, England or the USA and combines an innovative mixture of video, Super-8 film, atmospheric soundscapes and original music.

Videos of each episode – containing additional footage not shown on television – are available from good book and video shops, but the availability of individual videos varies with regional screening schedules.

Video destinations include: Alaska • American Rockies • Australia – The South-East • Baja California & the Copper Canyon • Brazil • Central Asia • Chile & Easter Island • Corsica, Sicily & Sardinia – The Mediterranean Islands • East Africa (Tanzania & Zanzibar) • Ecuador & the Galapagos Islands • Greenland & Iceland • Indonesia • Israel & the Sinai Desert • Jamaica • Japan • La Ruta Maya • Morocco • New York • North India • Pacific Islands (Fiji, Solomon Islands & Vanuatu) • South India • South West China • Turkey • Vietnam • West Africa • Zimbabwe, Botswana & Namibia

The Lonely Planet TV series is produced by:
Pilot Productions
Duke of Sussex Studios
44 Uxbridge St
London W8 7TG UK

Lonely Planet videos are distributed by:
IVN Communications Inc
2246 Camino Ramon
California 94583, USA

107 Power Road, Chiswick
London W4 5PL UK

Music from the TV series is available on CD & cassette.
For video availability and ordering information contact your nearest Lonely Planet office.

PLANET TALK

Lonely Planet's FREE quarterly newsletter

We love hearing from you and think you'd like to hear from us.

When...is the right time to see reindeer in Finland?
Where...can you hear the best palm-wine music in Ghana?
How...do you get from Asunción to Areguá by steam train?
What...is the best way to see India?

For the answer to these and many other questions read PLANET TALK.

Every issue is packed with up-to-date travel news and advice including:

* a letter from Lonely Planet co-founders Tony and Maureen Wheeler
* go behind the scenes on the road with a Lonely Planet author
* feature article on an important and topical travel issue
* a selection of recent letters from travellers
* details on forthcoming Lonely Planet promotions
* complete list of Lonely Planet products

To join our mailing list contact any Lonely Planet office.

Also available: Lonely Planet T-shirts. 100% heavyweight cotton.

LONELY PLANET ONLINE

Get the latest travel information before you leave or while you're on the road

Whether you've just begun planning your next trip, or you're chasing down specific info on currency regulations or visa requirements, check out the Lonely Planet World Wide Web site for up-to-the-minute travel information.

As well as travel profiles of your favourite destinations (including interactive maps and full-colour photos), you'll find current reports from our army of researchers and other travellers, updates on health and visas, travel advisories, and the ecological and political issues you need to be aware of as you travel.

There's an online travellers' forum (the Thorn Tree) where you can share your experiences of life on the road, meet travel companions and ask other travellers for their recommendations and advice. We also have plenty of links to other Web sites useful to independent travellers.

With tens of thousands of visitors a month, the Lonely Planet Web site is one of the most popular on the Internet and has won a number of awards including GNN's Best of the Net travel award.

http://www.lonelyplanet.com

LONELY PLANET PRODUCTS

Lonely Planet is known worldwide for publishing practical, reliable and no-nonsense travel information in our guides and on our web site. The Lonely Planet list covers just about every accessible part of the world. Currently there are eight series: *travel guides, shoestring guides, walking guides, city guides, phrasebooks, audio packs, travel atlases* and *Journeys* – a unique collection of travel writing.

EUROPE

Austria • Baltic States & Kaliningrad• Baltic States phrasebook • Britain • Central Europe on a shoestring • Central Europe phrasebook • Czech & Slovak Republics • Denmark • Dublin city guide • Eastern Europe on a shoestring • Eastern Europe phrasebook • Finland • France • Greece • Greek phrasebook • Hungary • Iceland, Greenland & the Faroe Islands • Ireland • Italy • Mediterranean Europe on a shoestring • Mediterranean Europe phrasebook • Paris city guide • Poland • Prague city guide • Portugal • Russia, Ukraine & Belarus • Russian phrasebook • Scandinavian & Baltic Europe on a shoestring • Scandinavian Europe phrasebook • Slovenia • Spain • St Petersburg city guide • Switzerland • Trekking in Greece • Trekking in Spain • Ukrainian phrasebook • Vienna city guide • Walking in Britain • Walking in Switzerland • Western Europe on a shoestring • Western Europe phrasebook

NORTH AMERICA

Alaska • Backpacking in Alaska • Baja California• California & Nevada • Canada • Florida • Hawaii • Honolulu city guide • Los Angeles city guide • Mexico • Miami city guide • New England • New Orleans city guide • Pacific Northwest USA • Rocky Mountain States • San Francisco city guide • Southwest USA • USA phrasebook • Washington, DC & the Capital Region

CENTRAL AMERICA & THE CARIBBEAN

Bermuda • Central America on a shoestring • Costa Rica • Cuba • Eastern Caribbean • Guatemala, Belize & Yucatán: La Ruta Maya • Jamaica

SOUTH AMERICA

Argentina, Uruguay & Paraguay • Bolivia • Brazil • Brazilian phrasebook • Buenos Aires city guide • Chile & Easter Island • Chile & Easter Island travel atlas • Colombia • Ecuador & the Galápagos Islands • Latin American Spanish phrasebook • Peru • Quechua phrasebook • Rio de Janeiro city guide • South America on a shoestring • Trekking in the Patagonian Andes • Venezuela

Travel Literature: Full Circle: A South American Journey

ANTARCTICA

Antarctica

ISLANDS OF THE INDIAN OCEAN

Madagascar & Comoros • Maldives & Islands of the East Indian Ocean • Mauritius, Réunion & Seychelles

AFRICA

Arabic (Moroccan) phrasebook • Africa on a shoestring • Cape Town city guide • Central Africa • East Africa • Egypt • Egypt travel atlas• Ethiopian (Amharic) phrasebook • Kenya • Kenya travel atlas • Morocco • North Africa • South Africa, Lesotho & Swaziland • Swahili phrasebook • Trekking in East Africa • West Africa • Zimbabwe, Botswana & Namibia • Zimbabwe, Botswana & Namibia travel atlas

Travel Literature: The Rainbird: A Central African Journey • Songs to an African Sunset: A Zimbabwean Story

MAIL ORDER

Lonely Planet products are distributed worldwide. They are also available by mail order from Lonely Planet, so if you have difficulty finding a title please write to us. North American and South American residents should write to Embarcadero West, 155 Filbert St, Suite 251, Oakland CA 94607, USA; European and African residents should write to 10 Barley Mow Passage, Chiswick, London W4 4PH; and residents of other countries to PO Box 617, Hawthorn, Victoria 3122, Australia.

NORTH-EAST ASIA

Beijing city guide • Cantonese phrasebook • China • Hong Kong, Macau & Guangzhou• Hong Kong city guide • Japan • Japanese phrasebook • Japanese audio pack • Korea • Korean phrasebook • Mandarin phrasebook • Mongolia • Mongolian phrasebook • North-East Asia on a shoestring • Seoul city guide • Taiwan • Tibet • Tibet phrasebook • Tokyo city guide

Travel Literature: Lost Japan

MIDDLE EAST & CENTRAL ASIA

Arab Gulf States • Arabic (Egyptian) phrasebook • Central Asia • Iran • Israel & the Palestinian Territories • Israel & the Palestinian Territories travel atlas • Istanbul city guide • Jerusalem city guide • Jordan & Syria • Jordan, Syria & Lebanon travel atlas • Middle East • Turkey • Turkish phrasebook • Yemen

Travel Literature: The Gates of Damascus • Kingdom of the Film Stars: Journey into Jordan

ALSO AVAILABLE:

Travel with Children • Traveller's Tales

INDIAN SUBCONTINENT

Bangladesh • Bengali phrasebook • Delhi city guide • Hindi/Urdu phrasebook • India • India & Bangladesh travel atlas • Indian Himalaya • Karakoram Highway • Nepal • Nepali phrasebook • Pakistan • Rajasthan • Sri Lanka • Sri Lanka phrasebook • Trekking in the Indian Himalaya • Trekking in the Karakoram & Hindukush • Trekking in the Nepal Himalaya

Travel Literature: In Rajasthan • Shopping for Buddhas

SOUTH-EAST ASIA

Bali & Lombok • Bangkok city guide • Burmese phrasebook • Cambodia • Ho Chi Minh city guide • Indonesia • Indonesian phrasebook • Indonesian audio pack • Jakarta city guide • Java • Laos • Lao phrasebook • Laos travel atlas • Malay phrasebook • Malaysia, Singapore & Brunei • Myanmar (Burma) • Philippines • Pilipino phrasebook • Singapore city guide • South-East Asia on a shoestring •South-East Asia phrasebook • Thailand • Thailand travel atlas • Thai phrasebook • Thai audio pack • Thai Hill Tribes phrasebook • Vietnam • Vietnamese phrasebook • Vietnam travel atlas

AUSTRALIA & THE PACIFIC

Australia • Australian phrasebook • Bushwalking in Australia • Bushwalking in Papua New Guinea • Fiji • Fijian phrasebook • Islands of Australia's Great Barrier Reef • Melbourne city guide • Micronesia • New Caledonia • New South Wales & the ACT • New Zealand • Northern Territory • Outback Australia • Papua New Guinea • Papua New Guinea phrasebook • Queensland • Rarotonga & the Cook Islands • Samoa • Solomon Islands • South Australia • Sydney city guide • Tahiti & French Polynesia • Tasmania • Tonga • Tramping in New Zealand • Vanuatu • Victoria • Western Australia

Travel Literature: Islands in the Clouds • Sean & David's Long Drive

THE LONELY PLANET STORY

Lonely Planet published its first book in 1973 in response to the numerous 'How did you do it?' questions Maureen and Tony Wheeler were asked after driving, bussing, hitching, sailing and railing their way from England to Australia.

Written at a kitchen table and hand collated, trimmed and stapled, *Across Asia on the Cheap* became an instant local bestseller, inspiring thoughts of another book.

Eighteen months in South-East Asia resulted in their second guide, *South-East Asia on a shoestring*, which they put together in a backstreet Chinese hotel in Singapore in 1975. The 'yellow bible', as it quickly became known to backpackers around the world, soon became *the* guide to the region. It has sold well over half a million copies and is now in its 9th edition, still retaining its familiar yellow cover.

Today there are over 180 titles, including travel guides, walking guides, language kits & phrasebooks, travel atlases and travel literature. The company is one of the largest travel publishers in the world. Although Lonely Planet initially specialised in guides to Asia, we now cover most regions of the world, including the Pacific, North America, South America, Africa, the Middle East and Europe.

The emphasis continues to be on travel for independent travellers. Tony and Maureen still travel for several months of each year and play an active part in the writing, updating and quality control of Lonely Planet's guides.

They have been joined by over 70 authors and 170 staff at our offices in Melbourne (Australia), Oakland (USA), London (UK) and Paris (France). Travellers themselves also make a valuable contribution to the guides through the feedback we receive in thousands of letters each year.

The people at Lonely Planet strongly believe that travellers can make a positive contribution to the countries they visit, both through their appreciation of the countries' culture, wildlife and natural features, and through the money they spend. In addition, the company makes a direct contribution to the countries and regions it covers. Since 1986 a percentage of the income from each book has been donated to ventures such as famine relief in Africa; aid projects in India; agricultural projects in Central America; Greenpeace's efforts to halt French nuclear testing in the Pacific; and Amnesty International.

'I hope we send the people out with the right attitude about travel. You realise when you travel that there are so many different perspectives about the world, so we hope these books will make people more interested in what they see. These are guidebooks, but you can't really guide people. All you can do is point them in the right direction.'
– Tony Wheeler

LONELY PLANET PUBLICATIONS

Australia
PO Box 617, Hawthorn 3122, Victoria
tel: (03) 9819 1877 fax: (03) 9819 6459
e-mail: talk2us@lonelyplanet.com.au

USA
Embarcadero West, 155 Filbert St, Suite 251,
Oakland, CA 94607
tel: (510) 893 8555 TOLL FREE: 800 275-8555
fax: (510) 893 8563
e-mail: info@lonelyplanet.com

UK
10 Barley Mow Passage, Chiswick,
London W4 4PH
tel: (0181) 742 3161 fax: (0181) 742 2772
e-mail: 100413.3551@compuserve.com

France:
71 bis rue du Cardinal Lemoine, 75005 Paris
tel: 1 44 32 06 20 fax: 1 46 34 72 55
e-mail: 100560.415@compuserve.com

World Wide Web: http://www.lonelyplanet.com